BEHAVIORAL NEUROSCIENCE MADE ACCESSIBLE

New and revised artwork and animations bring key concepts to life.

All-new *In the News* examples link research to everyday aspects and applications of behavioral neuroscience, with thought questions to stimulate critical thinking.

New and updated *Applications* demonstrate how brain discoveries can impact our lives.

A new *Research Spotlight* feature uncovers the inner workings of the research influencing our world.

New *Learning Objectives* help readers stay focused on the most important content.

New and updated coverage of

- optogenetics as a research technique
- reward, brain plasticity, and learning in addiction
- brain structures and chemical systems involved in aggression
- psychological disorders in line with the *Diagnostic and Statistical Manual* (*DSM*-5)
- recent findings on sleep and waking circuits

IN THE NEWS
LEARN A NEW LANGUAGE WHILE YOU STUDY PSYCHOLOGY

How would you like to learn a new language while doing your psychology homework? We have been told since we were young that we had to focus and practice to learn how to speak another language, but recent evidence suggests that our brains are just as good at acquiring language information passively when we divert our attention elsewhere (reported in Greenwood, 2017).

In one study, two groups of participants were trained to distinguish between several similar-sounding phonemes of native Hindi speakers. The focus group practiced for one continuous hour across two days, while the other group alternated between 10 minutes of active practice and 10 minutes of another task for an hour while the sounds continued in the background. Surprisingly, the researchers discovered the "distracted" group

were learning Spanish learned to distinguish among sounds better if they simply listened to the new language rather than trying to speak along with the new material. So there might be something to taking frequent breaks from intensive language study and, turn on a movie in that language while you do something else.

THOUGHT QUESTIONS

1. How could you apply the results of these studies to learning a new language in college?
2. Why do you think that listening by itself leads to better language learning than listening while repeating?

APPLICATION
Ultrasound Surgery

Source: AP Photo/The Canadian Press, Frank Gunn.

Brain disorders often require surgery, which has its own drawbacks. The use of focused ultrasound is making intervention noninvasive, safer, and more precise. The energy is focused on the target area by an acoustic lens, much the same way as a magnifying glass focuses beams of sunlight. An individual acoustic beam by itself has no effect, but when multiple intersecting beams of ultrasound are focused on a target they can produce important biological effects. The war...
a brain scan, wh...

the location. Targets can be as small as 1 mm³ or up to 150 mm³. Increasing the energy level generates enough heat to destroy the target, and the technique can be used to break up blood clots or destroy tumors and other diseased tissue, as well as to silence neural circuits to treat disabling tremors and unbearable pain (Monteith, Gwinn, & Newell, 2015).

Recent work suggests that these techniques can also be applied to neuropsychiatric disorders such as Alzheimer's and Parkinson's diseases, which historically have relied on drugs and invasive treatments (Leinenga, Langton, Nisbet, & Götz, 2016). The therapeutic effects are immediate and without the recovery and side effects typically seen with traditional surgery or radiation treatments. Researchers are also using the technique with transgenic mice that develop the brain pathology and memory deficits characteristic of Alzheimer's disease (Burgess et al., 2014). Their strategy is to activate glial cells and open the blood-brain barrier near memory structures, to allow

RESEARCH SPOTLIGHT
A Bug That Causes Road Rage?

When the protozoan parasite *Toxoplasma gondii* infects animals, it forms cysts in the brain that change the host's behavior. Rats, for example, become risk takers and lose their fear of cats; this makes it likely they will get eaten, which means *T. gondii* cysts will end up in the cat's feces and be spread to new hosts. About one third of the world's population is infected with *T. gondii*, including about 14% of the U.S. population, due to contaminated food and water; infected individuals are more likely to have slower reaction times and are more likely to have car accidents, and infection has been linked to some cases of psychiatric disorder, such as schizophrenia (Torrey, Bartko, & Yolken, 2012).

Following studies that found an association with aggression (Cook et al., 2015) and suicidal behaviors in women (Ling, Lester, Mortensen,

Langenberg, & Postolache, 2011), Emil Coccaro and his colleagues (2016) at the University of Chicago asked whether the parasite might contribute to intermittent explosive disorder (IED). IED is a form of problematic, impulsive aggressive behavior, such as we see in road rage, and it affects about 16 million Americans. The researchers found that individuals who tested positive for *T. gondii* were also more likely to score higher on measures of aggression. The rate of infection was 21.8% in the subjects with IED, compared with 16.7% among control subjects with psychiatric diagnoses and 9.1% of healthy control subjects. Coccaro said that these results "confirm that IED is a brain disorder and not a disorder of 'personality.'" Previous studies found that the cysts show up mostly in the amygdala, where they cause retraction of dendrites, and in the prefrontal cortex.

BEHAVIORAL NEUROSCIENCE BROUGHT TO LIFE

The *Brain & Behavior* **hallmark art program**, updated for the new edition, includes images, figures, and illustrations that enhance core concepts and reflect cutting-edge, evidence-based research. Select original illustrations throughout the book are paired with two sets of animations to increase student understanding and engagement:

Figures Brought to Life **animations** illustrate concept processes with animated versions of illustrations accompanied by easy-to-follow narration.

Stories of Brain & Behavior **animations** explain chapter concepts in a narrative and storytelling format.

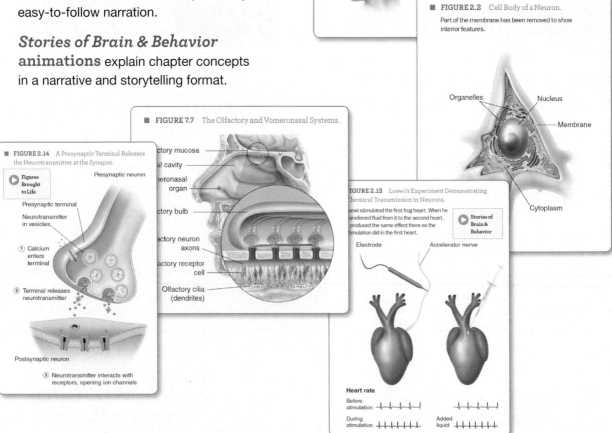

■ FIGURE 6.3 Thirst Control Signals and Brain Centers.

SFO
Median preoptic nucleus
Thalamus
OVLT
Nucleus of the solitary tract
Angiotensin II
Vagus nerve
Blood vessel

■ FIGURE 2.2 Cell Body of a Neuron.
Part of the membrane has been removed to show interior features.

Organelles
Nucleus
Membrane
Cytoplasm

■ FIGURE 7.7 The Olfactory and Vomeronasal Systems.

ctory mucosa
al cavity
eronasal organ
ctory bulb
actory neuron axons
actory receptor cell
Olfactory cilia (dendrites)

■ FIGURE 2.14 A Presynaptic Terminal Releases the Neurotransmitter at the Synapse.

▶ Figures Brought to Life

Presynaptic neuron
Presynaptic terminal
Neurotransmitter in vesicles
① Calcium enters terminal
② Terminal releases neurotransmitter
Postsynaptic neuron
③ Neurotransmitter interacts with receptors, opening ion channels

FIGURE 2.13 Loewi's Experiment Demonstrating Chemical Transmission in Neurons.
oewi stimulated the first frog heart. When he ansferred fluid from it to the second heart, produced the same effect there as the timulation did in the first heart.

▶ Stories of Brain & Behavior

Electrode
Accelerator nerve

Heart rate
Before stimulation
During stimulation
Added liquid

"Garrett's use of illustrations/art and examples are exemplary. The material is pitched at the right level and with optimal detail."

—**Robert Faux**, *Duquesne University*

RESOURCES
STUDENTS WILL USE

STUDY GUIDE AND COURSEPACK

Completely revised to accompany the best-selling *Brain & Behavior: An Introduction to Behavioral Neuroscience, Fifth Edition*, the **Study Guide** offers students even more opportunities to review, practice, and master course material. Featuring chapter outlines, learning objectives, summaries, guided reviews, short answer and essay questions, the guide reflects important updates made to the content in the main text to enhance student understanding.

SAGE coursepacks **Our Content Tailored to Your LMS**

Instructors! **SAGE coursepacks** makes it easy to import our quality instructor and student resource content into your school's learning management system (LMS). Intuitive and simple to use, **SAGE coursepacks** allows you to customize course content to meet your students' needs. Learn more at **sagepub.com/coursepacks**.

PEDAGOGY

- In-chapter pedagogy includes frequent **concept checks** and **marginal questions** to keep students on track.
- **End-of-chapter pedagogy** includes questions for discussion, quizzes, additional readings, key terms, and descriptions of online chapter resources and multimedia resources paired with learning objectives to boost understanding.

"Each chapter tells a story that the students can follow in a very systematic way with good flow in the writing style."
—Lorenz S. Neuwirth, *SUNY College at Old Westbury*

"I find the clinical applications most impressive."
—Andrea L. O. Hebb, *Dalhousie University*

Sara Miller McCune founded SAGE Publishing in 1965 to support the dissemination of usable knowledge and educate a global community. SAGE publishes more than 1000 journals and over 800 new books each year, spanning a wide range of subject areas. Our growing selection of library products includes archives, data, case studies and video. SAGE remains majority owned by our founder and after her lifetime will become owned by a charitable trust that secures the company's continued independence.

Los Angeles | London | New Delhi | Singapore | Washington DC | Melbourne

Brain&Behavior

FIFTH EDITION

To Duejean
taken from her family and friends by Alzheimer's disease.

—Bob Garrett

To my father
You were the smartest man I've ever known. I miss you every day.

—Gerald Hough

Brain&Behavior

An Introduction to Behavioral Neuroscience
FIFTH EDITION

BOB GARRETT

California Polytechnic State University, San Luis Obispo

GERALD HOUGH

Rowan University

Contributions by

MEGHAN C. KAHN

Indiana University Southeast

JOSHUA S. RODEFER

Valdosta State University

Los Angeles | London | New Delhi
Singapore | Washington DC | Melbourne

FOR INFORMATION:

SAGE Publications, Inc.
2455 Teller Road
Thousand Oaks, California 91320
E-mail: order@sagepub.com

SAGE Publications Ltd.
1 Oliver's Yard
55 City Road
London EC1Y 1SP
United Kingdom

SAGE Publications India Pvt. Ltd.
B 1/I 1 Mohan Cooperative Industrial
Area
Mathura Road, New Delhi 110 044
India

SAGE Publications Asia-Pacific Pte. Ltd.
3 Church Street
#10-04 Samsung Hub
Singapore 049483

Copyright © 2018 by SAGE Publications, Inc.

Printed in Canada

Cover and title page image: © iStock.com/Krle

ISBN 978-1-5063-4920-6

Acquisitions Editor: Abbie Rickard
Content Development Editor: Lucy Berbeo
Editorial Assistant: Jennifer Cline
Production Editors: David C. Felts, Kelly DeRosa
Copy Editor: Amy Marks
Typesetter: C&M Digitals (P) Ltd.
Proofreaders: Lawrence W. Baker, Scott Oney
Indexer: Diggs Publication Services
Cover Designer: Gail Buschman
Marketing Manager: Katherine Hepburn

This book is printed on acid-free paper.

17 18 19 20 21 10 9 8 7 6 5 4 3 2 1

Brief Contents

Detailed Contents

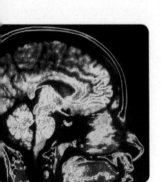

Scott Camazine/Science Source

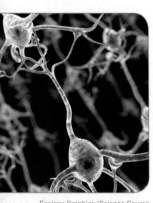

Equinox Graphics/Science Source

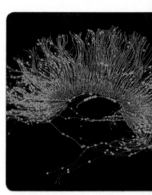

Callista Images/Cultura/Getty Images

Chapter 4 • The Methods and Ethics of Research   85

Oli Scarff/Staff/Getty Images
News/Getty

PART II. Motivation and Emotion: What Makes Us Go   115

Chapter 5 • Drugs, Addiction, and Reward   117

© Neeta Lind

© iStockphoto/CathyKeifer

Paul Gilham/Getty Images

Flashpop/DigitalVision/Getty Images

© Photo courtesy of Eric Schrader

Chapter 10 • Vision and Visual Perception   275

J. R. Eyerman/The LIFE Picture Collection/Getty

Chapter 11 • The Body Sense and Movement   313

Mads Perch/Stone/Getty

Chapter 12 • Learning and Memory   345

iStock/michellegibson

Chapter 13 • Intelligence and Cognitive Functioning   373

Hero Images/Hero Images/Getty

Chapter 14 • Psychological Disorders   405

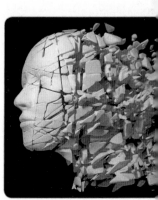

© iStockphoto.com/morkeman

MONEY SHARMA/Staff/AFP/Getty

Preface

A Message From the Authors

> *Anyone who stops learning is old, whether at twenty or eighty. Anyone who keeps learning stays young. The greatest thing in life is to keep your mind young.*
>
> —Henry Ford

Flip through this book and you'll see that its pages are chock-full of facts and applications—just a sampling gleaned from a vast supply that grows too fast for any of us to keep up with and that becomes obsolete just as fast. But sifting through those facts and reporting them is neither the most difficult nor the most important function of a good textbook. A greater challenge is that most students fail to share their instructors' infatuation with learning; perhaps they lack the genes, or the parental role models, or just the idea that learning can be fun. At any rate, they can find a text like this intimidating, and it is the textbook's role to change their minds.

The colorful illustrations, case studies, and research vignettes may capture students' interest, but sparking interest alone is not enough. That's why we've adopted a big-picture approach in writing the text, one that marshals facts into explanations and discards the ones left standing around with nothing to do. When you put facts to work that way, you begin to see students look up and say, "That makes sense," or "I've always wondered about that, but I never thought of it that way," or "Now I understand what was going on with Uncle Edgar."

We believe education has the capacity to make a person healthy, happy, and productive, and it makes a society strong. Education realizes that promise when it leads people to inquire and to question, when they *learn how to learn.* When 45% of the public believes in ghosts, and politics has become a game played by shouting the loudest or telling the most convincing lie, education more than ever needs to teach young people to ask, "Where is the evidence?" and "Is that the only possible interpretation?"

To those who would teach and those who would learn, this book is for you.

To the Student

Brain & Behavior is our attempt to reach out to students, to beckon them into the fascinating world of behavioral neuroscience. These are exceptionally exciting times, comparable in many ways to the renaissance that thrust Europe from the Middle Ages into the modern world. According to the American neurologist Stanley B. Prusiner,

> Neuroscience is by far the most exciting branch of science because the brain is the most fascinating object in the universe. Every human brain is different—the brain makes each human unique and defines who he or she is.

We know of no scientific discipline with greater potential to answer the burning questions about ourselves than behavioral neuroscience. We hope this textbook will convey that kind of excitement as you read about discoveries that will revolutionize our understanding of what it means to be human.

We want you to succeed in this course, but, more than that, we want you to learn more than you ever imagined you could and to go away with a new appreciation for the promise of behavioral neuroscience. So, we have a few tips we want to pass along. First, try to sit near the front of the class, because those students usually get the best grades. That is probably because they stay more engaged and are encouraged to ask more questions; but to ask good questions, you should always read the text before you go to class. And so you'll know where you're going before you begin to read, take a look at "After reading this chapter, you will be able to," then skim the chapter subheadings, and read the summary at the end of the chapter. Make sure you can define the terms, and visualize the pathways and brain areas as you come across them. Use the questions in the margins as you go through the text,

Stories of Brain & Behavior

answer the Concept Check questions, and be sure to test yourself at the end using the Test Your Understanding questions. As you read, pay special attention to the text in blue; these are definitions of the most important terms, which are defined again in the glossary at the end of the book. A "play button" icon like the one you see here will tell you which figures have been animated on the text's website to help sharpen your understanding. Then, don't forget to look up some of the books and articles in For Further Reading. Finally, carefully curated lists of web resources at the end of every chapter are fully hyperlinked on the Student Resources site at edge.sagepub.com/garrett5e, directing you to a wealth of additional information on the web. If you are considering a career in behavioral neuroscience, make sure you look at the For Further Thought questions at the end of each chapter. If you do all of these things, you won't just do better in this course; you will leave saying, "I really got something out of that class!" And when it's time to take the GRE (or MCAT or VCAT), or talk to your doctor, or interview for a biomedical job, or simply read the Science section of the *New York Times*, you'll be using the knowledge you gained in this text.

We wrote *Brain & Behavior* with you in mind, so we hope you will let us know where we have done things right and, especially, where we have not. We wish you the satisfaction of discovery and knowledge as you read what we have written *for you*.

To the Instructor

When Bob wrote the first edition of *Brain & Behavior*, he had one goal: to entice students into the adventure of behavioral neuroscience. There were other good texts out there, but they read as though they were written for students preparing for further neuroscience courses in graduate school. Those students will find this book adequately challenging, but Bob wrote *Brain & Behavior* so that anyone interested in behavior, including the newly declared sophomore major or the curious student who has wandered over from the history department, can have the deeper understanding that comes from a biological perspective as they take other courses in psychology.

It is not enough to draw students in with lively writing or by piquing their interest with case studies and telling an occasional story along the way; unless they feel they are learning something significant, they won't stay—they'll look for excitement in more traditional places. As Bob wrote, he remembered the text he struggled with in his first behavioral neuroscience class; it wasn't very interesting because neuroscientists knew much less about the biological underpinnings of behavior than they do now. Since that time, they have learned how the brain changes during learning, they have discovered some of the genes and brain deficiencies that cause schizophrenia, and they are beginning to understand how intricate networks of brain cells produce language, make us intelligent, and help us play the piano or find a mate. In other words, behavioral neuroscience has become a lot more interesting. So the material is there; now it is our job to communicate the excitement we have felt in discovering the secrets of the brain and to make a convincing case that behavioral neuroscience has the power to answer students' questions about behavior.

A good textbook is all about teaching, but there is no teaching if there is no learning. Over the years, our students have taught us a great deal about what they needed to help them learn. For one thing, we realized how important it is for students to build on their knowledge throughout the course, so we have made several changes from the organization of other texts. First, the chapter on neuronal physiology precedes the chapter on the nervous system, because we believe that you can't begin to understand the brain until you know how its neurons work. And we reversed the usual order of the vision and audition chapters, because audition provides a friendlier context for introducing the basic principles of sensation and perception. The chapters on addiction, motivation, emotion, and sex follow the introduction to neurophysiology; this was done to build student motivation before tackling sensation and perception. Perhaps more significant, some topics have been moved around among chapters so that they can be developed in a more behaviorally meaningful context. So we discuss language along with audition, the body senses with the mechanisms of movement, the sense of taste in the context of feeding behavior, and olfaction in conjunction with sexual behavior. Most unique, though, is the inclusion of a chapter on the biology of intelligence and another on consciousness. The latter is a full treatment of recent developments in the field, rather than being limited to the usual topics of sleep and split-brain behavior. These two chapters strongly reinforce the theme that behavioral neuroscience is personally relevant and capable of addressing important questions.

Brain & Behavior has several features that will motivate students to learn and encourage them to take an active role in their learning. It engages the student with interest-grabbing opening vignettes; illustrative case studies; and In the News, Application, and Research Spotlight features that take an intriguing step beyond the chapter content. Throughout each chapter, questions in the margins keep the student focused on key points, and a Concept Check at the end of each section serves as a reminder of the important ideas. At the end of each chapter, In Perspective emphasizes the importance and implications of what the student has just read, a summary helps organize that information, and Test Your Understanding questions assess the student's conceptual understanding as well as factual knowledge. Then, For Further Reading suggestions guide the student in exploring the chapter's topics more fully, and a list of websites points the way to related information on the Internet. We have found over the years that students who use the study aids in a class are also the best performers in the course.

New in the Fifth Edition

It has been just three years since publication of the fourth edition of *Brain & Behavior,* but that short time has witnessed unprecedented activity in the neurosciences. We (founding author Bob Garrett and new author Gerald Hough) have reviewed thousands of research articles to ensure that the fifth edition provides students with the most up-to-date coverage of behavioral neuroscience possible. We have undertaken the most ambitious revision of *Brain & Behavior* since the second edition. We have updated more than 300 references, added 30 new terms, revised more than 50 illustrations, freshened the overall look of the text, and polished its presentation. We completely rewrote several sections, not only to bring them up to date but also to provide better organization and clarity and to shift focus to the most significant aspects. We have, for example, added optogenetics as one of the research techniques in Chapter 4; recast the Chapter 5 discussion of reward, brain plasticity, and learning in addiction; in Chapter 8 developed recent thinking that aggression depends on both testosterone-to-cortisol ratio and the balance of activity among the hypothalamus, amygdala, and prefrontal cortex; revised the discussion of long-term potentiation in Chapter 12 to better emphasize the roles of dopamine, synaptic proteins, and neurogenesis; reconceptualized Chapter 14 to bring the discussion of psychological disorders into line with the fifth edition of the *Diagnostic and Statistical Manual of Mental Disorders* (*DSM-5*); and revised the final chapter to reflect current understanding of the sleep and waking circuits. To support these changes, we replaced all the In the News features, updated the Applications, and added a new feature, Research Spotlight, to highlight selected recent developments. In addition, we updated the online material and added new animations to better explain difficult concepts.

In recent years behavioral neuroscience has been dominated by two areas of research, and both continue to gain significance in explaining behavior. The first of these is genetics. New gene associations continue to be discovered, for example, linking autism spectrum disorder to genes for GABA and oxytocin receptors and genes concerned with the formation of synaptic proteins. At the same time, intelligence, schizophrenia, Down syndrome, and Alzheimer's disease are yielding additional secrets as researchers shift their attention to *de novo* mutations, copy number variations, and epigenetic influences. Also on the genetic front, the CRISPR technique of gene editing (the American Association for the Advancement of Science's 2015 breakthrough of the year) is showing great promise for medicine while generating increased concerns about modifying the human gene line.

The second research area, involving neural connectivity and networks, is continuing to reveal how the brain works and, in the case of disorders, how it fails to work. For example, we are beginning to appreciate the role of the salience network in consciousness, by detecting conditions that require attention and switching between the default mode network and the executive network. Other recent studies have found decreased connectivity in the cortex, corpus callosum, and thalamus in bipolar disorder, and both decreased and increased connectivity in different brain areas in depression.

At the same time, we are keenly aware of the need to translate research findings into applications whenever possible. Newly developing treatments featured in the text include the use of anti-inflammatory drugs and memory-inhibiting drugs to fight addiction; and treatment of Alzheimer's disease with nerve growth factor, brain-growth neurotrophic factor, and the drug aducanumab, which are in phase 1, phase 2, and phase 3 clinical trials, respectively. We also applaud the good news in two recent reports that prevalence of autism spectrum disorder appears to have leveled off and the risk for Alzheimer's disease has declined in several countries, including the United Kingdom (by 20%) and the United States (by 26%).

Acknowledgments

Revising a textbook like *Brain & Behavior* is incredibly hard work, and in spite of Bob's and Gerald's best efforts, the fifth edition would not be possible without the help of many others. Kudos to acquisitions editor Abbie Rickard and content development editor Lucy Berbeo for their insights, their patience, and their ability to keep us on schedule (almost). Aside from their challenges in dealing with the authors, they have managed a host of contributors, including Meghan C. Kahn, of Indiana University Southeast, who revised the Study Guide and wrote the In the News features; Joshua S. Rodefer, of Valdosta State University, who contributed Application and Research Spotlight features; Richard J. Addante, of California State University, San Bernardino, who reviewed the artwork; and an untold number of illustrators and animators. We also want to thank others who have made the project go so smoothly, including production editors David Felts and Kelly DeRosa, editorial assistant Jennifer Cline, cover designer Gail Buschman, marketing manager Katherine Hepburn, and marketing associate Tzveta Mihaylov.

Bob has had a number of mentors along the way, to whom he is forever grateful. A few of those special people are Wayne Kilgore, who taught the joys of science along with high school chemistry and physics; Garvin McCain, who introduced him to the satisfactions of research; Roger Kirk, who taught him that anything worth doing is worth doing over and over until it's right; and Ellen Roye and Ouilda Piner, who shared their love of language. These dedicated teachers showed him that learning was his responsibility, and they shaped his life with their unique gifts and quiet enthusiasm.

But of all of Bob's supporters, the most important was his wife, Duejean; love and thanks to her for fond memories and for her patient understanding and her appreciation of how important this project has been to him.

For Gerald, becoming a coauthor on this textbook, which he has used in his classes over the past decade, is an amazing privilege. He hopes that the instructors and students who use this book find that the overall presentation and helpfulness in assisting in the learning process are unchanged from the previous editions. His background in behavioral neuroethology (a mouthful for sure!) provides a background in understanding the neural bases of behavior. He would like to thank his academic mentors who have helped him find his way in a complex scientific world: Erich Klinghammer at Wolf Park in Battle Ground, Indiana, sowed the seeds for a love of wolves and understanding behavior in naturalistic settings; Susan Volman at The Ohio State University introduced him to the complexities of behavioral neuroscience through their investigation of how birds learn (and forget) songs at the neural level; and Verner Bingman gave him the opportunity to develop as a scholar and mentor to his students at Bowling Green State University in Ohio. He would also like to thank his family for letting him work on this important textbook: his wife of 25 years, Kerry; sons Alexander and Benjamin; and of course Melbourne the parakeet.

In addition, the following reviewers gave generously of their time and expertise throughout the development of this text; they contributed immensely to the quality of *Brain & Behavior*:

First edition: Susan Anderson, University of South Alabama; Patrizia Curran, University of Massachusetts–Dartmouth; Lloyd Dawe, Cameron University; Tami Eggleston, McKendree College; James Hunsicker, Southwestern Oklahoma State University; Eric Laws, Longwood College; Margaret Letterman, Eastern Connecticut State University; Doug Matthews, University of Memphis; Grant McLaren, Edinboro University of Pennsylvania; Rob Mowrer, Angelo State University; Anna Napoli, University of Redlands; Robert Patterson, Washington State University; Joseph Porter, Virginia Commonwealth University; Jeffrey Stern, University of Michigan–Dearborn; Aurora Torres, University of Alabama in Huntsville; Michael Woodruff, East Tennessee State University; and Phil Zeigler, Hunter College.

Second edition: M. Todd Allen, University of Northern Colorado; Patricia A. Bach, Illinois Institute of Technology; Wayne Brake, University of California–Santa Barbara; Steven I. Dworkin, University of North Carolina; Sean Laraway, San Jose State University; Mindy J. Miserendino, Sacred Heart University; Brady Phelps, South Dakota State University; Susan A. Todd, Bridgewater State College; and Elizabeth Walter, University of Oregon.

Third edition: John A. Agnew, University of Colorado Boulder; Michael A. Bock, American International College; Rachel E. Bowman, Sacred Heart University; Jessica Cail, Pepperdine University; Mary Jo Carnot, Chadron State College; Cheryl A. Frye, The University at Albany–State University of New York; Rebecca L. M. Fuller, Catholic University of America; Cindy Gibson, Washington College; Bennet Givens, Department of Psychology, The Ohio State University; Robert B. Glassman, Lake Forest College; Gerald E. Hough, Rowan University; Joseph Nuñez, Michigan State University; and Kimberly L. Thomas, University of Central Oklahoma.

Fourth edition: John A. Agnew, University of Colorado Boulder; Ben Allen, University of Pittsburgh; Scott L. Decker, University of South Carolina; Carol L. DeVolder, St. Ambrose University; Jeff Dyche, James Madison University; Cindy Gibson, Washington College; Deirdre C. Greer, Columbus State University; William Meil, Indiana University of Pennsylvania; Samar Saade Needham, California State University, Long Beach; M. Foster Olive, Arizona State University; Catherine Powers Ozyurt, Bay Path College; Allen Salo, University of Maine at Presque Isle; Justin P. Smith, University of South Dakota; Gretchen Sprow, University of North Carolina at Chapel Hill; and Sandra Trafalis, San Jose State University.

Fifth edition: Kurt T. Choate, Northeastern State University; Andrea L. O. Hebb, Saint Mary's University; Bryant Horowitz, East Los Angeles College, California State University, Northridge, and The Chicago School of Professional Psychology; Dwight J. Kravitz, The George Washington University; and Lorenz S. Neuwirth, SUNY College at Old Westbury.

—Bob Garrett and Gerald Hough

Supplemental Material

Student Study Guide

This affordable study guide and workbook to accompany *Brain & Behavior, Fifth Edition*, will help students get the added review and practice they need to improve their skills and master course material. Each part of the study guide corresponds to the appropriate chapter in the text and includes a chapter outline, chapter summary, study quiz, and chapter posttest.

Student Resources

Additional resources are available to students using *Brain & Behavior, Fifth Edition*. The interactive eBook includes animations of key figures in the text, and the SAGE edge site at edge.sagepub.com/garrett5e links to On the Web sites and other digital resources, eFlashcards, study quizzes (students can receive their scores immediately), and relevant SAGE journal articles.

Instructor Resources

A number of helpful teaching aids are available for professors new to teaching behavioral neuroscience and to using *Brain & Behavior, Fifth Edition*. Included are PowerPoint slides, a computerized test bank to allow for easy creation of exams, lecture outlines, suggested class activities and critical thinking questions, and video and Web resources for each chapter of the text.

About the Authors

Bob Garrett is a Visiting Scholar at California Polytechnic State University, San Luis Obispo. He was Professor of Psychology at DePauw University in Greencastle, Indiana, and held several positions there, including Chairperson of the Department of Psychology, Faculty Development Coordinator, and Interim Dean of Academic Affairs. He received his BA from the University of Texas at Arlington and his MA and PhD from Baylor University. He received further training in the Department of Physiology at Baylor University College of Medicine and at the Aeromedical Research Primate Laboratory, Holloman Air Force Base. Bob lives on a 3,200-acre ranch he shares with 47 other families in the hills outside San Luis Obispo. His two sons and three beautiful grandchildren all live nearby.

Gerald (Jerry) Hough is an Associate Professor of Biological Sciences and Psychology at Rowan University in Glassboro, New Jersey. He received his BA from Purdue University and his MS and PhD from The Ohio State University. He also worked in the lab of Verner Bingman at Bowling Green State University. He has taught undergraduate and graduate courses on anatomy, animal behavior, research methods, psychopharmacology, cognitive neuroscience, physiology, and learning. He has also served as the Undergraduate Advising Coordinator for Psychology, as the Chair of the IACUC, and in curriculum development for the Cooper Medical School at Rowan University. His research focus is in the neural bases of spatial and communication behaviors in birds, as well as the effect of aging on learning and memory. Gerald; his wife, Kerry; their two sons; and their pets live in southern New Jersey. A lifelong Cubs fan, he was able to experience the joy of a World Series Championship for the first time in 2016 with his family. Dad, wherever you are, they finally did it.

About the Contributors

Meghan C. Kahn is an Associate Professor of Psychology and Neuroscience at Indiana University Southeast in New Albany, Indiana. She teaches undergraduate courses on research methods and statistics, learning, neuroscience, sensation and perception, and neuroethics. She has served as the Psychology and Neuroscience Program Coordinator, an advisor for the campus chapter of Psi Chi, and a member of the Women's and Gender Studies committee. Her research focus is on the role of olfactory cues in spatial learning and conditional discrimination learning in pigeons. She received her BA from Alfred University and her MA and PhD from Bowling Green State University.

Joshua S. Rodefer is on faculty at Valdosta State University. He received his BS from Denison University (Granville, OH) and his PhD from the University of Minnesota before completing research fellowships at UNC–Chapel Hill and Harvard Medical School. His teaching is centered around undergraduate courses related to neuroscience and experimental methodology. He has mentored students in research related to cognition, behavioral pharmacology, and psychiatric disorders. In his spare time, Josh is an enthusiast about all things Pittsburgh, spends too much time planting trees, and has a never-ending appreciation of BBQ. He lives with his family and many adopted pets in south Georgia.

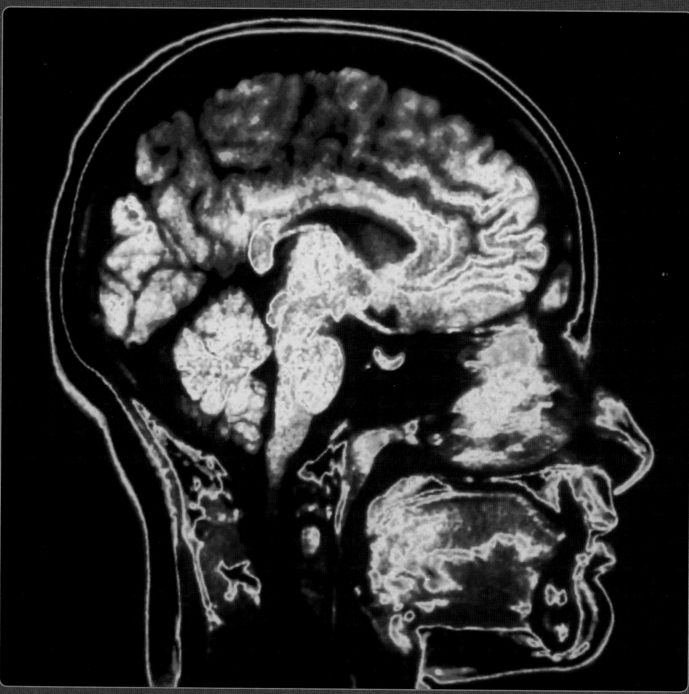

What Is Behavioral Neuroscience?

After reading this chapter, you will be able to:

- Define the mind-brain problem in behavioral neuroscience.

- Describe the contributions of philosophers and scientists to the development of behavioral neuroscience as a field of study.

- Identify the role of physiologists in the establishment of modern-day behavioral neuroscience.

- Compare the relative contributions of genes and environment in the development of behavioral characteristics.

- Critique the fixed nature of heredity in shaping behavior.

That device you carry in your pocket is a wonder of modern technology. It represents a very recent step in the evolution of long-distance communications, which began with smoke signals and drum beats and progressed through the telegraph, the wireless radio, and the landline telephone.

Mobile telephones appeared in vehicles in 1956, but a handheld mobile was not commercially available until 1983; dubbed the "brick," it weighed 1.75 pounds (0.79 kilograms) and cost $3,995 (Figure 1.1). Your four- or five-ounce phone operates over a vast cellular network to connect you to your friends and family and an estimated 4.8 billion people all around the world (there are actually more mobile devices on earth than there are people). Assuming you have a smartphone, you have access to many additional people by way of email, text, and video, as well as more than 1 billion websites on the Internet. Your phone also allows you to record memories in the form of notes and images, perform calculations, identify a tune or a flower, and determine the best route for your road trip.

The brain has many similarities. The neural cells (neurons) generate a tiny electrical signal that allows each one to communicate with a thousand other neurons, which in turn connect to thousands of others in a network of more than 80 billion neurons. One computational neuroscientist estimates that the brain's storage capability rivals that of the Internet; as a psychologist put it, if the brain were a video recorder it could store 300 *years* of video. But storage of memories and information is only one of the brain's many tasks. The brain is organized into specialized subnetworks that orchestrate your body's 640 muscles, generate thought and make decisions, perform calculations, keep track of where you are and help you navigate around your world, tell you when to drink and when and what to eat, and provide your humanly unique language capability and range of sensory capabilities. Like the cell phone, the brain has evolved over time and across species, but in this case as its capability has grown so has its size. Still, all of its amazing power is packed into just three pounds of tissue that consumes the same amount of energy as a 20-watt light bulb!

"
My cell phone is my best friend. It's my lifeline to the outside world.

—Carrie Underwood
"

Master the content.
edge.sagepub.com/garrett5e

■ **FIGURE 1.1** Lead Engineer Martin Cooper With the Motorola DynaTAC 8000X.

When the first hand-held cellular phone came out in 1984 it cost $4,000 (about $10,000 today), had a battery that took 10 hours to charge, and only had 30 minutes of talk time.

Source: Ted Soqui/Corbis Historical/Getty Images.

Mobile phones came into their own in the last decade of the 20th century, in terms of both their capabilities—such as built-in cameras, Bluetooth connectivity, and international calling—and their popularity, indicated by more sales worldwide in 1998 than for cars and PCs combined. The period was also seminal for the awakening field of neuroscience, so much so that in the United States it was designated as the Decade of the Brain. Planned as an effort to increase public awareness of the benefits of brain research, the Decade of the Brain was also a celebration of past achievements and a sober look at the future. At the threshold of a new millennium, we understood that we had an obligation to expand the horizons of human knowledge and advance the treatment of neurological diseases, emotional disorders, and addictions that cost the country a trillion dollars a year in care, lost productivity, and crime (Uhl & Grow, 2004). Since then, in the span of your lifetime, we have developed new treatments for depression, identified key genes responsible for the devastation of schizophrenia, developed agents that block addiction to drugs, found ways to slow the memory impairment of Alzheimer's, produced a map of the human genes, and literally peered into the brain itself to watch it work. These achievements seem remarkable for such a brief span of time, but in fact they have their roots in a 300-year scientific past and in 22 centuries of thought and inquiry before that. For that reason, we will spend a brief time examining those links to our past.

The Origins of Behavioral Neuroscience

The term *neuroscience* identifies the subject matter of the investigation rather than the scientist's training. A neuroscientist may be a biologist, a physiologist, an anatomist, a neurologist, a chemist, a psychologist, or a psychiatrist—or even a computer scientist or a philosopher. Psychologists who work in the area of neuroscience specialize in *behavioral neuroscience,* the branch of psychology that studies the relationships between behavior and the body, particularly the brain. (Behavioral neuroscience is the more modern term for *biological psychology;* sometimes the term *biopsychology, psychobiology,* or *physiological psychology* is also used.) For psychologists, *behavior* has a very broad meaning, which includes not only overt acts but also internal events such as learning, thinking, and emotion. Behavioral neuroscientists attempt to answer questions like "What changes in the brain when a person learns?" "Why does one person develop depression and another, under similar circumstances, becomes anxious while another seems unaffected?" "What is the physiological explanation for emotions?" "How do we recognize the face of a friend?" "How does the brain's activity result in consciousness?" Behavioral neuroscientists use a variety of research techniques to answer these questions, as you will see in Chapter 4. Whatever their area of study or their strategy for doing research, behavioral neuroscientists try to go beyond the mechanics of how the brain works to focus on the brain's role in behavior.

To really appreciate the impressive accomplishments of today's brain researchers, it is useful, perhaps even necessary, to understand the thinking and the work of their predecessors. Contemporary scientists stand on the shoulders of their intellectual ancestors, who made heroic advances with far less information at their disposal than is available to today's undergraduate student.

Writers have pointed out that psychology has a brief history but a long past. What they mean is that thinkers have struggled with the questions of behavior and experience for more than two millennia, but psychology arose as a separate discipline fairly recently; the date most people accept is 1879, when Wilhelm Wundt (Figure 1.2) established the first psychology laboratory in Leipzig, Germany. But biological psychology would not emerge as a separate science until psychologists offered convincing evidence that the biological approach could answer significant questions about behavior. To do so, they would have to come to terms with an old philosophical question about the nature of the mind. Because the question forms a thread that helps us trace the development of behavioral neuroscience, we will orient our discussion around this issue.

? What is behavioral neuroscience, and how does it relate to psychology?

" In the sciences, we are now uniquely privileged to sit side by side with the giants on whose shoulders we stand.

—Gerald Holton "

Prescientific Psychology and the Mind-Brain Problem

This issue is usually called "the mind-body problem," but it is phrased differently here to place the emphasis squarely where it belongs—on the brain. The *mind-brain problem* deals with what the mind is and what its relationship is to the brain. There can be no doubt that the brain is essential to our behavior, but does the mind control the brain, or is it the other way around? Alternatively, are mind and brain the same thing? How these questions are resolved affects how we ask all the other questions of neuroscience.

At the risk of sounding provocative, we argue that there is no such thing as *mind*. It exists only in the sense that, say, weather exists; weather is a concept used to include rain, wind, humidity, and related phenomena. We talk as if there is *a weather* when we say things like "The weather is interfering with my travel plans." But no one really thinks that there is *a weather*. Most, though not all, neuroscientists believe that we should think of the mind in the same way; it is simply the collection of things the brain does, such as thinking, sensing, planning, and feeling. But when we think, sense, plan, and feel, we get the compelling impression that there is *a mind* behind it all, guiding what we do. Most neuroscientists say this is just an illusion, that the sense of mind is nothing more than the awareness of what the brain is doing. Mind, like weather, is just a concept; it is not a *something*; it does not *do* anything.

This position is known as monism, from the Greek *monos*, meaning "alone" or "single." *Monism* is the idea that the mind and the body consist of the same substance. Idealistic monists believe that everything is nonphysical mind, but most monists take the position that the body and mind and everything else are physical; this view is called *materialistic monism*. The idea that the mind and the brain are separate is known as *dualism*. For most dualists, the body is material and the mind is nonmaterial. Most dualists also believe that the mind influences behavior by interacting with the brain.

This question did not originate with modern psychology. The Greek philosophers were debating it in the fifth century BCE (G. Murphy, 1949), when Democritus proposed that everything in the world was made up of atoms (*atomos*, meaning "indivisible"), his term for the smallest particle possible. Even the soul, which included the mind, was made up of atoms, so it, too, was material. Plato and Aristotle, considered the two greatest intellectuals among the ancient Greeks, continued the argument into the fourth century BCE. Plato was a dualist, whereas his student Aristotle joined the body and soul in his attempt to explain memory, emotions, and reasoning.

Defending either position was not easy. The dualists had to explain how a nonphysical mind could influence a physical body, and monists had the task of explaining how the physical brain could account for mental processes such as perception and conscious experience. But the mind was not observable, and even the vaguest understanding of nerve functioning was not achieved until the 1800s, so neither side had much ammunition for the fight.

■ **FIGURE 1.2**   Wilhelm Wundt (1832–1920).

Source: Weltrundschau zu Reclams Universum 1902.

 How do monists and dualists disagree on the mind-brain question?

The nature of the mind and soul is bodily.

—*Lucretius, c. 50 BCE*

What we call our minds is simply a way of talking about the functions of our brains.

—*Francis Crick, 1966*

Descartes and the Physical Model of Behavior

Scientists often resort to the use of models to understand whatever they are studying. A *model* is a proposed mechanism for how something works. Sometimes, a model is in the form of a theory, such as Charles Darwin's explanation that a species developed new capabilities because the capability enhanced the individual's survival and opportunity to reproduce. Other times, the model is a simpler organism or system that researchers study in an attempt to understand a more complex one. For example, researchers have used the rat to model everything from learning to Alzheimer's disease in humans, and the computer has often served as a model of cognitive processes.

In the 17th century, the French philosopher and physiologist René Descartes (Figure 1.3a) used a hydraulic model to explain the brain's activity (Descartes, 1662/1984). Descartes's choice of a hydraulic

 What is a model in science, and how is it useful?

■ **FIGURE 1.3**   Descartes (1596–1650) and the Hydraulic Model.

Descartes believed that behavior was controlled by animal spirits flowing through the nerves.

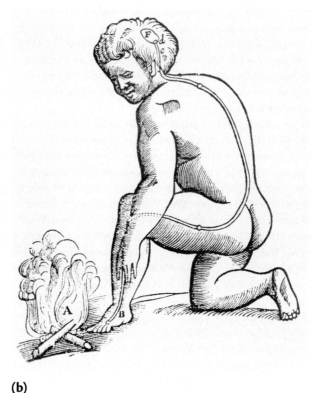

(a)   **(b)**

Sources: (a) Courtesy of the National Library of Medicine. (b) Bettmann/Getty Images.

model was influenced by his observation of the statues in the royal gardens at St. Germain. When a visitor stepped on certain tiles, the pressure forced water through tubes to the statues and made them move. Using this model, Descartes then reasoned that the nerves were also hollow tubes. The fluid they carried was not water, but what he called "animal spirits"; these flowed from the brain and inflated the muscles to produce movement. Sensations, memories, and other mental functions were produced as animal spirits flowed through "pores" in the brain. The animal spirits were pumped through the brain by the pineal gland (Figure 1.3b). Descartes's choice of the pineal gland was based on his conclusion that it was at a perfect location to serve this function. Attached just below the two cerebral hemispheres by its flexible stalk, it appeared capable of bending at different angles to direct the flow of animal spirits into critical areas of the brain. Thus, for Descartes, the pineal gland became the "seat of the soul," the place where the mind interacted with the body. Although Descartes assigned control to the mind, his unusual emphasis on the physical explanation of behavior foreshadowed the physiological approach that would soon follow.

Descartes lacked an understanding of how the brain and body worked, so he relied on a small amount of anatomical knowledge and a great deal of speculation. His hydraulic model not only represented an important shift in thinking; it also illustrates the fact that a model or a theory can lead us astray, at least temporarily. Fortunately, this was the age of the Renaissance, a time not only of artistic expansion and world exploration but also of scientific curiosity. Thinkers began to test their ideas through direct observation and experimental manipulation as the Renaissance gave birth to science. In other words, they adopted the method of *empiricism*, which means that they gathered their information through observation rather than logic, intuition, or other means. Progress was slow, but two critically important principles would emerge as the early scientists ushered in the future.

? What two discoveries furthered the early understanding of the brain?

Helmholtz and the Electrical Brain

In the late 1700s, the Italian physiologist Luigi Galvani showed that he could make a frog's leg muscle twitch by stimulating the attached nerve with electricity, even after the nerve and muscle had been removed from the frog's body. A century later in Germany, Gustav Fritsch and Eduard Hitzig (1870) produced movement in dogs by electrically stimulating their exposed brains. What these scientists showed was that animal spirits were not responsible for movement; instead, the cause was *nerves operated by electricity!* But the German physicist and physiologist Hermann von Helmholtz (Figure 1.4) demonstrated that nerves do not behave like wires conducting electricity. He was able to measure the speed of conduction in nerves, and his calculation of about 90 feet/second (27.4 meters/second) fell far short of the speed of electricity, which travels through wires at the speed of light (186,000 miles/second or 299,000 kilometers/second). It was obvious that researchers were dealing with a biological phenomenon and that the functioning of nerves and of the brain was open to scientific study. Starting from this understanding, Helmholtz's studies of vision and hearing gave "psychologists their first clear idea of what a fully mechanistic 'mind' might look like" (Fancher, 1979, p. 41). As you will see in later chapters, Helmholtz's ideas were so insightful that even today we refer to his theories of vision and hearing as a starting point before describing the current ones.

The Localization Issue

The second important principle to come out of this period—localization—emerged over the first half of the 19th century. *Localization* is the idea that specific areas of the brain carry out specific functions. Fritsch and Hitzig's studies with dogs gave objective confirmation to physicians' more casual observations dating as far back as 17th-century BCE Egypt (Breasted, 1930), but it was two medical case studies that really grabbed the attention of the scientific community. In 1848, Phineas Gage, a railroad construction foreman, was injured when a dynamite blast drove an iron rod through his skull and the frontal lobes of his brain (see Chapter 3). Amazingly, he survived with no impairment of his intelligence, memory, speech, or movement. But he became irresponsible and profane and was unable to abide by social conventions (H. Damasio, Grabowski, Frank, Galaburda, & Damasio, 1994). Then, in 1861, the French physician Paul Broca (Figure 1.5) performed an autopsy on the brain of a man who had lost the ability to speak after a stroke. The autopsy showed that damage was limited to an area on the left side of his brain now known as Broca's area (Broca, 1861).

By the mid-1880s, additional observations like these had convinced researchers about localization (along with some humorists, as the quote from Mark Twain shows). But a few brain theorists were already taking the principle of localization too far, and we should be on guard lest we make the same mistake. At the end of the 18th century, when interest in the brain's role in behavior was really heating up, the German anatomist Franz Gall had come up with an extreme and controversial theory of brain localization. According to *phrenology,* each of 35 different "faculties" of emotion and intellect—such as combativeness, inhabitiveness (love of home), calculation, and order—was located in a precise area of the brain (Spurzheim, 1908). Gall and his student Spurzheim determined this by feeling bumps on people's skulls and relating any protuberances to the individual's characteristics (Figure 1.6). Others, such as Karl Lashley (1929), took an equally extreme position at the other end of the spectrum; *equipotentiality* is the idea that the brain functions as an undifferentiated whole. According to this view, the extent of damage, not the location, determines how much function is lost.

We now know that bumps on the skull have nothing to do with the size of the brain structures beneath and that most of the characteristics Gall and Spurzheim identified have no particular meaning at the physiological level. But we also know that the brain is not equipotential. The truth, as is often the case, lies somewhere between these two extremes.

FIGURE 1.4   Hermann von Helmholtz (1821–1894).

Source: INTERFOTO/Alamy.

> *I never could keep a promise. . . . It is likely that such a liberal amount of space was given to the organ which enables me to make promises that the organ which should enable me to keep them was crowded out.*
>
> —Mark Twain,
> in Innocents Abroad

FIGURE 1.5   Paul Broca (1824–1880).

Source: Wikimedia Commons.

■ **FIGURE 1.6**   A Phrenologist's Map of the Brain.

Phrenologists believed that the psychological characteristics shown here were controlled by the respective brain areas.

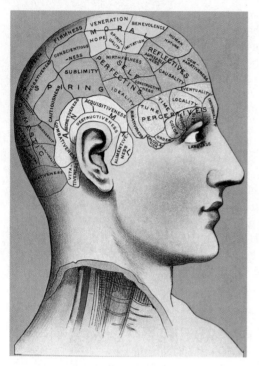

Source: Bettmann/Getty Images.

Today's research tells us that functions are as much *distributed* as they are localized; behavior results from the interaction of many widespread areas of the brain. In later chapters, you will see examples of cooperative relationships among brain areas in language, visual perception, emotional behavior, motor control, and learning. In fact, you will learn that neuroscientists these days are less likely to ask where a function is located than to ask how the brain integrates activity from several areas into a single experience or behavior. Nevertheless, the locationists strengthened the monist position by showing that language, emotion, motor control, and so on are controlled by *relatively* specific locations in the brain (Figure 1.7). This meant that the mind ceased being *the explanation* and became *the phenomenon to be explained.*

Understand that the nature and role of the mind are still debated in some quarters. For example, some neuroscientists believe that brain research will be unable to explain how a material brain can generate conscious experience, and that this will spell the final doom of materialism. These nonmaterial neuroscientists interpret the brain changes that occur during behavior therapy as evidence of the mind changing the brain (J. M. Schwartz, Stoessel, Baxter, Martin, & Phelps, 1996; see Chapter 14). Of course, what material neuroscientists see is the brain changing the brain (Gefter, 2008). Neuroscience has been able to explain a great deal of behavior without any reference to a nonmaterial mind, and as you explore the rest of this text you will begin to see why most brain scientists would describe themselves as material monists.

■ **FIGURE 1.7**   Some of the Brain's Functional Areas.

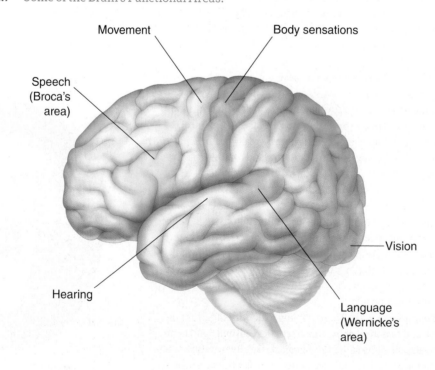

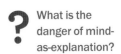

? What is the danger of mind-as-explanation?

Take a Minute to Check Your Knowledge and Understanding

- What change in method separated science from philosophy?
- What were the important implications of the discoveries that nerve conduction is electrical and that specific parts of the brain have (more or less) specific functions?
- Where do scientists stand on the localization issue?

Nature and Nurture

A second extremely important issue in understanding the biological bases of behavior is the *nature versus nurture* question, or how important heredity is relative to environmental influences in shaping behavior. Like the mind-brain issue, this is one of the more controversial topics in psychology, at least as far as public opinion is concerned. The arguments are based on emotion and values almost as often as they appeal to

? How are characteristics inherited?

evidence and reason. For example, some critics complain that attributing behavior to heredity is just a form of excusing actions for which the person or society should be held accountable. A surprising number of behaviors are turning out to have some degree of hereditary influence, so you will encounter this issue again in later chapters. Because there is so much confusion about heredity, we need to be sure you understand what it means to say that a behavior is hereditary before we go any further.

The Genetic Code

The *gene* is the biological unit that directs cellular processes and transmits inherited characteristics. Most genes are found on the chromosomes, which are located in the nucleus of each cell, but there are also a few genes in structures outside the nucleus, called mitochondria. Each body cell in a human has 46 chromosomes, arranged in 23 pairs (Figure 1.8). Each pair is iden-

■ **FIGURE 1.8** A Set of Human Chromosomes.

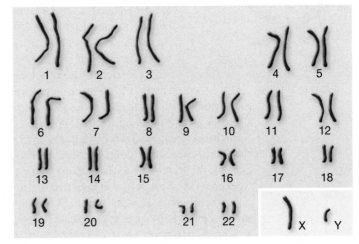

Sex chromosomes

Source: U.S. National Library of Medicine.

tifiably distinct from every other pair. This is important, because genes for different functions are found on specific chromosomes. The chromosomes are referred to by number, except for the sex chromosomes; in mammals, females have two X chromosomes, while males typically have an X and a Y chromosome. Notice that the members of a pair of chromosomes are similar to each other, again with the exception that the Y chromosome is much shorter than the X chromosome.

Unlike the body cells, the male's sperm cells and the female's ova (egg cells) each have 23 chromosomes. When these sex cells are formed by the division of their parent cells, the pairs of chromosomes separate so that each daughter cell receives only one chromosome from each pair. When the sperm enters the ovum during fertilization, the chromosomes of the two cells merge to restore the number to 46. The fertilized egg, or *zygote*, then undergoes rapid cell division and development on its way to becoming a functioning organism. For the first eight weeks (in humans), the new organism is referred to as an *embryo*, and from then until birth, as a *fetus*.

The mystery of how genes carry their genetic instructions began to yield to researchers in 1953, when James Watson and Francis Crick published a proposed structure for the deoxyribonucleic acid that genes are made of. *Deoxyribonucleic acid (DNA)* is a double-stranded chain of chemical molecules that looks like a ladder that has been twisted around itself; this is why DNA is often referred to as a *double helix* (Figure 1.9). Each rung of the ladder is composed of two of the four nucleotides—adenine, thymine, guanine, and cytosine

■ **FIGURE 1.9** Structure of a Strand of DNA.

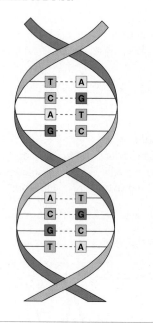

(A, T, G, C). The order in which these nucleotides appear on the ladder forms the code that carries all our genetic information. The four-letter alphabet these nucleotides provide is adequate to spell out the instructions for every structure and function in your body. How is a microscopic structure capable of such a daunting task? The accompanying Application will help you appreciate the remarkable complexity of DNA.

We only partially understand how genes control the development of the body and its activities, as well as how they influence many aspects of behavior. However, we do know that genes exert their influence in a deceptively simple manner: They provide the directions for making proteins. Some of these proteins are used in the construction of the body, and others are enzymes; enzymes act as catalysts, modifying chemical reactions in the body. It is estimated that humans differ among themselves in the sequences of nucleotides that make up our DNA by only about 0.5% (S. Levy et al., 2007); however, you will see throughout this text that this variation leads to enormous differences in development and behavior.

Because all but two of the chromosomes are paired, most genes are as well; a gene on one chromosome is paired with a gene for the same function on the other chromosome. The exception is that the shorter Y chromosome has only 1/25th as many genes as the X chromosome. Although paired genes have the same type of function, their effects often differ; these different versions of a gene are called *alleles*. In some cases the effects of the two alleles blend to produce a result; for example, a person with the allele for type A blood on one chromosome and the allele for type B blood on the other will have type AB blood.

In other cases, one allele of a gene may be dominant over the other. A *dominant* allele will produce its effect regardless of which allele it is paired with on the other chromosome; a *recessive* allele will have an influence only when it is paired with the same allele. Figure 1.10 illustrates this point. In the example, note that one parent is *heterozygous* for the blood type B allele, which means that the two alleles are different; the other parent is heterozygous for the blood type A allele. The A and B alleles are dominant over the o allele; as a result, each blood type (A, B, AB, or O) has an equal chance (one in four) of occurring in an offspring. Individuals with the same *phenotype* (an observable characteristic like blood type B) may differ by *genotype* (combinations of alleles like B and B, or B and O). You can see in the figure that A and B type parents have a one in four chance of having a child with different blood types; one of which will be *homozygous* (receiving two identical alleles) for the recessive o allele.

In the case of unpaired genes on the X chromosome, a recessive gene alone is adequate to produce an effect because it is not opposed by a dominant gene. A characteristic produced by an unpaired gene on the X chromosome is referred to as *X-linked*. With such a large discrepancy in the number of genes on the X and Y chromosomes, you can understand the potential for effects from X linkage. One example is that males are eight times more likely than females to have a deficiency in red-green color vision. See Chapter 10 for more on this deficiency.

Some characteristics—such as blood type and the degenerative brain disorder Huntington's disease—result from a single pair of genes, but many characteristics are determined by several genes; they are *polygenic*. Height is polygenic, and most behavioral characteristics such as intelligence and psychological disorders are also controlled by a large number of genes.

We have known from ancient times that animals could be bred for desirable behavioral characteristics such as hunting ability or a mild temperament that made them suitable as pets. Darwin helped establish the idea that behavioral traits can be inherited in humans as well, but the idea fell into disfavor as an emphasis on learning as the major influence on behavior became increasingly fashionable. In the 1960s and 1970s, however, the tide of strict environmentalism began to ebb, and the perspective shifted toward a balanced view of the roles of nature and nurture (Plomin, Owen, & McGuffin, 1994). By 1992, the American Psychological Association was able to identify genetics as one of the themes that best represent the present and the future of psychology (Plomin & McClearn, 1993).

Of the behavioral traits that fall under genetic influence, intelligence is the most investigated. Most of the behavioral disorders, including alcoholism and drug addiction, schizophrenia, major mood disorders, and anxiety, are partially hereditary as well (McGue & Bouchard, 1998). The same can be said for some personality characteristics (T. J. Bouchard, 1994) and sexual orientation (J. M. Bailey & Pillard, 1991; J. M. Bailey, Pillard, Neale, & Agyei, 1993; Kirk, Bailey, Dunne, & Martin, 2000).

However, you should exercise caution in thinking about these genetic effects. Genes do not provide a script for behaving intelligently or instructions for homosexual behavior. They control the production of

? Why do males more often show characteristics that are caused by recessive genes?

? What are some of the inheritable behaviors?

■ **FIGURE 1.10** Blood Types in the Offspring of Two Sets of Parents With Type A Blood.

The circles in the boxes indicate the genotypes of the parents whose genes are indicated on the outside. The text below the circles indicates the offspring's phenotype. Because the type A and type B alleles are dominant over the o allele, the A/o parent has type A blood and the B/o parent has type B. Each offspring will receive one allele from each parent, and their alleles can produce four different blood types; each of these blood types has an equal chance (one in four) of occurring in an offspring. Because the o allele is recessive, type O blood is possible only if the child is homozygous for o.

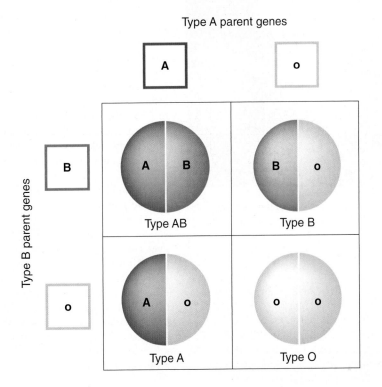

proteins; the proteins in turn affect the development of brain structures, the production of neural transmitters and the receptors that respond to them, and the functioning of the glandular system. We will offer specific examples in later chapters, where we will discuss this topic in more depth.

The Human Genome Project

After geneticists have determined that a behavior is influenced by genes, the next step is to discover which genes are involved. The various techniques for identifying genes boil down to determining whether people who share a particular characteristic also share a particular gene or genes that other people don't have. This task is extremely difficult if the researchers don't know where to look, because the amount of DNA is so great. However, the gene search received a tremendous boost in 1990 when a consortium of geneticists at 20 laboratories around the world began a project to identify all the genes in our chromosomes, or the human *genome*.

The goal of the *Human Genome Project* was to map the location of all the genes on the human chromosomes and to determine the genes' codes—that is, the order of bases within each gene. In 2000—just 10 years after the project began—the project group and a private organization simultaneously announced they had produced "rough drafts" (International Human Genome Sequencing Consortium, 2001; Venter et al., 2001); within another 5 years, the entire human genome had been sequenced (Gregory et al., 2006).

But when it comes to gene functioning, there is still more mystery than enlightenment. Only 21,000 of our genes—just 3% of our DNA—have turned out to be protein encoding (ENCODE Project Consortium, 2012). The lowly roundworm has 19,735 protein-coding genes (Hillier, Coulson, & Murray, 2005), so, clearly, the number of genes is not correlated with behavioral complexity. However, the amount of noncoding DNA—which we used to call noncoding DNA—*does* correlate with behavioral complexity (Andolfatto, 2005;

 What is the Human Genome Project, and how successful has it been?

Landing a person on the moon gave us an extraterrestrial perspective on human life . . . and now the human genome sequence gives us a view of the internal genetic scaffold around which every human life is molded.

—Svante Pääbo

APPLICATION
The Promise of DNA Computing

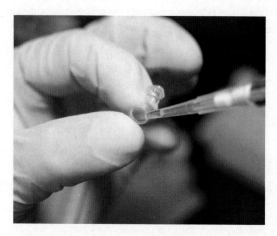

The pink blob of DNA in the end of the test tube could hold the entire content of 600 smartphones.

Source: Maggie Bartlett, National Human Genome Research Institute, National Institutes of Health.

Some researchers envision a day when computers will be constructed from DNA. They recognize that current technology is reaching size, heat, and speed limitations imposed by silicon-based components, and they believe DNA has several advantages. In one experiment, DNA strands performed basic computing operations almost three times as fast as the world's fastest supercomputer (Srivastava, 2003). DNA's small size so ideally suits it for parallel processing that just 1,018 strands could operate 10,000 times faster than today's supercomputers (J. Parker, 2003). Hypothetically, DNA could enable construction of a computer that would be able to investigate all possible solutions to a problem at the same time (Currin et al., 2017). Its capability would

be limited only by the amount of space it would take up and, since DNA is so dense, a blob the size of a sugar cube could store the data that would require a Walmart supercenter full of contemporary storage media. As a bonus, the life of the data would be centuries rather than the decades typical of current storage methods (Langston, 2016). But DNA computing on a grand scale won't be practical or cost-effective for some time. Ross King and his colleagues who study machine intelligence at the University of Manchester acknowledge the main problem is that they don't know how they can program these DNA computers . . . yet (Currin et al., 2017). Current efforts are focused instead on constructing relatively simple logic devices; these are the building blocks of computers, but their DNA versions could have useful applications on their own. For example, chemists at North Carolina State University have used DNA to construct an AND gate, a logic device that sends output only if both of its inputs are activated. Each input of their DNA version detects one of two genes that are biomarkers for multiple types of cancer; each of its two inputs is sensitive to one of the genes, and when both are activated the gate releases a fluorescent molecule (Hemphill & Deiters, 2013).

More recently, researchers in Singapore used DNA to construct a programmable multitasking processor that emulates a GPS device. On a map consisting of six locations and multiple possible routes, the processor can simultaneously determine the shortest routes between two starting points and two destinations (Shu, Wang, Yong, Shao, & Lee, 2015).

Siepel et al., 2005). So what is important about "junk" DNA? Some of it is, in fact, nonfunctional, remnants left behind during evolution. But 80% of the non-protein-coding DNA is biochemically active, and much of it controls the *expression* of other genes—the translation of their encoded information into the production of proteins, thus controlling their functioning (Pennacchio et al., 2006). For example, when a stretch of non-coding DNA known as *HACNS1*—which is unique to humans—is inserted into a mouse embryo, it turns on genes in the "forearm" and "thumb" (Figure 1.11; Prabhakar et al., 2008). DNA taken from the same area in chimpanzees and rhesus monkeys does not have that effect. The researchers speculate that the genes that *HACNS1* turns on led to the evolutionarily important dexterity of the human thumb.

A second question is what the genes do. The gene map doesn't answer that question, but it does make it easier to find the genes responsible for a particular disorder or behavior. For example, when geneticists were searching for the gene that causes Huntington's disease in the early 1980s, they found that most of the affected individuals in a large extended family shared a couple of previously identified genes with known locations

Do genes lock a person into a particular outcome in life?

on chromosome 4 whereas the disease-free family members didn't. This meant that the Huntington's gene was on chromosome 4 and near these two *marker* genes (Gusella et al., 1983). Actually finding the Huntington's gene still took another 10 years; now the gene map is dramatically reducing the time required to identify genes.

Identifying the genes and their functions will improve our understanding of human behavior and psychological as well as medical disorders. We will be able to treat disorders genetically, counsel vulnerable individuals about preventive measures, and determine whether a patient will benefit from a drug or have an adverse reaction, thus eliminating delays from trying one treatment after another. (See the accompanying Research Spotlight.)

Heredity: Destiny or Predisposition?

To many people, the idea that several, if not most, of their behavioral characteristics are hereditary implies that they are clones of their parents and their future is engraved in stone by their genes. This is neither a popular nor a comfortable view, and it creates considerable resistance to the concept of behavioral genetics. The view is also misleading; a hallmark of genetic influence is actually *diversity*.

Genes and Individuality

Although family members do tend to be similar to each other, children share only half of their genes with each of their parents or with each other. A sex cell receives a random half of the parent's chromosomes; as a result, a parent can produce 2^{23}, or 8 million, different combinations of chromosomes. Add to this the uncertainty of which sperm will unite with which egg, and the number of genetic combinations that can be passed on to offspring rises to 60 or 70 trillion! So sexual reproduction increases individuality in spite of the inheritability of traits. This variability powers what Darwin (Figure 1.12) called *natural selection*, which means that those whose genes endow them with more adaptive capabilities are more likely to survive and transmit their genes to more offspring (Darwin, 1859).

The effects of the genes themselves are not rigid; they can be variable over time and circumstances. Genes are turned on and turned off, or their activity is upregulated and downregulated, so that they produce more or less of their proteins or different proteins at different times. If the activity of genes were constant, there would be no smoothly flowing sequence of developmental changes from conception to adulthood. A large number of genes change their functioning late in life, apparently accounting for many of the changes common to aging (Ly, Lockhart, Lerner, & Schultz, 2000), as well as the onset of diseases such as Alzheimer's (Breitner, Folstein, & Murphy, 1986). The functioning of some genes is even controlled by experience, which explains some of the changes in the brain that constitute learning (C. H. Bailey, Bartsch, & Kandel, 1996). For the past quarter century, researchers have puzzled over why humans are so different from chimpanzees, our closest relatives, considering that 95%–98% of our DNA sequences are identical (R. J. Britten, 2002; M.-C. King & Wilson, 1975). Part of the answer appears to be that we differ more dramatically in which genes are *expressed*—actually producing proteins—in the brain (Enard et al., 2002).

Genes also have varying degrees of effects. Some determine the person's characteristics, whereas others only influence them. A person with the mutant form of the *huntingtin* gene *will* develop Huntington's disease, but most behavioral traits depend on many genes. For instance, a single gene will account for only a slight increase in intelligence or in the

■ **FIGURE 1.11**   Human Junk DNA Turns on Genes in a Mouse Embryo's Paw.

To determine where the DNA was having an effect, it was paired with a gene that produces a blue protein when activated. The blue area indicates that *HACNS1* is targeting genes in the area analogous to the human thumb.

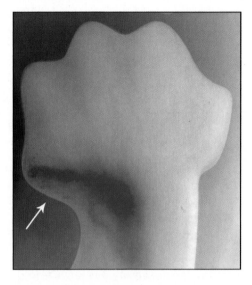

Source: From "Human-specific gain of function in a developmental enhancer," by S. Prabhakar et al., *Science*, 321, p. 1348. Reprinted with permission from AAAS.

■ **FIGURE 1.12**   Charles Darwin (1809–1882).

Source: From *Origins*, Richard Leakey and Roger Lewin.

RESEARCH SPOTLIGHT
Beyond the Human Genome Project

The completion of the Human Genome Project resulted in the successful sequencing of the 3 billion DNA base pairs of the human genome. The next logical steps included determining the functions of the genes and the remaining 97% of DNA, and turning this research knowledge into practical solutions and treatments that can benefit individual humans.

When the Human Genome Project ended in 2003, it was replaced by the Encyclopedia of DNA Elements (ENCODE) Project; its purpose is to determine all the functional elements of the human genome and make an initial assessment of what their functions are. Working at 32 institutions around the world, the project's teams had churned out more than 400 publications by 2012 (Maher, 2012; Pennisi, 2012); one of their surprising revelations was that 80% of the genome is biochemically active. In addition, ENCODE findings are already giving researchers new tools for understanding the etiology of a variety of diseases.

The Human Genome and ENCODE projects have catapulted us into a new era of genetic understanding (National Institutes of Health, 2016), but some geneticists believe the focus needs to be narrowed to the parts of the genes that direct protein production. These short sequences of DNA, or exons, make up the exome. The 180,000 exons of the human exome constitute only about 1% of the entire genome, so sequencing them is faster and cheaper, and scientists believe they contain 85% of all disease-causing mutations. Dutch scientists in 2012 reported that sequencing the exomes of 262 patients detected disease-causing mutations in half of the cases of blindness; 20% of the cases of intellectual disability; 20% of the deafness cases; and 15%–20% of the cases of movement disorders (European Society of Human Genetics, 2012). Lead researcher Marcel Nelen says that most of these patients have had "a long and worrying journey through different doctors and hospitals before they are diagnosed," and exome sequencing can shorten that route.

A methodological tool that evolved from the Human Genome Project is the genome-wide association study (GWAS). A GWAS study compares the genetic makeup of individuals who differ on a particular health condition. Over the past few decades, the health effects related to obesity have become increasingly obvious. G. Chen and colleagues (2017) hypothesized that there might be genetic factors in persons with African ancestry that account for the relatively higher rate of obesity seen in African Americans. Their genome-wide study found that individuals with a particular variant of the semaphorin-4D (*SEMA4D*) gene shared by 1% of continental Africans and African Americans average six pounds heavier than others without the allele.

risk for schizophrenia. The idea of risk raises the issue of vulnerability and returns us to our original question, the relative importance of heredity and environment.

Heredity, Environment, and Vulnerability

To assess the relative contributions of heredity and environment, we need to be able to quantify the two influences. *Heritability* is the percentage of the variation in a characteristic that can be attributed to genetic factors. There are various ways of estimating heritability of a characteristic. One technique involves a comparison of how often identical twins share the characteristic with how often fraternal twins share the characteristic. The reason for this comparison is that identical twins develop from a single egg and therefore have the same genes, while fraternal twins develop from separate eggs and share just 50% of their genes, like nontwin siblings. Heritability estimates are around 50% for intelligence (Devlin, Daniels, & Roeder, 1997), which means that about half of the population's differences in intelligence are due to heredity. Heritability has been estimated at 60%–90% for schizophrenia (Tsuang, Gilbertson, & Faraone, 1991) and 40%–50% for personality characteristics and occupational interests (Plomin et al., 1994). By way of comparison, the genetic influence on behavioral characteristics is typically stronger than it is for common medical disorders, as Figure 1.13 shows (Plomin et al., 1994).

Since about half of the differences in behavioral characteristics among people are attributable to heredity, approximately half are due to environmental influences. Keep in mind that heritability is not an absolute measure but tells us the proportion of variability that is due to genetic influence; the measure depends on the environmental circumstances of the group we're looking at as much as its genetic characteristics. For example, adoption studies tend to overestimate the heritability of intelligence because adopting parents are disproportionately from the middle class. Because the children's adoptive environments are unusually similar, environmental influence will appear to be lower and heritability higher than typical (McGue & Bouchard, 1998). Similarly, heritability will appear to be lower if we look only at a group of closely related individuals.

■ **FIGURE 1.13**   Twin Studies of Behavioral and Medical Disorders.

The concordance of (a) behavioral disorders and (b) medical disorders in identical and fraternal twins. Concordance is the proportion of twin pairs in which both twins have the disorder. Note the greater concordance in identical twins and the generally higher concordance for behavioral disorders than for medical disorders.

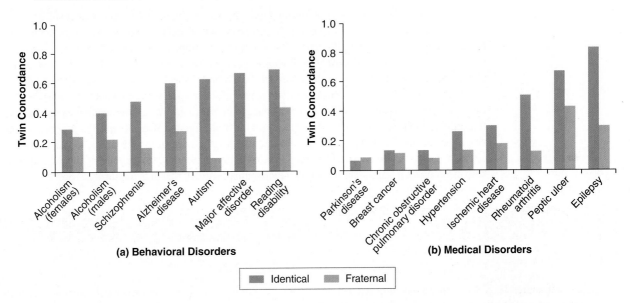

Source: From "The Genetic Basis of Complex Human Behavior," by R. Plomin, M. J. Owen, and P. McGuffin, *Science, 264*, p. 1734. © 1994 American Association for the Advancement of Science. Reprinted with permission from AAAS.

Researchers caution us that "we inherit dispositions, not destinies" (R. J. Rose, 1995, p. 648). This is because the influence of genes is only partial. This idea is formalized in the vulnerability model, which has been applied to disorders such as schizophrenia (Zubin & Spring, 1977). *Vulnerability* means that genes contribute a predisposition for a disorder, which may or may not exceed the threshold required to produce the disorder; environmental challenges such as neglect or emotional trauma may combine with a person's hereditary susceptibility to exceed that threshold. The general concept applies to behavior and abilities as well, though we wouldn't use the term *vulnerability* in those contexts. For example, the combination of genes a person receives determines a broad range for the person's potential intelligence; environmental influences then will determine where in that range the person's capability will fall. Psychologists no longer talk about heredity versus environment, as if the two are competing with each other for importance. Both are required, and they work together to make us what we are. As an earlier psychologist put it, "To ask whether heredity or environment is more important to life is like asking whether fuel or oxygen is more necessary for making a fire" (Woodworth, 1941, p. 1).

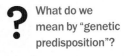

What do we mean by "genetic predisposition"?

With increasing understanding of genetics, we are now in the position to change our very being. This kind of capability carries with it a tremendous responsibility. The knowledge of our genetic makeup raises the question of whether it is better for a person to know about a risk that may never materialize, such as susceptibility to Alzheimer's disease. In addition, many people worry that the ability to do genetic testing on our unborn children means that some parents will choose to abort a fetus because it has genes for a trait they consider undesirable. Our ability to plumb the depths of the brain and of the genome is increasing faster than our grasp of either its implications or how to resolve the ethical questions that will arise. We will consider some of the ethical issues of genetic research in Chapter 4.

In Perspective

In the first issue of the journal *Nature Neuroscience,* the editors observed that brain science still has a "frontier" feel to it. The excitement of exploration is real and tangible, and the discoveries and accomplishments are remarkable for such a young discipline. The successes come from many sources: the genius of our intellectual ancestors, the development of new technologies, the adoption of empiricism, and, we believe, a coming to terms with the concept of the mind. Evidence of all these influences will be apparent in the following chapters.

Behavioral neuroscience still has a long way to go. For all our successes, we do not fully understand what causes schizophrenia, exactly how the brain is changed by learning, or why some people are more intelligent than others. The 1990s was declared the Decade of the Brain; Torsten Wiesel (whose landmark research in vision you will read about later) scoffed at the idea of dedicating a decade to the brain as "foolish. . . . We need at least a century, maybe even a millennium" (quoted in Horgan, 1999, p. 18). As you read the rest of this book, keep in mind that you are on the threshold of that century's journey, that millennium of discovery.

CHAPTER SUMMARY

The Origins of Behavioral Neuroscience

- Behavioral neuroscience (or biopsychology) developed out of physiology and philosophy as early psychologists adopted empiricism.
- Most psychologists and neuroscientists treat mind as a product of the brain, believing that mental activity can be explained in terms of the brain's functions.
- Localization describes brain functioning better than equipotentiality, but a brain process is more likely to be carried out by a network of structures than by a single structure.

Nature and Nurture

- We are learning that a number of behaviors are genetically influenced. One does not inherit a behavior itself, but genes influence structure and function in the brain and body in a way that influences behavior.
- Behavior is a product of both genes and environment. In many cases, genes produce a predisposition, and environment further determines the outcome.
- With the knowledge of the genome map, we stand on the threshold of unbelievable opportunity for identifying causes of behavior and diseases, but we face daunting ethical challenges as well. ■

STUDY RESOURCES

FOR FURTHER THOUGHT

- Why, in the view of most neuroscientists, is materialistic monism the more productive approach for understanding the functions of the mind? What will be the best test of the correctness of this approach?
- Scientists were working just as hard on the problems of the brain a half century ago as they are now. Why were the dramatic discoveries of recent years not made then?
- What are the implications of knowing what all the genes do and of being able to do a scan that will reveal which genes an individual has?

- If you were told that you had a gene that made it 50% likely that you would develop a certain disease later in life, what could you do with that knowledge?

TEST YOUR UNDERSTANDING

1. How would a monist and a dualist pursue the study of behavioral neuroscience differently?

2. What was the impact of the early electrical stimulation studies and the evidence that specific parts of the brain were responsible for specific behaviors?

3. The allele for type B blood is, like the one for type A, dominant over the allele for type O. Make a matrix like the one in Figure 1.10 to show the genotypes and phenotypes of the offspring of an AO parent and a BO parent.

4. A person has a gene that is linked with a disease but does not have the disease. We mentioned three reasons why this could occur; describe two of them.

5. Discuss the interaction between heredity and environment in influencing behavior, including the concept of vulnerability.

Select the best answer:

1. The idea that mind and brain are both physical is known as

   a. idealistic monism.
   b. materialistic monism.
   c. idealistic dualism.
   d. materialistic dualism.

2. A model is

   a. an organism or a system used to understand a more complex one.
   b. a hypothesis about the outcome of a study.
   c. an analogy, not intended to be entirely realistic.
   d. a plan for investigating a phenomenon.

3. Descartes' most important contribution was in

   a. increasing knowledge of brain anatomy.
   b. suggesting the physical control of behavior.
   c. emphasizing the importance of nerves.
   d. explaining how movement is produced.

4. Helmholtz showed that

   a. nerves are not like electrical wires because they conduct too slowly.
   b. nerves operate electrically.
   c. nerves do not conduct animal spirits.
   d. language, emotion, movement, and so on depend on the activity of nerves.

5. In the mid-1800s, studies of brain-damaged patients convinced researchers that

   a. the brain's activity was electrical.
   b. the mind was not located in the brain.
   c. behaviors originated in specific parts of the brain.

   d. the pineal gland could not serve the role Descartes described.

6. Localization means that

   a. specific functions are found in specific parts of the brain.
   b. the most sophisticated functions are located in the highest parts of the brain.
   c. any part of the brain can take over other functions after damage.
   d. brain functions are located in widespread networks.

7. X-linked characteristics affect males more than females because

   a. the X chromosome is shorter than the Y chromosome.
   b. unlike males, females have only one X chromosome.
   c. the responsible gene is not paired with another gene on the Y chromosome.
   d. the male internal environment exaggerates effects of the genes.

8. Two parents are heterozygous for a dominant characteristic. They can produce a child with the recessive characteristic

   a. if the child receives a dominant gene and a recessive gene.
   b. if the child receives two recessive genes.
   c. if the child receives two dominant genes.
   d. under no circumstance.

9. The Human Genome Project has

   a. counted the number of human genes.
   b. made a map of the human genes.
   c. determined the functions of most genes.
   d. cloned most of the human genes.

10. Heritability is greatest for

   a. intelligence.   b. occupational interest.
   c. personality.   d. schizophrenia.

11. If we all had identical genes, the estimated heritability for a characteristic would be

   a. 0%.   b. 50%.
   c. 100%.   d. impossible to determine.

1. b, 2. a, 3. b, 4. a, 5. c, 6. a, 7. c, 8. b, 9. b, 10. d, 11. a.

Answers:

ON THE WEB

The following websites are coordinated with this chapter's content. You can access these websites from the **SAGE edge Student Resources site**; select this chapter and then click on Web Resources. (**Bold** items are links.)

1. **Milestones in Neuroscience Research** traces the earliest roots of neuroscience with a timeline of events reaching back to 4000 BCE.

2. **Mind and Body** covers the history of the idea from René Descartes to William James. Most pertinent sections are I: 1–5 and II: 1–2.

3. You can search **Online Mendelian Inheritance in Man** by characteristic/disorder (e.g., schizophrenia), chromosomal location (e.g., 1q21–q22), or gene symbol (e.g., *SCZD9*) to get useful genetic information and summaries of research articles.

4. The Wikipedia article **Exome** includes links to descriptions of several research projects using exome sequencing.

The following journals are major sources of neuroscience articles (those that are not *open* access may require a subscription or university access):

Brain and Behavior (open access)

Brain, Behavior, and Evolution

Frontiers in Neuroscience (open access; also see related journals under "18 Sections")

Journal of Neuroscience

Nature

Nature Neuroscience

Nature Reviews Neuroscience

New Scientist (for the general reader)

PLoS Biology and *PLoS Genetics* (open access)

Scientific American Mind (for the general reader)

The Scientist (for the general reader)

Trends in Neurosciences

General information sites:

BrainFacts (various topics in neuroscience)

Brain in the News (neuroscience news from media sources)

The Human Brain (a collection of brain-related articles published in the magazine *New Scientist*)

Neuroguide (a small but growing offering of resources)

Science Daily (latest developments in science; see "Mind & Brain" and "Health & Medicine")

FOR FURTHER READING

1. "The Emergence of Modern Neuroscience: Some Implications for Neurology and Psychiatry," by W. Maxwell Cowan, Donald H. Harter, and Eric R. Kandel (*Annual Review of Neuroscience,* 2000, *23*, 343–391), describes the emergence of neuroscience as a separate discipline in the 1950s and 1960s, and details its most important accomplishments in understanding disorders.

2. "Neuroscience: Breaking Down Scientific Barriers to the Study of Brain and Mind," by E. R. Kandel and Larry Squire (*Science,* 2000, *290*, 1113–1120), is a briefer treatment of the recent history of neuroscience, with an emphasis on psychological issues; a timeline of events over more than three centuries is included.

3. *The Scientific American Brave New Brain*, by Judith Horstman (Jossey-Bass, 2010), describes how today's scientific breakthroughs will in the future help the blind to see and the deaf to hear, allow our brains to repair and improve themselves, help us postpone the mental ravages of aging, and give the paralyzed control of prosthetic devices and machinery through brain waves.

4. *Behavioral Genetics*, by Robert Plomin, John DeFries, Valerie Knopik, and Jenae Neiderhiser (Worth, 2012, 6th ed.), is a textbook on that topic; another text, *Evolutionary Psychology*, by William Ray (Sage, 2012), takes a neuroscience approach to the evolution of behavior.

5. "Tweaking the Genetics of Behavior," by Dean Hamer (available at http://apbio.savithasastry.com/Units/Unit%208/articles/cle_review_genesandbehavior.pdf), is a fanciful but thought-provoking story about a female couple in 2050 who have decided to have a child cloned and the decisions available to them for determining their baby's sex and her physical and psychological characteristics through genetic manipulation.

KEY TERMS

allele 8
behavioral neuroscience 2
deoxyribonucleic acid (DNA) 7
dominant 8
dualism 3
embryo 7
empiricism 4
equipotentiality 5
expression (of genes) 10
fetus 7
gene 7
genome 9
genotype 8
heritability 12
heterozygous 8
homozygous 8
Human Genome Project 9
localization 5
materialistic monism 3
mind-brain problem 3
model 3
monism 3
natural selection 11
nature versus nurture 7
phenotype 8
phrenology 5
polygenic 8
recessive 8
vulnerability 13
X-linked 8
zygote 7

⑤SAGE edge™   **edge.sagepub.com/garrett5e**

SAGE edge offers a robust online environment featuring an impressive array of free tools and resources for review, study, and further exploration, keeping both instructors and students on the cutting edge of teaching and learning.

1.1 Define the mind-brain problem in behavioral neuroscience.	▶ Understanding Consciousness
1.2 Describe the contributions of philosophers and scientists to the development of behavioral neuroscience as a field of study.	▶ Understanding Neurophysiology
1.3 Identify the role of physiologists in the establishment of modern-day behavioral neuroscience.	▶ Interview With Eric Kandel
1.4 Compare the relative contributions of genes and environment in the development of behavioral characteristics.	▶ How We Discovered DNA 📢 Inheritance: Nature-Nurture
1.5 Critique the fixed nature of heredity in shaping behavior.	📄 The Genetics of Success

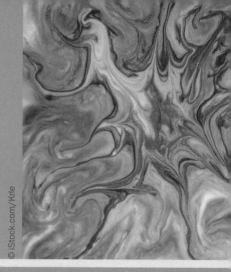

Part I

Neural Foundations of Behavior: The Basic Equipment

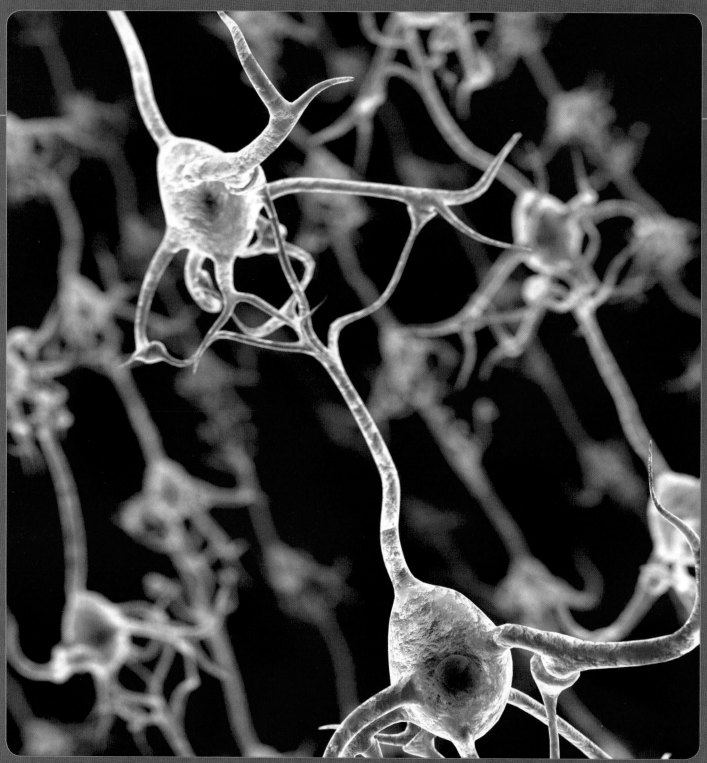

Communication Within the Nervous System

2

After reading this chapter, you will be able to:

- Identify the cells of the nervous system.

- Name the structures of neurons.

- Compare the functions of sensory, motor, and interneurons.

- Explain the roles of ions and the cell membrane in nervous system communication.

- Demonstrate how neurotransmitters are involved in communication between nervous system cells.

- Discuss how neurons work together to generate your experiences of the world.

- Illustrate the ways that excitation and inhibition are important to the functioning of the nervous system.

Things were looking good for Jim and his wife. She was pregnant with their first child, and they had just purchased and moved into a new home. After the exterminating company treated the house for termites by injecting the pesticide chlordane under the concrete slab, Jim noticed that the carpet was wet and there was a chemical smell in the air. He dried the carpet with towels and thought no more about it, not realizing that chlordane can be absorbed through the skin. A few days later, he developed headaches, fatigue, and numbness. Worse, he had problems with memory, attention, and reasoning. His physician referred him to the toxicology research center of a large university medical school. His intelligence test score was normal, but the deficiencies he was reporting showed up on more specific tests of cognitive ability. Jim and his wife had to move out of their home; at work, he had to accept reduced responsibilities because of his difficulties in concentration and adapting to novel situations. The chlordane had not damaged the structure of his brain as you might suspect, but it had interfered with the functioning of the brain cells by impairing a mechanism called the sodium-potassium pump (Zillmer & Spiers, 2001). Jim's unfortunate case reminds us that the nervous system is as delicate as it is intricate. Only by understanding how it works will we be able to appreciate human behavior, to enhance human performance, and to treat behavioral problems such as drug addiction and psychosis.

Master the content.
edge.sagepub.com/garrett5e

The Cells That Make Us Who We Are

To understand human behavior and the disorders that affect it, you must understand how the brain works. And to understand how the brain works, you must first have at least a basic understanding of the cells that carry messages back and forth in the brain and throughout the rest of the body. *Neurons* are specialized cells that convey sensory information into the brain; carry out the operations involved in thought, feeling, and action; and transmit commands out into the body to control muscles and organs. It is estimated that there are about 86 billion neurons in the human brain (Figure 2.1; Azevedo et al., 2009). This means that there are more neurons in your brain than stars in our galaxy. But as numerous and as important as they are, neurons make up only half of the brain's cells. The other half are glial cells, which we will discuss later in the chapter.

■ **FIGURE 2.1**   Estimated Numbers of Neurons in the Brain and Spinal Cord.

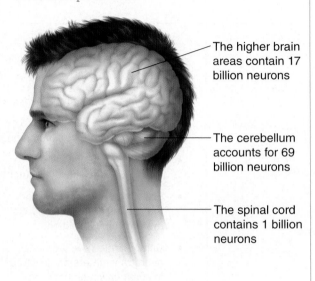

The higher brain areas contain 17 billion neurons

The cerebellum accounts for 69 billion neurons

The spinal cord contains 1 billion neurons

? What are the parts of the neuron?

■ **FIGURE 2.2**   Cell Body of a Neuron.

Part of the membrane has been removed to show interior features.

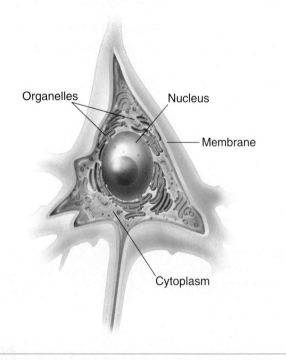

Organelles

Nucleus

Membrane

Cytoplasm

Neurons

Neurons are responsible for all the things we do—our movements, our thoughts, our memories, and our emotions. It is difficult to believe that anything so simple as a cell can measure up to this task, and the burden is on the neuroscientist to demonstrate that this is true. As you will see, the neuron is deceptively simple in its action but impressively complex in its function.

Basic Structure: The Motor Neuron

First let's look inside a neuron, because we want to show you that the neuron is a cell, very much like other cells in the body. Figure 2.2 is an illustration of the most prominent part of the neuron, the *cell body* or soma. The cell body is filled with a liquid called cytoplasm and contains a number of *organelles*. The largest of these organelles is the *nucleus,* which contains the cell's chromosomes. Other organelles are responsible for converting nutrients into fuel for the cell, constructing proteins, and removing waste materials. So far, this could be the description of any cell; now let's look at the neuron's specializations that enable it to carry out its unique role. Figure 2.3 illustrates a typical neuron. "Typical" is used guardedly here, because there are three major kinds of neurons and many variations within those types. The figure illustrates a *motor neuron*, which carries commands to the muscles and organs. It is particularly useful for demonstrating the structure and functions that all neurons have in common.

Dendrites are extensions that branch out from the cell body to receive information from other neurons. Their branching structure allows them to collect information from many neurons. The *axon* extends like a tail from the cell body and carries information to other locations, sometimes across great distances. The myelin sheath that is shown wrapped around the axon supports the axon and provides other benefits that we will consider later. Branches at the end of the axon culminate in swellings called *axon terminals.* The terminals contain chemical *neurotransmitters,* which the neuron releases to communicate with a muscle, an organ or the next neuron in a chain. In our examples, we will talk as if neurons form a simple chain, with one cell sending messages to a single other neuron, and so on; in actuality, a single neuron receives input from many neurons and sends its output to many others.

Neurons are usually so small that they can be seen only with the aid of a microscope. The cell body is the largest part of the neuron, ranging from 0.005 to 0.1 millimeter (mm) in diameter in mammals. (In case you are unfamiliar with metric measurements, a millimeter is about the thickness of a dime.) Even the giant neurons of the squid, favored by researchers for their conveniently large size, have axons that are only 1 mm in diameter. Typical axons are smaller; in mammals, they range from 0.002 to 0.02 mm in diameter. Axons may be as short as 0.1 mm or as long as 5 m in the tallest giraffes.

Other Types of Neurons

The second type of neuron is the sensory neuron. *Sensory neurons* carry information from the body and from the outside world into the brain and spinal cord. Motor and sensory neurons have the same components, but they are configured differently. A motor neuron's axon and dendrites extend in several directions from the cell body, which is why it is called a *multipolar* neuron. Sensory neurons can be either *unipolar* or *bipolar.* The sensory neuron in Figure 2.4a is called a unipolar neuron because of the single short stalk from the cell body that divides into two branches. Bipolar neurons have an axon on one side of the cell body and a dendritic process on the other (Figure 2.4b).

Motor and sensory neurons are specialized for transmission over long distances; their lengths are not shown here in the same scale as the rest of the cell.

The third type is neither motor nor sensory. *Interneurons* connect one neuron to another in the same part of the brain or spinal cord. Notice in Figure 2.4c that this neuron is also multipolar, but its axon appears to be missing; for some interneurons this is so, and when they do have axons, they are often so short that they are indistinguishable from dendrites. Because interneurons make connections over very short distances, they do not need the long axons that characterize their motor and sensory counterparts. In the spinal cord, interneurons bridge between sensory neurons and motor neurons to produce a reflex. In the brain,

■ **FIGURE 2.3**   Components of a Neuron.

The illustration is of a multipolar motor neuron.

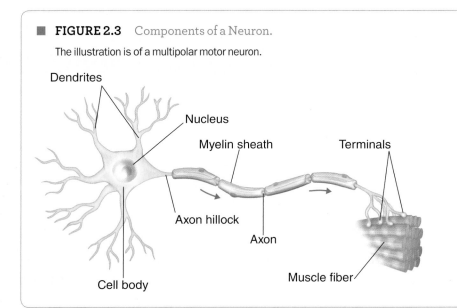

■ **FIGURE 2.4**   Sensory Neurons and an Interneuron.

Compare the location of the soma in relation to the dendrites and axon in these neurons and in the motor neuron.

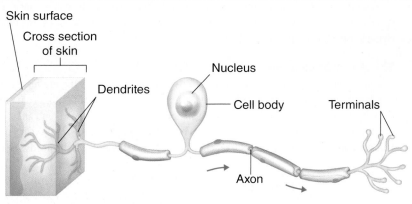

(a) Unipolar neuron (sensory)

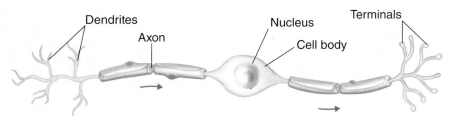

(b) Bipolar neuron (sensory)

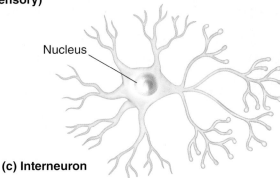

(c) Interneuron

TABLE 2.1   The Major Types of Neurons.

TYPE	FUNCTION	FORM AND LOCATION	DESCRIPTION
Motor	Conducts messages from brain and spinal cord to muscles and organs	Multipolar; throughout nervous system	Axon, dendrites extend in several directions from cell body
Sensory	Carries information from body and world to brain and spinal cord	Unipolar; outside brain	Single short stalk from cell body divides into two branches
		Bipolar; outside brain and spinal cord	Axon and dendritic processes are on opposite sides of cell body
Interneuron	Conducts information between neurons in same area	Multipolar; brain and spinal cord	Has short axon that communicates locally (with nearby neurons)

they connect adjacent neurons to carry out the complex processing that the brain is noted for. Considering the major role they play, it should come as no surprise that interneurons are the most numerous neurons.

The different kinds of neurons operate similarly; they differ mostly in their shape, which fits them for their specialized tasks. We will examine how neurons work in the next few sections. The types of neurons and their characteristics are summarized in Table 2.1.

The Neural Membrane and Its Potentials

? What accounts for the resting potential?

The most critical factor in the neuron's ability to communicate is the membrane that encloses the cell. The membrane is exceptionally thin—only about 8 micrometers (millionths of a meter) thick—and is made up of lipid (fat) and protein (Figure 2.5). Each lipid molecule has a "head" end and a "tail" end. The heads of the molecules are water soluble, so they are attracted to the seawater-like fluid around and inside cells. The tails are water insoluble, so they are repelled by the fluid. Therefore, as the heads orient toward the fluid and the tails orient away from the fluid, the molecules turn their tails toward each other and form a double-layer membrane.

The membrane not only holds a cell together but also controls the environment within and around the cell. Some molecules, such as water, oxygen, and carbon dioxide, can diffuse through the membrane freely. Many other substances are barred from entry. Still others are allowed limited passage through protein channels (shown in the figure in green) that open and close under different circumstances. This selective permeability contributes to the most fundamental characteristic of neurons, *polarization*, which means that there is a difference in electrical charge between the inside and outside of the cell. A difference in electrical charge between two points, such as the poles of a battery or the inside and outside of a cell, is also called a *voltage*.

The Resting Potential. Just as you would measure the voltage of a battery, you can measure a neuron's voltage (Figure 2.6). By arbitrary convention, the voltage is expressed as a comparison of the inside of the neuron with the outside. The difference in charge between the inside and outside of the membrane of a neuron at rest is called the *resting potential.* This voltage is negative and varies anywhere from −40 to −80 millivolts (mV) in different neurons but is typically

■ FIGURE 2.5   Cross Section of the Cell Membrane of a Neuron.

Notice how the lipid molecules form the membrane by orienting their heads toward the extracellular and intracellular fluids.

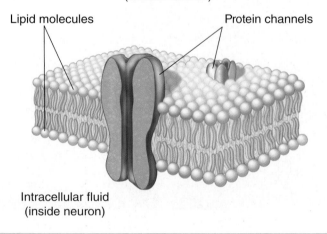

Extracellular fluid
(outside neuron)

Lipid molecules

Protein channels

Intracellular fluid
(inside neuron)

■ **FIGURE 2.6**   Recording Potentials in a Neuron.

Potentials are being recorded in the axon of a neuron, with an electrode inside the cell and one in the fluid outside. Due to the size of neurons, the electrodes have microscopically small tips. On the right, a highly magnified view shows the size of a microelectrode relative to that of neurons. Electrodes for recording inside neurons are even smaller.

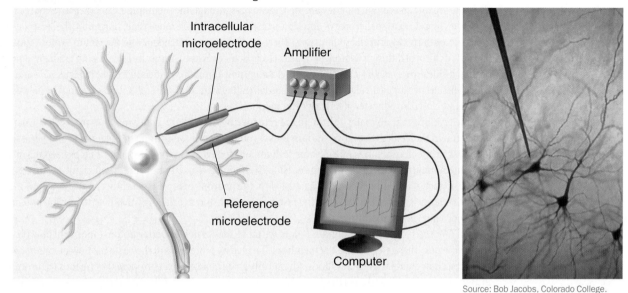

Source: Bob Jacobs, Colorado College.

around −70 mV. You should understand that neither the inside of the neuron nor the outside has a voltage, because a voltage is a *difference* and is meaningful only in comparison with another location. Note that this voltage is quite small—the voltage of a 1.5-V flashlight battery is 25 times greater. No matter; we're moving information, and very little power is required.

The resting potential is due to the unequal distribution of electrical charges on the two sides of the membrane. The charges come from *ions,* atoms that are charged because they have lost or gained one or more electrons. Sodium ions (Na^+) and potassium ions (K^+) are positively charged. Chloride ions (Cl^-) are negative, and so are certain proteins and amino acids that make up the organic anions (A^-). The fluid outside the neuron contains mostly Na^+ and Cl^- ions, and the ions inside the neuron are mostly K^+ and A^- (Figure 2.7). The inside of the neuron has more negative ions than positive ions, whereas the ions on the outside are mostly positive, and this makes the resting potential negative.

If you remember from grade-school science that molecules tend to diffuse from an area of high concentration to one of low concentration, then you are probably

■ **FIGURE 2.7**   Distribution of Ions Inside and Outside the Resting Neuron.

Ions on the outside are mostly Na^+ (red) and Cl^- (green) ions; inside, the ions are mostly K^+ ions (blue) and organic anions (dark green). In the middle of the membrane is an ion channel, which is closed and not allowing ions through; on the left, a sodium-potassium pump is discharging three Na^+ ions outside the neuron, while on the right an identical pump is returning two K^+ ions to the inside.

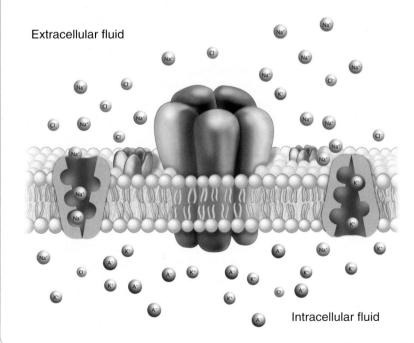

wondering how this imbalance in ion distribution can continue to exist. In fact, two forces do work to balance the location of the ions. Because of the *force of diffusion,* ions move through the membrane to the side where they are less concentrated. And, as a result of *electrostatic pressure,* ions are repelled from the side that is similarly charged and attracted to the side that is oppositely charged.

In spite of these two forces, a variety of other influences keep the membrane polarized. Both forces would move the organic anions out, but they are too large to pass through the membrane. Their negative charge then repels the chloride ions, so the force of diffusion is unable to move those ions inside. As a result, the "real players" then become the potassium and sodium ions. There is a slightly greater tendency for potassium to move outward (because its force of diffusion is stronger than its electrostatic pressure), while the force of both gradients attracts sodium inside. However, ions may cross the membrane only through channels like those in Figures 2.7 and 2.8, which are selective for particular ions. In the neuron's resting state, both the sodium channel and the potassium channel are closed, so only a few ions trickle through.

The few ions that do make it through are returned by the *sodium-potassium pump,* which consists of large protein molecules that move sodium ions through the cell membrane to the outside and potassium ions back inside. Its exchange rate of three sodium ions for every two potassium ions helps keep the inside of the membrane more negative than the outside. The pump is a metabolic process, which means that it uses energy; in fact, it accounts for an estimated 40% of the neuron's energy expenditure. But you will soon see that this energy is well spent, because the resting potential stores the energy to power the action potential, the major signal in the nervous system.

Ion Channels and Local Potentials. Before we move on, we need a better understanding of how the ion channels work. These are pores in the membrane formed by proteins, and they gate the flow of ions between the extracellular and intracellular fluids. Chemically gated channels can be opened by ligands (neurotransmitters or hormones), and electrically gated channels are opened by a change in the electrical potential of the membrane.

A neuron is usually stimulated by inputs that arrive on the neuron's dendrites and/or cell body from another neuron or from a sensory receptor. The effect may be excitatory or inhibitory, depending on the ligand and the characteristics of the receptors. An excitatory signal causes a slight partial depolarization, which means that the polarity in a small area of the membrane is shifted toward zero. This partial depolarization disturbs the ion balance in the adjacent membrane, so the disturbance flows down the dendrites and across the cell membrane. This looks at first like the way the neuron might communicate its messages through the nervous system; however, because a partial depolarization is decremental—it dies out over distance—it is effective over only very short distances. For this reason, the partial depolarization is often called the *local potential.* The ion channels in the axon are electrically gated, and they have unique physical properties. If the local potential exceeds the threshold for activating those channels, typically about 10 mV more positive than the resting potential, it will initiate an action potential.

Action Potentials. The *action potential* is an abrupt depolarization of the membrane that allows the neuron to communicate over long distances. The voltage across the resting neuron membrane is stored energy, just as the term resting *potential* implies. Imagine countless sodium ions being held outside the neuron against the combined forces of diffusion and electrostatic pressure (Figure 2.8a). A stimulus that partially depolarizes a segment of membrane causes voltage-gated sodium ion channels to open; this allows nearby sodium ions to rush into the axon at a rate 500 times greater than normal (Figure 2.8b). They are propelled into the cell's interior so rapidly that the movement is often described as explosive. A small area inside the membrane becomes fully depolarized to zero; the potential even overshoots to around +30 or +40 mV, making the interior at that location temporarily positive.

Just as abruptly as the neuron "fired," it begins to recover its resting potential. At the peak of the action potential, voltage sensors in the sodium channels detect the depolarization and close a gate, inactivating the channel and preventing further sodium ion influx (Catterall, 2010). The depolarization also causes voltage-gated potassium ion channels to open; the positive charge and the concentration of potassium ions inside the membrane combine to force potassium ions out. This outward flow of potassium ions returns the axon to its resting potential and a bit beyond (Figure 2.8c). The action potential lasts about 1 millisecond (one thousandth of a second); the actual duration varies among individual neurons. (Obviously, these channels are what make the neuron operate; the accompanying Application describes how they are exploited by nature and in research and medicine.)

Only the ions in a very thin layer on either side of the membrane have participated in the action potential; these dislocated ions diffuse into the surrounding fluid, and the membrane potential returns to its resting level (Figure 2.8d). Eventually, though, the ions must be returned to their locations or the neuron cannot continue firing; the sodium-potassium pump takes care of this. (Perhaps you can see now why Jim was in such a bad way after his bout with chlordane.)

? What is the role of the sodium-potassium pump following an action potential?

■ **FIGURE 2.8** Ion Movement and Voltages During the Neural Impulse.

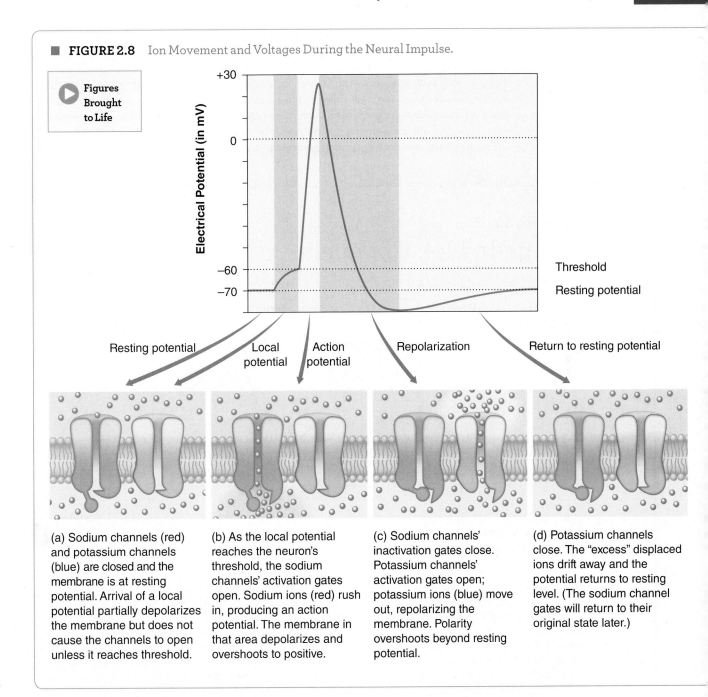

▶ Figures Brought to Life

(a) Sodium channels (red) and potassium channels (blue) are closed and the membrane is at resting potential. Arrival of a local potential partially depolarizes the membrane but does not cause the channels to open unless it reaches threshold.

(b) As the local potential reaches the neuron's threshold, the sodium channels' activation gates open. Sodium ions (red) rush in, producing an action potential. The membrane in that area depolarizes and overshoots to positive.

(c) Sodium channels' inactivation gates close. Potassium channels' activation gates open; potassium ions (blue) move out, repolarizing the membrane. Polarity overshoots beyond resting potential.

(d) Potassium channels close. The "excess" displaced ions drift away and the potential returns to resting level. (The sodium channel gates will return to their original state later.)

The depolarization that occurs during the action potential triggers nearby sodium channels to open as well. Thus, a new action potential is triggered right next to the first one. That action potential in turn triggers another farther along, creating a chain reaction of action potentials that move through the axon; thus, a signal flows from one end of the neuron to the other. Nothing physically moves down the axon. Instead, a series of events occurs in succession along the axon's length, much as a line of dominoes standing on end knock each other over when you tip the first one. When the action potential reaches the terminals, they pass the signal on to the next neuron in the chain (or to an organ or a muscle). The transmission of signals from neuron to neuron is covered later; for now, the action potential needs to be examined a bit further.

The action potential differs in two important ways from the local potential that initiates it. First, the local potential is a *graded potential,* which means that it varies in magnitude with the strength of the stimulus that produced it. The action potential, by contrast, is *ungraded*; it operates according to the *all-or-none law,* which means that it occurs at full strength or it does not occur at all. A larger graded potential does not produce a larger action potential; like the fuse of a firecracker, the action potential depends on the energy stored in the neuron, in this case due to the difference in ion concentrations between the two sides of the membrane.

How is an action potential different from a graded potential?

A second difference is that the action potential is *nondecremental*; it travels down the axon without any decrease in size, propagated anew and at full strength at each successive point along the way. The action potential thus makes it possible for the neuron to conduct information over long distances.

However, because the action potential is all-or-none, its size cannot carry information about the intensity of the initiating stimulus. One way stimulus intensity is represented is in the number of neurons firing. The voltage sensitivity of sodium channels varies among neurons, resulting in different thresholds; a more intense stimulus will recruit firing in neurons with higher thresholds and, therefore, in more neurons. There is, though, a way in which the individual neuron can encode stimulus strength, as you will see in the discussion of refractory periods.

 APPLICATION

Targeting Ion Channels

Modified Membrane Enables Light Control of Neuron Activity.

 Stories of Brain & Behavior

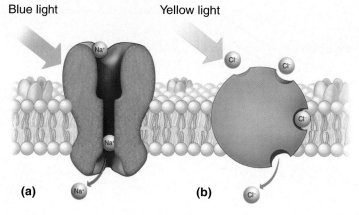

(a) Blue light activates a channel from green algae; the channel allows positive ions to flow inward, triggering neural impulses. (b) Yellow light activates a chloride pump from bacteria; chloride ions hyperpolarize the neuron.

Source: Adapted from "Controlling Neural Circuits With Light," by M. Häusser and S. L. Smith, 2007, *Nature*, 446, 617–619 (Figure 1a, p. 617).

The Japanese delicacy fugu, or puffer fish, produces an exciting tingling sensation in the diner's mouth; improperly prepared, it causes numbness and weakness and, in some cases, a paralysis of the respiratory muscles that has claimed the lives of a few thousand culinary risk takers. The fish's natural poison, tetrodotoxin (TTX), blocks sodium channels and prevents neurons from firing (Kandel & Siegelbaum, 2000a). Other *neurotoxins* (neuron poisons) are found in snake venoms, which block sodium, potassium (Benoit & Dubois, 1986; Fertuck & Salpeter, 1974), or calcium channels, and scorpion venom, which keeps sodium channels open, prolonging the action potential (Catterall, 1984; Chuang, Jaffe, Cribbs, Perez-Reyes, & Swartz, 1998; Pappone & Cahalan, 1987).

Interfering with neuron functioning can be useful, though; for example, most local anesthetics prevent neuron firing by blocking sodium channels (Ragsdale, McPhee, Scheuer, & Catterall, 1994), and some general anesthetics hyperpolarize the neuron by opening potassium channels and allowing the potassium ions to leak out (Nicoll & Madison, 1982; A. J. Patel et al., 1999). The cone snail of the South Seas can penetrate a wet suit with its proboscis and inject toxins that will kill a human in half an hour, but the various species' hundred or so toxins that target sodium, potassium, or calcium channels or block neurotransmitter receptors are in demand by researchers developing pain relievers and drugs for epilepsy (L. Nelson, 2004).

An exciting new research strategy known as *optogenetics* allows researchers to create light-responsive channels (as well as receptors) in neurons so that they can be controlled by light. Different types of channels are triggered by different wavelengths of light, which allows the researcher either to accelerate or to inhibit firing. The procedure is being used to understand the circuitry in a variety of behaviors and brain processes and is showing potential for use in therapeutic procedures.

Refractory Periods

With the sodium ion channels inactivated at the end of the action potential, the neuron cannot generate another impulse for a millisecond or so, a time referred to as the *absolute refractory period*. This delay in responsiveness has two important effects. First, the absolute refractory period limits how frequently the neuron can generate new action potentials. A neuron that requires a millisecond to recover can fire at most a thousand times a second; many neurons have much lower firing rate limits. A second effect of this recovery period is that the action potential can initiate new potentials only in the forward direction, not behind it. This is critical, because backward-moving potentials would "lock up" the neuron with a series of repeating action potentials traveling in both directions and block responses to newly arriving messages.

A second refractory period plays a role in intensity coding in the axon. The potassium channels remain open for a few milliseconds following the absolute refractory period. Although enough sodium ion channels have become active to support another action potential, the continued exit of potassium ions makes the neuron slightly more negative than usual (the "dip" in Figure 2.8). During the *relative refractory period*, another action potential can be generated, but only by a stronger-than-threshold stimulus. A stimulus that is greater than this temporarily higher threshold will cause the neuron to fire again earlier; with increasingly stronger stimuli the neuron will fire earlier and at a higher rate. Thus, the axon encodes stimulus intensity not in the size of its action potential but in its firing rate, an effect called the *rate law*.

What are the absolute and relative refractory periods?

Glial Cells

Glial cells are nonneural cells that provide a number of supporting functions to neurons. The name *glia* is derived from the Greek word for glue, which gives you some idea how the role of glial cells has been viewed in the past. However, glial cells do much more than hold neurons together. One of their most important functions is to increase the speed of conduction in neurons.

Myelination and Conduction Speed

Survival depends in part on how rapidly messages can move through the nervous system, enabling the organism to pounce on its prey, outrun a predator, or process spoken language quickly. The speed with which neurons conduct their impulses varies from 1 to 120 meters (m) per second (s), or about 270 miles per hour (435 km/hr). This is much slower than the flow of electricity through a wire (which can approach 300,000 km/hr), the analogy sometimes used to describe neural conduction. Because conduction speed is so critical to survival, strategies have evolved for increasing it. One way is to develop larger axons, which provide less resistance to the flow of electrical potentials. By evolving motor neurons with 0.5 mm thick axons, the squid has achieved conduction speeds of 30 m/s, compared with 1 m/s in the smallest neurons.

However, conduction speed does not increase in direct proportion to axon size. To reach our four-times-greater maximum conduction speed of 120 m/s, our axons would have to be $4^2 = 16$ times larger than the squid axon, or 8 mm in diameter (the size of a large pea)! Obviously, your brain would be larger than you could carry around. In other words, if axon size were the only way to achieve fast conduction speed, *you* would not exist. Vertebrates (animals with backbones) have developed another solution, myelination. Two types of glial cells produce *myelin,* a fatty tissue that wraps around the axon (like a jellyroll) to insulate it from the surrounding fluid and from other neurons. Only the axon is covered, not the cell body. Myelin is produced in the brain and spinal cord by a type of glial cell called *oligodendrocytes* and in the rest of the nervous system by *Schwann cells* (Figure 2.9). Almost 75% of the glial cells in the brain are myelin-producing oligodendrocytes (Pillay & Manger, 2007)

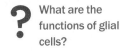

What are the functions of glial cells?

Because there are very few sodium channels under the myelin sheath, action potentials cannot occur there; conduction in myelinated areas is by graded potential (Waxman & Ritchie, 1985). However, myelin appears in segments about 1 mm long, with a gap of one or two thousandths of a millimeter between segments. The gaps in the myelin sheath are called *nodes of Ranvier* (see Figure 2.9). At each node of Ranvier, where the membrane is exposed and there are plenty of sodium channels, the graded potential triggers an action potential. Action potentials thus jump from node to node in a form of transmission called *saltatory conduction.*

This arrangement has three benefits. First, the insulating effect of myelin reduces an electrical effect of the membrane called capacitance. Because capacitance slows the movement of ions down the axon, the graded potential gets a big boost in speed. The overall effect of myelination is the equivalent of increasing the axon diameter 100 times (Koester & Siegelbaum, 2000). Second, the breaks in the myelination mean that

■ **FIGURE 2.9**   Glial Cells Produce Myelin for Axons.

A single oligodendrocyte provides myelin for multiple segments of the axon and for multiple neurons. A Schwann cell covers only one segment of an axon.

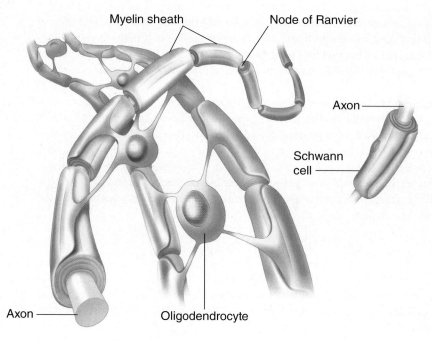

the signal is regenerated by an action potential at every node of Ranvier. Third, myelinated neurons use much less energy because there is less work for the sodium-potassium pump to do.

Some diseases, such as multiple sclerosis, destroy myelin. As myelin is lost, the capacitance rises, reducing the distance that graded potentials can travel before dying out. The individual is worse off than if the neurons had never been myelinated; because there are few voltage-sensitive sodium channels under the myelin sheath (Ritchie & Rogart, 1977), action potentials may not be generated in the previously myelinated area. Conduction slows or stops in affected neurons.

Other Glial Functions

There are several types of glial cells, and they make numerous contributions to neural functioning. During fetal development, radial glia form scaffolds that guide new neurons to their destinations. Later on, microglia provide energy to neurons and respond to injury and disease by removing cellular debris. Neurons form seven times as many connections in the presence of astrocytes, and they start to lose their synapses if astrocytes are removed from the culture dish (Pfrieger & Barres, 1997; Ullian, Sapperstein, Christopherson, & Barres, 2001; see Figure 2.10). Astrocytes also appear to play a key role in learning, as Figure 2.11 demonstrates (X. Han et al., 2013; Suzuki et al., 2011). Later in this chapter you will see that glial cells play a direct role in neural activity.

Mice receiving brain grafts of human glial cells rapidly learned a fear response ("freezing" to a tone which signaled an upcoming electric shock), while ungrafted controls showed little or no improvement.

CONCEPT CHECK

Take a Minute to Check Your Knowledge and Understanding

- How is information conducted in the axon?
- How does the all-or-none law limit information transmission?
- What benefits do the refractory periods provide?
- How does myelin speed up conduction in axons?

■ **FIGURE 2.10**   Glial Cells Increase the Number of Connections Between Neurons.

Neurons were cultured for 5 days in (a) the absence of glial cells and (b) the presence of glia. The number of neurons was similar in both cultures; the greater density on the right is due to increased connections among the neurons.

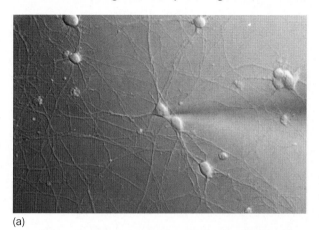

(a)

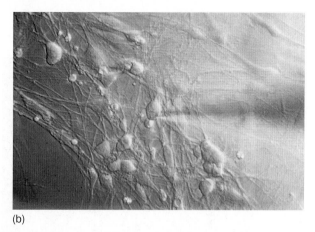

(b)

Source: From F. W. Pfrieger and B. A. Barres, "Synaptic Efficacy Enhanced by Glial Cells In Vitro," *Science*, Vol. 277, p. 1684, 1997. Reprinted with permission from AAAS.

How Neurons Communicate With Each Other

Before the late 1800s, microscopic examination suggested that the brain consisted of a continuous web. At that point, however, Camillo Golgi developed a new tissue-staining method that helped anatomists see individual neurons by randomly staining some entire cells without staining others (see the discussion of staining methods in Chapter 4). With this technique, the Spanish anatomist Santiago Ramón y Cajal (1937/1989) was able to see that each neuron is a separate cell. (See the accompanying In the News feature for more information about Ramón y Cajal's seminal work on describing the nervous system). The connection between two neurons is called a *synapse,* a term derived from the Latin word that means "to grasp." The neurons are not in direct physical contact at the synapse but are separated by a small gap called the *synaptic cleft.* Two terms will be useful to us in the following discussion: The neuron that is transmitting to another is called the *presynaptic* neuron; the receiving neuron is the *postsynaptic* neuron (Figure 2.12).

Chemical Transmission at the Synapse

Until the 1920s, physiologists assumed that neurons communicated by an electrical current that bridged the gap to the next neuron. The German physiologist Otto Loewi believed that synaptic transmission was chemical, but he did not know how to test his hypothesis. One night Loewi awoke from sleep with the solution to his problem (Loewi, 1953). He wrote his idea down so he would not forget it, but the next morning he could not read his own writing. He recalled that day as the most "desperate of my whole scientific life" (p. 33). But the following night he awoke again with the same idea; taking no chances, he rushed to his laboratory. There he isolated the hearts of two frogs. He applied electrical stimulation to the vagus nerve attached to one of the hearts, which slowed the heartbeat. Then he extracted a salt solution that he had placed in the heart beforehand to capture any chemical that might have been released. When he placed this salt solution in the second heart, that heart slowed, too, just as Loewi expected. Then he stimulated the accelerator nerve of the first heart, which

■ **FIGURE 2.11**   Human Glial Cells Enhance Conditioning in Mice.

Mice receiving brain grafts of human glial cells rapidly learned a fear response ("freezing" to a tone that signaled an upcoming electric shock), while ungrafted controls showed little or no improvement.

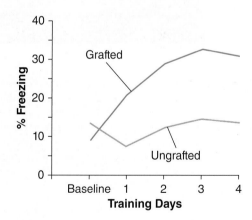

Source: Adapted from Figure 6B of "Forebrain Engraftment by Human Glial Progenitor Cells Enhances Synaptic Plasticity and Learning in Adult Mice," by Xiaoning Han et al., 2013, *Cell Stem Cell,* 12, p. 350.

IN THE NEWS
RAMÓN Y CAJAL'S WORK RECEIVED BY NEW AUDIENCE

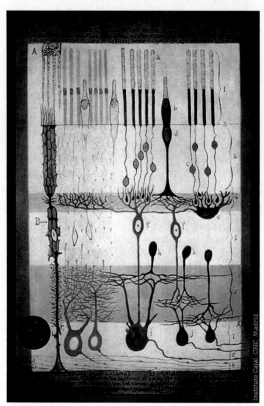

Paul Fearn/Alamy Stock Photo.

Santiago Ramón y Cajal's drawings of neurons have inspired neuroscientists for more than a century, but now they are touching a wider audience through an exhibition of his work at the Weisman Art Museum in Minneapolis (Hamilton, 2017). Although art and science are often portrayed as radically different disciplines, in the days before

microscopic photography, neuroanatomists relied on skilled artwork to portray what they observed of the nervous system. Ramón y Cajal had studied art and combined his skills not only to portray the structures he saw but also to alter our understanding of those structures. The scientific import of Ramón y Cajal's drawings has long been recognized, as evidenced by the 1906 Nobel Prize in Physiology or Medicine that he shared with Camillo Golgi for identifying the neuron as the main building block of the nervous system, but the artistry of his drawings received little prior attention. The "Beautiful Brain" exhibit and the related book, *The Beautiful Brain: The Drawings of Santiago Ramón y Cajal,* show how his drawings of neurons can provoke emotion, even in those with no training in the nervous system. Some of the drawings seem almost like trees, with dendritic spines extending out across the paper, while others show cell bodies looking like fruit. The exhibit's organizer, Lyndel King, also hopes that the exhibit will show people how art and science can work together to improve understanding.

THOUGHT QUESTIONS

1. How have Ramón y Cajal's drawings been important in the history of neuroscience?

2. In what ways do you think scientists and artists might be able to work together to promote knowledge?

For the news story and photographs of Ramón y Cajal's drawings, visit edge.sagepub.com/garrett5e and select the Chapter 2 study resources.

> *I awoke again, at three o'clock, and I remembered what it was. . . . I got up immediately, went to the laboratory, made the experiment . . . and at five o'clock the chemical transmission of the nervous impulse was conclusively proved.*
>
> —Otto Loewi

caused the heart to beat faster. When he transferred the solution from the first heart to the second, this time it speeded up (Figure 2.13). So Loewi demonstrated that transmission at the synapse is chemical and that neurons release at least two different chemicals that have opposite effects.

It turned out later that some neurons do communicate electrically by passing ions through channels that connect one neuron to the next; their main function appears to be synchronizing activity in nearby neurons (Bennett & Zukin, 2004). In addition, some neurons release a gas transmitter. Still, Loewi was essentially correct because most synapses are chemical. By the way, if this example suggests to you that the best way to solve a problem is to "sleep on it," keep in mind that such insight occurs only when people have paid their dues in hard work beforehand!

At chemical synapses, neurotransmitters are stored in the terminals in membrane-enclosed containers called *vesicles*; the term means, appropriately, "little bladders." When the action potential arrives at the terminals, it opens channels that allow calcium ions to enter the terminals from the extracellular fluid. The calcium ions cause the vesicles clustered nearest the membrane to fuse with the membrane. The membrane opens there, and the transmitter spills out and diffuses across the cleft in a process called *exocytosis* (Figure 2.14).

On the postsynaptic neuron, the neurotransmitter docks with specialized protein receptors that match the molecular shape of the transmitter molecules like a key in a lock (see Figure 2.14). Activation of these receptors causes ion channels in the membrane to open. *Ionotropic receptors* open the channels directly to produce the immediate reactions required for muscle activity and sensory processing; *metabotropic receptors* open channels indirectly and slowly to produce longer-lasting effects. Opening the channels is what sets

How does synaptic transmission differ from transmission in the axon?

off the graded potential that initiates the action potential. You will see in the next section that the effect this has on the postsynaptic neuron depends on which receptors are activated.

The chemical jump across the synapse takes a couple of milliseconds; that is a significant slowing compared with transmission in the axon. In a system that places a premium on speed, inserting these gaps in the neural pathway must have some compensating benefit. As you will see in the following sections, synapses add important complexity to the simple all-or-none response in the axon.

Excitation and Inhibition

Opening ion channels on the dendrites and cell body has one of two effects: It can cause the local membrane potential to shift in a positive direction toward zero, partially depolarizing the membrane, or it can shift the potential farther in the negative direction. Partial depolarization, or *hypopolarization,* is excitatory and facilitates the occurrence of an action potential; increased polarization, or *hyperpolarization*, is inhibitory and makes an action potential less likely to occur. The value of excitation is obvious, but inhibition can communicate just as much information as excitation does. Also, the message becomes more complex because input from one source can partially or completely negate input from another. In addition, inhibition helps prevent runaway excitation; one cause of the uncontrolled neural storms that sweep across the brain during an epileptic seizure is a deficiency in receptors for an inhibitory transmitter (Baulac et al., 2001).

What determines whether the effect on the postsynaptic neuron is facilitating or inhibiting? It depends on a combination of which transmitter is released and the type of

■ **FIGURE 2.12**   The Synapse Between a Presynaptic Neuron and a Postsynaptic Neuron.

Notice the separation between the presynaptic axon terminal and the postsynaptic neuron.

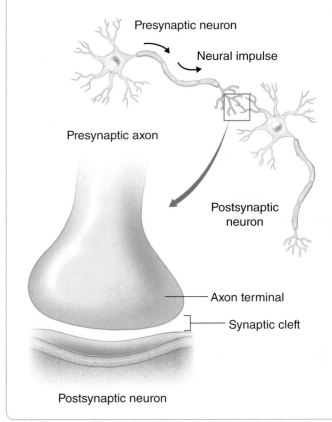

receptors on the postsynaptic neuron. A particular transmitter can have an excitatory effect at one location in the nervous system and an inhibitory effect at another; however, some transmitters typically produce excitation, and others most often produce inhibition. If the receptors open sodium channels, this produces hypopolarization of the dendrites and cell body, which is an *excitatory postsynaptic potential (EPSP)*. Other receptors open potassium channels, chloride channels, or both; as potassium moves out of the cell or chloride moves in, it produces a hyperpolarization of the dendrites and cell body, or an *inhibitory postsynaptic potential (IPSP)*.

At this point, there is only a graded local potential. This potential spreads down the dendrites and across the cell body to the *axon hillock* (where the axon joins the cell body). At the axon, a positive graded potential that surpasses threshold will produce an action potential; a negative graded potential will make it harder for the axon to fire. Most neurons fire spontaneously all the time, so EPSPs will increase the rate of firing and IPSPs will decrease the rate of firing (Figure 2.15). So now another form of complexity has been added at the synapse: The message to the postsynaptic neuron can be *bidirectional,* not just off-on.

What are the differences between an EPSP and an IPSP?

You should not assume that excitation of neurons always corresponds to activation of behavior or that inhibition necessarily suppresses behavior. An EPSP may activate a neuron that has an inhibitory effect on other neurons, and an IPSP may reduce activity in a neuron that has an inhibitory effect on other neurons, increasing their activity. An example of this paradox at the behavioral level is the effect of Ritalin. Ritalin and

■ **FIGURE 2.13**   Loewi's Experiment Demonstrating Chemical Transmission in Neurons.

Loewi stimulated the first frog heart. When he transferred fluid from it to the second heart, it produced the same effect there as the stimulation did in the first heart.

Stories of
Brain &
Behavior

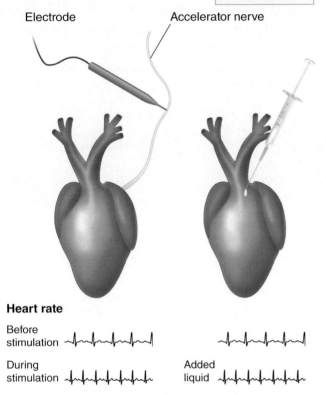

Electrode   Accelerator nerve

Heart rate

Before
stimulation

During
stimulation

Added
liquid

? What are summation and integration?

many other medications used to treat attention-deficit/hyperactivity disorder (ADHD) in children are in a class of drugs called stimulants, which increase activity in the nervous system. Yet they calm hyperactive individuals and improve their ability to concentrate and focus attention (D. J. Cox, Merkel, Kovatchev, & Seward, 2000; Mattay et al., 1996). They probably have this effect by stimulating frontal areas of the brain where activity has been found to be abnormally low (Faigel, Szuajderman, Tishby, Turel, & Pinus, 1995).

Next you will see that the ability to combine the inputs of large numbers of neurons expands the synapse's contribution to complexity even further.

Postsynaptic Integration

The output of a single neuron is not enough by itself to cause a postsynaptic neuron to fire or to prevent it from firing. In fact, an excitatory neuron may depolarize the membrane of the postsynaptic neuron by as little as 0.2 to 0.4 mV (Kandel & Siegelbaum, 2000b); remember that it takes an approximately 10-mV depolarization to trigger an action potential. However, a typical neuron receives input from approximately one thousand other neurons (Figure 2.16); because each neuron has numerous terminals, this amounts to as many as 10,000 synaptic connections in most parts of the brain and up to 100,000 in the cerebellum (Kandel & Siegelbaum, 2000a).

Because a single neuron has a relatively small effect, the postsynaptic neuron must combine potentials from many neurons to fire. This requirement is actually advantageous: It ensures that a neuron will not be fired by the spontaneous activity of a single presynaptic neuron, and it allows the neuron to combine multiple inputs into a more complex message. These potentials are combined at the axon hillock in two ways. *Spatial summation* combines potentials occurring simultaneously at different locations on the dendrites and cell body. *Temporal summation* combines potentials arriving a short time apart, from either the same or separate inputs. Temporal summation is possible because a local potential persists for a few milliseconds. Spatial summation and temporal summation occur differently, but they have the same result. Summation is illustrated in Figure 2.17.

As you can see in Figure 2.18, summation combines EPSPs so that an action potential is more likely to occur. Alternatively, summation of IPSPs drives the membrane's interior even more negative and makes it more difficult for incoming EPSPs to trigger an action potential. When both excitatory and inhibitory impulses arrive on a neuron, they will summate algebraically. The combined effect will equal the difference between the sum of the hypopolarizations and the sum of the hyperpolarizations. Spatial summation of two excitatory inputs and one inhibitory input is illustrated in Figure 2.19. The effect from temporal summation would be similar.

Because the neuron can summate inputs from multiple sources, it rises above the role of a simple message conductor—it is an *information integrator*. And, using that information, it functions as a *decision maker*, determining whether to fire or not. Thus, the nervous system becomes less like a bunch of telephone lines and more like a computer. In subsequent chapters, you will come to appreciate how important the synapse is in understanding how we see, how we learn, and how we succumb to mental illness.

Terminating Synaptic Activity

Usually, the transmitter must be inactivated; otherwise, it might "lock up" a circuit that must respond frequently, or leak over to other synapses and interfere with their functions. Typically, transmitters are taken back into the terminals by membrane proteins called transporters in a process called *reuptake;* they are repackaged in vesicles and used again. At some synapses, the transmitter in the cleft is absorbed by nearby astrocytes. Other transmitters are partially broken down through a process called inactivation. The neurotransmitter acetylcholine, for example, is inactivated by the enzyme acetylcholinesterase, which splits the molecule into its components of choline and acetate. Choline is then taken back into the terminals and used to make more acetylcholine.

Controlling how much neurotransmitter remains in the synapse is one way to vary behavior, and many drugs capitalize on this mechanism. Cocaine blocks the reuptake of dopamine; some antidepressant medications block the reuptake of serotonin, norepinephrine, or both, whereas others (*MAO inhibitors*) prevent monoamine oxidase from inactivating those transmitters as well as dopamine and epinephrine; and drugs for treating the muscular disorder myasthenia gravis increase acetylcholine availability by inhibiting the action of acetylcholinesterase.

Regulating Synaptic Activity

The previous description has been of a system that amounts to *"neuron A stimulates neuron B, neuron B stimulates neuron C,"* and so on. However, such a simple system cannot transmit the complex information required to solve a math equation, write a symphony, or care for a newborn. Not only that, but as messages flow from neuron to neuron, activity would soon drift out of control; some activity would fade out, while other activity would escalate until it engulfed an entire area of the brain. A nervous system that controls complex behavior must have several ways to regulate its activity.

The synapses described so far are referred to as *axodendritic* and *axosomatic* synapses, because their targets are dendrites and cell bodies. At *axoaxonic* synapses, a third neuron releases transmitter onto the terminals of the presynaptic neuron (see #1 in Figure 2.20). The result is *presynaptic excitation* or *presynaptic inhibition,* which increases or decreases, respectively, the presynaptic neuron's release of neurotransmitter onto the postsynaptic neuron. One way an axoaxonic synapse adjusts a presynaptic terminal's activity is by regulating the amount of calcium entering the terminal, which, you will remember, triggers neurotransmitter release.

Neurons also regulate their own synaptic activity in two ways. *Autoreceptors* on the presynaptic terminals sense the amount of transmitter in the cleft; if the amount is excessive, the presynaptic neuron reduces its output (Figure 2.20, #2). Postsynaptic neurons participate in regulation of synaptic activity as well. When there are

? What are the three ways of regulating synaptic activity?

■ **FIGURE 2.14**   A Presynaptic Terminal Releases the Neurotransmitter at the Synapse.

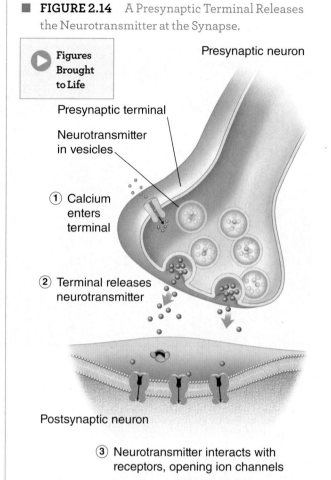

▶ Figures Brought to Life

Presynaptic neuron

Presynaptic terminal

Neurotransmitter in vesicles

① Calcium enters terminal

② Terminal releases neurotransmitter

Postsynaptic neuron

③ Neurotransmitter interacts with receptors, opening ion channels

■ **FIGURE 2.15**   Effect of Excitation and Inhibition on Spontaneous Firing Rate.

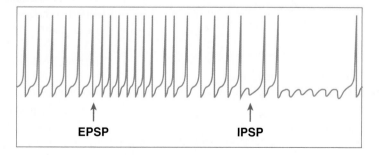

EPSP   IPSP

Source: Adapted from *Principles of Neural Science*, 4th ed., by E. R. Kandel et al., pp. 207–208. © 2002, McGraw-Hill Companies, Inc.

■ **FIGURE 2.16**   A Cell Body Virtually Covered With Axon Terminals.

Source: Dr. Don Fawcett/Visuals Unlimited/Getty Images.

■ **FIGURE 2.17**   Spatial and Temporal Summation.

Impulses arriving at different locations combine through spatial summation.

> **Stories of Brain & Behavior**

Impulses arriving a short time apart combine through temporal summation.

? What are two additional ways synapses add information complexity?

unusual increases or decreases in neurotransmitter release, postsynaptic receptors change their sensitivity or even their numbers to compensate (Figure 2.20, #3). You will see in Chapter 14 that receptor changes figure prominently in some psychological disorders, such as schizophrenia.

Glial cells also contribute to the regulation of synaptic activity. They surround the synapse and prevent neurotransmitter from spreading to other synapses, but some also remove neurotransmitter from the synaptic cleft and recycle it for the neuron's reuse (Figure 2.21). By varying the amount of transmitter they remove, glial cells influence postsynaptic excitability (Oliet, Piet, & Poulain, 2001). They can even respond to the neurotransmitter level in the synapse by releasing transmitters of their own. These gliotransmitters regulate transmitter release from the presynaptic neuron or directly stimulate the postsynaptic neuron to excite or inhibit it (M. Anderson & Hanse, 2010; E. A. Newman, 2003). Thus, rather than simply being neural "glue" as the name implies, glia should be considered active partners in neural transmission.

Neurotransmitters

Table 2.2 on page 40 lists twelve transmitters, grouped according to their chemical structure. This is an abbreviated list; there are other known or suspected transmitters, and there are doubtless additional transmitters yet to be discovered. This summary is intended to illustrate the variety in neurotransmitters and to give you some familiarity with the functions of a few of the major ones. You will encounter most of them again in the discussion of various behaviors in later chapters.

Having a variety of neurotransmitters multiplies the effects that can be produced at synapses; the fact that there are different subtypes of the receptors adds even more. For example, two types of receptors detect acetylcholine: the nicotinic receptor, so called because it is also activated by nicotine, and the muscarinic receptor, named for the mushroom derivative that can stimulate it. Nicotinic receptors are excitatory; they are found on muscles and, in lesser numbers, in the brain. Muscarinic receptors are more frequent in the brain, where they have an excitatory effect at some locations and an inhibitory one at others. Other transmitters have many more receptor subtypes than acetylcholine does.

For decades, neurophysiologists labored under the erroneous belief, known as *Dale's principle,* that a neuron was capable of releasing only one neurotransmitter. We now know that many neurons ply their postsynaptic partners with more than one chemical messenger (Vaaga, Borisovska, & Westbrook, 2014). These neurons may release two fast-acting neurotransmitters, a fast-acting neurotransmitter and a slow-acting monoamine, or a fast-acting neurotransmitter and a neuromodulator, which alters the effect of the transmitter. There is even evidence that some neurons release

■ **FIGURE 2.18**   Temporal and Spatial Summation.

An EPSP (point 1); temporal summation of two EPSPs (2); temporal summation of three EPSPs reaches threshold (3); spatial summation of EPSPs reaches threshold (4); an IPSP (5); temporal summation of two IPSPs (6).

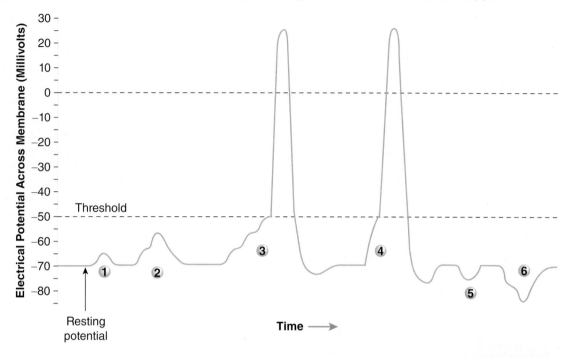

more than two neurotransmitters, for example, dopamine, gamma-amino-butyric acid (GABA), and glutamate.

The release can occur in three ways. In *corelease,* the transmitters are packaged in the same vesicles. However, this doesn't mean they're always released equally; in the example in Figure 2.22a, the fusion pores between the vesicle and terminal membranes have opened only partially, impeding the release of the larger messenger molecules while allowing the smaller molecules to exit freely (see M. Braun et al., 2007). In *cotransmission,* the transmitters are in separate vesicles. Vesicles containing different transmitters in the same terminal differ in sensitivity to calcium (Ca^{2+}); a low rate of neural impulses will trigger release of only one of the messengers, whereas a higher rate will release both of them (Figure 2.22b). Finally, the neuron may release different transmitters from its various terminals to produce different effects at separate destinations (Figure 2.22c).

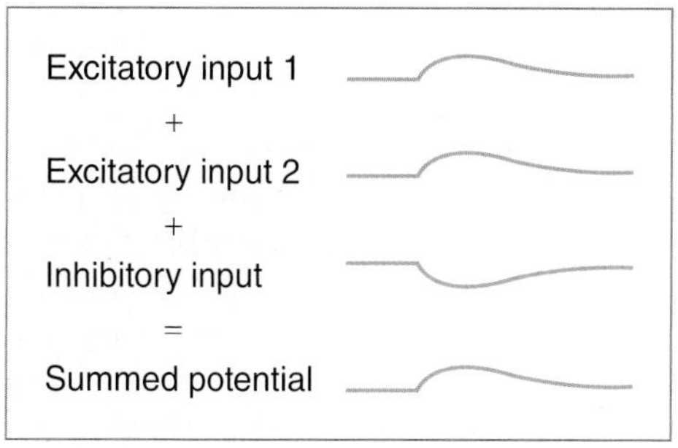

Corelease and cotransmission are not well understood, but we do know they play a significant role in neural functioning. For example, release of inhibitory GABA dampens the excitatory effects of glutamate during seizures (Trudeau, 2004) and counters the arousing effects of histamine to prevent hyperactivity and sustained wakefulness (Yu et al., 2015). In addition, direction-detecting cells in the retina of the eye release acetylcholine and GABA in response to any movement of a visual object, but they release only GABA when the movement is in the cell's "preferred" direction (Lee, Kim, & Zhou, 2010).

■ **FIGURE 2.19**   Spatial Summation of Excitatory and Inhibitory Potentials.

Note that inhibitory potentials cancel out excitatory potentials of equal strength (and vice versa).

Excitatory input 1
+
Excitatory input 2
+
Inhibitory input
=
Summed potential

Neural Codes and Neural Networks

Underlying this discussion has been the assumption that we can explain behavior by understanding what neurons do. But we cannot make good on that promise as long as we talk as if neural communication is limited to single chains of neurons that either fire or don't fire. In fact, neurons are capable of generating complex messages, which they send across intricate networks.

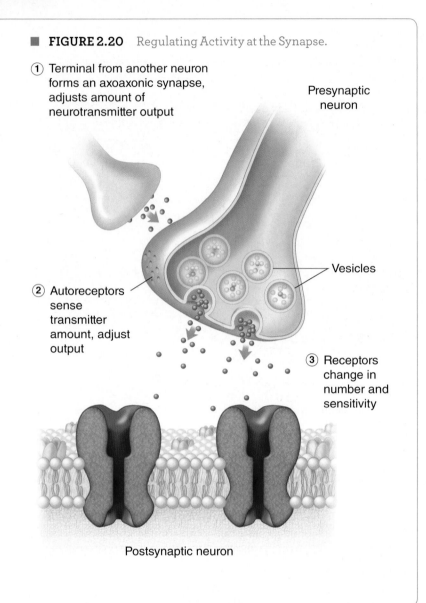

■ FIGURE 2.20 Regulating Activity at the Synapse.

① Terminal from another neuron forms an axoaxonic synapse, adjusts amount of neurotransmitter output

Presynaptic neuron

Vesicles

② Autoreceptors sense transmitter amount, adjust output

③ Receptors change in number and sensitivity

Postsynaptic neuron

Coding of Neural Messages

Neurons don't just produce a train of equally spaced impulses: They vary the intervals between spikes, they produce bursts of varying lengths, and the bursts can be separated by different intervals (Cariani, 2004). But do these temporal (time-related) variations in firing pattern form a code that the brain can use, or are they just "noise" in the system? The best way to answer this question is to look at sensory processes, because the researcher can correlate firing patterns with sensory input on one end and behavior on the other. A good example is an early study done by Patricia Di Lorenzo and her colleague Gerald Hecht (1993). First, they recorded the firing patterns in individual taste neurons of rats during stimulation with a sucrose (sugar) solution and quinine. As you can see in Figure 2.23a, these flavors produce different neural activity. Then they duplicated the temporal patterns in the form of electrical pulses (Figure 2.23b) and used these to stimulate the taste pathways of other rats. The assumption was that if the brain *uses* this information, the unanesthetized rats would behave as if they were actually *tasting* sweet sucrose or bitter quinine. As Figure 2.23c shows, that is exactly what happened: The rats licked a water tube at a high rate when they were receiving stimulation patterned after sucrose but almost stopped licking—even though they were water deprived—when the stimulation was patterned after quinine.

However, this coding apparently is not sufficient to carry the complex information involved in brain communication. An additional opportunity for coding is provided by the fact that neural information often travels over specialized pathways. For example, taste information is carried by at least five types of specialized fibers; Di Lorenzo and Hecht (1993) recorded the sucrose firing pattern from a "labeled line" specialized for sweet stimuli and the quinine pattern from another specialized for bitter stimuli. In later chapters, you will see that not only taste but also information about color and about the higher sound frequencies is transmitted over a limited number of labeled lines. However, even with temporal coding and labeled lines, a significant burden remains for the brain if it is to make sense of this information. This leads us to the topic of neural networks.

Neural Networks

Individual neurons cannot carry enough information to determine the taste of a bite of food or the color of an object. Color processing, for example, depends on four "labeled lines" carrying information about red, green, blue, and yellow light; we can distinguish millions of colors by comparing the relative activity in these four pathways. This kind of analysis requires complex interactions among a network of neurons. *Neural networks* are groups of neurons that function together to carry out a process; they are where the most complex neural processing—the "computing" work of the brain—occurs. Sometimes these networks involve a relatively small number of neurons in a single area, such as groups of neurons in a part of the rat's brain called the hippocampus. When rats navigate a maze, these networks store their preceding choices and calculate their next choice. The networks perform so reliably that the researcher can use their activity to predict which way the rat will turn after a delay (Pastalkova, Itskov, Amarasingham, & Buzsáki, 2008). As you will see in later chapters,

■ **FIGURE 2.21**   Glial Cell Interacting With Neurons at the Synapse.

An astrocyte, a type of glial cell, encloses the synapse, where it absorbs the neurotransmitter glutamate (Glu) from the synaptic cleft. It recycles the transmitter into its precursor glutamine (Gln) and returns the Gln to the presynaptic terminal for reuse. The glial cell can influence synaptic activity by granting or withholding transmitter absorption and by releasing its own transmitter in response to the neurotransmitter level in the synapse.

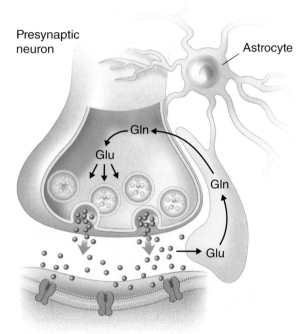

Source: Adapted with permission from "Energy on Demand," by P. J. Magistretti et al., 1999, *Science*, 283, p. 497. Copyright © 1999. Reprinted with permission from AAAS.

■ **FIGURE 2.22**   Neural Corelease and Cotransmission.

(a) In corelease, the neuron can limit exit of larger chemical messengers by partially opening the fusion pore. (b) When the messengers are in different vesicles in the same terminal, the vesicles' differential Ca^{2+} sensitivity provides release selectivity. (c) Packaging the transmitters in separate terminals allows the neuron to have different effects at the terminals' destinations.

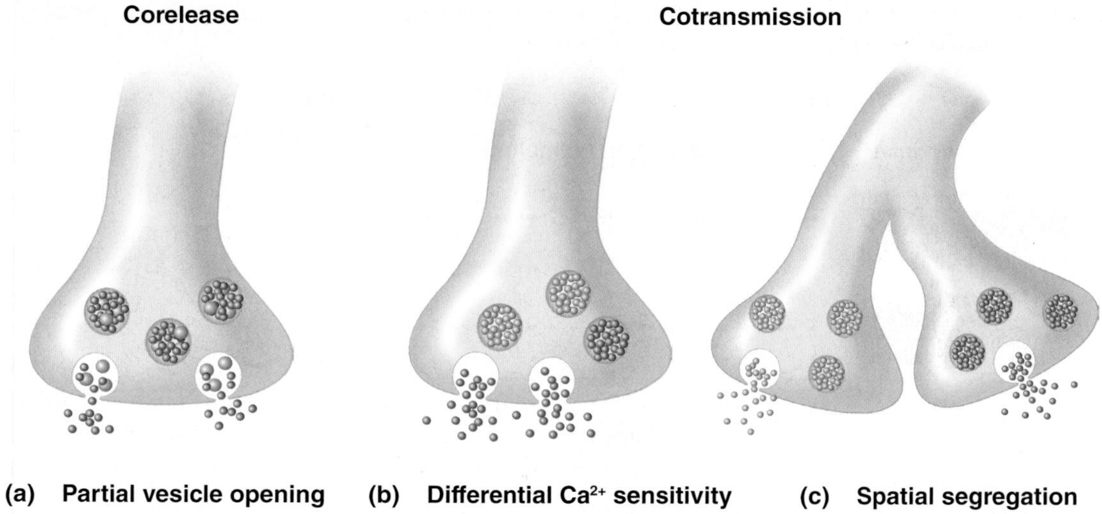

Corelease   **Cotransmission**

(a)   Partial vesicle opening   **(b)   Differential Ca^{2+} sensitivity**   **(c)   Spatial segregation**

Source: Adapted from "Dual-transmitter Neurons: Functional Implications of Co-release and Co-transmission," by C. E. Vaaga, M. Borisovska, and G. L. Westbrook, 2014, *Current Opinions in Neurobiology*, 29, 25–32.

TABLE 2.2   Some Representative Neurotransmitters.

NEUROTRANSMITTER	FUNCTION
Acetylcholine	Transmitter at muscles; in brain, involved in learning, etc.
Monoamines	
Serotonin	Involved in mood, sleep and arousal, aggression, depression, obsessive-compulsive disorder, and alcoholism.
Dopamine	Contributes to movement control and promotes reinforcing effects of food, sex, and abused drugs; involved in schizophrenia and Parkinson's disease.
Norepinephrine	A hormone released during stress. Functions as a neurotransmitter in the brain to increase arousal and attentiveness to events in the environment; involved in depression.
Epinephrine	A stress hormone related to norepinephrine; plays a minor role as a neurotransmitter in the brain.
Amino Acids	
Glutamate	The principal excitatory neurotransmitter in the brain and spinal cord. Vitally involved in learning and implicated in schizophrenia.
Gamma-aminobutyric acid (GABA)	The predominant inhibitory neurotransmitter. Its receptors respond to alcohol and the class of tranquilizers called benzodiazepines. Deficiency in GABA or receptors is one cause of epilepsy.
Glycine	Inhibitory transmitter in the spinal cord and lower brain. The poison strychnine causes convulsions and death by affecting glycine activity.
Neuropeptides	
Endorphins	Neuromodulators that reduce pain and enhance reinforcement.
Substance P	Transmitter in neurons sensitive to pain.
Neuropeptide Y	Initiates eating and produces metabolic shifts.
Gas	
Nitric oxide	One of two known gaseous transmitters, along with carbon monoxide. Can serve as a retrograde transmitter, influencing the presynaptic neuron's release of neurotransmitter. Viagra enhances male erections by increasing nitric oxide's ability to relax blood vessels and produce penile engorgement.

FIGURE 2.23   Response of Rats to Neural Stimulation Simulating the Taste of Sucrose and Quinine.

(a) Recordings from individual neurons during stimulation with sucrose and quinine. (b) Electrical stimulation mimicking the recorded neuronal activity; each dot represents a single neural impulse. (c) The average number of times the rats licked a drinking tube for water during delivery of the quinine simulation and the sucrose simulation.

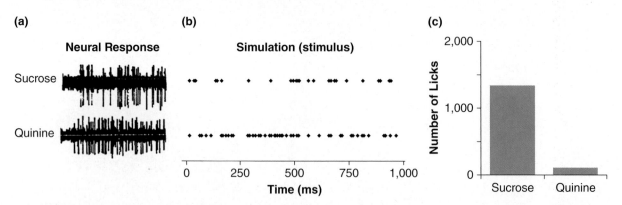

Sources: (a) and (b) Adapted from Figure 7 of "Temporal Coding in the Gustatory System," by R. M. Hallock and P. M. Di Lorenzo, 2006, *Neuroscience and Biobehavioral Reviews*, 30, p. 1156. Used with permission from Elsevier. (c) Adapted from Figure 4 of "Perceptual Consequences of Electrical Stimulation in the Gustatory System," by P. M. Di Lorenzo and G. S. Hecht, 1993, *Behavioral Neuroscience*, 107, p. 135.

Agonists and Antagonists in the Real World

Amazonian Indians tip their blowgun darts with the plant neurotoxin curare.

Source: By Jialiang Gao, https://commons.wikimedia.org/wiki/File:Yahua_Blowgun_Amazon_Iquitos_Peru.jpg, licensed under CC BY-SA 4.0 https://creativecommons.org/licenses/by-sa/4.0/.

Neurotransmitters are not the only substances that affect the nervous system. The many drugs and other compounds that mimic or increase the effect of a neurotransmitter are called *agonists*. Any substance that reduces the effect of a neurotransmitter is called an *antagonist*. Practically all drugs that have a psychological effect interact with a neurotransmitter system in the brain, and many of them do so by mimicking, or blocking, the effect of neurotransmitters (S. H. Snyder, 1984).

You have already seen that the effect of acetylcholine (ACh) is duplicated by nicotine and muscarine at the two kinds of acetylcholine receptors (nicotinic-ACh and muscarinic-ACh, respectively). Opioid drugs such as heroin and morphine also act as agonists, stimulating receptors for opiate-like transmitters in the body. The drugs naloxone and naltrexone act as an antagonists to opiates, occupying the receptor sites without activating them; consequently, naloxone and naltrexone can be used to counteract an overdose.

The plant toxin curare blocks nicotinic acetylcholine receptors at the muscle, causing paralysis (A. Trautmann, 1983). Indigenous tribes of Central and South America put curare on the tips of their darts and arrows to disable their game. A synthetic version of curare was used as a muscle relaxant during surgery before safer and more effective drugs were found (M. Goldberg & Rosenberg, 1987). It was even used occasionally in the past to treat the muscle spasms of tetanus (lockjaw), which, ironically, is caused by another neurotoxin.

other networks combine the activity of widespread brain areas to perform language functions (Chapter 9), to identify an object visually and locate it in space (Chapter 10), and, some researchers believe, to produce conscious awareness (Chapter 15).

Understanding these networks is the next big frontier in brain research. Their complexity and relative inaccessibility are challenging researchers' resolve and ingenuity, but recent developments in brain imaging capabilities make the goal more realistic. The *Human Connectome Project* is a large-scale, multi-university effort to map the brain's circuits. Its researchers are using a combination of four scanning techniques, behavioral measures, and genetic analysis to determine the brain's anatomical and functional connectivity (Van Essen et al., 2013). The maps will help researchers understand normal brain functioning in realms such as learning and consciousness, as well as disorders in functioning, including autism and schizophrenia (Figure 2.24). By the way, it took more than a decade to map the roundworm's brain, with just 300 neurons and 7,000 connections, so attempting it for the human brain is a very tall order.

While we're waiting for neuroscientists to explain how the brain works, the idea of neural networks provides a useful way of thinking about mental processes. The next time you are trying to remember a person's name that is "on the tip of your tongue," imagine your brain activating individual components of a neural network until one produces the name you're looking for. If you visualize the person's face as a reminder, imagine that the name and the image of the face are stored in related networks so that activating one memory activates the other. This is not just speculation: Electrode recordings from patients preparing for brain surgery show that the information triggered by the photo of a familiar person and by the person's written name converge on the same neurons in a critical memory area of the brain (Quian Quiroga, Kraskov, Koch, & Fried, 2009)—thanks, of course, to neural networks.

■ **FIGURE 2.24**   Image of White Matter Fiber Tracts.

This image is from the brain of an infant at risk for autism, based on having older siblings with autism. Those who were diagnosed with autism at 24 months had already begun to differ in tract development by the age of 6 months (Wolff et al., 2012). The study used a white matter imaging technique called diffusion tensor imaging; colors represent varying strengths of connection.

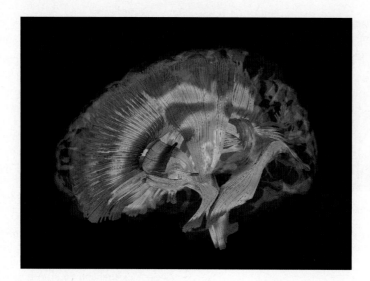

Source: Jason Wolff, PhD, University of North Carolina at Chapel Hill.

RESEARCH SPOTLIGHT
DHA for a Better Brain

The omega-3 fatty acid docosahexaenoic acid (DHA) is a critical component in neural membranes and is essential for optimal brain health and functioning. The best sources of DHA—fatty fish, such as salmon, and fish oil supplements—are readily available, but average intake in the United States is less than a third of the recommended level. Studies show that omega-3 oils improve cognitive development in children, protect adults from Alzheimer's disease, and improve the quality of life and memory in people affected by dementia (Blaylock, 2008).

Considerable research suggests that dietary DHA intake can speed neural recovery following injury, for example reducing recovery time from spinal cord injury in animals (Zhou-Hao, Yip, Priestley, & Michael-Titus, 2017) and by speeding tissue recovery and restoring cognitive function

following adolescent traumatic brain injury (Schober et al., 2016). DHA also improves cognition (Weiser, Butt, & Mohajeri, 2016). Brain scans of 8- to 10-year-old children while they worked on a sustained attention task showed that those with higher DHA levels had greater functional connectivity, the ability of different areas of the brain to communicate and work with each other (Almeida, Jandacek, Weber, & McNamara, 2016). Importantly, these positive beneficial effects of DHA continue into adulthood. After 12 months on a high DHA diet, elderly individuals (average age of 88) in nursing homes showed lower levels of depression and less cognitive impairment than the control group (Hashimoto et al., 2016). Interestingly, the psychological and mental state of their elderly caregivers also was greater than the caregivers of the control group participants.

CONCEPT CHECK

Take a Minute to Check Your Knowledge and Understanding

- How is information transmitted at the synapse?
- It can be said that integration transforms neurons from a "telephone line" into a computer. Explain.
- What difference would it make if there were no regulation of activity at the synapse?
- What is Dale's principle, and in what way is it incorrect?
- Explain why researchers' focus is shifting from localized neural activity to brainwide connections and activity.

In Perspective

It is impossible to understand the brain and impossible to understand behavior without first knowing the capabilities and the limitations of the neuron. Although more complexity is added at the synapse, a relatively simple device is the basis for our most sophisticated capabilities and behaviors. However, what happens at the individual neuron is not enough to account for human behavior; neurons work in concert with each other, in both local and brainwide networks. With modern tools and large cooperative efforts, researchers hope to understand how neurons work together to produce thought, memory, emotion, and consciousness. In Chapter 3, you will learn about some of the functional structures in the brain that are formed by the interconnection of neurons.

CHAPTER SUMMARY

The Cells That Make Us Who We Are

- There are three major kinds of neurons: motor neurons, sensory neurons, and interneurons. Although they play different roles, they have the same basic components and operate the same way.
- The neural membrane is electrically polarized. This polarity is the resting potential, which is maintained by forces of diffusion and electrostatic pressure in the short term and by the sodium-potassium pump in the long term.
- Polarization is the basis for the neuron's responsiveness to stimulation, in the form of the graded potential and the action potential.
- The neuron is limited in firing rate by the absolute refractory period and in its ability to respond to differing strengths of stimuli by the all-or-none law. More intense stimuli cause the neuron to fire earlier during the relative refractory period, providing a way to encode stimulus intensity (the rate law).
- Glial cells provide the myelination that enables neurons to conduct rapidly while remaining small. They also help regulate activity in the neurons and provide several supporting functions for neurons.

How Neurons Communicate With Each Other

- Transmission from neuron to neuron is usually chemical in vertebrates, involving neurotransmitters released onto receptors on the postsynaptic dendrites and cell body.
- The neurotransmitter can create an excitatory postsynaptic potential, which increases the chance that the postsynaptic neuron will fire, or it can create an inhibitory postsynaptic potential, which decreases the likelihood of firing.
- Through temporal and spatial summation, the postsynaptic neuron integrates its many excitatory and inhibitory inputs.
- Regulation of synaptic activity is produced by axoaxonic synapses from other neurons, adjustment of transmitter output by autoreceptors, and change in the number or sensitivity of postsynaptic receptors.
- Leftover neurotransmitter may be taken back into the presynaptic terminals, absorbed by glial cells, or broken down by an enzyme.
- The human nervous system contains a large number of neurotransmitters, detected by an even greater variety of receptors. A neuron can release combinations of two or more neurotransmitters.
- The computing work of the brain is done in complex neural networks. ∎

STUDY RESOURCES

FOR FURTHER THOUGHT

- What would be the effect if there were no constraints on the free flow of ions across the neuron membrane?
- What effect would it have on neural conduction if the action potential were decremental?
- Sports drinks replenish electrolytes that are lost during exercise. Electrolytes are compounds that separate into ions; for example, sodium chloride (table salt) dissociates into sodium and chloride ions. What implication do you think electrolyte loss might have for the nervous system? Why?
- Imagine what the effect would be if the nervous system used only one neurotransmitter.
- How similar to humans do you think computers are capable of becoming? How much is your answer based on how you think human behavior is controlled versus how capable you think computers are?

TEST YOUR UNDERSTANDING

1. Describe the ion movements and voltage changes that make up the neural impulse, from graded potential (at the axon hillock) to recovery.

2. Discuss the ways in which the synapse increases the neuron's capacity for transmitting information.

3. Describe neural networks and explain their importance.

Select the best answer:

1. The inside of the neuron is relatively poor in _____ ions and rich in _____ ions.

   a. chloride, phosphate   b. sodium, potassium
   c. potassium, sodium   d. calcium, sodium

2. The rate law

   a. explains how the intensity of stimuli is represented.
   b. does not apply to neurons outside the brain.
   c. describes transmission in myelinated axons.
   d. describes the process of postsynaptic integration.

3. Without the sodium-potassium pump, the neuron would become

   a. more sensitive because of accumulation of sodium ions.
   b. more sensitive because of accumulation of potassium ions.
   c. overfilled with sodium ions and unable to fire.
   d. overfilled with potassium ions and unable to fire.

4. There is a limit to how rapidly a neuron can produce action potentials. This is due to

   a. inhibition.
   b. facilitation.

   c. the absolute refractory period.
   d. the relative refractory period.

5. Saltatory conduction results in

   a. less speed with the use of more energy.
   b. greater speed with the use of less energy.
   c. less speed with the use of less energy.
   d. greater speed with the use of more energy.

6. General anesthetics open potassium channels, allowing potassium ions to leak out of the neuron. This

   a. increases firing in pain-inhibiting centers in the brain.
   b. increases firing in the neuron until it is fatigued.
   c. hypopolarizes the neuron, preventing firing.
   d. hyperpolarizes the neuron, preventing firing.

7. When the action potential arrives at the terminal button, entry of _____ ions stimulates release of transmitter.

   a. potassium   b. sodium
   c. calcium   d. chloride

8. All the following neurotransmitters are deactivated by reuptake except

   a. acetylcholine.   b. norepinephrine.
   c. serotonin.   d. dopamine.

9. An inhibitory neurotransmitter causes the inside of the postsynaptic neuron to become

   a. more positive.   b. more negative.
   c. more depolarized.   d. neutral in charge.

10. Excitatory postsynaptic potentials are typically produced by movement of _____ ions, whereas inhibitory postsynaptic potentials are typically produced by movement of _____ ions.

    a. potassium; sodium or chloride
    b. potassium; sodium or calcium
    c. sodium; calcium or chloride
    d. sodium; potassium or chloride

11. Which of the following is not an example of regulation of synaptic activity?

    a. A neuron has its synapse on the terminals of another and affects its transmitter release.
    b. Autoreceptors reduce the amount of transmitter released.
    c. A presynaptic neuron inhibits a postsynaptic neuron.
    d. Postsynaptic receptors change in numbers or sensitivity.

12. The graph below shows three graded potentials occurring at the same time.

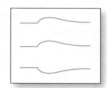

Assume that the resting potential is –70 mV and that each graded potential individually produces a 5-mV change. What is the membrane's voltage after the graded potentials arrive?

a. –65 mV   b. –70 mV

c. –75 mV   d. +75 mV

13. The presence of synapses in a neuron chain provides the opportunity for

a. increases in conduction speed.

b. modification of neural activity.

c. two-way communication in a pathway.

d. regeneration of damaged neurons.

14. Neural networks

a. are groups of neurons that function together.

b. are where the most complex work of the brain occurs.

c. must connect at least two brain areas to be considered a network.

d. All of these are true.

e. Not all of these are true.

Answers: 1. b, 2. a, 3. c, 4. c, 5. b, 6. d, 7. c, 8. a, 9. b, 10. d, 11. c, 12. a, 13. b, 14. e.

ON THE WEB

The following websites are coordinated with this chapter's content. You can access these websites from the **SAGE edge Student Resources site**; select this chapter and then click on Web Resources. (**Bold** items are links.)

1. **Neuroscience for Kids** (don't be put off by the name!) has a review of the resting and action potentials and an animation of their electrical recording. A YouTube animation of the **sodium-potassium pump** is an instructive illustration of how the mechanism works.

2. **The Schwann Cell and Action Potential** is a visually appealing animation of myelination and how it speeds conduction.

3. The animated video **The Origin of the Brain** describes how (and why) neurons and synapses evolved and ends with a demonstration of how simple circuits can "remember" and make "decisions."

4. **The Symphony Inside Your Brain** describes the Human Connectome Project and features a rotating scan of the major pathways of one hemisphere.

5. The **American Association for Artificial Intelligence** site covers a wide variety of topics, including artificial neural networks (which learn how to perform a task, rather than being programmed to do it), robots, cognitive science, and related ethical and social issues.

FOR FURTHER READING

1. *Synaptic Self,* by Joseph LeDoux (Penguin Books, 2003), takes the position that "your 'self,' the essence of who you are, reflects patterns of interconnectivity between neurons in your brain." A good read by a noted neuroscientist.

2. "Understanding Synapses: Past, Present, and Future," by Thomas Südhoff and Robert Malenka (*Neuron,* 2008, *60,* 469–476), will convince you of the importance of synapses and will provide a useful reference throughout the course.

3. "Tripartite Synapses: Astrocytes Process and Control Synaptic Information," by Gertrudis Perea, Marta Navarrete, and Alfonso Araque (*Trends in Neurosciences,* 2006, *32,* 421–431), reviews what we know about glial influence on synaptic activity.

4. "All My Circuits: Using Multiple Electrodes to Understand Functioning Neural Networks," by Earl Miller and Matthew Wilson (*Neuron,* 2008, *60,* 483–488), gives a good description of brainwide neural networks that play a variety of roles.

5. Written by well-known neuroscientist John E. Dowling (you will see some of his work in Chapter 10), *Neurons and Networks: An Introduction to Behavioral Neuroscience* (Harvard University Press, 2001) elaborates on the topics in this chapter. According to one student, the book "goes into depth without becoming murky."

6. Sebastian Seung's book *Connectome* (Houghton Mifflin Harcourt, 2012) describes the effort to map the brain using computers and artificial intelligence; you can read a summary and review in *New Scientist,* February 4, 2012, p. 46.

7. "The Human Brain Project," by Henry Markram (*Scientific American,* June 2012, 50–55), describes the author's plan to model the entire brain on a computer, along with the scientific and medical benefits and the awesome computing demands.

KEY TERMS

absolute refractory period 29
action potential 26
agonist 41
all-or-none law 27
antagonist 41
autoreceptor 35
axon 22
axon terminal 22
cell body 22
Dale's principle 36
dendrite 22
electrostatic pressure 26
excitatory postsynaptic potential
    (EPSP) 33
force of diffusion 26
glial cell 29
graded potential 27
Human Connectome Project 41
hyperpolarization 33

hypopolarization 33
inhibitory postsynaptic potential
    (IPSP) 33
interneuron 23
ion 25
ionotropic receptor 33
metabotropic receptor 33
motor neuron 22
myelin 29
neural network 38
neuron 21
neurotoxin 28
neurotransmitter 22
node of Ranvier 29
nondecremental 28
oligodendrocyte 29
optogenetics 28
polarization 24
postsynaptic 31

presynaptic 31
presynaptic excitation 35
presynaptic inhibition 35
rate law 29
relative refractory period 29
resting potential 24
reuptake 34
saltatory conduction 29
Schwann cell 29
sensory neuron 22
sodium-potassium pump 26
spatial summation 34
synapse 31
synaptic cleft 31
temporal summation 34
vesicle 32
voltage 24

edge.sagepub.com/garrett5e

SAGE edge offers a robust online environment featuring an impressive array of free tools and resources for review, study, and further exploration, keeping both instructors and students on the cutting edge of teaching and learning.

2.1 Identify the cells of the nervous system.

▶ Glial Cell Disorders
🔊 Glial Cell Function

2.2 Name the structures of neurons.

🔊 Historical Drawings of Neurons
▶ Neuron and Synapse Structures

2.3 Compare the functions of sensory, motor, and interneurons.

▶ Sensory Neurons, Interneurons, and Motor Neurons

2.4 Explain the roles of ions and the cell membrane in nervous system communication.

▶ A Light Switch for Neurons

2.5 Demonstrate how neurotransmitters are involved in communication between nervous system cells.

▶ How Does Synaptic Transmission Occur?

2.6 Discuss how neurons work together to generate your experiences of the world.

▶ How the Brain Generates Your Reality

2.7 Illustrate the ways that excitation and inhibition are important to the functioning of the nervous system.

▤ GABA, Brain Maturation, and Neurological Disorders

PRACTICE AND APPLY WHAT YOU'VE LEARNED

▶ **edge.sagepub.com/garrett5e**

HEAD TO THE STUDY SITE WHERE YOU'LL FIND

- **eFlashcards to strengthen your understanding of key terms**

- **Practice quizzes to test your comprehension of key concepts**

- **Videos and multimedia content to enhance your exploration of key topics**

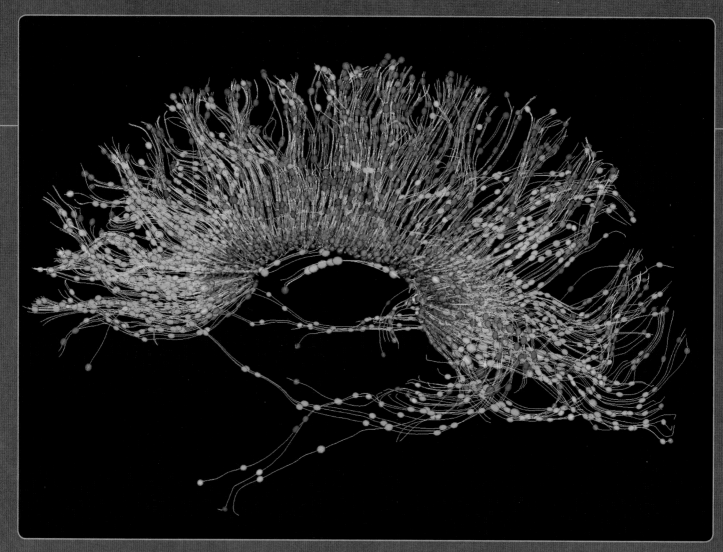

The Organization and Functions of the Nervous System

3

After reading this chapter, you will be able to:

- Identify the components of the central nervous system.

- Name the structures in the forebrain, midbrain, and hindbrain.

- Predict how damage to specific brain structures will impact specific behaviors.

- Describe the components that protect the brain from damage.

- Examine the functions of the peripheral nervous system divisions.

- Explain how the peripheral and central nervous systems interact in generating experiences and behavior.

- Summarize the changes that the nervous system undergoes during typical development.

- Illustrate the changes that occur in the nervous system as the result of experiences.

Karen is a college graduate and holds a job with considerable responsibility. She is married and leads a normal life except for occasional epileptic seizures. When her doctors ordered a brain scan to find the cause of her seizures, they were astounded. The normal person's brain has many folds on its surface, so it is wrinkled like a walnut; Karen's is perfectly smooth, like the one on the right in Figure 3.1. Notice, too, that the dark areas in the middle of the brain (ventricles) are enlarged, indicating a deficiency in the amount of brain tissue. People with her disorder are usually not only *lissencephalic* (literally, *smooth-brained*) and epileptic like Karen, but severely impaired intellectually as well (Barinaga, 1996; Eksioglu et al., 1996). So what really amazed Karen's doctors was not how abnormal her brain is, but that she functions not just normally but well above average. How do we explain why some people are able to escape the consequences of what is usually a devastating developmental error? The answer is that we do not know why; it is one of the mysteries that neuroscientists are attempting to solve in order to understand the brain's remarkable resilience.

You are now well versed in the functioning of neurons and how they interact with each other. What you need to understand next is how neurons are grouped into the functional components that make up the nervous system. In the next few pages, we will review the physical structure of the nervous system so that you will have a road map for more detailed study in later chapters. We will also include an overview of major functions to prepare you for the more detailed treatments to come in later chapters. First we will look at the two divisions of the nervous system before turning our attention to issues such as brain development.

The Central Nervous System

The nervous system is divided into two subunits. The *central nervous system (CNS)* includes the brain and the spinal cord. The second part is the peripheral nervous system,

SAGE edge

Master the content.
edge.sagepub.com/garrett5e

> *The Brain—is wider than the Sky—*
> *For—put them side by side—*
> *The one the other will contain*
> *With ease—and You—beside—*
>
> —*Emily Dickinson*

which we will examine later in the chapter. Before we go any further, we need to be sure you understand a couple of terms correctly. As we talk about the nervous system, be careful not to confuse *nerve* and *neuron*. A neuron is a single neural cell; a *nerve* is a bundle of axons running together like a multiwire cable.

However, the term *nerve* is used only in the peripheral nervous system; inside the CNS, bundles of axons are called *tracts*. Most of the neurons' cell bodies are also clustered in groups; a group of cell bodies is called a *nucleus* in the CNS and a *ganglion* in the peripheral nervous system. Table 3.1 should help you keep these terms straight.

Figure 3.2 is a photograph of a human brain. It will be easier to visualize the various structures of the brain if you understand that the CNS begins as a hollow tube and preserves that shape as it develops (Figure 3.3). The upper end of the tube develops three swellings, which will become the forebrain, midbrain, and hindbrain; the lower part of the tube develops into the spinal cord. The forebrain appears to be perched on top of the lower structures as it enlarges and almost completely engulfs them. By comparing the four drawings in this series, you can see that the mature forebrain obscures much of the lower brain from view. You will get a better idea of these hidden structures later when we look at an interior view of the brain.

The Forebrain

The major structures of the forebrain are the two cerebral hemispheres, the thalamus, and the hypothalamus. The outer layer of the hemispheres, the cortex, is where the highest-level processing occurs in the brain.

The Cerebral Hemispheres

The large, wrinkled *cerebral hemispheres* dominate the brain's appearance (Figure 3.4). They not only are large in relation to the rest of the brain but also are disproportionately larger than in other primates (Deacon, 1990). The *longitudinal fissure* that runs the length of the brain separates the two cerebral hemispheres, which are nearly mirror images of each other in appearance. Often the same area in each hemisphere has identical functions as well, but you will see that this is not always the case. The simplest form of *asymmetry* is that each hemisphere receives most of its sensory input from the *opposite* side of the body (or of the world, in the case of hearing and vision) and provides most of the control of the opposite side of the body.

Look again at Figures 3.2 and 3.4. The brain's surface has many ridges and grooves that give it a very wrinkled appearance; the term we use is *convoluted*. Each ridge is called a *gyrus;* the groove or space between two gyri is called a *sulcus* or, if it is large, a *fissure*. You can see how the gyri are structured in the cross section of a brain in Figure 3.5. The outer

■ **FIGURE 3.1** A Normal Brain and a Lissencephalic Brain.

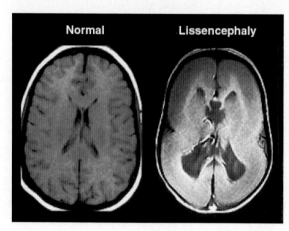

Source: Courtesy of Dr. Joseph Gleeson, University of California San Diego School of Medicine.

■ **FIGURE 3.2** View of a Human Brain.

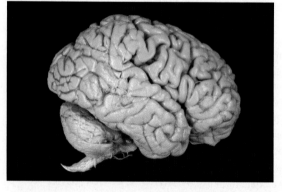

Source: © Dr. Fred Hossler/Visuals Unlimited/Getty Images.

> One of the key strategies of the nervous system is localization of functions: specific types of information are processed in particular regions.
>
> —Eric Kandel

TABLE 3.1 Terms for Axons and Cell Bodies in the Nervous System.

	PERIPHERAL	CENTRAL
Bundle of axons	Nerve	Tract
Group of cell bodies	Ganglion	Nucleus

■ **FIGURE 3.3**   The Brain Develops From a Tubular Structure.

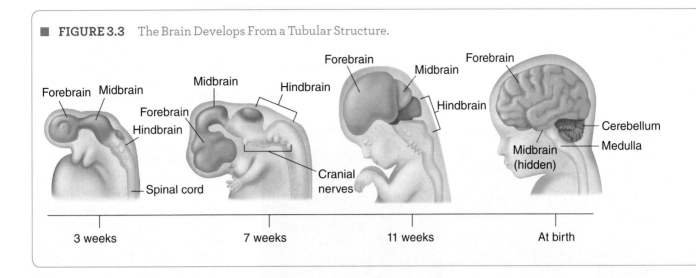

surface is the *cortex* (literally, "bark"), which is made up mostly of the cell bodies of neurons; because cell bodies are not myelinated, the cortex looks grayish in color, which is why it is referred to as gray matter. Remember that neural processing occurs where neurons synapse on the cell bodies of other neurons, which indicates why the cortex is so important. The cortex is only 1.5 to 4 millimeters (mm) thick, but the convolutions increase the amount of cortex by tripling the surface area. The convolutions also provide the axons with easier access to the cell bodies than if the developing cortex thickened instead of wrinkling. The axons come together in the central core of each gyrus, where their myelination gives the area a whitish appearance. Notice how the white matter of each gyrus joins with the white matter of the next gyrus, creating the large bands of axons that serve as communication routes, both within each hemisphere and between the two hemispheres.

You find yourself running to your early morning test, fretting about being late while rehearsing answers to the questions you expect on the exam. You interrupt your thoughts only to greet a fellow student, doing your best to conceal your disdain because of the silly questions he asks in class. Do you ever wonder how your brain pulls all this off?

Why is a wrinkled brain better than a smooth one?

■ **FIGURE 3.4**

Human Brain Viewed From Above.

This photo shows the cerebral hemispheres and longitudinal fissure. The blood vessels have been removed from the right hemisphere.

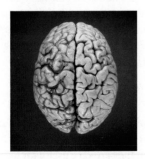

Source: © David Bassett/Science Source.

■ **FIGURE 3.5**   Section of Human Brain Showing Gyri and Sulci.

Source: Reproduced with permission from http://www.brains.rad.msu.edu, and http://brainmuseum.org, supported by the U.S. National Science Foundation.

■ **FIGURE 3.6** Layers and Columns of the Cortex.

(a) Photograph of a section of cortex, revealing its layered organization. (b) Photograph showing the columnar arrangement of cells in the cortex; the numbers on the left identify the cortical layers.

(a)

(b)

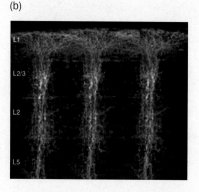

Source: (a) "Human-Specific Organization of Primary Visual Cortex: Alternating Compartments of Dense Cat-301 and Calbindin Immunoreactivity in Layer 4A," by Todd M. Preuss and Ghislaine Q. Coleman, *Cerebral Cortex, 12*(7), pp. 671–691, doi:10.1093/cercor/12.7.671. (b) Reconstructed neurons from the Blue Brain Project © BBP/EPFL.

It will take the rest of this book to *start* answering that question, but this is a good time to mention two ways the brain's organization helps it to be more efficient. First, the cortex in humans and most mammals is arranged in layers; the number of layers is usually six, though a particular layer may be absent in some areas. The layers stand out from each other because they are separated by fibers that serve the cell bodies, but they also differ in appearance: They vary in type and size of cells and in the concentration of cell bodies versus axons (see Figure 3.6a). There are differences in function as well. Some researchers have concluded that layers II and III are associational, IV is sensory, and V and VI have motor functions (Buxhoeveden & Casanova, 2002).

Second, the cells of the cortex are organized into groups of 80 to 100 interconnected neurons, which are arranged in columns running perpendicular to the cortical surface (Figure 3.6b; Buxhoeveden & Casanova, 2002). They provide a vertical unification of the cortex's horizontal layers, which contributes to their role as the primary information-processing unit in the cortex (Torii, Hashimoto-Torii, Levitt, & Rakic, 2009). The cells in a column have a similar function; for example, they may receive input from the same area on the skin's surface, while surrounding columns serve adjacent locations. In the visual cortex, the cells in a column may detect object edges at a particular orientation, while surrounding columns respond to edges at a slightly different orientation. Having similar functions grouped close together in well-connected columns helps the brain work quickly and efficiently.

Students often ask whether intelligent people have bigger brains. Bischoff, the leading European anatomist in the 19th century, argued that the greater average weight of men's brains was infallible proof of their intellectual superiority over women. When he died, his brain was removed and added to his extensive collection as his will had specified; ironically, it weighed only 1,245 grams (g), less than the average of about 1,250 g for women ("Proof?" 1942). There actually is a tendency for people with larger brains to be more intelligent (Willerman, Schultz, Rutledge, & Bigler, 1991), but the relationship is small and highly variable. What this means is that factors other than brain size are more important; otherwise, women would be less intelligent than men as Bischoff claimed, but we know from research that this is not the case. When we look at brain size more closely in Chapter 13, you will learn that Einstein's brain was even smaller than Bischoff's.

Across species, brain size is more related to body size than to intelligence; the brains of elephants and sperm whales are five or six times larger than ours. It is a brain's complexity, not its size, that determines its intellectual power. Look at the brains in Figure 3.7, and then compare them with the human brain in Figure 3.2. You can see two features that distinguish more complex, more highly evolved brains from less complex ones. One is that the higher brains are more convoluted; the greater number of gyri means more cortex. The other is that the cerebral hemispheres are larger in proportion to the lower parts of the brain. It is no accident that the cerebral hemispheres are perched atop the rest of the brain and the spinal cord. The CNS is arranged in a *hierarchy;* as you ascend from the spinal cord through the hindbrain and midbrain to the forebrain, the neural structures become more complex, and so do the behaviors they control.

The Four Lobes

The hemispheres are divided into four lobes—frontal, parietal, occipital, and temporal—each named after the bone of the skull covering it. The lobes are illustrated in Figure 3.8, along with the major functions located within them. These divisions are somewhat arbitrary, but they are very useful for locating structures and functions, so we will organize our discussion around them. Sometimes we need additional precision in locating structures, so you should get used to seeing the standard terms that are used; the most important ones are illustrated in Figure 3.9a. Also, throughout this text you will see illustrations of the nervous system from a variety of perspectives; until you get more comfortable with the structure of the nervous system, it may be difficult to tell what you are seeing. The images in Figure 3.9b will serve as a guide for understanding the orientation of most of these illustrations.

The *frontal lobe* is the area anterior to (in front of) the *central sulcus* and superior to (above) the *lateral fissure*. The functions here are complex and include some of the highest human capabilities. A considerable portion of the frontal lobes is also involved with the control of movement. And because the primary motor area is located along the posterior boundary of the frontal lobe, we start our discussion there. (You should continue to refer to Figure 3.8.)

The *precentral gyrus*, which extends the length of the *central sulcus*, is the location of the primary *motor cortex*, which controls voluntary (nonreflexive) movement. The motor area in one hemisphere controls the opposite side of the body, though it does exert a lesser control over the same side of the body. The parts of the body are "mapped onto" the motor area of each hemisphere in the form of a *homunculus*, which means "little man." All this means is that the cells that control the muscles of the hand are adjacent to the cells controlling the muscles of the arm, which are next to those controlling the shoulder, and so on (Figure 3.10). The homunculus is distorted in shape, however; the parts of the body that make precise movements, such as the hands and fingers, have more cortex devoted to their control. The *primary motor cortex,* like other functional areas of the brain, carries out its work in concert with adjacent *secondary* areas. The secondary motor areas are located just anterior to the primary area. Subcortical (below the cortex) structures, such as the basal ganglia, also contribute to motor behavior.

Looking back at Figure 3.8, locate Broca's area anterior to the motor area and along the lateral fissure. *Broca's area* controls speech production, contributing the movements involved in speech and grammatical structure. A patient with damage to this area was asked about a dental appointment; he replied, haltingly, "Yes . . . Monday . . . Dad and Dick . . . Wednesday 9 o'clock . . . 10 o'clock . . . doctors . . . and . . . teeth" (Geschwind, 1979). Similar problems occur in reading and writing. In another example of hemispheric asymmetry, language activity is controlled mostly by the left hemisphere in 9 out of 10 people.

The more anterior part of the frontal lobes—the prefrontal cortex in Figure 3.8—is functionally complex. It is the largest region in the human brain, twice as large as in chimpanzees, and it accounts for 29% of the total cortex (Andreasen et al., 1992; Deacon, 1990). The *prefrontal cortex* is involved in planning and organization, impulse control, adjusting behavior in response to rewards and punishments, and some forms of decision making (Bechara, Damasio, Tranel, & Damasio, 1997; Fuster, 1989; Kast, 2001). Symptoms of impairment are varied, depending on which part of the prefrontal area is affected (Mesulam, 1986), but malfunction often strikes at the capabilities we consider most human. Schizophrenia and depression, for example, involve dysfunction in the prefrontal cortex.

People with prefrontal damage often engage in behavior that normal individuals readily recognize will get them into trouble. In clinical interviews, they show good understanding of social and moral standards and the consequences of behavior—for example, they can describe several valid ways to develop a friendship, maintain a romantic relationship, or resolve an occupational difficulty—but they are unable to choose among the options. In real life, they suffer loss of friends, financial disaster, and divorce (A. Damasio, 1994). Research indicates that prefrontal damage impairs the ability to learn from reward and punishment and to control impulses (Bechara et al., 1997). In addition, those with prefrontal damage have reduced behavioral flexibility with respect to choosing possible actions based on a particular situation (Ragozzino, 2007).

? What functions are found in the frontal lobes?

■ **FIGURE 3.7**   Brains of Three Different Species.

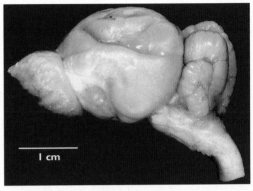

(a) Armadillo brain.

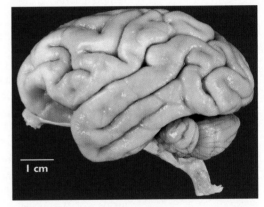

(b) Monkey brain.

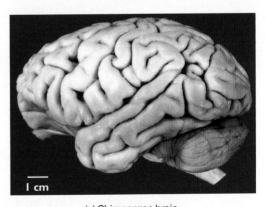

(c) Chimpanzee brain.

Source: Reproduced with permission from http://www.brains.rad.msu.edu, and http://brainmuseum.org, supported by the U.S. National Science Foundation.

■ FIGURE 3.8   Lobes and Functional Areas on the Surface of the Hemispheres.

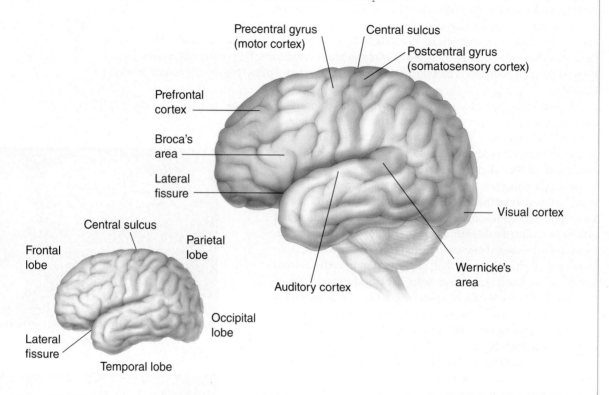

In spite of the effects of frontal lobe damage, during the 1940s and 1950s, surgeons performed tens of thousands of *lobotomies,* a surgical procedure that disconnects the prefrontal area from the rest of the brain. Initially, the surgeries were performed on patients with severe schizophrenia, but many overly enthusiastic doctors lobotomized patients with much milder problems. Walter Freeman, shown in Figure 3.11, did more than his share of the 40,000 lobotomies performed in the United States and zealously trained other psychiatrists in the technique (Valenstein, 1986). The surgery calmed agitated patients, but the benefits came at a high price; the patients often became emotionally blunted, distractible, and childlike in behavior. In a follow-up study of patient outcomes, 49% were still hospitalized, and less than a fourth of the others were living independently (A. Miller, 1967). Lack of success with lobotomy and the introduction of psychiatric drugs in the 1950s made the surgery a rare therapeutic choice. Now *psychosurgery,* the use of surgical intervention to treat cognitive and emotional disorders, is generally held in disfavor, unlike brain surgery to treat problems such as tumors. The accompanying Application describes the most famous case of accidental lobotomy.

What functions are found in the parietal lobes?

The *parietal lobes* are located superior to the lateral fissure and between the central sulcus and the occipital lobe. The *primary somatosensory cortex,* located on the postcentral gyrus, processes the skin senses (touch, warmth, cold, and pain) and the senses that inform us about body position and movement (see Figure 3.8 again). Like the motor cortex, the somatosensory area serves primarily the opposite side of the body. The somatosensory cortex also is organized as a homunculus, but in this case, the size of each area depends on the sensitivity in that part of the body. When we discuss the senses of vision and hearing in later chapters, you will learn that this mapping is a principle of brain organization. Also, this is a good place to point out that the sensory areas of the brain are often referred to as *projection areas,* as in *somatosensory projection area.*

Each of the lobes contains *association areas,* which carry out further processing beyond what the primary area does, often combining information from other senses. Parietal lobe association areas receive input from the body senses and from vision; they help the person identify objects by touch, determine the location of the limbs, and locate objects in space. Damage to the posterior parietal cortex may produce *neglect,* a disorder in which the person ignores objects, people, and activity on the side opposite the damage. This occurs much more frequently when the damage is in the right parietal lobe. The person may fail to shave or apply makeup on the left side of the face. In some cases, a stroke patient with a paralyzed arm or leg will deny that anything is wrong and even claim that the affected limb belongs to someone else.

■ **FIGURE 3.9**   Terms Used to Indicate Direction and Orientation in the Nervous System.

(a) *Dorsal* means toward the back, and *ventral* means toward the stomach. (This terminology was developed with other animals and becomes more meaningful when you imagine the human on all fours, face forward. *Anterior* means toward the front, and *posterior* means toward the rear. *Superior* is a location above another structure, and *inferior* means below another structure. *Lateral* means toward the side; *medial* indicates toward the middle.

(b) The *coronal plane* divides the brain vertically from side to side, the *sagittal plane* divides it vertically in an anterior-posterior direction, and the *horizontal plane* divides it between the top and bottom. We use these terms when we refer to an image (e.g., a sagittal view) or when the brain is cut along one of these planes (e.g., a horizontal section).

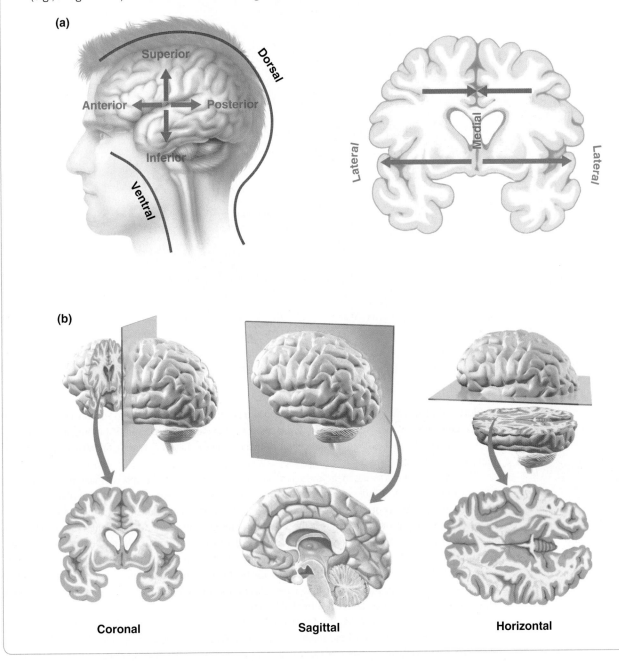

Coronal   **Sagittal**   **Horizontal**

The lateral fissure separates the temporal lobe from the frontal and parietal lobes. The *temporal lobes* contain the auditory projection area, visual and auditory association areas, and an additional language area (see Figure 3.8). The *auditory cortex,* which receives sound information from the ears, lies on the superior (uppermost) gyrus of the temporal lobe, mostly hidden from view within the lateral fissure. Just posterior to the auditory cortex is *Wernicke's area,* an association area that interprets language input arriving from the nearby

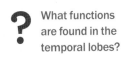 What functions are found in the temporal lobes?

■ **FIGURE 3.10**   The Motor Cortex.

This view shows a cross section (coronal) of the precentral gyrus. The distorted body proportions and facial features of the homunculus indicate the relative amount of motor cortex devoted to those body areas.

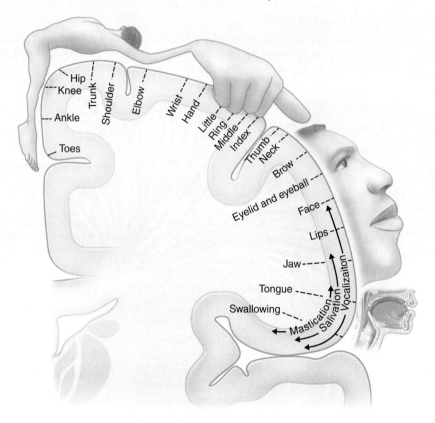

auditory and visual areas; it also generates spoken language through Broca's area and written language by way of the motor cortex. When Wernicke's area is damaged, the person has trouble understanding speech or writing; the person can still speak, but the speech is mostly meaningless. Like Broca's area, this structure is found in the left hemisphere in most people.

The *inferior temporal cortex,* in the lower part of the lobe as the name implies, plays a major role in the visual identification of objects. People with damage in this area have difficulty recognizing familiar objects by sight, even though they can give detailed descriptions of the objects. They have no difficulty identifying the same items by touch. They may also fail to recognize the faces of friends and family members, though they can identify people by their voices. The neurologist Oliver Sacks (1990) described a patient who talked to parking meters, thinking they were children. Considering his strange behavior, it seems remarkable that he was unimpaired intellectually. As you read about cases like this one and hear of patients who do things like denying ownership of their paralyzed leg, you may begin to understand that human capabilities are somewhat independent of each other because they depend on different parts of the brain.

When the neurosurgeon Wilder Penfield (1955) stimulated patients' temporal lobes, he often elicited what appeared to be memories of visual and auditory experiences. Penfield was doing surgery to remove malfunctioning tissue that was causing epileptic seizures. Before the surgery, Penfield would stimulate the area with a weak electrical current and observe the effect; this allowed him to distinguish healthy tissue and important functional areas from the diseased tissue he wished to remove (Figure 3.12).

The patients were awake because their verbal report was needed for carrying out this mapping; since brain tissue has no pain receptors, patients require only a local anesthetic for the surgery. Stimulation of primary sensory areas provoked only unorganized, meaningless sensations, such as tingling, lights, or buzzing sounds. But when Penfield stimulated the association areas of the temporal cortex, 25% of the patients reported hearing music or familiar voices

APPLICATION
The Case of Phineas Gage

In 1848, Phineas Gage, a 25-year-old railroad construction foreman in Cavendish, Vermont, was tamping explosive powder into a blasting hole when the charge ignited prematurely and drove the 3½-foot-long (1.15-m) tamping iron through his left cheek and out the top of his skull. Gage not only regained consciousness immediately and was able to talk and to walk with the aid of his men but also survived the accident with no impairment of speech, motor abilities, learning, memory, or intelligence. However, his personality was changed dramatically. He became irreverent and profane, and although Gage previously was the most capable man employed by the railroad, he no longer was dependable and had to be dismissed. He wandered about for a dozen years, never able to live fully independently, and died in the care of his family.

Almost a century and a half later, Hanna Damasio and her colleagues carried out a belated postmortem examination of Gage's skull (H. Damasio et al., 1994). Combining measurements from the skull with a three-dimensional computer rendering of a human brain, they reconstructed the path of the tamping iron through Gage's brain (see the accompanying figure). They concluded that the accident damaged the part of both frontal lobes involved in processing emotion and making rational decisions in personal and social matters. More recently, Jack Van Horn and colleagues at UCLA extended Damasio's work by calculating how much the white matter pathways—the myelinated axons that create the circuitry of the brain—would have been damaged by Gage's accident (Van Horn et al., 2012). They determined that whereas about 4% of the cerebral cortex was disrupted by the passage of the rod through his brain, the white matter pathways suffered greater damage, with more than 10% of the myelinated fibers damaged by the rod. At the time of Gage's accident, physiologists were debating whether different parts of the brain have specific functions or are equally competent in carrying out functions. Gage's experience had such an important influence in tipping the balance toward localization of function that in 1998 scientists from around the world gathered in Cavendish to commemorate the 150th anniversary of the event (Vogel, 1998).

(a) A reconstruction of where the rod passed through Gage's skull. (b) A normal brain showing the area where Gage's was damaged; the colors indicate motor, language, and body sensory areas that were unharmed. (c) Phineas Gage, with the tamping iron.

(a)

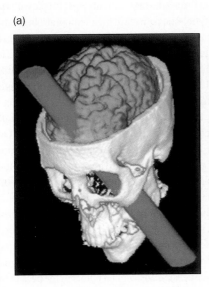

(b)

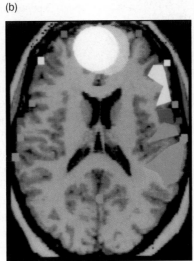

(c)

■ **FIGURE 3.11**   Lobotomy Procedure and a Lobotomized Brain.

(a) Walter Freeman inserts his instrument between the eyelid and the eyeball, drives it through the skull with a mallet, and moves it back and forth to sever the connections between the prefrontal area and the rest of the brain. (b) A horizontal view of a brain shows the gaps (arrows) produced by a lobotomy.

(a)

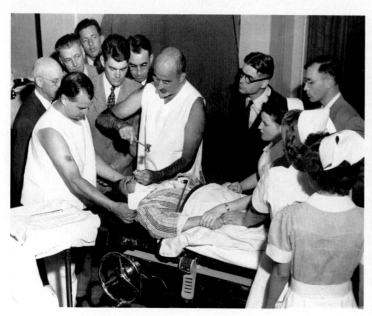

(b)

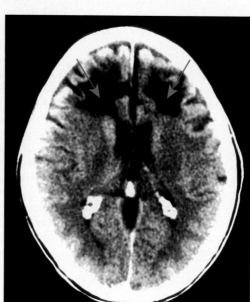

Source: (a) © Bettman/Getty Images. (b) © Living Art Enterprises, LLC/Science Source.

■ **FIGURE 3.12**   Brain of One of Penfield's Patients.

The numbered tags allowed Penfield to relate areas to patients' responses.

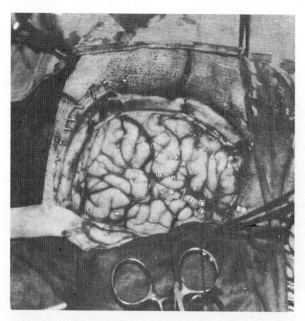

Source: From *The Excitable Cortex in Conscious Man*, by Wilder Penfield, 1958. Courtesy of Dennis Coon and Liverpool University Press, Liverpool, UK © 1958. Used with permission.

or, occasionally, reliving a familiar event. One time, the patient hummed along with the music she was "hearing," and the nurse, recognizing the tune, joined in by supplying the lyrics. (Does this not sound like a scene from a Monty Python movie—a sing-along during brain surgery?) People with epileptic activity or brain damage in their temporal lobes sometimes hear familiar tunes as well. Unfortunately, Penfield made no attempt to verify whether the apparent memories were factual or a sort of electrically induced dream; we will see in Chapter 12, however, that part of the temporal lobe has an important role in memory.

Finally, the *occipital lobes* are the location of the *visual cortex,* which is where visual information is processed (see Figure 3.8). The primary projection area occupies the posterior tip of each lobe; anterior to the primary area are four association areas that detect individual components of a scene, such as color, movement, and form; this information is then combined and processed further in other association areas, particularly in the temporal and parietal lobes. Just as the somatosensory and motor areas are organized to represent the shape of the body, the visual cortex contains a map of visual space because adjacent receptors in the back of the eye send neurons to adjacent cells in the visual cortex.

Now that you are familiar with the four lobes and some of the functions located in the cortex, we will direct our tour to structures below the surface.

The Thalamus and Hypothalamus

Deep within the brain, the *thalamus* lies just below the lateral ventricles, where it receives information from all the sensory systems except olfaction (smell) and relays it to the respective cortical projection areas. (Figure 3.13 is a sagittal view of a brain sliced down the middle to show the structures described in this section.) Many other neurons from the thalamus project more diffusely throughout the cortex and help arouse the cortex when appropriate. Actually there are two thalami, a right and a left, lying side by side. We will discuss additional functions for the thalamus in later chapters.

The *hypothalamus*, a smaller structure just inferior to the thalamus, plays a major role in controlling emotion and motivated behaviors such as eating, drinking, and sexual activity (see Figure 3.13). The hypothalamus exerts this influence largely through its control of the autonomic nervous system, which we will consider shortly. The hypothalamus also influences the body's hormonal environment through its control over the pituitary gland. In Figure 3.13, the pituitary appears to be hanging down on its stalk just below the hypothalamus. The pituitary is known as the *master gland* because its hormones control other glands in the body. The hypothalamus, which like the thalamus is paired, contains perhaps the largest concentration of nuclei important to behavior in the entire brain.

Just posterior to the thalamus is the pineal gland. You can see in Figure 3.13 why it was Descartes's best candidate for the seat of the soul (see Chapter 1): It is a single, unpaired structure, attached by its flexible stalk just below the hemispheres. In reality, the *pineal gland* secretes melatonin, a hormone that induces sleep. It controls seasonal cycles in nonhuman animals and participates with other structures in controlling daily rhythms in humans.

The Corpus Callosum

If you were to look inside the longitudinal fissure between the two cerebral hemispheres, you would see that the hemispheres are distinctly separate from each other. A couple of inches below the brain's surface, the longitudinal fissure ends in the *corpus callosum,* a dense band of fibers that carry information between the hemispheres. The corpus callosum is visible in Figure 3.13; you can see it from another perspective, along

 What functions are found in the occipital lobes?

 What functions do the thalamus and hypothalamus perform?

■ **FIGURE 3.13**   Sagittal View of the Interior Features of the Human Brain.

In this view, the cut has been made between the cerebral hemispheres. Everything above the midbrain is forebrain; everything below is hindbrain.

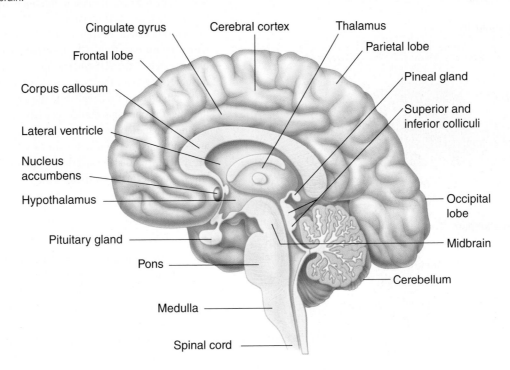

■ **FIGURE 3.14** A Patient With Severed Corpus Callosum Identifying Objects by Touch.

He cannot say what the object is because the right hemisphere, which receives the information from the hand, has been disconnected from the more verbal left hemisphere. Results are similar for visually presented stimuli and sound information.

■ **FIGURE 3.15** The Ventricles of the Brain.

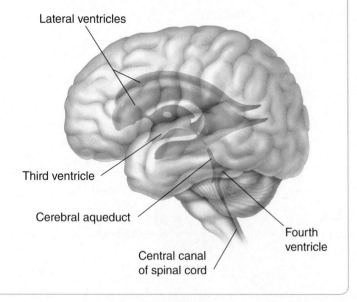

with a smaller band of crossing fibers, the anterior commissure, by looking back at Figure 3.5. You know that the two hemispheres carry out somewhat different functions, so you can imagine that they must communicate with each other constantly to integrate their activities. In addition, incoming information is often directed to one hemisphere—visual information appearing to one side of your field of view goes to the hemisphere on the opposite side, just as information from one side of your body does. This information is "shared" with the other hemisphere through the crossing fibers, especially the corpus callosum; the car that is too close on your left is registered in your right hemisphere, but if you are steering with your right hand, it is your left hemisphere that must react.

Occasionally, surgeons have to sever the corpus callosum in patients with incapacitating epileptic seizures that cannot be controlled by drugs. The surgery prevents the out-of-control neural activity in one hemisphere from engulfing the other hemisphere as well. The patient is then able to maintain consciousness during seizures and to lead a more normal life. These patients have been very useful for studying differences in the functions of the two hemispheres, because a stimulus can be presented to one hemisphere and the information will not be shared with the other hemisphere. Studies of these individuals have helped establish, for example, that the left hemisphere is more specialized for language than the right hemisphere and the right hemisphere is better at spatial tasks and recognizing faces (Gazzaniga, 1967; Nebes, 1974). An example is shown in Figure 3.14. We will explore this topic further when we discuss consciousness in Chapter 15.

The Ventricles

During development, the hollow interior of the nervous system develops into cavities called *ventricles* in the brain and the central canal in the spinal cord. The ventricles are filled with *cerebrospinal fluid,* which carries material from the blood vessels to the CNS and transports waste materials in the other direction. The *lateral ventricles* (Figures 3.13 and 3.15) extend forward deeply into the frontal lobes and in the other direction into the occipital lobes before they curve around into the temporal lobes. Below the lateral ventricles and connected to them is the *third ventricle;* it is located between the two thalami and the two halves of the hypothalamus, which form the ventricle's walls. The *fourth ventricle* is not in the forebrain, so we will locate it later.

The Midbrain and Hindbrain

The *midbrain* contains structures that have secondary roles in vision, hearing, and movement (Figures 3.13 and 3.16). The *superior colliculi,* for example, help guide eye movements and fixation of gaze, and the *inferior colliculi* help locate the direction of sounds. One of the structures involved in movement is the *substantia nigra,* which projects to the basal ganglia to integrate movements; its dopamine-releasing cells degenerate in Parkinson's disease (see Chapter 11). Another is the *ventral tegmental area,* which plays a role in the rewarding effects of food, sex, drugs, and so on (see Chapter 5). The midbrain also contains part of the reticular formation, which is described below. Passing through the midbrain is the cerebral aqueduct, which connects the third ventricle above with the fourth ventricle below (see Figure 3.15). Notice in Figure 3.16 that the brain takes on a more obvious tubular shape here, reminding us of the CNS's origins. Considering the shape of these structures and the appearance of the cerebral hemispheres perched on top, you can see why this part of the brain is referred to as the *brain stem.*

The hindbrain is composed of the pons, the medulla, and the cerebellum (see Figures 3.13 and 3.16). The *pons* contains centers related to sleep and arousal, which are part of the reticular formation. The *reticular formation* is a collection of many nuclei running through the middle of the hindbrain and the midbrain; besides its role in sleep and arousal, it contributes to attention and to aspects of motor activity, including reflexes and muscle tone. The word *pons* means "bridge" in Latin, which reflects not only its appearance but also the fact that its fibers connect the two hemispheres of the cerebellum; the pons also has pathways connecting higher areas of the brain with the brain stem. The *medulla* forms the lower part of the hindbrain; its nuclei are involved with control of essential life processes, such as cardiovascular activity and respiration (breathing).

The cerebellum is the second most distinctive-appearing brain structure (see Figures 3.2, 3.8, 3.13, and 3.20). Perched on the back of the brain stem, it is wrinkled and divided down the middle like the cerebral hemispheres—thus its name, which means "little brain." The most obvious function of the *cerebellum* is refining movements initiated by the motor cortex by controlling their speed, intensity, and direction. A person whose cerebellum is damaged has trouble making precise reaching movements and walks with difficulty because the automatic patterning of movement routines has been lost. It is not unusual for individuals with cerebellar damage to be arrested by the police because their uncoordinated gait is easily mistaken for drunkenness. The cerebellum also plays a role in motor learning, and research implicates it in other cognitive processes and in emotion (Fiez, 1996). With 70% of the brain's neurons in its fist-sized volume, it would be surprising if it did not hold a number of mysteries waiting to be solved.

We have admittedly covered a large number of structures. It may help to see them and their major functions summarized in Table 3.2. But as you review these functions, remember the caveat about localization from Chapter 1 that a behavior is seldom the province of a single brain location but instead results from the interplay of a whole network of structures.

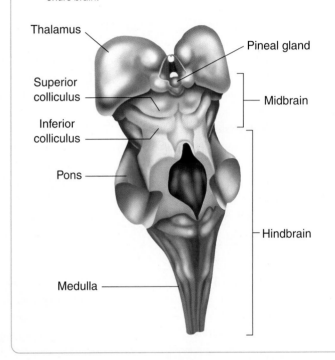

■ **FIGURE 3.16** The Brain Stem.

The brain stem includes posterior parts of the forebrain (thalamus, hypothalamus, etc.), the midbrain, and the hindbrain. The cerebellum has been removed to reveal the other structures. This is a dorsal view of the brain stem. Refer to Figure 3.13 for its orientation with respect to the entire brain.

TABLE 3.2 Major Structures of the Brain and Their Functions.

STRUCTURE	MAJOR FUNCTION
Forebrain	
Frontal lobes	
Motor cortex	Plans and executes voluntary movements
Basal ganglia	Smooths movement generated by motor cortex
Broca's area	Controls speech, adds grammar
Prefrontal cortex	Involved in planning, impulse control

(Continued)

TABLE 3.2   (Continued)

STRUCTURE	MAJOR FUNCTION
Forebrain	
Parietal lobes	
Somatosensory cortex	Projection area for body senses
Association area	Location of body and objects in space
Temporal lobes	
Auditory cortex	Projection area for auditory information
Wernicke's area	Language area involved with meaning
Inferior temporal cortex	Visual identification of objects
Occipital lobes	
Primary visual cortex	Projection area for visual information
Visual association cortex	Processes components of visual information
Corpus callosum	Communication between the hemispheres
Ventricles	Contain cerebrospinal fluid
Thalamus	Relays sensory information to cortex
Hypothalamus	Coordinates emotional and motivational functions
Pineal gland	Controls daily and seasonal rhythms
Midbrain	
Superior colliculi	Role in vision—for example, eye movements
Inferior colliculi	Role in hearing, such as sound location
Substantia nigra	Integrates movement
Ventral tegmental area	Contributes to rewarding effects of food, sex, and drugs
Hindbrain	
Medulla	Reflexively controls life processes
Pons	Contains centers related to sleep and arousal
Reticular formation	Involved with sleep, arousal, attention, some motor functions
Cerebellum	Controls speed, intensity, direction of movements

The Spinal Cord

The *spinal cord* is a finger-sized cable of neurons that carries commands from the brain to the muscles and organs and sensory information into the brain. Its role is more complicated than that, though. It controls the rapid reflexive response when you withdraw your hand from a hot stove, and it contains pattern generators that help control routine behaviors such as walking. Notice the appearance of the interior of the spinal cord in Figure 3.17; it is arranged just the opposite of the brain, with the white matter on the outside and the gray matter in the interior. The white exterior is made up of axons—ascending sensory tracts on their way to the brain and descending motor tracts on their way to the muscles and organs.

? What is the structure of the spinal cord?

Sensory neurons enter the spinal cord through the *dorsal root* of each spinal nerve. The sensory neurons are unipolar; clustering of their cell bodies in the dorsal root ganglion explains the dorsal root's enlargement. The sensory neuron in Figure 3.17 could be as much as 1 meter (m) long, with its other end out in a fingertip or a toe. The H-shaped structure in the middle of the spinal cord is made up mostly

■ **FIGURE 3.17**　Horizontal Cross Section of the Spinal Cord, With Reflex Circuit.

A sensory neuron from the hand transmits signals (1) via the dorsal root of the spinal nerve into the spinal cord, where it (2) forms a reflex arc with a motor neuron that (3) exits through the ventral root and (4) activates the biceps muscle to flex the arm and withdraw the hand. The sensory input also travels (5) up to the brain to produce a sensation. (6) A motor neuron from the brain connects to the motor neuron in the ventral horn; this adds a voluntary activation of the muscle, though more slowly. (In reality, many neurons would be involved.)

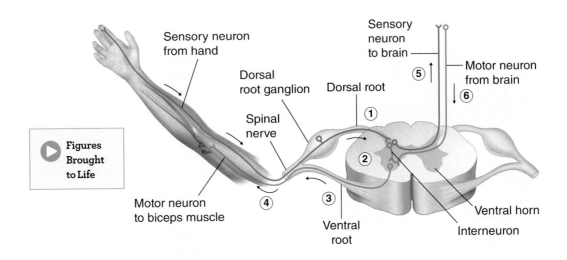

of unmyelinated cell bodies. The cell bodies of motor neurons are located in the *ventral horns,* which is why the ventral horns are enlarged. The axons of the motor neurons pass out of the spinal cord through the *ventral root.* The dorsal root and the ventral root on the same side of the cord join to form a spinal nerve that exits the spine between adjacent vertebrae (the bones that make up the spine).

Most of the motor neurons receive their input from the brain, either from the motor cortex or from nuclei that control the activity of the internal organs. Notice in Figure 3.17, however, that in some cases sensory neurons from the dorsal side connect with motor neurons, either directly or through an interneuron. This pathway produces a simple, automatic movement in response to a sensory stimulus; this is called a *reflex.* For example, when you touch a lighted match with your hand, input travels to the spinal cord, where signals are directed out to the muscles of the arm to produce reflexive withdrawal. Many people use the term *reflex* incorrectly to refer to any action a person takes without apparent thought; however, the term is limited to behaviors that are controlled by these direct sensory-motor connections. Besides not requiring thought, reflexive acts occur much more rapidly than the same response produced voluntarily. Reflexes originate in the brain as well as in the spinal cord, and reflexes also affect the internal environment—for example, reducing blood pressure when it goes too high.

Protecting the Central Nervous System

The brain and the spinal cord are delicate organs, vulnerable to damage from blows and jostling, to poisoning by toxins, and to disruption by mislocated or excessive neurotransmitters. Both structures are enclosed in a protective three-layered membrane called the *meninges.* The space between the meninges and the CNS is filled with cerebrospinal fluid, which cushions the neural tissue from the trauma of blows and sudden movement. The brain and spinal cord literally float in the cerebrospinal fluid, so the weight of a 1,200- to 1,400-g brain is in effect reduced to less than 100 g. The tough meninges and the cerebrospinal fluid afford

■ **FIGURE 3.18**   The Blood-Brain Barrier.

The tight junctions of the capillary walls prevent passage of large molecules into the brain. Small molecules, such as oxygen and carbon dioxide, pass through freely, as do fat-soluble substances, including most drugs. Water-soluble substances such as amino acids and glucose must be transported through the walls.

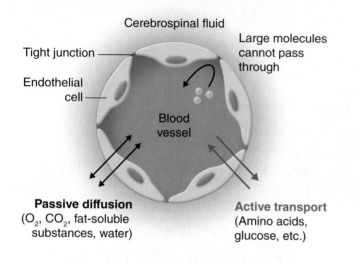

the brain some protection from occasional trauma, but the *blood-brain barrier,* which limits passage between the bloodstream and the brain, provides constant protection from toxic substances and from neurotransmitters circulating in the blood such as norepinephrine, which increases during stress.

Outside the brain, the cells that compose the walls of the capillaries (small blood vessels) have gaps between them that allow most substances to pass rather freely. In the brain, these cells are joined so tightly that easy passage is limited to small molecules such as carbon dioxide and oxygen and to substances that can dissolve in the lipid (fat) of the capillary walls (Figure 3.18). Fat solubility accounts for the effectiveness of most drugs, both therapeutic and abused. Most substances needed by the brain are water soluble and cannot pass through on their own, so glucose, iron, amino acids (the building blocks that proteins are made of), and many vitamins must be actively carried through the walls by specialized transporters.

Not all brain areas are protected by the barrier, however. This is particularly true of brain structures surrounding the ventricles. One of them is the area postrema; when you ingest something toxic, such as an excess of alcohol, the substance passes from the bloodstream into the area postrema. Because the area postrema induces vomiting, your stomach empties quickly—ideally before too much harm is done.

CONCEPT CHECK

Take a Minute to Check Your Knowledge and Understanding

- What is the advantage of the convoluted structure of the cortex?
- What has been the fate of psychosurgery; what clue from past experience did doctors have that lobotomy in particular might have undesirable consequences?
- Select one of the lobes or the midbrain or the hindbrain and describe the structures and functions located there.
- Describe the pathway of a reflex, identifying the neurons and the parts of the spinal cord involved.

The Peripheral Nervous System

The *peripheral nervous system (PNS)* is made up of the *cranial nerves,* which enter and leave the underside of the brain, and the *spinal nerves,* which connect to the sides of the spinal cord at each vertebra. From a functional perspective, the PNS can be divided into the somatic nervous system and the autonomic nervous system. The *somatic nervous system* includes the motor neurons that operate the skeletal muscles—that is, the ones that move the body—and the sensory neurons that bring information into the CNS from the body and the outside world. The *autonomic nervous system (ANS)* controls smooth muscle (stomach, blood vessels, etc.), the glands, and the heart and other organs. The diagram in Figure 3.19 will help you keep track of these divisions and relate them to the CNS. We dealt with the spinal nerves when we discussed the spinal cord, and we have said all we need to for now about the somatic system, so we will give the rest of our attention to the cranial nerves and the ANS.

The Cranial Nerves

The cranial nerves enter and exit on the ventral side of the brain (Figure 3.20). Whereas the spinal nerves are concerned exclusively with sensory and motor activities within the body, some of the cranial nerves convey sensory information to the brain from the outside world. Two of these, the olfactory nerves and the optic nerves, are often considered part of the brain. One reason for this special status is the brainlike complexity of the olfactory bulb and of the retina at the back of the eye; another is that their receptor cells originate in the brain during development and migrate to their final locations. As a consequence, the olfactory and optic nerves are sometimes referred to as *tracts.*

The Autonomic Nervous System

The functions of the ANS are primarily motor; its sensory pathways provide internal information for regulating its own operations. The ANS is composed of two branches. The *sympathetic nervous system* activates the body in ways that help it cope with demands such as emotional stress and physical emergencies. Your most recent emergency may have been when you overslept on the morning of a big exam. As you raced to class, your heart and breathing sped up to provide your body the resources it needed. Your blood pressure increased as well, and your peripheral blood vessels constricted, shifting blood supply to the internal organs, including your brain. Your muscles tensed to help you fight or flee, and your sweat glands started pouring out sweat to cool your overheating body. All this activity was just the sympathetic nervous system at work. The *parasympathetic nervous system* not only slows the activity of most organs to conserve energy but also activates digestion to renew energy.

The sympathetic branch rises from the middle (thoracic and lumbar) areas of the spinal cord (Figure 3.21). Most sympathetic neurons pass through the *sympathetic ganglion chain,* which runs along each side of the spine; there they synapse with postsynaptic neurons that rejoin the spinal nerve and go out to the muscles or glands they serve. (The others pass directly to ganglia in the body cavity before synapsing.) Because most of the sympathetic ganglia are highly interconnected in the sympathetic ganglion chain, this system tends to respond as a unit. Thus, when you were rush-

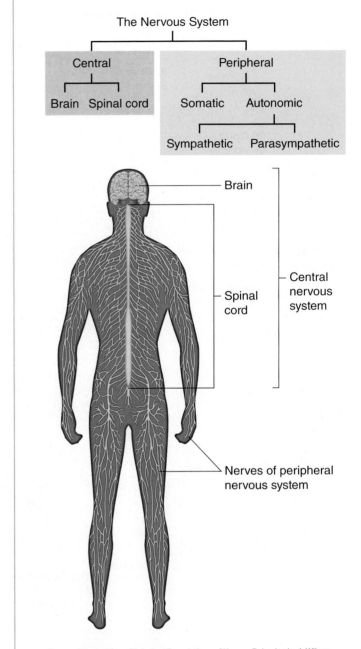

■ FIGURE 3.19   Divisions of the Nervous System.

Source: Adapted from *Biological Foundations of Human Behavior,* by J. Wilson, 2003, Belmont, CA: Wadsworth.

ing to your exam, your whole body went into hyperdrive. As you can see in Figure 3.21, the parasympathetic branch rises from the extreme ends of the PNS—in the cranial nerves and in the spinal nerves at the lower (sacral) end of the spinal cord. The parasympathetic ganglia are not interconnected but are located on or near the muscles and glands they control; as a result, the components of the parasympathetic system operate more independently than those of the sympathetic system.

Organs are innervated by both branches of the ANS, with the exception of the sweat glands, the adrenal glands, and the muscles that constrict blood vessels, which receive only sympathetic activation. It is not accurate to assume that one branch is active at a time and the other completely shuts down. Rather, both are active to some degree all the time, and the body's general activity reflects the balance between sympathetic and parasympathetic stimulation.

? What are the functions of the autonomic nervous system?

■ FIGURE 3.20   Ventral View of the Brain Showing the Cranial Nerves and Their Major Functions.

Brain landmarks are labeled to help you locate the nerves.

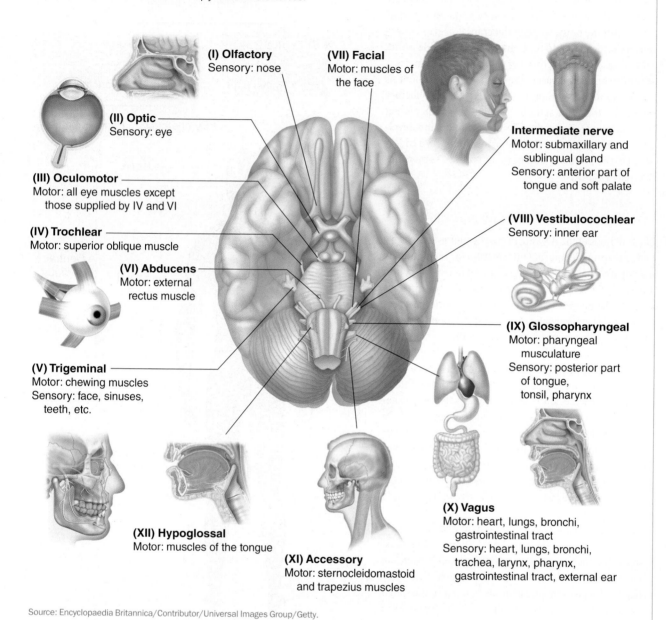

(I) Olfactory
Sensory: nose

(II) Optic
Sensory: eye

(III) Oculomotor
Motor: all eye muscles except
those supplied by IV and VI

(IV) Trochlear
Motor: superior oblique muscle

(VI) Abducens
Motor: external
rectus muscle

(V) Trigeminal
Motor: chewing muscles
Sensory: face, sinuses,
teeth, etc.

(VII) Facial
Motor: muscles of
the face

Intermediate nerve
Motor: submaxillary and
sublingual gland
Sensory: anterior part of
tongue and soft palate

(VIII) Vestibulocochlear
Sensory: inner ear

(IX) Glossopharyngeal
Motor: pharyngeal
musculature
Sensory: posterior part
of tongue,
tonsil, pharynx

(XII) Hypoglossal
Motor: muscles of the tongue

(XI) Accessory
Motor: sternocleidomastoid
and trapezius muscles

(X) Vagus
Motor: heart, lungs, bronchi,
gastrointestinal tract
Sensory: heart, lungs, bronchi,
trachea, larynx, pharynx,
gastrointestinal tract, external ear

Source: Encyclopaedia Britannica/Contributor/Universal Images Group/Getty.

Take a Minute to Check Your Knowledge and Understanding

- Which cranial nerves are sometimes referred to as tracts, and why?
- Why does the sympathetic system operate more as a unit than the parasympathetic system does?
- How do the branches of the ANS interact to regulate internal activity?

■ FIGURE 3.21   The Autonomic Nervous System.

A diagrammatic view of the parasympathetic and sympathetic nerves and their functions. The nerves exit both sides of the brain and spinal cord through the paired cranial and spinal nerves but are shown on one side for simplicity.

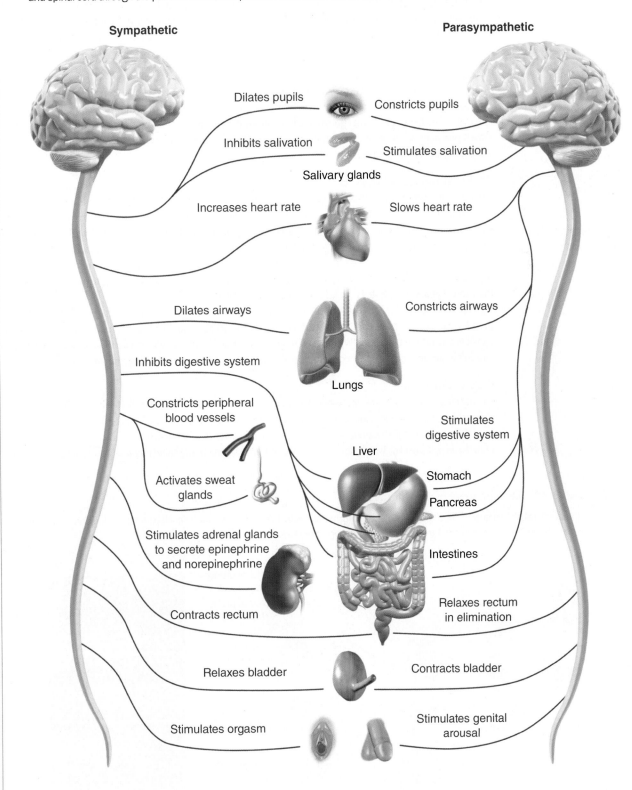

Development and Change in the Nervous System

Nothing rivals the human brain in complexity, which makes the development of the brain the most remarkable construction project that you or we can imagine. During development, its 100 billion neurons must find their way to destinations throughout the brain and the spinal cord; then they must make precise connections to an average of a thousand target cells each (Tessier-Lavigne & Goodman, 1996). How this is accomplished is one of the most intriguing mysteries of neurology, but it is a mystery that is being solved a little at a time.

The Stages of Development

You already know that the nervous system begins as a hollow tube that later becomes the brain and the spinal cord. The nervous system begins development when the surface of the embryo forms a neural groove (Figure 3.22). The edges of this groove curl upward until they meet, turning the groove into a neural tube. Development of the nervous system then proceeds in four distinct stages: cell proliferation, migration, circuit formation, and circuit pruning.

Proliferation and Migration

? How do neurons find their correct destination?

During *proliferation,* the cells that will become neurons divide and multiply at the rate of 250,000 new cells every minute. Proliferation occurs in the ventricular zone, the area surrounding the hollow tube that will later become the ventricles and the central canal. During *migration,* these newly formed neurons move from the ventricular zone outward to their final location. They do so with the aid of specialized *radial glial cells* (Figure 3.23 on page 69). Remember Karen from the beginning of the chapter? This is where development went awry in her brain. The neurons that would have formed her cortex failed to migrate properly and got off their radial glial cell scaffolds too early (J. W. Fox et al., 1998).

The functional role that a neuron will play depends on its location and the time of its "birth"; different structures form during different stages of fetal development. Prior to birth and for a time afterward, the neurons retain considerable functional flexibility, however. In fact, fetal brain tissue can be transplanted into a different part of an adult brain, and the transplanted neurons will form synapses and assume the function of their new location.

Circuit Formation

During *circuit formation,* the axons of developing neurons grow toward their target cells and form functional connections. For example, axons of motor neurons grow toward the spinal cord, and cells in the retina of the eye send their axons to the thalamus, where they form synapses with other neurons. To find their way, axons form *growth cones* at their tip, which sample the environment for directional cues (Figure 3.24 on page 70). Chemical

---

■ **FIGURE 3.22**   Development of the Neural Tube.

The photograph (a) shows how the neural groove closes to form the neural tube, which will then develop into the brain and spinal cord. Details are shown in end views in the drawing (b) and microscopic photos (c).

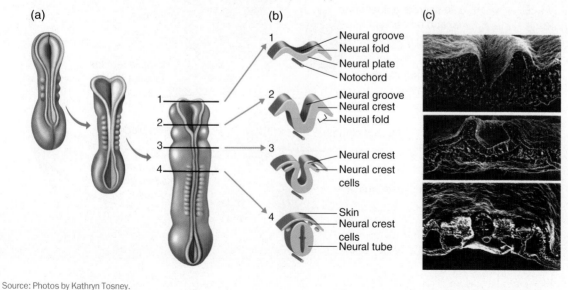

Source: Photos by Kathryn Tosney.

and molecular signposts attract or repel the advancing axon, coaxing it along the way (Tessier-Lavigne & Goodman, 1996). By pushing, pulling, and hemming neurons in from the side, the chemical and molecular forces guide the neurons to intermediate stations and past inappropriate targets until they reach their final destinations.

The path to the developing axon's destination is not necessarily direct, but thanks to changing genetic control, it is able to make direction changes along the way. This is most strongly illustrated by an axon whose destination is on the opposite side of the midline. Ordinarily, a migrating axon will grow parallel to the midline without crossing over, because it is repelled by a midline chemical that is under the control of the gene *Robo1*. But at the appropriate location, the gene *Robo3* becomes active; the axon is then attracted to the midline and turns and enters it. At that point, *Robo3* is downregulated; the axon is repelled again and, continuing in the same direction, exits the midline and will not recross (C. G. Woods, 2004).

Circuit Pruning

The brain produces extra neurons, apparently as a means of compensating for the errors that occur in reaching targets. This overproduction is not trivial: The monkey's visual cortex contains 35% more neurons at the time of birth than in adulthood, and the number of axons crossing the corpus callosum is four times what it will be later in life (LaMantia & Rakic, 1990; R. W. Williams, Ryder, & Rakic, 1987). The next stage of neural development, *circuit pruning,* involves the elimination of excess neurons and synapses. Neurons that are unsuccessful in finding a place on a target cell, or that arrive late, die; the monkey's corpus callosum alone loses 8 million neurons a day during the first 3 weeks after birth.

In a second step of circuit pruning, the nervous system refines its organization and continues to correct errors by eliminating large numbers of excessive synapses. For example, in mature mammals, neurons from the left and right eyes project to alternating columns of cells in the visual cortex, but the connections made during development are indiscriminate. Synapses are strengthened or weakened depending on whether the presynaptic neuron and the postsynaptic neuron fire together. Because a single neuron cannot by itself cause another neuron to fire, this is likely to happen when neighboring neurons are also firing and adding summating inputs through overlapping terminals. If a neuron is *not* firing at the same time as its neighbors, it has probably made its connection in the wrong neighborhood. It is thought that the postsynaptic neuron sends feedback to the presynaptic terminals in the form of *neurotrophins,* chemicals that enhance the development and survival of neurons.

In the visual system, sensory stimulation provides neuronal activation that contributes to this refinement. However, pruning of synapses begins in some parts of the visual system even before birth. How can this stimulation occur when visual input is impossible? The answer is that waves of spontaneous neural firing sweep across the fetal retina, providing the activation that selects which synapses will survive and which will not (Hooks & Chen, 2007; Huberman, 2007). In the first few years of the rhesus monkey's life, 40% of the synapses in the primary visual cortex are eliminated, at the stunning rate of 5,000 per second (Bourgeois & Rakic, 1993). This process of producing synapses that will later be eliminated seems wasteful, but targeting neurons' destinations more precisely would require prohibitively complex chemical and molecular codes. Later, the *plasticity* (ability to be modified) of these synapses decreases; a practical example is that recovery from injury to the language areas of the brain is greatly reduced in adulthood. However, the synapses in the cortical association areas are more likely to retain their plasticity, permitting later modification by experience—in other words, learning (Kandel & O'Dell, 1992; W. Singer, 1995).

As impressive as is the brain's ability to organize itself during development, mistakes do occur and for a variety of reasons. Periventricular heterotopia, the problem Karen had (see beginning of the chapter), is caused by any one of a variety of gene mutations that cause developing neurons to clump near the ventricles

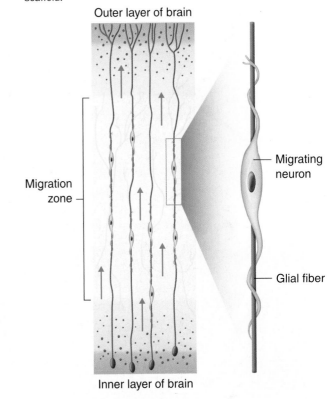

■ FIGURE 3.23 A Neuron Migrates Along Glial Scaffolding.

Left: Immature neurons migrate from the inner layer, where they were "born," to their destination between there and the outer layer. Right: A close-up of one of the neurons climbing a radial glial cell scaffold.

Outer layer of brain

Migration zone

Migrating neuron

Glial fiber

Inner layer of brain

Source: Adapted from illustration by Lydia Kibiuk, © 1995.

? What determines which synapses will survive?

■ **FIGURE 3.24**   Neurons With Growth Cones.

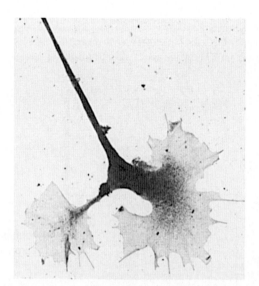

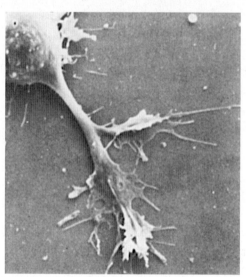

Source: Steven Rothman, MD.

rather than migrate to the cortex. *Fetal alcohol syndrome,* which often produces intellectual disability, is caused by the mother's use of alcohol during a critical period of brain development. The brains of individuals with fetal alcohol syndrome are often small and malformed, and neurons are dislocated (Figure 3.25). During migration, many cortical neurons fail to line up in columns as they normally would because the radial glial cells revert to their more typical glial form prematurely; other neurons continue migrating beyond the usual boundary of the cortex (Clarren, Alvord, Sumi, Streissguth, & Smith, 1978; Gressens, Lammens, Picard, & Evrard, 1992; P. D. Lewis, 1985). Exposure to ionizing radiation, such as that produced by nuclear accidents and atomic blasts, also causes intellectual impairment by interfering with both proliferation and migration. The offspring of women who were in the 8th through 15th weeks of pregnancy during the bombing of Hiroshima and Nagasaki and during the meltdowns at the Chernobyl and Fukushima nuclear generating stations were the most vulnerable, because the rates of proliferation and migration are highest then (Schull, Norton, & Jensh, 1990).

An additional step is required for full maturation of the nervous system: myelination. In the brain, it begins with the lower structures and then proceeds to the cerebral hemispheres, moving from occipital lobes to frontal lobes. Myelination starts around the end of the third trimester of fetal development but is not complete until late adolescence or beyond (Sowell, Thompson, Holmes, Jernigan, & Toga, 1999). This slow process has behavioral implications—for instance, contributing to the improvement through adolescence on cognitive tasks that require the frontal lobes (H. S. Levin et al., 1991). Considering the role of the prefrontal cortex in impulse control and the fact that this area is the last to mature (Sowell et al., 1999), it should come as no surprise that parents are often baffled by their adolescents' behavior.

How Experience Modifies the Nervous System

Stimulation continues to shape synaptic construction and reconstruction throughout the individual's life. For example, training rats to find their way through a maze or just exposing them to a complex living environment causes increased branching of synapses in the cortex (Greenough, 1975). Humans lose neurons as they age, but they develop *more* synapses (Buell & Coleman, 1979), presumably as the result of experience.

Experience-induced change can involve *reorganization,* a shift in connections that changes the function of an area of the brain. For example, in blind people who read Braille, the space in the brain devoted to the index (reading) finger increases, at the expense of the area corresponding to the other fingers on the same hand (Pascual-Leone & Torres, 1993). In a brain scan study, researchers discovered that blind individuals who excel at sound localization had recruited the unused visual area of their brains to aid in the task (Gougoux, Zatorre, Lassonde, Voss, & Lepore, 2005). This rewiring is not random: In blind individuals, trying to locate sounds or touch activated the area normally involved in visual localization; when cats deaf from birth located objects or detected motion visually they used areas that ordinarily perform those functions with sounds (Lomber, Meredith, & Kral, 2010; Renier et al., 2010). Much of our brain plasticity is lost after the age of two or three (Bedny, Konkle, Pelphrey, Saxe, & Pascual-Leone, 2010), but dramatic changes can occur in adulthood. And some of them take place rapidly, as we see in a study of individuals born with a condition called *syndactyly,* in which the fingers are attached to each other by a web of skin. Use of the fingers is severely limited, and the fingers are represented by overlapping areas in the somatosensory cortex. Figure 3.26 shows that after surgery, the representations of the fingers in the cortex became separate and distinct in just seven days (Mogilner et al., 1993).

 What kinds of changes occur in the brain due to experience?

■ **FIGURE 3.25** Fetal Alcohol Syndrome in the Mouse Brain.

(a) In this cross section of the normal cortex, the neurons (the dark spots) tend to line up in vertical columns. (b) In the alcohol-exposed brain, the neurons are arranged randomly.

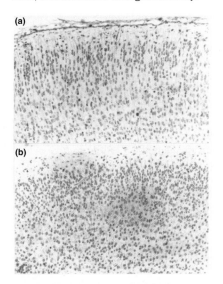

Source: From "Ethanol Induced Disturbances of Gliogenesis and Neurogenesis in the Developing Murine Brain: An *in Vitro* and an *in Vivo* Immunohistochemical and Ultrastructural Study," by P. Gressens, M. Lammans, J. J. Picard, and P. Evrard, *Alcohol and Alcoholism, 27,* pp. 219–226. © 1992. Used by permission of Oxford University Press.

■ **FIGURE 3.26** Changes in the Somatosensory Area Following Surgery for Syndactyly.

(a) The hand before (top) and after (bottom) surgery. (b) Images (coronal) showing brain areas responsive to stimulation of the fingers before and after surgery. (c) Graphic representation of the relative size and location of the responsive areas.

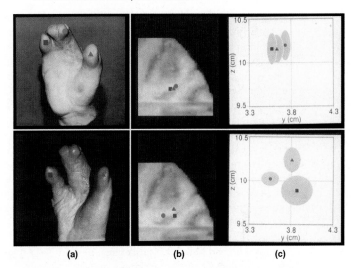

Source: From "Somatosensory Cortical Plasticity in Adult Humans Revealed by Magnetoencephalography," by A. Mogilner et al., 1993, *Proceedings of the National Academy of Sciences*, 90, pp. 3593–3597.

The 19th-century philosopher and psychologist William James speculated that if a surgeon could switch your optic nerves with your auditory nerves, you would then see thunder and hear lightning (James, 1893). James was expressing Johannes Müller's *doctrine of specific nerve energies* from a half century earlier—that each sensory projection area produces its own unique experience regardless of the kind of stimulation it receives. This is why you "see stars" when your skateboard shoots out from under you and the back of your head (where the visual cortex is located) hits the pavement.

But during early development, even this basic principle of brain operation can fall victim to reorganization. In people blind from birth, the visual cortex has nothing to do; as a result, some of the somatosensory pathways take over part of the area, so the visual cortex is activated by touch. But in this case, does the visual cortex produce a visual experience, or one of touch? To find out, researchers stimulated the visual cortex of blind individuals by applying an electromagnetic field to the scalp over the occipital area (L. G. Cohen et al., 1997). In sighted people, this disrupted visual performance, but in the blind individuals, the procedure distorted their sense of touch and interfered with their ability to identify Braille letters. Apparently, their visual area was actually processing information about touch in a meaningful way!

Reorganization does not always produce a beneficial outcome. When kittens were reared in an environment with no visual stimulation except horizontal stripes or vertical stripes, they didn't develop the ability to respond to objects in the other orientation. A cat reared, for example, with vertical stripes would play with a rod held vertically and ignore the rod when it was horizontal. Electrical recording indicated that the cells in the visual cortex that would have responded to horizontally oriented stimuli had reorganized their connections in response to the limited stimulation. In Chapter 11, we will explain the related phenomenon of *phantom pain,* in which people who have a limb amputated often experience pain that seems to be located in the missing limb. It appears to be caused by sensory neurons from a nearby part of the body growing into the somatosensory area that had served the lost limb (Flor et al., 1995).

IN THE NEWS

BREASTMILK CONSUMPTION IS GOOD FOR THE BRAIN

Breastfeeding can be difficult for mothers, particularly those who return to work shortly after giving birth, and societal support for breastfeeding remains mixed. However, there is increasing evidence that breastmilk provides nutrition that promotes healthy nervous system development. One study followed preterm infants (those born 10 or more weeks early) for their first seven years to determine the impacts of early breastmilk consumption (Belfort et al., 2016). The researchers discovered that the more breastmilk infants consumed during their first 28 days, the greater the volume of gray matter in their brains at the time of their due date (when they would have been born if they were full term). At the age of seven years the children who had high breastmilk consumption also had higher IQ scores, working memory performance, motor abilities, math performance, and increased intercranial volume. These findings are important because they suggests that breastmilk consumption may help infants make up for some of the in-utero brain development that they missed by being born early.

Other researchers have approached investigations of breastmilk benefits in the gut (reported in Yong, 2016), showing that human breastmilk provides hundreds of human milk oligosaccharides (complex sugars) that promote development of good bacteria in the gut and protect against infections. You might think of gut bacteria as being important solely for digestion, but a host of studies have found associations between the type of bacteria found in the gut and psychological functions including stress, anxiety, and cognition (Mayer, Knight, Mazmanian, Cryan, & Tillisch, 2014). In fact, neuroscientists are now looking at ways that the collection of bacteria found in the gut (the gut microbiome) can influence brain activity, via signals sent through the vagus nerve. This research is clarifying the mechanism by which breastmilk could have profound impacts on later brain functioning.

THOUGHT QUESTIONS

1. How do scientists think breastmilk is able to influence later brain functioning in children who had early breastmilk consumption?

2. What special characteristic of breastmilk seems important in promoting babies' health and development?

For the news story on the link between breastmilk consumption and healthy nervous system development, visit edge.sagepub.com/garrett5e and select the Chapter 3 study resources.

Damage and Recovery in the Central Nervous System

One reason neuroscientists are interested in the development of the nervous system is because they hope to find clues about how to repair the nervous system when it is damaged by injury, disease, or developmental error. It is difficult to convey the impairment and suffering that results from brain disorders, but the staggering financial costs in Table 3.3 will give you some idea. Here we will focus mostly on stroke and trauma and leave the other sources of injury for later chapters.

Stroke, also known as cerebrovascular accident, is caused by a loss of blood flow in the brain. Most strokes are ischemic, caused by blockage of an artery by a blood clot or other obstruction; hemorrhagic strokes occur when an artery ruptures. The neurons are deprived of oxygen and glucose, of course, but most of the damage is due to *excitotosis* (not to be confused with *exocytosis*, mentioned in Chapter 2). In excitotosis, dying neurons release excess glutamate, which overstimulates the surrounding neurons. The neurons then die as large amounts of calcium enter the cells. Further impairment is caused by edema, an accumulation of fluid that causes increased pressure on the brain. Stroke is the fourth leading cause of death in the United States (Centers for Disease Control and Prevention, 2015a) and a leading cause of long-term disability, including paralysis and loss of language and other functions (Heron et al., 2009). In the accompanying Application, we discuss a novel treatment for breaking up ischemic clots when recovery is most likely.

TABLE 3.3 Annual Costs of Brain Damage and Disorders in the United States.

DAMAGE OR DISORDER	COST (IN BILLION U.S. DOLLARS)	
	United States	30 European Countries
Psychiatric disorders (schizophrenia, depression, anxiety)	192.85	407.73
Head/spinal cord injuries	94.91	40.76 (brain injury only)
Stroke	27.03	79.09
Dementias and Alzheimer's Disease	170.86	129.84
Addictions	544.11	81.10
Total	1,029.76	738.52

Source: Olesen et al. (2011); Uhl and Grow (2004).

Note: Includes direct costs of care and treatment and indirect costs such as crime, lost wages, and financial assistance. Differences between the U.S. and European data are due to a variety of factors, including incidence rate, greater cost of direct health care in the United States, and which indirect costs were included in each study.

Traumatic brain injury (TBI) is caused by an external mechanical force such as a blow to the head, sudden acceleration or deceleration, or penetration. TBIs cause 52,000 deaths each year in the United States; about 35% of TBIs are caused by falls, and another 17% result from traffic accidents (Faul, Xu, Wald, & Coronado, 2010). Besides the direct damage to neurons, edema and ischemia (loss of blood supply due to blood clots) take an additional toll. Mild traumatic injury, or concussion as it is more commonly known, is the most common TBI. It results from blows and acceleration-deceleration that occur in automobile accidents, sports activities, and battlefield explosions. Whether or not these traumas are sufficient to cause loss of consciousness, they are often followed by headache, drowsiness, and memory loss, which usually go away if the individual rests for three weeks following the injury. Repeated concussions can cause cumulative brain damage. The expression "punch-drunk" refers to dementia pugilistica, the impairment suffered by boxers who didn't know when to quit. However, even a single concussion severe enough to cause brief unconsciousness or amnesia produces brain atrophy detectable one year later and correlated with memory and attention deficits (Y. Zhou et al., 2013).

TBI has been very much in the news recently because of its high incidence in sports. A research project at Boston University has found signs of Alzheimer's-like brain disease in autopsies of 87 out of 91 former National Football League (NFL) players (Breslow, 2015a); a suit by thousands of ex-players has resulted in a settlement that will cost the NFL upwards of $1 billion (Breslow, 2015b). But risk of brain damage isn't limited to professional contact sports. Even heading the ball in women's youth and college soccer can produce impacts 40 to 63 times the force of gravity (Hanlon & Bir, 2012; Lynall et al., 2016), and frequent heading is associated with white matter abnormalities and memory deficits (Lipton et al., 2013).

Limitations on Recovery

Nervous system repair is no problem for some species, particularly amphibians. For example, when Sperry (1943, 1945) severed the optic nerves of frogs, the eyes made functional reconnections to the brain even when the disconnected eye was turned upside down or transplanted into the other eye socket. *Regeneration,* the growth of severed axons, also occurs in mammals, at least in the PNS. So when you fell skateboarding, if you broke your arm so badly that a nerve was severed, the disconnected part of the cut axon would have died, but the part connected to the cell body would have survived and regrown. Myelin provides a guide tube for the sprouting end of a severed neuron to grow through (W. J. Freed, de Medinaceli, & Wyatt, 1985), and the extending axon is guided to its destination much as it would be during development (Horner & Gage, 2000).

But in the mammalian CNS, damaged neurons encounter a hostile environment. If your skateboarding accident severed neurons in your spinal cord, the axon stumps would sprout new growth, but they would make little progress toward their former target. This is partly because the CNS in adult mammals no longer

What limits central nervous system repair? How might repair be encouraged?

APPLICATION
Ultrasound Surgery

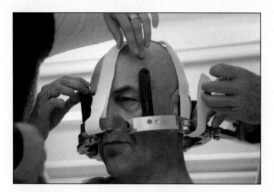

Source: AP Photo/The Canadian Press, Frank Gunn.

Brain disorders often require surgery, which has its own drawbacks. The use of focused ultrasound is making intervention noninvasive, safer, and more precise. The energy is focused on the target area by an acoustic lens, much the same way as a magnifying glass focuses beams of sunlight. An individual acoustic beam by itself has no effect, but when multiple intersecting beams of ultrasound are focused on a target they can produce important biological effects. The warming produced can be detected on a brain scan, which allows the surgeon to readjust the location. Targets can be as small as 1 mm^2 or up to 150 mm^2. Increasing the energy level generates enough heat to destroy the target, and the technique can be used to break up blood clots or destroy tumors and other diseased tissue, as well as to silence neural circuits to treat disabling tremors and unbearable pain (Monteith, Gwinn, & Newell, 2015).

Recent work suggests that these techniques can also be applied to neuropsychiatric disorders such as Alzheimer's and Parkinson's diseases, which historically have relied on drugs and invasive treatments (Leinenga, Langton, Nisbet, & Götz, 2016). The therapeutic effects are immediate and without the recovery and side effects typically seen with traditional surgery or radiation treatments. Researchers are also using the technique with transgenic mice that develop the brain pathology and memory deficits characteristic of Alzheimer's disease (Burgess et al., 2014). Their strategy is to activate glial cells and open the blood-brain barrier near memory structures, to allow immune cells to enter the brain and help clear away cellular damage caused by the disease.

> *In the adult centres the nerve paths are something fixed, ended and immutable.*
>
> *Everything may die, nothing may be regenerated. It is for the science of the future to change, if possible, this harsh decree.*
>
> —Santiago Ramón y Cajal, 1928

produces the chemical and molecular conditions that stimulate and guide neuronal growth. In addition, scar tissue produced by glial cells blocks the original pathway, glial cells also produce axon growth inhibitors, and immune cells move into the area and possibly interfere with regrowth (D. F. Chen, Schneider, Martinou, & Tonegawa, 1997; Horner & Gage, 2000; Thallmair et al., 1998).

Another way the nervous system could repair itself is by *neurogenesis,* the birth of new neurons. Neurogenesis occurs in several areas of adult animal brains (Kahn, Hough, Ten Eyck, & Bingman, 2003; C. D. Fowler, Liu, & Wang, 2007), but research indicates that it is most extensive in two places. One is the hippocampus, and the other is near the lateral ventricles, supplying the olfactory bulb (Gage, 2000). This research was done by administering bromodeoxyuridine (BrdU), which is taken up in the DNA of cells as they divide; the animals were then sacrificed, and the presence of BrdU in neurons in the brain indicated robust neurogenesis, especially in the hippocampus. In 1998, Peter Eriksson and his colleagues were able to use this technique with deceased cancer patients who had been given BrdU to track the spread of tumors, and they found the first evidence of neurogenesis in the adult human hippocampus. The use of BrdU in humans was banned shortly after that, making replication of the study difficult and leaving other researchers skeptical. Then a team at Stockholm's Karolinska Institute hit upon the idea of measuring carbon 14 (C14), which was absorbed by individuals around the world between 1945 and 1963 as a result of above-ground nuclear testing (Spalding et al., 2013). Cellular levels of C14 correspond to atmospheric levels, so the researchers were able to date the birth of new neurons and determine that our hippocampi add 1,400 new neurons every day. Neurogenesis in human olfactory bulbs has been controversial, apparently because it occurs at a much lower rate there than in other locations (Maheu et al., 2015).

These new neurons apparently contribute to the neural plasticity required in learning: Blocking neurogenesis in the hippocampus interferes with certain types of learning that involve that structure, and doing so in the olfactory bulbs impairs learning associations with odors (Lazarini & Lledo, 2011; Ming & Song, 2011). There is no guarantee that this neurogenesis contributes to brain repair following injury. However, neural precursor cells migrate to damaged areas in rats' brains following experimentally induced stroke and appear to replace damaged neurons (Parent, 2003). Furthermore, increased neurogenesis has been observed at damage sites in the brains of deceased Alzheimer's patients and Huntington's disease patients (Curtis et al., 2003; Jin et al., 2004). Results such as these suggest that if we could enhance neurogenesis, it might provide a means of self-repair.

Compensation and Reorganization

Although axons do not regenerate and neuron replacement is limited at best, considerable recovery of function can occur in the damaged mammalian CNS. Much of the improvement in function following injury is nonneural in nature and comes about as swelling diminishes and glia remove dead neurons (Bach-y-Rita, 1990). The simplest recovery that is neural in nature involves *compensation* as uninjured tissue takes over the functions of lost neurons. Presynaptic neurons sprout more terminals to form additional synapses with their targets (Fritschy & Grzanna, 1992; Goodman, Bogdasarian, & Horel, 1973), and postsynaptic neurons add more receptors (Bach-y-Rita, 1990). In addition, normally silent side branches from other neurons in the area become active within minutes of the injury (Das & Gilbert, 1995). These synaptic changes are similar to those occurring during learning; this would explain why physical therapy can be effective in promoting recovery after brain injury.

? **What forms of recovery are possible in the human CNS?**

A more dramatic form of neural recovery involves reorganization of other brain areas. During recovery of language ability following brain damage or surgery, the functions apparently are assumed by nearby brain areas or, in the case of massive damage, by the other hemisphere (Guerreiro, Castro-Caldas, & Martins, 1995). Occasionally, an entire hemisphere must be removed because it is diseased. The patients typically do not reach normal levels of performance after the surgery, but they often recover their language and other cognitive skills and motor control to a remarkable degree (Glees, 1980; J. Ogden, 1989). In these cases, malfunction in the removed hemisphere dated back to infancy, so presumably the reorganization began then rather than at the time of surgery in late adolescence or early adulthood. In rare instances, people are born entirely lacking a corpus callosum. A further tribute to the brain's plasticity is that 75% of these individuals develop normally and fewer than 12% are severely impaired (Sotiriadis & Makrydimas, 2012).

Recovery from aphasia and periventricular heterotopia challenges our understanding of how the brain works. Hydrocephalus provides another such example. *Hydrocephalus* occurs when the circulation of cerebrospinal fluid is blocked and the accumulating fluid interferes with the brain's growth, typically producing severe intellectual impairment. If detected in time, the condition can be treated by installing a drain that shunts the excess fluid into the bloodstream. However, the occasional individual somehow avoids impairment without this treatment. The British neurologist John Lorber described a 26-year-old college student with hydrocephalus whose ventricles were so enlarged that the cerebral walls (between his ventricles and the outer surface of his brain) were less than 1 mm thick, compared with the usual 45 mm (Figure 3.27). Yet he had a superior IQ of 126, had earned an honors degree in mathematics, and was socially normal (Lewin, 1980). It is unclear how these individuals can function normally in the face of such enormous brain deficits. What is clear is that somewhere in this remarkable plasticity lies the key to new revelations about brain function.

Possibilities for CNS Repair

In 1995, Christopher Reeve, the movie actor best known for his role as Superman, was paralyzed from the neck down when he was thrown from his horse during a competition. Three quarters of his spinal cord was destroyed at the level of the injury (J. W. McDonald et al., 2002). He had

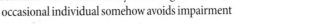

■ FIGURE 3.27 Normal Brain and Hydrocephalic Brain.

The ventricles are greatly enlarged and brain tissue is reduced in the brain on the right, compared with the normal brain on the left. The individual has an IQ of 75 (above the cutoff for intellectual impairment), is employed as a civil servant, and has a wife and two children.

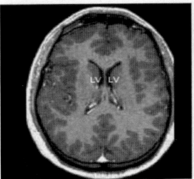
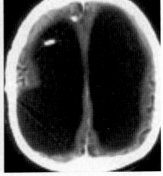

Source: Reprinted from "Brain of a White-Collar Worker," by L. Feuillet, H. Dufour, and J. Pelletier, 2007, *The Lancet*, 370, p. 262. © 2007, with permission from Elsevier.

■ **FIGURE 3.28**   Johnny Knox.

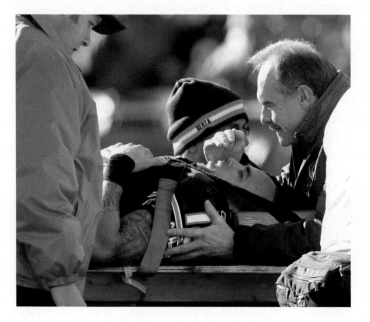

Source: Chicago Tribune/Contributor/Tribune News Service/Getty Images.

no motor control and almost no sensation below the neck; like 90% of similarly injured patients, he experienced little functional improvement over the next few years. Chicago Bears wide receiver Johnny Knox also suffered a severely damaged spinal cord, when a Seattle Seahawks lineman bent him backwards almost in half during a game in 2011 (Figure 3.28). Many people thought he would not be able to walk again due to the amount of damage; but unlike Reeve, through intensive treatment by properly trained staff at the time of injury and during the recovery process, and advances in spinal fusion surgery, he was able to regain the ability to walk despite shattering several vertebrae and severely bruising his spinal cord. Although we cannot yet repair severed spinal cords, we have made significant advances in helping injured ones heal.

In spite of Ramón y Cajal's declaration that there is no regeneration in the CNS, scientists nearly a century later are pursuing several strategies for inducing self-repair following damage like Reeve's and Knox's. These efforts include minimizing the initial damage, encouraging regrowth and new connections, and—the holy grail of stroke and spinal cord treatment—replacing lost neurons. As one example, administering a newly developed molecule shortly after induced stroke in rats reduced glutamate-induced excitotoxicity, which in turn reduced the area of damage by 40% and minimized the loss of motor functions (Bach et al., 2012). Although the brain releases gamma-aminobutyric acid (GABA) to defend against excitotoxicity, GABA's effect at receptors elsewhere on the neuron is to reduce later plasticity. Researchers at UCLA have found a way to block GABA's effect outside the synapse, while leaving its synaptic inhibition intact; as a result, mice treated with the drug recovered 50% more motor function than controls (Clarkson, Huang, MacIsaac, Mody, & Carmichael, 2010).

Several strategies for encouraging axon regrowth are under investigation. One option is to block receptors for the protein Nogo-A, which inhibits regeneration following injury. In monkeys with surgically induced spinal cord damage, a Nogo-A inhibitor produced axon growth across the injured area, and the monkeys recovered 80% of the use of their paralyzed hands (P. Freund et al., 2006; P. Freund et al., 2007). In rats with induced stroke, combining this Nogo-A blocker with inosine doubled the compensatory growth of axon branches into the spinal cord from the intact hemisphere; this restored the rats' skilled reaching to preoperative levels (Zai et al., 2011). The drug company Novartis has begun a phase 2 clinical trial to test the effectiveness of a Nogo-A blocker, indicating that its phase 1 safety trial was successful, though those results have not been published yet.

The most graphic axon regrowth results were in a study with rats whose severed spinal cords were treated with electrical stimulation and drugs that increased neural excitability (van den Brand et al., 2012). When the rats were suspended in a

■ **FIGURE 3.29**   Embryonic Stem Cells.

Because they can develop into any type of cell, stem cells offer tremendous therapeutic possibilities.

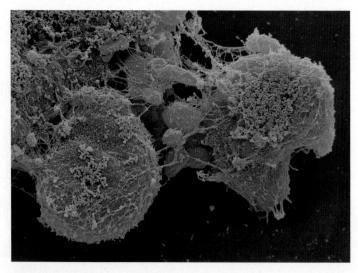

Source: David Scharf/Science Source.

sling, circuits in the lower spinal cord enabled them to step in response to a moving treadmill but not to walk voluntarily. But when the electrochemical stimulation was combined with the temptation of a chocolate treat, they were able after four to five weeks of training not only to walk but to sprint up rat-sized stairs. Compared with untrained rats and rats trained on the treadmill alone, they had an increase in axonal projections around the lesion site that equaled 45% of the original fibers, plus an almost fourfold increase in projections from the cortex to brain-stem motor areas.

The most exciting possibility involves the use of stem cells to replace injured neurons. *Stem cells* are undifferentiated cells that can develop into specialized cells such as neurons, muscle, or blood cells. Stem cells in the embryo (Figure 3.29) are *pluripotent,* which means that they can differentiate into any cell in the body. The developing cell's fate is determined by chemical signals from its environment that turn on specific genes and silence others. Later in life, stem cells lose most of their flexibility and are confined to areas with a high demand for cell replacement, such as the skin, the intestine, and bone marrow (the source of blood cells). In the brain, stem cells are the source of the neurogenesis we discussed earlier. When embryonic stem cells are placed into an adult nervous system, they tend to differentiate into neurons appropriate to that area; researchers are also learning how to coax adult stem cells to do the same. Researchers in Portugal and an international team operating in Panama have reported encouraging improvements in spinal cord patients treated with stem cells, including the ability to transfer to and from a wheelchair, the ability to step with assistance, and return of bowel and urinary control and sexual function (Ichim, 2010; Lima et al., 2006). By contrast, the U.S. biotech company Geron has called off its stem cell clinical trial; the company cited financial reasons, but critics have suggested that at this stage of our understanding it is too early even to venture into this form of treatment (Coghlan, 2011).

Five years after his injury, Christopher Reeve undertook an intensive rehabilitation program called activity-based recovery (J. W. McDonald et al., 2002). The therapy involved using electrical stimulation to exercise critical muscle groups. For example, electrodes placed over three muscles of each leg were activated sequentially to allow him to pedal a customized exercise bike. This effort appeared futile; no spinal cord patient classified as Grade A (the category of greatest impairment) had ever recovered more than one grade after two years. But after three years of this therapy, two thirds of Reeve's touch sensation had returned, and he was able to walk in an aquatherapy pool and make swimming movements with his arms; as a result, he was reclassified to Grade C. It even seemed possible that Reeve might achieve his goal of walking again, but he died of heart failure in October 2004. The Christopher Reeve Paralysis Foundation continues his work toward lifting Ramón y Cajal's decree. But since that day appears far off, researchers in the meantime are merging neurons with electronics to give back to patients control of their bodies (see the accompanying Research Spotlight on the next page).

> The word impossible *is not in the vocabulary of contemporary neuroscience.*
>
> —Pasko Rakic

CONCEPT CHECK

Take a Minute to Check Your Knowledge and Understanding

- Describe the four steps of nervous system development and the fifth step of maturation.
- Give three examples of changes in the brain resulting from experience.
- What are the obstacles to recovery from injury in the CNS and the strategies for overcoming them?

In Perspective

We could end this chapter by talking about how much is known about the brain and its functions. Or we could tell you about how little is known. Either point of view would be correct; it is the classic case of whether the glass is half full or half empty. As we said in Chapter 1, remarkable progress has been made during the past few years. The functions of most areas of the brain are known. We have a good idea how the brain develops and how neurons find their way to their destinations and make functional connections. And we're getting closer to understanding how the neurons form complex networks that carry out the brain's work.

But questions remain: How does the brain combine activity from widespread areas to bring about an action or a decision or a conscious experience. What is a thought? How do we fix a broken brain? But, of course, there is hope, and for good reason. You will see in the following chapters that a vast amount of knowledge has already been gathered and that researchers have a solid foundation for making remarkable advances in our lifetime and revolutionary ones in yours.

> *If the human brain were so simple that we could understand it, we would be so simple that we couldn't.*
>
> —Emerson Pugh

RESEARCH SPOTLIGHT

Mending the Brain With Computer Chips

Faced with the daunting challenge of coaxing axons to regrow and stem cells to take over the duties of brain cells, some researchers are turning to computer chips, and their results have been encouraging. For example, neuroscientists at Northwestern University simulated spinal injury in two monkeys by temporarily anesthetizing nerves in their arms at the elbow. Then they used an electrode array to pick up signals from the hand area of the motor cortex, which were then amplified and delivered to muscles in the forearm. With this arrangement the monkeys were able to grasp and pick up a ball and drop it into an opening almost as well as they had done before the anesthesia (Figure a; Ethier, Oby, Bauman, & Miller, 2012).

Moving these experimental accomplishments out of the laboratory and into the patient's everyday life will take years, but the potential of computer brain interfaces (BCI) is proceeding rapidly. The possibility of using thought to control external devices promises some degree of independence for individuals with limited limb mobility. After implantation of an electrode array in the arm area of his motor cortex, a 25-year-old quadriplegic (both arms and legs paralyzed) was able to move a cursor on a computer screen to read emails and to play a simple computer game (Hochberg et al., 2006). Later refinements have allowed two patients to control a robotic arm to pick up and manipulate objects, including drinking from a water bottle (see Figure b; Hochberg et al., 2012).

Although the ability to accomplish a task in and of itself may seem like an adequate goal, the reality is that being able to accomplish tasks with speed comparable to unimpaired individuals is often a practical limitation for technological advances to be adopted and implemented on a wider scale. Recent work by neurosurgeon Jaimie Henderson at Stanford, part of the Brain Gate consortium, implanted tiny electrode arrays onto the surface of the motor cortex in individuals who either were quadriplegic or had amyotrophic lateral sclerosis (ALS, also known as Lou Gehrig's disease). The individuals performed free typing tasks, assessed in terms of words per minute typed, and importantly

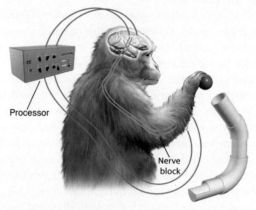

(a) A Monkey Uses Its Paralyzed Arm to Pick Up and Manipulate a Ball.

Source: Adapted from Figure 1 of "Restoration of Grasp Following Paralysis Through Brain-Controlled Stimulation of Muscles," by C. Ethier, E. R. Oby, M. J. Bauman, and I. E. Miller," *Nature, 485*, pp. 368–371.

(b) Paralyzed Woman Gives Herself a Drink for the First Time in 15 Years.

Source: Figure 2 of "Reach and Grasp by People With Tetraplegia Using a Neurally Controlled Robotic Arm," by L. R. Hochberg et al., *Nature, 485*, pp. 372–377.

without any word completion suggestions from software algorithms. These individuals typed up to eight words per minute, which may seem slow compared with professional writers but is approximately half as fast as individuals can type out messages on their cell phones.

CHAPTER SUMMARY

The Central Nervous System

- The CNS consists of the brain and the spinal cord.
- The CNS is arranged in a hierarchy, with physically higher structures carrying out more sophisticated functions.
- The cortex is the location of the most sophisticated functions; the convoluted structure of the cerebral hemispheres provides for the maximum amount of cortex.
- See Table 3.2 for the major structures of the brain and their functions.
- Although localization is an important functional principle in the brain, most functions depend on the interaction of several brain areas.
- The spinal cord contains pathways between the brain and the body below the head and provides for sensory-motor reflexes.
- The meninges and the cerebrospinal fluid protect the brain from trauma; the blood-brain barrier blocks toxins and blood-borne neurotransmitters from entering the brain.

The Peripheral Nervous System

- See Figure 3.19 for a summary of the divisions of the nervous system.

  ○ The PNS consists of the cranial and spinal nerves or, alternatively, the somatic nervous system and the ANS.

  ○ The somatic nervous system consists of the sensory nerves and the nerves controlling the skeletal muscles.

  ○ The sympathetic branch of the ANS prepares the body for action; the parasympathetic branch conserves and renews energy.

- Interconnection in the sympathetic ganglion chain means that the sympathetic nervous system tends to function as a whole, unlike the parasympathetic branch.

Development and Change in the Nervous System

- Prenatal development of the nervous system involves

  ○ *proliferation,* the multiplication of neurons by division;

  ○ *migration,* in which neurons travel to their destination;

  ○ *circuit formation,* the growth of axons to, and their connection to, their targets; and

  ○ *circuit pruning,* the elimination of excess neurons and incorrect synapses.

- Myelination continues through adolescence or later, with higher brain levels myelinating last.
- Experience can produce changes in brain structure and function.
- Although some recovery of function occurs in the mammalian CNS, there is little or no true repair of damage by either neurogenesis or regeneration; enhancing repair is a major research focus. ■

STUDY RESOURCES

FOR FURTHER THOUGHT

- Patients with damage to the right parietal lobe, the temporal lobe, or the prefrontal cortex may have little or no impairment in their intellectual capabilities, yet they show deficits in behavior that seem inconsistent for an otherwise intelligent individual. Does this modify your ideas about how we govern our behavior?
- Like the heroes in the 1966 science fiction movie *Fantastic Voyage,* you and your crew will enter a small submarine to be shrunk to microscopic size and injected into the carotid artery of an eminent scientist who is in a coma. Your mission is to navigate through the bloodstream to deliver a lifesaving drug to a specific area in the scientist's brain. The drug can be designed to your specifications, and you can decide where in the vascular system you will release it. What are some of the strategies you could consider to ensure that the drug will enter the brain and be effective?
- What strategy do you think has the greatest potential for restoring function in brain-damaged patients? Why?

TEST YOUR UNDERSTANDING

1. Describe the specific behaviors you would expect to see in a person with prefrontal cortex damage.

2. Describe compensation and reorganization in recovery from brain damage, giving examples.

3. In what ways does the brain show plasticity after birth?

Select the best answer:

1. Groups of cell bodies in the CNS are called

   a. tracts.   b. ganglia.
   c. nerves.   d. nuclei.

2. The prefrontal cortex is involved in all but which one of the following functions?

   a. Responding to rewards
   b. Orienting the body in space

c.   Making decisions

d.   Behaving in socially appropriate ways

3. Because the speech center is usually located in the left hemisphere of the brain, a person with the corpus callosum severed is unable to describe stimuli that are

a.   seen in the left visual field.

b.   seen in the right visual field.

c.   presented directly in front of him or her.

d.   felt with the right hand.

4. A person with damage to the inferior temporal cortex would most likely be unable to

a.   see.

b.   remember previously seen objects.

c.   recognize familiar objects visually.

d.   solve visual problems, such as mazes.

5. A particular behavior is typically controlled by

a.   a single structure.

b.   one or two structures working together.

c.   a network of structures.

d.   the entire brain.

6. When the police have a drunk-driving suspect walk a straight line and touch his nose with his finger, they are assessing the effect of alcohol on the

a.   motor cortex.   b.   corpus callosum.

c.   cerebellum.   d.   medulla.

7. Cardiovascular activity and respiration are controlled by the

a.   pons.   b.   medulla.

c.   thalamus.   d.   reticular formation.

8. All the following are involved in producing movement, except the

a.   hippocampus.   b.   cerebellum.

c.   frontal lobes.   d.   basal ganglia.

9. Damage would be most devastating to humans if it destroyed the

a.   pineal gland.   b.   inferior colliculi.

c.   corpus callosum.   d.   medulla.

10. If the ventral root of a spinal nerve is severed, the person will experience

a.   loss of sensory input from a part of the body.

b.   loss of motor control of a part of the body.

c.   loss of both sensory input and motor control.

d.   none of the above.

11. During a difficult exam, your heart races, your mouth is dry, and your hands are icy. In your room later, you fall limply into a deep sleep. Activation has shifted from primarily _____ to primarily _____.

a.   somatic, autonomic

b.   autonomic, somatic

c.   parasympathetic, sympathetic

d.   sympathetic, parasympathetic

12. In the circuit formation stage of nervous system development,

a.   correct connection of each neuron is necessary, since barely enough neurons are produced.

b.   axons grow to their targets and form connections.

c.   neurons continue dividing around a central neuron, and those neurons form a circuit.

d.   neurons that fail to make functional connections die.

13. Fetal alcohol syndrome involves

a.   loss of myelin.

b.   overproduction of neurons.

c.   errors in neuron migration.

d.   excessive growth of glial cells.

14. The study in which kittens reared in an environment with only horizontal or vertical lines were later able to respond only to stimuli at the same orientation is an example of

a.   compensation.   b.   reorientation.

c.   reorganization.   d.   regeneration.

15. If a peripheral nerve were transplanted into a severed spinal cord, it would

a.   fail to grow across the gap.

b.   grow across the gap but fail to make connections.

c.   grow across the gap and make connections but fail to function.

d.   bridge the gap and replace the function of the lost neurons.

1. d, 2. b, 3. a, 4. c, 5. c, 6. c, 7. b, 8. a, 9. d, 10. b, 11. d, 12. b, 13. c, 14. c, 15. a.

Answers:

ON THE WEB

The following websites are coordinated with this chapter's content. You can access these websites from the **SAGE edge Student Resources site**; select this chapter and then click on Web Resources. (**Bold** items are links.)

1.   The **Whole Brain Atlas** has images of normal and diseased or damaged brains. The **HOPES Brain Tutorial** will help you

visualize how the brain is organized. The final segment, Build a Brain, is best.

2.   The **History of Psychosurgery**, from trephining (drilling holes in the skull to let evil spirits out) to lobotomy to more recent experimental attempts, is the subject of this sometimes less than professional but very interesting website. At Lobotomy's Hall of Fame you will learn, for example, that sisters of

the playwright Tennessee Williams and President John F. Kennedy had lobotomies (the story that actress Frances Farmer had a lobotomy turned out to be a fabrication).

3. **Healthline's** interactive brain allows you to examine external and internal features and rotate them 360° for a better view; **brainline** adds functions of these areas and symptoms when they're damaged.

4. **The Dana Foundation** offers regular updates on the latest findings in neuroscience research.

5. Genetics Home Reference gives a good description of **periventricular heterotopia** and its genetic causes. The **National Organization on Fetal Alcohol Syndrome** has information and statistics on the disorder.

6. The **American Association of Neurological Surgeons** website has information on traumatic brain injury and incidence frequency for the riskiest sports.

7. Read a news article about the use of carbon 14 nuclear fallout to document **human adult neurogenesis**.

8. The **Miami Project to Cure Paralysis** at the University of Miami School of Medicine has summaries of basic and clinical research on central nervous system damage. The **Christopher and Dana Reeve Foundation** site provides information about spinal cord damage research.

9. The National Institutes of Health's **Stem Cell Information** site is a good resource for information about stem cells and their potential.

10. **BrainGate Lets Your Brain Control the Computer** is a video explanation of the BrainGate system, which shows the patient controlling a computer and a prosthetic hand. A second video shows a paralyzed woman **controlling a robotic arm** to drink coffee, and a third documents a man's **moderately successful stem cell treatment** for a spinal cord injury.

FOR FURTHER READING

1. In *The New Executive Brain* (Oxford University Press, 2009), Elkhonon Goldberg draws from recent discoveries and fascinating case studies to explore how the brain engages in complex decision making, deals with ambiguity, makes moral choices, and controls emotion.

2. *The Human Brain Book* by award-winning science writer Rita Carter (DK Publishing, 2009) ranges from brain anatomy and neural transmission to explorations of behavior, sensory processing, dreaming, and genius.

3. *The Scientific American Day in the Life of Your Brain*, by Judith Horstman (Scientific American, 2009), in 130 articles tackles the brain bases of creativity, hunger, sex, addictions, dreaming, biological clocks, and more.

4. *The Man Who Mistook His Wife for a Hat and Other Clinical Tales,* by Oliver Sacks (Harper Perennial, 1990), a collection of case studies, is as entertaining as it is informative, as it treats the human side of brain damage and disorder.

5. *Pictures of the Mind: What the New Neuroscience Tells Us About Who We Are,* by Miriam Boleyn-Fitzgerald (FT Press, 2010), uses brain imaging technology to reveal the resiliency and flexibility of the brain. Its topics range from brain damage to emotional disorders to addiction.

KEY TERMS

anterior 55
association area 54
auditory cortex 55
autonomic nervous system (ANS) 64
blood-brain barrier 64
Broca's area 53
central nervous system (CNS) 49
central sulcus 53
cerebellum 61
cerebral hemispheres 50
cerebrospinal fluid 60
circuit formation 68
circuit pruning 69
compensation 75
corpus callosum 59
cortex 51
cranial nerves 64
dorsal 55

dorsal root 62
fetal alcohol syndrome 70
fissure 50
frontal lobe 53
ganglion 50
growth cone 68
gyrus 50
hydrocephalus 75
hypothalamus 59
inferior 55
inferior colliculi 60
inferior temporal cortex 56
lateral 55
lateral fissure 53
longitudinal fissure 50
medial 55
medulla 61
meninges 63

midbrain 60
migration 68
motor cortex 53
neglect 54
nerve 50
neurogenesis 74
neurotrophins 69
nucleus 50
occipital lobe 58
parasympathetic nervous
    system 65
parietal lobe 54
peripheral nervous system (PNS) 64
pineal gland 59
plasticity 69
pons 61
posterior 55
precentral gyrus 53

$SAGE edge™   edge.sagepub.com/garrett5e

SAGE edge offers a robust online environment featuring an impressive array of free tools and resources for review, study, and further exploration, keeping both instructors and students on the cutting edge of teaching and learning.

3.1 Identify the components of the central nervous system. — Components of the CNS

3.2 Name the structures in the forebrain, midbrain, and hindbrain. — Structure and Circuitry of the Brain

3.3 Predict how damage to specific brain structures will impact specific behaviors. — Astrocytes and Brain Injury / The Story of Phineas Gage

3.4 Describe the components that protect the brain from damage. — What Protects the Brain from Damage?

3.5 Examine the functions of the peripheral nervous system divisions. — What Does the PNS Do?

3.6 Explain how the peripheral and central nervous systems interact in generating experiences and behavior. — Brain-Computer Interfaces

3.7 Summarize the changes that the nervous system undergoes during typical development. — How Brains Are Built

3.8 Illustrate the changes that occur in the nervous system as the result of experiences. — Brain Reorganization

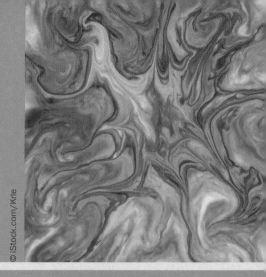

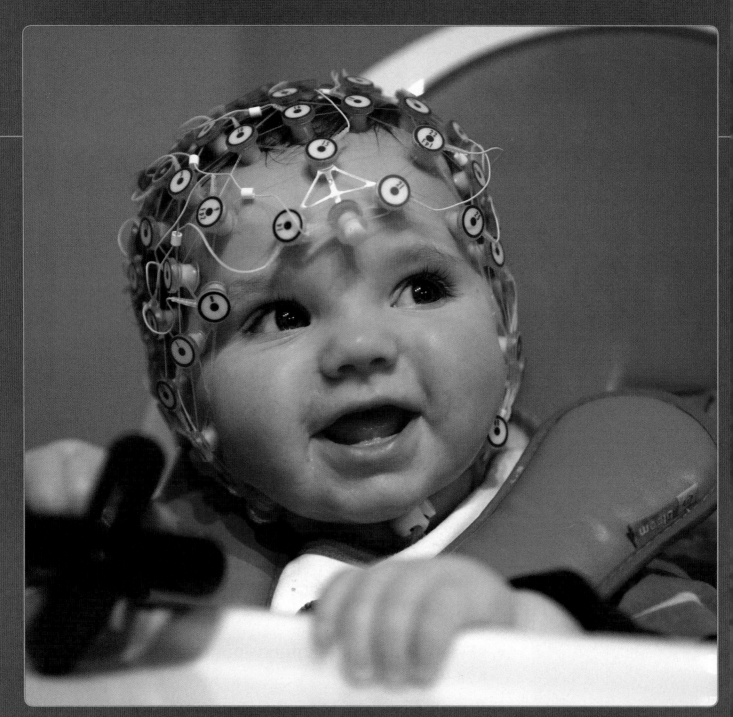

The Methods and Ethics of Research

4

After reading this chapter, you will be able to:

- Explain how scientific theories are generated.

- Demonstrate how scientists test hypotheses.

- Describe the differences between correlational and experimental studies.

- Assess the methods that scientists have for studying the role of brain structures in behavior.

- Compare the methods that scientists use to investigate the structure and function of brain cells.

- Identify the ethical protections that are in place for human participants.

- Summarize the ethical protections that exist for research animals.

- Examine the ethical concerns that have been raised about stem cell and gene therapy research.

Ashanthi DeSilva developed her first infection just two days after her birth. There would be many more. At the age of two, her frequent illnesses and poor growth were diagnosed as being due to *severe combined immunodeficiency* (SCID)—better known as the "bubble-boy disease" after an earlier victim who had to live in a sterile environment in a plastic tent (Figure 4.1). Her immune system was so compromised that she suffered from frequent infections and gained weight slowly; because traditional enzyme treatments were inadequate, at the age of four her parents enrolled her in a revolutionary experimental therapy. SCID is caused by a faulty gene, so the doctors transferred healthy genes into her immune cells (Blaese et al., 1995). Ashanthi is a grown woman now and living a normal life in suburban Cleveland (Springen, 2004), her health and normal resistance to disease a silent testimonial to the power of genetic research.

Just a few years ago, cures like Ashanthi's and the gene therapies and stem cell therapies that you will read about in this chapter and others seemed like miracles. These breakthroughs are products of the ingenuity of medical and neuroscience researchers, who have built on the accumulated knowledge of their predecessors. Their accomplishments are also the result of more powerful research methods, including research design as well as technology. This is the story of the role that research methodology plays in the field of biopsychology, and of the increasing ethical implications of our advancing knowledge. But first, we need to take a few minutes to review some important points about research in the context of behavioral neuroscience.

Master the content.
edge.sagepub.com/garrett5e

■ **FIGURE 4.1**   The Original "Bubble Boy."

The most famous patient with SCID was so vulnerable to life-threatening infections that he had to live in a sterile plastic tent. Thanks to research advances, genetic treatment is offering new hope.

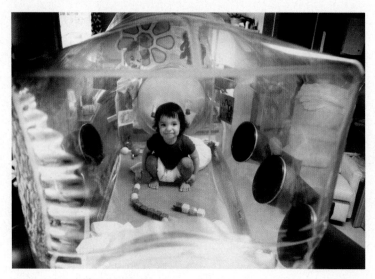

Source: Bettmann/Getty Images.

Science, Research, and Theory

Science is not distinguished by the knowledge it produces but *by its method of acquiring knowledge.* We learned in Chapter 1 that scientists' primary method is empiricism; this means that they rely on observation for their information rather than on intuition, tradition, or logic (alone). Descartes started out with the traditional assumption that there was a soul, and then he located the soul in the pineal gland because it seemed the logical place for the soul to control the brain. Aristotle, using equally good logic, had located the soul in the heart because the heart is so vital to life. (He thought that the brain's function was to cool the blood!) Observation—which is a much more formal activity in science than the term suggests—is more objective than alternative ways of acquiring knowledge; this means that two observers are more likely to reach the same conclusion about what is being observed (though not necessarily about its interpretation) than if they were using intuition or logic.

Biopsychologists, and scientists in general, have great confidence in observation and all the methods in their arsenal. But in scientific writings, you will often see statements beginning with "It appears that . . .," "Perhaps . . .," or "The results suggest. . . ." So you might well wonder, *Why do scientists always sound so tentative?*

Theory and Tentativeness in Science

Why are scientists so tentative?

One reason for the tentativeness is that the field is very complex, so it is always possible that a study is flawed or that new data will change how previous studies are interpreted. A second reason is that scientists base their conclusions on samples of subjects and samples of data from those subjects; the laws of probability tell us that even well-designed studies will occasionally include a few unusual participants or a slight but important shift in behavior may occur that has nothing to do with the variable under study.

Scientists recognize that knowledge is changing rapidly and the cherished ideas of today may be discarded tomorrow. A case in point is that, until recently, no one accepted that there was regrowth of severed axons or any neurogenesis in the mammalian central nervous system (Rakic, 1985), beliefs that you now know are incorrect. You seldom hear scientists using the words *truth* and *proof,* because these terms suggest final answers. Such uncertainty may feel uncomfortable to you, but centuries of experience have shown that certainty about truth can be just as uncomfortable. "Certainty" has an ugly way of stifling the pursuit of knowledge.

One way the researcher has of making sense out of ambiguity is through theory. A *theory* integrates and interprets diverse observations in an attempt to explain some phenomenon. For example, schizophrenia researchers noticed that people who overdosed on the drug amphetamine were being misdiagnosed as having schizophrenia when they were admitted to emergency rooms with hallucinations and paranoia. They also knew that amphetamine increases activity in neurons that release dopamine as the neurotransmitter. This led several researchers to propose that schizophrenia is due to excess dopamine activity in the brain.

A theory explains existing facts, but it also generates hypotheses that guide further research. One hypothesis that came from dopamine theory was that drugs that decrease dopamine activity would improve functioning in schizophrenia. This hypothesis was testable, which is a requirement for a good theory. The hypothesis was supported in many cases of schizophrenia, but not in others. We now realize that the dopamine theory is an incomplete explanation for schizophrenia. However, even a flawed theory inspires further research that will yield more knowledge and additional hypotheses. But remember that the best theory is still only a theory; theory and empiricism are the basis of science's ability to self-correct and its openness to change and renewal.

Now we will examine one of the knottiest issues of research, one that you will need to think about often as you evaluate the research evidence discussed throughout this text.

Experimental Versus Correlational Studies

Observation has a broad meaning in science. A biological psychologist might observe aggressive behavior in children on the playground to see if there are differences between boys and girls (*naturalistic observation*), report on the brain scan of a patient who had violent outbursts following a car accident that caused brain injury (*case study*), use a questionnaire to find out whether some women are more aggressive during the premenstrual period (*survey*), or stimulate a part of rats' brains with electricity to see what parts of the brain control aggressive behavior (*experiment*). These different research strategies fall into the broad categories of *correlational and experimental studies.*

An *experiment* is a study in which the researcher manipulates a condition (the independent variable) that is expected to produce a change in the subject's behavior (the dependent variable). The experimenter also eliminates *extraneous variables* that might influence the behavior or equates them across subjects—for example, by removing environmental distractions, instructing participants not to use caffeine or other stimulants beforehand, and "running" subjects at the same time of day. In a *correlational study,* the researcher does not control an independent variable but observes whether two variables are related to each other. When we use brain scans to determine that violent criminals more often have impaired frontal lobe activity, we are conducting a correlational study. If we *induce* the impairment in monkeys (independent variable) and then observe whether this increases aggression (dependent variable), we are doing an experiment.

Figure 4.2 illustrates some of the differences between a correlational and an experimental study of aggressive behavior. Based on observations that violent criminals often have impaired frontal lobe functioning, we might identify a large group of impaired individuals (using brain scans or behavioral and cognitive tests) and see if they have a record of violent crimes. We would very likely find that they do, but Figure 4.2a reveals a problem with interpretation: For all we know, the individuals' brain damage may have been incurred in the process of committing their violent acts rather than the other way around. Or both frontal lobe damage and violent behavior could stem from any number of third variables, such as physical abuse during childhood, long-term drug use, or a genetic predisposition to engage in risky behaviors. These variables are potentially *confounded* with each other, so we cannot separate their effects. In other words, *we cannot draw conclusions about cause and effect from a correlational study.*

? What is the advantage of experimental studies over correlational studies?

What about doing this research as an experimental study? For ethical reasons, of course, we would not induce brain damage in humans, but remember the study described in Chapter 3 in which researchers used an electromagnetic field to disrupt activity in the visual cortex of blind individuals. Let's use this *transcranial magnetic stimulation* to disrupt temporarily our hypothetical volunteers' frontal lobe functioning. Granted, we won't see them become physically violent in the laboratory, but we can borrow a technique from a similar study we will see later in Chapter 8, on emotion: We will administer several mild shocks to the subject under the pretense that the shocks are being controlled by another (fictitious) player, and we will record the intensity of shocks our participant delivers in retaliation. Because we selected our research participants and induced the brain impairment, we have *controlled* the confounding variables that plagued us in the correlational study. That is, the variables are likely to be similar between the impaired group and an unimpaired control group, especially if we make sure factors such as age and gender are similar between the groups. Now if we see higher levels of shock administered by subjects while their frontal activity is being disrupted, we can be fairly confident that the frontal lobe impairment is *causing* the increase in the aggressive behavior.

Of course, we could quibble about how well this study mirrors real brain damage and violent aggression;

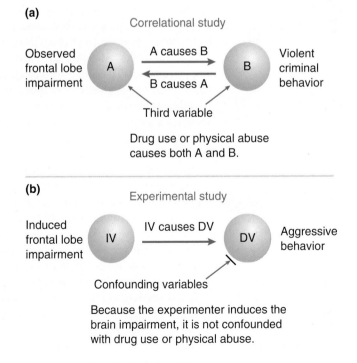

■ **FIGURE 4.2**   Correlational Versus Experimental Studies.

In a correlational study (a), we cannot tell whether *A* influences *B*, *B* influences *A*, or a third variable affects both. In an experimental study (b), the researcher manipulates the independent variable (IV), which increases assurance that it is the cause of the change in the dependent variable (DV). (The red arrows indicate possible interpretations of causation.)

(a)   Correlational study

Observed frontal lobe impairment   A   A causes B / B causes A   B   Violent criminal behavior

Third variable

Drug use or physical abuse causes both A and B.

(b)   Experimental study

Induced frontal lobe impairment   IV   IV causes DV   DV   Aggressive behavior

Confounding variables

Because the experimenter induces the brain impairment, it is not confounded with drug use or physical abuse.

the greater control afforded by experimental studies often carries a cost of some artificiality. Experimentation is the most powerful research strategy, but correlational studies also provide unique and valuable information, such as the observation that children of parents who have schizophrenia have a high incidence of the disorder even when they are reared in normal adoptive homes. To advance our understanding in biopsychology, we need correlational studies as well as experimental research, but we equally need to be careful about interpreting their results—a point you should keep in mind as we explore various research techniques and as we look at research in later chapters.

CONCEPT CHECK

Take a Minute to Check Your Knowledge and Understanding

- What is the value of empiricism? What is the value of theory?
- A scientist speaking to a group of students says, "I do not expect my research to find the truth." Why?
- What advantages do correlational studies have over experiments?
- You hear the newscaster say, "Physicians are urging people to stay active in retirement, because researchers have found that people who are more physically and socially active are less likely to develop Alzheimer's disease." What should you be thinking?

Research Techniques

The brain does not give up its secrets easily. If we remove a clock from its case and observe the gears turn and the spring expand, we can get a pretty good idea how a clock measures time. But if we open the skull, how the brain works remains just as much a mystery as before. This is where research technique comes in, extending the scientist's observation beyond what is readily accessible. Your understanding of the information that fills the rest of this book—and of the limitations of that information—will require some knowledge of how the researchers came to their conclusions. The following review of a few major research methods is abbreviated, but it will help you navigate through the rest of the book, and we will add other methods as we go along.

Staining and Imaging Neurons

? *What major discovery did Golgi staining enable?*

It didn't take long to exhaust the possibilities for viewing the nervous system with the naked eye, but the invention of the microscope took researchers many steps beyond what the pioneers in gross anatomy could do. Unfortunately, neurons are greatly intertwined and are difficult to distinguish from each other, even when magnified. The *Golgi stain* method randomly stains about 5% of neurons, placing them in relief against the background of seeming neural chaos (Figure 4.3a). As we saw in Chapter 2, the Italian anatomist Camillo Golgi developed this technique in 1875 and, shortly after, his Spanish contemporary Santiago Ramón y Cajal used it to discover that neurons are separate cells. Golgi and Ramón y Cajal jointly received the 1906 Nobel Prize in physiology and medicine for their contributions.

Other staining methods add important dimensions to the researcher's ability to study the nervous system. *Myelin stains* are taken up by the fatty myelin that wraps and insulates axons; the stain thus identifies neural pathways. In Figure 4.3b, the slice of brain tissue is heavily stained in the inner areas where many pathways converge, but it is stained lightly or not at all in the perimeter where mostly cell bodies are located. *Nissl stains* do the opposite; they identify cell bodies of neurons (Figure 4.3c).

Later-generation techniques are used to trace pathways to determine their origin or their destination—that is, which part of the brain is communicating with another. These procedures take advantage of the fact that neurons move materials up and down the axon constantly. For example, if we inject the chemical *fluorogold* into a part of the brain, it will be taken up by the terminals of neurons and transported up the axons to the cell bodies. Under light of the appropriate wavelength, fluorogold will fluoresce—radiate light—so it will show up under a microscope and tell us which brain areas receive neural input from the area we injected. For example, fluorogold injected into a rat's superior colliculi will show up a few days later among the neurons at the back of the eye.

? *What advantage does autoradiography have?*

These staining and tracing procedures reveal fine anatomy, but they do not tell us anything about function. *Autoradiography* makes neurons stand out visibly just as staining does, but it also reveals which neurons are active, and this information can be correlated with the behavior the animal was engaged in. In this procedure, the animal is injected with a substance that has been made radioactive, such as a type of sugar called 2-deoxyglucose (2-DG). Then, the researcher usually stimulates the animal, for instance, by

■ **FIGURE 4.3** Three Staining Techniques.

(a) Golgi stains highlight individual neurons. (b) Myelin stains emphasize white matter and, therefore, neural pathways (stained blue here). (c) Nissl stains emphasize the cell bodies of neurons (stained dark).

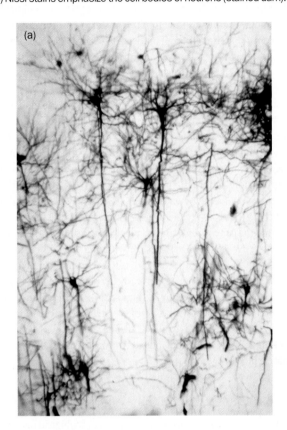

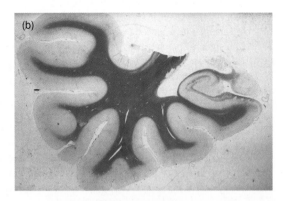

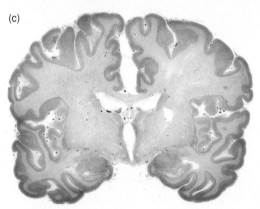

Sources: (a) © Dr. John D. Cunningham/Visuals Unlimited/Corbis. (b) © Biophoto/Science Source. (c) Reproduced with permission from http://www.brains.rad.msu.edu, and http://brainmuseum.org, supported by the U.S. National Science Foundation.

presenting a visual pattern or requiring the subject to learn a task. Active neurons take up more glucose, and because 2-DG is similar to glucose, the neurons involved in the activity become radioactively "labeled." In Chapter 10, you will see an example of this technique, in which vision researchers mapped the projections to the visual cortex from light-receptive cells in the eye (Tootell, Silverman, Switkes, & De Valois, 1982). After injecting monkeys with radioactive 2-DG, they presented the subjects with a geometric visual stimulus. The animals were euthanized (killed painlessly), and a section of their visual cortical tissue was placed on photographic film. The radioactive areas exposed the film and produced an image of the original stimulus. This confirmed that just as the somatosensory projection area contains a map of the body, the visual cortex maps the visual-sensitive retina and, thus, the visual world (Figure 4.4a).

A variation of this method is used to determine the location and quantity of receptors for a particular drug or neurotransmitter. Candace Pert used this procedure to find out whether there are receptors in the brain for opiate drugs (a class containing opium, morphine, and heroin), which seemed like the best explanation for the drugs' potency in relieving pain (Herkenham & Pert, 1982; Pert & Snyder, 1973). First, she soaked rat brains in radioactive *naloxone*, a drug that she knew counteracts the effects of opiates, on the assumption that it does so by blocking the hypothesized receptors. She then placed thinly sliced sections of the brains on photographic film. Sure enough, an image of the brain formed, highlighting the locations of opiate receptors (Figure 4.4b). This procedure not only established that the receptors exist but also implied that the brain makes its own opiates!

Instead of using radioactivity, *immunocytochemistry* uses antibodies attached to a dye to identify cellular components such as receptors, neurotransmitters, or enzymes. The technique takes advantage of the fact that antibodies, which attack foreign intruders in the body, can be custom designed to be specific to any cellular component. The dye, which is usually fluorescent, makes the antibodies' targets visible when the tissue

■ FIGURE 4.4 Autoradiographs.

(a) Monkeys were injected with radioactive 2-DG before they were presented with a geometric visual stimulus. The monkeys were euthanized, and slices of their brains were placed on photographic film; the pattern of radioactivity produced the image you see here. (b) An autoradiograph of a horizontal slice from a rat's brain that was soaked in a radioactive opiate antagonist, naloxone. White areas indicated opiate receptors. The slice is at the level of the thalamus; the front of the brain is at the top of the picture.

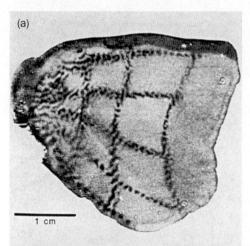

(a)

1 cm

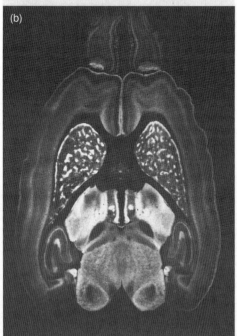

(b)

Sources: (a) From "Deoxyglucose Analysis of Retinotopic Organization in Primate Striate Cortex," by R. B. H. Tootell et al., *Science*, 218, pp. 902–904. Reprinted with permission from AAAS. (b) Republished with permission of The Society for Neuroscience, from "Light Microscopic Localization of Brain Opiate Receptors: A General Autoradiographic Method Which Preserves Tissue Quality," by M. A. Herkenham and C. B. Pert, 1982, *Journal of Neuroscience*, 2, pp. 1129–1149.

is removed and examined under a microscope. Night-migrating birds use the earth's magnetic field to navigate, and earlier evidence suggested that the magnetic detectors might be *cryptochromes,* which are molecules found in some neurons in the birds' retinas. Henrik Mouritsen and his colleagues (2004) in Germany have provided strong supporting evidence. Using immunocytochemistry, they found that during the day, cryptochromes were plentiful in the retinas of both garden warblers and zebra finches; at night, however, cryptochromes diminished virtually to zero in the nonmigratory finches but *increased* in the eyes of the night-migrating warblers (Figure 4.5).

But before they could do this study, Mouritsen's team had to decide which of two kinds of cryptochrome to focus their efforts on, CRY1 or CRY2. So they used another powerful research technique that determines where particular genes are active, in this case the *cry1* and *cry2* genes. Remember from Chapter 1 that genes control the production of proteins; the instructions for protein production are carried from the nucleus into the cytoplasm of a cell by *messenger ribonucleic acid (mRNA),* which is a copy of one strand of the gene's DNA. So, when we locate specific mRNA, we know that the gene is active in that place; this is done by in situ hybridization. *In situ hybridization* involves constructing strands of complementary DNA, which will dock with strands of mRNA. Because the complementary DNA is first made radioactive, autoradiography can then be used to determine the location of gene activity (Figure 4.6). The researchers found that the protein product CRY2 was being constructed in cell nuclei, whereas CRY1 was being constructed outside the nucleus. Because a magnetoreceptor was more likely to function outside the nucleus, they limited their study to that cryptochrome.

Light and Electron Microscopy

For more than three centuries, the progress of biological research closely paralleled the development of the light microscope. The microscope evolved from a device that used a drop of water as the magnifier, through the simple microscope with a single lens, to the compound microscope with multiple lenses. At that point, investigators were able to see the gross details of neurons: cell bodies, dendrites, axons, and the largest organelles. But the capability of the light microscope is limited, not due to the skills of the lens maker but due to the nature of light. Increases in magnification beyond about 1,500 times yield little additional information.

The electron microscope, by contrast, magnifies up to about 250,000 times and can distinguish features as small as a few hundred millionths of a centimeter. The *transmission electron microscope* works by passing a beam of electrons through a thin slice of tissue; different parts of the tissue block or pass electrons to different degrees, so the electrons produce an image of the object on photographic film or on a video screen. It uses magnets to bend the electron beams to magnify the image up to a million times; this allows us to see details such as the synaptic vesicles in an axon terminal. Engineers have enhanced the technique in the *scanning electron microscope.* The beam of electrons induces the specimen to emit electrons itself, and these are captured just as the conventional microscope collects reflected light. Magnification is half that of the transmission electron microscope, but the images have a three-dimensional (3-D) appearance that is helpful in visualizing details. You can see this feature in Figure 4.7, as well as in Figure 2.16.

Microscopic technology continues to evolve, for example, in the *confocal laser scanning microscope* and the *two-photon microscope.* These microscopes image specific kinds of tissue, depending on the fluorescent dye the tissue is stained with (a fluorescent dye emits light when radiated with light within a specific range of wavelengths). These microscopes have the advantage that they are not limited to very thin slices of tissue. They can be used with thicker tissue samples and can even image details in the upper layers of the exposed living brain; with optical probes, they can image neurons as deep as 1 centimeter below the surface. As an example, researchers using a dye specific for calcium were able to measure movement-related neural activity in the brains of mice running on a treadmill (Dombeck, Khabbaz, Collman, Adelman, & Tank, 2007). As the accompanying Research Spotlight reveals, techniques for viewing the brain are getting a significant boost.

Measuring and Manipulating Brain Activity

You learned in previous chapters that it is easy to stimulate the surface of the brain with electricity to produce movement, sensations, and even apparent memories. We can also record electrical activity from the surface of the brain or even from the scalp. Studying deeper structures will require more inventive techniques, which we will look at after we discuss electroencephalography.

Electroencephalography

In 1929, the German psychiatrist Hans Berger invented the electroencephalograph and used it to record the first electroencephalogram from his young son's brain. Since then, the technique has proved indispensable in diagnosing brain disorders such as epilepsy and brain tumors; it has also been valuable for studying brain activity during various kinds of behavior, from sleep to learning. The *electroencephalogram (EEG)* is recorded from two electrodes on the scalp over the area of interest; an electronic amplifier detects the combined electrical activity of all the neurons between the two electrodes (popularly known as "brain waves"; see Figure 4.8). Usually, the researcher applies a number of electrodes and monitors activity in multiple brain areas at the same time.

The *temporal* (time) *resolution* of the EEG is one of its best features; it can distinguish events only 1 millisecond (ms) apart in time, so it can track the brain's responses to rapidly changing events. However, its *spatial resolution,* or ability to detect precisely where in the brain the signal is coming from, is poor. This problem can be alleviated somewhat by applying electrodes directly to the brain, which removes the interference of the skull. Of course, this procedure is used

■ **FIGURE 4.5** Immunocyto-chemistry Reveals Cryptochromes in the Eyes of Migrating Birds.

Neurons that contain cryptochromes and are currently active are labeled in orange. The larger type of neurons (indicated by arrows) project to a brain area that responds to magnetic field stimulation.

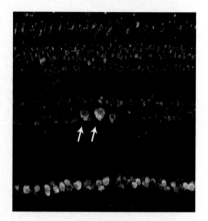

Source: From "Cryptochromes and Neuronal-Activity Markers Colocalize in the Retina of Migratory Birds During Magnetic Orientation," by H. Mouritsen et al., *PNAS, 101,* pp. 14294–14299. © 2004 H. Mouritsen. Used with permission.

■ **FIGURE 4.6** DNA, Proteins, and In Situ Hybridization.

Messenger RNA copies a strand of the DNA and then moves out into the cytoplasm, where it controls the development of proteins. Complementary radioactive DNA helps researchers locate gene activity.

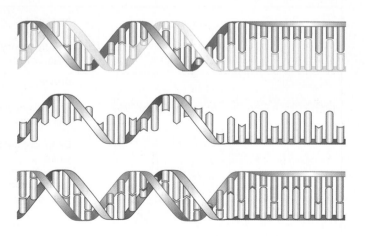

DNA

Messenger RNA moves out into the cytoplasm and directs construction of proteins.

Complementary radioactive DNA (red) docks with the messenger RNA.

■ **FIGURE 4.7** Scanning Electron Micrograph of a Neuron.

Notice the depth and detail this kind of imaging provides. (The white structures on and around the cell body are glial cells.)

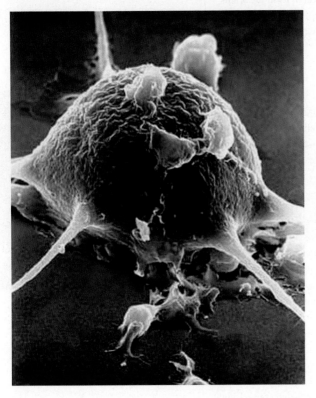

Source: © Dr. Robert Berdan, 2007.

only with animals or with humans undergoing surgery. So although the EEG provides relatively gross measurements, its advantages are good time resolution, ease of use, and lower cost than the imaging techniques we will consider shortly.

EEGs are most useful for detecting changes in arousal, as in the example in Figure 4.8. They are not good at detecting the response to a brief stimulus, such as a spoken word; the time resolution is adequate, but the "noise" of the brain's other ongoing activity drowns out the response, so the tracing looks much like the "awake" recording in the figure. However, by combining electroencephalography with the computer, the researcher can average the EEG over several presentations of the stimulus to produce an *event-related potential*, like the one in Figure 4.9. Averaging over many trials cancels out the ongoing noise, leaving only the unique response to the stimulus. In this example, Shirley Hill (1995) repeatedly presented a low-pitched tone to her research participants and occasionally interjected a high-pitched tone. Averaging showed a large dip in the electrical potential following the novel (high-pitched) stimulus. In Chapter 5, you will learn that this dip is smaller in alcoholics than in nonalcoholics, as well as in the young children of alcoholics, which suggests an inherited vulnerability to alcoholism. Another example is that biopsychologists have used the technique to confirm that spoken words produce a greater response in the left hemisphere, just as you would expect, than in the right hemisphere.

As computer analysis has become more sophisticated, it has allowed researchers to combine activity from several electrodes and generate dynamic, rapidly changing images of the brain's activity. Some innovative applications of this technology are described in the accompanying In the News feature.

■ **FIGURE 4.8** An Electroencephalograph and a Sample EEG.

An electroencephalograph records the electrical activity of the brain through electrodes applied to the scalp (a). The up-and-down fluctuations of the tracings on the computer screen (b) indicate the EEG frequency, and the height indicates the voltage. The computer does precise analyses of the signal for research or diagnostic purposes.

(a)   (b)

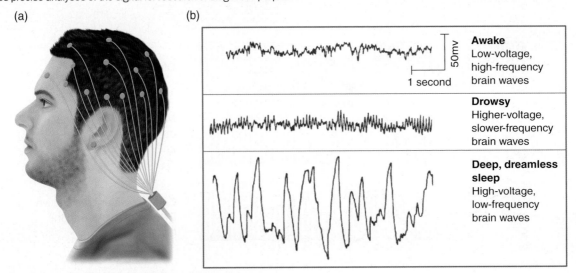

Source: (b) From *Current Concepts: The Sleep Disorders*, by P. Hauri, 1982, Kalamazoo, MI: Upjohn.

RESEARCH SPOTLIGHT
Looking Into the Brain

Neuroscientists have many holy grails, and one of them is the ability to peer into the brain, to visualize the neurons and their all-important connections. Chapter 2 described methods for imaging white-matter pathways, but the resolution is poorer than researchers would like. Light microscopy provides more detail, but brain tissue is mostly opaque so it must be sliced into very thin sections that limit ability to trace pathways. There have been attempts to make brain tissue transparent by extracting the lipids that make up the cell membranes, but the process also removes proteins and the cells fall apart.

Now a team at Stanford University led by psychiatrist and bioengineer Karl Deisseroth has come up with a solution in the form of a process they call, appropriately, CLARITY (Chung et al., 2013; Tomer, Ye, Hsueh, & Deisseroth, 2014). The brain is placed in a solution of acrylamide, which binds to the brain's proteins and holds them together while the lipids are removed. By then the tissue is totally transparent, as you can see in the figure. In the next step, the neurons are "labeled" with fluorescent antibodies, which attach to specific proteins and make particular structures visible; the third panel of the figure shows the

neurons in an intact mouse hippocampus (the curved structure in the image). The procedure has allowed the team to visualize lesions in the brain of a deceased Alzheimer's patient (K. Ando et al., 2014). The acrylamide increases the tissue's resilience, so that the labels can be removed and replaced with others to highlight different types of neurons. This means that the precious few brains available from people with particular disorders can be used over and over again.

More recently, a Caltech research team headed by Viviana Gradinaru (C. Xiao et al., 2016) has used CLARITY techniques to identify and label circuits of neurons involved in controlling motor activity that is commonly dysfunctional in people with Parkinson's disease. Once the specific neurons were traced from their place of origin to their destination, the researchers used optogenetic techniques (see Chapter 3) in a separate experiment to show that activation of these circuits could regulate the impaired motor function. These research findings provide specific targets to neurosurgeons who may then attempt to implant artificial stimulators into the brains of Parkinson's patients so that they can lead more productive lives with fewer motor impairments.

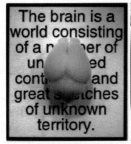
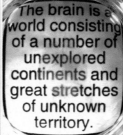
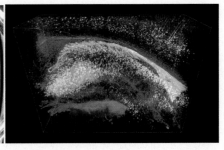

The first two images compare a mouse brain before and after clarification. The third image is a three-dimensional view of a hippocampus (the curved structure) stained to reveal neurons (green), connecting interneurons (red), and glia (blue).

Stimulation, Recording, and Stereotaxic Techniques

Most of the structures of interest to brain scientists are well below the surface of the brain; reaching them requires the use of various kinds of electrical, chemical, and light probes. Usually this work is done with animals, and the researcher uses a map of the brain called a *stereotaxic atlas* to determine where to locate the probe. To construct an atlas, first a large number of brains are sliced into very thin coronal sections; drawings are prepared that show the average location of brain structures on each section (Figure 4.10). The researcher typically uses a *stereotaxic instrument*, a device that allows precise positioning of an electrode or other probe in the brain. Figure 4.11 shows a stereotaxic instrument for rats; the instrument secures the anesthetized rat's head and allows the investigator to insert the probe through a small hole drilled in the skull at the precise location and depth specified by the atlas.

 What are the different ways a stereotaxic instrument is used?

■ **FIGURE 4.9** Event-Related Potential Produced by a Novel Tone.

A research participant responds to a novel stimulus, such as an occasional high-pitched tone among low-pitched tones, with a large dip in the event-related potential. Without averaging over several stimulus presentations, all we would see would be an EEG like the "awake" recording in Figure 4.8.

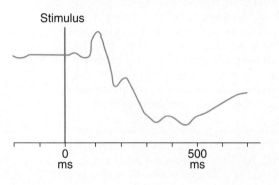

Often the probe is a fine-wire electrode, electrically insulated except at its tip, that is used to activate the structure with very low voltage electricity. While the still-anesthetized animal's brain is being stimulated, the researcher can monitor responses in other parts of the brain or in the body. If the animal must be awake to test the effect, the electrode can be anchored to the skull; the wound is closed, and after a couple of days of recovery, the rat's behavior can be observed during stimulation. In Chapter 5 you will learn about research in which animals were willing to press a lever to deliver electrical stimulation to certain parts of their own brains. (The stimulation isn't painful, because the brain lacks pain receptors.)

A similar electrode arrangement is used to record neural activity; the biopsychologist might subject the animal to a learning task, present visual or auditory stimuli, or introduce a member of the other sex while monitoring activity in an appropriate brain location. Electrodes ordinarily will record from all the surrounding neurons, but *microelectrodes* have tips so fine that they can record from a single neuron and can even be inserted into the neuron. Most microelectrodes are glass micropipettes filled with a solution that is similar to the intracellular fluid of the cell and electrically conducting. The tip can be as small as 1 micron (millionth of a meter). Stimulating and recording electrodes may be placed in the brain temporarily in an anesthetized animal, or they may be mounted in a socket cemented to the animal's skull to permit recording in the unanesthetized, behaving subject.

IN THE NEWS

Portable EEG Reveals Real-Life Brain Activity

Brain imaging studies provide invaluable dynamic images of the active, behaving brain, but the cumbersomeness of fMRI and PET equipment limits research to the artificial environment of the laboratory, with participants performing tasks that bear little resemblance to real life. In the past few years, portable EEG devices have allowed researchers to begin examining the brains of people in more naturalistic settings, providing insights into new brain-behavior interactions. One brand of equipment, the EMOTIV system, uses a simple headband with 5 to 14 electrodes to detect brain activity from several locations; it then sends these signals wirelessly to a computer for analysis (EMOTIV, n.d.). This type of equipment allows researchers to make recordings in real-life social situations. Suzanne Dikker and her colleagues discovered that when students interacted with each other in the classroom, their brain activity fell into similar, synchronized patterns (Cell Press, 2017). Cognitive psychologist David Strayer has even taken the equipment on three-day camping trips to study how the brain,

especially the prefrontal cortex, rejuvenates itself in the relaxing environment of nature (F. Williams, 2016). As behavioral evidence of this rejuvenation, an Outward Bound group performed 50% better on creative reasoning tasks by the third day. Now that studies of brain activity are no longer confined to the laboratory, the possibilities for insight into the neural correlates of human behavior seem limitless.

THOUGHT QUESTIONS

1. How has portable EEG technology helped advance our understanding of the nervous system?

2. In addition to the two examples mentioned here, what is another behavior that you believe could be better understood through the use of portable EEG technology?

For the news story visit edge.sagepub.com/garrett5e and select the Chapter 4 study resources.

■ FIGURE 4.10   A Plate From a Stereotaxic Atlas of the Rat Brain.

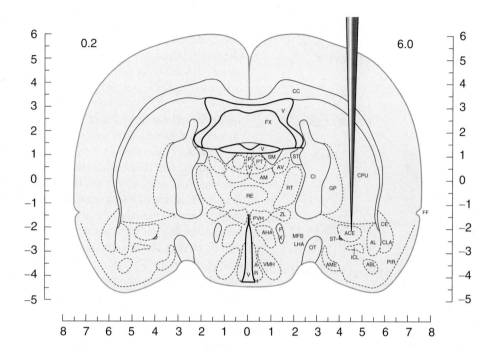

Each drawing is numbered to indicate the anterior/posterior location of the slice and the structures shown; the scales on the bottom and the sides of the drawing tell the researcher how far from the midline and how deep to insert the probe. (The electrode from Figure 4.11 is shown superimposed over the drawing, for illustrative purposes.)

Source: L. J. Pellegrino, A. S. Pellegrino, and A. J. Cushman, *A Stereotaxic Atlas of the Rat Brain*, 2nd edition, Kluwer Academic/Plenum Publishers. © 1979; with kind permission from Springer Science+Business Media B.V.

Optogenetic techniques (see Chapter 2) have significant advantages over electrical stimulation. The light-sensitive channels can be inserted in specific types of neurons, so the procedure offers more precise control than electrical stimulation, which activates all neurons in the area. And, unlike electrical stimulation, light activation doesn't interfere with simultaneous recording of the resulting neural activity. Neurons near the brain's surface can be stimulated through an opening in the skull, or the light can be directed to deeper structures via optical fibers. Both techniques allow the study of awake, freely moving subjects. The channels are usually introduced by inserting genes from algae or bacteria. Channels derived from these sources are activated by opsins, the same light-sensitive proteins that enable our eyes to detect light; in the original hosts, their roles include orientation to light and control of day-night rhythms, as well as vision (F. Zhang et al., 2011). Optogenetics is not limited to stimulation; by genetically introducing the appropriate sensors, researchers can detect and measure several aspects of neural activity, including membrane voltage, neurotransmitters, and release of transmitters from vesicles (Mancuso et al., 2010; Treger, 2015).

Optogenetics has turned out to be a very powerful technique. It has been used to study the neural bases of brain activities ranging from movement regulation to memory, the role of rhythmic neural activity in behavior

■ FIGURE 4.11   A Stereotaxic Instrument.

This device allows the researcher to locate an electrode precisely at the right horizontal position and depth in the animal's brain. (Although its eyes are open, the rat is deeply anesthetized.)

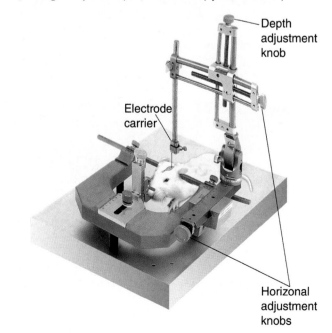

■ FIGURE 4.12 A Cannula for Microdialysis.

Neurochemicals in the surrounding fluid diffuse into the cannula through the porous membrane. Fluid is pumped in through the outer tube and flows out through the inside tube, carrying the neurochemicals with it.

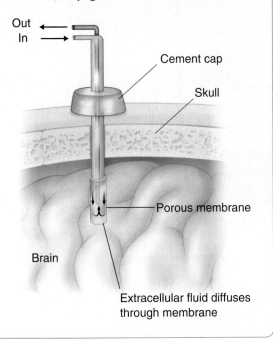

and information processing, and the contribution of neural activity to myelination and adult neurogenesis (Deisseroth, 2015). It is also helping us understand the recovery processes following stroke, as well as a wide range of disorders including Parkinson's disease, Alzheimer's disease, anxiety, depression, and addiction (Deisseroth, 2015; Steinberg, Christoffel, Deisseroth, & Malenka, 2015). Therapeutic applications are on the horizon, as well. The first clinical trials began in March 2016, when doctors injected light-sensitive algae into patients' eyes in hopes of restoring some vision to blind individuals ("RetroSense Therapeutics Doses First Patients," 2016).

Chemical stimulation of the brain can be carried out by inserting a small-diameter tube called a cannula. Chemical stimulation has a special advantage over electrical stimulation in that it acts only at the dendrites and cell bodies of neurons. This means that the researcher can simulate the effects of a neurotransmitter or block a transmitter's effects at the synapses. Often the tube is not used to deliver the drug but is cemented in place and used later as a guide for inserting a smaller drug-delivery cannula; this arrangement can be used for stimulation later on multiple occasions. The same technique is used for microdialysis, in which brain fluids are extracted for analysis, but a more elaborate dual cannula is required. As Figure 4.12 shows, the brain fluids seep through a porous membrane into the lower chamber of the cannula; a biologically neutral fluid (very similar to seawater) is pumped through one of the dual tubes, and it flushes the brain fluid out the other tube for analysis. In Chapter 5, you will see results from both of these techniques, when researchers deliver abused drugs to rats' brains or monitor the release of brain neurotransmitters after an animal is injected with a drug.

Some clinical situations require doctors to insert an electrode or cannula into the brain of a human patient—for example, to identify functional areas by recording electrical activity prior to brain surgery, to lesion malfunctioning tissue in patients with epilepsy, or to stimulate the brain in patients with Parkinson's disease. Sometimes, though, a patient undergoing brain surgery will volunteer to have unrelated measurements done at the time for research purposes. Placement of the probe can be done visually using one of the brain scanning techniques, but stereotaxic atlases of the human brain are published for this purpose, and there are human stereotaxic instruments as well, usually designed to mount on the head, as shown in Figure 4.13.

■ FIGURE 4.13 A Human Stereotaxic Instrument.

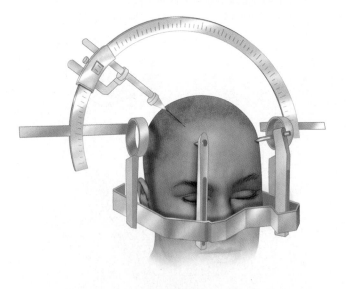

Ablation and Lesioning

Historically, one of the most profitable avenues of brain research has been the study of patients who have sustained brain damage. Brain damage can occur in a variety of ways: gunshot wounds, blows to the head, tumors, infection, toxins, and strokes. Although these "natural experiments" have been extremely valuable to neuroscientists, they also have major disadvantages. Most important, the damage doesn't coincide neatly with the functional area; it will affect a smaller area or overlap with other functional areas. Fortunately, the pattern of damage varies from patient to patient, so if the neuroscientist studies a large number of patients, it may be possible to identify the location of damage common to people with the same deficits.

Because of these and other difficulties in studying patients with brain damage, researchers often resort

Source: Adapted from *Biological Foundations of Human Behavior*, by J. Wilson, 2003, Belmont, CA: Wadsworth.

to producing the damage themselves in animals. In some cases, a whole area of the brain may be removed; removal of brain tissue is called *ablation*. Ablation can be done with a scalpel, but *aspiration* is a more precise technique, and it allows access to deeper structures. The skull is opened, and a fine-tipped glass micropipette connected to a vacuum pump is used to suck out neural tissue. Usually, however, lesioning is preferred in place of ablation because the damage can be controlled more precisely. *Lesions,* or damage to neural tissue, can be produced by electrical current, heat, or injection of a neurotoxin (using a stereotaxic instrument) or by using a knife or a fine wire to sever connections between areas. "Reversible lesions" can be produced by chilling a brain area or by injecting certain chemicals; this means that the animal's behavior can be observed before and during treatment and again after recovery.

Transcranial Magnetic Stimulation

Transcranial magnetic stimulation (TMS) is a relatively new noninvasive brain stimulation technique that uses a magnetic coil to induce a voltage in brain tissue. The device is held close to the scalp over the target area, as in Figure 4.14. TMS is pulsed at varying rates; frequencies of 1/s or lower decrease brain excitability, and frequencies of 5/s or higher increase excitability.

TMS has demonstrated its usefulness mostly as a research instrument. By making clever combination of TMS stimulation and brain imaging techniques (described in the next section), researchers have teased out the neural modifications that account for recovery in stroke patients (Gerloff et al., 2006) and confirmed that making visual-spatial judgments involves not just the parietal area but rather a broader network that includes frontal regions (A. T. Sack et al., 2007). Clinically, TMS has shown effectiveness in treating the symptoms of Parkinson's disease (Y. Chou, Hickey, Sundman, Song, & Chen, 2015), depression and pain (Lefaucheur et al., 2014), and migraine headache (Bhola et al., 2015).

A simpler and less expensive alternative, transcranial direct current stimulation (tDCS), involves application of direct current electrical stimulation through electrodes placed on the scalp (Sparing & Mottaghy, 2008). Unlike TMS, tDCS does not excite neurons to fire. Instead, it activates astrocytes (Monai et al., 2016), increasing neuronal excitability and functional connectivity (Cosmo et al., 2015). Studies indicate that it can improve attention (Coffman, Trumbo, & Clark, 2012) and memory (Prehn-Kristensen et al., 2014). The U.S. military reportedly is experimenting with tDCS for improving training and enhancing performance (E. Young, 2014).

Brain Imaging Techniques

In Broca's day, and in fact until fairly recently, a researcher had to wait for a brain-damaged patient to die in order to pinpoint the location of the damage. There was little motivation to do exhaustive observations of the patient's behavior when the patient might outlive the researcher or the body might not be available to the researcher at death. All that changed with the invention of imaging equipment that could produce a picture of the living brain showing the location of damage.

The first modern medical imaging technique came into use in the early 1970s. *Computed tomography (CT)* scanning produces a series of X-rays taken from different angles; a computer combines the series of two-dimensional horizontal cross sections, or "slices," so that the researcher can scan through them as if they are a 3-D image of the entire organ (Figure 4.15). "False colors" are often added to the achromatic image to make features more distinguishable. Imaging soft tissue such as the brain requires injecting a dye that will show up on an X-ray; the dye diffuses throughout the tiny blood vessels of the brain, so it is really the differing density of blood vessels that forms the image. A major drawback of earlier equipment was its extreme slowness, but newer models of CT scanners are fast, and they provide detailed images. CT scans are also popularly known as *CAT scans.*

Another imaging technique, *magnetic resonance imaging (MRI),* works by measuring the radio-frequency waves emitted by the nuclei of hydrogen atoms when they are subjected to a strong magnetic field. Most of that hydrogen is in the water that composes 78% of the brain, but the water content varies in different brain structures, so these emissions from hydrogen nuclei can be used to form a detailed image of the brain (Figure 4.16a). The MRI is reasonably fast, and it can image small areas. Recent increases in power permit more versatile imaging by

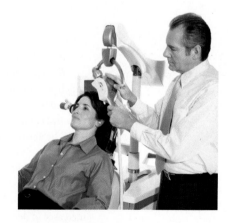

■ **FIGURE 4.14** A Therapist Uses TMS With a Patient.

Source: "Using Magnets as a Depression Treatment," *Design News*, October 11, 2010. Retrieved August 26, 2012, from http://www.designnews.com/document.asp?doc_id=229440.

■ **FIGURE 4.15**   Computed Tomography Scanning Procedure.

(a)
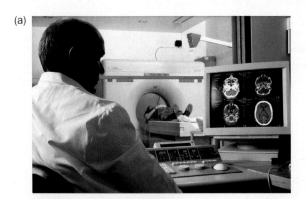

(b)
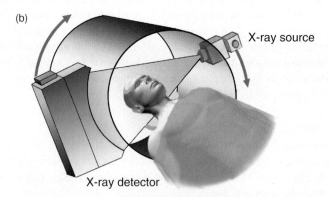

X-ray source

X-ray detector

(c)
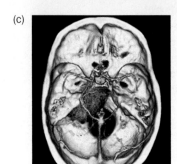

(a) The patient's head is positioned in a large cylinder, as shown here. (b) An X-ray beam and X-ray detector rotate around the patient's head, taking multiple X-rays of a horizontal slice of the patient's brain. (c) A computer combines X-rays to create an image of a horizontal slice of the brain. The scan reveals a tumor on the right side of the brain.

Sources: (a) Phanie/Science Source. (b) From Weiten. Psychology: Themes and Variations (with InfoTrac), 5E. © 2001 South-Western, a part of Cengage Learning, Inc. Reproduced by permission. www.cengage.com/permissions. (c) ZEPHYR/SCIENCE PHOTO LIBRARY/Getty Images.

detecting elements other than hydrogen, including sodium, phosphorus, carbon, nitrogen, and oxygen. MRI scanners can cost up to $3 million and require a suite costing hundreds of thousands more, but more sensitive magnetic field detectors are making low-power, portable scanners available for use in the field. A variant of MRI, *diffusion tensor imaging,* measures the movement of water molecules; because water moves easily along the length of axons, this technique is useful for imaging brain pathways and measuring their quality (Figure 4.16b). As you read through the rest of this text, you will learn how the ability to quantify white matter is helping us understand mental disorders and psychological functions such as intelligence and learning.

CT and MRI added tremendous capability for detecting tumors and correlating brain damage with behavioral symptoms. However, CT and MRI lack the ability to detect changing brain activity (as EEG does, for instance). The two remaining techniques add that capability.

Positron emission tomography (PET) involves injecting a radioactive substance into the bloodstream, which is taken up by parts of the brain according to how active they are. The scanner captures the positrons emitted by the radioactive substance to form an image that is color coded to show the relative amounts of activity (Figure 4.17). Radioactive 2-DG is often the substance that is injected because increased uptake of 2-DG by active neurons provides a measure of metabolic activity. Other radioactive substances can be used to monitor blood flow or oxygen uptake, and if a neurotransmitter is made radioactive, it can be used to determine the locations and numbers of receptors for the transmitter. Usually, the researcher produces a "difference scan" by subtracting the activity occurring during a neutral control condition from the activity that occurred during the test condition; this produces an image that uses a color scale to show where activity increased or decreased in the brain.

? What advantage do PET and fMRI have over CT and MRI?

PET equipment is expensive and requires a sophisticated staff to operate it; the facility must also be near a cyclotron, which produces the radioactive substance, and there are few of those around. The advantage that justifies this expense is that PET is able to track changing activity in the brain. However, PET cannot detect changes during behaviors that are briefer than 30 seconds. PET also does not image the brain tissue itself, so the results are often displayed overlaid on a brain image produced by another means, such as MRI.

■ **FIGURE 4.16**   Magnetic Resonance and Diffusion Tensor Images.

(a) A magnetic resonance image, which has detected a tumor (red arrow). (b) A diffusion tensor image reveals fibers connecting frontal, parietal, temporal, and occipital areas. Colors have been added to provide three-dimensional information; for example, the yellow fibers are ascending or descending vertically.

(a)

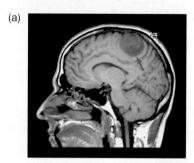

(b)

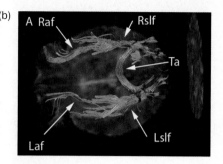

Sources: (a) © Living Art Enterprises/Photo Researchers/Getty Images. (b) Courtesy of Aaron Filer, MD, PhD.

A modification of MRI takes advantage of the fact that oxygenated blood has magnetic properties that are different from those of blood that has given up its oxygen to cells. *Functional magnetic resonance imaging (fMRI)* measures brain activation by detecting the increase in oxygen levels in active neural structures (Figure 4.18). MRI and fMRI have the advantage over PET and CT because they involve no radiation, so they are safe to use in studies that require repeated measurements. In addition, fMRI measures activity, like PET, and produces an image of the brain with good spatial resolution, like MRI; researchers can detect activity in cortical areas as small as 1 millimeter (Barinaga, 1997). The fMRI machines are particularly pricey though, which limits their usefulness for research. The techniques described here are summarized in Table 4.1.

Brain imaging has been referred to as "the predominant technique in behavioral and cognitive neuroscience" (Friston, 2009, p. 399). That said, you will not be surprised to see many examples of its use throughout this text—though none will be as unusual as the one in the accompanying Application. However, some investigators are urging caution in interpreting results; their focus has been mostly on fMRI, but their criticisms apply more broadly. For one thing, comparison of fMRI data with data from electrode recording in monkeys showed that fMRI misses a great deal of information; this is due to its lower sensitivity as well as to chance factors such as the distance of the neurons from a blood vessel (Logothetis, 2002). A related problem is that test-retest reliability is often low. For example, when researchers showed volunteers pictures of fearful faces, correlations of amygdala activity in sessions two weeks apart ranged from .4 to .7, indicating a disappointing level of consistency (Johnstone et al., 2005). (We discuss the meaning of correlations in more detail in the next section.)

Perhaps more important, some researchers have been criticized for the way they select their data. Ideally, researchers should decide in advance to obtain data from a specific area, such as the amygdala, but often researchers do not have enough information to make this selection beforehand and therefore scan the whole brain. Then they divide the scan into tiny cube-shaped areas called voxels and determine which voxels' activity is correlated with performance on a task or with a characteristic of the subjects. This involves calculating literally thousands of correlations; if you have even a basic understanding of probability, you know that this procedure

■ **FIGURE 4.17**   Positron Emission Tomography.

A PET scan detects concentrations of radioactivity where neural activity is high; the computer produces a color-coded image, shown here superimposed over a separate scan of a brain. Traditionally, red indicates the greatest amount of activity, followed by yellow, green, and then blue. The individual was working on a verbal task, so areas involved in language processing were activated.

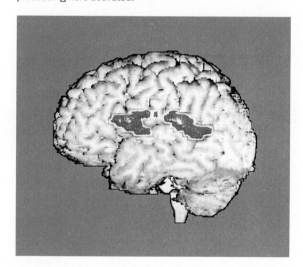

Source: © SPL/Science Source.

■ **FIGURE 4.18**   An fMRI Scan.

The colored areas were more active when research participants were processing words that were later remembered than when they processed words that were not remembered.

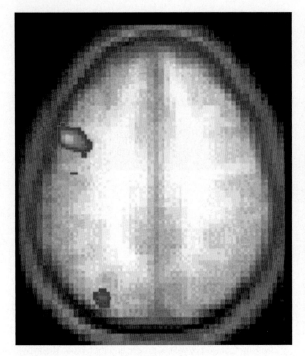 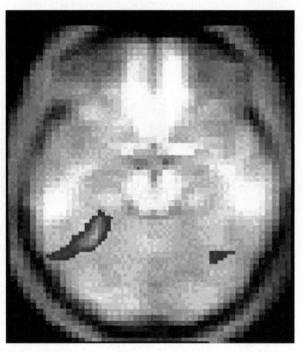

Source: From "Building Memories: Remembering and Forgetting of Verbal Experiences as Predicted by Brain Activity," by A. D. Wagner et al., *Science, 281*, pp. 1188–1191. © 1998 American Association for the Advancement of Science. Reprinted by permission from AAAS.

TABLE 4.1   Comparison of EEG and Imaging Techniques.

TECHNIQUE	DESCRIPTION	TIME	SPATIAL (MM)
EEG	Sums the electrical activity of neurons between two electrodes; detects fast-changing brain activity but is poor at localizing it	1 ms	10–15
CT	Forms 3-D image of brain by combining X-rays of cross sections of brain; images structure and damage	<1 ms	0.5
MRI	Measures variations in hydrogen concentrations in brain tissue; images structure and damage	3–5 s	1–1.5
PET	Image produced by emissions from injected substances that have been made radioactive; tracks changing activity, detects receptors, etc.	30 s	2–3
fMRI	Detects increases in oxygen levels during neural activity; tracks changing activity	1 s	1–2

APPLICATION
Scanning King Tut

In January 2005, King Tutankhamun, pharaoh of Egypt 3,000 years ago, was removed from his tomb in the Valley of the Kings for the first time in almost 80 years. The trip was a short one, to a nearby van where his mummified body was subjected to a CT scan to determine whether Tut's death at the age of 19 might have resulted from murderous intrigue within the royal family.

An X-ray conducted in the tomb 30 years earlier had found pieces of his skull inside the cranium, adding to the murder theory. But if Tut had died from a blow to the head, the bone fragments would have been caught up in the embalming material. Instead, the scan showed them lodged between the skull and the now solidified embalming fluid. More likely the archaeologist Howard Carter, who discovered Tut's tomb in 1922, damaged the skull while prying away the golden mask that was stuck to the skull by solidified resins. The scans also found no mineral deposits in the bone, which some poisons would leave behind, though other poisons could not be ruled out. The most promising evidence was that one leg had been broken, within days of his death judging by the lack of healing. The break was severe enough to cause an open wound, so King Tut's death could have been caused by an infection. A study by an interdisciplinary research team suggested that Tut's overall health was already a liability. By combining CT scans with genetic evidence from his and some of his relatives' mummies, they concluded that he may have had multiple disorders,

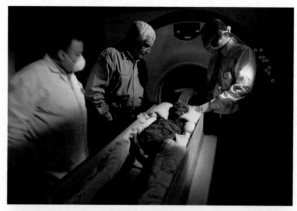

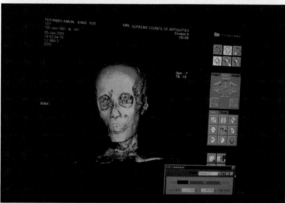

(Top) Egypt's Vice Minister of Culture Zahi Hawass (center) and technicians ready Tut's mummy for scanning. (Bottom) A resulting scan of Tut's head.

Sources: Kenneth Garrett/National Geographic/Getty Images.

including a weakened immune system, and that he probably needed the numerous ornamental canes left in his tomb to walk (Hawass, 2010).

guarantees finding several voxels whose activity correlates with the dependent variable even when no relationship exists. Thus, to ensure reliability of the results, the researcher should repeat the experiment focusing only on those areas to rule out the possibility the original correlations occurred by chance.

However, researchers sometimes choose the easier approach of simply reporting the correlations they found in that one session. In an analysis of 53 studies that reported correlations of fMRI activity with social or emotional measures (such as distress from social rejection), more than half used the flawed nonindependent approach, and they accounted almost entirely for the highest correlations (Vul, Harris, Winkielman, & Pashler, 2009; see also the similar results of Kriegeskorte, Simmons, Bellgowan, & Baker, 2009). Nikos Logothetis has warned that erroneous claims of brain areas specialized for everything from empathy to neuroticism are leading to a phrenology that is even more dangerous than the 19th-century variety because it is cloaked in the respectability of brain imaging (Spinney, 2002).

Still, these problems do not undermine the potential of imaging studies for understanding behavior. The fact that five people won Nobel Prizes for their work in developing scanning technology indicates the importance of

> *The single most critical piece of equipment is still the researcher's own brain. . . . What is badly needed now, with all these scanners whirring away, is an understanding of exactly what we are observing, and seeing, and measuring, and wondering about.*
>
> —Endel Tulving

RESEARCH SPOTLIGHT

Growing a Model Brain From Skin Cells

Rene Anand and his team at Ohio State University coaxed stem cells derived from human skin cells to develop into a nearly complete human brain comparable to that of a 5-week-old fetus (Caldwell, 2015). More appropriately called a brain organoid, it has all the major regions of a brain, functioning neurons, glial cells, a retina, and even a spinal cord.

Recently Jessica Mariani and her colleagues (2015) at Yale University used this strategy in an attempt to learn why autism develops in some individuals without a clear genetic cause. To do this they focused on a subtype of autism in which individuals have slightly enlarged heads, which affects about

20% of those with autism. They cultured stem cells from these autistic individuals to grow into organoids and compared them with organoids grown from non-autistic biological relatives. The scientists observed that after about a month of development, the organoids growing from autistic individuals were overproducing GABA-releasing neurons, due to overexpression of the *FOXG1* gene. This was the first clear identification of a neural mechanism that leads to the development of autism. Although there are still many hurdles ahead, having a cellular target during development may lead to earlier identification of factors that could result in developmental disorders like autism.

imaging techniques, and you can be sure that many important future developments in neuroscience will depend on brain imaging, just as they have for the past 20 years.

A deficiency of all these technologies is that they show what the brain is doing at the current time. To understand many brain processes and disorders such as schizophrenia, we also need to watch the brain as it develops. The accompanying Research Spotlight describes an important step in that direction.

Investigating Heredity

We looked at the interplay of heredity and environment in shaping behavior in Chapter 1. Now we need to understand some of the techniques scientists use to do genetic research. The idea that behavior can be inherited is an ancient one, but most of the methods for genetic research were introduced or came into maturity in the past three or four decades. Until then, the work was not much more sophisticated than observing that a characteristic runs in families.

Genetic Similarities: The Correlational Approach

In a *family study,* which determines how strongly a characteristic is shared among relatives, we would find that intelligent parents usually have intelligent children. However, as one researcher put it, "Cake recipes run in families, but not because of genes" (Goodwin, 1986, p. 3). This is a good example of the problem with correlational research. People who have similar genes often share a similar environment, so the effects of heredity are confounded with the effects of environment. Still, the fact that family members are similar in a characteristic tells researchers that it would be worthwhile to pursue more complicated and costly research strategies. We will look at ways to reduce the confounding of heredity with environment, but first we need a way to quantify the results.

Quantification is a simple matter for characteristics that can be treated as present or absent, such as schizophrenia. We can say, for instance, that the rate of schizophrenia is about 1% in the general population but increases to around 13% among the offspring of a schizophrenic parent (Gottesman, 1991). For variables that are measured on a numerical scale, such as height and IQ (intelligence quotient, a measure of intelligence), we express the relationship with a statistic called the *correlation coefficient. Correlation* is the degree of relationship between two variables, measured on a scale between 0.0 and ±1.0. The strength of the relationship is indicated by the absolute value—how close the correlation is to *either* 1.0 or −1.0. A positive correlation means that when one variable is high, the other tends to be high as well. For example, the correlation between the IQs of parents and their children averages about .42 across studies, and the correlation between brothers and sisters in the same family is about .47 (T. J. Bouchard & McGue, 1981). A negative value indicates the opposite tendency—when one value is high, the other tends to be low—not that the relationship is weaker. Now we can consider how to separate the effects of heredity from those of the environment.

Adoption studies eliminate much of the confounding of heredity and environment that occurs in family studies. *Adoption studies* compare the similarity between adopted children and their biological parents with their similarity to their adoptive parents. This kind of study is often called a *natural experiment*, but it lacks the control of a real experiment because we do not manipulate the adoption variable. As a result, environmental confounding can still occur. For example, families that must be split up by adoption may differ from the control families in important ways. Additional confounding occurs because children are often adopted into similar family environments and because adoption is frequently delayed until after critical developmental periods have passed. Nevertheless, the technique has yielded extremely valuable information, such as the fact that rearing children apart from their biological parents results in a drop in the correlation between their IQs from .42 to about .22 (T. J. Bouchard & McGue, 1981). The drop in correlation indicates a substantial influence of environment; the remaining correlation indicates genetic influence.

An environmental confound that adoption studies don't control is the prenatal environment, which can bring about long-term alterations in nervous system functioning. Animal researchers get around this problem by *cross-fostering*, implanting a fetus or an egg into another female. Of course, this strategy is unavailable in human research, or at least it was until *in vitro* fertilization became so widespread. British researchers examined the medical records of 800 children conceived by in vitro fertilization; in one-fourth of the cases, the egg or embryo was donated by another woman, so the offspring was unrelated to the mother. With this strategy, the researchers were able to conclude that the low birth weight previously observed in babies whose mothers smoked during pregnancy is environmental, whereas antisocial behavior (tantrums, fighting, lying, etc.) in children of smoking mothers has a genetic origin (F. Rice et al., 2009).

Twin studies assess how similar twins are in some characteristic; their similarity is then compared with that of nontwin siblings, or the similarity between identical twins is compared with the similarity between fraternal twins. Remember that fraternal twins are produced from two separately fertilized eggs (*dizygotic*), whereas identical twins result from a single egg that splits and develops into two individuals (*monozygotic*). Fraternal twins, like nontwin siblings, share only half their genes with each other; identical twins share 100% of their genes. Because both identical twins and fraternal twins share a common environment for the most part, a greater similarity between identical twins in a characteristic is probably due to their greater genetic similarity. Investigations of intelligence provide particularly good examples of the value of twin studies. For example, the correlation between fraternal twins' IQs is about .60, and for identical twins it increases to around .86 (T. J. Bouchard & McGue, 1981). (Of course, we have to select fraternal pairs that are of the same sex, because identical twins are of the same sex.) Criticisms of twin studies include the possibility that identical twins might be treated more similarly than fraternal twins, and the fact that they usually share the same placenta and sometimes the amniotic sac makes their prenatal environment more similar.

A useful measure for identifying genetic influence is *concordance rate*, the frequency with which relatives are alike in a characteristic. An example of this measure is that when one fraternal twin is schizophrenic, the second twin will also be diagnosed with schizophrenia about 17% of the time; in identical twins this measure almost triples, to 48% (Figure 4.19; Gottesman, 1991). But, because the correlation falls short of a perfect 1.0, even the identical twin

 How are adoption and twin studies superior to family studies?

■ **FIGURE 4.19**   The Genain Quadruplets.

Identical quadruplets, the sisters all became schizophrenic later in life. The chances of any four unrelated individuals all being schizophrenic is 1 in 100 million. The name *Genain* is a nickname derived from the Greek word meaning "dreadful gene."

Source: Associated Press.

TABLE 4.2   Comparison of Relationship Studies.

FAMILY STUDY	ADOPTION STUDY	TWIN STUDY
• Indicates how strongly a characteristic is shared among relatives • Can show that a characteristic follows family lines • Confounds heredity and environment	• Compares adopted children with their adoptive parents and their biological parents • Susceptible to confounding because the adoption variable is not manipulated	• Compares similarity of twins with that of nontwin siblings, or similarity of identical twins with similarity of fraternal twins • Allows comparison of two levels of genetic similarity

of a person with schizophrenia escapes schizophrenia about half of the time; for the same reason, identical twins will rarely have exactly the same IQ. The incomplete influence of heredity means that environmental effects are also operating. Family, adoption, and twin studies are compared in Table 4.2.

? What advantage does genetic engineering have over adoption and twin studies?

Genetic Engineering: The Experimental Approach

Although adoption and twin studies reduce confounding, they still share some of the disadvantages of correlational studies. *Genetic engineering* involves manipulation of the organism's genes or their functioning. Studies using this technology qualify as experiments. At present, genetic engineering is employed mostly with mice, because their genetic makeup is well known and their embryos are more successfully manipulated.

An obvious way to find out what a gene does is to disable it and see what effect this has on the animal. In the *knockout technique,* a nonfunctioning mutation is introduced into the isolated gene, and the altered gene is transferred into embryos. Subsequent mating of the resulting animals is required to produce animals that are homozygous for the gene. Another strategy is to disable the gene by interfering with its messenger RNA. The *antisense RNA* procedure blocks the participation of messenger RNA in protein construction. This is accomplished by inserting strands of complementary RNA into the animal, which dock with the gene's messenger RNA (Figure 4.20). The cell recognizes this newly formed molecule as abnormal and releases an enzyme that destroys the RNA.

In *gene transfer,* a gene from another organism is inserted into the recipient's cells. An important research tool is the *transgenic animal,* created by inserting the gene into the developing embryo. Again, mating of these animals is required to integrate the gene into all the cells. Researchers observe the effects in recipient animals to determine the transferred gene's function. One fascinating new way to investigate the connections in the nervous system is *Brainbow,* which is described in the accompanying Research Spotlight.

Gene therapy, the treatment of disorders by manipulating genes, does not allow the luxury of multiple generations to distribute the gene to all the cells. Typically the gene is carried into the individual by a vector, most often a disabled virus, which is injected directly into the diseased tissue or into the bloodstream near the target organ. Alternatively, the possibility of an immune response can be reduced by inserting the genes into cells removed from the patient's body, which are then returned to the patient. An adaptation of a strategy that bacteria use as a defense against an invading virus is enabling researchers to manipulate genes with much

■ **FIGURE 4.20**   Antisense RNA.

Antisense RNA is a strand of RNA that is complementary to a particular messenger RNA. The two will dock with each other, which disables the messenger RNA and halts production of its protein. The researcher observes differences in the animal to determine the gene's function.

RESEARCH SPOTLIGHT
The Brainbow Connection

Genetic engineering has enabled researchers to develop a major new technique for labeling and visualizing neurons, appropriately called *Brainbow*. Genes that produce phosphorescent proteins in three or four colors are inserted into an animal's genome; these combine in random combinations in neurons, labeling individual cells in as many as 100 different hues. Using light microscopy, the researcher is able to trace a neuron's path and view and photograph the connectome.

For more information, Brainbow images, and a related video, visit edge.sagepub.com/garrett5e and select the Chapter 4 study resources.

more precision. The bacteria send a strand of RNA to join with the virus's DNA; an enzyme then cuts the DNA, disabling the virus. The adaptation, known as CRISPR, can be used to delete or disable a defective gene or to insert a beneficial gene at the location.

In spite of some disastrous setbacks along the way, genetic engineering is becoming a therapeutic reality. Gene therapy for a type of SCID has just been approved by the European Commission after trial patients had a 100 percent survival rate, some as long as 13 years following treatment (Nield, 2016). A new gene insertion procedure has halted the brain myelin–destroying disease adrenoleukodystrophy (ALD) in all but one of 17 boys (J. Kaiser, 2016). A family's struggle to save their son from ALD was the subject of the 1992 movie *Lorenzo's Oil*. Though CRISPR has been used to treat diseases only in animal models so far, researchers recently took a major step when they were able to replace a blindness-causing gene mutation in stem cells that had been derived from a patient who had retinitis pigmentosa. Returning the stem cells to the patient might have cured the disease, but human trials have not been approved yet (Bassuk, Zheng, Li, Tsang, & Mahajan, 2016). In Chapter 12, you will see that doctors are having some success using gene transfer to treat Alzheimer's disease. Although these results are promising, the ability to manipulate our genome carries tremendous risks and raises important ethical questions.

> *There will be a gene-based treatment for essentially every disease within 50 years.*
>
> —W. French Anderson

CONCEPT CHECK

Take a Minute to Check Your Knowledge and Understanding

- Organize your knowledge: Make a table of the staining and labeling techniques and their functions.
- What different ways could be used to determine the function of a part of the brain?
- Name three procedures that can be used to identify receptors.
- What are the advantages and disadvantages of experimental studies and correlational studies?
- Describe the different genetic manipulation strategies discussed in this chapter.

Research Ethics

What are the main issues in research integrity?

As important a topic as research ethics is, it usually gets pushed into the background by the excitement of scientific accomplishments and therapeutic promise. To place ethics at the forefront where it belongs, the major scientific and medical organizations have adopted strict guidelines for conducting research, for the treatment of subjects, and for communicating the results of research (see, for example, American Psychological Association, 2010; "Policies on the Use of Animals and Humans in Neuroscience Research," n.d.; "Public Health Service Policy on Humane Care and Use of Laboratory Animals," 2015; "Research Involving Human Subjects," n.d.).

Plagiarism and Fabrication

The success of research in answering questions and solving problems depends not only on the researchers' skill in designing studies and collecting data but also on their accuracy and integrity in communicating results. Unfortunately, research is sometimes misrepresented intentionally; the two cardinal sins of research are plagiarism and the fabrication of data.

Plagiarism is the theft of another's work or ideas. Plagiarism denies individuals the credit they deserve and erodes trust among the research community. The infraction may be as simple as failing to give appropriate credit through citations and references (like those you see throughout this text), but occasionally a researcher literally steals another's work. In a recent high-profile case, for example, German education minister Annette Schavan resigned after the University of Düsseldorf revoked her Ph.D. due to plagiarism. According to the university, large parts of her 1980 dissertation were closely paraphrased from other sources without crediting those sources ("German Education Minister Quits," 2013).

Fabrication, or faking, of results is more serious than plagiarism because it introduces erroneous information into the body of scientific knowledge. As a result, the pursuit of false leads by others consumes scarce resources and sidetracks researchers from more fruitful lines of research. More important, fabrication in clinical research can slow therapeutic progress and harm lives. In 1998, Andrew Wakefield published a study implicating a preservative in some vaccines as a cause of autism. No one could replicate the results, and later investigation revealed numerous instances of data fabrication and misrepresentation in the research (Deer, 2011). The article was retracted and Wakefield lost his medical license, but the repercussions continue today. Many parents have become suspicious of vaccines and are failing to have their children immunized. As one result, although measles was declared eliminated from the United States in 2000, 1,400 people were infected between 2010 and 2016 (Centers for Disease Control and Prevention, 2016).

Although such cases are rare (E. Marshall, 2000b), they undermine confidence in scientific and medical research. Increasingly, concerned government agencies are taking steps to educate researchers about research ethics (R. Dalton, 2000), setting aside $1 million of grant money to support studies on research integrity (E. Marshall, 2000c) and discouraging ties between scientists and the companies whose products they are testing (Agnew, 2000). In a fascinating development, a social psychologist at the University of Pennsylvania has devised a statistical method to detect suspicious patterns in research data. Using this method, he accused a psychologist at the University of Rotterdam of data tampering, which led to a university investigation, withdrawal of two papers, and the psychologist's resignation (Enserink, 2012).

> Falsification is far more serious because it always corrupts the scientific record. It is a crime against science, indeed a crime against all humanity, when it legitimizes science that is false.
>
> —David Crowe

Protecting the Welfare of Research Participants

All the scientific disciplines that use live subjects in their research have adopted strict codes for the humane treatment of both humans and animals. The specifics of the treatment of human research participants and even the legitimacy of animal research are controversial, however. These are not abstract issues. As a student, you are a consumer of the knowledge that human and animal research produces, and you benefit personally from the medical and psychological advances, so you are more than just a neutral observer.

Research With Humans

In 1953, the psychologist Albert Ax performed a study that was as significant for its ethical implications as for its scientific results. He was attempting to determine whether all emotions result in the same general bodily arousal or each emotion produces a unique pattern of activation. To do so, he measured several physiological variables sensitive to emotional arousal, such as heart rate, breathing rate, and skin temperature, while inducing anger in the individuals at one time and fear at another. If Ax had told the research participants what would happen during the study, it would have altered their behavior, so he said he was doing a study of blood pressure.

 What are the principal ethical concerns in human research?

In the "anger" condition, the research participant was insulted by Ax's assistant, who complained at length that the person was not a very good experimental subject. The "fear" situation was more intense. During the recordings, the individual received a mild electrical shock through the recording electrodes, while sparks jumped from nearby equipment. The experimenter acted alarmed as he explained that there was a dangerous high-voltage short circuit. Later interviews indicated that both ruses worked. Ax (1953) reported that one participant kept pleading during the fear treatment, "Please take the wires off. Oh! Please help me." Another said of the anger treatment, "I was just about to punch that character on the nose" (p. 435). You will find the results of Ax's research described in Chapter 8; here we will look at the issues of informed consent and deception in relation to his study.

Occasionally, research involves some pain, discomfort, or even risk. Before proceeding with a study, current standards require the researcher to obtain the participant's informed consent. *Informed consent* means that the individual voluntarily agrees to participate after receiving information about any risks, discomfort, or other adverse effects that might occur. However, sometimes the nature of a study requires the researcher to use *deception,* failing to tell the participants the exact purpose of the research or what will happen during the study, or actively misinforming them. According to the American Psychological Association (APA), deception is acceptable only when the value of the study justifies it, alternative procedures are not available, and the individuals are correctly informed afterward. The APA's guidelines are also clear that psychologists should not deceive subjects about research that is reasonably expected to cause physical pain or severe emotional distress (American Psychological Association, 2010). Some researchers and subjects' rights advocates believe that deception is never justified. Ax's study would probably not be permitted today, but we will see in Chapter 8 that researchers have found interesting alternatives for doing this kind of research.

Research With Animals

Psychological and medical researchers have perhaps no more important resource than the laboratory animal. As the American Medical Association (1992) concluded, "Virtually every advance in medical science in the twentieth century, from antibiotics and vaccines to anti-depressant drugs and organ transplants, has been achieved either directly or indirectly through the use of animals in laboratory experiments" (p. 11). Psychologists have used animals to investigate behavior, aging, pain, stress, and cognitive functions such as learning and perception (D. Blum, 1994; F. A. King, Yarbrough, Anderson, Gordon, & Gould, 1988; N. F. Miller, 1985). It may seem that the best subjects for that purpose would be humans, but animals are useful because they live in a controlled environment and have a homogeneous history of experience, as well as a briefer development and life span. In addition, researchers feel that it is more ethical to use procedures that are painful or physically or psychologically risky on other animals than on humans. As a result, in the mid-1980s, U.S. scientists were using 20 million animals a year: 90% of them were rodents, mostly mice and rats, and around 3.5% were primates, mostly monkeys and chimpanzees (U.S. Congress Office of Technology Assessment, 1986).

What are the opposing views on animal research?

The preference for inflicting discomfort or danger on nonhuman animals rather than on humans is based on the assumption that the well-being of animals is less important than that of humans. Animal rights activists have called this dual ethical standard *speciesism* (H. A. Herzog, 1998), a term chosen to be intentionally similar to *racism*. Some activists work hand in hand with researchers to improve conditions for research animals; others have been more aggressive, breaking into labs, destroying equipment and records, and releasing animals (typically resulting in the animals' death). In Europe and Britain, death threats have forced some researchers to move their work behind high fences (Koenig, 1999; Schiermeier, 1998). At the University of California at Santa Cruz, one animal researcher's home was firebombed, and another's car was burned (G. Miller, 2008). Activists have been shifting their attacks from laboratories to the researchers themselves; since the 1990s, attacks on individuals have risen from 9% of incidents to 46% ("Animal Rights Extremists Increasingly Targeting Individuals," 2014).

Animal research guidelines provide for humane housing of animals, attention to their health, and minimization of discomfort and stress during research (American Psychological Association, 2010; "Guidelines for Ethical Conduct in the Care and Use of Animals," n.d.; "Policies on the Use of Animals and Humans in Neuroscience Research," n.d.). But critics point out that researchers sometimes do not live up to the standards of their professional organizations. The Behavioral Biology Center in Silver Spring, Maryland, was engaged in research that involved severing the sensory nerve in one arm of monkeys to study the reorganization that occurs in the brain. The lab's contributions drew the praise of neuroscientists and led to the design of routines for extensive exercise of an afflicted limb to help people recover from brain injuries. But in 1981, a student summer employee informed the police of what he considered to be abuse of the lab's animals, and the police carried out the first raid on a research laboratory in the United States ("A Brighter Day for Edward Taub," 1997; Orlans, 1993). The director, Edward Taub, was convicted of animal abuse because of poor postoperative care, but the conviction was overturned because the state lacked jurisdiction over federally supported scientific research. The National Institutes of Health withdrew Taub's funding, and Congress enacted more stringent animal protection laws. In spite of the controversy, Taub received the William James Award from the American Psychological Society. However, he points out that the award was for work that is no longer permitted and that animal welfare rules enacted by Congress prevent him from taking measurements in the brain of the one remaining monkey for the length of time that would be needed.

The conflict between animal welfare and research needs is obviously not a simple issue and is strongly felt on both sides (Figure 4.21). Although psychologists and neuroscientists do not condone mistreatment of research animals, most of them argue that the distress that does occur is justified by the benefits animal research has produced. The 2000 Nobel Prize in physiology or medicine was shared by three neuroscientists: Arvid Carlsson, for his discovery of the role of dopamine as a neurotransmitter in the brain; Paul Greengard, for identifying how dopamine and related neurotransmitters produce their effect on neurons;

Every one has heard of the dog suffering under vivisection, who licked the hand of the operator: this man, unless he had a heart of stone, must have felt remorse to the last hour of his life.

—*Charles Darwin*, The Descent of Man and Selection in Relation to Sex, *1871*

■ **FIGURE 4.21**   Animal Research Controversy.

The poster illustrates the contrasting views on animal research.

Source: Foundation of Biomedical Research.

and Eric Kandel, for his work on the molecular changes that occur in the brain during learning. The work of all three prize winners relied heavily on animal research.

It is unlikely that animal research will be banned as the more extreme activists demand, but animal care and use guidelines have been tightened and outside monitoring increased, and states have passed more stringent laws. In addition, researchers have become more sensitive to the welfare of animals, adopting more humane methods of treatment and turning to tissue cultures and computer simulations in place of live animals when possible. In a survey of articles published in major biomedical journals between 1970 and 2000, the proportion of studies using animal subjects had fallen by one third, and in the studies that did use animals, the average number had decreased by half (Carlsson, Hagelin, & Hau, 2004). The National Institutes of Health is furthering that trend by withdrawing all support from biomedical research on chimpanzees and relocating its animals to a retirement colony in Louisiana (National Institutes of Health, 2015).

Human research has typically generated less controversy than the use of animals, largely because scientists are more restrained in their treatment of humans, and humans are able to refuse to participate and to bring lawsuits. The balance of concern is shifting, though, particularly as treatments move from the research lab to the clinic.

Gene Therapy

? What are the problems with gene research and gene therapy?

Gene therapy has enjoyed glowing press reviews because of its potential for correcting humanity's greatest handicaps and deadly diseases. But a distinct chill fell over the research in 1999, when Jesse Gelsinger, an 18-year-old patient volunteer, became the first human to die as the direct result of gene research (Lehrman, 1999; E. Marshall, 2000a). The study was using a deactivated form of adenovirus, which causes the common cold, to transport a gene into the liver in an experimental attempt to correct a genetic liver enzyme deficiency. Gelsinger developed an immune reaction to the adenovirus, which resulted in his death.

The Food and Drug Administration (FDA), which was overseeing the study, reprimanded the researchers for not consulting with the FDA when most of the patients developed mild adverse reactions and for not informing the research participants that two monkeys had died in an earlier study after receiving much larger doses of adenovirus ("U.S. Government Shuts Down Pennsylvania Gene Therapy Trials," 2000). The university was assessed a $1 million fine, and the three principal investigators had restrictions placed on their human research until 2010 (Check, 2004). The case slowed gene therapy research across the country, but a positive outcome is that it has led to stricter supervision of human studies.

There are privacy issues as well, including the potential abuse of information in a person's DNA. In the United States, it is now illegal for insurers and employers to discriminate against people based on their DNA ("Genetic Information Nondiscrimination Act of 2008," n.d.). In the United Kingdom it is illegal to analyze a person's DNA without the person's consent ("Sneaky DNA Analysis to Be Outlawed," 2004). In the United States, 17 states limit nonconsensual analysis and 27 limit disclosure without consent (Congressional Research Service, 2008). An additional concern is that, because gene therapy is very expensive, it is likely to increase inequalities further between the haves and have-nots in our society. Some observers worry that its application will not be limited to correcting disabilities and disease but will be used to enhance the beauty, brawn, and intelligence of the offspring of well-to-do parents. The science fiction movie *Gattaca* (whose title is a play on the four letters of the genetic code) depicts a society in which privilege and opportunity are reserved for genetically enhanced "superior" individuals. Fortunately, the U.S. Congress wisely set aside 5% of the Human Genome Project budget to fund the study of the ethical, legal, and social implications of genetic research (Jeffords & Daschle, 2001).

There are more significant concerns that gene manipulation could affect the reproductive cells and change the genome of nonconsenting future generations. A gene-editing summit called by CRISPR co-discoverer Jennifer Doudna and 17 other scientists, the Alliance for Regenerative Medicine, and several U.S. government agencies has urged researchers to forgo gene editing that could modify the germ line until its safety and ethical implications can be determined (Alliance for Regenerative Medicine, 2015a, 2015b). How many laboratories will step back from ongoing projects remains to be seen. In the meantime, Chinese scientists have used the CRISPR technique to modify a gene in a human embryo (Liang et al., 2015), and a U.K. government agency has given a research team in London the go-ahead for a similar project (Joseph, 2016). Most countries, however, ban editing embryos for a pregnancy.

Stem Cell Therapy

You learned in Chapter 3 that embryonic stem cells are undifferentiated cells that have the potential for developing into any other body cell. Stem cells have been used successfully to treat spinal cord damage (J. W. McDonald et al., 1999) and brain damage (Ren et al., 2000) in rats; they have also tracked down tumors in the brains of mice and delivered *interleukin 12,* making it easier for immune cells to kill the tumors (Ehtesham et al., 2002). In humans, heart functioning improved in patients with congestive heart failure after injection of stem cells (A. N. Patel et al., 2004). Medical researchers hope that stem cells can eventually be used to grow human organs in the laboratory to supply organ transplants and to allow genetic researchers to watch a gene produce a diseased organ rather than working backward from the diseased patient to the gene. An estimated 28 million people in the United States alone have diseases that are potentially treatable by stem cell therapy (Perry, 2000).

So if stem cells hold such wonderful potential, why are they being discussed under the topic of *ethics*? Extracting stem cells destroys the embryo, so right-to-life advocates oppose this use of human embryos, even though most are "extras" resulting from fertility treatment and

■ **FIGURE 4.22**   Injecting Cells Into a Damaged Brain.

Although the procedure (a) is promising, it is controversial because of where the cells (b) come from, which is usually human embryos.

(a)

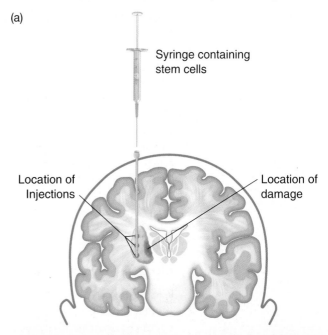

Syringe containing stem cells

Location of Injections

Location of damage

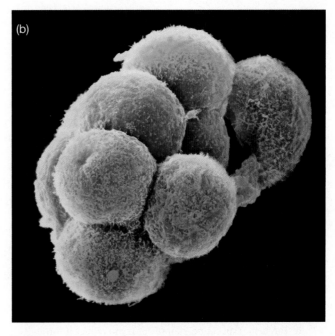

(b)

Sources: (a) From Coon, *Introduction to Psychology*, 9E. © 2001 South-Western, a part of Cengage Learning, Inc. Reproduced by permission. (b) © Science Source/SPL.

would otherwise be discarded (Figure 4.22). Stem cell research was crippled for years in the United States by the George W. Bush administration's refusal to fund research on stem cell lines derived from embryos after August 2001; however, the earlier lines were too contaminated for human use (M. J. Martin, Muotri, Gage, & Varki, 2005). This policy was reversed in 2009 by President Barack Obama and, after a three-year court battle, a federal appeals court ruled that government funding of research with human embryonic stem

What are the promise and problems associated with stem cell therapy?

cells does not violate existing U.S. law (J. Kaiser, 2012). Research with embryonic stem cells is still controversial in the United States, and future government leaders may slow (or stop) stem cell research; further, views differ across the European Union's 28 member nations as much as they do in the United States (Drumi, 2009). Due to this controversy and the limited availability of embryonic stem cells, other sources are being sought; for example, the stem cells used to treat the heart patients were taken from their own bone marrow. Mature cells can be turned into embryonic-like *induced pluripotent stem cells* by increasing the expression of four genes, but only about 10% of cells are transformed in this procedure. Israeli scientists discovered that the protein Mbd3 acts as a brake on reprogramming; by mutating the *Mbd3* gene or decreasing its expression, they have been able to increase the transformation rate to almost 100% (Rais et al., 2013).

Implementation of gene and stem cell therapies slowed following the Jesse Gelsinger case and after three children being treated for SCID developed leukemia and one died, apparently because the retrovirus used to transfer the gene activated a gene involved in cell proliferation ("Therapy Setback," 2005). Critics suggest that there are unknown dangers as well; for example, sometimes stem cells injected into animals have found their way into tissues throughout the body, and we don't know what all the consequences might be. There is no question the therapies are becoming safer, but when the implications of research are so far-reaching, restraint is as valuable as enthusiasm and commitment.

CONCEPT CHECK

Take a Minute to Check Your Knowledge and Understanding

- What are the effects of dishonesty in research?
- How do researchers justify their use of animals in research?
- What do you think about genetically modifying a nonviable embryo to learn how the gene causes a deadly disease? Modifying an embryo to prevent a severe mental deficiency, before implanting in the mother? Modifying an embryo to increase the child's intelligence or athletic ability?
- Why is there an ethical issue with human stem cell research? How might it be resolved?

In Perspective

Early progress in psychology and in biopsychology relied on the wit and perspiration of the pioneering researchers. Now they are aided by sophisticated equipment and methods that are escalating discovery at an unprecedented pace and taking research into areas that were barely conceivable a few decades ago.

Knowledge is power, and with power comes responsibility. For the scientists who study behavior, that responsibility is to the humans and animals that provide the source of our knowledge and to the people who may be healed or harmed by the new treatments resulting from research.

CHAPTER SUMMARY

Science, Research, and Theory

- Researchers respect uncertainty but try to reduce it through research and the use of theory.
- Of the many research strategies at their disposal, biopsychologists favor the experimental approach because of the control it offers and the ability to determine cause and effect.
- Correlational techniques have value as well, particularly when the researcher cannot control the situation.

Research Techniques

- Staining and labeling techniques make neurons more visible, emphasize cell bodies or axons, trace pathways to or

from a location, and identify active areas or specific structures such as receptors.
- Light microscopy is extremely useful, but electron microscopy reveals more detail, scanning electron microscopy adds three-dimensionality, and confocal and two-photon microscopy produce images at greater depths.
- The EEG sums the neural activity between two electrodes to assess arousal level and detect damage and some brain disorders. Event-related potentials measure averaged responses to brief stimuli.
- Brain functioning can be studied by observation of brain-damaged individuals, electrical and chemical stimulation (using stereotaxic techniques), destruction of neural

tissue (ablation and lesioning), and microdialysis of brain chemicals.

- Brain imaging using CT and MRI depicts structure, for example, to assess damage, whereas PET and fMRI are capable of measuring activity.
- Family studies, adoption studies, and twin studies are correlational strategies for investigating heredity. Family studies determine whether a characteristic runs in families, while adoption studies assess whether adopted children are more like their adoptive parents or their biological parents in a characteristic. Twin studies contrast the similarity of fraternal twins with the similarity of identical twins.
- Genetic engineering includes gene transfer and gene-disabling techniques (knockout and antisense RNA). Although experimental, it is already showing therapeutic promise.

Research Ethics

- A major concern in biopsychology is maintaining the integrity of research; plagiarism and fabrication of data are particularly serious infractions.
- Both the public and the scientific community are increasingly concerned about protecting the welfare of humans and animals in research. The various disciplines have standards for subject welfare, but the need for more monitoring and training is evident.
- Stem cell technology is promising for treating brain and spinal cord damage and a variety of diseases, but it is controversial because obtaining stem cells often involves destroying embryos. Gene therapy also holds much promise, but it has dangers and could be abused. ∎

STUDY RESOURCES

FOR FURTHER THOUGHT

- Pay close attention as you read through this text, and you will notice that human studies are more likely than animal studies to be correlational. Why do you think this is so?
- Genetic engineering is mostly a research technique now. What practical uses can you imagine in the future?
- Is it unreasonable coercion (a) to require a student in an introductory psychology course to participate in research, (b) to require a student in a research methods course to participate in research exercises during the laboratory sessions as a part of the educational experience, or (c) to offer money and a month's housing and meals to a homeless person to participate in a risky drug study?
- Do you think the rights of humans and animals are adequately protected in research? Why or why not? What do you think would be the effect of eliminating the use of animal subjects?

TEST YOUR UNDERSTANDING

1. Describe the four imaging techniques, including method, uses, and advantages and disadvantages.

2. Discuss the relative merits of experimental and correlational research, using family, twin, and adoption studies versus genetic engineering as the example.

3. Discuss the conflicts between research needs and animal rights.

4. In spite of their promise, stem cell research and gene therapy are controversial. Why?

Select the best answer:

1. You could best identify receptors for acetylcholine by using
   a. Golgi stain.
   b. Nissl stain.
   c. immunocytochemistry.
   d. electron microscopy.

2. If you needed to measure brain activity that changes in less than 1 s, your best choice would be
   a. EEG.
   b. CT.
   c. MRI.
   d. PET.

3. Your study calls for daily measurement of activity changes in emotional areas of the brain. You would prefer to use
   a. CT.
   b. MRI.
   c. PET.
   d. fMRI.

4. Science is most distinguished from other disciplines by
   a. the topics it studies.
   b. the way it acquires knowledge.
   c. its precision of measurement.
   d. its reliance on naturalistic observation.

5. Experiments are considered superior to other research procedures because they
   a. involve control over the variable of interest.
   b. permit control of variables not of interest.
   c. permit cause-and-effect conclusions.
   d. All of the above
   e. None of the above

6. A theory
   a. is the first step in research.
   b. is the final stage of research.
   c. generates further research.
   d. is an opinion widely accepted among researchers.

7. The best way to assess the relative contributions of heredity and environment would be to compare the similarity in behavior of
   a. fraternal versus identical twins.
   b. relatives versus nonrelatives.

c. siblings reared together versus those reared apart.

d. fraternal versus identical twins, half of whom have been adopted out.

8. The most sensitive way to determine whether a particular gene produces a particular behavior would be to

a. compare the behavior in identical and fraternal twins.

b. compare the behavior in people with and without the gene.

c. use genetic engineering to manipulate the gene and note the behavior change.

d. find out whether people with the behavior have the gene more often than people without the behavior.

9. Antisense RNA technology involves

a. inserting a gene into the subject's cells.

b. interfering with protein construction controlled by the gene.

c. introducing a nonfunctioning mutation into the subject's genes.

d. All of the above

10. The most popular research animals among the following are

a. rats.   b. pigeons.

c. monkeys. d. chimpanzees.

11. Speciesism refers to the belief that

a. humans are better research subjects than animals.

b. it is more ethical to do risky experiments on lower animals than on humans.

c. humans are the superior species.

d. All of the above

e. None of the above

12. The biggest obstacle to using stem cells would be eliminated if researchers could

a. get adult stem cells to work as well as embryonic ones.

b. get stem cells to differentiate into neurons.

c. get stem cells to survive longer.

d. get stem cells to multiply faster.

1. c, 2. a, 3. d, 4. b, 5. d, 6. c, 7. d, 8. c, 9. b, 10. a, 11. b, 12. a.

Answers:

ON THE WEB

The following websites are coordinated with this chapter's content. You can access these websites from the **SAGE edge Student Resources site**; select this chapter and then click on Web Resources. (**Bold** items are links.)

1. A video explains the **CLARITY** technique, flies you through a mouse brain, and examines neurons in the brain of a deceased boy with autism.

2. **Brain Imaging** compares the advantages and disadvantages of different imaging techniques, along with sample images. **fMRI 4 Newbies** is the whimsical title of a site filled with images and information, as well as humor (such as "Ten Things Sex and Brain Imaging Have in Common").

3. **A blog by Rene Anand** includes a photo and a scan of his model brain.

4. **Brainbow** is illustrated in a slide show of stunning images, and an animated video explains how the **CRISPR** technique works.

5. The American Psychological Association establishes **Ethical Principles of Psychologists and Code of Conduct**, covering research and publication, therapeutic practice, and conflict of

interest, as well as numerous other areas. The National Institutes of Health publishes its policies on the use of **human** and **animal** research.

6. You can download several *Scientific American* articles expressing contrasting opinions on the **Benefits and Ethics of Animal Research. Research With Animals in Psychology** is a rationale for the use of animals in behavioral research, provided by the Committee on Animal Research and Ethics of the American Psychological Association.

7. Several videos describe an idyllic life for retired chimps at **Chimp Haven.**

8. The Wikipedia article **Gene Therapy** describes the strategy and the successes of the technique and provides a timeline history of developments from 1990 to the present.

9. **The International Society for Stem Cell Research** website has news, recent research, photos and movie clips, and ethics essays related to stem cell research. **TriStem Corporation** is dedicated to creating stem cells from mature adult cells, and its website has informative articles and press releases along with several colorful images of stem cells.

FOR FURTHER READING

1. "Remote Control Brains," by Douglas Fox (*New Scientist*, July 27, 2007, 30–34), is a nontechnical review of the field of optogenetics, the strategy described in Chapter 2 for controlling neurons with light; "The Optogenetic Catechism," by Gero Miesenböck (*Science*, 2009, *326*, 395–399), is a more thorough treatment.

2. "Why You Should Be Skeptical of Brain Scans," by Michael Shermer (*Scientific American Mind,* October/November 2008, 66–71), is the layperson's guide to understanding why interpretations of brain scan research can be misleading.

3. Transgenic animals have almost exclusively been mice, but now the marmoset has become the first transgenic primate, enabling research with a subject considerably closer to humans ("Generation of Transgenic Non-human Primates With Germline Transmission," by Erika Sasaki et al., *Nature*, 2009, *459*, 523–528).

4. Opposing views of several writers on research deception are presented in the *American Psychologist*, July 1997, 746–747, and July 1998, 803–807.

5. "The World's First Neural Stem Cell Transplant," by K. Mossman (*Scientific American*, December 18, 2016), describes the first operation to inject stem cells into the brain of a human subject.

6. "Selling Stem Cells in the USA: Assessing the Direct-to-Consumer Industry," by Leigh Turner and Paul Knoepfler (*Cell Stem Cell*, 2016, *19*, pp. 154–157), reports the proliferation of clinics offering unauthorized and unproven treatments for dozens of diseases.

KEY TERMS

ablation   97
antisense RNA   104
autoradiography   88
computed tomography (CT)   97
concordance rate   103
correlation   102
correlational study   87
deception   106
diffusion tensor
    imaging   98
electroencephalogram (EEG)   91
event-related potential   92
experiment   87
fabrication   106

family study   102
functional magnetic resonance imaging
    (fMRI)   99
gene therapy   104
gene transfer   104
genetic engineering   104
Golgi stain   88
immunocytochemistry   89
in situ hybridization   90
informed consent   106
knockout technique   104
lesion   97
magnetic resonance imaging
    (MRI)   97

messenger ribonucleic acid
    (mRNA)   90
myelin stain   88
Nissl stain   88
plagiarism   106
positron emission tomography
    (PET)   98
scanning electron microscope   90
stereotaxic instrument   93
theory   86
transcranial magnetic stimulation
    (TMS)   97
transmission electron
    microscope   90

edge.sagepub.com/garrett5e

SAGE edge offers a robust online environment featuring an impressive array of free tools and resources for review, study, and further exploration, keeping both instructors and students on the cutting edge of teaching and learning.

4.1 Explain how scientific theories are generated.	▶ Why We Should Trust Scientists
4.2 Demonstrate how scientists test hypotheses.	▶ How Animations Help Test Hypotheses
4.3 Describe the differences between correlational and experimental studies.	▶ NASA Twin Study
4.4 Assess the methods that scientists have for studying the role of brain structures in behavior.	▶ Researching Human Spatial Recognition
4.5 Compare the methods that scientists use to investigate the structure and function of brain cells.	▶ How to Look Inside the Brain
4.6 Identify the ethical protections that are in place for human participants.	📣 Neuroethics of Brain Development ▶ Human Research Ethics
4.7 Summarize the ethical protections that exist for research animals.	📄 Attitudes Toward Animal Use in Science
4.8 Examine the ethical concerns that have been raised about stem cell and gene therapy research.	▶ The Stem Cell Debate

© iStock.com/Krie

PRACTICE AND APPLY WHAT YOU'VE LEARNED

▶ **edge.sagepub.com/garrett5e**

HEAD TO THE STUDY SITE WHERE YOU'LL FIND

- **eFlashcards to strengthen your understanding of key terms**
- **Practice quizzes to test your comprehension of key concepts**
- **Videos and multimedia content to enhance your exploration of key topics**

Part II

Motivation and Emotion: What Makes Us Go

Drugs, Addiction, and Reward

5

After reading this chapter, you will be able to:

- Identify the main classes of drugs.

- Describe the effects of each class of drugs on the nervous system.

- Predict how different drugs will affect behavior, based on the neural systems on which those drugs act.

- Illustrate how the brain changes during addiction.

- Discuss the role of learning in overdose and addiction.

- Explain how pharmacology can be used to treat addiction.

- Contrast the environmental and hereditary influences on addiction.

Honoré de Balzac (Figure 5.1) wrote a phenomenal 45 novels in 20 years. He was aided in his long writing marathons by large amounts of a stimulant drug whose effects pleased him so much that he advocated its use to others. However, he died at the age of 51 in part because of this unrelenting stimulation. What was the powerful drug that contributed both to his success and to his untimely death? According to his physician, Balzac died from a heart condition, aggravated by "the use or rather the abuse of coffee, to which he had recourse in order to counteract man's natural propensity to sleep" ("French Roast," 1996, p. 28).

There is good reason to consider caffeine an addictive drug. Coffee may have milder effects than the other drugs coming out of Colombia, but strength of effect and illegality are not the criteria for classifying a substance as addictive. As you will see, a drug's effect on the brain is the telling feature, and that is our reason for discussing drugs at this particular point: It provides the opportunity to tie together our preceding discussions of brain structures and neural (particularly synaptic) functioning.

Psychoactive Drugs

A *drug* is a substance that on entering the body changes the body or its functioning. Drugs fall into one of two general classes, according to their effect on a transmitter system. As we saw in Chapter 2, an *agonist* mimics or enhances the effect of a neurotransmitter. It can accomplish this by having the same effect on the receptor as the neurotransmitter, by increasing the transmitter's effect on the receptor, or by blocking the reuptake or the degradation of the transmitter. An *antagonist* may occupy the receptors without activating them,

$SAGE edge™

Master the content.
edge.sagepub.com/garrett5e

"
You illustrious Human Candles . . . who consume your own brilliant selves with the heat and light of your minds . . . I have discovered a horrible, rather brutal method that I recommend only to men of excessive vigor, men with thick black hair and skin covered with liver spots, men with big square hands and with legs shaped like bowling pins.

—*Balzac (1839/1996)*
"

■ FIGURE 5.1   Honoré de Balzac.

Source: © The Print Collector/Alamy.

simultaneously blocking the transmitter from binding to the receptors. Or it may decrease the availability of the neurotransmitter, for example, by reducing its production or its release from the presynaptic terminals.

Psychoactive drugs are those that have psychological effects, such as anxiety relief or hallucinations. The focus of this chapter is primarily on abused psychoactive drugs, although many of the principles discussed here are applicable more generally. We will discuss several psychotherapeutic drugs in the chapter on psychological disorders (Chapter 14). The effects of abused drugs are extremely varied, but whether they arouse or relax, expand the consciousness or dull the senses, addictive drugs produce a sense of pleasure in one form or another, at least initially. They also have several other effects in common; reviewing those effects will give us the language we need for a discussion of how the drugs work.

Most of the abused drugs produce *addiction,* which is identified by preoccupation with obtaining a drug, compulsive use of the drug in spite of adverse consequences, and a high tendency to relapse after quitting. Many abused drugs also produce withdrawal reactions. *Withdrawal* is a negative reaction that occurs when drug use is stopped. Withdrawal symptoms are due at least in part to the nervous system's having adapted to the drug's effects, so they are typically the opposite of the effects the drug produces. For example, the relaxation, constipation, chills, and positive mood of heroin are replaced by agitation, diarrhea, fever, and depression during withdrawal.

Regular use of most abused drugs results in *tolerance,* which means that the individual becomes less responsive to the drug and requires increasing amounts of the drug to produce the same results. Like withdrawal, tolerance results from compensatory adaptation in the nervous system, mostly a reduction in receptor number or sensitivity. Tolerance is one reason for overdose, because tolerance can develop in response to the drug's pleasurable effects without developing in response to others. Thus, if the drug abuser takes larger doses of heroin to achieve the original sense of ecstasy while the tendency to produce sleep and respiratory arrest are undiminished, overdose is nearly inevitable, and the consequences can be deadly.

Opiates

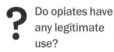

Do opiates have any legitimate use?

The *opiates* are drugs derived from the opium poppy (*Papaver somniferum,* see Figure 5.2). Opiates have a variety of effects: They are *analgesic* (pain relieving) and *hypnotic* (sleep inducing, which is where it gets its scientific name), and they produce a strong *euphoria* (sense of happiness or ecstasy). Their downside is their addictive potential due to the euphoria. *Opium* has been in use since around 5700 BCE (Merlin, 2003). Originally it was eaten, but when explorers carried the American Indians' practice of pipe smoking of tobacco back to their native countries, opium users adopted this technique. *Morphine* was extracted from opium poppies at the beginning of the early 1800s and has been extremely valuable as a treatment for the pain of surgery, battle wounds, and cancer. *Heroin* was synthesized from morphine in the late 1800s. At the turn of the century, it was marketed by the Bayer Drug Company of Germany as an over-the-counter analgesic until its dangers were recognized. It is now an illegal drug in the United States but is prescribed as a pain reliever in Great Britain and is used there and in a few European countries as a replacement drug in addiction treatment. Codeine, another ingredient of opium, has been used as a cough suppressant, and dilute solutions of opium, in the form of paregoric and laudanum (literally, "something to be praised"), were once used to treat diarrhea and to alleviate pain; paregoric was even used to quiet fretful children. Morphine continues to be used with cancer patients and is showing promise of safe use with milder pain in a time-release form that virtually eliminates the risk of addiction. Aside from morphine, opiates have mostly been replaced by synthetics. These are called *opioids,* to indicate that they are not derived from opium, at least not directly, though the term is increasingly used to include all substances that affect the endogenous receptors. Although the synthetic opioids are safer, they too are subject to abuse. You probably recognize OxyContin because of its reputation for abuse rather than for its pain-relieving ability.

Heroin is the most notoriously abused opiate, due to its intense effect: a glowing, orgasm-like sensation that occurs within seconds, followed by drowsy relaxation and contentment. Because heroin is highly soluble in lipids, it passes the blood-brain barrier easily; the rapid effect increases its addictive potential. The major danger of heroin use comes from overdose—either from the attempt to maintain the pleasant effects in the face of increasing tolerance or because the user unknowingly obtains the drug in a purer form than usual. In a 33-year

study of 581 male heroin addicts, 49% were dead at the end of the study, with an average age at death of 46 years (Hser, Hoffman, Grella, & Anglin, 2001). Nearly a fourth of those had died of drug overdoses (mostly from heroin); 19.5% died from homicide, suicide, or accident; and 15% died from chronic liver disease. Half of the survivors who could be interviewed were still using heroin, and the high likelihood of returning to usage even after 5 years or more of abstinence suggested to the researchers that heroin addiction may be a lifelong condition. Despite the representation of the horrors of heroin withdrawal in movies and on the Internet, it is best described as similar to a bad case of flu, so fear of withdrawal apparently is not the prime motivator for continued heroin addiction. Opioid addiction has become epidemic in the United States, with a two- to threefold increase in overdose deaths just between 2010 and 2012 (Rudd et al., 2014). The severity of the crisis has led to several corrective measures described in the accompanying Application.

As tolerance to a drug develops, it also becomes associated with the person's drug-taking surroundings and circumstances. This learned or *conditioned tolerance* does not generalize completely to a new setting; when the person buys and takes the drug in a different

■ **FIGURE 5.2** Opium Poppies.

Source: iStock/Satirus.

neighborhood, the usual dose can lead to overdose (Macrae, Scoles, & Siegel, 1987; Siegel, 1984). Heroin is a particularly good example of this situational tolerance effect; an amount of heroin that killed 32% of rats injected in their customary drug-taking environment killed 64% of rats injected in a novel environment (Siegel, Hinson, Krank, & McCully, 1982).

We saw in Chapter 4 that neuroscientist Candace Pert discovered why opioid drugs are so effective as pain relievers: The body has receptors that are specific for these drugs, because it manufactures its own *endogenous* (generated within the body) opioids, known as *endorphins*. One effect of endorphins is pain relief, as you will see in Chapter 11. Stimulation of endorphin receptors triggers some of the positive effects of opiates; others occur from indirect activation of dopamine pathways.

Depressants

Depressants are drugs that reduce central nervous system activity. The group includes *sedative* (calming) drugs, *anxiolytic* (anxiety-reducing) drugs, and hypnotic drugs. Alcohol, of course, is the most common and is the most abused in this class, so we start there.

 What are the uses and dangers of depressant drugs?

Alcohol

Ethanol, or *alcohol,* is a drug fermented from fruits, grains, and other plant products; it acts at many brain sites to produce euphoria, anxiety reduction, sedation, motor incoordination, and cognitive impairment (Koob & Bloom, 1988). Alcohol is the oldest of the abused drugs. There is evidence of beer making in the mountains of Iran as far back as 3500 BCE (Wilkins & Hill, 2006), but alcohol consumption likely began when early humans discovered the pleasant effects of eating fruit after it had fallen and fermented. Drunkenness from this source has even been reported in animals, from elephants to butterflies (Dudley, 2002)! Alcohol has historically played a cultural role in celebrations and ceremonies, provided a means of achieving religious ecstasy, and, especially in primitive societies, permitted socially sanctioned temporary indulgence in hostility and sexual misbehavior. In modern societies, controlled group drinking has been replaced by uncontrolled individual abuse.

APPLICATION
Government Agencies Act to Curb Overdose Deaths

Since the year 2004, the number of deaths in the United States due to overdose of prescription opioid pain relievers has almost doubled; for heroin the rate has increased fivefold (National Institute on Drug Abuse, 2015). One reason for the increase is that taking opioids paradoxically increases pain and prolongs it long after the injury has healed and the drug has been discontinued; recent work shows that the drugs produce an immune response that generates painful inflammatory signals in the spinal cord (P. M. Grace et al., 2016). Drug companies are working on formulations that will counteract this effect. But critics have also blamed the U.S. Food and Drug Administration (FDA) for approving the drugs too readily, as well as physicians' willingness to prescribe the drugs, which has closely paralleled the increase in deaths. Under pressure from public opinion and from Congress, the FDA (Dennis, 2016), the Centers for Disease Control

and Prevention (CDC), and the U.S. Department of Justice are overhauling their policies. Under this plan, the FDA will improve follow-up regarding safety and effectiveness of long-term opioid use; extend training of doctors; obtain outside advice before approving new opioid drugs that do not have "abuse deterrent" properties; and encourage development of painkillers that are difficult to crush, break, or dissolve (tactics that allow addicts to ingest large amounts quickly by injecting or snorting the drug). In addition, the CDC released new guidelines in 2016 that discourage primary care physicians from prescribing opioid medications for chronic pain (Dowell, Haegerich, & Chou, 2016). Moreover, the Drug Enforcement Administration (2016) is reducing manufacturing quotas by 25%–33% for the vast majority of all Schedule II opioids in an attempt to minimize the supplies of drugs for diversion and illicit use while providing adequate supplies for medical needs.

> *I had booze, and when I was drinking, I felt warm and pretty and loved—at least for a while.*
>
> —*Gloria, a recovering alcoholic*

Alcohol is valued by moderate users as a social lubricant and as a disinhibitor of social constraints, owing largely to its anxiolytic effect. Like many drugs, its effects are complex. At low doses, say, a couple of drinks, it turns off the inhibition the cortex normally exerts over behavior, resulting in behavioral stimulation, but it also has a direct stimulatory effect by increasing dopamine release (Hendler, Ramchandani, Gilman, & Hammer, 2013). As intake increases, alcohol begins to have a sedative or even hypnotic effect; behavior moves from relaxation to sleep or unconsciousness. Later, after the bout of drinking has ended, the alcohol is metabolized back to a low blood level and it becomes a stimulant again. That is why a few drinks in the evening may help you get to sleep at bedtime only to awaken you later in the night. And as discussed in the accompanying Application, some individuals have a condition called auto-brewery syndrome, in which they improperly metabolize sugar into alcohol, appearing to be intoxicated without imbibing alcohol.

Because it interferes with cognitive and motor functioning as well as judgment, alcohol-impaired driving accounts for one third of all U.S. traffic fatalities (National Highway Traffic Safety Administration, 2015). In the United States and Canada, a person is legally considered too impaired to drive when the blood alcohol concentration (BAC) reaches 0.08%. Alcohol is also closely linked with violent crime, accounting for an estimated 37% of violent victimizations (Greenfeld & Henneberg, 2001). Besides affecting judgment, alcohol reduces the anxiety that normally inhibits aggression (Pihl & Peterson, 1993).

Alcohol carries with it a host of health and behavioral problems. High levels of any depressant drug have the potential to shut down the brain stem, resulting in coma or death; a BAC of 0.30%–0.40% is life threatening, and BACs over 0.45% will usually be fatal ("BAC Measurement," n.d.). A common result of chronic alcoholism is cirrhosis of the liver, which in its severest form is fatal. In addition, the vitamin B1 deficiency that is associated with chronic alcoholism can produce brain damage and Korsakoff syndrome, which involves severe memory loss along with sensory and motor impairment (Figure 5.3). Binge drinkers are more likely to be impulsive and to have learning and memory impairments (Stephens & Duka, 2008). Alcohol is the fifth leading cause of premature death and disability globally, and first among people between the ages of 15 and 49 (National Institute on Alcohol Abuse and Alcoholism, 2016). In the United States, the death toll is 88,000 each year (Stahre, Roeber, Kanny, Brewer, & Zhang, 2014). Even abstinence can be dangerous for people with alcoholism. Alcohol withdrawal involves tremors, anxiety, and mood and sleep disturbances; more severe reactions are known as *delirium tremens*—hallucinations, delusions, confusion, and, in extreme cases, seizures and possible death.

Considering the health risks, violence, and disruption of homes and livelihoods, alcohol is more costly to society than any of the illegal drugs. Excessive drinking costs the United States $249 billion—about $2.05 per drink—three quarters of it resulting from binge drinking (Sacks, Gonzales, Bouchery, Tomedi, & Brewer, 2015). In view of all the dangers of drinking, it seems amazing now that in 1961 a speaker at a symposium of psychiatrists and physicians on drinking expressed the group's consensus that "alcohol is the safest, most available tranquilizer we have" ("Paean to Nepenthe," 1961, p. 68).

■ **FIGURE 5.3**   A Normal Brain and an Alcoholic Brain.

Both brains are from 53-year-old men. In the alcoholic brain, note the smaller corpus callosum, as well as the enlarged ventricles, sulci, and fissures, which indicate reduced brain tissue.

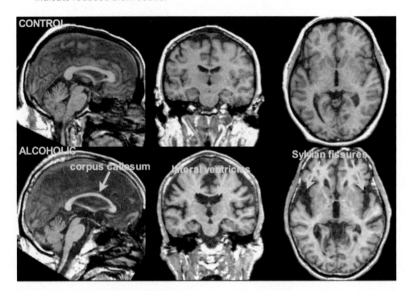

Source: From "Magnetic Resonance Imaging of the Living Brain," by Margaret J. Rosenbloom and Adolf Pfefferbaum, 2008, *Alcohol Research and Health, 31,* pp. 362–376.

Alcohol provides a good example of the complex effects that drugs have on multiple receptor and neurotransmitter systems. First, it inhibits the release of glutamate (Hoffman & Tabakoff, 1993; G. Tsai, Gastfriend, & Coyle, 1995). You may remember from Chapter 2, Table 2.2, that *glutamate* is the most prevalent excitatory neurotransmitter. Glutamate reduction produces a sedating effect; then there is a compensatory increase in the number of glutamate receptors, which probably accounts for the seizures that

---

APPLICATION

The Auto-Brewery Syndrome

The woman insisted she'd had very little to drink, but her BAC was 0.40%, so the policeman rushed her to the hospital (LaMotte, 2015). She should have been unconscious or worse, but she was only a bit woozy. In later testing with no alcohol, her BAC was double the legal limit at 9:15 a.m., triple the limit at 6 p.m., and more than four times the limit at 8:30 p.m. She was diagnosed with *auto-brewery syndrome,* also known as gut fermentation syndrome, which is a rare condition in which the intestines produce intoxicating levels of ethanol (Doucleff, 2013). With only 12 cases reported prior to 1972 (Iwata,

1972), there was skepticism about the legitimacy of the diagnosis (Logan & Jones, 2000). However, a recent review of cases has linked the symptoms to physiological conditions such as bowel dilation, short bowel syndrome, and an overabundance of intestinal yeast (B. T. Welch, Coelho Prabhu, Walkoff, & Trenkner, 2016). Treatments have included antibiotics, carbohydrate control, and antifungal therapy; the woman described above is being treated with antifungal medications and a yeast-free diet with no sugar, no alcohol, and low carbohydrates (Herbeck, 2015).

■ **FIGURE 5.4** The GABA$_A$ Receptor Complex.

The complex has binding sites for GABA, barbiturates, benzodiazepines, and alcohol.

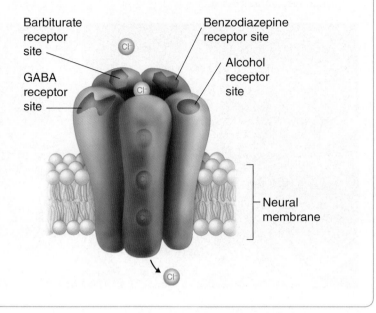

? What prenatal effects does alcohol have?

■ **FIGURE 5.5** Child With Fetal Alcohol Syndrome.

Besides intellectual impairment and behavioral problems, FAS individuals often have facial irregularities, including a short, upturned nose that is flattened between the eyes; a thin upper lip; and a lack of a groove between the nose and upper lip.

Source: © George Steinmetz.

sometimes occur during withdrawal. Alcohol also increases the release of *gamma-aminobutyric acid* (*GABA*), the most prevalent inhibitory neurotransmitter (Wan, Berton, Madamba, Francesconi, & Siggins, 1996). The combined effect at these two receptors is sedation, anxiety reduction, muscle relaxation, and inhibition of cognitive and motor skills. Alcohol also affects opiate receptors (in turn increasing dopamine release), serotonin receptors, and cannabinoid receptors, which are also excited by marijuana (Julien, 2008); these actions likely account for the pleasurable aspects of drinking.

Alcohol specifically affects the A subtype of GABA receptor. Because the GABA$_A$ receptor is important in the action of other drugs, we give it special attention here. It is actually a receptor complex, composed of five different kinds of receptor sites (Figure 5.4). One receptor, of course, responds to GABA. Its activation opens the receptor's chloride channel, and the influx of chloride ions hyperpolarizes the neuron. Other receptors in the complex respond to alcohol, to barbiturates, and to benzodiazepines; these drugs enhance the binding of GABA to its receptor and thus its ability to open the chloride channel. Now you can understand why it is so dangerous to mix alcohol with barbiturates or benzodiazepines.

Alcohol passes easily through the placenta, raising the BAC of a fetus to about the same level as the mother's. You saw in Chapter 3 that prenatal exposure to alcohol can result in fetal alcohol syndrome (FAS; see Figure 5.5), which is the leading cause of intellectual impairment in the Western world (Abel & Sokol, 1986). Besides being intellectually impaired, FAS children are irritable and have trouble maintaining attention. Regular alcohol abuse apparently is not required to produce damage. In one study, mothers who had FAS children did not drink much more on average than the mothers of normal children, but they did report occasional binges of five or more drinks at a time (Streissguth, Barr, Bookstein, Sampson, & Olson, 1999). Just having three or more drinks at any one time during pregnancy more than doubles the offspring's risk of a drinking disorder during adulthood (Alati et al., 2006). No safe level of alcohol intake during pregnancy has been established, so most authorities recommend total abstention. (Refer to Figure 3.25 to see the developmental effects of FAS on a mouse brain.)

Barbiturates and Benzodiazepines

Like alcohol, *barbiturates* in small amounts act selectively on higher cortical centers, especially those involved in inhibiting behavior; in low doses, they produce talkativeness and increased social interaction, and in higher doses, they are sedatives and hypnotics. Barbiturates have been used to treat insomnia and prevent epileptic seizures, and from 1912 to 1960, they were the drug of choice for treating anxiety and insomnia (Julien, 2008). They are not addictive in prescribed doses, but tolerance leads the person to increase the dosage, resulting in addictive symptoms similar to those of alcoholism. Like alcohol, barbiturates act at the GABA$_A$ complex, though at the barbiturate receptor, but unlike alcohol they can open chloride channels on their own in the absence of GABA. As a result, the line between therapeutic and toxic levels is a fine one, and their use has been fraught with accidental and intentional overdose (including famous cases such as Marilyn Monroe, Judy Garland, and Jimi Hendrix). As a result, barbiturates were mostly replaced by much safer benzodiazepines.

Benzodiazepines act at the benzodiazepine receptor on the GABA$_A$ complex to produce anxiety reduction, sedation, and muscle relaxation. They reduce anxiety by suppressing activity in the *limbic system,* a network of structures we will consider in more detail in the chapter on emotion (Chapter 8). Their effect in the brain stem produces relaxation, while GABA activation in the cortex and hippocampus results in confusion and amnesia (Julien, 2008). They are considerably safer than barbiturates because they do not open chloride channels on their own.

There are several benzodiazepine drugs, the best known of which are Valium (diazepam), Xanax (alprazolam), and Halcion (triazolam). One of the benzodiazepines, Rohypnol (roofies or rophies), has gained notoriety as the date rape drug. Because benzodiazepines are addictive and can produce mental confusion, safer alternatives have replaced them, and new drugs are actively being developed.

Stimulants

Stimulants activate the central nervous system to produce arousal, increased alertness, and elevated mood. They include a wide range of drugs, from the legal (caffeine) to the illegal (cocaine), which vary in the degree of risk they pose. The greatest danger lies in how they are used.

Cocaine

Cocaine, which is extracted from the South American coca plant, produces euphoria, decreases appetite, increases alertness, and relieves fatigue. It is processed with hydrochloric acid into cocaine hydrochloride, the familiar white powder that is usually administered intranasally ("snorted"), or mixed with water and injected. Pure cocaine, or *freebase,* can be extracted from cocaine hydrochloride by chemically removing the hydrochloric acid. When freebase is smoked, the cocaine enters the bloodstream and reaches the brain rapidly. Developed in the 1970s, a simpler chemical procedure yielded *crack,* which is less pure but produces pure cocaine vapor when it is smoked. The low cost of crack has spread its use into poor urban communities where users could not afford cocaine.

Cocaine has not always been viewed as a dangerous drug. The coca leaf has been chewed by South American Indians for centuries as a means of enduring hardship and impoverishment. When cocaine was isolated in 1855, it was initially injected as a local anesthetic. It soon found its way into over-the-counter medications (Figure 5.6), and from 1886 to 1906, Coca-Cola owed much of its refreshment to 60 milligrams of cocaine in every serving (M. S. Gold, 1997). Sigmund Freud, the father of psychoanalysis, championed the use of cocaine, giving it to his fiancée, sisters, friends, and colleagues and prescribing it to his patients. He even wrote an essay, which he called a "song of praise" to cocaine's virtues as an antidepressant, a fighter of chronic fatigue, and even a treatment for morphine addiction. He gave up the use of the drug, both personally and professionally, when he realized its dangers (Brecher, 1972). As a result of rising cocaine abuse and its links to criminal activity in the United States, Congress in 1914 enacted the Harrison Narcotics Act, which regulated its sale and use.

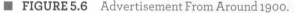

■ FIGURE 5.6   Advertisement From Around 1900.

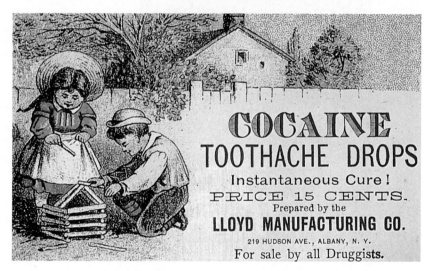

Source: The National Library of Medicine.

Cocaine blocks the reuptake of dopamine and serotonin at synapses, potentiating their effects. Dopamine usually has an inhibitory effect, so cocaine reduces activity in much of the brain, as the positron emission tomography (PET) scans in Figure 5.7 show (London et al., 1990). Presumably, cocaine produces euphoria and excitement because dopamine removes the inhibition the cortex usually exerts on lower structures. Reduced cortical activity is typical of drugs that produce euphoria, including benzodiazepines, barbiturates, amphetamines, alcohol, and morphine, although localized activation is often reported in frontal areas (R. Z. Goldstein & Volkow, 2002; London et al., 1990). Brain metabolism rises briefly during the first week of abstinence but then falls again during prolonged withdrawal; however, during craving, activity increases in several areas, as we will see later (R. Z. Goldstein & Volkow; S. Grant et al., 1996; Volkow et al., 1991, 1999).

Injection and smoking produce an immediate and intense euphoria, which increases the addictive potential of cocaine. After the end of a cocaine binge, the user crashes into a state of depression, anxiety, and cocaine craving that motivates a cycle of continued use. Withdrawal effects are typically mild, involving anxiety, lack of motivation, boredom, and lack of pleasure. Three decades ago, addiction was defined in terms of a drug's ability to produce withdrawal, and because cocaine's withdrawal symptoms are so mild, it was not believed to be addictive (Gawin, 1991). As usage increased in the population, we learned that cocaine is one of the most addictive of the abused drugs. The intensity of the drug's effect makes treatment for addiction very difficult, and no treatment is generally accepted as successful. Complicating rehabilitation is the fact that cocaine addicts typically abuse other drugs, and they have a very high rate of psychological disorders, including depression, anxiety, bipolar disorder, and posttraumatic stress disorder (Julien, 2008).

■ **FIGURE 5.7** A Normal Brain and a Brain on Cocaine.

The upper two scans show activity in a cocaine-free individual. The remaining scans show reduced activity in the brain of a cocaine abuser 10 days and 100 days after last cocaine use.

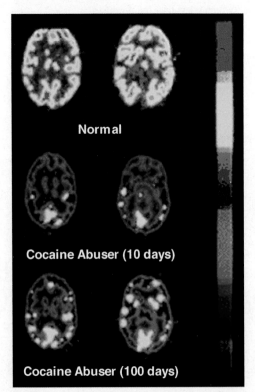

Source: Photo courtesy of Nora Volkow, PhD, from "Long-Term Frontal Brain Metabolic Changes in Cocaine Abusers," N. D. Volkow, R. Hitzemann, G.-J. Wang, J. S. Fowler, A. P. Wolf, and S. L. Dewey, 1992, *Synapse, 11,* pp. 184–190.

Cocaine provides a good example of selective tolerance: While increasing amounts of the drug are required to produce the desired psychological effects, the person becomes supersensitive to the effect that produces seizures. It is possible that the risks of cocaine relative to other drugs have been underestimated. In one study, rats were allowed to press a lever that caused heroin or cocaine to be injected into their bloodstream; after 1 month, 90% of rats receiving cocaine had died of self-administered overdose, compared with 36% of rats receiving heroin (Bozarth & Wise, 1985).

Cocaine users have impairments in memory and in executive functions, including impulse control, decision making, and assessment of emotional stimuli. These deficits are accompanied by reduced activity in the prefrontal cortex (Beveridge, Gill, Hanlon, & Porrino, 2008), and by a loss of gray matter in prefrontal and temporal areas during middle age that is almost twice as fast as in nonusers (3.1 ml/year versus 1.7 ml/year; Ersche, Jones, Williams, Robbins, & Bullmore, 2012). Also, like alcohol, cocaine passes through the placenta easily, where it interferes with fetal development. It is difficult to separate the effects of abused drugs on a child's development from the effects of frequently co-occurring poverty and neglect, but a Toronto group was able to control environmental factors by studying 26 cocaine-exposed children who had been adopted. Compared with control children matched for the mother's IQ and socioeconomic status, the cocaine-exposed children had lower IQs, poorer language development, and greater distractibility (Nulman et al., 2001). In addition, we have evidence from animal studies that prenatal exposure to cocaine results in abnormal circuit formation among dopamine neurons (L. B. Jones, 2000).

Amphetamines

Amphetamines are a group of synthetic drugs that produce euphoria and increase confidence and concentration. The group includes amphetamine sulfate (marketed as Benzedrine), the three to four times more potent dextroamphetamine sulfate (marketed as Dexedrine), and the still more powerful methamphetamine (known on the street as *meth, speed, crank,* and *crystal*). Like cocaine, methamphetamine can be purified to its smokable, freebase form called *ice*. Because they dull the appetite, reduce fatigue, and increase alertness, amphetamines have shown up in weight-loss drugs and have been used by truck drivers, pilots, soldiers, and students to postpone sleep. They have also been used to treat ailments such as narcolepsy, a disorder of uncontrollable daytime sleepiness.

Amphetamines increase the release of norepinephrine and dopamine, and they mimic the actions of epinephrine. Increased release of dopamine exhausts the store of transmitter in the vesicles, which accounts for the period of depression that follows. The effects of amphetamine injection are so similar to those of cocaine that individuals cannot tell the difference between the two (Cho, 1990).

Heavy use can cause hallucinations and delusions of persecution that are so similar to the symptoms of paranoid schizophrenia that even trained professionals cannot recognize the difference (resulting in occasional emergency room mistreatment). In laboratory studies, psychotic symptoms develop after one to four days of chronic amphetamine administration. In one study, a volunteer on amphetamine was convinced that a "giant oscillator" in the ceiling was controlling his thoughts. Another believed his ex-wife had hired an assassin to kill him and was perturbed when the doctor would not guard the window while he stood watch at the door (Griffith, Cavanaugh, Held, & Oates, 1972; S. H. Snyder, 1972). After an amphetamine psychosis subsides, the person may be left with a permanently increased sensitivity to the drug so that using even a small amount years later can revive symptoms (Sato, 1986).

Safety concerns have been raised in recent years by *bath salts,* a variety of synthetic derivatives of the *Catha edulis* plant (khat). Chewing khat leaves for their stimulant effects is popular in Middle Eastern countries; in the movie *Captain Phillips,* it was the mainstay of the Somali pirates as they held the captain of the *Maersk Alabama* for ransom. Although bath salts produce positive effects similar to those of amphetamines, they can also lead to hallucinations, delusions, paranoia, anxiety, or depression, as well as impaired memory, attention, and concentration; seizures and death have also been reported. As the popularity of bath salts has increased, there have been several media reports linking them to violent and sometimes bizarre crimes (Dolak, 2012).

Nicotine

Nicotine is the primary psychoactive and addictive agent in tobacco. Tobacco is ingested by smoking, chewing, or inhaling (as snuff, a finely powdered form). Nicotine has an almost unique effect (Schelling, 1992): When tobacco is smoked in short puffs, it has a stimulating effect; when inhaled deeply, it has a tranquilizing or depressant effect. In large doses, nicotine can cause nausea, vomiting, and headaches; in extremely high doses, it is powerful enough to produce convulsions and even death in laboratory animals.

The withdrawal reactions are well known because smokers "quit" so often. The most prominent symptoms are nervousness and anxiety, drowsiness, lightheadedness, and headaches. The United Kingdom annually observes a "No Smoking Day," similar to the "Great American Smokeout," in which people voluntarily abstain from smoking for a day; apparently as a result of impairment from withdrawal symptoms, the number of workplace accidents increases by 7% on that day (Waters, Jarvis, & Sutton, 1998). People who try to give up smoking are usually able to abstain for a while but then relapse; only about 20% of attempts to stop are successful after 2 years. Before bans on public and workplace smoking, about 80% of male smokers and two thirds of female smokers smoked at least one cigarette per waking hour (Brecher, 1972).

In part because usage is more continuous with tobacco than with other drugs, the health risks are particularly high. The health risks from smoking are not the result of nicotine but of some of the 4,000 other compounds present in tobacco smoke. For example, a metabolite of benzo-[*a*]pyrene damages a cancer-suppressing gene, resulting in lung cancer (Denissenko, Pao, Tang, & Pfeifer, 1996). Other cancers resulting from smoking occur in the larynx, mouth, esophagus, liver, and pancreas. Smoking can also cause Buerger's disease, constriction of the blood vessels that may lead to gangrene in the lower extremities, requiring progressively higher amputations. Although abstinence almost guarantees a halt in the

? What neurotransmitter system is involved in the effects of all stimulant drugs?

> Tobacco use is the greatest potentially remediable problem throughout the world.
>
> —R. Gregory Lande

disease's progress, surgeons report that it is not uncommon to find a patient smoking in the hospital bed after a second or third amputation (Brecher, 1972). Smoking is the leading preventable cause of death, accounting for 480,000 premature deaths annually in the United States and 6 million worldwide; the health and lost-productivity costs in the United States add up to $326 billion (Centers for Disease Control and Prevention, 2015b).

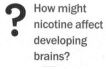 **How might nicotine affect developing brains?**

Cigarette package warnings aimed at expectant mothers are not just propaganda. Infants born to mothers who smoked during pregnancy have lower birth weight, a higher incidence of asthma, and up to 56% greater mortality (Gilliland, Li, & Peters, 2001; Kleinman, Pierre, Madans, Land, & Schramm, 1987; F. Rice et al., 2009). One study of 6- to 8-year-old children whose mothers smoked throughout pregnancy found reductions in cortical gray matter and overall brain volume, cortical thinning in prefrontal areas, and a tendency for depression (El Marroun et al., 2013). We cannot be sure from these results alone that maternal smoking *caused* the problems in offspring. In Chapter 4 we described a unique study of cross-fostered children that confirmed a causal relationship between maternal smoking and low birth weight but determined that the link with conduct disorder is genetic (F. Rice et al.). The association with conduct disorder probably arises because women with a genetic predisposition for impulse control problems are also more likely to smoke. A causal relationship for El Marroun's findings receives some credibility from the fact that children of women who quit smoking when they learned they were pregnant were no different from the children of nonsmoking mothers (El Marroun et al.), though there may be important genetic differences between mothers who were able to give up smoking and those who weren't. These findings illustrate why we shouldn't be too quick to accept the "obvious" interpretation when two variables are correlated.

As described in Chapter 2, nicotine stimulates nicotinic acetylcholine receptors. In the periphery, it activates muscles and may cause twitching. Centrally, it produces increased alertness and faster response to stimulation. Neurons that release dopamine contain nicotinic receptors, so they are also activated, resulting in a positive mood effect (Svensson, Grenhoff, & Aston-Jones, 1986).

Caffeine

Caffeine, the active ingredient in coffee and tea, produces arousal, increased alertness, and decreased sleepiness. It is hardly the drug that amphetamine and cocaine are, but as you saw in Balzac's case, it is subject to abuse. It blocks receptors for the neuromodulator adenosine, increasing the release of dopamine and acetylcholine (Silinsky, 1989; S. H. Snyder, 1997). Because adenosine has sedative and depressive effects, blocking its receptors contributes to arousal. Withdrawal symptoms include headaches, fatigue, anxiety, shakiness, and craving, which last about a week. Withdrawal is not a significant problem, because caffeinated beverages are in plentiful supply, but heavy drinkers may wake up with a headache just from abstaining overnight. Because 80% of Americans drink coffee, researchers at the Mayo Clinic once recommended intravenous administration of caffeine to patients recovering from surgery to eliminate postoperative withdrawal headaches ("Caffeine Prevents Post-op Headaches," 1996).

Psychedelics

Psychedelic drugs are compounds that cause perceptual distortions in the user. The term comes from the Greek words *psyche* ("mind") and *delos* ("visible"). "Visible mind" refers to the expansion of the senses and the sense of increased insight that users of these drugs report. Although the drugs are often referred to as *hallucinogenic,* they are most noted for producing perceptual distortions: Light, color, and details are intensified; objects may change shape; sounds may evoke visual experiences; and light may produce auditory sensations. Psychedelics may affect the perception of time, as well as self-perception; the body may seem to float or to change shape, size, or identity. These experiences are often accompanied by a sense of ecstasy, which makes recreational use of these substances common. Psychedelics fall into three classes in terms of their pharmacological effects: serotonin receptor agonists, serotonin releasers, and NMDA antagonists.

The "classic" psychedelics are similar in structure and function to the neurotransmitter serotonin (Jacobs, 1987), and they work by stimulating the 5-HT$_{2A}$ serotonin receptor. As you will see in this chapter and in later chapters, serotonin has a variety of psychological functions. Typical experiences include sensory distortions, such as warping of surfaces, repetitive geometric shapes, and intense colors. One of the best-known classic psychedelics, *lysergic acid diethylamide (LSD),* was popularized in the student peace movement of the 1960s and championed by the psychologist Timothy Leary. Although LSD is serotonergic, its ability to stimulate dopamine receptors makes it unusual among psychedelics. Other classic psychedelics include *psilocybin* and *psilocin* (LSD-like drugs from the mushroom *Psilocybe mexicana*); *DMT* (a chemical extracted from a native flowering vine in the Brazilian Amazon); and *mescaline,* the active ingredient in the "button" on the top of the peyote cactus. Some of these psychedelics have been authorized for religious use as protected First Amendment religious rights: The Native American Church uses peyote in religious ceremonies (Julien, 2008), and DMT-containing tea is permitted in several religions originating from Brazil ("Supreme Court Rules . . . ," 2006).

The serotonin releasers are referred to as empathogen-enactogens, because they produce feelings of openness, euphoria, empathy, and self-awareness. Chemically, they are substituted phenethylamines, a class that includes the neurotransmitters dopamine, epinephrine, and norepinephrine. Examples are the synthetic drugs ecstasy and 2C-B. *Ecstasy* is the street name of *methylenedioxymethamphetamine* (let's just call it MDMA!); it is a popular drug among young people, especially at dance clubs and "raves." Structurally similar to amphetamine, at low doses it is a *psychomotor stimulant* that increases energy, sociability, and sexual arousal; at higher doses it produces hallucinatory effects like serotonergic psychedelics (Liechti & Vollenweider, 2000). What's worse is that high doses are toxic to serotonergic neurons, at least in monkeys (Figure 5.8; McCann, Lowe, & Ricaurte, 1997), and it impairs serotonin function in the hippocampus even in new users (D. Wagner, Becker, Koester, Gouzoulis-Mayfrank, & Daumann, 2013). A meta-analysis of 422 studies showed small but persistent effects on cognitive performance, especially memory deficits (Rogers et al., 2009).

Although health effects are usually minimal, MDMA increases heart rate and blood pressure and causes hyperactivity, which leads to numerous deaths annually. One bright spot about MDMA is that evidence indicates that the drug, coupled with psychotherapy, may be useful for treating posttraumatic stress disorder (we will elaborate on this in Chapter 14).

NMDA receptor antagonist psychedelics are known as *dissociatives*, because they cause more intense depersonalization and a sense of unreality. For example, ketamine produces a feeling of being disconnected from one's body and the environment. A better known dissociative psychedelic is *phencyclidine (PCP, angel dust, or crystal)*, which was developed as an anesthetic but abandoned because it produced disorientation and hallucinations that were almost indistinguishable from the symptoms of schizophrenia (J. B. Murray, 2002). PCP increases activity in dopamine pathways and inhibits a subtype of glutamate receptors (Carlezon & Wise, 1996; E. D. French, 1994). Research with PCP has led scientists and psychologists to revise their theories of schizophrenia (Jentsch & Roth, 1999).

■ **FIGURE 5.8** Brain Damage Produced by the Drug Ecstasy.

These brain sections have been stained with a chemical that makes neurons containing serotonin turn white. Photos in the top row are from a normal monkey; those below are from a monkey given MDMA a year earlier.

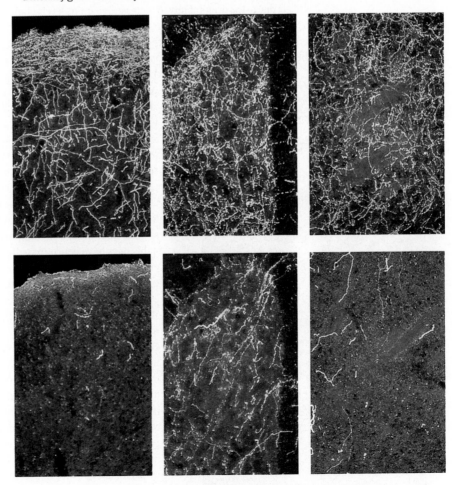

Source: From "Long-Lasting Effects of Recreational Drugs of Abuse on the Central Nervous System," by U. D. McCann, K. A. Lowe, and G. A. Ricaurte, 1997, *The Neuroscientist*, 3, pp. 399–411.

The field has seen a rapid expansion of synthetic or "designer" drugs, which are created from chemicals rather than natural ingredients. Synthetic drugs are a special problem because the ingredients themselves are often legal and their use is disguised, for example, by labeling them as "bath salts" or "plant food" and including the warning "not for human consumption." As lawmakers outlaw these drugs, underground chemists simply concoct new ones. Examples of synthetic psychedelics include LSD, MDMA, PCP, and 2C variants (including the most widely used 2C-B, commonly sold as ecstasy at raves). The organic chemist Alexander Shulgin, who discovered the 2C family of phenethylamines, created many of these new drugs in the late 20th century. Through his research (mostly using himself and his friends as subjects), he described the psychological effects of more than 100 different drugs (Shulgin & Shulgin, 1991, 1997).

Marijuana

Marijuana is the dried and crushed leaves and flowers of the Indian hemp plant, *Cannabis sativa* (Figure 5.9). The hemp plant was cultivated heavily in the United States during World War II as a source of material for making rope, and it is still found occasionally growing wild along midwestern roadsides. Marijuana is usually smoked but can be mixed in food and eaten. The major psychoactive ingredient is *delta-9-tetrahydrocannabinol (THC)*. THC is particularly concentrated in the dried resin from the plant, called *hashish*.

THC is a *cannabinoid,* a group of compounds that includes two known endogenous cannabinoids, anandamide and 2-arachidonyl glycerol, or 2-AG (Devane et al., 1992; di Tomaso, Beltramo, & Piomelli, 1996; Mechoulam et al., 1995). Cannabinoid receptors are found on axon terminals; cannabinoids are released by postsynaptic neurons and act as retrograde messengers, regulating the presynaptic neuron's release of neurotransmitter (R. I. Wilson & Nicoll, 2001). The receptors are widely distributed in the brain and spinal cord, which probably accounts for the variety of effects that marijuana has on behavior. The pleasurable sensation is likely due to the drug's ability to increase dopamine levels (Tanda, Pontieri, & Di Chiara, 1997). Receptors in the frontal cortex probably account for impaired cognitive functioning and distortions of time sense and sensory perception, receptors in the hippocampus disrupt memory, and those in the basal ganglia and cerebellum impair movement and coordination (Herkenham, 1992; Howlett et al., 1990; W. Y. Ong & Mackie,

■ **FIGURE 5.9** Marijuana Plants.

1999). Although drugs may reveal a great deal about brain functioning, the pattern of effects they produce is usually unlike normal functioning; drugs affect wide areas of the brain indiscriminately, whereas normal activation tends to be more discrete and localized.

Marijuana may have a greater impact on users than previously thought. Long-term heavy users have various brain anomalies, including reduced volume in the hippocampus and amygdala and impaired white matter connectivity in the hippocampus and corpus callosum (Yücel et al., 2008; Zalesky et al., 2012). These findings are correlational, leaving open the possibility that the deficits were preexisting and contributed to excessive marijuana use; however, several animal studies have shown that cannabis does have neurotoxic effects on the hippocampus (cited in Yücel et al., 2008). Longitudinal studies also get around the correlational issue; one study showed that individuals who smoked five joints a day had an average 4-point decline in IQ from childhood to young adulthood (Fried, Watkinson, James, & Gray, 2002). In another study, individuals who used marijuana from their teens to age 38 lost an average of 6 IQ points (Meier et al., 2012). Abstinence apparently led to recovery of the losses in the first study but not in the second, probably due to longer use. In addition, the illegality of marijuana led to the development of synthetic marijuana, often with life-threatening results. In the summer of 2016, 33 individuals in Brooklyn were hospitalized after taking a form of synthetic marijuana called K2 (Rosenberg & Schweber, 2016).

There has been much less research on prenatal effects of marijuana, most likely because the impairments are not as obvious as those caused by prenatal exposure to cocaine and alcohol. Indeed, the studies that have been done found no deficits until about 4 years of age. Then, and through adolescence, data reveal behavioral problems, including impulsiveness and hyperactivity; decreased performance on visual-spatial tasks; and deficits in attention, memory, and language comprehension (P. A. Fried, 1995; C.-S. Wu, Jew, & Lu, 2011). These studies also suffer from being correlational, but experiments with animals have produced similar results.

Legalization is the major controversy surrounding marijuana; it is a battle that is being waged on two very different fronts. Because of the drug's mild effects, many people contend that its use should be unrestricted. Others, citing reports that it reduces pain, the nausea of chemotherapy, and the severity of the eye disease glaucoma, believe it should be available by a doctor's prescription. The medical claims have been controversial but are gaining acceptance, and both public and governmental attitudes are changing, as the accompanying Application indicates.

Another controversy concerns whether marijuana is addictive. The importance of this debate is that it requires us to define just what we mean by the term *addiction*. Addiction has traditionally been equated with a drug's ability to produce withdrawal symptoms; because marijuana's withdrawal symptoms are very mild, its compulsive use was attributed to "psychological dependence," a concept also invoked to explain the habitual use of other drugs that do not produce dramatic withdrawal symptoms, like nicotine and caffeine. Withdrawal symptoms are mild because cannabinoids dissolve in body fats and leave the body slowly. However, monkeys will press a lever to inject THC into their bloodstream in amounts similar to doses in marijuana smoke inhaled by humans (Tanda, Munzar, & Goldberg, 2000). Researchers are reluctant to attribute drug self-administration in animals to psychological dependence and usually consider it evidence of addiction. Earlier we defined addiction in terms of the drug's hold on the individual, without reference to its ability to produce withdrawal symptoms. Next, we examine the reasons for taking this position.

What are the two controversies about marijuana?

APPLICATION
Changing Attitudes Toward Marijuana

Although marijuana remains illegal under federal law, the U.S. Department of Justice has not been prosecuting medical use in states that have legalized it, or recreational use as long as legalizing states maintain strict procedures for the sale of the drug. This reflects changing public attitudes toward marijuana as well as a desire to remove the criminal element and reduce demand for the more dangerous synthetic marijuana as well as other drugs. Data from the Pew Research Center (Geiger, 2016) suggest that a significant majority (57%) of U.S. adults support legalization of marijuana, while 37% of adults endorse marijuana remaining illegal. Perhaps not surprisingly, young adults have had a large impact on this shift in public perception; 71% of millennials support marijuana legalization. The youngest generation may be the most supportive of new attitudes toward legalized and medical marijuana, but individuals from Gen X (aged 36–51 in 2016) and Baby Boomers (aged 52–70 in 2016) have shown considerable increases as well. A majority (57%) of Baby Boomers support marijuana legalization, representing a nearly threefold

Source: iStock/rasilja.

increase from 17% in 1990 (Pew Research Center, 2015). So far, 29 states and Washington, D.C., have legalized marijuana for medical purposes, and recreational use has been approved in seven of those jurisdictions ("Marijuana Legalized for Fun . . . ," 2016; Wattles, 2016). Several other states are considering changes to their laws.

Addiction

Why does the avoidance of withdrawal symptoms fail to explain addiction?

It is an oversimplification to assume that chronic drug use is motivated primarily by the pleasurable effects of the drug. In fact, individuals who engage in compulsive drug taking often report that they no longer enjoy their drug experience. Their casual drug use has progressed into the compulsive disorder of addiction. The common belief that addiction is fueled by the drug user's desire to avoid withdrawal symptoms also has several flaws. First, it does not explain what motivates the person to use the drug until addiction develops. Second, we know that many addicts go through withdrawal fairly regularly to reset their tolerance level so they can get by with lower and less costly amounts of the drug. Third, it does not explain why many addicts return to a drug after a long period of abstinence and long after withdrawal symptoms have subsided. Finally, the addictiveness of a drug is unrelated to the severity of withdrawal symptoms (Leshner, 1997). Cocaine is a good example of severe addictiveness but mild withdrawal, while a number of drugs—including some asthma inhalers, nasal decongestants, and drugs for hypertension and angina pain—produce withdrawal symptoms but are not addictive (S. E. Hyman & Malenka, 2001).

The Neural Basis of Reward

Reward refers to the positive effect an object or a condition—such as a drug, food, sexual contact, or warmth—has on the user. Reward is accompanied by a tendency to repeat the behavior that brought about the reward and, typically, by feelings of pleasure. The most important reward circuit is the *mesolimbic pathway,* which consists of dopaminergic neurons originating in the *ventral tegmental area* and connecting to several targets in the limbic system, especially the *nucleus accumbens* (Figure 5.10). Microdialysis studies show that natural rewards—food, water, and sexual stimulation—increase dopamine levels in the nucleus accumbens of rats (Carelli, 2002; Damsma, Pfaus, Wenkstern, & Phillips, 1992). Other structures also participate in reward, including the amygdala, the hippocampus, the hypothalamus, and parts of the frontal cortex.

Electrical stimulation affects the same areas (Fibiger, LePiane, Jakubovic, & Phillips, 1987). In *electrical stimulation of the brain (ESB),* animals and, sometimes, humans learn to press a lever to deliver mild electrical stimulation to brain areas where the stimulation is rewarding. Drugs that block dopamine receptors interfere with learning to press a lever to obtain this stimulation (Wise, 2004). ESB is thought to reflect "natural" reward processes because, for example, effective sites are often in areas where experimenter-delivered stimulation evokes eating or sexual activity, and because self-stimulation rate in the posterior hypothalamus varies with experimenter-induced sexual motivation (Caggiula, 1970). The most sensitive areas are where the density of dopaminergic neurons is greatest (D. Corbett & Wise, 1980).

However, ESB has a much more powerful effect than natural rewards. Animals will ignore food and water and tolerate painful shock to stimulate their brains with electricity, sometimes pressing a lever thousands of times in an hour. Drugs are similarly powerful: Humans will sacrifice their careers, relationships, and lives in the interest of acquiring and using drugs. While food and sex increase dopamine in the nucleus accumbens by 50%–100%, drugs and electrical stimulation can have a three- to sixfold greater effect (A. G. Phillips et al., 1992; Wise, 2002).

The Neural Basis of Addiction

How is the reward system involved in addiction?

Rats will learn to press a lever to inject abused drugs into the reward areas (Bozarth & Wise, 1984; Hoebel et al., 1983), and lesioning the nucleus accumbens reduces reward effects for many drugs (Kelsey, Carlezon, & Falls, 1989). All abused drugs target the mesolimbic dopamine system and increase dopaminergic activity. If dopamine activity is blocked, rats will not learn to press a lever for a drug injection, and those that have learned previously will stop lever pressing after receiving the dopamine-blocking drug (Wise, 2004). In PET scan studies, human volunteers who had the greatest increase in dopamine in the general area of the nucleus accumbens during drug administration also experienced the most intense "highs" (Volkow, Fowler, & Wang, 2003). In one study, participants began reporting that they felt "high" when cocaine had blocked 47% of the dopamine reuptake sites in the nucleus accumbens (Volkow et al., 1997).

Drug researchers have expanded their attention to a broader area, the *mesolimbocortical dopamine system,* which consists of the mesolimbic pathway and the *mesocortical pathway,* dopaminergic neurons which project from the ventral tegmental area to several areas in the frontal cortex (see Figure 5.10). Through this system, chronic exposure to abused drugs changes the brain in several ways (Nestler, 2005). First, baseline levels of dopamine activity decrease in the system, resulting in tolerance and a decreased response to normal rewarding stimuli (Figure 5.11; Volkow, Fowler, Wang, & Swanson, 2004); however, the drug and drug-related stimuli produce greater increases in dopamine transmission. This sensitization to the drug and associated stimuli can last long after the person stops taking the drug, making the individual prone to relapse. Another effect is *hypofrontality,* reduced activity in several frontal regions—prefrontal cortex, anterior cingulate cortex, and orbitofrontal cortex—which control working memory, attention, behavioral

■ **FIGURE 5.10**   The Mesolimbic and Mesocortical Dopamine Systems.

The mesolimbic system projects from dopamine (DA) neurons in the ventral tegmental area (VTA) to the nucleus accumbens; the mesocortical system projects from DA neurons in the VTA to the frontal cortex. Together, they form the mesolimbocortical dopamine system, so named because it begins in the midbrain (mesencephalon) and projects to the limbic system and prefrontal cortex.

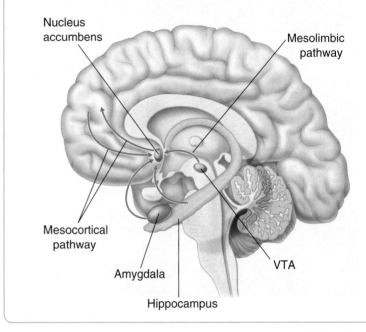

inhibition, and the individual's response to the environment. The impulsivity and compulsivity that characterize hypofrontality plus the decreased effectiveness of natural rewards refocus the individual's life on obtaining and taking the drug. Stopping the drug activates neurons in the amygdala that mediate fear and other aversive states, producing the negative emotions and many of the bodily symptoms that characterize withdrawal.

Although dopamine is the primary transmitter in the reward/addiction circuit, it is not the only one. Stimulants and nicotine act directly on dopaminergic neurons in the nucleus accumbens, but others increase dopamine transmission indirectly—alcohol through GABAergic neurons and opiate-releasing neurons, and opiates by stimulating opioid receptors and inhibiting GABAergic neurons. Regardless of a drug's initial effect, the final pathway involves the nucleus accumbens and increased dopamine transmission (Lüscher, 2016).

> *Drugs of abuse create a signal in the brain that indicates, falsely, the arrival of a huge fitness benefit.*
>
> —Randolph Nesse and Kent Berridge

Brain Plasticity and Learning in Addiction

Reward is an essential factor in early drug taking, but it does not appear to be what maintains long-term drug abuse (Volkow & Fowler, 2000; Wise, 2004). Rather, researchers believe that addictive behavior is maintained by *learning,* potentially lifelong changes in brain functioning that are initiated during the earlier stages. A key player in this process is glutamate, an excitatory transmitter involved in the remodeling of synapses during learning. A single administration of cocaine modifies glutamate receptors on dopamine neurons in the ventral tegmental area, increasing the effectiveness of glutamate activity for a week (Mameli et al., 2009) and sensitizing response to further drug exposure (S. Jones & Bonci, 2005). Chronic administration of amphetamine or cocaine leads to more enduring neural changes, in the form of increased dendrite length and greater synaptic complexity in the nucleus accumbens and prefrontal cortex (Robinson, Gorny, Mitton, & Kolb, 2001; Robinson & Kolb, 1997).

> *It is as if drugs have hijacked the brain's natural motivational control circuits.*
>
> —Alan Leshner

■ FIGURE 5.11 Reduced Dopamine D$_2$ Receptors in Drug Abusers.

The researchers imaged the brains using PET and an agent that binds to dopamine D$_2$ receptors. The predominance of yellow in place of red in the scans of the drug abusers' brains indicates fewer of the D$_2$ receptors than in the control subjects' brains.

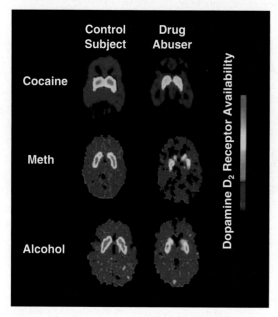

Source: From "Role of Dopamine, the Frontal Cortex, and Memory Circuits in Drug Addiction: Insight From Imaging Studies," by N. D. Volkow et al., *Neurobiology of Learning and Memory,* 78, pp. 610–624. © 2002 Nora Volkow. Used with permission from Elsevier.

> *The proneness to relapse is based on changes in brain function that continue for months or years after the last use of the drug.*
>
> —Charles O'Brien
>
> *The hardest thing I do every day is not take cocaine. You don't get cured of addiction— you're just in remission.*
>
> —Aaron Sorkin, screen-writer, producer, and playwright

The power of drug-induced learning is most obvious in craving, especially in its ability to persist years after drug use has ceased. Even viewing drug paraphernalia is enough to evoke craving in addicts (Garavan et al., 2000; S. Grant et al., 1996; Maas et al., 1998) and often triggers relapse; PET scans show that the sight of drug-related stimuli shifts the addict's typically low brain metabolism to hyperactive in areas involved in learning and emotion (Figure 5.12; R. Z. Goldstein & Volkow, 2002; S. Grant et al., 1996; Volkow, Fowler, & Wang, 2004). The hippocampus, which has inputs to the nucleus accumbens, is particularly important in learning associations with environmental stimuli like those involved in drug taking. After rats have given up pressing a lever because the drug delivery mechanism has been disconnected, electrical stimulation of the hippocampus results in a 30-minute-long release of dopamine in the nucleus accumbens and a return to lever pressing (Vorel, Liu, Hayes, Spector, & Gardner, 2001).

An intriguing feature of craving is that it increases progressively over the first weeks or months of drug abstinence, a phenomenon referred to as *incubation of craving* (Pickens et al., 2011). Incubation results from a number of factors, but changes in inputs to the nucleus accumbens are a good illustration of drug-induced plasticity. Over the course of addiction, glutamatergic pathways to the nucleus accumbens from the prefrontal cortex and the amygdala develop "silent" synapses. The synapses are capable of releasing glutamate, but they lack the necessary receptors on the postsynaptic side; during withdrawal, the synapses mature and become functional. Unsilencing of these pathways produces craving, as evidenced by the rats' increased drug seeking in the presence of drug-related cues (S.-Y. Lee et al., 2013; Ma et al., 2014).

Treating Drug Addiction

Synanon, the residential community for the treatment of addictions, supplied its residents with all their food, clothing, and other necessities including, until 1970, cigarettes—which alone cost $200,000 annually (Brecher, 1972). But then Synanon's founder and head Charles Dederich had a chest X-ray that showed a cloudy area in his lungs. He quit smoking and, realizing that residents as young as 15 were learning to smoke under his watch, stopped supplying cigarettes and banned their use on the premises. Giving up smoking was more difficult for the residents than expected. About 100 people left during the first 6 months rather than do without cigarettes. Some of the residents who quit smoking noticed that they got over withdrawal symptoms from other drugs in less than a week but the symptoms from smoking hung around for at least 6 months. As one resident said, it was easier to quit heroin than cigarettes.

Freud had a similarly difficult experience (Figure 5.13). He smoked as many as 20 cigars a day and commented that his passion for smoking interfered with his work. Although he quit cocaine with apparent ease, each time he gave up smoking he relapsed. He developed cancer of the mouth and jaw, which required 33 surgeries, but he continued smoking. After replacement of his jaw with an artificial one, he was in constant pain and sometimes unable to speak, chew, or swallow, but still he smoked. He quit smoking when he died of cancer in 1939 (Brecher, 1972).

The first step in quitting drug use is detoxification. This means giving up the drug and allowing the body to cleanse itself of the drug residues. This is admittedly difficult with nicotine or opiates, but withdrawal from alcohol is potentially life threatening; medical intervention with benzodiazepines to suppress the withdrawal syndrome may be necessary (C. P. O'Brien, 1997). Still, withdrawal is often easier than the subsequent battle against relapse. The addict's impulsiveness, accompanied by atrophy and reduced activity in the orbitofrontal cortex, are even more pronounced in those who relapse (Beck et al., 2012; Dom, Sabbe, Hulstijn, & van den Brink, 2005), making therapy all the more difficult. However, in spite of the challenges, the relapse rate is no higher for drug addiction than for other chronic diseases such as hypertension, asthma, and type 2 diabetes (McLellan, Lewis, O'Brien, & Kleber, 2000). Fortunately, the number of treatment options is increasing, reflecting our improving knowledge of how addiction works.

Treatment Strategies

Agonist treatments replace an addicting drug with another drug that has a similar effect; this approach is the most common defense against drug craving and relapse. For example, nicotine gum and nicotine patches provide controlled amounts of the drug without the dangers of smoking, and their use can be reduced systematically over time. Opiate addiction is often treated with a synthetic opioid called *methadone*. This treatment is controversial because it substitutes one addiction for another, but methadone is a milder and safer drug and the person does not have to resort to crime to satisfy the habit. As a side note, methadone was developed in World War II Germany as a pain-relieving replacement for morphine, which was not available; it was called *adolphine*, after Adolph Hitler (Bellis, 1981). Addicts who do not benefit from methadone are sometimes given pharmaceutical-grade prescription heroin or the synthetic pain reliever hydromorphone as a means of deterring street use and criminal activity (Oviedo-Joekes et al., 2016).

■ FIGURE 5.12 The Brain of a Cocaine Abuser During Craving.

PET scans are shown at two depths in the brain. Notice the increased activity during presentation of cocaine-related stimuli. Frontal areas and temporal areas are involved in learning and emotion.

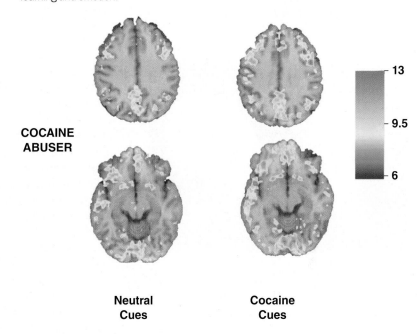

COCAINE ABUSER

Neutral Cues   **Cocaine Cues**

Source: From "Activation of Memory Circuits During Cue-Elicited Cocaine Craving," by S. Grant et al., 1996, *Proceedings of the National Academy of Sciences, USA*, 93, pp. 12040–12045. © 1996. National Academy of Sciences, U.S.A.

■ FIGURE 5.13 Sigmund Freud and Relapse of Smoking Addiction.

Notice in the graph that the two legal drugs have relapse rates equal to that of heroin.

(a)

(b)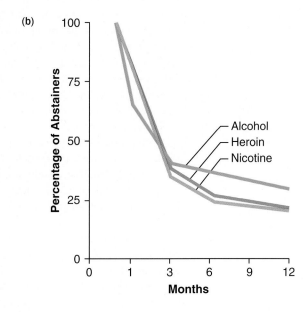

Source: (a) Bettmann/Getty Images. (b) Adapted with permission from "Nicotine Becomes Addictive," by R. Kanigel, 1988, *Science Illustrated*, Oct/Nov, pp. 12–14, 19–21. © 1988 *Science Illustrated*.

FIGURE 5.14 Effects of a GABA_A Receptor Blocker.

The two rats received the same amount of alcohol, but the one on the right received a drug that blocks the effect of alcohol at the GABA_A receptor.

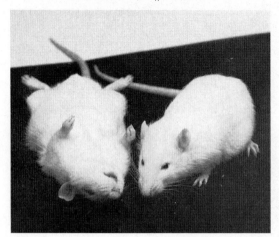

Source: From "New Drug Counters Alcohol Intoxication," by G. Kolata, 1986, *Science, 234*(4781), p. 1198. Reprinted with permission from AAAS.

Antagonist treatments, as the name implies, involve drugs that block the effects of the addicting drug. Drugs that block opiate receptors, such as naltrexone, are used to treat opiate addictions and alcoholism because they reduce the pleasurable effects of the drug. The potential for this type of treatment is illustrated dramatically in Figure 5.14 (Suzdak et al., 1986). However, antagonist treatment has a distinct disadvantage compared with agonist treatment. Because the treatment offers no replacement for the abused drug's benefit, success depends on the addict's motivation to quit and willingness to comply with treatment. That could be changing as the FDA continues to approve medication implants, which last three to six months.

Other receptor-targeting strategies are in the experimental stage. For example, the muscle relaxant baclofen activates GABA_B receptors on dopaminergic neurons and dampens the reward system (Addolorato et al., 2011; Bock, 2010); drugs that enhance activity at glutamate receptors help addicts "unlearn" the association between drug-related stimuli and craving (Cleva, Gass, Widholm, & Olive, 2010; "Cognitive Enhancement and Relapse Prevention in Cocaine Addiction," 2012). Baclofen is currently undergoing clinical trials. Genetic intervention is another possibility for turning down receptor functioning. Rats trained to binge drink stopped drinking almost immediately after researchers blocked a gene for the GABA_A receptor in their amygdalae (J. Liu et al., 2012).

Rather than blocking the effects of a drug, *aversive treatments* cause a negative reaction when the person takes the drug. For example, Antabuse interferes with alcohol metabolism, so drinking alcohol makes the person ill. Similarly, adding silver nitrate to chewing gum or lozenges makes tobacco taste bad. As with antagonist treatments, success depends on the addict's motivation and treatment compliance.

All of these approaches have problems: Alcoholics often fail to take Antabuse; methadone is itself addictive; naltrexone works with only a subset of addicts; and the anti-nicotine drugs Chantix and Zyban have been associated with hostility, depression, and suicidal thoughts. An attractive alternative is anti-drug vaccines. *Antidrug vaccines* consist of molecules that attach to the drug and stimulate the immune system to make antibodies that will degrade the drug. These treatments avoid the side effects that occur when receptors in the brain are manipulated. Another benefit is that the antibodies are expected to last from weeks to years, which means that therapeutic success will not depend on the addict's decision every morning to take an anti-addiction drug. In rats, vaccines reduced the amount of cocaine reaching the brain by 80% (Carrera et al., 1995) and the amount of nicotine by 65% (Pentel et al., 2000); early human trials showed promise as well, but larger, more definitive trials were disappointing (Martinez & Trifilieff, 2014). A significant problem with vaccines is that they do not reduce craving, and the number of antibodies produced is limited; the addict can increase drug intake and continue to get high.

Several abused drugs produce their own immune response in the brain when glia respond by initiating inflammation. Anti-inflammatory treatment is used to ease the symptoms of withdrawal but, because inflammation increases the excitability of dopaminergic neurons, it also may be effective against the addiction itself. Ibudilast, an inhibitor of glial activation, reduces self-administration of alcohol, methamphetamine, and opioids in rodents (Jacobsen, Hutchinson, & Mustafa, 2016), and clinical trials are under way with methamphetamine addiction ("Trial of Ibudilast for Methamphetamine Dependence (IBUD ph II)," 2016).

The number of drugs approved for treating addictions is quite limited, as Table 5.1 shows. Because addiction is so difficult to treat, researchers must remain open to novel approaches. One intriguing new avenue involves disrupting drug-related memory. Injecting the memory inhibitor Latrunculin A into the amygdalae of rats and mice disrupted their preference for the location where methamphetamine had been administered, without affecting other memories motivated by food reward or shock (E. J. Young et al., 2014). Another novel approach, described in the accompanying In the News feature, is an attempt to lessen withdrawal and keep addicts in treatment by applying electrical stimulation to the ear.

TABLE 5.1 Medications Approved by the U.S. Food and Drug Administration for Treating Drug Addictions.

DRUG	MEDICATION	ACTION
Alcoholism	Disulfiram (Antabuse)	Inhibits aldehyde dehydrogenase. Aversive treatment.
	Naltrexone	Opioid receptor antagonist. Supposedly blocks reward; effectiveness questioned.
	Acamprosate	GABA agonist, glutamate antagonist. Reduces craving, unpleasant effects of abstinence.
Nicotine	Nicotine gum, patch, etc.	Replaces nicotine.
	Bupropion (Zyban)	Blocks reuptake of dopamine, norepinephrine, and serotonin.
	Varenicline (Chantix)	Enhances general reward but reduces nicotine reward; reduces withdrawal effects.
Heroin/opiates	Naltrexone	Opioid receptor antagonist. Competes with opiates for receptor sites.
	Methadone	Replaces opiates at receptor.
	Buprenorphine, buprenorphine with naloxone	Replaces opiates at receptor.

Source: National Institute on Drug Abuse, 2014.

> Addiction will eventually be seen as analogous to other medical illnesses—as complex constructs of genetic, environmental, and psychosocial factors that require multiple levels of intervention for their treatment and prevention.
>
> —Eric Nestor and George Aghajanian

IN THE NEWS
TARGETING THE BRAIN TO LESSEN DRUG WITHDRAWAL

The current opioid epidemic in the United States is a major public safety problem that has law enforcement officials stymied. At the same time, it is a health concern that has sent doctors scrambling to find more effective treatments. One innovative approach involves reducing opioid withdrawal symptoms so that patients are more likely to remain in treatment. Adrian Miranda and Arturo Taca (2017) used a neurostimulation device called the BRIDGE, originally developed to treat pain, in order to electrically stimulate peripheral nerves in the ear. They believed these nerves might feed into brain areas involved in fear and pain and that stimulating them could modify the patient's emotional perceptions during withdrawal. Over the five days that opioid-addicted patients wore the BRIDGE, withdrawal symptoms such as sweating, tremors, anxiety, and restlessness decreased significantly.

This study was an important first step in suggesting that noninvasive neurostimulation might promote adherence to opioid treatment. Because treatment with the BRIDGE is nonpharmaceutical, it also avoids the controversy about replacing one addicting substance with another (as occurs when using methadone as a treatment).

THOUGHT QUESTIONS

1. What was Miranda and Taca's rationale for reducing withdrawal symptoms through use of the BRIDGE device?

2. How does the BRIDGE differ from other approaches to treating opioid addiction?

For the news story, visit edge.sagepub.com/garrett5e and select the Chapter 5 study resources.

Effectiveness and Acceptance of Pharmacological Treatment

Pharmacological intervention increases treatment effectiveness dramatically. Methadone combined with counseling produces abstinence rates of 60%–80% in heroin addiction, compared with 10%–30% for programs that rely on behavioral management alone (Landry, 1997). This is not an argument for pharmacological treatment alone. Drug addiction is almost always accompanied by environmental problems and emotional issues that must be dealt with, and therapeutic benefits are greater when medication is combined with psychosocial support (Strang et al., 2012).

A major difficulty in treating addiction is *comorbidity* with personality disorders, either mental or emotional. This means that drug abusers are likely to have other problems that complicate their rehabilitation. In a study of 43,000 people, 18% of drug abusers had an anxiety disorder, 20% had a mood disorder (most often depression), and 48% had a personality disorder (most often antisocial personality disorder) (B. F. Grant et al., 2004a, 2004b). These symptoms could be partly a by-product of the ravages of addiction, but drug abuse can also be the result of another disorder, for instance, when the person uses drugs as an escape or as a way to self-medicate the symptoms. However, it is more likely that the addiction and the personality disorder have a common genetic, neurological, or environmental cause.

Drug substitution treatment for addiction to heroin and other opioids has the strongest evidence of effectiveness (Strang et al., 2012), but giving a drug to combat a drug is controversial in some segments of society. Some people believe that recovery from addiction should involve the exercise of will and that recovery should not be easy. According to this perspective, Antabuse is okay because it causes the backslider to suffer, but methadone is not okay because it continues the pleasures of drug taking (Szalavitz, 2000). The counterargument is that the bottom line in drug treatment is effectiveness. Addiction costs an estimated $600 billion each year in the United States alone (National Institute on Drug Abuse, 2012). Even when the outcome of treatment is not abstinence, it can enable the addict to lead a healthy and productive lifestyle and avoid criminal activity. Besides the obvious social and personal benefits, treatment saves $7 for every dollar invested (Ettner et al., 2006).

> *Science has yet to defeat the mind/body problem—or those who view psychological problems as failures of will and values.*
>
> —Maia Szalavitz

CONCEPT CHECK

Take a Minute to Check Your Knowledge and Understanding

- What is wrong with the withdrawal explanation of addiction?
- Describe the roles of reward and brain plasticity in addiction.
- What are the strengths and weaknesses of the different types of pharmacological treatment of addiction?

The Role of Genes in Addiction

Much of the research on what predisposes a person to addiction has focused on alcoholism to the neglect of other drugs. This is understandable, because alcoholism is such a pervasive problem in our society. Also, alcoholics are readily accessible to researchers because their drug use is legal. We are beginning to accumulate the same kind of information for other drugs, but as you will see, the study of alcoholism has served as a good model for other addiction research.

Separating Genetic and Environmental Influences

The heritability of addiction was first established with alcoholism. However, the role of heredity in alcoholism was controversial for a long time, because studies yielded inconsistent results. One reason for the inconsistency is that researchers typically treated alcoholism as a unitary disorder; they would study whatever group they had access to, such as hospitalized alcoholics, and generalize to all alcoholics. An important breakthrough came when Robert Cloninger and his colleagues included in their study all 862 men and 913 women who had been adopted by nonrelatives at an early age (average, 4 months) in Stockholm, Sweden, between 1930 and 1949 (Bohman, 1978; Cloninger, 1987).

Cloninger identified two groups of alcoholics. Individuals with Type 1 alcoholism tended to be cautious and emotionally dependent; their problem drinking typically began after the age of 25 and was characterized

How do hereditary and environmental contributions differ in the two types of alcoholism?

by periods of abstinence followed by binge drinking fraught with guilt. Those with Type 2 alcoholism began drinking at a young age, drinking frequently and with little guilt. They showed signs of antisocial personality disorder: They were impulsive, uninhibited, confident, and socially and emotionally detached, and they frequently got into bar fights and were arrested for reckless driving. Most of them were male, and they made up most of the hospitalized population.

Later research showed that alcoholics do not always fit neatly into the two categories (Wennberg, Berglund, Berggren, Balldin, & Fahlke, 2014), but Cloninger produced groundbreaking revelations when he examined the offspring of the two groups. Those in the late-onset group were likely to become alcoholic only if they were reared in a home where there was alcohol abuse. But for the offspring of those with early-onset alcoholism, the rearing environment made no difference—evidence of a strong genetic influence that had eluded previous researchers. Cloninger highlighted the complexity of heredity and environment in addiction. A more recent example comes from research with the *Met158* allele of the *COMT* gene. The gene is responsible for an enzyme that metabolizes dopamine, and *Met158* is associated with an anxious, sensitive, and cautious personality. This greater anxiety and cautiousness apparently confers some protection from alcoholism in American Plains Indians, but among European Caucasian men, who tend to drink socially on a daily basis as a means of relaxing, *Met158* predisposes them to late-onset alcoholism (Enoch, 2006).

What Is Inherited?

Obviously, not everyone who tries a drug becomes addicted; percentages run about 4% for inhalants, 9% for marijuana, 15% for alcohol, 17% for cocaine, 23% for heroin, and 32% for tobacco (Anthony, Warner, & Kessler, 1994). About 50% of addiction is due to heredity; the rest is attributable to a host of environmental factors, including stress, social pressure, and drug exposure and availability (Wang, Kapoor, & Goate, 2012). Genetics research has implicated most of the major neurotransmitter systems (D. Dick & Agrawal, 2008), but, for obvious reasons, genes that influence activity in the dopamine reward system have received the most attention. Kenneth Blum and his colleagues (2017) have developed a Genetic Addiction Risk Score based on 11 alleles of 10 genes; these alleles reduce activity in the dopamine system and produce a reward deficiency syndrome. The amino acid nutrient compound KB220 influences dopamine homeostasis mechanisms to increase reward functioning; administering KB220 has resulted in improvement in prefrontal networks, activation of the nucleus accumbens, and reduced drug craving and relapse.

Genetic influences may increase an individual's vulnerability or provide protection; genes increase or decrease transmitter levels, regulate the number and sensitivity of receptors (for both neurotransmitters and the drug itself), and control metabolism of the drug. A study of 120,000 coffee drinkers is illustrative. The researchers identified eight gene locations that contribute to caffeine addiction (Coffee and Caffeine Genetics Consortium et al., 2015); their functions range from regulating the activity of dopamine, glutamate, and serotonin, to the rapid metabolism of caffeine so that the drinker is ready for another cup sooner. Four of the locations had previously been linked to smoking and obesity. Together, these gene locations explain only about 1.3% of the variation in caffeine intake. This suggests that many more genes are involved in caffeine addiction alone, and we can assume the same is true for other forms of dependence.

Whether drug use will lead to addiction depends largely on how the individual reacts to the drug. For example, people with a particular allele of the *CHRNA5* acetylcholine receptor gene get a pleasurable rush during early experimentation with tobacco and are more likely to become heavy smokers (Sherva et al., 2008). An allele of the opioid receptor gene *OPRMI* confers a similar euphoria from drinking and triples the risk of alcohol abuse (L. A. Ray & Hutchison, 2004); the risk is quadrupled in people resistant to the negative effects of alcohol (Schuckit, 1994). Many Asians are protected from alcoholism because they experience intense flushing, nausea, and increased heart rate when drinking. This is due to excess oxidation of the alcohol to its toxic metabolite, acetaldehyde, or to reduced conversion of the acetaldehyde to acetate. Three responsible gene variants are prevalent among Asians, and possession of one or more of them leads to a four- to ninefold reduction in alcohol dependence (Eng, Luczak, & Wall, 2007).

Impulsiveness, a major characteristic of the "addictive personality," is about 49% heritable (D. E. Gustavson, Miyake, Hewitt, & Friedman, 2014), and there is evidence linking impulsiveness to functional and structural brain anomalies in drug users. For example, individuals with two specific alleles of the *GABRA2* gene, which influences $GABA_A$ receptor functioning, are higher in impulsiveness and have more

■ **FIGURE 5.15** Evoked Potentials in Children at High Risk and Low Risk for Alcoholism.

Evoked potentials were elicited by high-pitched tones occurring among low-pitched tones. The usual dip of the P300 wave is diminished in the high-risk children.

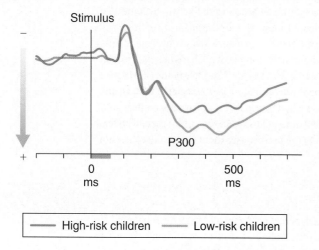

Source: Reprinted by permission of Elsevier Science from S. Y. Hill, D. Muka, S. Steinhauer, and J. Locke, "P300 Amplitude Decrements in Children From Families of Alcoholic Female Probands," *Biological Psychiatry, 38,* pp. 622–632. © 1995 Society of Biological Psychiatry. Used with permission from Elsevier.

symptoms of alcohol dependence (Villafuerte et al., 2012). When anticipating a reward or loss, they showed more activity in the insular cortex, an area involved in food and drug craving, than did non-addicted individuals. People addicted to stimulant drugs have abnormal white fiber connectivity in prefrontal areas associated with impulse control, along with gray matter increases in temporal lobe areas involved in both addiction and learning (Ersche, Jones, Williams, Turton, Robbins, & Bullmore, 2012). The same characteristics are also found in non-addicted siblings of addicted individuals, which suggests they are genetic in origin and predate the onset of addiction.

Alcoholics have a diminished P300 (P3) response, which is a dip in the EEG event-related potential that occurs about 300 milliseconds after an unexpected stimulus (Figure 5.15; Hesselbrock, Begleiter, Porjesz, O'Connor, & Bauer, 2001; S. Hill, 1995; W. G. Iacono, Carlson, Malone, & McGue, 2002). Reduced P3 has an estimated heritability of 64% (Hicks et al., 2007); in boys at age 17 it predicts the development of drug abuse disorders by the age of 20 (W. G. Iacono et al., 2002). Reduced P3 amplitude is seen in a variety of disorders characterized by behavioral disinhibition, the most distinctive characteristic of which is impulsivity. These include additional forms of drug abuse, as well as childhood conduct disorder and adult antisocial behavior.

This discussion would be incomplete if we left the impression that the link between genes and drug use is unidirectional; drugs also change the way our genes function. A recent study of smokers and former smokers found more than 7,000 genes whose functioning had been modified by the process of methylation (Joehanes et al., 2016); *methylation* is the attachment of a methyl group to DNA, which suppresses a gene's activity. The changes were found most reliably on genes associated with smoking-related diseases, including cardiovascular disease and certain types of cancer. Although most of these changes had disappeared after five years of nonsmoking, some persisted as long as 30 years, which may explain why smoking-related diseases can occur decades after a person stops smoking. Even more disturbing is that a mother's smoking has similar effects on the genes of her unborn fetus (Joubert et al., 2016). The genes affected are related to lung and nervous system development; smoking-related cancers; and birth defects associated with prenatal smoking, such as cleft lip and cleft palate.

Implications of Addiction Research

The study of drug abuse and addiction has practical societal importance, but it is worthwhile for other reasons as well, particularly in shedding light on other kinds of vulnerability and principles of behavioral inheritance. For example, the fact that genetic and environmental influences operate differently in different types of alcoholism and in different cultural settings demonstrates that no behavior is simple or simply explained. Even after we understand the relative roles of heredity and environment, there is further complexity, because we must also understand the mechanisms—the neurotransmitters, receptors, pathways, enzymes, and so on. In other words, the causes of addiction, and of behavior in general, are many and complex. Finally, we must look beyond simple appeals to willpower in explaining the self-defeating behavior of the addict, just as we must do when we try to understand other kinds of behavior. Our brief look at addiction is a good preparation for our inquiries into the physiological systems behind other human behaviors and misbehaviors.

Take a Minute to Check Your Knowledge and Understanding

- How did the failure to recognize two types of alcoholism create misunderstandings about hereditary and environmental influences and gender distribution in alcoholism?
- How can lowered sensitivity to a drug increase the chances of addiction?
- What are two kinds of evidence that some people are predisposed to alcoholism from birth?

In Perspective

The costs of drug abuse include untold suffering; loss of health, productivity, and life; and billions of dollars in expenses for treatment and incarceration. The only upsides are that the study of drug abuse reveals the workings of the synapses and brain networks and helps us recognize that powerful biological forces are molding our behavior. This knowledge in turn helps us understand the behaviors that are the subject of the remaining chapters, including the disorders covered there, and guides research into developing therapeutic drugs.

CHAPTER SUMMARY

Psychoactive Drugs

- Most abused drugs produce addiction, which is usually (but not always) accompanied by withdrawal symptoms when drug use is stopped.
- Tolerance can increase the dangers of drugs because tolerance to life-threatening effects may not develop.
- The opiates have their own receptors, which are normally stimulated by endorphins.
- The opiates are particularly addictive and dangerous.
- Depressants reduce activity in the nervous system. Some of them have important uses, but they are also highly abused.
- Stimulants increase activity in the nervous system. They encompass the widest range of effects and include nicotine, most notable for its addictiveness and its association with deadly tobacco.
- Psychedelic drugs are interesting for their perceptual/hallucinatory effects, which result from their transmitter-like structures.
- Marijuana is controversial not just in terms of the issue of legalization but also because it raises questions about what constitutes addiction.

Addiction

- The mesolimbocortical dopamine system is implicated by several lines of research as a reward center that plays a role in drug addiction, feeding, sex, and other behaviors.
- Dopamine may also contribute to addiction through its role in learning by modifying neural functioning.
- Treatment of addiction is very difficult; effective programs combine psychological support with pharmacological strategies, including agonist, antagonist, and aversive treatments and, potentially, drug vaccines and genetic intervention.

The Role of Genes in Addiction

- Research suggests that addiction is partially hereditary and that the inherited vulnerability is not necessarily drug specific.
- Heredity research indicates that there are at least two kinds of alcoholism, with different genetic and environmental backgrounds.
- Alcoholics often have dopamine and serotonin irregularities that may account for the susceptibility, and some have a deficiency in evoked potentials that appears to be inherited.
- Addicts have transmitter and receptor irregularities and structural and functional brain anomalies that appear to be genetic in origin. ■

STUDY RESOURCES

FOR FURTHER THOUGHT

- Is the legality or illegality of a drug a good indication of its potential for abuse?
- Is it morally right to treat addictions with drug antagonists, aversive drugs, and antidrug vaccines? Is your opinion the same for drug agonists?

- You work for an agency that has the goal of substantially reducing the rate of drug abuse in your state through education, family support, and individualized treatment. Based on your knowledge of addiction, what elements should the program include?

TEST YOUR UNDERSTANDING

1. Describe the two proposed roles for dopamine in addiction and give two pieces of evidence for each.

2. What are the practical and ethical considerations in using drugs to treat addiction?

3. Sally and Sam have alcoholism. Sally seldom drinks but binges when she does and feels guilty later. Sam drinks regularly and feels no remorse. What other characteristics would you expect to see in each, and what speculations can you make about their environments?

Select the best answer:

1. In the study of conditioned tolerance to heroin,
   a. human subjects failed to show the usual withdrawal symptoms.
   b. human subjects increased their drug intake.
   c. rats were unresponsive to the drug.
   d. rats tolerated the drug less in a novel environment.

2. Withdrawal from alcohol
   a. can be life threatening.
   b. is about like a bad case of flu.
   c. is slightly milder than with most drugs.
   d. is usually barely noticeable.

3. Alcohol, barbiturates, and benzodiazepines are deadly when taken together because they
   a. affect the thalamus to produce almost total brain shutdown.
   b. have a cumulative effect on the periaqueductal gray.
   c. affect the same receptor complex.
   d. increase dopamine release to dangerous levels.

4. Psychedelic drugs often produce hallucinations by
   a. inhibiting serotonin neurons.
   b. stimulating serotonin receptors.
   c. stimulating dopamine receptors.
   d. blocking dopamine reuptake.

5. Marijuana was the subject of disagreement among researchers because some of them
   a. believed it is more dangerous than alcohol or tobacco.
   b. believed it is highly addictive.
   c. thought it failed to meet the standard test for addictiveness.
   d. overstated its withdrawal effects.

6. Evidence in the text that addiction does not depend on the drug's ability to produce withdrawal symptoms is that
   a. they never occur together with the same drug.
   b. they are produced in different parts of the brain.
   c. either can be produced without the other in the lab.
   d. addiction occurs in the cortex, but withdrawal occurs in the peripheral nervous system.

   e. the same addictive drug can cause withdrawal in some people, but not others.

7. When rats trained to press a lever for electrical stimulation of the brain are given a drug that blocks dopamine receptors, lever pressing
   a. increases.
   b. decreases.
   c. increases briefly and then decreases.
   d. remains the same.

8. The best argument that caffeine is an addictive drug like alcohol and nicotine is that
   a. it is used regularly by most of the population.
   b. users progressively increase their intake.
   c. it affects the same processes in the brain.
   d. it stimulates dopamine receptors directly.

9. The most obvious indication that learning and brain plasticity are involved in addiction is seen in
   a. activity increases in the prefrontal cortex.
   b. loss of synapses between the hippocampus and the nucleus accumbens.
   c. craving.
   d. withdrawal.

10. Agonist treatments for drug addiction
    a. mimic the drug's effect.
    b. block the drug's effect.
    c. make the person sick after taking the drug.
    d. reduce anxiety so that there is less need for the drug.

11. Critics of treating drug addiction with drugs believe that
    a. getting over addiction should not be easy.
    b. drugs like Antabuse are dangerous themselves.
    c. the drugs are not very effective and delay effective treatment.
    d. a and b
    e. b and c

12. The type of alcoholism in which the individual drinks regularly is associated with
    a. behavioral rigidity.
    b. perfectionism.
    c. feelings of guilt.
    d. antisocial personality disorder.

13. Alcoholics often
    a. have reduced serotonin and dopamine functioning.
    b. are more sensitive to the effects of alcohol.
    c. are unusually lethargic and use alcohol as a stimulant.
    d. have an inherited preference for the taste of alcohol.

1. d, 2. a, 3. c, 4. b, 5. c, 6. b, 7. b, 8. c, 9. c, 10. a, 11. a, 12. d, 13. a.

Answers:

ON THE WEB

The following websites are coordinated with this chapter's content. You can access these websites from the **SAGE edge Student Resources site**; select this chapter and then click on Web Resources. (**Bold** items are links.)

1. The National Institute on Drug Abuse's (NIDA) **Heroin** page is a good source for research and other information on heroin and its effects. Check **The Effects of Drugs on the Nervous System** at the Neuroscience for Kids site for information on more than a dozen drugs.

2. The **Alcoholics Anonymous** site has information about AA, testimonials from members, and a quiz for teenagers (or anybody else) to help them decide if they have a drinking problem.

3. **Cocaine Anonymous** offers news, information, a self-test for addiction, and a directory of local groups.

4. NIDA's **Tobacco/Nicotine** page provides facts, publications, and links to other sites.

5. NIDA also has information on **LSD, Ecstasy,** and **PCP. "Travels in the New Psychedelic Bazaar"** addresses the history of synthetic psychedelics and the dangers they pose.

6. There's even a **Marijuana Anonymous**, and its site offers a variety of publications for the person who wants to stop using marijuana or for the student who wants to learn more. Of course, NIDA has its **Marijuana** page, too. And ProCon.org's **Medical Marijuana** page has arguments for and against the medical use of marijuana, along with discussions of legal issues and marijuana's use with each of 16 different diseases. See how **attitudes toward legalization of marijuana** have changed, and a list of 14 **states most likely to decriminalize use** next.

7. The **Web of Addictions** provides fact sheets, links to a variety of other information sites, contact information for support organizations and other organizations concerned with drug problems, and in-depth reports on special topics.

8. The **Substance Abuse and Mental Health Services Administration** website has a broad range of information for the general public and for professionals. The **NIDA** site provides news; research information; and information on prevention for parents, teachers, and students.

FOR FURTHER READING

1. Often used as a text in psychopharmacology and upper-level behavioral neuroscience courses, *Julien's Primer of Drug Action*, by Claire Advokat, Joseph Comaty, and Robert Julien (13th ed., Worth, 2014), covers principles of drug action, properties of specific drugs, pharmacotherapy for various disorders, and societal issues. It is a #1 best seller in Medicine and Psychology at Amazon, where it receives good reviews from students.

2. *Buzzed: The Straight Facts About the Most Used and Abused Drugs From Alcohol to Ecstasy*, by Cynthia Kuhn and Scott Swartzwelder (4th ed., Norton, 2014), gives technical information about drugs written in a style appropriate for college students. It covers drug characteristics, histories of the drugs, addiction, the workings of the brain, and legal issues.

3. *Dreamland: The True Tale of America's Opiate Epidemic*, by Sam Quinones (Bloomsbury, 2016), has received numerous awards, including the National Book Critics Award, for its account of the origins of the country's opiate crisis.

KEY TERMS

addiction 118
agonist treatment 133
alcohol 119
amphetamine 125
analgesic 118
antagonist treatment 134
antidrug vaccine 134
anxiolytic 119
aversive treatment 134
barbiturate 122
bath salts 125
benzodiazepine 123
caffeine 126
cannabinoids 128
cocaine 123

delirium tremens 121
depressant 119
drug 117
electrical stimulation of the brain (ESB) 130
endogenous 119
endorphins 119
euphoria 118
heroin 118
hypnotic 118
marijuana 128
mesocortical pathway 131
mesolimbic pathway 130
mesolimbocortical dopamine system 131

methadone 133
methylation 138
nicotine 125
nucleus accumbens 130
opiate 118
psychedelic drug 126
psychoactive drug 118
reward 130
sedative 119
stimulant 123
tolerance 118
ventral tegmental area 130
withdrawal 118

edge.sagepub.com/garrett5e

SAGE edge offers a robust online environment featuring an impressive array of free tools and resources for review, study, and further exploration, keeping both instructors and students on the cutting edge of teaching and learning.

5.1	Identify the main classes of drugs.	▶ Classes of Psychoactive Drugs
5.2	Describe the effects of each class of drugs on the nervous system.	▶ The Truth About Bath Salts
5.3	Predict how different drugs will impact behavior, based on the neural systems on which those drugs act.	▶ The Chemistry of Addiction
5.4	Illustrate how the brain changes during addiction.	▶ Why Bad Habits Are Hard to Break
5.5	Discuss the role of learning in overdose and addiction.	▶ Drug Addiction as a Learning Disorder
5.6	Explain how pharmacology can be used to treat addiction.	▶ An Evidence-Based View of Addiction and Drug Policy
5.7	Contrast the environmental and hereditary influences on addiction.	🔊 How We Think About Addiction 📄 Reefer Madness to Marijuana Legalization

PRACTICE AND APPLY WHAT YOU'VE LEARNED

▶ **edge.sagepub.com/garrett5e**

HEAD TO THE STUDY SITE WHERE YOU'LL FIND

- **eFlashcards to strengthen your understanding of key terms**

- **Practice quizzes to test your comprehension of key concepts**

- **Videos and multimedia content to enhance your exploration of key topics**

Motivation and the Regulation of Internal States

6

After reading this chapter, you will be able to:

- Summarize the psychological theories of motivation.

- Describe how temperature regulation and thirst reflect the concept of homeostasis.

- Explain the role of taste in choices of food.

- Identify the brain signals that control when we begin and end eating.

- Compare the roles of environment and heredity in risk for obesity.

- Examine how the environment and genetics impact risk for disordered eating.

- Discuss the role of neurotransmitters in eating disorders.

Master the content.
edge.sagepub.com/garrett5e

When Christopher was born, it was obvious there was something wrong (Lyons, 2001). He was a "floppy baby," lying with his arms and legs splayed lifelessly on the bed, and he didn't cry. Doctors thought he might never walk or talk, but he seemed to progress all right until grade school, when he was diagnosed with Prader-Willi syndrome. The disorder occurs when a small section of the father's chromosome 15 fails to transfer during fertilization. The exact contribution of those genes is not known, but the symptoms are clearly defined, and Christopher had most of them. He stopped growing at 5 feet, 3 inches (1.6 meters), he had learning difficulties, and he had difficulty with impulse control.

More obviously, Christopher could never seem to recognize when he had eaten enough, so he ate constantly. He even stole his brother's paper-route money to buy snacks at the corner store. At school, he would retrieve food from the cafeteria garbage can and wolf it down; his classmates would taunt him by throwing a piece of food in the trash to watch him dive for it. The only way to protect a person like Christopher is to manage his life completely, from locking the kitchen to institutionalization. State law did not permit institutionalization for Christopher, because his average-level IQ did not fit the criterion for inability to manage his affairs. He lived in a series of group homes but was thrown out of

I can stuff my face for a long time and I won't feel full.

—Christopher Theros

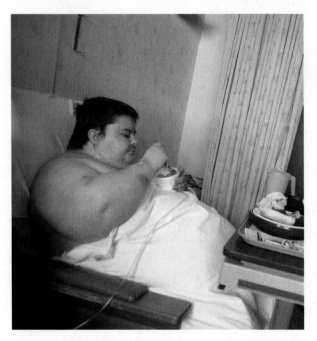

FIGURE 6.1   Christopher During a Hospital Stay.

Source: Courtesy of the *San Luis Obispo County Tribune*.

each one for rebelliousness and violence, behaviors that are characteristic of the disorder. When he died at the age of 28, he weighed 500 pounds (227 kg; Figure 6.1).

In Chapter 5, we puzzled over why people continue to take drugs that are obviously harming them. Now we are forced to wonder why a person would be so out of control that he would literally eat himself to death. When we ask why people (and animals) do what they do, we are asking about their motivation.

Motivation and Homeostasis

Motivation, which literally means "to set in motion," refers to the set of factors that initiate, sustain, and direct behaviors. The need for the concept was prompted by psychologists' inability to explain behavior solely in terms of outside stimuli. Assuming various kinds of motivation, such as hunger or achievement need, helped make sense of differing responses to the same environmental conditions.

Keep in mind, though, that *motivation is a concept psychologists have invented and imposed on behavior.* We should not expect to find a single "motivation center" in the brain or even a network whose primary function is motivation. The fact that we sometimes cannot distinguish motivation from other aspects of behavior, like emotion, is evidence of how arbitrary the term can be. Still, it is a useful concept for organizing ideas about the sources of behavior.

After a brief overview of some of the ways psychologists have approached the problem of motivation, we will take a closer look at temperature regulation, thirst, and hunger as examples before taking up the topics of sexual behavior in Chapter 7 and emotion and aggression in Chapter 8.

Theoretical Approaches to Motivation

Greeks relied heavily on the concept of instinct in their attempts to explain human behavior. An *instinct* is a complex behavior that is automatic, unlearned, and unmodifiable, and occurs in all the members of a species (Birney & Teevan, 1961). Migration and parental behavior are good examples of instinctive behaviors in animals. According to early instinct theorists, humans were guided by instincts, too, waging war because of an aggressive instinct, caring for their young because of a parental instinct, and so on. At first blush, these explanations sound meaningful. But if we say that a person is combative because of an aggressive instinct, we know little more about what makes the person fight than we did before; if we cannot then analyze the supposed aggressive instinct, we have simply dodged the explanation. Contemporary students of behavior have used stringent requirements of evidence to identify a few instincts in animals, such as homing and flight in birds. But most psychologists believe that, in human evolution, instincts have been for the most part replaced by learned behaviors.

Several theories have been proposed as a replacement to instinct. The first, drive theory, deals with motivation in terms of needs arising from physical conditions such as hunger, thirst, and body temperature. According to *drive theory,* the body maintains a condition of *homeostasis,* in which any particular system is in balance or equilibrium (C. L. Hull, 1951). Any departure from homeostasis, such as depletion of nutrients or a drop in temperature, produces an aroused condition, or *drive,* which impels the individual to engage in appropriate action such as eating, drinking, or seeking warmth. *Incentive theory* recognizes that people are motivated by external stimuli, not just internal needs (Bolles, 1975). Incentives can meet a biological need (such as food, clothing, or mates) or can be things that are valuable to the individual (such as money or good grades). According to the theory, motivation is mostly geared toward seeking and acquiring external rewards, or incentives. Then again, sometimes we do things without either an obvious drive or an incentive. The first author's wife once jumped out of an airplane for the thrill of plummeting toward the earth, only to be saved at the last minute by a flimsy parachute. Observations like this have led to the *arousal theory,* which states that people behave in ways that keep them at their preferred level of stimulation (Fiske & Maddi, 1961). Different people have different optimum levels of arousal, and some seem to have a need for varied experiences or the thrill of confronting danger (Zuckerman, 1971). This *sensation seeking* finds expression in anything from travel and unconventional dress to skydiving,

? What do homeostasis and drive mean?

drug use, risky behaviors, violence, and eating *fugu* (see Chapter 2). Both of these theories share a common neural mechanism of increased release of dopamine in the brain, which can result in addiction (see Chapter 5).

In the face of challenges to drive theory, psychologists have shifted their emphasis to drives as states of the brain rather than as conditions of the tissues (Stellar & Stellar, 1985). This approach nicely accommodates sexual behavior, which troubled drive theorists because it does not involve a tissue deficit. Even eating behavior is better understood as the result of a brain state. Hunger ordinarily occurs when a lack of nutrients in the body triggers activity in the brain. However, an incentive like the smell of a steak on the grill can also cause hunger, apparently by activating the same brain mechanisms that tissue deficits do. In addition, the person feels satisfied and stops eating long before the nutrients have reached the deficient body cells. Similarly, if the brain is not "satisfied," it little matters how much the person has eaten. In other words, if the information that reserves are excessive fails to reach the brain or to have its usual effect there, the person may, like Christopher, eat to obesity and still feel hungry. In the following pages, we will look at the regulation of body temperature, fluid levels, and energy supply from the perspective of drive and homeostasis.

Simple Homeostatic Drives

To sustain life, a number of conditions, such as body temperature, fluid levels, and energy reserves, must be held within a fairly narrow range. Accomplishing that requires a *control system.* A mechanical control system that serves as a good analogy is a home heating and cooling system. Control systems have a *set point,* which is the point of homeostasis (or equilibrium) to which the system returns. For the heating and cooling system, the set point is the temperature selected on the thermostat. The result of a departure in the room temperature from the set point is analogous to a drive; the thermostat initiates an action, turning on the furnace or the air conditioner. Larger deviations from the system's set point trigger stronger drives to return to it. When the room temperature returns to the preset range, the system is "satisfied" in the technical sense of the word; homeostasis has been achieved, so the system goes into a neutral state until there is another departure from the set point.

Temperature Regulation

Not only is the regulation of body temperature superficially similar to our thermostat analogy; it is almost as simple. All animals have to maintain internal temperature within certain limits to survive, and they operate more effectively within an even narrower range; this is their set point. How they respond to departures from homeostasis is much more variable than with the home heating and cooling system, however. *Ectothermic* animals, such as snakes and lizards, are unable to regulate their body temperature internally, so they adjust their temperature behaviorally by sunning themselves, finding shade, burrowing in the ground, and so on. *Endothermic* animals, which include mammals and birds, use some of the same strategies, such as building nests or houses, moving to warmer or cooler areas, and wearing clothing. However, endotherms are also able to use their energy reserves to maintain a nearly constant body temperature automatically. In hot weather, their temperature regulatory system reduces body heat by causing sweating, reduced metabolism, and dilation of peripheral blood vessels. In cold weather, it induces shivering, increased metabolism, and constriction of the peripheral blood vessels. To say that we make these adjustments because we *feel* hot or cold suggests that the responses are intentional behaviors, but, of course, that is not the case. So how do these behaviors occur?

In mammals, the major "thermostat" is located in the *preoptic area* of the hypothalamus, which contains separate warmth-sensitive and cold-sensitive cells (Figure 6.2; Nakashima, Pierau, Simon, & Hori, 1987). Some of these neurons respond directly to the temperature of the blood flowing through the area; others receive input from temperature receptors in other parts of the body, including the skin. The preoptic area integrates information from these two sources and initiates temperature regulatory responses, such as panting, sweating, shivering, increasing or decreasing blood flow to the extremities, and building winter fat reserves as insulation against the cold (for a summary, see Morrison, 2016). We will be talking about several nuclei in the hypothalamus in this chapter, so you may want to refer to Figure 6.2 often.

? How is body temperature regulated?

Thirst

The body is about 70% water, so it seems obvious that maintaining water balance is critical to life. Water is needed to maintain the cells of the body, to keep the blood flowing through the veins and arteries, to transport nutrients, and to dispose of waste. You can live for weeks without eating but for only a few days without water, in part because of the constant loss through evaporation, urination, and defecation. The design of your nose, which could have been just a pair of nostrils on your face, is testimonial to the body's efforts to conserve water. As you breathe, you exhale valuable moisture; but as your breath passes through the much cooler blood-rich passages of your nose, some of the moisture condenses and is reabsorbed. The next time you get a sinus cold that interferes with water absorption, you will be surprised by how much water your runny nose isn't recycling.

■ **FIGURE 6.2**   Selected Nuclei of the Hypothalamus.

The illustration shows only the right hypothalamus. The hypothalamus is a bilaterally symmetrical structure, which means that the left and right halves (separated by the third ventricle) are duplicates of each other. (The pituitary, and optic chiasm have been identified for use as landmarks.)

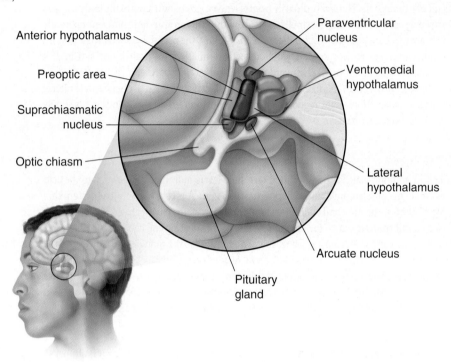

Source: Nieuwenhuys, R., Voogd, J., & vanHuijzen, C. (1988). *The human central nervous system* (3rd Rev. ed.). Berlin, Germany: Springer-Verlag.

? How does the body regulate its water reserves?

It is also obvious that you drink when your mouth and throat feel dry, but at most a dry mouth and throat determine only *when* you drink, not *how much* you drink. There are two types of thirst generated by a drop in water content, one from inside the body's cells (*osmotic*) and the other from the blood (*hypovolemic*). Drinking remedies both kinds of deficits, but the fluid levels in the two compartments vary independently and so the brain manages them separately. *Osmotic thirst* occurs when the fluid content decreases inside the body's cells. If you eat a salty meal, the excess blood solutes (salt and other dissolved substances) contrast with the lower solutes inside the cells. Since water flows freely across cell membranes, but solutes do not, water corrects this osmotic difference by leaving the cells and flowing into the bloodstream. *Hypovolemic thirst* occurs when the blood volume drops due to a loss of extracellular water. This can be due to breathing, sweating, vomiting, urination, defecation, or a loss of blood. That is why you might feel thirsty after donating blood, exercising, or spending a few hours at the beach. (For relative amounts of water loss at rest versus exercise, see Tam & Noakes, 2013, for a review.)

The reduced water content of cells that contributes to osmotic thirst is detected primarily in areas bordering the third ventricle, particularly in the *organum vasculosum lamina terminalis (OVLT*; Figure 6.3). Injecting saline (salt solution) into the bloodstream draws water out of the cells and induces drinking, but this effect is dramatically reduced when the OVLT is damaged (Thrasher & Keil, 1987). This is because the OVLT communicates the osmotic loss to the *median preoptic nucleus* of the hypothalamus, which triggers thirst.

Hypovolemia is detected by pressure receptors (baroreceptors) located where the large veins connect to the left and right atria of the heart; these receptors increase activity when blood pressure rises and decrease when blood pressure falls (Fitzsimons & Moore-Gillon, 1980). Information about the reduced blood volume that accompanies hypovolemia is conveyed by the vagus nerve to the *nucleus of the solitary tract (NST)* in the medulla. From there, the signal goes to the median preoptic nucleus of the hypothalamus (Figure 6.3; Stricker & Sved, 2000).

Lowered blood volume is also detected by kidney receptors, which trigger the release of the hormone renin. Renin then increases production of the hormone angiotensin II in the bloodstream. *Angiotensin II* informs the brain of the drop in blood volume. It stimulates the *subfornical organ (SFO),* a structure bordering the third

■ FIGURE 6.3   Thirst Control Signals and Brain Centers.

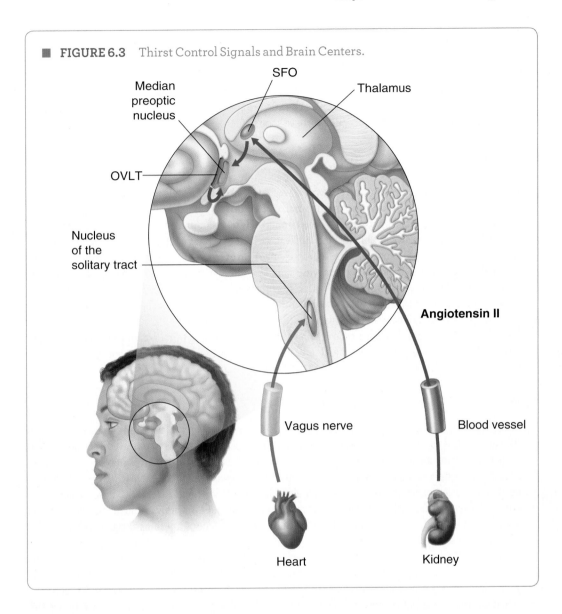

ventricle and one of the few areas not protected by the blood-brain barrier (see Figure 6.3). Again, thirst is induced by the nearby median preoptic nucleus (Fitzsimons, 1998; Stricker & Sved, 2000). Injecting angiotensin into the SFO increases drinking; lesioning the SFO blocks this effect but has no effect on thirst in response to osmotic thirst (J. B. Simpson, Epstein, & Camardo, 1978).

So far we've been talking about what *initiates* drinking; we still must ask how we know when to *stop* drinking. Based on what you've just learned, you might think that we stop drinking when the deficit is eliminated and the initiating signals subside. However, that takes 10 to 20 minutes to occur; if we continued to drink until the cellular need was satisfied, we'd be in danger of water intoxication, which would mean headache, confusion, alterations in behavior and personality, and possibly death. So how do we explain *satiety,* the satisfaction of appetite? Like humans, dogs drink an amount of water according to their cellular need and then stop (reviewed in G. Fink, Pfaff, & Levine, 2012). They will continue to drink this way even when a tube in the stomach allows the water to drain out as quickly as it is ingested, so we can rule out the intestines as the source of the stop signal. Injecting water directly into the stomach doesn't inhibit drinking, so the stomach isn't involved, either. Researchers concluded that the act of drinking somehow signals the brain about the intake of water; recent studies with mice revealed what that neural mechanism is (Zimmerman et al., 2016). The SFO not only assesses the fluid levels of the body but also anticipates the consequences of a water meal on those water reserves. Drinking inhibits thirst-activating neurons in the SFO, with activity beginning to decline with the very first lick of water. Cool water is more effective than warm water; salty water inhibits the SFO as much as pure water, but this is reversed about a minute later as receptors detect the water's concentration.

Take a Minute to Check Your Knowledge and Understanding

- How do temperature regulation and thirst qualify as homeostatic drives?
- Receptors are able to do their jobs because they are specialized for specific types of stimuli. What are the specializations of the receptors we have seen so far?

Hunger: A Complex Drive

Although hunger can be described in terms of drive and homeostasis just like temperature regulation and thirst, the differences almost overshadow the similarities. Hunger is more complicated in a variety of ways. Eating provides energy for activity, fuel for maintaining body temperature, and materials needed for growth and repair of the tissues. In addition, the set point is so variable that you might think there is none. This is not surprising, because the demands on our resources change with exercise, stress, growth, and so on. A changing set point is not unique to hunger, of course. For example, our temperature set point changes daily, decreasing during our normal sleep period (even if we fly to Europe and are awake during normal sleep time). It also increases during illness to produce a fever to kill invading bacteria. What is unusual about hunger is that the set point can undergo dramatic and prolonged shifts, for instance, in obesity.

Another difference is that the needs in temperature regulation and thirst are unitary, whereas hunger involves the need for a variety of different and specific kinds of nutrients. Making choices about what foods to eat can be more difficult than knowing when to eat and when to stop eating.

"
You are what you eat.

—popular adage
"

Gustation: The Role of Taste

Selecting the right foods is no problem for some animals. Some *herbivores* (plant-eating animals) can get all the nutrients they need from a single source; koalas, for instance, eat only eucalyptus leaves, and giant pandas eat nothing but the shoots of the bamboo plant. *Carnivores* (meat eaters) also have it rather easy; they achieve a balanced diet because their prey eats a balanced diet. We are *omnivores;* we are able to get the nutrients we need from a variety of plants and animals. Being able to eat almost anything is liberating but simultaneously a burden: We must distinguish among foods that may be nutritious, non-nutritious, or toxic, and we must vary our diet among several sources to meet all our nutritional requirements. Choosing the right foods and in the right amounts can be a real challenge.

It is possible that you plan your diet around nutritional guidelines, but probably you rely more on what you learned at the family table about which foods and what combinations of foods make an "appropriate" meal in your culture. Have you ever wondered where these traditions came from, or why they survive when each new generation seems to delight in defying society's other customs? Long before humans understood the need for vitamins, minerals, proteins, and carbohydrates, your ancestors were using a "wisdom of the body" to choose a reasonably balanced diet that ensured their survival and your existence. That wisdom is reflected in cultural food traditions, which usually provide a balanced diet (Rozin, 1976), sometimes by dictating unattractive (to us) choices such as grub worms or cow's blood. As you will see, the internal forces that guide our selection of a balanced diet are more automatic than the term *choice* usually suggests, but they are also subtle and easily overcome by the allure of modern processed foods, which emphasize taste over nutrition.

The simplest form of dietary selection involves distinguishing between foods that are safe and nutritious and those that are either useless or dangerous. This is where the sense of taste comes in. In humans, all taste experience is the result of just five taste sensations: sour, sweet, bitter, salty, and the more recently discovered umami (Kurihara & Kashiwayanagi, 1998). The first four need no explanation; umami is often described as "meaty" or "savory." These five sensations are called *primaries;* more complex taste sensations are made up of combinations of the primaries. There may be other taste primaries; recent research, for example, has found evidence that we can distinguish the taste of starches (Lapis, Penner, & Lim, 2016) and fats (Besnard, Passilly-Degrace, & Khan, 2016).

It is easy to see why we have evolved taste receptors with these particular sensitivities, because they correspond closely to our dietary needs. We will readily eat foods that are sweet, which include fruits and carbohydrates. We also prefer foods that are a bit salty; salt provides the sodium and chloride ions needed for cellular functioning and for neural transmission. Mountain gorillas get 95% of their sodium by eating decaying wood—while avoiding similar wood with lower sodium content (Rothman, Van Soest, & Pell, 2006). Umami receptors aid in our selection of proteins. One type responds to amino acids, and two respond to glutamate (Chaudhari, Pereira, & Roper, 2009), which is found in meats, cheese, and soy products (as well as in the flavor enhancer monosodium glutamate). Just as we are attracted to useful foods by taste, we avoid others. Overly sour foods are likely to be spoiled, and bitter foods are likely to be toxic. You do not have to understand these relationships, much less think about them; they operate quietly, in the neural background.

Taste receptors are located on taste buds, which in turn are found on the surface of papillae; papillae are small bumps on the tongue and elsewhere in the mouth (Figure 6.4). Taste neurons travel through the thalamus to the *insula,* the primary gustatory (taste) area in the frontal lobes. But on their way, they pass through the NST in the medulla, which we saw in Figure 6.3 in relation to drinking and will soon see plays an important role in feeding behavior. Back in Chapter 2, you saw research indicating that taste neurons encode different taste stimuli in unique time patterns of impulses, but there is another, more important, way the system informs the brain of what we are tasting. Each of the primary taste stimuli is detected by receptors that are specialized for that stimulus; information from the different receptors travels to the brain via separate pathways to distinct areas in the insular cortex (Figure 6.5; X. Chen, Gabitto, Peng, Ryba, & Zuker, 2011; Schoenfeld et al., 2004). You will see in later chapters that other sensory systems exploit this *labeled line* coding of stimuli and that the brain combines primary sensations into more complex sensory experiences.

Besides the nutritional and safety benefits we have already mentioned, the taste sense contributes to dietary selection in three additional ways: sensory-specific satiety, learned taste aversion, and learned taste preferences.

Sensory-Specific Satiety: Varying the Choices

When Bob Garrett was a youngster, a neighbor child joined the family for lunch. At the end of the meal, she enjoyed a bowl of homemade apple cobbler, then another, and another. Halfway through the third serving, she observed in puzzlement that the last serving wasn't nearly as good as the first. Barbara and Edmund Rolls call this experience sensory-specific satiety. *Sensory-specific satiety* means that the more of a particular food an individual eats, the less appealing the food becomes. Humans rate a food less favorably after they have consumed it, and they eat more if they are offered a variety of foods instead of a single food (Rolls, Rolls, Rowe, & Sweeney, 1981).

The effect sounds trivial, but it is not; sensory-specific satiety is the brain's way of encouraging you to vary your food choices, which is necessary for a balanced diet. Back in the 1920s, Clara Davis (1928) allowed three newly weaned infants to choose all their meals from a tray of about 20 healthy foods. They usually selected only two or three foods at one meal and continued choosing the same foods for about a week. Then they would switch to another two or three foods for a similar period. Their self-selected diet was adequate to prevent any deficiencies from developing over a period of six months. By the way, the "taste map" you've almost certainly seen suggesting that different tastes are detected at different locations on the tongue is a myth. It resulted from Harvard psychologist Edward G. Boring's misinterpretation of a 1901 German study that then became a part of scientific folklore.

Sensory-specific satiety takes place in the NST. Place a little glucose (one of the sugars) on a rat's tongue, and it produces a neural response there. But if glucose is injected into the rat's bloodstream first, sugar placed on the tongue has less effect in the NST (Giza, Scott, & Vanderweele, 1992). The brain automatically motivates the rat—or you—to switch to a new flavor and a different nutrient.

Learned Taste Aversion: Avoiding Dangerous Foods

Learned taste aversion, the avoidance of foods associated with illness or poor nutrition, was discovered when researchers were studying bait shyness in rats. Farmers know that if they put out poisoned bait in the barn, they will kill a few rats at first but the surviving rats will soon start avoiding the bait

? In what ways does taste contribute to selection of a proper diet?

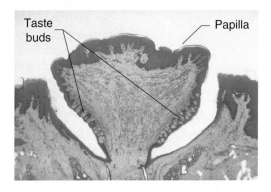

■ FIGURE 6.4   A Microscopic Photo of a Papilla With Taste Buds.

Source: © Southern Illinois University/Science Source.

■ FIGURE 6.5   Localization of Taste Responses in the Cortex.

The color-coded areas on this fMRI scan indicate where the insular cortex was activated as the subject tasted various liquids. The locations differed among subjects but were consistent over time for each subject. The location of the insular cortex is shown in the lower image.

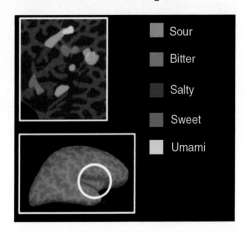

Source: From "Functional Magnetic Resonance Tomography Correlates of Taste Perception in the Human Primary Taste Cortex," by M. A. Schoenfeld et al., 2004, *Neuroscience,* 127, pp. 347–353. Used with permission from Elsevier.

(thus the term *bait shyness*). Rats eat small amounts of a new food; a poison will more likely make them ill instead of killing them, and they will avoid that food in the future. Learned aversion is studied in the laboratory by giving rats a specific food and then making them nauseous with a chemical like lithium chloride or with a dose of X-ray radiation. Later they refuse to eat that food.

Learned taste aversion helps wild animals and primitive-living humans avoid dangerous foods (see the accompanying Application). Modern-living humans experience learned taste aversions, too. In a study of people with strong aversions to particular foods, 89% could remember getting sick after eating the food, most often between the ages of 6 and 12 (Garb & Stunkard, 1974). However, in civilized settings, learned aversions have little value in identifying dangerous foods. Instead, we usually get sick following a meal because we left the food out of the refrigerator too long or because we happened to come down with stomach flu. Learned taste aversion appears to be one reason chemotherapy patients lose their appetite. Among children who were given a uniquely flavored ice cream before a chemo session, 79% later refused that flavor, compared with 33% of children receiving chemotherapy without the ice cream; the effect was just as strong four months later (I. L. Bernstein, 1978).

Learned taste aversion may not be very useful to modern humans for avoiding dangerous foods, but it may help us avoid non-nutritious ones. When rats are fed a diet that is deficient in a particular nutrient, such as thiamine (vitamin B), they start showing an aversion to their food; they eat less of it, and they spill the food from its container in spite of indications they are hungry, like chewing on the wire sides of their cage (Rozin, 1967). Even after recovery from the deficit, the rats prefer to go hungry rather than eat the previously deficient food. But aversion to a nutrient-deficient food is just the first step toward selecting a nutritious diet.

Learned Taste Preferences: Selecting Nutritious Foods

Although rats, and presumably humans, can detect salt, sugars, and fat directly by their taste (A. T. Beck & Galef, 1989), they must *learn* to select the foods containing other necessary nutrients. This apparently requires the development of a *learned taste preference,* which is a preference not for the nutrient itself but for the flavor of a food that contains the nutrient. In an early study, rats were fed a diet deficient in one of three vitamins (thiamine, riboflavin, or pyridoxine); later they learned to prefer a food enriched with that vitamin,

APPLICATION
Predator Control Through Learned Taste Aversion

Source: © Janet Haas/Rainbow.

The principles of classical conditioning and learned taste aversion have been put to practical use in an unlikely context: predator control. As a novel and humane (compared with extermination)

means of controlling the frequency of wolves and coyotes killing sheep, Carl Gustavson and colleagues fed captive predators sheep carcasses laced with lithium chloride (see the photo), which made them sick. When they were placed in a pen with sheep, the wolves and coyotes then avoided the sheep instead of attacking them. One coyote threw up just from smelling a lamb, and two hesitant wolves were chased away by a lamb that turned on them (Gustavson, Garcia, Hankins, & Rusiniak, 1974; Gustavson, Kelly, Sweeney, & Garcia, 1976). In a three-year study on 10 ranches in Saskatchewan, coyote predation of sheep decreased 87% (Gustavson, Jowsey, & Milligan, 1982). These interventions also have benefits for conservation efforts since other endangered species (e.g., California condors, black-footed ferrets) are spared the traditional uses of traps and poisons that are intended for predators but sometimes kill other animals.

which was flavored distinctively by adding anise (which tastes like licorice). When the anise was switched to the vitamin-deficient food, the rats began eating that food instead (E. M. Scott & Verney, 1947). This type of learning requires pairing of a taste with some benefit, such as recovery from a dietary deficiency, and usually requires constant pairing over a period of several days (T. R. Scott, 2011). A diet-deficient rat enhances its chances of learning which foods are beneficial by eating a single food at a time (Rozin, 1969). (Notice how similar this is to the sampling behavior of Davis's infants who were allowed to choose their own food.)

How much humans are able to make use of these abilities is unclear; certainly we often choose an unhealthy diet over a healthy one. These bad selections may not be due so much to a lack of *ability* to make good choices as they are to the distraction of tasty, high-calorie foods that are not found in nature. Even rats have trouble selecting the foods that are good for them when the competing foods are flavored with cinnamon or cocoa (A. T. Beck & Galef, 1989), and they become obese when they are offered human junk food (Rolls, Rowe, & Turner, 1980). Wisdom of the body is inadequate in the face of the temptation of French fries and ice cream.

Now a caveat: You have most likely read that taste is largely a matter of smell, and perhaps even tested the idea by holding your nose while tasting familiar foods. In this context, it is important to distinguish between *taste,* which is the experience you get from your taste receptors, and *flavor,* which depends on a combination of taste and smell. Smell does have a significant effect; how much depends on the specific food and, to our knowledge, has never actually been quantified (in spite of authoritative-sounding statements to the contrary). We will take up the topic of the sense of smell in Chapter 7.

Digestion and the Two Phases of Metabolism

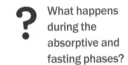

What happens during the absorptive and fasting phases?

Here we confront the inadequacy in our thermostat analogy again. To maintain consistent temperature, the thermostat calls on the furnace to cycle on and off frequently. Some species of animals do behave like the home furnace; they have to eat steadily, with only brief pauses, to provide the constant supply of nutrients the body needs. Humans do not; we eat a few discrete meals and fast in between. Eating discrete meals leaves us free to do other things with our time, but it requires a complex system for storing nutrient reserves, allocating the reserves during the fasting periods, and monitoring the reserves to determine the timing and size of the next meal.

The Digestive Process

Digestion begins in the mouth, where food is ground fine and mixed with saliva. Saliva provides lubrication and contains an enzyme that starts the breakdown of food. Digestion proceeds in the stomach as food is mixed with the gastric juices *hydrochloric acid* and *pepsin.* The partially processed food is then released gradually so that the small intestine has time to do its job. (Figure 6.6 shows the organs of the digestive system.)

The stomach provides another opportunity for screening toxic or spoiled food that gets past the taste test. If the food irritates the stomach lining sufficiently, the stomach responds by regurgitating the meal. Some toxins don't irritate the stomach, and they make their way into the bloodstream. If so, a part of the brain often takes care of this problem; the *area postrema* is one of the places in the brain that is outside the blood-brain barrier, so toxins can activate it to induce vomiting. The result can be surprisingly forceful; projectile vomiting usually means that you've got hold of something really bad. On the other hand, college students have been known to incorporate this adaptive response into a drinking game called "boot tag," the details of which I will leave to your imagination.

Digestion occurs primarily in the small intestine, particularly the initial 25 cm of the small intestine called the *duodenum.* There food is broken down into usable forms. Carbohydrates are metabolized into simple sugars, particularly *glucose.* Proteins are converted to *amino acids.* Fats are transformed into *fatty acids* and

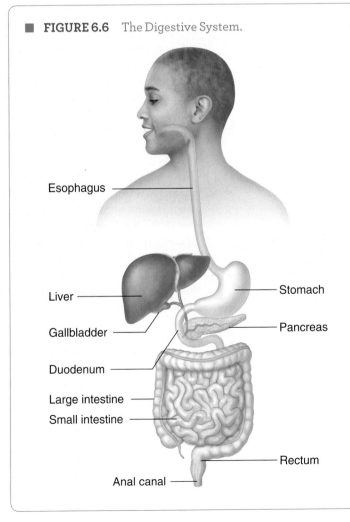

■ **FIGURE 6.6**   The Digestive System.

Esophagus

Liver

Gallbladder

Duodenum

Large intestine

Small intestine

Stomach

Pancreas

Rectum

Anal canal

■ **FIGURE 6.7**   Summary of the Absorptive and Fasting Phases.

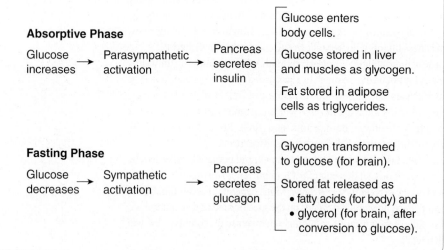

glycerol, either in the intestine or in the liver. The products of digestion are absorbed through the intestinal wall into the blood and transported to the liver via the *hepatic portal vein.* Digestion requires the food to be in a semiliquid mix, and the body can ill afford to give up the fluid; the large intestine's primary job is absorbing the excess water.

This process is under the control of the autonomic nervous system, so digestion is affected by stress or excitement, as you probably well know. If too much acid is secreted into the stomach, you'll take your course exam with an upset stomach. If food moves too slowly through the system, constipation will be the result. Too fast, and there isn't time to remove the excess water, so you may be asking to leave the room in the middle of your exam to go to the bathroom. Because diarrhea causes the body to lose water, you may have to drink more liquids to avoid dehydration. You also lose electrolytes, compounds that provide the ions your neurons and other cells need, which is why your doctor may recommend a sports drink as the replacement liquid.

The Absorptive Phase

The feeding cycle is divided into two phases, the absorptive phase and the fasting phase. For a few hours following a meal, the body lives off the nutrients arriving from the digestive system; this period is called the *absorptive phase.* Following a meal, the blood level of glucose, our primary source of energy, rises. The brain detects the increased glucose and shifts the autonomic system from predominantly sympathetic activation to predominantly parasympathetic activity. As a result, the pancreas starts secreting *insulin, a* hormone that enables body cells to take up glucose for energy and certain cells to store excess nutrients. (Actually, because of conditioning, just the sight and smell of food is enough to trigger insulin secretion, increased salivation, and release of digestive fluids into the stomach. Remember the incentive theory?)

The cells contain *insulin receptors,* which activate transporters that carry glucose into the cells. *Diabetes* results when the pancreas is unable to produce enough insulin (type 1 diabetes) or the body's tissues are relatively unresponsive to insulin (type 2 diabetes). The diabetic's blood contains plenty of glucose following a meal, but due to insulin resistance, the cells of the body are unable to make use of it and the diabetic is chronically hungry.

During the absorptive phase, the body is also busy storing some of the nutrients as a hedge against the upcoming period of fasting. Some of the glucose is converted into *glycogen* and stored in a short-term reservoir in the liver and surrounding the muscles. Any remaining glucose is converted into fats and stored in fat cells, also known as *adipose tissue.* Fats arriving directly from the digestive system are stored there as well. Storage of both glucose and fat is under the control of insulin. After a small proportion of amino acids is used to construct proteins and peptides needed by the body, the rest is converted to fats and stored.

The Fasting Phase

Eventually the glucose level in the blood drops. Now the body must fall back on its energy stores, which is why this is called the *fasting phase.* The autonomic system shifts to sympathetic activity. The pancreas ceases secretion of insulin and starts secreting the hormone *glucagon,* which causes the liver to transform stored glycogen back into glucose. Because the insulin level is low now, this glucose is available only to the nervous system. To meet the rest of the body's needs, glucagon triggers the breakdown of stored fat into fatty acids and glycerol. The fatty acids are used by the muscles and organs, while the liver converts glycerol to more glucose for the brain. During starvation, muscle proteins can be broken down again into amino acids, which are converted into glucose by the liver. The two phases of metabolism are summarized in Figure 6.7.

The oscillations of eating and fasting and the shifts in metabolism that accompany them are orchestrated for the most part by two particularly important areas in the hypothalamus. The *lateral hypothalamus* initiates eating and controls several aspects of feeding behavior as well as metabolic responses. It controls chewing and swallowing through its brainstem connections; salivation, acid secretion, and insulin production through autonomic pathways in the medulla and spinal cord; and cortical arousal, which likely increases locomotion and the possibility of encountering food (Currie & Coscina, 1996; Saper, Chou, & Elmquist, 2002; Willie, Chemelli, Sinton, & Yanagisawa, 2001). The *paraventricular nucleus (PVN)* initiates eating, though less effectively than the lateral hypothalamus, and regulates metabolic processes such as body temperature, fat storage, and cellular metabolism (Broberger & Hökfelt, 2001; Sawchenko, 1998). You can see where these structures are located in the brain in Figure 6.8, which we will refer to throughout this discussion.

After the body has lived for a few hours off of its stores, the falling level of nutrients signals the brain that it is time to eat again. However, by then you probably have already headed for lunch, cued by the clock rather than a brain center. In the modern, highly structured world, physiological motivations have been so incorporated into social customs that it is difficult to tell where the influence of one leaves off and the other begins. We will turn the power of research to answering the questions "What makes a person eat?" "How does a person know when to stop eating?" and "How does a person regulate weight?" As you will learn, the answers are not simple ones; even what you see here will be an abbreviated treatment.

■ FIGURE 6.8   Hunger Control Signals and Brain Centers.

▶ Figures Brought to Life

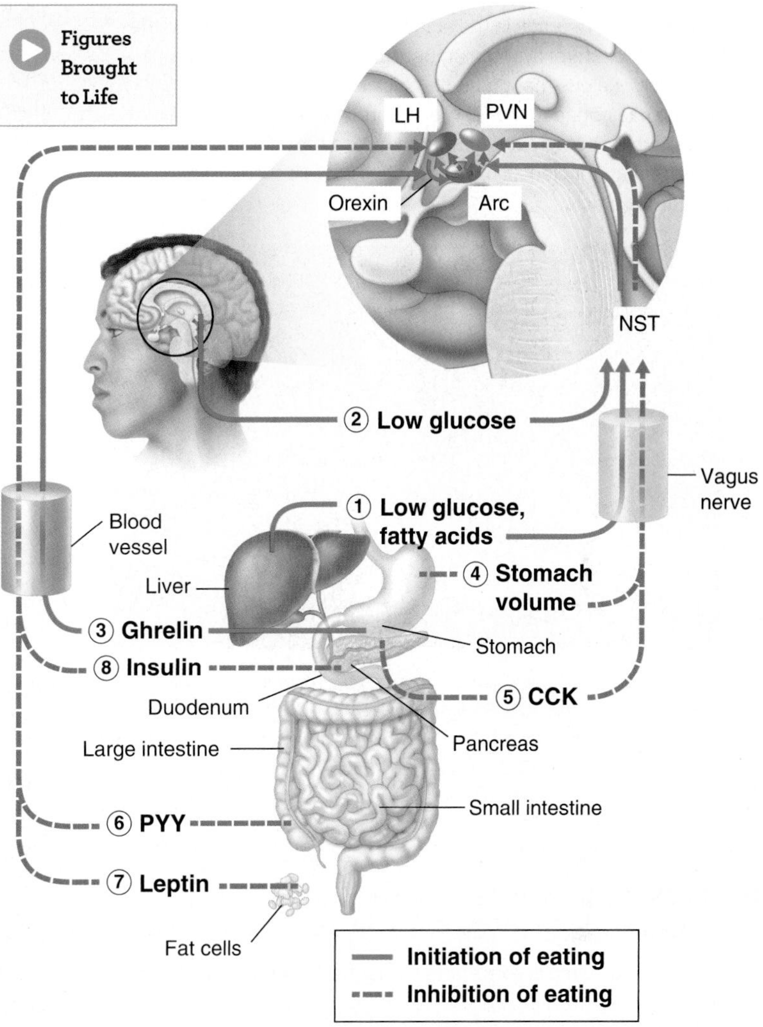

Note: PVN = paraventricular nucleus; LH = lateral hypothalamus; Arc = arcuate nucleus; NST = nucleus of the solitary tract; PYY = paraventricular nucleus; CCK = cholecystokinin.

Signals That Start a Meal

When we ask students in class what being hungry means, the favorite answer is that their stomach feels empty. Your stomach often does feel empty when you are hungry, but we don't eat to satisfy the stomach. The stomach is not even necessary for hunger to occur; people who have had their stomach removed because of cancer still report feeling hungry and still eat much as everybody else, though they have to take smaller meals (Ingelfinger, 1944). So what does make us feel hungry?

There are three major signals for hunger. One tells the brain of a low supply of glucose, or *glucoprivic hunger;* the second indicates a deficit in fatty acids, or *lipoprivic hunger;* and the third does informs us that the stomach's store of nutrients has been depleted. The liver monitors the glucose level and the fatty acids in the blood passing to it from the small intestine via the hepatic portal vein. As you can see in Figure 6.8 (#1), signals of glucose and fatty acid are carried by the vagus nerve from the liver to the NST in the medulla. Blocking the metabolism of fatty acids or creating a glucose deficit (by displacing it in the cells with 2-deoxyglucose, or 2-DG) causes an animal to start eating and to eat more than control animals. Lesioning the NST eliminates both of these increases; if the vagus nerve is cut, blocking fatty acids no longer increases feeding, nor does injection

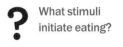

What stimuli initiate eating?

■ **FIGURE 6.9**   Immunohistochemical Labeling Highlights the Arcuate Nucleus.

NPY-releasing neurons in the arcuate nucleus send output to the PVN and the lateral hypothalamus, but they also inhibit neurons within the nucleus that ordinarily block eating. A fluorescent antigen has bound to the NPY receptors, making them appear white in this photograph; doing so has also defined the shape of the arcuate nucleus. (The dark space between the two nuclei is the third ventricle.)

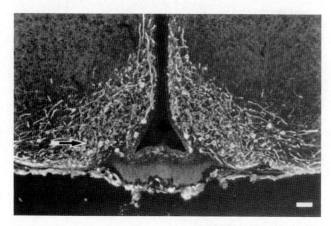

Source: From Figure 1 of "Hypothalamic and Vagal Neuropeptide Circuitries Regulating Food Intake," by C. Broberger and T. Hokfelt, 2001, *Physiology and Behavior*, 74, p. 670. Used with permission from Elsevier.

■ **FIGURE 6.10**   Ghrelin Levels in a Human Over a 24-Hour Period.

Notice that the ghrelin level started rising just before, and peaked at, the customary mealtimes.

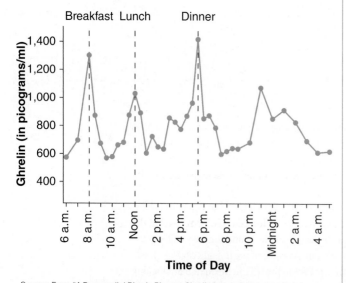

Source: From "A Preprandial Rise in Plasma Ghrelin Levels Suggests a Role in Meal Initiation in Humans," by D. E. Cummings et al., 2001, *Diabetes*, 50, p. 1716, fig. 2A. © 2001 American Diabetes Association.

of 2-DG in amounts that are effective with intact control animals (S. Ritter & Taylor, 1990). Larger amounts of 2-DG do increase feeding in vagotomized animals, after a delay of about an hour (Novin, VanderWeele, & Rezek, 1973; S. Ritter & Taylor); apparently the larger dosage depletes glucose in the brain, which has glucose receptors in the hypothalamus and the brain stem, including in the NST (Marty, Dallaporta, & Thorens, 2007).

The hypothalamus is the master regulator of the energy system. Information about glucose and fatty acid levels is relayed from the NST to the *arcuate nucleus,* a vital hypothalamic structure for monitoring the body's nutrient condition (see Figures 6.2, 6.8, and 6.9; Saper et al., 2002; Sawchenko, 1998). The arcuate nucleus sends neurons to the PVN and the lateral hypothalamus to regulate both feeding and metabolism.

The third major signal for hunger is *ghrelin,* a hormone that is synthesized in the stomach and released into the bloodstream as the stomach empties during fasting. Circulating ghrelin reaches the arcuate nucleus because it passes readily through the blood-brain barrier (Broberger & Hökfelt, 2001). Injecting ghrelin into rats' ventricles caused them to eat more and to gain weight four times faster than rats injected with saline (Kamegai et al., 2001). In humans, ghrelin levels in the blood rose almost 80% before each meal and dropped sharply after eating (Figure 6.10; Cummings et al., 2001). Ghrelin may account for the uncontrollable appetite of people like Christopher; ghrelin levels are 2.5 times higher in individuals with Prader-Willi syndrome than in lean controls and 4.5 times higher than the depressed levels found in equally obese individuals without the syndrome (Cummings et al., 2002).

All three of these hunger signals exert their influence through NPY/AgRP neurons in the arcuate nucleus; these neurons release *neuropeptide Y (NPY)* and *agouti-related protein (AgRP),* both of which excite neurons in the PVN and the lateral hypothalamus to increase eating and reduce metabolism (see Figure 6.8, #3; Horvath & Diano, 2004; Kamegai et al., 2001). Rats that receive NPY injections in the paraventricular nucleus double their rate of eating and increase their rate of weight gain sixfold (B. G. Stanley, Kyrkouli, Lampert, & Leibowitz, 1986). They are so motivated for food that they will tolerate shock to the tongue to drink milk and they will drink milk adulterated with bitter quinine (Flood & Morley, 1991). The fact that their weight gain is three times greater than their increase in food intake attests to NPY's ability to reduce metabolism. During extreme deprivation, NPY conserves energy further by reducing body temperature (Billington & Levine, 1992) and suppressing sexual motivation (J. T. Clark, Kalra, & Kalra, 1985). If you think about it, sexual activity is a particularly unnecessary luxury during food shortage because it expends energy and produces offspring that compete for the limited resources.

Signals That End a Meal

Just as with drinking, there must be a satiety mechanism that ends a meal well before nutrients reach the tissues. It might seem obvious that we stop eating when we feel "full," and that answer is partly right. R. J. Phillips and Powley (1996) used a small inflatable cuff to close the connection between the stomach and intestines of rats. Infusing glucose into the stomach reduced the amount of food the rats ate later, but saline had just as much effect as glucose; this meant that, in the stomach, volume and not nutrient value is important. Distension of the stomach activates stretch receptors that send a signal by way of the vagus nerve to the NST (see Figure 6.8, #4; Broberger & Hökfelt, 2001; B. R. Olson et al., 1993).

? What stimuli terminate eating?

But a full stomach cannot produce long-term satiation by itself; otherwise, drinking water would satisfy us. Humans and other animals also adjust the amount of food they eat according to the food's nutritional value. To a small extent, this involves oral factors and learning. A high-calorie soup produces a greater reduction in hunger if it is drunk than if it is infused into the stomach, and high-calorie drinks are more satisfying than noncaloric drinks (S. E. French & Cecil, 2001).

Optimal satiation, however, requires the interaction of mouth, stomach, and intestinal factors. When R. J. Phillips and Powley (1996) opened the cuff so that the stomach's contents could flow into the intestines, nutrient value did make a difference in the amount of food consumed in a subsequent 30-minute feeding period. Glucose reduced subsequent eating more than saline did, and higher concentrations of the glucose had a greater effect (Figure 6.11). The stomach and intestines respond to food by releasing peptides, which the brain uses to monitor nutrients. About a dozen different peptides have this function; different peptides are released in response to carbohydrates, fats, proteins, or mixtures of these nutrients. They induce the pancreas, liver, and gallbladder to secrete the appropriate enzymes into the duodenum to digest the specific nutrient, and at least some of them inform the brain as to which nutrient needs are being met (S. C. Woods, 2004), via either the vagus nerve or the bloodstream.

The best known of these satiety signals is *cholecystokinin (CCK)*, a peptide hormone released as food passes into the duodenum. CCK detects fats and causes the gallbladder to inject bile into the duodenum; the bile breaks down the fat so that it can be absorbed. When researchers injected CCK into the bloodstream of obese humans, they ate less at the next meal (Pi-Sunyer, Kissileff, Thornton, & Smith, 1982). CCK stimulates receptors on the vagus nerve; as Figure 6.8 (#5) indicates, the vagus conveys the signal to the NST, and from there it passes to the hypothalamus (S. C. Woods, 2004).

However, don't look for CCK to appear on the market as a weight loss drug. Although rats given CCK eat smaller meals, they eat more often and maintain their weight (West, Fey, & Woods, 1984). This means that CCK's role is limited to meal size; there must be other controls that exert a more long-term effect.

■ **FIGURE 6.11**   Effect of Nutrient Concentration on Later Meal Size.

In all trials except the baseline, the stomach was preloaded with 5 milliliters of saline or glucose solution before the subject was offered a glucose solution to drink. The connection between the stomach and small intestine (the pylorus) could be closed by inflating a small cuff. (a) With the pylorus closed, nutrient value made no difference. (b) With the pylorus open, the amount consumed diminished as nutrient values increased.

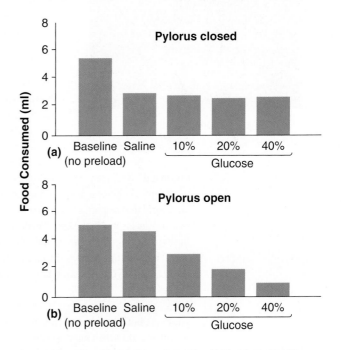

Source: Adapted from "Gastric Volume Rather Than Nutrient Content Inhibits Food Intake," by R. J. Phillips and T. L. Powley, *American Journal of Physiology*, 271, pp. R766–R799. © 1996 American Physiological Society. Used with permission.

Long-Term Controls

Another appetite-suppressing peptide hormone released in the intestines in response to food is *peptide* YY_{3-36} *(PYY)*. PYY is carried by the bloodstream to the arcuate nucleus, where it inhibits the NPY-releasing neurons (see Figure 6.8, #6; Batterham et al., 2002). Unlike CCK, PYY's nonneural route to the brain means that its action is too slow to limit the current meal; instead, it decreases caloric intake by about a third over the following 12 hours.

What are the signals for controlling body weight?

Over longer periods, humans and animals regulate their eating behavior by monitoring their body weight or, more precisely, their body fat. But how they sense their fat level has not always been clear. In 1952, G. R. Hervey surgically joined pairs of rats so that they shared a very small amount of blood circulation; animals joined like this are called *parabiotic*. Then Hervey operated on one member of each pair to destroy the *ventromedial hypothalamus*. This surgery increases parasympathetic activity in the vagus nerve and enhances insulin release (Weingarten, Chang, & McDonald, 1985). This creates a persistent absorptive phase in which most incoming nutrients are stored rather than being available for use; as a result, the animal has to overeat to maintain a normal energy level. The rat becomes obese, sometimes tripling its weight (Figure 6.12). Hervey's lesioned rats overate and became obese as expected, but their pairmates began to undereat and lose weight. In fact, in two of the pairs the lean rat starved to death. The message was clear: The obese rat was producing a blood-borne signal that suppressed eating in the other rat, a signal to which the brain-damaged obese rat was insensitive.

■ **FIGURE 6.12**   A Rat With Lesioned Ventromedial Hypothalamus.

Source: Neal Miller, Yale University.

What that signal was remained a mystery until a half-century later, when researchers discovered that fat cells secrete a hormone called *leptin* that inhibits eating. The amount of leptin in the blood is proportional to body fat; it is about four times higher in obese than non-obese individuals (Considine et al., 1996). Like cholecystokinin, leptin helps regulate meal size, but it does so in response to the long-term stores of fat rather than to the nutrients contained in the meal.

Insulin levels also are proportional to the size of fat reserves (M. W. Schwartz & Seeley, 1997) and provide a similar function. Together, leptin and insulin put the brakes on feeding in the arcuate nucleus, by inhibiting NPY/AgRP neurons (Berthoud & Morrison, 2008) and activating POMC neurons (which release proopiomelanocortin). POMC neurons then reduce feeding by inhibiting neurons in the PVN and lateral hypothalamus (see Figure 6.8, #7 and #8; Elmquist, 2001; Gao & Horvath, 2007; M. W. Schwartz & Morton, 2002). We now understand that when Hervey destroyed the ventromedial hypothalamus in rats, he also severed fibers passing through it and disconnected the arcuate nucleus from the PVN (see Figure 6.2 again to see how this could happen).

An additional contributor to the control of feeding and body weight is *orexin*, a neuropeptide that increases appetite and induces eating. Some researchers prefer to use the alternate term, *hypocretin*, but because the name orexin is derived from *orexis*, the Greek word for "appetite," it seems more appropriate here. Orexin is released when leptin or glucose is low and when ghrelin is high (Sakurai, 2007; Tsujino & Sakurai, 2009); thus, orexin is a hybrid that responds to both short-term and long-term indicators of nutrient reserves. Orexin-releasing neurons are located in the lateral hypothalamus; they project to the arcuate nucleus, where they increase feeding by activating NPY neurons and inhibiting POMC neurons.

Table 6.1 summarizes the factors that influence hunger and feeding that we have just covered, and the accompanying Research Spotlight makes the point that these pathways respond to more than just energy needs.

Until now, we have been considering the ideal situation, the regulation of feeding and weight when all goes well. But in many cases, people eat too much, they eat the wrong kinds of foods, or they eat too little. As we will see, these behaviors are not just personal preferences or inconvenient quirks of behavior; too often, they are health-threatening disorders.

CONCEPT CHECK

Take a Minute to Check Your Knowledge and Understanding

- What is the advantage of the ability to access stored nutrients between meals?
- How important are feeling "empty" and feeling "full" in the regulation of eating? Explain.
- You have lost weight during a long illness and now you are ravenous. What are your likely levels of glucose, fatty acids, ghrelin, insulin, and leptin?

TABLE 6.1 Summary of Feeding Signals.

STIMULUS	SIGNAL SOURCE	PATHWAY
START MEALS		
1. Glucose, fatty acids	Detected by liver as nutrients in blood are depleted.	Signal travels via vagus nerve to NST, then to arcuate nucleus in hypothalamus.
2. Glucose (in brain)	Low level detected by glucose receptors in the brain.	Detection occurs within the pathway, in hypothalamic and brain stem centers.
3. Ghrelin	Peptide released by stomach during fasting.	Circulates in bloodstream to arcuate nucleus.
END MEALS		
4. Stomach volume	Stretch receptors in stomach detect increased volume from food.	Signal travels via vagus nerve to NST, then to arcuate nucleus in hypothalamus.
5. CCK (and other nutrient indicators)	Stomach and intestines release peptides that aid digestion, signal brain of nutrient's presence.	CCK and others initiate activity in vagus to NST and hypothalamus; some may circulate in blood to brain.
LONG TERM		
6. PYY	Released by intestines.	Travels in bloodstream to arcuate nucleus; inhibits NPY neurons.
7. Leptin	Released by fat cells.	Travels in bloodstream to arcuate nucleus; inhibits NPY neurons.
8. Insulin	Released by pancreas.	Travels in bloodstream to arcuate nucleus; inhibits NPY neurons.
9. Orexin	Released by neurons from the lateral hypothalamus.	Released in the arcuate nucleus; activates NPY neurons and inhibits POMC neurons.

Note: Numbers refer to items in Figure 6.8 and in text. CCK = cholecystokinin; NPY = neuropeptide Y; NST = nucleus of the solitary tract; PYY = peptide YY_{3-36}.

Obesity

Between 1975 and 2014, the worldwide obesity rate doubled in men and tripled in women (Figure 6.13; NCD Risk Factor Collaboration, 2016). The number of people who are overfed and overweight now exceeds the number who are hungry and underweight, leading the World Health Organization to declare obesity a global epidemic. In developed countries the picture is staggering. In the United States, for example, the obesity rate is 38% for adults, 21% among adolescents, and 17% for children (Flegal, Kruszon-Moran, Carroll, Fryar, & Ogden, 2016; C. L. Ogden et al., 2016). There are many causes of obesity, but an abundance of food has also been accompanied by the availability of high-calorie junk food. Although the percentage of underweight people has decreased globally (Figure 6.13), the numbers of people who are *malnourished* has been reported as almost double the numbers who are *undernourished* (G. Gardner & Halweil, 2000).

Most researchers use the World Health Organization's BMI calculation to quantify leanness and obesity. *Body mass index (BMI)* is calculated by dividing the person's weight in kilograms by the squared height in meters. If you don't know your measurements in metric units, you can use the table in Figure 6.14, which also shows the World Health Organization categories based on health risks. BMI is an inaccurate measure in some individuals; because muscle is heavier than fat, a healthy, bulked-up athlete will have a high BMI score. A more complete analysis would include a body fat measure and the waist-to-hip ratio.

Obesity is most important because of its health risks. It is a major risk factor for diabetes, and as overweight and obesity increase, so does the incidence of diabetes. Rates of the disease more than doubled from 1990 to 2008, but in recent years have leveled off, with a little over 8% of the U.S. population diagnosed with diabetes (Geiss et al., 2014). Being overweight also increases the likelihood of high blood pressure, heart disease,

RESEARCH SPOTLIGHT
How Nicotine and Marijuana Affect Appetite

Monitoring the body's energy reserves is a complex task requiring intricately complex mechanisms. But this system is made up of multipurpose components, so they also respond to signals from a number of unrelated sources. That is why smoking tobacco helps people keep their weight down and cancer and AIDS patients smoke marijuana to keep theirs up.

Researchers at Yale and Baylor Colleges of Medicine traced nicotine's appetite-suppressing effects to a particular variety of nicotinic acetylcholine receptor in the arcuate nucleus, called a3β4 (Mineur et al., 2011). When nicotine stimulates these receptors, POMC neurons are activated and curtail appetite (Picciotto et al., 2013); mice given a drug that targets a3β4 ate half as much as untreated mice in the next two hours, and over a month their body fat dropped 15%–20%. Areas important in hunger and feeding—the arcuate nucleus, the paraventricular nucleus, and the ventromedial

hypothalamus—also have an abundance of cannabinoid receptors, whose activation induces feeding (Koch et al., 2015). Injecting anandamide or THC into these areas caused satiated mice to resume eating (Di Marzo, Ligresti, & Cristino, 2009). In human subjects, smoking marijuana cigarettes produced hunger-inducing increases in ghrelin levels and decreases in PYY.

There are several reasons for not smoking tobacco or marijuana, but understanding which cannabinoid and nicotinic receptors affect appetite should enable pharmaceutical researchers to develop safer substitutes; for example, there are already alternative ways of administering THC, such as with inhalers. The mechanisms of appetite regulation are obviously very complex, and targeting the nicotinic and cannabinoid receptors might not be the best approaches to weight control, but the problems have been so daunting that researchers are always looking for new solutions.

■ **FIGURE 6.13** Global Rates of Obesity and Underweight in Men and Women, 1975–2014.

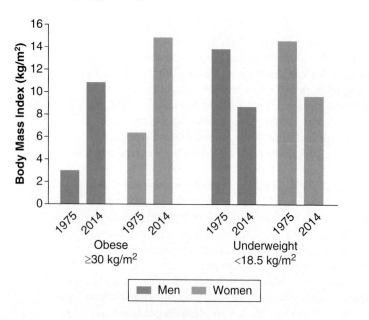

Source: Based on data from NCD Risk Factor Collaboration, 2016.

stroke, and colon cancer (Field et al., 2001; Must et al., 1999). Obesity is also linked to cognitive decline and risk for Alzheimer's disease. Swedish researchers found that in women with lifelong obesity, for every one-point increase in BMI there was a 13%–16% increase in the risk of temporal lobe shrinkage due to cell loss (Gustafson, Lissner, Bengtsson, Björkelund, & Skoog, 2004). The degeneration could have been the result of impaired blood flow to the brain or excess release of the stress hormone cortisol. The cost of obesity in the United States may be as high as $305 billion annually; according to one analysis, medical costs account for $190 billion, workplace absenteeism and reduced productivity cost $65 billion, and obesity-related health education adds another $50 billion (Blake, 2014). It is no wonder that researchers are open to even the most novel sources for treatments, like the one described in the accompanying Research Spotlight.

■ **FIGURE 6.14**   Body Mass Index Calculation Chart.

Below 18.5 (blue): underweight; 18.5–24 (green): normal; 25–29 (yellow): pre-obese; 30 and above (red): obese.

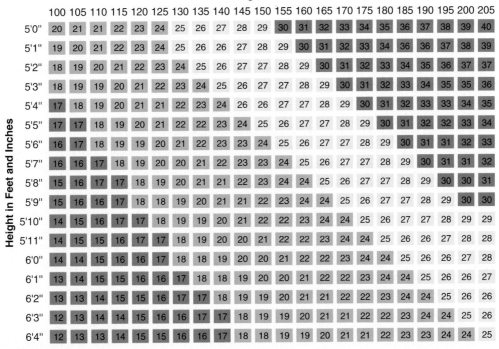

Source: Adapted from "Obesity: How Big a Problem?" by I. Wickelgren, *Science, 280*, pp. 1364–1367. Copyright 1998 American Association for the Advancement of Science. Reprinted with permission from AAAS.

 RESEARCH SPOTLIGHT

Diabetes, the Duck-Billed Platypus, and the Cone Snail

Insulin is often used to regulate blood sugar level in people with diabetes; the gut hormone glucagon-like peptide-1 (GLP-1) is an attractive alternative because it increases insulin naturally, but it is degraded too rapidly to be useful as a diabetes treatment. Enter the platypus, an animal so strange looking that when scientists first saw one in 1799 they believed it was a fake cleverly sewn together from several animals. The male of the species produces GLP-1, too, not only in the gut but also in a painful venom that it delivers from spurs on its hind feet when fighting other males during mating season. To serve that function, the platypus has evolved a more stable form of GLP-1, which is degraded by a different mechanism from the one in humans and would be more stable in the human body (Tsend-Ayush, 2016).

Another possible source for an insulin substitute is the venom of one species of marine cone snail (see Chapter 2). It is an insulin-like protein that produces hypoglycemic shock, a physiological state in which extremely low blood sugar induces a mild sedation in its prey (Safavi-Hemani et al., 2015). Just encountering the venom free-floating in seawater makes zebrafish sluggish, and injecting the venom immediately sends them into shock. The research has been funded in part by Sanofi, a pharmaceutical company that makes the long-acting insulin Lantus.

In other words, the diabetic patient's unlikely future best friends could be a duck-billed, web-footed, egg-laying mammal from Australia and a venomous snail hiding in a deceptively beautiful shell.

Health declines mean more than reduced quality of life. For every 5-point increase in BMI over 25, the risk of death increases by 31% (de Gonzalez et al., 2010); the result is a shortening of lifespan between 2 and 10 years, depending on the degree of overweight (Prospective Studies Collaboration, 2009). Between 1990 and 2008, longevity declined, likely due to the effects of obesity and drug use; this was the first time in a century that life expectancy failed to increase (Olshansky et al., 2012). The average loss of a tenth of a year was driven by larger losses in certain groups; for example, among people with less than a high school education the loss was three years for men and five years for women. But there was another 0.1-year decrease during 2015 alone; it could be just a statistical blip, but this time the loss was significant for all groups (Centers for Disease Control and Prevention, 2016a).

Just as obesity is detrimental to health, caloric restriction without malnutrition appears to be beneficial, even in people who aren't obese. As you would expect, limiting the number of calories by around 30% reduces cholesterol, triglycerides, and circulating levels of insulin and glucose. But it also lowers blood pressure and improves heart health and functioning (P. K. Stein et al., 2012; Trepanowski, Canale, Marshall, Kabir, & Bloomer, 2011), and in elderly subjects verbal memory improved 20% (Witte, Fobker, Gellner, Knecht, & Flöbel, 2009). Feeding restriction increases the lifespan of rats and mice by 20%–60% (Kennedy, Steffen, & Kaeberlein, 2007). Extending these results to primates has been difficult, because the 40- to 50-year lifespan of laboratory monkeys means that studies must last two or three decades. The handful of studies that have been conducted generally support disease reduction and life extension by restricting caloric intake (Colman et al., 2014). Some people believe the health benefits of dietary restriction will translate into longer lives for humans as well, but we'll have to wait a few more years to find out whether they're right. Because few people are willing to undergo the required diet restriction, biogerontologists are experimenting with drugs that produce similar changes in gene expression and improved health measures (Magalhães, Wuttke, Wood, Plank, & Vora, 2011).

The Myths of Obesity

Is obesity due to a lack of willpower?

"

Most forms of obesity are likely to result not from an overwhelming lust for food or lack of willpower, but from biochemical defects at one or more points in the system responsible for the control of body weight.

—Michael Schwartz and Randy Seeley

"

Because obesity is dangerous to the person's health as well as an occasion for social and career discrimination, it is important to ask why people become overweight and why obesity rates are rising so dramatically. Although the causes have been difficult to document, most authorities believe that the global increase in obesity has a simple explanation: People are eating more and richer foods and exercising less (J. O. Hill & Peters, 1998; J. O. Hill, Wyatt, Reed, & Peters, 2003). The cause of obesity seems straightforward enough, then: *Energy in* exceeds *energy out,* and the person gains weight. But we would miss the point entirely if we assumed that people become obese just because they cannot resist the temptation to overeat. Research has not supported the popular opinion that obesity is completely under voluntary control (Volkow & Wise, 2005) or that it can be characterized simply as lack of impulse control, inability to delay gratification, or maladaptive eating style (Rodin, Schank, & Striegel-Moore, 1989). In fact, as we will see later, obesity has a number of features in common with drug addiction.

Another popular belief is that obese children learn overindulgence from their family. Obesity does run in families, and body mass index and other measures are moderately related among family members. However, the evidence consistently points to genetic rather than environmental influences as more important (Grilo & Pogue-Geile, 1991). To the extent that environment does play a role, it is mostly from outside the family.

The Contributions of Heredity and Environment

Is obesity hereditary?

Two environmental influences on weight and obesity are obvious—diet and activity level. During the last three decades of the 20th century, advancing prosperity and improved agricultural production led to greater food availability, and per-capita calorie consumption increased by 1% or more per year in most areas of the world (Rosen, 1999). But this abundance turned out to be a mixed blessing, due to unhealthy dietary choices; for example, by the year 2000, half of calorie consumption in the United States consisted of carbohydrates, and fat made up another third (Wright, Kennedy-Stephenson, Wang, McDowell, & Johnson, 2004). This increased consumption added about 200 calories a day to the average U.S. diet (Wright et al., 2004), while decreasing energy demands on the job reduced daily energy expenditure by more than 100 calories (Church et al., 2011). As people drive rather than walk and spend more time on electronic devices and in front of televisions, activity levels are decreasing to the point that most world populations could be classified as sedentary within the next few years (Ng & Popkin, 2012). Physical activity begins to decline in adolescence, and reduced physical activity during that time is a strong predictor of obesity at age 25 (Pietiläinen et al., 2008).

A less obvious influence is sleep deprivation. Over the last century, average sleep time has decreased from around 9 hours per night to 6 hours and 40 minutes, a loss of 35%. Adults who sleep less than 6 hours a night on workdays have a 41% obesity rate, compared with 28% for 8-hour sleepers, and each hour of lost sleep during adolescence increases the risk of obesity by 80% (reviewed in McAllister et al., 2009). Sleep loss reduces leptin levels and increases ghrelin secretion, both of which cause a craving for high-calorie foods (Greer, Goldstein, & Walker, 2013). Remember that these hormone shifts also trigger the release of orexin, which is an additional reason appetite increases.

More surprising than the sleep connection is the possibility that some obesity is the result of infection. The human adenovirus-36, which causes respiratory and eye infections, is three times more prevalent among obese individuals (Atkinson et al., 2005), and in one study the presence of antibodies for four common viruses accounted for 9% of subjects' fat mass (Fernández-Real, Ferri, Vendrell, & Ricart, 2007). Animal research tells us that the viruses increase glucose uptake by fat cells; and because animals can be made obese by infecting them with the viruses, the viruses likely *cause* obesity in humans rather than being a result of it (McAllister et al., 2009). Bacteria also appear to play a role. When researchers transferred gut bacteria from obese humans to mice that had no gut microbes of their own, the mice increased their body fat by 10%, even though they were eating the same amount of food as mice that received microbes from the human donors' lean twins (Ridaura et al., 2013). Bacteria of the phylum *Firmicutes* are the likely culprit; animal studies suggest they enhance the ability to harvest energy from nutrients. In a study of childhood obesity, obese children had a higher ratio of *Firmicutes* to *Bacteriodetes,* the other major phylum of gut bacteria (Bervoets et al., 2013). *Bacteriodetes,* by contrast, may have a protective function. Cohousing the two mice treated with human microbes later in the study allowed them to eat each other's feces, which they have the unsavory habit of doing. In this situation, *Bacteriodetes* invaded the intestines of the overweight mice, dominated the *Firmicutes* in number, and prevented the mice from gaining further weight. However, that happened only in mice fed the usual high-fiber/low-fat lab chow, not a high-fat diet. Genetic analysis indicated the likely reason: The lean mice had more genes expressed that are involved in breaking down dietary fiber.

Both adoption studies and twin studies demonstrate the influence of heredity on body weight. Adopted children show a moderate relationship with their biological parents' weights and BMIs, and little or no similarity to their adoptive parents (Grilo & Pogue-Geile, 1991). In a meta-analysis of several studies involving 75,000 individuals, correlations for BMI averaged .74 for identical twins and .32 for fraternal twins (Maes, Neale, & Eaves, 1997). Even when identical twins are reared apart, the correlation drops only to .62 (Grilo & Pogue-Geile, 1991), still almost double that for fraternal twins reared together (Figure 6.15). Across 88 estimates from twin studies, heritability of BMI varied from .47 to .90 (Elks et al., 2012). The authors attributed the variation to methodological differences, but others have pointed out that heritability of obesity can vary greatly across populations (W. Yang, Kelly, & He, 2007). Interestingly, the correlation increased during childhood, likely due to increasing gene expression, and decreased through adulthood, possibly as subjects adopted individual dietary and exercise habits.

Forty years ago, it was known that the so-called *obesity gene* on chromosome 6 and the *diabetes gene* on chromosome 4 cause obesity in mice. Mice that are homozygous for the recessive obesity gene (*ob/ob*) or the recessive diabetes gene (*db/db*) have the same symptoms: overeating, obesity, and susceptibility to diabetes (Figure 6.16). To find out how the two genes produced these symptoms, Coleman (1973) used parabiotic pairings of the two kinds of mice and normals (Figure 6.17). When a *db/db* mouse was paired with a normal mouse, the normal mouse starved to death. The same thing happened to the *ob/ob* mouse when it was paired with the *db/db* mouse. These results suggested that the *db/db* mouse was producing a fat signal that it was incapable of responding to itself. The *ob/ob* mouse had no effect on a normal mouse, but its own rate of weight gain slowed. The *ob/ob* mouse apparently was sensitive to a fat signal that it did not produce. It was another 20 years before researchers discovered that the fat signal in Coleman's study

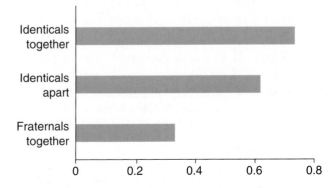

■ **FIGURE 6.15** Correlations of Body Mass Index Among Twins.

Notice that the correlation is higher for identical twins than for fraternal twins, even when the identicals are reared apart and the fraternals are reared together.

Source: Based on data from "The Nature of Environmental Influences on Weight and Obesity: A Behavior Genetic Analysis," by C. M. Grilo and M. F. Pogue-Geile, 1991, *Psychological Bulletin*, 110, pp. 520–537.

■ **FIGURE 6.16**   The Mouse on the Right Is an *ob/ob* Mouse.

Source: From "Positional Cloning of the Mouse *Obese* Gene and Its Human Homologue," by Y. Zhang et al., 1994, *Nature*, 335, pp. 11–16. Reprinted by permission of *Nature*, copyright 1994.

■ **FIGURE 6.17**   Effects of Leptin on *ob/ob, db/db,* and Normal Mice.

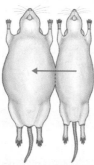 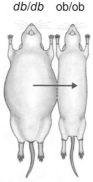

| *db/db* Normal | *ob/ob* Normal | *db/db* *ob/ob* |

Normal starves due to signal from *db/db*; *db/db* insensitive to normal's signal.

Normal unaffected, but its signal slows *ob/ob*'s weight gain.

ob/ob starves due to signal from *db/db*.

—— Strong leptin signal   —— Weak leptin signal

Source: Based on the results of Coleman (1973).

(and Hervey's 1952 lesioning study) was leptin. Following that discovery, they were able to test Coleman's hypothesis. Injecting leptin into *ob/ob* mice reduced their weight 30% in just 2 weeks, while *db/db* mice were not affected by the injections (Halaas et al., 1995). We now understand that the *ob* gene encodes the production of leptin, and the *db* gene is responsible for the receptor.

Those genes are rare in the population, however, and account for relatively few cases of obesity. By contrast, 16% of the population has two copies of the A allele of the *FTO* (fat mass and obesity–associated) gene, and this increases their risk of obesity by nearly 70%; even a single copy ups the risk by 30% (Frayling et al., 2007). Variants of the *MC4R* gene add 12% to the risk for obesity in women (Loos et al., 2008) and account for 6% of cases of severe childhood obesity (Farooqi et al., 2003). Both of these genes promote obesity by increasing calorie intake (Loos et al.; Speakman, Rance, & Johnstone, 2008). Other variants of *FTO* shift individuals into hunger mode by reducing leptin levels, while increasing ghrelin levels (Benedict et al., 2014), sensitivity of leptin receptors (Stratigopoulos et al., 2014), or insulin sensitivity (Heni et al., 2016). Four variants of the *Mrap2* gene found in severely obese individuals apparently interfere with functioning of the receptor for Mc4r, a protein involved in regulating appetite and energy expenditure (Asai et al., 2013). These mutations likely account for less than 1% of cases of obesity, however. More than 40 genetic variants are known to contribute to obesity and fat distribution (Herrera, Keildson, & Lindgren, 2011), and additional candidates turn up regularly. The research reminds us that there are many paths to obesity, including increased appetite, diminished satiety, reduced metabolism, and increased fat storage; accordingly, obesity results from the contributions of many genes.

All the known genes account for only a small proportion of obesity, and heritability measures leave room for significant environmental influence; indeed, we must recognize that the recent surge in obesity is due to nongenetic factors, such as diet and activity level. Even the tendency of overweight women to give birth to overweight babies cannot be attributed entirely to inheritance (M. H. Black, Sacks, Xiang, & Lawrence, 2013; Hochner et al., 2012); children born to women after they have lost weight through bariatric surgery are only one third as likely to be obese, compared with their siblings born before the surgery (J. Smith et al., 2009). The reason this discussion is occurring here is that environmental influences often work by altering gene activity. *Epigenetic* characteristics are inheritable traits that result from modifications of gene expression, rather than changes in the individual's DNA sequence. One mechanism of epigenetic change is *methylation,* the attachment of molecules called methyl groups to a gene, which makes it more difficult for the gene to function. A recent study found that body mass index is correlated with methylation of a handful of genes that had previously been linked to obesity and diabetes (A. P. Feinberg et al., 2010). In another study, methylation of the *RXRA* gene at birth accounted for more than 25% of variation in childhood weight; the methylation apparently was due to low carbohydrate intake by the mothers during early pregnancy (Godfrey et al., 2011).

You can see a graphic demonstration of the effects of methylation in Figure 6.18. Both mice have a mutation in the *agouti* gene, which is responsible for the agouti-related peptide mentioned earlier; the mutation produces obesity and an atypical yellow coat. But during pregnancy, the mother of the mouse on the right was fed supplements high in methyl groups (folic acid and vitamin B12); the resulting methylation downregulated the mutant gene (Waterland & Jirtle, 2003). But the most dramatic example comes from the Dutch *hunger winter* of 1944–1945, when Germany blockaded food shipments to western Holland and 20,000 people died from starvation. A study of young men whose mothers were exposed to famine during early pregnancy found that they were more often obese than unexposed control subjects (Ravelli, Stein, & Susser, 1976). More recent follow-up studies discovered the likely reason: In individuals exposed during early gestation, several genes that control prenatal growth showed modest increases or decreases in methylation, the remnants of epigenetic changes that occurred six decades earlier (Tobi et al., 2009; Tobi et al., 2012). Hunger winter offspring also had twice the typical rate of schizophrenia (Susser et al., 1996). In the following chapters, we will see growing evidence of the role of epigenetic influences on our lives and in our well-being. Meanwhile, the accompanying Application describes another influence on eating and weight gain that will likely also turn out to be epigenetic.

■ **FIGURE 6.18** Methylation Counters Effects of a Mutant Gene.

Both mice have a mutation in the *agouti* gene, but the mother of the mouse on the right received supplements high in methyl groups; the resulting methylation reduced expression of the mutant gene.

Source: Courtesy of Randy L. Jirtle, Duke University Medical Center.

APPLICATION
The Sweet Taste of Obesity

Source: iStock/mvp64.

People who are obese like sweet and fatty foods more than lean people do (Bartoshuk, Duffy, Hayes, Moskowitz, & Snyder, 2006). That's no surprise, but the fact that they are less sensitive to these tastes than the rest of us might surprise you. When asked to rate sweet stimuli, obese children rate them lower in flavor than other children do, plus they have trouble identifying all the primary flavors (Overberg, Hummel, Krude, & Wiegand, 2012). In addition, adults with lower sensitivity to the taste of fat consume more fatty foods and have higher BMIs (Stewart et al., 2010).

This might remind you of what we saw in Chapter 5: Both liking for cocaine and chronic drug use

are associated with a less sensitive dopamine reward system, and evidence suggests that this reduced sensitivity is a cause rather than a result of drug abuse. So, do people eat more sweet and fatty foods because their taste is blunted, or has a high-calorie diet modified the obese person's palate? Whereas taste ability is largely innate, personal taste preferences begin developing during the prenatal and postnatal periods (Beauchamp & Menella, 2009); for example, children whose mothers drank carrot juice regularly during either late pregnancy or initial breastfeeding ate more carrot-flavored cereal than other children (Menella, Jagnow, & Beauchamp, 2001). According to a study with rats, exposure to novel flavors produces long-term changes in the gustatory projection area (Swank & Sweatt, 2001).

So, experience can influence taste preferences, but to answer our question about what causes the relationship between obesity and taste sensitivity, we need to look at a study in which researchers induced lean rats to become obese by offering them access to a high-fat diet. After 10 weeks, the mice were 30%–40% heavier than their littermates; they also were less sensitive to sweet tastes, and fewer of their taste cells were physiologically responsive to the sweet stimuli (Maliphol, Garth, & Medler, 2013).

Obesity and Reduced Metabolism

Accounts of dieting are all too often stories of failure; overweight people report slavishly following rigorous diets without appreciable weight loss, or they lose weight and then gain it back within a year's time. One factor in the failures may be dieters' misrepresentation of their efforts, whether intentional or not. One group of diet-resistant obese individuals underreported the amount of food they consumed by 47% and overreported their physical activity by 51% (Lichtman et al., 1992).

But another critical element that can make weight loss difficult is a person's rate of energy expenditure. In the average sedentary adult, about 75% of daily energy expenditure goes into resting or *basal metabolism,* the energy required to fuel the brain and other organs and to maintain body temperature; the remainder is spent about equally in the two remaining components of metabolism, physical activity and digestion of food (Bogardus et al., 1986).

Differences in basal metabolism may be a key element in explaining differences in weight. When 29 women who claimed they could not lose weight were isolated and monitored closely while they were restricted to a diet of 1,500 kilocalories (kcal; a measure of food's energy value, popularly called *calorie*), 19 did lose weight, but 10 did not (D. S. Miller & Parsonage, 1975). The 10 who failed to lose weight turned out to have a low basal metabolism rate (BMR). Heredity accounts for about 40% of people's differences in BMR (C. Bouchard, 1989). When identical twins were overfed 1,000 calories a day for three months, the differences in weight gain within pairs of twins were only one third as great as the differences across pairs (C. Bouchard et al., 1990). As a result, some medical professionals have called for labeling obese individuals with low BMR as suffering from a disorder called *metabolic syndrome.*

However, a person's metabolism can shift when the person gains or loses weight. In an unusual *experimental* manipulation, researchers had both obese and never-obese individuals either lose weight or gain weight (Leibel, Rosenbaum, & Hirsch, 1995). Those who lost weight shifted to reduced levels of energy expenditure (resting plus nonresting), and the ones who gained weight increased their energy expenditure. This was expected, because your weight affects how much energy is required to move around and even to sit or stand. However, the energy expenditure changes were greater than the weight changes would require, suggesting that the individuals' bodies were *defending* their original weight (see Keesey & Powley, 1986). Individuals also defend against weight gain by increasing their physical activity, mostly through casual walking, fidgeting, and spontaneous muscle contraction (F. R. Levine, Eberhardt, & Jensen, 1999). Among volunteers overfed 1,000 calories a day, those who increased their energy expenditure the least gained 10 times as much weight.

So why doesn't this defense of body weight prevent people from becoming obese? One reason is that the body defends less against weight gain than against weight loss (J. O. Hill et al., 2003; J. O. Hill & Peters, 1998). Humans evolved in an environment in which food was sometimes scarce, so it made sense for the body to store excess nutrients during times of plenty and to protect those reserves during famine. Such a system is adaptive when humans are at the mercy of nature, but it is a liability when modern agriculture and global transportation provide a constant supply of more food than we need.

Obese people tend to be more sedentary, sitting for longer periods of time—two hours longer in one study (J. A. Levine et al., 2005). And compared with obesity-resistant individuals, those who are obesity prone respond to overfeeding by reducing their level of fat oxidation during the night (Schmidt, Kealey, Horton, VonKaenel, & Bessesen, 2013) and, three days following overfeeding, significantly decreasing the amount of time they spend walking (S. L. Schmidt, Harmon, Sharp, Kealey, & Bessesen, 2012).

Prolonged weight gain may reset a person's set point at a higher level. Barbara Rolls and her colleagues fattened rats on highly palatable, high-energy junk food (chocolate chip cookies, potato chips, and cheese crackers) for 90 days (Rolls et al., 1980). Surprisingly, when the rats were returned to their usual lab chow they did not lose weight. The rats maintained their increased weight for the four-month duration of the study—while eating the same amount of food as the control rats. They were defending a new set point. The researchers suggested that the variety of the foods offered, the length of the fattening period, and lack of exercise all contributed to the rats' failure to defend their original weight. In view of the difficulties in shedding excess weight, one obesity researcher pointed out that even modest weight loss reduces risk for chronic disease, and suggested that a goal of 10% weight reduction is more practical than a return to normal weight (Pi-Sunyer, 2003).

> "
> What is a wisdom of the body in times of deprivation becomes a foolishness in our modern environment.
>
> —Xavier Pi-Sunyer
> "

Treating Obesity

? How can obesity be treated effectively?

There is no greater testimony to the difficulty of losing weight than the lengths to which patients and doctors have gone to bring about weight loss. These include wiring the jaws shut, surgically reducing the

■ **FIGURE 6.19**   The Effect of Exercise on Weight Loss.

Dieters who also exercised lost 32% more weight than those who did not, and they lost 40% more body fat.

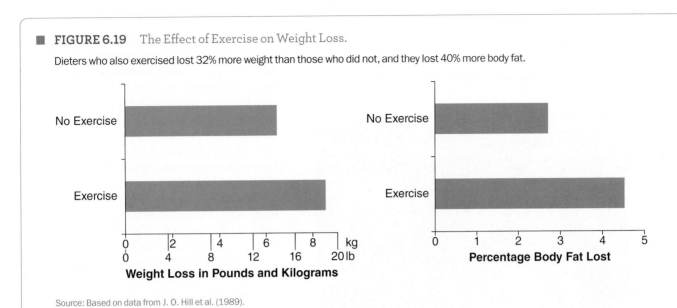

Source: Based on data from J. O. Hill et al. (1989).

stomach's capacity, and removing fat tissue. The standard treatment for obesity, of course, is dietary restriction. However, we have seen that the body defends against weight loss, and dieters are usually frustrated. Exercise burns fat, but it takes a great deal of effort to use just a few hundred calories. On the other hand, exercise during dieting may increase resting metabolic rate or at least prevent it from dropping (Calles-Escandón & Horton, 1992). Dieters who exercise lose more weight than dieters who do not exercise (Figure 6.19; J. O. Hill et al., 1989). In a study of formerly obese women, 90% of those who maintained their weight loss exercised, compared with 34% of those who regained their lost weight (Kayman, Bruvold, & Stern, 1990).

Another option in the treatment of obesity is medication. However, it has not been a particularly promising alternative. Lack of effectiveness is one problem, and because the drugs manipulate metabolic and other important body systems, they often have adverse side effects. The approval of dexfenfluramine in 1996 was the first by the FDA in 20 years. It was withdrawn just a year later, along with the older fenfluramine, after reports they caused heart valve leakage (Campfield, Smith, & Burn, 1998). Sibutramine was linked to increased risk of heart attack and stroke ("Abbot Laboratories Agrees to Withdraw . . . ," 2010), and rimonabant to serious psychiatric disorders (D. Taylor, 2009), resulting in withdrawal of both. In the United States, only orlistat remained available. Because it blocks fat absorption, it can cause digestive discomfort, and there have been rare reports of liver damage (U.S. Food and Drug Administration, 2010). After a lapse of 13 years, new drugs began arriving in 2012. Their mechanisms are varied; different ones enhance serotonin transmission, increase leptin, control blood sugar, and slow stomach emptying. Although these drugs are safer than most of their predecessors, their potential side effects include suicidal thoughts, dizziness, confusion, pancreatitis, and birth defects in offspring ("These 5 Weight-Loss Drugs . . . ," 2016; "Weight Loss Drugs . . . ," 2015). What is more, the drugs are no panacea; weight loss is modestly greater than with diet and exercise, which, by the way, are still part of the regimen.

Serotonin plays an interesting role in weight control. Carbohydrate regulation involves a feedback loop; eating carbohydrates increases serotonin levels, which inhibits a person's appetite for carbohydrates (Leibowitz & Alexander, 1998), apparently by reducing NPY activity (Dryden, Wang, Frankish, Pickavance, & Williams, 1995). Drugs that block serotonin reuptake reduce carbohydrate intake, but only in the group of obese individuals who crave carbohydrates and eat a large proportion of their diet in carbohydrates (Lieberman, Wurtman, & Chew, 1986; Wurtman, Wurtman, Reynolds, Tsay, & Chew, 1987). Serotonin also enhances mood in some people, and people who have trouble maintaining weight loss often say that they use food to make themselves feel better when they are upset (Kayman et al., 1990). A high-carbohydrate meal also improves mood only in carbohydrate cravers; it actually lowers the mood of noncravers and makes them feel fatigued and sleepy (Lieberman et al., 1986). So serotonin dysregulation may be an important contributor to obesity in a subset of people.

■ **FIGURE 6.20** A Leptin-Deficient Boy Before and After Treatment.

(a) At age 3.5 years when treatment began and (b) at age 8 and at normal weight.

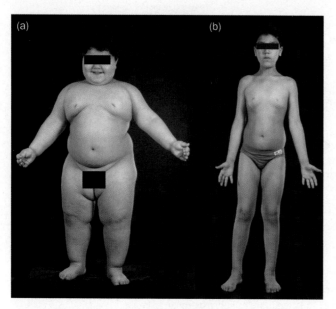

Source: Courtesy of Sadaf Farooqi and Stephen O'Rahilly.

■ **FIGURE 6.21** Diminished Number of Dopamine D$_2$ Receptors in Obese Individuals.

Less intense colors in the PET scan of obese individuals (showing the group average) reveal that D$_2$ receptors are reduced in the same areas as in individuals with drug addictions.

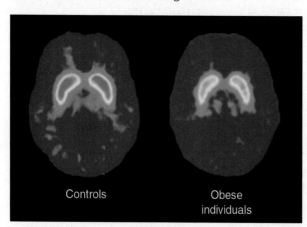

Source: Reprinted from "Brain Dopamine and Obesity," by G.-J. Wang et al., 2001, *Lancet*, 357, pp. 354–357, with permission from Elsevier.

By now you should be asking, "Why not try the body's own hormones as weight loss drugs?" And, of course, researchers have thought of that as well. Although gastric bypass patients who lost the most weight also showed elevated PYY levels (Buchwald et al., 2009), attempts to use PYY have so far been unsuccessful, because of either a lack of effect or extreme nausea (De Silva & Bloom, 2012). Leptin is particularly attractive to obesity researchers because, unlike food restriction, it increases metabolism (N. Levin et al., 1996), and it targets fat reduction while sparing lean mass (P. Cohen & Friedman, 2004). Leptin was administered to three severely obese children who produced no leptin at all due to a mutation in the *ob* gene (Farooqi et al., 2002). Their body weights decreased throughout treatment although they were increasing in age; more than 98% of the weight loss was in fat mass, while lean mass increased. Figure 6.20 shows how dramatic the effects were in one of the children. Unfortunately, leptin treatment benefits only the 5%–10% of obese people who are leptin deficient; the rest are resistant to leptin's effects, apparently as a result of long-term high-fat consumption (Enriori et al., 2007; Maffei et al., 1995). Many obesity researchers now believe that leptin's main role is in protecting the individual against weight loss during times of deprivation rather than against weight gain during times of plenty (Marx, 2003).

A more recent therapeutic approach involves treating obesity as an addictive behavior. Compulsive overeating and drug addiction share several behavioral and neurophysiological similarities, including high relapse rate, responsiveness to stress, dopamine release in response to cues, reduced numbers of dopamine D$_2$ receptors (Figure 6.21) with associated decreases in metabolism in prefrontal areas involved in impulse control, and continued drug taking and compulsive eating when the behaviors are self-destructive and no longer pleasurable (V. H. Taylor, Curtis, & Davis, 2009; Trinko, Sears, Guarnieri, & DiLeone, 2007; Volkow, Wang, Fowler, & Telang, 2008). In addition, signals that influence eating—orexin, insulin, leptin, and ghrelin—also increase or decrease activity in the reward system (Volkow, Wang, Tomasi, & Baler, 2013). Some drugs used in addiction treatment have shown promise for treating obesity as well. Obese patients taking Contrave, a combination of the anti-addiction drugs bupropion and naltrexone, lost 50% more weight than patients receiving a placebo; the manufacturer is in the final stages of obtaining FDA approval ("Orexigen Has Another Go," 2013; "Orexigen Therapeutics," 2009).

Unfortunately, lifestyle modification and approved drug therapies reduce body weight by only 5%–10% (Mitka, 2006), and most dieters regain their weight within a year (Bray, 1992). That much weight reduction can lead to significant health gains, but it is not enough for the morbidly obese, who are increasingly turning to bariatric surgery. The cost averages between $14,500 and $23,000 depending on the type of surgery ("Weight Loss Surgery Insurance Coverage and Costs," 2016), but the benefits can be remarkable. The most effective procedure, gastric bypass, reduces the stomach to a small pouch, which is then reconnected at a lower point on the intestine

PETS MAY PROVIDE PROTECTION AGAINST OBESITY

Many parents think a dog or cat can help their child learn responsibility or engage in more physical activity, but new research suggests that just exposure to pets, even while still in the womb, can be beneficial. Researchers at the University of Alberta Department of Pediatrics have been studying how prenatal and postnatal exposure to furry animals, such as cats and dogs, affects the types of bacteria found in the guts of infants (Tun et al., 2017). This is messy work requiring analysis of fecal samples, but it is rewarding researchers with evidence that the types of bacteria found in the gut are associated with risk for a variety of psychological and physical conditions. Infants with pet exposure had higher amounts of two "good" bacteria, *Oscillospira* and *Ruminococcus*, compared with infants without pet exposure. *Oscillospira* previously has been found in the guts of people with healthy BMIs, and *Ruminococcus* seems to protect against illness. With increasing rates of childhood obesity, the discovery that a household pet can promote helpful bacterial development in the guts of children suggests new possibilities in obesity and illness prevention.

THOUGHT QUESTIONS

1. How can pets influence risk for obesity in children?

2. How are bacteria such as *Oscillospira* and *Ruminococcus* potentially helpful to people?

For the news story, visit edge.sagepub.com/garrett5e and select the Chapter 6 study resources.

(Figure 6.22). This both limits meal size and reduces nutrient absorption in the digestive tract. The resulting weight loss averages 32% after 1 or 2 years and is maintained at 25% 10 years later (Sjöström et al., 2007). The weight loss engenders a cascade of additional benefits: remission of type 2 diabetes in 77% of patients, hypertension in 66%, and sleep apnea in 88% (Buchwald et al., 2004), as well as a 27% reduction in mortality at 15 years (Sjöström et al.). Reducing digestive capacity is not the only way bypass surgery brings about weight reduction; blood glucose control improves (Rubino et al., 2016); postmeal ghrelin levels are decreased and PYY is increased (Pournaras & le Roux, 2009), so the individual doesn't feel hungry; and even the balance of intestinal microbes improves (Kong et al., 2013). Surgery is a last resort, though, and its downsides highlight the need for obesity prevention and new strategies for weight management.

The best course of action, however, is to head off obesity before it begins, through exercise and healthy eating. But there is also more one can do, as the accompanying In the News feature suggests.

Not everyone with an eating disorder is overweight or obese. Some people try so hard to control their weight that they eat less than is needed to maintain health, or they eat normal or excess amounts and then vomit or use laxatives to avoid gaining weight. As you will see, anorexia and bulimia are as puzzling to researchers as obesity and often more deadly for the victims.

■ **FIGURE 6.22** Gastric Bypass Procedure.

A small area of the stomach is isolated from the rest. Then the small intestine is severed, and the cut end is attached to the pouch, reducing the length of the intestine and the amount of nutrient absorption.

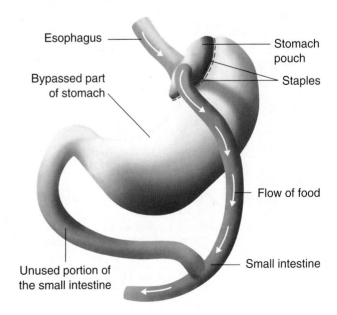

Source: Adapted from Ainsworth (2009).

CONCEPT CHECK

Take a Minute to Check Your Knowledge and Understanding

- What are the causes of obesity? Of the current surge in obesity?
- How does defense of body weight contribute to obesity?
- What are the problems in treating obesity?

Anorexia, Bulimia, and Binge Eating Disorder

Difficulties with eating and weight regulation affect women much more often than they do men. Though men are overrepresented among U.S. adults who are overweight or obese, women outnumber men two to one among the extremely obese (U.S. Department of Health and Human Services, 2012). Similarly, women are three times as likely to be diagnosed with anorexia nervosa or bulimia nervosa, and twice as likely to suffer from binge eating disorder (Figure 6.23; Hudson, Hiripi, Pope, & Kessler, 2007). The reasons are not well understood, so they will not be addressed here, but you should understand why the following discussion often refers only to women or girls.

? What are anorexia, bulimia, and binge eating disorder?

Anorexia nervosa is known as the "starving disease" because the individual restricts food intake to maintain weight at a level so low that it is threatening to health (Figure 6.24; Walsh & Devlin, 1998). The person may also exercise for hours a day or resort to vomiting to control weight loss. Anorexics often see themselves as fat even when they are emaciated. They are likely to deny the need for treatment and fail to comprehend the medical consequences of their disorder. There are two subgroups of anorexics. *Restrictors* rely only on reducing food intake to control their weight. *Binge-purgers* restrict their calorie intake as well, but they also resort to vomiting or using laxatives. If anorexia continues long enough, it leads to cessation of ovulation, loss of muscle mass, heart damage, and reduction in bone density. The death rate among anorexics is more than double that for female psychiatric patients; half of the deaths are from complications of the disease and another quarter from suicide (Sullivan, 1995).

Brain scans show deficits in brain volume, which appear to be only partially reversible following weight recovery (Castro-Fornieles et al., 2009; Lambe, Katzman, Mikulis, Kennedy, & Zipursky, 1997; Mainz, Schulte-Rüther, Fink, Herpertz-Dahlmann, & Konrad, 2012). Brain scans also reveal dysfunction in areas involved in reward, emotion, and processing of bodily information, including those responsible for body image (W. H. Kaye, Fudge, & Paulus, 2009). After 16 hours of fasting, healthy women showed activation of reward evaluation circuits; women in remission from anorexia (chosen to avoid confounding from starvation) did not, but they did activate cognitive control circuits, both when fasting and after eating (Wierenga et al., 2014). When choosing foods, they also activated the dorsal striatum, an area involved in habitual behavior, more than did healthy controls (Foerde, Steinglass, Shohamy, & Walsh, 2015). These results are consistent with patients' control over hunger and eating behavior, a control that relies on automatic learned behaviors rather than an assessment of bodily needs. The studies do not tell us whether these

■ **FIGURE 6.23** Prevalence by Sex of Overweight, Obesity, and Eating Disorders.

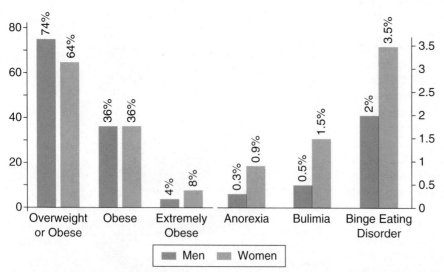

Source: Based on data from Hudson, Hiripi, Pope, and Kessler (2007); U.S. Department of Health and Human Services (2012).

brain anomalies are due to starvation or represent conditions that precede and contribute to the anorexia. However, the poor performance of anorexics on a behavioral test of frontal cortex functioning continues after recovery and is found in healthy sisters (Attia, 2009). In addition, the presence of obsessive-compulsive traits, harm avoidance, and perfectionism during childhood as well as after recovery suggests the presence of predisposing factors before the onset of illness (Kaye et al.).

Bulimia nervosa also involves weight control, but the behavior is limited to bingeing and purging. If the bulimic restricts food intake, it is only for a few days at a time, and restricting takes a backseat to bingeing and purging.

■ **FIGURE 6.24**   French Model Isabelle Caro in Late Stages of Anorexia.

Caro, who suffered from anorexia from the age of 13, fell into a coma when her weight dropped to 55 pounds. That experience led her to pose for photos that appeared in newspapers and on billboards as part of an Italian anti-anorexia campaign. She died 3 years later at the age of 28; her mother committed suicide over the guilt she felt.

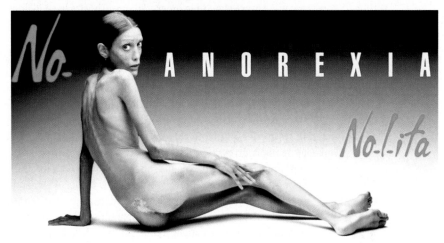

Source: Agencia el Universal/El Universal de Mexico/Newscom.

In fact, only 19% of bulimic women consume fewer calories than normal controls, whereas 44% overeat (Weltzin, Hsu, Pollice, & Kaye, 1991). Unlike anorexics, most bulimic women are of normal weight (Walsh & Devlin, 1998). However, there are indications that, like anorexics, they might also be battling hunger. Their ghrelin levels between meals are a third higher than in control subjects and decrease less following a meal; in addition, PYY levels do not rise as much following a meal (Kojima et al., 2005). Like anorexia, bulimia is also a dangerous disorder. Both anorexia and bulimia are difficult to treat; although three quarters of bulimics and a third of anorexics appear to be fully recovered after eight years, a third of these relapse (D. B. Herzog et al., 1999).

People with *binge eating disorder* (BED) frequently eat large amounts of food during a short period of time, and they feel they cannot control what or how much they eat. Because the individuals do not attempt to control weight by fasting, purging, or exercising, they typically are overweight, but this is not a requirement for diagnosis. They usually feel disgust and shame about their overeating, so they often choose to eat separately from others and do their bingeing in seclusion. BED has been recognized clinically only during the past two decades and was included as a disorder for the first time in the fifth edition of the *Diagnostic and Statistical Manual of Mental Disorders* (*DSM*-5; American Psychiatric Association, 2013). Although there has been much less research on this disorder than on anorexia and bulimia, recent reports suggest BED is caused by impairments in decision making, increased pleasure derived from food, and alterations in dopamine pathways characteristic of other impulsive and compulsive disorders such as substance abuse (Kessler, Hutson, Herman, & Potenza, 2016).

In addition to these three disorders, there are other eating disorders recognized by the *DSM*-5. These include night eating disorder (excessive eating between sleep bouts), pica (compulsive eating of dirt, rocks, and other non-food objects), rumination disorder (bringing back up and rechewing previously swallowed food), and avoidant/restrictive food intake disorder (ARFID; lack of interest in or concern about eating). Clearly, all are maladaptive and potentially harmful to the individual suffering from these disorders.

Environmental and Genetic Contributions

Both anorexics and bulimics are preoccupied with weight and body shape. Because increases in anorexia and bulimia seem to have paralleled an increasing cultural emphasis on thinness and beauty, some researchers have concluded that the cause is social. The male-female difference is consistent with this argument, because women are under more pressure to be slim while men are encouraged to "bulk

What is the evidence for social and genetic influences in anorexia and bulimia?

up." Cases are more common in Western, industrialized countries, where an impractical level of thinness is promoted by actors, models, and advertisers. Anne Becker of Harvard Medical School has been studying eating habits in the Pacific islands of Fiji since 1988 (Becker, Burwell, Gilman, Herzog, & Hamburg, 2002). Traditionally, a robust, muscled body has been valued for both sexes there. But when satellite television arrived in 1995, the tall, slim actors in shows like *Beverly Hills 90210* became teenage Fiji's new role models. By 1998, 74% of young island girls considered themselves too big or fat, even though they were not more overweight than others. Young girls who lived in homes that owned a TV were three times more likely to have an eating problem. Among 17-year-old girls, 11% admitted they had vomited to control weight, compared with just 3% in 1995.

There is little doubt that social pressure contributes to anorexia and bulimia. But the disorders are not unknown in non-Westernized societies, and anorexia has been reported for 300 years, long before the cultural emphasis on thinness. One indication that a sociocultural explanation is an oversimplification is that several studies show a genetic influence. Relatives of patients have a higher than usual incidence of the disorders, and the concordances for anorexia and bulimia are about three times greater for identical twins than for fraternals (Kendler et al., 1991; Kipman, Gorwood, Mouren-Simeoni, & Adès, 1999). Heritability has been estimated at 56% for anorexia (Bulik, Sullivan, Tozzi, Furberg, Lichtenstein, & Pedersen, 2006), 54%–83% for bulimia (Bulik et al., 2003), and 45% for binge eating disorder (K. S. Mitchell et al., 2010).

There has been no shortage of candidate genes, but definitive results have been elusive; this is due to a variety of reasons, including the apparent involvement of many small-effect genes, difficulty acquiring adequate numbers of patient volunteers, and the failure of studies to distinguish between the two subtypes of anorexia. The most promising results so far implicate a serotonin receptor gene and a dopamine receptor gene in anorexia; estrogen and cannabinoid genes that influence food intake in bulimia; and a serotonin transporter gene in binge eating disorder (Trace, Baker, Peñas-Lledó, & Bulik, 2013).

When researchers followed 772 female twins through adolescence, they made a surprising discovery (Klump, Burt, McGue, & Iacono, 2007). At age 11, genetic factors accounted for just 6% of disordered eating symptoms, such as weight preoccupation, body dissatisfaction, and binge eating, but by age 14 they accounted for 46% of the variance. Almost all of the nongenetic influence is unique to the individual (Bulik et al., 2006; Bulik, Sullivan, Wade, & Kendler, 2000; K. S. Mitchell et al., 2010), which suggests the possibility that adolescent hormonal changes, stress, and dieting (and, possibly, prenatal conditions) produce epigenetic changes in the genes that play a role in anorexia and bulimia. There has been relatively little research in this area, but epigenetic dysregulation of dopamine genes has been reported in women with anorexia and bulimia (Frieling et al., 2010).

Eating disorders typically are accompanied by comorbid psychological disorders; in a study of 2,436 female inpatients, almost all were diagnosed with depression, more than half had anxiety disorders, 22% had substance abuse disorders, and the rates of obsessive-compulsive disorder varied from 15% to 29% across the groups (Blinder, Cumella, & Sanathara, 2006). Studies have also confirmed genetic associations of eating disorders with depression and obsessive-compulsive disorder (Scherag, Hebebrand, & Hinney, 2009). Because you know the limitations of correlational studies, you should be thinking that there are three possible reasons for this relationship: The psychological disorders could trigger disordered eating, starvation or overeating could precipitate an emotional disorder, or both of these could be the result of a third underlying cause. For us, the immediate value is that this correlation leads us to look at transmitters involved in the two emotional disorders and in reward and substance abuse.

The Role of Serotonin, Dopamine, and Cannabinoids

What role does serotonin appear to have in anorexia and bulimia?

The involvement of serotonin and dopamine has been suggested by a large number of genetic studies. Researchers have focused most on serotonin, largely because it is involved so intimately in eating behavior and in the anxiety, depression, obsessiveness, and impulsive behavior that typically accompany anorexia and bulimia (W. Kaye, Gendall, & Strober, 1998). Antidepressants that block the reuptake of serotonin at synapses reduce bingeing and purging in patients with bulimia, and they lower the chance of relapse after recovery from anorexia. This finding led researchers to look for evidence of decreased serotonin activity. Instead, levels of serotonin metabolites in the cerebrospinal fluid were normal in the ill bulimia patients, and they rose to above normal after recovery (Figure 6.25). Levels did turn out to be low in patients with anorexia, but only during illness when their starvation diet provided too little tryptophan, the precursor to serotonin. After weight recovery (the only time antidepressants help them), metabolite levels were higher than normal. In addition, symptom improvement was unrelated to any reduction in depression, or even whether depression was present.

The key might not be in the general level of serotonin activity but in which of two types of serotonin receptor is more abundant. The $5HT_{1A}$ receptor responds to serotonin by inhibiting neural activity, whereas the $5HT_{2A}$ receptor increases activation. A preponderance of $5HT_{1A}$ receptors in the subgenual prefrontal cortex appears to interfere with the area's executive control over the amygdala; individuals with a higher ratio of 1A receptors respond more to photos depicting fearful or angry facial expressions than do subjects with a higher 2A ratio (Fisher et al., 2011). Imaging studies indicate that anorexia and bulimia patients have an imbalance in activity at serotonin receptors, with increased transmitter binding at the $5HT_{1A}$ receptors and diminished binding at $5HT_{2A}$ receptors in both groups (Bailer & Kaye, 2010). These receptors are of interest

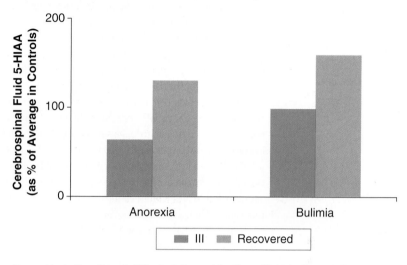

■ **FIGURE 6.25**   Cerebrospinal Fluid 5-HIAA in Anorexia and Bulimia.

Values are compared with levels in healthy control women, which are set at 100%. 5-HIAA (5-hydroxyindoleacetic acid) is a metabolite of serotonin, and the level found in cerebrospinal fluid is used to estimate serotonin activity.

Source: Adapted from Figure 1 of "Serotonin Neuronal Function and Selective Serotonin Reuptake Inhibitor Treatment in Anorexia and Bulimia Nervosa," by W. Kaye, K. Gendall, and M. Strober, *Biological Psychiatry*, 44, pp. 825–838. Copyright, 1998. Used with permission from Elsevier.

because of their role in anxiety, depression, compulsive behavior, and harm avoidance, and because 1A/2A imbalance is found in brain areas known to be involved in these symptoms. Bailer and Kaye also think this imbalance explains why people with anorexia have such a compelling urge to starve themselves. They point to evidence that experimentally depleting tryptophan reduces anxiety in both ill and recovered subjects and suggest that food restriction serves to reduce anxiety by depriving $5HT_{1A}$ receptors of serotonin. Tandospirone, which targets these receptors, improved symptoms of anorexia in one study, but only two patients were treated (Okita, Shiina, Nakazato, & Iyo, 2013). Drug treatment studies have been hampered by high dropout rates, and they have generated little support, leaving behavioral therapy as the treatment of choice (Zadka, 2015).

Anorexia patients' distinctive lack of enjoyment and ability to deny themselves not only food but other pleasures of life suggest that disordered reward systems might also be at work (Cassin & von Ranson, 2005). Individuals ill with and recovered from anorexia have low levels of dopamine metabolites in the cerebrospinal fluid, and evidence indicates that dopamine activity may be diminished in the ventral striatum, one of the areas important in reward. Similar measures in another brain area are associated with higher levels of harm avoidance in weight-recovered patients (W. H. Kaye et al., 2009). In addition, increasing dopamine activity by administering amphetamine produced euphoria in control subjects but increased anxiety in subjects recovered from anorexia (Bailer et al., 2012). Because eating increases dopamine release, this finding lends additional support to the idea that food restriction serves to reduce anxiety. The cannabinoid system, which plays a role in food intake and reward, also appears to be involved (Gérard, Pieters, Goffin, Bormans, & Van Laere, 2011). Both anorexic and bulimic patients have larger numbers of cannabinoid receptors in the insula, whose functions include the rewarding effects of food and responses to hunger; viewing pictures of food invokes atypical activity there in both groups.

CONCEPT CHECK

Take a Minute to Check Your Knowledge and Understanding

- What are the likely causes of anorexia and bulimia?
- How are anorexia and bulimia alike and different? (Don't forget the two types of anorexia.)

In Perspective

Temperature regulation, thirst, and hunger provide good examples of drive, homeostasis, and physiological motivation in general. Although they are explained best by drive theory, they also illustrate the point that it is ultimately the balance or imbalance in certain brain centers that determines motivated behaviors.

In addition, hunger in particular demonstrates that homeostasis alone does not explain all the facets of motivated behavior. For instance, we saw that the incentives of the sight and smell of food are enough to start the physiological processes involved in the absorptive phase. This suggests that incentives operate through physiological mechanisms and are themselves physiological in nature. We also know that there are important social influences on what and how much people eat, and sensation seeking may explain why some people are gourmets or enjoy the risks of eating puffer fish.

Most of the factors that determine our eating behavior are in turn influenced by genes. If it is true that we are what we eat, it is equally true that what we eat (and how much) is the result of who we are. But we will be reminded time and again throughout this text that heredity is not destiny, that we are the products of countless interactions between our genetic propensities and the environment.

Our interest in the motivation of hunger would be mostly theoretical if it were not for eating disorders, which can have life-threatening consequences. Despite their importance, we are unsure about the causes of obesity, anorexia, bulimia, and binge eating disorder, as well as what the best treatments are. We do know that, like the motivation of hunger itself, these disorders are complex and have a number of causes.

This chapter has given you an overview of what we mean by motivation. We will broaden that view in the next two chapters by looking at sexuality, emotion, and aggression.

CHAPTER SUMMARY

Motivation and Homeostasis

- Homeostasis and drive theory are key to understanding physiological motivation, but they are not adequate alone.
- Temperature regulation involves a simple mechanism for control around a set point.
- Thirst is a bit more complex, compensating for deficits both in the cells (osmotic thirst) and outside the cells (hypovolemic thirst).

Hunger: A Complex Drive

- Hunger is a more complex motivation, involving a variety of nutrients and regulation of both short-term and long-term nutrient supplies.
- Taste helps an individual select nutritious foods, avoid dangerous ones, and vary the diet.
- The feeding cycle consists of an absorptive phase, a period of living off nutrients from the last meal, and the fasting phase, when reliance shifts to stored nutrients.
- Eating is initiated when low blood levels of glucose and fatty acids are detected in the liver. The information is sent to the medulla and to the paraventricular nucleus of the hypothalamus, where neuropeptide Y is released to initiate eating.
- Feeding stops when stretch signals from the stomach, increasing glucose levels in the liver, and cholecystokinin released in the duodenum indicate that satiety has occurred.
- How much we eat at a meal is also regulated by the amount of fat we have stored, indicated by leptin and insulin levels.

Obesity

- Obesity is associated with malnutrition and with a variety of illnesses.
- A variety of factors, many of them outside the person's control, contribute to obesity.
- Obesity is partly inheritable, and the environmental influences that exist are not primarily from the family.
- As calorie intake decreases, metabolism decreases to defend against weight loss.
- Obesity is difficult to treat, but drugs that increase serotonin activity appear most promising, and bariatric surgery is beneficial for more extreme obesity.

Anorexia, Bulimia, and Binge Eating Disorder

- Anorexia involves restriction of food intake, and sometimes bingeing and purging, to reduce weight. Bulimia is a bingeing disease; weight increase is limited by purging or exercise.
- Both social pressure and heredity appear to be important in anorexia and bulimia.
- People with binge eating disorder eat excessively during a brief period of time; they are typically, but not always, overweight.
- Family and twin studies indicate a strong hereditary component, though few genes have been reliably identified. The large amount of individually unique environmental influence suggests epigenetic effects.
- Anomalies in serotonin, dopamine, and cannabinoid systems also are implicated. ■

STUDY RESOURCES

FOR FURTHER THOUGHT

- If a group of nuclei in the brain control a particular homeostatic need, what functions must those nuclei carry out?
- What do you think would happen if the brain had no way of monitoring stored fat levels?
- Several of the controls of eating seem to duplicate themselves. Is this wasteful or useful? Explain.
- What do you think a complete program of obesity treatment would look like?
- Can you propose another way to organize the three subgroups that make up anorexics and bulimics—perhaps even renaming the disorders?

TEST YOUR UNDERSTANDING

1. Describe either temperature regulation or thirst in terms of homeostasis, drive, and satisfaction, including the signals and brain structures involved in the process.

2. Describe the absorptive and fasting phases of the feeding cycle; be specific about what nutrients are available, how nutrients are stored, and how they are retrieved from storage.

3. Describe obesity as a problem of metabolism.

Select the best answer:

1. A problem that makes some people question drive theory is that

   a. an animal remains aroused after the need is satisfied.
   b. some people have stronger drives than others.
   c. not all motivation involves tissue needs.
   d. soon after a drive is satisfied, the system goes out of equilibrium again.

2. An animal is said to be in homeostasis when it

   a. recognizes that it is satisfied.
   b. feels a surge of pleasure from taking a drink.
   c. is in the middle of a high-calorie meal.
   d. is at its set point temperature.

3. Osmotic thirst is due to

   a. dryness of the mouth and throat.
   b. lack of fluid in the cells.
   c. reduced volume of the blood.
   d. stimulation of pressure receptors.

4. A structure in the medulla that is involved in taste as well as in hunger and eating is the

   a. nucleus of the solitary tract.
   b. paraventricular nucleus.

   c. area postrema.
   d. subfornical organ.

5. You have trouble with rabbits eating your garden. Several sprays are available, but they are washed off each day by the sprinklers. The solution with the best combination of kindness, effectiveness, and ease for you would be to

   a. spray the plants daily with a substance that tastes too bad to eat.
   b. spray the plants occasionally with a substance that makes the rabbits sick.
   c. spray the plants with a poison until all the rabbits are gone.
   d. forget about spraying; run outside and chase the rabbits away.

6. During the absorptive phase,

   a. fat is broken down into glycerol and fatty acids.
   b. insulin levels are low.
   c. glucagon converts glycogen to glucose.
   d. glucose from the stomach is the main energy source.

7. Neurons in the arcuate nucleus release NPY, which

   a. increases eating.
   b. increases drinking.
   c. breaks down fat.
   d. causes shivering.

8. A long-term signal that influences eating is

   a. glucose.
   b. 2-deoxyglucose.
   c. cholecystokinin.
   d. leptin.

9. Regarding environmental influences on weight,

   a. smoking increases appetite.
   b. the influence of infection appears to be minimal.
   c. sleep loss increases appetite.
   d. social influence is mostly from the family.

10. When we say that the body defends weight during dieting, we mean primarily that

    a. the person's metabolism decreases.
    b. the person eats less but selects richer foods.
    c. the person eats lower-calorie foods but eats larger servings.
    d. the body releases less NPY.

11. Studies comparing the weights of adopted children with their biological parents and their adoptive parents

    a. show that weight is influenced most by environment.
    b. show that weight is influenced most by heredity.
    c. show that heredity and environment have about equal influence.
    d. have not been in agreement.

12. If a *db/db* mouse is parabiotically attached to a normal mouse, the *db/db* mouse will

    a. gain weight while the normal loses.
    b. lose weight while the normal gains.
    c. be unaffected while the normal loses.
    d. be unaffected while the normal gains.

13. Epigenetic effects on offspring weight have resulted from the mother's

    a. drug use.
    b. activity level.
    c. diet.
    d. smoking.

14. Which of the following was not discussed as a factor in anorexia and/or bulimia?

    a. Increased numbers of nicotinic acetylcholine receptors.
    b. An imbalance in types of 5HT receptors.
    c. Reduced dopamine activity.
    d. Increased numbers of cannabinoid receptors.

15. Regarding anorexia and bulimia,

    a. both are characterized by a deficiency in hunger.
    b. evidence indicates that epigenetic changes occur during adolescence.
    c. they appear to be uniquely distinct from other disorders.
    d. antidepressants help with anorexia, but not bulimia.

Answers: 1. c, 2. d, 3. b, 4. a, 5. b, 6. d, 7. a, 8. d, 9. c, 10. a, 11. b, 12. c, 13. c, 14. a, 15. b.

ON THE WEB

The following websites are coordinated with this chapter's content. You can access these websites from the **SAGE edge Student Resources site**; select this chapter and then click on Web Resources. (**Bold** items are links.)

1. The National Institutes of Health site **Prader-Willi Syndrome** is a valuable resource for practical as well as technical information about the disorder. The **Prader-Willi Association** site has information about the association, facts about the disorder, and research information.

2. **ChartsBin** has a world map that is color coded to show the daily calorie intake per person in each country. Mouse over the country to see its name, calorie count, and changes since 1990.

3. The news article "**How the *FTO* Gene Causes Obesity**" appeared in *New Scientist*.

4. You've seen Alcoholics Anonymous's 12-step program applied to all the other drug addictions; now it's being used to manage compulsive overeating. **Overeaters Anonymous** has information about its organization and links to the sites of local help organizations.

5. The **National Eating Disorders Association** provides information about anorexia, bulimia, obesity, binge eating disorder, and other disorders, as well as information about treatments.

Internet Mental Health has information on diagnosis, treatment, and research related to anorexia and bulimia.

FOR FURTHER READING

1. In "Overfat and Underfat: New Terms and Definitions Long Overdue," Phillip Maffetone, Ivan Rivera-Dominguez, and Paul Laursen (*Frontiers in Public Health*, January 3, 2017) argue that 76% of the world's population is "overfat." This includes not only the obese and overweight but also people who are normal in weight but carry extra fat, particularly around the belly, increasing their risk for chronic and metabolic disease.

2. Researchers are continuing to discover maternal epigenetic influences on offspring risk of obesity, including stress (*Obesity Research*, 2015, *16*, 351–361), high-fat diet (*Diabetes*, 2016, *65*, 574–584), and poor sleep (*Diabetes*, 2014, *63*, 3230–3241).

3. There is no shortage of hypotheses about what causes anorexia, but if one possible cause is confirmed, it could lead to an additional treatment option. Researchers at the French National Institute of Health and Medical Research have found that antibodies to a protein produced by normal intestinal bacteria are elevated in anorexia patients, and that the antibodies also attack the satiety hormone melanotropin (*Translational Psychiatry*, 2014, *4*, e458.)

4. "Full Without Food," by Claire Ainsworth (*New Scientist*, September 5, 2009, 30–33), describes surgery for obesity and emphasizes its benefits for diabetics, as well as the possibility of creating drugs that mimic the effects of GLP-1, which is increased following the surgery.

KEY TERMS

absorptive phase 154

agouti-related protein (AgRP) 156

amino acids 153

angiotensin II 148

anorexia nervosa 170

arcuate nucleus 156

area postrema 153

arousal theory 146

basal metabolism 166

binge eating disorder 171

body mass index (BMI) 159

bulimia nervosa 171

cholecystokinin (CCK) 157

diabetes 163

diabetes gene 163

drive 146

drive theory 146

duodenum 153

epigenetic 164

fasting phase 154

fatty acids 153

ghrelin 156

glucagon 154

glucose 153

glycerol 154

glycogen 154

homeostasis 146

hypovolemic thirst 148

incentive theory 146

instinct 146

insulin 154

lateral hypothalamus 154

learned taste aversion 151

learned taste preference 152

leptin 158

median preoptic nucleus 148

motivation 146

neuropeptide Y (NPY) 156

nucleus of the solitary tract (NST) 148

obesity gene 163

orexin 158

organum vasculosum lamina terminalis (OVLT) 148

osmotic thirst 148

paraventricular nucleus (PVN) 155

peptide YY_{3-36} (PYY) 157

preoptic area 148

satiety 149

sensory-specific satiety 151

set point 147

subfornical organ (SFO) 148

$SAGE edge™ edge.sagepub.com/garrett5e

SAGE edge offers a robust online environment featuring an impressive array of free tools and resources for review, study, and further exploration, keeping both instructors and students on the cutting edge of teaching and learning.

6.1 Summarize the psychological theories of motivation. ▶ The Power of Motivation

6.2 Describe how temperature regulation and thirst reflect the concept of homeostasis. ▶ Thermoregulation

6.3 Explain the role of taste in choices of food. ▶ The Neurology of Taste

6.4 Identify the brain signals that control when we begin and end eating. ▶ What If You Stopped Eating? ▶ Why Dieting Usually Doesn't Work

6.5 Compare the roles of environment and heredity in risk for obesity. ▤ Diabetes Health Disparities

6.6 Examine how the environment and genetics impact risk for disordered eating. Genetics of Anorexia Nervosa

6.7 Discuss the role of neurotransmitters in eating disorders. ▶ Neuroscience of Eating Disorders

The Biology of Sex and Gender

7

After reading this chapter, you will be able to:

- Contrast sex with other motivated behaviors.

- Demonstrate the role of hormones and brain structures in sexual behavior.

- Identify hormonal and brain differences between females and males.

- Describe how behavioral differences between males and females are influenced by biology and environment.

- Explain the role of biological influences on gender identity.

- Assess the impact of biological influences on sexual orientation.

Master the content.
edge.sagepub.com/garrett5e

Bruce Jenner spent his early career as an athlete, playing football at Graceland College until a knee injury necessitated a change in sport to decathlon in 1968. After years of grueling training and competition, Jenner won a gold medal in decathlon at the 1976 Summer Olympics in Montreal and became a hero back home in the United States. Jenner even graced the cover of *Sports Illustrated* magazine and became the most widely known athlete to be on the cover of a Wheaties breakfast cereal box. Leaving athletics behind, he became better known as a sports commentator and occasional actor in films and television. During this time he had been married three times and fathered six children. Throughout the successes in athletics and as an actor, Jenner was struggling with a psychological disorder called gender dysphoria, which is the distress that people feel when their gender identity does not match their sex at birth. At times he dressed as a woman, and he was taking female hormones to try to better match his feelings of being female.

Source: Valerie Macon/AFP/Getty Images.

In April 2015, Jenner made news by coming out as a transgendered woman. Later that year, Jenner officially adopted her now-permanent feminine identity as Caitlyn Jenner, and in January 2017, she underwent gender reassignment surgery to replace the penis with a vaginal opening. Her memoir *The Secrets of My Life* and the documentary series *I Am Cait* detailed her gender transition; in recognition of her outspoken support for LGBT rights and the strength she demonstrated in discussing her gender identity struggles with the public, she received the Arthur Ashe Courage Award and *Out* magazine's Newsmaker of the Year award. Quite possibly the most interesting thing about Caitlyn Jenner's new gender and identity is that she still finds herself sexually attracted to women, underscoring the fact that gender identity does not always match a person's sexual orientation.

Humans have a great affinity for dichotomies, dividing their world into blacks and whites with few grays in between. No dichotomy is more significant for human existence than that of male and female: One's sex is often the basis for deciding how the person should behave, what the person can do, and with whom the person should fall in love. Not only are many of the differences between males and females imposed on them by society, but Caitlyn's experience suggests that typing people as male or female may not be as simple or as appropriate as we think. We will encounter even more puzzling cases later as we take a critical look at the designation of male versus female and the expectations that go with it. In the meantime, we need to continue our discussion of motivation by considering how sex is like and unlike other drives.

Sex as a Form of Motivation

To say that sex is a motivated behavior like hunger may be stating the obvious. But theorists have had difficulty categorizing sex with other physiological drives because it does not fit the pattern of a homeostatic tissue need. If you fail to eat or if you cannot maintain body temperature within reasonable limits, you will die. But no harm will come from forgoing sex; sex ensures the survival of the species but not of the individual.

There are, however, several similarities with other drives like hunger and thirst. They include arousal and satiation, the involvement of hormones, and control by specific areas in the brain. We will explore these similarities as well as some differences in the following pages.

Arousal and Satiation

How is sex like and unlike other drives?

The cycle of arousal and satiation is the most obvious similarity between sexual motivation and other motivated behaviors such as hunger and thirst. In the 1960s, William Masters and Virginia Johnson conducted groundbreaking research on the human sexual response. Until then, research had been limited to observing sexual behavior in animals or interviewing humans about their sexual activity. Masters and Johnson (1966) observed 312 men and 382 women and recorded their physiological responses during 10,000 episodes of sexual activity in the laboratory. This kind of research was unheard of at the time; in fact, the researchers had trouble finding journals that would publish their work. Their work on human sexual behavior was the subject of the recent Showtime cable series *Masters of Sex*.

Masters and Johnson identified four phases of sexual response (Figure 7.1). The *excitement phase* is a period of arousal and preparation for intercourse. Both sexes experience increased heart rate, respiration rate, blood pressure, and muscle tension. The male's penis becomes engorged with blood and becomes erect. The female's clitoris becomes erect as well, her vaginal lips swell and open, the vagina lubricates, her breasts enlarge, and the nipples become erect.

While hunger is mostly a function of time since the last meal, sexual arousal is more influenced by opportunity and sexual stimuli such as explicit conversation or the presence of an attractive person. In contrast to humans, sexual arousal in most mammal species is triggered by a surge in hormones. Another difference between sex and other drives is that we usually are motivated to reduce hunger, thirst, and temperature deviations, but we seek sexual arousal. This difference is not unique, though; for example, we might skip lunch to increase the enjoyment of a gourmet dinner.

During the *plateau phase,* the increase in sexual arousal levels off. Arousal is maintained at a high level for seconds or minutes, though it is possible to prolong this period. The testes rise in the scrotum in preparation for ejaculation; vaginal lubrication increases and the vaginal entrance tightens on the penis. During *orgasm,* rhythmic contractions in the penis are accompanied by ejaculation of seminal fluid containing sperm into the vagina. Similar contractions occur in the vagina. This period lasts just a few seconds but involves an intense experience of pleasure. Orgasm is similar to the pleasure one feels after eating or when warmed after a deep chill, but it is unique in its intensity; the *resolution* that follows is reminiscent of the period of quiet following return to homeostasis with other drives.

After orgasm, males have a *refractory phase,* during which they are unable to become aroused or have another orgasm for minutes, hours, or even days, depending on the individual and the circumstances. Females do not experience a refractory period and can have additional orgasms anytime during the resolution phase. When comparing the sex drive with other kinds of motivation, the male refractory period has an interesting parallel with sensory-specific satiety (see Chapter 6); it is called the Coolidge effect. According to a popular but probably questionable story, President Coolidge and his wife were touring a farm when Mrs. Coolidge asked the farmer whether the flurry of sexual activity among the chickens was the work of one rooster. The farmer answered yes, that the rooster copulated dozens of times each day, and Mrs. Coolidge said, "You might point that out to Mr. Coolidge." President Coolidge, so the story goes, then asked the farmer, "Is it a different hen each time?" The answer again was

FIGURE 7.1   Phases of the Sexual Response Cycle.

This is a typical response for a male; most females are capable of multiple orgasms.

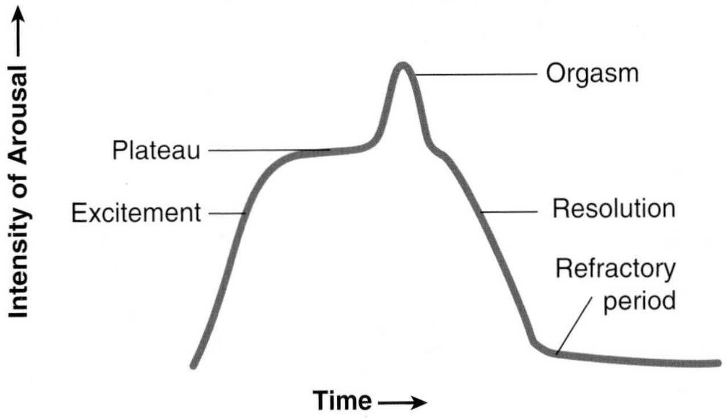

Source: From *Psychology: The Adaptive Mind* (2nd ed.), by J. S. Nairne, 2000, Wadsworth, a part of Cengage Learning, Inc.

yes. "Tell that to Mrs. Coolidge," the president replied. Whether the story is true or not, the *Coolidge effect*—a quicker return to sexual arousal when a new partner is introduced—has been observed in a wide variety of species. We will visit the subject again shortly.

The Role of Testosterone

As important as sex is to humans, it is ironic that so much of what we know about the topic comes from the study of other species. One reason is that research into human sexual behavior was for a long time considered off-limits, and funding was hard to come by. Another reason is that sexual behavior is more "accessible" in nonhuman animals; rats have sex as often as 20 times a day and are not at all embarrassed to perform in front of the experimenter. In addition, we can manipulate their sexual behavior in ways that would be considered unethical with humans. Hormonal control in particular is more often studied in animals because hormones have a clearer role in animal sexual behavior.

Castration, or removal of the gonads (testes or ovaries), is one technique used to study hormonal effects because it removes the major source of sex hormones; castration results in a loss of sexual motivation in nonhuman mammals of both sexes. Sexual behavior may not disappear completely, because the adrenal glands continue to produce both male and female hormones, though at a lesser rate than the gonads. The time course of the decline is also variable, ranging from a few weeks to five months in male rats (J. M. Davidson, 1966); across several species, animals who are sexually experienced are impaired the least and decline the slowest (B. Hart, 1968; Sachs & Meisel, 1994). Humans are less at the mercy of fluctuating hormone levels than other animals, but when they are castrated (usually for medical reasons, such as cancer), sexual interest and functioning decrease in both males and females (Bremer, 1959; Heim, 1981; Sherwin & Gelfand, 1987; Shifren et al., 2000). The decline takes longer in humans than in rats, but the rate is similarly variable.

Castration has been elected by some male criminals in the hope of controlling aggression or sexual predation, sometimes in exchange for shorter prison sentences. Castration is an extreme therapy; drugs that counter the effects of *androgens* (a class of hormones responsible for a number of male characteristics and functions) are a more attractive alternative. Those that block the production of the androgen *testosterone,* the major sex hormone in males, have been 80%–100% effective in eliminating deviant sexual behavior such as exhibitionism and pedophilia (sexual contact with children), along with sexual fantasies and urges (A. Rösler & Witztum, 1998; Thibaut, Cordier, & Kuhn, 1996). Chemical castration is either allowed on a voluntary basis or mandated for some offenses in nine states in the United States (M. Park, 2012) and in several other countries. The effects of castration indicate that testosterone is necessary for male sexual behavior, but the amount of testosterone required appears to be minimal; men with very low testosterone levels can be as sexually active as other men (Raboch & Stárka, 1973).

Frequency of sexual activity does vary with testosterone levels *within* an individual, but the testosterone increases appear to be the *result* of sexual activity rather than the cause. For example, testosterone levels are

Activity initiated by women peaks around the middle of the menstrual cycle, which is when ovulation occurs.

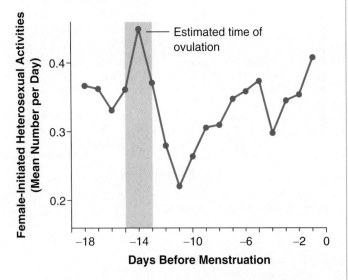

Source: From figure 2 from "Rise in Female-Initiated Sexual Activity at Ovulation and Its Suppression by Oral Contraceptives," by D. B. Adams, A. R. Gold, and A. D. Burt, 1978, *New England Journal of Medicine*, 299(21), pp. 1145–1150.

■ **FIGURE 7.3** Relationship Between Sexual Behavior and Salivary Testosterone Levels in Men and Women.

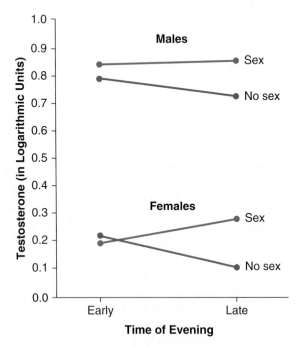

Source: From "Male and Female Salivary Testosterone Concentrations Before and After Sexual Activity," by J. M. Dabbs, Jr. and S. Mohammed, *Physiology and Behavior, 52*, pp. 195–197, Fig. 1. © 1992 Reprinted with permission from Elsevier Science.

high in males at the *end* of a period in which intercourse occurred, not necessarily before (J. M. Dabbs & Mohammed, 1992; Kraemer et al., 1976). A case report (which is anecdotal and does not permit us to draw conclusions) suggests that just the anticipation of sex can increase the testosterone level. Knowing that beard growth is related to testosterone level, a researcher working in near isolation on a remote island weighed the daily clippings from his electric razor. He found that the amount of beard growth increased just before planned visits to the mainland and the opportunity for sexual activity (Anonymous, 1970).

In most mammals, females are unwilling to engage in sex except during *estrus,* a period when the female is ovulating, sex hormone levels are high, and the animal is said to be in heat. Human females and females of some other primate species engage in sex throughout the reproductive cycle. Studies of sexual frequency in women have not shown a clear peak at the time of ovulation. However, initiation of sex is a better gauge of the female's sexual motivation than is her willingness to have sex; women do initiate sexual activity more often during the middle of the menstrual cycle, which is when ovulation occurs (Figure 7.2; D. B. Adams, Gold, & Burt, 1978; S. M. Harvey, 1987). The researchers attributed the effect to *estrogen,* a class of hormones responsible for a number of female characteristics and functions. Their reasons were that estrogen peaks at midcycle and the women did not increase in sexual activity if they were taking birth control pills, which level out estrogen release over the cycle.

However, testosterone peaks at the same time, and the frequency of intercourse during midcycle corresponds to the woman's testosterone level (N. M. Morris, Udry, Khan-Dawood, & Dawood, 1987). At menopause, when both estrogen and testosterone levels decline, testosterone levels show the most consistent relationship with intercourse frequency (McCoy & Davidson, 1985). How to interpret these observations is unclear, because testosterone increases in women as a *result* of sexual activity, just as it does in men (Figure 7.3; J. M. Dabbs & Mohammed, 1992). However, studies in which testosterone level was manipulated demonstrate that it also contributes to women's sexual behavior. Giving a dose of testosterone to women increases their arousal during an erotic film (Tuiten et al., 2000). More important, in women who had their ovaries removed, testosterone treatment increased sexual arousal, sexual fantasies, and intercourse frequency, but estrogen treatment did not (Sherwin & Gelfand, 1987; Shifren et al., 2000).

Brain Structures and Neurotransmitters

As neuroscientists developed a clearer understanding of the roles of various brain structures, motivation researchers began to shift their focus from drive as a tissue need to drive as a condition in particular parts of the brain. Sexual activity, like other drives and behaviors, involves a network of brain structures. This almost seems inevitable, because sexual activity involves reaction to a variety of stimuli, activation of several physiological systems, postural and movement responses, a reward experience, and so on. We do not understand yet how the sexual network operates as a whole, but we do know something about the functioning of several of its components. In this section, you will see some familiar terms, the names of hypothalamic structures you learned about in Chapter 6. This illustrates an important principle of brain functioning, that a particular brain area, even a very small one, often has multiple functions.

Two areas are important in sexual behavior in both sexes, the medial preoptic area of the hypothalamus and the medial amygdala. *The medial preoptic area (MPOA)* is one of the more significant brain structures involved in male and female sexual behavior. (Be careful not to confuse the medial preoptic area with the median preoptic nucleus, discussed in Chapter 6. They are both in the preoptic area, which you can locate in Figure 6.2.) Stimulation of the MPOA increases copulation in rats of both sexes (Bloch, Butler, & Kohlert, 1996; Bloch, Butler, Kohlert, & Bloch, 1993), and the MPOA is active when they copulate spontaneously (Pfaus, Kleopoulos, Mobbs, Gibbs, & Pfaff, 1993; Shimura & Shimokochi, 1990). The MPOA appears to be more responsible for performance than for sexual motivation; when it was destroyed in male monkeys, they no longer tried to copulate, but instead they would often masturbate in the presence of a female (Slimp, Hart, & Goy, 1978).

The *medial amygdala* also contributes to sexual behavior in rats of both sexes. Located near the lateral ventricle in each temporal lobe, the *amygdala* is involved not only in sexual behavior but also in aggression and emotions. The medial amygdala is active while rats copulate (Pfaus et al., 1993), and stimulation causes the release of dopamine in the MPOA (Dominguez & Hull, 2001; Matuszewich, Lorrain, & Hull, 2000). The medial amygdala's role apparently is to respond to sexually exciting stimuli, such as the presence of a potential sex partner (de Jonge, Oldenburger, Louwerse, & Van de Poll, 1992).

There are other areas that are involved in sexual behavior but only in the behaviors of a single sex. Especially significant for males is the *sexually dimorphic nucleus (SDN),* located in the preoptic area (de Jonge et al., 1989). The SDN is three to four times larger in male rats than in females (Figure 7.4; He, Ferguson, Cui, Greenfield, & Paule, 2013), and a male's level of sexual activity is related to the size of the SDN, which in turn depends, at least in part, on protection by testosterone from the cell death that occurs during the pruning stage shortly after birth (He et al., 2013). Destruction of the SDN reduces male sexual activity (de Jonge et al., 1989). The SDN's connections to other sex-related areas of the brain suggest that it integrates sensory and hormonal information and

 What is the role of testosterone in sexual behavior?

 What brain structures are involved in sexual behavior?

■ **FIGURE 7.4**   The Sexually Dimorphic Nuclei of the Rat.

(a) The SDN in the male is larger than (b) the SDN in the female. (c) The effects of testosterone and a masculinizing synthetic hormone on the female SDN.

(a) Adult male

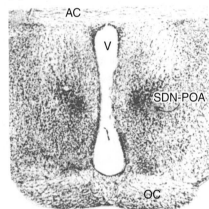

(b) Adult female

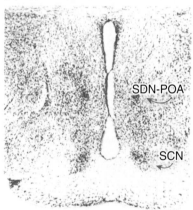

(c) Adult female exposed to testosterone

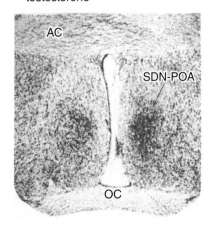

Diethylstilbestrol

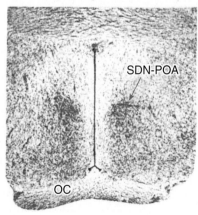

Source: From "The Neuroendocrine Regulation of Sexual Behavior," by R. A. Gorski, pp. 1–58, in G. Newton and A. H. Riesen (Eds.) *Advances in Psychobiology* (Vol. 2), 1974, New York: Wiley. Reprinted with permission of John Wiley & Sons, Inc.

■ **FIGURE 7.5**   Dopamine Levels in the Nucleus Accumbens During the Coolidge Effect.

Activity was recorded until the male lost interest in Female 1; then, Female 2 was presented. During the periods represented by the orange bars, the female was separated from the male by a clear screen. The line graph shows dopamine levels. Bars show the number of vaginal penetrations.

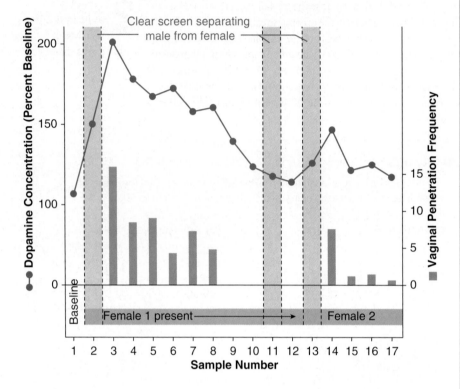

Source: From "Dynamic Changes in Nucleus Accumbens Dopamine Efflux During the Coolidge Effect in Male Rats," by D. F. Fiorino, A. Coury, and A. G. Phillips, 1997, *Journal of Neuroscience*, 17, p. 4852. © 1997 Society for Neuroscience. Reprinted with permission.

coordinates behavioral and physiological responses to sensory cues (Roselli, Larkin, Resko, Stellflug, & Stormshak, 2004). Two other hypothalamic structures are also important. The paraventricular nucleus (PVN; see Figure 6.2) is important for male sexual performance and, particularly, for penile erections (Argiolas, 1999). The *ventromedial hypothalamus* is active in females during copulation (Pfaus et al., 1993), and its destruction reduces the female's responsiveness to a male's advances (Pfaff & Sakuma, 1979).

For obvious reasons, we know much less about the brain structures involved in human sexual behavior. Functional MRI (fMRI) recording during masturbation has confirmed the involvement of the medial amygdala and PVN in human sexual activity (Komisaruk et al., 2004). PVN neurons are known to secrete the hormone/ neuromodulator *oxytocin*, which contributes to male and female orgasm and the intensity of its pleasure (Carmichael, Warburton, Dixen, & Davidson, 1994). We will see additional results from human research in the discussion of neurotransmitters. We also know that a few brain structures in humans differ in size between males and females. Because their contribution to sexual behavior is not clear and the size differences may also distinguish homosexuals from heterosexuals, we will defer discussion of these structures until we take up the subject of sexual orientation.

Sexual behavior involves several neurotransmitters, but dopamine has received the most attention. You saw in Chapter 5 that dopamine level increases in the nucleus accumbens during sexual activity, and in this chapter that stimulation of the medial amygdala releases dopamine in the MPOA. Dopamine activity in the MPOA contributes to sexual motivation in males and females of several species (E. M. Hull et al., 1999). In males, dopamine is critical for sexual performance: Initially, it stimulates D_1 receptors, activating the parasympathetic system and increasing motivation and erection of sexual tissues; as dopamine level increases, it activates D_2 receptors, which shifts autonomic balance to the sympathetic system, resulting in orgasm and ejaculation. D_2 activity also inhibits erection, which probably accounts in part for the sexual refractory period in males. Interestingly, dopamine release parallels sexual behavior during the Coolidge effect. As you can see in Figure 7.5, it increased in the male rat's nucleus accumbens in the presence of a female, dropped back to baseline as interest waned, and then increased again with a new female (Fiorino, Coury, & Phillips, 1997). The changes occurred even when the male and female were separated by a clear panel, so the dopamine level reflects the male's interest rather than the effects of sexual behaviors.

Our knowledge about the role of dopamine in human sexual behavior is less precise but nevertheless intriguing. Drugs that increase dopamine levels, such as those used in treating Parkinson's disease and stimulants, increase sexual activity in humans (Evans, Haney, & Foltin, 2002; Meston & Frolich, 2000). The dopamine system has been reported to be active in the ventral tegmental area in males during ejaculation (Holstege et al.,

2003) and in the nucleus accumbens in females during orgasm (Komisaruk et al., 2004). This activity likely reflects a reward response, but, significantly, the activated areas also have strong motor output to the pelvic floor muscles, which are important in orgasmic activity. Variations in the gene for the D_4 receptor (*DRD4*) are associated with sexual arousal and functioning (Ben Zion et al., 2006), and one variant is correlated with promiscuity and sexual infidelity (Garcia et al., 2010).

Ejaculation is also accompanied by serotonin increases in the lateral hypothalamus, which apparently contributes further to the refractory period (E. M. Hull et al., 1999). Injecting a drug that inhibits serotonin reuptake into the lateral hypothalamus increases the length of time before male rats will attempt to copulate again and their ability to ejaculate when they do return to sexual activity. Humans take serotonin reuptake blockers to treat anxiety and depression, and they often complain that the drugs interfere with their ability to have orgasms. The antianxiety drug buspirone, by contrast, decreases the release of serotonin and facilitates orgasms (Komisaruk, Beyer, & Whipple, 2008).

An interesting model for the regulation of gender-related aggressive and bonding behaviors has been proposed in the steroid/peptide theory of social bonds (van Anders, Goldey, & Kuo, 2011). According to this theory, the balance among testosterone, oxytocin, and vasopressin determine behaviors such as aggression and intimacy (Figure 7.6). As you probably guessed, a high testosterone level in either sex increases aggression, but it also impairs the formation of close social bonds. Oxytocin (involved in muscle contractions of sexual tissue and in social bonding) and vasopressin (a potent neuromodulator of brain activity) modulate the form of intimacy and aggression. Antagonistic aggression (which includes social dominance, partner acquisition, and defense of partners and territory) is seen in those with low levels of vasopressin, whereas protective aggression (such as defending children or partners) is seen in those with high levels of vasopressin. Intimacy increases oxytocin, but its interaction with testosterone levels determines whether that intimacy is sexual (if testosterone is high) or nurturing (if testosterone is low). Therefore, testosterone levels determine the relative amount of competitive versus nurturing behaviors an individual expresses, whereas oxytocin determines the relative amount of social bonding versus social isolation.

Odors, Pheromones, and Sexual Attraction

Sexual behavior results from the interplay of internal conditions, particularly hormone levels, with external stimuli. Sexual stimuli can be anything from brightly colored plumage or an attractive body shape to particular odors. Here we will examine the role of odors and pheromones in sexual attraction, with emphasis on how important they might be for humans.

Before we launch into this discussion, we need to have a basic understanding of the olfactory (smell) system. Olfaction is one of the two chemical senses, along with taste. Airborne

■ **FIGURE 7.6** The Steroid/Peptide Theory of Social Bonds.

In this theory, three important hormones interact to determine not only the strength of bonds with others but also the characteristics of those relationships. First, testosterone levels increase aggression and decrease social bonding, while vasopressin levels modify the form of aggression. Low levels of vasopressin cause attack-type behaviors (antagonistic), while high levels of vasopressin increase protective behaviors that result in stronger social bonds with others. Oxytocin regulates the level of intimacy and interacts with testosterone as well. Low testosterone with high oxytocin is correlated with more helpful, supporting intimacy and stronger social bonds, whereas high levels of both hormones lead to more sexualized relationships with others. Therefore, the strongest social bonds result from high levels of oxytocin and vasopressin and low levels of testosterone.

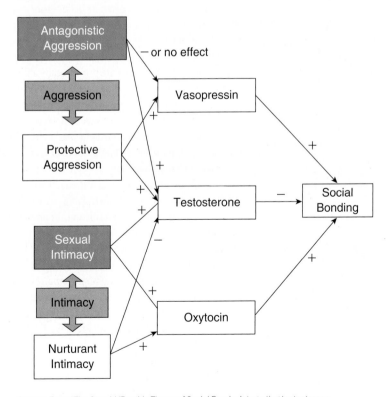

Source: From "The Steroid/Peptide Theory of Social Bonds: Integrating testosterone and peptide responses for classifying social behavioral contexts," by S. M. van Anders, K. L. Goldey, & P. X. Kuo. *Psychoneuroendocrinology*, 36(9). © Elsevier. Reprinted with permission.

■ **FIGURE 7.7**   The Olfactory and Vomeronasal Systems.

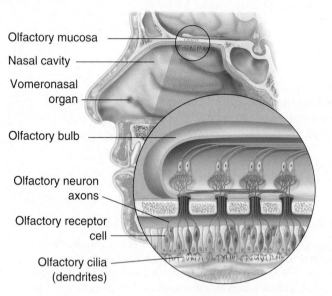

Olfactory mucosa

Nasal cavity

Vomeronasal organ

Olfactory bulb

Olfactory neuron axons

Olfactory receptor cell

Olfactory cilia (dendrites)

odorous materials entering the nasal cavity must dissolve in the mucous layer overlying the receptor cells; the odorant then stimulates a receptor cell when it comes in contact with receptor sites on the cell's dendrites (Figure 7.7). Axons from the olfactory receptors pass through openings in the base of the skull to enter the olfactory bulbs, which lie over the nasal cavity. From there, neurons follow the olfactory nerves to the nearby olfactory cortex tucked into the inner surfaces of the temporal lobes.

By varying the number of components in odor mixtures, researchers have calculated that humans can distinguish a trillion odors (Bushdid, Magnasco, Vosshall, & Keller, 2014). But we do not have a different receptor for each odor, and an individual neuron cannot produce the variety of signals required to distinguish among so many different stimuli. Researchers have discovered that humans have around 400 different receptor genes that produce an equal number of receptor types, but additional alleles of some of these genes brings the total to about 600 (Olender et al., 2012). Variation in these alleles among individuals suggests considerable variation in what different people can smell. We're pikers compared with dogs (800); mice (1,100); and the African elephant, which has 2,000 different receptor genes (Niimura, Matsui, & Touhara, 2016). Research has shown that elephants can distinguish people from different tribes by odor and can recognize up to 30 different family members.

There is a good argument to be made for the nose as a sexual organ. The most convincing evidence comes from the study of *pheromones,* airborne chemicals released by an animal that have physiological or behavioral effects on another animal of the same species. Most pheromones are detected by the *vomeronasal organ (VNO),* a cluster of receptors also located in the nasal cavity. The VNO is illustrated in Figure 7.7, although you will soon see that most researchers believe that it is no longer functional in humans, the victim of evolution as our ancestors developed color vision and came to rely on visual sexual signals (I. Rodriguez, 2004). However, a VNO may not be entirely necessary, because some pheromones and pheromone-like odors can be detected by the olfactory system when an animal's VNO has been blocked or eliminated surgically (Wysocki & Preti, 2004). The VNO's receptors are produced by a different family of genes, and the VNO and olfactory systems are separate neurally (P. J. Hines, 1997). Not surprisingly, in animals the VNO's pathway leads to the MPOA and the ventromedial nucleus of the hypothalamus, as well as to the amygdala (Keverne, 1999).

Pheromones can be very powerful, as you know if your yard has ever been besieged by all the male cats in the neighborhood when your female cat was "in heat." The female gypsy moth can attract males from as far as two miles away (Hopson, 1979). Pheromones provide cues for kin recognition in animals, influence cycling of sexual receptivity in female mice, initiate aggression in both males and females, and trigger maternal behavior in adults and suckling in infants (Wysocki & Preti, 2004). In pigs, the boar exudes androstenone, which elicits sexual posturing and receptivity in sows. In fact, pig farmers use androstenone as an aid in artificial insemination.

So, do pheromones play a role in human behavior? In spite of the eagerness with which the media and fragrance industry have embraced the topic, the best answer appears to be "maybe . . . maybe not." We certainly don't see pheromones controlling sexual behavior as powerfully as they do in animals; in fact, the best candidate for pheromone control of human behavior is the sucking and searching movements in infants in response to breast odors of a nursing woman (Wyatt, 2016; Wysocki & Preti, 2004). Early interest in the possibility of human pheromones was spurred by reports that women living together in dorms tended to have synchronized menstrual periods and that this was caused by sweat-borne compounds that altered the frequency of luteinizing hormone release (Preti, Cutler, Garcia, Huggins, & Lawley, 1986; Preti, Wysocki, Barnhart, Sondheimer, & Leyden, 2003; K. Stern & McClintock, 1998). Later studies have failed to demonstrate menstrual synchrony almost as often as they have succeeded, and the results have been questioned on methodological grounds (Z. Yang & Schank, 2006).

Several other studies have claimed evidence for an influence of pheromones, or at least body odors, on human behavior. This includes amygdala activation from smelling the sweat of first-time skydivers (Mujica-Parodi et al., 2009); increased intercourse opportunities when using aftershave or perfume containing underarm extracts that enhanced the person's sex-characteristic body odor (Cutler, Friedman, & McCoy,

? Is there evidence for pheromones in human sexual behavior?

APPLICATION
Of Love, Bonding, and Empathy

Prairie voles mate for life and share parenting duties.

Source: Todd Ahern/Emory University.

Prairie voles are a rare exception among mammals; they mate for life, and if they lose a mate they rarely take another partner. The bonding process (as reviewed in L. J. Young & Wang, 2004) begins with the release of dopamine in reward areas during mating. If dopamine activity is blocked by a receptor antagonist, partner preference fails to develop. Sexual activity also releases the neuropeptides oxytocin and vasopressin, which are likewise required for bonding to take place. Either can facilitate bonding in males or females, but oxytocin is more effective with females and vasopressin with males.

So does any of this apply to humans, who are also monogamous (more or less)? The most apparent parallel involves oxytocin. Oxytocin not only facilitates bonding but also causes smooth muscle contractions, such as those involved in orgasm and in milk ejection during breastfeeding. Blood levels of oxytocin increase dramatically as males and females masturbate to orgasm (M. R. Murphy, Checkley, Seckl, & Lightman, 1990). Oxytocin also contributes to social recognition, which is necessary for developing mate preferences. Male mice without the oxytocin gene fail to recognize females from one encounter to the next (J. N. Ferguson et al., 2000), and human males are better at recognizing previously seen photos of women after receiving oxytocin (Rimmele, Hediger, Heinrichs, & Klaver, 2009). Men given oxytocin also had more activity in the nucleus accumbens while viewing photos of their partners, and they increased their ratings of their partners' attractiveness, but not of other women they knew (Scheele et al., 2013).

Oxytocin's bonding effects are not limited to mates and sex partners. Mother-infant bonding is correlated with oxytocin levels during pregnancy and following birth (Feldman, Weller, Zagoory-Sharon, & Levine, 2007), and a gene for the oxytocin receptor is related to parenting sensitivity (Bakermans-Kranenburg & van IJzendoorn, 2008). Oxytocin also apparently explains empathetic behavior in prairie voles. Though we can't speculate about what the rodents are "feeling," they respond to a cagemate's earlier, unobserved stress with increased grooming, and they match the cagemate's fear response, anxiety-related behaviors, and corticosterone increase (Burkett et al., 2016). Consoling behavior did not occur if the animals received an infusion of an oxytocin receptor antagonist into the lateral ventricles.

1998; McCoy & Pitino, 2002); higher alcohol consumption and sociability in males after exposure to fertile female odors (Tan & Goldman, 2015); and men's higher attractiveness ratings of the scent of women's T-shirts when women were ovulating (Kuukasjärvi et al., 2004).

But there is no shortage of critics. They point out that no human secretion has been identified as a phero-mone, including the "putative human pheromones" regularly used in research studies (Wyatt, 2016; Wysocki & Preti, 2004). Although these compounds may have physiological effects, so do plant odors. Pepper oil, fennel oil, and rose oil can change blood pressure and catecholamine levels (including adrenaline), and the scent of lemon oil increases positive mood. In addition, pheromone studies are criticized for their small sample size, lack of statistical power, lack of replication, and publication bias—the tendency to publish positive results and shelve negative ones. In spite of these concerns, at least one of the critics agrees that we're able to identify family members by odor and that smell may influence our choice of sexual partner, but he attributes these abilities to a finely tuned sense of smell rather than pheromones (Wyatt).

In most animals, attraction is fleeting, lasting only through copulation or, at best, till the end of the mating season. For a few species, though, pair bonding occurs for years or for a lifetime, as we see in the accompanying Application.

Take a Minute to Check Your Knowledge and Understanding

- What change in thinking helped researchers see sex as similar to other biological drives?
- What roles do estrogen and testosterone play in sexual behavior in humans?
- In what ways do sensory stimuli influence sexual behavior?

The Biological Determination of Sex

Now we need to talk about differences between the sexes and the anomalies (exceptions) that occur. *Sex* is the term for the biological characteristics that divide humans and other animals into the categories of male and female. *Gender* refers to the behavioral characteristics associated with being male or female. For our purposes, it will be useful to make two further distinctions: *Gender role* is the set of behaviors society considers appropriate for people of a given biological sex, whereas *gender identity* is the person's subjective feeling of being male or female. The term *sex* cannot be used to refer to all these concepts, because the characteristics are not always consistent with each other. Thus, classifying a person as male or female can sometimes be difficult. You might think that the absolute criterion for identifying a person's sex would be a matter of chromosomes, but you will soon see that it is not that simple.

Chromosomes and Hormones

You may remember from Chapter 1 that when cells divide to produce sex cells, the pairs of chromosomes separate, and each gamete—the sperm or egg—receives only 23 chromosomes. This means that a sex cell has only one of the two sex chromosomes. In mammals, an egg will always have an X chromosome, but a sperm may have either an X chromosome or a Y chromosome. The procreative function of sexual intercourse is to bring the male's sperm into contact with the female's egg, or *ovum*. When the male ejaculates into the female's vagina, the sperm use their tail-like flagella to swim through the uterus and up the fallopian tubes, where the ovum is descending. As soon as one sperm penetrates and enters the ovum, the ovum's membrane immediately becomes impenetrable so that only that sperm is allowed to fertilize the egg. The sperm makes its way to the nucleus of the ovum, where the two sets of chromosomes are combined into a full complement of 23 pairs. After fertilization, the ovum begins dividing, producing the billions of cells that make up the human fetus.

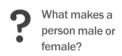
What makes a person male or female?

If the sperm that fertilizes the ovum carries an X sex chromosome, the fetus will develop into a female; if the sperm's sex chromosome is Y, the child will be a male (Figure 7.8).

For the first month, XX and XY fetuses are identical. Later, the primitive *gonads* (testes and ovaries, the primary reproductive organs) in the XX individual develop into *ovaries,* where the ova (eggs) develop. The *Müllerian ducts* develop into the uterus, the fallopian tubes, and the inner vagina, while the Wolffian ducts, which would become the male organs, wither and are absorbed (Figure 7.9). The undifferentiated external genitals become the clitoris, the outer segment of the vagina, and the labia, which partially enclose the entrance to the vagina (Figure 7.10).

If the fetus receives a Y chromosome from the father, the *SRY* (sex-determining region Y) gene on that chromosome produces a protein that causes the primitive gonads to develop into *testes,* the organs that will produce sperm. The testes begin secreting two types of hormones (Haqq et al., 1994). *Müllerian inhibiting hormone* defeminizes the fetus by causing the Müllerian ducts to degenerate. Testosterone, the most prominent of the androgens, masculinizes the internal organs: The *Wolffian ducts* develop into the seminal vesicles, which store semen, and the vas deferens, which carry semen from the testes to the penis. A derivative of testosterone, *dihydrotestosterone,* masculinizes the external genitals. The same structures that produce the clitoris and the

■ **FIGURE 7.8** Female and Male X and Y Chromosomes.

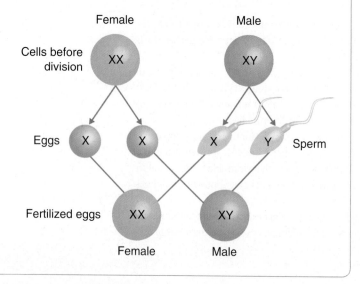

■ **FIGURE 7.9**   Development of Male and Female Internal Organs.

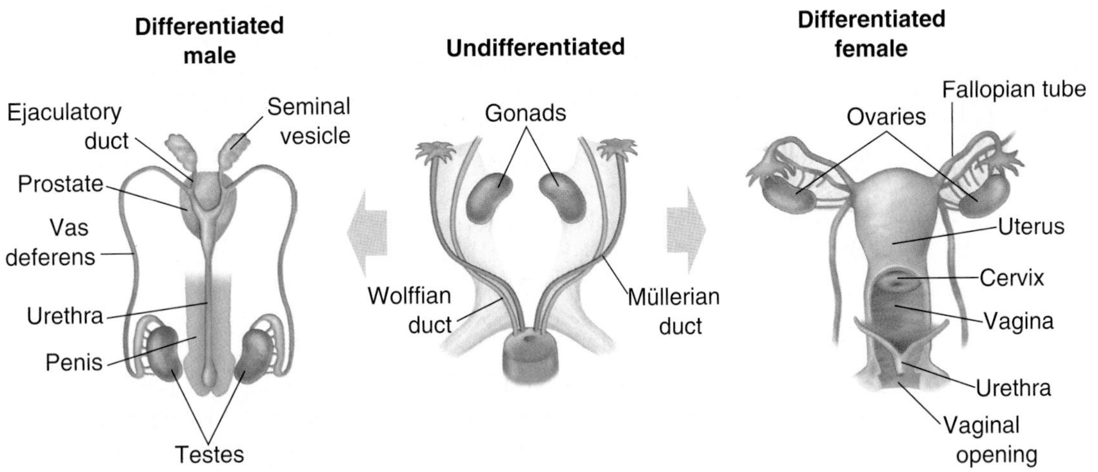

Differentiated male

Ejaculatory duct
Seminal vesicle
Prostate
Vas deferens
Urethra
Penis
Testes

Undifferentiated

Gonads
Wolffian duct
Müllerian duct

Differentiated female

Fallopian tube
Ovaries
Uterus
Cervix
Vagina
Urethra
Vaginal opening

Source: Adapted from *Our Sexuality* (7ed.), by R. Crooks and K. Baur, 1999, Fig. 3.2 p. 46. Stamford, CT: Cengage Learning.

labia in the female become the penis and the scrotum, into which the testes descend during childhood.

In the absence of a Y chromosome (and *SRY* gene), the primitive gonads of the XX fetus develop into ovaries. The ovaries won't begin producing estrogens until later, but in humans *default sex* is female, and the uterus, vagina, clitoris, and labia will all develop without benefit of hormones. You should understand that it is not entirely accurate to speak of hormones as being "male" or "female." The testes and ovaries each secrete both androgens and estrogens, although in differing amounts; the adrenal glands of the kidney also secrete small amounts of both kinds of hormones.

The hormonal effects we have been discussing are called *organizing effects*. *Organizing effects* mostly occur prenatally and shortly after birth; they affect structure and are lifelong in nature. Organizing effects are not limited to the reproductive organs; they include sex-specific changes in the brains of males and females as well, at least in nonhuman mammals. *Activating effects* can occur at any time in the individual's life; they are reversible changes that can come and go as hormone levels change. Some of the changes that occur during puberty are examples of activating effects.

■ **FIGURE 7.10**   Differentiation of Male and Female Genitals.

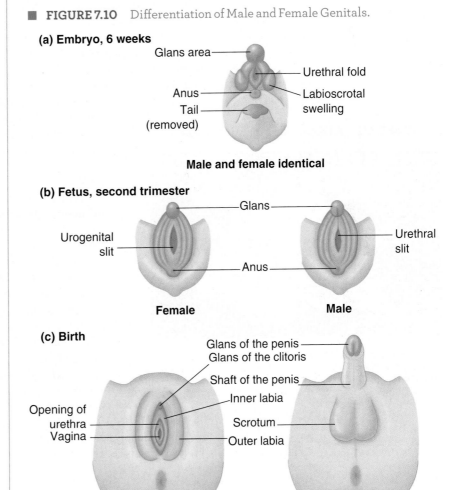

(a) Embryo, 6 weeks

Glans area
Anus
Tail (removed)
Urethral fold
Labioscrotal swelling

Male and female identical

(b) Fetus, second trimester

Glans
Urogenital slit
Urethral slit
Anus

Female   **Male**

(c) Birth

Glans of the penis
Glans of the clitoris
Shaft of the penis
Inner labia
Opening of urethra
Vagina
Scrotum
Outer labia

Female   **Structures with common origins**   **Male**

Source: Based on Netter (1983).

During childhood, differences between boys and girls other than in the genitals are relatively minimal. Boys tend to be heavier and stronger, but there is considerable overlap. Boys also are usually more active and more aggressive, and interests diverge at an early age. Marked differences appear about the time the child enters puberty, usually during the preteen years. At puberty, a surge of estrogens from the ovaries and testosterone from the testes completes the process of sexual differentiation that began during prenatal development. Organizing effects include maturation of the genitals and changes in body size. Activating effects include breast development in the girl and muscle increases and hair growth in the boy. In addition, the girl's ovaries begin releasing the ova that have been there since birth (i.e., she begins to *ovulate*), and she starts to menstruate. Boys' testes start producing sperm, and ejaculation becomes possible. More important from a behavioral perspective, sexual interest increases dramatically, and in the majority of cases, preference for same-sex company shifts to an attraction to the other sex, along with an interest in sexual intimacy.

Prenatal Hormones and the Brain

Several characteristics and behaviors can be identified as male typical and others as female typical. This does not mean that the behaviors are somehow more appropriate for that sex but simply that they occur more frequently in one sex than in the other. These differences are not absolute. For example, consider the stereotypical sexual behavior of rats: The male mounts the female from behind, while the female curves her back and presents her hindquarters in a posture called *lordosis*. However, females occasionally mount other females, and males will sometimes show lordosis when approached by another male.

? What is the effect of "sexualizing" the brain?

The same hormonal influence responsible for the development of male gonads and genitals affects behavior as well. A male rat will display lordosis (arching of the back) and accept the sexual advances of other males if he was castrated shortly after birth or if he was given a chemical that blocks androgens just before birth and for a short time postnatally (after birth). Similarly, a female rat given testosterone during this critical period will mount other females at a higher rate than usual as an adult (Figure 7.11; Gorski, 1974). These behaviors apparently result from the influence of testosterone on the size and function of several brain structures; in other words, the presence of testosterone masculinizes certain brain structures. That statement is somewhat misleading, though, because it is *estradiol,* the principal estrogen hormone, that carries out the final step of masculinization. When testosterone enters a neuron, it is converted to estradiol by a chemical process called *aromatization*. At the critical time when brain masculinization occurs, aromatase increases in the areas that are to be masculinized (Horvath & Wikler, 1999).

Until recently, it was believed that feminization of the brain, like the sex organs, required only the absence of testosterone; now we know that just as masculinization of the male brain requires estradiol, so does feminization of the female brain. Female knockout mice born unable to produce estradiol display less sexual interest and receptivity toward males or females as adults than do other mice, even when they are given replacement estrogens (Bakker, Honda, Harada, & Balthazart, 2002, 2003). Just as the male brain must be masculinized and the female brain feminized, the male brain must also be defeminized. Again, estrogens are necessary; male knockout mice lacking the estrogen receptor showed normal male sexual behavior but also were receptive to advances of other males (Kudwa, Bodo, Gustafsson, & Rissman, 2005).

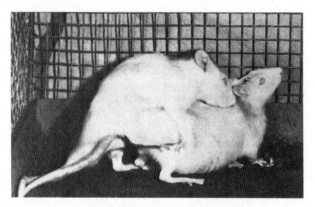

■ **FIGURE 7.11**   A Female Rat Mounting a Male.

Source: From "Sex-Hormone-Dependent Brain Differentiation and Sexual Functions," in G. Dörner (Ed.), *Endocrinology of Sex* (pp. 30–37). Leipzig: J. A. Barth. Copyright © 1974 Gunther Dörner. Used with permission.

This sexualization of the brain is reflected in behavioral differences, affecting not only sexual activity but also play behavior, spatial activity, and learning performance (see Collaer & Hines, 1995). Do hormones have a similar influence in humans? In the following pages we will try to answer that question.

CONCEPT CHECK

Take a Minute to Check Your Knowledge and Understanding

- How is the sex of a fetus determined, and what affects prenatal and postnatal sexual development?
- What effect do sex hormones have on differentiation of the brain and behavior?

Gender-Related Behavioral and Cognitive Differences

In his popular book *Men Are From Mars, Women Are From Venus*, John Gray (1992) said that men and women communicate, think, feel, perceive, respond, love, and need differently, as if they are from different planets and speaking different languages. How different are men and women? This question is not easily answered, but it is not for lack of research on the topic. The results of studies are often ambiguous and contradictory. One reason is that different researchers measure the same characteristic in different ways. Also, the research samples are often too small to yield reliable results, and the subjects are usually not selected in a manner that ensures accurate representation of the population. Whether the differences that do exist are influenced by biology or are solely the product of experience is controversial. Contemporary parents often make efforts to rear their children equally, but it can be difficult to separate oneself from ingrained societal expectations; parents who claimed equality as a childrearing value were found to verbalize differently and play differently with a child dressed as a girl than when the same child was dressed as a boy (Culp, Cook, & Housley, 1983). Differential rearing, of course, could account for marked differences in behavior, temperament, and self-expectations.

Some Demonstrated Male-Female Differences

Back in 1974, Eleanor Maccoby and Carol Jacklin reviewed more than 2,000 studies and concluded that the evidence firmly supported three differences in cognitive performance and one difference in social behavior: (1) Girls have greater verbal ability than boys, (2) boys excel in visual-spatial ability, (3) boys excel in mathematical ability, and (4) boys are more aggressive than girls. Later research has supported these differences to some extent, but with qualifications. First, there is considerable overlap between males and females in these characteristics. Second, the differences are rather specific. For example, females excel in verbal fluency and writing but not in reading comprehension or vocabulary (Eagly, 1995; Hedges & Nowell, 1995), and male spatial performance exceeds females' most on tasks requiring mental rotation of a three-dimensional object (like the one in Figure 7.12) and less on other spatial tasks (Hyde, 1996). More significantly, the differences have narrowed during the ensuing four-plus decades, particularly for the cognitive abilities.

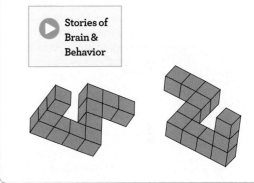

■ **FIGURE 7.12**   A Spatial Rotation Task.

People are presented several pairs of drawings like these and asked whether the first could be rotated so that it looks like the second. Males are typically better at this kind of task than females. (In case you're wondering, the answer in this case is no.)

▶ Stories of Brain & Behavior

Origins of Male-Female Differences

The best evidence that the three cognitive differences mentioned earlier are partially the result of experience is that they have decreased over the years, presumably as gender roles and expectations have changed (Hedges & Nowell, 1995; Hyde, 1996; Voyer, Voyer, & Bryden, 1995). In fact, testing of 7 million students indicates that the gender difference in average mathematical performance has disappeared in the United States, although boys are slightly overrepresented at both the lower and higher extremes (Hyde, Lindberg, Linn, Ellis, & Williams, 2008). Similar trends were found in a study of 89 countries, and data suggested that progress is due to increasing gender equality (Kane & Mertz, 2012). In addition, the dramatic variation in murder rate in different countries suggests there is also a strong cultural influence on aggression; for example, the murder rate in 2014/2015 was 57.15 per 100,000 of population in Venezuela, 4.88 in the United States, 0.92 in the United Kingdom, and 0.31 in Japan ("List of Countries," n.d.).

Although environmental influences play a significant role, gender differences in cognition and behavior also owe a great deal to biology. Most often, researchers attribute the differences to the effects of estrogen and testosterone, particularly on the organizational development of the brain during gestation. Supporting this view is the fact that gender differences in the volume of different brain areas correspond to the density of sex hormone receptors in those areas (J. M. Goldstein et al., 2001). Because the effects of sex hormones on brain development are most evident in people with atypical sexual development, we will hold that discussion for the next section and focus here on activating effects occurring after birth.

Males who produce low amounts of testosterone during the developmental years are impaired later in spatial ability (Hier & Crowley, 1982), and testosterone replacement in older men improves their spatial functioning (Janowsky, Oviatt, & Orwoll, 1994). Individuals born men who take estrogens because they

? How do we explain the differences in verbal and spatial abilities and in aggression?

IN THE NEWS

GTEx PROJECT PROVIDES NEW INSIGHT INTO THE DIFFERENCES BETWEEN THE SEXES

In the years since completion of the Human Genome Project, researchers have focused on understanding how differences in genes' ability to create proteins, or *gene expression,* can provide insight into typical versus atypical human functioning. The Genotype-Tissue Expression (GTEx) Project, which began in 2010, aims to identify differences in gene expression in tissues and organs that have been donated from hundreds of different people, with the hope of better understanding diseases (National Human Genome Research Institute, 2016). Researchers at the Weizmann Institute of Science have recently used some of the GTEx data to determine why human males and females differ in disease risk, behavior, and body type in spite of sharing most genes (Gershoni & Pietrokovski, 2017). Of the approximately 20,000 genes that they examined, the researchers identified more than 6,500 that were expressed differently in at least one tissue of males compared with females. Sex-based gene expression differences were found not just in the reproductive organs and mammary glands but also in the heart, the skin, the liver, and parts of the

brain. These differences in gene expression likely relate to sex differences not only in fat storage, body hair, and milk production and release but also in medical issues such as drug responsiveness, heart muscle disease, and risk for Parkinson's disease. Of particular interest, there were more mutations in male-specific genes than female-specific genes, suggesting that natural selection acts less strongly on males than females, possibly since males can create many more offspring in a lifetime (due to both gestation time and the Coolidge effect).

THOUGHT QUESTIONS

1. Why might so many genes be expressed differently in males and females?

2. What sorts of sex differences in behavior might be explained by gene expression differences?

For the news story, visit edge.sagepub.com/garrett5e and select the Chapter 7 study resources.

identify as females (transgender women) increase their scores on verbal fluency tasks, but they lose spatial performance; transgender men taking testosterone lose verbal ability but improve in spatial performance (for references, see Hulshoff Pol et al., 2006). Men kill 30 times as often as women do (Daly & Wilson, 1988), and testosterone is usually blamed for this difference. However, whether testosterone is the cause or the result of aggression is questioned because a variety of studies show, for example, that winning a sports competition increases testosterone and losing decreases it (Archer, 1991). Aggression in males is partly inheritable; genetic effects account for about half the variance in aggression, and aggression is moderately correlated in identical twins even when they are reared apart (Rushton, Fulker, Neale, Nias, & Eysenck, 1986; Tellegen et al., 1988). The source of aggression is a complex subject, and we will deal with it more thoroughly in Chapter 8.

Differences in brain functioning are also cited as bases for gender differences. Jerre Levy (1969) hypothesized that women outperform men on verbal tests because they are able to use both hemispheres of the brain to solve verbal problems rather than mostly the left hemisphere. This idea has obviously been controversial; there has been some support from fMRI studies, but there have also been negative findings, and a meta-analysis of fMRI studies during language tasks found no lateralization differences between males and females (Sommer, Aleman, Bouma, & Kahn, 2004). This doesn't settle the issue, according to Harrington and Farias (2008), who claim that many fMRI studies are not as methodologically rigorous as they could be, and point out that gender differences should be expected only on some types of tasks. A more recent strategy has been to measure functional connectivity. Some support for Levy's hypothesis comes from studies that found greater connectivity within hemispheres in males and greater connectivity between the hemispheres in females (Ingalhalikar et al., 2014; Tomasi & Volkow, 2012).

A meta-analysis of spatial performance did confirm gender differences, with males relying primarily on the right hemisphere and females showing no hemisphere preference (J. M. Vogel, Bowers, & Vogel, 2003). Imaging studies indicate that men use parietal areas to perform spatial rotations, whereas women rely more on frontal areas (reviewed in Andreano & Cahill, 2009), and that men's scores on the task are correlated with the amount of cortical surface in the parietal lobes (Koscik, O'Leary, Moser, Andreasen, & Nopoulos, 2009). In an fMRI study, men performed a spatial memory task by activating the right hippocampus, whereas women relied on the left hippocampus and reported using a verbal strategy (Frings et al., 2006).

There are also several other indications that male and female brains work differently. Males and females have different patterns of brain activation during learning (Andreano & Cahill, 2009), pain (Naliboff et al., 2003), and stress (J. Wang et al., 2007). Males are genetically more resistant to pain, and males and females respond differently to different pain medications (J. Bradbury, 2003). Men are less affected by stress (Matud, 2004), and, as you will see in subsequent chapters, males are more susceptible to autism, Tourette syndrome, and attention-deficit/hyperactivity disorder, whereas women are more likely to suffer from depression and Alzheimer's disease. Research described in the accompanying In the News feature suggests that some of these differences may be due to male-female differences in expression of their genes.

The value of studying these differences is not to determine whether one sex is smarter or more aggressive or healthier than the other but to understand what contributes to the characteristics in either sex. Keep in mind that aside from physical strength and possibly aggressiveness, the differences are small and do not justify discrimination in society or in the workplace. We are far more alike than we are different; this is a reason to use the term *other sex* instead of *opposite sex*. There are real differences, though, and an understanding of their origins could help us enhance intellectual development, reduce violence, and cure or manage diseases. From a scientific perspective, that knowledge also helps us understand how the brain develops, an issue that we will continue to pursue in the next two sections.

CONCEPT CHECK

Take a Minute to Check Your Knowledge and Understanding

- What are the origins of male-female differences in verbal and spatial abilities?
- What are the arguments for environmental origins and for biological origins of male-female differences in cognitive abilities and behaviors?

Biological Origins of Gender Identity

For decades, sex researchers have argued about what shapes an individual's gender identity, with some believing it is formed in the first few years of life by a combination of rearing practices and genital appearance (Money & Ehrhardt, 1972) and others claiming that chromosomes and hormones are more important (M. Diamond, 1965). Our earlier discussion of the effects of XY and XX chromosomes was the simple version of the sex-determination story; in reality, development sometimes takes an unexpected turn. As you will soon see, the results not only challenge our definition of what is male and what is female but also tell us a great deal about the influence of biology on gender.

> There is no one biological parameter that clearly defines sex.
>
> —Eric Vilain

Gender Dysphoria

Individuals who believe they have been born into the wrong sex are referred to as *transgender*. They may dress and live as the other sex, take hormones to feminize or masculinize their bodies, or undergo surgery for sex reassignment. It is estimated that 0.1%–0.5% of people in the United States and the United Kingdom have taken some steps to transition to the other sex (Gates, 2011). Distress that people may feel due to the perception that their sex does not match their gender is called *gender dysphoria*. The best therapeutic outcomes have resulted from the requested hormonal and surgical treatment rather than psychotherapy alone (Saraswat, Weinand, & Safer, 2015). Gender dysphoria is estimated to occur in 0.005%–0.014% of adult males and in 0.002%–0.003% of adult females (American Psychiatric Association, 2013). Gender dissatisfaction that appears as early as three or four years of age appears to be due mostly to family environmental influences (Knafo, Iervolino, & Plomin, 2005); among adolescents the heritability is estimated at 62%, with the remainder due to nonfamily environmental influence (Coolidge, Thede, & Young, 2002). Specific genes that have been identified are alleles of the *CYP17* gene and the *AR* gene. The first increases testosterone levels in

What influences affect gender identity and gender-related behavior?

■ **FIGURE 7.13**   BSTc Size in a Male-to-Female Transgender Individuals.

Representative images of the stained BSTc in a (a) heterosexual male, (b) heterosexual female, (c) homosexual male, and (d) male-to-female transgender individual.

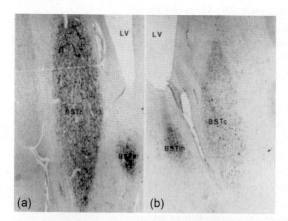

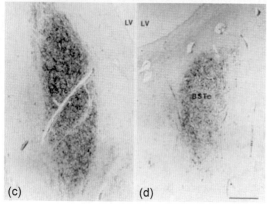

Source: Figure 2, "A Sex Difference in the Human Brain and Its Relation to Transsexuality," by J.-N. Zhou, M. A. Hofman, L. J. Gooren, and D. F. Swaab, 1995, *Nature*, 378, pp. 68–70. Reprinted by permission of Nature, copyright 1995.

female-to-male transgender individuals (Bentz et al., 2008) and the second reduces sensitivity to androgen in male-to-female transgender individuals (Hare et al., 2009); the researchers believe these genes lead to masculinization of the female brain and a failure to masculinize the male brain.

How could an individual's genitals and brain develop at variance with each other? They differentiate sexually at different times during gestation, the genitals during the first two months and the brain during the last half, presumably allowing them to fall under the influence of independent processes (Bao & Swaab, 2011). Several studies suggest that the brains of transgender individuals have followed a different developmental path, finding that various brain structures are more like those of their identified sex than of their birth sex in size, shape, or patterning (reviewed in Saraswat et al., 2015). The *third interstitial nucleus of the anterior hypothalamus (INAH3)* is larger in men than in women and is thought to be the human counterpart of the sexually dimorphic nucleus. It and the bed nucleus of the stria terminalis (BSTc, which controls autonomic, neuroendocrine, and behavioral responses) are larger in males than in females, but they have been reported to be female sized in male-to-female transgender individuals (Figure 7.13; Garcia-Falgueras & Swaab, 2008; Kruijver et al., 2000; J. N. Zhou, Hofman, Gooren, & Swaab, 1995). INAH3 is believed to correspond to the sexually dimorphic nucleus in animals. Female-typical brain responses have also been reported in male-to-female transgender individuals. In a study with presumed pheromones, an androgen derivative found in male sweat (4, 16-androstadien-3-one, or AND) activated the anterior hypothalamus, whereas an estrogen-like compound found in female urine (estratetraenol, or EST) did not (Berglund, Lindström, Dhejne-Helmy, & Savic, 2008). In a second study, when male-to-female transgender individuals viewed an erotic video, their pattern of brain responses resembled those of women rather than men (Gizewski et al., 2009). The studies are vulnerable to a variety of criticisms, however: Some, though not all, of the studies are potentially contaminated because the subjects were undergoing hormone treatment; studies have rarely been replicated, and results from attempts have been inconsistent; and "data-snooping" brain scans—measuring a large number of structures because the researcher doesn't know what to look for—increases the probability of incorrectly identifying one of them as different, especially in the small samples that are typical of research on transgender individuals.

For a variety of reasons, obtaining reliable data on gender identity has not been easy; the sexual variations described in the sections that follow serve as "natural experiments" that provide valuable, and sometimes dramatic, additional information.

46 XY Difference in Sexual Development

At puberty Jan had failed to develop breasts or to menstruate; instead, her voice deepened, and her body became muscular, while her clitoris grew to a length of 4 centimeters (1½ inches) and her vaginal lips partially closed, giving the appearance of a male scrotum. Once comfortable with her tomboyishness, she was now embarrassed by her appearance and increasingly masculine mannerisms; she withdrew from peers, and her school performance began to suffer. To everyone's surprise, her doctor discovered two undescended testes in her abdomen and no ovaries. After a psychiatric evaluation, Jan's parents and doctors offered Jan the opportunity to change to a male sexual identity. She immediately went home and changed into boy's clothing and got a boy's haircut. The family moved to another neighborhood where they were unknown. At the new high school, Jack became an athlete, excelled as a student, was well accepted socially, and began dating girls. Surgeons finished closing the labia and moved the testes into the newly formed scrotum. He developed into a muscular, 6-foot-tall male with a deep voice and a heavy beard. At the age of 25 he married, and he and his wife reported a mutually satisfactory sexual relationship (Imperato-McGinley, Peterson, Stoller, & Goodwin, 1979).

Today Jack would be diagnosed with *46 XY difference in sexual development* (46 XY DSD), meaning that he had a typical number of chromosomes, including an X and a Y chromosome, but his sexual development was atypical for those chromosomes. The term adopted by practitioners in 2006 used the word *disorder* in place of *difference*. Some observers contend that sexual development is a continuum, and prefer the term *difference* in place of *disorder*; in respect for that view, we will use DSD here to mean "difference in sexual development." These variations in development have a variety of causes. The reason for Jack's unusual development was a deficiency in an enzyme (17α-hydroxysteroid) that converts testosterone into dihydrotestosterone; dihydrotestosterone masculinizes the external genitalia before birth. The large surge of testosterone at puberty enabled his body partially to carry out that process.

A deficiency in another enzyme, 5α-reductase, also reduces dihydrotestosterone levels and delays genital development; this deficiency is genetic and is most likely to occur when there is frequent intermarriage among relatives. Of 18 such individuals in the Dominican Republic who were reared unambiguously as girls, all but one made the transition to a male gender identity after puberty, and 15 were living or had lived with women (Imperato-McGinley, Peterson, Gautier, & Sturla, 1979). The men said they realized they were different from girls and began questioning their sex between the ages of 7 and 12. Although their transition argues for the influence of genes and hormones on gender identity, such a conclusion must be tentative because the individuals had a great deal to gain from the switch in a society that puts a high premium on maleness (Cohen-Kettenis, 2005).

Eden Atwood (Figure 7.14) is a widely acclaimed jazz singer. She has recorded and performed all over the world and with the biggest names in jazz. Ms. Atwood is also remarkable for having been born with XY chromosomes and two testes. Her *androgen insensitivity syndrome,* a form of 46 XY DSD, is caused by a genetic absence of androgen receptors, which results in insensitivity to androgen. Müllerian inhibiting hormone suppresses development of most of the female internal organs, but because the individual is unaffected by androgens, the testes do not descend and the external genitals develop as more or less feminine (depending on the degree of insensitivity), with a shallow vagina. If the genitals are mostly feminine, the child is reared as a girl, and at puberty her body is further feminized by estrogen from the testes and adrenal glands. The condition may not be recognized until menstruation fails to occur at puberty or when unsuccessful attempts to become pregnant lead to a more complete medical examination. In the absence of testosterone's influence, androgen-insensitive individuals tend to have well-developed breasts and a flawless complexion. Because these characteristics are often combined with long, slender legs, androgen-insensitive males repeatedly turn up among female fashion models (J. Diamond, 1992).

■ **FIGURE 7.14**   Eden Atwood.

ZUMA Press, Inc. / Alamy

46 XX Difference in Sexual Development

A female fetus may be partially masculinized by excess androgen and by some hormone treatments during fetal development, resulting in *46 XX difference in sexual development*. The internal organs are female, because no Müllerian inhibiting hormone is released, but the external genitals are virilized to some extent; that is, they have some degree of masculine appearance. In extreme cases, the clitoris is as large as a newborn male's penis, and the external labia are partially or completely fused to give the appearance of an empty scrotum.

Figure 7.15 illustrates one cause of 46 XX DSD; *congenital adrenal hyperplasia (CAH),* which results from an enzyme defect that causes the individual's adrenal glands to produce large amounts of androgen during fetal development and after birth until the problem is treated. Postnatal hormone levels can be normalized by administering corticosteroids, and the parents often choose reconstructive surgery to reduce the size of the clitoris and eliminate labial fusion, giving the genitals a more feminine

■ **FIGURE 7.15** Female Infant With Congenital Adrenal Hyperplasia.

Parents of children with ambiguous genitalia often have difficulty knowing whether to rear them as boys or as girls. (The unusual pigmentation of the skin is due to excess excretion of sodium, or *salt wasting*, which often occurs with CAH.)

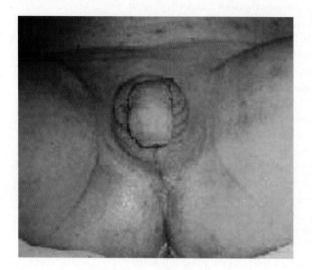

Source: Used with permission of Thomas A. Wilson, MD, The School of Medicine at Stony Brook University Medical Center.

appearance. If masculinization is more pronounced, the parents may decide to rear the child as a boy; in that case, the surgeons usually finish closing the labia and insert artificial testes in the scrotum to enhance the masculine appearance. Recent work indicates that the most common cause of CAH, 21-hydroxylase deficiency, can be detected in the womb and treated with a synthetic corticosteroid to reduce genital ambiguity (Nimkarn & New, 2010).

Obviously, sex cannot always be neatly divided between male and female. Some experts believe that two categories are not sufficient to describe the variations in masculinity and femininity. Anne Fausto-Sterling (1993) advocates at least five sexual categories. The ones between male and female are often referred to as *intersex conditions,* a term that is not used in the medical profession but is preferred by many individuals. It would be easy to get caught up in the unusual physical characteristics of these individuals and to be distracted from our question: What makes a person male or female? This question is the topic of the accompanying Application as well as the next few pages.

Cognitive and Behavioral Effects

As mentioned earlier, reversing the sex hormone balance during prenatal development changes the brain and later behavior in nonhuman animals. Is it possible that masculinization and feminization of the developing brain account for sex differences in behavior and cognitive abilities in humans as well? If so, then we would expect the behavior and abilities of individuals who have experienced an excess or a deficit of androgen during prenatal development to be at odds with their chromosomal sex.

That is indeed the case. Androgen-insensitive males are like females in that their verbal ability is higher than their spatial performance, and their spatial performance is lower than that of other males (Imperato-McGinley, Pichardo, Gautier, Voyer, & Bryden, 1991; Masica, Money, Ehrhardt, & Lewis, 1969). And though there have been contradictory results, evidence favors increased spatial ability in CAH women (Puts, McDaniel, Jordan, & Breedlove, 2008). Androgen-insensitive 46 XY individuals also are typically feminine in behavior, have a strong childbearing urge, and are decidedly female in their sexual orientation (M. Hines, 1982; Money, Schwartz, & Lewis, 1984; J. M. Morris, 1953). Although 95% of CAH women reared as girls accept a female identity, they also show behavioral shifts in the masculine direction (Dessens, Slijper, & Drop, 2005). They have been reported to be tomboyish in childhood (M. Hines); to prefer boys' toys, such as trucks and building blocks (Berenbaum, Duck, & Bryk, 2000); and to draw pictures more typical of boys, using darker colors and including mechanical objects and excluding people (Iijima, Arisaka, Minamoto, & Arai, 2001). They also more often report male-dominated occupational choices (30% vs. 13%), interest in rough sports (74% vs. 50%), and interest in motor vehicles (14% vs. 0%; Frisén et al., 2009). There is evidence that these effects are due to androgen levels before birth rather than during postnatal development (Berenbaum et al., 2000). Homosexual or bisexual orientation has been reported to be as high as 37% (Money et al., 1984) and at 19% in a recent larger study (Frisén et al.).

Some critics claim that humans are sexually neutral at birth, and they attribute the cognitive and behavioral effects we have just seen to feminine or ambiguous rearing in response to the child's genital appearance. (You may be beginning to appreciate the deficiencies of natural experiments.) However, some of the findings are difficult to explain from a socialization perspective. For example, the anti-miscarriage drug diethylstilbestrol (DES) given to women in the 1950s and 1960s has an androgen-like effect in the brain but does not virilize the genitals, yet DES-exposed daughters reported increased homosexual fantasy and behavior (Ehrhardt et al., 1985; Meyer-Bahlburg et al., 1995). In another study, girls exposed to a similar drug and who had nonvirilized genitals scored higher in aggression than their unexposed sisters (Reinisch, 1981). In addition, the fact that androgen-insensitive 46 XY individuals perform even lower on spatial tests than their unaffected sisters and female controls (Imperato-McGinley et al., 1991) can be explained by insensitivity to androgens but not by "feminine rearing."

? What are the behavioral implications of 46 XX and 46 XY DSD?

"
The evidence accumulated so far strongly suggests that man is no exception with regard to the influence of sex steroids on the developing brain and subsequent behavior.

—Anke Ehrhardt and Heino Meyer-Bahlburg
"

APPLICATION
Sex, Gender, and Sports

Cameron Spencer/Getty Images Sport/Getty.

When Caster Semenya of South Africa won the gold medal in the 800-meter race at the 2009 World Championships in Athletics, her strong performance and masculine physique aroused suspicions about her gender. Fueled by years of media reports that some female competitors might actually be men, the International Association of Athletics Federations (IAAF) and the International Olympic Committee (IOC) had introduced routine gender testing in the 1960s (J. L. Simpson et al., 1993). However, physical examination was soon rejected as unacceptable to many women, and chromosome testing turned out to be inadequate as a measure of performance advantage. For example, Barr body analysis, which identifies cells with XX chromosomes, rejects androgen-insensitive XY individuals though they receive no benefit from testosterone, but it would pass XXY males, who do benefit. The IOC and the IAAF ended routine testing in the 1990s, though both reserved the authority to request gender identification on an individual basis.

Semenya agreed to an IAAF request to undergo extensive gender testing. In the meantime, reports were leaked that Semenya had two testes and triple the normal level of testosterone for a female. The IAAF said that if the reports turned out to be accurate, it would pay for corrective surgery; the surgery would remove the internal testes, which have a high risk for cancer, and eliminate the source of the extra testosterone. When the IAAF received the report, it did not reveal the results to the public, but nearly a year after the championships, Semenya was cleared to compete again—as a woman. Some sexual activists argue that if society would place less emphasis on gender, whether a person is male or female wouldn't matter, but this case suggests there is a need for better understanding of what it means to be male or female.

The IOC tried to skirt the gender issue in 2012 by announcing it would bar athletes from competing as females if they had normal male levels of androgens and were responsive to androgens. However, this policy on hyperandrogenism was suspended in 2015 when female Indian sprinter Dutee Chand, who had a high testosterone level, brought suit in the Court of Arbitration for Sport (Branch, 2015). The court decided that evidence demonstrating testosterone-related increased athletic performance in women was lacking and gave the IAAF until 2017 to provide data supporting its claim for hormone-induced enhanced female performance.

Sources: "Caster Semenya Must Wait…," 2010; S. Hart, 2009; Macur, 2012; O'Reilly, 2010; Powers, 2010.

Ablatio Penis and Other Natural Experiments

The "neutral-at-birth" theorists claim that individuals reared in opposition to their chromosomal sex generally accept their sex of rearing and that this demonstrates that rearing has more effect on gender role behavior than chromosomes or hormones (studies reviewed in M. Diamond, 1965). Diamond, who advocates a "sexuality-at-birth" hypothesis, argues that the reason individuals with ambiguous genitals accept their assigned gender is that sex of rearing is usually decided by whether the genital appearance is predominantly masculine or feminine, which in turn reflects the influence of prenatal hormones. According to Diamond, there was no case in the literature where an *unambiguously* male or female individual was successfully reared in opposition to the biological sex. He and others (such as Money, Devore, & Norman, 1986) have described several instances in which individuals assigned as one sex successfully shifted to their chromosomal and gonadal sex in later years, long after the assumed window for forming gender identity (the first few years of life) had closed. Failures in predicting the later gender identity of a child with ambiguous genitals has led several experts (along with the advocacy group Accord Alliance) to advocate waiting until the child can give

> "
> *Gender identity is sufficiently incompletely differentiated at birth as to permit successful assignment of a genetic male as a girl.*
>
> —John Money
>
> *An extensive search of the literature reveals no case where a male or female without some sort of biological abnormality . . . accepted an imposed gender role opposite to that of his or her phenotype.*
>
> —Milton Diamond
> "

informed consent, or at least indicates a clear gender preference; others are reluctant to see the child subjected to the social difficulties that result from an ambiguous appearance.

In 1966, an eight-month-old boy became the most famous example of resistance to sexual reassignment when the surgeon using electrocautery to perform a circumcision turned the voltage too high and destroyed the boy's penis (called *ablatio penis*). After months of consultation and agonizing, Bruce's parents decided to let surgeons transform his genitals to feminine-appearing ones. While sounding radical even today, this has remained the recommended practice for *ablatio penis* cases. The neutral-at-birth view was widely accepted then, and the psychologist John Money counseled the parents that they could expect their son to adopt a female gender identity (M. Diamond & Sigmundson, 1997). Bruce would be renamed Brenda, and "she" would be reared as a girl. This case study had two characteristics lacking in other "natural experiments": The child was normal before the accident, and he happened to have an identical twin brother who served as a control.

Over the next several years, Money (1968; Money & Ehrhardt, 1972) reported that Brenda was growing up feminine, enjoying her dresses and hairdos, and choosing to help her mother in the house, while her "typical boy" brother played outside. But developmental progress was not nearly as smooth as Money claimed (M. Diamond & Sigmundson, 1997). Brenda was in fact a tomboy who played rough-and-tumble sports and fought, preferred her brother's toys and trucks over her dolls, and even preferred to urinate in a standing position. She had private doubts about her sex beginning in the second grade, decided she was a boy at age 11, and decided to switch to living as a male at 14. Only then did Brenda's father tell her the story of her sexual transition in infancy. Then, said Brenda, "everything clicked. For the first time things made sense and I understood who and what I was" (p. 300).

Brenda changed her name to David and requested treatment with testosterone, removal of the breasts that had developed under estrogen treatment, and construction of a penis. The person who was isolated and teased as a girl was accepted and popular as a boy, and he attracted girlfriends. At age 25, he married Jane and adopted her three children. Although he was limited in his sexual performance, he and Jane engaged in sexual play and occasional intercourse.

■ **FIGURE 7.16**   David Reimer, 1965–2004.

But life was still not ideal. He brooded about his childhood and was often angry or depressed; after 14 years, Jane told him they should separate for a while. Troubled by his past and his present, and perhaps a victim of heredity—his mother had attempted suicide, his father became an alcoholic, and his twin brother died of an overdose of antidepressants—one spring day in 2004 David Reimer took his own life (Figure 7.16; Colapinto, 2004).

Although only seven cases of ablatio penis have been examined in the literature, there are numerous instances of male infants born with a missing or underdeveloped penis, not involving hormonal causes. These include malformation of the pelvic area (cloacal exstrophy) and absence of a penis (penile agenesis). All of these conditions require decisions about surgical intervention and gender rearing (Meyer-Bahlburg, 2005). In 311 such individuals reared as male, all accepted that role, with only one indicating possible gender dysphoria. Of the 77 reared as females, 22% transitioned later to male and 13% more exhibited possible gender dysphoria. In another study of individuals with cloacal exstrophy who were assigned a female gender shortly after birth, most exhibited male-like behaviors and had switched to a male persona later in life (Reiner & Gearhart, 2004). The accompanying Application describes a recent case that highlights the need for better understanding when a child's gender must be chosen.

CONCEPT CHECK

Take a Minute to Check Your Knowledge and Understanding

- How do the sexual anomalies require you to rethink the meaning of male and female?
- What reasons can you give for thinking that the brains of people with sexual anomalies have been masculinized or feminized contrary to their chromosomal sex?

Sexual Orientation

Sex researchers, along with the rest of us, spend a great deal of time arguing about why some people are attracted to members of the same sex. Whether we know it or not, we are also asking why most people are heterosexual. The answer to that question may seem obvious, but the fact that a behavior is nearly universal and widely accepted does not mean that it requires no explanation. People who are attracted to members of their own sex may be able to tell us not only about homosexuality but also about the basis for sexual orientation in general.

It is difficult to estimate how many people are homosexual; the numbers vary from study to study and from one country to another, due to differences in definition and sampling methods, as well as reluctance to admit membership in a stigmatized group. In a review of nine studies, the average rate in the United States was 3.5%, with Canada, Australia, the United Kingdom, and Norway ranging from 1.2% to 2.1% (Gates, 2011). In the United States, prevalence was equally divided between men and women. Although almost two thirds of the nonheterosexual men identified themselves as exclusively homosexual, only one third of nonheterosexual women did so. Interestingly, when Gallup asked Americans what percentage of the U.S. population they thought was gay or lesbian, the average answer was 23% (Newport, 2015). That response hasn't changed significantly since 2002, in spite of increasing acceptance of homosexuality and access to greater information. Homosexual experiences are fairly common, especially during adolescence and in the absence of heterosexual opportunities. Almost 8% of the population have had at least one same-sex sexual encounter, and as many as 11% report same-sex attraction (Gates, 2011). As Ellis and Ames (1987) point out, these experiences do not make a person homosexual any more than occasional heterosexual activity makes a person heterosexual. About 1% of people express no interest in sex at all (Bogaert, 2004). *Asexuality* is gaining acceptance as an additional category of preference.

Research does not support the belief that gay men are necessarily feminine and lesbians are masculine; only about 44% of gays and 54% of lesbians fit those descriptions (Bell, Weinberg, & Hammersmith, 1981). Even then, they usually identify with their biological sex, so gender role, gender identity, and sexual orientation are somewhat independent of each other and probably have different origins.

 Why is it difficult to measure sexual orientation rates?

APPLICATION
Who Chooses a Child's Sex?

Source: Barcroft/Barcroft Media/Getty Images.

M.C. was born diagnosed with ovotesticular DSD; he had a normal penis and a scrotum and testosterone levels were high, but there was a small vaginal opening below his penis. His physicians recommended corrective surgery, but even though he was identified as male at birth, four months later

they decided he would be reassigned as a girl. Because M.C. was a ward of the state, the South Carolina Department of Social Services approved the surgery, which was performed at the age of 16 months, just 3 months before he was adopted by Pam and Mark Crawford. M.C. behaved more like a boy than a girl; he wanted a haircut like his dad, and he wanted to use the men's restroom and to be referred to as a boy. At the age of 7 he chose to begin living as a boy, an identity supported by his family, friends, school, pediatrician, and religious leaders. M.C.'s adoptive parents filed a legal suit against the Medical University of South Carolina, the Greenville Health System, and the Department of Social Services, on the grounds that the decision should have been left to the boy. Defense attorneys got the case dismissed from federal court by arguing that the doctors had no way of knowing at the time that they were violating M.C.'s constitutional rights, but the state case is proceeding. (For sources, see On the Web at the end of the chapter.)

It is not clear what causes homosexuality, which means that we do not know how to explain heterosexuality either. There is considerable evidence for biological influences on sexual orientation, or else the topic would not appear in this chapter. But because social influences are commonly believed to be more important, we will consider this position first.

The Social Influence Hypothesis

It has been argued that homosexuality arises from parental influences or is caused by early sexual experiences. Bell and his colleagues (1981) expected to confirm these influences when they studied 979 gay and 477 heterosexual men. But they found no support for frequently hypothesized environmental influences, such as seduction by an older male or a dominant mother and a weak father.

Several developmental experiences do seem to differentiate homosexuals from heterosexuals, and these have been considered evidence for a social learning hypothesis (Van Wyk & Geist, 1984). But these experiences—such as spending more time with other-sex playmates in childhood, learning to masturbate by being masturbated by a member of the same sex, and homosexual contact by age 18—can just as easily be interpreted as reflecting an early predisposition to homosexuality. In fact, Bell and his associates (1981) concluded that adult homosexuality "is just *a continuation of the earlier homosexual feelings and behaviors from which it can be so successfully predicted*" (p. 186; italics in the original). However, they did find more evidence for an influence of learning on bisexuality than on exclusive homosexuality. This suggests that there might be a biological influence that varies in degree, with experience making the final decision in the individuals with weaker predispositions for homosexuality.

Among homosexuals, 70% remember feeling "different" as early as four or five years of age (Bell et al., 1981; Savin-Williams, 1996). Memories of feelings are suspect, because they are easily distorted in light of today's circumstances. Memories of behavior are somewhat more reliable, and home videos from childhood are better yet. These behavioral measures show a high rate of *gender nonconformity,* including mannerisms and dress typical of the other sex, a tendency to engage in activities usually preferred by the other sex, and an atypical preference for other-sex playmates and companions while growing up (Bell et al., 1981; Rieger, Linsenmeier, Gygax, & Bailey, 2008). If we are to entertain a biological hypothesis of sexual orientation, though, we must come up with some reasonable explanation for how it is formed and how it is altered. There are three biological approaches to the question: *genetic, hormonal,* and *neural.*

Genetic and Epigenetic Influences

Twin and family studies provide the most documented evidence for a biological basis for sexual orientation. Homosexuality is seen two to seven times more often among the siblings of homosexuals than it is in the general population (J. M. Bailey & Bell, 1993; J. M. Bailey & Benishay, 1993; Hamer, Hu, Magnuson, Hu, & Pattatucci, 1993). Studies in the early 1990s reported concordances of about 50% in identical twins for both men and women (J. M. Bailey & Pillard, 1991; J. M. Bailey et al., 1993). However, when subjects were recruited without regard to their sexual preference, concordances for men fell to 37% in one study and 18% in another, and women's concordances dropped to 30% and 22% (J. M. Bailey, Dunne, & Martin, 2000; Långström, Rahman, Carlström, & Lichtenstein, 2010). Presumably the earlier data suffered from volunteer bias, due to homosexual individuals' greater willingness to volunteer if they had a homosexual sibling.

The search for specific genes has been frustrating, which is not uncommon when multiple genes are involved; because any number of combinations of the genes can produce the behavior, a particular gene can have a significant effect in one study and go undetected in the next. The most successful research on male homosexuality has involved a stretch of DNA on the X chromosome. Dean Hamer and his associates (1993) focused

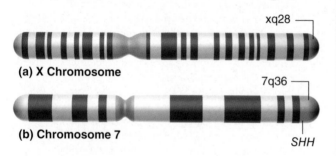

■ **FIGURE 7.17**   Possible Locations of Genes for Male Homosexuality.

(a) The X chromosome, showing the Xq28 region. (b) Chromosome 7, indicating region 7q36 and the relative location of the *SHH* gene.

(a) **X Chromosome**   xq28

(b) **Chromosome 7**   7q36   *SHH*

Source: Based on data from "Genetic and Environmental Effects on Same-Sex Sexual Behavior: A Population Study of Twins in Sweden," by N. Långström, Q. Rahman, E. Carlström, and P. Lichtenstein, 2010, *Archives of Sexual Behavior,* 39, pp. 75–80.

their attention there because gay men have more gay relatives on the mother's side of the family than on the father's side, and the mother contributes only X chromosomes to her sons. They found that 64% of the pairs of gay brothers they studied shared identical genetic material at one end of the X chromosome, in the region designated as Xq28 (Figure 7.17a). The location received additional confirmation in a meta-analysis of the five studies available in 1999 (Hamer, 1999), a whole-genome study in 2005 (Mustanski et al., 2005), and a recent unusually large study of 409 pairs of homosexual brothers (Sanders et al., 2015). The gene itself has not been identified yet, however. The Sanders study also supported linkage at 8q12, which had been tentatively identified a decade earlier. A whole-genome study implicated a stretch of DNA on chromosome 7 in the 7q36 region (Mustanski et al.), and a later study of Chinese homosexual men implicated an allele of the *SHH* gene there (Figure 7.17b; B. Wang et al., 2012). *SHH* contributes to the patterning of organ development, from growth of fingers to organization of the brain, but it is also involved in male-male sexual activity, at least in fruit flies. Female sexual orientation, by contrast, does not appear to be linked to 7q36 (S. Hu et al., 1995; Ngun & Vilain, 2014).

Evidence that homosexuality is influenced by genes presents a Darwinian contradiction; how could homosexuality survive when its genes are unlikely to be passed on by the homosexual individual? Italian researchers have offered an intriguing proposal; the birth rate is higher in women on the mother's side of the family of male homosexuals, so they conclude that genes responsible for homosexuality also increase the women's birth rate—compensating for the homosexual's lack of productivity (Camperio Ciani, Corna, & Capiluppi, 2004; Iemmola & Camperio Ciani, 2009). A later analysis indicated that this effect is best explained by two genes, at least one of which is on the X chromosome; the researchers also suggested that the genes increase attraction to men, in both men and women (Camperio Ciani, Cermelli, & Zanzotto, 2008).

In the face of recent data indicating that environmental influences are stronger than previously thought, we need to look further for the sources. As you can see in Figure 7.18, unique environmental factors are much greater than shared (family) influences (Långström et al., 2010). At the age of three or four, when prehomosexual feelings and behaviors typically appear, there has been little opportunity for social influences outside the family to come into play; this means that the prenatal environment is the more likely source of these unique influences. A variety of epigenetic mechanisms have been proposed as a prenatal factor. In females, one of each pair of X chromosomes in every cell is turned off by methylation; which of the two X chromosomes gets turned off usually varies randomly from cell to cell. However, inactivation of the same chromosome occurred in 90% of the cells in 13% of women with a homosexual son and 23% of the mothers of two or more gay sons, compared with only 4% of women with no gay sons (Bocklandt, Horvath, Vilain, & Hamer, 2006). Another suggestion is that an epigenetic modification of testosterone sensitivity that occurs in a parent as compensation for an atypical testosterone level could be passed on to the offspring (W. R. Rice, Friberg, &

Gravilets, 2012). If a man with low testosterone transfers his increased sensitivity to a daughter, or a woman with high testosterone transfers her decreased sensitivity to a son, it could have significant effects on the offspring's sexual and gender development. In the most promising effort so far, researchers at UCLA studying identical twins discordant for homosexuality identified a pattern of methylation in five DNA regions; the pattern predicted which individuals were homosexual with 70% accuracy (Ngun et al., 2015). The researchers cautioned that it is too early to know how well this predictive ability will generalize outside the sample.

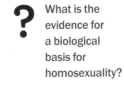

What is the evidence for a biological basis for homosexuality?

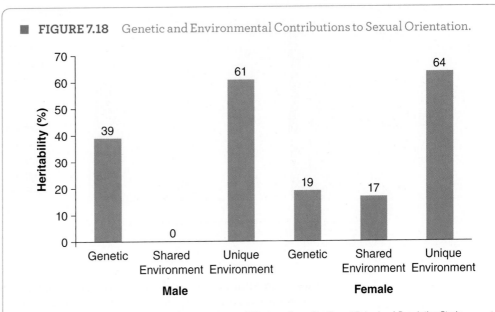

■ **FIGURE 7.18**   Genetic and Environmental Contributions to Sexual Orientation.

Source: Based on data from "Genetic and Environmental Effects on Same-Sex Sexual Behavior: A Population Study of Twins in Sweden," by N. Långström, Q. Rahman, E. Carlström, and P. Lichtenstein, 2010, *Archives of Sexual Behavior*, 39, pp. 75–80.

Prenatal Influences on Brain Structure and Function

? Which brain structures are different in homosexual males?

For early researchers, the most obvious biological explanation was that homosexuality is due to atypical sex hormone levels. Their attempts to reverse male homosexuality by administering testosterone not only were not successful but often increased homosexual activity (for references, see A. C. Kinsey, Pomeroy, Martin, & Gebbard, 1953). Later studies measured hormonal levels and found no evidence of either a deficit or an excess of sex hormones (Gartrell, 1982; Meyer-Bahlburg, 1984). However, by manipulating hormonal levels during gestation and shortly after birth, researchers were able to produce same-sex preference in rats, hamsters, ferrets, pigs, and zebra finches (for references, see LeVay, 1996).

Critics say this effect has no bearing on human behavior, claiming that spontaneous homosexual behavior occurs in animals only when members of the other sex are unavailable and that it does not represent a shift in sexual orientation. However, about 10% of male sheep prefer other males as sex partners, and some form pair bonds in which they take turns mounting and copulating anally with each other (Perkins & Fitzgerald, 1992). A few female gulls observed on Santa Barbara Island off the coast of California form "lesbian" pairs—courting, attempting copulation, taking turns sitting on their nest, and sharing parenting if some of the eggs were fertilized during an "unfaithful" interlude with a male (Hunt & Hunt, 1977; Hunt, Newman, Warner, Wingfield, & Kaiwi, 1984). A shortage of males could be a contributing factor, but the gulls' behavior is atypical of opportunistic homosexuality in that the majority of birds stay paired for more than one season.

If sex hormones play a role in human sexual orientation, they probably do so by altering brain development during gestation. It is difficult to measure prenatal hormone levels in humans, so researchers have looked for evidence for hypo- or hyper-masculinization of homosexuals' brains by examining differences known or thought to be influenced by sex hormones during development. A few differences in brain structures have been reported, including equal-sized cerebral hemispheres in gay males and straight women, with a larger right hemisphere in lesbian females and heterosexual men (Savic & Lindström, 2008); and a female-sized INAH3 (Figure 7.19; LeVay, 1991) and suprachiasmatic nucleus (Swaab & Hofman, 1990) in gay men. In rats, blocking the effects of testosterone in male rats during the prenatal period and shortly after birth increased the number of vasopressin-secreting cells; as adults, the rats preferred the company of a sexually active male rather than an estrous female, and they showed lordosis and accepted mounting from the male (Swaab, Slob, Houtsmuller, Brand, & Zhou, 1995). From a functional perspective, a few studies have reported that homosexual males perform better on verbal tests and poorer on spatial tests than do heterosexual men (Figure 7.20; Collaer, Reimer, & Manning, 2007; C. M. McCormick & Witelson, 1991; Rahman, Abrahams, & Wilson, 2003). Evidence that homosexual women perform like men has been inconsistent (Collaer et al., 2007; Gladue, Beatty, Larson, & Staton, 1990; Rahman et al., 2003). Also, some studies have reported that homosexual men and women respond to presumed pheromones similarly to members of the other sex (Figure 7.21; Savic, Berglund, & Lindström, 2005; W. Zhou et al., 2014). Finally, relative finger length is considered a marker of fetal androgen exposure, and the ratio of index finger to ring finger length has been reported to be male typical in lesbian women (T. J. Williams et al., 2000).

■ **FIGURE 7.19**   INAH3 in a Heterosexual Man (Left) and a Homosexual Man (Right).

The arrows indicate the boundaries of the structure. Note the smaller size in the homosexual brain.

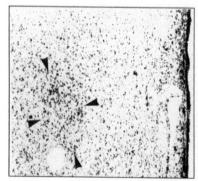 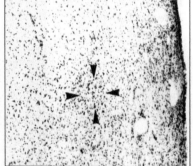

Source: From "A Difference in Hypothalamic Structure Between Heterosexual and Homosexual Men," by S. LeVay, *Science*, 253, pp. 1034–1047. © 1991, American Association for the Advancement of Science (AAS). Reprinted with permission from AAAS.

> *The most powerful sex organ is between the ears, not between the legs.*
>
> —Milton Diamond

You will notice that most of the differences relate to males; this is partly due to an unfortunate research focus on male homosexuality and partly because the results have more often been negative when studying females. The latter may be because homosexual women are more often bisexual, which could lead to disparate results; for that reason, studies should divide nonheterosexual women into two groups. Something else you might have picked up on is that these studies are several years old. That is not damning in itself, but it should be disturbing that most of these lines of research—on such a socially controversial topic—have

■ **FIGURE 7.20** Sex-Atypical Cognitive Performance in Homosexual Men and Women.

(a) Spatial performance of gay men was lower than that of heterosexual men; the homosexual women's performance was slightly, but significantly, higher than that of heterosexual women. (b) Verbal fluency was higher in homosexual males than in all others, including heterosexual females; performance was lower for both heterosexual males and homosexual females, who did not differ significantly from each other.

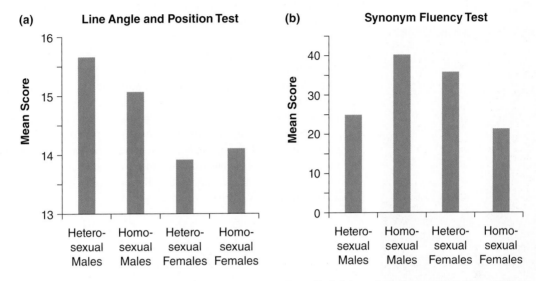

Sources: (a) Based on data from "Sexual-Orientation-Related Differences in Verbal Fluency," by Q. Rahman, S. Abrahams, and G. D. Wilson, 2003, *Neuropsychology, 17*, pp. 240–246. (b) Based on data from "Visuospatial Performance on an Internet Line Judgment Task and Potential Hormonal Markers: Sex, Sexual Orientation, and 2D:4D," by M. L. Collaer, S. Reimers, and J. T. Manning, *Archives of Sexual Behavior, 36*, pp. 177–192.

not seen replication. We are faced with the dilemma whether to draw conclusions based on either a single study or a few studies with inconsistent results, or to suspect that subsequent studies have yielded negative results, which often don't find their way into print. At this point we lack a clear idea of what forces determine human sexual preference. What does seem likely is that the answer will turn out to be a multiplicity of factors, rather than any single influence.

Social Implications of the Biological Model

As is often the case, the research we have been discussing has important

■ **FIGURE 7.21** Responses of Heterosexual Women, Homosexual Men, and Heterosexual Men to a Presumed Male Pheromone.

Heterosexual women and homosexual men responded to the testosterone derivative AND in the MPOA/anterior hypothalamus, but heterosexual men did not.

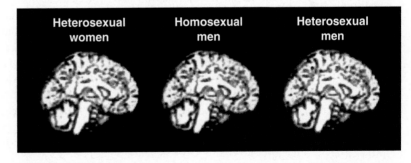

Source: From "Smelling of Odorous Sex Hormone-Like Compounds Causes Sex-Differentiated Hypothalamic Activations in Humans," by I. Savic et al., *Neuron, 31*, pp. 661–668, fig. 1. © 2002.

social implications. If homosexuality is a choice, as argued by some, then U.S. civil rights legislation does not apply to homosexuals, because protection for minorities depends on the criterion of unalterable or inborn characteristics (Ernulf, Innala, & Whitam, 1989). About 75% of homosexuals believe that homosexuality is inborn, and that they have no choice (Leland & Miller, 1998). When Congressman Barney Frank of Massachusetts (Figure 7.22) was asked if he ever considered whether switching to the straight life was a possibility, he replied, "I wished it was. But it wasn't. I can't imagine that anybody believes that a 13-year-old in 1953 thinks, 'Boy, it would be really great to be a part of this minority that everybody hates and to have a really restricted life'" (Dreifus, 1996, p. 25).

■ **FIGURE 7.22**   Former U.S. Congressman Barney Frank.

In 2012, Frank became the first member of Congress to marry someone of the same gender while in office.

But some people in the gay community think that promoting this view is not in their best interest. For them, the biological model is associated too closely with the old medical "disease" explanation of homosexuality. They fear that homosexuals will be branded as defective, or even that science may find ways to identify homosexual predisposition in fetuses and that parents will have the "problem" corrected through genetic manipulation or abortion. Emotions are so strong among some homosexuals that the researcher Dick Swaab was physically attacked in Amsterdam by members of the Dutch gay movement, who felt threatened by his biological findings (Swaab, 1996).

Other gay and lesbian rights activists welcome the biological findings because they think that belief in biological causation will increase public acceptance of homosexuality. Polls indicate they are right; in a survey of four different cultures, 56%–85% of people who believed homosexuals are "born that way" held significantly more positive views (Ernulf et al., 1989). In the United States, moral acceptance of homosexuality has risen from 40% in 2001 to 60% in 2016, and in the past 20 years belief that same-sex marriage should be legal has increased from 27% to 61% ("Gay and Lesbian Rights," 2016). The nature-nurture debate will not be settled to everyone's satisfaction anytime soon, but most researchers believe that when we understand the origins of homosexuality and heterosexuality, they will include a combination of heredity, hormones, neural structures, and experience (LeVay, 1996).

CONCEPT CHECK

Take a Minute to Check Your Knowledge and Understanding

- How has the social influence hypothesis fared in explaining homosexuality?
- What is the evidence that homosexuality has a biological cause?
- Organize your knowledge: Make a table of the structural and functional brain differences that may distinguish homosexual from heterosexual individuals. Include a brief explanation and critique.

> As for being gay, I never felt I had much choice ....I am who I am. I have no idea why.
>
> —Congressman Barney Frank

? Why is the search for a biological basis of homosexuality a social issue?

In Perspective

The fact that sex is not motivated by any tissue deficit caused researchers to look to the brain for its basis. What they found was a model for all drives that focused on the brain rather than on tissue that lacked nutrients or water or was too cold. This view changed the approach to biological motivation, and it meant that gender identity and gender-specific behavior and abilities might all be understood from the perspective of the brain.

The fact that a person's sexual appearance, gender identity, and behavior are sometimes in contradiction with each other or with the individual's chromosomes makes sex an elusive concept. Research is helping us understand that many differences between the sexes are cultural inventions and that many differences thought to be a matter of choice have biological origins. As a result, society is slowly coming around to the idea that distinctions should not be made on the basis of a person's sex, sexual appearance, or sexual orientation. These issues are emotional, as are the important questions behind them: Why are we attracted to a particular person? Why are we attracted to one sex and not the other? Why do we feel male or female? The emotion involved often obscures an important point: that the answers keep leading us back to the brain, which is why some have called the brain the primary sex organ.

CHAPTER SUMMARY

Sex as a Form of Motivation

- Although there is no tissue deficit, sex involves arousal and satiation like other drives, as well as hormonal and neural control. Also like the other drives, sex can be thought of as a need of the brain.

- The key elements in human sexual behavior are testosterone, structures in the hypothalamus, and sensory stimuli such as certain physical characteristics and pheromones.

The Biological Determination of Sex

- Differentiation as a male or a female depends on the combination of X and Y chromosomes and the presence or absence of testosterone.
- Testosterone controls the differentiation not only of the genitals and internal sex organs but also of the brain.

Gender-Related Behavioral and Cognitive Differences

- Evidence indicates that females exceed males in verbal abilities and that males are more aggressive and score higher in visual-spatial abilities. Males also score more often at the extremes of mathematical ability.
- With the possible exception of mathematical ability, it appears that these differences are at least partly due to differences in the brain and in hormones.

Biological Origins of Gender Identity

- Transgender individuals and people with sexual variations challenge our idea of male and female.
- The cognitive abilities and altered sexual preferences of people with sexual anomalies suggest that the human brain is masculinized or feminized before birth.

Sexual Orientation

- The idea that sexual orientation is entirely learned has not fared well.
- Evidence indicates that homosexuality, and thus heterosexuality, is influenced by genes, prenatal hormones (and possibly other factors), and brain structures.
- The biological view is controversial among homosexuals, but most believe that it promotes greater acceptance, and research suggests that this is the case. ■

STUDY RESOURCES

FOR FURTHER THOUGHT

- Do you think the cognitive differences between males and females will completely disappear in time? If not, would they in an ideal society? Explain your reasons.
- Some people believe that parents should have their child's ambiguous genitals corrected early, and others think it is better to see what gender identity the child develops. What do you think, and why?
- Do you think neuroscientists have made the case yet for a biological basis for homosexuality? Why or why not?

TEST YOUR UNDERSTANDING

1. Compare sex with other biological drives.

2. Describe the processes that make a person male or female (limit your answer to typical development).

3. Discuss sex as a continuum of gradations between male and female rather than a male versus female dichotomy. Give examples to illustrate.

4. Identify any weak points in the evidence for a biological basis for homosexuality (ambiguous results, gaps in information, and so on) and indicate what research needs to be done to correct the weaknesses.

Select the best answer:

1. Before undergoing her gender reassignment surgery, Caitlyn Jenner took estrogen supplements to start developing breasts and a more female-typical body shape. The changes to her body as a result of the estrogen supplements were _____ effects.

   a. activating
   b. organizing
   c. activating and organizing
   d. none of the above

2. Of the following, the best argument that sex is a drive like hunger and thirst is that

   a. almost everyone is interested in sex.
   b. sexual motivation is so strong.
   c. sexual behavior involves arousal and satiation.
   d. sexual interest varies from one time to another.

3. Pheromones

   a. synchronize menstrual cycles in women living together.
   b. contribute to aggressive behavior in animals.
   c. have a questionable role in human behavior.
   d. both a and b
   e. both b and c

4. A likely result of the Coolidge effect is that an individual will

   a. be monogamous.
   b. have more sex partners.
   c. prolong a sexual encounter.
   d. prefer attractive mates.

5. The part of the sexual response cycle that most resembles homeostasis is

   a. excitement.   b. the plateau phase.
   c. orgasm.   d. resolution.

6. The increase in testosterone on nights that couples have intercourse is an example of

   a. an organizing effect.
   b. an activating effect.

c.   cause.
d.   effect.

7. The sex difference in the size of the sexually dimorphic nucleus is due to

a.   experience after birth.
b.   genes.
c.   sex hormones.
d.   both genes and experience.

8. The most prominent structure in the sexual behavior of female rats is the

a.   MPOA.   b.   medial amygdala.
c.   ventromedial nucleus.   d.   sexually dimorphic nucleus.

9. The chromosomal sex of a fetus is determined

a.   by the sperm.
b.   by the egg.
c.   by a combination of effects from the two.
d.   in an unpredictable manner.

10. The main point of the discussion of cognitive and behavioral differences between the sexes was to

a.   illustrate the importance of experience.
b.   make a case for masculinization and feminization of the brain.
c.   make the point that men and women are suited for different roles.
d.   explain why men usually are dominant over women.

11. The term that describes a person with XX chromosomes and masculine genitals is

a.   homosexual.
b.   XX SCID

c.   androgen-insensitive male.
d.   XX DSD.

12. The best evidence that the *brains* of people with sexual variations have been masculinized or feminized contrary to their chromosomal sex is (are) their

a.   behavior and cognitive abilities.
b.   genital appearance.
c.   physical appearance.
d.   adult hormone levels.

13. Testosterone injections in a gay man would most likely

a.   have no effect.
b.   increase his sexual activity.
c.   make him temporarily bisexual.
d.   reverse his sexual preference briefly.

14. Evidence that lesbianism has a biological origin is

a.   that there is a high concordance among identical twins.
b.   weaker than it is for male homosexuality.
c.   that a brain structure is larger in lesbians and men than in heterosexual women.
d.   both a and b
e.   both b and c

15. Environmental influences on sexual orientation are

a. insignificant in size.
b. mostly from peers.
c. mostly within the family.
d. most likely prenatal.

Answers:
1.a, 2.c, 3.e, 4.b, 5.d, 6.d, 7.c, 8.c, 9.a, 10.b, 11.d, 12.a, 13.b, 14.b, 15.d.

ON THE WEB

The following websites are coordinated with this chapter's content. You can access these websites from the **SAGE edge Student Resources site**; select this chapter and then click on Web Resources. (**Bold** items are links.)

1. **The Scientist** and **Brain Facts** discuss sex differences in the brain, including structure, cognitive abilities, disorders, and medical treatment.

2. **Medscape** provides information on a variety of variations in sexual development.

3. **Profiles of Two Women With AIS** is a video interview with Eden Atwood and a young girl about living with androgen insensitivity syndrome.

4. **Intersex** and **Intersex Initiative** are two sites that provide a wealth of information about intersex conditions and treatment. **The Interface Project** presents the stories of people with intersex conditions, including Eden Atwood.

5. **CNNHealth** posted the story of M.C.; the **Atlantic** elaborated and described additional cases with similar issues.

6. **Facts About Homosexuality and Mental Health** describes research and changing attitudes regarding the mental health of homosexual individuals. Also available are links to additional information.

7. **Asexual Visibility and Education Network** (AVEN) provides information about asexuality and the opportunity to chat on a variety of related topics.

FOR FURTHER READING

1. *Why Is Sex Fun? The Evolution of Human Sexuality,* by Jared Diamond (Basic Books, 1997), takes an evolutionary approach to answer questions such as why humans have sex with no intention of procreating and why the human penis is proportionately larger than in other animals.

2. *Sex Differences in Cognitive Abilities,* 4th ed., by Diane Halpern (Psychology Press, 2011), updates research on cognitive differences and attempts to separate well-reasoned, data-supported conclusions from politicized pseudoscience.

3. *Brain Storm: The Flaws in the Science of Sex Differences,* by Rebecca M. Jordan-Young (Harvard University Press, 2011), criticizes studies of sex-related brain differences, claiming they fail to meet the standards of scientific research.

4. *Our Sexuality,* 13th ed., by Robert Crooks and Karla Baur (Cengage Learning, 2017), has become a classic textbook in the field, covering anatomy and physiology, gender issues, orientation, sexual difficulties, and more.

5. *Sexing the Body: Gender Politics and the Construction of Sexuality,* by Anne Fausto-Sterling (Basic Books, 2000), argues for a more flexible view of sex and gender than our traditional either/or approach, including accepting gradations between male and female and allowing intersexed individuals to make their own gender selection.

6. *As Nature Made Him: The Boy Who Was Raised as a Girl,* by John Colapinto (HarperCollins, 2000), tells the story of John Reimer. Described by reviewers as "riveting," with a touching description of his suffering and of his parents' and brother's support of him.

7. *Making Sense of Intersex: Changing Ethical Perspectives in Biomedicine,* by Ellen Feder (Indiana University Press, 2014), makes the argument that decisions about the treatment of children with intersex conditions should be the collective responsibility of the children, their parents, and their doctors.

8. "The Pheromone Myth: Sniffing Out the Truth," by Richard Doty (*New Scientist,* February 24, 2010, 28–29), is based on the author's book *The Great Pheromone Myth* (Johns Hopkins University Press, 2010), in which he dismisses pheromones in mammals as nothing more than learned odor preferences or, in some cases, the result of bad research.

KEY TERMS

activating effects 189
amygdala 183
androgen insensitivity syndrome 195
androgens 181
castration 181
congenital adrenal hyperplasia (CAH) 195
Coolidge effect 181
dihydrotestosterone 188
estrogen 182
estrus 182
46 XX difference in sexual development 195

46 XY difference in sexual development 195
gender 188
gender dysphoria 193
gender identity 188
gender nonconformity 200
gender role 188
gonads 188
medial amygdala 183
medial preoptic area (MPOA) 183
Müllerian ducts 188
Müllerian inhibiting hormone 188
organizing effects 189

ovaries 188
oxytocin 184
pheromones 186
sex 188
sexually dimorphic nucleus (SDN) 183
testes 188
testosterone 181
third interstitial nucleus of the anterior hypothalamus (INAH3) 194
transgender 193
ventromedial hypothalamus 184
vomeronasal organ (VNO) 186
Wolffian ducts 188

edge.sagepub.com/garrett5e

SAGE edge offers a robust online environment featuring an impressive array of free tools and resources for review, study, and further exploration, keeping both instructors and students on the cutting edge of teaching and learning.

7.1 Contrast sex with other motivated behaviors.

▶ Motivation, Eating, and Sexual Behaviors

7.2 Demonstrate the role of hormones and brain structures in sexual behaviorr.

▶ The Science Behind Monogamy

7.3 Identify hormonal and brain differences between females and males.

▶ Are Women Less Monogamous Than Men?
🗩 Neuroimaging and Gender Stereotypes

7.4 Describe how behavioral differences between males and females are influenced by biology and environment.

▤ How We Understand Sex Differences

7.5 Explain the role of biological influences on gender identity.

▶ Why Is Gender Identity So Important?

7.6 Assess the impact of biological influences on sexual orientation.

▶ Science and Sexual Orientation

© iStock.com/Krle

PRACTICE AND APPLY WHAT YOU'VE LEARNED

▶ **edge.sagepub.com/garrett5e**

HEAD TO THE STUDY SITE WHERE YOU'LL FIND

- **eFlashcards to strengthen your understanding of key terms**

- **Practice quizzes to test your comprehension of key concepts**

- **Videos and multimedia content to enhance your exploration of key topics**

Emotion and Health

8

After reading this chapter, you will be able to:

- Describe the brain structures and neurotransmitters involved in emotion.

- Explain how the body and the peripheral nervous system contribute to the experience of emotion.

- Identify the adaptive and maladaptive components of the stress response.

- Discuss the contributions of genetics and environment to stress responses.

- Compare the affective and sensory components of pain.

- Examine the brain structures and chemical systems involved in aggression.

When Jane was 15 months old, she was run over by a vehicle. The injuries seemed minor, and she appeared to recover fully within days of the accident. By the age of 3, however, her parents noticed that she was largely unresponsive to verbal or physical punishment. Her behavior became progressively disruptive, and by the age of 14 she had to be placed in the first of several treatment facilities. Although her intelligence was normal, she often failed to complete school assignments. She was verbally and physically abusive to others, she stole from her family and shoplifted frequently, and she engaged in early and risky sexual behavior that resulted in pregnancy at the age of 18. She showed little if any guilt or remorse; empathy was also absent, which made her dangerously insensitive to her infant's needs. Because her behavior put her at physical and financial risk, she became entirely dependent on her family and social agencies for financial support and management of her personal affairs.

Magnetic resonance imaging (MRI) revealed that there was damage to Jane's prefrontal cortex, which is necessary for making judgments about behavior and its consequences. People who sustain damage to this area later in life show an understanding of moral and social rules in hypothetical situations, but they are unable to apply these rules in real-world situations, so they regularly make choices that lead to financial losses and the loss of friends and family relationships (Bechara, Damasio, Damasio, & Lee, 1999). People like Jane, whose injury occurred in infancy, cannot even verbalize these rules when confronted with a hypothetical situation, and their moral development never progresses beyond the motivation to avoid punishment; they not only make a mess of their own lives but also engage in behavior that harms others as well, like stealing (S. W. Anderson, Bechara, Damasio, Tranel, & Damasio, 1999).

Master the content.
edge.sagepub.com/garrett5e

> "
> My own brain is to me the most unaccountable of machinery—always buzzing, humming, soaring, roaring, diving, and then buried in mud. And why? What's this passion for?
>
> —Virginia Woolf
> "

Emotion enriches our lives with, as the writer Virginia Woolf put it, its "buzzing, humming, soaring, and roaring." It also motivates our behavior: Anger intensifies our defensive behavior, fear accelerates flight, and happiness encourages the behaviors that produce it. Emotion adds emphasis to experiences as they are processed in the brain, making them more memorable (A. K. Anderson & Phelps, 2001); as a result, we are likely to repeat the behaviors that bring joy and avoid the ones that produce danger or pain. Although Jane was intelligent, her injury left her unable to learn from her emotional experiences. According to Antonio Damasio (1994), reason without emotion is inadequate for making the decisions that guide our lives and, in fact, make up our lives.

Emotion and the Nervous System

If asked what *emotion* means, you would probably think first of what we call "feelings"—the sense of happiness or excitement or fear or sadness. Then you might think of the facial expressions that go along with these feelings: the curled-up corners of the mouth during a smile, the knit brow and red face of anger. Next you would probably visualize the person acting out the emotion by fleeing, striking, embracing, and so on. Emotion is all these and more; a working definition might be that *emotion* is an increase or a decrease in physiological activity that is accompanied by feelings that are characteristic of the emotion and often accompanied by a characteristic behavior or facial expression. Having said that mouthful, we suspect you will understand why Joseph LeDoux (1996) wrote that we all know what emotion is until we attempt to define it. We will talk about these different facets of emotion in the following pages, along with some practical implications in the form of aggression and health.

Autonomic and Muscular Involvement in Emotion

To the neuroscientist, the most obvious component of emotional response is sympathetic nervous system activation. You may remember from Chapter 3 that the sympathetic system activates the body during arousal; it increases heart rate and respiration rate, increases sweat gland activity, shuts down digestion, and constricts the peripheral blood vessels, which raises the blood pressure and diverts blood to the muscles. As you will see in the section on stress, the sympathetic system also stimulates the adrenal glands to release various hormones, particularly *cortisol*. At the end of arousal, the parasympathetic system puts the brakes on most bodily activity, with the exception that it activates digestion. In other words, the sympathetic nervous system prepares the body for "fight or flight"; in contrast, the parasympathetic system generally reduces activity and conserves and restores energy (Figure 8.1).

Of course, muscular activation is involved in the external expression of emotion, such as smiling or fleeing or attacking. It is also a part of the less obvious responses of emotion, such as the bodily tension that not only prepares us to act but also produces a headache and aching muscles when we try to write a paper the night before it is due. Autonomic and muscular arousal are adaptive, because they prepare the body for an emergency and help it carry out an appropriate response. They are also an important part of the emotion itself, though the exact nature of their contribution has been the subject of controversy. Fortunately, as you will see from the following discussion, competing theories are one of the engines driving research and scientific advancement.

The Role of Feedback From the Body

A bit over a century ago, the American psychologist William James (1893) and Danish physiologist Carl Lange (1885/2010) independently proposed what has come to be known as the *James-Lange theory*: Emotional experience results from the physiological arousal that precedes it, and different emotions are the result of different patterns of arousal. In our discussion of research ethics in Chapter 4, we talked about an experiment by Albert Ax (1953) in which subjects either were made angry by an insulting experimenter or were frightened by the possibility of a dangerous electric shock. Consistent with the James-Lange theory, the two emotions were accompanied by different patterns of physiological activity. Seventy years after James and Lange, Stanley Schacter and Jerome Singer (1962) took a contrary position in their *cognitive theory*; they stated that the identity of the emotion is based on the cognitive assessment of the situation, and physiological arousal contributes only to the emotion's intensity. Their research demonstrated how easily people could misidentify emotions depending on the environmental context. For example, young men who were interviewed by an attractive woman while crossing a swaying footbridge 230 feet above a rocky river included

? What effect does the autonomic nervous system have during emotions?

? How do the James-Lange and cognitive theories disagree? What evidence is there for each?

> We feel sorry because we cry, angry because we strike, afraid because we tremble.
>
> —William James, 1893

more sexual content in brief stories they wrote later and were more likely to call the phone number the young woman gave them than were men who were interviewed 10 minutes after crossing the bridge (D. G. Dutton & Aron, 1974).

Studies like these have not determined that one theory is right and the other is wrong. Barlassina and Newen (2013) argue that neither is adequate; in their *integrative embodiment theory of emotions* they maintain that bodily sensations are a critical component of emotions, but these perceptions must be integrated with cognitive information. Nevertheless, incorrect theories can be useful if they generate research, and the competition between these two has produced valuable insights into emotion. A good example is the contribution of facial expressions to emotional experience. Experimenters have had to be very inventive in doing facial expression studies; obviously, they can't just tell people to smile or frown and then ask them what emotion they're feeling. Paul Ekman and his colleagues (Levenson, Ekman, & Friesen, 1990) instructed subjects to contract specific facial muscles to produce different expressions (Figure 8.2); for example, to produce an angry expression, subjects were told to pull their eyebrows down and together, raise the upper eyelid, and push the lower lip up with the lips pressed together (p. 365). The posed facial expressions for happiness, fear, anger, disgust, sadness, and surprise each resulted in the experience of the intended emotion, along with a distinct pattern of physiological arousal.

Induced facial poses also influence how the person interprets the environment. Volunteers rate a stimulus as more painful when they are making a sad face than a happy or neutral one (Salomons, Coan, Hunt, Backonja, & Davidson, 2008), and college students rate *Far Side* cartoons as more amusing when they are holding a pen between the teeth, which induces a sort of smile, than when they hold the pen between the lips, producing a frown (Strack, Martin, & Stepper, 1988). More strikingly, women who have had their corrugator muscles paralyzed by injecting botulinum toxin (Botox) to remove frown lines are unable to frown, and they report less negative mood—even if they don't perceive themselves as more attractive (M. B. Lewis & Bowler, 2009). In addition, when these women attempt to imitate angry expressions, they produce less activation of the amygdala than women who have not had Botox treatment (Figure 8.3; Hennenlotter et al., 2009).

Some researchers suggest that feedback from emotional expressions has another role besides contributing to our emotional experience in that it also helps us understand other people's emotions; this ability is critical to social communication and to societal success. This view is supported by studies of mirror neurons. *Mirror neurons* are neurons that respond both when we engage in a specific act and while observing the same act in others. They were first discovered when researchers noticed that neurons that were active while monkeys reached for food also responded when the monkeys saw the researcher picking up a piece of food (di Pellegrino, Fadiga, Fogassi, Gallese, & Rizzolatti, 1992); similar correlations have

■ **FIGURE 8.1** Comparison of Sympathetic Activity During Emotional Arousal With Parasympathetic Activity During Relaxation.

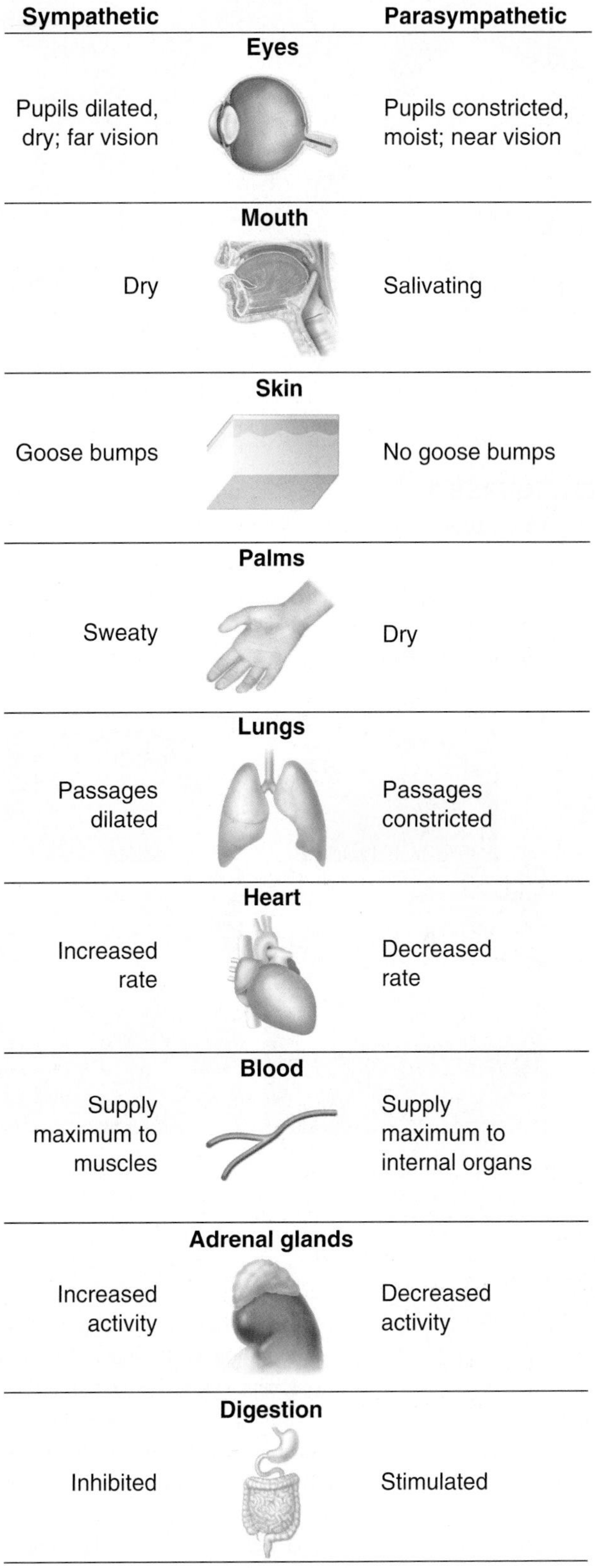

Sympathetic	Parasympathetic
Eyes	
Pupils dilated, dry; far vision	Pupils constricted, moist; near vision
Mouth	
Dry	Salivating
Skin	
Goose bumps	No goose bumps
Palms	
Sweaty	Dry
Lungs	
Passages dilated	Passages constricted
Heart	
Increased rate	Decreased rate
Blood	
Supply maximum to muscles	Supply maximum to internal organs
Adrenal glands	
Increased activity	Decreased activity
Digestion	
Inhibited	Stimulated

Source: Created for this book by Epicstudios, Inc.

■ **FIGURE 8.2**   Emotional Expressions Posed Using Ekman's Instructions.

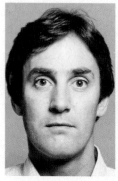

Source: © Don Francis/Mardan Photography.

■ **FIGURE 8.3**   Disabling Corrugator Muscle Reduces Amygdala Response to Simulated Anger.

A woman treated with Botox (a) is unable to produce the facial expression of anger and shows little activation of the amygdala (b). A control subject makes the expected facial expression (c) and produces much greater amygdala activation (d).

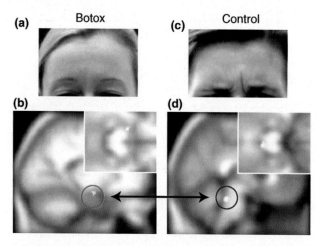

Source: Adapted from "The Link Between Facial Feedback and Neural Activity Within Central Circuitries of Emotion—New Insights From Botulinum Toxin-Induced Denervation of Frown Muscles," by A. Hennenlotter et al., 2009, *Cerebral Cortex, 19,* pp. 537–542. By permission of Oxford University Press.

been observed in other brain areas, including those involved in emotions (see review in Bastiaansen, Thioux, & Keysers, 2009). Observing another person's emotional expressions activates emotional areas in our own brains, and the amount of activity is related to scores on a measure of empathy (Chakrabarti, Bullmore, & Baron-Cohen, 2006). The accompanying In the News feature describes research showing that our socioeconomic class affects our empathic ability.

Our observation of other people's emotions is not entirely passive; we also mimic their gestures, body posture, tone of voice, and (often imperceptibly) facial expressions (Bastiaansen et al., 2009). Just as feedback during our own emotional activity adds to our own emotional experience, feedback from imitated expressions may help us empathize with the emotions of others. Indeed, interfering with facial mimicry by engaging the required muscles in other activities (such as chewing gum) impairs subjects' ability to recognize happiness and disgust in photos (Oberman, Winkielman, & Ramachandran, 2007). Women who have Botox treatments also rate facial photos and sentences as less emotional than before treatment (Baumeister, Papa, & Foroni, 2016). People with autism typically have trouble understanding other people's emotions, perhaps in part because their imitation of emotional expressions is delayed by about 160 milliseconds (Oberman, Winkielman, & Ramachandran, 2009).

A system this complex requires an equally complex control system. We will turn our attention now to the brain structures responsible for emotion.

The Emotional Brain

In the late 1930s and 1940s, researchers proposed that emotions originated in the *limbic system,* a network of structures arranged around the upper brain stem (Figure 8.4). As complex as this system is with its looping interconnections, we now know that this hypothesis is an oversimplification; emotion involves structures at all levels of the brain, from the prefrontal area to the brain stem (A. R. Damasio et al., 2000). Also, we know that some of the limbic structures are more involved in non-emotional functions. For example, the hippocampus and mammillary bodies have major roles in learning. The concept of a limbic system is less important as a description of how emotion works than for spawning a tremendous volume of research that has taken us in diverse directions, which we will explore over the next several pages.

Much of what we know about the brain's role in emotion comes from lesioning and stimulation studies with animals; this research is limited because we do not know what the animal is experiencing. Robert Heath did some of the earliest probing of the limbic system in humans in 1964 when he implanted electrodes in the brains of patients in an attempt to treat epilepsy, sleep disorders, or pain that had failed to respond to conventional treatments. Researchers knew from animal studies that the hypothalamus has primary control over the autonomic system and that it produces a variety of emotional expressions, such as the threatened cat's hissing and bared teeth and claws. Stimulation of the hypothalamus in Heath's patients produced general autonomic

? What are some of the brain structures involved in emotions, and what are their functions?

discharge and sensations such as a pounding heart and feelings of warmth, but it also evoked feelings of fear, rage, or pleasure, depending on the location of the electrode in the hypothalamus. Septal area stimulation also produced a sense of pleasure, but in this case the feeling was accompanied by sexual fantasies and arousal. During septal stimulation one patient went from near tears while talking about his father's illness to a broad smile as he described how he planned to take his girlfriend out and seduce her. When asked why he changed the subject, he replied that the thought just came into his head.

Now researchers are more likely to use one of the scanning techniques to study the brain centers of emotion. Typically, they do MRI scans to determine the location of damage in patients with emotional deficits, or they use positron emission tomography (PET) or functional magnetic resonance imaging (fMRI) while healthy subjects relive an emotional experience, examine facial expressions of emotion, or view an emotional video. Two of the most reliable brain-emotion associations have been the amygdala's role in fear and the location of disgust in the insular cortex and the basal ganglia (Figure 8.5; F. C. Murphy, Nimmo-Smith, & Lawrence, 2003; Phan, Wager, Taylor, & Liberzon, 2002). We will consider the amygdala in some detail later. The insula is the area we identified in Chapter 6 as the cortical projection site for taste; a number of writers have remarked on the fact that taste and disgust share the same brain area and that *dis-gust* means, roughly, "bad taste." In Chapter 3, we identified the basal ganglia as being

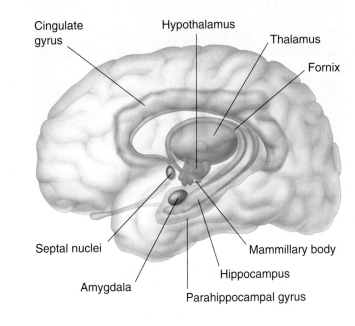

■ **FIGURE 8.4**   Structures of the Limbic System.

■ **FIGURE 8.5**   Location of the Amygdala, Insula, and Basal Ganglia.

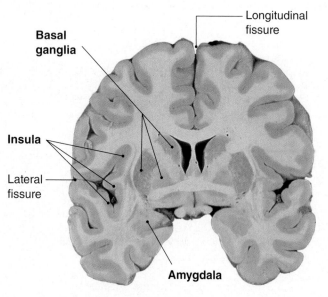

Source: Photo courtesy of Dana Copeland.

■ **FIGURE 8.6**   Size Differences in the Anterior Cingulate Gyrus.

A larger anterior cingulate gyrus (highlighted in red) is associated with a higher level of the personality characteristic of harm avoidance.

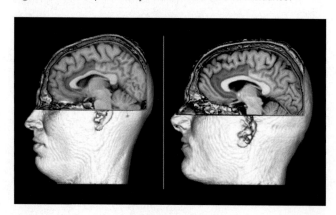

Source: From "Anatomical Variability of the Anterior Cingulated Gyrus and Basic Dimensions of Human Personality," by J. Pujol et al., *Neuroimage, 15*, pp. 847–855, fig. 1, p. 848. © 2002. Used with permission from Elsevier.

involved in motor functions. Interestingly, people with Huntington's disease or obsessive-compulsive disorder, both of which involve abnormalities in the basal ganglia, have trouble recognizing facial expressions of disgust (Phan et al., 2002).

Another significant structure in emotion is the *anterior cingulate cortex,* a part of the cingulate gyrus that is important in attention, cognitive processing, emotion, and possibly consciousness. You can see the cingulate gyrus in Figure 8.4 and the anterior cingulate gyrus in Figure 8.6. The anterior cingulate cortex is believed to combine emotional, attentional, and bodily information to bring about conscious emotional experience (Dalgleish, 2004). Consequently, it is involved in emotional activity regardless of which emotion is being experienced, although some studies have also linked parts of the structure to specific emotions, such as sadness and happiness (F. C. Murphy et al., 2003; Phan et al., 2002). Interestingly, an MRI investigation found that the right anterior cingulate was larger in people with high scores on *harm avoidance,* which involves worry about possible problems, fearfulness in the face of uncertainty, and shyness with strangers (Pujol et al., 2002).

Before we go too far in assigning emotions to specific brain structures, we need to understand that any specific emotion involves activity in a network that includes many brain areas. This is well illustrated in a study that combined the results of 55 PET and fMRI investigations (Phan et al., 2002). As you can see in Figure 8.7, places activated during a specific emotion cluster somewhat in particular areas, but they are also scattered across wide areas of the brain. This is partly due to different methods of inducing the emotions in the studies, but it also reflects the complexity of emotion. With the understanding that no emotion can be relegated to a single part of the brain, we will look more closely at three areas that have particularly important roles in emotional experience and behavior: the prefrontal cortex, the amygdala, and the right hemisphere.

The Prefrontal Cortex

The prefrontal cortex (see Figure 3.8 for location) is the final destination for much of the brain's information about emotion before action is taken. You saw in Chapter 3 that damage to the prefrontal area or severing its connections with the rest of the brain impairs people's ability to make rational judgments. Later in this chapter you will learn that people with deficiencies in the area are unable to restrain violent urges, and in Chapter 14 you will see that abnormalities in the prefrontal area also figure prominently in depression and schizophrenia. These deficits have a variety of causes, including injury, infection, tumors, strokes, and developmental errors. What the victims have in common is damage to the prefrontal area that includes the ventromedial cortex and the orbitofrontal cortex (see Figure 8.8).

■ **FIGURE 8.7** Brain Areas Activated During Different Emotions.

Each colored square represents the location identified in a single study for a particular emotion. In spite of the clustering of control of each emotion in a general area, the scattered dots of the same color indicate that each emotion relies on activity in multiple areas.

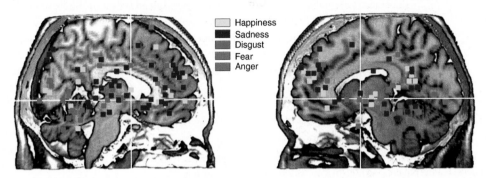

Happiness
Sadness
Disgust
Fear
Anger

Source: Reprinted from "Functional Neuroanatomy of Emotion: A Meta-Analysis of Emotion Activation Studies in PET and fMRI," by K. L. Phan, T. Wager, S. F. Taylor, and I. Liberzon, *Neuroimage, 16*, pp. 331–348. Copyright 2002, with permission from Elsevier.

■ **FIGURE 8.8** Location of Damage That Impairs Emotion-Based Decision Making.

In (a) the location of the ventromedial cortex and the orbitofrontal cortex is shown. In (b) you can see where damage occurred in four patients who showed judgment problems. The horizontal line shows where the scan in (c) was taken. In (b) and (c), the different colors indicate the number of patients with damage in the area, according to the code on the color bar. All shared damage in the ventromedial cortex, but some had damage in the orbitofrontal cortex as well.

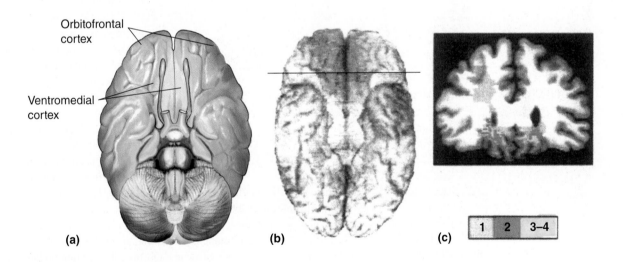

Orbitofrontal cortex

Ventromedial cortex

(a)   (b)   (c)

1 2 3–4

Sources: (b) and (c) from "Different Contributions of the Human Amygdala and Ventromedial Prefrontal Cortex to Decision-Making," by A. Bechara, H. Damasio, A. R. Damasio, & G. P. Lee, 1999, *Journal of Neuroscience, 19*, pp. 5473–5481.

The prefrontal cortex makes the final decision whether to produce a given behavior, using information supplied by other brain areas about the relative value of the choices, the likelihood of success, and the cost of failure. From this description it is easy to see why most research on decision making is done in the form of studies of risk taking. A good example is a gambling task study in which patients with ventromedial damage and healthy volunteers chose cards from four decks to win play money (Bechara et al., 1999). Initially both groups chose more often from the two "risky" decks, which usually resulted in large rewards but occasionally

? How does loss of emotion impair "rational" decision making?

led to large penalties, for an overall loss. Over time, the control subjects shifted to the two "safe" decks, whose cards produced lower rewards and smaller penalties for an overall gain; the patients typically did not make the shift, however, even after they figured out how the game worked (Figure 8.9a).

To assess the subjects' emotional responses during the task, the researchers used the *skin conductance response (SCR),* a measure of sympathetic nervous system activity obtained by recording changes in the skin's electrical conductance that occurs during sweat gland activation. Both groups showed emotional reactions—increases in skin conductance—when their choices resulted in wins or losses. And over time, the control subjects began to show anticipatory SCRs just before drawing a card from a risky deck, even before they were able to verbalize that those stacks were risky. (This is the example of unaware emotional influence we promised earlier.) The patients, however, did not produce anticipatory SCRs to the four decks; although their bad choices were eliciting emotional responses, their prefrontal damage made them unable to process the consequences of risky behavior and use that information to guide their choices (Figure 8.9b).

More recently, studies of risk taking have mapped out some of the circuitry involved in decision making. Functional MRIs showed that teenagers identified as risk takers had stronger functional connectivity of the right prefrontal cortex with the nucleus accumbens and the amygdala than did their non-risk-taking age-mates (DeWitt, Aslan, & Filbey, 2014). The nucleus accumbens and amygdala, of course, are involved in the evaluation of rewarding and emotional stimuli, respectively. While the prefrontal cortex dampens impulsive and risky behavior, the nucleus accumbens and amygdala appear to play the role of instigators. For example, in a simulated driving task fMRI showed significantly increased activity in the nucleus accumbens when the teenage subjects chose to run through a yellow light (Telzer, Ichien, & Qu, 2015). Activity in the nucleus accumbens is exceptionally high during adolescence. Meyer and Bucci (2016) pursued the hypothesis that this increased activity, along with the delayed development of the orbitofrontal cortex, plays a causal role in teen impulsiveness and risk taking. They manipulated receptors to increase activation of the nucleus accumbens while simultaneously decreasing activity in the orbitofrontal cortex of adult rats; the rats then performed comparably to adolescent rats, taking twice as long to learn to withhold a conditioned response when a stimulus indicated that it would not be followed by a reward.

Studies have also identified another part of the brain that participates in risk evaluation, the posterior parietal cortex (PPC). Patients with damage to this area had difficulty adjusting their betting according to the chances of winning; they often made large bets when the odds were low and small bets when the chances of winning were strongly favorable (Studer, Manes, Humphreys, Robbins, & Clark, 2015). In two additional studies, willingness to make risky choices was correlated with the amount of gray matter volume in the PPC (Gilaie-Dolan et al., 2014), and across subjects aged 18 to 88, risk taking and PPC gray matter volume declined together (Grubb, Tymula, Gilaie-Dolan, Glimcher, & Levy, 2016).

In the rest of us, who like to think of ourselves as normal, the prefrontal cortex's connections to other parts of the brain determine whether we are novelty-seeking adventurers or are more restrained, as the accompanying Application explains.

■ **FIGURE 8.9**   Comparison of Gambling Task Behavior in Controls and Patients With Damage to the Prefrontal Cortex.

The controls shifted from preferring cards from the risky decks to preferring cards from the safe decks, but the patients did not. (b) Also, as the task progressed, only the controls showed anticipatory skin conductance responses (SCR) before choosing from the risky decks.

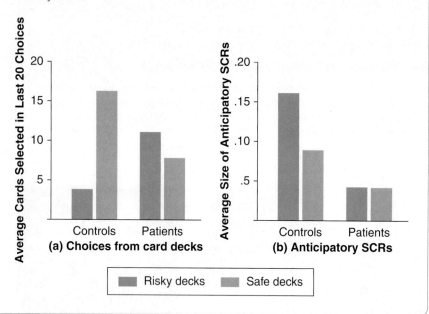

APPLICATION
Why Bob Doesn't Jump Out of Airplanes

Source: iStock/vuk8691.

In our discussion of sensation seeking in Chapter 6, we mentioned the first author's wife's skydiving adventure. Why did she enjoy leaping out of a perfectly good airplane at 14,000 feet, while he preferred to stay on the ground and take photos of her descent? Why did she like to travel to exotic places, like Thailand and Patagonia, while he would rather stay at home and write about behavioral neuroscience? Once again, research comes to the rescue. Psychologists at the University of Arizona (M. X. Cohen, Schoene-Bake, Elger, & Weber, 2009) used a questionnaire to categorize 20 volunteers as novelty seekers (agreeing to statements like "I like to try new things just for fun") or reward dependent (agreeing to statements like "I'd rather stay home than go out"). Novelty seekers are higher in exploratory drive and impulsivity, whereas those who are reward dependent are particularly sensitive to rewards and spend a lot of time pursuing activities that have been rewarding in the past.

Next, the researchers used diffusion tensor imaging to measure the density of the subjects' white-matter tracts. Their analysis focused on the hippocampus, amygdala, and striatum, because animal research has indicated that these structures form a looping circuit that is important in novelty seeking. There were strong white-matter connections within this loop in the human novelty seekers, but the reward-dependent volunteers' strongest connections were between the striatum and prefrontal areas, which tend to put the brakes on risky behavior. Just before the skydiving experience, the jump videographer interviewed Bob's wife about why she was making the jump, then turned the camera on Bob and asked why he chose not to. He answered lamely, "I just don't need to." Today, armed with the results of this study, his answer would be, "My prefrontal cortex won't let me!"

The Amygdala

The prefrontal areas receive much of their emotional input from the amygdala (see Figure 8.4 again), a small limbic system structure in each temporal lobe that is involved in emotions, especially negative ones. The amygdala has other functions as well. In Chapter 7 you learned that the amygdala responds to sexually exciting stimuli, and in Chapter 12 you will see that it participates in memory formation, especially when emotion is involved. Some amygdala neurons fire when the individual judges the facial expression in a photo to be fearful, and others respond to happy faces (S. Wang et al., 2014). So the amygdala's role may involve responding to emotionally significant stimuli in general (Phan et al., 2002).

Although the amygdala participates in other emotions, its role in fear and anxiety has been researched the most thoroughly. *Fear* is an emotional reaction to a specific immediate threat; *anxiety* is an apprehension about a future, and often uncertain, event. Stimulating the amygdala produces fear in human subjects

The individual on the left has the short allele of the *SLC6A4* gene, which reduces serotonin activity and increases fear responsiveness; the one on the right has two copies of the long allele.

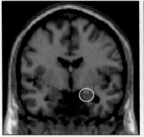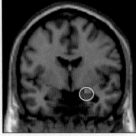

Source: From "Serotonin Transporter Genetic Variation and the Response of the Human Amygdala," by Hariri et al., *Science, 297,* pp. 400–403. Copyright 2002. Reprinted by permission of AAAS.

(Gloor, Olivier, Quesney, Andermann, & Horowitz, 1982). The amygdala contains receptors for benzodiazepines, which are used to treat anxiety, and injection of this type of drug directly into the amygdala reduces signs of both fear and anxiety in animals (M. Davis, 1992). A person with one version of the *SLC6A4* gene has decreased serotonin activity; as a result, the person is prone to fear and anxiety and, as Figure 8.10 shows, the amygdala is hyperreactive to fear stimuli (Hariri et al., 2002).

Rats with amygdala damage are so fearless they will not only approach a sedated cat but also climb all over its back and head (D. C. Blanchard & Blanchard, 1972). One rat even nibbled on the stuporous cat's ear, provoking an attack—and after the attack ended, the rat climbed right back onto the cat. A few humans have sustained damage to both amygdala structures, usually as a result of infection or disease, and they also show a variety of deficits; like the rats, for example, they are unusually trusting of strangers (Adolphs, Tranel, & Damasio, 1998). Bechara's study of prefrontal patients included a group of patients with bilateral amygdala damage (Bechara et al., 1999). The two groups performed similarly in most ways, with one notable exception: While neither group produced anticipatory SCRs when choosing from the risky decks, the amygdala patients also didn't respond to monetary gains and losses. Apparently the ventromedial patients were unable to make use of emotional information from the amygdala, but the amygdala patients couldn't even generate an emotional response to rewards and punishments. As a result, patients with bilateral amygdala damage often live in supervised care, because their actions can easily bring harm to themselves and others. Ventromedial patients are less impaired, which suggests that the amygdala sends its information to additional decision-making areas, suggesting a broad scope to this network.

SM is one of the best characterized patients with bilateral amygdala damage (Figure 8.11); she reports very little feeling of fear and—in spite of having been held up at knifepoint, nearly killed in an act of domestic violence, and threatened with death on other occasions—her behavior never reflected any sense of desperation or urgency (Feinstein, Adolphs, Damasio, & Tranel, 2011). Researchers were unable to find any stimulus that could evoke fear in her; she was undisturbed by horror movies or a haunted house that produced screams in her companions, and she showed an unusual compulsion to touch snakes she had been told were deadly. Interestingly, during a test that involved inhaling carbon dioxide, which produces a feeling of suffocation, she and a similar patient experienced full-blown panic attacks (Feinstein et al., 2013). The researchers' interpretation was that the amygdala monitors external threats from the environment, and that fear triggered internally—in this case by the sense of suffocation—has another neural basis.

Hemispheric Specialization in Emotion

The specialization of the cerebral hemispheres we have seen in other functions is also evident in emotion. Although both hemispheres are involved in the *experience* of emotions, the left frontal area is more active when the person is experiencing positive emotions, and the right frontal area is more active during negative emotion (R. J. Davidson, 1992). This is consistent with a study done with epilepsy patients who had numerous electrodes placed in their brains as part of a presurgical evaluation. Stimulation in the right amygdala evoked negative emotions (identified by the conscious patients as fear, anxiety, or sadness) at 100% of the locations; in the left amygdala the locations were split almost evenly between negative emotions and positive ones (joy and happiness; Lanteaume et al., 2007). People with damage to the left hemisphere often express more anxiety and sadness about their situation, whereas those with right-hemisphere damage are more likely to be unperturbed or even euphoric, even when dealing with an associated paralysis of an arm or a leg (Gainotti, 1972; Gainotti, Caltagirone, & Zoccolotti, 1993; W. Heller, Miller, & Nitschke, 1998). The same difference in emotions occurs when each of the cerebral hemispheres is anesthetized briefly in turn by injecting a short-acting barbiturate into the right or left carotid artery (Rossi & Rosadini, 1967). (This technique is sometimes used in evaluating patients prior to brain surgery.) In fact, when the right hemisphere is anesthetized, individuals can describe negative events in their lives but can barely recall having felt sad or angry or fearful, even with incidents as intense as their mother's death, the discovery of a spouse's affair, or the wife's threatening to kill the individual (E. D. Ross, Homan, & Buck, 1994).

Although both hemispheres are involved in experiencing emotion, the right is more specialized for its expression (Heller et al., 1998). Autonomic responses to emotional stimuli such as facial expressions and emotional scenes are greater when the stimuli are presented to the right hemisphere (using the strategy described by Spence, Shapiro, & Zaidel, 1996, p. 298). Much of the emotional suppression in patients with right-hemisphere damage is due to decreased autonomic response (Gainotti et al., 1993).

Perception of nonverbal aspects of emotion is impaired in patients with right-hemisphere damage; for example, they often have difficulty recognizing emotion in others' facial expressions (Adolphs, Damasio, Tranel, & Damasio, 1996). Verbal aspects are unimpaired, however; the same patients can under-

■ **FIGURE 8.11**   SM's Brain, Compared With a Normal Brain.

In SM's brain (left), you see only two dark voids (in the red circles) where each amygdala was before disease caused their deterioration. The brain on the right is normal, for comparison.

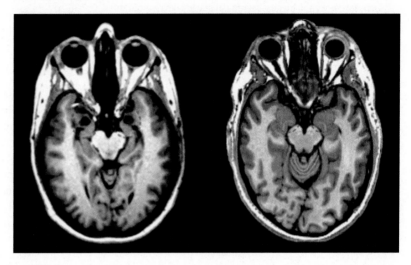

Source: From "Human Brain Is Divided on Fear and Panic: New Study Contends Different Areas of Brain Responsible for External Versus Internal Threats," by John Riehl, April 2, 2013, *Iowa Now*, retrieved from http://now.uiowa.edu/2013/01/human-brain-divided-fear-and-panic.

stand the emotion in a verbal description like "Your team's ball went through the hoop with one second left to go in the game," but they have trouble identifying the emotion in descriptions of facial or gestural expressions such as "Tears fell from her eyes" or "He shook his fist" (Blonder, Bowers, & Heilman, 1991). Patients with right-hemisphere damage also have trouble recognizing emotion from the tone of the speaker's voice (Gorelick & Ross, 1987), and their own speech is usually emotionless as well (Heilman, Watson, & Bowers, 1983). When asked to say a neutral sentence like "The boy went to the store" in a happy, sad, or angry tone, they speak instead in a monotone and often add the designated emotion to the sentence verbally, for example, ". . . and he was sad."

CONCEPT CHECK

Take a Minute to Check Your Knowledge and Understanding

- Describe the role of the autonomic nervous system in emotion (including the possible identification of emotions).
- Organize your knowledge: List the major parts of the brain described in this section that are involved in emotion, along with their functions.
- How are the effects of prefrontal and amygdala damage alike, and how are they different?

Stress, Immunity, and Health

Stress is a term that has two meanings in psychology. Stress is a condition in the environment that makes unusual demands on the organism, such as threat, failure, or bereavement. Stress is also an internal condition, your response to a stressful situation; you *feel* stressed, and your body reacts in several ways. Whether a situation is stressful to the person is often a matter of individual differences, either in perception of the situation or in physiological reactivity. For some people, even the normal events of daily life are stressful, whereas others thrive on excitement and would feel stressed if they were deprived of regular challenges. In other words, stress in this sense of the term is in the eye of the beholder.

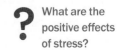

What are the positive effects of stress?

■ **FIGURE 8.12**   The Hypothalamus-Pituitary-Adrenal Axis.

The hypothalamus releases corticotropin-releasing hormone (CRH), which stimulates the synthesis and release of adrenocorticotropic hormone (ACTH) from the pituitary gland, which then binds to the adrenal cortex and triggers release of several stress hormones (cortisol, epinephrine, and norepinephrine). These hormones trigger a response from target organs, reducing the stress, and decreasing subsequent release of hormones in this pathway.

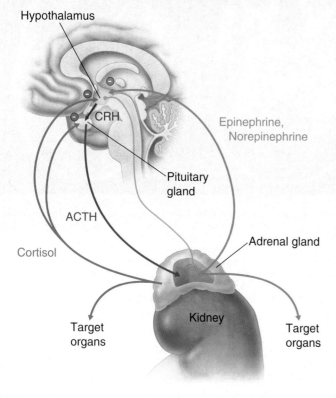

■ **FIGURE 8.13**   Macrophages Preparing to Engulf Bacteria.

A macrophage, a type of white blood cell, is stretching out projections which will eventually engulf and digest bacterial cells.

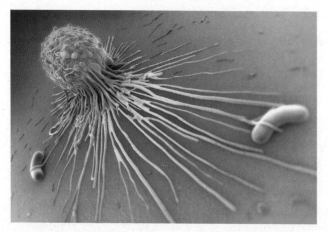

Source: Science Picture Co/Science Source.

Stress as an Adaptive Response

Ordinarily, the body's response to a stressful situation is positive and adaptive. In Chapter 3, you saw that the stress response includes activation of the sympathetic branch of the autonomic nervous system, which is largely under the control of the hypothalamus. The resulting increases in heart rate, blood flow, and respiration rate help the person deal with the stressful situation. Stress also activates the *hypothalamus-pituitary-adrenal axis,* a group of structures that help the body cope with stress (Figure 8.12). The hypothalamus activates the pituitary gland, which in turn releases hormones that stimulate the adrenal glands to release the stress hormones epinephrine, norepinephrine, and cortisol. The first two hormones increase output from the heart and liberate glucose from the muscles for additional energy. The hormone *cortisol* also increases energy levels by converting proteins to glucose, increasing fat availability, and increasing metabolism. Cortisol provides a more sustained release of energy than the sympathetic nervous system does, for coping with prolonged stress.

Brief stress increases activity in the *immune system* (Herbert et al., 1994), the cells and cell products that kill infected and malignant cells and protect the body against foreign substances such as bacteria and viruses. Of course, this is highly adaptive because it helps protect the person from any infections that might result from the threatening situation. The immune response involves two major types of cells. *Leukocytes,* or white blood cells, recognize invaders by the unique proteins that every cell has on its surface and kills them. These proteins in foreign cells are called *antigens.* A type of leukocyte called a *macrophage* ingests intruders (Figure 8.13). Then it displays the intruder's antigens on its own cell surface; this attracts *T cells,* another type of leukocyte that is specific for particular antigens, which kill the invaders. *B cells,* a third type of leukocyte, fight intruders by producing antibodies that attack a particular cell type. *Natural killer cells,* the second type of immune cells, attack and destroy certain kinds of cancer cells and cells infected with viruses; they are less specific in their targets than T or B cells. The brain and spinal cord are considered "immune privileged," in that the central nervous system is protected from most infectious agents by the blood-brain barrier. When these agents do make their way in, they are dealt with by *microglia,* which act in most ways like macrophages. Table 8.1 summarizes the characteristics of these immune cells.

Some antibodies are transferred from mother to child during the prenatal period or postnatally through the mother's milk. Most antibodies, though, result from a direct encounter with invading cells, for example, during exposure to measles. Vaccinations work because injection of a weakened form of the disease-causing bacteria or virus triggers the B cells to make antibodies for that disease.

TABLE 8.1   Major Types of Immune Cells.

LEUKOCYTES				
MACROPHAGES	**T CELLS**	**B CELLS**	**NATURAL KILLER CELLS**	**MICROGLIA**
Ingest invaders; display antigens, which attract T cells.	Multiply and attack invaders.	Make antibodies, which destroy intruders.	Attack cells containing viruses, certain kinds of tumor cells.	Ingest invaders; display antigens to attract T cells in brain, spinal cord.

The preceding is a description of what happens when all goes well. In the immune deficiency disease AIDS (acquired immune deficiency syndrome), by contrast, T cells fail to detect invaders, and the person dies of an infectious disease. In *autoimmune disorders,* the immune system runs amok and attacks the body's own cells. In the autoimmune disorder multiple sclerosis, for instance, the immune system destroys myelin in the central nervous system.

Negative Effects of Stress

We are better equipped to deal with brief stress than with prolonged stress. Chronic stress can interfere with memory, increase or decrease appetite, diminish sexual desire and performance, deplete energy, and cause mood disruptions. Although brief stress enhances immune activity, prolonged stress compromises the immune system. After the nuclear accident at the Three Mile Island electric generating plant, nearby residents had elevated stress symptoms and performed less well on tasks requiring concentration, compared with people who lived outside the area (Baum, Gatchel, & Schaeffer, 1983). Amid concerns about continued radioactivity and the long-term effects of the initial exposure, residents had reduced numbers of B cells, T cells, and natural killer cells as long as six years after the accident (McKinnon, Weisse, Reynolds, Bowles, & Baum, 1989).

Disease symptoms were not measured at Three Mile Island, but other studies have shown that health is compromised when stress impairs immune functioning. Recently widowed women experienced decreased immunity and marked health deterioration in the year following the spouse's death (Maddison & Viola, 1968). Also, students had reduced immune responses, more infectious illnesses, and slower wound healing at exam times than at other times of the year (Glaser et al., 1987; Marucha, Kiecolt-Glaser, & Favagehi, 1998). In a rare experimental study, healthy individuals were given nasal drops containing common cold viruses and then were quarantined and observed for infections. In Figure 8.14, you can see that their chance of catching a cold depended on the level of stress they reported on a questionnaire at the beginning of the study (S. Cohen, Tyrrell, & Smith, 1991). In a follow-up study, it turned out that only stresses that had lasted longer than a month increased the risk of infection (S. Cohen et al., 1998).

The cardiovascular system is particularly vulnerable to stress. Stress increases blood pressure, and prolonged high blood pressure can damage the heart or cause a stroke. Some people are more vulnerable to health effects from stress than others. Researchers classified young children as normal reactors or excessive reactors based on their blood pressure increases while one hand was immersed in ice water. Forty-five years later, 71% of the excessive reactors had high blood pressure, compared with 19% of the normal reactors (Wood, Sheps, Elveback, & Schirger, 1984).

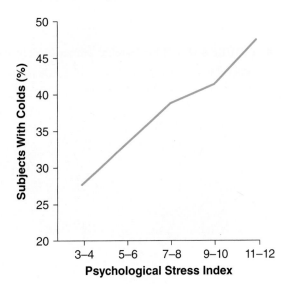

■ **FIGURE 8.14**   Relationship Between Stress and Vulnerability to Colds.

ct anto

■ **FIGURE 8.15**   Increase in Cardiac Deaths on the Day of an Earthquake.

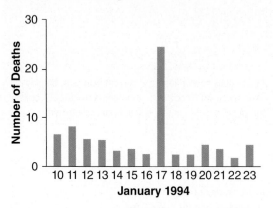

Stress can even produce death. This fact has not always been accepted in the scientific and medical communities, but in 1942 the physiologist Walter Cannon determined that reports of apparent stress-related deaths were legitimate. He even suggested that *voodoo death,* which has been reported to occur within hours of a person being "hexed" by a practitioner of this folk cult, is also due to stress. We now know that fear, loss of a loved one, humiliation, or even extreme joy can result in sudden cardiac death. In *sudden cardiac death,* stress causes excessive sympathetic activity that sends the heart into fibrillation, contracting so rapidly that it pumps little or no blood. When one of the largest earthquakes ever recorded in a major North American city struck the Los Angeles area in 1994, the number of deaths from heart attacks increased fivefold (Figure 8.15; Leor, Poole, & Kloner, 1996). The stress doesn't have to be as extreme as an earthquake: During the 2006 soccer World Cup games in Germany, cardiac emergencies in that country tripled in men and almost doubled in women (Wilbert-Lampen et al., 2008); and when the Los Angeles Rams were defeated in the 1980 Super Bowl, cardiac deaths in the team's hometown increased 15% in men and 27% in women (Kloner, McDonald, Leeka, & Poole, 2011). In 2016, when the Chicago Cubs (Gerald Hough's favorite team) won the World Series after 108 years, a 108-year-old fan died of a heart attack just days after the team's final win (Leavitt, 2016). Heart attack rates even increase during the first three days following the spring change to daylight savings time, as people cope with earlier wake times and minor sleep deprivation, and then drop slightly when the autumn transition gives them an extra hour of sleep (T. S. Janszky & Ljung, 2008).

Extreme stress can also lead to brain damage (Figure 8.16). Hippocampal volume was reduced in Vietnam combat veterans suffering from posttraumatic stress disorder (PTSD; Bremner et al., 1995) and in victims of childhood abuse (Bremner et al., 1997), and cortical tissue was reduced in torture victims (T. S. Jensen et al., 1982). The abused individuals had short-term memory deficits, and some of the torture victims showed slight intellectual impairment. There is some evidence that the damage is caused by cortisol; implanting cortisol pellets in monkeys' brains damaged their hippocampi (Sapolsky, Uno, Rebert, & Finch, 1990), and elderly humans who had elevated cortisol levels over a five-year period had an average 14% decrease in hippocampal volume (Lupien et al., 1998). However, individuals with PTSD have *lowered* cortisol levels. Rachel Yehuda (2001) points out that they also have an increased number and sensitivity of the glucocorticoid

> *In [emotional] pain there is as much wisdom as in pleasure.*
>
> —Friedrich Nietzsche

■ **FIGURE 8.16**   Hippocampal Damage in a Stressed Monkey.

Compare the number of cells between the arrows in the hippocampus of a control monkey (a) and the number in the same area in a monkey that died spontaneously of apparent stress (b).

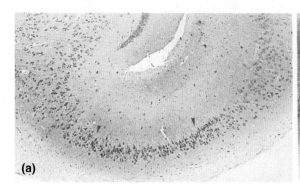
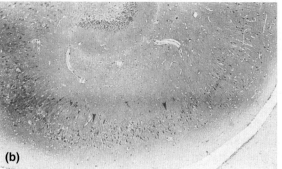

(a)   (b)

receptors that respond to cortisol. She suggests that PTSD involves increased sensitivity to cortisol rather than an increase in cortisol level. Although there is a compensatory decrease in cortisol release, it is not adequate to protect the hippocampus. The accompanying Research Spotlight describes remarkable evidence of brain damage following recent globally significant disasters.

Several studies suggest that reducing stress can improve health. T cell counts increased in AIDS patients after 20 hours of relaxation training (D. N. Taylor, 1995); similar training was associated with reduced death rates in elderly individuals (C. N. Alexander, Langer, Newman, Chandler, & Davies, 1989) and in cancer patients (Fawzy et al., 1993; Spiegel, 1996). However, evidence that survival rate in these studies is related to immune function improvement is sketchy (Fawzy et al., 1993); it is possible that study participation led the elderly subjects and cancer patients to make lifestyle changes. At any rate, it may be more practical to block stress hormones and bolster immunity chemically. Researchers at Tel Aviv University have found that the psychological and physiological stress of cancer surgery suppresses immunity, allowing the spread of cancer during the postoperative period; combining an anti-anxiety drug with an anti-inflammatory drug greatly increased the survival rate of mice following tumor removal, and clinical trials are under way with humans (Glasner et al., 2010; "New Method to Manage . . . ," 2012).

> **?** In what ways do personality characteristics influence immune functioning?

Social, Personality, and Genetic Factors

Social support was associated with dramatically lower death rates in several different populations (reviewed in House, Landis, & Umberson, 1988) and with lower stress and reduced stress hormone levels among Three Mile Island residents (Fleming, Baum, Gisriel, & Gatchel, 1982). People who are hostile are at greater risk for heart disease (T. Q. Miller, Smith, Turner, Guijarro, & Hallet, 1996), while cancer patients who have a "fighting spirit" may live longer than patients who accept their illness or have an attitude of hopelessness (Derogatis, Abeloff, & Melisaratos, 1979; Greer, 1991; Temoshok, 1987). Because of the high association between mood disorder and cancer, some observers have suggested that depression is a predisposing factor; however, the opposite is more likely, because animal research indicates that immune system cytokines released by tumors can produce depressive-like behaviors (Pyter, Pineros, Galang, McClintock, & Prendergast, 2009).

Social and personality influences must work through physiological mechanisms, which, unfortunately, are seldom assessed in these studies. An exception is an investigation of individual differences in immune response. Recall that there is a greater association of positive emotion with the left prefrontal area and negative emotion with the right. Six months after volunteers were given influenza vaccinations, the ones with higher EEG activity in the left prefrontal area had a five times greater increase in antibodies than those with higher activation on the right (Figure 8.17; Rosenkranz et al., 2003). In other research, men who had tested positive for human immunodeficiency virus (HIV) infection had HIV levels that were eight times higher if they were introverted (socially inhibited) rather than extroverted (S. W. Cole, Kemeny, Fahey, Zack, & Naliboff, 2003). The introverted patients' HIV levels also decreased less during treatment and their T cells did not increase at all.

The researchers point out that introverted individuals have elevated levels of epinephrine and norepinephrine, which activate the sympathetic nervous system during stress, and that norepinephrine increases the rate at which the HIV virus multiplies in the laboratory. Unfortunately, they didn't measure sympathetic activity specifically, but total autonomic activity (assessed from variability of heart rate, skin conductance, and other measures) was higher among the introverted HIV patients. This correlational study doesn't tell us which among introversion, norepinephrine, and HIV infection is the initial cause, but it does suggest that norepinephrine is an important mediator of the effects.

Personality characteristics such as introversion are moderately heritable, and so is vulnerability to stress; for example, a study of 300 Swedish twins concluded that 32% of workplace stress is genetic (Judge, Ilies, & Zhang, 2012). One gene implicated in stress is *NPY*, which encodes the production of neuropeptide Y (which you know from

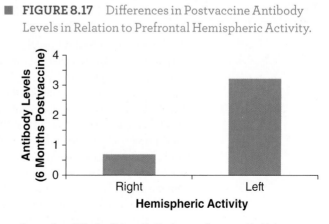

■ **FIGURE 8.17** Differences in Postvaccine Antibody Levels in Relation to Prefrontal Hemispheric Activity.

Source: From "Affective Style and In Vivo Immune Response," by M. A. Rosenkranz et al., *PNAS, 100*, pp. 11148–11152. © 2003.

RESEARCH SPOTLIGHT

One Aftermath of Disaster Is Stress-Related Brain Damage

Three years after the 9/11 terrorist attacks on the World Trade Center killed more than 2,600 people, researchers compared fMRI scans of people living within 1.5 miles (2.4 kilometers) of the towers with those of volunteers living 200 miles (322 kilometers) away (Ganzel, Kim, Glover, & Temple, 2008). Although the near residents' symptoms of PTSD were not serious enough to merit diagnosis, they had reduced gray-matter volume in the hippocampus, amygdala, prefrontal cortex, anterior cingulate cortex, and insula; in addition, amygdala activation was greater when they viewed facial expressions of fear (see figure).

Two studies of people affected by the devastating Japanese earthquake of 2011 have the rare advantage of being able to

examine before-and-after brain scans. After the earthquake, researchers recruited 42 subjects who had received MRI scans as part of previous research and scanned them again (Sekiguchi et al., 2013). The subjects most likely to have PTSD symptoms had lower gray-matter volume in the anterior cingulate cortex (ACC) prior to the quake and lower gray-matter volume in the orbitofrontal cortex (OFC) after. The researchers believed that, due to the ACC's involvement in processing fear and anxiety, its small volume was a predisposing factor to developing OFC damage and PTSD symptoms. A year later, the 37 original subjects who could be located showed decreased right hippocampal volumes, but they had not developed clinical PTSD and their OFC volumes had increased (Sekiguchi et al., 2014).

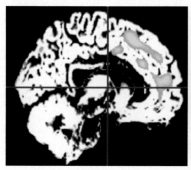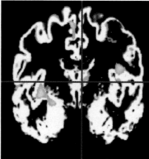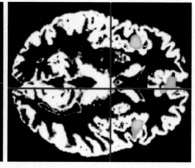

Source: "Resilience After 9/11: Multimodal Neuroimaging Evidence for Stress-Related Change in the Healthy Adult Brain," by B. L. Ganzel, P. Kim, G. H. Glover, and E. Temple, 2008, *NeuroImage, 40,* pp. 788–795. Used with permission from Elsevier.

its involvement in appetite); people with a low-functioning version of the gene show greater brain activity in response to negatively charged words, report more negative feelings in anticipation of a painful stimulus, and are more prone to depression (Mickey et al., 2011). But what may be as important as the genes we have is the ability of stress to modify the expression of those genes. German researchers took repeated blood samples from subjects undergoing a stressful interview and found that methylation of the oxytocin receptor gene *OXTR* increased during the first 10 minutes and then decreased below initial levels 90 minutes afterward, presumably increasing and then decreasing the number of oxytocin receptors (Unternaehrer et al., 2012). Besides playing a role in sexual experience and bonding, oxytocin increases during stress and reduces some of the physiological effects, including blood pressure and heart rate. The researchers suggest that the receptor changes observed would mobilize the body's resources initially and then support longer-term coping with the effects of stress. Stress effects are known to sometimes carry over to the offspring, apparently due to epigenetic changes of this sort. Male mice repeatedly separated from their mothers during the first 14 days after birth showed depressive symptoms as adults (passivity in response to stressful situations); the same behaviors were seen in the offspring, along with methylation changes in genes known to be involved in responses to stress (Franklin et al., 2010).

Pain as an Adaptive Emotion

Eighty percent of all visits to physicians are at least partly to seek relief from pain (Gatchel, 1996), and we spend billions each year on nonprescription pain medications. These observations alone qualify pain as a major health problem.

A world without pain might sound wonderful, but in spite of the suffering it causes, pain is valuable for its adaptive benefits. It warns us that the coffee is too hot, that our shoe is rubbing a blister, that we should take our skis back to the bunny slope for more practice. People with *congenital insensitivity to pain* are born unable to sense pain; they injure themselves repeatedly because they are not motivated to avoid dangerous situations, and they die from untreated conditions like a ruptured appendix. Mild pain tells us to change our posture regularly; a woman with congenital insensitivity to pain suffered damage to her spine because she could not respond to these signals, and resulting complications led to her death (Sternbach, 1968).

Pain is one of the senses, a point we consider in more detail in Chapter 11. Here we focus on the feature that makes pain unique among the senses: It is so intimately involved with emotion that we are justified in discussing it as an emotional response. In fact, when we tell someone about a pain experience, we are usually describing an emotional reaction; it is the emotional response that makes pain adaptive.

You know it, and Harvard psychologists have confirmed it: Pain someone inflicts on you intentionally hurts more than pain you experience accidentally (K. Gray & Wegner, 2008). As Beecher (1956) observed, "The intensity of suffering is largely determined by what the pain means to the patient" (p. 1609). In our society, childbirth is considered a painful and debilitating ordeal; in other cultures, childbirth is a routine matter, and the woman returns to work in the fields almost immediately. After the landing at the Anzio beachhead in World War II, 68% of the wounded soldiers denied pain and refused morphine; only 17% of civilians with similar "wounds" from surgery accepted their pain so bravely (Beecher, 1956). The soldiers were not simply insensitive to pain, because they complained bitterly about rough treatment or inept blood draws. According to Beecher, who was the surgeon in command at Anzio, the surgery was a major annoyance for the civilians, but the soldiers' wounds meant they had escaped the battlefield alive. Spiritual context can also have a powerful influence on the meaning of pain. Each spring in some remote villages of India, a man is suspended by a rope attached to steel hooks in his back; swinging above the cheering crowd, he blesses the children and the crops. Selection for this role is an honor, and the participant seems not only to be free of pain but also in a "state of exaltation" (Ghosh & Sinha, 2007; Kosambi, 1967). Figure 8.18 shows an example of culturally sanctioned self-torture.

The pain pathway has rich interconnections with the limbic system, where pain becomes an emotional phenomenon. Besides the somatosensory area, pain particularly activates the anterior cingulate cortex, which in turn is intimately connected with other limbic structures (D. D. Price, 2000; Talbot et al., 1991). The brain scan in Figure 8.19 shows increased activity in the anterior cingulate cortex as well as the somatosensory area during painful heat stimulation. But what evidence is there that activity in the anterior cingulate cortex represents the emotional aspect of pain? First of all, in humans and monkeys some of the neurons respond to the anticipation of pain as well as to painful stimulation (Hutchison,

■ **FIGURE 8.18**   Voluntary Ritualized Torture in Religious Practice.

Cultural values help determine a person's reaction to painful stimulation.

Source: ©Alain Evrard/Photo Researchers.

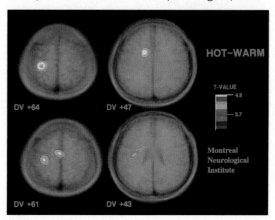

■ **FIGURE 8.19**   PET Scan of Brain During Painful Heat Stimulation.

The bright area near the midline is the cingulate gyrus; the one to the left is in the somatosensory area. The four views were taken simultaneously at different depths in the same brain. (The frontal lobes are at the top of the figure.)

Source: Reprinted with permission from "Multiple Representations of Pain in Human Cerebral Cortex," J. D. Talbot et al., *Science, 251,* pp. 1355–1358. Copyright 1991. Reprinted by permission of AAAS.

What makes pain an emotional response?

> Pain is a more terrible lord of mankind than even death itself.
>
> —Albert Schweitzer

Davis, Lozano, Tasker, & Dostrovsky, 1999; Koyama, Tanaka, & Mikami, 1998). More convincingly, as pain unpleasantness increases with repetitions of the same painful stimulus or due to hypnotic suggestion, activity increases in the ACC but not in the somatosensory area (D. D. Price, 2000; Rainville, Duncan, Price, Carrier, & Bushnell, 1997). Estimating the pain of others also activates the ACC but not the somatosensory cortex (Jackson, Meltzoff, & Decety, 2005; T. Singer et al., 2004). Interestingly, acetaminophen may owe some of its pain-alleviating ability to a dampening of emotion. Compared with control subjects receiving a placebo, volunteers who took a typical dose of acetaminophen showed blunted emotional reactions to photos (Durso, Luttrell, & Way, 2015) and rated the physical and emotional pain of others lower (Mischkowski, Crocker, & Way, 2016).

If pain continues, it also recruits activity in prefrontal areas where, presumably, the pain is evaluated and responses to the painful situation are planned (D. D. Price, 2000). The location of pain emotion in separate structures may explain the experience of two groups of patients. In pain insensitivity disorders, it is the emotional response that is diminished rather than the sensation of pain; the person can recognize painful stimulation, but simply is not bothered by it (Melzack, 1973; D. D. Price, 2000). The same is true for people who underwent prefrontal lobotomy back when that surgery was used to manage untreatable pain; when questioned, the patients often said they still felt the "little" pain but the "big" pain was gone.

CONCEPT CHECK

Take a Minute to Check Your Knowledge and Understanding

- Describe the positive and negative effects of stress, indicating why the effects become negative.
- Discuss the emotional aspects of pain, including the brain structures involved.

Biological Origins of Aggression

Both motivation and emotion reach a peak during aggression. Aggression can be adaptive, but it also takes many thousands of lives annually and maims countless others physically and emotionally. The systematic slaughter of millions in World War II concentration camps and the terrorist attack that destroyed the World Trade Center are dramatic examples, but we should not allow such catastrophic events as these to blind us to the more common thread of daily aggression running throughout society.

Aggression is behavior that is intended to harm. Researchers agree that there is more than one kind of aggression, but they do not agree on what the different kinds are, partly because the forms of aggression differ among species. Most often, researchers make a distinction between predatory aggression and affective aggression. *Predatory aggression* occurs when an animal attacks and kills its prey or when a human makes a premeditated, unprovoked attack on another. Predatory aggression is cold and emotionless, whereas *affective aggression* is characterized by its impulsiveness and emotional arousal. Although these terms have been useful in animal research, the terms *instrumental* and *impulsive* seem more descriptive of aggression seen in humans. *Instrumental aggression* is unprovoked and emotionless, and is intended to bring about some gain for the aggressor, for example, to intimidate or rob the victim. *Impulsive aggression* occurs in response to a threat, real or imagined, and is characterized by heightened emotionality. These two types of aggression are sometimes referred to as *proactive* and *reactive*, for obvious reasons.

The Brain's Role in Aggression

The primary neural instigator of aggressive behavior is the hypothalamus; electrical stimulation there reliably induces attack in rats, cats, and monkeys (reviewed in Falkner & Lin, 2014). Specific areas of the hypothalamus have been identified by using more precisely controllable techniques such as optogenetic stimulation; the most important are the anterior hypothalamic area, the medial hypothalamic area, and the ventrolateral part of the ventromedial hypothalamus. We know that the hypothalamus is important in human aggression as well, in part because back in the days of psychosurgery electrical lesions were made in the hypothalamus to treat extreme aggressiveness. Although there has not been the systematic identification of specific areas that we've seen with animals, there is some indication that the structures are organized very similarly from mice through humans (Haller, 2013).

RESEARCH SPOTLIGHT

A Bug That Causes Road Rage?

When the protozoan parasite *Toxoplasma gondii* infects animals, it forms cysts in the brain that change the host's behavior. Rats, for example, become risk takers and lose their fear of cats; this makes it likely they will get eaten, which means *T. gondii* cysts will end up in the cat's feces and be spread to new hosts. About one third of the world's population is infected with *T. gondii,* including about 14% of the U.S. population, due to contaminated food and water; infected individuals have slower reaction times and are more likely to have car accidents, and infection has been linked to some cases of psychiatric disorder, such as schizophrenia (Torrey, Bartko, & Yolken, 2012).

Following studies that found an association with aggression (Cook et al., 2015) and suicidal behaviors in women (Ling, Lester, Mortensen, Langenberg, & Postolache, 2011), Emil Coccaro and his colleagues (2016) at the University of Chicago asked whether the parasite might contribute to intermittent explosive disorder (IED). IED is a form of problematic, impulsive aggressive behavior, such as we see in road rage, and it affects about 16 million Americans. The researchers found that individuals who tested positive for *T. gondii* were also more likely to score higher on measures of aggression. The rate of infection was 21.8% in the subjects with IED, compared with 16.7% among control subjects with psychiatric diagnoses and 9.1% of healthy control subjects. Coccaro said that these results "confirm that IED is a brain disorder and not a disorder of 'personality.'" Previous studies found that the cysts show up mostly in the amygdala, where they cause retraction of dendrites, and in the prefrontal cortex.

Whether the individual becomes aggressive is not up to the hypothalamus alone; the amygdala is a central part of a circuit that detects and responds to threats (E. F. Coccaro, Sripada, Yanowitch, & Phan, 2011). Stimulation of the amygdala has been reported to produce anger in humans, but only in aggressive patients, and lesioning of the amygdala improved "intractable aggression" in 33%–100% of cases (Mpakopoulou, Gatos, Brotis, Paterakis, & Fountas, 2008). PET scan studies have consistently found reduced activity in the temporal lobes (where the amygdala is located) of aggressive individuals, but in fMRI studies amygdala activity has sometimes been reduced and sometimes enhanced; one hypothesis for this discrepancy is that amygdala responsiveness is characteristic of impulsive aggression, and reduced activation is seen in instrumental aggression (E. F. Coccaro et al.). Evidence of this is that individuals with borderline personality disorder or intermittent explosive disorder, both marked by impulsive aggression, typically have enhanced amygdala activity, whereas individuals with disorders that are typified by emotionless, instrumental aggression—for example, psychopathy and antisocial personality disorder—are more likely to have diminished responses in the amygdala. In addition, children who play violent video games and watch violent television shows (and are therefore presumed to have become somewhat immune to the emotional effects of violence) are likely to have reduced activity in the amygdala (R. J. Nelson & Trainor, 2007).

You're already familiar with the role of the prefrontal cortex in controlling risky behavior, and there is considerable evidence that diminished prefrontal functioning is important in aggression. Men have less gray matter in the prefrontal cortex than women, which in one study accounted for 77% of their greater antisocial behavior (Raine, Yang, Narr, & Toga, 2009). Impulsive aggression apparently occurs because diminished frontal activity is inadequate to inhibit circuits in the hypothalamus and amygdala (Bufkin & Luttrell, 2005; R. J. Nelson & Trainor, 2007). In a study of convicted murderers, prefrontal activity was reduced in those whose crimes were impulsive, but it was essentially normal among instrumental murderers (Raine et al., 1998). And though prefrontal gray matter was reduced by 22% in psychopaths who had been convicted of crimes, those who admitted to crimes but had escaped detection had no deficits (Y. Yang et al., 2005). Thus, although the prefrontal cortex deters most of us from engaging in hostile and aggressive behavior, it fails to do so in others. In still others it may provide the impulse control and planning ability needed to carry out instrumental aggression.

Hormones and Neurotransmitters in Aggression

No discussion of the neural bases of aggression is complete without considering the role of hormones and neurotransmitters. When the topic of hormones comes up, we immediately think of testosterone, largely because men are typically more violent than women. According to the Federal Bureau of Investigation (2010), 90.3% of murders are committed by males. So we will look at testosterone first, while acknowledging that it also plays a role in female aggression, and then consider emerging evidence that serotonin and cortisol are equally important as counters to testosterone.

Testosterone

? How is testosterone related to aggression?

The importance of testosterone in animal aggression is well established. For example, castration of an alpha male rat causes a significant decrease in aggressiveness along with loss of his dominant position; testosterone replacement prevents these losses (D. J. Albert, Walsh, Gorzalka, Siemens, & Louie, 1986). Male monkeys with high testosterone more often engage in aggression that asserts dominance, such as threatening other monkeys or displacing them from their position (Virkkunen, Goldman, & Linnoila, 1996; Virkkunen & Linnoila, 1993). A testosterone-aggression link has been reported in females as well, but few animal studies have even raised this question.

Obviously, it is more difficult to observe aggression in humans, so researchers often resort to simulations in the laboratory. For example, testosterone levels were highly correlated with the intensity of shocks college males delivered to a provocative fictitious confederate (Berman, Gladue, & Taylor, 1993). In a series of studies, high testosterone—whether endogenous or administered—was associated with increased responses to anger stimuli and decreased reactivity to fear stimuli (Montoya, Terburg, Bos, & van Honk, 2012), both of which would support aggressive behavior. Studies of real-life aggression have relied on self-report or criminal records. Testosterone levels were higher in male prisoners convicted of violent crimes, such as rape and murder, and in prisoners rated as tougher by their peers (Figure 8.20; J. M. Dabbs, Carr, Frady, & Riad, 1995; J. J. Dabbs, Frady, Carr, & Besch, 1987). In female inmates, testosterone levels were correlated with the violence of their crimes and with aggressive dominance while in prison (J. J. Dabbs & Hargrove, 1997).

The role of testosterone in human aggression has been controversial, and some observers have argued that elevated testosterone is the *result* of aggressive arousal rather than the cause. It is true that testosterone increases after winning a sports event (Archer, 1991; Mazur & Lamb, 1980), while *watching* one's team win a sports event (Bernhardt, Dabbs, Fielden, & Lutter, 1998), and even after receiving an MD degree (Mazur & Lamb, 1980). But that doesn't eliminate the possibility that testosterone contributes to aggression, and there are other potential reasons that studies sometimes come up with negative results. For one thing, correlations are typically low and highly variable across groups (J. Archer, Graham-Kevan, & Davies, 2005), which means that small studies could come up with differing results. More important, though, we are learning that it makes little sense to study testosterone alone because its effect depends on serotonin and cortisol, which we will discuss next.

Serotonin and Cortisol

We have already seen some indication of the importance of serotonin in motivation. Usually its role is inhibitory, suppressing motivated behaviors; when serotonin activity is low, appetite increases for food, water, sex, and drugs of abuse (Pihl & Peterson, 1993). Now we will add aggression to the list. Serotonin is important because it plays a crucial role in the inhibition that the prefrontal cortex exerts on aggression. Studies have found low serotonin levels in a variety of groups showing impulsive aggression, and

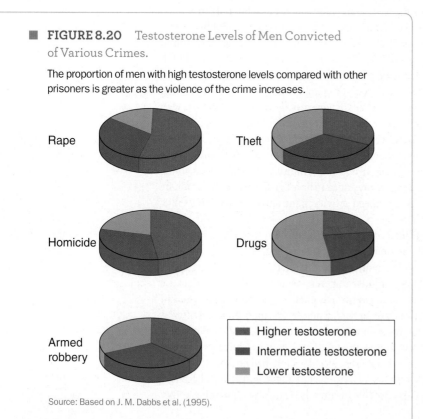

■ **FIGURE 8.20**   Testosterone Levels of Men Convicted of Various Crimes.

The proportion of men with high testosterone levels compared with other prisoners is greater as the violence of the crime increases.

Rape

Theft

Homicide

Drugs

Armed robbery

■ Higher testosterone
■ Intermediate testosterone
■ Lower testosterone

Source: Based on J. M. Dabbs et al. (1995).

low binding of serotonin at receptors in the prefrontal cortex and amygdala is associated with higher aggressiveness; treatment with antidepressants that increase serotonin levels increases prefrontal activation and reduces aggression (R. J. Nelson & Trainor, 2007). Remember in the study of monkeys that those with high testosterone were aggressive; in the same study, the monkeys with low serotonin were impulsive, taking dangerously long leaps among the treetops and allowing occasional aggression to escalate into greater violence (Higley et al., 1996). The most aggressive monkeys had both low serotonin and high testosterone levels. A similar relationship with aggression was seen in violent alcoholic offenders (Virkkunen, Goldman, & Linnoila, 1996; Virkkunen & Linnoila, 1993) and in normal males (Kuepper et al., 2010).

Cortisol, a steroid hormone, is released in response to stress and helps the body cope by regulating many of the changes that occur, such as blood pressure, blood sugar, and immune responses. In a study of male prisoners, those who were nonpsychopathic had high cortisol levels, whereas those diagnosed as psychopathic had low cortisol, just as we would expect in individuals who tend to be calculating and unemotional (Cima, Smeets, & Jelicic, 2008). But if we left the discussion here, we would miss the point of cortisol's broader role; along with dampening the physical responses to stress, it also inhibits aggression. In a group of late-adolescent males who had committed violent crimes, testosterone levels were correlated with aggression severity only if cortisol

 APPLICATION

Neurocriminology, Responsibility, and the Law

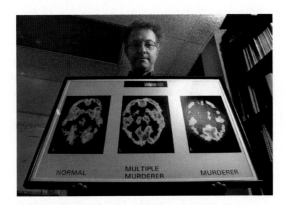

Adrian Raine.

Source: Lawrence K. Ho/Los Angeles Times/Getty Images.

In 1999, Donta Page robbed a young Denver woman and then raped and killed her. During the trial, British psychologist Adrian Raine testified that Page had a "perfect storm" of predisposing factors: a family history of mental illness; a distinct lack of activation in the prefrontal cortex (Glenn & Raine, 2014); and a childhood of poor nutrition, lead exposure, parental neglect, repeated physical and sexual abuse, and head injuries (Raine, 2013). As a result of Raine's testimony, Page received a life sentence rather than the death penalty.

Raine (who is cited frequently in this chapter) is a pioneer in the emerging field of neurocriminology, which uses neuroscience to understand and prevent criminal behavior. He raises the question

of whether we should hold criminals like Page to the same level of accountability we expect of other people. For emphasis, he points out that violence in the United States has closely tracked the rise and fall of lead in gasoline, which can statistically account for 91% of the changes in violence from the 1970s to the present ("Criminologist Believes Violent Behavior . . . ," 2013).

In spite of Page's impairments, his crime didn't have to happen. Earlier in 1999, he had come before the parole board while serving time for robbery. Had Raine been called on to testify then, he would have told the board that Page was at high risk for violence and should not be returned to society (Raine, 2013). Instead, Page was set free after serving 4 years of a 20-year term, and he murdered the young woman just 4 months later. Applying the expertise of neurocriminology earlier in a criminal's career could reduce later violence through treatment and more enlightened decisions about sentencing and parole. Obstacles standing in the way of this approach are the lack of research funding and outmoded attitudes of officials and the public when it comes to brain disorders, mental illness, and responsibility. A positive outcome of the December 2012 Sandy Hook school shooting is that the parents of one victim, six-year-old Avielle Richman, established the Avielle Foundation to foster more constructive attitudes and to encourage neuroscience research on the causes of violence (T. Smith, 2013).

was low (J. M. Dabbs, Jurkovic, & Frady, 1991). Since that study, numerous others have verified the relationship between a high testosterone-to-cortisol ratio and aggression in a variety of populations (see Montoya et al., 2012, for references) and, in at least one study, in girls as well as in boys (Platje et al., 2015). And as discussed in the accompanying Application, biological explanations for criminal behavior (called neurocriminology) are increasingly being used to explain violent acts and identify individuals for proper treatment instead of incarceration.

We are now beginning to see a counterbalanced system of opposed hormones and transmitters, just as we did with the neural structures involved in aggression. As you know, serotonin controls aggression through its inhibitory influence on the hypothalamus and amygdala; and cortisol exerts its inhibition by increasing expression of genes in the amygdala to facilitate fear and avoidance, whereas testosterone upregulates other genes there to facilitate aggression (Montoya et al., 2012). According to one hypothesis, these three factors work in concert to determine both whether and how aggression will occur (Montoya et al.). A high testosterone-to-cortisol ratio predisposes to aggression; low serotonin then predisposes to impulsive aggression, whereas high serotonin, if it does not suppress the behavior, channels it into planned, instrumental aggression.

Two other transmitters are worthy of note because they will show up in the next section. Dopamine levels increase during aggression in animals, and antidopaminergic drugs alleviate aggression in some psychiatric patients, but the precise role of dopamine is not understood (Narvaes & de Almeida, 2014). The contribution of dopamine could be due to its involvement in competitive motivation and risk taking. Gamma-aminobutyric acid (GABA) is, of course, the main inhibitory neurotransmitter in mammalian brains, and most studies report an inhibitory effect on aggression, but there have been contradictory results, possibly because its influence also depends on the other players.

Heredity and Environment

About 50% of the variability in aggressive behavior can be accounted for by genes, with the remaining half mostly due to nonshared (nonfamily) environmental influences (Tuvblad & Baker, 2011). Numerous genes have been implicated, including 18 involved in the development of neurons and another 7 related to formation of the forebrain. But those studied most often have functions in serotonin and dopamine transmission (Fernàndez-Castillo & Cormand, 2016). Examples are the serotonin transporter gene, *5HTT* (also known as *SLC6A4*), and the dopamine transporter gene, *DAT1* (or *SLC6A4*); transporter genes encode proteins that return the neurotransmitter to the presynaptic neuron. The *MAOA* gene encodes monoamine oxidase A, an enzyme that degrades serotonin and dopamine, as well as noradrenalin. The short alleles of this gene, known collectively as *MAOA-L*, result in low levels of monoamine oxidase; their association with impulsive aggression has earned them the nickname "warrior genes." Considering the role of testosterone in aggression, it is not surprising that some studies have identified the androgen receptor gene, *AR*, as important; two alleles may distinguish between impulsive and instrumental aggression (Waltes, Chiocchetti, & Freitag, 2016).

Research has also identified environmental conditions that predispose individuals to aggressive behavior, including maltreatment, family adversity, and low socioeconomic status (Tuvblad & Baker, 2011). Environmental influences and heredity interact in interesting and complicated ways. The best known example is *MAOA-L*, whose link to aggression has been replicated more than any other. Two studies of incarcerated criminals have confirmed that this allele leads to violent behavior *only* in individuals who were subjected to childhood physical abuse (Figure 8.21; Caspi et al., 2002; Gorodetsky et al., 2014).

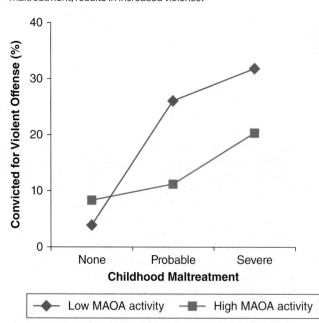

■ **FIGURE 8.21**   Genetic Influence on Violent Behavior in Victims of Childhood Maltreatment.

Low MAOA activity due to the *MAOA-L* allele, coupled with childhood maltreatment, results in increased violence.

Source: Based on data from "Role of Genotype in the Cycle of Violence in Maltreated Children," by A. Caspi et al., 2002, *Science, 292*, p. 852.

Take a Minute to Check Your Knowledge and Understanding

- Make a table with the following column headings: Prefrontal Cortex, Amygdala, Testosterone, Serotonin, and Cortisol. Under each heading, indicate the structure's or hormone's contribution to aggression (including interactions with others in the table).
- Now write your own theory of what causes impulsive and instrumental aggression.
- Do you think *T. gondii* is intentionally ensuring its own success when it induces a rat to get itself eaten? Explain from an evolutionary perspective.

In Perspective

Emotion has been difficult for neuroscientists to get a handle on because it is so complex physiologically and because so much of emotion is a subjective, private experience. With improved research strategies and new technologies like PET scans, old questions about the role of brain structures are finally yielding to research. A good example is the ability to separate the emotion of pain from its sensory aspects at the neural level. On another front, research has confirmed the influence of emotion on health, a topic that was practically relegated to fringe psychology not too long ago.

We have focused mostly on the negative aspects of emotion because they have received the most attention from researchers and we know more about them. Stress, pain, anger, and aggression are viewed as some of our greatest burdens, but they are permanently etched into our behavior because they helped ensure our ancestors' survival. Because they are part of our biology, we can sometimes treat these problems with medication and might one day be able to use genetic interventions. But society also needs to ask itself whether fewer students would show up at school with a weapon if we started thinking of it as an environmental problem, or if terrorism could be reduced through better international understanding, and whether we need to appreciate the role of hormones, genes, and the brain when judging the accountability of a murderer. In the meantime, if you find thoughts about the negative aspects of emotion a bit depressing, you might want to take a short break while you hold your pen between your teeth; brightening your corner of the world is a good place to start.

CHAPTER SUMMARY

Emotion and the Nervous System

- The autonomic nervous system increases bodily arousal during an emotional event and decreases it afterward.
- The James-Lange and cognitive theories differ as to the role of bodily feedback in emotional experience. There is evidence that bodily feedback, especially from facial expressions, contributes to emotions; also, mimicking other people's expressions may help us understand others' emotions.
- The limbic system is a network of several structures that have functions in emotion. We now know that emotion involves additional structures at all levels of the brain.
- The amygdala has a variety of functions, but its role in fear has received the most attention. Rats and humans with damage to both amygdalae lack fear and often fail to act in their own best interest.
- The prefrontal cortex combines emotional input with other information to make decisions. People with prefrontal cortex damage have trouble following moral and social rules, and they have impaired ability to learn from the consequences of their behavior.

- Damage to the right hemisphere particularly blunts emotions and impairs the person's ability to recognize emotion in faces and in voices.

Stress, Immunity, and Health

- Although the body's response to stress can result in damage, it is generally adaptive, mobilizing the body for action and increasing immune system activity.
- Prolonged stress interferes with mental, physical, and emotional functioning; compromises the immune system; and even damages the brain.
- Social support, personality, and attitudes are related to immune functioning and health, including cancer survival. However, these social and personality factors may not influence immune functioning; instead, they may be indicators of the individual's physiological functioning.
- Pain is also an adaptive response; it informs us of danger to the body, and the emotion that accompanies it motivates us to take action.

Biological Origins of Aggression

- Researchers usually distinguish two types of aggression in animals, predatory and affective; in humans, the two types are known as instrumental and impulsive.
- Aggression arises from the hypothalamus and, at least in the case of impulsive aggression, from the amygdala. The prefrontal cortex typically inhibits aggression, but in aggressive individuals its role in planning and impulse control may distinguish instrumental from impulsive aggression.
- Testosterone is involved in both male and female aggression, although in humans the causal link for testosterone has been questioned.
- Serotonin and cortisol inhibit aggression. According to one hypothesis, high testosterone and low cortisol predispose a person to aggression, and low serotonin further disposes

one to impulsive aggression, whereas high serotonin channels it into planned, instrumental aggression.
- The role of dopamine in aggression is not well understood, but antidopaminergic drugs alleviate aggression in some psychiatric patients. GABA has been reported to inhibit aggression, but there have been contradictory results.
- Heritability of aggressive behavior is about 50%, with most of the remainder due to nonshared environmental influences.
- Genes that contribute to aggression include several involved in neuronal and forebrain development. Others include serotonin and dopamine transporter genes, the *MAOA-L* allele, and the androgen receptor gene. Gene-environment interaction is illustrated by the finding that *MAOA-L* contributed to aggression only in individuals who had been abused as children. ∎

STUDY RESOURCES

FOR FURTHER THOUGHT

- Do you think we rely more on bodily feedback or the stimulus situation in identifying emotions? Why?
- Stress and pain involve considerable suffering, but they are necessary. Explain. What differentiates between good and bad stress and pain?
- You are an adviser to a government official charged with reducing aggression in your country. From what you have learned in this chapter, what would you recommend?
- The legal plea of "not guilty by reason of insanity" has historically required that the defendant did not *know* right from wrong—as evidenced, for example, by the defendant's failure to flee or try to conceal the crime. Critique this standard in terms of what you know about controlling behavior.

TEST YOUR UNDERSTANDING

1. Discuss the James-Lange and cognitive theories, including evidence for the theories.

2. Explain the roles of the amygdala and the prefrontal cortex in guiding our everyday decisions and behavior.

3. Describe the role the brain plays in animal and human aggression, including structures and their functions.

Select the best answer:

1. The James-Lange theory and the cognitive theory disagree on whether
   a. specific brain centers are involved in specific emotions.
   b. there is any biological involvement in human emotions.
   c. bodily feedback determines which emotion is felt.
   d. individuals can judge their emotions accurately.

2. Some people with brain damage do not seem to learn from the consequences of their behavior and must have supervised care. Based on the location of their damage, you would expect that they would particularly be lacking in
   a. sadness.
   b. joy.
   c. fear.
   d. motivation.

3. A person with partial paralysis seems remarkably undisturbed about the impairment. The paralysis
   a. probably is on the right side of the body.
   b. probably is on the left side of the body.
   c. probably involves both sides of the body.
   d. is as likely to be on one side as the other.

4. Stress can
   a. reduce immune system function.
   b. impair health.
   c. mobilize the immune system.
   d. both a and b
   e. a, b, and c

5. Long-term exposure to cortisol may affect memory by
   a. reducing blood flow to the brain.
   b. destroying neurons in the hippocampus.
   c. inhibiting neurons.
   d. redirecting energy resources to the internal organs.

6. AIDS is a deficiency of the
   a. immune system.
   b. autonomic system.
   c. central nervous system.
   d. motor system.

7. Indications are that if pain did not have an emotional component, we would probably

    a. be deficient in avoiding harm.
    b. avoid harm by using learning and reasoning.
    c. be more aggressive.
    d. generally lead happier lives.

8. A structure described in the text as being involved in both aggression and flight is the

    a. amygdala.
    b. anterior cingulate cortex.
    c. lateral hypothalamus.
    d. periaqueductal gray.

9. According to research, you would have your best chance of showing that testosterone increases aggression in humans if you injected testosterone into

    a. males rather than females.
    b. people with high cortisol.
    c. people with low serotonin.
    d. people who were being confronted by another person.

10. Based on information in the text, the chance of violent criminal behavior is increased in males who

    a. have high testosterone.
    b. were abused as children.
    c. have a gene for low MAOA.
    d. both a and b
    e. both b and c

1. c, 2. c, 3. b, 4. e, 5. b, 6. a, 7. a, 8. d, 9. c, 10. e.

Answers:

ON THE WEB

The following websites are coordinated with this chapter's content. You can access these websites from the **SAGE edge Student Resources site**; select this chapter and then click on Web Resources. (**Bold** items are links.)

1. Here you can link to a variety of sites, from the University of California to YouTube, to see **Brain and Emotion Videos.**

2. You can get a feel for what an active emotion research laboratory is like by visiting lab sites at **Boston College** and the **University of Maryland**. You can read descriptions of their research programs and download published articles.

3. The **National Center for Posttraumatic Stress Disorder** site has information on the disorder and on subtopics such as "Returning From War" and "Issues Specific to Women."

4. Various stress tests (some validated by research and some not) are available to assess the potential for stress to affect your health and well-being. You can take a test for **Type A personality**, which research indicates contributes to heart attacks; or the historically significant **Holmes-Rahe Stress Inventory**, designed to assess health risk from recent stressful events (positive as well as negative).

FOR FURTHER READING

1. *Descartes' Error*, by Antonio Damasio (Penguin Books, 2005), is a timeless classic that develops the premise that our rational decision making is largely dependent on input from emotions.

2. *Behave: The Biology of Humans at Our Best and Worst* is Robert Sapolsky's highly acclaimed latest treatment of violence, aggression, and competition (Penguin Group, 2017).

3. "Empathy Overkill," by Helen Thomson (*New Scientist*, March 13, 2010, 43–45), describes research with people with "mirror synesthesia," who intensely feel what they see others experiencing, and people with echopraxia, who greatly exaggerate the action mimicking that the rest of us engage in subtly.

4. *The Sickening Mind*, by Paul Martin (Flamingo, 2016), is about the interplay of emotion, stress, and immunity in shaping our health.

5. *The Better Angels of Our Nature: Why Violence Has Declined*, by Steven Pinker (Penguin Books, 2012), argues that in spite of what we see in the news, violence is declining worldwide and we may be living in the most peaceful era of human existence. Pinker attributes this in part to increasing empathy, as a result of literacy, travel, and a broader worldview.

6. *The Anatomy of Violence: The Biological Roots of Crime*, by Adrian Raine (Pantheon, 2013), describes his work and that of others over the past three decades, teasing out the biological causes of crime and what can be done, while establishing the new field of neurocriminology.

KEY TERMS

 **edge.sagepub.com/garrett5e**

SAGE edge offers a robust online environment featuring an impressive array of free tools and resources for review, study, and further exploration, keeping both instructors and students on the cutting edge of teaching and learning.

8.1 Describe the brain structures and neurotransmitters involved in emotion.

Recognizing Emotions From Facial Expressions

8.2 Explain how the body and the peripheral nervous system contribute to the experience of emotion.

How Emotions Are Made
Biology of Our Best and Worst Selves

8.3 Identify the adaptive and maladaptive components of the stress response.

How Stress Affects Your Brain

8.4 Discuss the contributions of genetics and environment to stress responses.

Psychology of Stress

8.5 Compare the affective and sensory components of pain.

Why Things Hurt

8.6 Examine the brain structures and chemical systems involved in aggression.

Neuroscience of Aggression vs. Altruism

Part III

Interacting With the World

Hearing and Language

9

After reading this chapter, you will be able to:

- Summarize how the nervous system processes sound stimuli.

- Identify the brain structures involved in hearing.

- Describe the role of specific brain structures in language ability.

- Explain how lateralization is important to the brain organization of language processing.

- Predict the brain regions that are impaired in specific language disorders.

- Contrast the communication abilities of other animals with human language.

The only way Heather Whitestone knew the music had started for her ballet number in the 1995 Miss America talent competition was because she could feel the vibrations through the floor. Heather was profoundly deaf, and she became the first person with deafness or any other handicap to win the title of Miss America (Figure 9.1).

Her hearing was normal until she contracted meningitis at the age of 18 months; the problem was not the meningitis but the strong antibiotics that destroyed the sound receptor cells in her ears. A hearing aid helped some, and she read lips and received twice-weekly speech therapy. By the time she reached high school, she could participate in mainstream classes without a sign language interpreter, and she graduated with a 3.6 grade point average. A cochlear implant was an option, but since she had been deaf so long, it was possible she would not tolerate the strange new sounds. Besides, she was satisfied with her level of adjustment—that is, until she married and had a son. Heather realized she could not share many of her son's experiences because she could not hear what he was hearing. Then one day she saw her husband running to their son when the boy hurt himself and she had not even heard him crying. It was then she decided to have the surgery.

The implant bypassed the dead receptor cells to stimulate the neurons in her inner ear directly. After the surgery, she could understand her son's speech much better, so he didn't have to repeat himself so many times. Best of all, she could hear him cry, even when he was playing outside in the backyard.

Nothing attests to the value of hearing more than the effects of losing it. Like Heather, the person is cut off from much of the discourse that our social lives depend on. There is no music,

⑤SAGE edge™

Master the content.
edge.sagepub.com/garrett5e

no song of birds, and no warning from thunder or car horns. When hearing is lost abruptly in later life, the effect can be so depressing that it eventually leads to suicide.

With the topics of hearing and language, we begin the discussion of how we carry on transactions with the world. This communication involves acquiring information through the senses, processing the sensory information, communicating through language, moving about in the world, and acting on the world. We have already touched on the senses of taste, smell, and pain in the context of hunger, sexual behavior, and emotion. Before we explore additional sensory capabilities, we need to establish some basic concepts.

First, every sensory system must have a specialized receptor. A *receptor* is a cell, often a specialized neuron that is suited by its structure to respond to a form of energy, such as sound. A receptor's function is to convert that energy into a specific pattern of neural responses. You will see examples of two kinds of receptors in this and the next chapter, but receptors come in a wide array of forms to carry out their functions.

For a sensory receptor to do its job, there must also be an adequate stimulus. An *adequate stimulus* is the energy form for which the receptor is specialized. Due to the imperfect specialization of receptors, other stimuli will often produce responses as well. For example, if you apply gentle pressure to the side of your eyeball (through the lid), you will see a circular dark spot caused by mechanically stimulating normally light-sensitive receptors inside your eye.

You will remember from Chapter 3 that, according to Müller's doctrine of specific nerve energies, the neural mechanism determines the kind of sensory experience you will have. A sensory system will register its peculiar type of experience even if the stimulus is inappropriate. So, when the neurosurgeon stimulates the auditory cortex, the patient hears a buzzing sound or even voices or music, and when your skateboard shoots out from under you and your head hits the pavement, you really do see "stars." You will learn in this and the next two chapters that it is the *pattern* of the stimulation—that is, the amplitude and timing of neural impulses—that makes sensory information meaningful.

Most people consider audition and vision the most important senses. As a result, there has been more research on these two senses than on others and we know more about them, so we will give them the most attention. Because audition is a more mechanical sensory mechanism than vision, it is a good place to begin our formal discussion of *sensation,* the acquisition of sensory information, and *perception,* the interpretation of sensory information.

Hearing

The fact that the auditory mechanism is less complex does not mean that hearing is a simple matter. The *cochlea,* where the auditory stimulus is converted into neural impulses, contains thousands of moving parts. Our range of sensitivity to intensity, from the softest sound we can hear to the point where sound becomes painful, is ten trillion to one. Our ability to hear low-intensity sounds is limited more by interference from the sound of blood coursing through our veins and arteries than by the auditory mechanism itself. In addition, we can hear frequencies ranging from about 20 hertz (Hz, cycles per second) up to about 20,000 Hz, and we can detect a difference in frequencies of only 2 or 3 Hz. To give you some idea of what these frequencies relate to in real life, the piano—the most versatile of musical instruments—has a range of about 27 to 4000 Hz. Upper ranges are more impressive for some animals: 60,000 Hz (60 kHz) for dogs, 79 kHz for cats, and an astonishing 300 kHz in a species of moth (Moir, Jackson, & Windmill, 2013)—15 times higher than for humans.

The Adequate Stimulus for Hearing

The adequate stimulus for audition is vibration in a conducting medium. Normally for humans the conducting medium is air, but we can also hear vibrations in water, as well as those conducted through our

---

> *To be deaf is a greater affliction than to be blind.*
>
> —Helen Keller

? How is a stimulus translated into information the brain can use?

? What is the difference between sensation and perception?

■ **FIGURE 9.1**   Heather Whitestone Using Sign Language.

Her communication and her quality of life improved when she received a cochlear implant.

Source: Allan Tannenbaum/The LIFE Images Collection/ Getty Images.

skulls. The air is set to vibrating by the vibration of the sound source—a person's vocal cords, a bell that has been struck, or a stereo speaker. As the sound source vibrates, it alternately compresses and decompresses the air (Figure 9.2).

If we used a microphone to convert a sound to an electrical signal, we could display the signal on a computer, like the one we used to measure the action potential in Chapter 2; the oscillations of the sound wave would form a graph of the compressions and decompressions, and we could see what the sound "looks like." In Figure 9.3 the up-and-down squiggles represent the increasing and decreasing pressure of different sounds (over a brief fraction of a second). One way sounds differ is in frequency. *Frequency* refers to the number of cycles or waves of alternating compression and decompression of the vibrating medium that occur in a second (expressed in hertz). Figure 9.3a and b have the same frequency—indicated by the number of waves in the same time—so we would hear these two sounds as the same, or nearly the same, pitch. Figure 9.3c and d would also sound about the same as each other, but higher in pitch than Figure 9.3a and b. *Pitch* is our psychological perception of the frequency of a sound—more waves per second correspond to higher perceived pitch.

Sounds also differ in amplitude (the physical energy). The sounds represented by Figure 9.3a and c have the same amplitude (the height of the wave), so they would sound about equally loud; Figure 9.3b and d would sound less loud but like each other. *Amplitude,* or *intensity,* is the term for the physical energy in a sound; *loudness* is the term for our perception of sound energy. Sound intensity is usually measured in decibels (dB); this is a logarithmic scale, so a doubling of amplitude corresponds to a 6 dB increase in loudness. This means the 10 trillion-fold difference between barely detectable to damaging is about 140 dB in intensity difference.

Pitch does not correspond exactly to frequency, nor is the amplitude of a sound exactly the same as its loudness; this is due to the way our sensitivity varies across the range of sounds. For example, we are most sensitive to sounds between 1000 and 4000 Hz—the range within which most conversation occurs—and equally intense sounds outside this range would seem less loud to us (Figure 9.4). Similarly, the amplitude of a sound influences our experience of pitch. Because the physical stimulus and the psychological experience are not always perfectly related, we need to use the terms *intensity* versus *loudness* and *frequency* versus *pitch* carefully.

The sounds we hear can also be classified as either pure tones or complex sounds. A pure tone, generated for example by striking a tuning fork, would produce a tracing on an oscilloscope that looks like one of the graphs in Figure 9.3a–d. Notice that these four waveforms are a very regular shape, called a sine wave. They are *pure tones:* Each has only one frequency. Figure 9.3e and f represent *complex sounds* that mix several frequencies. The random combination of frequencies in Figure 9.3e would be perceived as "noise." Depending on the combination and amplitude of frequencies, a complex sound might seem musical like the last waveform in Figure 9.3f, which was produced by a clarinet. The two waveforms may not look very different to you, but they would certainly sound different. Although what is considered *pleasantly* musical depends on experience and culture (and one's age!), we would recognize even the most foreign music as music.

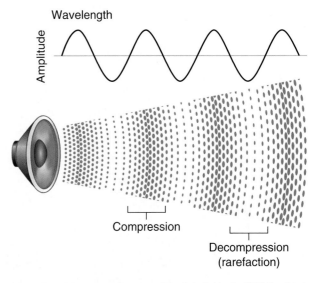

■ **FIGURE 9.2** Alternating Compression and Decompression of Air by a Sound Source.

The speaker's diaphragm moves in and out, alternately compressing and decompressing the surrounding air. The dark areas represent high pressure (a denser concentration of air molecules), and the light areas represent low pressure.

Source: From *Sensation and Perception*, 5th ed., by Goldstein, 1999. Reprinted with permission of Wadsworth, a division of Thomson Learning.

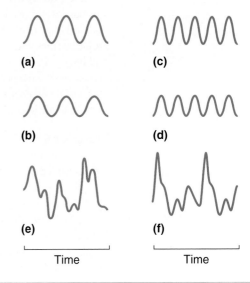

■ **FIGURE 9.3** Examples of Pure and Complex Sounds.

(a) and (b) are pure tones of the same frequency but different amplitudes, as are (c) and (d). (a) and (c) have the same amplitudes but different frequencies, as do (b) and (d). Both (e) and (f) are complex sounds—noise and a clarinet note, respectively.

■ **FIGURE 9.4**   Human Audiogram.

Humans have the best sensitivity between 1000 and 4000 Hz, where the frequencies of language are found (red bar on bottom).

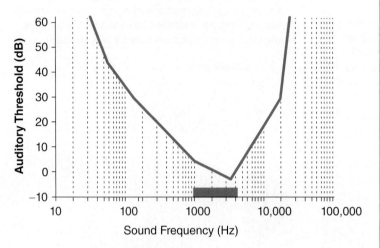

Source: Adapted from: "On Minimum Audible Fields," by L. J. Sivian and S. D. White, 1933, *Journal of the Acoustical Society of America*, 4, 288–321.

The Auditory Mechanism

To hear, we must get information about the sound to the auditory cortex. This requires a series of events, including sound reception, amplification, and conversion into neural impulses that the brain can use. Before we get to the functional aspects of encoding sound and how we extract meaningful information from a complex auditory environment, we will first begin with a survey of the structures of brain areas involved in processing sound.

The Outer and Middle Ear

The term *ear* refers generally to all the structures shown in Figure 9.5. The flap that graces the side of your head is called the outer ear or *pinna*. The outer ear filters the sound and then amplifies it slightly by funneling it from the larger area of the pinna into the smaller area of the auditory canal. It also selects for sounds in front; this makes it easier to focus on a sound, such as the conversation you're having, while excluding irrelevant sounds around you. Dogs and cats have muscles that enable them to turn their ears toward a sound that is not directly in front of them; you may be able to wiggle your ears a bit by twitching your scalp muscles, but you must turn your head to orient toward a sound. A unique aspect of your pinna is that its unique shape and filtering properties allow you to map sound objects in the world around you—if you wear earbuds that bypass your pinna, sound objects appear to be located within your own head rather than out in the world.

The separation between the outer and middle ear is the eardrum or *tympanic membrane,* a very thin membrane stretched across the end of the auditory canal; its vibrations transmit sound energy to the three middle ear bones (or ossicles). A muscle called the *tensor tympani* can stretch the eardrum tighter or loosen it to adjust the sensitivity to changing sound levels. The second part of the middle ear is the *ossicles,* tiny bones that operate in lever fashion to transfer vibration from the tympanic membrane to the cochlea. The *malleus, incus*, and *stapes* are named for their shapes, as you can see from their English equivalents *hammer, anvil*, and *stirrup.* By concentrating the energy collected from the larger tympanic membrane onto the much smaller base of the stirrup, which rests on the end of the cochlea, the ossicles amplify the sound approximately 30-fold. The amplification is more than enough to compensate for the loss of energy as the vibration passes from air to the denser liquid inside the cochlea. The ossicles are not passive players in the auditory process: The muscles attached to them tighten the joints to increase sensitivity to soft sounds and loosen the connections to dampen loud sounds. In addition to these sound-related structures, the middle ear also contains the *Eustachian tube,* connecting the middle ear to the back of your mouth, which equalizes the air pressure of the middle ear with the outside world. Pressure differences between the middle ear and the outside world put pressure on the tympanic membrane, which hurts. Therefore, your ears hurt when you dive deep in a pool, or climb up a mountain; yawning or chewing gum can open a blocked Eustachian tube, causing a "pop" as the pressure suddenly equalizes and the tympanic membrane returns to its normal shape.

The Inner Ear

Just like a membrane separates the outer and middle ears, membranes separate the air-filled middle and the fluid-filled inner ear (called the *oval* and *round windows*). You can also see the parts of the inner ear in Figure 9.5. The snail-shaped structure is the cochlea, where the ear's sound-analyzing structures are located. You can see from the cochlea's shape where it got its name, which means "land snail" in Latin. Figure 9.5a shows a more highly magnified view. It is a tube that is about 35 millimeters (mm) long in humans and coiled 2½ times. This tube is subdivided by membranes into three fluid-filled chambers or canals (Figure 9.5b). In this illustration, the end of the cochlea has been removed, and you are looking down the three canals from the base end. The stirrup (see Figure 9.5a) rests on the *oval window,* a thin,

■ FIGURE 9.5 Structures of the Outer, Middle, and Inner Ear.

(a) The outer ear—pinna and auditory canal; the middle ear—tympanic membrane and three ossicles; and the inner ear—the cochlea and auditory nerve. (b) A section of the cochlea, showing the three fluid-filled canals. (c) Schematic showing the organ of Corti, including three rows of outer hair cells (pink) and one row of inner hair cells (green). (d) How hair cell movements translate into auditory nerve action potentials. When hair cells bend to the left, potassium (K) inflow causes hair cells to increase their firing rates. When hair cells bend to the right, K outflow causes hair cells to decrease their firing rates.

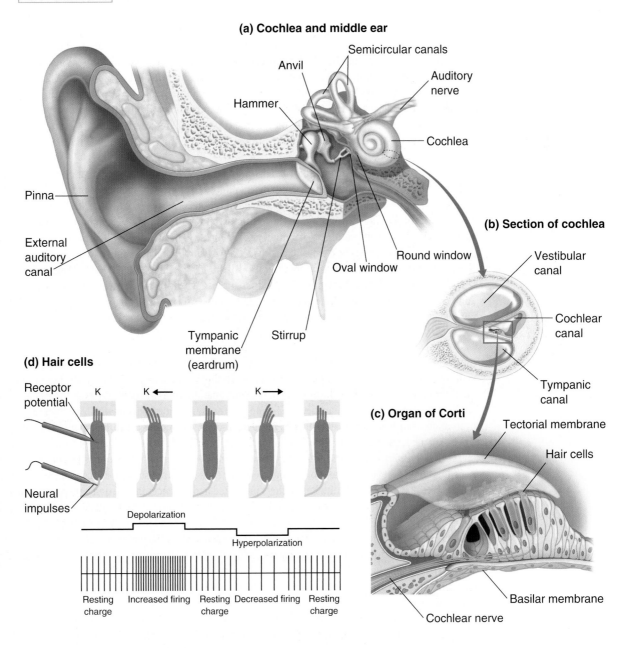

Source: (d) Koeppen & Stanton: *Berne & Levy Physiology* (6th Edition), Copyright 2008 by Mosby/Elsevier Inc.

flexible membrane on the face of the vestibular canal. The *vestibular canal* (scala vestibuli) is the point of entry of sound energy into the cochlea. The vestibular canal connects with the *tympanic canal* at the far end of the cochlea through an opening called the *helicotrema*. (You might not need to remember this term, but it just *sounds* too wonderful to leave out!) The helicotrema allows the pressure waves to travel through the cochlear fluid (called endolymph) into the tympanic canal more easily. Liquids are essentially incompressible; at the end of the tympanic canal another thin membrane, the *round window,* flexes outward with each sound wave and allows the fluid to move. The vestibular organs on top of the cochlea do not participate in hearing; we will talk about them in Chapter 11.

All this activity in the vestibular and tympanic canals bathes the *cochlear canal,* where the auditory receptors are located, in vibration. The vibration passes to the *organ of Corti,* the sound-analyzing structure that rests on the *basilar membrane.* The organ of Corti consists of four rows of specialized cells called hair cells, their supporting cells, and the *tectorial membrane* above the hair cells (Figure 9.5c). To visualize these structures, remember that you are looking down a long tube; imagine the four rows of hair cells as picket fences or rows of telephone poles and the tectorial membrane as a shelf overlying the hair cells.

How is the auditory stimulus converted to a neural impulse?

The hair cells are the receptors for auditory stimulation (Figure 9.5d). Vibration of the basilar membrane and the cochlear fluid bends the hair cells back and forth, forward movement opens potassium and calcium channels (not sodium channels, as in neurons), and the inflow of ions depolarizes the hair cell membrane (whereas backward movement closes the channels and hyperpolarizes the membrane). Depolarization results in neurotransmitter release and stimulation of the auditory neuron connected to the hair cells. The hair cells are very sensitive; the amount of movement required to produce a sensation is equivalent to the Eiffel Tower leaning just the width of your thumb (Hudspeth, 1989), about the distance the tower sways in a strong wind.

The human cochlea has two sets of hair cells: a single row of about 3,500 inner hair cells and three rows of about 12,000 outer hair cells ("inner" and "outer" refer to their location relative to the center of the coiled cochlea; see Figure 9.5c). The less numerous *inner hair cells* receive 90%–95% of the auditory neurons, and they provide most of the information about auditory stimulation (Dallos & Cheatham, 1976). A strain of mouse lacking inner hair cells due to a mutant gene is unable to hear (Deol & Gluecksohn-Waelsch, 1979). The *outer hair cells* increase the cochlea's sensitivity both by amplifying its output and by sharpening the frequency tuning at the location of peak vibration (Hudspeth, 2008; Z. Xiao & Suga, 2002). Damage to the outer hair cells by noise or chemical ablation causes a dramatic loss of hearing but also a loss of frequency selectivity along the basilar membrane. Why are these apparently non-sensory cells so important? Apparently, the outer hair cells' tugging on the tectorial membrane increases stimulation of the inner hair cells.

Pathway to the Auditory Cortex and Beyond

The work of the auditory system is hardly finished when we have converted sound into electrical impulses. Neurons from the two cochleas make up part of the auditory nerves (eighth cranial nerves), one of which enters the brain on each side of the brain stem. The information from the cochleas passes through the lateral lemniscus to various brain stem nuclei (see Figure 9.6a) to the inferior colliculi (which are involved in sound localization, as we will discuss later), then to the medial geniculate nucleus of the thalamus (where attentional processes interact with ascending auditory information), and finally to the auditory cortex in each temporal lobe. As you'll see in Chapters 10 and 11, the crossover of sensory information for opposite-side brain processing is a common occurrence. Therefore, a sound on your right side is registered primarily, but not exclusively, in the left hemisphere of the brain. Researchers interested in differences in function between the two hemispheres have used an interesting strategy, called the *dichotic listening task,* to stimulate one side of the brain. They present an auditory stimulus through headphones to one ear and present white noise (which contains all frequencies and sounds like radio static) to the other ear to occupy the nontargeted hemisphere. This technique has helped researchers determine that the left hemisphere is dominant for language in most people and that the right hemisphere is better at other tasks, such as identifying melodies. The auditory cortex is on the superior (upper) gyrus of the temporal lobe of each hemisphere; part of it is hidden inside the lateral fissure, as you can see in Figure 9.6a.

The area is *tonotopically organized,* which means that neurons from adjacent receptor locations project to adjacent cells in the cortex, and they convey similar frequencies. In this case, the projections form a sort of map of the unrolled basilar membrane (Merzenich, Knight, & Roth, 1975), just as the somatosensory cortex contains a map of the body. When we study vision in Chapter 10, we will see that this organization is typical in the senses.

Beyond the primary auditory cortex are additional processing areas, as many as nine in some mammals; these secondary auditory areas are involved in processing complex sounds and understanding their meaning.

■ FIGURE 9.6 The Auditory Pathway and the Auditory Cortex.

Auditory information from the cochlea ascends through many brain areas before arriving at the auditory cortex. Most auditory information crosses to the opposite (contralateral) hemisphere between the cochlear nucleus and trapezoid body, but some stays on the same side (ipsilateral) as the cochlea.

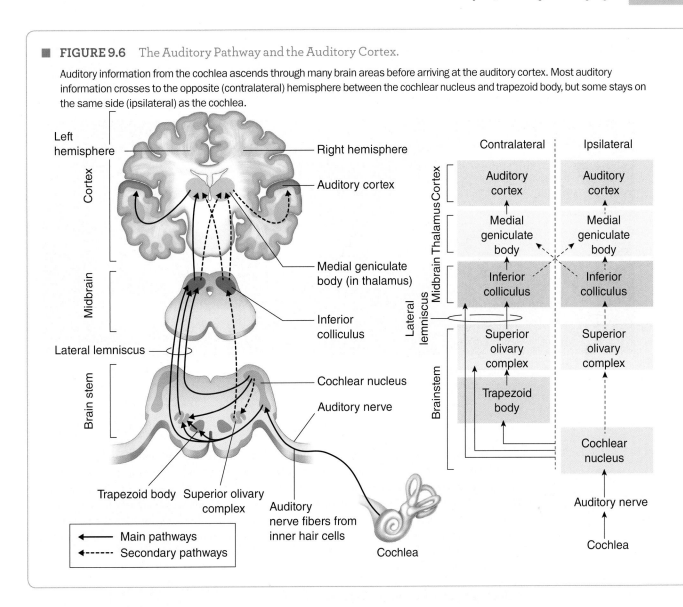

For example, some of the cells adjacent to the monkey's primary auditory area respond selectively to calls of their own species, and some of those react only to one type of call (Wollberg & Newman, 1972). The human primary auditory cortex has a secondary area surrounding it (Figure 9.6b), but auditory information also travels well beyond the auditory areas, following the *dorsal stream* or the *ventral stream* (Alain, Arnott, Hevenor, Graham, & Grady, 2001; Rauschecker & Tian, 2000).

The dorsal stream flows from the auditory cortex through the parietal area, where the brain combines information from other senses to locate the sound in relation to the body and the visual scene. The information then proceeds to the frontal lobes, where it can be used for directing eye movements toward sound sources and for planning movements. The ventral stream is active when the individual is identifying sounds; the call-specific cells of the monkey's auditory system are part of this system. Because of their specialties, the ventral and dorsal streams have been dubbed the "what" and "where" systems of audition. These two pathways are illustrated in Figure 9.7. We will consider the communication roles of the dorsal and ventral streams later, in the section on language, and you will see in Chapter 10 that vision has similar systems.

Frequency Analysis

Now that we have gone over the anatomy of the auditory system and processing areas in the brain, we can examine some of the functional aspects of the auditory system. Before we get to the more complex concepts on how our brains extract information from the cochlea to determine the location and meaning of sound, we

■ **FIGURE 9.7**   The Dorsal "Where" and Ventral "What" Streams of Auditory Processing

The red areas were active when subjects determined the locations of sounds. Green areas were activated when they identified sounds. Localization and identification followed dorsal "where" and ventral "what" streams, respectively, with both terminating in frontal areas. (Functional MRI data were superimposed over a smoothed brain.)

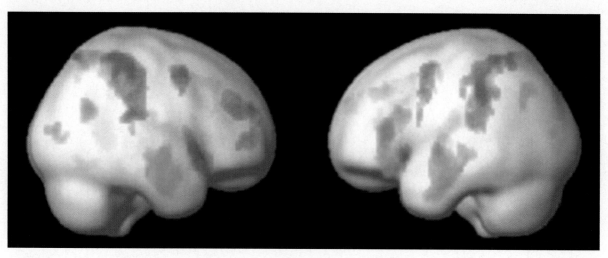

Source: From "Distinct Pathways Involved in Sound Recognition and Localization: A Human fMRI Study," by P. P. Maeder, R. A. Meuli, M. Adriani, A. Bellmann, E. Fornari, J.-P. Thiran, A. Pittet, and S. Clarke, 2001, *NeuroImage, 14*, pp. 802–816. Used with permission from Elsevier.

first must discuss how the vibrations of the conducting medium are converted into neural impulses by the cochlea. To do this, the cochlea is built to extract both frequency and intensity information from the sound through the movement of hair cells spread out across the length of the cochlea. More than 50 years ago, Ernest Wever (1949) described 17 versions of the two major theories of frequency analysis, which indicates the difficulty we have had in figuring out how people experience pitch. We will discuss a few versions that have been important historically. Besides introducing you to these two important theories, we will describe what we know about how the auditory mechanism works and give you some idea of how theories develop in response to emerging evidence.

Telephone and Frequency Theories

How do the frequency and place theories explain frequency analysis?

The most obvious explanation of how the auditory system analyzes frequency is the *frequency theory,* which assumes that the auditory mechanism transmits the actual frequency of a sound to the auditory cortex for analysis there. William Rutherford proposed an early version in 1886; it was called the *telephone theory* because he believed that individual neurons in the auditory nerve fired at the same frequency as the rate of vibration of the sound source. Half a century later, it was possible to test the theory with electrical recording equipment. Ernest Wever and Charles Bray (1930) performed one of the most intriguing investigations of auditory frequency analysis found in the scientific literature. They attached an electrode to the auditory nerve of an anesthetized cat and recorded from the nerve while they stimulated the cat's ear with various sounds. Because the simple equipment used to record neural activity at that time was limited to very low frequencies, Wever and Bray ran the amplified neural responses into a telephone receiver in a soundproof room and listened to the output. Sounds produced by a whistle were transmitted with great fidelity. When someone spoke into the cat's ear, the speech was intelligible, and the researchers could even identify who the speaker was. They concluded the auditory nerve was "following," or firing at the same rate as, the auditory stimulus frequencies. It appeared that the telephone theory was correct, but with the benefit of our more modern understanding of neural functioning, you and I know that single neurons cannot possibly fire at such high rates. (See the discussion of refractory periods in Chapter 2 if you don't remember.)

Obviously, Wever and Bray were not recording from a single neuron, but from all the neurons in contact with the hook-shaped copper electrode they placed in contact with the auditory nerve. Thus, they were monitoring the *combined* activity of hundreds, perhaps thousands of neurons. Wever explained their finding later in his *volley theory,* which states that groups of neurons follow the frequency of a sound at higher frequencies when a single neuron cannot (Wever, 1949). A group of neurons can follow high frequencies because different neurons "take turns" firing. The term *volleying* is analogous to playing volleyball, where players take turns when striking the ball to keep it aloft. Volleying is illustrated in Figure 9.8, where each of the neurons synchronizes its firing to the wave peaks of the tone; no single neuron can fire on every peak, but at least one neuron will be firing on each wave peak. In this theory, the brain then combines information from many neurons to determine the tone's frequency. In Wever and Bray's study, volleying in the auditory nerve was unable to keep up with the sound frequency beyond 5200 Hz, a figure that subsequent research has shown to be accurate (J. E. Rose, Brugge, Anderson, & Hind, 1967). So even with volleying, frequency following can account for only one-fourth of the range of frequencies we hear.

■ **FIGURE 9.8**   Illustration of Volleying in Neurons.

No single neuron can respond to each peak of a high-frequency sound, but a group of neurons can. The representative neurons 1–5 would be in the cochlea, whereas the summation neuron might be in the auditory midbrain.

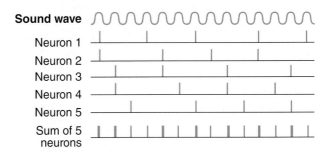

Place Theory

In the 19th century, Hermann von Helmholtz (1863/1948) proposed that the basilar membrane was like a series of piano strings, stretched progressively more loosely with distance down the membrane. Then he invoked a principle from physics called *resonance* to explain how we discriminate different frequencies. Resonance is the vibration of an object in sympathy with another vibrating object. If you pluck the strings of a violin, you will notice that the strings begin to vibrate. The thinner, more tautly stretched E string vibrates faster and has a higher pitch and frequency than the thicker, less tautly stretched G string. According to Helmholtz, resonance would cause the narrow base end of the membrane to resonate more to high-frequency sounds, the middle portion to moderate frequencies, and the wider apex (tip) to low frequencies. Helmholtz's proposal was a type of *place theory,* which states that encoding sound frequency depends on the location of maximal vibration on the basilar membrane; the more a particular section of membrane vibrates, the higher the levels of firing in the hair cells found there. Place theory in its evolving versions has been the most influential explanation of frequency analysis for a century and a half. It is an example of a scientific idea that has become almost universally accepted but continues to be referred to as a theory.

A century later, Georg von Békésy (a communications engineer from Budapest) began a series of innovative experiments that won him the Nobel Prize for physiology in 1961. Békésy constructed mechanical models of the cochlea and observed the responses of the basilar membrane in cochleas he removed from deceased subjects as diverse as elephants and humans. When he stimulated these cochleas with a vibrating piston, he could see under the microscope that vibrations peaked at different locations along the basilar membrane; a wavelike peak hovered near the base when the frequency was high and moved toward the apex when Békésy (1951) decreased the frequency. But Helmholtz was wrong about the basilar membrane being like a series of piano strings; Békésy (1956) determined that its frequency selectivity is due to differences in elasticity, with the membrane near the stirrup 100 times stiffer than at the apical end.

Figure 9.9a shows how frequency sensitivity is distributed along the membrane's length (see Figure 9.5 again for the location of the basilar membrane). Recordings from single auditory neurons have confirmed that place information about frequency is preserved in all lower levels of auditory processing, from the cochlea to the auditory cortex. In other words, these structures contain a *tonotopic map*, which means that each successive area responds to successively higher frequencies (Figure 9.9a and b).

You can see from the *tuning curves* in Figure 9.9c that each neuron responds most to a narrow range of frequencies (Palmer, 1987), due to the neuron's place of origin in the cochlea. However, each neuron also responds to a lesser extent to a range of frequencies around its "primary" frequency, mirroring the pattern of vibration in the basilar membrane. So how can neurons that make such imperfect discriminations inform the brain about the frequency of a sound with the 2- to 3-Hz sensitivity that has been observed? The answer is lateral inhibition; the more highly stimulated neurons inhibit activity in adjacent neurons with slightly different primary frequencies (G. Wu, Arbuckle, Liu, Tao, & Zhang, 2008). As a result, some neurons in the auditory cortex are many times more discriminating than neurons in the auditory nerve (E. L. Bartlett, Sadagopan, & Wang, 2011; Bitterman, Mukamel, Malach, Fried, & Nelken, 2008). This neural sharpening of information is a characteristic of most sensory systems, as we will see when we discuss sound localization and in Chapter 10 when we talk about vision.

■ FIGURE 9.9   Frequency Sensitivity of the Basilar Membrane and Auditory Cortex.

In (a), notice that the basilar membrane is narrower at the base end of the cochlea and widens toward the apex, the opposite of the cochlea's shape. Its frequency selectivity is preserved in the tonotopic map seen in the auditory cortex. In (b), the part of the auditory cortex at the left end of this view receives neurons from the apex of the cochlea, and the other end responds to signals from the base. The auditory cortex thus forms a "map" of the basilar membrane so that each successive area responds to progressively higher frequencies. In (c), we show the frequency sensitivities of three representative neurons in the auditory cortex. The lowest point of each curve indicates that neuron's primary frequency and the lowest amplitude of sound that will activate the neuron. Other frequencies within the curve will also activate that neuron, but activation decreases with distance from the primary frequency.

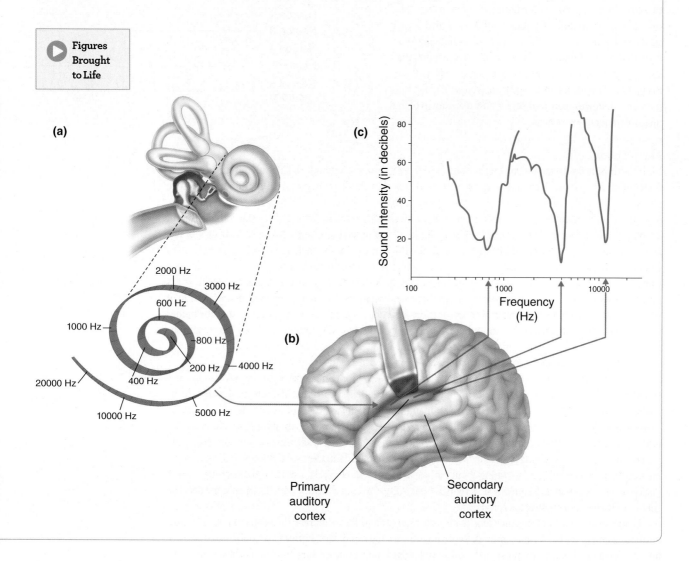

Place analysis is the reason we can hear with some clarity through bone conduction. The vibrations enter the cochlea from all sides during bone conduction, rather than through the oval window, but Békésy (1951) demonstrated with his cochleas that the tonotopic response of the basilar membrane is independent of sound source. As he moved his vibrating piston from the base around to the side of the cochlea, or to the apex or anywhere else, the peak of vibration remained in the same location. Thomas Edison was nearly deaf, yet his second most famous invention was the phonograph. He compensated for his impaired hearing by grasping the edge of the phonograph's wooden case between his teeth and listening to the recording through bone conduction. You can still see the bite marks on one of his phonographs in the museum at his winter home and laboratory in Fort Myers, Florida. Figure 9.10 shows a device that takes advantage of bone conduction.

Combining Theories

At low frequencies, the whole basilar membrane vibrates about equally, and researchers have been unable to find neurons that are specific for frequencies below 200 Hz (Kiang, 1965). Wever (1949) suggested a *frequency-volley-place theory:* Individual neurons follow the frequency of sounds up to about 500 Hz by firing at the same rate as the sound's frequency; then between 500 and 5000 Hz, the frequency is tracked by volleying, and place analysis takes over beyond that point. While volleying does occur in the auditory nerve, studies do not show that the brain uses that information in frequency analysis. Therefore, most researchers subscribe to a simpler *frequency-place theory:* Frequency following by individual neurons accounts for frequencies up to about 200 Hz, and all remaining frequencies are represented by the place of greatest activity.

Fortunately, we can sum up the auditory system's handling of intensity coding much more simply. As we

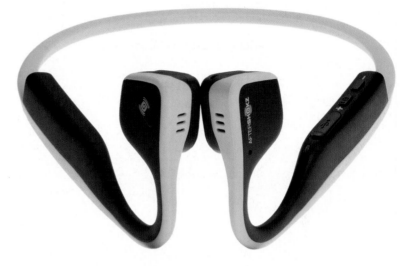

■ **FIGURE 9.10** A Bluetooth Headset That Works by Bone Conduction.

Like other Bluetooth headsets, the Trekz Titanium headset can connect to all your auditory devices. However, rather than using speakers, this device transmits sound directly to the cochlea through the skull, which means your ears are unobstructed.

Source: Hugh Threlfall/Alamy Stock Photo.

learned in Chapter 2, a more intense stimulus causes a neuron to fire at a higher rate. The auditory system relies on this strategy for distinguishing among different intensities of sound. However, this is not possible at lower frequencies, where firing rate is the means of coding frequency. Researchers believe that at the lower frequencies, the brain relies on the number of neurons firing as increases in stimulus intensity recruit progressively higher-threshold neurons into activity.

Restoring Hearing

For individuals who have damage to the middle ear bones, or a mild loss of hair cells due to aging, a simple hearing aid does an excellent job in compensating for the loss of amplification. However, 90% of hearing impairment cases involve loss of hair cells, and, because hair cells don't regenerate, these individuals may be candidates for a cochlear implant, like Heather Whitestone's and the ones worn by the two children in the opening photograph. An implant uses a microphone to pick up sounds and send them to a speech processor located behind the ear; then a transmitter on the surface of the skin sends the signal to a receiver that is surgically embedded under the skin. From there, the signal travels through a wire to an electrode array threaded through the cochlea; these electrodes deliver signals representing the different frequencies of a sound to different membrane locations. Activating different neurons with different frequencies mimics the functioning of the basilar membrane and hair cells in an unimpaired individual; in other words, it relies on the principle of place analysis.

Most cochlear implant recipients hear effectively enough to use a telephone, which is more difficult than face-to-face conversation; most children can be mainstreamed in school, and they rate their quality of life comparably with their peers (Loy, Warner-Czyz, Tong, Tobey, & Roland, 2010). Early implantation works best, because adjustment to an enriched auditory world can be surprisingly difficult and because neurons from other sensory areas can take over the unused auditory cortex over time (D. S. Lee et al., 2001). In adults, success also depends on having learned language before deafness occurred. Children, by contrast, can use the implants regardless of whether they learned language previously (Francis, Koch, Wyatt, & Niparko, 1999).

Conventional implants have a number of disadvantages: They cannot be worn in the shower or while swimming, they are bulky and cumbersome, and the wearer is likely to experience some amount of social

RESEARCH SPOTLIGHT
Beyond Cochlear Implants

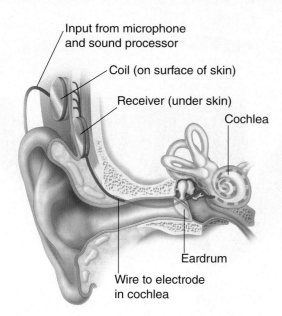

Input from microphone and sound processor

Coil (on surface of skin)

Receiver (under skin)

Cochlea

Eardrum

Wire to electrode in cochlea

A major problem people have with cochlear implants is difficulty following conversations in a crowded or noisy environment. A recent study with marmosets suggests that although implants restore basic functionality to the cochlea, they don't provide the signal complexity the auditory cortex requires (Johnson et al., 2016). Imagine, for example, what your photos would look like if your smartphone was limited to displaying them in a few hundred pixels instead of the usual few million. You would see the outlines of objects and some of the features, but most of the detail would be gone.

Because hearing is less than optimal with current cochlear implants, researchers continue to improve them. One potential improvement involves adding neurotrophins (see Chapter 3) to the cochlear implant itself to help regenerate and repair weak neurons (Pinyon et al., 2014). In the future, gene replacement may be an additional option. In genetically deaf mice, replacement of the *VGLUT3* gene improved glutamate transmission between the intact hair cells and auditory neurons (Akil et al., 2012) and inserting genes to replace damaged hair cells improved hearing to the point of ability to hear a loud conversation (György et al., 2017). Gene therapy carries some risks that could prevent its use in humans, but a drug has produced similar results, both increasing the number of supporting cells and coaxing them to develop into hair cells (McLean et al., 2017). Another possibility is the use of stem cells, which can be induced to develop into hair cells or auditory neurons; inserting the latter into chemically nerve-deafened guinea pigs partially restored their hearing (Chen et al., 2012). The first FDA-approved stem cell study to treat hearing loss is under way in a Phase 1 safety trial with infants, using stem cells from their own previously banked umbilical cord blood (Arcila, 2016).

stigma. Researchers at Harvard University and the Massachusetts Institute of Technology are developing a fully implantable device (Yip et al., 2015). A tiny sensor mounted on the malleus detects the movement of the ossicles and a processor-on-a-chip turns the vibrations into signals that are delivered to the cochlear nerve. The device consumes very little power, and it is anticipated that it would be charged overnight by sleeping on a special pillow. But there are additional problems with the quality of reproduction; the accompanying Research Spotlight describes some of the ongoing efforts to improve cochlear implants and eventually make them obsolete.

Analyzing Complex Sounds

 How does the auditory system handle complex sounds?

You may have realized that we rarely hear a pure tone. The speech, music, and noises that are so meaningful in our everyday lives are complex, made up of many frequencies. Yet we have an auditory mechanism that appears to be specialized for responding to individual frequencies. But a solution to this enigma was suggested even before Helmholtz proposed his place theory. The French mathematician Joseph Fourier had demonstrated 40 years earlier that any complex waveform—sound, electrical, or whatever—is in effect composed of two or more component sine waves. *Fourier analysis* is the analysis of a complex waveform into its sine wave components (Figure 9.11). A few years later, Georg Ohm, better known for Ohm's law of electricity, proposed that the ear performs a Fourier analysis of a complex sound and sends information about each of the component frequencies to the cortex. Current researchers agree that the basilar membrane acts as the auditory Fourier analyzer, responding simultaneously along its length to the sound's component frequencies.

Not only do we rarely hear a pure sound, but we also seldom hear a single complex sound by itself. At a party, we hear the music playing loudly, mixed in with several conversations going on all around us, as well as general sounds of people moving about, dancing, eating, and drinking. Despite the number of complex sounds assaulting our cochleas, we can separate our conversations with other partygoers from the other noises in the room. And we do more than that; we periodically sample the other sounds regularly enough to enjoy the music and to hear snippets of conversation across the room. The ability to sort out and focus on meaningful auditory messages from a complex background of sounds is referred to as the *cocktail party effect*.

The cocktail party effect is an example of selective attention; the brain must select the important part of the auditory environment for emphasis and suppress irrelevant background information. In the auditory system, this first happens in the superior olivary nucleus. When we look at attention more closely in Chapter 15, we will see that selective attention enhances activity in one part of the sensory cortex and reduces it in others.

To find out what happens in the brain during the cocktail party effect, researchers turned to patients who had EEG electrodes placed directly on the cortex to determine where their seizure-causing lesions were located. When these subjects attended to one of two speech sources, that speech was tracked closely in the auditory cortex, while the competing speech was somewhat suppressed; in higher-order areas, including those concerned with language, the unattended speech dropped out completely (Horton, D'Zmura, & Srinivasan, 2013; Zion Golumbic et al., 2013). Although outer hair cells have very few ascending connections to the brain, they receive many descending fibers; stimulating those fibers in bats increases hair cell activity in specific areas of the basilar membrane, which enhances frequency sensitivity in those areas (Z. Xiao & Suga, 2002). By measuring evoked otoacoustic emissions in humans, French researchers confirmed that attention to a tone causes frequency-specific changes in outer hair cell activity (Maison, Micheyl, & Collet, 2001).

Beyond distinguishing one sound from another, it is important to be able to *identify* a sound. Here it is useful to think in terms of an *auditory object*—a sound we identify as distinct from other sounds. Identifying an auditory object involves distinguishing characteristics such as pitch, rhythm, and tempo and depends on our ability to separate sounds by their directional location. Understand that identifying an auditory object does not imply that we recognize what the sound is; memory helps provide that function, enabling us to recognize an oncoming train or the voice of a friend. Dolphins can even recognize the signature whistle of former tank mates from as far back as 20 years, the typical dolphin lifespan in the wild (Bruck, 2013). Recognizing environmental sounds primarily requires posterior temporal areas and, to a lesser extent, the frontal cortex (J. W. Lewis et al., 2004), while recognizing individuals' voices involves the secondary auditory cortex in the superior temporal area (Kriegstein & Giraud, 2004; Petkov et al., 2008). More generally, these sound objects activate the "what" pathway (see Figures 9.12 and 9.7). In a few pages, you will see that these areas are also important in producing and understanding language.

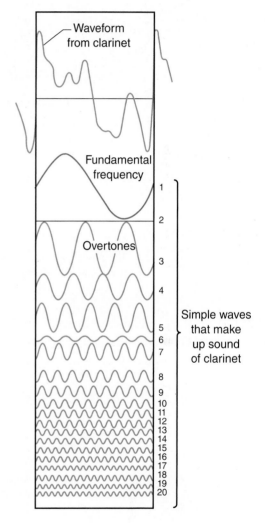

■ **FIGURE 9.11** Fourier Analysis of a Clarinet Note.

The dominant component is a relatively high-amplitude, low-frequency sine wave; the other components are progressively higher frequencies at lower intensities. If we produced sounds at each of these frequencies and amplitudes at the same time, the combined waveform when displayed on an oscilloscope would look like the waveform at the top, and the result would sound like the clarinet note.

Source: From "How Much Distraction Can You Hear?" by P. Milner, *Stereo Review*, June 1977, pp. 64–68. © 1977.

■ **FIGURE 9.12**   Areas Involved in Identifying Environmental Sounds.

Recognized sounds activated the areas in yellow; unrecognized sounds activated other areas (blue), mostly in the right hemisphere. Notice that the activity occurs mostly in the ventral and frontal "what" pathway.

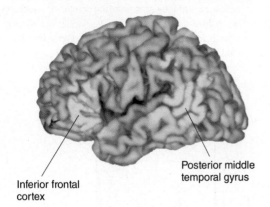

Inferior frontal cortex

Posterior middle temporal gyrus

Source: From "Human Brain Regions Involved in Recognizing Environmental Sounds," by J. W. Lewis et al., 2004, *Cerebral Cortex, 14*, pp. 1008–1021, by permission of Oxford University Press.

■ **FIGURE 9.13**   Sound Localizing Device Used by 19th-Century Sailors.

By listening through devices on a long rod (called a topophone), sailors effectively increased the distance between their ears and enhanced the binaural cues.

PROFESSOR MAYER'S TOPOPHONE.

Source: From "Navigation in Fog," *Scientific American*, July 3, 1880, p. 3.

? How does the brain determine the locations of sounds?

Locating Sounds

The most obvious way to locate a sound is to turn your head until the sound is loudest. This is not very effective, because the sound may be gone before the direction is located. Three additional cues permit us to locate sounds quickly and accurately, including those that are too brief to allow turning the head. All three of these cues are *binaural,* meaning that they involve the use of two ears; the brain determines the location based on acoustic differences between the two ears. These cues are useless when a sound source is in the median plane (equidistant from the person's ears), but if the sound is shifted to one side, the stimulus will differ between the ears. Animals with ears that are very close together (such as mice) are at a disadvantage in locating sounds because the differences are so small. Grasshoppers and crickets have evolved a compensation for their small head size: Their auditory organs are on their legs, as far apart as possible. Nineteenth-century sailors used a novel application of this strategy when they needed to locate a distant sound source: They listened through tubes attached to funnels at the ends of a long rod called a topophone (Figure 9.13). The following paragraphs describe the three binaural differences: *intensity, timing,* and *phase.*

Binaural Cues

When a sound source is on one side, the head blocks some of the sound energy. The sound shadow this creates produces an *interaural intensity (or level) difference (IID or ILD),* so that the near ear receives a more intense sound the more it is to that side (Figure 9.14). Some of the neurons of the lateral superior olivary nucleus (LSO, located in the brain stem) respond to differences in IID at the two ears using a simple subtraction mechanism (far ear being excitatory, near ear

■ **FIGURE 9.14**   Differential Intensity and Timing as Cues for Sound Localization.

The sound is reduced in intensity and arrives later at the distant ear.

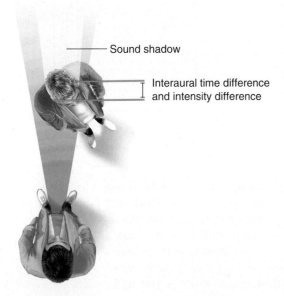

Sound shadow

Interaural time difference and intensity difference

Source: From "Navigation in Fog," *Scientific American*, July 3, 1880, p. 3.

being inhibitory). Because low-frequency sounds tend to pass through solid objects (like the head), this cue works best when the sound is above 2000 Hz.

The second binaural cue for locating sounds is *interaural timing difference (ITD)* at the two ears. A sound that is directly to a person's left or right takes about 0.5 milliseconds to travel the additional distance to the second ear (see Figure 9.14 again); humans can detect an ITD difference as small as 10 microseconds (millionths of a second; Hudspeth, 2000), which means we can locate sound sources that move by as little as a degree horizontally. This computation is done in the medial superior olivary nucleus (MSO, Masterton, Jane, & Diamond, 1966). Although components of our auditory system can respond to smaller angles of separation, we cannot distinguish such small intervals consciously; this kind of precision involves automatic processing by specialized circuits, as we will see shortly.

At low frequencies, a sound arriving from one side of the body will be at a different phase of the wave at each ear, referred to as an *interaural phase difference (IPD)* (Figure 9.15). As a result, at a given moment one eardrum will be pushed in more or less than the other or, at very low frequencies, one will be pushed in while the other is being pulled out. Some of the neurons in the superior olivary nucleus respond only when the inputs from the two ears have different IPD values. Above about 1500 Hz, a sound will have begun a new wave by the time it reaches the second ear, introducing something called phase ambiguity, which makes localizing sounds more difficult. This, like timing differences, is also computed in the MSO.

■ **FIGURE 9.15** Phase Difference as a Cue for Sound Localization.

(a) At lower frequencies, the sound reaches each ear at a different phase of the same pressure wave; the different stimulation of the two ears can be used to locate the sound's direction. (b) At higher frequencies, the sound has begun a new wave by the time it reaches the second ear; the phase difference is useless for locating the sound.

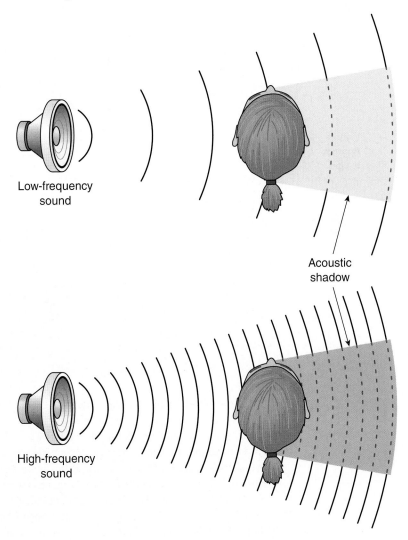

Low-frequency sound

Acoustic shadow

High-frequency sound

A Brain Circuit for Detecting Time Differences

Of the neural circuits for binaural sound localization, the one for ITD has been studied the most thoroughly. The circuit has been mapped in the barn owl, which is extremely good at sound localization; in fact, it can locate a mouse in darkness just from the sounds it makes rustling through the grass. The circuit is in the *nucleus laminaris*, the avian (bird) counterpart of the mammalian LSO. Electrical recording has revealed the function of its *coincidence detectors*, neurons that fire most when they receive input from both ears at the same time (C. E. Carr & Konishi, 1990). Figure 9.16 is a simplified diagram of the Jeffress model of sound localization (Jeffress, 1948), with delay lines and coincidence detectors, confirmed through neuronal mapping in the barn owl. When the sound comes directly from the left side of the figure (Speaker A), Detector A will receive stimulation simultaneously from the two ears and the simultaneous inputs will cause the neuron to fire at a high rate. The stimulation is simultaneous because the connection between the near ear and the coincidence detector acts as a delay line, compensating for the delay in the sound reaching the distant ear. Likewise, Detector B will fire at its highest rate when the sound comes from Speaker B. When the sound source is equidistant from the two ears, Detector C is most active, and so on. Note that these relationships hold whether

■ **FIGURE 9.16**   A Circuit for Detecting Interaural Timing Differences.

The circuit's arrangement compensates for the greater travel time to the more distant ear. Try tracing the flow of activity through this diagrammatic representation of the circuit to determine which detector will fire most when sound comes from each of the speakers. (The speakers are at the same horizontal level as the ears.)

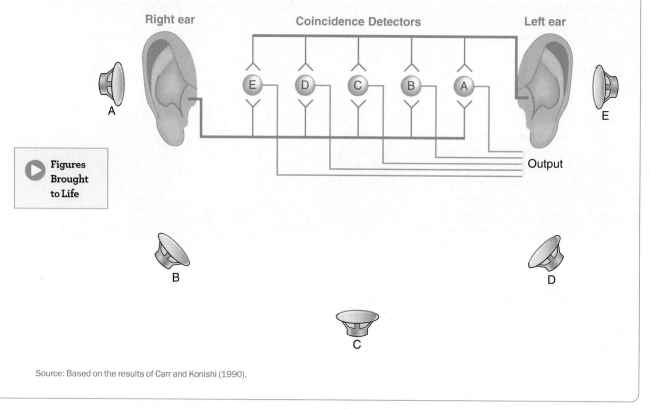

Figures Brought to Life

Source: Based on the results of Carr and Konishi (1990).

the sound comes from in front of the observer, behind, above, or below. This circuit is another example of the neural enhancement of small sensory differences that we referred to earlier.

These circuits can determine the direction of a sound, but that is not very useful by itself; it must be integrated with information from the visual environment and information about the position of the body in space. In Chapter 3, you learned that combining all this information is the function of association areas in the parietal lobes. So, unlike identifying sounds, locating sounds in space occurs in the dorsal "where" stream.

The ultimate in sound localization is *echolocation*, a sort of sonar that bats, dolphins, whales, and even some cave-dwelling birds use to avoid obstacles and to detect prey and predators. Bats are so proficient that they can use the echoes of their ultrasonic chirps to catch insects while avoiding obstacles in total darkness (see Ulanovsky & Moss, 2008, for more information about these amazing mammals). We are currently using knowledge gained from echolocating mammals not only to demonstrate people who can echolocate but also to design new devices that use sound to help people see, which is the subject of the accompanying Application.

If this were the end of our discussion of audition, it would also be the end of the chapter and, obviously, it is not. In humans, the most elaborate processing of auditory information occurs in language, which is our next topic.

CONCEPT CHECK

Take a Minute to Check Your Knowledge and Understanding

- Trace an auditory stimulus from the pinna to the auditory neurons in the cortex.
- Explain how, according to place theory, the frequency of sound is coded. How does the cochlea handle complex sounds?
- Explain how the circuit for detecting interaural timing difference works.

APPLICATION
I Hear a Tree Over There

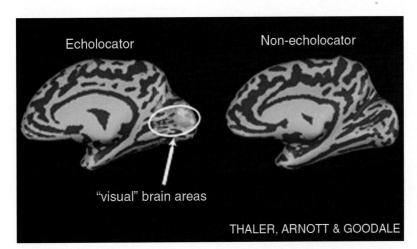

Source: From "Neural Correlates of Natural Human Echolocation in Early and Late Blind Echolocation Experts," by Thaler, L., Arnott, S. R., and Goodale, M. A., 2011, *PLoS ONE* 6(5), e20162, doi: 10.1371/journal. pone.0020162.

Some blind individuals have a remarkable ability to avoid obstacles in their paths, often without any awareness of how they do so. In 1749, the French philosopher Denis Diderot (1916) studied one of these adept individuals and concluded that he relied on air currents deflected by the obstacles. By the time Karl Dallenbach and his colleagues tackled the question at Cornell University, 14 theories had been proposed (Supa, Cotzin, & Dallenbach, 1944) to explain how blind subjects could detect a wall from 4–17 feet away. They concluded that the subjects accomplished this by listening to the sounds of their footsteps reflected by the obstacle as they approached. Their performance was still surprisingly good when they listened from another room through headphones as an experimenter carrying a microphone walked toward the wall.

Blind individuals may use echolocation passively—simply listening for reflected sounds in their environment—or actively, by scuffing their feet or tapping a cane on the pavement, but these efforts can be thwarted by thick carpeting or a blanket of snow. Researchers have demonstrated that humans echolocate better when they actively vocalize instead of passively listen (Flanagin et al., 2017), and Daniel Kish is a living example of this principle. Daniel lost his eyes to cancer at the age of one, but he grew up surprisingly normally, even riding a bicycle to school (Kish, 2013). It wasn't until he was 11 that a friend pointed out to him that he was using echolocation, clicking his tongue two to three times a second and listening for the echoes. As an adult, he bikes in busy traffic, travels by plane without assistance, and hikes in the woods, where he can recognize trees by the difference in the way the leaves and the trunks reflect the sounds. An fMRI study showed that blind individuals engage part of the visual cortex during echolocation, an area that is well suited for processing spatial information (see figure; Thaler, Arnott, & Goodale, 2011).

A team at University of California, Berkeley, took inspiration from bat echolocation to create a device that emits ultrasonic sweeps, whose echoes provide higher spatial resolution than sounds in our normal range of hearing; the device then converts the echoes to sound frequencies we can hear. Even untrained individuals could use the echoes to locate objects and determine their distance (Sohl-Dickstein et al., 2015).

Language

Now that we have gone over the basics of the auditory system, let's apply this knowledge to a behavior we all need to learn: language. Few would question the importance of language in human behavior. Keep in mind the meaning of the term *language*: It is not limited to speech but includes the generation and understanding of written, spoken, and gestural communication. Communication through language has important survival value and is inestimably important to human social relationships. A person who cannot communicate his or her thoughts to others suffers a high degree of isolation; one who cannot comprehend the communications of

> *"For humans, the most important aspect of hearing is its role in processing language.*
>
> —A. J. Hudspeth

■ **FIGURE 9.17**   Language-Related Areas of the Cortex.

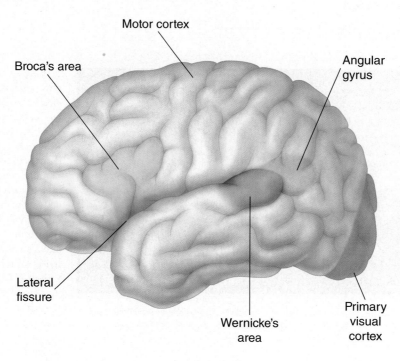

others is worse off still. These capabilities not only require learning; they also depend on specific structures of the brain, and damage to these structures can deprive a person of some or all of these functions.

Every language is characterized by a consistent set of rules, called grammar. This grammar can be quite flexible yet still convey the ideas and meaning of the speaker, which is called semantics. For instance, the *Star Wars* character Yoda frequently speaks with altered grammar in sentences like "See you I do," but the semantic meaning is clear. The individual sounds that comprise a language are called phonemes. Phonemes are small units of speech sound that distinguish one word from another—for example, the beginning sounds that distinguish *book, took*, and *cook*. Phonemes can be combinations of consonants and vowels (and even clicks!) and vary in languages from less than 20 in Polynesian languages (like Hawaiian) to over 80 in Taa (spoken in Botswana and Namibia).

In 1861, the French physician Paul Broca reported his observations of a patient who for 21 years had been almost unable to speak. Tan, as the hospital staff knew him because that was one of the few sounds he could make, died shortly after he came under Broca's care. The autopsy revealed that Tan's brain damage was in the posterior portion of the left frontal lobe. After studying eight other patients, Broca concluded that *aphasia*—language impairment caused by damage to the brain—results from damage to the frontal area anterior to the motor cortex, now known as *Broca's area*. Nine years later, a German doctor named Carl Wernicke identified a second site where damage produced a different form of aphasia. Located in the posterior portion of the left temporal lobe, this site is known as Wernicke's area. See Figure 9.17 to locate Broca's and Wernicke's areas and the other structures to be discussed here. Most of our understanding of the brain structures involved in language comes from studies of brain-damaged individuals, so this is where we will start.

Broca's Area

Broca's aphasia is language impairment caused by damage to Broca's area and surrounding cortical and subcortical areas. The symptoms can best be understood by examining the speech of a stroke patient; as you read this interview, you will see why the disorder is also referred to as *expressive aphasia*.

? What are the differences between Broca's aphasia and Wernicke's aphasia?

Doctor: What happened to make you lose your speech?

Mr. Ford: Head, fall, Jesus Christ, me no good, str, str . . . oh Jesus . . . stroke.

Doctor: I see. Could you tell me, Mr. Ford, what you've been doing in the hospital?

Mr. Ford: Yes, sure. Me go, er, uh, P.T. nine o'cot, speech . . . two times . . . read . . . wr . . . ripe, er rike, er, write . . . practice . . . getting better. (H. Gardner, 1975, p. 61)

Mr. Ford's speech was not nearly as impaired as Tan's; he can talk, and you can get a pretty good idea of his meaning, but he showed the classic symptoms associated with damage to Broca's area. First, his speech was *non-fluent*. Although well-practiced phrases such as "yes, sure" and "oh, Jesus" come out easily, his speech was halting, with many pauses between words. Second, he had trouble finding the right words, a symptom known as *anomia* ("without name"). He had *difficulty with articulation*; he mispronounced words, like "rike" for *write*. Finally, notice that his speech was *agrammatic*; it had content words (nouns and verbs) but lacked grammatical, or function, words (articles, adjectives, adverbs, prepositions, and conjunctions). The hardest phrase for a Broca's aphasic to repeat is "No ifs, ands, or buts" (Geschwind, 1972).

Broca believed that Broca's aphasia impaired motor instructions for vocalizing words. But Mr. Ford could recite the days of the week and the letters of the alphabet, or sing "Home on the Range." So, vocalization is not lost, but the ability to translate information into speech patterns is compromised. The problem is "upstream" from speech in the brain, so reading and writing are impaired as much as speech is. Comprehension is also as impaired as speech when the meaning depends on grammatical words. For example, the patient can answer questions like "Does a stone float on water?" but not the question "If I say, 'The lion was killed by the tiger,' which animal is dead?" (H. Gardner, 1975).

Wernicke's Area

In *Wernicke's aphasia,* the person has difficulty understanding and producing spoken and written language. This is often called *receptive aphasia,* but that term is misleading because the same problems with understanding language also show up in producing it. For example, the person's speech is *fluent* but meaningless. A patient asked to describe a picture of two boys stealing cookies behind a woman's back said, "Mother is away here working her work to get her better, but when she's looking the two boys looking in the other part. She's working another time" (Geschwind, 1979). This meaningless speech is called *word salad,* for obvious reasons.

Because the speech of the Wernicke's patient is articulate and has the proper rhythm, it sounds normal to the casual listener. The first time one of us met a person with Wernicke's aphasia, he was knocking on the social worker's door at the nursing home, and he thought it was because his thoughts were elsewhere that he failed to understand one of the residents when she spoke. But then his "Pardon me" elicited "She's in the frimfram," and he realized the problem was hers rather than his. He responded with a pleasantry, and she gave a classic word-salad reply. That began a long relationship of conversations, but the difference was that neither of us ever understood the other; another difference was that it did not matter, because she seemed strangely unaware that anything was amiss.

The Wernicke-Geschwind Model

Of course, language requires more than just these two areas. Wernicke suggested, and Norman Geschwind later elaborated on, a model for how Broca's area and Wernicke's area interact to produce language (Geschwind, 1970, 1972, 1979). The model is illustrated in Figure 9.18 and in the following examples. Answering a verbal question involves a progression of activity from the auditory cortex to Wernicke's area, and then to Broca's area. Broca's area then formulates articulation of the verbal response and sends the result to the facial area of the motor cortex, which produces the speech. If the response is to be written, Wernicke's area sends output to the angular gyrus instead, where it elicits a visual pattern. When a person reads aloud, the visual information is translated into an auditory form by the angular gyrus and then passed to Wernicke's area, where a response is generated and sent to Broca's area for directing the muscles of the throat, mouth, and lungs. The idea that visual information must be converted to an auditory form for processing arose in part from the fact that language evolved long before writing was invented, and Wernicke's area was believed to operate in an auditory fashion.

 What is the Wernicke-Geschwind model?

This system has long been the primary model for how language operates. It is relatively simple and seems to explain the various aphasias. Modern imaging techniques have confirmed the participation of Broca's and Wernicke's areas in language. One study has traced the progression of activity while subjects produced a verbal response to written material, from the visual cortex to Wernicke's area and then to Broca's area (Dhond, Buckner, Dale, Marinkovic, & Halgren, 2001). However, there are problems. One is that language functions are not limited to Broca's and Wernicke's areas; damage to the basal ganglia, thalamus, and subcortical white matter also produce aphasias (Hécaen & Angelergues, 1964; Mazzocchi & Vignolo, 1979; Naeser et al., 1982). Broad cortical areas also play an important role, though possibly only because they are storage sites for information. For example, noun use (naming objects) produces activity just below the auditory cortex and Wernicke's area in the inferior/anterior temporal lobe (H. Damasio, Grabowski, Tranel, Hichwa, & Damasio, 1996). Verb use (describing what is happening in a picture) is impaired by damage to the left premotor cortex, which sends output to the motor cortex. This area is also activated while naming tools and by imagining body movements (Hauk, Johnsrude, & Pulvermüller, 2004). Apparently when tool names are learned, they are stored near the brain structure that would produce the action. And there is evidence that object categories are stored in different areas as well (Caramazza & Mahon, 2006).

■ **FIGURE 9.18**   The Wernicke-Geschwind Model of Language.

Verbal input arrives in the auditory cortex and then travels to Wernicke's area for interpretation. Written input arrives there via the visual cortex and angular gyrus. If a verbal response is required, Wernicke's area sends output to Broca's area for articulation of the response, and the facial area of the motor cortex produces the speech.

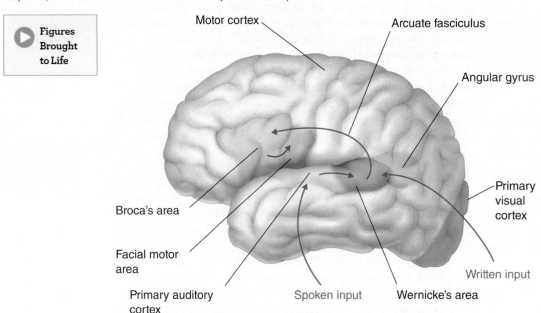

Source: Adapted from "Specializations of the Human Brain," by N. Geschwind, *Scientific American*, 241(9), pp. 180–199.

Electrical stimulation studies (Mateer & Cameron, 1989; Ojemann, 1983) and studies of brain damage (Hécaen & Angelergues, 1964) have also shown that the various components of language functioning are scattered throughout all four lobes (Figure 9.19). This does not mean that there is no specialization of the cortical areas; for example, articulation errors are still more likely to result from frontal damage and comprehension problems from damage in the temporal lobes (Hécaen & Angelergues; Mazzocchi & Vignolo, 1979). However, it does mean that each function depends on a network of interconnected structures rather than a single structure. We do know that, like vision, there are processing streams in the cortex devoted to language. The dorsal stream passes through frontal sensorimotor areas that deal with planning speech, rhyming, and working memory, whereas the ventral stream that passes through the left temporal gyrus helps us comprehend language (Hickok & Poeppel, 2007).

Other challenges to classic theory include studies that question, for example, how the language structures are interconnected (Dick & Tremblay, 2012), indicating that spoken words are processed anterior to the auditory cortex rather than in Wernicke's area (DeWitt & Rauschecker, 2012). The Wernicke-Geschwind view therefore has turned out to be too simple, but it has also helped researchers organize their thinking about language and has generated volumes of research—which, after all, is how we make scientific sense of our world.

Reading, Writing, and Their Impairments

Although aphasia affects reading and writing, these functions can be impaired independently of other language abilities when the visual inputs to the language network are interrupted. In language disorders, a complete absence of behavior has the prefix "a-," while impairment of behavior has the prefix "dys-." *Alexia* is the inability to read, and *agraphia* is the inability to write. Presumably, they are due to disruption of pathways in the *angular gyrus* that connect the visual projection area with the auditory and visual association areas in the temporal and parietal lobes (see Figure 9.17 again). The PET scans in Figure 9.20 show that activity increases in this area during reading.

Reading and writing are also impaired in learning disorders. The most common learning disorders are *dyslexia,* an impairment of reading; dysgraphia, difficulty in writing; and *dyscalculia,* a disability with

■ **FIGURE 9.19**   Frequency of Language Deficits Resulting From Damage in Each Area.

Language functions are more widely distributed than originally thought.

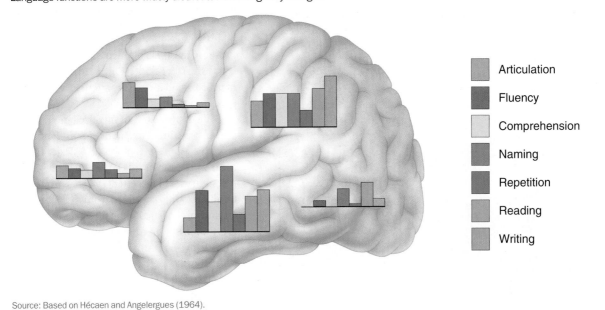

Articulation
Fluency
Comprehension
Naming
Repetition
Reading
Writing

Source: Based on Hécaen and Angelergues (1964).

■ **FIGURE 9.20**   PET Scans During Reading.

Viewing letterlike forms (a) and strings of consonants (b) did not activate the area between the primary visual cortex and language areas, but reading pronounceable nonwords (c) and real words (d) did.

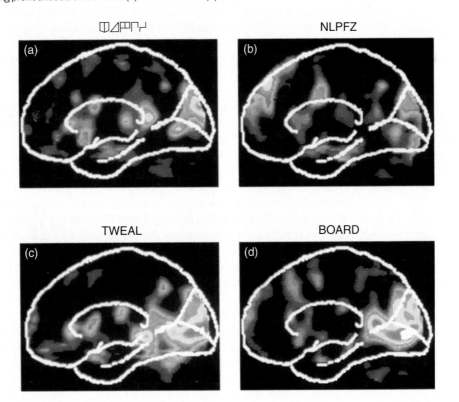

Source: From "Activation of Extrastriate and Frontal Cortical Areas by Visual Words and Word-Like Stimuli," S. E. Petersen, P. T. Fox, A. Z. Snyderand, and M. E. Raichle, *Science, 249*, pp. 1049–1044. Reprinted with permission from AAAS.

■ **FIGURE 9.21**   Left- Versus Right-Hemisphere Language Processing in Nonimpaired and Dyslexic Readers.

Dyslexic readers have much less left hemisphere processing of language, compared to normal readers. Node C (green), an executive decision area in the frontal lobe, has strong connectivity with the language centers on the left side of the brain (red) in non-impaired readers. Dyslexic readers, in contrast, have stronger connections to bilateral posterior areas (blue).

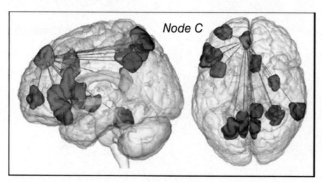

Node C

Source: Figure 3C from "Disruption of Functional Networks in Dyslexia: A Whole-Brain, Data-Driven Analysis of Connectivity," by E. S. Finn, X. Shen, et al., 2014, *Biological Psychiatry*, 76, pp. 397–404. With permission from Society of Biological Psychiatry.

arithmetic. Because of its importance and the amount of research that has been done, we will focus on dyslexia. Dyslexia can be *acquired,* through damage, but its origin is more often *developmental.* Developmental dyslexia is partially genetic, with an estimated heritability between 40% and 60% (Gayán & Olson, 2001). Of the seven most reliably identified genes involved in dyslexia (Scerri & Schulte-Körne, 2010), four are involved in neuron guidance and migration, and two contribute to cell functioning.

The implications of impaired brain development are far-reaching. The public is most familiar with the *visual-perceptual* symptoms of dyslexia: The individual reads words backwards ("now" becomes "won"), confuses mirror-image letters (*p* and *q*, *b* and *d*), and has trouble fixating on printed words, which seem to move around on the page. Some researchers have attributed this to slowness in responding to low-contrast, rapidly changing visual stimuli (Livingstone, Rosen, Drislane, & Galaburda, 1991); presumably, words jump around and reverse themselves because the reader has difficulty detecting and correcting for rapid, unintentional eye movements (called saccades), which affects both reading performance and learning to read in the first place (Bucci, Bremond-Gignac, & Kapoula, 2008).

What problems have been found in the brains of people with dyslexia?

However, individuals with dyslexia also have trouble tracking the frequency and amplitude changes that distinguish speech sounds from each other (J. Stein, 2001); supposedly this impairs the dyslexic's ability to associate speech sounds with letters when learning to read and explains his or her slowness in reading nonwords. According to the *phonological hypothesis,* individuals with dyslexia have impairment in processing, storing, and/or retrieving phonemes. When a group of dyslexic college students was administered a battery of tests, 10 had auditory deficits and 2 had a visual function deficit, but all 16 suffered from a phonological deficit (Ramus et al., 2003). Almost all researchers in the field now agree that phonological impairment is the crucial problem, and even suggest that at least some of the visual processing problems are a consequence, rather than a cause, of reading impairment (Habib, 2003; Olulade, Napollello, & Eden, 2013).

These difficulties are accompanied by several functional and structural irregularities in the brain. Kindergartners who had a delayed EEG response when a string of repeated auditory or speech sounds was interrupted by a novel sound were more likely to have reading difficulties in the fifth grade (Maurer et al., 2009). In addition, kindergartners who scored poorly on a phonological awareness test used to measure risk for dyslexia had a smaller left arcuate fasciculus, which connects Wernicke's area with Broca's area (Saygin et al., 2013). The *planum temporale,* where Wernicke's area is located, averages about 13% larger in the left hemisphere than the right in nondyslexics but is equally sized in people with dyslexia (J.S. Bloom, Garcia-Barrera, Miller, Miller, & Hynd, 2013). In at least some dyslexic brains, many of the neurons in the left planum temporale lack the usual orderly arrangement, and some of them have migrated past their normal destination and into the outermost layer of the cortex (Galaburda, 1993). One study found that young individuals with dyslexia must "sound out" the words in their minds, rather than visually recognizing the words in a much faster fashion, due to reduced connections in the left word form areas (Figure 9.21; Finn et al., 2014). These brain anomalies suggest that at least some of the origins of developmental dyslexia are prenatal.

The incidence of dyslexia is twice as great in some cultures as in others; this seems to suggest a cultural explanation for the disorder, but in fact the discrepancies support a brain-based phonological hypothesis. Italian and Spanish are phonologically simpler languages, with an almost one-to-one correspondence between phonemes and spelling. Predictably, dyslexia is much rarer in Italy and Spain than in French- and English-speaking countries, where the same spelling may have several pronunciations (*cough, tough, dough, slough*). PET imaging shows that Italians suffering from dyslexia have the same brain impairments seen in French and English speakers (Figure 9.22; Paulesu et al., 2001).

■ **FIGURE 9.22**   Activation of Language Areas in Individuals With Dyslexia From Three Countries.

Here (a) shows activation due to reading in control subjects; (b) shows activation due to reading in dyslexics; (c) indicates the area significantly less activated in dyslexics than in control subjects; and (d) shows that dyslexia is associated with the same deficiency in individuals from France, Italy, and the United Kingdom.

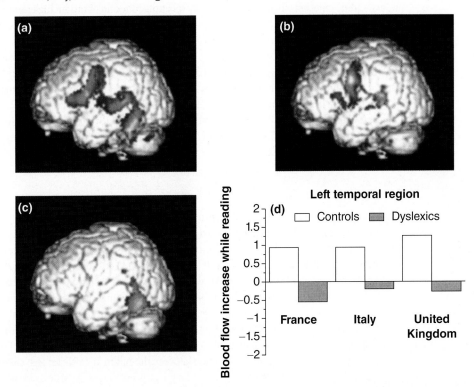

Source: From "Dyslexia: Cultural Diversity and Biological Unity," by E. Paulesu, J.-F. Démonet, F. Fazio, E. McCrory, V. Chanoine, N. Brunswick, S. F. Cappa, G. Cossu, M. Habib, C. D. Frith, and U. Frith, *Science, 291*, pp. 2165–2167. Reprinted with permission from AAAS.

Recovery From Aphasia and Lateralization of Language

There is usually some recovery from acquired aphasia during the first one or two years, more so for Broca's aphasia than for Wernicke's aphasia (I. P. Martins & Ferro, 1992). Initial improvement is due to reduction of the swelling that often accompanies brain damage rather than to any neural reorganization. Just how the remaining recovery occurs is not well understood, but it is a testament to the brain's plasticity.

The right hemisphere can take over language functions following left-hemisphere damage, if the injury occurs early in life. A two-year-old girl had a left-hemisphere stroke; her language was impaired, but she developed normal language capability by the age of seven. Then at the age of 56, she had a right-hemisphere stroke, which resulted in a second aphasia from which she had only minimal recovery (Guerreiro et al., 1995). Right-hemisphere language was confirmed by fMRI in all five individuals of a group who had been born with inadequate blood supply to the language areas of the left hemisphere (Vikingstad et al., 2000). Rasmussen and Milner (1977) used the *Wada technique* and electrical stimulation to determine the location of language control in patients before removing lesioned tissue that was causing epileptic seizures. (The Wada technique involves anesthetizing one hemisphere at a time by injecting a drug into each carotid artery; when the injection is into the language-dominant hemisphere, language is impaired.) Individuals whose left-hemisphere injury occurred before the age of five were more likely to have language control in the right hemisphere, supporting the hypothesis of right-hemisphere compensation. Patients whose left-hemisphere damage occurred later in life more often continued to have language control in the left hemisphere; there was, however, evidence in some cases that control had shifted into the border of the parietal lobe. Since language functions are scattered widely in the left hemisphere, perhaps the compensation involves enhancing already-existing activity rather than establishing new functional areas.

The ability of the right hemisphere to assume language functions may result in part because it normally makes several contributions to language processing. The most obvious right-hemisphere role in language is *prosody,* the use of intonation, emphasis, and rhythm to convey meaning in speech. An example of one aspect of prosody is the *difference* between "You put the cat out when it's freezing" spoken as a statement and spoken as an emotion-filled question. We saw in Chapter 8 that people with right-hemisphere damage have trouble understanding emotion when it is indicated by speaking tone and in producing emotional speech the same way. An fMRI study found that right-hemisphere activity increased while individuals detected angry, happy, sad, or neutral emotions from the intonation of words (Buchanan et al., 2000).

The right hemisphere also is important in understanding information from language that is not specifically communicated by the meaning of the words, such as when the meaning must be inferred from an entire discourse or when the meaning is figurative rather than literal. For example, interpreting the moral of a story activates the right hemisphere (Nichelli et al., 1995), as does understanding a metaphor or determining the plausibility of statements such as "Tim used feathers as paperweights" (Bottini et al., 1994). Interestingly, the right-hemisphere regions involved in all these activities correspond generally to the structures we have identified in left-hemisphere language processing.

A Language-Generating Mechanism?

> *Man has an instinctive tendency to speak, as we see in the babble of our young children.*
>
> —Charles Darwin

When Darwin suggested that we have an instinctive tendency to speak, what he meant was that infants seem very ready to engage in language and can learn it with minimal instruction. Children learn language with such alacrity that by the age of six they understand about 13,000 words, and by the time they graduate from high school, their working vocabulary is at least 60,000 words (Dronkers, Pinker, & Damasio, 2000). This means that children learn a new word about every 90 waking minutes. The hearing children of deaf parents pick up language just about as fast as children with hearing parents (Lenneberg, 1969), despite minimal learning opportunities. Not only are preadolescent children particularly sensitive language learners, but they are also believed to be the driving force in the development of creole language (which combines elements of two languages, allowing communication between the cultures). In Nicaragua, children in the school for the deaf, where sign language is not taught, have devised their own sign language with unique gestures and grammar (Senghas, Kita, & Özyürek, 2004).

Noam Chomsky (1980) and later Steven Pinker (1994) interpreted children's readiness to learn language as evidence of a *language acquisition device,* a hypothesized part of the brain dedicated to learning and controlling language. Not all researchers agree with this idea (see below), but most accept that there are biological reasons why language acquisition is so easy. This ease cuts across forms of language. For example, both hearing and deaf infants of signing parents babble in hand movements (Figure 9.23); the deaf infants' babbling proceeds into signing through the same stages and at about the same pace that children of speaking parents learn vocal language (Petitto, Holowka, Sergio, & Ostry, 2001; Petitto & Marentette, 1991). The researchers suggest that the ease of children's language acquisition is due to a brain-based sensitivity to rhythmic language patterns, a sensitivity that does not depend on the form of the language. Rhythm problems in childhood appear to correlate to reading disorders as adults (K. W. Carr, White-Schwoch, Tierney, Strait, & Kraus, 2014). And new evidence suggests that when musicians improvise passages within a larger ensemble, they use language centers as if they are participating in a musical conversation with the group (Donnay, Rankin, Lopez-Gonzalez, Jiradejvong, & Limb, 2014). As the accompanying In the News feature explains, we are predisposed to learn language as adults, even when we are not focused on it.

Innate Brain Specializations

More than 90% of right-handed people are left-hemisphere dominant for language. This is also true for two-thirds to three-quarters of left-handers; the remainder is about equally divided between right-hemisphere dominant and mixed (Knecht et al., 2000; B. Milner, 1974). In the large majority of autopsied brains, the left-hemisphere Broca's area is larger (Falzi, Perrone, & Vignolo, 1982), and the lateral fissure (Yeni-Komshian & Benson, 1976) and planum temporale

■ **FIGURE 9.23** Babies of Signing Parents Babble With Their Hands.

Unlike the meaningless hand movements of other infants (which they also make at other times), their babbling is like their parents' signing. Babbling hand movements are slower and restricted to the space in front of the infants' bodies, and they correspond to the rhythmic patterning of adult sign-syllables.

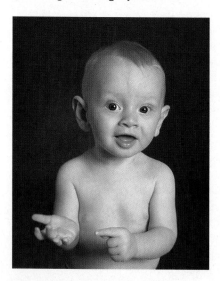

Source: Petitto, Holowka, Sergio, & Ostry, "Language rhythms in baby hand movements." *Nature*, 413, 35–36. Photo courtesy of Dr. Laura-Ann Petitto, University of Toronto.

IN THE NEWS

LEARN A NEW LANGUAGE WHILE YOU STUDY PSYCHOLOGY

How would you like to learn a new language while doing your psychology homework? We have been told since we were young that we had to focus and practice to learn how to speak another language, but recent evidence suggests that our brains are just as good at acquiring language information passively when we divert our attention elsewhere (reported in Greenwood, 2017).

In one study, two groups of participants were trained to distinguish between several similar-sounding phonemes of native Hindi speakers. The focus group practiced for one continuous hour across two days, while the other group alternated between 10 minutes of active practice and 10 minutes of another task for an hour while the sounds continued in the background. Surprisingly, the researchers discovered the "distracted" group learned the discrimination task as well as the "focused" group. In another study, students who

were learning Spanish learned to distinguish among sounds better if they simply listened to the new language rather than trying to speak along with the new material. So there might be something to taking frequent breaks from intensive language study and turn on a movie in that language while you do something else.

THOUGHT QUESTIONS

1. How could you apply the results of these studies to learning a new language in college?

2. Why do you think that listening by itself leads to better language learning than listening while repeating?

For the news story, visit edge.sagepub.com/garrett5e and select the Chapter 9 study resources.

(Geschwind & Levitsky, 1968; Rubens, 1977; Wada, Clarke, & Hamm, 1975) are longer. These differences are not the result of usage. By the 20th week of gestation, the left temporal lobe is already beginning to enlarge relative to the right (Kasprian et al., 2010), and the left planum temporale is larger by the 29th week (Wada et al., 1975). At birth or shortly after, speech causes a greater increase in cerebral blood flow than nonspeech sounds, speech sounds activate the same left-hemisphere language areas as in adults, and sentence melody activates the right hemisphere (reviewed by Friederici, 2006). Congenitally deaf individuals also have larger left temporal lobes, though the lack of auditory experience does result in fewer connections between language areas and auditory centers (Shibata, 2007).

Storing Multiple Languages

Additional evidence for a language acquisition device comes from studies of individuals who communicate with sign language. Left-hemisphere damage impairs sign-language ability more than right-hemisphere damage does (Hickok, Bellugi, & Klima, 1996), and communicating in sign language activates the classical left-hemisphere language areas (Figure 9.24; Neville et al., 1998; Petitto et al., 2000). This was true of both congenitally deaf and normally hearing signers (all of whom had used sign language from infancy), but the finding is especially interesting in the deaf individuals, because it cannot be the result of the brain simply using pathways already established by an auditory language. It is also interesting because Wernicke's area has traditionally been considered auditory in nature, which required the conversion of written words into an auditory form. Either the posterior language area is inherently more versatile than some theorists have thought, or the area underwent reorganization during infancy that enabled it to handle visual language.

Either way, language seems to be a specialized capability of a limited subset of brain structures.

But what happens if a person learns a second language after childhood, when the brain is less plastic (Figure 9.25); will the brain then recruit other areas to handle the task? Two imaging studies indicate that this does happen, to some extent. In the first study, bilingual individuals silently "described" events from the previous day in each of their two languages; the languages activated separate areas in the frontal lobes, with centers that were 4.5–9 mm apart in different individuals. This was not true of subjects who learned their second

■ **FIGURE 9.24**   Language Areas in Hearing and Deaf Individuals.

(a) fMRI results while hearing subjects read written English. (b) Activation in subjects deaf from birth while processing sign language. Yellow areas were significantly activated and those in red more so.

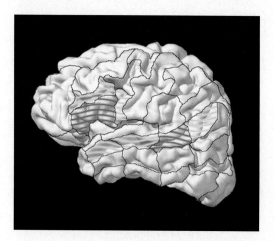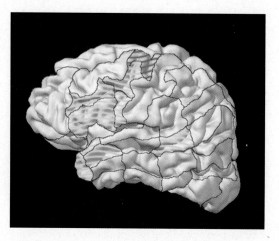

Source: From "Cerebral Organizations for Language in Deaf and Hearing Subjects: Biological Constraints and Effects of Experience," by H. J. Neville et al., 1998, *Proceedings of the National Academy of Sciences, USA, 95*, pp. 922–929. © 1998 National Academy of Sciences, U.S.A.

■ **FIGURE 9.25**   Brain Areas Activated by Different Languages in Bilingual Individuals.

Green circles represent areas activated by listening to English, and yellow circles indicate activation while listening to Spanish. These images are from different subjects, selected to represent the variability among 11 subjects. Although the patterns are different, in every case the languages activate separate areas.

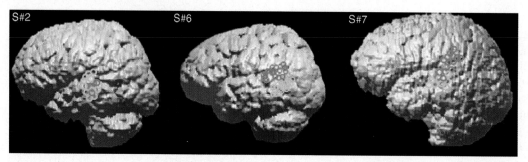

Source: From "Mapping of Receptive Language Cortex in Bilingual Volunteers by Using Magnetic Source Imaging," by P. G. Simos, E. M. Castillo, J. M. Fletcher, D. J. Francis, F. Maestu, J. I. Breier, W. W. Maggio, & A.C. Papanicolaou, 2001, *Journal of Neurosurgery, 95*, pp. 76–81.

language simultaneously with the first (K. H. S. Kim, Relkin, Lee, & Hirsch, 1997). The second study produced similar results in the temporal lobe when subjects heard and read words in their two languages (Figure 9.26; Simos et al., 2001). This separation is so distinct that capability can be impaired in one of the languages while the other is unaffected (called bilingual aphasia; Gomez-Tortosa, Martin, Gaviria, Charbel, & Auman, 1995; M. S. Schwartz, 1994). A colleague who is originally from Lebanon told one of us an interesting story about his mother. She lives in the United States, and she was fluent in English until a stroke impaired her ability to speak English, but not Arabic. Her nearby family members spoke only English, so when they needed to talk with her they had to telephone a relative in another city to translate! These observations are not as inconsistent with the hypothesis of a single language acquisition device as they might seem. In both the K. H. S. Kim et al. (1997) and the Simos et al. (2001) studies, the second-language locations were in the same area as Broca's and Wernicke's areas, respectively.

We still cannot say that they evolved specifically to serve language functions. You will see in the next section that some primates show similar enlargements in the left hemisphere, and their possession of language is

■ **FIGURE 9.26**   The Critical Period of Language Acquisition.

Children can readily learn new languages when young, but they slowly lose this ability starting at puberty. The mean score is a relative measure of English mastery; the age of arrival is when the individual arrives in the United States and begins to learn English.

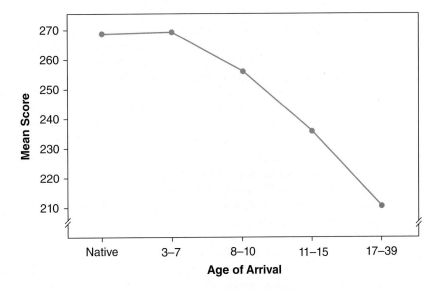

Source: From "Critical period effects in second language learning: the influence of maturational state on the acquisition of English as a second language," by J. S. Johnson & E. L. Newport, 1989, *Cognitive Psychology*, 21, pp. 60–99.

questionable at best. A reasonable interpretation of these data is that certain brain areas evolved simply to handle rapidly changing information and complex discriminations, which language in its various forms requires. The strongest proponent of this "language as use" theory is Vyvyan Evans, who cites agrammatic languages in native Australia, and the lack of new spontaneous languages forming in isolated groups of humans, as evidence that language may simply be the result of our vast capacity to learn. Another view is that the language areas are primarily specialized for different aspects of general learning: the frontal area for "procedural" or how-to learning that coincides with the rules of grammar and verb tenses, and the temporal area for "declarative" or informational learning and, thus, the storage of word meanings and information about irregular word forms (Ullman, 2001). Even if these learning structures have been "borrowed" to serve language functions and the concept of a dedicated language acquisition device isn't meaningful, it is still clear that the human brain is uniquely well fitted for creating, refining, and learning language. We will explore the possible evolutionary roots of this ability in the context of animal language.

Language in Nonhuman Animals

Research has refuted most of humans' claims to uniqueness, including tool use, tool making, and self-recognition. Determining whether we have exclusive ownership of language has been more difficult. Animal language intrigues us both because we're curious whether we have any company "at the top" and because we want to trace the evolutionary roots of language. Because language (like all behaviors) leaves no fossils behind, the origin of language is "a mystery with all the fingerprints wiped off" (Terrence Deacon, quoted by Holden, 2004a). Without this evidence, we are left with comparing the behavior and brains of our nonhuman relatives. The rationale behind animal language research is that any behavior or brain mechanism we share with other animals must have originated in common ancestors, or through similar mechanisms. Although dolphins, whales, and gorillas have been the subjects of mammalian research, the major contenders for a coprocessor of language have been the chimpanzee and bonobo. The reason is that humans and these ape species diverged from common ancestors a relatively recent 5 million years ago and we still share 99% of our genetic material (Prufer et al., 2012).

A major obstacle has been deciding what we mean by *language*. Linguists agree that the vocalizations animals use to announce intentions or states (like finding food, detecting danger, and being hungry) are only signals and have little to do with language. Even the human toddler's request of "milk" may initially be just a learned signal to indicate hunger and, like the monkey's alarm call, indicate no language understanding. As you will see in the following discussion, some of the results obtained in language research with animals are equally difficult to interpret.

? What skills have chimps achieved in language studies?

The first hurdle was deciding how to communicate with chimpanzees. An early study that attempted to teach a home-reared chimpanzee (Viki) to talk failed because chimpanzees lack a larynx for forming words (Hayes & Hayes, 1953; Kellogg, 1968). Since chimpanzees normally communicate using gestures, later researchers turned to American Sign Language (ASL) with better success. Over a four-year period, the chimpanzee Washoe learned to use 132 signs; she could request food or to be tickled or to play a game, and she would sign "sorry" when she bit someone (Fouts, Fouts, & Schoenfeld, 1984). And these gestures were transferrable to others: Washoe's adopted son, Loulis, learned 47 signs from her and three other chimps. The chimps regularly carried on sign-language conversations among themselves, most requesting hugs or tickling, asking to be chased, and signing "smile" (Fouts et al., 1984). But critics argued that no chimpanzee had learned to form a sentence; they concluded that expressions such as "banana me eat banana" are just a "running-on" of words, and Washoe's signing "water bird" in the presence of a swan was not the inventive characterization of "a bird that inhabits water" but the separate identification of the bird and the water it was on (Terrace, Petitto, Sanders, & Bever, 1979).

Results were more remarkable with bonobos, a near relative of chimpanzees and equally close to humans. When Duane and Sue Savage-Rumbaugh trained the bonobo Mutata to communicate by pressing symbols on a panel, her son Kanzi spontaneously began to communicate with the symbols and eventually learned 150 of them without any formal instruction (Figure 9.27; S. Savage-Rumbaugh, 1987; S. Savage-Rumbaugh, McDonald, Sevcik, Hopkins, & Rubert, 1986). Kanzi uses the board to request specific food items or to be taken to specific locations on the 55-acre research preserve, asks one person to chase a specific other person, and responds to similar requests from trainers. His communication skills have been estimated at the level of a two-year-old child (E. S. Savage-Rumbaugh et al., 1993).

Clearly, chimps and bonobos use predominantly gestural communication mechanisms, while we use a vocal mechanism. How did our spoken language evolve from a gestural one? There are two theories that have the most support. One theory, described by Corballis (2002), suggests that vocal language was a replacement for gestural language, to communicate over longer distances. Another theory, put forth by Dunbar (1996),

■ **FIGURE 9.27** Language Research With Chimpanzees and Bonobos.

(a) A researcher converses with a chimp using American Sign Language. (b) A bonobo communicates through the symbol board.

Sources: (a) © Susan Kuklin/Science Source. (b) © Frans Lanting Studio/Alamy Stock Photo.

suggests a more social role in communication; as groups of apes grew large, the grooming signals used to bond with others were replaced by vocal ones so that the hands could be used for other things like foraging. Dunbar's theory explains why most of us are right-handed and why speech is processed in the left hemisphere—gestural language controlled by the left hemisphere became vocal language in the same areas. Taken together, both theories explain why our greatest successes in communicating with chimps and bonobos have come through ASL—while we communicate primarily using vocalizations, primates communicate primarily using gestures.

What about other, nonrelated animals? There is evidence that birds evolved a very human-like language system, even though birds and humans are evolutionarily separated by over 350 million years. Even Charles Darwin, in his book *The Descent of Man and Selection in Relation to Sex* (1871), comments on the similarities between birdsong and human speech. Irene Pepperberg (1993) emphasized concept learning with her African gray parrot, Alex, but his communication skills turned out to be equally interesting. Using speech, Alex could tell his trainer how many items she was holding, the color of an item, or whether two items differed in shape or color. He also could respond to complex questions, such as "What shape is the green wood?" In addition, birds learn language in similar ways to us (see Marler, 1997, for a review); birds can have geographically distinct song *dialects,* which are regionally stable variations in language (Marler & Tamura, 1964); and can even learn grammatical patterns like us (Gentner, Fenn, Margoliash, & Nusbaum, 2006). Some birds, like the mockingbird, can even learn new "words" throughout adulthood and can control their vocal apparatus in ways that mimic other species' patterns (Zollinger & Suthers, 2004).

So do we share language ability with animals? The behavior of animals like Loulis, Kanzi, and Alex requires us to rethink our assumptions about human uniqueness, but no animal has yet turned in the critical language performance, and as far as we know, no animals in the wild have developed anything resembling a true language. But what some researchers do see in the animals' performance is evidence of evolutionary foundations of our language abilities (Gannon, Holloway, Broadfield, & Braun, 1998).

Neural and Genetic Antecedents

An approach of some researchers has been to determine whether other animals share with us any of the brain organization associated with human language. The results have been intriguing. In the chimpanzee, as with humans, there is a greater ratio of white to gray matter in the left hemisphere than in the right (Cantalupo et al., 2009), and the left lateral fissure is longer and the planum temporale is larger (Gannon et al., 1998; Yeni-Komshian & Benson, 1976). Japanese macaque monkeys respond better to calls of their own species when the recorded calls are presented through headphones to the right ear (and, therefore, primarily to the left hemisphere) than when they are presented to the left ear. There is no left-hemisphere advantage for the (nonmeaningful) calls of another monkey species (M. R. Petersen, Beecher, Zoloth, Moody, & Stebbins, 1978). Dolphins and the Rumbaughs' chimps Austin and Sherman responded more quickly when symbols or command gestures were presented to their left hemisphere (Hopkins & Morris, 1993; Morrel-Samuels & Herman, 1993). Songbirds and parrots have language centers functionally analogous to Broca's and Wernicke's areas (called RA and HVC, respectively; Vu, Mazurek, & Kuo, 1994). Finally, birds also have a dominant side of the brain for controlling song: dominant-side lesions to HVC in both canary and zebra finch brains severely disrupted their songs (Nottebohm, 1977; H. Williams, Crane, Hale, Esposito, & Nottebohm, 1992).

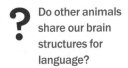

Do other animals share our brain structures for language?

Many researchers consider hand and face gestures to be more analogous to human speech than animal vocalizations are. They think that our ancestors communicated this way, aided in forming this simple but effective prelanguage by emerging language structures (Holden, 2004a; MacNeilage, 1998). Chimpanzees, our best living window into that ancestral past, communicate primarily through hand and face gestures (Figure 9.28), and one-third of the hand gestures used by chimpanzees in the wild are like those used by humans, such as beckoning to an individual or waving an individual away (A. I. Roberts, Vick, Roberts, Buchanan-Smith, & Zuberbühler, 2012). These researchers also believe that the ability to imitate gestures was critical to the development of language in humans; in fact, research indicates that children initially learn speech not by imitating sounds but by imitating the actions of the mouth (Goodell & Studdert-Kennedy, 1993), and the amount of gesturing at 14 months predicts vocabulary size at 54 months (Rowe & Goldin-Meadow, 2009). Now language theorists think they have identified the mechanism for the imitative development of language in mirror neurons, which you learned about in Chapter 8.

Mirror neurons were first discovered in the area of the monkey brain that corresponds to Broca's area; they respond not only to monkeys' hand movements but also to communicative mouth gestures such as

■ **FIGURE 9.28** A Chimpanzee Communicating With Face and Hand Gestures.

Source: Karl Ammann/The Image Bank/Getty.

■ **FIGURE 9.29** Overlap Between Language Areas and Areas Involved in Imitation.

Yellow indicates Broca's and Wernicke's areas and nearby areas that are active during imitation of acts by others. The overlapping brown areas are also active, and red indicates additional areas involved in imitation.

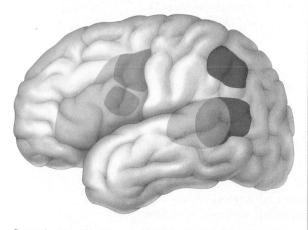

Source: Image provided courtesy of Dr. Marco Iacoboni. Adapted from "The Origin of Speech," by C. Holden, 2004, *Science*, 303, p. 1318.

lip smacking (Ferrari, Gallese, Rizzolatti, & Fogassi, 2003). In humans, they are in Broca's area and Wernicke's area and in the parietal lobe (Grèzes, Armony, Rowe, & Passingham, 2003; Holden, 2004a). Human mirror neurons are most active during imitation of another's movement (Iacoboni et al., 1999), which has encouraged the belief that they figure prominently in imitative ability and, thus, in the evolution of language (Figure 9.29). However, the fact that we share mirror neurons with monkeys and chimpanzees does not imply that monkeys and chimpanzees also share our language abilities. In fact, the evolutionary clues we do have suggest that language developed well after the split that led to humans and chimpanzees (Holden, 2004a). In addition, the involvement of songbird HVC neurons in both the perception and the production of song is highly analogous to mirror neurons in human language centers (Prather et al., 2008), suggesting that any species with mirror neurons may be capable of eventually evolving language. Whatever brain foundations of language we share with other animals required extensive refinement, such as expansion of the brain, including the language areas; migration of the larynx lower in the throat, which increased vocalization range; and the development of imitative ability, which is poor in nonhuman primates (Holden, 2004a).

Suggesting that language is a product of evolution means, of course, that genes are involved. *KIAA0319,* one of the genes contributing to dyslexia, also plays a role in the development of speech and language (M. L. Rice, Smith, & Gayán, 2009), and *CNTNAP2* and *ATP2C2* have been implicated in language impairment (Newbury, Fisher, & Monaco, 2010; Vernes et al., 2008). *ROBO1*, a gene that controls axon guidance in fetal speech and hearing areas (C. Johnson, Drgon, McMahon, & Uhl, 2009), has been implicated in a particularly severe type of dyslexia (Hannula-Jouppi et al., 2005) and is also found in avian brain areas involved in song learning (R. Wang et al., 2015). But the most researched and best understood language gene is *FOXP2*. A mutation of this gene results in reduced gray matter in Broca's area, along with articulation difficulties, problems identifying basic speech sounds, grammatical difficulty, and trouble understanding sentences (C. S. L. Lai, Fisher, Hurst, Vargha-Khadem, & Monaco, 2001; Pinker, 2001; Vargha-Khadem, Gadian, Copp, & Mishkin, 2005). We also share this gene with chimpanzees, but the human version differs in two apparently very important amino acids. The human version has been found in Neanderthal remains (J. Krause et al., 2007), and other fossil and archaeological evidence suggests to some researchers that the Neanderthals had the capacity for language. According to the researchers, the Neanderthals' increased nerve supply (assessed from the size of the bony pathways) enabled the voluntary control of the tongue and respiratory muscles necessary for speech; their auditory system specialized them for sensitivity in the speech range; and the spread of complex tool designs implied the imitative ability involved in learning speech (Dediu & Levinson, 2013). In a recent study, mice genetically altered to carry a human form of *FOXP2* enhanced their ability to turn thoughts into actions through increased dopamine activity in the striatum (an area involved in fine movements and memory; Schreiweis et al., 2014). Although the evidence is circumstantial and the interpretation subjective, it does appear that modern language has roots in the far distant past. However, not all the innovation has been in the human ancestral line, as the accompanying In the News feature reveals.

IN THE NEWS

LANGUAGE DIALECTS: YOU ARE FROM WHAT YOU SAY

Did you know your state (or country) of origin could be deduced by the words you say? While someone from the United Kingdom might say "knackered" when tired, and folks from Australia call a charcoal grill a "barbie," there is evidence of strong regional dialects in the United States itself. A book by a statistician, Joshua Katz, of North Carolina State University, demonstrates that there are some remarkably precise and predictable dialect boundaries in American English (Katz, 2016).

Do you call a carbonated beverage "pop," "soda," or "coke"? The "pop" crowd tends to be in the northern United States. The "soda" group includes the desert Southwest, the Northeast, and for some reason the area around St. Louis. The "coke" bunch is in the South, east of New Mexico. Do you call the thing you drink water out of in school a "bubbler"? You're from Wisconsin. Do you call something diagonally across an intersection "catty-corner," or do you say "kitty-corner"? That separates those who grew up in the South (catty) from those who grew up in the North and West (kitty). Sometimes a particular word can originate from a very small area. In Putnam and Westchester counties in New York, where Gerald grew up, there was a rather unique name for a sandwich with meats, vegetables, and cheese: They call it

a "wedge" because of the slice taken out of the bread roll. The best meatball wedge in the area came from Rodak's restaurant in Mahopac, New York. Good stuff. Gerald is from New York, so he enjoys bottles of "soda," refers to a group of people as "you guys," and wears "sneakers." Bob, on the other hand, grew up in Texas, so he calls these things "coke," "y'all," and "tennis shoes." If you want to learn about geographical language oddities (like the Deep South term "the devil beating his wife" for when it rains when the sun is shining) and other dialectical differences, be sure to read Katz's book, *Speaking American* (2016).

So where do we get these localized differences in language, seeing that we all learn the same basic language rules and vocabulary in school? We learn these differences during the sensitive period of our language development, when a group of people decide to call something a unique term, and it passes from person to person through cultural learning until most of the people in that area use the same term. Once learned, we carry these regional differences with us for the rest of our lives, which serves as a reminder of where we began our journeys. They indicate the background we've each had and the experiences we went through, and they provide clues to how little we seem to travel from our birth areas.

CONCEPT CHECK

Take a Minute to Check Your Knowledge and Understanding

- In what ways is the Wernicke-Geschwind model correct? In what ways is it incorrect?
- What are the different roles of the left and right hemispheres in language (in most people)? (See Chapter 8 for part of the answer.)
- What clues are there in dialects for the movements of people?

In Perspective

Our guess is that at the beginning of this chapter you would have said that vision is the most important sense. Perhaps now you can appreciate why Helen Keller thought her deafness was a greater handicap than her blindness. Hearing alerts us to danger, brings us music, and provides for the social interactions that bind humans together. Small wonder that during evolution, the body invested such resources in the intricate mechanisms of hearing.

Hearing has important adaptive functions with or without the benefit of language, but from our vantage point as language-endowed humans, it is easy to understand Hudspeth's (2000) claim that audition's most important role is in processing language. The person who is unable to talk is handicapped; the person who is unable to understand and to express language is nearly helpless. No wonder we put so much research effort into understanding how language works.

Some of the most exciting directions that language research has taken have involved attempts to communicate with our closest nonhuman relatives, and to make sense of the chirps and warbles of birds. Whether they possess language capabilities depends on how we define language. It is interesting how the capabilities we consider most characteristic of being human—such as language and consciousness—are the hardest to define. As so often happens, studying our animal relatives, however distant they may be, helps us understand ourselves.

CHAPTER SUMMARY

- Sensation requires a receptor that is specialized for the kind of stimulus. Beyond sensation, the brain carries out further analysis, called perception.

Hearing

- The auditory mechanism responds mostly to airborne vibrations, which vary in frequency and intensity.
- Sounds are captured and amplified by the outer ear and transformed into neural impulses in the inner ear by the hair cells on the basilar membrane. The signal is then transmitted through the brain stem and the thalamus to the auditory cortex in each temporal lobe.
- Frequency discrimination depends mostly on the basilar membrane's differential vibration along its length to different frequencies, resulting in neurons from each location carrying frequency-specific information to the brain. At lower frequencies, neurons fire at the same rate as the sound's frequency; it is possible that intermediate frequencies are represented by neurons firing in volleys, though research has not indicated that the brain utilizes this information.
- Although the cochlea is specialized for responding to pure tones, the basilar membrane apparently performs a Fourier analysis on complex sounds, breaking down a sound into its component frequencies.
- When different sounds must be distinguished from each other, stimulation from the brain probably adjusts the sensitivity of the hair cells to emphasize one sound at the expense of others. Selective attention also results in differential activity in areas of the cortex.

- Locating sounds helps us approach or avoid sound sources and to attend to them despite competition from other sounds.
- The brain has specialized circuitry for detecting the binaural cues of differences in intensity, timing, and phase at the two ears.

Language

- Researchers have identified two major language areas in the brain, with Broca's area involved with speech production and grammatical functions and Wernicke's area with comprehension.
- Damage to either area produces different symptoms of aphasia, and damage to connections with the visual cortex impairs reading and writing. Developmental dyslexia may involve planum temporale abnormalities, reduced activity in the posterior language area, or deficiencies in the auditory and visual pathways.
- Although damage to the left frontal or temporal lobes is more likely to produce the expected disruptions in language, studies have shown that control of the various components of language is distributed across the four lobes.
- Although some animals have language-like brain structures and have been taught to communicate in simple ways, it is controversial whether they possess true language. Their study suggests some possible evolutionary antecedents of language. Several genes with language functions have been identified, the best known being a variant of *FOXP2*, which was shared by Neanderthals.
- Since language is learned, there are regional differences, called dialects, that give clues as to the origin of individuals. ■

STUDY RESOURCES

FOR FURTHER THOUGHT

- Write a modified Wernicke-Geschwind theory of language control, based on later evidence.

- Would you rather give up your hearing or your vision? Why?
- Make the argument that chimps possess language, though at a low level. Then argue the opposite, that their behavior does not rise to the level of language.

TEST YOUR UNDERSTANDING

1. Describe the path of sound information from the outer ear to the auditory neurons, telling what happens at each point along the way.

2. State the telephone theory, the volley theory, and the place theory. Indicate a problem with each, and state the theory that is currently most widely accepted.

3. Summarize the Wernicke-Geschwind model of language function. Include structures, the effects of damage, and the steps in reading a word aloud and in repeating a word that is heard.

Select the best answer:

1. An adequate and an inadequate stimulus, such as light versus pressure on the eyeball, will produce similar experiences because
   a. they both activate visual receptors and the visual cortex.
   b. the receptors for touch and vision are similar.
   c. touch and vision receptors lie side by side in the eye.
   d. our ability to discriminate is poor.

2. Frequency is to pitch as
   a. loudness is to intensity.
   b. intensity is to loudness.
   c. stimulus is to response.
   d. response is to stimulus.

3. The sequence of sound travel in the inner ear is
   a. oval window, ossicles, basilar membrane, eardrum.
   b. ossicles, oval window, basilar membrane, eardrum.
   c. eardrum, ossicles, oval window, basilar membrane.
   d. eardrum, ossicles, basilar membrane, oval window.

4. Place analysis depends most on the physical characteristics of the
   a. hair cells.   b. basilar membrane.
   c. tectorial membrane. d. cochlear canal.

5. The fact that neurons are limited in their rate of firing by the refractory period is most damaging to which theory?
   a. telephone   b. volley
   c. place   d. volley-place

6. The place theory's greatest problem is that
   a. neurons cannot fire as frequently as the highest frequency sounds.
   b. neurons specific for frequencies above 5000 Hz have not been found.
   c. the entire basilar membrane vibrates about equally at low frequencies.
   d. volleying does not follow sound frequencies above about 5000 Hz.

7. An auditory neuron's tuning curve tells you
   a. which frequency it responds to.
   b. which part of the basilar membrane the neuron comes from.
   c. at what rate the neuron can fire.
   d. how much the neuron responds to different frequencies.

8. A cochlear implant works because
   a. the tympanic membrane is intact.
   b. the hair cells are intact.
   c. it stimulates the auditory cortex directly.
   d. it stimulates auditory neurons.

9. An auditory object is
   a. a vibrating object in the environment.
   b. a sound recognized as distinct from others.
   c. the sound source the individual is paying attention to.
   d. none of the above

10. As a binaural sound location cue, difference in intensity works
    a. poorly at low frequencies.
    b. poorly at medium frequencies.
    c. poorly at high frequencies.
    d. about equally at all frequencies.

11. In the following diagram of coincidence detectors, which cell would respond most if the sound were directly to the person's left?

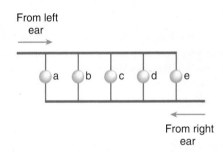

12. On returning home from the hospital, an elderly neighbor drags one foot when he walks and uses almost exclusively nouns and verbs in his brief sentences. You guess that he has had a mild stroke located in his
    a. left temporal lobe.   b.   right temporal lobe.
    c. left frontal lobe.   d.   right frontal lobe.

13. Most researchers agree that dyslexia is primarily a problem of
    a. development in Broca's area.
    b. development in the visual area.
    c. visual processing.
    d. phonological processing.

14. Evidence providing some support for a language acquisition device comes from studies showing that American Sign Language activates
    a. the left hemisphere.
    b. the left and right hemispheres.
    c. both frontal lobes.
    d. the occipital lobe.

15. The most reasonable conclusion regarding language in animals is that

    a. they can use words or signs but do not possess language.
    b. they can learn language to the level of a six-year-old human.
    c. language is "built in" for humans but can be learned by animals.
    d. some animals have brain structures similar to human language structures.

16. The role of mirror neurons in language development is supposedly in the

    a. imitation of word sounds.
    b. imitation of gestures and mouth actions.
    c. development of grammar.
    d. use of prosody.

Answers:

1. a, 2. b, 3. c, 4. b, 5. a, 6. c, 7. d, 8. d, 9. b, 10. a, 11. e, 12. c, 13. d, 14. a, 15. d, 16. b.

ON THE WEB

The following websites are coordinated with this chapter's content. You can access these websites from the **SAGE edge Student Resources site**; select this chapter and then click on Web Resources. (**Bold** items are links.)

1. **National Institute on Deafness and Other Communication Disorders (or NIDCD)**, a division of the National Institutes of Health, is an excellent resource site for information on deafness, language, and speech disorders, as well as information for student and teacher activities. The site **Hereditary Hearing Loss** provides an overview of the genetics of hereditary hearing loss.

2. Two animations, **Hearing and How it Works** and **Auditory Transduction**, give a good picture of what happens in the middle and inner ear. **Dancing Hair Cell** is a highly magnified video of an outer hair cell shortening and lengthening in rhythm with Linda Ronstadt's "Quiéreme Mucho."

3. **Biointeractive: The Cochlea** features an animation of the basilar membrane responding to pure tones and music. The video is a good demonstration of place analysis, although for simplicity's sake it suggests that the basilar membrane around the area of greatest vibration does not vibrate at all.

4. **Cochlear Implant** is an animated explanation of the process of hearing and how cochlear implants restore hearing. A YouTube video captures the excitement of a **young woman** when her new implant is turned on.

5. To communicate over long distances on Isla Gomera, one of the Canary Islands, people use complex whistles; you can see **a video from UNESCO** on YouTube. The whistles are processed in the left-hemisphere language areas by whistlers, but not by others (Carreiras, Lopez, Rivero, & Corina, 2005).

!Kung hunters of the Kalahari Desert communicate solely with clicks while stalking game, and some researchers believe clicks formed the first vocal language. (The ! symbol denotes a click, which is part of the name.) Hear South African singer **Miriam Makeba** demonstrate the click language and sing her famous "Click Song." In addition, the host for *The Daily Show*, comedian Trevor Noah, speaks Xhosa, which also contains click syllables as can be seen in **this YouTube interview** on the BBC.

6. You can see a video of **Daniel Kish describing his use of echolocation** to "see" using sound in this fascinating TED talk.

7. The **National Aphasia Association** has information about aphasia and about research on the disorder, as well as resources. **Stroke Family** has information about recovering speech after a stroke, including free mini guides, with emphasis on how the family can help.

8. The **International Dyslexia Association** provides information on the disorder.

9. At **Friends of Washoe** you can learn about the lives and personalities of Washoe and her family, including Loulis. Note especially Tatu's signing and her awareness of time, including seasonal holidays. Sadly, Alex passed away in 2007, but Dr. Pepperberg continues her language research with two other parrots (Athena and Griffin). See the **Alex Foundation**'s descriptions of the birds and the research, and a video of **Alex performing**. A **BBC article from 2015** describes the remarkable similarity between birdsong and human language.

10. The **dialect quiz** can be taken on the *New York Times*'s website, and the results can be shared on several social media platforms.

FOR FURTHER READING

1. In *Auditory Neuroscience: Making Sense of Sound* (MIT Press, 2012), Israel Nelken and Andrew King draw on physics, psychophysics, and neuroscience to explain hearing, speech processing, sound localization, and auditory scene analysis. They end with a description of auditory prostheses.

2. *The Language Instinct* (Harper Perennial, 2007) is a reprint of Stephen Pinker's classic on the evolution of language. Pinker's expertise and lively writing style garnered one reviewer's evaluation as "an excellent book full of wit and wisdom and sound judgment."

3. *The Evolution of Social Communication in Primates* (Springer, 2014), edited by Marco Pina and Nathalie Gontier, is a fascinating series of articles about the origin of language in primates from philosophical, social, and evolutionary perspectives.

4. *Speaking American: How Y'all, Youse, and You Guys Talk: A Visual Guide*, by Joshua Katz (Houghton Mifflin Harcourt, 2016), is an excellent summary of the many regional language dialects in the United States and includes examples from specific cities nationwide.

5. "Genetics of Speech and Language Disorders," by Changsoo Kang and Dennis Drayna (*Annual Review of Genomics and Human Genetics*, 2011, *12*, 145–164), describes the progress made in identifying genes responsible for these disorders.

KEY TERMS

adequate stimulus 240
agraphia 258
alexia 258
amplitude 241
angular gyrus 258
aphasia 256
auditory object 251
basilar membrane 244
binaural 252
Broca's aphasia 256
cochlea 240
cochlear canal 244
cocktail party effect 251
coincidence detectors 253
complex sound 241
dialect 267

dyslexia 258
Eustachian tube 242
frequency 241
frequency-place theory 249
frequency theory 246
inner hair cells 244
intensity 241
interaural intensity difference (IID) 252
interaural phase difference (IPD) 253
interaural timing difference (ITD) 253
language acquisition device 262
loudness 241
organ of Corti 244
ossicles 242
outer hair cells 244
perception 240

phonological hypothesis 260
pinna 242
pitch 241
place theory 247
planum temporale 260
prosody 262
pure tone 241
receptor 240
sensation 240
tectorial membrane 244
telephone theory 246
tonotopically organized 244
tympanic membrane 242
volley theory 246
Wernicke's aphasia 257

edge.sagepub.com/garrett5e

SAGE edge offers a robust online environment featuring an impressive array of free tools and resources for review, study, and further exploration, keeping both instructors and students on the cutting edge of teaching and learning.

9.1 Summarize how the nervous system processes sound stimuli.	▶ Making Complex Sounds Visible
9.2 Identify the brain structures involved in hearing.	🔊 Your Brain on Sound
9.3 Describe the role of specific brain structures in language ability.	▶ Babies and Sign Language ▶ Language and Communication Disorders
9.4 Explain how lateralization is important to the brain organization of language processing.	▶ Right Brain vs. Left Brain
9.5 Predict the brain regions that are impaired in specific language disorders.	🔊 Music, Rhythm, and Language
9.6 Contrast the communication abilities of other animals with human language.	📄 Phylogenetic Roots of Language

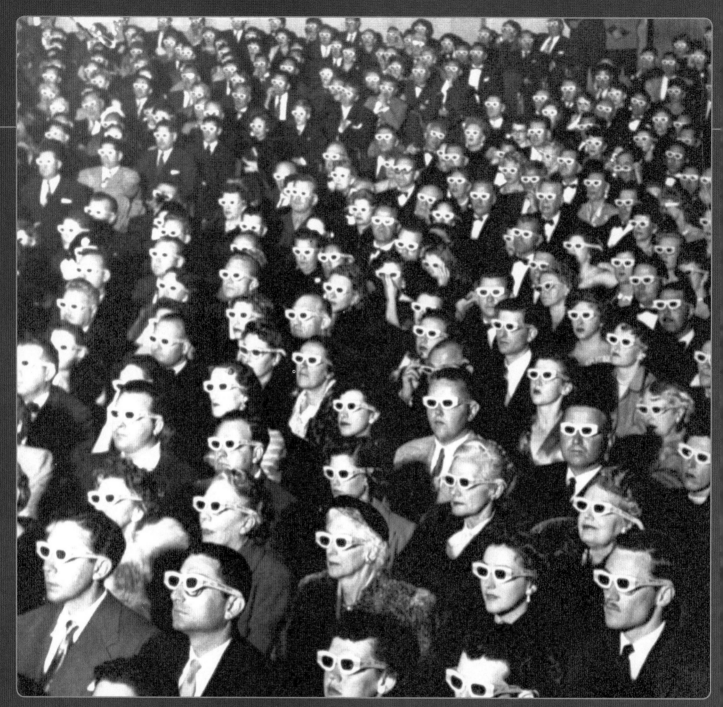

Vision and Visual Perception

After reading this chapter, you will be able to:

- Describe the functions of structures within the eye.

- Illustrate the processing pathways of visual information from the eye up to cortical brain areas.

- Compare the major theories of color processing.

- Contrast the major theories of form processing.

- Discuss how visual information is segregated and reconstructed in the visual system.

- Identify how action potentials and synaptic transmission can produce a variety of visual experiences.

- Predict how damage to specific portions of the visual system will impact a person's visual perceptions.

Jonathan I. was in his car when a small truck hit it. In the emergency room, he was told that he had a concussion. For a few days, he was unable to read, saying that the letters looked like Greek, but fortunately this alexia soon disappeared. Jonathan was a successful artist who had worked with the renowned Georgia O'Keeffe, and he was eager to return to his work. Driving to his studio, he noticed that everything appeared gray and misty, as if he were driving in a fog. When he arrived at his studio, he found that even his brilliantly colored paintings had become gray and lifeless.

His whole world changed. People's appearance was repulsive to him, because their skin appeared "rat colored"; he lost interest in sex with his wife for that reason. Food was unattractive, and he came to prefer black and white foods (coffee, rice, yogurt, black olives). His enjoyment of music was diminished, too; before the accident, he used to experience *synesthesia, in which musical tones evoked a sensation of changing colors,* and this pleasure disappeared as well. Even his migraine headaches, which had been accompanied by brilliantly colored geometric hallucinations, became "dull." He retained his vivid imagery, but it too was without color.

Over the next two years, Jonathan seemed to forget that color once existed, and his sorrow lifted. His wife no longer appeared rat colored, and they resumed sexual activity. He turned to drawing and sculpting and to painting dancers and race horses, rendered in black and white but characterized by movement, vitality, and sensuousness. However, he preferred the colorless world of darkness and would spend half the night wandering the streets (O. Sacks & Wasserman, 1987).

Master the content.
edge.sagepub.com/garrett5e

> *From the patterns of stimulation on the retina we perceive the world of objects and this is nothing short of a miracle.*
>
> —Richard Gregory

Vision enables us to read and to absorb large amounts of complex information. It helps us navigate in the world, build structures, and avoid danger. Color helps distinguish objects from their background, and it enriches our lives with natural beauty and works of art. We suspect that in contrast to Helen Keller's belief that deafness was a greater affliction than blindness, most of you would consider vision the most important of our senses. Apparently, researchers share that opinion, because vision has received more research attention than the other senses combined. Thus, we understand a great deal about how the brain processes visual information. In addition, studies of vision are providing a valuable model for understanding complex neural processing in general.

Light and the Visual Apparatus

Vision is an impressive capability. There are approximately 97 million light receptors in the human eye (Curcio, Sloan, Kalina, & Hendrickson, 1990), and a complex network of cells connecting them to each other and to the optic nerve. The optic nerve itself boasts a million axons (Mikelberg, Drance, Schulzer, Yidegiligne, & Wels, 1989), compared with 30,000 in the auditory nerve. The optic nerve transmits information to the brain at an estimated 100 million bits per second, comparable to Ethernet data transmission rates (Koch et al., 2006). What our brain does with the information it receives from the eye is equally remarkable. The topics of vision and visual perception form an exciting story, one of high-tech research and conflicting theories, and dedicated scientists' lifelong struggles to understand our most amazing sense.

The Visible Spectrum

To understand vision, we need to start at the beginning by describing the *adequate stimulus*, as we did with audition. To say that the stimulus for vision is light seems obvious, but the point needs some elaboration. Visible light is a part of the electromagnetic spectrum. The *electromagnetic spectrum* includes a variety of energy forms, ranging from gamma rays at one extreme of frequency to the radiations of alternating current circuits at the other (Figure 10.1); the portion of the electromagnetic spectrum that we can see is represented by the colored area in the figure.

The visible part of the electromagnetic spectrum accounts for only 1/70 of the frequency range. Most of the frequencies are not useful for producing images; for instance, AM, FM, and analog television waves pass right through objects. Some of the other energy forms, such as X-rays and radar, can be used for producing images, but they require powerful energy sources and special equipment for detecting the images. Heat-producing objects give off infrared energy, which some nocturnal animals (such as the sidewinder rattlesnake) use to detect their prey in darkness. Humans can convert infrared images to visible ones with the aid of specialized equipment, and this capability is very useful to the military and law enforcement for detecting heat-producing individuals, heat-producing vehicles, and armament at night. Sometimes this ability can be used to deceive heat-detecting equipment; during the first Gulf War, the Iraqi army set up plywood silhouettes of tanks with heaters behind them to distract Allied airplanes. But infrared is best for detecting nearby objects—distant ones have blurred edges

■ **FIGURE 10.1**   The Electromagnetic Spectrum.

The visible part of the spectrum is the middle (colored) area, which has been expanded to show the color experiences usually associated with the wavelengths. Only 0.0035% of the electromagnetic spectrum is visible to humans.

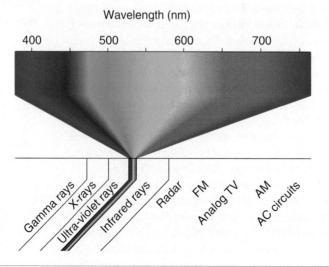

and fuzzy detail. The electromagnetic energy within our detectable (visible) range produces well-defined images because it is reflected from objects with minimal distortion. We are adapted to life in the daytime, and we sacrifice the ability to see in darkness in exchange for crisp, colorful images of faces and three-dimensional objects in daylight. In other words, our sensory equipment is adapted for detecting the energy that is most useful to us, just as the night-hunting sidewinder rattlesnake is equipped to detect the infrared radiation emitted by its prey and a bat's ears are specialized for the high-frequency sound waves it bounces off small insects.

Light is a form of oscillating energy and travels in waves just as sounds do. We could specify visible light (and the rest of the electromagnetic spectrum) in terms of frequency, just as we did with sound energy, but the numbers would be extremely large. So, we describe light in terms of its wavelength—the distance the oscillating energy travels in one complete cycle. (We could do the same with sound, but those numbers would be just as inconveniently small.) The unit of wavelength is the nanometer (nm), which is a billionth of a meter; visible light ranges from about 380 to 800 nm. Notice in Figure 10.1 that different wavelengths correspond to different colors of light; for example, when light in the range of 500 to 570 nm strikes the receptors in our eye, we normally report seeing green. Later in the chapter, we will qualify this relationship when we examine why wavelength does not always correspond to the color we see (just like our pitch perception isn't perfectly aligned with sound frequency).

The Eye and Its Receptors

The eye is a spherically shaped structure filled with a clear, thick liquid (Figure 10.2a). The white outer covering, or sclera, is opaque except for the cornea, which is transparent. Behind the cornea is the iris, which

■ **FIGURE 10.2**   The Human Eye and Retina.

In (a), the major parts of the eye are shown. In (b), the major pathway of visual information is shown (photoreceptor to bipolar cells to ganglion cells). (Note how the connections to the cones "fan out" away from the fovea, making the cones there more accesssible to light.)

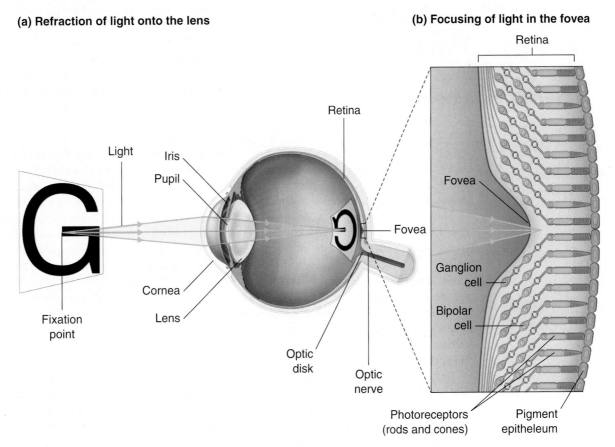

(a) Refraction of light onto the lens

(b) Focusing of light in the fovea

Source: Modified from Figure 26-1 in Eric R. Kandel, James H. Schwartz, Thomas M. Jessell, Steven A. Siegelbaum, A. J. Hudspeth, & Sarah Mack. *Principles of Neural Science* (5th Edition), 2012.

■ **FIGURE 10.3**   Accommodation of the Lens.

When you are looking at something far away, the muscles surrounding the lens relax, and the lens flattens (a). When you focus on something close, the muscles contract and make the lens more round. This is called accommodation (b).

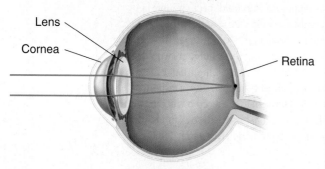

(a) Object far—eye relaxed

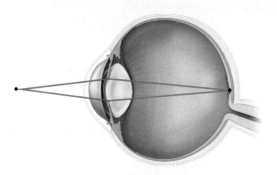

(b) Object near—eye accommodation

Source: Schwartz, B. L. & Krantz, J. H. (2015).

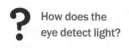

How does the eye detect light?

gives your eye its color. The iris is a circular muscle that controls the amount of light entering your eye by contracting reflexively in bright light and relaxing in dim light. You can observe this response in yourself by watching in a mirror while you change the level of light in the room. The pupil is not a real structure, but simply a hole in the iris muscle; it looks black because light that enters your eye doesn't come out. Behind the iris is the lens. Notice in the figure that the lens reflects the image upside down and backwards onto the retina. You can demonstrate this by touching the side of your eye through your closed lid—you'll be manually stimulating the retina on one side, but you'll see a flashing spot on the other side of your eye—if you move your finger down, the spot moves up. Because the normally flat lens is a transparent yet remarkably flexible tissue, the muscles attached to it can contract to make the lens rounder to focus on a near object through a process called *accommodation* (Figure 10.3).

The *retina,* the light-sensitive tissue at the rear of the eye, is made up of two main types of light-sensitive receptor cells, called rods and cones, and the neurons that are connected to them. As you can see in Figure 10.4, the receptors—collectively referred to as *photoreceptors*—are at the very back of the eye. Light must pass through the neural cells to reach the photoreceptors over much of the retinal surface, but this presents little problem because the neural cells are very small and transparent (see Figure 10.2b). The photoreceptors connect to *bipolar cells,* which in turn connect to *ganglion cells,* whose axons form the optic nerve. The photoreceptors are filled with light-sensitive chemicals called *photopigments*. The photopigment absorbs energy from the light that causes some of the molecules to break down into two components, and the ensuing chemical reaction ultimately results in a neural response. The two components then recombine to maintain the supply of photopigment.

The rods and cones are named for their shapes, as you can see by looking at Figure 10.4 again. The human eye contains about 92 million rods and about 4.6 million cones (Curcio et al., 1990). The two types of receptors contain different kinds of photopigments; rods and cones function similarly, but their chemical contents and their neural connections give them different specializations.

The rod photopigment is called *rhodopsin*; the name refers to its color (from the Latin *rhodon,* "rose"), not to its location in rods. Rhodopsin absorbs light much faster than cone photopigment, so it is used exclusively for low-light situations. In very bright light, the rhodopsin in your eyes remains broken down most of the time, so the rods are not useful. The brief delay in adjusting to a darkened movie theater is due to the time it takes the rhodopsin to resynthesize. *Iodopsin,* the cone photopigment, requires a high light intensity level, so your cones function well in daylight but are nonfunctional in dark situations. Three varieties of iodopsin, located in different cone types, respond best to different wavelengths of light; this means that cones detect only certain different wavelengths, whereas rods differentiate only among different levels of light and dark (which is why you cannot recognize colors in dim light).

Rods and cones also differ in their retinal distribution and in their amount of neural interconnection. Cones are most concentrated in the *fovea,* a 1.5-millimeter-diameter circle in the middle of the retina, and drop off rapidly with distance from that point. Rods are most concentrated at 20 degrees from the fovea; from that point, they decrease in number in all directions and fall to zero in the fovea. In the center of the fovea, there is one ganglion cell for each cone; the number of cones per ganglion cell increases with distance from the center but remains small compared with rods. Because few cones share ganglion cells, the fovea has higher *visual acuity,* or ability to distinguish details. In contrast, many rods share a single ganglion cell; this reduces their resolution but enhances their already greater sensitivity to dim light. The area of the retina from which a ganglion cell (or any other cell in the visual system) receives its input is the cell's *receptive field.* So, we can say that receptive fields are smaller in the fovea and larger in the periphery. Table 10.1 summarizes the characteristics of these two visual systems.

The receptors' response to light is different from what you might expect, because they are most active when they are *not* being stimulated by light. In darkness, the photoreceptor's sodium and calcium channels are open, allowing these ions to flow in freely. Thus, the membrane is partially depolarized; the receptor releases a continuous flow of glutamate, and this *inhibits* activity in the bipolar cells. The chemical response that occurs when light strikes the photopigments closes the sodium and calcium channels, reducing the release of glutamate in proportion to the amount of light. The bipolar cells release more neurotransmitters, which increases the firing rate in the ganglion cells. (The photoreceptors and bipolar cells do not produce action potentials.) In neural terms, ganglion cells undergo what is called "release from inhibition."

If you look again at Figure 10.4, you can see that the rods and cones are highly interconnected by *horizontal cells.* In addition, *amacrine cells* connect across many ganglion cells. This might suggest to you that the retina does more than transmit information about points of light to the brain. You might also suspect that a great deal of processing goes on in the retina itself. You will soon see that both are true. With such complexity, it's no wonder most vision scientists consider the retina to be part of the brain and refer to the optic nerve as a tract!

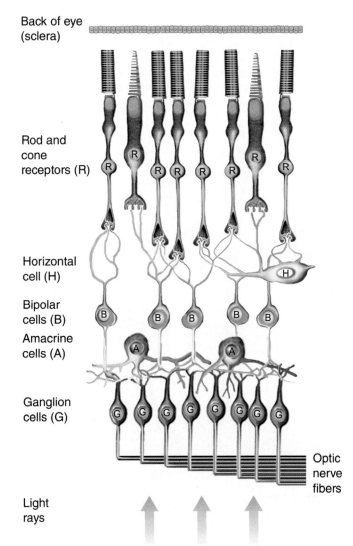

■ **FIGURE 10.4**   The Cells of the Retina.

Source: Adapted from "Organization of the Primate Retina," by J. E. Dowling and B. B. Boycott, *Proceedings of the Royal Society of London, B166,* Fig. 23 on p. 104. Copyright 1966 by the Royal Society.

TABLE 10.1   Summary of the Characteristics of the Rod and Cone Systems.

	ROD SYSTEM	CONE SYSTEM
Function	Functions best in dim light, poorly or not at all in bright light.	Functions best in bright light, poorly or not at all in dim light.
	Detail vision is poor.	Detail vision is good.
	Does not distinguish colors.	Subset distinguishes among colors.
Location	Mostly in periphery of retina.	Mostly in fovea and surrounding area.
Receptive field	Large, due to convergence on ganglion cells; contributes to light sensitivity.	Small, with one or a few cones converging on a single ganglion cell; contributes to detail vision.

■ **FIGURE 10.5**   Projections From the Retinas to the Cerebral Hemispheres.

Notice how images of objects in the left and right sides of the visual field fall on the opposite sides of the two retinas; the information from the two eyes then travels to the visual cortex in the hemisphere opposite the object, where it is combined. (The distance between the two lateral geniculate nuclei is greatly exaggerated.). The inset demonstrates the separation of information from each eye into separate ocular dominance columns (white from left eye, gray from right eye).

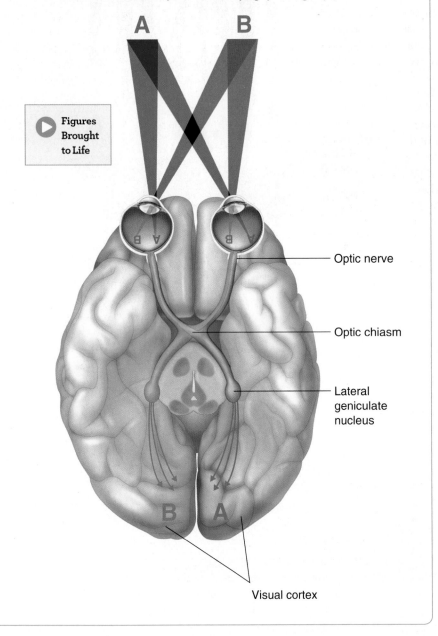

▶ Figures Brought to Life

Optic nerve

Optic chiasm

Lateral geniculate nucleus

Visual cortex

Pathways to the Brain

The axons of the ganglion cells join and pass out of each eye to form the two optic nerves (Figure 10.5). Where the nerve exits the eye, there are no receptors, so it is referred to as the *blind spot* (see Figure 10.2a). This point is located about 20 degrees toward the outside and down slightly from the usual focal point of each retina. The blind spots of the two eyes fall at different points in a visual scene, so you do not notice that any of your visual world is missing; besides, your brain is good at "filling in" missing information, even when a small part of the visual system is damaged. The two optic nerves run to a point just in front of the pituitary, where they join for a short distance at the *optic chiasm* before separating again and traveling to their first synapse in the *lateral geniculate nuclei* of the thalamus. At the optic chiasm, axons from the nasal sides of the eyes cross to the other side and go to the occipital lobe in the opposite hemisphere. Neurons from the outside half of the eyes (the temporal side) do not cross over but go to the same side of the brain.

It seems like splitting the output of each eye between the two hemispheres would cause a major distortion of the image. However, if you look closely at Figure 10.5, you can see that the arrangement keeps related information together. Notice that the letter *A*, which appears in the person's left *visual field* (the part of the environment being registered on the retina), casts an image on the right half of *each* retina. The information from the right half of each eye will be transmitted to the right hemisphere. An image in the right visual field will similarly be projected to the left hemisphere. This is how researchers who study differences in the functions of the two cerebral hemispheres can project a visual stimulus to one hemisphere. They present the stimulus slightly to the left or to the right of the midline; the exposure time is too brief to allow the subject to shift the eyes toward the stimulus, and with brief exposures the information does not transfer to the other hemisphere.

? How does information about an object on your right end up in your left hemisphere?

Although it appears that information from both eyes is integrated at the lateral geniculate nuclei (LGN) in Figure 10.5, information from each eye is processed in separate areas of the primary visual cortex (V1). If you close one eye in a research animal, and then stain V1 for cytochrome oxidase (which indicates metabolic activity), only the areas of V1 that were actively processing visual information would be darkly stained. When you look at the tissue under a microscope, you can see clear light and dark bands that appear like a fingerprint. These stripes are called ocular (left and right) dominance columns.

There is a good reason you have two forward-facing eyes, instead of one like the mythical Cyclops or one on each side of your head like many animals. The approximately 6-centimeter (cm) separation of your eyes produces *retinal disparity,* a discrepancy in the location of an object's image on the two retinas. Figure 10.6 shows how the image of distant objects in a scene falls toward the nasal side of each retina and closer objects cast their image in the temporal half. Retinal disparity is detected in the visual cortex, where different neurons fire depending on the amount of lateral displacement. Then in the anterior parietal cortex this information is combined with information about an object's shape and location to provide information about the distance of objects (J.-B. Durand et al., 2007). There are several good demonstrations of retinal disparity; the simplest is to hold your finger a foot (30 cm) in front of you and alternately close one eye and then the other while you notice how your finger moves relative to the background. The ViewMaster 3-D viewer you may have had as a child took advantage of your brain's retinal disparity detectors by presenting each eye with an image photographed at a slightly different angle. 3-D movies use the same principle, but differently polarized lenses in the special glasses separate the two images. A striking 3-D effect can also be obtained without a viewer from stereograms such as those created by Magic Eye.

As the rest of the story of vision unfolds, you will notice three themes that will help you understand how the visual system works: inhibition, modularity, and hierarchical processing. You will learn that neural *inhibition* is just as important as excitation, because it sharpens information beyond the processing capabilities of a system that depends on excitation alone. You will also learn that, like hearing and language, the visual system carries out its functions in discrete specialized structures, or *modules,* which pass information to each other in a serial, *hierarchical* fashion.

? How does retinal disparity help us see 3-D?

CONCEPT CHECK

Take a Minute to Check Your Knowledge and Understanding

- In what ways is human vision adapted for our environment?
- How are the rod and cone systems specialized for different tasks? The two visual pathways?

■ **FIGURE 10.6**   Retinal Disparity.

The image of an object to which the eyes are oriented (A) falls on the fovea, while the image of a more distant object (B) is displaced to the inside of each retina and the image of a closer object (C) is displaced to the outside. This provides information to the brain for depth perception.

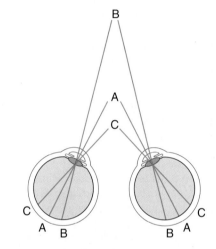

Source: Schwartz, B. L. & Krantz, J. H. (2015).

Color Vision

In Figure 10.1, you saw that there is a correspondence between color and wavelength; this would suggest that color is a property of the light reflected from an object and, therefore, of the object itself. However, wavelength does not always predict color, as Figure 10.7 illustrates. The circle on the left and the circle on the right appear to be different colors, although they reflect exactly the same wavelengths. Just as with the auditory terms *pitch* and *loudness,* the term *color* refers to the observer's experience rather than a characteristic of the object. Thus, it is technically incorrect to say that the light is red or that a book is blue, because *red* and *blue* are experiences that are imposed by the brain. However, in the interest of simplicity, we will be rather casual about this point in future discussions, as long as we understand that "red" and "blue" are experiences rather than object characteristics. To understand the experience of color, we must now examine the neural equipment that we use to produce that experience. Our understanding of color vision has been guided over the past two centuries by two competing theories: the trichromatic theory and the opponent process theory.

■ **FIGURE 10.7**   Independence of Wavelength and Color.

Although the circles are identical, they appear to differ in color due to the color contrast with their backgrounds.

APPLICATION
Restoring Lost Vision

The World Health Organization (2013) estimates that 285 million people worldwide suffer from blindness or impaired vision, but researchers now have several promising strategies for restoring lost vision such as camera-based electrode grids, photosensitive polymer implants, and stem cell therapy. The camera-based electrode grids use a strategy that is like the cochlear implants discussed in Chapter 9, where a glasses-mounted camera converts images into a grid of electrode impulses delivered to the retina. Several other systems are in clinical trials, including one that uses a light-sensitive chip mounted behind the retina. One of its advantages is that it allows the recipient to look around by moving the eyes rather than turning the head (Stingl et al., 2013).

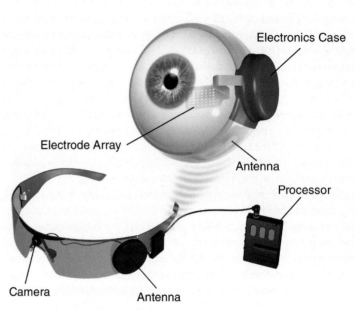

Source: Copyright © 2013 Second Sight Medical Products, Inc.

Of course, the ideal treatment would be to make the damaged retina respond to light on its own, and research teams are making impressive progress to accomplish this. Fortunately, ganglion cells usually survive when diseases such as retinitis pigmentosa damage the rods and cones. A recently designed retinal prosthetic uses photosensitive polymers embedded just behind the retina; the light-sensitive polymers convert light to electrical signals that are picked up by the ganglion cells (see figure). After six months, rats with degenerative blindness had increased levels of activity in the visual cortex and could detect (Maya-Vetencourt et al., 2017). An optogenetic method seeks to restore vision in people who have lost their retinal receptors by inserting a synthetic light-sensitive glutamate channel (called

LiGluR6) into ganglion cells to make them work like photoreceptors (Caporale et al., 2011). In a human clinical trial, retinal stem cell injections produced improved vision or stabilization after six months (W. T. Schmidt, 2015). Finally, there are promising results using gene therapy (see Chapter 2). In one study, vision was restored in mice with damaged retinas when a virus encoding a synthetic form of rhodopsin (channelrhodopsin) was injected (Bi et al., 2006). In another, injection of a pigment gene (*RPE65*) into retinas with a damaged gene has been found safe and effective in restoring vision in animals (Amado et al., 2010). While these methods are not ready for routine implementation in humans, they are demonstrating promise for individuals with vision loss.

Trichromatic Theory

After observing the effect of passing light through a prism, Sir Isaac Newton proposed in 1672 that white light is composed of seven fundamental colors that cannot themselves be resolved into other colors. If there are seven "pure" colors, this would suggest that there must be seven receptors and brain pathways for distinguishing color, just as there are five primary tastes (or six, if the fat receptor is confirmed). In 1852, Hermann von Helmholtz (whose place theory was discussed in Chapter 9) revived an idea of Thomas Young from a half-century earlier. Because combining different amounts of just three colors of light can produce any color, Young and Helmholtz recognized that this must be due to the nature of the visual mechanism rather than the nature of light. They proposed a *trichromatic theory*—now known as the

Young-Helmholtz theory—that just three color processes account for all the colors we are able to distinguish. They chose red, green, and blue as the primary colors because observers cannot resolve these colors into separate components as, for example, you can see red and blue in the color purple. When you watch television or look at an electronic device screen, you see an application of trichromatic color mixing: All the colors you see on the screen are made up different intensities of tiny red, green, and blue dots (pixels) of light. This is illustrated in the color cube in Figure 10.8.

Opponent Process Theory

The trichromatic theory accounted for some of the observations about color perception very well, but it ran into trouble explaining why yellow also appears to observers to be a pure color. Ewald Hering (1878) "solved" this problem by adding yellow to the list of physiologically unique colors. But rather than assuming four color receptors, he asserted that there are only two—one for red *and* green and one for blue *and* yellow. *Opponent process theory* attempts to explain color vision in terms of opposing neural processes. In Hering's version, the photochemical in the red-green receptor is broken down by red light and regenerates in the presence of green light. The chemical in the second type of receptor is broken down in the presence of yellow light and regenerates in the presence of blue light.

Hering proposed this arrangement to explain the phenomenon of *complementary colors,* colors that cancel each other out to produce a neutral gray or white. (Note the spelling of this term; *complementary* means "completing.") In Figure 10.9, the visible spectrum is represented as a circle. This rearrangement of the spectrum makes sense, because violet at one end of the spectrum blends naturally into red at the other end just as easily as the colors adjacent to each other on the spectrum blend into each other. Another reason the color circle makes sense is that any two colors opposite each other on the circle are complementary; mixing equal amounts of light from across the circle results in the sensation of a neutral gray tending toward white, depending on the brightness. An exception to this rule is the combination of red and green; they produce yellow, for reasons you will understand shortly.

Another indication of complementarity is that overstimulation of the eye with one light makes the eye more sensitive to its complement. Stare at a red stimulus for a minute, and you will begin to see a green edge around it; then look at a white wall or a sheet of paper, and you will see a green version of the original object. This experience is called a *negative color aftereffect*; the butcher decorates the inside of the meat case with parsley or other greenery to make the beef look redder. Negative color aftereffect is what one would expect if the wavelengths were affecting the same receptor in opposed directions, as Hering theorized. The flag in Figure 10.10 is a very good interactive demonstration of complementary colors and negative aftereffects.

If this discussion of color mixing seems inconsistent with what you understood in the past, it is probably because you learned the principles of color mixing in an art class. The topic of discussion there was *pigment mixing,* whereas we are talking about *mixing light.* An object appears red to us because it reflects mostly long-wavelength (red) light, while it *absorbs* other wavelengths of light. The effect of light mixing is *additive,* whereas pigment mixing is *subtractive.* If we mix lights, we add wavelengths to the stimulus, but as we mix paints more wavelengths are absorbed. For example, if you mix equal

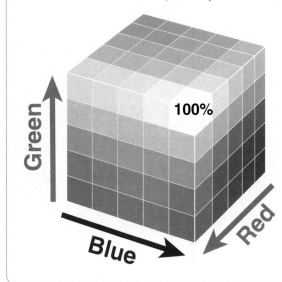

■ **FIGURE 10.8** Color Cube Demonstrating Trichromatic Theory.

All colors are possible by mixing different levels of green, blue, and red. Yellow is a result of high green and red levels with low blue levels, for example.

? How do we distinguish colors?

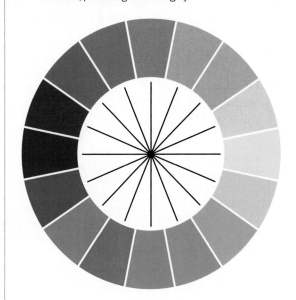

■ **FIGURE 10.9** The Color Circle.

Colors opposite each other are complementary; that is, equal amounts of light in those colors cancel each other out, producing a neutral gray.

■ **FIGURE 10.10**   Complementary Colors and Negative Color Aftereffect.

Stare at the dot in the center of the flag for about a minute, and then look at a white surface (the ceiling or a sheet of paper); you should see a traditional red, white, and blue flag.

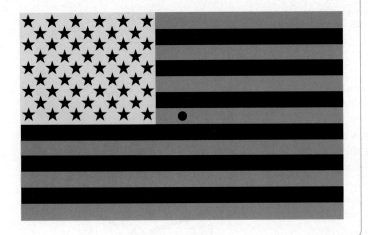

amounts of all wavelengths of light, the result will be white light; mixing paints in the same way produces black because each added pigment absorbs additional wavelengths of light until the result is total absorption and blackness (Figure 10.11).

Now, back to color vision theory. Although Hering's theory did a nice job of explaining complementary colors and the uniqueness of yellow, it received little acceptance. One reason was that researchers had trouble with Hering's assumption of a chemical that would break down in response to one light and regenerate in the presence of another. His theory was, in fact, in error on that point, but developments 100 years later would bring Hering's thinking back to the forefront.

A Combined Theory

The trichromatic and opponent process theories appear to be contradictory. Sometimes this means that one position is wrong and the other is right, but often it means that each of the competing theories is partly correct but just too simple to accommodate all the known facts. Hurvich and Jameson (1957) resolved the conflict with a compromise: They proposed that three types of color receptors—red sensitive, green sensitive, and blue sensitive—are interconnected in an opponent process fashion at the ganglion cells.

Figure 10.12 is a simplified version of how Hurvich and Jameson thought this combined color-processing strategy might work. Long-wavelength light excites "red" cones and the red-green ganglion cell to give the perception of red. Medium-wavelength light excites the "green" cones and inhibits the red-green cell, reducing its firing rate below its spontaneous level and signaling green to the brain. Likewise, short-wavelength light excites "blue" cones, which inhibits the yellow-blue ganglion cell, leading to a perception of blue. Light midway between the sensitivities of the "red" and "green" cones would stimulate both cone types. The firing rate in the red-green ganglion cell would not change, because equal stimulation and excitation from the two cones would cancel out; however, the cones' connections to the yellow-blue ganglion cell are both excitatory, so their combined excitation would excite the ganglion cell to produce a perception of yellow. If all three cones are stimulated at equal intensities, both ganglion cell types receive equal amounts of excitatory and inhibitory stimulation and, therefore, produce a perception of a shade of gray equal to the intensity of the light. According to this combined theory, there are

■ **FIGURE 10.11**

Mixing Lights Is Additive; Mixing Paints Is Subtractive.

The combination of all three primaries (or all colors) of light produces white; the same combination of pigments produces black, which is the lack of color.

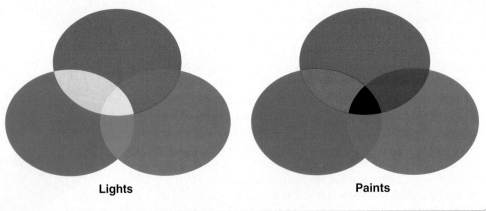

three color processes at the receptors and four beyond the ganglion cells.

This scheme does explain very nicely why yellow would appear pure just like red, green, and blue do. Also, it is easy to understand why certain pairs of colors are complementary instead of producing a blended color. For example, you could have a color that is reddish blue (purple) or greenish yellow (chartreuse) but not a reddish green or a bluish yellow. You can try this out in any drawing program: make a gradient that is red on one side and green on the other, and you'll see that where they meet is gray. Negative aftereffects can be explained as overstimulation "fatiguing" a ganglion cell's response in one direction, causing a rebound in the opposite direction and a subtle experience of the opposing color. By the way, this is our first example of the significance of all that interconnectedness we saw back in Figure 10.4.

Evidence for this combined trichromatic/opponent process theory would be almost a decade away, however, because it depended on the development of more precise measurement capabilities. Support came in two forms. First, researchers produced direct evidence for three color receptors in the retina (K. Brown & Wald, 1964; Dartnall, Bowmaker, & Mollon, 1983; Marks, Dobelle, & MacNichol, 1964). The researchers shone light of selected wavelengths through individual receptors in eyes that had been removed from humans for medical reasons or shortly after their death; they measured the light that passed through to determine which wavelengths had been lost through absorption. The absorbed wavelengths indicated the ones the receptor's photochemical was sensitive to. Figure 10.13 shows the results from a study of this type. Note that there are three distinct color response curves (plus a response curve for rods), just as Hurvich and Jameson predicted. We should point out that the "red" cone's sensitivity is actually closer to orange, but tradition is tradition, so we continue to refer to its preferred color as red.

Let's look at three additional features of these results. Like the tuning curves for frequency we saw in Chapter 9, these curves are not very sharp; each receptor has a sensitivity peak, but its response range is broad and overlaps with that of its neighbors. This means that the medium-wavelength cones could be active because the stimulus is "green" light or because they are being stimulated with intense "blue" light. The system must *compare activity in all three types of cones* to determine which wavelengths you are seeing. This "comparison" does not occur at the level of awareness; it is an automatic neural process, like the one that sharpens frequency discrimination and the activity of coincidence detectors in sound localization.

The second feature is related to the evolution of color vision. Notice that in Figure 10.13 the medium- and long-wavelength curves (green and red, respectively) are distant from the short-wavelength curve (blue) but are very close to each other. Genetic research indicates that the genes for the photopigments in the medium- and long-wavelength cones evolved from a common precursor gene relatively recently (*only* about 35 million

■ **FIGURE 10.12** Hurvich and Jameson's Proposed Interconnections of Cones Provide Four Color Responses and Complementary Colors.

According to their theory, excitation of "red" receptors activates red-green ganglion cells to produce the experience of red; excitation of "green" receptors inhibits the same ganglion cells, resulting in an experience of green. A sensation of yellow occurs when "red" and "green" receptors stimulate yellow-blue ganglion cells equally. Inhibition of those ganglion cells by "blue" receptors produces a sensation of blue.

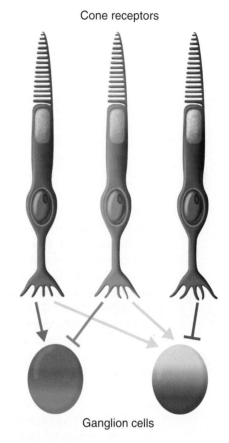

Source: Based on the findings of De Valois et al. (1966).

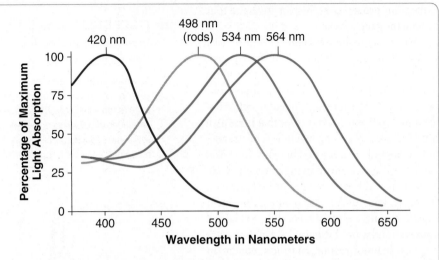

Source: Adapted from "Visual Pigments of Rods and Cones in Human Retina," by Bowmaker and Dartnall, 1980, *Journal of Physiology, 298,* pp. 501–511. Copyright 1980, with permission from John Wiley & Sons, Inc.

■ **FIGURE 10.13** Relative Absorption of Light of Various Wavelengths by Visual Receptors.

Note that each type of cone responds best to wavelengths corresponding to blue, green, and red light, though each responds to other wavelengths as well.

years ago), but the genes for the short-wavelength cones and for the rod receptors split off from their precursor much earlier. Indeed, the "red" and "green" genes are adjacent to each other on the X chromosome, and they are 98% identical in DNA (Gegenfurtner & Kiper, 2003). Because the genes are on the X chromosome, red-green color blindness is a sex-linked trait and tends to affect males many times more than females. (See the discussion of X-linked traits in Chapter 1.)

Third, a recent finding suggests that the bulk of red- and green-sensitive cones respond equally to all wavelengths of light, and only a subset respond to these particular colors (Figure 10.14; Sabesan, Schmidt, Tuten, & Roorda, 2016). Presumably, this ensures that we see the fine details of objects clearly regardless of color, and the need for sharpness overrules the need for precise color perception. This tendency to detect all wavelengths in the majority of cones may be useful for some proposed retinal damage therapies (see the earlier Application on restoring vision), in that improving any cone function (regardless of color sensitivity) will increase light perception in those with vision loss.

Trichromatic vision is certainly beneficial in appreciating art, but we might well ask what evolutionary benefits compelled its development. An obvious advantage was an enhanced ability to distinguish ripe red fruit among green foliage, and to distinguish young, tender leaves from darker ones. In addition, comparisons of primate genomes indicate intriguing parallels between the appearance of genes for trichromacy, the decreases in olfactory and pheromone receptor genes, and the development of visual sexual signals such as the reddened and swollen sexual skin in female baboons and Old World monkeys (Gilad, Wiebe, Przeworski, Lancet, & Pääbo, 2004; J. Zhang & Webb, 2003). The importance of the red-green end of the spectrum is suggested by the fact that only 10% of human cones have their sensitivity in the blue end of the spectrum (see Figure 10.14). Analyzing 5,000 photographs from the savannas of Botswana, researchers concluded that this balance matches the distribution of colors in the environment in which humans are believed to have evolved (Garrigan et al., 2010).

Additional confirmation of the trichromatic/opponent process theory came when researchers found color-opponent cells in monkeys, both in the retina and in the lateral geniculate nucleus of the thalamus (De Valois, 1960; De Valois, Abramov, & Jacobs, 1966; Gouras, 1968). Figure 10.15 shows two types of opponent cells, one that is excited by red and inhibited by green (R+G−) and one that is excited by yellow and inhibited by blue (Y+B−); Russell De Valois and his colleagues (1966) identified two additional types that were the inverse of the previous two: green excitatory/red inhibitory (G+R−) and blue excitatory/yellow inhibitory (B+Y−).

A surprise was that some of the color-opponent ganglion cells receive their input from cones that are arranged in two concentric circles (Gouras, 1968; Wiesel & Hubel, 1966). The cones in the center and those in the periphery have color-complementary sensitivities (see Figure 10.15). Of course, the yellow response is provided by the combined output of "red" and "green" cones. Why all this complexity? First, the opposition of cones at the ganglion cells provides wavelength discrimination that individual cones are incapable of producing (E. B. Goldstein, 1999)—an example of the "neural comparison" we referred to earlier. The concentric-circle receptor fields also enhance information about color contrast in objects. This mode of information sharpening will become clearer when we look at how the retina distinguishes the edge of an object.

A theory is considered successful if it is consistent with the known facts, can explain those facts, and can predict new findings. The combined trichromatic and opponent process color theory meets all three criteria: (1) It is consistent with the observation that all colors can be produced by using red, green, and blue light. (2) It can explain why observers regard red, green, blue, *and* yellow as pure colors. It also explains complementary colors, negative aftereffects, and the impossibility of color experiences such as greenish red. (3) It predicted the discovery of three photopigments and of the excitatory/inhibitory neural connections at the ganglion cells.

Color Blindness

Color blindness (or the more accurate term, color vision deficiency) occurs when an individual has a poor or absent response from one or more cone types. It is an intriguing curiosity; but more than that, it has played an important role in our understanding of color perception by scuttling inadequate theories and providing the inspiration for new ones. There are very few completely color-blind people—about 1 in every

FIGURE 10.14 Cones Respond to More Than Specific Colors.

The inner circles denote the cones' color preferences, either red or green. (Blue-sensitive cones were not tested but are indicated by solid blue dots.) The proportion of red or green in the outer circle indicates how much the cone is specialized for that color, *versus* its ability to detect all wavelengths (indicated in white).

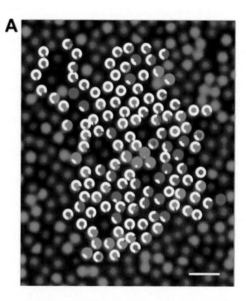

Source: Figure 1a from Sabesan, R., Schmidt, B. P., Tuten, W. S., & Roorda, A. (2016). The elementary representation of spatial and color vision in the human retina. *Science Advances*, 2, e1600797-e1600797.

FIGURE 10.15 Receptive Fields of Color-Opponent Ganglion Cells.

The cones in the center and the cones in the periphery respond to colors that are complementary to each other. The center cones excite the ganglion cell, and the cones in the periphery inhibit it.

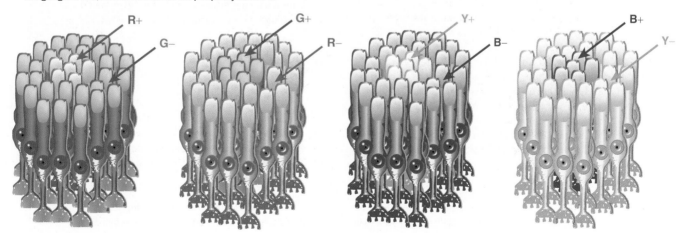

Source: Based on the findings of De Valois et al. (1966).

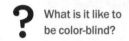

FIGURE 10.16 A Test for Color Blindness.

This is one of the plates from the Ishihara test for color blindness. Most people see the number 74; the person with color deficiency sees the number 21.

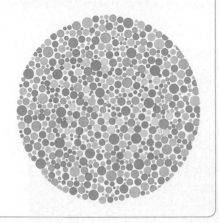

 What is it like to be color-blind?

100,000. They usually have an inherited lack of cones; limited to rod vision, they see in shades of gray, they are very light sensitive, and they have poor visual acuity. More typically a person is partly color-blind, due to a defect in one of the cone systems rather than a lack of cones.

There are two major types of retinal color blindness. A person who is red-green color-blind sees these two colors but is unable to distinguish between them (this is either protanopia with absence of red receptors, or deuteranopia with absence of green receptors). We know something about what color-blind people experience by noting which colors color-blind people confuse and from studying a few rare individuals who are color-blind in only one eye. When a red-green color-blind colleague of one of the authors was describing his experience of color, he explained that green grass appeared to be the same color as peanut butter! We're not sure what peanut butter actually looked like to him, but he said that he found grass and trees "very beautiful." People in the much rarer second color-blind group do not perceive blue (tritanopia, due to a defect on Chromosome 7), so their world appears in variations of red and green. Many partly color-blind individuals are unaware that they see the world differently from the rest of us. Color vision deficiencies can be detected by having the subject match or sort colored objects or with a test like the one illustrated in Figure 10.16.

Red-green color-blind individuals show a deficiency in either the red end of the spectrum or in the green portion; this suggests that the person lacks either the appropriate cone or the photochemical. Acuity is normal in both groups, so there cannot be a lack of cones. Some are unusually sensitive to green light, and the rest are sensitive to red light; this suggests that in one case the normally red-sensitive cones are filled with

---

IN THE NEWS

BEING A COLOR-BLIND SPORTS FAN

Having color vision deficiency is not easy, and nowhere is it more problematic than in fast-paced team sports like football. It can be hard enough to keep track of the action as 22 men run around the field executing complicated plays, but it is much more difficult if you can't tell the two teams apart.

NFL teams typically use different uniform colors and styles to distinguish between the home and visiting teams, but in 2015 a new fad in uniform design called Color Rush made this task much more difficult. In Color Rush the jerseys, pants, and socks are all the same vibrant color (or color accent). For most of us it was easy to distinguish between the fluorescent orange uniforms worn by the Buffalo Bills and the fluorescent green uniforms of the New York Jets in their November 2015 game. But for someone with red-green color blindness, the orange Bills uniforms looked exactly like the green Jets uniforms. See http://goo.gl/CsFzqk for what this looked like to a colorblind individual. Because of this confusion, the NFL instituted a new

policy requiring that one team wear white uniforms instead of the Color Rush jerseys. This is not just a problem with sports but is true in advertisements, TV shows, and other forms of media like safety signs. For this reason, most commercial image editing software products have tools to simulate color blindness, so that color issues can be detected during the production process.

THOUGHT QUESTIONS

1. How do cone deficiencies impact the perceptions of humans?

2. What steps can be taken to ensure that all people, including people who experience color blindness, can clearly perceive information in sporting events and advertisements?

For more information, visit edge.sagepub.com/garrett5e and select the Chapter 10 study resources.

green-sensitive photochemical and in the other the normally green-sensitive cones are filled with red-sensitive chemical. The In the News feature offers one example of the kind of difficulties this deficiency can pose for an individual.

Take a Minute to Check Your Knowledge and Understanding

- Summarize the three color vision theories described here.
- What is the benefit of the color-opposed concentric circle receptor fields?
- What causes color blindness?

Form Vision

Just as the auditory cortex is organized as a map of the cochlea, the visual cortex contains a map of the retina. Russell De Valois and his colleagues demonstrated this point when they presented the image in Figure 10.17a to monkeys that had been injected with radioactive 2-deoxyglucose. The animals were sacrificed and their brains placed on photographic film. Because the more active neurons absorbed more radioactive glucose, they exposed the film more darkly in the autoradiograph in Figure 10.17b; this produced an image of the stimulus that appears to be wrapped around the monkey's occipital lobe (Tootell et al., 1982).

This result tells us that, just as there is a tonotopic map of the basilar membrane in the auditory cortex, we have a *retinotopic map* in the visual cortex, meaning that adjacent retinal receptors activate adjacent cells in the visual cortex. However, this does not tell us how we see images; transmitting an object's image to the cortex like a television picture does not amount to perception of the object. Object perception is a two-stage affair. In this section we will discuss *form vision,* the detection of an object's boundaries and features (such as texture). We will discuss the second component, object recognition, a bit later. The story that unfolds here is about more than perception; it provides a model for understanding how the brain processes information in general. It is also a story that begins not in the cortex but in the retina itself.

■ **FIGURE 10.17** Deoxyglucose Autoradiograph Showing Retinotopic Mapping in Visual Cortex.

Monkeys were given radioactive 2-deoxyglucose and then shown the design in (a). They were sacrificed, and a section of their visual cortical tissue was placed on photographic film. The exposed film showed a pattern of activation (b) that matched the design.

(a)

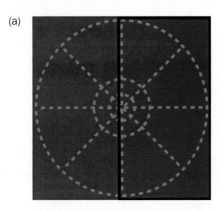

(b)

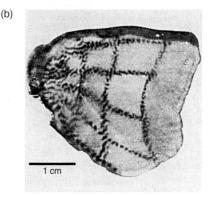

1 cm

Source: From "Deoxyglucose Analysis of Retinotopic Organization in Primate Striate Cortex," by R. B. H. Tootell et al.," *Science*, 218, pp. 902–904. Reprinted with permission from AAAS.

Contrast Enhancement and Edge Detection

Detecting an object's boundaries is the first step in form vision. The nervous system often exaggerates especially important sensory information. In the case of boundaries, the retina uses *lateral inhibition,* where each neuron's activity inhibits the activity of its neighbors and in turn they inhibit its activity, to enhance the contrast in brightness that defines an object's edge. To demonstrate this enhancement for yourself, look at the

APPLICATION
Neural Bases of Visual Illusions

(a)

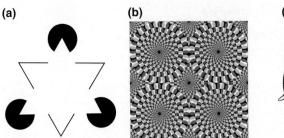

(b)

(c)

As you have been learning in this chapter, visual signals are processed at multiple levels; the Mach band illusion, for example, occurs at the retinal level, whereas other features of the visual world are not processed until the cortex. Illusions are more than entertaining novelties; they also can tell us how the visual mechanism converts retinal stimulation into a meaningful visual experience. This includes how we distinguish the edges or boundaries of objects, separate objects from each other, and make sense of the contents of an image. Look at the Kanizsa triangle (a) for instance. The white triangle you see is an illusion, created when the cortical area V2 "fills in" the triangle's boundaries that are suggested by the missing portions of the circles and the actual triangle (von der Heyde, Peterhans, & Baumgartner, 1984). Further up the visual processing pathway, the medial temporal lobe (MT) is responsible for extracting motion information. The middle image (b), called the Fraser-Wilcox or peripheral drift illusion, fools your brain into thinking the circles are rotating even though you obviously are looking at a printed page. This is because the MT interprets the rapid high-contrast alternations between the yellow and blue, which are processed by the same ganglion cells, as being in motion. Finally, the cortex is responsible for combining features from the two processing streams into a singular experience. In the last image in the figure (c), how many legs does the elephant have? Is there anything odd about them? It may take a bit of study to see why the elephant is clearly an impossible animal—understanding what you're seeing here requires the contribution of your frontal lobes (Shepard, 1990). If you want to see more visual illusions, especially moving ones, check out the Illusion of the Year website listed at the end of the chapter.

Hermann grid illusion in Figure 10.18a and the Mach band illusion in Figure 10.18b. The Hermann grid is the more dramatic of the two illusions, but the simplicity of the Mach band graphic makes it easier to explain, so we will focus on it. Each bar in the Mach band image is consistent in brightness across its width, but it looks a bit darker on the left and a bit lighter on the right than it does in the middle. (If you don't see a difference at the edges, you may notice that the bars seem slightly curved. This is because the illusion suggests subtle shadowing on the left side of each bar.) An illusion is not simply an error of perception, but an exaggeration of a normal perceptual process, which makes illusions very useful in studying perception. See the Application for more on visual illusions.

> *Deceptions of the senses are the truths of perception.*
>
> —Johannes Purkinje

Figure 10.19 will help you understand how your retinas produce the illusion using lateral inhibition. In this case, the inhibition is delivered by horizontal cells to nearby synapses of receptors with bipolar cells. The critical point in the illustration is at ganglion cells 7 and 8. Ganglion cell 7 is inhibited less than ganglion cells 1 to 6; this is because the receptors to its right are receiving very little stimulation and producing low levels of inhibition. This lesser inhibition of ganglion cell 7 creates a sensation of a lighter band to the left of the border, as indicated at the bottom of the illustration. Similarly, ganglion cell 8 is inhibited more than its neighbors to the right, because the receptors to its left are receiving greater stimulation and producing more inhibition. As a result, the bar appears darker to the right of the border.

Actually, this description is more appropriate for the eye of the horseshoe crab, where lateral inhibition was originally confirmed by electrical recording; in fact, the graph in Figure 10.18d was based on data from the horseshoe crab's eye (Ratliff & Hartline, 1959). The principle is the same in the mammalian eye, but each ganglion cell's receptive field is made up of several receptors arranged in circles, like the color-coded circular fields we saw earlier (Kuffler, 1953). Light in the center of the field has the opposite effect on the ganglion cell from light in the surround. In *on-center* cells, light in the center increases firing, and light in the *off surround* reduces firing below the resting levels. Other ganglion cells have an *off center* and an *on surround*. Figure 10.20 illustrates these two types of ganglion cells.

These ganglion cells are good at detecting spots of light or darkness, but their contribution to vision is as light–dark contrast detectors (Hubel, 1982). Look at the illustrations in Figure 10.21. Light falling across the entire field will have little or no effect on the ganglion cell's firing rate, because the excitation and inhibition cancel each other out (Figure 10.21a). Light that falls only on the off surround will suppress firing in the ganglion cell (Figure 10.21b). But the ganglion cell's firing will be at its maximum when the stimulus falls on all of the on center and only a part of the off surround, as in Figure 10.21c. Figure 10.21d represents what happens in an off-center ganglion cell when its receptors are stimulated by an object that is darker than the background (or by a shadow). Because the dark image falls across the entire off center but only part of the on surround, the cell's activity is high. We are so accustomed to thinking of vision in terms of light stimulation that we neglect the importance of dark stimulation. The fact is that off ganglion cells outnumber on cells two to one in the human retina, and for good reason. When researchers analyzed photos taken in several settings ranging from the streets of Philadelphia to

■ **FIGURE 10.18**   Demonstration of Lateral Inhibition.

(a) In the Hermann grid illusion, lateral inhibition causes you to see small, grayish blotches at the intersections of the large squares. (b) The Mach band illusion is another example. Each band is consistent in brightness across its width, as shown in the graph of light intensity in (c). But where the bands meet, you experience a slight enhancement in brightness at the edge of the lighter band and a decrease in brightness at the edge of the darker band (e.g., at points B and C). This effect is represented graphically in (d). Exaggeration of brightness contrast at edges helps us see the boundaries of objects.

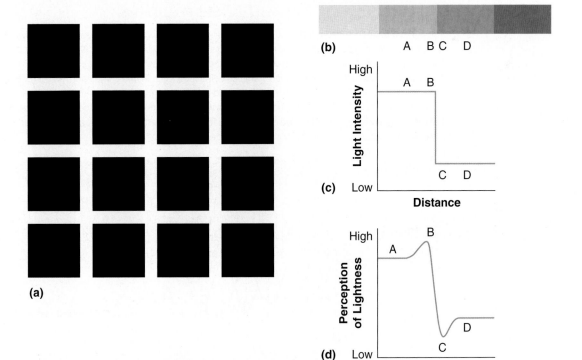

Sources: (a) Based on Hermann (1870). (b) From *Mach Bands: Quantitative Studies on Neural Networks in the Retina* (fig. 3.25, p. 107), by F. Ratcliff, 1965. San Francisco: Holden-Day. Copyright © Holden-Day Inc.

the plains of Africa, they found that dark-on-light contrasts were 10%–20% more numerous than light contrasts (Ratliff, Borghuis, Kao, Sterling, & Balasubramanian, 2010). When they created a mathematical model of the ideal system for processing these scenes, it predicted the smaller and more numerous off cells found in the retina. We will see the significance of this light–dark contrast mechanism in the next section.

Hubel and Wiesel's Theory

How do we detect objects' boundaries?

Cells in the lateral geniculate nucleus have circular receptive fields just like the ganglion cells from which they receive their input. The receptive fields of visual neurons in the cortex, however, turn out to be surprisingly different. David Hubel and Torsten Wiesel (1959) were probing the visual cortex of anesthetized cats as they projected visual stimuli on a screen in front of a cat. Their electrode was connected to an auditory amplifier so they could listen for indications of active cells. One day, they were manipulating a glass slide with a black dot on it in the projector and getting only vague and inconsistent responses

> when suddenly over the audio monitor the cell went off like a machine gun. After some fussing and fiddling we found out what was happening. The response had nothing to do with the black dot. As the glass slide was inserted its edge was casting onto the retina a faint but sharp shadow, a straight dark line on a light background. (Hubel, 1982, p. 517)

Hubel and Wiesel then began exploring the receptive fields of these cortical cells by projecting bars of light on the screen. They found that an actively responding cell would decrease its responding when the stimulus was moved to another location or rotated to a slightly different angle. Figure 10.22 shows the changes in response in one cell as the orientation of the stimulus was varied. Hubel and Wiesel called these cortical cells simple cells. *Simple cells* respond to a line or an edge that is at a specific orientation and at a specific place on the retina.

■ **FIGURE 10.19**   The Neural Basis of the Mach Band Illusion.

The bar at the top represents the middle two bands from Figure 10.18b. Red arrows indicate excitation, and gray arrows indicate inhibition. All ganglion cells are activated, but ganglion cell 7 is activated most; like 1 through 6, it receives more stimulation from the brighter stimulus, but it receives less inhibition from the receptors to the right. Likewise, ganglion cell 8 receives minimal stimulation, plus it receives more inhibition from the receptors to the left than do cells 9 through 15. As a result, the light bar appears lighter at its border with the dark bar, which in turn appears darker at its border. (Cells between the receptors and ganglion cells have been omitted for simplicity. Also, you would see some gradation of contrasts, because the inhibitory connections extend farther than the adjacent cell.)

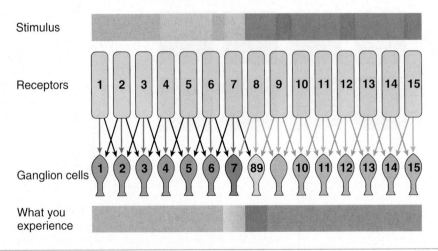

■ FIGURE 10.20 Effect of Light on Center and Surround of Receptive Field.

The receptive fields and ganglion cells are shown in cross section. The connecting cells between the receptors and the ganglion cells have been omitted for simplicity.

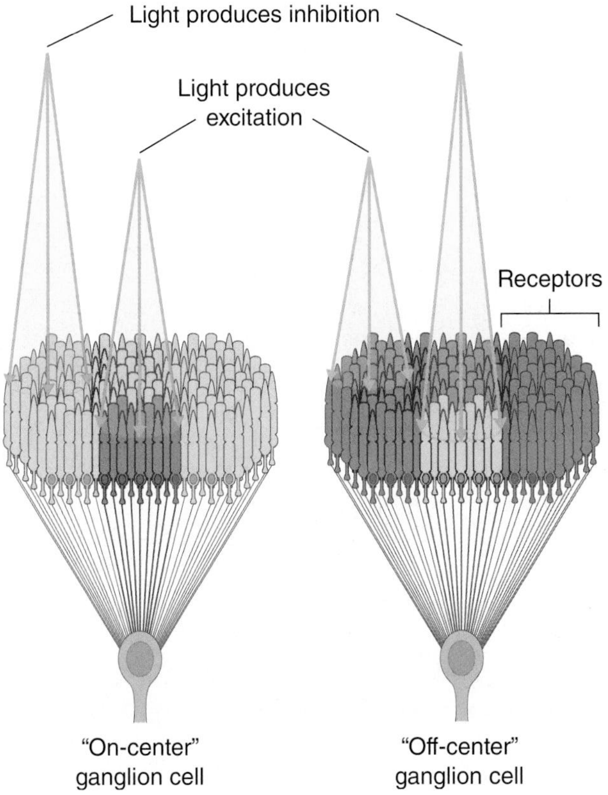

Light produces inhibition

Light produces excitation

Receptors

"On-center" ganglion cell

"Off-center" ganglion cell

■ FIGURE 10.21 Effects of a Border on an On-Center and an Off-Center Ganglion Cell.

The receptors shown in (a)–(c) are connected to an on-center ganglion cell, and those in (d) are connected to an off-center cell. The vertical marks on the blue bars indicate neural responses; the yellow line underneath indicates when the light was on, and the dark line indicates presence of the dark image. Notice that the greatest activity occurs in the ganglion cell when the (appropriate) stimulus falls on all of the center but less than the entire surround.

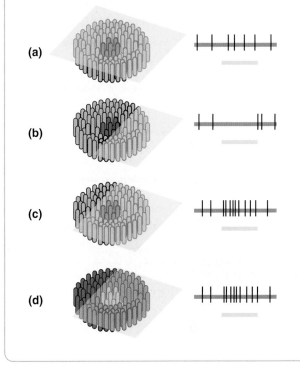

(a)

(b)

(c)

(d)

How can we explain the surprising shift in specialization in these cortical cells? Imagine several contrast-detecting circular fields arranged in a straight line, like those in Figure 10.23. (Notice that the fields overlap each other; by now you shouldn't be surprised that receptors would share their output with multiple ganglion cells.) Then, connect the outputs of their ganglion cells to a single cell in the cortex—one of Hubel and Wiesel's simple cells. You now have a mechanism for detecting not just spots of light–dark contrast but a contrasting edge, such as in the border of an object that is lighter or darker than its background. Fields with on centers would detect a light edge, like the one in the figure, and a series of circular fields with off centers would detect a dark edge.

In other layers of the cortex, Hubel and Wiesel found *complex cells,* which continue to respond when a line or an edge moves to a different location, as long as it is not too far from the original site. They explained the complex cell's ability to continue responding in essentially the same way they explained the sensitivity of simple cells. They assumed that complex cells receive input from several simple cells that have the same orientation sensitivity but whose fields are adjacent to each other on the retina. This arrangement is illustrated in Figure 10.24. Notice that as the edge moves horizontally, different simple cells will take over, but the same complex cell will continue responding. However, if the edge rotates to a different orientation, this complex cell

■ **FIGURE 10.22**   Responses to Lines at Different Orientations in a Simple Cell Specialized for Vertical Lines.

The vertical hatch marks represent neural responses, and the yellow line underneath indicates when the stimulus occurred. Notice that the response was greatest when the line was closest to the cell's "preferred" orientation (vertical) and least when the orientation was most discrepant. In the last example, the response was diminished because the stimulus failed to cover the cell's entire field (indicated by the stimulus being off-center of the crosshair).

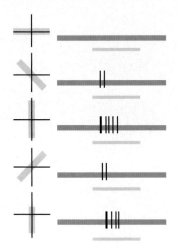

Source: From "Receptive Fields of Single Neurons in the Cat's Striate Cortex," by D. H. Hubel and T. N. Wiesel, 1959, *Journal of Physiology*, 148, pp. 574–591, Fig 3. © 1959 by The Physiology Society. Reprinted with permission from John Wiley & Sons, Inc.

■ **FIGURE 10.23**   Hubel and Wiesel's Explanation for Responses of Simple Cells.

When the edge is in this position, the ganglion cell for each of the circular fields increases its firing. (The fields shown here have on centers.) The ganglion cells are connected to the same simple cell, which also increases firing, indicating that an edge has been detected. This particular arrangement would be specialized for a vertical light edge.

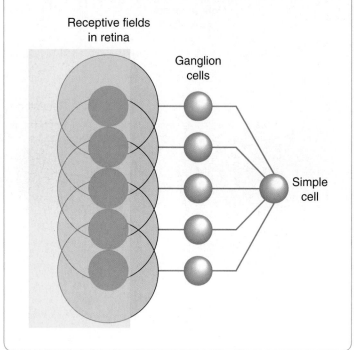

will stop responding, and another complex cell specific for that orientation will take over. Connecting several simple cells to a single complex cell enables the complex cell not only to keep track of an edge as it moves but also to *detect* movement.

The feasibility of this kind of arrangement has received support from an interesting source—artificial neural networks. Lau, Stanley, and Dan (2002) trained a network so that its output "neurons" gave the same responses to bar-shaped stimuli as those recorded from complex cells in cats. Then they examined the hidden processing layer and found that those "neurons" had rearranged their connections to approximate simple cells, complete with "on" and "off" regions in their receptive fields as well as directional sensitivity. In an earlier study, a neural network was trained to recognize curved visual objects (Lehky & Sejnowski, 1990). Its "neurons" spontaneously developed sensitivity to bars or edges of light even though they had never been exposed to such stimuli, suggesting that the Hubel-Wiesel model is a very versatile one.

But so far, Hubel and Wiesel had seen only the beginnings of the intricate neural organization that makes visual perception possible. They lowered electrodes perpendicularly through a monkey's striate cortex; as the electrode passed through simple and complex cells, the cells' preferred width and length changed, but they had the same orientation (Hubel & Wiesel, 1974). As the researchers moved the electrode slightly to the side, the preferred orientation of those cells shifted slightly but systematically in a clockwise or counterclockwise direction; over a distance of 0.5–1.0 mm, the orientation would progress through the complete circle. A complete 360-degree "set" of preferred orientations tends to be organized

■ **FIGURE 10.24** Hubel and Wiesel's Explanation for Responses of Complex Cells.

A complex cell receives input from several simple cells, each of which serves a group of circular fields (as in Figure 10.23). As a result, the complex cell continues to respond as the illuminated edge moves to the left or to the right. (Ganglion cells have been eliminated for simplicity.)

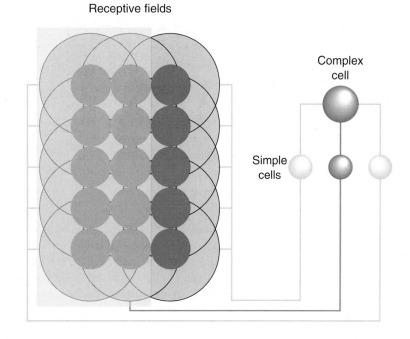

Receptive fields

Complex cell

Simple cells

around a common point, forming what are called orientation pinwheels or whorls (Figure 10.25a and b; Yacoub, Harel, & Ugurbil, 2008). This arrangement is repeated in the adjacent cortex, with the input coming from an adjacent part of the retina. This sort of organization is typical of the cortex's efficiency in processing and transmitting information. Connections mostly run up and down in columns, with much shorter lateral connections. In addition, similar functions are clustered together, increasing communication speed and reducing energy requirements.

Hubel and Wiesel shared the Nobel Prize for their work in 1981. However, their model has limitations—some would say problems. For one thing, it accounts for the detection of boundaries, but it is questionable whether edge detection cells can also handle the surface details that give depth and character to an image.

Spatial Frequency Theory

Although some cortical cells respond best to edges (Albrecht, De Valois, & Thorell, 1980; De Valois, Thorell, & Albrecht, 1985; von der Heydt, Peterhans, & Dürsteler, 1992), other cells apparently are not so limited. Think of an edge as an abrupt or high-frequency change in brightness. The more gradual changes in brightness across the surface of an object are low-frequency changes. According to De Valois, some complex cells are "tuned" to respond to the high frequencies found in an object's border, while others are tuned to low frequencies, for example, in the slow transition from light to shadow that gives depth to the features of a face (De Valois et al., 1985). Some cells respond better to "gratings" of alternating light and dark bars—which contain a particular combination of spatial frequencies—than they do to lines and edges. According to *spatial frequency theory,* visual cortical cells do a Fourier frequency analysis of the luminosity variations in a scene (see Chapter 9 to review Fourier analysis). According to this view, different visual cortical cells have a variety of sensitivities, not just those required to detect edges (Albrecht et al., 1980; De Valois et al., 1985).

A few photographs should help you understand what we mean by spatial frequencies, as well as the importance of low frequencies. The picture in Figure 10.26a was prepared by having a computer average the amount of light over large areas in a photograph; the result was a number of high-frequency transitions, and the image is not very meaningful. In Figure 10.26b, the computer filtered out the high frequencies,

■ **FIGURE 10.25**

Orientations in Primary
Visual Cortex.

(a) Preferred angle of a bar of
light rotates around a fixed spot,
forming what is called an orientation
"pinwheel." (b) Orientation
expressed as an angular graph.
The colors are added to visualize the
changes in orientation angle.

(a)

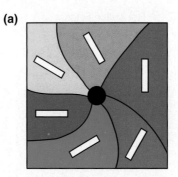

(b)

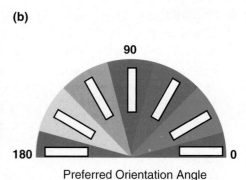

90

180   0

Preferred Orientation Angle

? Is spatial frequency theory a better explanation?

producing more gradual changes between light and dark (low frequencies). It seems paradoxical that blurring an image would make it more recognizable, but blurring eliminates the sharp boundaries. You can get the same effect from Figure 10.26a by looking at it from a distance or by squinting. In Figure 10.26c, the Spanish artist Salvadore Dali incorporated the illusion in one of his more famous paintings. A real-life example in Figure 10.27 suggests what our visual world might be like if we were limited to high frequencies or low frequencies.

So far, we have dealt only with the simplest aspects of visual perception. But we also are able to recognize an object as an object, assign it color under varied lighting conditions, and detect its movement. Attempting to explain these capabilities will provide challenge enough for the rest of this chapter.

CONCEPT CHECK

Take a Minute to Check Your Knowledge and Understanding

- Explain how the opponent arrangement of a ganglion cell's field enhances brightness contrast.
- How did Hubel and Wiesel explain our ability to detect an edge, the orientation of an edge or a line, and an edge or a line that changed its location?
- How do Hubel and Wiesel's theory and the spatial frequency theory differ?

■ **FIGURE 10.26**   Illustration of High and Low Frequencies in a Visual Scene.

(a) An image limited to abrupt changes in brightness (high spatial frequencies) is not as meaningful as (b) one that has both high- and low-frequency information. The image in (b) is the same image as (a), except that the edges have been blurred. (c) Salvador Dali's 1976 painting *Gala Contemplating the Mediterranean Sea Which at Twenty Meters Becomes a Portrait of Abraham Lincoln.* Look closely and you will see (a) rather than Dali's wife Gala; squint your eyes and you will see (b).

(a)

(b)

(c)

Sources: (a) and (b) From "Masking in Visual Recognition: Effects of Two-Dimensional Filtered Noise," by L. D. Harmon and B. Julesz, *Science, 180,* pp. 1194–1197. Reprinted with permission from AAAS. (c) © 2010 Salvador Dalí, Gala-Salvador Dalí Foundation/Artists Rights Society (ARS), New York.

■ **FIGURE 10.27**   The Role of High and Low Frequencies in Vision.

(a) The original photo; (b) the same photo with low frequencies removed; (c) the photo with high frequencies removed. Notice how high-frequency changes in contrast define borders and fine details, while low frequencies reveal distinguishing characteristics through shadow and texture.

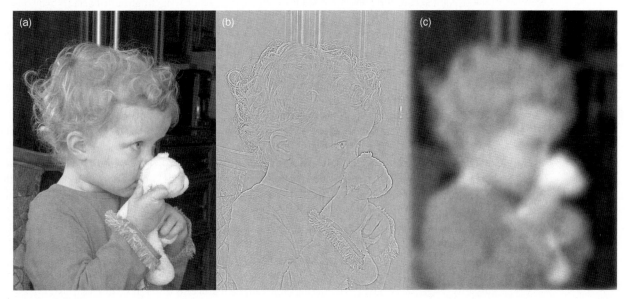

Source: © Bob Garrett.

The Perception of Objects, Color, and Movement

One of the more interesting characteristics of the visual system is how it dissects an image into its various components and analyzes them in different parts of the brain. The separation begins in the retina and increases as visual information flows through all four lobes of the brain, with locations along the way carrying out analyses of color, movement, and other features of the visual scene. Thus, we will see how visual processing is, as mentioned earlier, both modular and hierarchical. *Modular processing* refers to the segregation of the various components of processing into separate locations. *Hierarchical processing* means that lower levels of the nervous system analyze their information and pass the results on to the next higher level for further analysis.

Some neuroscientists reject the modular notion, arguing that any visual function is instead *distributed,* meaning that it occurs across a relatively wide area of the brain. One study found evidence that sensitivity to faces, for example, is scattered over a large area in the temporal lobe (Haxby et al., 2001). Research has not resolved the modular-distributed controversy, leaving researchers to quarrel over the interpretation of studies that seem to support one view or the other (J. D. Cohen & Tong, 2001). Vision may well involve a mix of modular and distributed functioning, rather like the arrangement we saw for language. With this thought in mind, we will consider what is known about the pathways and functional locations in the visual system.

The Two Pathways of Visual Analysis

Most visual information follows two routes from the retina through the brain, which make up the *parvocellular system* and the *magnocellular system* (Livingstone & Hubel, 1988; P. H. Schiller & Logothetis, 1990). Parvocellular ganglion cells are smaller than magnocellular cells, account for the large majority of ganglion cells, and are most numerous in the fovea. They have circular receptive fields that are small and color opponent, which suits them for the specialties of the *parvocellular system,* the discrimination of fine detail and color. Magnocellular ganglion cells have large circular receptive fields that are brightness opponent and respond rapidly but only briefly to stimulation. As a result, the *magnocellular system* is specialized for brightness contrast and for movement.

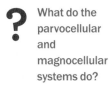

What do the parvocellular and magnocellular systems do?

We see evidence of differences in the two systems in our everyday lives. The simplest example is that at dusk our sensitivity to light increases, but we lose our ability to see color and detail. You cannot read a newspaper under such conditions or color coordinate tomorrow's outfit, because the high-resolution, color-sensitive parvocellular system is nearly nonfunctional. The magnocellular system's sensitivity to movement is most obvious in your peripheral vision. Hold your arms outstretched to the side while you look straight ahead, and move your hands slowly forward while wriggling your fingers. When you just notice your fingers moving, stop. Notice that you can barely see your fingers but you are very sensitive to their movement. Figure 10.28 is a striking demonstration of another capability of the magnocellular system, depth perception. Notice that you see considerable depth in (a); this is because the bicycle differs from the background in brightness, so the image stimulates primarily the magnocellular system. The bicycle in (b) looks "flat"; the image has color contrast but little brightness contrast, so it stimulates the magnocellular system minimally.

? What are the functions of the ventral and dorsal streams?

Both pathways travel to the lateral geniculate nucleus and then to the primary visual cortex, which is also known as V1. Although the two systems are highly interconnected, the parvocellular system dominates the *ventral stream,* which flows from the visual cortex into the temporal lobes, and the magnocellular system dominates the *dorsal stream* from the visual cortex to the parietal lobes (Figure 10.29). Like the two auditory pathways, the ventral stream is often referred to as involved with the "what" of visual processing, and the dorsal stream with the "where." Most of the research on this topic has been done with monkeys, but the two pathways have been confirmed with PET scans in humans (Ungerleider & Haxby, 1994).

Beyond V1, the ventral stream passes through V2 and into V4, which is mostly concerned with color perception. It then projects to the inferior temporal cortex, which is the lower boundary of the temporal lobe; this area shows a remarkable specialization for object recognition, which we will examine shortly.

Magnocellular neurons arrive in V1 in areas that are responsive to orientation, movement, and retinal disparity (Poggio & Poggio, 1984). The dorsal stream then proceeds through V2 to V5, also known as MT because it is on the middle temporal gyrus in the monkey; neurons there have strong directional sensitivity, which contributes to the perception of movement. The dorsal stream travels then to the posterior parietal cortex, the area just behind the somatosensory cortex; its role is primarily to locate objects in space, but the behavioral implications of its functions are far more important than that simple statement suggests.

■ **FIGURE 10.28**

Color Contrast and Brightness Contrast Stimulate Different Visual Systems.

Image (a) has considerable brightness contrast, so it mostly stimulates the magnocellular system, giving an appearance of depth. Image (b) consists of color contrast, which provides little stimulation to the magnocellular system.

(a)

(b)

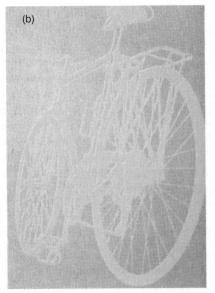

■ **FIGURE 10.29**   The Ventral "What" and Dorsal "Where" Streams of Visual Processing.

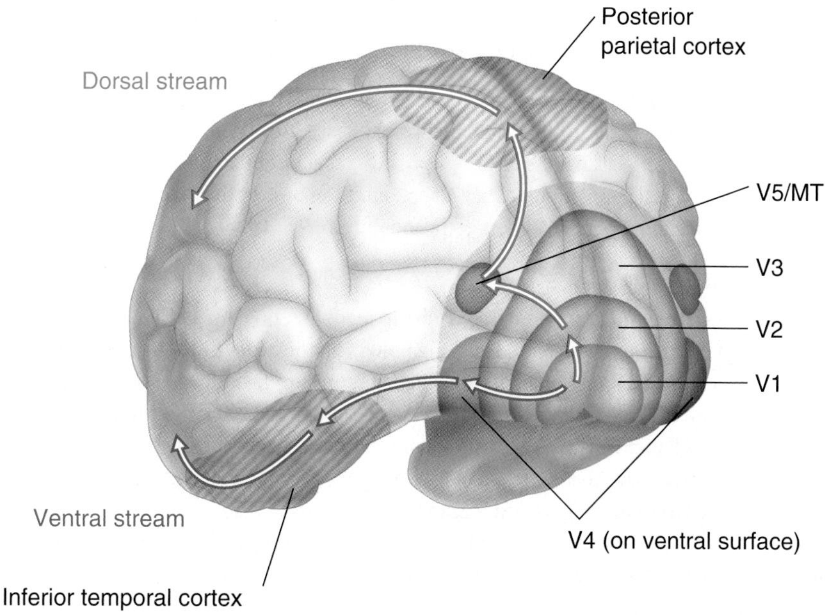

Movement perception is a good example of how modular and distributed processing work together. V5/MT and a nearby area that receives input from MT, known as MST (for medial superior temporal area), appear to be the most important areas for perceiving movement. They receive most of their input from the magnocellular pathway, including complex cells that are sensitive to movement; they also respond when the motion is only implied in a photograph of an athlete in action or a picture of a cup falling off a table (reviewed in Culham, He, Dukelow, & Verstraten, 2001). At the same time, there are many other areas that are specialized for particular kinds of movement. Viewing movement of the human body or its parts activates dorsal stream areas adjacent to V5/MT and MST, in the parietal and frontal lobes, and in the ventral stream in the temporal lobes (Vaina, Solomon, Chowdhury, Sinha, & Belliveau, 2001; Wheaton, Thompson, Syngeniotis, Abbott, & Puce, 2004).

Images move across your retinas every time you move your eyes, but you don't see the world moving around you. (Imagine trying to read, otherwise.) This is because the activity of movement-sensitive cells in MT and MST is suppressed during eye movements (Thiele, Henning, Kubischik, & Hoffmann, 2002). These cells are sensitive to movement in a particular direction, and some of them reverse their preferred direction of movement as the head moves, which allows them to continue responding to real movement of objects. The brain's visual movement areas are close to an area that analyzes input from the vestibular organs, which monitor body motion (Thier, Haarmeier, Chakraborty, Lindner, & Tikhonov, 2001); you are already indirectly familiar with this fact if you get motion sickness in a moving car when you read or when you watch roadside objects too closely.

The functions of the ventral and dorsal streams are best illustrated by a comparison of patients with damage in the two areas. People with damage in the temporal cortex (ventral stream) have trouble visually identifying objects, but they can walk toward or around the objects and reach for them accurately (Kosslyn, Ganis, & Thompson, 2001). People with damage to the dorsal stream have the opposite problem. They can identify objects, but they have trouble orienting their gaze to objects, reaching accurately, and shaping their hands to grasp an object using visual cues (Ungerleider & Mishkin, 1982). So the dorsal stream is also a "how" area that is important for action.

From the parietal and temporal lobes, the dorsal and ventral streams both proceed into the prefrontal cortex. One function of the prefrontal cortex is to manage this information in memory while it is being used to carry out the functions that depend on the two pathways (Courtney, Ungerleider, Keil, & Haxby, 1997; F. A. Wilson, Ó Scalaidhe, & Goldman-Rakic, 1993). As one example, we will see in Chapter 11 that the prefrontal cortex integrates information about the body and about objects around it during the planning of movements.

Disorders of Visual Perception

Because the visual system is somewhat modular, damage to a processing area can impair one aspect of visual perception while all others remain normal. This kind of deficit is often called an *agnosia,* which means "lack of knowledge." Because the disorders provide a special opportunity for understanding the neural basis of higher-order visual perception, we will orient our discussion of the perception of objects, color, movement, and spatial location around disorders of those abilities.

Object and Face Agnosia

Object agnosia is the impaired ability to recognize objects. In Chapter 3, we described Oliver Sacks's (1990) agnosic patient who patted parking meters on the head, thinking they were children; he was also surprised when carved knobs on furniture failed to return his friendly greeting. Dr. P. was intellectually intact; he continued to perform successfully as a professor of music, and he could carry on lively conversations on many topics. Patients with object agnosia are able to see an object, describe it in detail, and identify it by touch. But they are unable to identify an object by sight or even to recognize an object from a picture that they have just drawn from memory (Gurd & Marshall, 1992; Zeki, 1992).

Object agnosia is caused by damage to the inferior temporal cortex (see Figure 10.29); this part of the ventral stream is where information about edges, spatial frequencies, texture, and so on is reassembled to form perceptions of objects. Cells have been located there in monkeys and humans that respond selectively to geometric figures, houses, animals, hands, faces, or body parts (Figure 10.30a; Desimone,

■ **FIGURE 10.30**   Stimuli Used to Produce Responses in Hand- and Face-Sensitive Cells in Monkeys.

(a) The stimuli are ranked in order of increasing ability to evoke a response in a hand-sensitive cell. (b) The spikes recorded from a face-sensitive cell indicate the degree of response from the stimulus shown below.

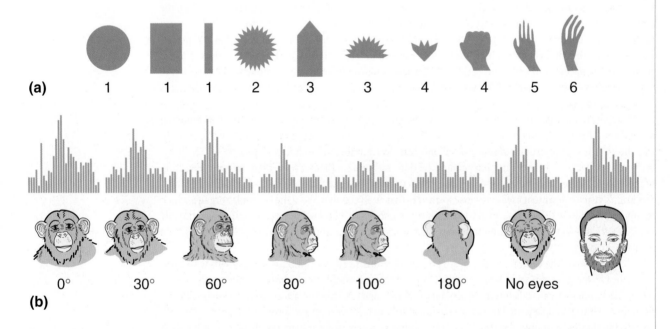

Sources: (a) From "Visual Properties of Neurons in Inferotemporal Cortex of the Macaque," by C. G. Gross et al., 1972, *Journal of Neurophysiology, 35*. Reprinted with permission. (b) From "Stimulus-Selective Properties of Inferior Temporal Neurons in the Macaque," by R. Desimone et al., p. 2057. in *Journal of Neuroscience, 4,* 1984.

Albright, Gross, & Bruce, 1984; Downing, Jiang, Shuman, & Kanwisher, 2001; Gross, Rocha-Miranda, & Bender, 1972; Kreiman, Koch, & Fried, 2000; Sáry, Vogels, & Orban, 1993). Some of these cells require very specific characteristics of a stimulus, such as a face viewed in profile; others continue to respond in spite of changes in rotation, size, and color (Figure 10.30b; Miyashita, 1993; Tanaka, 1996; Vogels, 1999). The latter group of cells likely receive their input from cells with narrower sensitivities (Tanaka, 1996), like those in V1 that detect edges. The inferior temporal cortex also has a columnar organization reminiscent of what we saw in V1; a column of object-responsive cells might respond to variations on a star-like shape, for example, and a column adjacent to one that responds to a frontal view of a face is activated by a face in profile (Tanaka, 2003).

Like Dr. P., many object agnosic patients also suffer from *prosopagnosia,* an impaired ability to visually recognize familiar faces. The problem is not memory, because they can identify individuals by other characteristics like their speech or mannerisms. Nor is their visual acuity impaired; they often have no difficulty recognizing facial expressions, gender, and age (Tranel, Damasio, & Damasio, 1988). However, they are unable to recognize the faces of friends and family members or even their own image in a mirror (Benton, 1980; A. R. Damasio, 1985). Prosopagnosia has a variety of causes, including stroke, carbon monoxide poisoning, and Alzheimer's disease. Damage usually impairs the ability to recognize both objects and faces, but the occasional case is reported of a patient with prosopagnosia alone (Benton, 1980) or of object agnosia with spared face identification (Behrmann, Moscovitch, & Winocur, 1994).

While some processing of face information occurs in the inferior temporal cortex, recognizing individual faces requires additional structures. In humans, a part of the fusiform gyrus on the underside of the temporal lobe is so important to face recognition that it is referred to as the *fusiform face area (FFA).* This area

 FIGURE 10.31 Location of Brain Damage in Patients With Prosopagnosia.

The color of the area indicates how often damage was observed there in patients with prosopagnosia.

Percent Overlap

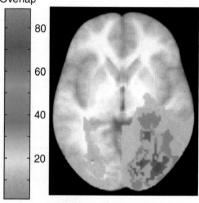

Source: From "Behavioral Deficits and Cortical Damage Loci in Cerebral Achromatopsia," by S. E. Bouvier and S. A. Engel, 2006, *Cerebral Cortex, 16,* pp. 183–191, by permission of Oxford University Press.

starts assisting us in recognizing caregiver faces at about two years of age (Bushnell, 2001) but can be developmentally delayed in individuals with autism (Scherf, Behrmann, Minshew, & Luna, 2008). Damage that results in prosopagnosia is usually in the right hemisphere (Figure 10.31; Bouvier & Engel, 2006; Gauthier, Skudlarski, Gore, & Anderson, 2000; Gauthier, Tarr, Anderson, Skudlarski, & Gore, 1999), but face processing is a cooperative effort involving both sides of the brain. Facelike images produce activity in the left fusiform gyrus that strengthens as the resemblance to a face increases; about two seconds later, the right fusiform gyrus increases its activity only when the image is of a human face (Meng, Cherian, Singal, & Sinha, 2012). Another area that has been implicated in face recognition is the medial temporal lobe, which is important in memory and seems to be involved in decision making between familiar and unfamiliar faces, even when features are shared between those two groups of faces (Quian Quiroga, Kraskov, Mormann, Fried, & Koch, 2014).

Until recently, researchers thought the only way prosopagnosia occurred was through brain damage. Then medical student Martina Grueter began to recognize the symptoms in her husband's behavior and made congenital prosopagnosia the subject of her MD thesis (Grueter, 2007). An estimated 2.5% of the population has symptoms of the disorder without any history of brain damage (Kennerknecht et al., 2006); thus, they make errors in recognizing familiar faces, and they learn new faces slowly (Grüter, Grüter, & Carbon, 2008). Afflicted individuals include noted primatologist Jane Goodall, actor Brad Pitt, and Oliver Sacks, the neurologist who studied Dr. P. Face recognition ability has a heritability of about 39% (Zhu et al., 2010), so its deficiency in the absence of brain damage has a genetic origin. The defect, though, does not appear to be in the fusiform face area; fMRI shows that the FFA responds just as much to faces in prosopagnosics as it does in normal individuals. Instead, connections of the FFA to more anterior temporal and frontal cortex areas are diminished (Avidan & Behrmann, 2009), suggesting that face recognition is a distributed function, despite modularity of its components.

These capabilities might be "hardwired" at birth to some extent, but they also are amenable to learning. When researchers showed monkeys pictures of the faces of lab workers, neurons in the inferior temporal cortex increased their firing rates according to the monkeys' familiarity with the workers (M. P. Young & Yamane, 1992). Isabel Gauthier and her colleagues (1999) trained humans to identify faces, using pictures

■ **FIGURE 10.32**   Activity in the Fusiform Face Area While Viewing Faces and "Greebles."

Viewing faces activated a part of the fusiform gyrus (indicated by the white squares) both in "greeble novices" and in "greeble experts," who had learned to distinguish individual greebles from each other. Viewing greebles activated the area only in greeble experts. (Red indicates more activation than yellow.)

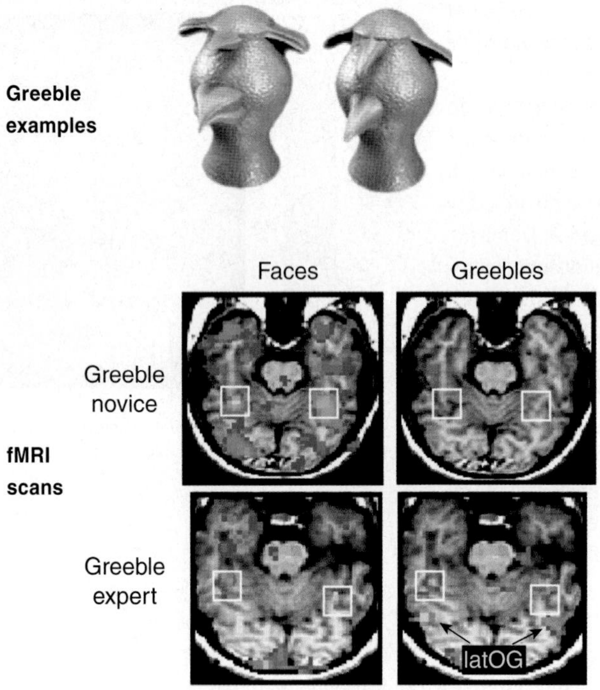

Greeble examples

Faces   Greebles

Greeble novice

fMRI scans

Greeble expert

latOG

Source: From "Activation of the Middle Fusiform 'Face Area' Increases With Expertise in Recognizing Novel Objects," by I. Gauthier et al., *Nature Neuroscience, 2*, pp. 568–573. © 1999 Nature Publishing Group.

"I was having a wonderful conversation with a woman at a party, but then I went to get us some drinks. When I returned, I had forgotten what she looked like, and I was unable to find her the rest of the evening.

—A young man with prosopagnosia"

? How is color coding different from wavelength coding?

of fictitious creatures they called "greebles" to ensure initial unfamiliarity. The fMRI scans in Figure 10.32 show that pictures of human faces activated the FFA but greebles did so only after the person had learned to recognize individual creatures.

Prosopagnosics do respond emotionally to photographs of familiar faces they do not recognize, as indicated by EEG evoked potentials and skin conductance response (Bauer, 1984; Renault, Signoret, Debruille, Breton, & Bolger, 1989; Tranel & Damasio, 1985). This "hidden perception" is not without precedent. Patients blinded by damage to V1 show a surprising ability to track the movement of objects and discriminate colors, all the while claiming to be guessing (Zeki, 1992). Cortically blind individuals also can identify emotions expressed in faces they do not otherwise see (Tamietto et al., 2009), and they can avoid obstacles while walking. This ability to respond to visual stimuli that are not consciously seen is called *blindsight*. Imaging studies have found that blindsight depends on pathways passing through the superior colliculus directly to extrastriate areas, bypassing V1 (reviewed in de Gelder & Tamietto, 2007; Tamietto et al., 2010).

A nearby area in the inferior temporal cortex has an intriguingly similar "object" recognition function; the *visual word form area (VWFA)* responds to written words as a whole. Its importance in reading was demonstrated in a patient whose VWFA was disconnected from adjacent language areas by surgery intended to remove tissue that was causing epileptic seizures (Gaillard et al., 2006). Before surgery, the patient could recognize familiar words of any length in less than a second; following surgery, the time had almost doubled for three-letter words and increased by an additional 100 milliseconds for each additional letter, indicating that he was deciphering words letter by letter. Performance in identifying faces, tools, and houses was unaffected. The VWFA is typically underactivated in adult dyslexics during reading (McCandliss & Noble, 2003), but, consistent with what we saw in Chapter 9, the authors suggest that this is not the cause of the dyslexia but the result of phonological deficits that interfere with learning rapid word recognition. It is clear that the VWFA could not have evolved as a dedicated whole-word detector, because written language is a relatively recent invention; still, it serves that function so precisely that two words evoke activity in different subareas, even when the words differ by just one letter (Glezer, Jiang, & Riesenhuber, 2009). What is intriguing about the VWFA is that, for whatever reason, the area has evolved special capabilities that suit it for learning to identify words as if they are unique visual "objects."

Color Agnosia

Let's return to Jonathan I., whose plight was described at the beginning of the chapter. Jonathan's problem was *color agnosia*, which is the loss of the ability to perceive colors due to brain damage. But before we can discuss this disorder, we need to revisit the distinction between wavelength and color. As one of the authors walked past a colleague's slightly open office door, he was astonished to see that his colleague's face was a distinct green! Opening the door to investigate, he understood why: The light from the colleague's desk lamp was reflecting off a bright green brochure he was reading. Immediately his face appeared normal again. This ability to recognize the so-called natural color of an object despite the illuminating wavelength is called *color constancy*. An example of this can be seen in Figure 10.33. Although both eyes are the same color gray, the colored shading pushes the brain's interpretation of color in the opponent direction. If not for color constancy, objects would seem to change colors as the sun shifted its position through the day or as we went indoors into artificial (or colored) light. Imagine having to survive by identifying ripe fruit if the colors kept changing.

When the author reinterpreted his colleague's skin color, it was not because he *understood* that his friend's face was bathed in green light; it occurred automatically as soon as his eyes took in the whole scene. Monkeys, who do not understand the principles of color vision, apparently have the same experience. When Zeki (1983) illuminated red, white, green, and blue patches with red light, each patch set off firing in V1 cells that preferred long-wavelength (red) light, regardless of its actual color; however, cells in V4 responded only when the patch's actual color matched the cell's color "preference." Zeki concluded that cells in V1 are *wavelength coded,* whereas cells in V4 are *color coded.* Schein and Desimone (1990) suggested how V4 cells provide color constancy. They have large circular receptive fields that are color opposed; so if, for example, a green light falling on the center increases the cell's firing rate, green light falling simultaneously in the surround reduces or eliminates the increase. In other words, the cells "subtract out" the color of any general illumination. It is our V4 cells that allow us to see our friend's face as normal pink rather than as the color that it might reflect.

We have no brain scan to tell us where Jonathan I.'s damage was located, but we know that cortical color blindness, or *cerebral achromatopsia,* occurs when people have lesions between V1 and the fusiform face area (Heywood & Kentridge, 2003; Witthoft et al., 2013); this is where V4 is located, but it is unclear whether the deficiency can be attributed to V4 malfunction. Unlike Jonathan I., many patients are unaware their color vision is impaired, just as we saw in Chapter 9 with Wernicke's aphasia.

Movement Agnosia

Although movement is detected by neurons in V1 and beyond, area V5/MT is the place where that information is integrated; MT (for middle temporal area) also helps direct reaching movements and eye movements when tracking objects (Born & Badley, 2005; Whitney et al., 2007). A 43-year-old woman known in the literature as LM suffered a stroke that caused bilateral damage in the general area of MT; the result was *movement agnosia,* an impaired ability to detect movement (Vaina, 1998; Zihl, von Cramon, & Mai, 1983). Although her vision was otherwise normal, she could distinguish between moving and stationary objects only in her peripheral view, she had difficulty making visually guided eye and finger movements, and she had trouble detecting the movement of people if there were more than two people in the room. She was often surprised to notice that an object had changed position (Zihl et al., 1983). You might think that perceiving a change in position would be the same thing as perceiving movement, but she had no sense of the object traveling through the intermediate positions. When she poured coffee, she could not tell that the liquid was rising in the cup, so she would keep pouring until the cup overflowed! When she tried to cross a street, a car would seem far away, but then suddenly very near.

Later analyses indicated that LM's most severe impairment was in her ability to detect radial movement (Vaina, 1998). We experience radial movement when the image of an approaching car expands outwardly, or radially. Radial movement also tells us that we are approaching an object when we walk or drive, because all the environmental objects around the central point appear to move outward; this effect provides information about our *heading* and is important for personal navigation. A patient with impaired perception of radial movement could not catch a ball that was thrown to him, and he frequently bumped into people in his wheelchair. Scans done while subjects perform a task involving radial movement or heading detection implicate the MST area (for medial superior temporal area, where it is located), which receives its input from MT (Peuskens, Sunaert, Dupont, Van Hecke, & Orban, 2001; Vaina).

Neglect and the Role of Attention in Vision

The posterior parietal cortex combines input from the visual, auditory, and somatosensory areas to help the individual locate objects in space and to orient the body in the environment. Damage impairs abilities such as reaching for objects, but it also often produces *neglect,* in which the patient

■ **FIGURE 10.33** Color Constancy.

In both images, all the eyes are gray. However, our cortex corrects for the right-sided tint; it tells us what color eye would produce the sensation we're experiencing, if it were seen through a blue or red glass. Punch a small circle in a piece of paper so that you see only the eye and verify it yourself! The suggestion of the colored earring enhances the effect, but doesn't produce it, as you can see if you cover the earring.

■ **FIGURE 10.34**   Drawings Copied by a Left-Field Neglect Patient.

Source: Schwartz, B. L. & Krantz, J. H. (2015).

ignores visual, touch, and auditory stimulation on the side opposite the injury. The term *neglect* seems particularly appropriate in patients who ignore food on the left side of the plate, shave only the right side of the face, or fail to dress the left side of the body. The manifestations are largely, but not entirely, visual, and they are more likely to occur on the left side of the body, following right-hemisphere damage. (Because the symptoms affect one side of space, the term *hemispatial neglect* is often used.)

Neglect is not due to any defect in visual processing, but rather it is due to a deficit in attention; it illustrates the fact that to the extent attention is impaired, so is visual functioning. Two patients with this condition, caused by right parietal tumors, were asked to report whether words and pictures presented simultaneously in the left and right visual fields were the same or different. They said that the task was "silly" because there was no stimulus in the left field to compare, yet they were able to answer with a high level of accuracy (Volpe, LeDoux, & Gazzaniga, 1979). Their performance is superior to that of blindsighted individuals, which supports the contention that neglect is a deficit in attention rather than in vision.

> "I knew the word "neglect" was a sort of medical term for whatever was wrong but the word bothered me because you only neglect something that is actually there, don't you? If it's not there, how can you neglect it?
>
> —P. P., a neglect patient"

Patients' drawings and paintings help us understand what they are experiencing. When asked to copy drawings, they will neglect one side while completing the other side in detail, like the example in Figure 10.34. The two portraits in Figure 10.35 were painted by Anton Raderscheidt two and nine months after a stroke that damaged his right parietal area. Notice that the first painting has very little detail and the left half of the image is missing. In the later painting, he was using the whole canvas, and the portrait looks more normal; but notice that the left side is still much less developed than the right, with the eyeglasses and face melting into ambiguity (Jung, 1974).

■ **FIGURE 10.35**   Self-Portraits Demonstrating Left Visual Field Neglect.

A self-portrait done two months after the artist's stroke, which affected the right parietal area, is incomplete, especially on the left side of the canvas. (b) One done nine months after the stroke is more complete but still shows less attention to detail on the left side.

RESEARCH SPOTLIGHT
When Binding Goes Too Far

Before his accident, Jonathan I. saw a "tumult" of changing colors whenever he listened to music. For other people with synesthesia, letters may have colors, days of the week may have personalities, visual motion might produce sounds, or words might have tastes. *Synesthesia* is a condition in which stimulation in one sense triggers an experience in another sense or a concept evokes an unrelated sensory experience. Over 60 varieties of synesthesia have been documented, and most synesthetes report more than one form (Brang & Ramachandran, 2011). Synesthesia was thought to be rare, based on the number of people who came forward to report these experiences, but when Julia Simner and her colleagues (2006) tested 1,700 non-self-referred individuals, almost 5% showed characteristics of synesthesia. A third of those were projectors, who experience the unrelated color or sound or taste, and the rest were associators, who have a persistent mental association between, for example, a word and a color but don't report that they see the color. Synesthesia is a neurological phenomenon; fMRI studies show that area V4 is active when grapheme/color synesthetes view letters and numbers and when auditory word/color synesthetes listen to spoken words (see figure; Hubbard, Arman, Ramachandran, & Boynton, 2005; Nunn et al., 2002).

There are two competing hypotheses as to why synesthetes "overbind" sensory information: Either there is excess connectivity among the involved brain areas, or there is inadequate inhibition in otherwise normal pathways. Studies favor the connectivity hypothesis; a diffusion tensor imaging MRI study (suited for imaging white matter) indicated more pronounced connections in grapheme/color synesthetes in the inferior temporal, parietal, and

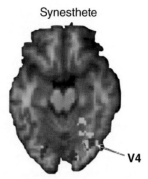
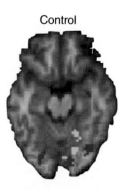

Synesthete   Control

Spoken words activate left-hemisphere area V4 in a synesthete but not in a control. Why do you think this activity occurred mostly in the left hemisphere?

Source: From "Functional Magnetic Resonance Imaging of Synesthesia: Activation of V4/V8 by Spoken Words," by J. A. Nunn et al., 2002, *Nature Neuroscience, 5*, pp. 371–375.

frontal cortex—all areas involved in processing and integrating visual information (Rouw & Scholte, 2007). Also, genetic studies suggest synesthesia runs in families, and at least four of the five chromosomal areas implicated contain genes for axon guidance and cortical development (Asher et al., 2009; Thomson et al., 2011).

By all rights, synesthesia could be considered a developmental brain disorder, but other than being a bit of a distraction it is relatively benign and, like Jonathan I., many synesthetes enjoy their enriched sensory experience. Besides, they often have no idea they are different from others. Julian Asher, who led the genetic study described above, discovered his synesthesia when, as a child attending the symphony with his parents, he remarked, "Oh, they turned the lights off so you could see the colors" ("Seeing Color," 2000).

The Problem of Final Integration

We have seen how the brain combines information about some aspects of an object, but many researchers wonder where *all* the information about the object is brought together; how the brain combines information from different areas into a unitary whole is known as the *binding problem*. Imagine watching a person walking across your field of view; the person is moving, shifting orientation, and changing appearance as the lighting increases and decreases under a canopy of trees. At the same time, you are walking toward the person, but your brain copes easily with the changing size of the person's image and the apparent movement of environmental objects toward you. It seems logical that a single center at the end of the visual pathway would combine all the information about shape, color, texture, and movement, constantly updating your perception of this image as the same person. In other words, the result would be a complete and dynamic awareness. Presumably, damage to that area would produce symptoms that are similar to blindsight but that affect all stimuli.

It has been suggested that our ultimate understanding of an object occurs in a part of the superior temporal gyrus that receives input from both neural streams (Baizer, Ungerleider, & Desimone, 1991) or in the part of the parietal cortex where damage causes neglect (Driver & Mattingley, 1998). Other investigators suspect frontal areas where both streams converge. But these ideas are highly speculative, and there is no convincing evidence for a master area where all perceptual information comes together to produce awareness (Crick, 1994; Zeki, 1992). The variety of hypothesized awareness centers suggests another possibility, that visual awareness is *distributed* throughout the network of 32 areas of cortex concerned with vision and their 305 interconnecting pathways (Van Essen, Anderson, & Felleman, 1992). This thinking is exemplified on a small scale in the interaction between V5/MT and V1. After a stimulus occurs, activity continues back and forth between these areas for a few hundred milliseconds, and disrupting this interchange eliminates awareness of movement (reviewed in McKeefry, Gouws, Burton, & Morland, 2009).

Actually, the brain's task is a balancing act between combining relevant information and segregating inconsequential information, as the accompanying Research Spotlight on synesthesia shows. We will spend more time examining how the brain sorts out and uses information when we talk about consciousness in Chapter 15.

CONCEPT CHECK

Take a Minute to Check Your Knowledge and Understanding

- Explain why higher-order processing is required to recognize the natural color of objects; how does it work?
- Draw a diagram of the brain, add lines showing the two major visual pathways, and label the various areas; for the higher-order processing areas, include their functions.

In Perspective

Very few subjects in the field of behavioral neuroscience can match the interest that researchers have bestowed on vision. As a result, we know more about the neuroanatomy and functioning of vision than any other neural system. Still, many challenges remain in the field of vision research.

Researchers' fascination with vision goes beyond the problems of vision itself. Our understanding of the networks of neurons and structures in the visual system provides a basis for developing theories to explain other functions as well, including the integration of complex information into a singular awareness. Whatever directions future research might take, you can be sure that vision will continue to be one of the most important topics.

CHAPTER SUMMARY

Light and the Visual Apparatus

- The human eye is adapted to the part of the electromagnetic spectrum that is reflected from objects with minimal distortion. Wavelength is related to the color of light but is not synonymous with it.

- The retina contains rods, which are specialized for brightness discrimination, and cones, which are specialized for detail vision and discrimination of colors. The cells of the retina are highly interconnected to carry out some processing at that level.

- The optic nerves project to the two hemispheres so that information from the right visual field goes to the left visual cortex, and vice versa.

Color Vision

- There are three types of cones, each containing a chemical with peak sensitivity to a different segment of the electromagnetic spectrum.
- Connections of the cones to ganglion cells provide for complementary colors and for perception of yellow as a unique color.
- The most common cause of partial color blindness is the lack of one of the photochemicals.

Form Vision

- Form vision begins with contrast enhancement at edges by ganglion cells with light-opponent circular fields.

- These ganglion cells contribute to cortical mechanisms that detect edges (Hubel and Wiesel's theory) or that perform a Fourier analysis of a scene (spatial frequency theory).

The Perception of Objects, Color, and Movement

- Most visual information follows two somewhat separate paths through the brain, which are part of the magnocellular and parvocellular systems.
- Structures along the way are specialized for different functions, including color, movement, object perception, and face perception.
- We do not know how or where the components of vision are combined to form the perception of a unified object. One suggestion is that this is a distributed function. ■

STUDY RESOURCES

FOR FURTHER THOUGHT

- Red and green are complementary colors and blue and yellow are complementary because their receptors have opponent connections to their ganglion cells. How would you explain the fact that bluish green and reddish yellow (orange) are also complementary?
- Considering what you know about the retina, how would you need to direct your gaze to read a book or to find a very faint star?
- Explain why the visual system analyzes an object's edges, texture, and color and then detects the object, instead of the other way around.
- Are Hubel and Wiesel's theory and the spatial frequency theory opposed or complementary theories?
- Cones in the bird retina detect blue, green, red, and ultraviolet. Can you imagine what they might gain from detecting ultraviolet reflections from objects in their environment? Then check http://en.wikipedia.org/wiki/Bird_vision (see the section "Ultraviolet Sensitivity"); you might be surprised by some of the benefits!
- How could you design traffic signs, uniforms, and safety equipment to make them recognizable to individuals with color vision deficiencies?

TEST YOUR UNDERSTANDING

1. Summarize the trichromatic and Hurvich-Jameson theories, indicating what facts about color vision each accounts for.

2. Compare the specialized sensitivities of simple and complex visual cortical cells; describe the interconnections among ganglion cells, simple cells, and complex cells that account for their specializations (according to Hubel and Wiesel).

3. The visual system appears to be more or less hierarchical and modular. What does this mean? (Use examples to illustrate.)

Select the best answer:

1. The receptive field of a cell in the visual system is the part of the _____ from which the cell receives its input.

   a. external world   b. retina
   c. temporal lobe   d. cortex

2. Mixing red and green lights produces a sensation of yellow because red-sensitive and green-sensitive cones

   a. excite yellow/blue ganglion cells.
   b. have opposite effects at yellow/blue ganglion cells.
   c. excite red/green ganglion cells.
   d. have opposite effects at red/green ganglion cells.

3. If our experience of color were entirely due to the wavelength of light reflected from an object, we would not experience

   a. complementary.   b. the color yellow.
   c. primary colors.   d. color constancy.

4. The parvocellular system is specialized for

   a. fine detail and movement.
   b. color and fine detail.
   c. color and movement.
   d. movement and brightness contrast.

5. What would be the effect on vision if there was a problem with your horizontal cells?

   a. Impaired color vision
   b. Detection of shapes in a complex background
   c. Impaired edge detection in the Mach band illusion
   d. Impaired night vision, but intact day vision

6. Cutting the optic nerve between the right eye and the chiasm would cause a loss of vision in

    a. the left visual field.
    b. the right visual field.
    c. half of each visual field.
    d. neither field, due to filling in.

7. People with red-green color blindness

    a. cannot see either red or green.
    b. see red and green as black.
    c. confuse red and green because they lack either "red" or "green" cones.
    d. confuse red and green because they lack one of the photopigments.

8. A light edge has enhanced apparent brightness next to a dark edge because the neurons stimulated by the light edge are inhibited

    a. less by their "dark" neighbors.
    b. more by their "dark" neighbors.
    c. less by their "light" neighbors.
    d. more by their "light" neighbors.

9. The ability of complex visual cortical cells to track an edge as it changes position appears to be due to

    a. input from receptors with similar fields.
    b. input from ganglion cells with similar fields.
    c. input from simple cells with similar fields.
    d. input from other complex cells.

10. According to the spatial frequency theory of visual processing, edges are detected by

    a. line-detecting cells in the visual cortex.
    b. edge detectors located in the visual cortex.
    c. cells that respond to low spatial frequencies.
    d. cells that respond to high spatial frequencies.

11. The circles represent the receptive field of a ganglion cell; the rectangle represents light. Unlike the illustrations in this chapter, the receptive field has an *off center*. In which situation will the ganglion cell's rate of firing be greatest?

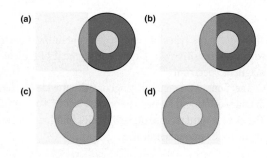

12. Studies of object, color, and movement agnosias indicate that

    a. the visual system is unstable and malfunctions with no apparent cause.
    b. components of the visual image are processed separately.
    c. color, object identification, and movement information are integrated in one place.
    d. all functions are processed in one place but the results are distributed to other parts of the brain.

13. Movement perception is the primary function in visual area

    a. V1.   b. V2.
    c. V4.   d. V5.

14. A person who has trouble identifying objects visually probably has damage in the

    a. temporal lobe.   b. parietal lobe.
    c. occipital lobe.   d. frontal lobe.

Answers: 1. b, 2. a, 3. d, 4. b, 5. c, 6. c, 7. d, 8. a, 9. c, 10. d, 11. b, 12. b, 13. d, 14. a.

ON THE WEB

The following websites are coordinated with this chapter's content. You can access these websites from the **SAGE edge Student Resources site**; select this chapter and then click on Web Resources. (**Bold** items are links.)

1. **Webvision** is essentially an online text covering numerous topics in vision. **Photoreceptors**, a part of that site, details the structure of rods and cones with high magnification images; some animations are also available.

2. Each year, there is a contest for the best visual Illusion of the Year. On this website, you can see all of the entrants for this year's contest, as well as prior years' entries.

3. Videos show the **Argus II** implantable retina; the **surgery** to implant the Argus (not for the squeamish); an **Alpha IMS** recipient describing what he sees; a blind man who "sees" using **BrainPort**, which transmits a video image to an array of electrodes on his tongue; and **Corey Haas**, whose improved vision allows him to live a normal life after gene therapy.

4. **Causes of Color** is a well-designed site with numerous exhibits on color in the real world and sections on color vision.

5. **Colorblindness** has very helpful information and illustrations, and the third page has an interactive demonstration of seven forms of color blindness. **Neitzvision** features color-blindness demonstrations and the research of Jay and Maureen Neitz, including a recent study in which inserting a human gene for the long-wave receptor turned dichromatic (red-green color-blind) monkeys into trichromats.

6. The **Colblindor** website demonstrates different types of color blindness and lets you drag and drop your own images to see how they would look to a person with each of those color deficiencies.

7. Akiyoshi Kitaoka's **Color Constancy website** has many interesting examples of how prevailing colors of light in an image affect our perception of individual colors. In addition, she has some rather interesting examples of illusions of motion.

8. **Faceblind** is the website of prosopagnosia research centers at Dartmouth, Harvard, and University College, London.

Prosopagnosia, at Wikipedia, features a rotating brain that provides a 3-D view of the fusiform face area's location.

9. **Blindsight: Seeing Without Knowing It** is a *Scientific American* article with a fascinating video of a man using blindsight to walk down a hallway filled with obstacles.

10. **Hearing Motion** is a video about motion synesthesia research, and **Exactly Like Breathing** is a collection of interviews of synesthetes. **Synesthesia** is a Wikipedia article written by two researchers, and *Neurophilosophy* has an article on the **genetics of synesthesia** and another on **tactile-emotion synesthesia**.

FOR FURTHER READING

1. "The Case of the Colorblind Painter," by Oliver Sacks (in Sacks's *An Anthropologist on Mars,* 1995, Vintage Books), is a compelling narrative of the case of Jonathan I.

2. "Visual Object Recognition: Do We (Finally) Know More Now Than We Did 20 Years Ago?" by Isabel Gauthier and Michael Tarr (*Annual Review of Vision Science,* 2016, *2,* 377–396) updates research on how we continue to recognize an object in spite of changes in orientation, lighting, and the like; "The Functional Neuroanatomy of Human Face Perception," by Kalanit Grill-Spector, Kevin Weiner, Kendrick Kay, and Jesse Gomez (*Annual Review of Vision Science,* to be published October 2017), reviews recent research on the ventral face network; and "Neuronal Mechanisms of Visual Attention," by John Maunsell (*Annual Review of Vision Science,* 2015, *1,* 373–391), marshals recent research to provide a clearer understanding of how representations in the visual system change as attention shifts from one target to another.

3. *Vision and Art,* by Margaret Livingstone (2014, Harry N. Abrams, Publisher), explores how great painters use the science of vision to fool the brain with Mona Lisa's mysterious smile and Monet's swaying *Poppy Field.*

4. *Seeing Through Illusions,* by Richard Gregory (2009, Oxford University Press), explains how illusions tell us not only how the brain works but also about its evolutionary past.

KEY TERMS

accommodation 278	fusiform face area (FFA) 301	receptive field 279
binding problem 305	hierarchical processing 297	retina 278
blindsight 302	iodopsin 278	retinal disparity 281
color agnosia 302	lateral inhibition 289	retinotopic map 289
color blindness 287	magnocellular system 297	rhodopsin 278
color constancy 302	modular processing 297	simple cell 292
complementary colors 283	movement agnosia 303	spatial frequency theory 295
complex cell 293	negative color aftereffect 283	synesthesia 275
distributed 297	object agnosia 300	trichromatic theory 282
dorsal stream 298	opponent process theory 283	ventral stream 298
electromagnetic spectrum 276	parvocellular system 297	visual acuity 279
form vision 289	photopigment 278	visual field 280
fovea 278	prosopagnosia 301	visual word form area (VWFA) 302

$SAGE edge™

edge.sagepub.com/garrett5e

SAGE edge offers a robust online environment featuring an impressive array of free tools and resources for review, study, and further exploration, keeping both instructors and students on the cutting edge of teaching and learning.

10.1	Describe the functions of structures within the eye.	▶ Transplanting Photoreceptors 📣 Strangers in the Mirror
10.2	Illustrate the processing pathways of visual information from the eye up to cortical brain areas.	▶ How We See Color
10.3	Compare the major theories of color processing.	▶ Neuroscience of Color Vision
10.4	Contrast the major theories of form processing.	▶ Teaching a Computer to Understand Pictures
10.5	Discuss how visual information is segregated and reconstructed in the visual system.	▶ Optical Illusions Spotlight How the Brain Works
10.6	Identify how action potentials and synaptic transmission can produce a variety of visual experiences.	▶ Light and Neuronal Activity
10.7	Predict how damage to specific portions of the visual system will impact a person's visual perceptions.	📄 Recognition of Biological Motion in Children With Autism ▶ New Glasses for Color-Deficient Individuals

© iStock.com/Krle

PRACTICE AND APPLY WHAT YOU'VE LEARNED

▶ **edge.sagepub.com/garrett5e**

HEAD TO THE STUDY SITE WHERE YOU'LL FIND

- **eFlashcards to strengthen your understanding of key terms**

- **Practice quizzes to test your comprehension of key concepts**

- **Videos and multimedia content to enhance your exploration of key topics**

Mads Perch/Stone/Getty Images

The Body Senses and Movement

11

After reading this chapter, you will be able to:

- Identify the receptors involved in each type of skin sensation.

- Describe the methods by which the brain gets information about the body and the environment.

- Illustrate how the cortical areas for sensation correspond to portions of the body.

- Assess the mechanisms by which pain is generated.

- Summarize the brain structures involved in the production of movement.

- Predict how movement is impaired in specific movement disorders.

Master the content.
edge.sagepub.com/garrett5e

The time for quietly soldiering on is through. The war against Parkinson's is a winnable war, and I have resolved to play a role in that victory.

—Michael J. Fox

O ne morning, Michael woke up with a strange sensation: His pinkie would not stop twitching. Stretching, even holding it straight, would stop the wiggle for a little while, but it would always start moving again uncontrollably after a minute or two. Over time, his twitching pinkie grew to a hand tremor, which eventually took over his arm. After seeing numerous physical therapists, doctors, and neurologists, he eventually received a diagnosis of this strange involuntary twitching: Parkinson's disease.

Michael was only 29, and Parkinson's disease is rare at such a young age. His doctors intimated that because of the progressive nature of the tremors, shuffling walk, and dyskinesia (uncontrollable movements), he had at most 10 more good working years as an actor before the symptoms would prevent him from acting again. As we'll see later, Michael's Parkinson's was a result of decreased dopamine levels, the neurotransmitter responsible for smooth movements. He was told that taking synthetic dopamine (L-dopa) would temporarily reduce, or even eliminate, the movement symptoms. Initially, he didn't tell anyone but his wife and threw himself into acting while he still was able to appear healthy to viewers. In the next few years, he played both major and minor roles in six films, recorded voices for seven animated films, and starred in a major television show called *Spin City*. Eventually, the tremors and movement problems became noticeable enough that he admitted he had the disease to the public (M. J. Fox, 2002).

After his diagnosis was made public. Michael could have simply asked for privacy and spent his time feeling sorry for himself. He did neither. Instead, he created one of the largest foundations dedicated to a cure for a single disorder—the Michael J. Fox Foundation for Parkinson's Research. In 1999, he testified in front of Congress advocating for more federal funds dedicated to Parkinson's research (which typically receives a fraction of the funding that cancer and Alzheimer's disease receive), and he has fostered countless scientific advances through his foundation. But more than that, he has grown comfortable with his disorder, treating his symptoms with L-dopa only when *he* wants to, and not just to look normal to others. As a result, he is not shy about showing the ravages of the disease on his own body, going off his L-dopa treatment in front of Congress to demonstrate how lack of dopamine changes your posture, movement, and speech while leaving your mind completely intact.

The Body Senses

We get information about our body from the somatosensory system and from the vestibular system. The somatosenses include proprioception; the skin senses, which tell us about conditions at the surface of our body; and the interoceptive system, concerned with sensations in our internal organs. The vestibular system informs the brain about body position and movement. The interoceptive system operates mostly in the background and participates less directly in behavior, so we will limit our attention to the other systems.

Proprioception

? What is proprioception, and why is it important?

Proprioception (from the Latin *proprius,* "belonging to one's self") is the sense that informs us about the position and movement of our limbs and body. Its sensors report tension and length in muscles and the angle of the limbs at the joints. Proprioception is not as glamorous a sense as vision or audition, or even touch. However, without it we would have a great deal of difficulty, like Michael J. Fox, in maintaining posture, moving our limbs, and grasping objects. Oliver Sacks tells the story of Christina, who lost all sense of proprioception following a bout with neuritis, an inflammation of the nerves that is often caused by a viral infection. Deprived of proprioceptive feedback, for the first month she was floppy as a rag doll, unable even to sit upright. After a year of rehabilitation she was able to resume a reasonably normal life, relying solely on vision to sit and stand erect and to walk. Ian Waterman, who is similarly afflicted, crumples helplessly onto the floor if someone turns the lights out (J. Cole, 1995). In other words, proprioception does more than provide information; it is critically important in the control of movement.

The Skin Senses

? Why are there so many kinds of skin receptors?

The commonly accepted *skin senses* are touch, warmth, cold, texture, and pain. However, three studies involving mice have found evidence that itch, until now believed to be a variant of pain, has its own receptors, neural pathway (spinothalamic tract), and receptor proteins (Han et al., 2012; Mishra & Hoon, 2013; Pandey et al., 2017); itch (which also goes by the interesting name of *pruriception*) will most likely be added to the list of skin senses. Whatever the actual number of skin senses, the important point here is that each is distinct from the others, with its own receptors and separate "labeled line" pathway to the brain. To demonstrate this for yourself, move the point of a lead pencil slowly across your face. You will feel the touch of the pencil continuously, but the lead will feel cold only occasionally—because touch and cold are monitored by different receptors. Although their range is limited to the surface of our body, changes there are often due to external stimulation, so the skin senses inform us about both our body and the world. (We experience these sensations deeper in the body as well, but less often and with less sensitivity.) The skin sense receptors are illustrated in the diagram of a section of skin in Figure 11.1.

There are two general types of receptors. *Free nerve endings* are simply processes at the ends of neuronal dendrites; they detect warmth, cold, and pain. All the other receptors are *encapsulated receptors,* which are more complex structures enclosed in a membrane; their role is to detect touch. Why are there so many receptors just for touch? Because touch is a complex sense that conveys several types of information. In the superficial layers of the skin, Meissner's corpuscles respond with a brief burst of impulses, while Merkel's disks give a more sustained response. Located near the surface of the skin as they are, they detect the texture and fine detail of objects. They also detect movement and come into play when you explore an object with gentle strokes of your hand or when a blind

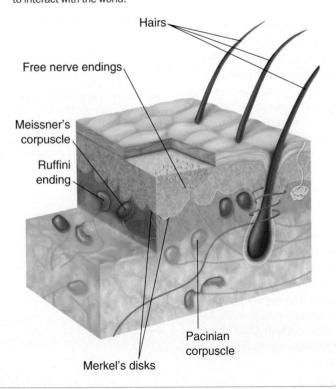

■ **FIGURE 11.1** Receptors of the Skin.

The different endings of the receptors account for their varied specialties, which provide the brain with the rich information it needs to interact with the world.

person reads Braille. Pacinian corpuscles and Ruffini endings are in the deeper layers, where they detect stretching of the skin and contribute to our perception of the shape of grasped objects (Gardner, Martin, & Jessell, 2000). Because the density of the skin receptors varies throughout the body, so does sensitivity—as much as 10-fold in fact. The fingertips and the lips are the most sensitive, and the upper arms and calves of the legs are the least sensitive (S. Weinstein, 1968).

The other three skin senses are detected by free nerve endings, but this statement is a bit misleading; those nerve endings have distinctly different receptors that make the neurons stimulus specific (Basbaum, Bautista, Scherrer, & Julius, 2009). We can respond to a wide range of temperatures; at least two different receptors detect different levels of warmth, and another receptor responds to cooling of the skin. These receptors are all members of the *transient receptor potential (TRP)* family of protein ion channels. Detection of pain also requires several receptors, mostly because of the variety of pain sources; these sources are categorized as thermal, chemical, and mechanical. Two TRP receptors respond to painful heat; a receptor for painful cold has not been conclusively identified, but the coolness receptor does not account for this sensation. Chemical receptors react to a wide range of chemical irritants. Best known is the TRPV1 heat pain receptor, which also responds to capsaicin, the ingredient in chili peppers that makes spicy foods painfully hot. Ointments containing capsaicin alleviate the joint pain of arthritis, apparently because continued stimulation of the receptors depletes the neuropeptide that the neurons use to signal pain. This receptor also responds to the pain-inducing acid released in bone cancer, and a TRPV1 antagonist relieves this pain (Ghilardi et al., 2005). The TRPM8 coolness receptor produces the cool sensation of mint in toothpaste and candies, as well as the cooling effect of menthol and camphor on the skin; menthol and camphor creams are useful for treating muscle pain, skin irritations, and canker sores in the mouth. TRPA1 receptors are responsible for the painful irritation caused by vehicle exhaust, tobacco smoke, hydrogen peroxide, and tear gas, and they account for the pungency of mustard, garlic, and wasabi, as well as the tingle you get from a carbonated drink. As we will see shortly, the body produces its own irritants when tissues are damaged; these continue to produce pain well after the stimulus is past. The receptors for mechanical pain have not been determined, which is unfortunate because persistent hypersensitivity to touch is a major problem following tissue or nerve injury.

The Vestibular Sense

In Chapter 8, you saw that the cochlea in the ear is connected to a strange-looking appendage above it, the vestibular organ. The *vestibular sense* helps us maintain balance, and it provides information about head position and movement. The organs are the semicircular canals, the utricle, and the saccule (see Figure 11.2a). The physical arrangement of the semicircular canals, three loops arranged in different planes of orientation, makes them especially responsive to movement of the head in three directions. At the base of each canal is a gelatinous (jellylike) mass called a cupula, which has a tuft of hair cells protruding into it (Figure 11.2b). During acceleration (an increase in the rate of movement), the head (and the cupula) moves but the fluid does not, which causes the cupula to bend in the opposite direction of head movement proportionally to the rate of acceleration. This displacement bends the hairs attaching the cupula to the semicircular canal, which depolarizes them and increases the neuronal rate of firing. Moving the head in the opposite direction bends the hairs in the other direction, which hyperpolarizes the neuron and decreases the firing rate.

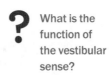

What is the function of the vestibular sense?

The system responds only to acceleration and stops responding when speed stabilizes. Just as the coffee sloshes out of your cup when you start up from a traffic light and then levels off in the cup when you reach a stable speed, the fluid in the canals also returns to its normal position. Otherwise, you would continue to sense the movement throughout an automobile trip or, worse yet, during a 500-mile per hour (805-km/hr) flight in an aircraft!

The utricle and saccule monitor head position in relation to gravity (detect where "up" is). In Figure 11.2c, you can see that the receptors (the hair cells) are covered with a gelatinous mass embedded with small calcium crystals called otoliths. When the head tilts, gravity shifts the mass and the hair cells are depolarized or hyperpolarized, depending on the direction of tilt. The hair cell receptors in the utricle are arranged in a horizontal patch, whereas the saccule's receptors are on its vertical wall; together, the two organs can detect tilt in any direction.

Consider what would happen without a functioning vestibular system. Mr. MacGregor, one of Oliver Sacks's patients, lost his vestibular sense to the neural degeneration of Parkinson's disease (Sacks, 1990). When he walked, his body canted to the left, tilted a full 20 degrees. Strangely, Mr. MacGregor wasn't aware of his tilt, even when his friends told him he was in danger of falling over. Once Sacks showed him a videotape, though, he was convinced. A retired carpenter, he put his expertise to work; three inches in front of his glasses he attached a miniature spirit level—a fluid-filled glass tube with a bubble in it that carpenters use to make sure their work is level with the world. By glancing at this makeshift device occasionally, he could walk without any slant, and after a few weeks, checking his tilt became so natural that he was no longer aware he was doing it.

But the vestibular sense is not just for adjusting the body's position. When we reach for an object, we must know not just where the object is in three-dimensional space but also the position of our body and the relation of our hand and arm to our body. The brain combines information about the object's spatial location with inputs from the vestibular sense and from proprioception to tell us what arm and hand movements are required. Proprioception also triggers reflexive eye movements that keep focusing our gaze to a target object as we turn our head or as our body bobs up and down when we walk; otherwise, the world would become a meaningless blur and tracking moving objects would be very difficult. Movement encoded by the vestibular nerve is processed by the vestibular nuclei in the midbrain, which then send information to the ocular nerves to produce compensatory eye movements. When people have balance problems, one of the first clinical signs is a failure of the person to fixate on an object when moving.

The semicircular canals and the utricle and saccule also send projections to the cerebellum and the brain stem, and there is also a pathway to the cortex, specifically, to an area called the parieto-insular-vestibular (PIV) cortex. This is the likely location where excessive eye movements, from reading in a moving car for example, cause dizziness and nausea. The same thing happens with excessive body motion, for example, during a rough boat ride or from spinning around quickly. Doing the latter eventually causes the vestibular fluid to move with

■ **FIGURE 11.2**   The Vestibular Organs.

(a) The inner ear, showing the cochlea and the vestibular organs. (b) Enlarged view of a cupula in a semicircular canal. During acceleration, the flow of endolymph displaces the cupula, triggering a neural response. (c) Receptors of the utricle and saccule. Tilting the head causes the gelatinous material to shift, stimulating the hair cells. The weight of the otoliths (calcium carbonate crystals) magnifies the shift.

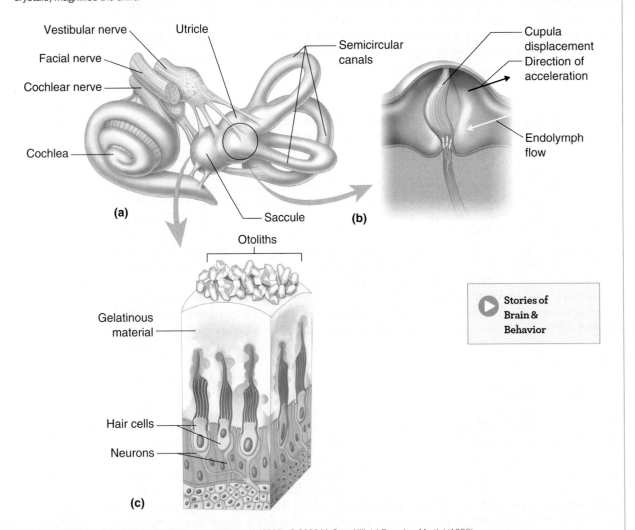

Stories of Brain & Behavior

Sources: (a) Iurato (1967). (b) Based on Goldberg and Hudspeth (2000). © 2000 McGraw-Hill. (c) Based on Martini (1988).

the head (like stirring a glass of water with a straw; at first the water resists movement, but eventually the water moves with the straw). When that happens and you stop, the fluid keeps moving, which makes the cupula continue to bend and makes you feel like you're spinning in the opposite direction. Figure skaters and gymnasts train themselves to focus on a single point when spinning and then turn their heads quickly to maintain that focus, which keeps the fluid from spinning. If you easily get motion or seasickness, chances are that you have a more sensitive PIV cortex. Taking an antihistamine drug (like Dramamine) can decrease PIV activation and, therefore, reduce nausea.

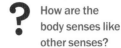

? How are the body senses like other senses?

The Somatosensory Cortex and the Posterior Parietal Cortex

The body is divided into segments called *dermatomes,* each served by a spinal nerve, as Figure 11.3 shows. The divisions are not as distinct as illustrated, because each dermatome overlaps the next by one third to one half. This way, if one nerve is injured, the area will not lose all sensation. Body sense information enters the spinal cord (via spinal nerves) or the brain (via cranial nerves) and travels to the thalamus. From there, the body sense neurons go to their projection area, the *somatosensory cortex,* located in the parietal lobes just behind the primary motor cortex and the central sulcus (Figure 11.4a). As with the auditory system, most of the neurons cross from one side of the body to the other side of the brain, so the touch of an object held in the right hand is registered mostly in the left hemisphere. Because not all neurons cross over, touching the object also stimulates the right somatosensory cortex, though much less.

Sensory systems have many organizational and functional similarities; a comparison of the somatosensory cortex with the visual cortex will illustrate this point. First, it contains a *somatotopic map* of the body, with adjacent body parts represented in adjacent parts of the cortex, just as the visual cortex contains a map of the retina and the auditory cortex contains a map of the cochlea (Figure 11.4b). Second, some of the cortical cells have complex receptive fields on the skin. Some of them have excitatory centers and inhibitory surrounds like those we saw in the visual system (Mountcastle & Powell, 1959). Some of them are quite large, as in Figure 11.5a, while smaller excitatory-inhibitory fields sharpen the localization of excitation and help distinguish two points touching the skin. In Figure 11.5b and c, we see that other somatosensory neurons with complex fields are feature detectors; they have sensitivities for orientation, direction of movement, shape, surface curvature, or texture (Carlson, 1981; Gardner & Kandel, 2000; Warren, Hämäläinen, & Gardner, 1986). Apparently, these neurons combine inputs from neurons with simpler functions, just as complex visual cells integrate the inputs of multiple simple cells (Iwamura, Iriki, & Tanaka, 1994). One type of receptive field includes multiple fingers; the cells' firing rate depends on how many fingers are touched, so they give an indication of the size of a held object.

A third similarity is that somatosensory processing is hierarchical. The *primary somatosensory cortex* consists of four areas, each of which contains a somatotopic map of the body and plays a role in processing sensory information from the body. The thalamus sends its output to two of these subareas, which extract some information and pass the result on to the other two areas, which in turn send their output to the secondary somatosensory cortex. At this point in processing, information from the right and left sides of the body is mostly segregated.

■ **FIGURE 11.3** Dermatomes of the Human Body.

For sensory functions, the body is divided into segments called dermatomes, each served by a spinal or cranial nerve. The labels identify the nerve; letters indicate the part of the spinal cord where the nerve is located (cervical, thoracic, lumbar, or sacral), and the numbers indicate the nerve's position within that section. Areas I, II, and III on the face are innervated by branches of the trigeminal (fifth) cranial nerve.

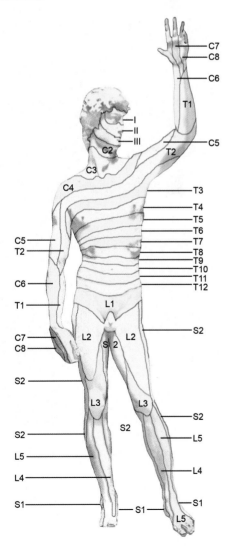

What processing occurs at each level of the somatosensory system?

The *secondary somatosensory cortex* receives input from the left and the right primary somatosensory cortices, so it combines information from both sides of the body. Neurons in this area are particularly responsive to stimuli that have acquired meaning, for instance, by association with reward (Hsiao, O'Shaughnessy, & Johnson, 1993). The secondary somatosensory cortex sends connections to the part of the temporal lobe that includes the hippocampus. The hippocampus is important in learning, so these connections likely contribute to memory formation when somatosensory information is involved (Gardner & Kandel, 2000).

The primary somatosensory cortex projects to the posterior parietal cortex as well as to the secondary somatosensory cortex. As you saw in Chapter 10, the *posterior parietal cortex* is an association area that brings together the body senses, vision, and audition (K. H. Britten, 2008). See Figure 11.4 again for the location of the posterior parietal cortex in relation to the somatosensory cortex. Here, the brain determines the body's orientation in space; the location of the limbs; and the location in space of objects detected by touch, sight, and sound. When you take a bite of apple pie, your posterior parietal cortex combines visual information about the forkful of pie with information about where your arm and hand are in relation to your body, how your head is oriented in relation to your body, and where your eyes are oriented in relation to your head. In other words, it integrates the body with the world. The posterior parietal cortex is composed of several subareas, which are responsive to different sense modalities and make different contributions to a person's interaction with the world. Some cells combine proprioception and vision to provide information about specific postures, for example, the location and positioning of the arm

■ FIGURE 11.4 The Primary and Secondary Somatosensory Areas.

(a) The primary and secondary somatosensory cortex and the posterior parietal cortex. The primary motor cortex is shown as a landmark. (b) A slice from the somatosensory cortex, showing its somatotopic organization. The size of the body parts in the figure is proportional to the area of the cortex in which they are represented. (The pictorial representation of the body on the cortex is called a *homunculus*.)

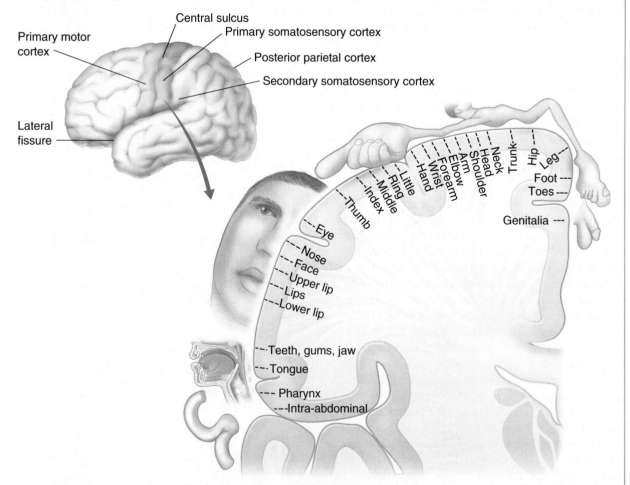

FIGURE 11.5 Receptive Fields in the Monkey Somatosensory System.

(a) Excitatory and inhibitory areas of the receptive field of a single touch neuron in the somatosensory cortex. (b) Receptive field of a somatosensory neuron that responded most to a horizontal edge. The recordings to the right indicate the strength of the neuron's response to edges of different orientations. (c) Receptive field of a neuron responsive to movement across the fingertip in one direction but not the other.

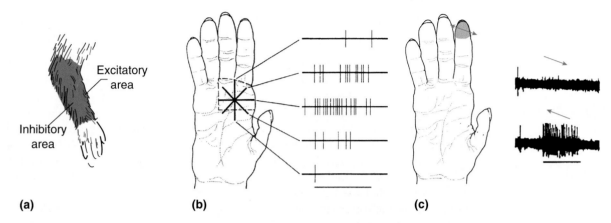

Sources: (a) From "Neural Mechanisms Subserving Cutaneous Sensibility, With Special Reference to the Role of Afferent Inhibition in Sensory Perception and Discriminiation," by V. B. Mountcastle and T. P. S. Powell, 1959, *Bulletin of the Johns Hopkins Hospital, 105*, p. 224, Figure 14. © The Johns Hopkins University Press. Reprinted with permission of the Johns Hopkins University Press. (b) and (c) From "Movement-Sensitive Cutaneous Receptive Fields in the Hand Area of the Post-central Gyrus in Monkeys," by J. Hyvärinen and A. Poranen, *Journal of Physiology, 283*, pp. 523–537. Copyright 1978, with permission from Elsevier.

and the hand (Bonda, Petrides, Frey, & Evans, 1995; Graziano, Cooke, & Taylor, 2000; Sakata, Takaoka, Kawarasaki, & Shibutani, 1973). Others contribute to reaching and grasping movements and eye movements toward targets of interest (Batista, Buneo, Snyder, & Andersen, 1999; Colby & Goldberg, 1999). The posterior parietal cortex's contribution is not solely perceptual, because many of its neurons fire before and during a movement. It does not itself produce movements but passes its information on to frontal areas that do (Colby & Goldberg).

A unified body image is critical to our ability to function and even to our self-concept, so you can imagine that any disruption would have significant consequences. You saw in Chapter 10 that damage to the right posterior parietal cortex can produce neglect and that some stroke patients will deny ownership of a paralyzed arm or leg (called xenomelia). A few people with no apparent brain damage—or mental or emotional

FIGURE 11.6 Stimulating the Temporoparietal Junction Creates a Shadow "Person."

The pink arrow and dots indicate the locations that elicited an imaginary second person that mirrored the actions and positions of the patient. Other colored dots indicate associated functions (red was motor, green was language, and blue was somatosensory) and the trigger area for seizures (stars).

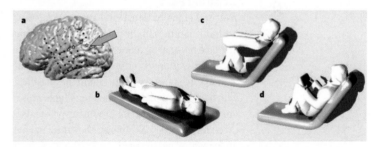

Source: From "Induction of an Illusory Shadow Person," by S. Arzy et al., *Nature, 443*, pp. 287, fig. 1. © 2006. Reprinted by permission of Nature Communications.

disorder, for that matter—are so convinced that a limb doesn't belong to them that they ask to have it amputated; this disorder is called *body integrity identity disorder,* or apotemnophilia (McGeoch et al., 2009). When the limb is touched, there is no response in the superior parietal area. Skin conductance response to stimulation is doubled in that limb, though, which indicates a high level of emotional feeling about the limb. A related phenomenon involving the same brain area incorporates the entire body into the illusion; in an *out-of-body experience,* the individual hallucinates seeing his or her body from another location, for example, from a position above the detached body. Causes include traumatic damage and epilepsy affecting the junction between the parietal and temporal lobes; the experience can also be produced by electrical stimulation in that area (Blanke & Arzy, 2005). In a particularly spooky clinical example, a woman whose temporoparietal junction was stimulated to see if that was the source of her epileptic seizures reported a ghostly form right behind her that mimicked her body posture and movements precisely (Figure 11.6; Arzy, Seeck, Ortigue, Spinelli, & Blanke, 2006).

Pain and Its Disorders

In Chapter 8, we learned about the emotional aspect of pain and how it motivates our behavior. Now we need to put pain in the context of the body senses and see how it works as a sensory mechanism. In spite of our attention to pain earlier, there are still a few surprises left.

Detecting Pain

Pain begins when certain free nerve endings are stimulated by intense pressure or temperature, by damage to tissue, or by various chemicals. Tissue injury also causes the injured cells to release a wide array of signaling molecules, referred to as the "*inflammatory soup*"; these include histamine, proteins (bradykinin), lipids (prostaglandins), neurotransmitters (serotonin), and cytokines (Julius & Basbaum, 2001; Kidd & Urban, 2001). Some of these stimulate pain receptors, but they also produce the familiar swelling and redness of inflammation, and they enhance excitability of the pain neurons so much that the neurons respond even to light touch. This effect is adaptive because it encourages guarding of the injured area, but the resulting pain can be more troublesome than the original injury. From the injured area, pain information travels to the spinal cord over large, myelinated A-delta fibers and small, lightly myelinated or unmyelinated C fibers. Because A-delta fibers transmit more rapidly than C fibers, you notice a *sharp, stinging pain* almost immediately when you are injured, followed by a longer lasting *dull, aching pain* (Basbaum & Jessell, 2000). Sharp pain receptors tend to be superficially located and are much more densely packed, which makes localizing the source of the sharp pain easier. Dull pain receptors are deeper and respond to a wider array of painful stimuli, and the sensations are harder to localize (Raja, Meyer, Ringkamp, & Campbell, 1999). Sharp pain makes a good danger signal and motivates you to take quick action, while dull pain hangs around for a longer time to remind you that you have been injured.

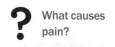

What causes pain?

In the spinal cord, pain neurons release the neurotransmitter glutamate; as stimulation becomes more intense, they release both glutamate and *substance P*, a neuropeptide that increases pain sensitivity (Cao et al., 1998). In Chapter 2, we saw that neuropeptides enhance the primary neurotransmitter's effect at the synapse; in mice lacking substance P or its receptors, mild pain is unaffected but sensitivity to moderate and intense pain is impaired (Cao et al.). As with the other body senses, pain information passes through the thalamus to the somatosensory cortex; however, the anterior cingulate cortex and the insula carry out additional processing of the emotional implications of pain, and the prefrontal cortex is concerned with pain of longer duration.

Treating Pain

We saw in Chapter 2 that local anesthetics—those that are applied to or injected into the painful area—block sodium channels in the pain neurons and reduce their ability to fire. General anesthetics, which may be injected or inhaled, render the patient unconscious. They work in the central nervous system, though their mechanism is poorly understood. We know that they affect the functioning of several proteins, but we don't know which ones are important to the anesthesia. The most frequently used pain drugs are aspirin, ibuprofen, naproxen, and acetaminophen (Table 11.1). The first three drugs (also called NSAIDs) block inflammatory enzymes required for producing prostaglandins, so they primarily reduce swelling and peripheral pain. Acetaminophen weakly blocks the same enzymes so it has little anti-inflammatory benefit; its major effect is in the central nervous system. Ameliorating intense pain often requires more powerful substances called opiates, and morphine extracted from the opium poppy is the acknowledged gold standard, but their addictiveness and patients' rapidly developing tolerance have spurred the development of numerous alternatives (refer to Chapter 5 for more on these drugs). The MDAN series of drugs, for example, targets the mu opioid receptor while blocking the delta opioid receptor; these drugs are reportedly 50 times more potent than morphine, without producing either tolerance or addiction (Dietis et al., 2009). One such drug (NKTR-181) just finished phase 3 clinical trials with promising results in decreasing chronic lower back pain without causing drowsiness or euphoria (Anson, 2017).

Efforts are under way on a variety of other fronts, as well. Tanezumab, an antibody for nerve growth factor, has shown safety and effectiveness in clinical trials with chronic back pain and the inflammatory pain of joint arthritis (M. T. Brown et al., 2013; Cattaneo, 2010). An experimental drug that blocks the TRPV1 receptor produces modest reduction of bone cancer pain in mice, but much smaller doses significantly increase the effectiveness of morphine when the two are used in combination (Niiyama, Kawamata, Yamamoto, Furuse, & Namiki, 2009). There has also been some preliminary success with gene therapy; patients whose pain from

TABLE 11.1   Medications for Pain.

DRUG CLASS	EXAMPLES	METHOD OF ACTION	SIDE EFFECTS
Nonsteroid anti-inflammatory drug (NSAID)	Naproxen, ibuprofen, aspirin	Decreases swelling in tissues	Increased risk of bleeding, stomach irritation, allergic reaction
COX-2 inhibitor (selective NSAID)	Celecoxib	Decreased inflammation	Slight risk of heart attack
Acetaminophen	Tylenol	Blocks pain signals in CNS	Liver problems
Opiates (narcotics)	Morphine, codeine, hydromorphone, oxycodone, fentanyl	Stimulates opiate receptors, blocks pain messages in CNS	Depressed breathing, sleepiness, addiction, tolerance, euphoria

cancer was not relieved by 200 mg per day of morphine experienced an 80% reduction following treatment with a gene that increases endorphin production (D. J. Fink et al., 2011). The fact that pain ultimately occurs in the brain has inspired a novel approach that is also showing promise; chronic pain patients given continuous functional magnetic resonance imaging (fMRI) feedback of activity in their cingulate gyrus learned to reduce pain-related brain activity and their experience of pain (deCharms et al., 2005).

Internal Mechanisms of Pain Relief

People sometimes feel little or no pain in spite of serious injury; they may even fail to realize they are injured until someone calls it to their attention. In the account of his search for the mouth of the Nile River, the explorer and missionary David Livingstone (1858/1971) gave an intriguing example (Figure 11.7):

> Starting, and looking half round, I saw the lion just in the act of springing upon me. I was upon a little height; he caught my shoulder as he sprang, and we both came to the ground below together. Growling horribly close to my ear, he shook me as a terrier dog does a rat. The shock produced a stupor similar to that which seems to be felt by a mouse after the first shake of the cat. It caused a sort of dreaminess, in which there was no sense of pain nor feeling of terror, though quite conscious of all that was happening. It was like what patients partially under the influence of chloroform describe, who see all the operation, but feel not the knife. (p. 12)

You learned in earlier chapters that the reason opiate drugs are so effective at relieving pain is that they operate at receptors for the body's own pain relievers. Researchers combined the words *endogenous* ("from

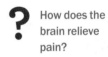

How does the brain relieve pain?

within") and *morphine* to come up with the name *endorphins* for this class of neurochemicals. *Endorphins* function both as neurotransmitters and as hormones, and they act at opiate receptors in many parts of the nervous system. Pain is one of the stimuli that release endorphins, but it does so only under certain conditions. Rats subjected to inescapable electric shock were highly tolerant of pain 30 minutes later; rats given an equal number of shocks that they could escape by making the correct response had only a slight increase in pain resistance (S. F. Maier, Drugan, & Grau, 1982). We are sure you can see the benefit of eliminating pain in situations of helplessness like Livingstone's and preserving pain when it can serve as the motivation to escape. An injection of naloxone eliminates the analgesia induced by inescapable shock but not the milder analgesia that follows escapable shock; the fact that naloxone blocks opiate receptors by occupying them indicates that the analgesia of inescapable shock is endorphin based. (You may be wondering how you would determine a rat's pain

■ **FIGURE 11.7**   David Livingstone Attacked by a Lion.

Endorphins allowed him to endure the pain of a lion's attack.

Source: Hulton Archive; Livingstone, 1858/1971.

FIGURE 11.8 Activation of Opiate Receptors in the Brain by a Placebo.

(a) Activity in cortical and brain stem areas (in red) during opiate drug treatment for pain. (b) A similar pattern of activity occurs during placebo treatment of pain. Pain alone did not produce this result. The blue dots indicate the location of the anterior cingulate cortex, which, as you saw in Chapter 8, is involved in emotional aspects of pain.

(a)   **(b)**

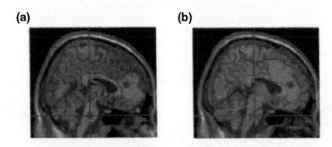

Source: From "Placebo and Opiod Analgesia—Imaging a Shared Neuronal Network," by P. Petrovic et al., *Science*, *295*, pp. 1737–1740, fig. 4 a and b, p. 1739. © 2004. Reprinted by permission of AAAS.

resistance, since it cannot verbally report its pain sensation. One way is to place the rat's tail under a heat lamp and record how long it takes the rat to flick its tail away.)

Several kinds of stimulation result in endorphin release and pain reduction, including physical stress (Colt, Wardlaw, & Frantz, 1981), acupuncture (Watkins & Mayer, 1982), and vaginal stimulation in female rats (Komisaruk & Steinman, 1987) and women (Whipple & Komisaruk, 1988). Analgesia resulting from vaginal stimulation probably serves to reduce pain during birth or intercourse. Even the pain relief from placebo, which doctors once took as evidence that the pain was not "real," is often the result of increasing endorphins, as revealed both by naloxone blockage of opiate receptors and by PET scans (Figure 11.8; Amanzio, Pollo, Maggi, & Benedetti, 2001; Petrovic, 2005; Petrovic, Kalso, Petersson, & Ingvar, 2002). So convincing yourself that the pain is diminishing may actually decrease the pain!

Not all stimulation-induced pain relief comes from endorphins. For example, naloxone does not reduce the analgesic effect of hypnosis, and naloxone blocks analgesia produced by acupuncture needles inserted at distant points from the pain site but not when the needles are placed near the site (Watkins & Mayer, 1982). Research indicates that the acupuncture needle causes a 24-fold increase in adenosine, which acts as a local anesthetic (N. Goldman et al., 2010). (Note, by the way, that this study's first author was a 16-year-old girl.)

The Descending Pain Inhibition Circuit

During a spring break in New Orleans, Bob was touring one of the Civil War–era plantation houses for which the area is noted. In a glass case was an assortment of artifacts that had been found on the plantation grounds. An odd part of the collection was a few lead rifle slugs with what were obviously deep tooth marks on them. When makeshift surgery had to be performed with only a large dose of whiskey for anesthesia, the unfortunate patient would often be given something to bite down on like a piece of leather harness or a relatively soft lead bullet. (You can probably guess the common expression that is associated with this practice.) As a toddler, when you scraped your knee you clenched your teeth and rubbed the area around the wound. And—tribute to your childhood wisdom—it really did help and got you through the pain without the benefit of either a lead bullet or whiskey. You might think that tooth clenching and rubbing simply take attention from the pain. Ronald Melzack and Patrick Wall (1965) had another idea. In their *gate control theory,* they hypothesized that pressure signals arriving in the brain trigger an inhibitory message that travels back down the spinal cord, where it closes a neural "gate" in the pain pathway.

How can we "gate" pain?

Research has confirmed the general idea of their theory, and we now know that a descending pathway in the spinal cord is one of the ways the brain uses endorphins to control pain. Pain causes the release of endorphins in the *periaqueductal gray (PAG),* a brain stem structure with a large number of endorphin synapses (Basbaum & Fields, 1984). As you can see in Figure 11.9, endorphin release inhibits the release of substance P, closing the pain "gate" in the spinal cord. (Note that enkephalin, the type of endorphin in the spinal cord, reduces substance P release by *presynaptic* inhibition, as described in Chapter 2.) Activation of the endorphin circuit apparently has multiple neural origins, including the cingulate cortex during placebo analgesia and the amygdala in the case of fear-induced analgesia (Petrovic, 2005). Brain imaging shows that placebo reduces pain through this circuit, and so does simple distraction (Petrovic, 2005; Petrovic et al., 2002; Tracey et al., 2002). Electrical stimulation of the PAG is also a very effective pain reliever, but it has the drawback of implanting electrodes in the brain (Bittar et al., 2005). Women, unfortunately, have fewer mu opioid receptors in the PAG than men, so they receive less pain-relieving benefit from opiate drugs (Loyd, Wang, & Murphy, 2008). The PAG also contains cannabinoid receptors, which respond to endogenous cannabinoids and the active ingredient in marijuana (see Chapter 5), and they account for some forms of stimulation-induced pain relief (Hohmann et al., 2005).

Pain's Extremes: From Congenital Insensitivity to Chronic Pain

Congenital insensitivity to pain (or congenital analgesia) is a very rare condition. This is fortunate, because those who are afflicted not only unknowingly hurt themselves but also often engage in risky and dangerous behavior that most other people avoid. One family with several afflicted members was discovered when researchers learned of a boy in northern Pakistan who entertained on the street by piercing his arms with knives; before he could be studied, he died when he celebrated his 14th birthday by jumping off a roof (J. J. Cox et al., 2006). Several genes have been identified as responsible for the different kinds of pain insensitivity. People with a mutation in the *SCN9A* gene have nonfunctioning versions of a specific sodium channel, so their pain neurons are disabled (J. J. Cox et al.). Mutations in the *PRDM12* gene also prevent the development of pain-sensing neurons (Y.-C. Chen et al., 2015). Those with a mutation in the gene for nerve growth factor (*NGFB*), which stimulates development of sensory nerves, have a significant loss of unmyelinated neurons and less severe loss of myelinated fibers (Einarsdottir et al., 2004). Another cause of insensitivity is illustrated in the case of a 16-year-old boy whose most significant characteristic was elevated opioid levels in his cerebrospinal fluid (Manfredi et al., 1981).

Chronic pain is much more common, and its victims often experience lifelong suffering. How many people are afflicted is difficult to determine, because studies include different populations and use different criteria. As a result, estimates have ranged from 10% to 55%; averages for two different criteria were 11.8% and 35.5% (Harstall & Ospina, 2003). Practitioners often attempt to distinguish chronic from acute pain in terms of duration, with standards varying from 1 month to 1 year. However, it makes more sense to define *chronic pain* as pain that persists after healing has occurred or beyond the time in which healing would be expected to occur.

Whether pain becomes chronic is largely unrelated to the severity of injury. Chronic pain patients are often clinically depressed; this could logically be attributed to the pain, but evidence indicates that in patients who exaggerate the extent and intensity of their pain, the depression precedes the injury (Bortsov, Platts-Mills et al., 2013). Also, the strength of functional connectivity between the nucleus accumbens and the frontal cortex, measured shortly after back pain began, predicted with 85% accuracy which patients would continue to suffer pain one year later (Baliki et al., 2012). Both areas are important in evaluating and dealing with stressful events, and their connection likely determines how emotionally the person reacts to pain. Several genes play a role as well. A different allele of the *SCN9A* sodium channel gene mentioned earlier lowers pain threshold and contributes to two types of neuropathic pain (T. Z. Fischer & Waxman, 2010). Variations in the *COMT* gene also regulate pain sensitivity, as well as responsiveness to pain relievers, and they figure in several pain syndromes (Andersen & Skorpen, 2009). Six variations of a glucocorticoid gene were associated with increased pain intensity in patients following motor vehicle collisions, while a variant of a D_2 dopamine receptor gene reduced severity (Bortsov, Smith, et al., 2013; Qadri et al., 2012).

The nervous system undergoes extensive functional and structural changes during chronic pain. The pain pathways increase their sensitivity, new connections sprout where peripheral neurons make connections in the spinal cord, and normal spinal inhibitory mechanisms are depressed (Woolf & Salter, 2000). The brain also participates in these changes. Brain stem pathways become more responsive (M. Lee, Zambreanu, Menon, &

? How does chronic pain differ from regular pain?

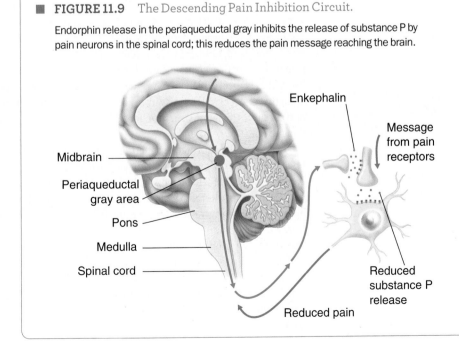

■ **FIGURE 11.9** The Descending Pain Inhibition Circuit.

Endorphin release in the periaqueductal gray inhibits the release of substance P by pain neurons in the spinal cord; this reduces the pain message reaching the brain.

Enkephalin

Message from pain receptors

Midbrain

Periaqueductal gray area

Pons

Medulla

Spinal cord

Reduced substance P release

Reduced pain

■ **FIGURE 11.10**   Gray Matter Loss, Then Gain, in Patients With Chronic Hip Pain Before and After Replacement Surgery.

Magnetic resonance imaging shows areas where patients lost more gray matter than controls in the anterior cingulate cortex, insula, and brain stem. (A) Yellow represents the amount of loss in chronic pain patients compared to pain-free controls, and (B) orange represents postsurgical gain compared to presurgical size in patients with chronic hip pain.

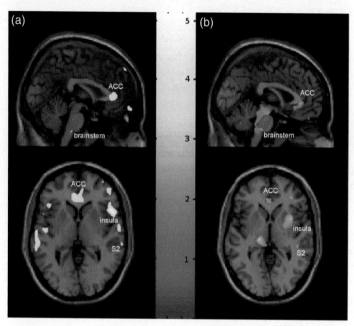

Source: From "Brain Gray Matter Decrease in Chronic Pain is the Consequence and Not the Cause of Pain," by Rodriguez-Raecke et al., *Journal of Neuroscience, 29,* pp. 13746–13750, fig. 1. © 2009 Society for Neuroscience. Used with permission.

Tracey, 2008); activation increases in the prefrontal cortex, anterior cingulate cortex, and insula (Baliki et al., 2006); and the amount of somatosensory cortex devoted to the painful area expands (Flor, Braun, Elbert, & Birbaumer, 1997). There is considerable loss of gray matter, equivalent to 10–20 years of additional aging in patients with chronic back pain (Figure 11.10; Apkarian, Sosa, Sonty, et al., 2004) and 9.5 years of additional aging per year of suffering with fibromyalgia (Kuchinad et al., 2007). Evidence of the functional disruption this causes is that chronic pain patients perform poorly, almost randomly, on the gambling test used to assess prefrontal impairment (described in Chapter 8; Apkarian, Sosa, Krauss, et al., 2004). One piece of good news is that cortical decline may be partially reversible; patients with chronic hip pain increased their gray matter volumes after receiving a hip replacement and going four months without pain (Rodriguez-Raecke, Niemeier, Ihle, Ruether, & May, 2009).

Phantom Pain

If damage to the right parietal cortex can eliminate recognition of a paralyzed left arm or leg, shouldn't removing a person's arm or leg eliminate all consciousness of the limb? Not if there are cortical areas still devoted to the missing body parts. Most amputees continue to experience the missing limb, not as a memory, but as vividly as if it were real (Melzack, 1992). A phantom leg seems to bend when the person sits down and then to become upright during standing; a phantom arm even feels as though it is swinging in coordination with the other arm during walking.

? **What causes phantom pain?**

In about 75% of amputees, we see what is undeniably the strangest manifestation of chronic pain (Kern, Busch, Rockland, Kohl, & Birklein, 2009; Richardson, Glenn, Nurmikko, & Horgan, 2006). *Phantom pain,* pain that is experienced in a missing limb, is not simply pain at the stump but is felt in the missing arm or leg itself. The classical explanation was that the cut ends of nerves continue to send impulses to the part of the brain that once served the missing limb. Peripheral input is a factor in some cases, but anesthetizing these nerves relieves phantom pain in no more than half of patients (Birbaumer et al., 1997; Flor, 2008), so something else must be going on.

Following the clue that stimulating the face often produces sensations in a phantom arm, a team of researchers in Germany used brain imaging to map face and hand somatosensory areas in upper-limb amputees (Flor et al., 1995). In patients with phantom pain, neurons from the face area appeared to have invaded the area that normally receives input from the missing hand (Figure 11.11). The area activated by touch on the lips was shifted an average of 2.05 centimeters (cm) in the hemisphere opposite the amputation, compared with 0.43 cm for the patients without phantom pain, a fivefold difference. It is unclear how much the results were due to intrusion of foreign neurons or to activation of existing neurons. However, facial stimulation can evoke sensations in the phantom arm within 24 hours after amputation, which indicates that "unmasking" of existing but ordinarily silent inputs is at least a partial explanation (Borsook et al., 1998). We usually think of neural plasticity as adaptive, but sometimes it can lead to malfunction and, in this case, truly bizarre results. As you can imagine, treating phantom pain poses special problems, so we will give it special attention in the accompanying Application.

■ **FIGURE 11.11**　Reorganization of the Somatosensory Cortex in a Phantom Pain Patient Following Arm Amputation.

The symbols represent the location of sensitivity to touch of the fingers (squares) and the lips (circles); black symbols are from a patient with phantom pain and white symbols from a patient without phantom pain. By looking at the homunculus superimposed on the left hemisphere (opposite the intact arm), you can see that the circles and the squares are in their normal locations. In the right hemisphere, opposite the amputated arm, lip sensitivity in the patient with the phantom pain (black circle) has migrated well into the area ordinarily serving finger sensitivity.

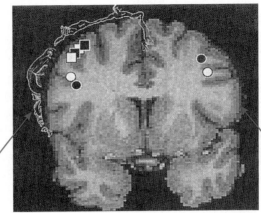

From side of body with intact arm

From side of body with amputated arm

Source: From "Phantom-limb Pain as a Perceptual Correlate of Cortical Reorganization Following Arm Amputation," by H. Flor et al., 1995, *Nature, 375*, pp. 482–484. Copyright © 1995.

CONCEPT CHECK

Take a Minute to Check Your Knowledge and Understanding

- What is the contribution of each of the three classes of body senses?
- In what ways are the somatosensory cortex and the visual cortex organized similarly?
- In what circumstances does the brain reduce pain?

Movement

A popular view of the brain is that it is mostly preoccupied with higher cognitive processes, such as thinking, learning, and language. However, a surprising proportion of the brain is devoted to planning and executing movements. We are talking about more than simply moving the body from one place to another; consider the surgeon's coordinated hand movements during a delicate operation, the control of mouth and throat muscles and diaphragm required to sing an aria, or a baseball outfielder's ability to track a fast-moving fly ball and arrive in time to catch it. Studies of the control of movement provided one of the earliest windows into the brain's organization and functioning, and it is that facet of the research that will interest us most. Before we launch into that topic, we need some understanding of the equipment the brain has to work with.

The Muscles

We have three types of muscles. The ones you are most familiar with are the *skeletal muscles,* which move the body and limbs but can fatigue if overused; they are also called *striated* muscles because of their striped cellular appearance. *Smooth muscles* produce rhythmic contractions in the internal organs; for example, they move food through the digestive system, constrict blood vessels, and void the bladder. *Cardiac muscles* are the non-fatiguing muscles that make up the heart. Because our focus is on movement, we will concentrate on the skeletal muscles. Anyway, despite differences in appearance, the muscles function similarly.

APPLICATION
Treating Pain in Limbs That Aren't There

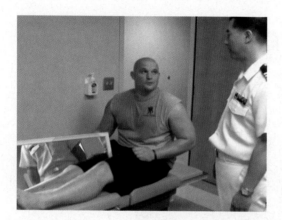

Source: © Walter Morris/Medill News Service.

Most treatments for phantom pain are ineffective and fail to consider the mechanisms producing the pain. Surgery and pharmacological interventions are typically no better than placebo and benefit less than 30% of patients (Flor, 2008). Postsurgical reorganization of cortical wiring is a likely cause of phantom limb pain (Yanagisawa et al., 2016), and several studies suggest that therapies that work either prevent or reverse the cortical reorganization that occurs following amputation (Birbaumer et al., 1997). Use of a functional prosthesis (as opposed to a purely cosmetic one) prevents cortical reorganization and reduces pain occurrence (Lotze et al., 1999); newer hand prostheses that have pressure sensors in the fingers to help amputees adjust their grip to different objects should reduce phantom pain even better (Friedrich-Schiller-Universität Jena, 2010). When a prosthesis is impractical, training to discriminate electrical stimuli applied to the stump reverses cortical reorganization and reduces pain in 60% of patients (Flor, Denke, Schaefer, & Grüsser, 2001).

One promising behavioral technique is mirror therapy. The patient places the stump out of sight on one side of a mirror and the good limb on the other side, so the reflection of the good limb appears to replace the one that is missing (see figure). Then the patient is told to move the two limbs in unison. In one later study, 100% of patients using the mirror box experienced decreases in pain (Chan et al., 2007); another study confirmed that pain relief is accompanied by reversal of cortical reorganization (Flor, Diers, Christmann, & Koeppe, 2006). For obvious reasons, mirror therapy is most effective if it is used soon after injury (Foeli, Bekrater-Bodmann, Diers, & Flor, 2013), but a new augmented reality technique has shown effectiveness in patients more than five years on average since their amputation and previous treatment (Ortiz-Catalan et al., 2016). Instead of a mirror image, patients see themselves on a video screen with their amputated arm replaced by a virtual one; electrodes on the stump send electrical signals from the muscles to a computer to make the virtual arm move (see image). After 12 sessions, the patients' pain decreased by 50%.

These techniques may work because of the greater responsiveness of the mirror neuron system in phantom limb patients. Bob saw this firsthand in a colleague, Ed, who had lost both legs in an accident. As they watched a construction worker walking the girders of a new building, Bob felt a bit of anxiety and a sympathetic tension in his legs as he imagined himself up there balancing on the narrow beams but, to his surprise, Ed exclaimed, "That makes my ankles hurt!" Researchers believe that simulated feedback therapy works because the image triggers exaggerated activity in mirror neurons in the hemisphere that once served the missing limb (Chan et al., 2007; Ramachandran & Altschuler, 2009). Without contradictory feedback from the missing limb, the mirror neuron activity is interpreted as actual touch or movement, and with continued practice the brain's reorganization is reversed.

Like other tissues of the body, a muscle is made up of many individual cells, or muscle fibers. The muscle cells are controlled by motor neurons that synapse with a muscle cell at the neuromuscular junction using the neurotransmitter acetylcholine (Figure 11.12). The number of cells served by a single axon determines the precision of movement possible. The biceps muscles have about a hundred muscle fibers per axon, but the ratio is around three to one in the eye muscles, which must make very precise movements in tracking objects (Evarts, 1979).

A muscle fiber is made up of myosin and actin filaments. When a motor neuron releases acetylcholine, the muscle fiber is depolarized, which opens calcium channels; the calcium influx initiates a series of actions by the myosin that contract the muscle. Small protrusions along the myosin filaments attach to the surrounding actin filaments; they then make a stroking movement that causes the actin filaments to slide along the myosin filaments, which shortens the muscle fibers. This sequence repeats rapidly, contracting the muscle (Figure 11.13).

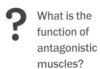

What is the function of antagonistic muscles?

Skeletal muscles are anchored to bones by tendons, which are tough fibrous bands of connective tissue. You can see in Figure 11.14 that by pulling against their attachments the muscles are able to operate the limbs like levers to produce movement. Muscles can only contract; a limb is both flexed and extended by pulling on the joint from one side or the other. You can see that limbs have *antagonistic muscles* that produce opposite movements at a joint.

In this case, the biceps muscle decreases the arm angle to flex the arm, and the triceps increases the angle, extending the arm. Rather than one muscle relaxing while the other does all the work, movement involves opposing contraction from both muscles. The simultaneous contraction of antagonistic muscles creates a smoother movement, allows precise stopping, and maintains the limb angle with minimal tremor. Standing requires coordinating the countering effects of antagonistic muscles in the legs, as well as muscles in the torso. The amount of contraction in a muscle varies from moment to moment, so the balance between two antagonistic muscles is constantly shifting, constantly correcting. If maintaining the balance between opposed pairs of muscles required conscious, voluntary activity, we would find it very difficult to hold a camera still enough to get a sharp picture or even to stand or sit erect. Adjustments this fast must be controlled by reflexes at the level of the spinal cord.

■ **FIGURE 11.12**   Muscle Fibers Innervated by a Motor Neuron.

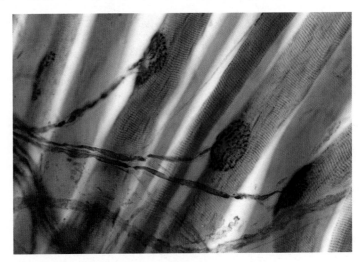

Source: © Ed Reschke/Photolibrary/Getty Images.

The Spinal Cord

In Chapter 3, we introduced the idea of the spinal reflex. Everyone is familiar with the reflex that makes you quickly withdraw your hand from a hot stove. When you step on a sharp object, you reflexively withdraw your foot and simultaneously make a variety of reflexive postural adjustments to avoid losing your balance. The advantage of reflexes is that we can make the appropriate adjustments quickly, without the delay of having to figure out the right action.

What do spinal reflexes and central pattern generators do?

The monosynaptic reflex illustrated in Figure 11.15 should also be familiar. Your doctor taps the patellar tendon, which connects the quadriceps muscle to the lower leg bone. This stretches the muscle, which is detected by muscle stretch receptors called *muscle spindles* and relayed to the spinal cord. There the sensory neurons synapse on motor neurons, which return to the quadriceps and cause it to contract and extend the lower leg. (There is an inhibitory interneuron in the spinal cord that relaxes the antagonistic hamstring muscle in the back of the leg, but this isn't shown in the figure.) The function of the stretch reflex is not just to amuse your doctor. It enables a muscle to resist very quickly if the muscle is stretched by activity in its antagonistic partner; this helps, for example, to maintain an upright posture. It also allows a muscle to respond quickly to an increased external load, for example, when you are holding a stack of books in front of you and a friend

■ **FIGURE 11.13**   Myosin and Actin Cause a Muscle to Contract.

Protrusions from the myosin filament extend to the actin filament and attach, then flex, causing the actin to slide alongside the myosin; this shortens the muscle, producing a contraction. The protrusions then withdraw from the actin and repeat the process in rapid succession.

Stories of Brain & Behavior

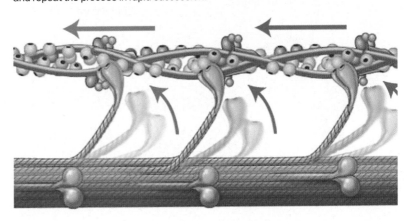

Source: Adapted from Figure 10.7, *Principles of Anatomy and Physiology* (11th ed.), by Gerard J. Tortora and Bryan H. Derrickson, 2006, Hoboken, NJ: John Wiley & Sons.

■ **FIGURE 11.14**   Antagonistic Muscles of the Upper Arm.

When the biceps muscle contracts, it flexes the arm (left); contracting the triceps muscle extends the arm.

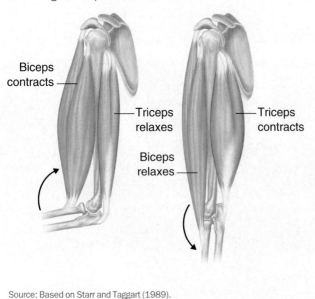

Source: Based on Starr and Taggart (1989).

unexpectedly drops another book on top of it. *Golgi tendon organs,* receptors that detect tension in a muscle, trigger a spinal reflex that inhibits the motor neurons and limits the contraction. This prevents muscles from contracting so strongly that they might be damaged.

More complex patterns of motor behavior are also controlled in the spinal cord. It has been known for at least a century that cats with severed spinal cords, eliminating control from the brain, can make rhythmic stepping movements, and walk when they are suspended with their feet on a treadmill (J. G. Jones, Tansey, & Stuart, 2011). This behavior depends on *central pattern generators (CPGs),* neuronal networks that produce a rhythmic pattern of motor activity, such as those involved in walking, swimming, flying, and breathing. Central pattern generators are in the spinal cord and in the brain, and have been found in all vertebrate animals. In humans, they are most obvious in infants below the age of one year, who can make stepping movements when held with their feet on a treadmill (Lamb & Yang, 2000). In adults, CPGs provide an important bit of automaticity to routine movements. They can be elicited in individuals with spinal cord injury to produce rhythmic stepping movements (Dimitrijevic, Gerasimenko, & Pinter, 1998), and researchers are working on ways to recruit them during therapy (Boulenguez & Vinay, 2009; Dietz, 2009; Edgerton & Roy, 2009). Spinal reflexes produce quick, reliable responses, and CPGs provide basic routines the brain can call up when needed, freeing the brain for more important matters (Figure 11.16). But reflexes and CPGs cannot provide all our movement capabilities, so we

■ **FIGURE 11.15**   The Patellar Tendon Reflex, an Example of a Stretch Reflex.

The hammer stretches the tendon, causing a reflexive contraction of the extensor muscle and a kicking motion. This is a highly simplified representation; many more neurons are involved.

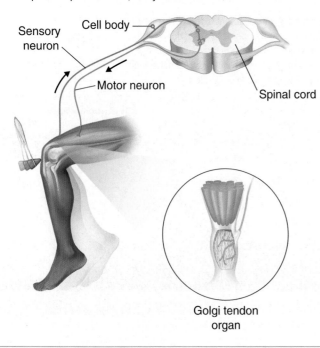

■ **FIGURE 11.16**   The Stepping Reflex.

The stepping reflex is present in young infants. If you support their weight and allow their feet to touch a flat surface, they will raise and lower their legs as though they are walking.

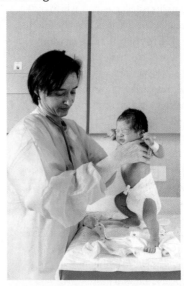

Source: © Phanie/Phanie/SuperStock.

will turn our attention to the contributions the brain makes to movement.

The Brain and Movement

In the motor system, we again see a hierarchical organization consisting of the forebrain, brain stem, and spinal cord. The motor cortex organizes complex acts and executes movements while modulating activity in the brain stem and spinal cord. The brain stem in turn modulates the activity of the spinal cord (Ghez & Krakauer, 2000). We will start with the cortex and give it most of our attention.

The motor cortex consists of the *primary motor cortex* and two major secondary motor areas, the *supplementary motor area* and the *premotor cortex* (Figure 11.17). Like the primary area, the secondary areas contain a map of the body, with greater amounts of cortex devoted to the parts of the body that produce finer movements (Figure 11.18). The sequence of processing in the motor cortex is just the opposite of what we see in the sensory areas: Planning of movement begins in the association areas, and the primary motor cortex is the final cortical motor area. Along the way, a movement is modified by inputs from the somatosensory cortex, the posterior parietal cortex, the basal ganglia, and the cerebellum. As with many other functions, the prefrontal cortex plays an executive role, so it will receive our attention first. We will be covering several brain areas and their functions in the next few pages. It would be a good idea to review the summary in Table 11.2 before reading further, so that you will have an idea of where we are going.

The Prefrontal Cortex

You already know two functions of the prefrontal cortex that suit it for its role in movement control: First, it plans actions with regard to their consequences; second, it receives information from the ventral visual stream about object identity, which is useful in identifying targets of motor activity. As an initial step in motor planning, the *prefrontal cortex* integrates auditory and visual information about the world with information about the body (from the posterior parietal cortex); it then holds the information in memory while selecting the appropriate movement and its target (see Figure 11.17). Considering its activities, it really makes more sense to say that the role of the prefrontal cortex is not so much in planning movements as in planning *for* movements.

These functions are typically investigated in monkeys while they perform some variation of a

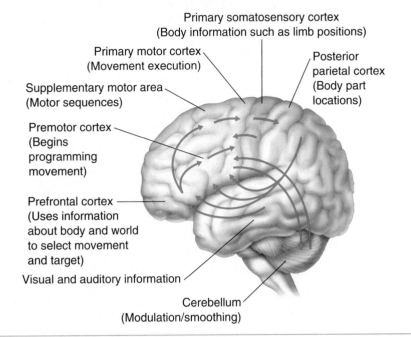

■ **FIGURE 11.17** The Motor Areas of the Cortex and Cerebellum.

Connections between the primary motor cortex and the basal ganglia are not shown.

Primary somatosensory cortex
(Body information such as limb positions)

Primary motor cortex
(Movement execution)

Posterior parietal cortex
(Body part locations)

Supplementary motor area
(Motor sequences)

Premotor cortex
(Begins programming movement)

Prefrontal cortex
(Uses information about body and world to select movement and target)

Visual and auditory information

Cerebellum
(Modulation/smoothing)

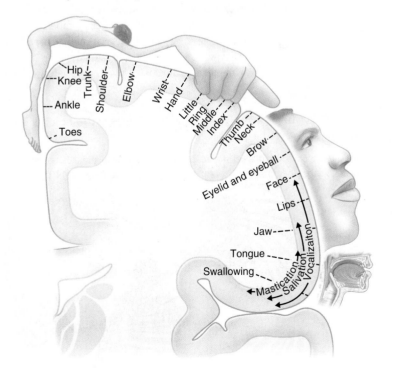

■ **FIGURE 11.18** The Primary Motor Area.

The homunculus shows the relative amount of cortex devoted to different parts of the body.

Hip, Knee, Ankle, Toes, Trunk, Shoulder, Elbow, Wrist, Hand, Little, Ring, Middle, Index, Thumb, Neck, Brow, Eyelid and eyeball, Face, Lips, Jaw, Tongue, Swallowing, Mastication, Salivation, Vocalization

Source: Adapted from *The Cerebral Cortex of Man* by W. Penfield and T. Rasmussen, 1950, New York: Macmillan. © 1950 Gale, a part of Cengage Learning, Inc. Reproduced by permission.

TABLE 11.2   The Major Brain Areas of Movement and Their Functions.

STRUCTURE	FUNCTIONS
Prefrontal cortex	Selects the appropriate behavior and its target, using a combination of bodily and external information.
Premotor cortex	Combines information needed for movement programming, such as the target being reached for and its location, which arm to use, and the arm's location.
Supplementary motor area	Assembles sequences of movements, such as eating or playing the piano; coordinates movements between the two sides of the body (e.g., task sharing between the hands).
Primary motor cortex	Executes voluntary movements by organizing the activity of unspecialized cells; adds force and direction control.
Basal ganglia	Uses information from secondary areas and the somatosensory cortex to integrate and smooth movements; apparently involved in learning movement sequences.
Cerebellum	Maintains balance, refines movements, controls compensatory eye movements. Involved in learning motor skills.

?

What is the relationship between the primary motor area and the association areas?

delayed match-to-sample task. The monkey is presented with a visual stimulus; then, after a delay of a few seconds in which the stimulus is absent, the monkey is presented two or more stimuli and required to select the original stimulus (by reaching for it) to obtain a reward, such as a sip of juice. Some cells in the prefrontal cortex start firing when the first stimulus is presented and continue to fire throughout the delay, suggesting that they are "remembering" the stimulus. At response time, another group of prefrontal cells starts firing before activity starts in the premotor areas; this indicates that the prefrontal cortex selects the target of behavior and the appropriate motor responses (Goldman-Rakic, Bates, & Chafee, 1992; Hoshi, Shima, & Tanji, 2000; Rainer, Rao, & Miller, 1999).

The Secondary Motor Areas

The *premotor cortex* begins programming a movement by combining information from the prefrontal cortex and the posterior parietal cortex (Krakauer & Ghez, 2000). A good example comes from a study in which monkeys were cued to reach for one of two targets, A or B, in different locations and to use the left arm on some trials and the right arm on others. Some premotor neurons increased their firing rate only if target A was cued, and other neurons were selective for target B. Other cells fired selectively depending on which arm was to be used. Still other cells combined the information of the first two kinds of cells; they increased their firing only when a target was cued *and* a particular arm was to be used (Hoshi & Tanji, 2000). Two other cell types combine visual and somatosensory information to provide visual guidance of reaching and object manipulation. The first responds to visual stimuli on or near a specific part of the body, as in Figure 11.19a;

■ **FIGURE 11.19**   Receptive Fields of Two Types of Premotor Neurons That Responded to Both Visual and Body Information.

(a) The receptive field of a cell that responded when a visual stimulus was in the area outlined near the face. (b) The visual field of the second type of neuron when the arm was out of sight. Middle and right, the visual field as the monkey's arm moved forward and across.

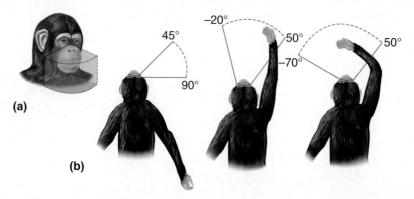

Source: Adapted from Figure 1 in "Coding of Visual Space by Premotor Neurons," by M. S. A. Graziano, G. S. Yap, and C. G. Gross, *Science, 266,* pp. 1054–1057. Copyright © 1979.

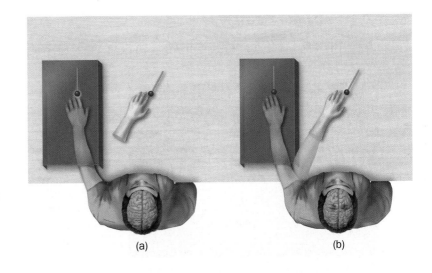

■ FIGURE 11.20

The Premotor Cortex and the Rubber Hand Illusion.

(a) The hidden left hand is stroked in synchrony with the fake hand, which is in full view. (b) After a few seconds, the individual feels that the sensation is coming from the rubber hand and reports a sense of ownership of the rubber hand. Apparently, the touch field and the visual field have become coordinated in the brain (indicated by the light blue outline and the yellow circle). fMRI recording shows that the premotor cortex is active during this illusion (indicated by the red circles).

(a)   (b)

Source: From "Probing the Neural Basis of Body Ownership," by M. Botvinick, *Science, 305,* pp. 782–783, unnumbered figure on page 782. Illustration copyright © 2004 Taina Litwak. Used with permission.

another shifts the location of its visual receptive field to coincide with the location of the monkey's hand as it moves (Figure 11.19b; Graziano, Hu, & Gross, 1997; Graziano, Yap, & Gross, 1994).

A fascinating demonstration of the role these specialized cells play occurs in a bizarre phenomenon known as the "rubber hand illusion." The individual sits at a table with the left hand hidden from view; the experimenter strokes the hidden left hand with a brush while simultaneously stroking a rubber hand, which is in full view (Figure 11.20). After a few seconds, the sensation seems to be coming from the rubber hand, which the subject identifies as "my hand." A study used fMRI to determine where the illusion occurs in the brain (Ehrsson, Spence, & Passingham, 2004). The posterior parietal cortex, which combines the visual and touch information, was active whether the two hands were stroked in synchrony or in asynchrony. The premotor area, by contrast, became active only when the stroking was simultaneous, and only after the individual began to experience the illusion; moreover, the strength of activation was related to the intensity of the illusion reported by the subject.

Output from the prefrontal cortex flows to the *supplementary motor area,* which assembles sequences of movements, such as those involved in eating or in playing the piano. In monkeys trained to produce several different sets of movement sequences, different neurons increase their firing during a delay period depending on which sequence has been cued for performance (Shima & Tanji, 2000; Tanji & Shima, 1994). An important form of movement sequencing is the coordination of movements between the two sides of the body. For example, when a monkey's supplementary motor cortex is damaged in one hemisphere, its hands tend to duplicate each other's actions instead of sharing the task (C. Brinkman, 1984). Humans with similar damage also have trouble carrying out tasks that require alternation of movements between the two hands (Laplane, Talairach, Meininger, Bancaud, & Orgogozo, 1977). Coordinating the actions of the limbs is one of the biggest problems to be overcome on the way to developing mechanized prostheses, as the accompanying Research Spotlight explains.

The Primary Motor Cortex

The *primary motor cortex* is responsible for the organization and execution of voluntary movements; its cells fire most during the movement instead of prior to it (G. E. Alexander & Crutcher, 1990; Riehle & Requin, 1989). Individual motor cortex cells are not reserved for a specific movement but contribute their function to a range of related behaviors (Saper, Iverson, & Frackowiak, 2000); the primary motor cortex orchestrates the activity of these cells into a useful movement and contributes control of the movement's force and direction (Georgopoulos, Taira, & Lukashin, 1993; Maier, Bennett, Hepp-Reymond, & Lemon, 1993). This orchestration was particularly evident in a stimulation study by Graziano, Taylor, and Moore (2002). Instead of using the usual brief pulses of electricity, which produce only muscle twitches, they increased the duration to a half-second and saw complex, coordinated responses in the monkeys, such as grasping, moving the hand to the mouth, and opening the mouth. The primary motor cortex can put these complex movement

RESEARCH SPOTLIGHT
Brain-Computer Interfaces

Source: Larry French/Getty Images Entertainment/Getty Images

Brain-controlled devices have been a science fiction trope for many years, such as the Russian thought-powered fighter jet in the 1977 book *Firefox* by Craig Thomas (and the 1982 movie starring Clint Eastwood). So far, most of the success with brain-computer interfaces has been limited to movement of a single body part, such as using a robotic arm to take a drink of coffee or eat a bit of chocolate (see the video in the "On the Web" section at the end of this chapter). Todd Kuiken at the Rehabilitation Institute of Chicago has developed a procedure called targeted reinnervation. The nerves that once served the muscles of the amputated limb are redirected to a "spare" muscle; the electrical signals generated when the individual activates this muscle are amplified and used to operate a motorized prosthesis. These devices, while much more advanced than the crude prosthetic limbs of a decade ago, are still in their infancy. They can restore motor function of a lost limb, but they lack

both the sense of touch and the ability to regulate the amount of force used to pick up an object without damaging it. Kuiken and other research teams are now developing prosthetic hands with pressure sensors in the fingers that stimulate the reinnervated muscle groups and provide feedback that is perceived by the brain as touch sensations. An artificial leg developed by Hubert Egger at the University of Linz in Austria can provide amputees with the feeling of the texture of the ground the individual is standing on (Schwartz, 2015).

How about making these artificial limbs more realistic by using synthetic materials that act like natural tissues in the way they bend, flex, and change with increasing force? Hugh Herr, at the MIT Biomechatronics group, lost both legs from frostbite while mountain climbing. He is designing synthetic limb prosthetics with these more natural and flexible materials. The limbs use residual nerve signals to control the actions of the limbs, but the strength of those signals can modify the flexibility and force of the artificial limb (Humphries, 2015). More recently, Dario Farina and colleagues (2017) developed new prosthetic arms that are controlled by undamaged spinal motor neurons, allowing more signals to be received and permitting more extensive range of movements than traditional prosthetics permit. Volunteers in Farina's study were able to open and close their hand, move their elbow joint, and move their wrist from side to side. More extensive clinical trials are the next step in developing these new prosthetics and making them available outside the research laboratory.

sequences together with the aid of input from the secondary motor areas, the somatosensory cortex, and the posterior parietal area (see Figure 11.17) (Krakauer & Ghez, 2000). Presumably, information from the somatosensory and posterior parietal areas provides feedback needed for refining movements on the fly.

The Basal Ganglia and Cerebellum

What do the basal ganglia and cerebellum add?

The basal ganglia and cerebellum produce no motor acts themselves. Rather, they modulate the activity of cortical and brain stem motor systems; in that role, they are necessary for posture and smooth movement (Ghez & Krakauer, 2000). The *basal ganglia*—the caudate nucleus, putamen, and globus pallidus—use information from the primary and secondary motor areas and the somatosensory cortex to integrate and smooth movements. The basal ganglia send output directly to the primary motor cortex and supplementary motor area, and to the premotor cortex via the thalamus. As you can see in Figure 11.21, these structures border the thalamus; they apparently smooth movements through both facilitating and inhibitory outputs to the thalamus (DeLong, 2000). The basal ganglia also are especially active during complex sequences of movements (Boecker et al., 1998). It appears that they are involved in learning movement sequences so that the movements can be performed as a unit (Graybiel, 1998). In fact, one of the symptoms of Parkinson's disease, which is caused by degeneration in the basal ganglia, is impaired learning, whether motor behavior is involved or not (Knowlton, Mangels, & Squire, 1996). Malfunction in the basal ganglia results in postural abnormalities and involuntary movements in Parkinson's disease and Huntington's disease, which can be treated using deep brain stimulation (see Wichmann & DeLong, 2016).

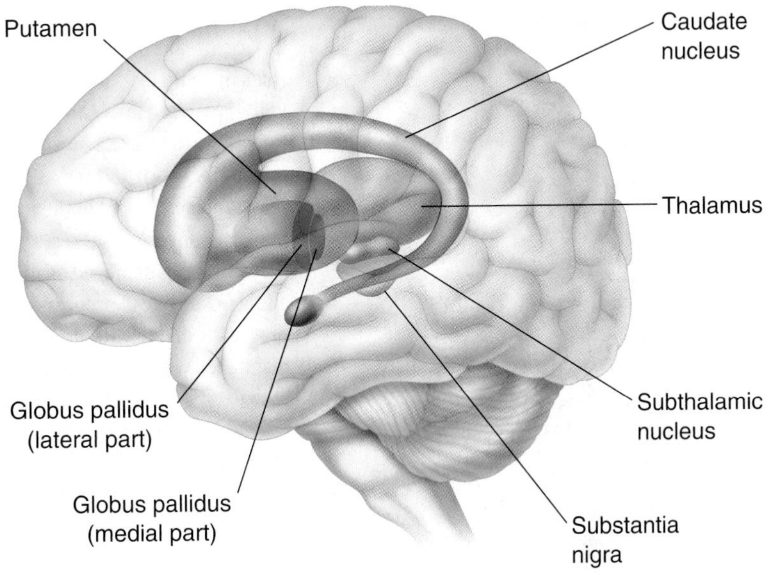

When the *cerebellum* receives information from the motor cortex about an intended movement, it determines the order of muscular contractions and their precise timing. It also uses information from the vestibular system to maintain posture and balance, refine movements, and control eye movements that compensate for head movements (Ghez & Thach, 2000). Once an intended movement has been modified, the cerebellum sends the information back to the primary motor cortex. We can see the contribution of the cerebellum in the deficits

■ **FIGURE 11.21** The Basal Ganglia.

The basal ganglia include the caudate nucleus, putamen, and globus pallidus.

Putamen

Caudate nucleus

Thalamus

Globus pallidus (lateral part)

Globus pallidus (medial part)

Subthalamic nucleus

Substantia nigra

that occur when it is damaged. For example, we begin to shape our hand for grasping while the arm is moving toward the target, but a person with cerebellar damage reaches, pauses, and then shapes the hand. A normal individual touches the nose in what appears to be a single, smooth movement; cerebellar damage results in exaggerated, wavering corrections. The effects of cerebellar damage on coordination and accuracy in limb movements is like the effect of alcohol; the drunk driver who is pulled over by the police has trouble walking a straight line, standing on one foot with the eyes closed, or touching the nose with the tip of the finger. People with damage to the cerebellum are often mistakenly believed to be drunk.

The cerebellum lives up to the meaning of its name, "little brain," by applying its expertise to a variety of tasks. It is necessary for learning motor skills (D. A. McCormick & Thompson, 1984), but it also participates in nonmotor learning (Canavan, Sprengelmeyer, Diener, & Hömberg, 1994) and in making time and speed judgments about auditory and visual stimuli (Keele & Ivry, 1990). Also, patients with cerebellar damage have difficulty shifting visual attention to another location in space (whether this involves eye movements or not), taking 0.8–1.2 seconds compared with 0.1 second for normal individuals (Townsend et al., 1999). We should think of the cerebellum in terms of its general functions rather than strictly as a motor organ.

Disorders of Movement

You might think that anything as complex as the movement system would be subject to malfunction; if so, you would be correct. Predictably, movement disorders are devastating to their victims. We will consider as representatives of these diseases Parkinson's disease, Huntington's disease, myasthenia gravis, and multiple sclerosis.

Parkinson's Disease

As we mentioned at the beginning of this chapter, *Parkinson's disease* is characterized by motor tremors, rigidity, loss of balance and coordination, and difficulty in moving, especially in initiating movements (Olanow & Tatton, 1999; Youdim & Riederer, 1997). Parkinson's affects about 0.3% of the population in industrialized countries and 1% of people over the age of 60 years (Nussbaum & Ellis, 2003). The symptoms are caused by deterioration of the *substantia nigra*, whose neurons send dopamine-releasing axons to the *striatum*, which is composed of the basal ganglia's caudate nucleus and putamen and the nucleus accumbens. In something less than 10% of cases, the disease is *familial*, meaning that it occurs more frequently among relatives of a person with the disease than it does in the population (Greenamyre & Hastings, 2004). If a member of a twin pair is diagnosed with Parkinson's disease before the age of 51, the chance of an identical twin also having Parkinson's

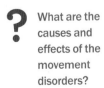

What are the causes and effects of the movement disorders?

■ **FIGURE 11.22**   Lewy Bodies in a Brain With Parkinson's Disease.

A neuron containing two stained Lewy bodies, abnormal clumps of protein.

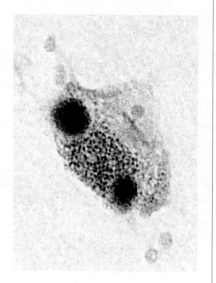

Source: From "α-Synuclein in Lewy Bodies," by M. G. Spillantini et al., 1997, *Nature* 8/28/1997. Copyright © 1997. Used with permission.

? How can we treat symptoms of Parkinson's disease?

is six times greater than it is for a fraternal twin (Tanner et al., 1999). The same study found no evidence of a genetic influence in individuals whose symptoms developed later in life; we will look at possible non-genetic causes shortly. Geneticists have located 28 chromosomal regions that are most likely related to Parkinson's disease, and 6 of those regions contain genes whose mutations are known to cause the disease on their own (reviewed in Klein & Westenberger, 2012). These six play many roles in cellular functioning and protein synthesis, and at least two are associated with the presence of *Lewy bodies,* abnormal clumps of protein that form within neurons (Figure 11.22). Lewy bodies are often found in Parkinson's patients as well as in patients with Alzheimer's disease (Glasson et al., 2000; Spillantini et al., 1997). Lewy bodies probably contribute to the cognitive deficits and depression that often accompany Parkinson's disease; they may represent the brain's attempt to remove proteins that have been damaged by toxins. The patient's complement of genes helps determine age of onset, rate of progression, and whether cognitive loss will be a part of the disease progression. Actor Robin Williams and television personality Casey Kasem had been diagnosed with Parkinson's disease, and each showed signs of the disorder dementia with Lewy bodies (DLW) prior to their deaths (McKeith, 2015; Savica, 2014).

Several environmental influences have been implicated in Parkinson's disease. One cause is subtle brain injury; being knocked unconscious once increases the risk by 32%, and the risk rises by 174% for those knocked out several times. Other research points to a variety of toxins, including industrial chemicals, carbon monoxide, herbicides, and pesticides (Olanow & Tatton, 1999). Numerous studies show an association between pesticide use and Parkinson's, but the human studies are correlational, and establishing a causal relationship has been difficult (reviewed in Moretto & Colosio, 2013). Pesticide exposure produces some of the symptoms of Parkinson's in animals, though with very high dosages. These studies also suggest that specific genes increase sensitivity to the toxic effects, providing another example of the interaction between hereditary and environmental effects. While firm conclusions have eluded us, a study in California's highly agricultural Central Valley that found a tripling of risk with occupational exposure to the pesticides ziram, maneb, and paraquat (A. Wang et al., 2011) suggests extreme caution while we try to sort things out.

Interestingly, the risk of Parkinson's disease is reduced as much as 80% in coffee drinkers (G. W. Ross et al., 2000). The risk also drops by 50% in smokers (Fratiglioni & Wang, 2000), but of course no benefit of smoking outweighs its dangers. Rat studies indicate that cigarette smoke may prevent the accumulation of neurotoxins (Soto-Otero, Méndez-Alvarez, Sánchez-Sellero, Cruz-Landeira, & López-Rivadulla, 2001) and that caffeine reduces the effect of neurotoxins by blocking adenosine receptors, which we saw in Chapter 5 results in increased dopamine and acetylcholine release (J.-F. Chen et al., 2001). In heavy coffee drinkers, a variant of the glutamate receptor gene *GRIN2A* reduces Parkinson's risk by 59% (Hamza et al., 2011). There has been some clinical success in treating Parkinson's with adenosine and glutamate receptor antagonists (Gasparini, Di Paolo, & Gomez-Mancilla, 2013; Hickey & Stacy, 2012).

Parkinson's disease is typically treated by administering *levodopa (L-dopa),* which is the precursor for dopamine. Parkinson's tends to be more severe in men than in women, presumably because estrogen indirectly raises dopamine levels (Haaxma et al., 2007). Dopamine will not cross the blood-brain barrier but L-dopa will, and the brain converts it to dopamine. Dopamine agonists can also be helpful, and even placebos increase dopamine release (de la Fuente-Fernández et al., 2001). But these treatments increase dopamine throughout the brain, which causes side effects ranging from restlessness and involuntary movements to hallucinations. Also, as more neurons die, more drug is required, increasing the side effects. While L-dopa remains the standard, its side effects mean that some patients are forced to use other drugs. Unfortunately, these drugs also treat only some of the symptoms and with limited benefit.

Early attempts showed that implanted embryonic neural cells could survive in the striatum and produce dopamine (Figure 11.23; C. R. Freed et al., 2001; Greene & Fahu, 2002). However, behavioral improvement was not clinically significant, and some of the patients developed involuntary movements, apparently due to excess dopamine. More recent work using adult neural stem cells resulted in more than 80% improvement in motor behavior ratings; the improvement held up for three years but had disappeared at the end of five years (Lévesque, Neuman, & Rezak, 2009). Clinical application is hampered by immune reactions to stem cells and by the development of tumors at the implant site. Recent work indicates that immune response is minimal with stem cells taken from the individual (Morizane et al., 2013), and tumor development can be avoided by allowing the stem cells to mature into an early form of neural cell before implanting (Doi et al., 2012). Gene therapy has also been tried experimentally, with the intent of increasing dopamine levels or reducing excess activity in affected brain areas. Results have been mixed in the handful of clinical trials conducted at the phase 1 and phase 2 levels; so far, no procedure has reached the critical phase 3 level that could establish its effectiveness sufficiently for approval by the U.S. Food and Drug Administration (FDA) (Denyer & Douglas, 2012). To avoid previous disappointments, the British company Oxford Biomedica has used a procedure called ProSavin to deliver a combination of three genes into the striatum to increase dopamine production there; all 15 drug-resistant patients improved in motor capability and maintained improvement for the full year of this phase 1/phase 2 safety and dosage trial (Palfi et al., 2014). These procedures are still in their infancy; we need to remember that the first several heart transplant operations failed, but they are almost routine today.

Frustration with therapeutic alternatives is creating something of a revival in surgical treatments, which were largely abandoned when drugs for Parkinson's disease became available (Cosgrove & Eskandar, 1998). Strategically placed lesions in the subthalamic nucleus and the globus pallidus, both in the basal ganglia (see Figure 11.21), have provided some improvement for patients who have difficulty using dopaminergic drugs (Cosgrove &

■ **FIGURE 11.23**   Transplanted Embryonic Cells in the Brain of a Parkinson's Patient.

The patient died in a car accident seven months after her surgery. (a) Her right putamen (part of the striatum) was removed and placed on a photograph of the magnetic resonance image of her brain made at the time of surgery. The red lines indicate the angle at which the needles were inserted into the brain to inject the fetal cells (right side of the brain) and as a control procedure (left side). The dark area on the putamen along the needle track is due to the staining of new dopamine cells and shows that the axons had grown 2–3 millimeters from the cell bodies. The image in (b) is an enlargement of the putamen.

(a)
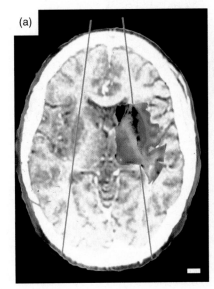

(b)

Source: From "Transplantation of Embryonic Dopamine Neurons for Severe Parkinson's Disease," by C. R. Freed et al., 2001, *New England Journal of Medicine, 334*, pp. 710–719, fig. 3a and b, p. 717.

Eskandar). Michael J. Fox had such lesions, and they vastly improved his ability to control his movement (M. J. Fox, 2002). These two structures produce a rhythmic bursting activity like the rhythmic activity in parkinsonian tremors, which apparently explains why destroying them reduces this symptom (Perkel & Farries, 2000). But the surgery can damage adjacent structures, resulting in other deficits, such as weakness in a part of the body. More recently, physicians are turning to a less drastic procedure known as *deep brain stimulation (DBS)*, in which electrical stimulation through implanted electrodes is used to trigger dopamine release in areas deprived of that neurotransmitter. While effective, there is a higher risk of weight gain and sensitivity to the pleasurable aspects of food seen in some dopamine-increasing drugs (see the accompanying Application).

Huntington's Disease

Like Parkinson's disease, *Huntington's disease* is a degenerative disorder of the motor system involving cell loss in the striatum and cortex. Years before a diagnosis, Huntington's disease begins with mild, infrequent jerky movements that result from impaired error correction (M. A. Smith, Brandt, & Shadmehr, 2000). Later, involuntary movements appear, first as fidgeting and then as movements of the limbs and, finally, writhing of the body and facial grimacing. Because these movements sometimes resemble a dance, Huntington's disease is also called Huntington's chorea, from the Greek word *choreia*, which means "dance." The patient loses the ability to carry out daily activities. Death usually follows within 15–30 years after the onset of the disease.

Unlike Parkinson's disease, cognitive and emotional deficits are a universal characteristic of Huntington's disease. These deficits include impaired judgment, difficulty with a variety of cognitive tasks, depression, and personality changes. The motor symptoms are due to the degeneration of inhibitory GABA-releasing neurons in the striatum, whereas defective or degenerated neurons in the cortex probably account for the psychological symptoms (Figure 11.24; J. B. Martin, 1987; Tabrizi et al., 1999).

This is a scary thing. . . . There is a test available, but I haven't had the guts to take it yet.

—Shana Martin, at risk for Huntington's disease

Deep Brain Stimulation and Parkinson's Disease

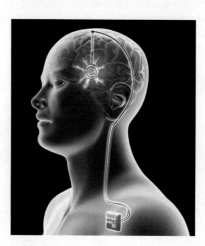

Source: ALFRED PASIEKA/Science Photo Library/Getty.

Although almost 30 years old, an effective treatment for the motor tremors and repetitive movements seen in Parkinson's disease patients continues to be a procedure called deep brain stimulation (DBS). The mechanism by which DBS works is to block electrical signals that are responsible for the tremors associated with Parkinson's. In this technique, neurosurgeons implant electrodes into the brain and run insulated wires under the skin down the neck into the upper chest area. There, the wires are attached to a pacemaker-like device that is also implanted into the patient's chest. In this way, a precise set of electrical pulses can be sent to the target area (usually the basal ganglia) to "reset" activity in the brain area(s) and restore normal function. After a set of stimulations, tremor usually dissipates within seconds (Blahak et al., 2009), whereas effective treatment for dystonia

(uncontrollable repetitive muscle contractions) may take additional months of treatment.

So what does DBS do in the brain? There's a lot of debate as to what exactly the stimulation does to improve motor function. Early research concluded the stimulation temporarily knocked out neurons in the stimulation site (like a reversible lesion; Wichmann, Bergman, & DeLong, 1994), but later teams suggested the added electrical charges made dendritic inputs stronger (McIntyre, Grill, Sherman, & Thakor, 2004). Other findings suggest an increase in chemical neurotransmitters such as adenosine (Bekar et al., 2008) and dopamine (Gale et al., 2013). Improved motor functioning, allowing L-dopa reduction, has been reported for as long as 10 years (reviewed in Fasano, Daniele, & Albanese, 2012). Results are mixed regarding reducing cognitive deficits, which often are more disabling and resistant to treatment than the motor symptoms. DBS usually improves or eliminates impulse control problems in the 13%–16% of patients affected, possibly due to L-dopa reduction.

This improvement does carry some risk: Some studies have reported the onset of pathological gambling, hypersexuality, and compulsive eating. Recent work has suggested that side effects of DBS of the subthalamic nucleus include increased impulsivity and sensitivity to food rewards, resulting in undesired weight gain, which indicates that the neurons and circuits play a role in multiple behaviors. In addition, there is some loss of verbal fluency after DBS, and apathy increases in some patients.

Huntington's disease results from a mutated form of the *huntingtin* gene (Huntington's Disease Collaborative Research Group, 1993). The loss of neurons is probably due to the accumulation of the gene's protein, also known as huntingtin, whose function is unknown (DiFiglia et al., 1997). In normal individuals, the gene has less than 26 repetitions of the bases cytosine, adenine, and guanine (CAG repeats; see Chapter 1). The more repeats the person has beyond 26, the earlier in life the person will succumb to the disease (F. O. Walker, 2007). Because the gene is dominant, a person who has a parent with Huntington's has a 50% chance of developing the disease. This is an unusual example of a human disorder resulting from a single gene.

Numerous drugs are used to treat the various symptoms, including antidepressants and antipsychotics, but only one (Tetrabenazine) has been approved specifically for Huntington's disease by the FDA. It reduces the excess dopamine that causes the abnormal movements. Drugs that silence the *huntingtin* gene are showing promise in animals; a single injection of one of these drugs normalized movement in mice for the nine-month duration of the study and significantly reduced *huntingtin* protein levels for eight weeks in monkeys (Kordasiewicz et al., 2012). Grafting of fetal striatal cells has so far produced only modest and temporary improvement (Cicchetti et al., 2009), but a recent method using human stem cells overexpressing neural growth factors has shown some promise in improving function in a mouse model (Pollock et al., 2016).

Autoimmune Diseases

Myasthenia gravis (MG) is a disorder of muscular weakness caused by reduced numbers or sensitivity of acetylcholine receptors. The muscle weakness can be so extreme that the patient has to be maintained on a respirator. In fact, 25 years ago the mortality rate from MG was about 33%; now few patients die from the disease, thanks to improved treatment (Rowland, 2000a).

The loss of receptors was demonstrated in an interesting way. The venom of the many-banded Formosan krait, a very poisonous snake from Taiwan, paralyzes prey by binding to the acetylcholine receptor. When the venom's toxin is labeled with radioactive iodine and applied to a sample of muscle tissue, it allows researchers to identify and count the acetylcholine receptors. The MG patients turned out to have 70%–90% fewer receptors than normal individuals (Fambrough, Drachman, & Satyamurti, 1973). Drugs that inhibit the action of acetylcholinesterase give temporary relief from the symptoms of myesthenia gravis (Figure 11.25; Rowland, Hoefer, & Aranow, 1960). Remember from Chapter 2 that acetylcholinesterase breaks down acetylcholine at the synapse; these inhibitors increase the amount of available neurotransmitter at the neuron-muscle junction.

Although immune system therapy has sometimes been used (Shah & Lisak, 1993), removal of the thymus (thymectomy) has now become a standard treatment for MG (Rowland, 2000a). The thymus is the major source of lymphocytes that produce antibodies. Improvement can take years, but thymectomy eliminates symptoms completely in almost 80% of patients and reduces them in another 13%–17% (Ashour et al., 1995; Jaretzki et al., 1988).

Multiple sclerosis (MS) is a motor disorder with many varied symptoms, caused by deterioration of myelin (demyelination) and neuron loss in the central nervous system. In Chapter 2, you saw that demyelination causes slowing or elimination of neural impulses. Demyelination thus reduces the speed and strength of move-

ments. Even before that happens, impulses traveling in adjacent neurons, which should arrive simultaneously, become desynchronized because of differential loss of myelin. An early sign of the disorder is impairment of functions that require synchronous bursts of neural activity, like tendon reflexes and vibratory sensation (Rowland, 2000b). As the disease progresses, unmyelinated neurons die, leaving areas of *sclerosis*, or hardened scar tissue (Figure 11.26). As a result, the person experiences muscular weakness, tremor,

■ **FIGURE 11.24** Loss of Brain Tissue in Huntington's Disease.

Left, a section from a normal brain; right, a section from a person with Huntington's disease. The enlarged lateral ventricle in the diseased brain is due to loss of neurons in the caudate nuclei (arrows).

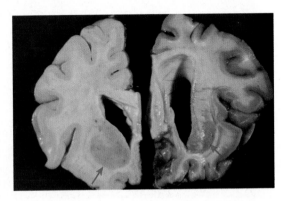

Source: Courtesy of Robert E. Schmidt, Washington University.

■ **FIGURE 11.25** Effect of an Acetylcholinesterase Inhibitor on Myasthenia Gravis.

(a) Patients often have drooping eyelids, as shown here. This patient also could not move his eyes to look to the side. (b) The same patient one minute after injection of an acetylcholinesterase inhibitor. The eyes are open and able to move freely.

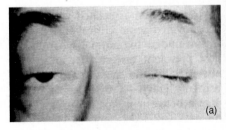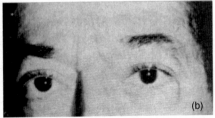

Source: From "Mysathenic Syndromes," by L. P. Rowland, P. F. A. Hoefer, and H. Aranow Jr., 1960, *Research Publications-Association for Research in Nervous and Mental Disease, 38*, pp. 547–560.

■ **FIGURE 11.26** The Brain of a Deceased Multiple Sclerosis Patient.

The arrows indicate areas of sclerosis, or hardened scar tissue (dark areas).

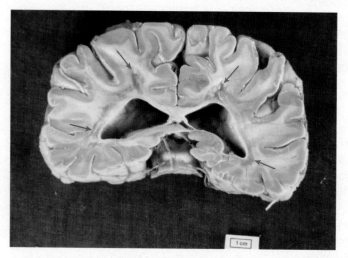

Source: Science Source.

pain, impaired coordination, urinary incontinence, and visual problems. Studies indicate that neuron loss is more important than previously thought and suggest that the loss results from a degenerative process in addition to the demyelination (DeLuca, Ebers, & Esiri, 2004; De Stefano et al., 2003).

Like myasthenia gravis, multiple sclerosis is an autoimmune disease. Injecting foreign myelin protein into the brains of animals produces symptoms like those of MS (Wekerle, 1993), and T cells that are reactive to myelin proteins (see Chapter 8) have been found in the blood of MS patients (Allegretta, Nicklas, Sriram, & Albertini, 1990). A genome-wide study has implicated various immune system genes in MS (International Multiple Sclerosis Genetics Consortium, 2007), but some environmental condition may be needed to trigger the immune attack on myelin. One possibility is that the immune system has been sensitized by an earlier viral infection; for example, studies have found antibodies for Epstein-Barr virus in MS patients (H. J. Wagner et al., 2000), and patients more often had mumps or measles during adolescence (Hernán et al., 2001).

Although many drugs are available to treat the various symptoms of the disease, only a few drugs modify the problematic immune activity in MS patients; these immune-suppressing drugs slow the progression but do not repair the harm already done. A drug that blocks voltage-gated potassium channels, dalfampridine, helps demyelinated axons transmit signals by increasing the strength of action potentials; it improves motor performance, particularly walking (Jeffrey, 2010), but it can increase the risk of seizures (U.S. Food and Drug Administration, 2012). In a multicenter stem cell study, 281 patients with progressive MS were treated by harvesting stem cells from their bone marrow, wiping out their immune systems using chemotherapy, and then injecting the stem cells back; 46% of the patients had no additional symptoms five years afterwards (Muraro et al., 2017).

CONCEPT CHECK

Take a Minute to Check Your Knowledge and Understanding

- Explain how antagonistic muscles and spinal reflexes maintain posture.
- What contribution does each of the cortical motor areas make to movement?
- Make a diagram showing how you think the neurons would be interconnected to carry out the target and arm selection task described in the Hoshi & Tanji study on page 330.
- What are the genetic and environmental causes of the movement disorders described in this chapter?

In Perspective

Unless we have a disorder like Michael J. Fox does (described in the chapter introduction), we usually take our body senses and our capability for movement for granted. And yet just standing upright is a remarkable feat. Granted, a mechanical robot could do it easily, but only if it had a rigid body like R2D2's. If the robot had our flexibility of movement and posture, it would have to devote a fair amount of its computer brain to making split-millisecond adjustments to avoid toppling over. Then another chunk of its computer would be required just to locate a visual object in space, to reach out smoothly and quickly for the object, and to shape its hand for grasping, deciding whether to use the whole hand or the finger and thumb and how much pressure to apply, and so on. You get the idea. Better let a human do it, because all that fancy equipment comes standard on the basic model.

Now you see why so much of the brain is concerned with the sensory and motor components of movement. And when the system becomes damaged, even the easiest behaviors become quite difficult. It is a wonder that we have enough left over for the demands of learning, intelligence, and consciousness, but as you will see in the remaining chapters, we do.

CHAPTER SUMMARY

The Body Senses

- The body senses include proprioception, which tells us about the position and movement of our limbs and body; the skin senses, which inform us about the conditions in the periphery of our body; and the vestibular sense, which contributes information about head position and movement and helps us maintain balance.
- The skin senses—touch, warmth, cold, and pain—tell us about conditions at the body surface and about objects in contact with our body.
- The body senses are processed in a series of structures in the primary and secondary somatosensory cortex and in the posterior parietal cortex, with several similarities to visual processing. Pain processing also extends into additional areas.
- In their quest to find better ways of relieving pain, researchers have learned how the nervous system detects painful stimulation and found that the body has its own ways of relieving pain. Chronic pain presents particularly difficult challenges.

Movement

- There are three types of muscles: cardiac (heart); smooth (internal organs); and skeletal muscles, which move the body by tugging against their attachments to bones.
- Spinal reflexes produce quick responses and provide postural adjustments. Central pattern generators provide routines such as rhythmic walking movements.
- Cortical motor areas assess spatial and body information and construct movements by passing information through a succession of brain areas.
- The basal ganglia and cerebellum refine movements produced by the motor cortex.
- Several diseases attack the motor system at various points of vulnerability. Major causes that have been implicated are heredity, toxins, and autoimmune disorders. ■

STUDY RESOURCES

FOR FURTHER THOUGHT

- Of proprioception, the vestibular sense, pain, and the other skin senses, which do you think you could most afford to give up? Why?
- If pain is beneficial, why does the body have pain relief mechanisms?
- Imagine a robot with a humanlike body. It is programmed to walk, reach, grasp, and so on. It has visual and auditory capabilities, but no body senses. What would its movement be like?
- Judging by the examples given of movement disorders, what are the points of vulnerability in the motor system?

TEST YOUR UNDERSTANDING

1. Explain how endorphins relieve pain, describing the receptors and the pathway from the periaqueductal gray; include how we determine whether pain relief is endorphin based.

2. Walking barefoot, you step on a sharp rock. You reflexively withdraw your foot, plant it firmly on the ground again, and regain your posture. Describe these behaviors in terms of the sensory/pain mechanisms and reflexes involved.

3. Trace the progress of a movement through the parietal and frontal lobes, giving the names of the structures and a general idea of the processing occurring in each.

4. Compare the symptoms, causes, and treatment options for Parkinson's and Huntington's diseases.

Select the best answer:

1. Proprioception gives us information about
   a. conditions at the surface of our skin.
   b. conditions in the internal organs.
   c. the position and movement of our limbs and body.
   d. balance and the head's position and movement.

2. The skin senses include
   a. touch, warmth, and cold.
   b. touch, temperature, and pain.
   c. touch, temperature, movement, and pain.
   d. touch, warmth, cold, and pain.

3. Sharp pain and dull pain are due primarily to
   a. different kinds of injury.
   b. pain neurons with different characteristics.
   c. the passage of time.
   d. the person's attention to the pain.

4. According to Melzack and Wall, pressing the skin near a wound reduces pain by
   a. triggering inhibition in the pain pathway.
   b. triggering pain messages from nearby areas.
   c. releasing endorphins into the brain.
   d. releasing histamine into the wound area.

5. Endorphins
   a. activate the same receptors as opiate drugs.
   b. occupy receptors for pain neurotransmitters.

    c.   block reuptake of pain neurotransmitters.

    d.   inhibit brain centers that process pain emotion.

6. Both congenital pain insensitivity and chronic pain involve

    a.   developmental alterations of brain areas responsible for the emotion of pain.

    b.   alterations in the myelination of pain fibers.

    c.   gene-mediated alterations of pain sensitivity.

    d.   variations in the amount of substance P available.

7. Research suggests phantom pain is due to

    a.   the patient's anxiety over the limb loss.

    b.   memory of the pain of injury or disease that prompted the amputation.

    c.   activity in severed nerve endings in the stump.

    d.   neural reorganization in the somatosensory area.

8. Without a posterior parietal cortex, we would be most impaired in

    a.   moving.

    b.   making smooth movements.

    c.   orienting movements to objects in space.

    d.   awareness of spontaneously occurring movements.

9. If the nerves providing sensory feedback from the legs were cut, we would

    a.   be able to walk but not run.

    b.   have trouble standing upright.

    c.   lose strength in our legs.

    d.   quickly lose muscle mass in our legs.

    e.   not be able to move our legs.

10. A monkey is presented a stimulus and then must wait a few seconds before it can reach to the correct stimulus. Activity in the secondary motor area during the delay suggests that this area

    a.   prepares for the movement.

    b.   initiates the movement.

    c.   executes the movement.

    d.   all of these

11. Cells in the premotor cortex would be particularly involved when you

    a.   remember a visual stimulus during a delay period.

    b.   catch a fly ball.

    c.   start to play a series of notes on the piano.

    d.   execute a movement.

12. The primary motor cortex is most involved in

    a.   combining sensory inputs.

    b.   planning movements.

    c.   preparing movements.

    d.   executing movements.

13. The basal ganglia and the cerebellum produce

    a.   no movements.

    b.   movements requiring extra force.

    c.   reflexive movements.

    d.   sequences of movements.

14. Parkinson's disease is characterized most by

    a.   deterioration of the myelin sheath.

    b.   dancelike involuntary movements.

    c.   deterioration of dopamine-releasing neurons.

    d.   immune system attack on acetylcholine receptors.

15. Results of removing the thymus gland suggest that myasthenia gravis is a(n) _____ disease.

    a.   genetic

    b.   autoimmune

    c.   virus-caused

    d.   degenerative

1. c, 2. d, 3. b, 4. a, 5. a, 6. c, 7. d, 8. c, 9. b, 10. a, 11. b, 12. d, 13. d, 14. c, 15. b.

Answers:

ON THE WEB

The following websites are coordinated with this chapter's content. You can access these websites from the **SAGE edge Student Resources site**; select this chapter and then click on Web Resources. (**Bold** items are links.)

1. **C-Span archived a recording of Michael J. Fox's 1999 testimony before Congress.** In this video, he has not taken his daily L-dopa dose and, therefore, is exhibiting "off his L-dopa" symptoms.

2. The **Vestibular Disorders Association** has information about vestibular problems and provides additional resources such as newsletters, books, and videotapes.

3. The **American Pain Foundation** offers information for pain patients, testimonials from people suffering pain from an assortment of causes, and links to numerous other pain sites.

The **International Association for the Study of Pain** has links to more technical resources on pain.

4. In BrainFacts.org's **Searching for Answers** videos, patients and their families describe what it is like to live with Huntington's disease, Parkinson's disease, and amyotrophic lateral sclerosis (ALS, or Lou Gehrig's disease). You can get information about a variety of movement disorders from the **Neuromuscular Disease Center, National Parkinson Foundation, Huntington's Disease Association,** and **National Multiple Sclerosis Society.**

5. In an interview with Katie Couric, actor **Michael J. Fox** talks about living with Parkinson's disease and about his views on stem cell research. A University of Sheffield **news release** describes the groundbreaking study that screened 2,000 potential drugs for Parkinson's disease.

6. Todd Kuiken is now **testing a prosthetic arm** that includes sensors and stimulators to provide sensation of touch. A new type of brain-controlled limb replacement, designed in **collaboration between Johns Hopkins Medical School and the U.S. Department of Defense DARPA**, has been mounted directly to an amputee's skeleton and can be controlled simply by thought. Finally, **Hugh Herr is using bioengineering techniques to design prosthetic limbs** that are more natural in design and function.

FOR FURTHER READING

1. *Lucky Man*, by Michael J. Fox (Hyperion, 2002), details the actor's initial diagnosis, struggle to balance life and work, and how he decided that helping others was more important than helping himself.

2. *Awakenings*, by Oliver Sacks (Vintage Books, 1999), describes Dr. Sacks's early experiments in using L-dopa to treat the symptom of parkinsonism in patients with sleeping sickness. The movie with Robin Williams was based on this book.

3. *Phantoms in the Brain*, by V. S. Ramachandran and Sandra Blakeslee (HarperPerennial, 1999), called "enthralling" by the *New York Times* and "splendid" by Francis Crick, uses numerous (often strange) cases to explain people's perception of their bodies.

4. *Wall and Melzack's Textbook of Pain*, edited by Stephen McMahon, Martin Koltzenburg, Irene Tracey, and Dennis Turk (Saunders, 6th ed., 2013), and *The Massachusetts General Hospital Handbook of Pain Management*, edited by Jane Ballantyne and in current use at the hospital (Lippincott Williams and Wilkins, 3rd ed., 2005), are technical references on pain and pain management.

5. *Oxford Textbook of Movement Disorders*, by David Burn (Oxford University Press, 2013), covers the science of movement disorders, along with their diagnosis and treatment.

KEY TERMS

antagonistic muscles 327
basal ganglia 332
body integrity identity disorder 319
cardiac muscles 325
central pattern generator (CPG) 328
chronic pain 323
deep brain stimulation (DBS) 335
dermatome 317
endorphins 321
familial 333
gate control theory 322
Golgi tendon organs 328
Huntington's disease 335

inflammatory soup 320
levodopa (L-dopa) 334
Lewy bodies 334
multiple sclerosis 337
muscle spindles 327
myasthenia gravis 337
out-of-body experience 319
Parkinson's disease 333
periaqueductal gray (PAG) 322
phantom pain 324
posterior parietal cortex 318
premotor cortex 330
primary motor cortex 331

primary somatosensory cortex 317
proprioception 314
secondary somatosensory cortex 318
skeletal muscles 325
skin senses 314
smooth muscles 325
somatosensory cortex 332
somatotopic map 317
striatum 333
substance P 320
substantia nigra 333
supplementary motor area 331
vestibular sense 315

 **edge.sagepub.com/garrett5e**

SAGE edge offers a robust online environment featuring an impressive array of free tools and resources for review, study, and further exploration, keeping both instructors and students on the cutting edge of teaching and learning.

11.1 Identify the receptors involved in each type of skin sensation.	▶ The Neuroscience of Touch
11.2 Describe the methods by which the brain gets information about the body and the environment.	📣 Brain Matters: The Vestibular System ▶ Cutaneous Sensory Information Pathways
11.3 Illustrate how the cortical areas for sensation correspond to portions of the body.	▶ The Homunculus
11.4 Assess the mechanisms by which pain is generated.	▶ Pain and the Anterolateral System
11.5 Summarize the brain structures involved in the production of movement.	▶ The Real Reason the Brain Evolved
11.6 Predict how movement is impaired in specific movement disorders.	📄 The Rubber Hand Illusion in Children With Autism ▶ How Deep Brain Stimulation Works

Part IV

Complex Behavior

Learning and Memory

12

After reading this chapter, you will be able to:

- Explain how the brain is involved in the different types of memory.

- Diagram the neural involvement in processing of information that is stored in memory.

- Describe the changes that occur in the brain as learning proceeds.

- Examine how memory changes during aging.

- Contrast the impacts of normal aging and disorders on memory.

At the age of seven, Henry Molaison's life was forever changed by a seemingly minor incident: He was knocked down by a bicycle and was unconscious for five minutes. Three years later, he began to have minor seizures, and his first major seizure occurred on his 16th birthday. Still, Henry had a reasonably normal adolescence, taken up with high school, science club, hunting, and roller-skating, except for a two-year furlough from school because the other boys teased him about his seizures.

After high school, he took a job in a factory, but eventually the seizures made it impossible for him to work. He was averaging 10 small seizures a day and 1 major seizure per week. Because anticonvulsant medications were unable to control the seizures, Henry and his family decided on an experimental operation that held some promise. In 1953, when Henry was 27, a surgeon removed much of both of his temporal lobes, where the seizure activity was originating. The surgery worked, for the most part: With the help of medication, the petit mal seizures were mild enough not to be disturbing, and major seizures were reduced to about one a year. Henry returned to living with his parents. He helped with household chores, mowed the lawn, and spent his spare time doing difficult crossword puzzles. Later, he worked at a rehabilitation center, doing routine tasks like mounting cigarette lighters on cardboard store displays.

Henry's intelligence was not impaired by the operation; his IQ test performance even went up, probably because he was freed from the interference of the abnormal brain activity. However, there was one important and unexpected effect of the surgery. Although he could

SAGE edge™

Master the content.
edge.sagepub.com/garrett5e

Discovering the physical basis of learning in humans and other mammals is among the greatest remaining challenges facing the neurosciences.

—T. H. Brown, Chapman, Kairiss, & Keenan, 1988

345

recall personal and public events and remember songs from his earlier life, Henry had difficulty learning and retaining new information. He could hold new information in memory for a short while, but if he were distracted or if a few minutes passed, he could no longer recall the information. When he worked at the rehabilitation center, he could not describe the work he did. He did not remember moving into a nursing home in 1980, or even what he ate for his last meal. And although he watched television news every night, he could not remember the day's news events later or even recall the name of the president (Corkin, 1984; B. Milner, Corkin, & Teuber, 1968).

Henry's inability to form new memories was not absolute. Although he could not find his way back to the new home his family moved to after his surgery if he was more than two or three blocks away, he was able to draw a floor plan of the house, which he had navigated many times daily (Corkin, 2002). Over the years, he became aware of his condition, and he was very insightful about it. In his own words,

> Every day is alone in itself, whatever enjoyment I've had, and whatever sorrow I've had. . . . Right now, I'm wondering. Have I done or said anything amiss? You see, at this moment everything looks clear to me, but what happened just before? That's what worries me. It's like waking from a dream; I just don't remember. (B. Milner, 1970, p. 37)

Over a period of 55 years, Henry would be the subject of a hundred scientific studies that he could not remember; he was known to the world as patient HM to protect his privacy. In the next several pages, you will see why many consider HM's surgery the most significant single event in the study of learning.

Learning as the Storage of Memories

Some one-celled animals "learn" surprisingly well, for example, to avoid swimming toward a light where they have received an electric shock before. I have placed the term *learn* in quotation marks because such simple organisms lack a nervous system; their behavior changes briefly, but if you take a lunch break during your subject's training, when you return, you will have to start all over again. Such a temporary form of learning may help an organism avoid an unsafe area long enough for the danger to pass or linger in a place where food is more abundant. But without the ability to make a permanent record, you could not learn a skill, and experience would not help shape who you are. We will introduce the topic of learning by examining the problem of storage.

Amnesia: The Failure of Storage and Retrieval

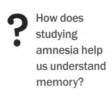

How does studying amnesia help us understand memory?

HM's symptoms are referred to as *anterograde amnesia,* an impairment in forming new memories. (*Anterograde* means "moving forward.") This was not HM's only memory deficit; the surgery also caused *retrograde amnesia,* the inability to remember events prior to impairment. His retrograde amnesia extended from the time of surgery back to about the age of 16; he had a few memories from that period, but he did not remember the end of World War II or his own graduation, and when he returned for his 35th high school reunion, he recognized none of his classmates. Better memory for earlier events than for recent ones may seem implausible, but it is typical of patients who have brain damage like HM's. How far back the retrograde amnesia extends depends on how much damage there is and which specific structures are damaged.

HM's surgery damaged or destroyed the hippocampus, nearby structures that along with the hippocampus make up the *hippocampal formation*, and the amygdala. Figure 12.1 shows the location of these structures. Because they are on or near the inside surface of the temporal lobe, they form part of what is known as the medial temporal lobe (remember that *medial* means "toward the middle"). Because HM's surgery was so extensive, it is impossible to tell which structures are responsible for the memory functions that were lost. Studies of patients with varying degrees of temporal lobe damage have helped determine which structures are involved in amnesia and, therefore, in memory. Henry died in 2008 at the age of 82, but he continues to contribute, as the accompanying Application explains.

The hippocampus consists of several substructures with different functions. The part known as *CA1* provides the primary output from the hippocampus to other brain areas; damage in that part of both hippocampi results in moderate anterograde amnesia and only minimal retrograde amnesia. If the damage includes

■ FIGURE 12.1   Temporal Lobe Structures Involved in Amnesia.

(a) HM's brain (top left) and a normal brain (below). You can see that the amygdala (A), hippocampus (H), and other structures labeled in the normal brain are partly or completely missing in HM's brain. (b) Structures of the medial temporal lobe, which are important in learning. (The frontal lobe is to the left.)

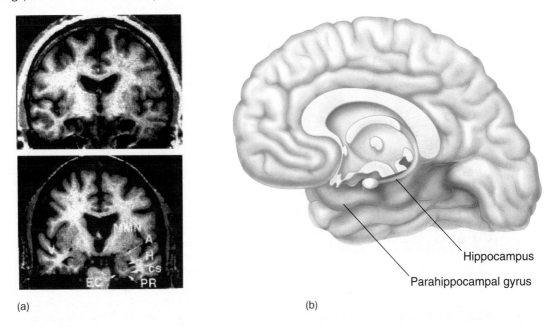

Hippocampus

Parahippocampal gyrus

(a)   (b)

Sources: (a) From "HM's Medial Temporal Lobe Lesion: Findings From Magnetic Resonance Imaging," by S. Corkin, D. G. Amaral, R. G. González, K. A. Johnson, and B. T. Hyman, 1997, *Journal of Neurosicence, 17,* pp. 3964–3979. Copyright © 1997 by the Society for Neuroscience. Used with permission. (b) Adapted with permission from "Remembrance of Things Past," by D. L. Schacter and A. D. Wagner, *Science, 285,* pp. 1503–1504. Illustration: K. Sutliff. © 1999 American Association for the Advancement of Science. Reprinted with permission from AAAS.

the rest of the hippocampus, anterograde amnesia is severe. Damage to the entire hippocampal formation results in retrograde amnesia extending back 15 years or more (J. J. Reed & Squire, 1998; Rempel-Clower, Zola, Squire, & Amaral, 1996; Zola-Morgan, Squire, & Amaral, 1986). More extensive retrograde impairment occurs with broader damage or deterioration, like that seen in Alzheimer's disease, Huntington's disease, and Parkinson's disease, apparently because memory storage areas in the cortex are compromised (Squire & Alvarez, 1995).

Mechanisms of Consolidation and Retrieval

HM's memory impairment consisted of two problems: consolidation of new memories and, to a lesser extent, retrieval of older memories. *Consolidation* is the process in which the brain forms a more or less permanent physical representation of a memory. *Retrieval* is the process of accessing stored memories—in other words, the act of remembering. When a rat presses a lever to receive a food pellet or a child is bitten by a dog or you skim through the headings in this chapter, the experience is held in memory at least for a brief time. But just like the phone number that is forgotten when you get a busy signal the first time you dial, an experience does not necessarily become a permanent memory; and if it does, the transition takes time. Until the memory is consolidated, it is particularly fragile. New memories may be disrupted just by engaging in another activity, and even older memories are vulnerable to intense experiences such as emotional trauma or electroconvulsive shock treatment (a means of inducing convulsions, usually in treating depression). Researchers divide memory into two stages, *short-term memory* and *long-term memory.* Long-term memory, at least for some kinds of learning, can be divided into two stages that have different durations and occur in different locations (Figure 12.2), as we will see later (McGaugh, 2000).

An animal study clearly demonstrates that the hippocampus participates in consolidation. Rats were trained in a water maze, a tank of murky water from which they could escape quickly by learning the location of a

> ❝ Most memories, like humans and wines, do not mature instantly. Instead they are gradually stabilized in a process referred to as consolidation.
>
> —Yadin Dudai ❞

The Legacy of HM

Source: Wikimedia Commons.

Not only did Henry Molaison devote much of his life to numerous scientific investigations, but his brain will continue to be the subject of study for many years to come (Lafee, 2009). Soon after his death, Molaison's preserved brain was in a plastic cooler strapped in a seat on a flight from Boston to San Diego; in the next seat was Jacopo Annese, director of the Brain Observatory at the University of California at San Diego. After several months of preparation, Annese and his colleagues dissected Molaison's brain into slices as thin as the width of a hair (70 μm). The 53-hour, uninterrupted procedure was recorded and live-streamed over the web to allow scientific scrutiny and to increase public awareness and engagement (Annese et al., 2014). Each slice of HM's brain was microscopically photographed with such resolution that the data from each *one* would fill 200 DVDs. The data were then combined into a three-dimensional reconstruction of the brain, which is available online. Scientists can navigate through it to the area of their interest and then zoom in to the level of individual neurons. HM's memory problems made him perhaps the most studied subject in neuroscience. Ironically, the man who could not remember will never be forgotten.

■ **FIGURE 12.2**   Stages of Consolidation.

Making a memory permanent involves multiple stages and different processes.

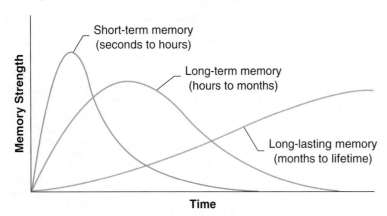

Source: Reprinted with permission from "Memory—A Century of Consolidation," by J. L. McGaugh, *Science, 287*, pp. 248–251. Copyright 2000 American Association for the Advancement of Science.

platform submerged just under the water's surface (Figure 12.3; Riedel et al., 1999). Then, for seven days the rats' hippocampi were temporarily disabled by a drug that blocks receptors for the neurotransmitter glutamate. Eleven days later—plenty of time for the drug to clear the rats' systems—they performed poorly compared with control subjects (Riedel et al.). Researchers have been able to "watch" the consolidation happening in humans, using brain scans and event-related potentials. Presenting words or pictures activated the hippocampus and adjacent cortex; how well the material was remembered later could be predicted from how much activation occurred in those areas during stimulus presentation (Figure 12.4; Alkire, Haier, Fallon, & Cahill, 1998; Brewer, Zhao, Desmond, Glover, & Gabrieli, 1998; Fernández et al., 1999).

Animals that were given the glutamate-blocking drug at the time of testing instead of immediately after training also had impaired recall in the water maze, indicating that the hippocampus has a role in retrieval as well as consolidation. Researchers have used PET scans to confirm that the hippocampus also retrieves memories in humans (D. L. Schacter, Alpert, Savage, Rauch, & Albert, 1996; Squire et al., 1992). Figure 12.5 shows increased activity in the hippocampi while the research participants recalled words learned during an experiment. The involvement of the hippocampus in

■ **FIGURE 12.3**   A Water Maze.

The rat learns to escape the murky water by finding the platform hidden just below the surface.

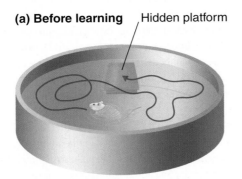

(a) Before learning   Hidden platform   **(b) After learning**

■ **FIGURE 12.4**   Hippocampal Activity Related to Consolidation.

The arrow is pointing to the hippocampal region. Reds and yellows indicate positive correlations of activity at the time of learning with later recall; blues indicate negative correlations.

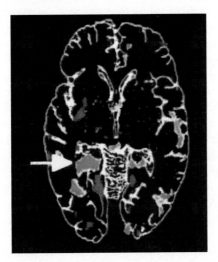

Source: From "PET Imaging of Conscious and Unconscious Memory," by M. T. Alkire, R. J. Haier, J. H. Fallon, and S. J. Barker, 1996, *Journal of Consciousness Studies, 3*, pp. 448–462.

■ **FIGURE 12.5**   Hippocampal Activity in the Human Brain During Retrieval.

(a) As participants tried to recall visually presented words that had been poorly learned (35% recall rate), the prefrontal and visual areas, but not the hippocampi, were highly activated compared with the baseline condition. (b) However, the successful recall of well-learned words (79% recall rate) activated both hippocampal areas.

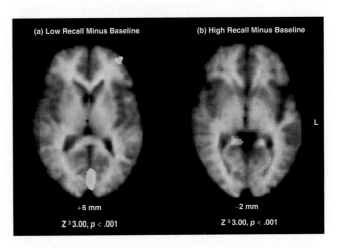

Source: Reprinted with permission from "Conscious Recollection and the Human Hippocampal Formation: Evidence From Positron Emission Tomography," by D. L. Schacter et al., *Proceedings of the National Academy of Sciences, USA, 93*, pp. 321–325. Copyright 1996 National Academy of Sciences, USA.

retrieval seems inconsistent with HM's ability to recall earlier memories. But the memories that patients with hippocampal damage can recall are of events that occurred at least two years before their brain damage. Many researchers have concluded that the hippocampal mechanism plays a time-limited role in consolidation and retrieval, a point we will examine shortly. This diminishing role of the hippocampus would explain why older memories suffer less than recent memories after hippocampal damage.

The prefrontal area is also active during learning and retrieval, and some researchers think that it directs the search strategy required for retrieval (Buckner & Koutstaal, 1998). Indeed, the prefrontal area is active during effortful attempts at retrieval, whereas the hippocampus is activated during successful retrieval (see

Figure 12.5; D. L. Schacter et al., 1996). We will look at the role of the frontal area again when we consider working memory and Korsakoff syndrome.

We saw in Chapter 5 that rewards such as drugs increase activity in dopamine neurons. Because reward plays a crucial role in learning, we might suspect that dopamine has some function in learning, and that is indeed the case. Blocking dopamine receptors in guinea pigs shortly after learning impairs consolidation and memory (K.-N. Lee & Chirwa, 2015), and increasing dopamine levels by injecting the dopamine precursor levodopa improves memory in humans (Chowdhury, Guitart-Masip, Bunzeck, Dolan, & Düzel, 2012). Novel experience, such as exploring an unfamiliar environment, increases dopamine activity; placing rats in a novel environment before or after learning improves learning (S.-H. Wang, Redondo, & Morris, 2010). In humans, learning can be increased by dopamine-enhancing stimulation as simple as viewing novel photographs from *National Geographic* (Fenker, Frey, Schuetze, & Heipertz, 2008).

Dopamine-enhancing stimulation is effective whether it occurs before or after the learning experience; this is because dopamine directly affects consolidation of long-term memory, rather than by improving short-term memory (Lisman, Grace, & Duzel, 2011). Dopamine release initiates the synthesis of proteins in the postsynaptic neuron. These plasticity-related proteins are necessary for consolidation to occur, as we will see later, and drugs that block their synthesis inhibit learning (Clopath, 2012).

Dopamine does not signal rewards so much as it signals *errors in prediction*. Firing increases in dopamine neurons only if the reward is unexpected—either of greater value than usual or occurring when it has been infrequent (Schultz, 2016). If the reward is expected, the firing rate remains the same and it declines if the reward is less than expected. In other words, evolution has tailored learning specifically to help us cope with changes in our environment and in our circumstances.

Where Memories Are Stored

The hippocampal area is not the permanent storage site for memories. If it were, patients like HM would not remember anything that happened before their damage occurred. According to most researchers, the hippocampus stores information temporarily in the hippocampal formation; then, over time, a more permanent memory is consolidated elsewhere in the brain. A study of mice that had learned a spatial discrimination task supported the hypothesis: Over 25 days of retention testing, metabolic activity progressively decreased in the hippocampus and increased in the cortical areas (Bontempi, Laurent-Demir, Destrade, & Jaffard, 1999).

? Is there a place where memories are stored?

To explore further the relationship between these two areas, Remondes and Schuman (2004) severed the pathway that connects CA1 of the hippocampus with the cortex. The lesions did not impair the rats' performance in a water maze during training or 24 hours (hr) later, but after 4 weeks the rats had lost their memory for the task. The results supported the hypothesis that short-term memory depends on the hippocampus but long-term memory requires the cortex and an interaction over time between the two. To pin down the window of vulnerability of the memory, the researchers lesioned two additional groups of animals at different times *following* training. Those lesioned 24 hr after training were impaired in recall four weeks later, but those whose surgery was delayed until three weeks after training performed as well as the controls. This progression apparently takes longer in humans. Christine Smith and Larry Squire (2009) used fMRI to image the brain's activity while subjects recalled news events from the past 30 years. Activity was greatest in the hippocampus and related areas as subjects recalled recent events, declined as they recalled events as far back as 12 years, and stabilized after that. At the same time, activity increased progressively with older memories in the prefrontal, temporal, and parietal cortex. So, your brain works rather like your computer when it transfers volatile memory from RAM to the hard drive—it just takes a lot longer.

In Chapter 3, you learned that when Wilder Penfield (1955) stimulated association areas in the temporal lobes of surgery patients, he often evoked visual and auditory experiences that seemed like memories. We speculated that memories might be stored there, and more recent research has supported that idea, with memories for sounds activating auditory areas and memories for pictures evoking activity in the occipital region (Figure 12.6; M. E. Wheeler, Petersen, & Buckner, 2000). You also saw in Chapter 9 that when we learn a new language, it is stored near Broca's area. Naming colors (which requires memory) activates temporal lobe areas near where we perceive color; identifying pictures of tools activates the hand motor area and an area in the left temporal lobe that is also activated by motion and by action words (A. Martin, Haxby, Lalonde, Wiggs, & Ungerleider, 1995; A. Martin et al., 1996); and spatial memories appear to be stored in the parietal area and verbal memories in the left frontal lobe (F. Rösler, Heil, & Henninghausen, 1995). Thus, all memories are not stored in a single area, nor is each memory distributed throughout the brain. Rather, different memories are in different cortical areas, apparently according to where the information they are based on was processed.

An interesting example is the cells involved in place memory. *Place cells,* which increase their rate of firing when the individual is in a specific location in the environment, are found in the hippocampus. Each cell has a place field (overlapping somewhat with others), and together these cells form a map of the environment. This map develops during the first few minutes of exploration; the cells' fields are then remapped on entering a new environment, but they are restored on returning to the original location (Figure 12.7; Guzowski, Knierim, & Moser, 2004; M. A. Wilson & McNaughton, 1993). The fields are dependent on spatial cues in the environment, including visual, tactile, and even olfactory cues (Shapiro, Tanila, & Eichenbaum, 1997). Place cells do more than indicate an individual's current location. For example, they contribute the context of location that is so important in memories of events (D. M. Smith & Mizumori, 2006). They also provide spatial memory required for planning navigation; as rats paused at choice points in a maze with which they were well experienced, cells with place fields in the alternative sections fired in sequence, as if the rats were simulating the two choices (Johnson & Redish, 2007). Functional MRI has confirmed that humans have place cells; their activity is so precise that the investigators could determine the subject's "location" in a computer-generated virtual environment (Hassabis et al., 2009).

Two Kinds of Learning

Learning researchers were in for a revelation when they discovered that HM could readily learn some kinds of tasks (Corkin, 1984). One was mirror drawing, in which the individual uses a pencil to trace a path around a pattern, relying solely on a view of the work surface in a mirror. HM improved in mirror-drawing ability over three days of training, and he learned to solve the Tower of Hanoi problem (Figure 12.8). But he could not remember learning either task, and on each day of practice he denied even having seen the Tower puzzle before (N. J. Cohen, Eichenbaum, Deacedo, & Corkin, 1985; Corkin, 1984). What this means, researchers realized, is that there are two categories of

FIGURE 12.6 Functional MRI Scans of Brains During Perception and Recall.

Memories of pictures and sounds evoked responses in the same general areas (arrows) as the original stimuli.

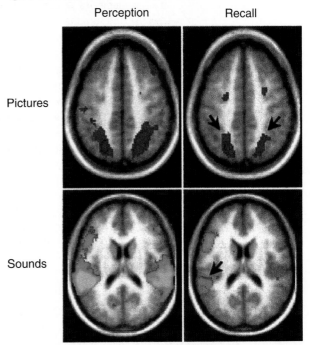

Source: From "Memory's Echo: Vivid Remembering Reactivates Sensory-Specific Cortex," by M. E. Wheeler et al., *Proceedings of the National Academy of Sciences, USA, 97,* pp. 11125–11129, fig. 1c, d, e, f, p. 11127. © 2000 National Academy of Sciences, USA.

What are the two kinds of learning?

FIGURE 12.7 Recordings From Place Cells in a Rat in a Circular Runway.

The recordings are from seven different place cells, indicated by different colors. Note that each cell responds when the rat is in a particular part of the runway. (Due to cue similarities in a circular apparatus, cells occasionally respond on the opposite side of the circle.)

Source: Reprinted by permission from Macmillan Publishers Ltd. From "Neural Plasticity in the Ageing Brain," by S. N. Burke and C. A. Barnes, 2006, *Nature Reviews Neuroscience, 7,* pp. 30–40. Nature Publishing Group.

memory processing. *Declarative memory* involves learning that results in memories of facts, people, and events that a person can verbalize or declare. For example, you can remember being in class today, where you sat, who was there, and what was discussed. Declarative memory includes a variety of subtypes, such as *episodic memory* (events), *semantic memory* (facts), *autobiographical memory* (information about oneself), and *spatial memory* (the location of the individual and of objects in space). *Nondeclarative memory* involves memories for behaviors; these memories result from procedural or skills learning, emotional learning, and stimulus-response conditioning. Learning mirror tracing or how to ride a bicycle or solve the Tower of Hanoi problem are examples of nondeclarative learning or, more specifically, procedural or skills learning; remembering practicing the tasks involves declarative learning. Another way of putting it, which is admittedly a bit oversimplified, is that declarative memory is informational, while nondeclarative memory is more concerned with the control of behavior. Just as we have *what* and *where* pathways in vision and audition, we have a *what* and a *how* in memory.

The main reason to distinguish between the two types of learning is that they have different origins in the brain; studying them can tell us something about how the brain carries out its tasks. For years, it looked like we were limited to studying the distinction in the rare human who had brain damage in just the right place; hippocampal lesions did not seem to affect learning in rats, so researchers thought that rats did not have an equivalent of declarative memory. But it just took selecting the right tasks. R. J. McDonald and White (1993) used an apparatus called the radial arm maze, a central platform with several arms radiating from it (Figure 12.9). Rats with damage to both hippocampi could learn the simple conditioning task of going into any lighted arm for food. But if every arm was baited with food, the rats could not remember which arms they had visited and repeatedly returned to arms where the food had already been eaten.

Conversely, rats with damage to the *striatum* could remember which arms they had visited but could not learn to enter lighted arms. Because Parkinson's disease and Huntington's disease damage the basal ganglia (which include the striatum), people with these disorders have trouble learning procedural tasks, such as mirror tracing or the Tower of Hanoi problem (Gabrieli, 1998). Incidentally, the term *declarative* seems inappropriate with rats; researchers have often preferred the term *relational memory,* which implies that the individual must learn relationships among cues, an idea that applies equally well to humans and animals.

You already know that the amygdala is important in emotional behavior, but it also has a significant role in nondeclarative emotional learning. Bechara and his colleagues (1995) studied a patient with damage to both amygdalae and another with damage to both hippocampi. The researchers attempted to condition an emotional response in the patients by sounding a loud boat horn when a blue slide was presented but not when the slide was another color. The patient with amygdala damage reacted emotionally to the loud noise, indicated by increased skin conductance responses (see Chapter 8). He could also tell the researchers which slide was followed by the loud noise, but the blue slide never evoked a skin conductance increase; in other words, conditioning was absent. The patient with hippocampal damage showed an emotional response and conditioning, but he could not tell the researchers which color the loud sound was

■ **FIGURE 12.8**   The Tower of Hanoi Problem.

The task is to relocate the rings in order onto another post by moving them one at a time and without ever placing a larger ring over a smaller one.

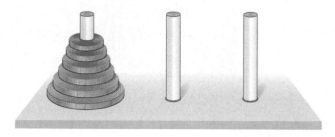

■ **FIGURE 12.9**   A Radial Arm Maze.

The rat learns where to find food in the maze's arms. The arms are often enclosed by walls.

Source: Mauro Fermariello/Science Source.

paired with. This neural distinction between declarative learning and nondeclarative emotional learning may well explain how an emotional experience can have a long-lasting effect on a person's behavior even though the person does not remember the experience.

The amygdala has an additional function that cuts across learning types. Both positive and negative emotions enhance the memorability of any event; the amygdala strengthens even declarative memories about emotional events, apparently by increasing activity in the hippocampus. Electrical stimulation of the amygdala activates the hippocampus, and it enhances learning of a non-emotional task, such as a choice maze (McGaugh, Cahill, & Roozendaal, 1996). In humans, memory for both pleasant and aversive emotional material is related to the amount of activity in both amygdalae while viewing the material (Cahill et al., 1996; Hamann, Ely, Grafton, & Kilts, 1999).

Working Memory

The brain stores a tremendous amount of information, but information that is merely stored is useless. It must be available, not just when it is being recalled into awareness but when the brain needs it for carrying out a task. *Working memory* provides a temporary "register" for information while it is being used. Working memory holds a password you just looked up long enough for you to type it in; it also holds information retrieved from long-term memory while it is integrated with other information for use in problem solving and decision making. Without working memory, we could not do long division, plan a chess move, or even carry on a conversation.

Why is working memory important?

Think of working memory as like the RAM in your computer. The RAM holds information temporarily while it is being processed or used, but the information is stored elsewhere on the hard drive. But we should not take any analogy too far. Working memory has a very limited capacity (with no upgrades available), and information in working memory fades within seconds. So, if you make a mistake entering the password you just looked up, you'll probably have to look it up again.

The *delayed match-to-sample task* described in Chapter 11 provides an excellent means of studying working memory. During the delay period, cells remain active in one or more of the association areas in the temporal and parietal lobes, depending on the nature of the stimulus (Constantinidis & Steinmetz, 1996; Fuster & Jervey, 1981; Miyashita & Chang, 1988). Cells in these areas apparently help maintain the memory of the stimulus, but they are not the location of working memory. If a distracting stimulus is introduced during the delay period, the altered firing in these locations ceases abruptly, but the animals are still able to make the correct choice (Constantinidis & Steinmetz, 1996; E. K. Miller, Erickson, & Desimone, 1996). Cells in the prefrontal cortex have several attributes that make them better candidates as working memory specialists. Not only do they increase firing during a delay, but they also maintain the increase despite a distracting stimulus (E. K. Miller et al., 1996). Some respond selectively to the correct stimulus (di Pellegrino & Wise, 1993; E. K. Miller et al.). Others respond to the correct stimulus, but only if it is presented in a specific position in the visual field; they apparently integrate information from cells that respond only to the stimulus with information from cells that respond to the location (Rao, Rainer, & Miller, 1997). Prefrontal damage impairs humans' ability to remember a stimulus during a delay (D'Esposito & Postle, 1999). All these findings suggest that the prefrontal area plays the major role in working memory.

> *The person recalls in almost photographic detail the total situation at the moment of shock, the expression of face, the words uttered, the position, garments, pattern of carpet, recalls them years after as though they were the experience of yesterday.*
>
> —G. M. Stratton, 1919

Although the prefrontal cortex serves as a temporary memory register, its function is apparently more than that of a neural blackboard. In Chapters 3 and 8, you learned that damage to the frontal lobes impairs a person's ability to govern his or her behavior in several ways. Many researchers believe that the primary role of the prefrontal cortex in learning is as a central executive. That is, it manages certain kinds of behavioral strategies and decision making and coordinates activity in the brain areas involved in the perception and response functions of a task, all the while directing the neural traffic in working memory (Wickelgren, 1997).

CONCEPT CHECK

Take a Minute to Check Your Knowledge and Understanding

- What determines the symptoms and the severity of symptoms of amnesia?
- Describe the two kinds of learning and the related brain structures.
- Working memory contributes to learning and to other functions. How?

Brain Changes in Learning

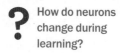

How do neurons change during learning?

Learning is a form of neural plasticity that changes behavior by remodeling neural connections. Specialized neural mechanisms have evolved to make the most of this capability. We will look at them in the context of long-term potentiation.

■ **FIGURE 12.10** LTP and LTD in the Human Brain.

The graphs show excitatory postsynaptic potentials in response to a test stimulus before and after repeated stimulation. (a) 100-hertz (Hz) stimulation produced LTP. (b) 1-Hz stimulation produced LTD, which blocked the potentiation established earlier.

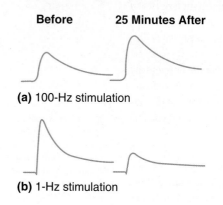

Before   **25 Minutes After**

(a) 100-Hz stimulation

(b) 1-Hz stimulation

Source: From "Long-Term Modifications of Synaptic Efficacy in the Human Inferior and Middle Temporal Cortex," by W. R. Chen et al., *Proceedings of the National Academy of Sciences, USA, 93,* pp. 8011–8015. Copyright 1996 National Academy of Sciences, USA. Used with permission.

Long-Term Potentiation

More than 50 years ago, Donald Hebb (1940) stated what has become known as the *Hebb rule:* If an axon of a presynaptic neuron is active while the postsynaptic neuron is firing, the synapse between them will be strengthened. We saw this principle in action during the development of the nervous system, when synaptic strengthening helped determine which neurons would survive; some of that plasticity is retained in the mature individual. Researchers have long believed that to understand learning as a physiological process, they would have to figure out what happens at the level of the neuron and, particularly, at the synapse.

Long-term potentiation (LTP) is a persistent strengthening of synapses that results from the simultaneous activation of presynaptic neurons and postsynaptic neurons (Cooke & Bliss, 2006). LTP can be induced in the laboratory by stimulating both neurons at the same time, or by stimulating the presynaptic neuron adequately to cause the postsynaptic neuron to fire. As you can see in Figure 12.10a, the postsynaptic neuron's response to a test stimulus is much stronger following induction of LTP. What is remarkable about LTP is that it can last for hours in tissue cultures and months in laboratory animals (Cooke & Bliss). LTP has been studied mostly in the hippocampus, but it also occurs in several other areas, including the visual, auditory, and motor cortex. So LTP appears to be a characteristic of much of neural tissue, at least in the areas most likely to be involved in learning.

Neural functioning requires weakening synapses as well as strengthening them. *Long-term depression (LTD)* is a decrease in the strength of synapses that occurs when stimulation of presynaptic neurons is insufficient to activate the postsynaptic neurons (Cooke & Bliss, 2006). Potentiation can be depressed in a postsynaptic neuron by applying a low-frequency pulse to the presynaptic neuron for a few minutes, causing the presynaptic neuron to fire but not the postsynaptic neuron (Figure 12.10b). LTD is believed to be the mechanism the brain uses to modify memories and to clear old memories to make room for new information (Stickgold, Hobson, Fosse, & Fosse, 2001).

Activity in presynaptic neurons also influences the sensitivity of nearby synapses. If a weak synapse and a strong synapse on the same postsynaptic neuron are active simultaneously, the weak synapse will be potentiated; this effect is called *associative long-term potentiation* (Figure 12.11). Associative LTP is usually studied in isolated brain tissue with artificially created weak and strong synapses, but it has important behavioral implications, which is why it interests us. Electric shock evokes a strong response in the lateral amygdala, where fear is registered, while an auditory stimulus produces only a minimal response there. Rogan, Stäubli, and LeDoux (1997) repeatedly paired a tone with shock to the feet of rats. Because of this procedure, the tone alone began to evoke a significantly increased response in the amygdala, as well as an emotional "freezing" response in the rats. You may recognize this scenario as an example of *classical conditioning;* we could easily change the labels in Figure 12.11 from "Strong synapse" to "Electric shock" and from "Weak synapse" to "Auditory tone." Researchers believe that associative LTP is the basis of classical conditioning, and Rogan et al.'s results support that view. LTP, LTD, and associative LTP can all be summed up in the expression "Cells that fire together wire together."

How LTP Happens

LTP has been studied most often in the neurons connecting CA1 and CA3 of the hippocampus, and we will use those findings as our model here without going into the variations that occur in other areas of the brain. LTP is induced through a cascade of events at the synapse. In CA1 (and in most locations) the neurotransmitter involved is glutamate, which is detected by two types of receptors: the AMPA (alpha-amino-3-hydroxy-5-methyl-4-isoxazole propionic acid) receptor and the NMDA (N-methyl-d-aspartic acid) receptor. Initially, glutamate activates AMPA receptors but not NMDA receptors, because they are blocked by magnesium ions

■ **FIGURE 12.11**   Associative LTP.

(a) Initially, the weak synapse produces only a very small excitatory postsynaptic potential.
(b) Simultaneous activation of a strong synapse along with activity in the weak synapse induces
associative LTP. (c) Following associate LTP, the much larger excitatory postsynaptic potential
indicates that the weak synapse has been potentiated.

▶ Figures Brought to Life

(a) Stimulation by weak synapse (test)

(b) Stimulation by weak and strong synapse (induction)

(c) Stimulation by strengthened synapse (test)

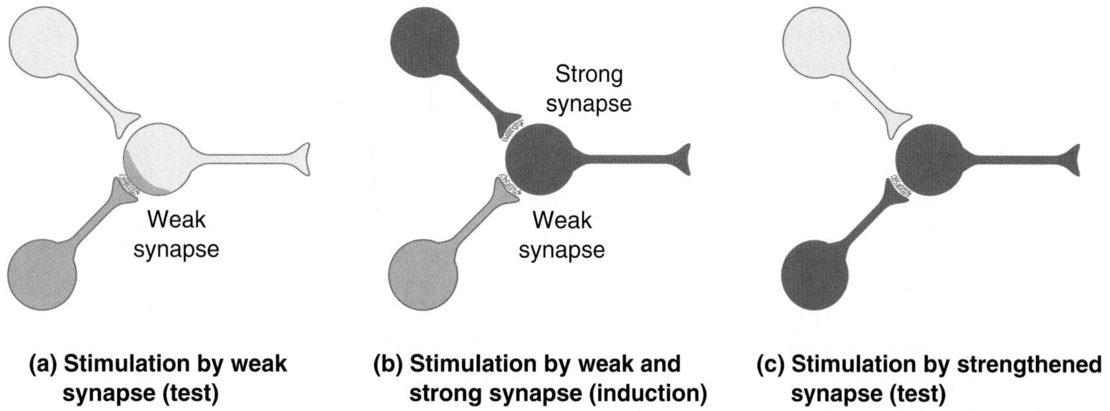

■ **FIGURE 12.12**   Participation of Glutamate Receptors in LTP.

(a) Initially, glutamate activates the AMPA receptors but not the NMDA receptors, which are blocked by magnesium ions.
(b) However, if the activation is strong enough to partially depolarize the postsynaptic membrane, the magnesium ions are ejected.
The NMDA receptor can then be activated, allowing sodium and calcium ions to enter.

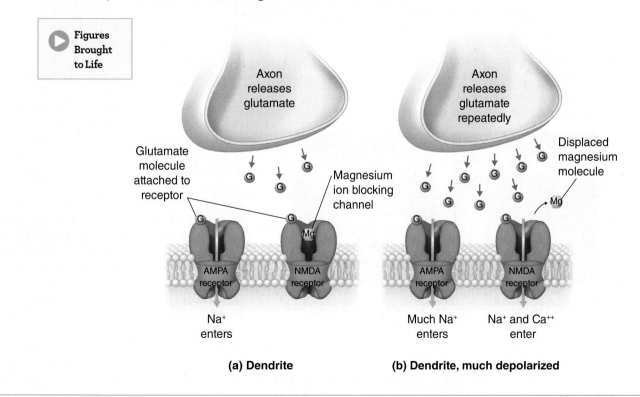

▶ Figures Brought to Life

(a) Dendrite

(b) Dendrite, much depolarized

(Figure 12.12). During LTP induction, activation of the AMPA receptors by the first few pulses of stimulation
partially depolarizes the membrane, and this dislodges the magnesium ions. The resulting large influx of calcium ions activates a host of *protein kinases,* enzymes that alter or activate other proteins (Lüscher & Malenka,
2012). One of the protein kinases, CaMKII (calcium/calmodulin-dependent kinase II) is required for LTP.

■ **FIGURE 12.13**   Retention in Normal and αCaMKII-Deficient Mice Over Time.

Mice given foot shocks in a conditioning chamber were later tested for memory of the foot shocks by observing emotional "freezing" when they were returned to the chamber. Note that in the mice heterozygous for the mutant gene, memory had begun to decay after three days and they failed to form permanent memory.

Source: Reprinted by permission from Macmillan Publishers Ltd. From "αCaMKII-Dependent Plasticity in the Cortex Is Required for Permanent Memory," by P. W. Frankland, C. O'Brien, M. Ohno, A. Kirkwood, & A. J. Silva, 2001, *Nature, 411,* pp. 309–313. Figure 1. Nature Publishing Group.

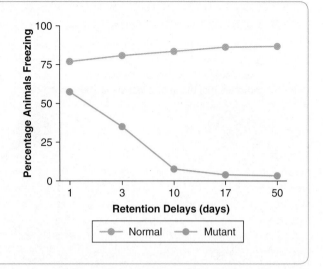

Mice with two mutant, nonfunctioning genes for the alpha form of CaMKII fail to show LTP; those with one mutant and one functioning gene do show LTP, but it is not consolidated into long-term memory (Figure 12.13; Frankland, O'Brien, Ohno, Kirkwood, & Silva, 2001). Several plasticity-related genes are activated as well (Kelleher, Govindarajan, & Tonagawa, 2004); they along with newly activated proteins begin producing structural changes in the synapse (Lüscher & Malenka).

How does the brain grow during learning?

Within 45–60 minutes after LTP, postsynaptic neurons develop dramatically increased numbers of *dendritic spines,* outgrowths from the dendrites that partially bridge the synaptic cleft and make the synapse more sensitive (Figure 12.14; N. Toni, Buchs, Nikonenko, Bron, & Muller, 1999). Existing spines also enlarge or split down the middle to form two spines (Matsuzaki, Honkura, Ellis-Davies, & Kasai, 2004). Another important structural change is the appearance of new AMPA receptors, which increase synaptic strength (Lüscher & Malenka, 2012). These come from a pool of silent receptors that are transported into the spines from within the dendrite; they can recycle between the cytoplasm and the membrane or in the other direction within mere tens of minutes. A further change that occurs in support of learning is the generation of new neurons in the hippocampus; though the rate of neurogenesis is relatively low in adults, over the life span new neurons add up to an estimated 10%–20% of the population (Jacobs, van Praag, & Gage, 2000). Numerous studies show that learning is impaired by blocking neurogenesis and enhanced by increasing new cell birth. New neurons are more active than mature ones, have a lower threshold for LTP induction, and are better at making fine discriminations, such as distinguishing between the contexts in which reward occurs and does not occur (Yau, Li, & So, 2015). It also appears that the

■ **FIGURE 12.14**   Increase in Dendritic Spines Following LTP.

(a) A single synaptic spine on a dendrite (white) and a presynaptic terminal (red). (b) The same spine split into two following LTP.

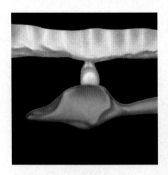
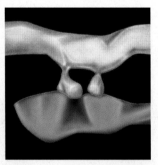

Source: Reprinted by permission from Macmillan Publishers Ltd. Based on "LTP Promotes Formation of Multiple Spine Synapses Between a Single Axon Terminal and a Dendrite," by N. Toni et al., *Nature, 402* (6706), pp. 421–425. Nature Publishing Group.

How do the roles of the hippocampus and the cortex differ?

new neurons contribute to the shift in memory from the hippocampus to cortex and interfere with the LTP established in the hippocampus to clear the way for new memories (Kitamura & Inokuchi, 2014). Blocking neurogenesis with X-radiation prolongs hippocampal LTP and delays completion of the transfer to the cortex by as many as 28 days.

With all that growth, you might suspect that there would be some increase in the volume of the brain areas that are involved in LTP. In fact, this does happen to some extent. London taxi drivers, who are noted for their ability to navigate the city's complex streets entirely from memory, spend about two years learning the routes before they can be licensed to operate a cab. Maguire and her colleagues (2000) used MRI to scan the brains of 16 drivers. The posterior part of their hippocampi, known to be involved in spatial navigation, was larger than in males of similar age. (Overall hippocampal volume did not change; their anterior hippocampi were smaller.) The difference was greater for cabbies who had been driving for the longest time, which we would expect if the difference was caused by experience.

Consolidation and Sleep

The hippocampus can acquire learning "on the fly" while the event is in progress, but a longer time is needed for long-term storage of declarative memories in the cortex. Many researchers now believe that the hippocampus transfers information to the cortex during times when the hippocampus is less occupied, even during sleep (Lisman & Morris, 2001; McClelland, McNaughton, & O'Reilly, 1995). During sleep, neurons in the rats' hippocampus and cortical areas repeat the pattern of firing that occurred during learning (Louie & Wilson, 2001; Y.-L. Qin, McNaughton, Skaggs, & Barnes, 1997). Human EEG and PET studies showed the hippocampus repeatedly activating the cortical areas that participated in the daytime learning, and this reactivation was accompanied by significant task improvement the next morning without further practice (Figure 12.15; Maquet et al., 2000; Wierzynski, Lubenov, Gu, & Siapas, 2009). Even a daytime nap of around 90 minutes is enough to evoke this kind of activity in the hippocampus and improve performance on a word-association test (Studte, Bridger, & Mecklinger, 2015). Presumably, "offline" replay provides the cortex the opportunity to undergo LTP at the more leisurely pace it requires (Lisman & Morris, 2001). During sleep, more than 100 genes increase their activity; many of those have been identified as major players in protein synthesis, synaptic modification, and memory consolidation (Cirelli, Gutierrez, & Tononi, 2004).

Changing Our Memories

As hard as the brain works to make memories "permanent," it is still important that these records not be inscribed in stone. Things change; the waterhole we learned was reliable over several visits is now becoming progressively more stagnant, so we must range in other directions until we find a new source of water. And sometimes erroneous learning must be corrected; the first two redheads we knew were hot tempered, and it will take meeting additional redheads to change what we have learned. A memory needs to be stable to be useful, but at the same time it must remain malleable; there are several ways the brain accomplishes this.

■ **FIGURE 12.15** PET Scans of Brain Activity During Sleep Following Learning.

Areas previously active during learning are also more active during sleep in the trained subjects, but not in the untrained subjects.

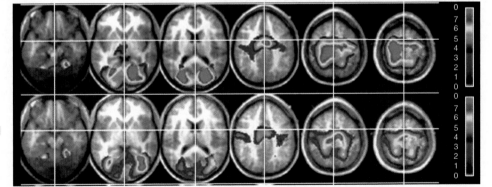

Source: Reprinted by permission from Macmillan Publishers Ltd. From "Experience-Dependent Changes in Cerebral Activation During Human REM Sleep," by P. Maquet et al., 2000, *Nature Neuroscience, 3*, pp. 831–855, fig. 2, p. 833. Nature Publishing Group.

Extinction

The first is *extinction*. The experimenter sounds a tone just before delivering a puff of air to your eye; after just a few trials, you blink just because you hear the tone. This doesn't happen simply because you understand that the air blast is coming; it occurs more quickly than you can make a voluntary response. Then the experimenter sounds the tone several times without administering the puff of air. Slowly the tone loses its power to make you blink. The memory is not gone; if the experimenter repeats the puff of air, you will be back to blinking every time you hear the tone. Nor is this an example of forgetting. Rather, extinction involves new learning; one indication is that, like LTP, extinction requires activation of NMDA receptors, and blocking these receptors eliminates extinction (Santini, Muller, & Quirk, 2001).

Forgetting

Most memories dissipate at least somewhat over time if they are not used frequently. We invariably regard memory loss from *forgetting* as a defect, but researchers are finding clues that the brain actively removes useless information to prevent the saturation of synapses with information that is not called up regularly or has not made connections with other stored memories. One way the brain cleans house apparently involves the enzyme protein phosphatase 1 (PP1), a product of the *PP1* gene. To study PP1's effect, researchers created transgenic mice (see Chapter 4) with genes for a particularly active form of PP1 inhibitor (Genoux et al., 2002). The genes were inducible, which means that the researchers could activate them at any time. Mice were trained in a water maze, and then the genes were turned on in the transgenic animals; 6 weeks later, the control subjects' memory for the task was completely absent, while the transgenic mice had forgotten very little. You may remember from your introductory psychology course that for most tasks, spreading out practice sessions (*distributed practice*) leads to better learning

---

APPLICATION
Total Recall

Source: iStock/michellegibson

Most of us would like to remember more and forget less. But a few years ago, Jill Price wrote to neuropsychologist James McGaugh at the University of California, Irvine, asking for help because she couldn't forget; she can remember what she did and what was happening in the world for practically every day of her life, and she is often tormented by bad memories (J. Marshall, 2008; E. S. Parker, Cahill, & McGaugh, 2006). Two years later two men with similar memory capabilities came forward, but unlike Price, Brad Williams and Rick

Baron can keep their memories at bay (Elias, 2008; D. S. Martin, 2008). Williams uses his memory in his work as a radio news reporter; Baron is unemployed but supports himself in part by winning contests that utilize his memory for facts. The researchers are eager to understand what fuels this unusual ability, because the knowledge could help the memory impaired. Of the 33 super-memory people confirmed by McGaugh's lab, 11 have undergone MRI scans; these revealed structural differences in nine brain areas, as well as greater white matter connections between areas (LePort et al., 2012).

The interesting thing is that these individuals do no better than other people on memorization tests; they just don't suppress their memories once they're formed. So what might be going on in these individuals? One indication is that inadequate inhibition might be involved because they show signs of compulsive behavior. Each is a devoted collector—years of TV guides, rare record albums, hundreds of TV show tapes—and Baron arranges all the bills in his wallet according to the city of the Federal Reserve Bank where they were issued and how the sports teams in that city did.

ENHANCING SOLDIERS' LEARNING WITH NEUROSTIMULATION

In 2016, the U.S. military began a new project aimed at applying knowledge of how learning occurs in the brain in order to improve performance in a variety of tactical areas (DARPA Public Affairs, 2017). The Targeted Neuroplasticity Training (TNT) program is funding research at several academic institutions to develop invasive and noninvasive methods for coaxing the brain to form connections in areas involved in cognitive functioning. Arizona State University scientist Stephen Helms Tillery will be using a technology called transdermal electrical neuromodulation, a noninvasive method of electrically activating parts of the nervous system by stimulating nerves through the skin (B. Wang, 2017). Helms Tillery's work will focus on stimulating the trigeminal nerve to activate a brain nucleus called the locus coeruleus, which releases the neurotransmitter norepinephrine. Scientists know that norepinephrine is activated as part of the "fight or flight" response and people show enhanced sensory functioning as part of their response to stress. Participants in Helms Tillery's studies will receive neuromodulation while performing a variety of perceptual and decision-making tasks, with the goal of increasing activity in related brain areas and improving performance on these tasks. Eventually, the military plans to use trigeminal nerve stimulation to enhance training of marksmen and drone pilots. Researchers at other institutions will be stimulating the vagus nerve, either through transdermal electrical neuromodulation or using invasive methods, to promote language learning; the technique could be useful, for example, in training intelligence experts (DARPA Public Affairs, 2017). Because military applications of neuroenhancements are controversial, the TNT program has funded a workshop on the ethical implications of this and related investigations.

THOUGHT QUESTIONS

1. How might neuromodulation impact the performance of military personnel in combat or noncombat roles?

2. How can electrical stimulation through the skin be used to activate portions of the brain?

3. What is one ethical issue that you think should be considered in these types of neuroscience applications?

For the news story, visit edge.sagepub.com/garrett5e and select the Chapter 12 study resources.

than *massed practice.* When the inhibitor genes were turned on during training, this advantage disappeared, which suggests that the reason distributed practice is superior is that PP1's effects accumulate over massed practice trials. Another gene involved in forgetting is *Drac1(V12).* Its protein product, Rac, causes memory to decay after learning. Interestingly, continued training suppresses Rac, which means that additional practice has a dual benefit (Shuai et al., 2010).

Efficient memory involves a balance between remembering and forgetting. Later in this chapter we will see how devastating memory impairment can be. The accompanying Application shows that there is another side to the coin as well.

Reconsolidation

Consolidation is a progressive affair extending over a relatively long period of time. During that time, the memory is vulnerable to disruption from several sources, including electroconvulsive shock and drugs that interfere with protein synthesis. In recent years, researchers have come to realize that each time a memory is retrieved, it must be *reconsolidated,* and during that time the memory becomes even more vulnerable (Dudai, 2004). For example, Nader, Schafe, and LeDoux (2000) conditioned a fear response (freezing) to a tone in mice by pairing the tone with electric shock to the feet. The antibiotic anisomycin blocks protein synthesis; it will eliminate the fear memory if it is injected shortly after learning, but injection 24 hours after training has no effect. However, as many as two weeks later, anisomycin eliminated the fear learning if the researchers induced retrieval of the memory by presenting the tone again (without the shock). You might very well wonder why the brain would give up protection of a consolidated memory during retrieval. Apparently, reopening a memory provides the opportunity to refine it, correct errors, and modify your emotional response to people who rubbed you the wrong way the first time you met them (J. L. C. Lee, 2009; McKenzie & Eichenbaum, 2011). Reconsolidation may even have therapeutic usefulness. It can be used to eliminate a learned fear response in humans, and (as you will see in Chapter 14) could provide an effective tool for erasing fear memories in people with posttraumatic stress disorder (D. Schiller et al., 2010). Although retrieval makes a memory vulnerable, reconsolidation during the labile period apparently strengthens the memory. Rats given several brief exposures to the training apparatus during the first few days after they learned a shock avoidance task showed no forgetting when tested 55 days after training (Inda, Muravieva, & Alberini, 2011).

Of course, there is no way to guarantee that reconsolidation will always be adaptive; the opportunity to correct errors also allows the introduction of new errors. We have long known that memories get "reconstructed" over time, usually by blending with other memories. Reconstruction can be a progressive affair. Evidence suggests that one reason for the "recovery" of *false* childhood memories during therapy may be therapists' repeated attempts to stimulate recall at successive sessions. Laboratory research has shown that people's agreement with memories planted by the experimenter can increase over multiple interviews (E. F. Loftus, 1997). In one study, researchers using doctored photographs found that after being questioned three times, 50% of subjects were describing a childhood ride in a hot air balloon that never happened (Wade, Garry, Read, & Lindsay, 2002). More recently, Loftus and her colleagues (D. M. Bernstein, Laney, Morris, & Loftus, 2005) were able to shift their subjects' food preferences by giving them a bogus computer analysis of their responses to a food questionnaire. For example, in a follow-up questionnaire, about 20% of the subjects agreed with the analysis that they had, in fact, been made sick by eating strawberry ice cream as children and reported that they would avoid it in the future.

CONCEPT CHECK

Take a Minute to Check Your Knowledge and Understanding

- Make a list of the changes that occur in neurons during learning.
- Describe LTP, LTD, and associative LTP.
- Consolidated memory is both stable and vulnerable. Explain.

Learning Deficiencies and Disorders

Learning may be the most complex of human functions. Not surprisingly, it is also one of the most frequently impaired. Learning can be compromised by accidents and violence that damage the structures we have been studying. But more subtle threats to learning ability come from aging and from disorders of the brain, including Alzheimer's disease and Korsakoff syndrome, which we will discuss in this section.

Effects of Aging on Memory

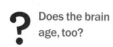
Does the brain age, too?

Old Man: Ah, memory. It's the second thing to go.

Young Man: So what's first?

Old Man: I forget . . .

You may or may not find humor in this old joke, but declining memory is hardly a laughing matter to the elderly. The older person might mislay car keys, forget appointments, or leave a pot on the stove for hours. Working memory and the ability to retrieve old memories and to make new memories may all be affected (Fahle & Daum, 1997; Small, Stern, Tang, & Mayeux, 1999). Although we usually associate aging with brain cell loss, significant deficits occur only in the midbrain, basal forebrain (lower frontal lobes), and some prefrontal areas. Some parts of the prefrontal cortex and hippocampus also decline in volume, likely due to a decrease in synaptic density. These areas, of course, are critical for learning, memory, and cognitive functioning (Mora, 2013).

Deficits occur at the molecular level as well. One study, for example, examined the brains of deceased individuals and found 17 genes in the dentate gyrus of the hippocampus that undergo changed levels of expression with aging (Pavlopoulos et al., 2013). Downregulation of one of these genes results in less abundant production of the protein RbAp48 in humans and mice. This protein turns out to be important for memory: Young mice engineered to produce reduced RbAp48 showed dysfunction in the dentate gyrus and performed like old mice on memory tests. In the study described earlier, Genoux and his colleagues (2002) found that aged mice were significantly impaired on the learning task after just one day without practice, but performance in old mice with the enhanced PP1 inhibitor genes was still robust four weeks later. If we could find simple, safe ways to manipulate gene expression in humans, we could reduce many of the burdens of aging.

Some elderly people seem immune to the effects of aging on learning and cognition. Certainly, a part of this is genetic, but there have been many research efforts to identify environmental interventions that could benefit the rest of the population. Housing animals in an enriched environment reduces age-related changes in dendritic branching, neurogenesis, spine density, and cortical thickness; physical exercise and calorie restriction have similar effects in animals' brains and, in humans, improve cognitive functioning (Mora, 2013). We are beginning to appreciate the value of diet as well; consumption of fruits and vegetables containing flavonoids, for example, is associated with better language and episodic memory and slower cognitive decline in the elderly (Vauzour, 2014). In animals, flavonoids have been found to activate cellular learning mechanisms, enhance LTP, and increase hippocampal neurogenesis. There have been additional attempts to improve memory and general cognitive performance in the elderly through training, but these have not met with much success (Salthouse, 2006), despite the hype for commercial training programs. There could be many reasons for the lack of effect, including how meaningful and engaging the training tasks are and the amount of time spent in training. One promising effort is the Synapse Project, in which elderly individuals showed gains in episodic memory capabilities after spending 16 hours a week for three months learning digital photography or quilting, tasks that are both interesting and cognitively demanding (D. C. Park et al., 2014).

Alzheimer's Disease

Substantial loss of memory and other cognitive abilities (usually, but not necessarily, in the elderly) is referred to as *dementia*. The most common cause of dementia is *Alzheimer's disease*, a disorder characterized by progressive brain deterioration and impaired memory and other cognitive abilities. Alzheimer's disease was first described by the neuroanatomist and neurologist Alois Alzheimer in 1906, after autopsying the brain of a 56-year-old patient with memory problems. Alzheimer's is primarily a disorder of the aged, but it can strike early in life. Of the nearly 5 million people in the United States with Alzheimer's, 4.7 million are over the age of 65 (Hebert, Weuve, Scherr, & Evans, 2013). The earliest and most severe symptom is usually impaired declarative memory. Initially, the person is indistinguishable from a normally aging individual, though the symptoms may start earlier; the person has trouble remembering events from the day before, mislays items, forgets names, and must search for the right word in a conversation. Later, the person repeats questions and tells the same story again during a conversation. As time and the disease progress, the person eventually fails to recognize acquaintances and even family members. Alzheimer's disease is not just a learning disorder but a disorder of the brain, so ultimately most behaviors suffer. Language, visual-spatial functioning, and reasoning are particularly affected, and there are often behavioral problems such as aggressiveness and wandering away from home. Alzheimer's researcher Zaven Khachaturian (1997) eloquently described his mother's decline: "The disease quietly loots the brain, nerve cell by nerve cell, like a burglar returning to the same house each night" (p. 21). Eventually, Alzheimer's is fatal; it is the sixth leading cause of death in the United States (S. L. Murphy, Xu, & Kochanek, 2013).

The Diseased Brain: Plaques and Tangles

There are two notable characteristics of the Alzheimer's brain, though they are not unique to the disease. *Plaques* are clumps of beta amyloid (Aβ), a type of protein, that cluster among axon terminals and interfere with neural transmission (Figure 12.16a). The main component is Aβ42, so called because it is 42 amino acids long; Aβ42 is particularly "sticky," so it clumps easily to form the plaques. In addition, abnormal accumulations of the protein tau form *neurofibrillary tangles* inside neurons; tangles are associated with the death of brain cells (Figure 12.16b). Plaques and tangles move through the brain in a predictable succession of stages, beginning with the medial cortex and progressing to the limbic areas, particularly the hippocampus, and then to the neocortex, the outer layers of cortex responsible for our highest functions (H. Braak & Braak, 1991). This accounts for the pattern of changing symptoms as the disease advances. Recently we've learned that this sequence parallels a progressive variation in two significant factors in those areas: the relative level of expression of inflammatory genes and the balance between proteins that promote or inhibit the aggregation (accumulation and clumping) of plaques and tangles (Figure 12.17; Freer et al., 2016). Interestingly, this differential

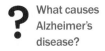
? What causes Alzheimer's disease?

■ **FIGURE 12.16**   Neural Abnormalities in the Brain of a Person With Alzheimer's.

(a) The round clumps in the photo are plaques, which interfere with neural transmission. (b) The dark, twisted features are neurofibrillary tangles, which are associated with death of neurons.

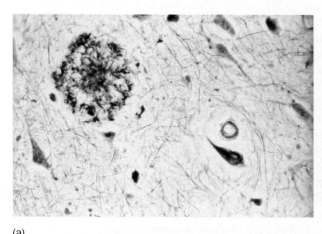

(a)

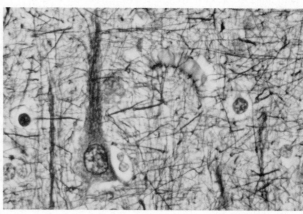

(b)

Sources: (a) © Dr. M. Goedert/Science Source. (b) © SPL/Science Source.

vulnerability among brain areas was discovered in healthy brains. Studying the progress of the disease can be difficult; we don't get a chance to look at the afflicted human brain until the disease is well advanced and, as the Research Spotlight explains, the laboratory models have been less than satisfactory.

Figure 12.18 compares the brain of a deceased Alzheimer's patient with a normal brain. Notice the decreased size of the gyri and the increased width of the sulci in the diseased brain. Internally, enlarged ventricles tell a similar story of severe neuron loss. Many of the lesions are in the temporal lobes; because of their location, they effectively isolate the hippocampus from its inputs and outputs, which partly explains the early memory loss (B. T. Hyman, Van Horsen, Damasio, & Barnes, 1984). However, plaques and tangles also attack the frontal lobes, accounting for additional memory problems as well as attention and motor difficulties. The occipital lobes and parietal lobes may be involved as well; disrupted communication between the primary visual area and the visual association areas in the parietal and temporal lobes explains the visual deficits that plague some Alzheimer's sufferers.

Although amyloid plaques have been considered the hallmark of Alzheimer's disease, the number of amyloid deposits is only moderately related to the degree of cognitive impairment (Selkoe, 1997), and about 25% of the elderly have plaques but suffer no dementia (Mintun et al., 2006). Researchers, however, are beginning to distinguish between insoluble forms of amyloid and soluble forms, which reach 70-fold higher levels in the brains of people with Alzheimer's (M. E. Larson & Lesné, 2012), and in mice have been linked

■ **FIGURE 12.17**   Alzheimer's Disease Progress Parallels Aggregation Difference Scores.

In (a), the darker the colors, the earlier plaques and tangles appear in that area; gray areas are unaffected. In (b), the darker the colors, the more aggregation promoters exceed aggregation-inhibiting proteins. Note the similarity in the images.

Progression of Alzheimer's Disease

Aggregation Difference Score

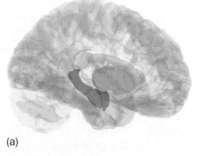

(a)

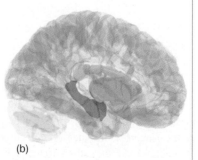

(b)

Source: Excerpted from Figure 3 from "A Protein Homeostasis Signature in Healthy Brains Recapitulates Tissue Vulnerability to Alzheimer's Disease," by R. Freer, P. Sormanni, G. Vecchi, P. Ciryam, C. M. Dobson, & M. Vendruscolo, Science Advances, 2 (8), e1600947.

Alzheimer's in a Dish

Studying Alzheimer's disease in the laboratory has been difficult because the models used so far don't duplicate the pathology completely. Mice can be genetically engineered to produce the amyloid plaques, but not the neurofibrillary tangles; and cultures of neurons from Alzheimer's patients' brains produce amyloid and tau, but not the plaques and tangles. Researchers at Massachusetts General Hospital realized that the two-dimensional liquid cultures used in the laboratory are very different from the gelatinous environment of the brain, so they started using a three-dimensional gel to grow their cultures; to this they added stem cells that carried two gene variants known to cause Alzheimer's (S. H. Choi et al., 2014). After six weeks, the culture had both the typical amyloid and the toxic form of amyloid, and was complete with plaques and tangles. When they blocked the formation of plaques, they obtained the first direct evidence that plaque formation is a precursor to the development of the synapse-damaging tangles. The researchers say that the 3-D culture will allow them to screen hundreds of thousands of potential new drugs in a few months' time.

to memory failure, loss of synapses, and failure of LTP in the hippocampus (Gong et al., 2003). More recently we have learned that a modified form of tau, called *acetylated* tau (because of an added acetyl group), is particularly important because it depletes KIBRA, a protein required for inserting extra receptors into the neuronal membrane during learning (Tracy et al., 2016). Increasing KIBRA levels in cultured neurons reversed the effects of acetylated tau and restored their ability to strengthen connections, suggesting a new therapeutic approach.

Heredity and Environment

Heredity is an important factor in Alzheimer's disease. The first clue to a gene location came from a comparison of Alzheimer's with Down syndrome (Lott, 1982). Down syndrome individuals also have plaques and tangles, and they invariably develop Alzheimer's disease if they live to the age of 50. Because Down syndrome is caused by an extra chromosome 21, researchers zeroed in on that chromosome; there they found mutations in the *amyloid precursor protein* (*APP*) gene (Goate et al., 1991). When aged mice were genetically engineered with an *APP* mutation that increased plaques, both LTP and spatial learning were impaired (Chapman et al., 1999).

Three additional genes that influence Alzheimer's had been confirmed by the end of the 1990s; all of those affect amyloid production or its deposit in the brain (Selkoe, 1997). As you can see in Table 12.1, the genes fall into two classes, those associated with early-onset Alzheimer's disease (often before the age of 60) and one found in patients with late-onset Alzheimer's. The ε4 allele of the *APOE* gene is particularly interesting because it contributes to so many Alzheimer's cases. It increases risk by three- to eightfold and is associated with plaques and tangles, but how it contributes to pathology is not well understood. Two studies indicate that carriers without dementia have lower cerebral blood flow (Thambisetty, Beason-Held, An, Kraut, & Resnick, 2010) and that 2- to 25-month-old children with the allele have reduced growth in temporal and parietal areas, which are affected in patients with Alzheimer's (Dean et al., 2014).

The four genes in the table account for just a little over half the cases of Alzheimer's disease, so there are likely many rare or small-effect genes as well as environmental influences. Discovery of additional genes had to await whole-genome studies with large numbers

■ **FIGURE 12.18**   Normal Brain (Left) and Alzheimer's Brain

The illustration shows the most obvious differences, the reduced size of gyri and increased size of sulci produced by cell loss in the diseased brain.

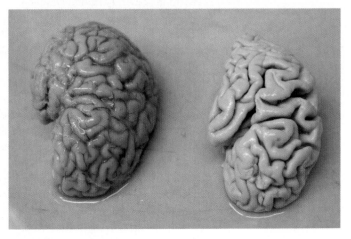

Source: REUTERS/Denis Balibouse.

TABLE 12.1   Known Genes for Alzheimer's Disease.

GENE	CHROMOSOME	AGE OF ONSET (YEARS)	PERCENTAGE OF CASES
APP	21	45–66	<0.1
Presenilin 1	14	28–62	1–2
Presenilin 2	1	40–85	<0.1
ApoE4	19	>60	>50

Sources: Marx (1998); Selkoe (1997).

of individuals. Such studies have the advantage that they allow gene searches without the need for a preconceived target area. Prior to 2009, 11 genes had been associated with Alzheimer's, but a whole-genome study of 74,000 individuals was able to add 11 additional gene locations (Lambert et al., 2013). Although the genes themselves have not been identified yet, genes near the loci are involved in amyloid and tau pathways, inflammation, immune response, cell migration, and cellular functions.

Genome-wide studies have also made it possible to do broad searches for epigenetic changes, and in the past few years the focus has been shifting in that direction. A recent study conclusively identified seven genes that were differentially methylated in Alzheimer's patients by taking the unusual step of verifying their results in a second group of subjects (De Jager et al., 2014). If we could identify the environmental conditions that trigger these changes, then preventive measures could reduce the incidence of Alzheimer's. A meta-analysis identified several environmental risks for dementia, including exposure to pesticides, fertilizers, herbicides, and insecticides; airborne particulate matter; second-hand smoke; and electromagnetic fields (Killin, Starr, Shiue, & Russ, 2016). On the health side, we can add vitamin D deficiency (Killin et al.), sedentary lifestyle, diabetes, obesity, smoking, and hypertension (Baumgart et al., 2015). In addition, studies with combat soldiers, football players, and boxers have established a strong link between traumatic brain injury and Alzheimer's-like brain pathology and dementia (Vincent, Roebuck-Spencer, & Cernich, 2014). A meta-analysis found a 5-fold increase in Alzheimer's disease with *Chlamydophila pneumoniae* bacterial infection and a 10-fold increase with spirochete infection (Maheshwari & Eslick, 2015). Indeed, there is increasing evidence that beta amyloid can be triggered by infection and acts as an antimicrobial agent; in the first study in living models, human beta amyloid protected human neural cells from *Candida* infection and round-worms from infection by *Candida* and *Salmonella*, and significantly extended the survival time of mice after *Salmonella* infection (Kumar et al., 2016).

Treatment of Alzheimer's Disease

The Alzheimer's Association (2017) estimates that the cost of caring for Alzheimer's and other dementia patients in the United States in 2017 will be $259 billion. By 2050, the U.S. population is expected to increase by 50%, while the number of people over the age of 85 increases sixfold (Bureau of the Census, 2001). As a result, experts have been predicting that Alzheimer's rates will almost triple (Figure 12.19; Hebert et al., 2013. In the past few years, however, at least nine studies have shown a declining risk for Alzheimer's in the wealthiest nations (Langa, 2015), including a 20% drop in the United Kingdom (Matthews et al., 2015) and a 26% decrease in the United States (Langa et al., 2017). One contributing factor is increasing educational levels (see the discussion of the cognitive reserve hypothesis in the next section), and the researchers believe that more effective treatment of health risks such as cardiovascular disease make up the rest of the difference.

Five drugs are currently approved for the treatment of Alzheimer's in the United States, but one of those is rarely prescribed due to side effects (Patoine & Bilanow, n.d.). Three of the ones in regular use are cholinesterase inhibitors; they restore acetylcholine transmission by interfering with the enzyme that breaks down acetylcholine at the synapse. Acetylcholine-releasing neurons are significant victims of degeneration in Alzheimer's disease; blocking acetylcholine activity impairs learning in humans (Newhouse, Potter, Corwin, &

Lenox, 1992), and in rats it interferes with learning by eliminating hippocampal theta (J. A. Deutsch, 1983), rhythmic neural activity that is necessary for LTP to occur. The fourth drug, memantine (marketed in the United States as Namenda), was the first approved for use in patients with moderate and severe symptoms. Some of the neuron loss in Alzheimer's occurs when dying neurons trigger the release of the excitatory transmitter glutamate; the excess glutamate produces excitotoxicity, overstimulating NMDA receptors and killing neurons. Memantine limits the neuron's sensitivity to glutamate, reducing further cell death. Studies indicate moderate slowing of deterioration and improvement in symptoms (Reisberg et al., 2003; U.S. Food and Drug Administration, 2003). Unfortunately, these drugs provide only modest relief for the memory and behavioral symptoms of Alzheimer's, and they are little or no help when degeneration is advanced.

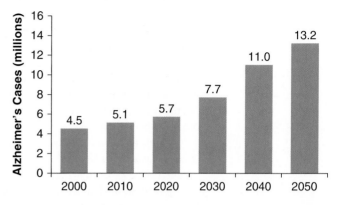

■ **FIGURE 12.19**   Projected Increases in Alzheimer's Disease in the United States.

Note that numbers begin to escalate rapidly after 2020.

Source: Based on data from Hebert et al. (2013).

In their quest for more effective treatments, researchers are mounting efforts on three major fronts: removing beta amyloid or blocking its formation, preventing tau from forming tangles, and reducing inflammation. However, no new drug has been approved by the FDA since 2003, and the disappointments continue to accumulate. The failure of two large trials of anti-amyloid antibodies, one of which was at the final phase 3 level, has some researchers now thinking that once symptoms have appeared the treatment is too late; they are shifting to pretreatment in asymptomatic individuals who are at genetic risk (Callaway, 2012). Similarly, a phase 3 trial attempting to treat inflammation with injections of immunoglobulin has come up empty-handed (Weill Cornell Medical College, 2014). However, the tangle-preventing drug LMTX is now in phase 3 clinical trials, after reducing symptom progression by 90% in phase 2 trials (TauRx Therapeutics, n.d.).

Stem cell and gene therapy are obvious treatment possibilities, and although work is in the early stages, progress is being made. A Florida stem cell research company has a phase 1 human safety trial under way; if nothing else, the researchers expect benefits from the anti-inflammatory effects of stem cells (Stem Cells Portal, 2017). On the gene therapy front, a Chinese team has demonstrated that neural stem cells can be used to deliver RNA to silence the gene responsible for the key enzyme in beta amyloid production (Z. Liu et al., 2013); in the United States, researchers have increased axonal sprouting among degenerating neurons by inserting a gene for nerve growth factor into patients' brains (Tuszynski et al., 2015). *Brain-derived neurotrophic factor (BDNF)* prevents the death of neurons and stimulates their functioning; individuals with the highest levels of BDNF were 33% less likely to develop dementia and Alzheimer's disease than those with the lowest levels (G. Weinstein et al., 2014). BDNF is in phase 1 clinical trials; and nerve growth factor (NGF), which has similar effects, is in phase 2 trials (Tuszynski & Nagahara, 2016). Researchers also continue to focus on removing plaques from the brain. After much promise from animal studies and multiple failures with humans, one drug (aducanumab) has been successful in reducing both soluble and insoluble beta amyloid and slowing cognitive decline; the drug is now in phase 3 trials (Sevigny et al., 2016). Another approach showing promise in animals is ultrasound stimulation of the brain; it cleared plaques in the brains of mice engineered to duplicate some characteristics of Alzheimer's, apparently by stimulating glia to ingest the plaques, resulting in reversal of lost memory capability (Leinenga & Götz, 2015).

Detecting Alzheimer's Disease

The aging individual dealing with memory problems typically wonders "Am I getting Alzheimer's?" No single test can diagnose Alzheimer's, but a battery of physical, neurological, and cognitive tests can do a reasonably good job, mostly by ruling out other forms of dementia that may be more treatable, if not reversible. The physician may also order an MRI to look for atrophy in the temporal and parietal areas. For many years, patients were told that a definite diagnosis could be made only on autopsy, after examining the brain for plaques and tangles, but recent advances in PET scanning and measurement of biomarkers is changing that. Using new tracers that specifically target plaques, PET scans can identify 75%–90% of individuals who are confirmed to have Alzheimer's at the time of autopsy; measuring Aβ42 and tau in the cerebrospinal fluid is equally accurate (Fraller, 2013). Biological assessment should lead to more appropriate treatment planning by differentiating better between Alzheimer's and other dementias; in addition, it will be possible to monitor therapeutic progress, detecting changes before they translate into cognitive gains. But because current treatments only slow the progress of Alzheimer's, researchers are interested in detecting the disease well before it is full-blown and before irreversible damage has occurred. PET scanning for amyloid predicts about one-third of individuals with mild cognitive impairment who will be diagnosed with Alzheimer's during the next several months; among the normal elderly, 25% with high amyloid levels are diagnosed within three years, while those with low levels have a 98% chance of remaining cognitively stable (Gelosa & Brooks, 2012). Biomarkers found in cerebrospinal fluid and blood have shown 90%–100% accuracy in predicting progression to Alzheimer's over the next five to six years (De Meyer et al., 2010; Khan & Alkon, 2010; S. Ray et al., 2007).

A study of Roman Catholic sisters that has been going on since 1986 revealed cognitive differences as many as five decades before some of them were diagnosed with Alzheimer's (Riley, Snowdon, Desrosiers, & Markesbery, 2005). Autobiographical essays were available for 180 of the study participants, written when they joined the order at an average age of 22. These were scored for idea density, defined as the number of ideas expressed for every 10 words. Almost 80% of the sisters with the lowest density scores eventually developed Alzheimer's, compared with 10% among those who scored the highest. A surprising finding was the number of participants with high density scores and no symptoms of Alzheimer's who had neurofibrillary tangles when they were autopsied (Iacono et al., 2009; Riley et al., 2005). Also, the sisters who remained healthy were just as likely as the ones with Alzheimer's to have one or more *ApoE4* alleles (Riley et al.). So, what protected some of the women from Alzheimer's? This question leads us to the reserve hypothesis.

Resistance to Alzheimer's: The Reserve Hypothesis

According to the *reserve hypothesis,* individuals with greater cognitive or brain capacity can compensate for brain changes due to aging, brain damage, or disorders such as Alzheimer's. There is some evidence for compensation in the elderly through *brain reserve,* either by means of greater activation in the network involved or by recruiting other brain areas (reviewed in Y. Stern, 2012). However, most studies have focused on *cognitive reserve,* by assessing experiential factors and cognitive capabilities. For example, the risk of developing the symptoms of dementia decreases by 46% with higher educational and occupational levels and higher IQ and mental activity in earlier life. This compensation is an effortful activity; fMRI showed that older people with more beta amyloid deposits produced more activation in their brains' memory areas, and they were more accurate in recalling material when they did so (Elman et al., 2014). The protection this affords is temporary, however; the delay may last the rest of the individual's life but, if not, decline occurs more rapidly than in other Alzheimer's patients.

The elderly fare better if they have a history of both mental and physical activity, so they are frequently advised to stay active to stave off mental decline. However, choosing an active lifestyle may simply be a reflection of general fitness, rather than the cause of better cognitive health later; we should be careful about assuming cause until we have adequate experimental evidence and, so far, the results have been mixed. The most consistently positive results have been with exercise; cognitive training has not been very promising, except for complex computer games and role-playing games.

Korsakoff Syndrome

What are the symptoms of Korsakoff syndrome?

Another form of dementia is *Korsakoff syndrome,* brain deterioration that is almost always caused by chronic alcoholism. The deterioration results from a deficiency in the vitamin *thiamine* (B1), which has two causes: (1) The alcoholic consumes large quantities of calories in the form of alcohol in place of an adequate diet, and (2) the alcohol reduces absorption of thiamine in the stomach. The most pronounced symptom is anterograde amnesia, but retrograde amnesia is also severe; impairment is to declarative memory, while nondeclarative memory remains intact. The hippocampus and temporal lobes are unaffected; but the mammillary bodies (see Figures 3.20 and 8.4) and the medial part of the thalamus are reduced in size, and structural and functional abnormalities occur in the frontal lobes (Gebhardt, Naeser, & Butters, 1984; Kopelman,

1995; Squire, Amaral, & Press, 1990). A bizarre accident demonstrated that damage limited to the thalamic and mammillary areas can cause anterograde amnesia; a 22-year-old college student received a penetrating wound to the area when his roommate accidentally thrust a toy fencing foil up his left nostril, producing an amnesia that primarily affected verbal memory (Squire, Amaral, Zola-Morgan, Kritchevsky, & Press, 1989). Thiamine therapy can relieve the symptoms of Korsakoff syndrome somewhat if the disorder is not too advanced, but the brain damage itself is irreversible.

Some Korsakoff patients show a particularly interesting characteristic in their behavior, called *confabulation;* they fabricate stories and facts to make up for those missing from their memories. Non-Korsakoff amnesiacs also confabulate, and so do normal people occasionally when their memory is vague. However, Korsakoff patients are champions at this kind of "creative remembering," especially during the volatile early period, when their symptoms have just heated up. We will talk about what causes confabulation shortly; in the meantime, try to refrain from assuming that confabulation involves intentional deception.

For some, confabulation becomes a way of life. Mary Frances could converse fluently about her distant past as a college and high school English teacher and recite Shakespeare and poetry that she had written. But, robbed of the memory of more recent years by Korsakoff disease, she constantly invented explanations for her nursing home surroundings. One time, she was just "visiting" at the home, and she watched patiently through the glass front doors for her brother who would pick her up shortly for an automobile trip to Florida. Another time, she complained that she was stranded in a strange place and needed to get back to her "post"; she had in fact been in the army in World War II as a speechwriter for General Clark. On another occasion, she thought that she was in prison—probably suggested by the real memory that she had been a prisoner of war—and she was querying the nurse about what she had "done wrong."

Confabulation occurs following damage to a specific area in the frontal lobes (Turner, Cipolotti, Yousry, & Shallice, 2008). A Korsakoff patient studied by Benson and his colleagues (1996) did poorly on cognitive tests that are sensitive to impairment in frontal lobe functioning, and a brain scan showed that activity levels were reduced in the frontal area as well as in the diencephalon, the lower part of the forebrain that includes the thalamus and hypothalamus. Four months later, he had ceased confabulating, and the scan of the frontal area had returned to normal; however, his amnesia and deficient diencephalic activity continued. Confabulating amnesic patients have more trouble than nonconfabulating amnesiacs in suppressing irrelevant information they have learned earlier (Schnider & Ptak, 1999). Consequently, Benson and colleagues (1996) suggest that confabulation is due to an inability to distinguish between current reality and earlier memories. We will take up this topic again in Chapter 15.

CONCEPT CHECK

Take a Minute to Check Your Knowledge and Understanding

- What changes occur in the brain during aging?
- What is the role of plaques and tangles in Alzheimer's disease?
- How are Alzheimer's disease and Korsakoff syndrome similar and different?

In Perspective

Learning is a form of neural plasticity. However, that simple statement ignores a variety of complex features that characterize learning. For example, different kinds of learning can be impaired selectively, as we see in patients who can learn and yet have no recollection of having learned. Our exploration of learning has been an abbreviated one, in part because many mysteries are waiting to be solved.

Despite all we know about the learning process, we have little ability to enhance it. Researchers tell us that blueberries can reduce learning deficits in aging rats and that wearing a nicotine patch can improve memory, but they can do disappointingly little to help the Alzheimer's patient. Curing learning disorders and improving normal learning ability are little more than aspirations today. But there is good reason to think the mysteries will be solved eventually, perhaps with your help.

CHAPTER SUMMARY

Learning as the Storage of Memories

- Brain damage can cause amnesia by impairing the storage of new memories (anterograde) or the retrieval of old memories (retrograde).
- The hippocampus is involved in both consolidation and retrieval. The prefrontal area may play an executive role.
- Memories are stored near the area where the information they are based on is processed.
- There are at least two kinds of learning: declarative, mediated by the hippocampus, and nondeclarative, which involves the striatum and amygdala.
- Working memory holds new information and information retrieved from storage while it is being used.

Brain Changes in Learning

- LTP increases synaptic strength, and LTD reduces it.
- LTP is necessary for learning; diminishing it impairs learning, and increasing it enhances learning.
- The hippocampus manages new declarative memories, but they are transferred later to the cortex.

- Changes at the synapse include protein activation and increases in the number of AMPA receptors and the number of dendritic spines. Increased neurogenesis in the hippocampus appears to aid memory transfer to the cortex.

Learning Deficiencies and Disorders

- Aging usually involves some impairment of learning and memory, but in the normally aging brain, substantial loss of neurons and synapses is limited to a few areas.
- Alzheimer's disease is a hereditary disorder that impairs learning and other brain functions, largely through the destruction of acetylcholine-producing neurons. Plaques and tangles are associated with cell death, but evidence they are the cause is not yet clear. Treatment usually involves increasing acetylcholine availability, but experimental treatments take other approaches.
- Korsakoff syndrome is caused by a vitamin B deficiency resulting from alcoholism. Anterograde and retrograde amnesia are effects. ■

STUDY RESOURCES

FOR FURTHER THOUGHT

- If you were building an electronic learning and memory system for a robot, is there anything you would change from the human design? Why or why not?
- What are the learning and behavioral implications of impaired working memory?
- What implication does the experiment in which mice were injected with the antibiotic anisomycin at the time of retrieval have for your study conditions as you review material for an exam?
- Which direction of research for the treatment of Alzheimer's do you think holds the greatest promise? Why?

TEST YOUR UNDERSTANDING

1. Discuss consolidation, including what it is, when and where it occurs, and its significance in learning and memory.

2. Make the argument that LTP provides a reasonably good explanation of learning, including some of learning's basic phenomena.

3. Compare Alzheimer's disease and Korsakoff syndrome in terms of causes, symptoms, and brain areas affected.

Select the best answer:

1. Anterograde amnesia means that the patient has trouble remembering events that occurred

   a. more than a few minutes earlier.
   b. before the brain damage.
   c. since the brain damage.
   d. since the brain damage and for a few years before.

2. If you are positive you know who the 14th president of the United States is, but cannot remember at this very moment, you are having a problem with

   a. consolidation.
   b. retrieval.
   c. amnesia.
   d. dementia.

3. The main neurotransmitter implicated in memory formation is

   a. serotonin.
   b. epinephrine.
   c. endorphin.
   d. dopamine.

4. If HM's striatum had also been damaged, he would also not have remembered

a. declarative memories of childhood events.
b. skills learned before his surgery.
c. skills learned after his surgery.
d. emotional experiences after his surgery.

5. In the course of adding a long column of entries in your checkbook, you have to carry a 6 to the next column. If you forget the number in the process, you're having a problem with

a. consolidation.
b. LTP.
c. retrieval.
d. working memory.

6. The researcher sounds a tone and then delivers a puff of air to your eye. After several times, the tone alone causes you to blink. This behavior is probably explained by

a. LTP.
b. associative LTP.
c. LTD.
d. associative LTD.

7. Synaptic changes during learning involve

a. activation of proteins.
b. increased number of dendritic spines.
c. increased number of receptors.
d. all of the above.

8. When do most of the genes linked to memory consolidation increase their activities?

a. During sleep.
b. During times of relaxation.
c. During long bouts of studying.
d. When you are distracted.

9. Memories are vulnerable to the insertion of "false facts" through suggestions or ideas that fill in the gaps. This usually occurs during the process of

a. extinction.
b. consolidation.
c. retrieval.
d. reconsolidation.

10. When researchers injected anisomycin, which blocks protein synthesis, into the brains of mice two weeks after fear conditioning, the results demonstrated that

a. protein increase improves memory.
b. antibiotics can improve memory.
c. memories are particularly vulnerable during recall.
d. once recalled, a memory takes longer to reconsolidate.

11. The aged brain is characterized by substantial _____ throughout the cortex.

a. loss of neurons
b. loss of synapses
c. decrease in metabolism
d. all of the above
e. none of the above

12. Alzheimer's disease is most closely associated with

a. plaques and tangles.
b. a single gene.
c. environmental toxins.
d. all of the above

13. The feature most common between Alzheimer's disease and Korsakoff syndrome is the

a. symptoms.
b. age of onset.
c. degree of hereditary involvement.
d. degree of environmental contribution.

1. c, 2. b, 3. d, 4. c, 5. d, 6. b, 7. d, 8. a, 9. d, 10. c, 11. e, 12. a, 13. a.

Answers:

ON THE WEB

The following websites are coordinated with this chapter's content. You can access these websites from the **SAGE edge Student Resources site**; select this chapter and then click on Web Resources. (**Bold** items are links.)

1. The Institute for Brain and Society's **H.M.** page has information about the famous amnesiac and the project to digitize his brain and make it available for continued scientific study. **New Scientist TV** describes the preparation of HM's brain and provides a video of the slicing and staining procedure. Having trouble visualizing the hippocampus? See it in a rotating transparent brain at **Wikipedia**.

2. The professional journal *Learning and Memory* provides free access to published articles from the preceding year and earlier.

The **American Psychological Association** is a good source of information on learning and memory and other topics. Many of the articles are brief updates appearing in the APA *Monitor on Psychology*. Just type the name of a topic in the search window.

3. The **Alzheimer's Association** has information about the disease, help for caregivers, and descriptions of research it is funding.

4. The National Institute of Neurological Disorders and Stroke's **Wernicke-Korsakoff Syndrome Information Page** describes the disorder, treatments, and research. The **Family Caregiver Alliance** has a useful fact sheet on Korsakoff syndrome, including characteristics, prevalence, diagnosis, and treatment.

FOR FURTHER READING

1. *The Cognitive Neuroscience of Memory*, by Scott Slotnick (Cambridge University Press, 2017), covers the brain mechanisms underlying long-term memory and its failure, working memory, and diseases of memory.

2. *The Cognitive Neuroscience of Memory Consolidation*, edited by Nikolai Axmacher and Björn Rasch (Springer, 2017), provides an in-depth treatment of that topic.

3. In "Neurogenesis Erases Existing Memories," by Leonie Welberg (*Nature Reviews Neuroscience*, 2014, *15*, 428–429), the author presents evidence that hippocampal neurogenesis not only promotes the formation of new memories but also induces forgetting of established ones.

4. "Place Cells, Grid Cells, and Memory," by May-Britt Moser, David C. Rowland, and Edvard Moser (*Cold Spring Harbor Perspectives in Biology*, 2015, *7*, a021808, available at http://cshperspectives.cshlp.org/content/7/2/a021808.full), goes beyond place cells to describe a whole network that provides our maps of space.

5. "Secrets of an Age-Resistant Memory," by Jessica Hamzelou (*New Scientist*, September 10, 2016), describes a project studying people who qualify as "superagers" by being over the age of 80 but performing like 55-year-olds on memory tests.

KEY TERMS

Alzheimer's disease 361
anterograde amnesia 346
associative long-term potentiation 354
brain-derived neurotrophic factor
    (BDNF) 365
confabulation 367
consolidation 347
declarative memory 352

dementia 361
dendritic spines 356
Hebb rule 354
Korsakoff syndrome 366
long-term depression (LTD) 354
long-term potentiation (LTP) 354
neurofibrillary tangles 361
nondeclarative memory 352

place cells 351
plaques 361
reserve hypothesis 366
retrieval 347
retrograde amnesia 346
working memory 353

 **SAGE edge™**   edge.sagepub.com/garrett5e

SAGE edge offers a robust online environment featuring an impressive array of free tools and resources for review, study, and further exploration, keeping both instructors and students on the cutting edge of teaching and learning.

12.1 Explain how the brain is involved in the different types of memory.	🔊	Memory and Forgetting
12.2 Diagram the neural involvement in processing of information that is stored in memory.	📄	BDNF and Memory Formation and Storage
12.3 Describe the changes that occur in the brain as learning proceeds.	▶	How Reliable Is Your Memory?
	▶	The Connection Between Memory and Sleep
12.4 Examine how memory changes during aging.	▶	What Is Alzheimer's?
12.5 Contrast the impacts of normal aging and disorders on memory.	▶	Can We Reverse the Effects of Aging?

Hero Images/Getty Images

Intelligence and Cognitive Functioning

13

After reading this chapter, you will be able to:

- Describe how scientists have defined intelligence.

- Critique the scientific methods for measuring intelligence.

- Identify how the structure of the nervous system relates to intelligence.

- Appraise the relative contributions of heredity and environment to intelligence.

- Assess the impact of the typical aging process on cognitive functioning.

- Compare the impacts of intellectual disability, autism, and attention-deficit/hyperactivity disorder on intelligence.

Master the content.
edge.sagepub.com/garrett5e

Some people are calling Cambridge's theoretical physicist Stephen Hawking the most brilliant person living today. Following in Einstein's footsteps, he has developed theories of the origin of the universe that are altering the way scientists think. He lectures around the world, mixing high-powered physics with a keen sense of humor. He has achieved all this despite having Lou Gehrig's disease (*amyotrophic lateral sclerosis*, or *ALS*), a degenerative disease that impairs voluntary movement. Confined to a wheelchair and able to make only small facial movements, he writes and speaks by moving a cursor on the screen of a computer equipped with a voice synthesizer (Figure 13.1).

When we consider people like Hawking, we are forced to wonder what makes one person more intelligent than another. Is it genes, upbringing, hard work, or opportunity? And is the ultra-intelligent brain in some way different? Unfortunately, we have a problem with the presumption of *who* is smarter. Is Hawking more intelligent than Einstein, or has he just had the advantage of more predecessors' accomplishments to build on? Is Marilyn vos Savant smarter than her husband because at the age of 10 she made the highest score recorded on an intelligence test (Yam, 1998) while he had trouble testing well enough to get into medical school, or is he smarter because he invented the Jarvik artificial heart? We cannot attempt to understand the biological bases of intelligence without having some appreciation of our limitations in measuring it or even defining what it is.

■ **FIGURE 13.1** Stephen Hawking.

His great intellect resides in a body that can communicate only by moving a cursor on a computer screen.

Source: Jemal Countess/Singer/Getty Images Entertainment/Getty Images.

The Nature of Intelligence

There are many ideas about what intelligence is, which is the first clue that we don't have consensus about what it is. Most definitions say something to the effect that *intelligence* is the ability to reason, to understand, and to profit from experience. That is what we *think* intelligence is; the problem comes when we try to translate that abstract definition into the behaviors that would indicate the presence of intelligence. That is what we must do to measure intelligence, which is the first step toward determining its biological basis.

What Does "Intelligence" Mean?

Understanding how we measure intelligence is important because we are in effect defining intelligence as *what that test measures.* The measure of intelligence is typically expressed as the *intelligence quotient (IQ).* The term originated with the scoring on early intelligence tests designed for use with children. The tests produced a score in the form of a *mental age,* which was divided by the child's chronological age and multiplied by 100. The tests were designed to produce a score of 100 for a child performing at the average for his or her chronological age. The scoring is completely different now, partly because the tests were extended to adults, who do not increase consistently in intellectual performance from year to year. The base score is still 100, a value selected arbitrarily and preserved artificially by occasional adjustments to compensate for any drift in performance in the population. Most people are near the average, as Figure 13.2 shows, with relatively few people at either of the extremes. For example, only 2% of the population score above 130 points or below 70 points.

The first intelligence test was devised by Alfred Binet in 1905, to identify French schoolchildren who needed special instruction (Binet & Simon, 1905). Predicting school performance is still what most intelligence tests do best, and intelligence tests have found their greatest use in the school setting. The correlation between IQ scores and school grades typically falls in the range of .40 to .60 (Kline, 1991). (If you've forgotten what a correlation coefficient means, see pages 112–113.) However, IQ is also related to job performance, income, and socioeconomic level and, negatively, to juvenile delinquency (Neisser et al., 1996).

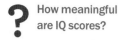

How meaningful are IQ scores?

Critics believe that scores on traditional intelligence tests are closely related to academic performance and to higher socioeconomic levels mostly because the tests were designed to reflect that kind of success. According to these critics, the tests overemphasize verbal ability, education, and Western culture. A few tests are designed to be culture-free, like the Raven Progressive Matrices (Raven, 2003). These tests are mostly nonverbal, and the tasks require no experience with a particular culture. They have an obvious advantage for testing people from a very different culture or language background or with impaired understanding of language. Some researchers also believe that these tests give them a better representation of "pure" intelligence.

Claiming that true intelligence is much more than what the tests measure, these critics often point to instances where practical intelligence or "street smarts" is greater than conventional intelligence. For example, as young Brazilian street vendors conducted their business, they were adept at performing calculations that they were unable to perform in a classroom setting (Carraher, Carraher, & Schliemman, 1985). In another study, expert racetrack gamblers used a highly complex algorithm involving seven variables to predict racetrack odds, but their performance was unrelated to their IQ; in fact, four of them had IQs in the low to mid-80s (Ceci & Liker, 1986). More recently, Robert Sternberg (2000) compared the scores that the presidential candidates George W. Bush, Al Gore, and Bill Bradley made on the verbal section of the Scholastic Aptitude Test (SAT) when they applied for college; the SAT has many items similar to those on conventional intelligence tests. Two of the candidates scored above average for college applicants but not markedly so, and one had a score that was below average. To Sternberg, their success raises questions about the narrowness of what intelligence tests measure.

Sternberg (1988) argues that intelligence does not exist in the sense we usually conceive of it but is "a cultural invention to account for the fact that some people are able to succeed in their environment better than others" (p. 71). Perhaps intelligence is, like the mind, just a convenient abstraction we invented to describe a group of processes. If so, we should not expect to find intelligence residing in a single brain location or even in a neatly defined network of brain structures. And to the extent we find processes or structures that are directly involved in intelligence, their performance may not be highly correlated with scores on traditional intelligence tests.

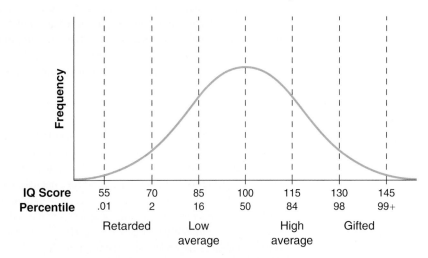

■ **FIGURE 13.2** Distribution of IQ Scores in the Population.

Source: From *Psychology: The Adaptive Mind* (2nd ed.), by J. S. Nairne, 2000, Wadsworth, a part of Cengage Learning, Inc. Reproduced by permission.

The Structure of Intelligence

Another controversy that is critical to a biological understanding of intelligence is whether intelligence is a single capability or a collection of several independent abilities. Intelligence theorists tend to fall into one of two groups, *lumpers* or *splitters.* Lumpers claim that intelligence is a single, unitary capability, which is usually called the *general factor,* or simply *g.* General factor theorists admit that there are separate abilities that vary somewhat in strength in an individual, but they place much greater weight on the underlying g factor. They point out that a person who is high in one cognitive skill is usually high in others, so they believe that a measure of g is adequate by itself to describe a person's intellectual ability. General intelligence is sometimes assessed by the overall IQ score from a traditional intelligence test, such as the Wechsler Adult Intelligence Scale, whose 11 subtests measure more specific abilities. But many g theorists prefer to use other tests like the Raven Progressive Matrices, because they emphasize reasoning and problem solving and are relatively freer of influence from specific abilities such as verbal skills.

Splitters, by contrast, hold that intelligence is made up of several mental abilities that are more or less independent of each other. Therefore, they are more interested in scores on the subtests of standard IQ tests or scores from tests of specific cognitive abilities. They may agree that there is a general factor, but they give more emphasis to separate abilities and to differences among them in an individual. An accurate description of a person's intelligence would require the scores on all the subtests of these abilities. These theorists point to cases of brain damage in which one capability is impaired without affecting others and to the savant's exceptional ability in a single area. Splitters disagree with each other, though, on how many abilities there are; a review of intelligence tests identified more than 70 different abilities that can be measured by available tests (Carroll, 1993).

CONCEPT CHECK

Take a Minute to Check Your Knowledge and Understanding

- What do IQ scores tell us, and not tell us, about a person's capabilities?
- What difference does it make to our search for a biological basis for intelligence whether intelligence is a "real" entity or an invented concept?
- What is the lumper–splitter controversy?

The Biological Origins of Intelligence

With this background, we are now ready to explore the origins of intelligence. Based on our introduction, we will avoid two popular assumptions—that intelligence tests are the only way to define intelligence and that intelligence is a single entity. Instead, we will consider performance and achievement as additional indicators of intelligence, and we will first examine the evidence of a biological basis for a general factor and then consider the relationship between brain structures and individual abilities.

The Brain and Intelligence

How are intelligent brains different?

Is a more intelligent brain different in any identifiable way from other brains? Anyone asking this question would naturally wonder how Albert Einstein's brain was different from other people's. Fortunately, the famous scientist's brain was preserved, and it has been made available from time to time to neuroscientists (Figure 13.3). In cursory examinations, it turned out to be remarkably unremarkable. In fact, at 1,230 grams (g) it was almost 200 g lighter than the average weight of the control brains (Witelson, Kigar, & Harvey, 1999). The number of neurons did not differ from normal, and studies have disagreed about whether the neurons were more densely packed or the cortex was thinner, perhaps because the samples were taken from different locations (B. Anderson & Harvey, 1996; Kigar, Witelson, Glezer, & Harvey, 1997). One study found a higher ratio of glial cells to neurons in the left parietal lobe (M. C. Diamond, Scheibel, Murphy, & Harvey, 1985). The comparison brains averaged 12 years younger than Einstein's at the time of death, and we know that glial cells continue proliferating throughout life (T. Hines, 1998), but the number of glial cells was not elevated in Einstein's right parietal lobe or in either frontal sample. Each of Einstein's hemispheres was a full centimeter wider than those of control brains, due to larger parietal lobes (Witelson et al., 1999), and there were intriguing variations in some of the parietal gyri (Falk, 2009). These anomalies are interesting because the parietal lobes are involved in mathematical ability and visual-spatial processing, and Einstein reported that he performed his mathematical thinking not in words but in images. Remember, though, that in Chapter 12 we saw that London taxi drivers have enlarged posterior hippocampi, and no one has suggested that large hippocampi explain why they became taxi drivers. In fact, a later follow-up study found that drivers who qualified at the end of their training increased in hippocampal volume, but drivers who failed to qualify did not (Woollett & Maguire, 2011). Whether Einstein's large parietal lobes or intense mathematical activity came first is uncertain (assuming they are related).

> *The contrast between the popular estimate of my powers and achievements compared to the reality is simply grotesque.*
>
> —Albert Einstein

■ **FIGURE 13.3**   Albert Einstein and His Brain.

The brain of the genius looks just like yours; it took careful study to find differences.

(a)

(b)
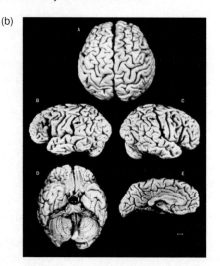

Sources: (a) Wikimedia Commons/Ferdinand Schmutzer. (b) Figure 1. "The Exceptional Brain of Albert Einstein," by Witelson, S. F., Kigar, D. L., & Harvey, T. The Lancet, 353(9170), 2149–2153.

It is interesting that the strongest finding in the examination of Einstein's brain seems to be related to a specific ability rather than to overall intelligence. British researcher John Duncan and his colleagues (2000) sought the location of general intelligence in the brains of more ordinary folk. They used tasks that required reasoning and that are known to correlate with general intelligence more than with any specific ability. Although verbal and spatial tasks had different patterns of activation, prefrontal activation was common to both tasks; the authors concluded that general intelligence may be located there. But general intelligence is likely more complex than what happens in one area of the brain. A team of researchers scanned the brains of 241 individuals with brain damage and correlated the location of their lesions with their scores on a set of intelligence subtests chosen to measure g (Gläscher et al., 2010). They found that g requires a distributed system, a network that spans the frontal, parietal, and temporal lobes (Figure 13.4). They concluded that g involves the brain's ability to pull together different kinds of processing, such as visual-spatial processing and working memory. The ability to integrate these functions depends on the quality of connections between the areas, which is highly heritable, up to 84% in some parts of the brain (Chiang et al., 2009).

> Words and language . . .
> do not seem to play
> any part in my thought
> processes.
>
> —Albert Einstein

Brain Size

Popular wisdom is that smart people have bigger brains, and that is true—to an extent, at least. A meta-analysis of 88 studies including more than 8,000 individuals found a correlation between intelligence and brain size of .24 (Pietschnig, Penke, Wicherts, Zeiler, & Voracek, 2015). This means that variations in brain size account for about 6% (0.24^2) of people's differences in intelligence. And lest we give too much importance to brain size, Einstein's 1,230-gram brain was a bit more than 100 g under the average for a male of his age (Harrison, Freemantle, & Geddes, 2003). Nevertheless, brain size is a factor in intelligence, but we can't generalize this across species; elephants have much larger brains, and not many people think elephants are smarter than we are. More important than brain size is our compact primate neural organization that packs more neurons into a smaller space; on top of that, we have the largest brains of all the primates and, so far as we know, the largest number of neurons (Pietschnig et al.).

But if brain size accounts for just 6% of our differences in intelligence, then other factors must be more important. Men's brains are 11% larger on average than women's, yet men and women score equally on intelligence tests. Men may have a size advantage, but women apparently compensate with a different structural organization. They have a greater ratio of gray matter to white matter than do men (Haier, Jung, Yeo, Head, & Alkire, 2005), which increases their number of neurons. Women also have stronger connections between the hemispheres and more complex convolutions, and they rely on different parts of the brain than men to achieve comparable results in intelligence testing (Pietschnig et al.).

Gray matter and white matter volumes are more specific measures than overall size of the brain, and both are predictive of intelligence. The correlation of gray matter volume with IQ has been measured at .37 (Narr et al., 2007); in men, the correlation is strongest in the frontal and parietal lobes, whereas women show the strongest gray matter relationship in frontal areas, including Broca's area (Haier et al., 2005). White matter volume, which indicates the extent of connectivity within the brain, has a correlation of .26; variations in white matter volume are more important for women's cognitive performance than for men's (Figure 13.5). Note in Figure 13.5 that the widespread distribution of significant areas suggests that intellectual ability depends on a broad network of neural structures.

■ **FIGURE 13.4**

Brain Areas Involved in General Intelligence.

A view of the cortical surface (left) and subcortical areas (right) shows a g-related network extending throughout much of the brain.

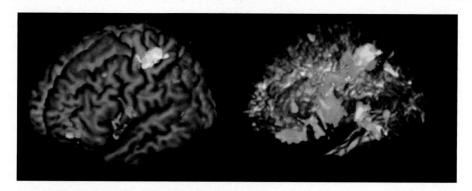

Source: From "Distributed Neural System for General Intelligence Revealed by Lesion Mapping," by J. Gläscher et al., 2010, *Proceedings of the National Academy of Sciences, 90*, pp. 4705–4709.

■ **FIGURE 13.5**

Correlations Between Gray Matter and White Matter Volumes and IQ.

Notice that gray matter volume is correlated with IQ in more areas in men than in women, and white matter volume is correlated with IQ in more locations in women than in men. (Lighter colors indicate stronger relationships.)

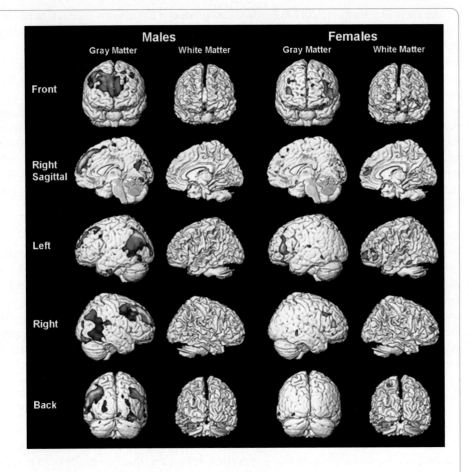

Source: Montreal Neurological Institute.

Processing Speed and Efficiency

Cognitive processes require the person to apprehend, select, and attend to meaningful items from a welter of stimuli arriving at the sensory organs. Then the person must retrieve information from memory, relate the new information to it, and then manipulate the mental representation of the combined information. All of this takes time. Back in 1883, when there were no intelligence tests, Sir Francis Galton attempted to relate measures of intellectual achievement like course grades and occupational status to people's reaction times, but he couldn't find a relationship. Later researchers have shown that IQ scores are correlated with reaction time and, even more so, with *nerve conduction velocity* (Figure 13.6; T. E. Reed & Jensen, 1992). Neural conduction speed depends on the integrity of the white matter tracts; white matter integrity is correlated with intelligence and explains 10% of the variance (Penke et al., 2012). White matter integrity declines with age, and intelligence along with it (Bennett & Madden, 2014). Faster nerve conduction may make its contribution through improved processing efficiency.

White matter integrity and nerve conduction velocity are vital in determining how well information travels throughout the brain. One of the most important contributors to both and, therefore, to transmission efficiency is myelination, which increases conduction speed and protects against "cross-talk" between neurons. Humans have a greater proportion of white matter (myelinated processes) to gray matter than other animals, and IQ varies among individuals with the degree of myelination (Willerman, Schultz, Rutledge, & Bigler, 1994). In addition, myelination, speed of information processing, and intelligence all follow a curvilinear time path, increasing from childhood to maturity and then declining in old age.

One indicator of the role of brain efficiency in intelligence is that individuals who are higher in IQ use less brain energy. This was indicated by a lower rate of glucose metabolism during a challenging task, playing the computer game Tetris (Haier, Siegel, Tang, Abel, & Buchsbaum, 1992). And, as you can see in Figure 13.7, individuals with mild intellectual disability (IQs between 50 and 70) require 20% more neural activity to perform an attention-demanding task than do individuals with IQs of 115 or higher (Haier et al., 1995). You might think the more intelligent brain would be the more active one during a task, but remember that we are talking about efficiency.

Improved technology, particularly the availability of diffusion tensor imaging, has shifted the conversation toward brain networks and network efficiency. After reviewing 37 imaging studies related to intelligence, Rex Jung and Richard Haier (2007) proposed the Parieto-Frontal Integration Theory (P-FIT). According to their theory, information processing takes place in four stages, primarily in the parietal and frontal lobes: (1) After sensory information has been processed in secondary areas, it is passed on to (2) parietal areas, which abstract the information and integrate it, and then (3) these areas interact with frontal areas in problem solving and evaluation. (4) Finally, the anterior cingulate cortex selects the response and inhibits alternative responses. Subsequent studies have lent support to the theory, identifying these areas as central to intelligence and the parietal cortex as the main hub (Langer et al., 2012; Y. Li et al., 2009). In addition, the brains of more intelligent individuals were more efficient, with more numerous interconnections within clusters of neural activity and shorter paths between clusters.

Specific Abilities and the Brain

Brain size, speed, and efficiency can reasonably be viewed as contributors to general intelligence; now we will consider evidence for individual components of intelligence. The statistical method called *factor analysis* has been useful in identifying possible components. The procedure involves giving a group of people several tests that measure cognitive abilities that might be related to intelligence; the tests may be intelligence tests, or they may be measures of more limited abilities such as verbal skills or reaction time. Then correlations are calculated among all combinations of the tests to locate "clusters" of abilities that are more closely related with each other than with the others. Performance on practically all tests of cognitive ability is somewhat related, which is consistent with the hypothesis of a general factor. However, factor analysis has also identified clusters of more specific abilities. Three capabilities have emerged frequently as major components of intelligence: *linguistic, logical-mathematical,* and *spatial* (A. R. Jensen, 1998).

Several authors have argued that each of the cognitive abilities depends on a complex network or module in the brain that has evolved in ways that support that function. In other words, they believe that the brain is hardwired for functions like mathematics and language (Dehaene, 1997; Pinker, 1994). We have already seen examples of modular functions in earlier chapters; for example, the language (linguistic) module is made up of a network of structures located mainly in the left frontal and temporal lobes (see Chapter 9). Spatial ability depends mostly on functions in the parietal lobes. An MRI study at the University of Iowa revealed structural differences related to male spatial superiority on the Mental Rotations Test, a standard measure of spatial ability (Koscik et al., 2009). Women in the study had greater gray matter volume (relative to white matter) in the parietal lobes, but this was correlated with poorer spatial performance. Men, by contrast, had greater cortical surface area in the parietal

■ **FIGURE 13.6** Relationship Between IQ Scores and Nerve Conduction Velocity.

The research participants were divided into five groups according to their nerve conduction velocity. Group 1 had the lowest nerve conduction velocity and Group 5 the highest. Nerve conduction velocity was calculated as elapsed time between a stimulus and the occurrence of the evoked potential divided by the distance between the eyes and the back of the head.

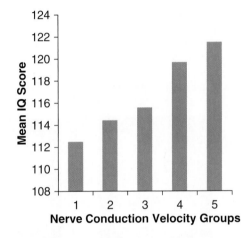

Source: Adapted from "Conduction Velocity in a Brain Nerve Pathway of Normal Adults Correlates With Intelligence Level," by T. E. Reed and A. R. Jensen, *Intelligence, 16,* pp. 259–272. Copyright 1992, with permission from Elsevier Science.

■ **FIGURE 13.7** Greater Efficiency in the More Intelligent Brain.

During an attention-demanding task, PET scans showed 20% more activity (indicated by more reds and yellows) in (a) the brain of an individual with intellectual disability than in (b) the brain of a person with above-average IQ.

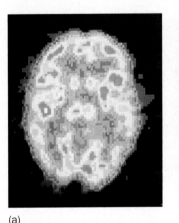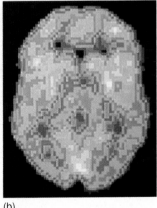

(a)   (b)

Source: From "Brain Size and Cerebral Glucose Metabolic Rate in Nonspecific Mental Retardation and Down Syndrome," by R. J. Haier et al., 1995, *Intelligence, 20,* pp. 191–210.

lobes (after correction for brain size), and this was correlated with better performance. Previous work has indicated that greater cortical surface area translates to a larger number of neurons.

Mathematical ability in humans depends on the prefrontal cortex and the parietal cortex. That fact by itself makes no distinction between mathematical ability and general intelligence; most likely the distinction lies in specifics of the interconnections and how the brain can recruit activity in the structures. For example, subjects who performed better on tests of basic arithmetic had greater cross-connection activity between the two parietal lobes during problem solving (J. Park, Park, & Polk, 2012). In addition, the areas are activated selectively according to the task and progressively as difficulty increases. The left prefrontal cortex is most active when an individual performs calculations from memory, such as 2×4 and $2 + 4$; the area is probably the storage site of arithmetic facts. Both parietal areas come into play during estimation of values (Figure 13.8a; Dehaene, Spelke, Pinel, Stanescu, & Tsivkin, 1999); this makes sense, because visual-spatial representations of quantity, such as finger counting and the "number line," are an almost universal stage in learning exact calculation. Calculation recruits both left and right prefrontal areas and both parietal cortices; activation increases further in the parietal lobes with increasing difficulty (incorporating an additional step to the calculation), and in the prefrontal areas as speed demands increase (Figure 13.8b; Menon, Rivera, White, Glover, & Reiss, 2000). Studies of brain damage support these conclusions. Individuals with damage to the left frontal language area can arrange numbers in rank order and estimate results, but they cannot perform precise calculations; those with parietal damage are impaired in the opposite direction (Butterworth, 1999; Dehaene & Cohen, 1997). Katherine Keller and Vinod Menon (2009) also observed frontal and parietal activation as their subjects did multistep mental arithmetic; but they also looked at the occipital areas and found activation there, demonstrating that people recruit additional resources as needed (in this case, visualization; Figure 13.8c). Four clusters in the right hemisphere were more activated in men than in women, but this did not translate to greater calculation accuracy; so, although brain differences sometimes result in performance differences, once again we see evidence of males and females using different brain strategies to achieve comparable results.

Obviously, neither of these areas is dedicated exclusively to numeric functions. This is consistent with the suggestion in Chapter 9 that the language areas may simply use processing strategies that make them particularly suited to the demands of the task, rather than being dedicated to language processing. However, Wynn (1998) argues that the brain has a specialized mechanism for numbers by pointing to evidence that even infants and lower primates seem to have an inborn ability to estimate quantities. The infants she studied saw two objects placed one at a time behind a screen. They acted surprised—which means that they looked for a longer time—when the screen was removed to reveal three objects or only one object instead of the expected two (Wynn, 1992). Rhesus monkeys tested in the wild responded to the task the same way (Hauser, MacNeilage, & Ware, 1996). Monkeys can rank-order groups of objects that differ in number by touching their images on a computer monitor in the correct order (Brannon & Terrace, 1998), and chimpanzees have learned

? Are there separate components of intelligence?

■ **FIGURE 13.8**   Brain Locations Involved in Mathematical Performance.

(a) Calculations from memory (such as 2×4) activate primarily left prefrontal cortex; estimation involves both parietal cortices. (b) Non-rote calculation involves all four areas, and activation increases with difficulty (for example, $5 - 2$ versus $6 + 3 - 5$). (c) Activation of all four areas plus occipital areas during multistep mental arithmetic.

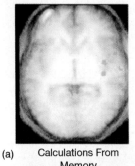
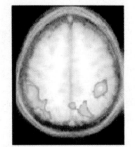

(a) Calculations From Memory	Estimation

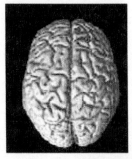
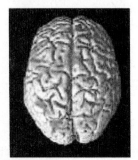

(b) Easy Calculation	Difficult Calculation

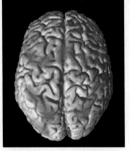

(c) Mental Arithmetic

Sources: (a) From "Sources of Mathematical Thinking: Behavioral and Brain-Imaging Evidence," by S. Dehaene, E. Spelke, P. Pinel, R. Stanescu, & S. Tsivkin, 1999, *Science, 284*, pp. 970–973. Reprinted with permission of AAAS. (b) From "Dissociating Prefrontal and Parietal Cortex Activation During Arithmetic Processing," by V. Menon, S. M. Rivera, C. D. White, G. H. Glover, and A. L. Reiss, 2000, *NeuroImage, 12*, pp. 357–365.

RESEARCH SPOTLIGHT
We Aren't the Only Tool Users

A chimp dines on termites "fished" from their mound with a stick.

Source: Ingo Arndt/Minden Pictures/Getty.

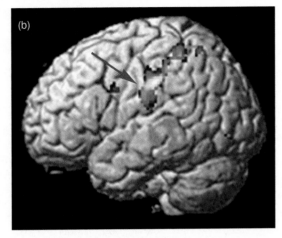

Source: From "The Representation of Tool Use in Humans and Monkeys: Common and Uniquely Human Features," by R. Peeters et al., 2009, *Journal of Neuroscience, 29*, pp. 11523–11539.

Humans have been fascinated with how intelligent animals' behavior can seem. Termites build earthen mounds that are so well ventilated they stay cool under the African sun. Dolphins cooperate with each other to herd schools of fish into their pod mates' waiting mouths. Kanzi communicates with symbols, Alex mastered simple concepts (see Chapter 9), and monkeys and chimpanzees can "count."

Especially intriguing is the concept of tool use. Chimpanzees have long been known to "fish" for termites by punching a hole in the nest and inserting a small green twig that the termites climb onto in defense of the nest, only to be slurped up by the chimp (Figure a; Holden, 2004b). Congo chimps add a unique twist: They fray the end of the twig, enabling them to pick up 20 times as many termites (Sanz, Cali, & Morgan, 2009).

New Caledonian and Hawaiian crows cut and shape twigs and use them to extract food from crevices, and they have been observed to spontaneously shape wire into hooks to retrieve food (Rutz et al., 2016; Weir, Chappell, & Kacelnik, 2002). But Santino, a chimp in a Swedish zoo (Osvath, 2009), may demonstrate the greatest ingenuity. Santino occasionally threw stones at visitors, but zookeepers weren't concerned because there was so little ammunition on his island. Then stone throwing increased dramatically, so a caretaker watched to figure out where the stones were coming from. Each morning, Santino retrieved stones from the moat and placed them strategically for launching at the visitors. He was also seen dislodging chunks of concrete from a wall, after first tapping where there were cracks and listening for the hollow sound that meant a piece was loose enough to be removed.

So what do these research observations tell us? First, animals are more intelligent than we've given them credit for. Second, some of our capabilities aren't unique after all. But we also have a chance to discover where we are truly different. For example, watching someone retrieve an object with the hand activates mirror neurons that are similarly located in humans and in monkeys (Peeters et al., 2009). However, when a human sees the object being retrieved with a tool, an additional area is activated in the anterior parietal lobe (Figure b); yet no such area for tool use showed up in the monkeys, even the ones that were trained for three to six weeks to use the same tools. Apparently we have developed some additional specialized structures, either through evolution or individual experience.

to do the same with numerals (Kawai & Matsuzawa, 2000). The accompanying Research Spotlight offers some additional insight into animal intelligence.

An impartial observer would have to say that there is evidence for characteristics that contribute to an overall intelligence and for somewhat independent capabilities as well. An either–or stance is not justified now; it makes sense to continue the two-pronged approach of looking for biological bases for both general intellectual ability and separate capabilities.

■ **FIGURE 13.9**   Correlations of IQ Scores Among Relatives.

Percentages indicate the degree of genetic relatedness. "Together" and "apart" refer to whether related children are raised in the same household.

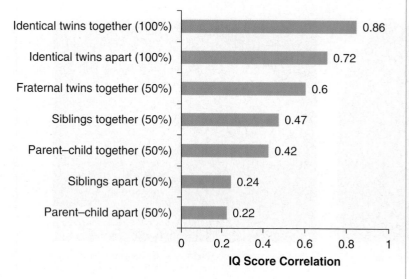

Source: Data from "Familial Studies of Intelligence: A Review," by T. J. Bouchard and M. McGue, 1981, *Science, 212*, pp. 1055–1059.

Heredity and Environment

We saw in Chapter 1 that intelligence is the most investigated of the genetically influenced behaviors. Our understanding of the genetic underpinnings of intelligence hardly lives up to the amount of effort, however; this is because intelligence is so complex and poorly understood itself and because many genes are involved. In addition, environment accounts for half of the differences among us in intelligence, yet the environmental influences have themselves not been clearly identified (Plomin, 1990).

Heritability of Intelligence

Figure 13.9 shows the IQ correlations among relatives, averaged from many studies and several thousand people. You can see that IQ is more similar in people who are more closely related (T. J. Bouchard & McGue, 1981). Separating family members early in life does not eliminate the correlation; in fact, identical twins reared apart are still more similar in IQ than are fraternal twins reared together. Interestingly, the relative influence of heredity *increases* with age, from 41% in childhood to 55% in adolescence and 66% in adulthood (Haworth et al., 2009). Intuition tells us that environment should progressively overtake genetic effects as siblings go their separate ways and their experiences diverge, but J. R. Gray and Thompson (2004) suggest that the genes that influence intelligence also influence the individual's choices of environment and experience.

? Which is more important, heredity or environment?

Researchers have documented genetic influence on several of the functions that contribute to intelligence, including working memory, processing speed, and reaction time in making a choice (Ando, Ono, & Wright, 2001; Luciano et al., 2001; Posthuma, de Geus, & Boomsma, 2001). Most of the differences among individuals in the major structural contributors to intelligence are accounted for by genetic factors; estimated heritabilities in one twin study were 90% for brain volume, 82% for gray matter, and 88% for white matter (Figure 13.10; Baaré et al., 2001). General intelligence has higher heritability than more specific abilities, such as verbal and spatial abilities (McClearn et al., 1997), which is an additional argument for a stronger biological basis for g (J. R. Gray & Thompson, 2004).

Locating the specific genes is another matter. Two genes that have received special interest underwent accelerated evolution following our separation from chimpanzees. The *ASPM* gene is a major determinant of brain size (J. Zhang, 2003), while the *PACAP* precursor gene plays a role in neurogenesis and neural signaling and may have contributed to the formation of human cognitive abilities (Y. Wang et al., 2005). But the search for genes has been fraught with one replication failure after another. One reason is that effect sizes for individual genes are small, on the order of around 1%, which means that unless samples are very large, the genes will be missed. However, small samples often yield false positives that don't hold up on further scrutiny. Recently, a large consortium of researchers has been combining genetic data with brain scanning to locate genes responsible for the structural foundations of intelligence. One of these studies has identified a genetic variant associated with brain size (the C allele of rs10784502; its possessors scored on average 1.29 points higher on IQ tests, and having two of the C alleles doubled the gain; J. L. Stein et al., 2012). A second study identified 24 genetic variations on six genes, which were related to the structural integrity of major brain pathways; some of these were associated with intelligence, and individuals with multiple of these variants scored several points higher than others on intelligence tests (Chiang et al., 2012). Another group identified a gene linking cortical thickness to intelligence; individuals with a particular variant had a thinner cortex in the left hemisphere and performed less well on intelligence tests (Desrivières et al., 2014). This variant, however, accounted for only 0.5% of the variation in IQ.

■ **FIGURE 13.10** Genetic Control of Gray Matter Volume in Identical and Fraternal Twins.

Red indicates areas where the correlation between twins in gray matter was most significant; green indicates lesser correlation and blue, no statistically detectable relationship. Notice the markedly greater similarity (greater abundance of red) between identical twins. (W indicates Wernicke's area and S/M the somatosensory and motor areas.)

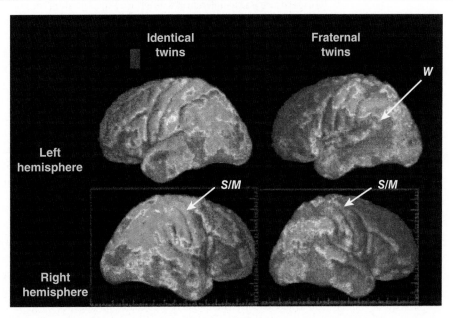

Source: Reprinted by permission from Macmillan Publishers Ltd. From "Genetic Influences on Brain Structure," by Paul M. Thompson et al., 2001, *Nature Neuroscience, 4*(12), pp. 1253–1258. © 2001 Nature Publishing Group.

The Genetic Controversy

The conclusion that intelligence is highly heritable has not been greeted with unquestioning acceptance. The heritability of intelligence is controversial on a variety of fronts; these controversies illustrate both the pervasive misunderstanding of genetic influence and the difficulty in resolving questions of heredity. Critics fear that inheritance of intelligence implies that intelligence is inborn and unchangeable (Weinberg, 1989). Nothing could be further from the truth, however; as Weinberg points out, genes do not fix behavior but set a range within which the person may vary. By way of illustration, height is about 90% heritable (Plomin, 1990), yet the average height has increased dramatically over the past few decades, due to improved nutrition. Similarly, IQ scores increased at the rate of 5–25 points over just a generation (termed *the Flynn effect*; Flynn, 1987), so test constructors have been adjusting the test norms occasionally to maintain an average of 100 points. Although the environmental causes have not been identified, such rapid increases cannot be due to genetic changes. However, we know that the world is a much more stimulating, information-filled place and education has changed dramatically; and, as Flynn points out, in 1900 the median year of schooling was 6 years, compared with 13 years now, and schools taught by memorization and recitation (Flynn, te Nijenhuis, & Metzen, 2014).

Some researchers argue that the correlation of IQ among relatives does not mean that intelligence is inherited. They suggest, for example, that identical twins' similarity in appearance and personality lead others to treat them similarly, even when they are reared apart, and this similar treatment results in similar intellectual development. Although physical features and behavior do affect how others react to a child, there is little evidence that these responses in turn influence intelligence. To test this possibility, researchers compared the IQs of twins who had been either correctly or incorrectly perceived by their parents as fraternal or identical. If similar environmental treatment accounts for IQ similarity, then the parents' perception of their twins' classification should be more important than the twins' actual genetic classification. Instead, the studies showed that only the true genetic relationship influenced IQ similarity in the twins, not the parents' perception (Scarr & Carter-Saltzman, 1982).

In another controversy, a debate has raged since the 1930s over whether IQ differences between ethnic groups are genetically based. The question is not whether the ethnic groups differ in IQ scores, but how much the differences are due to heredity and to environment. Arthur Jensen (1969) has argued that environment and socioeconomic differences are inadequate to account for the observed IQ differences among groups. He and Philippe Rushton cite studies indicating that IQ differences are consistent around the world, with East Asians averaging 106 points whether in the United States or in Asia, Whites about 100, and African Americans at 85 and sub-Saharan Africans around 70 (Rushton & Jensen, 2005). In addition, they say that the

IQ gaps correspond to differences in brain size. Their position has practical as well as theoretical implications. For example, extreme hereditarians believe that intervention efforts like Head Start not only do not work but also cannot work.

Other intelligence researchers countered that Jensen and Rushton ignored or misinterpreted the most relevant data (Nisbett, 2005). For example, African Americans with more African ancestry scored as high on cognitive tests as those with mixed ancestry (Scarr, Pakstis, Katz, & Barker, 1977). Another study suggests that socioeconomic class is more important than ethnic origin; it found that IQ runs about 20–30 points lower in the lowest social classes than in the highest social classes (Locurto, 1991). Higher intelligence test results are not always found for Asians (Naglieri & Ronning, 2000), and their higher academic achievement is typically attributed to cultural and motivational differences (Dandy & Nettelbeck, 2002). A task force appointed by the American Psychological Association to study the intelligence debate concluded that there is not much direct evidence regarding the genetic hypothesis of IQ differences between African Americans and Whites, and what little there is does not support the hypothesis (Neisser et al., 1996).

Environmental Effects

Most intelligence researchers agree that intelligence is the result of the joint contributions of genes and environment; it has even been said that intelligence is 100% hereditary and 100% environmental, because both are necessary. However, it has been more difficult than expected to identify just which environmental conditions influence intelligence, other than those that cause brain damage. We will give environmental influences more attention here than usual because intelligence is a good arena for illustrating the difficulties in sorting out heredity from environment. One problem is similar to the one we have encountered in identifying specific genes: The environmental influences are many and, for the most part, individually weak (A. R. Jensen, 1981). Even a twin study that looked at major environmental events such as severe infant and childhood illness failed to find an effect (Loehlin & Nichols, 1976). A second problem is that environmental influences are often hopelessly confounded with genetic effects. For example, family conditions such as socioeconomic level and parental education are moderately related to the offspring's intelligence (T. J. Bouchard & Segal, 1985), but these characteristics also reflect the parents' genetic makeup, which they pass on to their children.

The best way to demonstrate environmental influences is by environmental intervention. Although the Head Start program has produced long-term benefits in mathematics, educational attainment, and career accomplishments, the average increase of 7.42 IQ points compared with controls eventually disappears. The Abecedarian Project, which began at birth, produced IQ gains that were as strong 10 years later as those in the Head Start program after 2 years (Ramey et al., 2000). Apparently, intervention must occur at an earlier age; a new Early Head Start program now takes children from birth through age five. Adoption has a better chance of demonstrating any environmental influences on intelligence, because it alters the child's entire environment (Scarr & Weinberg, 1976). Adopted children's IQs are more highly correlated with the intelligence of their biological parents than with the intelligence of their adoptive parents (Scarr & Weinberg; Turkheimer, 1991), but this does not mean that the children's IQs do not go up or down according to the adoptive environment. When African American children were adopted from impoverished homes into middle-class homes, by the age of six their IQs had increased from the 90-point average for African American children in the geographic area to 106. The beneficial effects persisted a decade later (Scarr & Weinberg; Weinberg, Scarr, & Waldman, 1992).

Does this mean there was no genetic effect at all? No. In fact, the correlation between the children's IQs and their biological parents' educational levels (used in the absence of IQ scores) *increased* over the 10-year follow-up period, while correlations with their adoptive parents' educational levels *decreased* (Weinberg et al., 1992). It may puzzle you how the children's IQs could be correlated with their biological parents' intelligence if the children's IQs had moved into the adoptive parents' range. Although we usually think that correlation indicates similarity within pairs of scores (e.g., a parent's and a child's IQs), this is not necessarily the implication; rather, it means that the scores have similar rank orders in their groups. In other words, the parent with the highest IQ has the child with the highest IQ, the parent with the second highest IQ has the child with the second highest IQ, and so on. Now move the children into a new household and raise each child's IQ by 10 points; the biological parent with the highest IQ still has the child with the highest IQ and the parent with the second highest IQ. . . . You get the point. The correlation tells us that the children's IQs are still tied to their biological parents' intelligence, as if by an elastic string that can stretch but nevertheless affects *how much* the IQ can change; that elastic string in this case is the influence of genes.

Though it has been difficult to identify specific environmental influences that increase intelligence, we have had some success identifying influences that have a deleterious effect. One example is prenatal exposure to pesticides. In

Enhancing Intelligence and Cognitive Performance

Source: iStock/picmax13.

Most of us feel the need for a bit of an edge as we deal with a demanding world. Drugs have long been the go-to solution; 34% of college students, for example, reported using stimulants ordinarily prescribed for attention-deficit/hyperactivity disorder (DeSantis, Webb, & Noar, 2008). The benefits of these drugs are modest and the drugs can impair some types of cognitive functioning while they are enhancing others (Husain & Mehta, 2011). Manipulating genes might seem an alternative, but remember that the known genes have a very small individual influence. Neuroscientists have created mutant strains of mice that were smarter at one task or another, but these mice also had their problems. One strain was overly fearful, and another solved some problems well but struggled with simpler ones ("Small, Furry... and Smart," 2009).

Faced with these realities, researchers have sought more benign strategies. They have reported long-term improvement in solving mathematical problems following electrical stimulation to the scalp over the prefrontal cortex (Snowball et al., 2013) and demonstrated cognitive gains after subjects played video games that required extensive use of working memory (Anguera et al., 2013; Jaeggi, Buschkuekhl, Jonides, & Shah, 2011). Furthermore, working memory training increased functional connectivity in the frontal-parietal networks (Jolles, van Buchem, Crone, & Rombouts, 2013; Mackey, Singley, & Bunge, 2013). Given these successes, some researchers have suggested the better question is not whether the techniques work but which training regimens produce the best real-life benefits (Jaeggi et al., 2011).

Recently, two strategies have advanced to clinical trials. In studies of older (age 50 and over) individuals, both extensive training on various cognitive tasks (A. Corbett et al., 2015) and consumption of cocoa flavanols (nutrients in foods like cocoa, tea, grapes, and apples) for three months showed beneficial effects to cognition (Brickman et al., 2014). Another study reminds us of the importance of early stimulation. Psychologists visited the homes of Jamaican children aged 9–24 months who were stunted in growth (bottom 5th percentile for height; Gertler et al., 2014). Researchers played with the children weekly, provided books and toys, and taught the mothers better ways to interact with their children. Compared to nonstunted control children, those who received early stimulation had better grades and higher IQs, showed less depression, and got into fewer fights; later in adulthood they had 25% higher earnings.

The bottom line is that there is no magic pill to increase intelligence; the most promising approaches appear to be very basic—early stimulation, adequate diet, and practice, practice, practice.

an agricultural community in California, children whose mothers who had high levels of organophosphate pesticide residue in their blood during pregnancy averaged 7.0 IQ points lower, compared with children of mothers with the lowest residue measures (M. F. Bouchard et al., 2011). The exposed children also scored lower on tests of working memory, processing speed, verbal comprehension, and perceptual reasoning. Similarly, children with the highest levels of prenatal exposure to chlorpyrifos scored 2.7 points lower in IQ and 5.3 points lower on a test of working memory (Rauch et al., 2011). Until it was banned for indoor use in 2001, chlorpyrifos was one of the most widely used insecticides for household pest control.

■ FIGURE 13.11   Worldwide Relationship Between Intelligence and Infectious Disease.

Although the relationship is not perfect (in which all the dots would fall on the line), you can see that high IQ scores are associated with low levels of infection and low IQ scores are associated with high levels of infection.

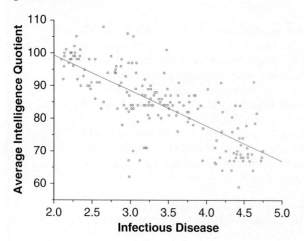

Source: Adapted from "Parasite Prevalence and the Worldwide Distribution of Cognitive Ability," by C. Eppig, C. L. Fincher, and R. Thornhill, 2010, *Proceedings of the Royal Society B: Biological Sciences, 277* (1701), pp. 3801–3808.

Although childhood illness in general was not a predictor of later intelligence, infection does seem to be important. A study in a north Manhattan, New York, community designed to identify risk factors for stroke found that people with multiple risk-associated pathogens also had lower cognitive ability (Katan et al., 2013). Researchers at the University of New Mexico concluded that the level of infectious diseases is the best predictor of national differences in intelligence (Eppig, Fincher, & Thornhill, 2010). After controlling for confounding variables, including education, climate, and economy, the correlation between national average IQ and infectious disease ranged from −.76 to −.82, depending on the method of estimating intelligence (Figure 13.11). The investigators believe that fighting off infections during childhood robs the body of energy needed for normal brain development. Not only might disease prevalence partly account for racial differences in intelligence, but the researchers also suggest that reduction in the incidence of infectious diseases explains some of the IQ increase seen in the Flynn effect.

We want to understand the antecedents of intelligence to enhance cognitive functioning and prevent the disorders that diminish it. We have already seen in Chapter 12 that this is a daunting challenge in the case of Alzheimer's disease, and the accompanying Application reveals that enhancing performance in normally functioning individuals is not so easy, either.

CONCEPT CHECK

Take a Minute to Check Your Knowledge and Understanding

- What is the likely neural basis of general intelligence and of separate components of intelligence?
- Suppose you read a quote from a researcher that "intelligence is not a matter of a place in the brain, but how well the brain does its job." Explain why someone would say this.
- What are the relative contributions of heredity and environment to intelligence? Why is it so difficult to identify the genetic influences? The environmental influences?
- How can adopted children's IQs increase into the range of their adoptive homes and yet be more highly correlated with their parents' intelligence? (*Hint:* Draw a diagram, with made-up IQ scores of children from several families.)

Deficiencies and Disorders of Intelligence

Intelligence is as fragile as it is complex. Accordingly, the list of conditions that can impair intelligence is impressively, or depressingly, long. To give you a feel for the problems that can occur in this most revered of our assets, we will add a few thoughts to what we have already covered in Chapter 12 on aging, take a brief look at intellectual disability, then spend more time on autism in recognition of its half-century-long challenge to neuroscientists' investigative skills, and finish with attention-deficit/hyperactivity disorder.

Effects of Aging on Intelligence

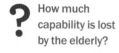

How much capability is lost by the elderly?

In Chapter 12, we discussed the most widely known cognitive disorder of aging, Alzheimer's disease. Here, we will limit our attention to normal declines in cognitive abilities that are associated with aging. One source of normal decline is the reduced activity of numerous genes involved in long-term potentiation and memory storage due to age-related damage (T. Lu et al., 2004). Genes involved in synaptic functioning and plasticity, including those responsible for glutamate and GABA receptors and for synaptic vesicle release and recycling, are particularly affected.

Although intelligence and cognitive abilities do typically decline with age, the amount of loss has been overestimated. One reason is that people are often tested on rather meaningless tasks, like memorizing lists of words; when the elderly are tested on meaningful material the decline is moderate (Kausler, 1985). Another reason for the overestimation is that early studies were *cross-sectional,* comparing people at one age with different people at another age; you have already seen that more recent generations have an IQ test performance advantage over people from previous generations. When the comparison is done *longitudinally*—by following the same people through the aging process—the amount of loss diminishes (Schaie, 1994). Also, the loss depends on the type of intelligence measured. *Crystallized intelligence*—skills and overlearned knowledge—remains stable or improves; vocabulary, for example, improves through the seventh decade (Harada, Love, & Triebel, 2013). Problem solving, reasoning, and the ability to process and learn new information make up *fluid intelligence,* which declines beyond the third decade.

Apparently, performance speed is particularly vulnerable during aging, and its loss turns out to be important. Schaie (1994) found that statistically removing the effects of speed from test scores significantly reduced elderly individuals' performance losses. We saw earlier that working memory is especially important to intellectual capability. A study of people ranging in age from 18 to 82 showed that speed of processing accounted for all but 1% of age-related differences in working memory (Salthouse & Babcock, 1991).

You know that a determinant of general intelligence is the ability to integrate activity between brain areas. Even in healthy aging there is a loss of coordination in the *default mode network,* portions of the frontal, parietal, and temporal lobes that are active when the brain is at rest or focused internally rather than on the outside world; activity in the default mode network is thought to represent preparedness for action (Andrews-Hanna et al., 2007; Broyd et al., 2009). To the extent this coordination diminishes, cognitive ability does as well. Imaging reveals that the loss is due to a decline in white matter connections among the areas. In the elderly, those with better whole brain network efficiency (clustering and short path length) had higher processing speed and superior executive functions, including impulse control and decision making (Wen et al., 2011).

The brain does have ways of compensating, such as the increased metabolism that is seen in subjects with mild intellectual disability and the recruitment of frontal areas in people with dyslexia during reading (see Chapter 9). Studies of elderly individuals who are "aging gracefully" indicate that they are holding their own through additional neural effort (Helmuth, 2002). For example, a memory task activated only the right prefrontal cortex in young adults and in older adults who performed poorly, but older adults who performed as well as the young adults used both prefrontal areas to perform the tasks (Figure 13.12; Cabeza, Anderson, Locantore, & McIntosh, 2002). The increase in frontal activity is in proportion to decreases in other areas, which supports the idea that the shift serves a compensatory function (S. W. Davis, Dennis, Daselaar, Fleck, & Cabeza, 2008). Compensation may not be limited to frontal activity; it has also been observed in the parahippocampal area during a memory recognition task (van der Veen, Nijhuis, Tisserand, Backes, & Jolles, 2006). This less-than-efficient adaptation might not be the only pathway to graceful aging; elderly subjects initially coped with a task via compensation, but after just five hours of training on the task, they showed brain patterns like those of young subjects (Erickson et al., 2007).

Some of the loss in performance is due to nonphysical causes and is reversible; for example, older people often lack opportunity to use their skills. In one study, aged individuals regained part of their lost ability through skills practice, and many of them returned to their predecline levels; they still had some advantage over controls seven years later (Schaie, 1994). Elderly people also improved in memory test scores when their self-esteem was bolstered by presenting them with words that depict old age in positive terms such as *wise, learned,* and *insightful* (B. Levy, 1996).

Loss in performance that has a physical basis may be reduced if not reversed. Diet appears to be one factor; for example, in a study of 6,000 people over the age of 65, cognitive decline was 13% less in those who ate two or more fish meals per week, compared with people who ate fish less than once per week (M. C. Morris, Evans, Tangney, Bienias, & Wilson, 2005). Evidence in this study and others suggested that the important factor was the overall pattern of fat intake. Vitamin supplements might also help. In elderly individuals with mild cognitive impairment, a combination of B vitamins reduced the rate of brain atrophy 50% and slowed cognitive decline, compared with subjects given a placebo (de Jager, Oulhai, Jacoby, Refsum, & Smith, 2012; Douaud et al., 2013). The B vitamins slow gray matter atrophy by reducing homocysteine, a toxic compound that is elevated in people with a diet high in animal proteins.

Interestingly, the sex hormones provide some protection against the cognitive effects of aging. In menopausal women, estrogen replacement therapy reduces the decline in verbal and visual memory as well as

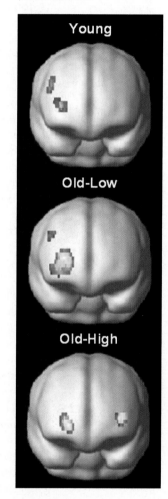

■ **FIGURE 13.12**

Compensatory Brain Activity in High-Performing Older Adults.

A memory task activated the right prefrontal area in young and in low-performing older adults. Older adults who performed as well as the young showed activation in both prefrontal areas.

Source: From "Aging Gracefully: Compensatory Brain Activity in High-Performing Older Adults," by R. Cabeza et al., *NeuroImage, 17,* pp. 1394–1402, fig. 2, p. 1399. © 2002 Elsevier.

lowering the risk of Alzheimer's disease (Sherwin, 2003; van Amelsvoort, Compton, & Murphy, 2001). The importance of estrogen is supported by the fluctuations in performance that occur during the menstrual cycle. First, remember from Chapter 7 that women tend to be superior to men on some types of verbal tasks and that men typically outperform women on tasks requiring spatial ability. During the part of the month when estrogen is high, women perform higher on verbal tasks; then during menstruation estrogen drops and so does performance on the verbal tasks, but spatial performance improves (Kimura & Hampson, 1994; Maki, Rich, & Rosenbaum, 2002).

How does estrogen produce these effects? We are not sure, but we do know that neurons throughout the brain have estrogen receptors; estrogen levels during the menstrual cycle are correlated with cortical excitability (M. J. Smith et al., 1999), increased glucose metabolism (Reiman, Armstrong, Matt, & Mattox, 1996), blood flow in areas involved in cognitive tasks (Dietrich et al., 2001), and responsiveness to acetylcholine, which is important in memory and cognitive functioning (O'Keane & Dinan, 1992). Finally, untreated menopausal women are more impaired than women receiving estrogen replacement on tests of working memory, response switching, and attention, which tells us that estrogen improves functioning in prefrontal areas (Keenan, Ezzat, Ginsburg, & Moore, 2001).

So what about the male of the species? Men who maintain testosterone production past the age of 50 have better preserved visual and verbal memory and visual-spatial functioning (Moffat et al., 2002). The effects of replacement therapy have been variable, owing apparently to the form of the testosterone preparation used. However, numerous studies have shown improvement in spatial, verbal, and working memory (Cherrier, Craft, & Matsumoto, 2003; Cherrier et al., 2005; Gruenewald & Matsumoto, 2003). Interestingly, testosterone improves only spatial memory; additional memory improvement requires that the testosterone be delivered in the form of dihydrotestosterone, which can be converted to estrogen in the brain by the process of aromatization (Cherrier et al., 2003, 2005). When it comes to cognitive abilities, we could be tempted to consider estrogen a wonder drug.

So, losses are smaller than believed, and they differ across people and across skills. In addition, practice, esteem enhancement, and an active lifestyle may slow cognitive decline during aging. Obviously, we cannot stereotype the older person as a person with diminished abilities.

Intellectual Disability

Intellectual impairment was previously referred to as retardation, but that term has taken on such negative meaning in popular usage that practitioners and authorities are shifting to the term *intellectual disability*. *Intellectual disability (ID)* is a limitation in intellectual functioning (reasoning, learning, problem solving) and adaptive behavior that is developmental in origin. The criteria set by the *Diagnostic and Statistical Manual of Mental Disorders,* 5th edition (*DSM*-5), are an IQ at or below 70; deficits in adaptive functioning, such as communication, social participation, and independent living; and onset during the developmental period (American Psychiatric Association, 2013). Looking back at Figure 13.2, you can see that 2% of the population falls in this IQ range, and a lower percentage would meet both criteria. Table 13.1 describes the areas of impairment that contribute to a diagnosis of functional impairment. Not only is any definition arbitrary, but it is situational and cultural as well; a person considered to have an intellectual disability in our society might fare reasonably well in a simpler environment. The situational nature is illustrated by the fact that many individuals shed the label as they move from a childhood of academic failure into adulthood and demonstrate their ability to live independent lives.

TABLE 13.1   Areas of Impairment Leading to a Diagnosis of Intellectual Disability.

DOMAIN	INCLUDES. . .
Conceptual	Skills in language, reading, writing, math, reasoning, knowledge, and memory
Social	Empathy, social judgment, interpersonal communication skills, ability to make and retain friendships
Practical	Self-management in areas such as personal care, job responsibilities, money management, recreation, and organizing school and work tasks

Intellectual disability has an estimated prevalence of just over 1% worldwide, with a higher incidence in low- and middle-income countries (Maulik, Mascarenhas, Mathers, Dua, & Saxena, 2011). It can result from childhood infections, birth complications, extreme malnutrition and, as you saw in Chapter 5, maternal alcohol abuse during pregnancy. Although intelligence is highly heritable, no reliable estimates of the heritability of ID exist. Determining which genes are at fault has also been difficult, in part because ID is made up of a large number of disorders. Another problem is that while milder forms of ID involve common forms of inheritance, severe ID more often results from *de novo* mutations, those that appear spontaneously in the individual rather than being passed down from the parents (Vissers, Gilissen, & Veltman, 2016). Nevertheless, more than 700 genes have been convincingly linked to ID; however, this very fact means that we can expect additional genes to have small effects and to be difficult to isolate.

The most common genetic cause of intellectual disability is Down syndrome, with a prevalence of 1 in every 700 births (S. E. Parker et al., 2010). Usually caused by the presence of an extra 21st chromosome, *Down syndrome* typically results in individuals with IQs in the 40–55 range, although some are less impaired (Figure 13.13). Recall that the amyloid precursor protein gene that is involved in early-onset Alzheimer's disease is located on chromosome 21 and that it was discovered because Down syndrome individuals also develop amyloid plaques (Goate et al., 1991; Murrell, Farlow, Ghetti, & Benson, 1991). Ninety-five percent of people with Down syndrome have the entire extra chromosome (called *complete trisomy 21*). In 1% of cases some of the body's cells have the extra chromosome, but not all of them do (*mosaic trisomy 21*). In a few cases only an end portion is present and is attached to another chromosome (*translocation trisomy 21*). A strain of mouse (Ts65Dn) engineered with a third copy of 55% of chromosome 21 has been a useful model for studying Down syndrome. As in people with that disorder, its glial cells secrete less of two proteins that support neuron survival. Treating pregnant Ts65Dn females with these proteins eliminates the developmental delays that would ordinarily be seen in their offspring (Toso et al., 2008). Conceivably this strategy could be used with pregnant women when amniocentesis (genetic testing of the amniotic fluid) reveals that the fetus has a third 21st chromosome. Another therapeutic possibility is postnatal correction of inadequate norepinephrine release in the hippocampus, a deficiency that is believed to contribute to learning impairment. After treatment with a drug that increased norepinephrine levels, Ts65Dn mice performed as well as normal mice (Salehi et al., 2009). However, it may be an oversimplification to focus only on the effects of chromosome 21 genes. DNA methylation differs by more than 10% between subjects with Down syndrome and controls, and the degree of methylation difference is correlated with cognitive function (Dekker, De Deyn, & Rots, 2014). Although the differentially methylated genes were found on other chromosomes, the authors attributed the hypermethylation to the presence of the third chromosome 21.

 What causes intellectual disabilities?

■ FIGURE 13.13 Down Chromosomes and *Born This Way*.

(a) Chromosomes of a person with Down syndrome (female). The arrow points to the three 21st chromosomes. (b) Some individuals with Down syndrome are more fortunate than others. The documentary series *Born This Way* follows seven young people with Down syndrome in southern California as they pursue their various careers and dreams.

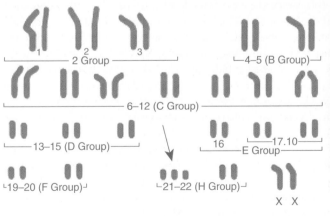

(a)

(b)

Sources: (a) © www.nads.org, 2007. (b) Everett Collection Inc/Alamy Stock Photo.

■ **FIGURE 13.14**   The Hydrocephalic Brain.

(a) Normal brain. (b) Hydrocephalic brain. Notice the large lateral ventricles and the small amount of cortex around the perimeter in the hydrocephalic brain.

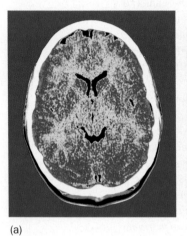

(a)

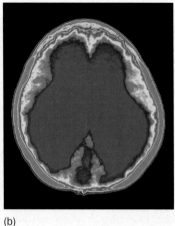

(b)

Sources: (a) © Du Cane Medical Imaging Ltd./Science Source. (b) © Mehau Kulyk/Science Source.

Another frequent genetic cause of intellectual disability is *fragile X syndrome*, which is due to a mutation in the fragile X mental retardation 1 gene (*FMR1*). The *FMR1* gene normally contains between 6 and 45 repetitions of the nucleotide sequence C, G, G. If the number of CGG repeats reaches 200, the gene is turned off, and no protein is made. Fragile X syndrome is the result, with IQs typically below 75. An intermediate number of CGG repeats results in reduced protein production, accompanied by a slight increase in the chance of intellectual disability. Males are affected more often, and when fragile X does occur in females, the symptoms are usually milder. In *FMR1* knockout mice, unusual numbers of dendrites and immature spines indicate a failure to prune excess synapses (Bagni & Greenough, 2005).

Phenylketonuria is due to an inherited inability to metabolize the amino acid phenylalanine; the excess phenylalanine interferes with myelination during development. Newborn infants are routinely tested for phenylalanine in the urine or blood, and intellectual disability can be prevented by avoiding foods containing phenylalanine. The artificial sweetener aspartame is a familiar example of a substance that is high in phenylalanine. Without dietary treatment, the individual is severely or profoundly disabled, with an adult IQ around 20 points.

Hydrocephalus occurs when cerebrospinal fluid builds up in the cerebral ventricles; the increased fluid volume crowds out neural tissue, usually causing intellectual disability (Figure 13.14). As we saw in Chapter 3, hydrocephalus can also be treated if caught early, by installing a shunt that prevents the accumulation of the excess cerebrospinal fluid. Also in that chapter, you learned that some individuals seem not to be harmed by the dramatic loss of cortex; in fact, half of those whose ventricles fill 95% of the cranium have IQs over 100 (Lewin, 1980).

Zika virus, one of the infectious causes of intellectual disability, can have a devastating effect on brain development and intelligence. The accompanying In the News feature describes the effect of Zika on neural development.

Autism Spectrum Disorder

Autism spectrum disorder (ASD) is a set of neurodevelopmental disorders characterized by social deficits, communication difficulties, and repetitive behaviors. In *DSM*-5, autism spectrum disorder includes the previously used diagnoses of autism, Asperger syndrome, pervasive developmental disorder not otherwise specified, and childhood disintegrative disorder (American Psychiatric Association, 2013). For simplicity, we will refer to the disorder as *autism* or *ASD*. The prevalence of ASD was 1 in 150 children (3.7%) in the years 2000 and 2002 but increased to 1 in 68 in 2010 (1.4%) (Figure 13.15; Centers for Disease Control and Prevention, 2016a). Rates in North America, Asia, and Europe are similar, averaging between 1% and 2%. At least some of the increase can be attributed to improved detection, broader diagnostic criteria, and doctors' greater willingness to use the label because of decreasing stigmatization of autism and because the diagnosis will qualify the family for increased services and financial assistance (Rutter, 2005). Some observers believe the increase is real and due, for example, to rising environmental toxins, but the position of most authorities is that we simply don't know how much the actual rate has increased or why. The good news is that there was no further increase between 2010 and 2012, but it is too early to tell whether that signifies a trend. One statistic is not in dispute: The prevalence is almost five times higher among males than females (Centers for Disease Control and Prevention, 2016a).

Cognitive and Social Impairment

In a study of cognitive abilities in children with ASD, 55% had intellectual disability (defined as IQ < 70), and 16% had moderate to severe disability, with IQs below 50 (Charman et al., 2011). Impairment was

IN THE NEWS

ZIKA VIRUS IMPACTS NEURAL DEVELOPMENT

During the summer of 2016, the outbreak of Zika virus became an increasing public health concern when babies born to Zika-infected mothers showed smaller than normal brains, a condition called microcephaly. Even with the knowledge from dozens of early investigations, there are many unanswered questions regarding Zika's effects. Although Zika infection has been clearly linked to microcephaly, studies still must be done to determine the mechanisms by which Zika impacts fetal development (Tang et al., 2016). In addition, not all infants born to infected mothers show signs of microcephaly (Children's National Health System, 2017). Fortunately, the infant brain retains much of the fetal brain's plasticity, which leaves open the possibility that ways could be found of altering postnatal brain development, particularly of cortical areas, to compensate for the disruption caused by the virus.

Tang and colleagues (2016) have investigated how Zika affects the brain by infecting stem cells, then coaxing them to develop into neural tissue. The results were clear: Infection resulted in reduced overall neural cell numbers, both by increasing cell death and by disrupting the cell cycle (Tang et al., 2016). Other scientists have evaluated brain development using MRIs to see how often the fetal brain is impacted by the mother's infection (Children's National Health System, 2017); in a preliminary report on a sample of 48 fetuses, only 3 showed abnormal development. Other studies are planned to determine the long-term consequences of exposure and whether exposed babies born with normal-appearing brains might still be affected neurologically.

THOUGHT QUESTIONS

1. How do scientists think Zika virus might result in microcephaly in exposed infants?

2. What potential insights into neural development might come about through long-term studies of infants who were exposed prenatally to Zika virus?

For the news story, visit edge.sagepub.com/garrett5e and select the Chapter 13 study resources.

---

not universal, however; 28% had average intelligence (IQs of 85–115), and 3% scored above 115. Autistic individuals share a common core of impairment in communication, imagination, and socialization (Frith, 1993). Trouble understanding verbal and nonverbal communication often makes testing difficult, raising questions about the meaningfulness of test results. In some cases, nonverbal tests such as the Raven Progressive Matrices are used or IQ is estimated from an assessment of adaptive behavior, but these do not eliminate the deficits. Difficulty with imagination also is common, in the form of an inability to pretend or to understand make-believe situations. Use of language is also very literal—"Can you pass me the salt?" is met with "Yes" with no compliance—and in some cases this literalism extends to an obsessive interest in facts, like that seen in the movie *Rain Man.*

These characteristics make it difficult to socialize with others, which is what sets apart children with autism the most. They usually prefer to be alone and ignore people around them (Figure 13.16). Their interaction with others often is limited to requests for things they want; they otherwise treat people as objects, sometimes even walking or climbing over them. Verbalization is usually limited, and the child often repeats what others say (echolalia).

What is autism like?

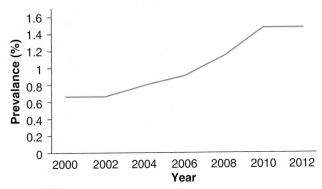

■ **FIGURE 13.15** Prevalence of Autism Spectrum Disorder, 2000–2012.

Prevalence increased sharply from 2002 to 2010 but remained the same in 2012.

Source: Based on data from "Autism Spectrum Disorder (ASD)," by Centers for Disease Control and Prevention, 2016a.

■ **FIGURE 13.16**   Individuals With Autism Typically Feel Threatened by Social Interaction.

A typical symptom in children with autism is the need for order in their world, often expressed by meticulously lining up their toys.

Source: iStock/UrsaHoogle.

Some researchers believe that much of the social behavior problem is that the person with autism lacks a *theory of mind,* the ability to attribute mental states to oneself and to others. In other words, the autistic person cannot infer what other people are thinking. One man with autism said that people seem to have a special sense that allows them to read other people's thoughts (Rutter, 1983), and an observant autistic youth asked, "People talk to each other with their eyes. What is it that they are saying?" (Frith, 1993). In a study that measured this deficiency, children watched hand puppet Anne remove a marble from a basket where puppet Sally had placed it, and put it in a box while Sally was out of the room. On Sally's return, children were asked where she would look for the marble. Normal four year olds had no problem with this task, nor did Down syndrome children with a mental age of five or six. But 80% of children with autism with an average mental age of nine answered that Sally would look in the box (Frith, Morton, & Leslie, 1991).

There are two hypotheses as to how we develop a theory of mind. According to the "theory theory," we build hypotheses over time based on our experience. Simulation theory holds that we gain insight into people's thoughts and intentions by mentally mimicking the behavior of others. This view gets some support from studies of the mirror neurons we talked about in Chapters 8 and 9. Individuals who score higher on a measure of empathy tend to have more activity in these mirror neurons (Gazzola, Aziz-Zadeh, & Keysers, 2006). Researchers have suggested that impaired mirror functions reduce the autistic person's ability to empathize and to learn language through imitation. Children with autism engage in less contagious yawning than other children do (Senju et al., 2007), and they show neural deficiencies during mirroring tasks. For example, they can imitate others' facial expressions, but mirror neuron activity while doing so is either delayed or nonexistent (Dapretto et al., 2005; Oberman et al., 2007). Other studies show reduced activation in the inferior frontal cortex and motor cortex, suggesting weakness in the dorsal stream connections that provide input to those areas (Nishitani, Avikainen, & Hari, 2004; Villalobos, Mizuno, Dahl, Kemmotsu, & Müller, 2005). This interpretation was supported in a study of individuals diagnosed with Asperger syndrome, the former term for high-functioning autism. When they imitated facial expressions, transmission over the dorsal stream (occipital to superior temporal to posterior parietal to frontal) was delayed by 45–60 milliseconds compared with normal controls (Nishitani et al., 2004).

Brain Anomalies in Autism

Autism was long thought to be purely psychological in origin, because no specific brain defects had been found. The problem was blamed on a lack of maternal bonding or a disastrous experience of rejection that caused the child to retreat into a world of aloneness (Frith, 1993). But no evidence could be found for this kind of influence; autistic children often had exemplary homes, and children with extremely negative experiences did not become autistic. The frequent association with intellectual disability and epilepsy implied that autism was a brain disorder. Later work found subtle but widespread brain anomalies, especially in the brain stem, the cerebellum, and the temporal lobes (Happé & Frith, 1996). The location of the damage varied among individuals, which suggests that there are various pathways to autism.

There are many anomalies in the brains of individuals with autism, but the most striking characteristic is the atypical sequencing of brain development. The autistic brain undergoes dramatic growth during the first year of life, with the overgrowth focused in frontal and temporal areas that are important for the social, emotional, and language functions that are impaired in the disorder (Courchesne et al., 2007; Redcay & Courchesne, 2005). The excess growth ends around three to five years of age, but by then the brain has already reached normal adult size. In adulthood, these areas are under-activated during tasks that would ordinarily engage them, for example, when viewing animations that require the viewer to understand the mental state of the actor (Castelli, Frith, Happé, & Frith, 2002). Despite comparable overall brain volumes, adult patients have increased cortical volume and thickness and more gray matter volume in prefrontal and temporal areas, with reductions in other areas (Ecker et al., 2012; Greimel et al., 2013; Raznahan et al., 2010).

Several studies have reported white matter and connectivity reductions in the brains of individuals with ASD, particularly in the corpus callosum and other long-distance connections (Figure 13.17; Aoki, Abe, Nippashi, & Yamasue, 2013; Wilkinson, Wang, van der Kouwe, & Takahashi, 2016). These findings have led to the hypothesis that underconnectivity is a fundamental characteristic of the disorder. However, additional research has reported hyperconnectivity. One thorough study replicated its results with two different methodologies and found strong evidence of overconnection over both short and long distances in the brain (Supekar et al., 2013). An interesting observation supports an association between ASD and hyperconnectivity: Synesthesia is found 2.6 times more often in people with ASD than in the general population (Baron-Cohen et al., 2013), and we saw in Chapter 10 that evidence favors hyperconnectivity between sensory areas as an explanation. So how do we reconcile these disparate results? Studies by researchers at San Diego State University suggest two possible reasons. One study reported frontal underconnectivity in milder cases of ASD and temporal-occipital overconnectivity in more severe cases (Keown et al., 2013); indeed, Supekar and his colleagues noted that children with greater functional connectivity had more severe social deficits. More severely affected individuals are less likely to be included in studies because of their inability to cooperate with the scanning procedure. The other study

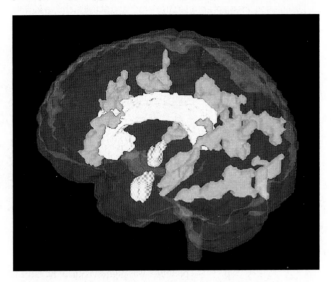

Source: From "White Matter Structures in Autism: Preliminary Evidence From Diffusion Tensor Imaging," by N. Barnea-Goraly et al., 2004, *Biological Psychiatry*, 55, pp. 323–326.

■ FIGURE 13.17   Areas of Decreased White Matter in Adolescent Males With Autism.

Areas of decrease are shown in dark gray. The corpus callosum (white) and the amygdalae (checkered gray) are shown for reference.

found underconnectivity in several areas, including prefrontal cortex, but hyperconnectivity in the temporal lobe; the researchers pointed out that the underconnectivity occurred in earlier-maturing parts of the cortex and overconnectivity was associated with a later-maturing area (Nair et al., 2013). This study raises the possibility of both under- and overconnectivity occurring to varying degrees within an individual or an individual exhibiting one or the other, in both cases depending on the time progression of the disorder.

Biochemical Anomalies in Autism

As researchers looked for genetic links to autism, several of the genes that turned up pointed in turn to serotonin, glutamate, GABA, and oxytocin (Freitag, Staal, Klauck, Duketis, & Waltes, 2010; Sutcliffe, 2008). Serotonin has received considerable attention because of its contribution to neural development. Prenatal serotonin activity is regulated by cortisol levels, and cortisol is increased in the mother by psychological stress, depression, type 2 diabetes, inflammatory disorders, and obesity (Rose'Meyer, 2013). Neuroimaging studies have found diminished serotonin synthesis in children with ASD, and treatment with serotonin reuptake inhibitors, such as Prozac, decreases repetitive and obsessive behavior in some autistic individuals. The antipsychotic drug risperidone antagonizes dopamine as well as serotonin, and its stronger therapeutic track record implicates that neurotransmitter. According to an analysis of 22 previously published studies, several autism symptoms improve during treatment with risperidone (Sharma & Shaw, 2012). High levels of the excitatory transmitter glutamate have also been found in autism (Hassan et al., 2013). Treatment with glutamate antagonists alone has produced unremarkable results, but pairing the anti-Alzheimer's drug memantine with risperidone decreased irritability more than risperidone alone (Ghanizadeh & Moghimi-Sarani, 2013).

In Chapter 7 we saw that oxytocin facilitates bonding and social recognition; for that reason, it is known as the "sociability molecule." Most studies have found that oxytocin is reduced in individuals with autism, though not in all (reviewed in Anagnostou et al., 2014, and S. Y. Lee et al., 2015). Even studies using a single dose of oxytocin have reported improvements in repetitive behaviors, self-injury, empathy, social interaction, and ability to recognize mental or emotional state from photos of the eyes. Results of an fMRI study indicated that oxytocin improves trust by reducing activity in fear areas in the amygdala and midbrain (Figure 13.18; Baumgartner, Heinrichs, Vonlanthen, Fischbacher, & Fehr, 2008). In two studies with high-functioning ASD participants, oxytocin improved brain functioning by increasing previously deficient activity in the right anterior insula during an emotion inference task (Aoki et al., 2014) and increasing functional connectivity between anterior cingulate

■ **FIGURE 13.18**   Reduced Response to Betrayal of Trust Following Oxytocin.

Compared with subjects receiving a placebo, those who received nasally administered oxytocin responded less to betrayal of trust in an investment simulation. Areas of comparatively reduced activity (shown in yellow) were the caudate nucleus (Cau), amygdala (Amy), and midbrain (MB).

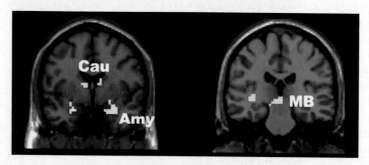

Sources: From "Oxytocin Shapes the Neural Circuitry of Trust and Trust Adaptation in Humans," by T. Baumgartner et al., 2008, *Neuron, 58*, pp. 639–650, fig 4.

cortex and dorsomedial prefrontal cortex (Watanabe et al., 2015). Research with mice indicated that oxytocin enhances social reward by increasing serotonin activity in the nucleus accumbens (Dölen, Darvishzadeh, Huang, & Malenka, 2013).

The Environment and Autism

Parental treatment has been ruled out as the cause of autism, but numerous other environmental conditions have been identified as contributing factors. One's suspicions immediately turn to environmental pollutants, such as those generated by automobile traffic, agricultural practices, and industrial activity. Researchers usually assess such effects by studying people living near agricultural fields or a busy highway, but two studies are notable for employing more meaningful measures of pollution. Using localized estimates of traffic pollution based on Environmental Protection Agency data, traffic volume, and climatic conditions during each child's gestational period and first year of life, researchers found that living in homes where traffic pollution was highest tripled the rate of autism (Volk, Lurmann, Penfold, Hertz-Picciotto, & McConnell, 2014). Recognizing that ASD occurs in geographic clusters, University of Chicago researchers used county-level data on genital malformation in male children as a surrogate for environmental exposure and found that the incidence of ASD increased 283% for every percentage point increase in incidence of malformations (Rzhetsky et al., 2014).

Other environmental influences originate in the mother herself. For example, infection during the second trimester of pregnancy tripled the chance of bearing a child who would later be diagnosed with ASD (Zerbo et al., 2015). Ten percent of women who have a child with autism have immune molecules in the blood that react with proteins in the brain; this rate is four times higher than in the general population of women of childbearing age (Brimberg, Sadiq, Gregersen, & Diamond, 2013). Other researchers identified six brain proteins that anti-brain antibodies attach to; all of them are involved in neuronal development (Braunschweig et al., 2013). Maternal metabolic conditions, including obesity, diabetes, and hypertension, may also be associated with ASD; mothers of autistic children were 40% more likely to be obese and 47% more likely to have any one of these conditions (Krakowiak et al., 2012; also see the earlier discussion of serotonin). The news is not all bad: Mothers who took folic acid during pregnancy were half as likely to bear a child who would later be diagnosed with autism (Surén et al., 2013). In addition, as the accompanying Application explains, there is no evidence that vaccines are linked to autism.

Heredity and Autism Spectrum Disorders

Siblings of children with autism are 25 times more likely to be diagnosed with autism than other children (Abrahams & Geschwind, 2008); the number would be even higher, but parents tend to stop having children after the first autism diagnosis. For the identical twin of a child with autism, the risk of autism is at least 60%. However, relatives frequently have autistic-like cognitive and social characteristics. When these symptoms are also considered, the concordance for identical twins jumps to 92%, compared with 10% for fraternal pairs (A. Bailey et al., 1995). In the largest study to date, researchers examined data from all two million children born in Sweden between 1982 and 2006 and estimated the heritability of ASD to be 50% and of autism at 54%, with the remainder due to nonshared (nonfamilial) environmental influence (Sandin et al., 2014).

As you might expect, genes that have been identified contribute to neuron development and migration, synapse formation, and neurotransmitter activity (Freitag et al., 2010; Sutcliffe, 2008). For example, several genes that code for synaptic proteins have been implicated (J. Chen, Yu, Fu, & Li, 2014); synaptic proteins are required for the formation and functioning of synapses. Genes for $GABA_A$ and $GABA_B$ receptors and for both AMPA and NMDA glutamate receptors have also been linked to ASD, and a $GABA_B$ receptor agonist improves social function and behavior. But once again, it has been difficult to identify the specific genes involved. So-called common variants—genes that occur in 5% or more of the population—have weak effects individually, requiring multiple "hits" to have an effect (Anney et al., 2012). Small effect is not the only reason identifying autism genes is difficult;

APPLICATION
Childhood Vaccines and Autism

Source: From Wakefield et al. (1998). Retrieved from http:// vaccines.procon.org/sourcefiles/retracted-lancet-paper.pdf.

In 1998 Andrew Wakefield and several colleagues published a paper in which they linked the measles, mumps, and rubella (MMR) vaccine to autism. Years later, two reviews of all the available studies concluded that there was no credible link between autism and the MMR vaccine or the mercury-derived preservative (thimerosal) used in some vaccines (Demicheli, Jefferson,

Rivetti, & Price, 2005; Immunization Safety Review Committee, 2004). In early 2010 the General Medical Council, which oversees doctors in Britain, decided that Wakefield's study was methodologically flawed and that he had acted unethically. *The Lancet,* which published the study, called the report "the most appalling catalog and litany of some of the most terrible behavior in any research" and took the rare action of withdrawing the study (M. Park, 2010). More recently, a comprehensive meta-analysis examined scientific data from more than 1.25 million children and concluded that there was no relationship between vaccines, components of vaccines, or multiple vaccine administrations and the development of autism or autism spectrum disorder (L. E. Taylor, Swerdfeger, & Eslick, 2014).

Many parents whose children's first signs of autism coincided with a round of childhood vaccinations say they find these reports unconvincing. More than 5,000 families have brought suit; a U.S. federal court has denied the claims in four test cases ("Vaccine Court Finds...," 2010), but that does not signal the end of litigation or of the controversy. In the meantime, there has been a disturbing decrease in the rate of childhood immunization in several countries in spite of the health risks, leading to large outbreaks of measles and other childhood diseases that could have been prevented.

a recent genetic analysis estimates that half of all autism cases are the result of *de novo* mutations (Iossofov et al., 2015). There is a limited window of opportunity to identify the genes because the mutations appear spontaneously and typically are not passed on because the individuals are unlikely to reproduce.

Of course, oxytocin genes come into play as well. Several studies have reported a relationship between the oxytocin receptor genes (*OXTR*) and ASD; evidence suggests that downregulation of the gene in some subgroups of ASD results in increased activity in the temporal-parietal junction, which participates in social perception (S. Y. Lee et al., 2015). Also, individuals with ASD who had a mutant allele of *CD38* had lower oxytocin levels than others with ASD.

Irene Voineagu and her colleagues (2011) identified over 500 genes that were expressed at different levels between the frontal and temporal cortices of healthy brains, and only 8 in ASD brains. ASD genes are particularly expressed in superficial layers of the cortex, where they interfere with the development of connections between the layers and between the hemispheres (Parikshak et al., 2013). As you have seen before, environmental influences almost certainly exert their effect through epigenetic modification of gene expression; this fact offers a glimmer of hope in that drugs designed to reverse those modifications might be used as a treatment for autism (Siniscalco, Cirillo, Bradstreet, & Antonucci, 2013). An additional important factor in understanding genetic influence in autism and other disorders is that some genes exert control over many additional genes. The *RORA* gene, for example, codes for the protein RORA1, which regulates the activity of more than 2,500 other genes;

some of these are involved in neuron and synapse development and synaptic transmission, and at least 6 have been associated with ASD (Sarachana & Hu, 2013).

Researchers attempting to explain the higher incidence of ASD in males have most often looked to the X chromosome. They have had little luck pinning down the responsible genes, but now researchers at Emory University have a promising candidate. In their study, mutations in the *AFF2* gene occurred five times more frequently in boys with ASD than in boys without ASD (Mondal et al., 2012). Male vulnerability may not be the whole story, however; females may enjoy some protection. Girls with ASD had very long copy number variations (differences in how often a segment of DNA is repeated) more often than boys with ASD; this implied that it takes more mutations to produce ASD in a female, which suggested a "female protective model" (Jacquemont et al., 2014). Although cortical levels of the RORA protein are decreased in both males and females with autism, levels are higher in unaffected females than in unaffected males (V. W. Hu, Sarachana, Sherrard, & Kocher, 2015). The apparent reason is that the *RORA* gene is upregulated by estrogen and downregulated by testosterone (Sarachana & Hu). We're also learning that male–female differences in vulnerability may be qualitative as well as quantitative. One study found that adult males and females with autism had markedly different patterns of white and gray matter increases compared to neurotypical controls (M.-C. Lai et al., 2013).

Autistic Savants and High-Functioning Autism

A *savant* is a person with exceptional intellectual skills, beyond the level of "typical" genius, like Leonardo da Vinci or Albert Einstein. However, the term is more frequently used to describe individuals who have one or more remarkable skills but whose overall functioning is below normal; half of these individuals with islands of exceptional capabilities are *autistic savants* (Treffert & Christensen, 2006). Some can play a tune on the piano after hearing it once, another can memorize whole books, while others take cube roots of large numbers in their heads or calculate the day of the week for any date thousands of years in the past or future. Stephen Wiltshire's remarkable talent is for architectural art; after brief helicopter flights, he has produced a detailed drawing of a 4-square-mile (10-square-kilometer) area of London and a 98-foot-long (30-meter-long) mural of Hong Kong's Victoria Harbor and the surrounding cityscape (see Figure 13.20; Stephen Wiltshire MBE—Biography, n.d.). A few "ordinary" individuals can perform similar feats, but the savant's performance is typically faster, more automatic, and without insight into how it is done (A. W. Snyder & Mitchell, 1999). The savant's exceptional capability may be limited in scope, however; some who are calendar calculators cannot even add or subtract with accuracy (Sacks, 1990).

The source of the autistic savant's enhanced ability is unknown. Dehaene (1997) suggests that it is due to intensely concentrated practice, but more typically the skill appears without either practice or instruction, as in the case of a three-year-old autistic girl who began drawing animated and well-proportioned horses in perfect perspective (Selfe, 1977). Allan Snyder and John Mitchell (1999) believe that these capabilities are within us all and are released when brain centers that control executive or integrative functions are compromised. This, they say, gives the savant access to speedy lower levels of processing that are unavailable to us. But, lacking the executive functions, the savants perform poorly on apparently similar tasks that require higher-order processing. The idea gains some credibility from the case of a man impaired in his left temporal and frontal areas by dementia; despite limited musical training, he began composing classical music, some of which was performed publicly (B. L. Miller, Boone, Cummings, Read, & Mishkin, 2000; also see Figure 13.19). The best-known savant was Kim Peek, the model used by Dustin Hoffman

■ **FIGURE 13.19** Savant-Like Ability Following Brain Impairment.

(a) The scan is from a 64-year-old woman with dementia in the left frontal-temporal area, which shows less activity than the right. (b) After the onset of her dementia, she began to create remarkable paintings like the one here.

(a)

(b)

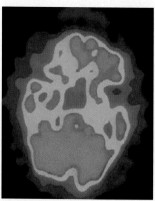 

Source: From "Emergence of Artistic Talent in Frontal-Temporal Dementia," by B. L. Miller et al., *Neurology, 51,* pp. 978–982. Copyright © 1998. Reprinted by permission of Wolters Kluwer.

in his portrayal of Raymond Babbitt in *Rain Man*; Peek's brain had several anomalies, particularly in the left hemisphere (Figure 13.20; Treffert & Christensen, 2006). A few researchers have attempted to unleash savant-like capabilities by using transcranial electrical or magnetic stimulation to inhibit neural activity in the frontal-temporal area (Snyder, 2009). Most of the results have been unremarkable, but 40% of subjects receiving excitatory right-hemisphere stimulation along with inhibitory left-hemisphere stimulation were able to solve a problem that none of the control subjects could solve (Chi & Snyder, 2012). Whatever the explanation, the phenomenon adds to the argument that intellectual ability involves multiple and somewhat independent modules.

If these savants have an island of exceptional ability, autism is an island of impairment in high-functioning individuals with ASD. As an infant, Temple Grandin would stiffen and attempt to claw her way out of her affectionate mother's arms (Sacks, 1995). She was slow to develop language and social skills, and she would spend hours just dribbling sand through her fingers. A speech therapist unlocked her language capability, starting a slow emergence toward a normal life. Even so, she did not develop decent language skills until the age of six and did not engage in pretend play until she was eight.

As an adult, Grandin earned a doctorate in animal science; she teaches at Colorado State University and designs humane facilities for cattle, while lecturing all over the world on her area of expertise and on autism. Still, her theory of mind is poorly developed, and she must consciously review what she has learned to decide what others would do in a social situation. She says that she is baffled by relationships that are not centered on her work and that she feels like "an anthropologist on Mars."

■ **FIGURE 13.20** Stephen Wiltshire With One of His Drawings.

He completed this drawing after observing the site only briefly.

Source: Dan Kitwood/Staff/Getty Images News/Getty.

Attention-Deficit/Hyperactivity Disorder

Attention-deficit/hyperactivity disorder (ADHD) is characterized by impulsiveness, inability to sustain attention, learning difficulty, and hyperactivity. Behaviorally, what we see is fidgeting and inability to sit still, difficulty organizing tasks, distractibility, forgetfulness, blurting out answers in class, and risk taking (Smalley, 1997). Diagnosticians recognize three types of ADHD; combined inattention and hyperactivity-impulsiveness is most common, but some individuals are predominantly inattentive or predominantly hyperactive-impulsive. ADHD is the most common among childhood-onset behavioral disorders. A meta-analysis of 179 studies estimated prevalence at 7.2% worldwide (Thomas et al., 2015); boys are more than twice as likely as girls to be diagnosed (Visser et al., 2014). Although ADHD is often thought of as a learning disorder (and many children with ADHD do have at least one learning disability), its effects are felt in every aspect of a person's life. Besides having the expected difficulties with life and work, these individuals have greatly increased rates of antisocial personality disorder, criminal behavior, and drug abuse (Biederman, 2004); in fact, 35% of people seeking treatment for cocaine abuse have a history of childhood ADHD (F. R. Levin, Evans, & Kleber, 1998). People with ADHD are also twice as likely to die prematurely, mostly from accidents (Dalsgaard, Østergaard, Leckman, Mortensen, & Pedersen, 2015).

Drugs are usually prescribed to control the symptoms of ADHD, and from 2002 to 2010 the prescription rate jumped 46% in the United States (Chai et al., 2012), while in Denmark it went up a whopping 630% (Dalsgaard, Nielsen, & Simonsen, 2013). With 69% of diagnosed children taking medication (Visser et al.), some observers have raised concerns that children are being overdiagnosed and overmedicated as an easy solution to classroom behavioral problems. The link with drug abuse fostered concerns that treating children with stimulant drugs such as methylphenidate (Ritalin) and amphetamine was leading to addiction later in life. However, research that followed children with ADHD into adolescence and adulthood revealed that, at worst, stimulant treatment made no difference (Barkley, Fischer, Smallish, & Fletcher, 2003) and that it might even be protective against drug abuse (Figure 13.21; Wilens, Faraone, Biederman, & Gunawardene, 2003). The more positive outcome for the treated individuals could have been due to the reduction of symptoms, or it could have been the result of other factors, such as the support of parents who opted for treatment, but at least these results do not support fears that the medications act as gateway drugs.

■ **FIGURE 13.21**   Relative Odds of Avoiding Substance Abuse Disorder in Individuals Receiving Stimulant Treatment for ADHD as Children, Compared With Those Not Receiving Stimulant Treatment.

Individuals with ADHD who were treated with a stimulant drug as children were as much as 4.6 times as likely to be free of alcohol abuse disorder as individuals who did not receive stimulant treatment and up to 8.1 times as likely to be free of a drug abuse disorder. Values below 1 indicate that treated individuals in that study were at greater risk.

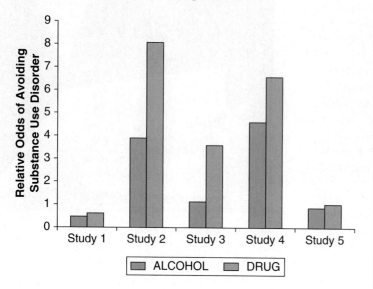

Source: Based on data from Wilens et al. (2003).

Although ADHD is considered a childhood disorder, in a 13-year-long study of 2,040 twins in the United Kingdom, 22% of the children diagnosed with ADHD continued to meet criteria at age 18 (Agnew-Blais et al., 2016). *DSM*-5 diagnostic criteria require onset during childhood, but 68% of the 18 year olds who met diagnostic criteria without regard to age of onset had not done so in any of the four previous screenings. These results are not unique to the United Kingdom; they were confirmed in an even larger study in Brazil (Caye et al., 2016) and are supported by an earlier study in New Zealand. Unfortunately, the data can't tell us whether adult-onset ADHD is a different form or if these individuals were simply able to compensate for their impairments through childhood. We do know, however, that the adult-onset ADHD group had higher IQs than the childhood-onset group and was preponderantly female.

Brain Anomalies in ADHD

Numerous studies have reported one difference or another in the brains of individuals with ADHD, but the results have been inconsistent. Brain MRIs cost anywhere between $1,000 and $5,000, so study samples are usually small; brain differences in psychological disorders are typically slight, on the order of just a few cubic centimeters of volume, so reliable detection of these differences requires large samples. Now a nine-country international group has solved that problem by compiling data from 1,700 people diagnosed with ADHD and 1,500 people without (Hoogman et al., 2017). They found reductions in overall brain volume and in five specific structures involved in emotion, motivation, and reward processing: the caudate nucleus, putamen, nucleus accumbens, amygdala, and hippocampus. The amygdala had the most pronounced deficit, which is important because the amygdala has functions not only in emotion but also in response inhibition. Reductions were greatest in children and leveled off in adults, which lent support to the brain maturation theory of ADHD.

White matter integrity also is reduced in children with ADHD, both in interhemispheric connections and in anterior-posterior pathways (Figure 13.22a; Ameis et al., 2016). They share this characteristic with children diagnosed with ASD and obsessive-compulsive disorder. In fact, the children with greater white matter impairment also had more impairment in functioning, regardless of their diagnosis. Because of this reduced connectivity, activity is segregated into localized clusters rather than being integrated across larger areas (Griffiths et al., 2016). There is a hub of local connections centered around the amygdala; the researchers suggested that the ADHD brain may be configured to respond impulsively instead of having the neural organization to regulate and inhibit responses. Other studies have found overall reductions in brain volume, particularly in prefrontal and parietal-temporal areas and the cerebellum, along with reductions in cortical thickness (Figure 13.22b; Proal et al., 2011). The reductions were observable in adults at 33-year follow-up, though there was some evidence of mitigation of the deficiencies in those who were symptom free.

Genes, Neurotransmitters, and ADHD

To say that ADHD runs in families would be an understatement: Heritability averages 76% across studies (Biederman & Faraone, 2005; Brikell, Kuja-Halkola, & Larsson, 2015), and concordances have been variously estimated at 58%–83% for identical twins and 31%–47% for fraternal twins (Wender, Wolf, & Wasserstein, 2001). Like autism, ADHD is a complex, multisymptom disorder, and different individuals display different combinations of symptoms. Whole-genome studies have implicated genes involved in cell migration, synaptic excitability, and neuronal plasticity (Jain et al., 2012). Another study found 222 copy number variations (CNVs) in ADHD patients that were not found in control subjects (Elia et al., 2010). These CNVs were in or near genes involved in synaptic transmission, neural development, and learning and other psychological functions. Numerous CNVs are in chromosomal locations that have been identified in autism and schizophrenia (N. M. Williams et al., 2010); participation of a gene in more than one disorder should not be surprising, since different disorders share some symptoms. And remember that we are not talking about a gene for autism or a gene for ADHD or a gene for schizophrenia, but genes that regulate brain growth, receptor development, and so on.

However, the genes most frequently implicated in ADHD are involved with neurotransmission. In fact, it is difficult to discuss the genetics of ADHD without simultaneously discussing neurotransmitters. A review of genetic studies identified 24 "hot genes," each of which had been linked to ADHD in at least five studies (Li, Chang, Zhang, Gao, & Wang, 2014). The large majority of these genes are involved with dopamine, serotonin, and norepinephrine transmission, including synthesis, transport, and receptors. In addition, one gene's protein contributes to the construction of the nicotinic acetylcholine receptor. For the past half-century, ADHD has been treated mostly with the stimulant drugs methylphenidate and amphetamines. These drugs increase dopamine and norepinephrine activity by blocking reuptake at the synapse, which supports a role for both transmitters. Most research, however, links ADHD to reduced activity in dopamine pathways, including the prefrontal cortex (Ernst et al., 1998) and the striatum (K.-H. Krause, Dresel, Krause, King, & Tatsch, 2000). These structures' functions include executive control, impulse inhibition, working memory, movement, learning, and reward—all functions that are affected in ADHD. The significance of reward may be less immediately obvious, but several researchers believe that impaired reward contributes to impulsiveness because the allure of later rewards is too weak to overcome the temptation of immediate gratification (Castellanos & Tannock, 2002; Tripp & Wickens, 2009). Some 20%–30% of patients do not respond to the traditional medications or cannot tolerate them (Biederman & Faraone, 2005). Two drugs sometimes used in their place, modafinil and atomoxetine, block norepinephrine reuptake, adding support for its role in ADHD as suggested by genetic studies.

■ **FIGURE 13.22**   White Matter Reduction and Cortical Thinning in the ADHD Brain.

(a) Red and yellow colors indicate where white matter is significantly reduced in the brains of individuals with ADHD, compared with controls. (b) Areas where the cortex is thinner in individuals with ADHD than in controls. Transitions from purple to red indicate greater thinning.

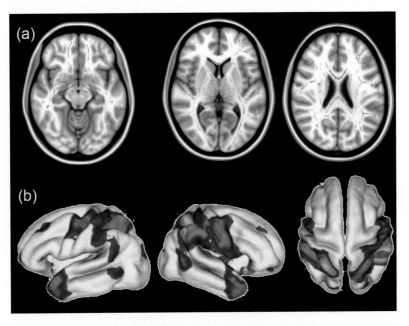

Source: From "Cortical Abnormalities in Children and Adolescents With Attention-Deficit Hyperactivity Disorder," by E. R. Sowell et al., *Lancet, 362*, figs. 2 & 3, pp. 1702–1703. © 2003 Elsevier Ltd.

The Environment and ADHD

What appears to be an environmental cause of ADHD often turns out to be an indication of a genetic predisposition in the parents. This includes correlations of ADHD with maternal smoking and stress during pregnancy (A. Rodriguez & Bohlin, 2005); parental abuse of alcohol, stimulants, and cocaine; and parental mood and anxiety disorders (Chronis et al., 2003). Confirmed environmental influences include brain injury, stroke, and complications during pregnancy and birth (Biederman & Faraone, 2005; Castellanos & Tannock, 2002), along with some toxins. Lead, for example, is a known neurotoxin; although eliminating lead in gasoline and paint has reduced levels in the environment, it is occasionally found in children's costume jewelry and imported candies as well as in the soil and water. A recent study confirmed higher blood levels of lead in children diagnosed with ADHD, and lead levels were correlated with teacher and parent ratings of symptoms (Nigg, Nikolas, Knottnerus, Cavanagh, & Friderici, 2010). Another source of concern is air pollution; children whose mothers were exposed during pregnancy to high levels of polycyclic aromatic hydrocarbon from sources such as traffic and fossil-fuel-burning electric plants had increased levels of ADHD symptoms, especially inattentiveness, at age nine (Perera et al., 2014).

As with autism, another culprit is organophosphate pesticides; children with above average urinary levels of a metabolite of these pesticides are twice as likely to be diagnosed with ADHD compared with children with undetectable levels (M. F. Bouchard, Bellinger, Wright, & Weisskopf, 2010). Even chemicals found in cosmetics, perfumes, and shampoo are turning out to be a problem; mothers who had higher levels of phthalates in their urine during the third trimester of pregnancy reported that their children had significantly more trouble with attention, aggression, and depression (S. M. Engel et al., 2010). How phthalates cause this result is unknown, but they may disrupt thyroid hormones that are important during brain development.

Although these examples are distinctly environmental, it is important to remember that environmental insults often exert their influence by changing gene functioning. For example, inducing concussion in rats altered over 1,200 genes, 16 of which are linked to ADHD (Q. Meng et al., 2017). Another example is dietary: High fat and sugar in women's diets during pregnancy was associated with increased methylation of the *IGF2* gene, which is involved in development of brain areas implicated in ADHD, along with higher symptoms of ADHD (Rijlaarsdam et al., 2017). In addition, genes can influence whether an environmental condition has an effect; in children with ADHD who had a specific mutation in the *C282Y* gene, "safe" levels of lead exposure were associated with increased symptoms (Nigg, Elmore, Natarajan, Friderici, & Nikolas, 2016).

CONCEPT CHECK

Take a Minute to Check Your Knowledge and Understanding

- Make a list of the kinds of intellectual disability described and their causes.
- What neural and biochemical differences have been found in the brains of people with ASD?
- Why are males more prone to ASD than females?

In Perspective

As important as the assessment of intelligence is in our society for determining placement in school, opportunities for continued education, and employability and promotability, it is remarkable that so much disagreement remains about what intelligence is. This lack of agreement makes it more difficult to study the brain functions that make up intelligence. Nevertheless, we have identified several features that appear to contribute to greater mental power; brain size, neural conduction speed, processing efficiency, and working memory are among these. Although it would be an error to overlocalize any function in the brain, we also know that some areas have a special role in important cognitive functions related to intelligence. It remains to be seen whether any characteristic of these areas, such as size, explains why some people have a particularly strong talent in one area, such as creative writing or mathematics. Some people hope that we will eventually have objective brain measures that will tell us exactly how intelligent a person is or whether a child has ASD.

When we reach that point, perhaps another dream will be realized: the ability to diminish or even reverse some of the defects that rob the intellectually disabled, the autistic, and the aged of their capabilities. We may even be able to increase the intelligence of normal individuals. We can only hope that our capacity to make the ethical decisions required keeps pace with our ability to manipulate the human condition.

CHAPTER SUMMARY

The Nature of Intelligence

- Intelligence is usually assessed with tests designed to measure academic ability.
- Some people show strong abilities not tapped by these tests; our understanding of intelligence should be broader than what tests measure.
- Intelligence theorists are divided over their emphasis on a general factor or multiple components of intelligence.

The Biological Origins of Intelligence

- Probable contributors to general intelligence are brain size, neural conduction speed, processing speed, quality of neural connections, and processing efficiency.
- The involvement of different brain areas suggests multiple components of intelligence.
- About half of the variation in intelligence among people is due to heredity. The closer the family relationship, the

more correlated are the IQs. Apparently, many genes are involved; there are several leads to specific genes, but little certainty.

- Research has not supported a genetic basis for ethnic differences in intelligence. Adoption has resulted in dramatic increases in IQ above the ethnic group mean.

- Although half of the variation in intelligence is due to environment, demonstrating which environmental conditions are important has been difficult. Judging by experience with Head Start and similar programs, any influence must be early and intense. Adoption can have dramatic effects if the difference in environments is large.

Deficiencies and Disorders of Intelligence

- Loss of intellectual functioning with age is less than previously believed and, like decreases in learning ability, it is not inevitable. Diminished speed of processing appears to be most important.

- Intellectual disability has many causes, including disease, fetal alcohol syndrome, Down syndrome, fragile X syndrome, phenylketonuria, and hydrocephalus.

- Down syndrome, caused by a third 21st chromosome, produces mild to moderate intellectual disability.

- Intellectual disability due to phenylketonuria, the inability to metabolize phenylalanine, is severe to profound.

- Hydrocephalus can usually be treated to avoid serious impairment, but there are hydrocephalic individuals with no apparent deficiencies.

- ASD is partially hereditary, with several gene locations implicated; heritability is around 50%, and the environmental contribution consists mostly of pollution and maternal illnesses in the third trimester.

- ASD involves abnormalities in several brain areas and possible weak connections among them.

- ASD may involve anomalies in serotonin, glutamate, GABA, and oxytocin functioning.

- Pollutants, infections, and maternal factors can increase the chances of ASD.

- ADHD is a partially genetic disorder characterized by hyperactivity, impulsiveness, and impaired attention and learning; heritability averages 76%. ADHD is associated with a variety of anomalies in functioning and in dopamine, serotonin, norepinephrine, and acetylcholine transmission. Several gene locations have been implicated.

- A variety of environmental influences have been associated with ADHD, including brain injury, environmental pollution, and pesticides. ∎

STUDY RESOURCES

FOR FURTHER THOUGHT

- Environmental influences on intelligence have been hard to identify. Does this mean that we are stuck with our genetic destiny?
- Intelligence is subject to physical disorders and genetic and environmental deviations. Speculate about why intelligence is so vulnerable.
- As you look at autism and ADHD, you see several similarities in the causes. Why, for example, do you think one child exposed to organophosphate pesticides would develop ASD and another might be diagnosed with ADHD?

TEST YOUR UNDERSTANDING

1. Describe the uncertainties about the measurement of intelligence and how this affects the search for biological bases of intelligence.

2. Discuss the brain characteristics that appear to contribute to general intelligence.

3. Discuss what we know about brain and biochemical differences in autistic individuals.

Select the best answer:

1. A problem with most intelligence tests is that they
   a. are not based on theory.
   b. are each based on a different theory.
   c. assess a limited group of abilities.
   d. try to cover too many abilities in one test.

2. Lumpers and splitters disagree on the significance of _____ in intelligence.
   a. heredity
   b. environment
   c. the g factor
   d. early education

3. It is likely that _____ is/are important to general intelligence.
   a. size of neurons
   b. processing speed
   c. processing efficiency
   d. a, b, and c
   e. b and c

4. Research with adults, children, chimpanzees, and monkeys suggests that we are born with
   a. a mechanism for number or quantity.
   b. the ability to do the same things as savants.

c. many times more intellectual capacity than we use.

d. time-limited abilities that inevitably deteriorate with age.

5. Research suggests that, normally, environmental effects on intelligence

a. are almost nonexistent.

b. are significant but difficult to identify.

c. are less important than the effect of heredity.

d. are more important than the effect of heredity.

6. Some observers claim the high correlation between identical twins' IQs occurs because they evoke similar treatment from people. This was refuted by a study in which the correlation

a. held up when the twins were reared separately.

b. was unaffected by parents' misidentification of twins as fraternal or identical.

c. was just as high in mixed-sex as in same-sex identical pairs.

d. increased as the twins grew older, though they lived apart.

7. The best evidence that ethnic differences in intelligence are not genetic is that

a. the various groups perform the same on culture-free tests.

b. no well-done research has shown an IQ difference.

c. no genes for an ethnic difference in intelligence have been found.

d. adoption into a more stimulating environment reduces the difference.

8. Apparently, the most critical effect on intelligence during aging is loss of

a. speed.

b. motivation.

c. neurons.

d. synapses.

9. Sam has dramatically reduced brain tissue and enlarged ventricles, but his IQ is 105; his disorder is most likely

a. hydrocephalus.

b. phenylketonuria.

c. Down syndrome.

d. autism.

10. Most mild intellectual disability is believed to be caused by

a. an impoverished environment.

b. brain damage sustained during birth.

c. a combination of a large number of genes.

d. a combination of environmental and hereditary causes.

11. Research with autism spectrum disorders suggests that autism involves

a. a single gene.

b. several genes.

c. heredity alone.

d. primarily environment.

12. Impaired sociability in autistic individuals may involve low levels of

a. risperidone.

b. serotonin.

c. thalidomide.

d. oxytocin.

13. ADHD is associated with reduced or impaired

a. gray matter.

b. intelligence.

c. dopamine activity.

d. theory of mind.

Answers: 1. c, 2. c, 3. e, 4. a, 5. b, 6. b, 7. d, 8. a, 9. a, 10. d, 11. b, 12. d, 13. c.

ON THE WEB

The following websites are coordinated with this chapter's content. You can access these websites from the **SAGE edge Student Resources site**; select this chapter and then click on Web Resources. (**Bold** items are links.)

1. **Stephen Hawking's website** features a brief biography, information about his professional accomplishments, and downloadable copies of public lectures.

2. At **Not Exactly Rocket Science** you can read about tool use in chimpanzees and see a video of chimps making and using fishing sticks. **Nature's Tools: How Birds Use Them** is an excerpt from a BBC wildlife film that shows a New Caledonian crow fishing for grubs.

3. **Brain Drain: Are We Evolving Stupidity?** is a *New Scientist* article about studies indicating a slight worldwide decline in IQ in recent years. Some observers worry that medical and societal support may be keeping maladaptive genes in the pool, while others say the evidence is sparse and sometimes contradictory, and may be due to chance.

4. *The Bell Curve* **Flattened**, an article in the online magazine *Slate*, refutes ideas about genetic racial differences in intelligence that were presented in the controversial book *The Bell Curve*.

5. You can get information about various kinds of intellectual disability from the **The Arc**, the **American Association on Intellectual and Developmental Disabilities**, the **National Fragile X Foundation**, and the National Library of Medicine's **Williams Syndrome** page.

6. Sources of information on autism and autism spectrum disorders include the National Institute of Mental Health's website **Autism Spectrum Disorder**, Internet Mental Health's **Autism Spectrum Disorder** site, and the **Autism Research Institute's** section on Treating Autism (see menu item). **Mapping**

Connectivity has information about connectivity mapping in autism, with photos illustrating seven methods used.

7. The Wisconsin Medical Society's **Savant Syndrome 2013—Myths and Realities** may dispel some of your notions about savantism and even about intelligence. Then, two videos of **Kim Peek** are guaranteed to impress you.

8. **Temple Grandin's website** features her professional work along with a brief description of her.

9. The **Attention Deficit Disorder Association** has high-quality articles on ADHD, and the National Institute of Mental Health explores a number of topics at its **Attention-Deficit/Hyperactivity Disorder** site.

FOR FURTHER READING

1. *Possessing Genius: The Bizarre Odyssey of Einstein's Brain*, by Carolyn Abraham (St. Martin's, 2001), tells the story of the study of Einstein's brain and the controversy about how it came to be removed in the first place and about its caretaker, Thomas Harvey (coauthor of all the Einstein brain studies cited here).

2. "Representation of Number in the Brain," by Andreas Nieder and Stanislas Dehaene (*Annual Review of Neuroscience*, 2009, *32*, 185–208), reviews research on the basis of number understanding in children, adults, and nonhuman primates.

3. *Smarter: The New Science of Building Brain Power*, by Dan Hurley (Plume, 2014), describes scientists' efforts toward cognitive enhancement. "Anyone who doubts that environment can make a real difference to cognition should start with this book."—James Flynn, noted writer on intelligence.

4. *Autism Spectrum Disorder: The Complete Guide to Understanding Autism*, by Chantal Sicile-Kira (TarcherPerigee, 2014), endorsed by Temple Grandin, is written for both professionals and the public.

5. *Thinking in Pictures: My Life With Autism*, by Temple Grandin (Vintage, 2010), is a perspective from the point of view of an autistic individual and a scientist. *Born on a Blue Day: Inside the Extraordinary Mind of an Autistic Savant*, by Daniel Tammet (Free Press, 2006), chronicles his life, while his *Embracing the Wide Sky: A Tour Across the Horizons of the Mind* (Free Press, 2009) adds relevant scientific information.

KEY TERMS

attention-deficit/hyperactivity disorder (ADHD) 397
autism spectrum disorder 390
autistic savant 396

default mode network 387
Down syndrome 389
fragile X syndrome 390
intellectual disability 388

intelligence 374
intelligence quotient (IQ) 374
phenylketonuria 390
theory of mind 392

edge.sagepub.com/garrett5e

SAGE edge offers a robust online environment featuring an impressive array of free tools and resources for review, study, and further exploration, keeping both instructors and students on the cutting edge of teaching and learning.

13.1 Describe how scientists have defined intelligence.	Straight Talk About IQ
13.2 Critique the scientific methods for measuring intelligence.	Are Crows the Ultimate Problem Solvers?
13.3 Identify how the structure of the nervous system relates to intelligence.	The Evolution of Intelligence
13.4 Appraise the relative contributions of heredity and environment to intelligence.	The Genetics of Intelligence / The Heredity of Intelligence
13.5 Assess the impact of the typical aging process on cognitive functioning.	Cognition and Healthy Brain Aging
13.6 Compare the impacts of intellectual disability, autism, and attention deficit/hyperactivity disorder on intelligence.	The World Needs All Kinds of Minds

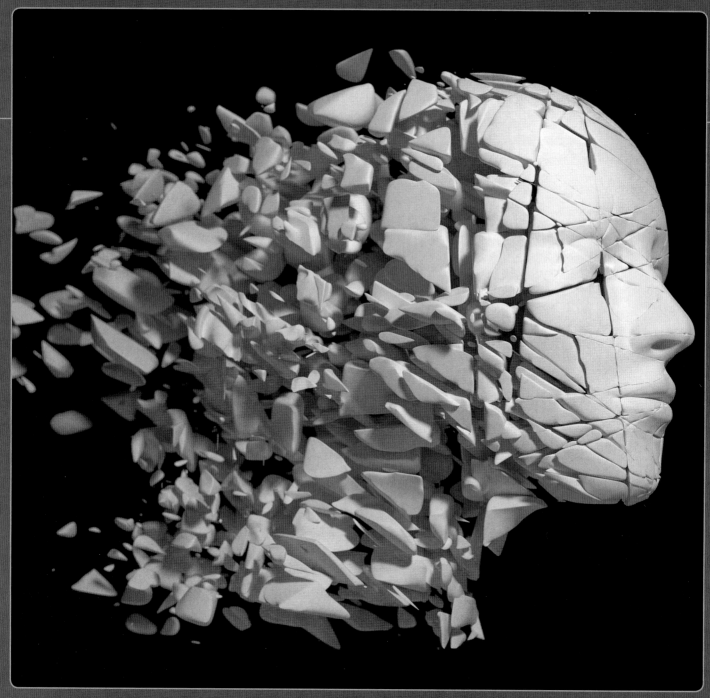

Psychological Disorders

14

After reading this chapter, you will be able to:

- Name and describe the various categories of psychological disorders.

- Understand the characteristics and neurological causes of schizophrenia.

- Describe how heredity and environment interact to produce psychological disorders.

- Understand the symptoms and causes of the affective disorders.

- Understand and describe the symptoms and physiological causes of the anxiety disorders.

- Explain the causes and features of the various personality disorders.

Master the content.
edge.sagepub.com/garrett5e

ob Garrett stood by his chair and waited for the students to take their places around the table, eagerly tying up the loose ends of conversations that the trek across campus hadn't given them time to finish. As the bell in the East College tower tolled the start of the hour and he was about to call the class to order, Ned got up from his seat and approached him.

"I forgot to give the bookstore cashier her pen after I used it to write a check. Can I take it back?"

"I think she can wait until class is over," he answered. Ned accepted that judgment and returned to his seat, but he seemed restless for the remainder of the hour. As soon as class was over, he was one of the first out of the door. Bob couldn't help but smile at Ned's youthful impetuousness.

> *Canst thou not minister to a mind diseas'd*
> *Pluck from the memory a rooted sorrow*
> *Raze out the written troubles of the brain*
>
> —William Shakespeare, Macbeth

The next day he understood that Ned's behavior had a completely different origin. Around 10 o'clock the night before, his dorm mates found him huddled on the stair landing, fending off an imaginary alien spaceship circling over his head and firing projectiles at him. He was taken to the hospital and sedated; then his parents took him back to his hometown, where he spent several months in a hospital psychiatric ward. He was diagnosed with paranoid schizophrenia. Fortunately, medication helped, and he was able to move to a home school with a comprehensive program of support and rehabilitation.

Ned has now spent two thirds of his life at the home. A few years ago he wrote to Bob, and they have kept up a regular correspondence since; his primary motivation is that he remembers his brief time in college as the happiest in his life. It is not that the home is unpleasant. He is on the baseball, basketball, and golf teams; he works part time outside the home; and he has a girlfriend. Questions he asks in his letters reveal a healthy curiosity, usually provoked by something he has read or seen on television about the brain. Once he talked candidly about his diagnosis, and about how he prefers to believe that someone slipped him a dose of LSD on that fateful night. There is no evidence that happened, but even if it did, it only precipitated, rather than caused, the decades-long debilitation that followed. Despite Ned's apparently good adjustment—and we see only the face that he wants to put on his situation—the preadolescent intellectual maturity of his letters and the barely legible scrawl of his handwriting suggest the havoc that schizophrenia has wreaked in his brain. Ned is unable to function outside the home's protective environment and professional support, and he will never be able to leave.

Researchers estimate that one out of every four adults in the United States suffers from a diagnosable mental illness, and that 46% will fall victim during their lifetime (R. C. Kessler et al., 2005). We aren't sure how many people are mentally ill, because researchers rely primarily on self-reports, which are notoriously

TABLE 14.1   Mental Disorders.

DISORDER	SYMPTOMS
Schizophrenia	Perceptual, emotional, and intellectual deficits; positive and negative symptoms
Affective Disorders	
Major depressive disorder	Sadness, hopelessness, decreased enjoyment, loss of energy and appetite, slow thought, sleep disturbance
Bipolar disorder	Alternating depression and either anxiety, irritation, or mania
Seasonal affective disorder	Depression that worsens in the winter and improves in the summer
Anxiety, Trauma, and Stress-Related Disorders	
Generalized anxiety disorder	Feeling of stress and unease most of the time
Panic disorder	Sudden and intense attack of anxiety with no obvious trigger
Phobia	Fear or stress when confronted with a particular situation
Posttraumatic stress disorder	Prolonged stress reaction to a stressful event characterized by recurrent thoughts, images, nightmares, impaired concentration, and overreaction to sudden events
Personality Disorders	
Obsessive-compulsive disorder	Recurrent, uncontrollable thoughts (obsessions) paired with ritualistic behaviors that remove anxiety (compulsions)
Tourette syndrome	Involuntary motor and sound tics, grimaces, blinks, grunts, and imitation
Borderline personality disorder	Unstable mood, self-image, anxiety, self-harm, and anger that leads to impulsive acts due to apparently common events

inaccurate. In late-life interviews people recalled bouts of mental illness 2–12 times less often, depending on the type of illness, than they had reported them in three interviews over the previous 25 years (Takayanagi et al., 2014). The monetary cost in terms of treatment and lost wages amounts to $467 billion a year in the United States (Insel, 2015) and $2.5 trillion globally (Trautmann, Rehm, & Wittchen, 2016). According to the World Health Organization (2008), mental disorders are the leading cause of disability among people aged 15 to 44 in the United States and Canada (Figure 14.1). An obvious benefit of research is the development of improved therapeutic techniques; in addition, because the disorders involve malfunctions in neurotransmitter systems and brain structures, studying them helps researchers understand normal neural functioning as well. In this chapter, we will make good use of what you have already

■ **FIGURE 14.1**   Psychological Disorders Impair a Person's Ability to Cope.

Source: Cheryl Chan/Moment/Getty.

learned about brain structure and neurotransmitter activity as we examine schizophrenia, mood disorders, and anxiety disorders, and in turn this survey will further expand your knowledge of how the brain works.

The *Diagnostic and Statistical Manual of Mental Disorders,* 5th edition (*DSM-5*; American Psychiatric Association, 2013), provides the framework for therapists, clinicians, and researchers in assessing an individual's unique history and symptoms and arriving at a diagnosis from a long list of disorders (for example, see Table 14.1). Many of these disorders have been discussed in prior chapters, such as substance-related disorders (Chapter 5), eating disorders (Chapter 6), sexual and gender dysfunctions (Chapter 7), aggressive and disruptive disorders (Chapter 8), and neurodevelopmental and cognitive disorders (Chapters 12 and 13). This chapter will focus on several of the remaining disorders: schizophrenia spectrum disorders, affective disorders, anxiety disorders not covered in Chapter 8, and obsessive-compulsive disorders.

Schizophrenia

Schizophrenia is a debilitating disorder characterized by perceptual, emotional, and intellectual deficits; loss of contact with reality; and inability to function in life. Schizophrenia is a *psychosis,* which simply means that the individual has severe disturbances of reality, orientation, and thinking. Schizophrenia is the most severe of the mental illnesses, and it is particularly feared because of the bizarre behavior it produces in many of its victims. All social classes are equally vulnerable; though patients themselves "drift" to lower socioeconomic levels, when they are classified by their parents' socioeconomic level, the classes are proportionately represented (Huber, Gross, Schüttler, & Linz, 1980). Schizophrenia is diagnosed in about 1% of the population worldwide; in the United States the rate is 1.2%, or roughly 3.8 million people (Nemade & Dombeck, 2009). The economic burden of schizophrenia amounts to $156 billion annually in the United States, which included direct health care costs (24%), unemployment (38%), and caregiving (34%) (Cloutier et al., 2016). Fortunately, schizophrenia is one of the few psychological disorders that appear to be on the decline. Critics have attributed the apparent reduction to methodological flaws in studies, but a study of all people born in Finland between 1954 and 1965 found a significant decline in each successive age-group, totaling 29% for women and 33% for men (Suvisaari, Haukka, Tanskanen, & Lönnqvist, 1999). This decrease has been noted in other countries such as Canada (Woogh, 2001) and Japan (Toshitani et al., 2006), but as of 2017 there hasn't been a systematic study in the United States.

 What is schizophrenia, and what causes it?

Characteristics of the Disorder

The term *schizophrenia* was coined in 1911 by the Swiss psychiatrist Eugen Bleuler (Figure 14.2) from the combination of two Greek words meaning "split mind." Contrary to popular belief, schizophrenia has

■ **FIGURE 14.2**   Eugen Bleuler (1857–1939).

A pioneer in the field, he introduced
the term *schizophrenia*.

Source: © Bettmann/Getty Images.

■ **FIGURE 14.3**   Risk for Schizophrenia
by Age.

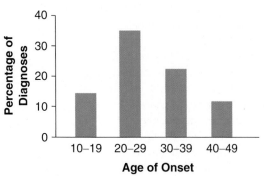

Source: Data from Huber et al. (1980).

nothing to do with multiple personalities; the term refers to the distortion of thought and emotion, which are "split off" from reality. The schizophrenic has some combination of several symptoms: hallucinations (internally generated perceptual experiences, such as voices telling the person what to do); delusions (false, unfounded beliefs, such as that one is a messenger from God); paranoia, characterized by delusions of persecution; disordered thought; inappropriate emotions or lack of emotion; and social withdrawal. Note that Ned had a hallucination of a spaceship, the paranoid delusion that it was attacking him, and a possible delusion about the LSD.

In the past, people with schizophrenia were subdivided into diagnostic categories based on which of these symptoms was predominant, such as *paranoid* or *catatonic*. However, patients often have overlapping symptoms and can receive multiple diagnoses, so there is little belief that these categories represent distinct disease processes. Also, as neuroscience and evidence-based practices progress, we are realizing that two people can have the same symptom with different causes or the same brain defect with different symptoms. As a result, the National Institute of Mental Health encourages researchers to shift their focus from diagnostic categories to underlying neural and genetic mechanisms (G. Miller, 2010). As a first step in that direction, the *DSM*-5 eliminated these subgroups of schizophrenia as diagnostic categories (American Psychiatric Association, 2013).

Schizophrenia afflicts men and women about equally often, and there is no difference in incidence between urban and rural environments (Saha, Chant, & McGrath, 2005). Men usually show the first symptoms during their teens or twenties, as Ned did, while the onset for women ordinarily comes about a decade later (Figure 14.3). *Acute* symptoms develop suddenly and are typically more responsive to treatment; the prognosis is reasonably good despite brief relapses. Symptoms that develop gradually and persist for a long time with poor prognosis are called *chronic*. The media has frequently overplayed the bizarre features of schizophrenia; many patients are able to function reasonably well, especially if they are fortunate enough to be among those who respond to antipsychotic drugs. Among patients studied 20 years after their first psychiatric admission, 22% were fully recovered, another 43% were improved, and the symptoms of the remaining 35% had remained the same or worsened; 56% were fully employed (Huber et al., 1980). A more recent meta-analysis of over 114 studies performed by Warner (2005) is consistent with this earlier study (20%–25% fully recovered).

In the late 1700s and early 1800s, doctors began to view mental illness as a medical problem; at that time, the mentally ill were literally released from their chains and given treatment (Figure 14.4; Andreasen, 1984). By the early 20th century, it was widely assumed that schizophrenia had a physiological basis. But when the search for biological causes produced little success, the emphasis shifted in the 1940s to the social causes of schizophrenia, especially in America, where Freud's theory of psychoanalysis was in its ascendancy and biologically oriented psychiatrists were in the minority (Andreasen; Wender, Rosenthal, Kety, Schulsinger, & Welner, 1974). Until the 1960s, research techniques were not up to the task of demonstrating the validity of the physiological position. It was then that increasing knowledge of neurotransmitters, the advent of brain scanning techniques, and improved genetic studies shifted the explanation for schizophrenia back to the realm of biology and permanently changed the perception of mental illness.

■ **FIGURE 14.4**   Philippe Pinel Freeing Mental Patients From Their Chains.

Patients were warehoused without treatment; sometimes care consisted of throwing in fresh straw and food once a week. Pinel was convinced that they would benefit from humane treatment and in 1794 freed the mental patients of Paris from their chains.

Source: © Rapho Agence/Photo Researchers.

> *I'm a paranoid schizophrenic and for us life is a living hell. . . . Society is out to kill me. . . . I tried to kill my father. I went insane and thought he ruled the world before me and caused World War Two.*
>
> —*Ross David Burke in* When the Music's Over: My Journey Into Schizophrenia

Heredity

Schizophrenia is a familial disorder, which means that the incidence of schizophrenia is higher among the relatives of people with schizophrenia than it is in the general population (Gottesman, McGuffin, & Farmer, 1987; Tsuang et al., 1991). Of course, this association could be due to environmental influence or to heredity; in fact, in the 1940s supporters for both the genetic and environmental bases argued for their positions from the same data (Wender et al., 1974). However, studies of twins and adoptees provided compelling evidence for a genetic influence.

Twin and Adoption Studies

In Figure 14.5, you can see that the shared incidence of schizophrenia increases with the genetic closeness of the relationship and that the concordance rate for schizophrenia is three times as high in identical twins as in fraternal twins (Lenzenweger & Gottesman, 1994). In other words, identical twins of people with schizophrenia are three times as likely to develop the disorder as the fraternal twins of patients. The heritability for schizophrenia has been estimated at between .60 and .90 (Tsuang et al., 1991). This means that 10%–40% of the variability is due to environmental factors.

Information from adoption studies gives a more impressive indication of genetic influence; these studies show that adopting out of a home with schizophrenia provides little or no protection from developing schizophrenia symptoms. The incidence of schizophrenia *and* schizophrenia-like symptoms was 28% among individuals adopted out of Danish homes in which there was one parent with schizophrenia, compared with 10% in matched adoptees from homes without an individual with symptoms (Lowing, Mirsky, & Pereira, 1983). Other studies have produced similar findings.

Discordance among identical twins has been used as an argument that schizophrenia is environmentally produced. To address this issue, Gottesman and Bertelsen (1989) compared the incidence of schizophrenia in the offspring of affected and normal identical twins; they found that the offspring of the

■ **FIGURE 14.5**   Concordances for Schizophrenia Among Relatives.

Genetic Relatedness	Relationship	Risk
100%	Identical twin	48%
—	Offspring of two patients	46%
50%	Fraternal twin	17%
50%	Offspring of one patient	17%
50%	Sibling	9%
25%	Nephew or niece	4%
0%	Spouse	2%
0%	Unrelated person in the general population	1%

Source: From *Introduction to Psychology, Gateways to Mind and Behavior* (with InfoTrac), 9th edition by Coon, 2001. Reprinted with permission of Wadsworth, a division of Thomson Learning.

unaffected identical twins were just as likely to be schizophrenic as the offspring of the affected twins (Figure 14.6). This result would not have occurred unless the normal twins were carrying genes for schizophrenia. Discordance does raise the question, however, of whether some environmental factors determine whether the person's schizophrenic genes will remain "silent." Refer back to Chapter 6 for the discussion of these *epigenetic* effects on genes.

The Search for the Schizophrenia Genes

Although we have known for a long time that schizophrenia is partially genetic, identifying the genes involved has been difficult. One reason has been researchers' inconsistency in including the spectrum disorders in their diagnosis of schizophrenia (Heston, 1970; Lowing et al., 1983). When identical twins are discordant for schizophrenia, 48%–54% of the nonschizophrenic twins have spectrum disorders (Heston; Onstad, Skre, Torgersen, & Kringlen, 1991). If the spectrum disorders are due to the same genes, then classifying these individuals as nonschizophrenic means that the genes will not appear to distinguish between schizophrenia and normality. A second problem is that schizophrenia apparently involves the cumulative effects of multiple genes, each of which has a small effect by itself. Evidence indicates that the number of variants contributing to schizophrenia is in the thousands (Wray & Visscher, 2010). A person's risk of schizophrenia presumably increases with the number of these genes inherited. This view is supported by the fact that risk has been found to increase with the number of relatives who are schizophrenic and with the degree of the relatives' disability (Heston, 1970; Kendler & Robinette, 1983).

Recent genome-wide studies have identified at least 108 genes suspected of a role in producing schizophrenia (Schizophrenia Working Group, 2014). These genes are typically related to neurodevelopment and plasticity, neurotransmission (such as dopamine, glutamate, and calcium channels), immune responses, and hormonal activity, such as the *DISC1* (disrupted in schizophrenia 1) gene. This gene appears to change how neurons develop and migrate by disrupting a messenger system in neurons in areas involved in learning, memory, and mood (J. Y. Kim et al., 2009; Millar et al., 2000; Millar et al., 2005). Although many genes such as *DISC1* have been linked to schizophrenia, they have small individual effects and together may account for less than 5% of the variability in susceptibility. Copy number variations (CNVs) have much larger effects; for example, a duplication of a segment of DNA on chromosome 7 produces a 10-fold increase in risk (Mulle et al., 2014). But CNVs are individually rare and make an even smaller contribution than common genes. The large majority of CNVs are inherited, but *de novo* mutations are more often implicated in diseases. Along with epigenetic modifications, they help account for discordance in identical twins, who otherwise have identical genomes. Epigenetic studies of schizophrenia are in their infancy. Though they have produced interesting results, our knowledge is based on small numbers of subjects and tissues taken from widely varying brain locations. According to one group of reviewers, some of the current results may be harder to interpret than early small-sample gene association studies (Dempster, Viana, Pidsley, & Mill, 2013).

Schizophrenia is a very old disease (see W. J. Ray, 2014, for a review). Disorders with psychotic-like symptoms have been reported for 4,000 years, and similar rates in disparate and long-separated societies suggest that the genes were present before humans left Africa some 100,000 years ago. So why wouldn't genes as detrimental as those that produce schizophrenia be eliminated through evolution? One suggestion is that the genes that in combination can produce schizophrenia individually confer an evolutionary advantage. Ten or fifteen centuries ago, these individual genes might have helped individuals cope with the demands of burgeoning social culture. It has been pointed out that many gifted Nobel recipients, the likes of Albert Einstein, Bertrand Russell, and John Nash (featured in the film *A Beautiful Mind*), either had some schizophrenic traits or had relatives thought to have schizophrenia. In addition, an individual's overall risk for schizophrenia (as well as for bipolar disorder) is highly correlated with intellectual and artistic creativity (Power et al., 2015). Therefore, our amazing human ability to express, integrate, and create comes with an increased risk for psychotic disorders that can be triggered by the same genes and circuits.

The Vulnerability Model

Most researchers agree that genes determine only the person's vulnerability for the illness; both heredity and environment are needed to explain the *etiology* (causes) of schizophrenia (Zubin & Spring, 1977) as well as most other disorders. According to the *vulnerability model,* some threshold of causal forces must be exceeded for the illness to occur; environmental challenges combine with a person's genetic vulnerability to exceed that threshold. The environmental challenges may be external, such as bereavement, job difficulties, or divorce, or they may be internal, such as maturational changes, poor nutrition,

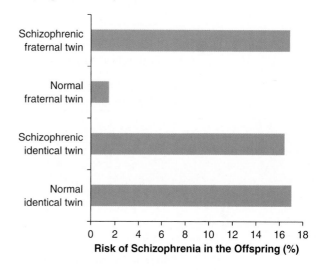

■ **FIGURE 14.6**   Risk of Schizophrenia in the Offspring of Normal and Schizophrenic Twins.

Offspring of the normal fraternal twin of a schizophrenic do not have an elevated risk. The offspring of the normal identical twin of a schizophrenic are as likely to become schizophrenic as the offspring of the schizophrenic identical twin.

Source: Based on data from Gottesman and Bertelsen (1989).

infection, or toxic substances. There is mounting evidence that these environmental influences work in part by epigenetic means, that is, by upregulating and downregulating gene functioning (Tsankova, Renthal, Kumar, & Nestler, 2007). Vulnerability is viewed as a continuum, depending on the number of affected genes inherited. At one extreme, a small percentage of genetically predisposed individuals will become schizophrenic under the normal physical and psychological stresses of life; at the other extreme are individuals who will become schizophrenic only under the severest stress such as the trauma of battle (Fowles, 1992) or because of a constantly stressful life with poor social support and family environments (see Lange et al., 2017).

Two Kinds of Schizophrenia

Researchers disagree on whether schizophrenia represents one disease or many, but most authorities do agree that the symptoms fall into two major categories: positive and negative. *Positive symptoms* involve the presence or exaggeration of behaviors, such as delusions, hallucinations, disorganized thinking, and abnormal motor behaviors. *Negative symptoms* are characterized by the absence or insufficiency of normal behaviors and include lack of affect (emotion), inability to experience pleasure, lack of motivation, poverty of speech, and impaired attention and social interactions.

Crow (1985) theorized that positive and negative symptoms are due to two different syndromes of schizophrenia, with different causes and different outcomes. His Type I and Type II schizophrenias are described in Table 14.2. Subsequent research has supported this distinction in many respects. Positive symptoms are more often acute, and they are more likely to respond to antipsychotic drugs than are negative symptoms (Fowles, 1992). Negative symptoms tend to be chronic; these patients show poorer adjustment prior to the onset of the disease (Andreasen, Flaum, Swayze, Tyrrell, & Arndt, 1990); poorer prognosis after diagnosis (Dollfus et al., 1996); more intellectual and other cognitive deficits, suggestive of a brain disorder (Andreasen et al., 1990); and greater reduction in brain tissue (Fowles). These findings led researchers to think in terms of two distinct groups of patients, a view we will modify shortly.

"
What consoles me is that I am beginning to consider madness as an illness like any other, and that I accept it as such.

—Vincent van Gogh, 1889, in a letter to his brother, Theo
"

TABLE 14.2   Positive Versus Negative Schizophrenia.

ASPECT	TYPE I (POSITIVE)	TYPE II (NEGATIVE)
Characteristic symptoms	Delusions, hallucinations, etc.	Poverty of speech, lack of affect, etc.
Response to antidopaminergic drugs	Good	Poor
Symptom outcome	Potentially reversible	Irreversible?
Intellectual impairment	Absent	Sometimes present
Suggested pathological process	Increased D_2 dopamine receptors	Cell loss in temporal lobes

Source: From "The Two-Syndrome Concept: Origins and Current Status," T. J. Crow, 1985, *Schizophrenia Bulletin, 11,* pp. 471–486, with permission of Oxford University Press.

The Dopamine Hypothesis

Little could be done to treat psychotic patients until the mid-1950s, when a variety of antipsychotic medications arrived on the scene. For the first time in history, the population of hospitalized mental patients decreased in size. As is often the case in medicine, and more particularly in mental health, these new drugs had not been designed for this purpose—researchers had too little understanding of the disease to do so. Doctors tried chlorpromazine with a wide variety of mental illnesses because it calmed surgical patients, and it turned out to help those with schizophrenia as well. However, it was not clear *why* chlorpromazine worked, because tranquilizers have little or no usefulness in treating schizophrenia.

So, investigators tried reverse engineering. You will remember from Chapter 5 that amphetamine overdose causes psychotic behavior indistinguishable from schizophrenia, complete with hallucinations and paranoid delusions. In time, researchers determined that amphetamine produces these symptoms by increasing dopaminergic activity. This discovery eventually led to the *dopamine hypothesis,* that schizophrenia involves excessive dopamine activity in the brain. According to the theory, blockade of the D_2 type of dopamine receptors is essential for a drug to have an antipsychotic effect, and a drug's effectiveness is directly related to the drug's blocking potency. The theory has considerable support; schizophrenic patients typically have higher dopamine activity in the striatum (Abi-Dargham et al., 2000), and drugs that block dopamine receptors are effective in treating the positive symptoms of schizophrenia (S. H. Snyder, Bannerjee, Yamamura, & Greenberg, 1974). In fact, the effective dosage for most antipsychotic drugs is directly proportional to their ability to block dopamine receptors (Figure 14.7; Seeman, Lee, Chau-Wong, & Wong, 1976). What exactly does dopamine do to trigger the symptoms of schizophrenia? One theory, called the *aberrant salience hypothesis,* suggests that heightened levels of dopamine increase attentional and motivational circuits to make ordinary environmental features seem significant. Therefore, an individual projects his or her own thoughts and imaginings as real-world events and experiences (Howes & Nour, 2016).

Beyond the Dopamine Hypothesis

However, the drugs did not help 30%–40% of schizophrenic patients, and—troublesome for the dopamine theory—nonresponsive patients experienced just as much D_2 receptor blockade as responders. In fact, in some of them the blockade exceeded 90%, while some responders showed remarkably low levels of receptor blocking (Kane, 1987; Pilowsky et al., 1993). Furthermore, some patients appear to have a *dopamine deficiency,* especially those with chronic, treatment-resistant symptoms (Grace, 1991; Heritch, 1990; Okubo et al., 1997).

Another problem for the drugs was that the side effects could be permanently disabling. Prolonged use of antidopamine drugs often produces *tardive dyskinesia,* tremors and involuntary movements due to long-term blocking of dopamine receptors and resultant neuron death in the basal ganglia. Once dyskinesia

■ FIGURE 14.7 Relationship Between Receptor Blocking and Clinical Effectiveness of Schizophrenia Drugs.

The horizontal axis is the average daily doses prescribed by physicians; the horizontal red lines represent typical ranges of doses used. Values on the vertical axis are amounts of the drugs required to block 50% of the dopamine receptors.

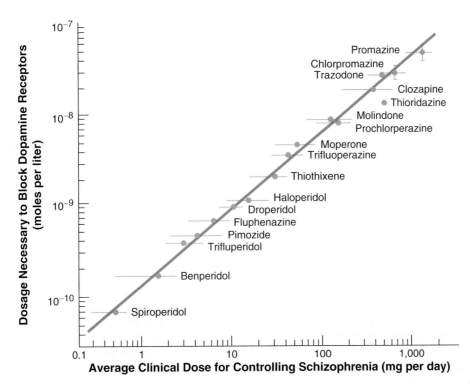

Source: Reprinted by permission from "Antipsychotic Drug Doses and Neuroleptic/Dopamine Receptors," by P. Seeman et al., *Nature, 261,* p. 718, fig. 1. Copyright 1976 Macmillan Publishers, Ltd.

develops, it persists even after the person stops taking the drug. Seventy years ago, this effect was believed to be so inevitably linked to the therapeutic benefit that the "right" dose was the one that caused some degree of motor side effects. Thus, the drugs used to treat schizophrenia became known as *neuroleptics,* because the term means "to take control of the neuron" (Julien, 2008). The effect appears to be due to a compensatory increase in the sensitivity of D_2 receptors in the basal ganglia. (This is a good illustration of the fact that drugs do not affect just the part of the brain we want to treat.)

Since the early 1990s, we have seen the introduction of several new antipsychotic substances that are referred to as *atypical* or *second-generation* drugs. Atypical antipsychotics block D_2 receptors less strongly, while also targeting non-dopamine receptors; as a result, they produce motor problems only at much higher doses, but they still reduce psychotic symptoms. Fortunately, avoiding motor side effects does not require a therapeutic compromise. The major atypical antipsychotics are at least equivalent to the first-generation drugs, and some are 15%–25% more effective; what is more, they often bring relief to treatment-resistant patients (Iqbal & van Praag, 1995; Leucht et al., 2009; Pickar, 1995; Siever et al., 1991). So, is the dopamine hypothesis just another example of a beautiful hypothesis slain by ugly facts? Not entirely; although atypical antipsychotics mostly target other receptors, those that lack at least a modest effect at D_2 receptors are therapeutically ineffective (H. M. Jones & Pilowsky, 2002). So, successful therapy apparently requires D_2 blockade *and* other effects. For a summary of the types of drugs prescribed for individuals with schizophrenia, and their side effects, see the accompanying Research Spotlight.

And what are these other effects? One involves serotonin. The serotonergic system is suspect largely because of the 5-HT$_{2A}$ receptor's involvement in schizophrenic-like responses to hallucinogenic drugs, such as psilocybin and LSD. The number of 5-HT$_{2A}$ receptors is upregulated in the brains of deceased schizophrenic subjects (González-Maeso et al., 2008), and atypical antipsychotics block serotonin 5-HT$_2$ receptors by as much as 90%

Antipsychotics and Their Side Effects

Antipsychotic medication is generally classified in two different categories: first-generation antipsychotics (FGA), and second-generation (atypical) drugs (SGA). Each has its own unique qualities and side effects. Although each is effective in preventing the positive symptoms of schizophrenia, they are less likely to affect the negative symptoms.

FGA drugs include Thorazine (chlorpromazine) and Haldol (haloperidol). Potent D_2 blockers, they help alleviate positive symptoms in most individuals with schizophrenia. They have four major categories of side effects (Preston, O'Neal, & Talaga, 2013). The first is called extrapyramidal effects and is a result of excessive blocking of dopamine receptors; impaired movement such as tardive dyskinesia, shuffling gait, tremors, and a blank facial expression are a result of damage to the basal ganglia (the "extrapyramidal" region) and mimic Parkinson's disease. Although many of these side effects are immediately apparent with FGAs, the tardive dyskinesia is seen only after prolonged use. This is common for Haldol. Anticholinergic side effects are due to blocking acetylcholine receptors and the parasympathetic

nervous system and includes dry mouth and eyes, constipation, and sedation; this is common for Thorazine. Antiadrenergic side effects are caused by blocking the sympathetic nervous system and can result in low blood pressure and lightheadedness.

SGA drugs include clozapine, Abilify (aripiprazole), Latuda (lurasidone), and Seroquel (quetiapine). They weakly block D_2 receptors but strongly block serotonin receptors. Because dopamine is not strongly blocked, there is a much smaller risk of extrapyramidal effects and tardive dyskinesia. However, these drugs carry their own set of undesirable side effects. They tend to cause sleepiness, can result in weight gain, and are more effective in reducing the negative symptoms of schizophrenia. Two major side effects that rarely occur are agranulocytosis (a life-threatening blood disorder; Idänpään-Heikkilä, Alhava, Olkinuora, & Palva, 1977) and serotonin syndrome (which causes sweating, high body temperature, seizures, headaches, and confusion; Buckley, Dawson, & Isbister, 2014). Both are life threatening and must be treated by medical administration of either blood factors (for agranulocytosis) or serotonin agonists (for serotonin syndrome).

(H. M. Jones & Pilowsky, 2002; Kapur, Zipursky, & Remington, 1999). But serotonin has not received nearly as much attention as glutamate activity, which also is affected by atypical antipsychotics. The drug phencyclidine (PCP), which inhibits the NMDA (N-methyl-d-aspartic acid) subtype of glutamate receptor, mimics schizophrenia far better than amphetamine does, particularly in producing negative as well as positive symptoms (Sawa & Snyder, 2002). Glycine activates the NMDA receptor, and adding it or similar compounds to antipsychotic medications reduces both kinds of symptoms (Lisman et al., 2008). According to the *glutamate theory,* hypofunction of NMDA receptors results in increases in glutamate and downstream increases in dopamine, which together produce positive and negative symptoms of schizophrenia (Lisman et al.; Sendt, Giaroli, & Tracy, 2012). Indeed, genes that underlie glutamate signaling are correlated with the severity of schizophrenia and related disorders (N. L. O'Brien et al., 2014). However, it has been difficult to develop drugs that target NMDA receptors or reduce glutamate levels, and that are both therapeutically effective and well tolerated (Sendt et al.). Those that do work produce modest results, and a couple of them are in final phase 3 clinical trials.

Obviously, it would be a mistake to focus entirely on a single neurotransmitter, considering the complex interactions among them. The glutamate theory provides some recognition of this fact, and it is showing considerable usefulness in explaining schizophrenia and some promise in guiding drug development. While we wait for the glutamate story to unfold, we have additional clues about the origins of schizophrenia from structural and functional anomalies in the brain.

Brain Anomalies in Schizophrenia

Malfunctions have been identified in virtually every part of the brain in people with schizophrenia. The most consistent finding has been enlargement of the ventricles; another is hypofrontality, or reduced activity in the frontal lobes. We will examine each of these defects in turn.

■ **FIGURE 14.8**   Ventricle Size in People With and Without Symptoms of Schizophrenia.

In two identical twins (a) the lateral ventricles are larger in the one with schizophrenia. However, (b) shows that while this difference is true on average (indicated by the dotted lines), ventricle size is normal in several patients and increased in several controls.

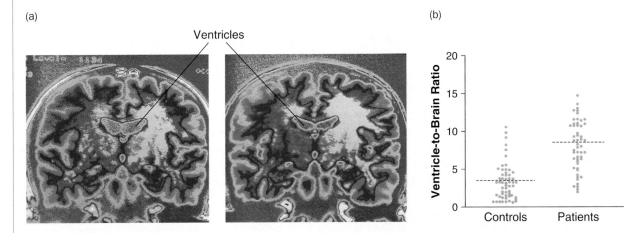

(a)   (b)

Brain Tissue Deficits and Ventricular Enlargement

A signature characteristic of schizophrenia is a decrease in brain tissue, both gray and white matter, with deficits reported in at least 50 different brain areas (Honea, Crow, Passingham, & Mackay, 2005). The number of sites and the variability across studies attest to the multifaceted nature of schizophrenia, but the frequency with which deficiencies are found in the frontal and temporal lobes indicates that they are particularly important. These tissue losses are accompanied by alterations in neural functioning but not necessarily in the expected direction: Activity is decreased in the dorsolateral prefrontal cortex but increased in the orbitofrontal cortex and in a subregion of the hippocampus (Schobel et al., 2009). In fact, the hippocampal activation is so characteristic of schizophrenia that in a group of people having brief psychotic symptoms, it identified with 70% accuracy those who would later be diagnosed with full-blown schizophrenia (Schobel et al.).

An indication of the tissue deficits seen in schizophrenia is ventricular enlargement; this is because the ventricles expand to take up space normally occupied by brain cells (Figure 14.8). Both deficiencies are usually subtle, on the order of less than a tablespoonful increase in ventricular volume (Suddath et al., 1989) and a 2% decrease in brain volume (Haijma et al., 2012; Harrison et al., 2003), but these figures belie the functional importance of the losses. In fact, an often-distinguishing feature between identical twins discordant for schizophrenia is the size of their ventricles (Suddath, Christison, Torrey, Casanova, & Weinberger, 1990). Ventricular enlargement is not specific to schizophrenia; enlarged ventricles are also associated with several other conditions, including old age, dementia (loss of cognitive abilities), Alzheimer's disease, Huntington's chorea (Weinberger & Wyatt, 1983), and alcoholism with dementia (D. M. Smith & Atkinson, 1995). Nor are enlarged ventricles an inherent characteristic of schizophrenia. As you can see in Figure 14.8a, several controls have enlarged ventricles, and many of the patients have ventricle sizes in the normal range. We will look more closely at the tissue deficits later when we consider their origins.

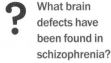

What brain defects have been found in schizophrenia?

Hypofrontality

Earlier, we saw that prefrontal functioning can be assessed by using the gambling task; an alternative technique is the *Wisconsin Card Sorting Test,* which requires individuals to change strategies in midstream, first sorting cards using one criterion but then changing to another. Many people with schizophrenia perform poorly on the test, persisting with the previous sorting strategy. Normal individuals show increased activation in the prefrontal area during the test; schizophrenic patients typically do not, despite normal activation in other areas (D. R. Weinberger, Berman, & Zec, 1986). Figure 14.9 shows a normal brain practically lighting up during the test, in comparison with the schizophrenic brain, especially in the frontal area called the *dorsolateral prefrontal cortex*. This *hypofrontality* apparently involves prefrontal dopamine *deficiency*, because administering amphetamine increases blood flow in the prefrontal cortex and improves performance on the Wisconsin Card Sorting Test (Daniel et al., 1991). Traumatic injury to the dorsolateral prefrontal cortex causes impairments like the symptoms of schizophrenia: flat affect, social withdrawal, reduced intelligence and problem-solving ability, diminished motivation and work capacity, and impaired attention and concentration (Weinberger et al., 1986). Because of the frontal lobes' involvement in planning actions, recognizing the consequences of actions, and managing working memory, it is not surprising that frontal dysfunction would cause major abnormalities in thinking and behavior.

Neural Connections and Synchrony

Recent attention has been shifting away from localized deficits and focusing instead on disrupted coordination of neural activity across brain areas. For example, in normal controls performing a working-memory task, activity in the hippocampal formation varies together with prefrontal activity, but this coordination is absent in people with schizophrenia (Meyer-Lindberg et al., 2005). The hypofrontality seen during the Wisconsin Card Sorting Test has been attributed to disrupted communication between the hippocampus and the prefrontal cortex (Weinberger, Berman, Suddath, & Torrey, 1992). Inadequate coordination between brain areas is at least partly due to white matter reduction; white matter loss has been consistently reported in the brains of people with schizophrenia, particularly in prefrontal and temporal areas (Begré & Koenig, 2008; Ellison-Wright & Bullmore, 2009). Diffusion tensor imaging shows that the quality of connections is compromised throughout much of the brain (B. R. Lee et al., 2013). Recent studies also documented an overall decrease in cortical thickness, changes in neuronal maturation, and reduced cortical folding in the cingulate-frontal-temporal circuit, suggesting that hypofrontality may be a result of decreased gray and white matter in frontal-associated circuits (Alexander-Bloch et al., 2014; Nanda et al., 2014). Reduced connectivity between frontal and posterior regions of the brain correlates with positive and negative symptoms as well as with performance on the Wisconsin Card Sorting Test.

■ **FIGURE 14.9**   Blood Flow in Normal and Schizophrenic Brains During Card Sorting Test.

(a) The upper images are of the left and right hemispheres of a normal brain; the schizophrenic brain is below. Red and yellow represent greatest activation. Note especially the activity in the dorsolateral prefrontal cortex, whose location is identified in (b).

(a)

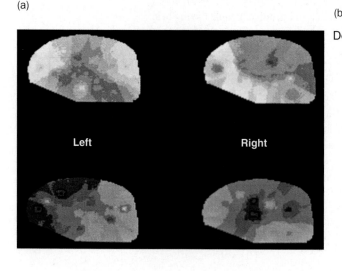

(b)

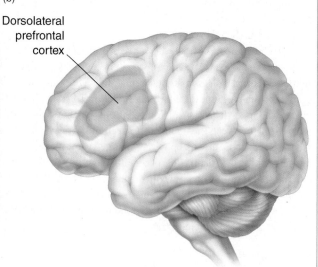

Dorsolateral prefrontal cortex

Source: (a) From "Physiologic Dysfunction of Dorsolateral Prefrontal Cortex in Schizophrenia: I. Regional Cerebral Blood Flow Evidence," by D. R. Weinberger, K. F. Berman, and R. R. Zec, 1986, *Archives of General Psychiatry, 43*, pp. 114–124.

Brain functioning is coordinated by synchronized firing that links the activity of neurons within a cortical area, across areas, and even between hemispheres. This synchronization is widely believed to be critical to perceptual binding and cognitive performance, and it is one of the functions disrupted in schizophrenia (Uhlhaas & Singer, 2010). Synchronized activity in frontal-thalamocortical circuits occurred at lower frequencies in patients (Ferrarelli et al., 2012), perhaps because the reduced white matter connections cannot support coordination at higher frequencies. Frequency reduction averaged 10 Hz in the frontal cortex; the deficit was greatest in the prefrontal area, and the frequency loss there was correlated with positive and negative symptoms. To some extent we can correlate the patterns of synchrony with the symptoms of schizophrenia; in patients with positive symptoms, for example, oscillation synchrony is enhanced within limited areas but is deficient between areas (Uhlhaas & Singer). This enhanced synchrony, which indicates hyperexcitability, is seen in the occipital area in visual hallucinators (Spencer et al., 2004) and in the left auditory cortex in auditory hallucinators (Spencer, Niznikiewicz, Nestor, Shenton, & McCarley, 2009). At the same time, auditory hallucinators fail to show normal synchrony between frontal and temporal areas while talking (Ford, Mathalon, Whitfield, Faustman, & Roth, 2002).

It may surprise you to learn that hallucinations are associated with activity in the respective sensory areas. Scans of the brains of people with schizophrenia show that language areas are active during auditory hallucinations and visual areas are active during visual hallucinations (Figure 14.10; McGuire, Shah, & Murray, 1993; McGuire et al., 1995; Silbersweig et al., 1995). Because these areas are activated in normal individuals when they are engaged in "inner speech" (talking to oneself) and imagining visual scenes, it appears that the hallucinating schizophrenic is not simply imagining voices and images but is misperceiving self-generated thoughts.

One of the most documented symptoms of schizophrenia is the inability to suppress environmental sounds. With *sensory gating* impaired, the intrusion of non-attended stimuli such as traffic noise or a distant conversation is not just annoying but can be interpreted by the person with schizophrenia as threatening. Impaired sensory gating can be a useful diagnostic tool for schizophrenia. Most people will "gate out" the second of two clicks presented a half-second apart, indicated by a reduction in the P50 EEG wave, but individuals with schizophrenia typically have an abnormal P50 wave (Figure 14.11). This deficit is also associated with reduced synchrony across wide areas of the brain (M. H. Hall, Taylor, Salisbury, & Levy, 2010). Atypical antipsychotics improve gating, but nicotine normalizes it (Adler et al., 2004; Kumari & Postma, 2005). The smoking rate declined in the United States from 42% in 1965 to about 15% in 2015 (Centers for Disease Control and Prevention, 2015b), but the rate remained about 80% among people with schizophrenia (Keltner & Grant, 2006), in an apparent attempt at self-medication. Besides sensory gating, nicotine improves several negative symptoms, including impaired visual tracking of moving objects, working memory, and other cognitive abilities (Sacco, Bannon, & George, 2004; Sacco et al., 2005; Tregellas, Tanabe, Martin, & Freedman, 2005). Nicotine appears to compensate for diminished functioning of nicotinic acetylcholine receptors (S. I. Deutsch et al., 2005), increase glutamate and GABA release, and increase dopamine levels in the prefrontal cortex where it is depleted in hypofrontality (Kumari & Postma; Sata et al., 2008). Three studies have linked schizophrenia with one of the genes responsible for nicotinic receptors (De Luca, Wang, et al., 2004; S. I. Deutsch et al., 2005).

■ **FIGURE 14.10** Brain Activation During Visual and Auditory Hallucinations in a Patient With Schizophrenia.

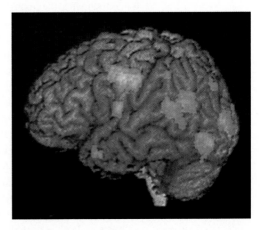

Source: From "A Functional Neuroanatomy of Hallucinations in Schizophrenia," by D. A. Silbersweig et al., *Nature, 378*, pp. 176–179. Reprinted by permission of Nature, copyright 1995.

■ **FIGURE 14.11** Absence of P50 Gating in Schizophrenia.

Two clicks are presented 500 milliseconds apart; healthy control subjects show a reduced P50 EEG wave to the second click, a sign of gating (a, left), but those with schizophrenia do not (a, right). After several drug treatments that decrease schizophrenia symptoms, the gating improves (b).

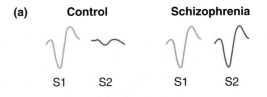

(a) **Control**   **Schizophrenia**

S1   S2   S1   S2

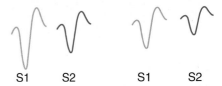

(b) Sz After Treatment 1   Sz After Treatment 2

S1   S2   S1   S2

Source: Figure 1 from "Translational utility of rodent hippocampal auditory gating in schizophrenia research: a review and evaluation," by J. Smucny, K. E. Stevens, A. Olincy, & J. R. Tregellas, 2015, *Translational Psychiatry, 5,* pp. e587.

There may very well be other changes to the brain due to schizophrenia. A large coalition of European researchers and pharmaceutical companies is undertaking a €16.5 million ($18.8 million) study called PRISM (Psychiatric Ratings Using Intermediate Stratified Markers); they will follow individuals with schizophrenia and other neurological disorders to determine the biological roots of the negative symptom of social withdrawal that is common to the groups (Underwood, 2016).

Environmental Origins of the Brain and Transmitter Anomalies

An obvious potential cause of brain defects would be head injury. Several studies have reported an association between schizophrenia and brain damage that occurred within a few years prior to diagnosis (reviewed in David & Prince, 2005). However, the studies have been criticized for several methodological inadequacies, including reliance on patients' and relatives' memory of the injuries, casual diagnosis of schizophrenia, and failure to consider accident proneness and preinjury symptoms as confounding factors (David & Prince, 2005; Nielsen, Mortensen, O'Callaghan, Mors, & Ewald, 2002). A later study of almost 114,000 Danish citizens found a correlation between severe head injury and schizophrenia; injury occurring between 11 and 14 years of age increased the likelihood of schizophrenia by 65% (Orlovska et al., 2014). However, researchers cannot separate the effects of the physical injury to the brain from the emotional effects of the stress and anxiety caused by the injury experience.

The evidence is stronger for a variety of influences at the time of birth or during the prenatal period. These include both physical complications (Cannon, Jones, & Murray, 2002) and emotional stresses on the mother, such as death of the father (Huttunen, 1989) and military invasion (van Os & Selten, 1998). Prenatal stress in mice results in upregulation of 5-HT_{2A} receptors and downregulation of $mGlu_2$ receptors, both of which are seen in the brains of schizophrenia patients (Holloway et al., 2013). One indication that birth and pregnancy complications contribute to brain deficits is that they are associated with enlarged ventricles later in life (Pearlson et al., 1989). They are a possible explanation for the difference in ventricle size between identical twins (Bracha, Torrey, Gottesman, Bigelow, & Cunniff, 1992).

It is easy to see how birth complications, such as being born with the umbilical cord around the neck, could differentiate between twins, but different experiences in the womb require some explanation. Identical twins may share the same placenta and amniotic sac or they may have their own, depending on whether the developing organism splits in two before or after the fourth day of development. Identical twins who did not share a placenta had an 11% concordance rate for schizophrenia, compared with 60% for those who shared a placenta, presumably due to the sharing of infections (J. O. Davis, Phelps, & Bracha, 1995). In spite of the importance of prenatal factors, some researchers believe that they produce schizophrenia only in individuals who are already genetically vulnerable (Schulsinger et al., 1984).

The *winter birth effect* refers to the fact that more people who develop schizophrenia are born during the winter and spring than during any other time of the year. The effect has been replicated in a large number of studies, some with more than 50,000 schizophrenic patients as subjects (T. N. Bradbury & Miller, 1985). The important factor in winter births is not cold weather, but the fact that infants born between January and May would have been in the second trimester of prenatal development in the fall or early winter, when there is a high incidence of infectious diseases (C. G. Watson, Kucala, Tilleskjor, & Jacobs, 1984). There is good evidence that the mother's exposure to *viral infections* during the fourth through sixth months of pregnancy (second trimester) increases the risk of schizophrenia. This appears to be caused not by the virus itself but by the immune reaction that it triggers. This conclusion is supported by a markedly higher level of interleukin-1β in the spinal fluid of first-episode patients, indicating that an immune response has occurred (Figure 14.12; Söderlund et al., 2009). Because the patients were infection free at the time, the infection must have occurred earlier, possibly during the prenatal period.

Several illnesses have been implicated, but the effect of influenza has been researched most frequently, and a higher incidence of schizophrenic births has been confirmed following influenza outbreaks in several countries.

■ **FIGURE 14.12**   Interleukin-1β Levels in Schizophrenia Patients and Controls.

Elevated levels of this protein at the time of a first schizophrenic episode indicated that strong immune reactions had occurred in the past.

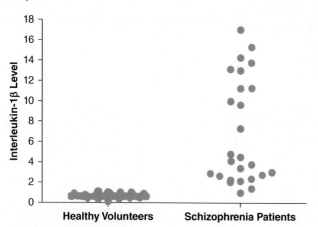

Source: From "Activation of Brain Interleukin-1β in Schizophrenia," by J. Söderland et al., 2009, *Molecular Psychiatry, 14,* pp. 1069–1071. Copyright © 2009 Nature Publishing Group. Used with permission.

Figure 14.13 shows that during years of high influenza infection the birth rate of people later diagnosed with schizophrenia increases during winter and spring; also, there is a peak of such births a few months after the start of epidemics. However, these studies could not confirm that the individual mothers had been exposed to the influenza virus; by analyzing the blood specimens drawn from expectant mothers, Alan Brown and his colleagues (2004) found a sevenfold increased risk for schizophrenia and spectrum disorders when influenza antibodies were present, and they estimated that influenza infection accounts for 14% of schizophrenia cases. As was the case with stress, maternal infection with the influenza virus upregulates 5-HT$_{2A}$ receptors and downregulates mGlu$_2$ receptors in the frontal cortex of the offspring (Moreno et al., 2011). Injecting pregnant mice with a drug that activates the immune system produced the same result, suggesting that immune responses are responsible for the receptor alterations in schizophrenia (Holloway et al., 2013).

Prenatal starvation is another pathway to schizophrenia that until recently was the subject of controversy. The idea came about after the rate of schizophrenia doubled among the offspring of mothers who were pregnant during Hitler's 1944–1945 food blockade of the Netherlands (Susser et al., 1996). However, the interpretation was questionable because the sample was small and because toxins in the tulip bulbs the women ate to survive could have been to blame. But now data from a much larger sample of adults born during the 1959–1961 famine in China have confirmed the association, with an increase in schizophrenia from 0.84% to 2.15% (St. Clair et al., 2005).

Most of the environmental influences we have been discussing occur during pregnancy or birth; one, however, relates to the father. There is a greater risk of schizophrenia if the father's age at the time of conception exceeds 25, and by paternal age of 50 the risk has increased by two thirds (B. Miller et al., 2010). The mechanism for this effect is unknown, but chances are it is epigenetic, due either to the normal aging process or to an accumulation of external environmental insults. Epigenetic effects in general can be traced to a variety of environmental influences, including toxins, diet, starvation, drugs, and stress; they likely account for most of the environmental influences we have been talking about. The fact that obesity in the Dutch hunger winter offspring was linked to epigenetic changes (see Chapter 6) makes us suspect the same mechanism in the cases of schizophrenia in that group. This is a relatively new area of investigation, so there has been little documentation of epigenetic influences in schizophrenia.

Schizophrenia as a Developmental Disease

The defects in the brains of people diagnosed with schizophrenia apparently occur early in life, some at the time of birth or before. In some cases, it appears that many neurons in the temporal and frontal lobes failed to migrate to the outer areas of the cortex during the second trimester; they are disorganized and mislocated in the deeper

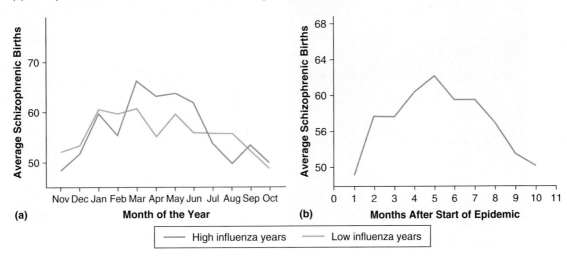

■ **FIGURE 14.13** Relationship of Schizophrenic Births to Season and Influenza Epidemics in England and Wales (1939–1960).

(a) Schizophrenic birth rates by month during years of high and low influenza incidence.
(b) Schizophrenic birth rate as a function of time from beginning of epidemic.

Source: From "Schizophrenia Following Pre-natal Exposure to Influenza Epidemics Between 1939 and 1960," by P. C. Sham et al., *British Journal of Psychiatry, 160,* pp. 461–466. Copyright 1992. Reprinted with permission of the publisher.

(a)   (b)

■ **FIGURE 14.14**

Neural Disorganization
in Schizophrenia.

The neurons in the normal
hippocampus have an orderly
arrangement (a), but in the brain of
an individual with schizophrenia you
can see that they have migrated in a
haphazard fashion (b).

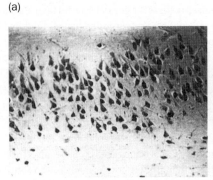 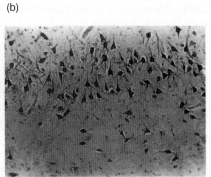

Source: © Arne Scheibel, UCLA.

white layers (Figure 14.14; Akbarian, Bunney, et al., 1993; Akbarian, Viñuela, et al., 1993). The hippocampus and prefrontal cortex are 30%–50% deficient in reelin, a protein that functions as a stop factor for migrating neurons (Fatemi, Earle, & McMenomy, 2000; Guidotti et al., 2000). In addition, neurons generated from stem cells derived from skin cells of individuals with schizophrenia exhibited impairment of signaling molecules that are responsible for neuronal differentiation (Topol et al., 2016). These observations and the association of schizophrenia with birth trauma and prenatal viral infection all argue for early damage to the brain *or* a disruption of development.

This view is supported by behavioral data. Home movies of children who later became schizophrenic revealed more negative facial expressions and physical awkwardness than in their healthy siblings; the movies were rated by judges who were unaware of the children's later outcome (Walker, Lewine, & Neumann, 1996). Among New Zealanders followed from age 3 to 32, those who later developed schizophrenia had deficits in learning, attention, and problem solving during childhood, and for each year of life they fell an additional two to three months further behind other children (Reichenberg et al., 2010).

Gray matter deficit and ventricular enlargement are ordinarily present at the time of patients' diagnosis (Degreef et al., 1992). Most of the evidence indicates that the loss of brain volume occurs rapidly and dramatically in adolescence or young adulthood and then levels off (B. T. Woods, 1998). Adolescence is a particularly significant period in the development of schizophrenia. This is a time when symptoms of schizophrenia often begin to develop and a time of brain maturation, including frontal myelination and connection of temporal limbic areas (D. R. Weinberger & Lipska, 1995). Thompson, Vidal, et al. (2001) identified a group of adolescents who had been diagnosed with schizophrenia and used MRIs to track their brain development. At the age of 13, there was little departure from the normal amount of gray matter loss that occurs with circuit pruning, but over the next five years, loss occurred in some areas as rapidly as 5% per year (Figure 14.15). The nature of the symptoms varied as the loss progressed from parietal to temporal to frontal areas. Studies have found no evidence of dying neurons or of the inflammation that would be expected with an ongoing degenerative disease; instead, gray matter deficits have been attributed to loss of synapses (Jarskog, Glantz,

■ **FIGURE 14.15**   Gray Matter Loss in Schizophrenic Adolescents.

There is some loss in the brains of normal adolescents due to circuit pruning, but the rate of loss is much greater in schizophrenic adolescents. Red and pink areas represent 3%–5% losses annually.

Rate of Gray Matter Loss

Normal
Adolescents

Schizophrenic
Subjects

Average
Annual
Loss

0%
-1%
-2%
-3%
-4%
-5%

Source: From "Mapping Adolescent Brain Change Reveals Dynamic Wave of Accelerated Gray Matter Loss in Very Early-Onset Schizophrenia," by P. M. Thompson, *PNAS, 98,* pp. 11650–11655, fig. 1A, p. 11651, and fig. 5, p. 11653. © 2001 National Academy of Sciences, U.S.A. Used with permission.

Gilmore, & Lieberman, 2005; D. A. Lewis & Levitt, 2002; D. R. Weinberger, 1987). This apparent severe pruning may reflect the elimination of circuits that have already been diminished (D. A. Lewis & Levitt) by a lack of gluta-mate activity (Coyle, 2006) or through neuronal cell death pathways (Jarskog et al., 2005); this view is supported by the fact that the diagnosis of schizophrenia preceded significant gray matter reductions in the schizophrenic adolescents.

Take a Minute to Check Your Knowledge and Understanding

- What is the interplay between heredity and environment in schizophrenia?
- Describe the two symptom categories of schizophrenia.
- How are dopamine irregularities and brain deficits proposed to interact?
- What role does glutamate play in schizophrenia?

Affective Disorders

The affective (mood) disorders include *depressive disorders, mania,* and *bipolar disorders* (Figure 14.16). Almost all of us occasionally experience *depression,* an intense feeling of sadness; we feel depressed over grades, a bad relationship, or loss of a loved one. This *reactive* depression can be severe, but major depres-sion goes beyond the normal reaction to life's challenges. In *major (or unipolar) depressive disorder (MDD),* a person often feels sad to the point of hopelessness for weeks at a time; loses the ability to enjoy life, relation-ships, and sex; and experiences loss of energy and appetite, slowness of thought, and sleep disturbance. In some cases, the person is also agitated or restless. Stress is often a contributing factor, but major depression can occur for no apparent reason. *Mania* involves excess energy and confidence that often leads to grandiose schemes; decreased need for sleep, increased sexual drive, and abuse of drugs are common.

What are the affective disorders?

The *DSM*-5 now considers bipolar disorder to be a cluster of disorders, separate from depressive disorders and serving as a bridge between depression and schizophrenia (American Psychiatric Association, 2013). Bipolar disorder was once called "manic-depressive" disorder, but as you will learn in this chapter, mania is not always a characteristic of this group of disorders. In *bipolar disorder,* a person alternates between peri-ods of depression and either mania (bipolar I) or hypomania (bipolar II); mania can occur in the absence of depression, but this is rare and the treatment is the same as for bipolar I disorder. In addition, bipolar I patients often demonstrate psychotic features such as delusions, hallucinations, paranoia, or bizarre behav-ior, which has led psychologists to consider bipolar I as a bridge disorder between schizophrenia and depres-sion. Finally, there is a third major category of bipolar disorder called cyclothymic disorder, in which individuals cycle rapidly between hypomania and mild depression. Two quotes provide some insight into the disorders from the patients' own per-spectives (National Institute of Mental Health, 1986):

Depression: I doubt completely my ability to do anything well. It seems as though my mind has slowed down and burned out to the point of being virtually useless. . . . [I am] haunt[ed] . . . with the total, the desperate hope-lessness of it all. . . . If I can't feel, move, think, or care, then what on earth is the point?

Mania: At first when I'm high, it's tremendous . . . ideas are fast . . . like shooting stars you follow until brighter ones appear . . . all shyness disappears, the right words and gestures are suddenly there. . . . Sensuality is perva-sive, the desire to seduce and be seduced is irresistible. Your marrow is infused with unbelievable feelings of ease, power, well-being, omnipotence, euphoria . . . you can do anything . . . but, somewhere this changes.

■ **FIGURE 14.16**   Major Categories of Affective Disorders.

Individuals with BPI alternate between mania and major depression, those with BP II between milder hypomania and major depression, those with Cyclothymic disorder switch rapidly between hypomania and mild depression, and those with MDD alternate between normal mood and major depression.

BP I = bipolar I disorder; BP II = bipolar II disorder; cyclo = cyclothymic disorder; MDD = major depressive disorder.

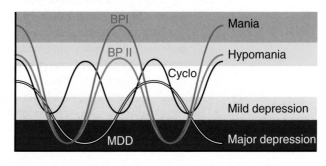

The most recent data indicate that 3 out of 10 people will suffer a mood disorder in their lifetimes, most likely depression (Kessler, Petukhova, Sampson, Zaslavsky, & Wittchen, 2012). Women are two to three times more likely than men to suffer from MDD during their lifetimes; bipolar disorder occurs equally often in both sexes (Gershon, Bunney, Leckman, Van Eerdewegh, & DeBauche, 1976; P. W. Gold, Goodwin, & Chrousos, 1988) at a rate of about 4.5% (Kessler, Merikangas, & Wang, 2007). The risk for MDD increases with age in men, whereas women experience their peak risk between the ages of 35 and 45; the period of greatest risk for bipolar disorder is in the early 20s to around the age of 30. Getting a handle on the economic burden of these disorders is difficult, because it depends on what costs are included and what assumptions are made. Estimates of the annual cost for all mood disorders in the United States have varied from $24 billion to $234 billion (Dilsaver, 2011; Greenberg et al., 2003; Uhl & Grow, 2004). Regardless of the economic cost, by 2020 depression will be the second largest cause of disability world-wide (Patel, 2009).

Heredity

As with schizophrenia, there is strong evidence that affective disorders are partially heritable. Part of that evidence is the increased incidence of affective disorders among patients' relatives. When one identical twin has an affective disorder, the probability that the other twin will have the illness as well is about 69%, compared with 13% in fraternal twins (Gershon et al., 1976). Lack of complete concordance in identical twins indicates that there is an environmental contribution. However, the concordance rate drops surprisingly little when identical twins are reared apart (J. Price, 1968), which may mean that the most important environmental influences occur in the prenatal period or shortly after.

Genetic liability differs by gender; a Swedish twin study estimated heritability at 29% for men and 42% for women (Kendler, Gatz, Gardner, & Pedersen, 2006). These results were consistent with studies in the United States and Australia, as well as with studies that identified different chromosomal locations for risk factors in men and women. In one study, seven genes were exclusive to men, nine were exclusive to women, and only three were shared between men and women (Zubenko, Hughes, Stiffler, Zubenko, & Kaplan, 2002). The sex disparity suggests one reason disorder genes can be difficult to locate in a clinical group, and it may explain the higher frequency of depression in women and the higher rate of suicide in men.

Once again, the genes we are interested in are many and of small effect, requiring much larger sample sizes than are typically employed. Researchers are more and more resorting to meta-analyses, which pool the results of many studies. One finding is that the *5-HTTLPR portion of the SLC6A4* serotonin transporter gene has been associated with an increased vulnerability to depression, along with a 15% reduction in gray matter in the amygdala and a 25% reduction in the subgenual anterior cingulate cortex (Pezawas et al., 2005). People with the short variation show an exaggerated amygdala response to fearful facial expressions (Hariri et al., 2002), apparently due to a loss of feedback from the cingulate cortex that would ordinarily dampen amygdala activity (Pezawas et al., 2005). According to some studies, these deficiencies increase susceptibility to stress, which leads to depression (Figure 14.17; Canli et al., 2006; Caspi et al., 2003). Although a meta-analysis that pooled 56 studies produced a strong confirmation of the linkage (Karg, Burmeister, Shedden, & Sen, 2011), not all studies have confirmed it. One reason may be that studies rarely consider gene interactions such as epistasis, the suppression of one gene's effect by another. In this case, the *VAL66MET* allele of the gene for brain-derived neurotrophic factor (BDNF), a protein that encourages neuron growth and survival, protects against the effects of the *5-HTTLPR* short allele on brain development (Pezawas et al., 2008). A later meta-analysis confirmed that *VAL66MET* also reduces vulnerability to depression (Hosang, Shiles, Tansey, McGuffin, & Uher, 2014).

Whole-genome studies have been extremely beneficial because researchers can explore the genome without any hypothesis or even an educated guess about what to look for. But the statistical procedure used to confirm an association must be corrected for the increased probability of a chance "hit" due to the millions of comparisons performed, which makes it even harder to find genes that have a small effect. One solution is to increase the effect size by targeting a limited group of subjects; a gene location on chromosome 3 was identified only when researchers limited their search to patients with severe depression (Breen et al., 2011). Another approach is to limit the search to the genes known to be involved in a relevant pathway; knowledge that the immune system is dysregulated in depression led researchers to discover several candidate immune system genes (Bufalino, Hepgui, Aguglia, & Pariaante, 2013).

A common characteristic of depression is disruption of the circadian (day–night) cycle, which is controlled by numerous genes (Bunney et al., 2015). At last count, at least 11 circadian genes were disrupted in patients with major depression (J. Z. Li et al., 2013). These genes are in the pineal gland (which secretes the sleep-inducing hormone melatonin), the pituitary gland (which controls hormone levels in the body), and most important, the anterior cingulate cortex (which, as we discussed in Chapter 8, is involved in autonomic functions, reward, decision making, and emotion). It is this last area that probably causes the alteration in mood we see in affective disorders.

Despite similarities between depression and bipolar disorder, they are genetically independent of each other (P. W. Gold et al., 1988; Moldin, Reich, & Rice, 1991). In fact, there is a much higher genetic correlation between bipolar disorder and schizophrenia (68%) than mood disorders (43%; Cross-Disorder Group of the Psychiatric Genomics Consortium, 2013). Bipolar disorder is more heritable than either depression or schizophrenia, with estimates of 85% and 93% (Kieseppä, Partonen, Haukka, Kaprio, & Lönnqvist, 2004; McGuffin et al., 2003). Few genes have been confirmed, however, apparently again because of small sample sizes. An unusually large genome-wide study that included 9,747 patients confirmed three previously discovered genes and added two more (Mühleisen et al., 2014). The genes' functions involve a calcium channel at the nodes of Ranvier and cellular functioning and signaling. The Cross-Disorder Group study, with 33,332 patients, reported that some genes are shared among five disorders: bipolar disorder, major depressive disorder, schizophrenia, autism spectrum disorders, and attention-deficit/hyperactivity disorder (Cross-Disorder Group of the Psychiatric Genomics Consortium). Genetic sharing is one of the arguments for considering these disorders as a continuum. Whether that is appropriate or not, you should understand that all five of these disorders do have a variety of functional and structural characteristics in common. Finally, mutations have been found in bipolar patients in three genes that control circadian rhythms, none of which overlapped with the five associated with depression (McGrath et al., 2009; Soria et al., 2010).

The Monoamine Hypothesis of Depression

The first effective treatment for depression was discovered accidentally, and theory again followed practice rather than the other way around. *Iproniazid* was introduced as a treatment for tuberculosis, but it was soon discovered that the drug produced elevation of mood (Crane, 1957) and was an effective antidepressant (Schildkraut, 1965). Iproniazid was later abandoned as an antidepressant because of its side effects, but its ability to increase activity at the monoamine receptors led researchers to the *monoamine hypothesis,* that depression involves reduced activity at norepinephrine and serotonin synapses. You may remember that the

What is the monoamine hypothesis?

■ **FIGURE 14.17** The Role of Stress and the Serotonin Transporter Gene in Depression.

(a) In individuals with either one or two copies of the so-called short allele, the percentage who were diagnosed at age 26 with depression increased with the number of stressful life events in the past five years. (b) In those with two copies of the long allele, the number of stressful events made no difference. Life events were assessed from a checklist of 14 employment, financial, housing, health, and relationship stressors.

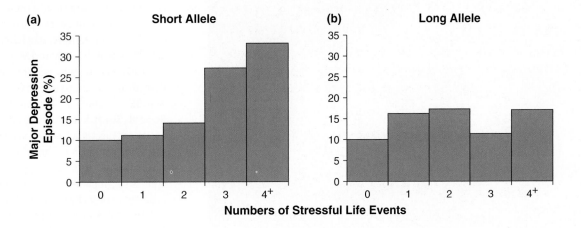

Source: From "Influence of Life Stress on Depression: Moderation by a Polymorphism in the 5-HTT Gene," by A. Caspi et al., *Science, 301,* pp. 386–389, fig. 3, p. 389. © 2003. Reprinted by permission of AAAS.

monoamines also include dopamine, but because dopamine agonists such as amphetamines produced inconsistent therapeutic results, researchers have limited their interest to norepinephrine and serotonin.

All the effective antidepressant drugs increase the activity of norepinephrine or serotonin, or both, at the synapses. They do this in different ways. Some block the destruction of excess monoamines by enzymes in the terminals (*monoamine oxidase inhibitors*), whereas others block reuptake at the synapse (*tricyclic antidepressants*). *Atypical (second-generation)* antidepressants affect a single neurotransmitter; for example, Prozac (fluoxetine) is one of several *selective serotonin reuptake inhibitors*. Finally, some antidepressants have a mixed effect on multiple neurotransmitter systems and are effective for specific combinations of disorders. For instance, Cymbalta (duloxetine) is one of several *serotonin and norepinephrine reuptake inhibitors*. This last group's effectiveness truly supports the monoamine hypothesis. The synaptic effects of antidepressants can occur within hours, but symptom improvement usually takes two to three weeks through the gradual modification of cortical circuits.

Additional evidence to support the monoamine hypothesis is that serotonin and norepinephrine are involved in behaviors that are disturbed in affective disorders. Serotonin plays a role in mood, activity level, sleep and daily rhythms, feeding behavior, sexual activity, body temperature regulation, and cognitive function (Meltzer, 1990; Siever et al., 1991). Because the noradrenergic system is involved in responsiveness and sensitivity to the environment, reduced norepinephrine activity may contribute to the depressed individual's slowed behavior, lack of goal-directed activity, and unresponsiveness to environmental change (Siever et al.).

Earlier, we saw that nicotine provides some relief from symptoms of schizophrenia. Nonnicotine ingredients in tobacco smoke also have been found to act as monoamine oxidase inhibitors. This would explain why smoking is so frequent among those with depression and why they have difficulty giving up smoking (J. S. Fowler et al., 1996; Khalil, Davies, & Catagnoli, 2006). We mention a therapeutic effect of smoking for the second time only to illustrate again how people may self-medicate without being aware they are doing it and why some people have so much trouble quitting; if it sounds as though the benefits of smoking outweigh the cost to the smoker's health, reread the section on nicotine in Chapter 5. Figure 14.18 is a dramatic demonstration of the extensive effect of smoking on monoamine oxidase inhibitor levels throughout the body.

Treatment resistance and the delay required for drugs to take effect are serious issues, especially if the patient is suicidal. Experiments with ketamine, which was developed as an anesthetic but gained infamy as a club drug, suggest that these problems might be avoidable. In a study with patients who had shown resistance to at least two antidepressant drugs, a single injection of ketamine alleviated depression in 68%, and the improvement lasted seven days in 46% of the patients (Murrough et al., 2013). Relapse time is highly variable, though, and ketamine appears to be most valuable as a temporary treatment (aan het Rot et al., 2010). Ketamine also interests us because its effect is not on norepinephrine or serotonin; instead, it has its antidepressant effect by activating AMPA receptors (Zanos et al., 2016), implicating glutamate function in depression as well as in schizophrenia.

About 30%–50% of depressed patients fail to respond to drug therapy, a statistic made worse by the fact that the placebo response rate alone is 30% (Depression Guideline Panel, 1993). Lack of response is

■ **FIGURE 14.18**   Monoamine Oxidase Levels in the Body of a Nonsmoker and a Smoker.

PET scans were done using a radioactive tracer that binds to monoamine oxidase B. Levels were reduced 33%–46% in smokers. Monoamine oxidase reduction can have beneficial, detrimental, or neutral effects, depending on the location and other conditions.

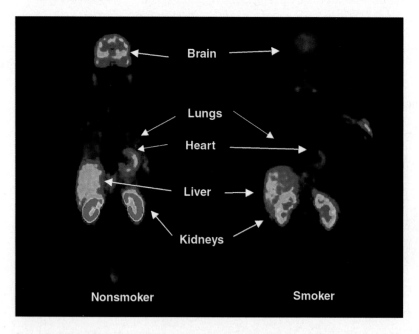

Source: From "Low Monoamine Oxidase B Levels in Peripheral Organs of Smokers," by J. S. Fowler et al., *PNAS, 100*, fig. 2, p. 11602. © 2003 National Academy of Sciences, U.S.A. Used with permission.

partly related to symptom severity; patients with mild or moderate symptoms receive little or no relief, but for patients with severe depression the benefit of medications is substantial (Fournier et al., 2010). So how do we treat drug-resistant forms of depression? Cognitive-behavioral therapy is generally about as effective as antidepressants, and when it was added to the usual treatment in resistant patients, depression scores improved by 50% or more in 46% of patients, compared with 22% in those who remained in typical treatment (Wiles et al., 2013). One thing that must be clear to you by now is how much therapeutic effectiveness depends on designing drugs to affect the right receptors and avoiding effects at sites that would produce side effects. This is the subject of the accompanying Application.

APPLICATION
Targeting Drugs to Specific Receptors

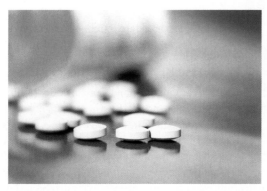

Source: iStock/BCFC.

As we have already mentioned, the most prescribed class of antidepressant medications today is the selective serotonin reuptake inhibitors (SSRIs). Although mood disorders are most commonly linked to serotonin (5-HT), abnormal function of other receptors and neurotransmitters can cause similar behavioral changes. For instance, there could be an imbalance of norepinephrine or dopamine. Newer antidepressant medications are designed to stimulate different classes of receptors or to bind to only one of several receptor subtypes. For instance, a class of drugs called SNRIs increases the amounts of both serotonin and norepinephrine, which is useful for individuals with depression as well as emotional pain. Examples of these drugs include Cymbalta, Effexor, and Pristiq. Another class is the NDRIs, a relatively new class of drugs that raise norepinephrine as well as dopamine levels. These drugs are useful for treating some types of depression as well as attention-deficit/ hyperactivity disorder (ADHD). Examples of this group include Focalin, Ritalin, Concerta, and Wellbutrin. One drug that targets a specific receptor subtype is the atypical antipsychotic

Pimavanserin (in clinical trials), which specifically treats psychosis associated with Parkinson's disease by stimulating 5-HT_{2A} receptors and leaving the other serotonin receptor subtypes alone (Friedman, 2013). Another drug, Cariprazine, stimulates the D_2 receptor family and not the D_1 subfamily, which improves mania symptoms of both schizophrenia and bipolar I (Tohen, 2015). One of the oddest atypical antidepressants is Remeron (mirtazapine), which is classified as a norepinephrine and specific serotonergic antidepressant (NaSSA). This drug enhances the release of norepinephrine, increases serotonin release by presynaptic neurons, and modulates serotonin receptors in a complex way: It blocks 5-HT2 and 5-HT3 receptors so that the increased serotonin can bind only to 5-HT1 receptors (Antilla & Leinonen, 2001). The 5-HT2 and 5-HT3 receptors are associated with anxiety, changes in appetite, sexual dysfunction, and memory problems, so targeting only the 5-HT1 receptors provides effective antidepressant relief without as many side effects as with SSRIs (Schreiber, Melon, & DeVry, 1998).

As we just indicated, there are many types of each receptor in your nervous system. You have at least seven different serotonin receptor families, two dopamine receptor families, and at least five norepinephrine receptors (two alpha and three beta). Many of these receptors are found not only in the brain but also throughout the body, and stimulating them broadly using tricyclic antidepressants, MAOIs, or even SSRIs triggers most of the unpleasant side effects of those drugs. The future of psychopharmacology will therefore be in designer drugs that interact only with a subset of receptors that match an individual's symptoms and neurobiology.

Electroconvulsive Therapy

In extreme cases of treatment nonresponse or because of suicidal behaviors, an alternative is electroconvulsive therapy. *Electroconvulsive therapy (ECT)* involves applying 70–130 volts of electricity to the head of an anesthetized patient, which produces a seizure accompanied by convulsive contractions of the neck and limbs and lasting about a half minute to a minute (Figure 14.19). Without the seizure activity in the brain that produces the convulsions, the treatment does not work. Within a few minutes, the patient is conscious and coherent, though perhaps a bit confused; the patient does not remember the experience. Usually ECT is administered two to three times a week for a total of 6–12 treatments.

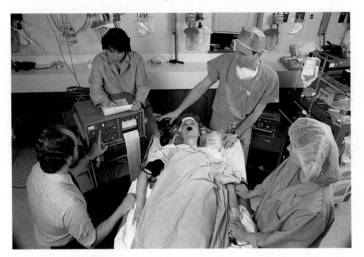

■ **FIGURE 14.19**   A Patient Being Readied for Electroconvulsive Therapy.

Source: James D. Wilson/Woodfin Camp & Associates.

ECT is the most controversial of the psychiatric therapies. Producing convulsions by sending a jolt of electricity through the brain *sounds* inhumane, and in fact the procedures used in the early days of ECT treatment often resulted in bone fractures and long-term memory deficits. Now patients are anesthetized and given muscle relaxants that eliminate injury and reduce emotional stress. The numbers of treatments and the voltage have been reduced, and stimulation is delivered in brief pulses rather than continuously. Though bilateral electrode placement produces a faster response that is desirable with suicidal patients, unilateral right hemisphere placement is usually favored because it minimizes cognitive side effects, such as temporary memory impairment (Kellner, Tobias, & Wiegand, 2010). These changes have made ECT safer and more effective (Weiner & Krystal, 1994). Follow-up studies indicate that memory and cognitive impairment induced by ECT dissipates within a few months (Crowe, 1984; Weeks, Freeman, & Kendell, 1980) and that cognitive performance even improves over pretreatment levels as the depression lifts (Sackeim et al., 1993). Brain scans and autopsies of patients and actual cell counts in animal subjects show no evidence of brain damage following ECT (reviewed in Devanand, Dwork, Hutchinson, Bolwig, & Sackheim, 1994).

ECT is usually reserved for patients who do not respond to the medications or who cannot take them due to extreme side effects or because of pregnancy. In a recent analysis of 13 studies that compared ECT with antidepressant drugs, 79% of patients responded to ECT, compared with 54% of patients treated with antidepressants (Pagnin, de Queiroz, Pini, & Cassano, 2004). ECT works especially well when depression or mania is accompanied by psychosis (Depression Guideline Panel, 1993; Potter & Rudorfer, 1993), and it works rapidly, which is beneficial to suicidal patients who cannot wait for weeks while a drug takes effect (Rudorfer, Henry, & Sackeim, 1997). The disadvantage of ECT is that its benefit is often short term, but the patient can usually be maintained on drug therapy once a round of ECT has been completed.

ECT is effective with depression, mania, and schizophrenia, which suggests that its effects are complex, and research bears this out. Several changes occur at the brain's synapses. Like the drugs, ECT increases the sensitivity of postsynaptic serotonin receptors (Mann, Arango, & Underwood, 1990); in addition, the sensitivity of autoreceptors on the terminals of norepinephrine- and dopamine-releasing neurons is reduced, so the release of those transmitters is increased. A temporary slowing of the EEG, which is correlated with therapeutic effectiveness, suggests that ECT synchronizes neuronal firing over large areas of the brain (Ishihara & Sasa, 1999; Sackeim et al., 1996). This reduced excitability is likely due to the fact that ECT increases diminished GABA concentrations (Sanacora et al., 2003). However, as you will see in the next section, both antidepressants and ECT now appear to trigger dramatic remodeling of the depressed brain.

Antidepressants, ECT, and Neural Plasticity

Although antidepressant drugs and ECT have been used to treat depression for more than half a century, we are not sure how they work. Most puzzling is the delay between neurotransmitter changes and symptom relief; hypotheses that changes in receptor sensitivity account for the delay have not been successful (Yamada, Yamada, & Higuchi, 2005). A promising lead is that antidepressant drugs, lithium, and ECT all increase neuronal birth rate in the hippocampus, at least in rodents and presumably in humans as well (Figure 14.20;

Inta et al., 2013; Mendez-David, Hen, Gardier, & David, 2013; Sairanen, Lucas, Ernfors, Castrén, & Castrén, 2005). Although increased neurogenesis can be detected within hours of antidepressant treatment, the time required for new hippocampal neurons to migrate to their new locations and form functional connections closely matches the delay in symptom improvement (Sairanen et al., 2005).

After new cell development was blocked by X radiation, antidepressants no longer had an effect in mice, suggesting that neurogenesis is required for antidepressant action (Santarelli et al., 2003). An increase in cell numbers is not the basis, however, because cell death also accelerates; some researchers have suggested that the therapeutic effect is due to the greater plasticity of new cells (Gould & Gross, 2002), a point we saw in Chapter 12 in relation to their lower threshold for LTP. However, when researchers used a drug instead of X radiation to block neurogenesis, antidepressant effect was not diminished (Bessa et al., 2009). All three of the antidepressant drugs used increased dendritic remodeling and synaptic contact; this led the researchers to conclude that antidepressant drugs work by enhancing plasticity rather than by promoting neurogenesis. There is additional evidence for a plasticity hypothesis: Both antidepressants and ECT modify activity in a large number of genes, especially in the hippocampus; most of those genes contribute to neural plasticity and neuron survival, as well as to neurogenesis (Altar et al., 2004; Yamada et al., 2005). Neurogenesis might contribute to antidepressant effect, but it appears that restoration of plasticity is more important.

Rhythms and Affective Disorders

As we mentioned earlier, several circadian rhythm genes are implicated in depression, so it should be no surprise that depressed people often have problems with their biological rhythms. The *circadian rhythm*—the one that is a day in length—tends to be phase advanced in patients with affective disorders; this means that the person feels sleepy early in the evening and then wakes up in the early morning hours, regardless of the previous evening's bedtime (Dew et al., 1996). The person also enters rapid eye movement sleep earlier in the night and spends more time in this state than normal (Kupfer, 1976). As you will learn in Chapter 15, *rapid eye movement (REM) sleep* is the stage of sleep during which dreaming occurs; the excess REM sleep is at the expense of the other stages of sleep. Patients with unipolar depression share this early onset of REM sleep with 70% of their relatives, and relatives with reduced REM latency are three times more likely to be depressed than relatives without reduced latency (Giles, Biggs, Rush, & Roffwarg, 1988).

? What are the roles of daily rhythms and seasons?

Circadian Rhythms and Antidepressant Therapy

Some patients who are unresponsive to antidepressant medication can get relief from their depression by readjusting their circadian rhythm. They can do this simply by staying up a half hour later each night until

---

■ **FIGURE 14.20**   Increased Neurogenesis in the Hippocampus During Antidepressant Treatment.

(a) Antidepressant treatment produced a 60% increase in neurogenesis, compared with administration of inert material (vehicle). (b) Brown dots are new cells (preneurons).

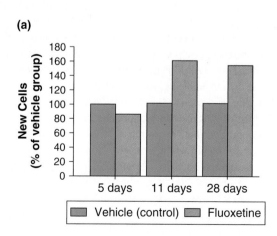

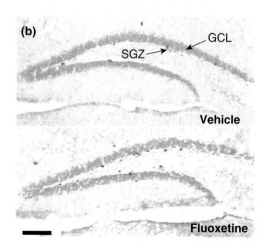

Source: From "Requirement of Hippocampal Neurogenesis of the Behavioral Effects of Antidepressants," by L. Santarelli et al., *Science, 301,* 805–809, fig. 2a and 2b, p. 806. © 2003. Reprinted with permission from AAAS.

they reach the desired bedtime. In some patients, this treatment results in a relief from depression that lasts for months (D. A. Sack, Nurnberger, Rosenthal, Ashburn, & Wehr, 1985).

Some depressed patients also benefit temporarily from sleep deprivation. This was initially seen with REM sleep deprivation, which is accomplished by waking the person every time the EEG indicates that sleep has moved into the REM stage (J. C. Wu & Bunney, 1990). Interestingly, most antidepressant drugs also suppress REM sleep (G. W. Vogel, Buffenstein, Minter, & Hennessey, 1990). Later research showed that depressed individuals also improve following non-REM sleep deprivation (Landsness, Goldstein, Peterson, Tononi, & Benca, 2011) or total overnight sleep deprivation (Giedke & Schwärzler, 2002). To find out why, researchers at Tufts University School of Medicine dosed mice with a drug that mimics adenosine, a compound that builds up in the brain during wakefulness and produces sleepiness. Twelve hours later the mice showed increased resistance to treatments that produce depressive-like behavior (Hines, Schmitt, Hines, Moss, & Haydon, 2013). The mice slept normally, perhaps because the drug targeted only the A1 type of adenosine receptor; a similar drug might provide humans the antidepressant benefits of sleep deprivation without the sleepiness.

Seasonal Affective Disorder

There is another rhythm that is important in affective disorders; some people's depression rises and falls with the seasons and is known as *seasonal affective disorder (SAD).* This is on a *circannual rhythm,* one that follows the changes of the seasons. Most SAD patients are more depressed during the fall and winter, and then improve in the spring and summer, which parallels onset for schizophrenia as well (Owens & McGorry, 2003). Others are more depressed in the summer and feel better during the winter. Members of either group may experience a mild mania-like activation called hypomania during their "good" season. While depressed, they usually sleep excessively, and they often have increased appetites, especially for carbohydrates, and gain weight. The length of day and the amount of natural light appear to be important in winter depression; symptoms improve when the patient travels farther south (or north, if the person lives in the Southern Hemisphere) even for a few days, and some report increased depression during cloudy periods in the summer or when they move to an office with fewer windows. Summer depression appears to be temperature related: Traveling to a cooler climate, spending time in an air-conditioned house, and taking several cold showers a day improves the symptoms. About 10% of all cases of affective disorder are seasonal, and 71% of SAD patients are women (Faedda et al., 1993). Although seasonal influences on affective disorder have been known for 2,000 years and documented since the mid-1850s, summer depression has received relatively little attention, so we will restrict our discussion to winter depression.

■ **FIGURE 14.21**   A Woman Uses a High-Intensity Light to Treat Her Seasonal Affective Disorder.

Source: Science & Society Picture Library / Contributor/SSPL/Getty.

A treatment for winter depression is *phototherapy*—having the patient sit in front of high-intensity lights for a couple of hours or more a day (Figure 14.21). Patients begin to respond after two to four days of treatment with light that approximates sunlight from a window on a clear spring day; they relapse in about the same amount of time following withdrawal of treatment (Rosenthal et al., 1985). The fact that midday phototherapy is effective suggests that the increased amount of light is more important than extending the length of the shortened winter day; the observation that suicide rate is related to a locale's *amount* of clear sunlight rather than the number of hours of daylight supports this conclusion (Wehr et al., 1986). Phototherapy resets the circadian rhythm (Lewy, Sack, Miller, & Hoban, 1987), so it is also helpful with circadian rhythm problems including jet lag, delayed sleep syndrome, and difficulties associated with shift work (Blehar & Rosenthal, 1989).

Physiological mechanisms for disorders of circadian and circannual rhythms include both neurotransmitter and prefrontal cortex changes. Lowered serotonin activity is involved in winter depression. Drugs that increase serotonin activity alleviate the depression and reduce carbohydrate craving (O'Rourke, Wurtman, Wurtman, Chebli, & Gleason, 1989). As we saw in Chapter 5, eating carbohydrates increases brain serotonin levels. So, rather than thinking that SAD patients lack willpower when they binge on junk food and gain weight, it might be more accurate to think of them as self-medicating with carbohydrates. But what areas of the brain change seasonally? A recent study suggests that the dorsolateral prefrontal cortex contains genes activated on a seasonal basis (Lim et al., 2017).

Bipolar Disorder and Related Disorders

The mystery of major depression is far from solved, but bipolar disorder is even more puzzling. Bipolar patients vary greatly in their symptoms: The depressive cycle usually lasts longer than mania, but either may predominate. There are three major forms of bipolar disorder: bipolar I (major depressive episodes with occasional manic episodes), bipolar II (major depression with mild hypomanic episodes), and cyclothymic disorder (frequent alternation between hypomanic and mild depressive episodes that are not severe enough for a diagnosis of bipolar II). Some patients cycle between depression and mania regularly (this is called *rapid cycling*), whereas others are unpredictable; cycles usually vary from weeks to months in duration, although some patients switch as frequently as every 48 hours (Bunney, Murphy, Goodwin, & Borge, 1972). Stress often precipitates the transition from depression into mania, followed by a more spontaneous change back to depression; the prospect of discharge from the hospital is particularly stressful and often will precipitate the switch into mania. However, as bipolar disorder progresses, manic episodes tend to occur independently of life's stresses (P. W. Gold et al., 1988).

It appears that bipolar disorder involves increased sensitivity to dopamine and either decreased sensitivity to serotonin or a more general dysregulation in the dopaminergic system (Miklowitz & Johnson, 2006). Drugs used to treat the disorder include several atypical antipsychotics, as well as carbamazepine, valproate, and lithium. Carbamazepine and valproate stabilize electrical activity in the brain and are typically used as anticonvulsants for the treatment of epilepsy. *Lithium,* a metal administered in the form of lithium carbonate, is the medication of choice for bipolar illness; it is most effective during the manic phase, but it also prevents further depressive episodes. Examination of lithium's effects has not identified any critical neurotransmitters, partly because lithium affects several transmitter systems (Worley, Heller, Snyder, & Baraban, 1988). It may be that lithium stabilizes neurotransmitter and receptor systems to prevent the large swings seen in manic-depressive cycling; its dual role as an antidepressant argues for a normalizing effect rather than a directional one (Gitlin & Altshuler, 1997). Closer examination, however, has revealed a specific effect on mania; lithium and valproate indirectly inhibit protein kinase C (PKC), a family of intracellular messengers that regulate neural excitability. The breast cancer drug tamoxifen is used to block estrogen receptors, but it also inhibits PKC. In a phase 2 clinical trial, 90% of patients receiving tamoxifen with lithium were considered in remission, versus 55% receiving lithium alone (Amrollahi et al., 2011). Tamoxifen itself may not be practical as a treatment for bipolar disorder because it antagonizes estrogen activity; if the drug continues to prove effective, an alternative that targets PKC only will have to be found.

? What brain irregularities are involved in affective disorders?

Brain Anomalies in Affective Disorders

As with schizophrenia, affective disorders are associated with structural abnormalities in several brain areas. Again, a larger ventricle size suggests loss of brain tissue, but the reductions are small and are not always found (Depue & Iacono, 1989). A review of numerous studies of depression reveals volume deficits in prefrontal areas, especially the dorsolateral cortex and the anterior cingulate cortex as well as in the hippocampus, but an increased volume in the amygdala (R. J. Davidson, Pizzagalli, Nitschke, & Putnam, 2002). Volume reduction apparently precedes depression rather than being a degenerative consequence of it; it is evident at the time of patients' first episode, and it can even be detected in the nondepressed offspring of patients (M. C. Chen, Hamilton, & Gotlib, 2010; Peterson et al., 2009; Zou et al., 2010).

These structural alterations are accompanied by changes in activity level. Not surprisingly, total brain activity is reduced in unipolar patients (Sackeim et al., 1990) and in bipolar patients when they are depressed (Baxter et al., 1989). Gray matter is particularly reduced in the hippocampus, the orbitofrontal cortex that regulates emotions (Figure 14.22; Egger et al., 2008),

■ **FIGURE 14.22** Reduction in Gray Matter in Elderly Depressed Patients.

Elderly patients with depression exhibited significant declines in gray matter in the amygdala (a), orbitofrontal cortex (b), and hippocampus (b, c). Yellow indicates severity of loss compared to elderly patients without depression.

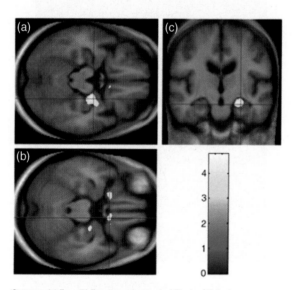

Sources: (a) From "A Functional Anatomical Study of Unipolar Depression," by W. C. Drevets et al., *Journal of Neuroscience, 12,* pp. 3628–3641. © 1992 Society for Neuroscience. Used with permission. (b) From "Reduction of Prefrontal Cortex Glucose Metabolism Common to Three Types of Depression," by L. R. Baxter et al., 1999, *Archives of General Psychiatry, 46* (14), pp. 243–249.

■ **FIGURE 14.23**   Increased Activity in the Ventral Prefrontal Cortex (PFC) and Amygdala in Depression.

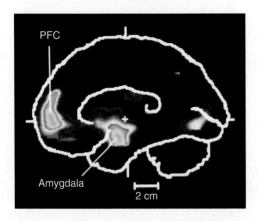

Source: From "A Functional Anatomical Study of Unipolar Depression," by W. C. Drevets et al., *Journal of Neuroscience, 12,* pp. 3628–3641. © 1992 Society for Neuroscience. Used with permission.

■ **FIGURE 14.24**   Glucose Metabolism Increase During Mania in a Rapid-Cycling Bipolar Patient.

The middle row shows the sudden increase in activity during a manic episode, just a day after the previous scan during depression. In the bottom row, the patient had returned to the depressed state.

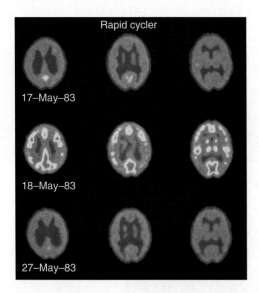

Source: From "Cerebral Metabolic Rates for Glucose in Mood Disorders: Studies With Positron Emission Tomography and Fluorodeoxyglucose F18," by L. R. Baxter et al., 1985, *Archives of General Psychiatry, 42,* pp. 441–447.

basal forebrain (Ribiez et al., 2013), prefrontal cortex, and cingulate cortex (Arnone, McIntosh, Ebmeier, Munafò, & Anderson, 2012). These decreases in brain tissue volume have been postulated to be predictors not only for depression but also for the likelihood that the person will improve following antidepressant treatment (Ribiez et al.). What *is* surprising is that some areas are *more* active in depressed patients. In unipolar depression, blood flow is higher in the amygdala and a frontal area connected to the amygdala called the *ventral prefrontal cortex* (Figure 14.23). The ventral prefrontal area may also be a "depression switch," because activation comes and goes with bouts of depression. The amygdala continues to be active between episodes and returns to normal only after the remission of symptoms. Activity in the amygdala corresponds to the *trait* of depression—the continuing disorder—whereas activation of the ventral prefrontal area indicates the *state* of depression, which subsides from time to time in some individuals (Drevets, 2001; Drevets et al., 1992; Drevets & Raichle, 1995).

It is also not surprising that during a manic episode, brain metabolism increases from its depressed level by 4%–36% (Figure 14.24; Baxter et al., 1989). The *subgenual prefrontal cortex* is particularly interesting because it has been suggested as a possible "switch" controlling bipolar cycling (Figure 14.25). Its metabolic activity is reduced during both unipolar and bipolar depression, but increases during manic episodes (Drevets et al., 1997). The structure is a part of the cingulate cortex, located at the midline; it is in a good position to act as a bipolar switch, because it has extensive connections to emotion centers such as the amygdala and the lateral hypothalamus and it helps regulate neurotransmitters involved in affective disorders. Imaging studies also implicate the anterior parts of the limbic system (Strakowski, 2011). Even when bipolar subjects were asymptomatic and working on a cognitive task, activity increased in limbic and associated areas (Strakowski, Adler, Holland, Mills, & DelBello, 2004). The researchers suggested that individuals with bipolar I disorder are unable to suppress emotion networks during emotionally neutral activities.

Both depressed and bipolar patients have anomalies in functional brain connectivity. Connectivity is reduced in the cortex, corpus callosum, and thalamus in individuals with bipolar disorder (Barysheva, Jahanshad, Foland-Ross, Altshuler, & Thompson, 2013). In depression, increased as well as decreased connectivity has been reported. For example, one study reported decreased connectivity between frontal areas and the ventral striatum, but increased connectivity between frontal areas and the dorsal striatum (Furman, Hamilton, & Gotlib, 2011). Treatment has been shown to increase deficient connectivity between some areas (Heller et al., 2013) and to decrease excess connectivity in others (Perrin et al., 2012). In both cases, the changes in connectivity were accompanied by symptom improvement.

Suicide

Suicide accounts for more deaths than homicide or war; it is the 13th leading cause of death worldwide and the 4th among those aged 15–44 years (World Health Organization, 2002). Ninety percent of people who attempt suicide have a diagnosable psychiatric illness; mood disorder alone accounts for 60% of all completed suicides (Figure 14.26; Mann, 2003). Bipolar patients are most at risk; about

■ **FIGURE 14.25**   Activity in the Subgenual Prefrontal Cortex in Depression and Mania.

(a) The dark areas (at the end of the red lines) indicate decreased activity during depression in the subgenual prefrontal cortex.
(b) Comparison of groups shows that activity in the subgenual PFC is lower during depression and higher during mania, which suggests that it controls cycling between depression and mania.

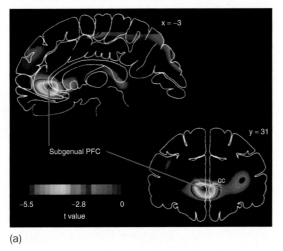

(a)

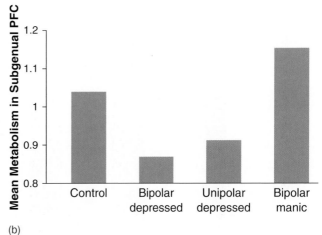

(b)

Sources: (a) From "Subgenual Prefrontal Cortex Abnormalities in Mood Disorders," by W. C. Drevets et al., *Nature, 386*, 824–827. © 1997 Macmillian Publishing Inc. (b) From "Neurimaging and Neuropathological Studies of Depression: Implications for the Cognitive-Emotional Features of Mood Disorders," by W. C. Drevets, *Current Opinion in Neurobiology, 11*, pp. 240–249, fig. 4b. © 2001 with kind permission of Elsevier.

20% of people who have been hospitalized for bipolar disorder commit suicide. According to the *stress-diathesis model,* the suicidal individual has a predisposition, known as a diathesis, and then stress such as a worsening psychiatric condition acts as an environmental "straw that breaks the camel's back" (Mann, 2003). The stresses can be physical, as well as psychological, as the accompanying *In the News* feature illustrates.

The predisposition is at least partly genetic; a study of depressed patients located six chromosome sites that were associated with suicidal risk but independent of susceptibility for mood disorders (Zubenko et al., 2004). Psychiatric patients who attempt suicide also are more likely to have low levels of the serotonin metabolite 5-hydroxyindoleacetic acid (5-HIAA) than non-attempters, which means that their serotonin activity is particularly decreased. When a group of patients at risk for suicide was followed for one year, 20% of those who were below the group median in 5-HIAA level had committed suicide; none of the patients above the median had (Träskman, Åsberg, Bertilsson, & Sjöstrand, 1981). Other studies have confirmed the association between lowered serotonin and suicidality (see Figure 14.27; Mann, 2003; Roy, DeJong, & Linnoila, 1989; M. Stanley, Stanley, Traskman-Bendz, Mann, & Meyendorff, 1986). Lowered 5-HIAA is found in suicide attempters with a variety of disorders and probably reflects impulsiveness rather than the patient's specific psychiatric diagnosis (Mann et al., 1990; M. Stanley et al., 1986; Träskman et al., 1981); this view was supported by a later study in which impulsive suicide attempters were found to have

■ **FIGURE 14.26**   Suicide Rates for Three Disorders in Men and Women.

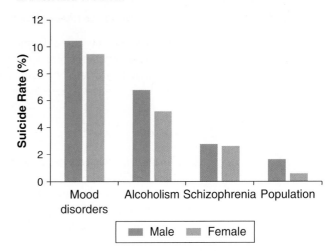

Source: From "Catamnestic Long-Term Study on the Course of Life and Aging of Schizophrenics," by L. Ciompi, 1980, *Schizophrenia Bulletin, 6*, pp. 607–618, fig. 2, p. 610. Copyright © Oxford University Press. Used with permission.

■ **FIGURE 14.27**   Serotonin Levels and Suicide.

Serotonin level, as assessed by the metabolite 5-HIAA, was lower in depressed patients who attempted suicide than in those who did not, and even lower in those who reattempted.

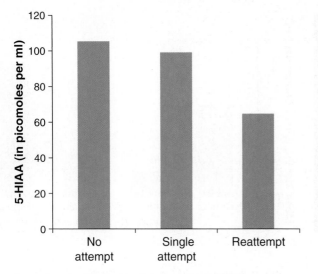

Source: Based on data from Roy, DeJong, and Linnoila (1989).

lower 5-HIAA than either nonimpulsive attempters or controls (Spreux-Varoquaux et al., 2001).

However, antidepressants *can* increase the risk of suicide. A variety of explanations have been offered, including the agitation that often accompanies SSRI use (Fergusson et al., 2005) and disappointment over slow improvement and side effects (Mann, 2003). Concern about the vulnerability of children and adolescents resulted in a 22% decrease in SSRI prescriptions for youths in the United States and the Netherlands; unfortunately, this turned out to be a case of throwing out the baby with the bathwater, since youthful suicides increased 14% in the United States in one year and 49% in the Netherlands over two years (Gibbons et al., 2007). Some observers believe that the suicidal acts of individuals on antidepressants is the result of rebounding energy levels, which allow those with suicidal ideation the ability to carry out suicidal thoughts. Rather than reducing prescriptions wholesale, therapists need to be selective and to monitor their patients for suicidal tendencies.

Research has identified heritable characteristics that distinguish people at risk for suicide from others, referred to as *endophenotypes*. The most reproduced personality indicators have been impulsivity and aggression (Courtet, Gottesman, Jollant, & Gould, 2011). Disadvantageous decision making, indicated by measures such as the Iowa Gambling Task, suggest a prefrontal deficiency, and this has been verified in terms of reduced neural activity and altered prefrontal serotonergic functioning. The heritability of suicidal behavior (ideation as well as attempts) has been estimated in various studies at 38%–55% (Brent & Melhem, 2008). Locating genes that predispose a person to suicide has been difficult, in part because of confounding with so many instigators to suicide; these include mental illness, physical illness, and life disappointments. Most studies have pointed to serotonin-related genes and genes involved with brain-derived neurotrophic factors, and a few other genes have been implicated, but there has been little confirmation (S.-J. Tsai, Hong, & Liou, 2011).

CONCEPT CHECK

Take a Minute to Check Your Knowledge and Understanding

- State the monoamine hypothesis; what is the evidence for it?
- How is affective disorder related to circadian rhythms?
- What brain differences are involved in the affective disorders?
- What are some of the factors in suicide?

Anxiety, Trauma, and Stress-Related Disorders

As discussed in Chapter 8, anxiety is the anticipation of some future threat. Anxiety disorders include several illnesses. The major ones—phobia, generalized anxiety, and panic disorder—have lifetime risks of about 13%, 9%, and 6.8%, respectively (Kessler et al., 2012). But their significance lies less in their prevalence than in the disruptiveness of their symptoms. The panic disorder patient or the phobic patient may be unable to venture out of the house, much less hold down a job.

Heredity

Family and twin studies indicate that the anxiety disorders are genetically influenced, with heritability ranging between 20% and 47%, depending on the disorder (Abramowitz, Taylor, & McKay, 2009; P. E. Arnold,

---

IN THE NEWS

HEIGHTENED SUICIDE RISK AFTER CONCUSSION

Concerns about the cognitive and emotional impacts of brain injury have received a lot of public attention due to well-publicized studies of retired National Football League (NFL) players and military veterans who had been injured due to improvised explosive devices. It now seems clear that the type of repeated injuries that occur in contact sports such as football can result in chronic traumatic encephalopathy (CTE), a progressive degenerative disease of the brain resulting from trauma (Kutner, 2017). One possible effect researchers are investigating is whether head injury increases a person's risk for suicide. Most media attention has focused on the suicides of retired NFL players such as Junior Seau and Dave Duerson, whose brains showed signs of CTE, but evidence is accumulating from other populations to support a suicide–brain injury link. A study of veterans who had experienced a concussion or cranial fracture found that they were twice as likely to commit suicide as other veterans (Brenner, Ignacio, & Blow, 2011), and a 20-year study reported a tripling of the suicide rate in civilians who had a concussion (Fralick, Thiruchelvam, Tien, & Redelmeier, 2016). Although more investigations are needed, the current data suggest that people who have experienced even one brain injury need to be monitored for long-term affective changes to prevent suicide.

THOUGHT QUESTIONS

1. What evidence has shown a link between head injury and suicide risk?

2. How do the types of head injuries experienced by football players differ from those experienced by military veterans and civilians who did not play a contact sport?

3. Which information presented here do you find most convincing of a connection between head injuries and suicides?

For the news story, visit edge.sagepub.com/garrett5e and select the Chapter 14 study resources.

Zai, & Richter, 2004; Hettema, Neale, & Kendler, 2001). Understanding the hereditary underpinnings of anxiety is difficult because of significant genetic overlap with other disorders. More than 90% of individuals with anxiety disorders have a history of other psychiatric problems (Kaufman & Charney, 2000). The overlap with mood disorders is particularly strong; 50%–60% of patients with major depression also have a history of one or more anxiety disorders (Kaufman & Charney), and panic disorder is found in 16% of bipolar patients (Doughty, Wells, Joyce, Olds, & Walsh, 2004). Some neural commonality between these two groups is suggested by the effectiveness of antidepressants in treating both mood disorders and anxiety disorders. The anxieties themselves appear to fall into three genetically related clusters, with generalized anxiety, panic, and agoraphobia (fear of crowds and open places) in one group; animal phobias and situational phobias in the second; and social phobia overlapping genetically with both groups (Hettema, Prescott, Myers, Neale, & Kendler, 2005).

 What causes anxiety disorders?

Genetic research has most often implicated genes responsible for serotonin production, serotonin reuptake, and various subtypes of serotonin receptors (reviewed in P. E. Arnold et al., 2004; Rothe et al., 2004; You, Hu, Chen, & Zhang, 2005). Other leads include genes for monoamine oxidase (Tadic et al., 2003), for the adenosine receptor (P. E. Arnold et al.; Lam, Hong, & Tsai, 2005), and for cholecystokinin and its receptor (P. E. Arnold et al.).

Generalized Anxiety, Panic Disorder, and Phobia

Anxiety is often confused with fear; however, as we saw in Chapter 8, fear is a reaction to real objects or events present in the environment, whereas anxiety involves anticipation of events or an inappropriate reaction to the environment. A person with generalized anxiety has a feeling of stress and unease most of the time and overreacts to stressful conditions. In panic disorder, the person has a sudden and intense attack of anxiety, with symptoms such as rapid breathing, high heart rate, and feelings of impending disaster. A person with a phobia experiences fear or stress when confronted with a situation—for instance, crowds, heights, enclosed spaces, open spaces, or specific objects such as dogs or snakes.

Neurotransmitters

Benzodiazepines were the most frequently used anxiolytic (antianxiety) drugs in the past (Costall & Naylor, 1992) but now are considered a second line of defense because of their addiction potential. You may remember from our earlier discussion of drugs in Chapter 5 that benzodiazepines increase receptor sensitivity to the inhibitory transmitter gamma-aminobutyric acid (GABA), which is a major neurotransmitter in anxiety. A deficit in benzodiazepine receptors may be one cause of anxiety disorder. Marczynski and Urbancic (1988) injected pregnant cats with a benzodiazepine tranquilizer. When the offspring were one year old, they were restless and appeared anxious in novel situations. When their brains were studied later, several areas of the brain had compensated for the tranquilizer by reducing the number of benzodiazepine receptors.

Anxiety also appears to involve lower activity at serotonin synapses. Antianxiety drugs initially suppress serotonin activity, but then they apparently produce a compensatory increase. The idea that a serotonergic increase is involved in anxiety reduction is supported by the fact that antidepressants are now the drug of choice for treating anxiety and related disorders.

Posttraumatic Stress Disorder

Posttraumatic stress disorder (PTSD) is a prolonged stress reaction to a traumatic event; it is typically characterized by recurrent thoughts and images (flashbacks), nightmares, lack of concentration, and overreactivity to environmental stimuli, such as loud noises. Because of recent news coverage, we usually associate PTSD with combat experiences, but it can be triggered by all kinds of trauma, including robbery, sexual assault, hostage situations, and automobile accidents. Men are more often exposed to such traumas, but women are almost four times as likely to develop PTSD when they do experience trauma (Fullerton et al., 2001). PTSD symptoms are resistant to traditional drug and psychotherapy treatments; an alternative approach is exposure therapy, which allows the individual to confront anxiety-provoking stimuli in the safety of the therapist's office. Exposure therapy is essentially an extinction process, and fear memories are notoriously resistant to extinction, especially in the 30% of people who have the *VAL66MET* allele (which we saw is also involved in depression). We know this gene plays a causal role in fear extinction, because when it was inserted into mice they showed the same increased resistance (Soliman et al., 2010). Brain imaging of human subjects during extinction trials showed why; connections between the prefrontal cortex and the amygdala that are important in fear conditioning and extinction were hypoactive in carriers of the allele.

In their search for better therapies, researchers are resorting to novel approaches; some, for example, believe that therapists could take a lesson from the phenomenon of reconsolidation that you learned about in Chapter 12. A team led by Daniela Schiller (2010) used a mild electric shock to condition an emotional reaction (measured by skin conductance response) to a blue square. A day later, the response was extinguished by repeatedly presenting the blue square alone. However, two subgroups of subjects received a "reminder" of the fear memory, one 10 minutes before extinction began and the other six hours before; the reminder was intended to start reconsolidation, a window of opportunity that was expected to remain open during extinction for the 10-minute group but to be closed by the time the six-hour group's extinction trials began. It worked: The skin conductance response was almost entirely absent in the 10-minute group but had recovered to near training levels in the other two groups; the effect persisted for a year. Researchers hope this technique of *fear erasure* can be used to help relieve PTSD sufferers of their lingering fear and anxiety.

Anomalies in Brain Functioning

For the most part, the various anxiety disorders share a commonality of functional brain anomalies. Not surprisingly, the amygdala is hyperresponsive; the anterior cingulate cortex is hyperactive in general anxiety, panic disorder, and phobias, and the insular cortex is overly responsive in phobias and PTSD (Etkin & Wager, 2007; Morey et al., 2012; Shin & Liberzon, 2010). PTSD is distinguished by *decreased* activity in the medial prefrontal cortex and, according to some studies, in the hippocampus. Some structures have been reported to be smaller in people with anxiety disorders, particularly in those with PTSD. Researchers have usually assumed these variations were the result of the anxiety disorders, but we will see that this is not always the case.

Whether trauma is followed by PTSD is unrelated to either the severity of the traumatic event or the individual's distress at the time (Harvey & Bryant, 2002; Shalev et al., 2000); the key apparently is the person's vulnerability. Mark Gilbertson and his colleagues (2002) used magnetic resonance imaging to measure hippocampal volumes in Vietnam combat veterans and their noncombat identical twins. Those who suffered from PTSD had smaller hippocampi than did PTSD-free veterans, as expected, but so did the PTSD subjects' noncombat twins (Figure 14.28). Hippocampal reduction is often associated with childhood abuse, and Elizabeth Binder and her coworkers (2008) found that previously abused individuals were twice as likely to succumb to PTSD following traumatic events. Two mutations of the *FKBP5* gene are more common among PTSD patients who were abused and apparently contribute to the vulnerability (Binder et al.). A smaller anterior cingulate cortex (ACC) may also be a vulnerability factor. After the Japanese earthquake and tsunami in 2011, researchers at Tohoku University asked 42 local residents who had previously received MRI scans to return and have their brains imaged again. Though none of

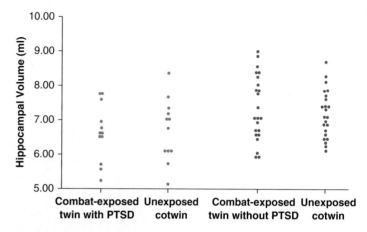

■ **FIGURE 14.28**   Hippocampal Volume Is Reduced in Combat Veterans and Their Twins.

Similar reduction in unexposed identical twins of PTSD patients suggests that hippocampal reduction is a predisposing factor.

Source: From "Smaller Hippocampal Volume Predicts Pathologic Vulnerability to Psychological Trauma," by M. W. Gilbertson et al., *Nature Neuroscience, 5*, pp. 1242–1247. Copyright © 2002 Nature Publishing Group. Used with permission.

the residents had full-blown PTSD, those with the highest scores had lower gray matter volumes in the orbitofrontal cortex and in the ACC, compared with control subjects (Sekiguchi et al., 2013). Reduced volume in the orbitofrontal cortex had occurred since the first scan, but the high-scoring subjects had lower ACC volume at the time of the first scan; this suggests that a smaller ACC is a vulnerability factor for PTSD. This makes sense, because the ACC is involved in the processing of fear and anxiety and in eliminating fear-related memories.

Of course, these structures operate as part of circuits, rather than in isolation from each other or other parts of the brain. Chad Sylvester and his colleagues (2012) have identified four networks whose faulty performance they believe contributes to anxiety (Figure 14.29). The *ventral attention network* orients to attention-demanding stimuli and in people with anxiety disorders contributes to excessively stimulus-driven attention. Once a response to a situation is formulated, a *salience network* provides error detection by comparing the intended response with appropriate responses. A mismatch would signal the need for increased executive control, the domain of the *frontoparietal network*. Finally, the *default mode network* engages in self-monitoring, future planning, and emotion regulation; underactivity in this network results in poor emotional regulation.

Take a Minute to Check Your Knowledge and Understanding

- What neurotransmitter deviations are involved in anxiety disorders?
- What brain anomalies are associated with anxiety disorders?
- What are the environmental, physiological, and genetic contributors to PTSD?

Personality Disorders

The personality disorders are a group of 10 related disorders characterized by a relatively inflexible pattern of behavior that is different from one's peers, has an onset around puberty to young adulthood, and causes distress or inability to function in society. Typical behavior patterns include distrust and suspicion (paranoid), unstable social and interpersonal relationships (asocial, avoidant, dependent, borderline), problems with control and attention (obsessive-compulsive), and emotional dysfunctions (histrionic, narcissistic). An abnormal psychology course will likely cover most of these personality disorders, but in this text we

■ **FIGURE 14.29**   Networks Involved in Anxiety.

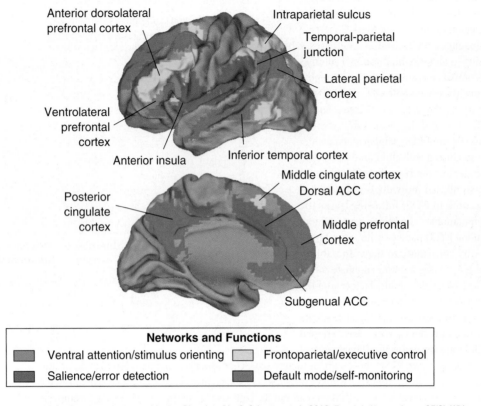

Source: From "Functional Network Dysfunction in Anxiety and Anxiety Disorders," by C. Sylvester et al., 2012, *Trends in Neuroscience, 35*(9). With permission from Elsevier.

will concentrate on two types: obsessive-compulsive disorder and related disorders, and borderline personality disorder.

? What is obsessive-compulsive disorder, and what causes it?

Obsessive-Compulsive Disorder

Obsessive-compulsive disorder (OCD) consists of two behaviors, obsessions and compulsions, which occur in the same person. The disorder affects about 2.6% of the population over their lifetimes (Kessler et al., 2012). An *obsession* is a recurring, uncontrollable thought; a person may be annoyed by a tune that mentally replays over and over or by troubling thoughts such as wishing harm to another person. Normal people have similar thoughts, but for the obsessive individual, the experience is extreme and feels completely out of control. Just as the obsessive individual is a slave to thoughts, the compulsive individual is a slave to actions. *Compulsions* are ritualistic behaviors that must be done to remove the anxiety of the obsession, such as touching a door frame three times before passing through the door, endless bathing and hand washing, or checking to see if appliances are turned off and the door is locked (Rapoport, 1991). Prominent examples of this disorder are depicted in the films *As Good as It Gets* and *The Aviator* and in the television show *Monk*.

One psychiatrist described a patient who tired of returning home to check whether she had turned her appliances off and solved the problem by taking her coffeemaker and iron to work with her (Begley & Biddle, 1996). The playwright and humorist David Sedaris (1998) wrote that his short walk home from school during childhood took a full hour because of his compulsion to stop every few feet and press his nose to the hood of a particular car, lick a certain mailbox, or touch a specific leaf that demanded his attention. Once home, he had to make the rounds of several rooms, kissing, touching, and rearranging various objects before he could enter his own room. About a fourth of OCD patients have a family member with OCD, suggesting a genetic involvement; boys are afflicted more often than girls, but the ratio levels off in adulthood (Swedo, Rapoport, Leonard, Lenane, & Cheslow, 1989).

What about individuals who are obsessed with neatness, organization, and generally making sure that their world is "where it should be?" This is not OCD, but a related disorder called obsessive-compulsive personality disorder (OCPD), in which the person does not experience the distress and anxiety over obsessively cleaning and organizing that someone with OCD would experience. Instead, those feelings of perfection are perceived to be rational and reasonable. OCPD is much harder to treat, compared to OCD.

Imaging studies of OCD patients reveal increased activity in the orbitofrontal cortex, especially the left orbital gyrus, and in the caudate nuclei (Whiteside, Port, & Abramowitz, 2004). It is unclear whether these increases cause OCD or are merely activation increases associated with symptoms of OCD, such as worry. However, both drug treatment and behavior therapy reduce activation of the caudate nucleus and, in at least one study, the orbital gyrus (Figure 14.30; Porto et al., 2009; J. M. Schwartz et al., 1996; Swedo, Schapiro, et al., 1989). White matter reductions indicate that there are deficient connections between the cingulate gyrus and a circuit involving the basal ganglia, thalamus, and cortex, which apparently result in a loss of impulse control (Insel, 1992; Szeszko et al., 2005). An indication of dysfunction in this network is that orbitofrontal activity does not increase when OCD patients are required to reverse a previously correct choice; their unaffected relatives show the same deficit, suggesting that it is genetic (Chamberlain et al., 2008).

OCD occurs with several diseases that damage the basal ganglia (H. L. Leonard et al., 1992), which, you will remember, are involved in motor activity. There is growing evidence that the disorder can be triggered in children by a bacterial infection that results in an autoimmune attack on the basal ganglia; vulnerability to the immune malfunction apparently is hereditary (P. D. Arnold & Richter, 2001; P. E. Arnold et al., 2004). OCD has also been reported in cases of head injury (McKeon, McGuffin, & Robinson, 1984). Two of the most famous obsessive-compulsive individuals had a strong germ phobia (called mysophobia): the multimillionaire Howard Hughes (R. Fowler, 1986) and the star of the television show *Deal or No Deal,* comedian Howie Mandel (Mandel, 2010). In Hughes's case, some signs of disorder during childhood and his mother's obsessive concern with germs suggest either genetic vulnerability or environmental influence. However, symptoms of OCD did not begin until after a series of airplane crashes and automobile accidents that left him almost unrecognizable (Figure 14.31). When a business associate died, Hughes gave explicit instructions that flowers for the funeral were to be delivered by an independent messenger who would not have any contact with the florist or with Hughes's office—even to the point of sending a bill—to prevent "backflow" of germs (Bartlett & Steele, 1979). Assistants were required to handle his papers with gloves, sometimes several pairs, and he in turn grasped them with a tissue. He instructed his assistants not to touch him, talk directly to him, or even look at him; his defense for this behavior was that everybody carries germs and he wanted to avoid germs (R. Fowler).

■ **FIGURE 14.30**   Brain Structures Involved in Obsessive-Compulsive Disorder.

Scans of OCD patients show that (a) activity is elevated in the caudate nucleus (a part of the basal ganglia) and in the orbital gyrus, and that (b) behavior therapy reduces this activity in the caudate nucleus.

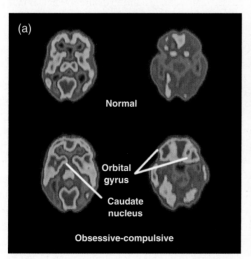
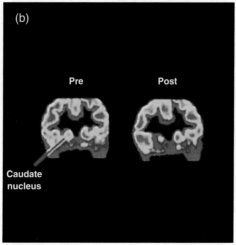

Sources: (a) From "Local Cerebral Glucose Metabolic Rates in Obsessive Compulsive Disorder," by L. R. Baxter et al., 1987, *Archives of General Psychiatry, 44*(14), pp. 211–218. (b) From "Systematic Changes in Cerebral Glucose Metabolic Rate After Successful Behavior Modification Treatment of Obsessive-Compulsive Disorder," by J. M. Schwartz et al., 1996, *Archives of General Psychiatry, 53*(14), pp. 109–113.

■ **FIGURE 14.31**   Howard Hughes.

Hughes was an extraordinarily successful businessman and dashing man-about-Hollywood, but he spent his later years crippled by symptoms of OCD. His life was documented in the Warner Brothers film *The Aviator*.

Source: Bettmann/Getty Images.

■ **FIGURE 14.32**   Excessive Grooming and the *Sapap3* Gene.

The mouse lacking the *Sapap3* gene (top) has groomed to the point of creating lesions on the neck and face and even damaging the eye.

Source: Courtesy of Jing Lu, Jeff Welch, and Guoping Feng.

Researchers believe that OCD patients are high in serotonergic activity. This was suggested by the fact that people with OCD are inhibited in action and feel guilty about aggressive impulses; sociopaths, by contrast, feel no guilt after committing impulsive crimes, and they have lowered serotonin activity. But the only drugs that consistently improve OCD symptoms are antidepressants that inhibit serotonin reuptake (Insel, Zohar, Benkelfat, & Murphy, 1990). So, if OCD patients do have high serotonergic activity, then reuptake inhibitors must work by causing a compensatory reduction in activity; there is some evidence that treatment does decrease the sensitivity of serotonin receptors (Insel et al., 1990), but the nature of serotonin involvement remains uncertain (Graybiel & Rauch, 2000).

Patient response to serotonin reuptake inhibitors is usually only partial, and some patients do not respond at all; a third of these patients benefit from antipsychotics, and an antiglutamate drug produces modest relief (Abramowitz et al., 2009), suggesting the involvement of these transmitters. For treatment-resistant patients, psychosurgery is an option. Forty-seven percent of patients went into remission following cingulotomy, which involves lesioning the ACC, and another 22% improved (Sheth et al., 2013). A less drastic procedure is deep brain stimulation (DBS), targeting the internal capsule, a bundle of fibers that connect the frontal lobe with the thalamus and other areas. A DBS device was approved by the U.S. Food and Drug Administration (2009) after it produced a 40% reduction in symptoms in OCD patients.

A meta-analysis of 113 studies found associations with two serotonin genes and, in males only, two genes involved in degradation of dopamine and serotonin (S. Taylor, 2013). There were trends for two dopamine-related genes and a glutamate-related gene, but these were not statistically significant. The rate of disorders in relatives of people with OCD suggests a genetic association with anxiety disorders, depression, tic disorders such as Tourette syndrome (discussed later), and grooming disorders such as hair pulling and skin picking (Bienvenu et al., 2012).

OCD-Related Disorders

The symptoms of OCD, particularly washing and "grooming" rituals and preoccupation with cleanliness, suggest to some researchers that it is a disorder of "excessive grooming" (H. L. Leonard, Lenane, Swedo, Rettew, & Rapoport, 1991; Rapoport, 1991). Dogs and cats sometimes groom their fur to the point of producing bald spots and ulcers in a disorder known as *acral lick syndrome*. Some chimpanzees and monkeys engage in excessive self-grooming and hair pulling, and 10% of birds in captivity compulsively pull out their feathers, occasionally to the point that the bird is denuded and at risk for infection and hypothermia. Clomipramine, an antidepressant that inhibits serotonin reuptake, is effective in reducing all these behaviors (Grindlinger & Ramsay, 1991; Hartman, 1995; Rapoport, 1991).

If you think that the excessive grooming idea sounds far-fetched, consider the human behaviors of nail biting and obsessive hair pulling (trichotillomania), in which the person pulls hairs out one by one until there are visible bald spots or even complete baldness of the head, eyebrows, and eyelashes. There are several similarities between hair pulling and OCD: Both behaviors appear to be hereditary, and hair pullers have a high frequency of relatives with OCD; both symptoms also respond to serotonin reuptake inhibitors (Leonard et al., 1991; Swedo et al., 1991). However, trichotillomania and OCD sufferers appear to differ from each other in their versions of the *Sapap3* gene (Bienvenu et al., 2008). The gene's normal role is most likely a protective one, since mice that lack the gene groom to the point of self-injury; their behavior is relieved by a serotonin reuptake inhibitor (Figure 14.32; J. M. Welch et al., 2007).

Hoarders are dedicated collectors, stashing away just about anything from string to old newspapers. People with OCD are often hoarders as well, but hoarding disorder is considered distinct from OCD. David Tolin and his colleagues (2012) placed people with hoarding disorder in an fMRI scanner and had them look at pictures of junk mail and newspapers and decide whether to keep or discard them. The subjects had brought 50 of the items from home, and another 50 were provided by the experimenters. Hoarders, people with OCD, and healthy controls all were willing to discard more than 40 of the 50 items that were not theirs.

APPLICATION
Of Hermits and Hoarders

Searchers climb over debris piled almost to the ceiling in the Collyer home.

Source: *New York Daily News*/Contributor/*New York Daily News/Getty Images*.

There is greater awareness about hoarding disorder because of documentary TV series such as *Hoarders,* which profiles extreme hoarders; in one segment, the home is so cluttered that people take meals in bed (Weiss, 2010). In each episode, clinicians and professional organizers, with the aid of friends and family, assist the hoarder in the cleanup of his or her home. The intervention is usually precipitated by a crisis, such as a threat to remove the children for health and safety reasons. Hoarding can be so extreme that it poses broader dangers as well; for example, 14 firefighters were injured when 150 of them were called to put out a fire in a New York City apartment filled with floor-to-ceiling junk (Newman, 2006).

But the most severe hoarders that we know about may be the Collyer brothers, Homer and Langley. They grew up in a Fifth Avenue New York City mansion with their eccentric first-cousin parents; their father, a gynecologist, canoed to work at Bellevue Hospital and the family gave up their telephone, electricity, and gas to "simplify" their lives (Weiss, 2010). Homer became an attorney, and Langley graduated from Columbia University in mechanical engineering and chemistry and then tried a career as a concert pianist. After their parents died, the two brothers became reclusive hermits. Homer was confined to the home by blindness and arthritis, but Langley busied himself with nighttime treks through the neighborhood collecting odds and ends off the streets. On March 21, 1947, responding to a tip about an odor, police broke into the mansion through a second-story window after finding the foyer blocked by a solid wall of junk ("Collyer Brothers," n.d.). They found Homer dead of starvation and no sign of Langley. The home was so cluttered that Langley had made tunnels through the debris in order to move from room to room; some of those tunnels were rigged with booby traps as a defense against intruders. Authorities removed the contents from the home; 18 days after Homer's body was discovered, Langley was found just 10 feet away, crushed under one of his own traps. There was so little of value in the 130 tons of material that was removed from the home that an auction brought little money. For the next decade, children grew up with their mothers' admonition, "Clean up your room or you'll end up like the Collyer brothers!" (Weiss, p. 251).

■ **FIGURE 14.33** Increased Dopamine Activity in the Caudate Nuclei in Tourette Syndrome.

These two scans have not been superimposed over images of a brain; you can refer to Figure 14.30b to see where the caudate nuclei are located in the brain.

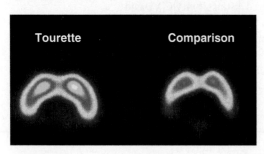

Source: From "[123I]α-CIT SPECT Imaging of Striatal Dopamine Transporter Binding in Tourette's Disorder," by R. T. Malison et al., 1995, *American Journal of Psychiatry, 152,* pp. 1359–1361. Copyright © 1995 American Psychiatric Publishing. Used with permission.

When it came to their own items, the healthy controls discarded 40 and those with OCD discarded 37, but the hoarders gave up only 29. More telling, during this part of the study the hoarders reported "not feeling right" and showed more activity than the others in the ACC, which evaluates behavior and detects errors, and in the insula, which is important to a sense of self. Apparently, giving up these possessions was threatening; this can lead to really bizarre behavior, as the accompanying Application reveals.

Another disorder associated with OCD is *Tourette syndrome,* whose victims suffer from a variety of motor and phonic (sound) tics. They twitch and grimace, blink their eyes rapidly, throw punches at the air, cough, grunt, bark, echo what others say, mimic people's facial expressions and gestures, and (rarely) blurt out derogatory remarks and profanity. Both OCD and Tourette sufferers can manage their symptoms for short periods; for instance, Tourette patients are usually symptom free while driving a car, having sex, or performing surgery (yes, some of them are surgeons!). But neither OCD nor Tourette is a simple matter of will: Children often suppress compulsive rituals at school and "let go" at home, or they suppress tics during the day and then tic during their sleep. Neurologist Oliver Sacks (1990) graphically describes a woman on the streets of New York who was imitating other people's expressions and gestures as she passed them on the sidewalk:

Suddenly, desperately, the old woman turned aside, into an alley-way which led off the main street. And there, with all the appearances of a woman violently sick, she expelled . . . all the gestures, the postures, the expressions, the demeanours, the entire behavioural repertoires, of the past forty or fifty people she had passed. (p. 123)

Symptoms begin between the ages of 2 and 15 years and usually progress from simple to more complex tics, with increasing compulsive or ritualistic qualities. The incidence of Tourette is difficult to determine; in recent studies the numbers have varied from 3 to 8 per 1,000 persons. In a survey of 64,000 children in the United States, the rate was 3 out of every 1,000, with three times as many males as females (Scahill, Bitsko, Visser, & Blumberg, 2009). Tourette syndrome is genetically influenced, with a concordance rate of 53% for identical twins and 8% for fraternal twins (R. A. Price, Kidd, Cohen, Pauls, & Leckman, 1985). Tourette shares some genetic roots with OCD; a third of patients with early-onset OCD also have Tourette syndrome (do Rosario-Campos et al., 2005), and 30% of adults with Tourette are also diagnosed with OCD (R. A. King, Leckman, Scahill, & Cohen, 1998). Recent studies have identified a mutation of the *SLITRK1* gene in Tourette and found a mutation of the *Hdc* gene in a man and his eight offspring, all of whom have the disorder (Abelson et al., 2005; Ercan-Sencicek et al., 2010). The genes function in neural development and transmission, and both are highly active in brain areas involved in Tourette.

Tourette syndrome, like OCD, involves increased activity in the basal ganglia. But unlike OCD, the most frequently prescribed drug for Tourette is an antidopaminergic drug, haloperidol, though newer antidopamine drugs are also being used. One effect dopamine has is motor activation, and Malison and his colleagues (1995) found that dopamine activity is elevated in Tourette sufferers in the caudate nuclei of the basal ganglia (Figure 14.33). There has been some success treating Tourette with deep brain stimulation to the thalamus, which suppressed tics and produced feelings of calmness (Okun et al., 2013).

Borderline Personality Disorder

To finish up our tour of the psychological disorders, we end with one of the most intriguing personality disorders: borderline personality disorder (BPD). This condition, which affects 0.5–5.9% of the population (Grant et al., 2008), is characterized by unstable interpersonal relationships, poor self-image, and impulsivity. Individuals with this condition have an intense fear of abandonment and rejection and an equally strong desire to be loved. They often switch between intense feelings of "love" and "hate," they engage in risky behaviors such as gambling and speeding, and they are at a very high risk for suicide and suicidal thoughts. In fact, 8%–10% of individuals with BPD kill themselves, and they are prone to taking medication far beyond the recommended dose in committing suicide.

■ **FIGURE 14.34**   Integrative Model of Borderline Personality Disorder.

Although environmental support can prevent the imbalances that result in epigenetic changes to plasticity genes resulting in borderline personality disorder (blue), poor environmental features turn on genes that result in impulsivity and poor emotional control, which leads to the poor behavioral choices characteristic of the disorder (orange).

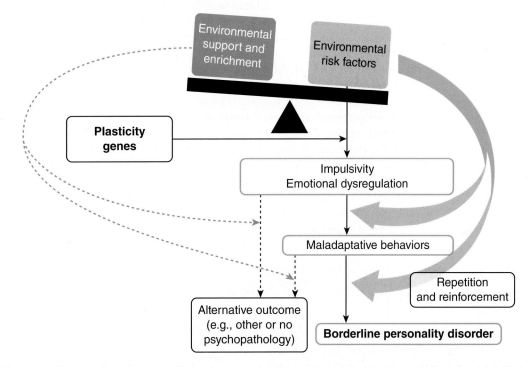

Source: Figure 2 from "Genetics of borderline personality disorder: systematic review and proposal of an integrative model," by A. Amad et al., 2014, *Neuroscience and Biobehavioral Reviews, 40,* pp. 6–19. Copyright © 2014 Elsevier. Used with permission.

BPD has a strong genetic basis, with a heritability about 40% (Amad, Ramoz, Thomas, Jardri, & Gorwood, 2014). Genes linked to BPD include ones responsible for serotonin receptors, serotonin transporters such as 5HTTLPR, dopamine transporters such as DAT1, and enzymes that make neurotransmitters (such as tyrosine hydroxylase), as well as genes that influence neuronal survival (brain-derived neurotrophic factor) and neuronal death (see Amad et al., 2014, for a review of the research that led to these conclusions). Therefore, BPD appears to be caused by dysfunction of both serotonin and dopamine neurotransmitter systems, as well as by decreases in neuronal number. Of interest was a finding that the *MAOA* gene (discussed in Chapter 8) is linked to both aggressive behaviors and borderline personality disorder (Craig & Halton, 2009). Even with these genetic correlates, the remaining 60% of the disorder likelihood is environmental; indeed, psychiatrists believe the genes predispose an individual toward the imbalance of BPD but that a set of environmental events must happen to activate the epigenetic changes that result in the disorder (Figure 14.34).

CONCEPT CHECK

Take a Minute to Check Your Knowledge and Understanding

- Describe the symptoms of OCD and the related disorders.
- What are the distinguishing characteristics of borderline personality disorder?
- What treatments are used with these disorders?

In Perspective

The past several decades have seen enormous progress in research, and we now know a great deal about the physiological causes of disorders. We owe these breakthroughs to advances in imaging techniques and genetics research technology and to our greatly improved understanding of the physiology of synapses, not to mention the persistence of dedicated researchers. The result is that we can now describe at the biological level many disorders that previously were believed to be "psychological" in origin or that were only suspected of having an organic basis.

Despite these great research advances, we cannot reliably distinguish the schizophrenic brain from a normal one, or diagnose psychological disorders from a blood test. We may be able to someday, but in the meantime, we rely on changes in behavior of the individuals for a disorder diagnosis. This can be difficult, because these disorders frequently share common features (for example, schizophrenia, mood disorders with psychotic features, and bipolar I disorder). We know, at least to some extent, the physiological components of mental illness, but we do not understand the unique combination of physiological and environmental factors that determines who will suffer from a disorder and who will not. If that is true, our treatments will remain a pale hope rather than a bright promise.

We have been reminded repeatedly that genetic vulnerability is not the same thing as fate. In most cases, the genes produce an illness only with the cooperation of the environment. This point is emphasized by the fact that psychotherapy and cognitive-behavioral therapy play an important role in treatment, enhancing and frequently exceeding the benefit that drugs can provide (see Durand & Barlow, 2006). While we search for genetic treatments of the disorders, we must remind ourselves once again that heredity is not destiny; improving the physical and psychological welfare of the population would go a long way toward preventing mental illness or reducing its severity.

Just before the dawning of this new age of research, one frustrated schizophrenia researcher concluded, "Almost everything remains to be done" (Heston, 1970, p. 254). Since then our knowledge of both the brain and its participation in the symptoms of mental illness has increased dramatically, but as you can see, much of our understanding remains tentative. The pace is quickening, and we are confident that in this second decade of the new millennium, we will be celebrating even more impressive advances than in the past.

CHAPTER SUMMARY

Schizophrenia

- Schizophrenia is characterized by a mix of positive and negative symptoms such as hallucinations, delusions, thought disorder, and social and emotional withdrawal.
- Twin and adoption studies indicate that heritability is .60 to .90. Genetic influences involve many small-effect genes and rarer copy number variations with stronger effects. Genes apparently determine the level of vulnerability.
- Positive and negative symptoms may be distinguished by excess dopamine activity versus brain deficits.
- Although there is evidence for the dopamine hypothesis, it is an incomplete explanation. The glutamate hypothesis is getting more attention because NMDA receptor antagonists produce symptoms of schizophrenia and drugs that activate NMDA receptors relieve them.
- The brain irregularities include ventricular enlargement (due to tissue deficits), hypofrontality, and impaired connections; these apparently arise from prenatal insults and impaired postnatal development, in interaction with genetic vulnerability. Reduced connectivity and impaired synchrony between areas are also involved.
- Maternal effect from illnesses such as influenza and prenatal starvation are examples of environmental influences.

Affective Disorders

- The affective disorders include depression, mania, and bipolar disorder, an alternation between mania and depression.
- The affective disorders are also highly heritable, especially for women. Some genes are shared with schizophrenia, ASD, and ADHD.

- The most prominent explanation of affective disorders is the monoamine hypothesis—an imbalance in serotonin and epinephrine.
- Electroconvulsive therapy is a controversial but very effective last-resort therapy that has value when medications fail and as a temporary suicide preventative; both drugs and ECT increase neurogenesis and neural plasticity.
- People with affective disorders often have circadian rhythm disruptions. Others respond to circannual changes with winter depression or summer depression.
- Bipolar disorder is now considered to be a separate group of disorders, and is the bridge disorder between schizophrenia and depression.
- Bipolar disorder is less understood than unipolar depression. Response to atypical antipsychotics suggests involvement of dopamine and, possibly, serotonin.
- A number of brain anomalies distinguish depressed people from bipolar patients and both from normal people.
- Depression, low serotonin activity, and several genes are associated with suicide risk.

Anxiety, Trauma, and Stress-Related Disorders

- The anxiety disorders are characterized mostly by brain hyperresponsiveness, but activity is decreased in some areas in posttraumatic stress disorder.
- Anxiety involves low serotonin activity; GABA transmission and benzodiazepine receptor deficiency may also be involved.
- The anxiety disorders are partially hereditary, and the serotonin system is most often implicated. There is considerable overlap with mood disorders.

Personality Disorders

- In obsessive-compulsive disorder, activity is increased in the orbitofrontal cortex; deficient connections with the cingulate gyrus apparently reduce impulse control.
- OCD is associated with grooming disorders.
- Tourette syndrome shares some genetic roots with OCD, but OCD appears to involve high serotonin activity, whereas Tourette is treated with dopamine antagonists.

- In borderline personality disorder, there is a strong tendency for impulsivity, rapid emotional swings, and a series of damaging and maladaptive behaviors like cutting, suicide, and risky behaviors.
- BPD is thought to occur through the epigenetic activation of genes related to serotonin, dopamine, and aggression systems.

STUDY RESOURCES

FOR FURTHER THOUGHT

- Now that we are nearing the end of the text, summarize what you know about the interaction of heredity and environment. Give examples from different chapters and include the concept of vulnerability.
- Give an overall view of what produces deviant behavior (going back to earlier chapters as well as this one). What effect does this have on your ideas about responsibility for one's behavior?
- Behavior is vulnerable to a number of disturbances, involving both genetic and environmental influences. Consider the different ways complexity of the brain contributes to this vulnerability.

TEST YOUR UNDERSTANDING

1. Explain the dopamine theory of schizophrenia. What are its deficiencies? What alternative or complementary explanations are available?

2. Describe the monoamine hypothesis of depression; include the evidence for it and a description of the effects of the drugs and ECT used to treat depression.

3. Describe the similarities and associations among OCD, Tourette, and "grooming" behaviors.

Select the best answer:

1. If you were diagnosed with schizophrenia, you should prefer _____ symptoms.
   - a. positive
   - b. negative
   - c. chronic
   - d. bipolar

2. The fact that schizophrenia involves multiple genes helps explain
   - a. vulnerability to winter viruses.
   - b. the onset late in life.
   - c. positive symptoms.
   - d. different degrees of vulnerability.

3. All drugs that are effective in treating schizophrenia
   - a. interfere with reuptake of dopamine.
   - b. have some effect at D_2 receptors.
   - c. stimulate glutamate receptors.
   - d. inhibit serotonin receptors.

4. Schizophrenia apparently involves
   - a. tissue deficits.
   - b. frontal dysfunction.
   - c. disrupted connections.
   - d. a and b
   - e. a, b, and c

5. Which disorder is the bridge between schizophrenia and depressive disorders?
   - a. Borderline personality disorder
   - b. Obsessive-compulsive disorder
   - c. Bipolar disorder
   - d. Posttraumatic stress disorder

6. The monoamine hypothesis states that depression results from
   - a. reduced activity in norepinephrine and serotonin synapses.
   - b. increased activity in norepinephrine and serotonin synapses.
   - c. reduced activity in norepinephrine, serotonin, and dopamine synapses.
   - d. increased activity in norepinephrine, serotonin, and dopamine synapses.

7. ECT appears to relieve depression by
   - a. producing amnesia for depressing memories.
   - b. the same mechanisms as antidepressant drugs.
   - c. punishing depressive behavior.
   - d. increasing EEG frequency.

8. A frontal area hypothesized to switch between depression and mania is the
   - a. dorsolateral prefrontal cortex.
   - b. caudate nucleus.
   - c. ventral prefrontal cortex.
   - d. subgenual prefrontal cortex.

9. Studies indicate that risk for suicide is related to

   a. low norepinephrine and serotonin.
   b. high norepinephrine and serotonin.
   c. low serotonin.
   d. low norepinephrine.

10. The anxiety disorders are associated genetically with

   a. schizophrenia and depression.
   b. schizophrenia.
   c. depression.
   d. none of these

11. Of these, the best predictor of PTSD following trauma is

   a. a history of childhood abuse.
   b. being male.
   c. the severity of the trauma.
   d. the intensity of the reaction to the trauma.

12. Both OCD and Tourette syndrome involve compulsive rituals, probably because they involve

   a. increased dopamine.
   b. increased activity in the basal ganglia.
   c. a stressful home life.
   d. all of these

13. Instability of emotion is a hallmark of

   a. bipolar II disorder
   b. PTSD
   c. OCPD
   d. borderline personality disorder

1.a, 2.d, 3.b, 4.e, 5.c, 6.a, 7.b, 8.d, 9.c, 10.c, 11.a, 12.b, 13.d.

Answers:

ON THE WEB

The following websites are coordinated with this chapter's content. You can access these websites from the **SAGE edge Student Resources site**; select this chapter and then click on Web Resources. (**Bold** items are links.)

1. **I and I, Dancing Fool, Challenge You the World to a Duel** is Ian Chovil's account of his schizophrenia, bizarre delusions, and homelessness. Coping much better on olanzapine, he now works part time educating the public about the illness.

   An online version of the **Wisconsin Card Sorting Test** is available at PsyToolkit's website. In addition, that free site has many other psychological experiments you can perform.

2. PsychCentral offers an online **Depression Screening Test** to help a person assess his or her symptoms.

3. **MD Junction** and **DailyStrength** provide discussion groups for people affected by SAD and information about the disorder.

4. The **Depression and Bipolar Support Alliance** site is a place to learn about mood disorders and ongoing research and to take a mood disorders questionnaire.

5. At **Hoarders,** you can watch entire episodes of the reality TV series; if you don't have time for that, sample a few and read descriptions of the people for insights into the lives of hoarders and their families.

6. The **Tourette Association of America** is a good resource for information on this disorder.

7. **The Mighty** has a great selection of resources on borderline personality disorder, as well as autism, mental illness, and how these affect parents and caregivers.

FOR FURTHER READING

1. *When the Music's Over: My Journey Into Schizophrenia,* by Ross Burke (Plume/Penguin, 1995), is the author's account of his battle with schizophrenia, published by his therapist after Burke ended the battle with suicide.

2. *An Unquiet Mind,* by Kay Jamison (Knopf, 1995), tells the story of her continuing battle with bipolar disorder, which rendered her "ravingly psychotic" three months into her first semester as a psychology professor. With the aid of lithium, she has become an authority on mood disorders.

3. *Abnormal Psychology,* by William Ray (SAGE, 2015), is a text written with a neuroscience perspective.

4. *Here's the Deal: Don't Touch Me,* by Howie Mandel (Bantam, 2010), is a fascinating memoir of the comedian's lifelong struggle with OCD, and the effect it has had not only on his own life but also on the lives of those around him.

5. "All in the Mind of a Mouse," by Carina Dennis (*Nature,* 2005, *438,* 151–152), is an intriguing look at the creative ways researchers are using mice to study human psychological disorders.

6. "I Hate You—Don't Leave Me," by Jerold J. Kreisman (TarcherPerigee, 2010), is an amazing view into what someone with borderline personality disorder goes through, written by

a clinician who founded the world's first care facility specifically for individuals struggling with the disorder.

7. If you are interested in the most up-to-date description of medications currently being prescribed to combat various disorders, the *Handbook of Clinical Psychopharmacology for Therapists* (7th edition), by John Preston and colleagues (New Harbinger Publications, 2012), is a wonderful and inexpensive resource.

KEY TERMS

aberrant salience hypothesis 412
acute 408
bipolar disorder 421
chronic 408
circadian rhythm 427
circannual rhythm 428
depression 421
dopamine hypothesis 412
electroconvulsive therapy (ECT) 426
glutamate theory 414
lithium 429

major depressive disorder (MDD) 421
mania 421
monoamine hypothesis 423
negative symptoms 411
neuroleptics 413
obsessive-compulsive disorder
    (OCD) 436
phototherapy 428
positive symptoms 411
posttraumatic stress disorder
    (PTSD) 434

psychosis 407
rapid eye movement (REM) sleep 427
schizophrenia 407
seasonal affective disorder (SAD) 428
tardive dyskinesia 412
Tourette syndrome 440
vulnerability model 411
winter birth effect 418
Wisconsin Card Sorting Test 415

edge.sagepub.com/garrett5e

SAGE edge offers a robust online environment featuring an impressive array of free tools and resources for review, study, and further exploration, keeping both instructors and students on the cutting edge of teaching and learning.

14.1 Name and describe the various categories of psychological disorders.	▶	Types of Psychological Disorders
14.2 Understand the characteristics and neurological causes of schizophrenia.	▶	Understanding Brain Disorders
14.3 Describe how heredity and environment interact to produce psychological disorders.	📄	Genetic Influence on Human Psychological Traits
14.4 Understand the symptoms and causes of the affective disorders.	📢 ▶	Bipolar Disorder and Lithium The Neuroscience of Depression
14.5 Understand and describe the symptoms and physiological causes of the anxiety disorders.	▶	OCD and Anxiety Disorders
14.6 Explain the causes and features of the various personality disorders.	▶	Personality Disorders: Causes and Symptoms

Sleep and Consciousness

15

After reading this chapter, you will be able to:

- Summarize the characteristics of the rhythms that occur during sleep and waking.

- Describe the neural controls of sleep and waking rhythms.

- Examine the functions of sleep and shorter rhythms.

- Assess the causes of sleep disorders.

- Explain how researchers are approaching the issue of consciousness.

- Indicate the neural processes that contribute to consciousness.

Kenneth Parks got up from the couch where he had been sleeping and drove 14 miles to his in-laws' home. There he struggled with his father-in-law before stabbing his mother-in-law repeatedly, killing her. He then drove to the police station, where he told the police that he thought he had "killed some people." In court, his defense was that he was sleepwalking. Based on the testimony of sleep experts and the lack of motive—Ken had an affectionate relationship with his in-laws—the jury acquitted him of murder (Broughton et al., 1994).

Were Ken's actions possible for someone who was sleepwalking? Was he really asleep and therefore not responsible? This case raises the question of what we mean by *consciousness*. Many psychologists, and especially neuroscientists, avoid the topic because they think that consciousness is inaccessible to research. This has not always been so; consciousness was a major concern of the fledgling discipline of psychology near the end of the 19th century. But the researchers' technique of *introspection* was subjective: The observations were open only to the individuals doing the introspecting, who often disagreed with each other. This failing encouraged the development of behaviorism, which was based on the principle that psychology should study only the relationships between external stimuli and observable responses. Behaviorism was a necessary means of cleansing psychology of its subjective methods, but its purge discarded the subject matter along with the methodology. The interests of psychologists would not shift back to include internal experience until the emergence of the field of *cognitive psychology* in the 1950s and 1960s.

Many cognitive psychologists were finding it difficult to understand psychological functions such as learning and perception without taking account of various aspects of consciousness. Still, few of them tackled the subject of consciousness itself. The problem seemed too big, there was no clear definition of consciousness, and the bias that consciousness was a problem for philosophers still lingered. Gradually, some of them began to ally themselves with philosophers, biologists, and computer experts to develop new research strategies for exploring this

Master the content.
edge.sagepub.com/garrett5e

"

Studying the brain without studying consciousness would be like studying the stomach without studying digestion.

—John R. Searle
"

last frontier of psychology. The greatest inroads have been made in the study of sleep, largely because sleep is readily observable. Also, because sleep is open to study by objective techniques, it has not had the stigma among researchers that characterizes other aspects of consciousness. We will begin this last leg of our journey with the topic of sleep and dreaming.

Sleep and Dreaming

Each night, we slip into a mysterious state that is neither entirely conscious nor unconscious. Sleep has intrigued humans throughout history: Metaphysically, dreaming suggested to our forebears that the soul took leave of the body at night to wander the world; practically, sleep is a period of enforced nonproductivity and vulnerability to predators and enemies.

In spite of thousands of research studies, we are still unclear on the most basic question—What is the function of sleep? The most obvious explanation is that sleep is *restorative*. Support for this idea comes from the observation that species with higher metabolic rates typically spend more time in sleep (Zepelin & Rechtschaffen, 1974). A less obvious explanation is the *adaptive* hypothesis; according to this view, the amount of sleep an animal engages in depends on the availability of food and on safety considerations (Webb, 1974). Elephants, for instance, which must graze for many hours to meet their food needs, sleep briefly. Animals with low vulnerability to predators, such as the lion, sleep much of the time, as do animals that find safety by hiding, like bats and burrowing animals. Vulnerable animals that are too large to burrow or hide—for example, horses and cattle—sleep very little (Figure 15.1). In a study of 39 species, the combined factors of body size and danger accounted for 80% of the variability in sleep time (Allison & Cicchetti, 1976).

? Why do we sleep?

An interesting new idea is that the brain cleanses itself of toxins during sleep. Researchers at the University of Rochester in New York recently discovered a network of channels formed by glia, which transport cerebrospinal fluid (CSF) through the brain. By injecting a colored dye in the brains of mice as they slept and a dye of another color when they woke up, the researchers determined that large amounts of CSF flowed through the brain during sleep but not during the awake state. The researchers then injected β-amyloid proteins into the brains of the mice and found that the CSF cleared the proteins out of cells twice as fast during sleep (Xie et al., 2013). (Students note: This is one more argument for getting enough sleep!)

Whatever the function of sleep may be, its importance becomes apparent when we look at the effects of sleep deprivation. These effects are nowhere more evident than in shift work. Shift workers sleep less than day workers, and their work performance suffers as a result (Tepas & Carvalhais, 1990). Also, they typically fail to adjust their sleep-wake cycles adequately, because their sleep is disturbed during the day and they conform to the rest of the world's schedule on weekends. With their work and sleep schedules at odds with their biological rhythms, shift workers find that sleep intrudes into their work and daytime arousal interferes with their sleep. Another study with mice may give us a clue why this happens. After just a few days of sleeping three to five hours a day, the mice had lost 25% of the neurons in the locus coeruleus, a part of the brain that is important for alertness (J. Zhang et al., 2014).

In long-term sleep deprivation studies, impairment follows a rhythmic cycle—performance declines during the night and then shows some recovery during the daytime (Horne, 1988). The persistence of this rhythm represents a safety hazard of gigantic proportions when people try to function at night. The largest number of single-vehicle traffic accidents attributed to "falling asleep at the wheel" occur around 2 a.m. (Mitler et al., 1988), and the number of work errors peaks at the same time (Broughton, 1975). In addition, the Three Mile Island nuclear plant accident took place at 4 a.m.; the Chernobyl nuclear plant meltdown began at 1:23 a.m.; the Bhopal, India, chemical plant leakage, which poisoned more than 2,000 people, began shortly after midnight; and the *Exxon Valdez* ran aground at 12:04 a.m., spilling 11 million gallons of oil into fragile Alaskan waters (Alaska Oil Spill Commission, 1990; Mapes, 1990; Mitler et al., 1988).

Travel across time zones also disrupts sleep and impairs performance, particularly when you travel eastward. It is difficult to quantify the effects of *jet lag*, but three researchers have attempted to do so in a novel way by comparing the performance of baseball teams. When East Coast and West Coast teams played at home, their percentage of wins was nearly identical—50% and 49%, respectively. When they traveled across the continent but had time to adjust to the new time zone, they showed a typical visitor's disadvantage, winning 45.9% of their games. Teams traveling west without time to adjust won about the same, 43.8% of their games, whereas teams traveling east won only 37.1% (Recht, Lew, & Schwartz, 1995). Sleep quality is better when you extend the day's length by traveling west, rather than shorten it as you do when you travel east. One way of looking at this effect is that it is easier to stay awake past your bedtime than it is to go to sleep when you are not sleepy. We will examine a more specific explanation in the next section, when we consider circadian rhythms.

■ **FIGURE 15.1** Time Spent in Daily Sleep for Different Animals.

Observations support the hypothesis that sleep is an adaptive response to feeding and safety needs.

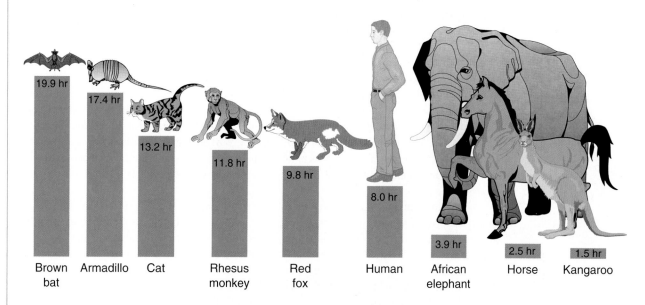

Source: Based on data from "Animal Sleep: A Review of Sleep Duration Across Phylogeny," by S. S. Campbell and I. Tobler, 1984, *Neuroscience and Biobehavioral Reviews*, 8, pp. 269–300.

Circadian Rhythms

We saw in Chapter 14 that a *circadian rhythm* is a rhythm that is about a day in length; the term *circadian* comes from the Latin *circa,* meaning "approximately," and *dia,* meaning "day." We operate on a 24-hour (hr) cycle, in synchrony with the solar day. We sleep once every 24 hr, and body temperature, alertness, urine production, steroid secretion, and a variety of other activities decrease during our normal sleep period and increase during our normal waking period, even when we reverse our sleep-wake schedule temporarily.

The main biological clock that controls these rhythms in mammals is the *suprachiasmatic nucleus (SCN)* of the hypothalamus. Lesioning the SCN in rats abolishes the normal 24-hr rhythms of sleep, activity, body temperature, drinking, and steroid secretion (Abe, Kroning, Greer, & Critchlow, 1979; Stephan & Nunez, 1977). The SCN is what is known as a *pacemaker,* because it keeps time and regulates the activity of other cells. We know that the rhythm arises in the SCN, because rhythmic activity continues in isolated SCN cells (Earnest, Liang, Ratcliff, & Cassone, 1999; Inouye & Kawamura, 1979). Lesioned animals do not stop sleeping, but instead of following the usual day-night cycle, they sleep in naps scattered throughout the 24-hr period. So the SCN controls the timing of sleep, but sleep itself is controlled by other brain structures, which we will discuss later. The SCN is shown in Figure 15.2, and you can check Figure 6.2 to see its location.

The SCN is *entrained* to the solar day by cues called *zeitgebers* ("time-givers"). If humans are kept in isolation from all time cues in an underground bunker or a cave, they usually lose their synchrony with the day-night cycle; in many studies, zeitgeber-deprived individuals "drifted" to a day that was about 25 hr long, with a progressively increasing delay in sleep onset (Figure 15.3; Aschoff, 1984). For a long time, researchers believed that alarm clocks and the activity of others were the most important influences that entrain our activity to the 24-hr day, but research points more convincingly to light as the primary zeitgeber.

The *difference* in light intensity between the light and dark periods is important for entraining the day-night cycle. One group of night workers worked under bright lights and slept in complete darkness during the day (*light discrepant*); a second group worked under normal light and slept in the semidarkness that is typical of the day sleeper (*similar light*). The light-discrepant workers scored higher in performance and alertness than the similar-light workers. Their physiological measures also synchronized with the new sleep-wake cycle; for example, their body temperature dropped to its low value around 3:00 p.m., when they were asleep, but the

? Why are circadian rhythms important?

Early to bed and early to rise, makes a man healthy, wealthy, and wise.

—*Benjamin Franklin*

similar-light group's low continued to occur at 3:30 a.m. in spite of being awake and working (Czeisler et al., 1990). If you're thinking the take-home from this study is that you should keep the lights as bright as possible when you're awake, you would be wrong. Compared with dim light, exposure to normal room light for the 8-hr period before bedtime reduces the duration of melatonin release by 90 minutes each night (Gooley et al., 2010). *Melatonin* is a hormone that induces sleepiness. The typically sleep-deprived state in modern society appears to be due in part to living under bright lights and spending evenings in front of a computer.

Just how much we rely on a regular lighting schedule for entrainment was underscored in a study of four Greenpeace volunteers living in isolation during the four-month darkness of the Antarctic winter; their sleep times and physiological measures free-ran on a roughly 25-hr interval, even though they had access to time information and social contact with each other (Kennaway & van Dorp, 1991). According to some observers, it is this "slow-running" clock that makes phase delays (going to sleep later) easier than phase advances (going to sleep earlier). So adjustment after westward travel is easier than after traveling east, and workers who rotate shifts sleep better and produce more if the rotation is to later shifts rather than to earlier ones (Czeisler, Moore-Ede, & Coleman, 1982). Some people seem to be relatively insensitive to the environmental cues that entrain most of us to a 24-hr day and operate on a 25-hr clock under normal circumstances; and like a clock that runs too slowly, their physical and cognitive functioning moves in and out of phase with the rest of the world, resulting in insomnia and impaired functioning.

Why the internal clock would operate on a 25-hr cycle is unclear, especially since animals kept in isolation typically run on a 24-hr cycle (Czeisler et al., 1999). Some researchers believe that it has something to do with the 24.8-hr lunar cycle, which influences the tides and activity cycles of a number of marine species (T. S. Kaiser, Neumann, & Heckel, 2011; Tessmar-Raible, Raible, & Arboleda, 2011). Czeisler and his colleagues (1999) suggested that the 25-hr cycle in isolation studies is no more than an artifact of allowing the individuals to control the room lighting. Bright light late in the day causes the cycle to lengthen, so Czeisler kept the light at a level that was too low to influence the circadian rhythm while people lived on a 28-hr sleep-wake schedule. Under that condition, their body temperature cycle averaged 24.18 hr, which led Czeisler to conclude that the *biological* rhythm is approximately 24 hr long. By the way, if you think a lunar influence on sleep is hard to believe, Swiss researchers have preliminary evidence for it. Near the time of the full moon, volunteers sleeping in a windowless laboratory slept 20 minutes less, produced half as much melatonin, and had 30% less of one stage of sleep than at other times of the month (Cajochen et al., 2013). The researchers believe this observation represents an inherent biological rhythm, but they admit that the results could have been influenced by exposure to brighter evening light before their subjects entered the laboratory.

■ **FIGURE 15.2** The Suprachiasmatic Nucleus.

(a) The nuclei, indicated by the arrows, took up more radioactive 2-deoxy-glucose in the scan because the rat was injected during the "light-on" period of the day; (b) the rat was injected during the "light-off" period.

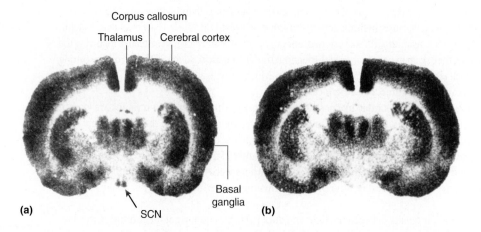

Source: Reprinted with permission from W. J. Schwartz and H. Gainer, "Suprachiasmatic Nucleus: Use of 14C-labeled Deoxyglucose Uptake as a Functional Marker," *Science, 197,* 1089–1091. Copyright 1977 American Association for the Advancement of Science.

The SCN regulates the pineal gland's secretion of melatonin. Melatonin is often used to combat jet lag and to treat insomnia in shift workers and in the blind (Arendt, Skene, Middleton, Lockley, & Deacon, 1997). Light resets the biological clock by suppressing melatonin secretion (Boivin, Duffy, Kronauer, & Czeisler, 1996). Most totally blind individuals are not entrained to the 24-hr day and suffer from insomnia in spite of regular schedules of sleep, work, and social contact. These individuals do not experience a decrease in melatonin production when exposed to light; however, totally blind people *without* insomnia do show melatonin suppression by light, even though they are unaware of the light (Czeisler et al., 1995).

Animal studies explain how some blind individuals are able to entrain to the light-dark cycle and, thus, how the rest of us do so as well. Light information reaches the SCN by way of a direct connection from the retinas called the *retinohypothalamic pathway*; however, mice lacking rods and cones still show normal entrainment and cycling, so the signal must arise from some other retinal light receptors (M. S. Freedman et al., 1999; Lucas, Freedman, Muñoz, Garcia-Fernández, & Foster, 1999). Ganglion cells ordinarily receive information about light from the receptors, but about 1% of ganglion cells respond to light directly and send neurons into the retinohypothalamic pathway (Berson, Dunn, & Takao, 2002; Hannibal, Hindersson, Knudsen, Georg, & Fahrenkrug, 2002; Hattar, Liao, Takao, Berson, & Yau, 2002). These ganglion cells contain melanopsin, which is a light-sensitive substance, or photopigment (Dacey et al., 2005; Panda et al., 2005; Qiu et al., 2005). The melanopsin is located in their widely branching dendrites, which suits the cells for detecting the overall level of light, as opposed to contributing to image formation (Figure 15.4). A study has confirmed that human retinas have melanopsin in some of their ganglion cells (Dkhissi-Benyahya, Rieux, Hut, & Cooper, 2006).

■ **FIGURE 15.3**   Sleep and Wake Periods During Isolation From Time Cues.

Each dark bar indicates the timing and length of sleep during a day. During the unscheduled period (without time cues), the subject's activity assumed a 25-hr rhythm and began to advance around the clock. When light-dark periods were scheduled, he resumed a normal sleep and activity rhythm.

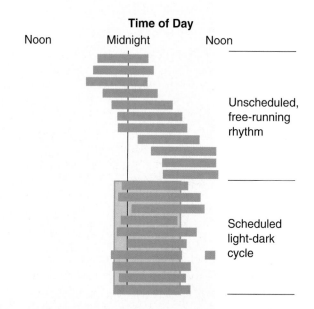

Source: From *Introduction to Psychology, Gateways to Mind and Behavior* (with InfoTrac) 9th edition, by D. Coon, 2001. Reprinted with permission of Wadsworth, a division of Thomson Learning.

However, synchronizing the rhythm does not account for the rhythm itself. The internal clock consists of a few genes and their protein products (Clayton, Kyriacou, & Reppert, 2001; Hastings, Reddy, & Maywood, 2003; Shearman et al., 2000); the genes fall into two groups, one group that is turned on while the other is turned off. When the genes are on, their particular protein products build up. Eventually, the accumulating proteins turn their genes off, and the other set of genes is turned on. This feedback loop provides the approximately 24- or 25-hr cycle, which then must be reset each day by light. This process is not limited to neurons in the SCN; there are additional clocks, located outside the brain and controlling the activities of the body's organs (Hastings et al., 2003). These clocks operate independently of the SCN, but the SCN entrains them to the day-night cycle. Feeding is an example of an activity that is controlled independently. According to the researchers, local clocks that affect blood pressure and heart activity explain why there is a large increase in the risk of heart attack, stroke, and sudden cardiac death after waking in the morning. The clock in the SCN does not always operate properly, as we saw in Chapter 14 with some depressed patients.

Rhythms During Waking and Sleeping

Riding on the day-long wave of the circadian rhythm are several *ultradian rhythms,* rhythms that are shorter than a day in length. Hormone production, urinary output, alertness, and other functions follow regular cycles throughout the day. For example, the dip in alertness and performance in the wee hours of the morning is mirrored by another in the early afternoon, which cannot be accounted for by postlunch sleepiness, because it also occurs in people who skip lunch (Broughton, 1975). Incidentally, this dip coincides with the time of siesta in many cultures and a rest period in nonhuman primates. The *basic rest and activity cycle* is a rhythm that is about 90–100 minutes (min) long. When people wrote down what they were thinking every 5 min for

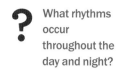

What rhythms occur throughout the day and night?

■ **FIGURE 15.4**   Retinal Ganglion Cells Containing Melanopsin.

The cells were labeled with a fluorescent substance that reacts to melanopsin. Notice the widespread dendrites, which contain melanopsin.

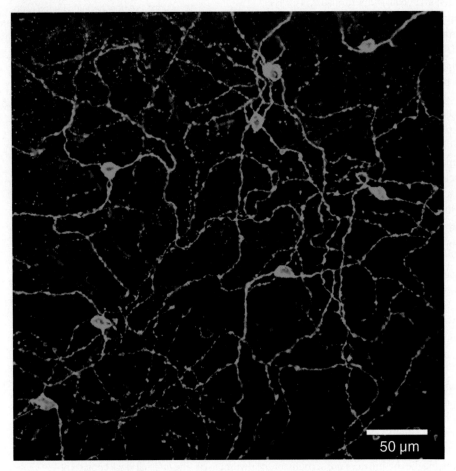

50 μm

Source: From "Melanopsin-Containing Retinal Ganglion Cells: Architecture, Projections, and Intrinsic Photosensitivity," by S. Hattar, H. W. Liao, M. Takao, D. M. Berson, and K. W. Yau, *Science*, *295*, pp. 1065–1070. © 2002 American Association for the Advancement of Science (AAAS). Reprinted with permission from AAAS.

10 hr, the contents showed that they were daydreaming on a 90-min cycle; EEG recordings verified that these were periods of decreased brain activity (Kripke & Sonnenschein, 1973).

The common view of sleep is that it is a cessation of activity that occurs when the body and brain become fatigued. Sleep, however, is an active process. This is true in two respects. First, you will soon see that sleep is a very busy time; a great deal of activity goes on in the brain. Second, sleep is not like a car running out of gas but instead is turned on by brain structures and later turned off by other structures.

The most important measure of sleep activity is the EEG. When a person is awake, the EEG is a mix of *alpha* and *beta* waves. Alpha is activity whose voltage fluctuates at a frequency of 8–12 hertz (Hz) and moderate amplitude; beta has a frequency of 13–30 Hz and a lower amplitude. Beta waves, which are associated with arousal and alertness, are progressively replaced by alpha waves as the person relaxes (Figure 15.5). It may seem strange that the amplitude of the EEG is lower during arousal. Remember that the EEG is the sum of the electrical activity of all the neurons between the two recording electrodes. When a person is cognitively aroused, neurons under the electrodes are mostly desynchronized in their firing as they carry out their separate tasks; with the neurons firing at different times, the EEG has a high frequency, but the amplitude is rather low. As the person relaxes, the neurons have less processing to do and fall into a pattern of synchronized firing. The rate is low, but the cumulative amplitude of the neurons firing at the same time is high.

As the person slips into the light first stage of sleep, the EEG shifts to *theta* waves, with a frequency of 4–7 Hz (Figure 15.5). About 10 min later, Stage 2 begins, indicated by the appearance of *K complexes* and *sleep*

■ **FIGURE 15.5** Electroencephalogram and the Stages of Sleep.

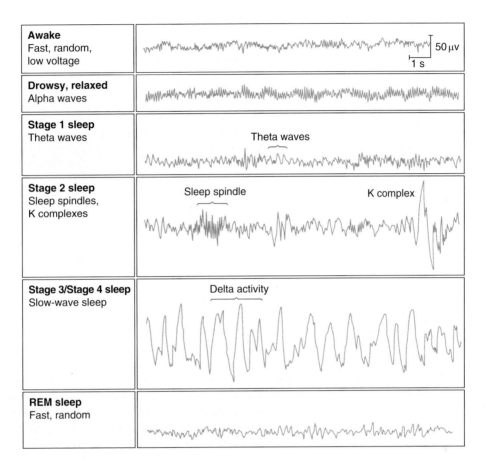

spindles. K complexes are sharp, large waves that occur about once a minute; sleep spindles are brief bursts of 12- to 14-Hz waves that appear to serve a gating function, preventing disruptive stimuli from reaching the cortex and waking the sleeper (Dang-Vu, McKinney, Buxton, Solet, & Ellenbogen, 2010). Stages 3 and 4 are known as *slow-wave sleep* and are characterized by large, slow delta waves at a frequency of 1–3 Hz. The person moves around in bed during this period, turning over and changing positions. Sleepwalking, bedwetting, and night terrors, disturbances that are common in children, occur during slow-wave sleep, too. Night terrors are not nightmares but involve screaming and apparent terror, which are usually forgotten in the morning; they are not a sign of a disorder unless they continue beyond childhood. After Stage 4, the sleeper moves rather quickly back through the stages in reverse order. But rather than returning to Stage 1, the sleeper enters rapid eye movement sleep.

Rapid eye movement (REM) sleep is so called because the eyes dart back and forth horizontally during this stage. The EEG returns to a pattern similar to a relaxed waking state, but the person does not wake up; in fact, the sleeper is not easily aroused by noise but does respond to meaningful sounds, such as the sleeper's name. It is easy to see why some researchers call this stage *paradoxical sleep,* because *paradoxical* means "contradictory." During REM sleep, respiration rate and heart rate increase. Males experience genital erection, and vaginal secretion increases in females. In spite of these signs of arousal, the body is very still—in fact, in a state of muscular paralysis or *atonia.* A complete cycle through the stages of sleep—like the daydreaming cycle—takes about 90 min to complete. The night's sleep is a series of repetitions of this ultradian rhythm, although the length of REM sleep periods increases and the amount of slow-wave sleep decreases through the night (Figure 15.6).

■ **FIGURE 15.6**   Time Spent in Various Sleep Stages During the Night.

As the night progresses, deep sleep decreases, and time in REM sleep (dark bars) increases.

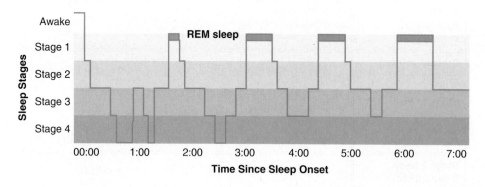

If people sleeping in the laboratory are awakened by the researcher during REM sleep, about 80% of the time they report dreaming. Dreams also occur during the other, *non-REM sleep* stages, but they are less frequent, less vivid, and less hallucinatory. Even people who say that they do not dream report dreaming when they are awakened from REM sleep; their non-REM sleep dreams are less frequent, though, and they often describe their experience as "thinking" (H. B. Lewis, Goodenough, Shapiro, & Sleser, 1966). Apparently, "non-dreamers" just fail to remember their dreams in the morning; in fact, we ordinarily remember a dream only if we wake up before the short-term memory of the dream has faded (Koulack & Goodenough, 1976). High-density EEG recording (using 256 channels) has revealed high-frequency activity (10–50 Hz) in areas related to the dream content—in the right posterior parietal cortex when the dream concerned a specific spatial setting, in Wernicke's area when speech was involved, and in the fusiform face area when people's faces were a part of the dream (Siclari et al., 2017).

The Functions of Sleep

What are the functions of REM and slow-wave sleep?

The effects of sleep loss leave no doubt about the importance of sleep. You have seen, for example, that the early morning hours are particularly vulnerable times for traffic accidents and major disasters. Cognitive impairment suffers especially; reducing sleep time to 6 hr or 4 hr for 14 days reduced alertness and working memory performance, with deficits equivalent to one night or two nights of total sleep deprivation, respectively (Van Dongen, Maislin, Mullington, & Dinges, 2003). Early research efforts were based on the idea that the main function of sleep is rest and restoration, with the major focus on non-REM sleep. One reason is that after total sleep deprivation, Stage 4 non-REM sleep is recovered before REM sleep (Anders & Roffwarg, 1973). Another reason is that slow-wave sleep increases following exercise; after athletes competed in a 92-kilometer race, slow-wave sleep was elevated for four consecutive nights (Shapiro, Bortz, Mitchell, Bartel, & Jooste, 1981). However, this effect appears to be due to overheating rather than fatigue. The night after people ran on treadmills, slow-wave sleep increased, at the expense of REM sleep; but if they were sprayed with water while they ran, their body temperature increased less than half as much and there was no change in slow-wave sleep (Horne & Moore, 1985). Horne & Harley (1989) believed that the slow-wave sleep increases are more related to the increase in the temperature of the brain than the increase in body temperature; heating only the head and face with a hair dryer was sufficient to increase slow-wave sleep later. According to Horne (1992), slow-wave sleep promotes cerebral recovery, especially in the prefrontal cortex, and there is evidence it restores processes involved in cognitive functioning. M. H. Bonnet and Arand (1996) gave people either caffeine or a placebo before a 3.5-hr nap. The caffeine group had reduced slow-wave sleep during the nap; although they felt more vigorous and no sleepier than the placebo group, they performed less well on arithmetic and vigilance tasks during a subsequent 41-hr work period.

To find out what functions REM sleep serves, researchers deprived volunteers of REM sleep by waking the research participants every time EEG and eye movement recordings indicated that they were entering a REM period. When this was done the subjects showed a "push" for more REM sleep. They went into REM more frequently as the study progressed and had to be awakened more often; then, on uninterrupted recovery nights, they tended to make up the lost REM by increasing their REM from about 20% of total sleep time to 25% or 30% (Dement, 1960). To psychoanalytically oriented theorists, these results were evidence of a psychological need for dreaming; but because REM sleep is so pervasive among birds and mammals, most neuroscientists believe that any explanation must be a biological one, and they treat dreaming as merely the by-product of spontaneous neural activity in the brain.

One hypothesis is that REM sleep promotes neural development during childhood. Infant sleep starts with REM rather than non-REM sleep, and the proportion of sleep devoted to REM is around 50% during infancy and decreases through childhood until it reaches an adult level during adolescence (Roffwarg, Muzio, & Dement, 1966). According to this hypothesis, excitation that spreads through the brain from the pons during REM sleep encourages differentiation, maturation, and myelination in higher brain centers, similar to the way spontaneous waves of excitation sweep across the retina during development to help organize its structure (see Chapter 3). There is some evidence from studies of the immature visual systems of newborn cats that REM sleep, and particularly these waves from the pons, regulates the rate of neural development (Shaffery, Roffwarg, Speciale, & Marks, 1999). The fact that sleep is associated with the upregulation of a number of genes involved in neural plasticity (see Chapter 12), as well as other genes that contribute to the synthesis and maintenance of myelin and cell membranes (Cirelli et al., 2004), is certainly consistent with this neurodevelopmental hypothesis. In addition, it suggests our next topic, which deals with the role of sleep beyond the developmental period. In the words of Giulio Tononi and Chiara Cirelli, sleep is "the price we pay for plasticity" (2014, p. 12).

Sleep, Plasticity, and Memory

In Chapter 12, you learned that a period of sleep following learning enhances later performance (Figure 15.7). REM sleep has received the most attention; it increases during the sleep period following learning, and REM sleep deprivation after learning reduces retention (see review in Dujardin, Guerrien, & Leconte, 1990; Karni, Tanne, Rubenstein, Askenasy, & Sagi, 1994; C. Smith, 1995). How much REM sleep increases depends on how well the subject learned (Hennevin, Hars, Maho, & Bloch, 1995). Observation of hippocampal activity after learning suggests why REM sleep is important. Replay during REM sleep of neural activity that occurred during learning (see Chapter 12) is synchronized with spontaneous theta-frequency (4–7 Hz) activity in the hippocampus (Stickgold, Hobson, Fosse, & Fosse, 2001); in other words, the peaks of one wave coincide with the peaks of the other. (You may remember from Chapter 12 that hippocampal theta is necessary for LTP to

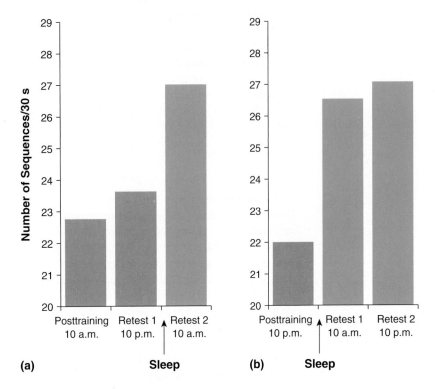

■ **FIGURE 15.7**   Improvement in Learning Following Sleep.

Participants learned a motor skill task and were retested twice at 10-hr intervals. There was no statistically significant improvement for individuals who remained awake during the interval (a, Retest 1), but performance improved following sleep (a, Retest 2, and b, Retest 1 and Retest 2).

Source: Adapted from "Practice With Sleep Makes Perfect: Sleep-Dependent Motor Skill Learning," by M. P. Walker, T. Brakefield, A. Morgan, J. A. Hobson, and R. Stickgold, 2003, *Neuron, 35*, pp. 205–211.

■ **FIGURE 15.8**   Correlation of Slow-Wave and REM Sleep With Overnight Task Improvement.

These graphs show the correlation of slow-wave sleep (SWS) and REM sleep with improvement on a visual discrimination task at the beginning of the next day's practice. They indicate that SWS has more effect during the first quarter of the night, whereas REM is important during the fourth quarter.

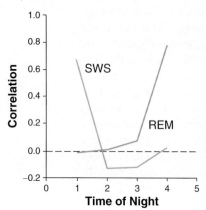

occur.) After four to seven days, the time during which memories become independent of the hippocampus, the replay shifts out of phase with the theta activity, with the peaks of one wave coinciding with the troughs of the other. This suggests that a period of consolidation is followed by one of deleting connections—representing old memories, inaccurate connections, or both.

Some research suggests that consolidation is a multistep process requiring a combination of slow-wave and REM sleep. Overnight improvement on a visual discrimination task in humans was correlated with the percentage of slow-wave sleep during the first quarter of the night *and* the percentage of REM sleep in the last quarter of the night (Figure 15.8; Stickgold, Whidbee, Schirmer, Patel, & Hobson, 2000). Even a 60- to 90-min nap that included both REM and slow-wave sleep produced significant improvement in performance (Mednick, Nakayama, & Stickgold, 2003). According to Ribeiro and his colleagues (2004), neuronal replay is strongest during non-REM sleep, and ample evidence from animal and human studies indicates the importance of non-REM sleep for learning (Hairston & Knight, 2004). For example, applying a 0.75-Hz oscillating current over the frontal and temporal areas or sounding tones timed to coincide with individual EEG waves increases slow-wave activity and improves the recall of word associations learned prior to sleep (L. Marshall, Helgadóttir, Mölle, & Born, 2006; J. L. Ong et al., 2016; Papalambros et al., 2017; Westerberg et al., 2015). Replay during non-REM sleep is accompanied by 200-millisecond bursts of fast-frequency (100–120 Hz) activity known as *ripples,* which are generated by the hippocampus and activate the default mode network, which is otherwise quiescent during non-REM sleep (Kaplan et al., 2016; M. P. Walker & Robertson, 2016). The number of ripples increases after intensive learning, and this increase predicts the success of memory consolidation; electrical stimulation of the hippocampus suppresses ripples and impairs learning.

In their synaptic homeostasis hypothesis, Tononi and Cirelli (2013, 2014) argue that there is far better evidence for synaptic pruning during sleep than for consolidation; they believe this pruning improves the accuracy of information that was stored during waking by eliminating inaccurate connections. According to them, ripples, slow waves, and sleep spindles down-select synapses that were activated rarely during waking or that fit less well with old memories, whereas synapses that were strengthened repeatedly during waking or that are better integrated with older memories are protected. Luisa de Vivo and her colleagues (2017) used three-dimensional electron microscopy to observe 6,920 synapses in mice and confirmed that, during sleep, synaptic spines decreased at smaller, less stable synapses, whereas stronger synapses were spared.

Brain Structures of Sleep and Waking

We have seen one of the ways sleep can be regarded as an active process: A great deal of activity goes on in the brain during sleep; in fact, the brain's energy use is not significantly lower in sleep than during waking, and may even increase during slow-wave sleep (Dworak, McCarley, Kim, Kalinchuk, & Basheer, 2010). For the second aspect of this active process, we turn to the brain structures involved in turning sleep on and off. There is no single sleep center or waking center; sleep and waking depend on a variety of structures that integrate the timing of the SCN with homeostatic information about physical conditions such as fatigue, brain temperature, and time awake. Sleep is a homeostatic process, in that a period of deprivation is followed by a period of sleep; the balance between the two is brought about by mutually inhibiting wake and sleep centers. The network of structures governing sleep and waking is complex, so you will want to trace its connections carefully in Figures 15.9 and 15.11. Except where noted, the following discussion is taken from the thorough review of the literature by Clifford Safer and his Harvard colleagues (Saper, Fuller, Pedersen, Lu, & Scammell, 2010). We will begin with the structures that produce wakefulness.

? What brain structures are responsible for sleep and waking?

Waking and Arousal Controls

The waking network consists of two major pathways (Figure 15.9); we will start with the *brainstem arousal centers*, which send their activating signals to higher levels of the brain. This ascending pathway is itself made up of two branches. The first consists of *pedunculopontine and laterodorsal tegmental nuclei (PPT/LDT)*, which fire most rapidly during wakefulness and REM sleep and most slowly during non-REM sleep, apparently driving the cortical activation seen outside non-REM sleep. The second branch includes the *locus coeruleus, raphe nuclei, tuberomammillary nucleus,* and *parabrachial nucleus.* A distinction between the two branches is that although they both send projections to the prefrontal cortex, basal forebrain, and lateral hypothalamus, the PPT/LDT also has connections to the thalamus. Figure 15.10 shows how firing varies with sleep and waking in two of these areas.

Although lesions of these brain stem structures produce a loss of wakefulness, both animals and humans recover normal sleep-wake cycles within a period of weeks or months; this underscores the additional contribution of the *forebrain arousal centers.* The *basal forebrain* produces wakefulness and desynchronization of the EEG; disabling the basal forebrain with an anesthetic results in deep non-REM sleep. Similarly, orexin (hypocretin)-releasing neurons in the *lateral hypothalamus* both sustain wakefulness and suppress REM sleep. Like the brain stem centers, the forebrain arousal centers innervate the prefrontal cortex; the prefrontal cortex in turn sends descending projections back to the basal forebrain, hypothalamus, and brain stem.

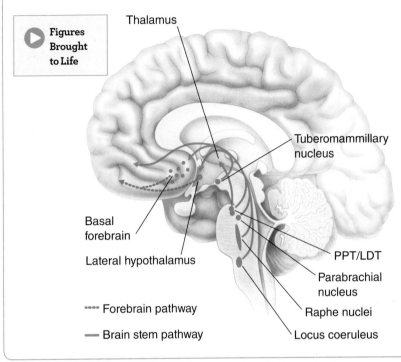

■ **FIGURE 15.9** Structures of Waking and Arousal.

Several interacting structures and pathways produce waking, maintain arousal during waking, and increase arousal during REM sleep.

Figures Brought to Life

Thalamus

Tuberomammillary nucleus

Basal forebrain

Lateral hypothalamus

PPT/LDT

Parabrachial nucleus

Raphe nuclei

Locus coeruleus

···· Forebrain pathway

— Brain stem pathway

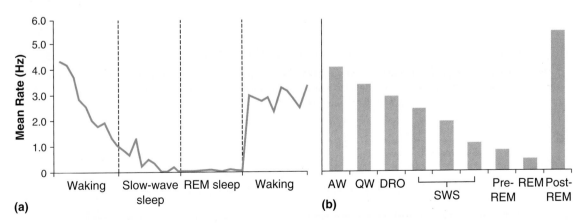

■ **FIGURE 15.10** Firing Rates in Brain Stem Arousal Centers During Waking and Sleep.

(a) Activity in the locus coeruleus; (b) activity in the raphe nuclei. Note that these nuclei are most active during waking, relatively quiet during non-REM sleep, and (unlike the PPT/LDT) almost silent during REM sleep. AW, alert waking; QW, quiet waking; DRO, drowsy; SWS, slow-wave sleep; pre-REM, 60 seconds before REM; post-REM, first second after REM ends.

Sources: (a) Copyright 1981 by the Society for Neuroscience; (b) From "Activity of Serotonin-Containing Nucleus Centralis Superior (Raphe Medianus) Neurons in Freely Moving Cats," by M. E. Trulson et al., *Experimental Brain Research, 54,* 33–44, fig. 2. © 1984. With kind permission from Springer Science and Business Media.

■ **FIGURE 15.11** Brain Mechanisms Regulating Sleep.

Sleep is brought about primarily by suppressing activity in arousal structures (shown in green).

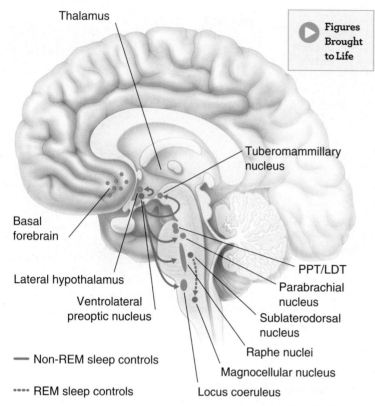

Thalamus

Tuberomammillary nucleus

Basal forebrain

Lateral hypothalamus

Ventrolateral preoptic nucleus

PPT/LDT

Parabrachial nucleus

Sublaterodorsal nucleus

Raphe nuclei

Magnocellular nucleus

Locus coeruleus

— Non-REM sleep controls

···· REM sleep controls

▶ Figures Brought to Life

Non-REM Sleep Controls

The most important structure in the non-REM sleep network is the *ventrolateral preoptic nucleus (VLPO;* Figure 15.11). Many of the VLPO's neurons fire two to four times faster during non-REM sleep than during wakefulness, and double that again as sleep deepens further. Lesions indicate that the VLPO's core is partly responsible for non-REM sleep and the extended VLPO contributes to REM sleep. The VLPO sends inhibitory signals to the lateral hypothalamus and the second branch of the brain stem arousal network; Saper and his colleagues suggest that the VLPO and the ascending arousal system are the basis for switching between the awake and sleep states. Rats with lesions of the VLPO still sleep about 50% as much as normal rats, which means there must be other sleep centers inhibiting the arousal systems. At least one has been identified; the *parafacial zone* in the medulla contributes to non-REM sleep by sending inhibition to the parabrachial nucleus (Anaclet et al., 2014).

REM Sleep Controls

High-voltage *PGO waves,* so called because of their path of travel from the *pons* through the lateral *geniculate* nucleus of the thalamus to the *occipital* area, begin about 80 seconds before the start of a REM period and apparently are what initiate the EEG desynchrony of REM sleep (Figure 15.12; Mansari, Sakai, & Jouvet, 1989; Steriade, Paré, Bouhassira, Deschênes, & Oakson, 1989). PGO waves are as characteristic of REM sleep as rapid eye movements are. Their arousal of the occipital area may account for the visual imagery of dreaming. PGO waves are synchronized with bursts of firing in PPT/LDT nuclei, while firing in the other arousal centers (locus coeruleus, raphe nucleus, and tuberomammillary nucleus) almost disappears. This suggests that the PPT/LDT might interact with the PGO nuclei to regulate alternation between non-REM and REM sleep.

The most important REM sleep center in the pons is the *sublaterodorsal nucleus (SLD),* which appears to govern switching in and out of REM sleep. Lesioning the SLD reduces REM sleep in rats; in cats it eliminates

■ **FIGURE 15.12** PGO Waves, EEG Desynchrony, and Muscle Atonia.

The records are of electrical activity in the lateral geniculate nucleus (LG), eye movements (EOG, electrooculogram), electroencephalogram (EEG), and muscle tension (EMG, electromyogram). Notice that PGO waves signal the beginning of EEG desynchrony, rapid eye movements, and atonia several seconds later.

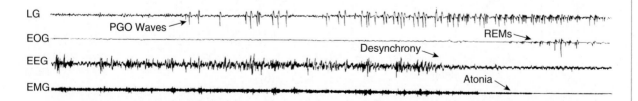

LG

PGO Waves

EOG

REMs

EEG

Desynchrony

EMG

Atonia

output to the magnocellular nucleus in the medulla, which is responsible for the atonia of REM sleep. The cats seemed to be acting out their dreams (assuming that cats dream), and their movements often woke them up (Shouse & Siegel, 1992).

Sleep Disorders

Insomnia

Insomnia is the inability to sleep or to obtain adequate-quality sleep, to the extent that the person feels inadequately rested. Insomnia is important not only as a nuisance but also because sleep duration has important implications for health. In a study of 1.1 million men and women, sleeping less than 6 hr a night was associated with decreased life expectancy (Kripke, Garfinkel, Wingard, Klauber, & Marler, 2002). However, the surprise in the study was that sleeping more than 8.5 hr was associated with as great an increase in risk of death as sleeping less than 4.5 hr. Lack of sleep may also be a factor in the obesity epidemic. In a long-term study of sleep behavior, people who slept less than 8 hr a night had a higher body mass index, along with lower leptin and higher ghrelin levels (Taheri, Lin, Austin, Young, & Mignot, 2004).

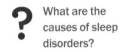

? What are the causes of sleep disorders?

The failure to get enough sleep is part of the lifestyle of industrialized countries, but many people who try to get an adequate amount of sleep complain that they have difficulty either falling asleep or staying asleep. In a survey by the National Sleep Foundation (2002), over half the respondents reported that they had trouble sleeping or woke up unrefreshed at least a few nights a week, and a third had experienced at least one symptom of insomnia every night or almost every night in the past year. Insomnia is one of the few disorders that is essentially self-diagnosed, and several studies suggest that the reported frequencies might be misleading. Although insomniacs may overestimate the time required to get to sleep and the amount of time awake through the night (Rosa & Bonnet, 2000), there are several indications that their sleep quality suffers from hyperarousal. These include excess high-frequency EEG during non-REM sleep (Perlis, Smith, Andrews, Orff, & Giles, 2001) and disturbance of the hypothalamic-pituitary-adrenal axis (see Chapter 8), with increased secretion of cortisol and adrenocorticotropic hormone during the night (Vgontzas et al., 2001).

Insomnia can be brought on by a number of factors, such as stress, but it also occurs frequently in people with psychological problems, especially affective disorders (Benca, Obermeyer, Thisted, & Gillin, 1992). Some loss of gray matter in the orbitofrontal cortex and the parietal cortex has been reported in insomniacs (Altena, Vrenken, Van Der Werf, van den Heuvel, & Van Someren, 2010); this could be a cause of their insomnia, or it could reflect the association with psychological disorders. Another study found reduced white matter integrity in several right hemisphere areas, the thalamus, and the corpus callosum; deficiencies in the thalamus and corpus callosum were correlated with the duration of patients' insomnia and with self ratings of depression (S. Li et al., 2016). Another frequent cause is the *treatment* of insomnia; most sleep medications are addictive, so attempts to do without medication or to reduce the dosage produce a rebound insomnia; this can happen after as little as three nights with some benzodiazepines (Kales, Scharf, Kales, & Soldatos, 1979). Insomnia can manifest itself as delayed sleep onset, nighttime waking, or early waking; a disruption of the circadian rhythm is often the culprit (M. Morris, Lack, & Dawson, 1990).

People with sleep difficulties often show a shift in their circadian rhythm; this can be the result of bad sleep habits, but it is more likely the cause. Normally, people fall asleep when their body temperature is decreasing in the evening and wake up when it is rising. But if your body temperature is still high at bedtime (phase delay), you will experience sleep-onset insomnia; if your body temperature rises too early (phase advance) you will wake up long before the alarm clock goes off (Figure 15.13). Sleep is also more efficient if you go to bed when your body temperature is low; for example, a volunteer living in isolation from time cues averaged a 7.8-hr sleep length when he went to bed during his temperature minimum and a 14.4-hr sleep length when sleep began near his temperature peak (Czeisler, Weitzman, & Moore-Ede, 1980). Your *chronotype*—when your internal clock is synchronized to the 24-hr day—depends partly on your genes and partly on your environment (Roenneberg et al., 2004). People with advanced sleep phase disorder feel compelled to go to sleep around 7:30 in the evening and then wake up around 4:30 a.m. A mutation in the circadian clock gene *CKI* has been linked to the disorder (Xu et al., 2005); more recently, three mutations in another clock gene, *PER2*, have also been identified (Chong, Ptáček, & Fu, 2012). Delayed sleep phase syndrome—late bedtime and rising—has been associated with the *PER3* clock gene (S. N. Archer et al., 2003).

It is usually easier for people to delay sleep at night than to rise early, which led to a treatment that seems completely counterintuitive. The patients had a 5- to 15-year history of sleep-onset insomnia so severe that they were not even going to bed until 4:15 a.m., on average. Rather than require them to retire earlier, the researchers had the patients *stay up 3 hr later* each day than the day before. After about a week of this routine—for example,

■ **FIGURE 15.13** Effects of Disrupted Circadian Rhythm on Sleep.

Ordinarily, a person falls asleep while the body temperature is decreasing and awakens as it is rising (a). If body temperature is phase delayed (b), the person has trouble falling asleep; if body temperature is phase advanced (c), the person wakes up early. (Sleep period is the time in bed, whether the person is sleeping or not.)

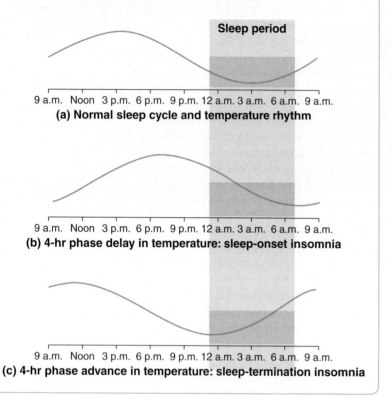

Sleep period

9 a.m. Noon 3 p.m. 6 p.m. 9 p.m. 12 a.m. 3 a.m. 6 a.m. 9 a.m.
(a) Normal sleep cycle and temperature rhythm

9 a.m. Noon 3 p.m. 6 p.m. 9 p.m. 12 a.m. 3 a.m. 6 a.m. 9 a.m.
(b) 4-hr phase delay in temperature: sleep-onset insomnia

9 a.m. Noon 3 p.m. 6 p.m. 9 p.m. 12 a.m. 3 a.m. 6 a.m. 9 a.m.
(c) 4-hr phase advance in temperature: sleep-termination insomnia

going to bed at 8 a.m., 11 a.m., 2 p.m., 5 p.m., 8 p.m., and 11 p.m. on successive nights—their average sleep-onset time had shifted from 4:50 a.m. to 12:20 a.m., and their average waking time had shifted from 1:00 p.m. to 7:55 a.m. All five patients were able to give up the sleeping pills they had become dependent on, and improvement was long lasting (Czeisler et al., 1981). Phototherapy is also sometimes used to reset the circadian clock.

Sleepwalking

Some of the sleep disorders are related to specific sleep stages. As we saw earlier, bedwetting, night terrors, and sleepwalking occur during slow-wave sleep. Although sleepwalking is most frequent during childhood, about 3%–8% of adults sleepwalk (A. Dalton, 2005). Kenneth Parks's story in the opening vignette is not unique. The sleepwalking defense was first used in 1846 when Albert Tirrell was acquitted of the murder of his prostitute mistress and the arson of her brothel, and the plea has been successful in a few more recent instances as well (A. Dalton, 2005). Sleepwalking can be triggered by stress, alcohol, and sleep deprivation; Ken's jury was convinced that he was not responsible because he was sleep deprived due to stress over gambling debts and the loss of his job for embezzling; there was a personal and family history of sleepwalking, sleep talking, and bedwetting; and he produced a high level of slow-wave sleep during sleep monitoring (Broughton et al., 1994).

Vulnerability for sleepwalking is at least sometimes genetic. Children of sleepwalkers are 10 times more likely to sleepwalk than children without sleepwalking relatives, and people with a version of a gene that is also implicated in narcolepsy are 3.5 times as likely to sleepwalk as others (Lecendreux et al., 2003). The gene is a member of the human leukocyte antigen (HLA) family, a group of genes that target foreign cells for attack by the immune system, and the authors suspect that cells important in sleep regulation have been attacked by the individual's immune system.

A less known non-REM sleep behavior is sexsomnia, engaging in sexual behavior while asleep. Although usually the worst consequence is embarrassment, the behavior has sometimes led to criminal charges (often leading to acquittal on grounds of nonresponsibility). The prevalence of sexsomnia is uncertain, but 11% of men and 4% of women seeking treatment for sleep disorders reported engaging in sexual behavior while asleep (American Academy of Sleep Medicine, 2010). Patients with sexsomnia didn't differ from the other patients in fatigue, depression, smoking, or caffeine consumption, but they were twice as likely to admit using illicit drugs.

Somewhere in between people who commit mayhem during sleepwalking and those who simply wander about the house are those who suffer from a *sleep-related eating disorder,* the subject of the accompanying Application.

Narcolepsy

When stabilization of the sleep switch fails, the result is *narcolepsy,* a disorder in which individuals fall asleep suddenly during the daytime and go directly into REM sleep. Another symptom of narcolepsy is *cataplexy,* in which the person has a sudden experience of one component of REM sleep, atonia, and falls to the floor paralyzed but fully awake. People with narcolepsy do not sleep more than others; rather, the boundaries are lost between sleep and waking (Nobili et al., 1996). Dogs also develop the disorder, and the study of canine narcolepsy has identified a mutated form of the gene that is responsible for the orexin receptor (Figure 15.14; Lin et al., 1999).

APPLICATION
In the Still of the Night

Shirley Koecheler raids the refrigerator at night (Black & Robertson, 2010). She would like to quit because she's gaining weight, but she isn't aware she's doing it until she wakes up in the morning to a crumb-filled bed and an uncomfortably full stomach. She even had her husband hide the Easter candy, but the next morning she found the wrappers from the chocolate bunnies in the wastebasket. Shirley's 24-year-old daughter Amy is also a sleep eater and has been since she was a toddler; the difference is that she doesn't gain weight. Anna Ryan, like Shirley, started sleep eating in adulthood; she didn't even know about the nighttime kitchen forays that added 60 pounds to her weight in a year and a half until she went to a sleep clinic to find out why she was exhausted every morning. Sleep eaters, usually women, ordinarily pass up healthy snacks for high-calorie junk food; they have also been known to eat soap, glue, frozen pizza, paper, and even egg shells (Epstein, 2010).

Source: iStock/Artfoliophoto.

Sleep-related eating likely has multiple causes. In some instances, the individuals have other sleep disorders, such as sleep apnea, or a history of substance abuse. Some individuals who take pharmacological sleep aids (e.g., Ambien or benzodiazepines such as zolpidem) have reported drug-induced sleep-related eating, although the clinical features of these individuals seem to differ from those who have sleep-related eating as a primary diagnosis (Komada et al., 2016).

A reliable and effective treatment has not yet been found. Amy has responded well to a drug used to prevent seizures; she still sleep eats occasionally, but it's no longer the problem it once was. It took Anna and her doctor months of trial and error to find a combination of drugs that works, but now she sleeps through the night and is losing weight.

Other researchers studied the effect of orexin as a feeding stimulant in mice by disabling both copies of the gene responsible for producing orexin, but what they observed was more interesting than eating behavior (Chemelli et al., 1999). Occasionally, the mice would suddenly collapse, often while walking around or grooming; the mice were narcoleptic! Most narcoleptic humans (those with cataplexy) turned out to have the same deficiency as the mice; they had low or undetectable levels of orexin, due to a loss of orexin-secreting neurons in the hypothalamus (Higuchi et al., 2002; Kanbayashi et al., 2002). The neurons are destroyed by an autoimmune reaction, which in some cases can be traced to an allele of the *HLA* immune system gene (Hallmayer et al., 2009). Narcolepsy's concordance of 25%–31% in identical twins (Mignot, 1998) leaves plenty of room for environmental influence. Identifying the nongenetic causes has been difficult, but one appears to be the H1N1 influenza (swine flu) virus (De la Herran-Arita et al., 2013; Han et al., 2011). The onset of narcolepsy tends to be seasonal, nearly seven times more frequent shortly after winter; it also increased threefold following the 2009 H1N1 epidemic in China, and lab study has shown that the virus can trigger the immune reaction.

REM Sleep Behavior Disorder

An apparent opposite of cataplexy is *REM sleep behavior disorder;* affected individuals are uncharacteristically physically active during REM sleep, often to the point of injuring themselves or their bed partners. A study of 93 patients, 87% of whom were male, found that 32% had injured themselves and 64% had assaulted their spouses

■ **FIGURE 15.14**   Cataplexy in a Dog.

Sleep researcher William Dement holds Tucker before (a) and during (b) an attack of cataplexy. Tucker is paralyzed but awake.

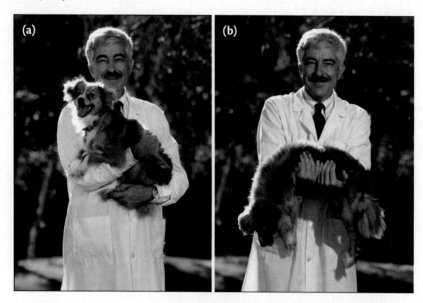

Source: Courtesy of Stanford University Center for Narcolepsy.

(E. J. Olson, Boeve, & Silber, 2000). A 67-year-old man had tied himself to his bed with a rope at night for 6 years because he had a habit of leaping out of bed and landing on furniture or against the wall. One night, he was awakened by his wife's yelling because he was choking her; he was dreaming that he was wrestling a deer to the ground and was trying to break its neck (Schenck, Milner, Hurwitz, Bundlie, & Mahowald, 1989). REM sleep behavior disorder is often associated with a neurological disorder, such as Parkinson's disease or a brain stem tumor (E. J. Olson et al., 2000). Lewy bodies have been found in patients' brains, and two thirds of patients develop Parkinson's about 10 years later (Boeve et al., 2003). These findings have contributed to the hypothesis that Parkinson's disease is preceded by the development of Lewy bodies in the medulla, where inhibition of the magnocellular nucleus ordinarily produces atonia; the Lewy bodies then progress upward through the brain before reaching the substantia nigra years later, when the full-blown disease appears (Braak et al., 2003).

Sleep as a Form of Consciousness

At the beginning of this discussion, we said that sleep is neither entirely conscious nor unconscious. Francis Crick (1994), who shared a Nobel Prize for the discovery of DNA's structure in 1962 before turning to neuroscience and the study of consciousness, believed that we are in a state of diminished consciousness during REM sleep and that we are unconscious during non-REM sleep. Certainly there are some elements of consciousness in the dream state, particularly in people who are *lucid dreamers.* You have probably had the occasional experience of realizing during a bad dream that it is not actually real and will end soon. That kind of experience is common for lucid dreamers—they are often aware during a dream that they are dreaming. People can be trained to become aware of their dreaming and to signal to the researcher when they are dreaming by pressing a handheld switch (Salamy, 1970). They can even learn to *control* the content of their dreams; they may decide before sleeping what they will dream about, or they may interact with characters in their dream (Gackenbach & Bosveld, 1989). This ability tells us that the sleeping person is not necessarily as detached from reality as we have thought. This point is further illustrated by sleepwalkers, who have driven cars; wandered the streets; brandished weapons (Schenck et al., 1989); and strangled, stabbed, and beaten people to death, all presumably during non-REM sleep.

So it is not clear where or whether the transition from consciousness to nonconsciousness occurs during sleep. The idea of a dividing line is blurred even further by reports that surgical patients can sometimes remember the surgical staff's conversations while they were anesthetized, and they show some memory later for verbal material presented at the time of surgery (Andrade, 1995; Bonebakker et al., 1996). Whether you draw the line of consciousness between waking and sleeping or between REM and non-REM sleep or between sleep and coma depends more on your definition of consciousness than on any clear-cut distinctions between these conditions. Perhaps it is better to think of sleep as a different state of consciousness along a continuum of consciousness. We can then concentrate on what the differences between waking and sleeping tell us about consciousness rather than worrying about classifications.

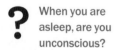

When you are asleep, are you unconscious?

"
The world shall perish not for lack of wonders, but for lack of wonder.

—*J. B. S. Haldane*
"

Take a Minute to Check Your Knowledge and Understanding

- Describe the circadian and ultradian rhythms discussed here.
- What, according to research, are the functions of REM and slow-wave sleep?
- Make a table showing the brain structures involved in sleep and waking, with their functions.
- Describe the sleep disorders and their causes.

The Neural Bases of Consciousness

Although strict behaviorists had banned consciousness as neither observable nor necessary for explaining behavior, over the last half of the 20th century researchers began to find that various components of consciousness *were* necessary as they studied memory, attention, mental imagery, and emotion. Still, they carefully avoided using the word *consciousness* as they talked about awareness, attention, or cognition. Then, a few respected theorists began musing about consciousness in print and even suggesting that it was an appropriate subject for neuroscientists to study. Other scientists slowly began to come out of their closets, while their more cautious colleagues warned them not to allow consciousness to become a back door for the reentry of the mind or for the proverbial homunculus, the "little man" inside the head who pulls all the levers. In the words of one team of writers, "consciousness is not some entity deep inside the brain that corresponds to the 'self,' some kernel of awareness that runs the show" (Nash, Park, & Willwerth, 1995).

So just what do we mean by *consciousness*? Actually, the term has a variety of connotations. We use it to refer to a state—a person is conscious or unconscious, and we use it in the sense of conscious experience, or awareness of something. *Consciousness* has additional meanings for researchers, though few try to define the term; Francis Crick (1994) suggested that any attempt at definition at this point in our knowledge would be misleading and would unduly restrict thinking about the subject. While agreeing on a definition is impractical, most researchers would likely be comfortable with the following assertions about consciousness. The person is aware, at least to some extent; as a part of awareness, the person holds some things in attention, while others recede into the background. Consciousness also involves memory, at least of the short-term variety, and fully conscious humans have a sense of self, which requires long-term memory. Consciousness varies in level, with coma and deep anesthesia on one extreme, alert wakefulness on the other, and sleep in between. There are also altered states of consciousness, including hypnosis, trances, and meditative states. Over the next several pages we will see how theorists have attempted to explain the neural bases of consciousness.

> "
> *The explanation of consciousness is essential for explaining most of the features of our mental life because in one way or another they involve consciousness.*
>
> —John R. Searle
> "

Network Explanations of Consciousness

One way researchers have sought the neural origins of consciousness is by identifying the structures where damage or stimulation can produce unconsciousness. We have long known that lesions to the thalamus can result in loss of consciousness; the intralaminar nuclei of the thalamus are especially important, most likely because they are responsible for the ability of the thalamus and cortical areas to work as a system (Tononi, 2005). A more recently identified area is a very small region of the brain stem called the rostral dorsolateral pontine tegmentum. Among 12 veterans whose wartime head injuries had rendered them unconscious, 10 had lesions there, whereas only one of 24 controls did (D. B. Fischer et al., 2016).

Consciousness does not reside in these structures, of course; they exert their influence through their connections with higher levels of the brain; the most important are with the anterior cingulate cortex and the anterior insular cortex (Figure 15.15). These structures have numerous functions related to awareness and arousal, from attention and response selection to pain and emotional behavior (Medford & Critchley, 2010). For example, they are less active in response to emotional stimuli in individuals with depersonalization disorder, which is characterized by a sense of unreality in experience of self and surroundings. More important for our purposes, they are core components in the *salience network,* which detects significant stimuli that require attention. The salience network switches back and forth between the default mode network, which you will remember is active when the brain is at wakeful rest, and the *central executive network,* which is goal and task oriented and externally directed (Figure 15.16; Uddin, 2015).

> "
> *One is always a long way from solving a problem until one actually has the answer.*
>
> —Stephen Hawking
> "

■ **FIGURE 15.15**   The Anterior Cingulate Cortex, Insular Cortex, and Claustrum.

(a) The cingulate cortex (highlighted) is the gyrus overlying the corpus callosum; the anterior cingulate cortex is the area in a lighter color. (b) The insular cortex forms the inner wall of the lateral fissure; the claustrum is nearby, separated only by a narrow band of white matter.

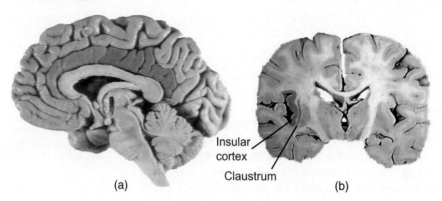

Insular cortex

Claustrum

(a)   (b)

Sources: (a) PEIR Digital Library: http://peir.path.uab.edu/library/picture.php?/19085 (color added to cingulate cortex). (b) Callisto Science: http://www.callisto-science.org/NSI/Neuroscience_Image_Database/Images/sol04139.jpg (background color removed; color added to insular cortex and claustrum).

■ **FIGURE 15.16**   The Default Mode, Salience, and Central Executive Networks.

By detecting whether conditions require attention, the salience network switches back and forth between the internally directed default mode network and the task-oriented, externally directed central executive network. ACC, anterior cingulate cortex; AIC, anterior insular cortex; DLPFC, dorsolateral prefrontal cortex; PCC, posterior cingulate cortex; PPC, posterior parietal cortex; VMPFC, ventromedial prefrontal cortex.

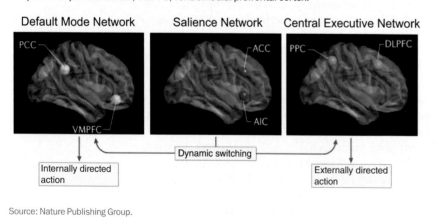

Source: Nature Publishing Group.

According to most theorists, consciousness occurs when functioning becomes coordinated between widespread networks, enabling them to share and integrate information (Baars, 2005; Dehaene & Naccache, 2001; Tononi, 2005). For example, when stimuli reach awareness they produce widespread activity in the prefrontal and parietal cortex (Figure 15.17; reviewed in Baars, 2005; see Dehaene et al., 2001; Sergent, Baillet, & Dehaene, 2005). By contrast, during deep sleep, coma, vegetative states, epileptic loss of consciousness, and general anesthesia, coordinated activity among brain areas disappears and auditory and pain stimuli fail to evoke activity beyond the primary areas. Many theorists believe that gamma frequency oscillations (30-90 Hz) between the thalamus and the cortex not only are the most likely means of achieving this coordination but also are necessary for consciousness (Ribary, 2005). This is difficult to demonstrate, but human imaging shows that during anesthesia-induced loss of consciousness, functional connectivity is disrupted between the thalamus and the cortex, and activity decreases in the frontal-parietal network and in the default mode network (Akeju et al., 2014). In addition, 40-Hz or 100-Hz stimulation of the central thalamus in mice arouses them from sleep and produces widespread activation of the forebrain, whereas stimulation at 10 Hz reduces forebrain activity, inhibits sensory cortex, and produces behavioral arrest (J. Liu et al., 2015). These results are consistent with Giulio Tononi's hypothesis that consciousness depends on the brain's ability to integrate information, an ability that is impaired by diminishing connectivity (Tononi, 2008). According to the accompanying In the News feature, LSD owes its ability to alter consciousness in part to changes it produces in network functioning.

Distribution of consciousness suggests that there is no *center* of consciousness, but some researchers believe that there must be an *executive*, an area that coordinates or orchestrates the activity of all the other structures. Researchers have proposed a variety of locations for this executive, including the thalamus (Crick, 1994), the anterior cingulate cortex (Posner & Rothbart, 1998), and the claustrum (see Figure 15.15 again; Crick & Koch, 2005). Both lesions and stimulation of the claustrum have been associated with loss of consciousness (Chau, Salazar, Krueger, Cristofori, & Grafman, 2015; Koubeissi, Bartolomei, Beltagy, & Picard, 2014). But what intrigues some consciousness researchers is that the claustrum has reciprocal connections with all the primary sensory and motor areas as well as the limbic system, and imaging showed it had the highest density of connections with all areas examined (Torgerson, Irimia, Goh, & Van Horn, 2015). Crick and Koch hypothesized that the claustrum binds information from multiple brain regions; Smythies, Edelstein, and Ramachandran (2012, 2014) have taken this a step further by hypothesizing that the claustrum does this by detecting neural synchrony between areas, and then it responds by sending out signals to initiate action. Whether this hypothesis is correct or not, support for a broad executive role for any structure remains weak. Just as consciousness appears to be distributed, its controls might be as well. And considering the complexity of consciousness that you see in Figure 15.18, those controls are likely to be numerous. These issues are not purely academic. As the accompanying Application shows, a better understanding of consciousness is a practical necessity. Following that, we will tackle the three components of consciousness we mentioned earlier.

Awareness

As an abstract concept, awareness is difficult to define and more difficult to study. Researchers have typically adopted the shorthand definition that awareness is equivalent to the content of consciousness (Chau et al., 2015) and focused their attention on *awareness of something*. Taking this approach has helped identify brain areas as potential locations of awareness. One strategy is to monitor the brain's activity in a scanner while flashing a series of words on a screen so briefly that they are at the threshold of detectability. If a person doesn't consciously notice the word, only the visual cortex is activated; as soon as the person becomes aware of the word, the lateral prefrontal cortex and posterior parietal cortex become active. These two areas and the thalamus

■ **FIGURE 15.17** Map of Event-Related Potentials to Masked and Unmasked Visually Presented Words.

When briefly presented words were masked by following them with nonmeaningful visual stimuli, activation was largely confined to the primary visual area (as well as slightly delayed) and did not produce awareness. Unmasked words produced additional subsequent activity, which spread through the frontal and parietal cortex, accompanied by awareness.

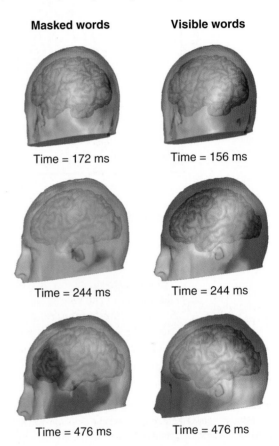

Masked words   **Visible words**

Time = 172 ms   Time = 156 ms

Time = 244 ms   Time = 244 ms

Time = 476 ms   Time = 476 ms

Source: From "Cerebral Mechanisms of Word Masking and Unconscious Repetition Priming," by S. Dehaene et al., *Nature Neuroscience, 4*, pp. 752–758, fig. 3, p. 755. © 2001 Macmillan Publishing. Used with permission.

have more interconnections with each other and the rest of the brain than any other region. These and other observations have led Daniel Bor and Ankil Seth to propose that the *prefrontal-parietal network* is important to awareness and to consciousness in general (Bor, 2013; Bor & Seth, 2012).

What happens when part of this network is damaged? There are many possibilities, but the case of a man who often attributed one object's color or direction of movement to another object after both parietal lobes were damaged is particularly instructive (L. J. Bernstein & Robertson, 1998). What this tells us is that brain damage impaired his ability to bind the spatial, color, and movement information together into an integrated percept. Increasingly, researchers are becoming convinced that binding involves synchronization of neural activity. Synchronized activity occurs mostly in the gamma frequency range. Early studies found that during visual stimulation, 50%–70% of neurons in the visual area of cats fired in synchrony at an average rate of 40 Hz (Engel, König, Kreiter, & Singer, 1991; Engel, Kreiter, König, & Singer, 1991). For an illustration of 40-Hz synchrony, see Figure 15.19. In response to a moving stimulus, activity synchronized between V1, the primary visual area, and V5, the area that detects movement (Engel, Kreiter, et al., 1991). This makes sense, because studies have indicated that visual awareness requires feedback to

 How does the brain solve the "binding problem"?

■ **FIGURE 15.18**   Awareness and Arousal in Normal and Impaired Consciousness.

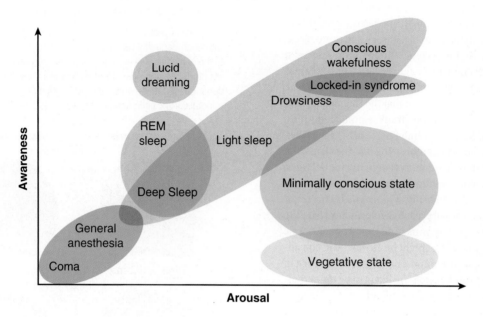

Source: Adapted from "The Neural Correlate of (Un)awareness: Lessons From the Vegetative State," by S. Laureys, 2005, *Trends in Cognitive Sciences, 9,* pp. 556–559.

V1 from extrastriate areas like V5 (reviewed in Tong, 2003). (You may want to refer to Figure 10.29 for the location of V1 and V5.)

Later investigations revealed that activity is coordinated over much wider areas. For example, when researchers presented a light that had previously been paired with shock to the finger, activity became synchronized between the visual cortex and the finger area of the somatosensory cortex (Figure 15.20; Miltner, Braun, Arnold, Witte, & Taub, 1999). In a learning study, at the moment each subject became aware that one tone was associated with a visual stimulus and another was not, neural activity in the left prefrontal cortex became coordinated with activity in other parts of the brain, including the right prefrontal cortex, auditory association areas, visual cortex, and cerebellum (McIntosh, Rajah, & Lobaugh, 1999). Another study better illustrates the integrative nature of this synchrony. Words were presented in various colors and at various locations on a screen; whether the subject became aware of the word's color or of its location—indicated by being able to recall it later—depended on whether a frontal or temporal area was activated during the presentation. But if the individual registered both the color and the location, additional activity occurred in a part of the parietal cortex (Uncapher, Otten, & Rugg, 2006).

Gaillard and his colleagues (2009) had the opportunity to record EEG activity from electrodes implanted in the brains of patients being evaluated for surgery to eliminate epileptic seizures; they recorded a cascade of awareness-defining events. Whether words reached awareness or not, they evoked coordinated gamma activity in the occipital area lasting

■ **FIGURE 15.19**   Forty-Hertz Oscillations in Neurons.

Top: Recording of the combined activity of all neurons in the vicinity of the electrode. *Bottom:* Activity recorded at the same time from two neurons adjacent to the electrode. By visually lining up the peaks and valleys of the two tracings, you can see that the two neurons are firing in synchrony with all the others in the area. (The upper tracing appears smoother because it is the sum of the activity of many neurons and because random activity is equally often positive and negative and cancels itself out.)

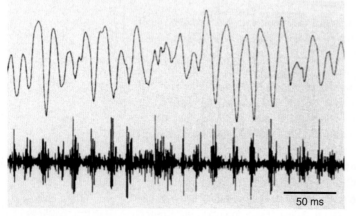

50 ms

Source: Courtesy of Wolf Singer, Max-Planck-Institut für Hirnforschung.

■ FIGURE 15.20 Synchronized Activity Among Areas Involved in Learning.

Numbered circles indicate the location of EEG electrodes; colored areas, from anterior to posterior, are the primary somatosensory cortex, secondary somatosensory cortex, and visual cortex. A light was paired several times with a shock to the middle finger. After that, presenting the light alone produced 40-Hz (average) EEG activity, which was synchronized between the visual cortex and the somatosensory cortex. The arrows indicate the pairs of electrodes between which synchrony was observed. Synchrony occurred (a) in the right hemisphere when shock had been applied to the left hand and (b) in the left hemisphere when shock had been applied to the right hand.

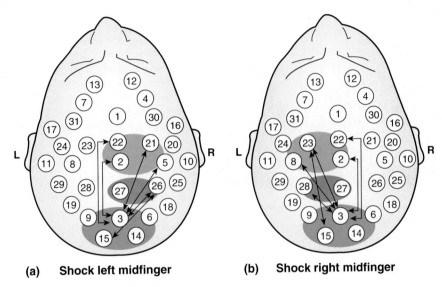

(a) **Shock left midfinger**   (b) **Shock right midfinger**

Source: Adapted from "Coherence of Gamma-Band EEG Activity as a Basis for Associative Learning," by W. H. Miltner et al., *Nature*, 397, pp. 434–436. © 1999 Nature Publishing. Reprinted by permission.

about 300 milliseconds; if the words were recognized, this localized activity was followed by synchronized activity among occipital, parietal, and temporal areas. In addition, neurons in one area appeared to be triggering firing among neurons in the other areas.

It is important to emphasize that much of our behavior is guided by processes that are outside awareness. A simple example would be our constant use of proprioceptive information to sit erect, to walk, and to reach accurately for objects in our environment. You learned in previous chapters that people with impaired facial recognition (prosopagnosics) are aroused by familiar faces that they do not otherwise recognize, that people with blindsight locate objects they deny seeing, and that patients with hippocampal damage improve over time on tasks that they deny having performed before. A more esoteric example is that by relying on nonvisual photoreceptors among the ganglion cells, blind people can tell whether a light is on or off better than chance, though they report that they don't see it (Vandewalle et al., 2013). In one study, research participants were able to learn and use a pattern for predicting the location of a target on a computer screen, but not one of them was able to state what the pattern was—even when offered a reward of $100 for doing so. Through subtle training procedures, people have learned to associate a particular facial feature with a particular personality characteristic without being aware they had done so; in fact, when questioned, they did not believe that such a relationship existed (reviewed in Lewicki, Hill, & Czyzewska, 1992). We like to believe that our behavior is rational and guided by conscious decisions; perhaps we invent logical-sounding explanations for our behavior when we are not aware of its true origins. So what is the benefit of conscious awareness? This is actually a matter of debate, but one apparent advantage is that it enables a consistency and a planfulness in our behavior that would not be possible otherwise.

Attention

Separating attention and awareness is difficult, and it is even controversial whether we can do so. However, it is instructive to think of awareness as referring to the *content* of consciousness and attention as a *process*—the act of attending, or the act of selecting among the contenders for our awareness. *Attention* is the brain's means of allocating its limited resources by focusing on some neural inputs to the exclusion of others.

APPLICATION
Determining Consciousness When It Counts

PET scans reveal metabolic activity corresponding to patients' level of consciousness.

Source: iStock/kupicoo.

A disturbing aspect of brain damage is that it often deprives patients of the ability to communicate with family and caregivers. The worst are in a *coma* and completely unresponsive to stimulation. Those who are in a *vegetative state* respond reflexively to stimulation and cycle through wakefulness and sleep, but they do not interact voluntarily with their environment. The *minimally conscious* occasionally show voluntary responses, such as following visual movement or crying when they hear a family member's voice, but they don't reliably communicate. In contrast, patients with *locked-in syndrome* are fully conscious; however, they are paralyzed and are able to communicate only with eye movements or finger twitches, if at all.

Physicians often rely on clinical observation for diagnosis rather than neurobehavioral testing. Thus, an estimated 40% of patients classified as being in a vegetative state are actually minimally conscious (Schnakers et al., 2009). Brain scans do a much better job (see figure), but they are expensive and not always available. J.-R. King and his associates (2013) developed a device that uses EEG to distinguish whether a series of beeps activates the auditory area or a larger network, signaling some level of consciousness. In a preliminary test, the device distinguished among patients who were in a vegetative state, in a minimally conscious state, or conscious. Determining level of consciousness is critical not only for care decisions but also for developing ways of communicating with patients and restoring function.

When patients were asked to imagine two different activities during an fMRI, five out of six patients classified as being in a vegetative state produced distinctive activity in different regions of the brain (Monti et al., 2010). One of the patients, considered in a vegetative state for five years, was able to answer questions correctly by thinking about one of the activities for "yes" and the other for "no." Adapting the task to EEG will allow locked-in patients to communicate in complex sentences by focusing on letters one at a time on a keyboard display (Sellers, Ryan, & Hauser, 2014).

Detecting consciousness might also identify patients who could benefit from therapies as they develop. Both dopamine (Fridman et al., 2010) and GABA (Chatelle et al., 2014) agonists have improved consciousness and communication in minimally conscious patients. When Schiff and his colleagues (2007) electrically stimulated the thalamus of a man who had been unreliably responsive for six years following brain injury, he ate without tube feeding, watched movies, and communicated with gestures and phrases. After noninvasive ultrasound stimulation of the thalamus, another patient became fully conscious and was communicating with nods and headshakes and offering a fist-bump to one of his doctors (Monti, Schnakers, & Korb, 2016).

It's hardly necessary to tell you how important attention is. When you are paying attention to a fascinating book, you may not notice all the hubbub around you. Some stimuli "grab" your attention, though; for example, the voice of a friend calling your name stands out above all the din. Also, what is attended to is easily remembered, and what escapes attention may be lost forever. The practical importance of attention is demonstrated in studies showing a fourfold increase in automobile accidents while drivers are using a cell phone (McEvoy et al., 2005; Redelmeier & Tibshirani, 1997). This is not due to the driver having one hand off the wheel, because the risk was just as high when the driver was using a speaker phone; clearly, the problem was attention.

Although you are aware of the importance of attention, you probably do not realize just how powerful it is. An interesting demonstration is the *Cheshire cat* effect, named after the cat in *Alice in Wonderland,* who would fade from sight until only his smile remained. Have a friend stand in front of you while you hold a mirror in your left hand so that it blocks your right eye's view of your friend's face but not the left eye's (Figure 15.21). Then hold your right hand so that you can see it in the mirror. (This works best if you and your friend stand in the corner of a room with blank walls on two sides.) Your hand and your friend's face will appear to be in the same position, but your friend's face, or part of it, will disappear. If you hold your hand steady, you will begin to see your friend's face again, perhaps through your "transparent" hand; move your hand slightly, and the face disappears again. By experimenting, you should be able to leave your friend with only a Cheshire cat smile. Your brain continues to receive information from both your hand and your friend's face throughout the demonstration; but because the two eyes are sending the brain conflicting information, telling it that two objects are in the same location, *binocular rivalry* occurs. The brain attends to one stimulus for a time and then switches to the other. Attention also switches when your hand or your friend's head moves and demands attention.

Attention is not just a concept; it is a physiological process, and changes in attention are accompanied by changes in neural activity. When an observer attends to an object, firing synchronizes between the brain areas involved, such as prefrontal with parietal neurons or parietal neurons with visual areas, depending on the task (Buschman & Miller, 2007; Saalmann, Pigarev, & Vidyasagar, 2007). When attention shifts, for example, during binocular rivalry, activity shifts from one group of neurons in the visual cortex to another, even though the stimulus inputs do not change (Leopold & Logothetis, 1996). When research participants focused on an object's color, PET scans showed that activity increased in visual area V4; activation shifted to the inferior temporal cortex when they attended to the object's shape, and it changed to area V5 during attention to its movement (Chawla, Rees, & Friston, 1999; Corbetta, Miezin, Dobmeyer, Shulman, & Petersen, 1990). We know that the shifts were due to attention, because activation also increased in V4 during attention to color even when the stimuli were uncolored and in V5 during attention to movement when the stimuli were stationary (Chawla et al., 1999).

So our experience of attention is a reflection of changes in brain activity. The increases in cortical activity described here are at least partly due to the modulation of activity in the thalamus, which is the gateway for sensory information to the cortex (except for olfaction). The cortex can selectively inhibit thalamic neurons and determine which information will reach it (John, 2005). When human subjects attended to a stimulus, neural responses to that stimulus increased in the lateral geniculate nucleus of the thalamus, and responses to ignored stimuli decreased (O'Connor, Fukui, Pinsk, & Kastner, 2002). (Remember that you saw similar results in Chapter 9.)

Attention involves a number of structures, and imaging suggests that they are organized into two networks: a dorsal one that allocates attention under goal-directed control and a ventral one that responds to stimulus demands (Asplund, Todd, Snyder, & Marois, 2010). However, the anterior cingulate cortex (ACC) may play an executive role (Figure 15.15). In individuals undergoing cingulate lesioning as a treatment for obsessive-compulsive disorder, 19% of ACC neurons either increased or decreased their firing rate during attention-demanding cognitive tests (K. D. Davis, Hutchison, Lozano, Tasker, & Dostrovsky, 2000). (You have to admire the brave souls who were willing to submit to mental arithmetic during brain surgery!) The ACC is also active during the Stroop word-color test, in which subjects must read color names as quickly as possible (Peterson et al., 1999). This is a difficult task, because some of the words are printed in a conflicting color; the researchers believe that the ACC modulates activity in attentional pathways to focus attention on the word's meaning and suppress attention to its color.

The Sense of Self

Consciousness is usually studied in relation to external reality—for example, object recognition or object awareness; this is in keeping with psychology's preference during much of its history for studying phenomena

■ **FIGURE 15.21**
Setup for Demonstrating the Cheshire Cat Effect.

Your view will alternate between your hand and your friend's face.

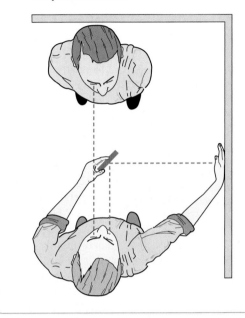

? What is the neural basis of attention?

Neural scientists are thus beginning to address aspects of the fundamental question of consciousness by focusing on a specific, testable problem: What neural mechanisms are responsible for focusing visual attention?

—Eric R. Kandel

Where does our sense of self come from?

that are "out there," where we can observe them objectively. But an important aspect of consciousness is what we call the self; the sense of self includes an identity—what we refer to as "I"—and the sense of *agency,* the attribution of an action or effect to ourselves rather than to another person or external force.

The sense of self is shared with few other species. We have learned this by using a cleverly simple technique developed for children. When the researcher puts a spot of rouge on a child's nose or forehead and places the child in front of a mirror, infants younger than about 15 months reach out and touch the child in the mirror or kiss it or hit it; older children will show self-recognition and use the mirror to examine the mysterious spot on their faces (M. Lewis & Brooks-Gunn, 1979). Chimpanzees are also able, after a time, to recognize themselves in the mirror; they examine the rouge spot, and they use the mirror to investigate parts of their body they have never seen before, like their teeth and their behinds (Figure 15.22). Elephants, orangutans, porpoises, and—get this—magpies also recognize themselves, but monkeys do not (Gallup, 1983; Plotnik, de Waal, & Reiss, 2006; Prior, Schwarz, & Güntürkün, 2008; Reiss & Marino, 2001). Although monkeys learned how a mirror works and would turn to face a person whose reflection they saw in the mirror, after 17 years of continuous exposure to a mirror in their cage, they still treated their reflections like an intruder (Gallup & Povinelli, 1998). Stroke or the dementia of old age can impair mirror self-recognition in humans; the person may treat the mirror image as a companion, as an intruder who must be driven from the home, or as a stalker who appears in automobile and shop windows (T. E. Feinberg, 2001).

Investigators have had some success in identifying neural correlates of the sense of self. Frontal-temporal damage, for example, impairs episodic memory and may produce a detachment from the self (M. A. Wheeler, Stuss, & Tulving, 1997). The anterior cingulate cortex and the insula (see Figure 15.15) are active when people recognize their own faces, identify memories as their own, or recognize descriptions of themselves (Devue et al., 2007; Farrer et al., 2003; G. R. Fink et al., 1998). Studies have also revealed that the medial parietal cortex and posterior cingulate cortex are responsible for self-related memory, whereas the medial prefrontal cortex and anterior cingulate cortex function together in self-evaluation (Lou, Changeux, & Rosenstand, 2016). For example, applying transcranial magnetic stimulation (TMS) over the parietal area reduced subjects' advantage in remembering words they had used to describe themselves compared to the words they had used to describe their best friend; TMS over the medial prefrontal cortex had no effect (Lou, Luber, Stanford, & Lisanby, 2010). By contrast, TMS over the medial prefrontal cortex (but not parietal cortex) reduced and even reversed subjects' tendency to describe themselves more positively than their best friend (Luber, Lou, Keenan, & Lisanby, 2012).

Farrer and Frith and their colleagues suggest that the sense of agency is mediated by the anterior insula and the inferior parietal area (Farrer et al., 2003; Farrer & Frith, 2002). When the subjects believed that they were controlling movements of a virtual hand or a cursor on a computer screen, activity increased in both the left and right insulas; when it became obvious that the experimenter was controlling the movement, activity shifted to the angular gyrus (in the inferior parietal cortex), particularly on the right (Figure 15.23). In other research, activity increased in the inferior parietal cortex as the discrepancy increased between the person's movements and feedback from the movements; Farrer and her colleagues (2008) interpret this as

■ **FIGURE 15.22**   A Chimp Demonstrates Concept of Self.

(a)

(b)

Source: Gallup and Povinelli (1998). Photos courtesy of Cognitive Evolution Group, University of Louisiana at Lafayette.

evidence that the angular gyrus contributes to the sense of agency by detecting discrepancies between actions and consequences. Later work found that sense of agency occurred during a task when the inferior parietal cortex initiated gamma-frequency communication with frontal cortical areas (Ritterband-Rosenbaum, Nielsen, & Christensen, 2014). People with schizophrenia who believe their behavior is controlled by another person or agent show heightened parietal activity compared with other schizophrenia patients and controls (Spence et al., 1997).

We do not find in these studies, nor should we expect to find, a brain location for the self; instead, what we see is scattered bits and pieces. We should regard the self as a concept, not an entity, and the sense of self as an amalgamation of several kinds of information, mediated by networks made up of many brain areas. Body image, memory, and the activity of mirror neurons are among the contributors to the sense of self; we will examine these topics and then consider two disorders of the self.

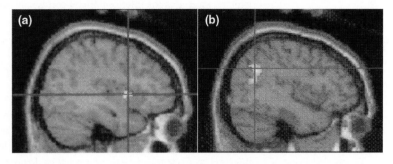

■ **FIGURE 15.23** Brain Areas Involved in the Sense of Agency.

Attributing an effect (movement of a computer cursor) to oneself activated the insula (a); attributing the movement to another person activated the angular gyrus in the inferior parietal cortex (b).

Source: From "Experiencing Oneself vs. Another Person as Being the Cause of an Action: The Neural Correlates of the Experience of Agency," by C. Farrer et al., *NeuroImage*, 15, pp. 596–603, fig. 2 and fig. 3, p. 598. © 2002 with permission from Elsevier, Ltd.

Body Image

Body image contributes to a sense of self because we have an identification with our body and with its parts; it is *our* body, *our* hand, *our* leg. A good example of the importance of body image to the sense of self is the phantom limb phenomenon. You learned in Chapter 11 that most amputees have the illusion that their missing arm or leg is still there (Figure 15.24). The illusion occurs in 80% of amputees and may persist for the rest of the person's life, which attests to the power of the body image. Distortions in the phantom sometimes add credibility to this point: One man was unable to sleep on his back because his phantom arm was bent behind him, and another had to turn sideways when walking through a door because his arm was extended to the side (Melzack, 1992). Researchers once thought that phantoms occurred only after a person developed a *learned* body image, but we now know that phantoms can occur in young children and even in people born with a missing limb. Because the body image is part of the equipment we are born with, it becomes an important part of the self—even when it conflicts with reality.

The "replacement" of a limb by a phantom does not prevent a feeling of loss, which can extend to the sense of self. This point was illustrated very graphically by S. Weir Mitchell, a Civil War physician who saw numerous amputees and presented some of his observations in the fictionalized account *The Case of George Dedlow* (S. W. Mitchell, 1866). Mitchell's hero, who has lost both arms and both legs in battle, says,

> I found to my horror that at times I was less conscious of myself, of my own existence, than used to be the case. . . . I felt like asking someone constantly if I were really George Dedlow or not. (p. 8)

In Chapter 11 we saw an example of a more extensive loss in the case of Christina. Watching a home movie of herself made before the disease had destroyed her proprioceptive sense, she exclaimed,

> Yes, of course, that's me! But I can't identify with that graceful girl any more! She's gone, I can't remember her, I can't even imagine her. It's like something's been scooped right out of me, right at the centre. (Sacks, 1990, p. 51)

■ **FIGURE 15.24** Maps of a Patient's Phantom Hand.

Touching the arm above the stump produced sensations of the missing hand. The same thing happened on the face, confirming what we saw in Chapter 11, that neurons from the face have invaded the hand area in the somatosensory cortex.

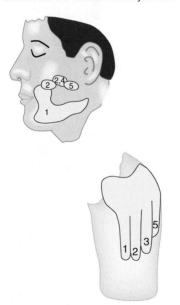

Source: Figure 2.2 from *Phantoms in the Brain* by V. S. Ramachandran, MD, PhD, and Sandra Blakeslee. Copyright © 1998 by V. S. Ramachandran and Sandra Blakeslee. Reprinted by permission of HarperCollins Publishers, Inc.

Although information about the body is processed in the somatosensory cortex, body image is a phenomenon that develops primarily in adjacent parietal areas. An example comes from earlier attempts to eliminate phantoms by surgery; lesions in the somatosensory area had no effect, but lesioning the right posterior parietal cortex did suppress the sensations (Berlucchi & Aglioti, 1997). One of the functions of the insula is the integration of internal with external information; damage to the posterior part of the insula, which is located in the inferior parietal cortex, can produce a variety of symptoms, including denial that a paralyzed limb belongs to the patient or perception of an extra limb (Berlucchi & Aglioti; Karnath & Baier, 2010). In Chapter 11, we saw that damage to the inferior parietal area can also cause the most extreme of body image illusions, the out-of-body experience (Blanke & Arzy, 2005).

Memory

Without long-term memory, it is doubtful there can be a self, because there is no past and no sense of who the person is. In the words of the memory researcher James McGaugh, memory "is what makes us us" (A. Wilson, 1998). Loss of short-term memory is not as disruptive; patients like HM (described in Chapter 12) have a lifetime of information about their past and about themselves as a background for interpreting current experience, even if they do not remember events that have occurred since their brain damage. However, for Alzheimer's and Korsakoff patients, memory loss extends back several years before the onset of illness, as well as after the onset. Oliver Sacks's patient Jimmie had lost 40 years of memories to Korsakoff syndrome; restless, unable to say whether he was miserable or happy, he reported that he had not felt alive for a very long time (Sacks, 1990).

Mary Frances, whom you met in Chapter 12, took another approach, explaining her situation with one false scenario after another. Another confabulator was Mr. Thompson, who took an unauthorized day's liberty from the hospital. At the end of the day, the cabdriver told the staff that he had never had so fascinating a passenger: "He seemed to have been everywhere, done everything, met everyone. I could hardly believe so much was possible in a single life" (Sacks, 1990, p. 110). According to Sacks, Mr. Thompson had to "make himself (and his world) up every moment" by turning everyone on the ward into characters in his make-believe world and weaving story after story as he attempted to create both a past and a present for himself.

The confabulated stories amnesiacs tell can usually be traced back to fragments of actual experiences. This is consistent with the hypothesis introduced in our earlier discussion, that confabulation is a failure to suppress irrelevant memories due to damage in the frontal area (Benson et al., 1996; Schnider, 2003; Schnider & Ptak, 1999). But, like Mr. Thompson, confabulators often prefer an embellished past to an ordinary one (Fotopoulou, Solms, & Turnbull, 2004); this together with the involvement of the anterior cingulate cortex (Turner et al., 2008) makes one suspect that the confabulation is also serving the self-image. The motivated nature of confabulation suggests the importance of real or imagined memories to the person's identity. As the movie director Luis Buñuel (1983) said as he contemplated his own failing memory,

> You have to begin to lose your memory, if only in bits and pieces, to realize that memory is what makes our lives. Life without memory is no life at all. . . . Our memory is our coherence, our reason, our feeling, even our action. Without it, we are nothing.

Self, Theory of Mind, and Mirror Neurons

A sense of self requires the distinction between our self and other selves and, arguably, some understanding of other selves. We saw in the discussion of autism that an ability to attribute mental states to others is called theory of mind and that researchers who study mirror neurons believe they are critical to our development of that comprehension (see Chapter 13). They give mirror neurons considerable credit for social understanding (Gallese & Goldman, 1998), empathy (Gazzola et al., 2006), and the ability to understand the intentions of others (Iacoboni et al., 2005). When volunteers watched a video clip, their mirror neurons responded more as a model reached for a full cup beside a plate of snacks (implying the intent to eat) than when the model reached for an empty cup beside an empty plate (implying the intent to clean up). The two scenes without the model produced no differences (Figure 15.25; Iacoboni et al., 2005).

Malfunction in the mirror neuron system is one reason suggested for the autistic individual's failure to develop a distinction between self and others, along with empathy and theory of mind (Cascio, Foss-Feig, Burnette, Heacock, & Cosby, 2012; J. H. G. Williams, 2008). Children with autism spectrum disorder took twice as long as control subjects to develop the rubber hand illusion, and the delay was correlated negatively with an empathy measure (Cascio et al., 2012). Justin Williams and his associates suggest that the problem is

■ **FIGURE 15.25** Different Intentions Distinguished by Mirror Neurons.

The implied intention of the actor in the photo on the left is to drink; in the photo on the right, it is to clean up. Different neurons were active as research participants viewed these two scenes, suggesting that mirror neurons can distinguish among intentions.

Source: From "Grasping the Intentions of Others With One's Own Mirror Neuron System," by M. Iacoboni, 2005, *PLoS Biology, 3,* pp. 529–535, fig. 1 upper right and lower right, p. 530. Used under the Creative Commons Attribution (CC BY) license.

not in the mirror neurons themselves but in the regulation of their function by the anterior cingulate cortex (J. H. G. Williams, Whiten, Suddendorf, & Perrtt, 2001).

Split Brains and Dissociative Identity Disorder: Disorders of Self

Chapter 3 describes a surgical procedure that separates the two cerebral hemispheres by cutting the corpus callosum. This surgery is used to prevent severe epileptic seizures from crossing the midline and engulfing the other side of the brain. Besides providing a unique opportunity to study the differing roles of the two hemispheres, split-brain patients also raise important questions about consciousness and the self. Gazzaniga (1970) described a patient who would sometimes find his hands behaving in direct conflict with each other—for instance, one pulling up his pants while the other tried to remove them. Once the man shook his wife violently with his left hand (controlled by the more emotional right hemisphere), while his right hand tried to restrain the left. If the person with a severed corpus callosum is asked to use the right hand to form a specified design with colored blocks, performance is poor because the left hemisphere is not very good at spatial tasks; sometimes the left hand, controlled by the more spatially capable right hemisphere, joins in to set the misplaced blocks aright and has to be restrained by the experimenter.

Different researchers interpret these studies in different ways. At one extreme are those who believe that the major or language-dominant hemisphere is the arbiter of consciousness and that the minor hemisphere functions as an automaton, a nonconscious machine. At the other extreme are the researchers who believe that each hemisphere is capable of consciousness and that severing the corpus callosum divides consciousness into two selves. Sixty years of research have prompted most theorists to take positions somewhere along the continuum between those extremes.

Gazzaniga, for instance, points to the right hemisphere's differing abilities, such as the inability to form inferences, as evidence that the right hemisphere has only primitive consciousness (Gazzaniga, Ivry, & Mangun, 1998). He says the left hemisphere not only has language and inferential capability but also contains a module that he calls the "brain interpreter." The role of the *brain interpreter* is to integrate all the cognitive processes going on simultaneously in other modules of the brain. Gazzaniga was led to this notion by observing the split-brain patient PS performing one of the research tasks. PS was presented a snow scene in the left visual field and a picture of a chicken's foot in the right and asked to point to a picture that was related to what he had just seen. With the right hand he pointed to the picture of a chicken, and with the left he selected a picture of a shovel (Figure 15.26). When asked to explain his choices, he (his left hemisphere) said that the chicken went with the foot and the shovel was needed to clean out the chicken shed. Unaware that the right hemisphere had viewed a snow scene, the left hemisphere gave a reasonable but inaccurate explanation for the left hand's choice. Although the right hemisphere has less verbal capability than the left, it can respond to simple commands; if the command "Walk" is presented to the right hemisphere, the person will get up and start to walk away. When asked where he or she is going, the patient will say something like "I'm going to get a Coke." According to Gazzaniga, these confabulations are examples of the brain interpreter making sense of its inputs, even though it lacks complete information.

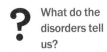

What do the disorders tell us?

■ FIGURE 15.26   Split-Brain Patient
Engaged in the Task Described in the Text.

His verbal explanation of his right hand's selection
was accurate, but his explanation of his left hand's
choice was pure confabulation.

Source: Gazzaniga (2002). Based on an illustration by John W.
Karpelou, BioMedical Illustrations.

Perhaps researchers who view the right hemisphere's consciousness as primitive are confusing consciousness with the ability to verbalize the contents of consciousness. Assigning different levels of consciousness to the two hemispheres may be premature when our understanding of consciousness is itself so primitive. Research with split-brain patients tells us to avoid oversimplifying such a complex issue.

Another disorder of self is *dissociative identity disorder* (DID; formerly known as multiple personality), which involves shifts in consciousness and behavior that appear to be distinct personalities or selves. You may be familiar with this disorder from the movie *The Three Faces of Eve*. Shy and reserved, Eve White would have blackouts while her alter ego, Eve Black, spent the night on the town dancing and drinking with strange men. The puritanical Eve White would have to deal with the hangover, explain a closetful of expensive clothes she didn't remember buying, and sometimes fend off an amorous stranger she found herself with in a bar (Lancaster, 1958; Thigpen & Cleckley, 1957). Eve, whose real name was Chris Sizemore, went on to develop 22 different personalities before she successfully integrated them into a single self (Figure 15.27; Sizemore, 1989). The causes of DID are not understood, but 90%–95% of patients report childhood physical and/or sexual abuse (Lowenstein & Putnam, 1990; C. A. Ross et al., 1990). Most therapists believe that the individual creates alternate personalities ("alters") as a defense against persistent emotional stress; the alters provide escape and, often, the opportunity to engage in prohibited forms of behavior (Fike, 1990; C. A. Ross et al., 1990).

Although DID is listed as a diagnostic category in the *Diagnostic and Statistical Manual of Mental Disorders,* 5th edition (*DSM*-5; American Psychiatric Association, 2013), a dramatic spike in cases has aroused suspicions not only about overdiagnosis but about the legitimacy of the disorder. DID had been reported occasionally since the middle 1600s (E. L. Bliss, 1980), but the number of cases jumped from 500 in 1979 to 5,000 in 1985 (Braun, 1985); the *DSM*-5 estimates the prevalence at 1.5% of American adults. Although some therapists believe that DID was underdiagnosed earlier (Putnam, 1991), critics say that the patients intentionally create the alternate personalities to provide an explanation for bizarre and troubling behavior, as a defense for criminal behavior, or at the urging of an overzealous therapist (Spanos, 1994). The case of Sybil (made famous by a book and a TV movie) is alleged to have been an elaborate hoax. According to writer Debbie Nathan (2011), it was motivated by Sybil's need for more attention from her therapist and her therapist's pursuit of professional recognition and a lucrative book deal. The possibility of numerous bogus cases justifies a certain amount of caution in interpreting the research in this area; at the same time there are a few research studies that indicate some intriguing physiological manifestations among individuals who report multiple personalities.

Consistent with a history of maltreatment and trauma during the childhood of people with DID, one study found a 19% reduction in the size of the hippocampus and a 32% reduction in the amygdala (Vermetten, Schmahl, Lindner, Loewenstein, & Bremner, 2006). From this perspective, it seems more

■ FIGURE 15.27   Chris Sizemore.

The story of her struggle with multiple personalities was the basis for the movie
The Three Faces of Eve.

Source: Debra Lex/Contributor/The LIFE Images Collection/Getty.

■ **FIGURE 15.28**   Hippocampal Activity During the Switch Between Multiple Personalities.

The scans show inhibition of the parahippocampus and hippocampus during the switch from the primary personality to the alter (a) and increased activity in the right hippocampus during the switch back (b, c). The brain levels of these three scans are shown in (d). (The brain is viewed from below, so right and left are reversed on the page.)

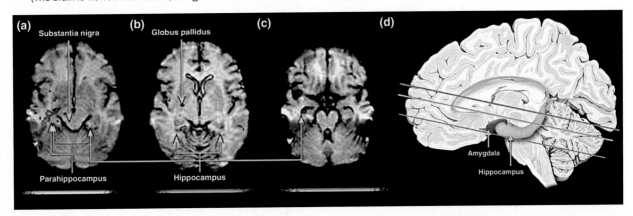

Source: From "Functional Magnetic Resonance Imaging of Personality Switches in a Woman With Dissociative Identity Disorder," by G. E. Tsai et al., *Harvard Review of Psychiatry*, 7(15), pp. 119–122. © 1999. Reprinted by permission of Wolters Kluwer Health.

appropriate to think of the alters not as personalities but as different ways of coping with a traumatic development. Physiological measures support this interpretation; alters respond differently in skin conductance, EEG, visual event-related potentials, and cardiovascular measures (Reinders et al., 2006). Brain scans show reduced activity in the orbitofrontal cortex, along with increases in the other frontal areas (Sar, Unal, & Ozturk, 2007) and differences in activation between alters while listening to personally relevant traumatic material (Reinders et al.).

Guochuan Tsai and his colleagues used functional magnetic resonance imaging to study a 33-year-old DID patient as she switched between her primary and an alter personality (Tsai, Condie, Wu, & Chang, 1999). During the switch from the primary to the alter, activity was inhibited in the hippocampus and parahippocampal area, particularly on the right side; during the switch back, the right hippocampus increased in activity (Figure 15.28). The hippocampal activity led the researchers to suggest that learning mechanisms are involved in development of the disorder. Imagining a new personality did not have the same effect even though it required as much effort. Several observations are consistent with the idea that learning structures are involved, and possibly impaired, in dissociation: Childhood abuse, which is frequent in patients' backgrounds, can produce hippocampal damage (Bremner et al., 1997); an association has been reported between identity dissociation and epileptic activity in the temporal lobes, where the hippocampi are located (Mesulam, 1981); and differences in temporal lobe activity have been found between personalities in the same individual (Saxe, Vasile, Hill, Bloomingdale, & Van der Kolk, 1992; Sheehan, Thurber, & Sewall, 2006).

> [T]here is a particular problem with finding endings in science. Where do these science stories really finish? Science is truly a relay race, with each discovery handed on to the next generation.
>
> —Richard Holmes, *in* The Age of Wonder

CONCEPT CHECK

Take a Minute to Check Your Knowledge and Understanding

- Summarize the "coordination" explanation for consciousness described here.
- What four changes in the brain accompany shifts of attention?
- What roles do body image and memory play in the sense of self?
- What controversy about consciousness have the split-brain studies produced?
- What physical differences have been found between alternate personalities in patients with dissociative identity disorder?

In Perspective

There was a time when the topic of sleep was totally mysterious and dreaming was the province of poets and shamans. Now sleep and dreaming are both yielding to the scrutiny of neuroscience. Although we are still unclear about the functions of sleep, we are learning how various structures in the brain turn it off and on, and how our body dances not only to a daily rhythm but also to another that repeats itself 16 times a day and controls our fluctuations in alertness, daydreaming, and night dreaming.

IN THE NEWS

LSD PROVIDES NEW INSIGHTS INTO CONSCIOUSNESS

As you learned in Chapter 5, the psychedelic drug lysergic acid diethylamide (LSD) had been studied previously by psychologists such as Timothy Leary for its ability to produce altered states of consciousness. Research on the effects of LSD had been halted for several decades due to bans on this illegal substance, but there is renewed interest in understanding LSD's effects on subjective experience. By using modern brain imaging techniques such as magnetoencephalography (MEG), arterial spin labelling (ASL), and blood oxygen level–dependent measures (BOLD) while participants experience the effects of LSD, researchers have gained new insight into the neural bases of human consciousness. Robin Carhart-Harris and colleagues (2016) discovered that the consciousness-altering effects of LSD were associated with modifications of brain networks; for example, increased connectivity between the visual cortex and other brain areas was correlated with visual hallucinations. The researchers also observed decreased alpha wave power, particularly in the posterior cingulate cortex, which they interpreted as an indication of reduced filtering of information. Of particular interest, decreased connection between the parahippocampus and the retrosplenial cortex was related to participants' loss of a sense of self and of meaning, indicating the circuit's role in those two processes. Further studies of altered consciousness under psychedelic drugs may provide insight into disruptions of consciousness that occur in psychological disorders such as schizophrenia.

THOUGHT QUESTIONS

1. How can modern brain imaging techniques reveal new information about people's experiences while under the influence of a drug such as LSD?

2. How can studies of people under the influence of drugs help scientists better understand typical brain function?

For more information, visit edge.sagepub.com/ garrett5e and select the Chapter 15 study resources.

Consciousness is also giving up its secrets as researchers bring modern technologies to bear on awareness, attention, and memory. In other words, what was once a taboo topic is becoming accessible to the research strategies of science and is providing a whole new arena of opportunities to observe the brain at work.

In this final chapter we have explored a unique field of research. The study of sleep has demonstrated neuroscience's ability to unravel mysteries and dispel superstition. The investigation of consciousness has been more daring, taking scientists where none had gone before. That is the job of science, to push back darkness, whether by finding a treatment for depression or by explaining humanity's most unique characteristics and capabilities. But we have traveled a road filled with questions and uncertain facts, and the words of the schizophrenia researcher that "almost everything remains to be done" still seem appropriate. If all this ambiguity has left you with a vaguely unsatisfied feeling, that is good; you may have the makings of a neuroscientist. And we have left the most exciting discoveries for you.

CHAPTER SUMMARY

Sleep and Dreaming

- Circadian rhythms are rhythms that repeat on a daily basis, affecting the timing of sleep and several bodily processes. The suprachiasmatic nucleus is the most important control center but not the only one. The rhythm is primarily entrained to light.
- Several ultradian rhythms occur within the day. One involves alternating periods of arousal during waking and stages that vary in arousal during sleep.

- REM sleep is when most dreaming occurs, but it has also been implicated in neural development and learning.
- Slow-wave sleep may restore cerebral and cognitive functioning; it participates in learning and memory, possibly in the form of both consolidation and pruning.
- Waking, sleep, and sleep's stages are controlled by separate, complex networks of brain structures.
- Insomnia, sleepwalking, narcolepsy, and REM sleep behavior disorder represent the effects of psychological disturbances in

some cases and malfunction of the sleep-wake mechanisms in others.

- Sleep is an active period, a state of consciousness that is neither entirely conscious nor unconscious.

The Neural Bases of Consciousness

- Any very specific definition of consciousness is premature, but normal consciousness includes awareness, attention, and a sense of self.
- How awareness comes about is unclear, but research has shown that it involves the thalamus, anterior cingulate cortex, insula, claustrum, and coordinated activity in brainwide networks.

- Attention allocates the brain's resources, actually shifting neural activity among neurons or brain locations.
- Body image, memory, and mirror neurons are important contributors to a sense of self.
- Split-brain surgery provides an interesting research opportunity into consciousness, which has prompted debates about each hemisphere's contribution to consciousness and to the self.
- Dissociative identity disorder involves what appear to be distinct personalities or selves. Reports indicate that the different states include different physical and physiological characteristics.

STUDY RESOURCES

FOR FURTHER THOUGHT

- Animals cycle on a 24-hr schedule, either sleeping at night and being active during the day or vice versa. An alternative would be to sleep when fatigue overtakes the body, regardless of the time. What advantages can you think of for a regular schedule?
- Machines and, probably, some simpler animals function just fine without awareness. Awareness places a significant demand on neural resources. What adaptive benefits do you see?
- Do you think we will be able to understand consciousness at the neural level? Why or why not? Will computers and robots achieve consciousness?

TEST YOUR UNDERSTANDING

1. Discuss the functions of sleep, including the REM and slow-wave stages of sleep.

2. Discuss attention as a neural phenomenon.

3. Discuss the function of confabulation in the behavior of split-brain patients and Korsakoff patients.

Select the best answer:

1. The most important function of sleep is

   a. restoration of the body.
   b. restoration of the brain.
   c. safety.
   d. a, b, and c
   e. uncertain.

2. The body's own rhythm, when the person is isolated from light, is

   a. approximately 24 hr long.
   b. approximately 25 hr long.

   c. approximately 28 hr long.
   d. unclear because of conflicting studies.

3. Jim is totally blind, but he follows a 24-hr day-night cycle like the rest of us and seems comfortably adapted to it. Animal studies suggest that he relies on

   a. a built-in rhythm in his SCN.
   b. nonvisual receptors in his eyes.
   c. clocks and social activity.
   d. a and b
   e. b and c

4. According to most neuroscientists, dreams are

   a. a way of resolving the day's problems.
   b. a replay of daytime learning.
   c. symbolic representations of emotional material.
   d. a by-product of neural activity.

5. Evidence that REM sleep specifically enhances consolidation is that

   a. REM increases after learning.
   b. REM deprivation interferes with learning.
   c. performance improves following REM sleep.
   d. a and b
   e. a, b, and c

6. An "executive" sleep and waking center is located in the

   a. rostral pons.
   b. lateral hypothalamus.
   c. preoptic area of the hypothalamus.
   d. magnocellular nucleus.
   e. none of the above

7. The magnocellular nucleus is responsible for

   a. initiating sleep.
   b. waking the individual.
   c. switching between REM and non-REM sleep.
   d. producing atonia during REM.

8. Cataplexy is

    a. sleep without a REM component.
    b. a waking experience of atonia.
    c. a more severe form of narcolepsy.
    d. clinically significant insomnia.

9. Evidence supporting a network theory of consciousness is

    a. the broader effect of a sensory stimulus during consciousness.
    b. that an executive for the networks has been identified.
    c. that there are several centers of consciousness.
    d. none of these

10. Neuroscientists generally agree that binding of spatial, color, and movement information into a single percept involves

    a. the insula.
    b. the anterior cingulate cortex.
    c. synchronization of neural activity between brain areas.
    d. activation of the default mode network.

11. An EEG at 40 Hz is associated with

    a. binding.   b. dreaming.
    c. consolidation.   d. attention.

12. The part of the brain where attention is shifted among stimuli may be the

    a. basal forebrain.   b. magnocellular nucleus.
    c. thalamus.   d. raphe nuclei.

13. An explanation offered for confabulation links it to damage to the

    a. locus coeruleus.   b. temporal lobes.
    c. pulvinar.   d. frontal areas.

14. Some evidence for the credibility of dissociative identity disorder is

    a. the high frequency of its diagnosis.
    b. different patterns of physiological measures.
    c. patients' lack of incentive to fake the symptoms.
    d. location of the damage in a particular brain area.

1. e, 2. d, 3. b, 4. d, 5. c, 6. e, 7. d, 8. b, 9. a, 10. c, 11. a, 12. c, 13. d, 14. b.

Answers:

ON THE WEB

The following websites are coordinated with this chapter's content. You can access these websites from the **SAGE edge Student Resources site**; select this chapter and then click on Web Resources. (**Bold** items are links.)

1. **The National Sleep Foundation** has links to sites of sleep research and support organizations, results of the annual poll Sleep in America, and information on sleep disorders.

2. **The Sleep Well** is the website of William Dement, noted sleep researcher.

3. The NOVA video **Sleep** is an entertaining treatment of the role of sleep in memory.

4. The American Academy of Sleep's **Sleep Education** page is a good source for information about sleep disorders and treatments.

5. **ABC News** video cameras caught Amy and Anna raiding the refrigerator—while they were asleep!

6. **Science of Consciousness** is a directory of thousands of articles on the topic.

7. Charlie Rose interviews neuroscientist **V. S. Ramachandran**, and the website TED presents a lecture by consciousness expert **Dan Dennett**.

FOR FURTHER READING

1. *Sleep Disorders for Dummies,* by Max Hirshkowitz and Patricia Smith (Wiley, 2004), is a guide for anyone who has trouble sleeping.

2. *Self Comes to Mind: Constructing the Conscious Brain,* by Antonio Damasio (Random House, 2010), discusses the brain bases of consciousness.

3. "The Source of Consciousness," by Ken Paller and Satoru Suzuki (*Trends in Cognitive Sciences, 2014, 18,* 387–389), explains why we should be optimistic about discovering the bases of consciousness and why the research should be funded.

4. "What's the Point of Consciousness," by Bob Holmes (*New Scientist,* May 13, 2017, 28–31), explores whether animals might be conscious and the evolution and function of consciousness.

5. "Forty-Five Years of Split-Brain Research and Still Going Strong," by Michael Gazzaniga (*Nature Reviews Neuroscience,* 2005, *6,* 653–659), is a useful and extensive summary of what we have learned from the research.

6. "The Patient's Journey: Living With Locked-In Syndrome," by Nick Chisholm and Grant Gillett (*British Medical Journal,* 2005, *331,* 94–97), is Nick's account of his partial recovery

from locked-in syndrome, a disorder that leaves the patient completely conscious but unresponsive, unable to vocalize, open the eyes, or signal to doctors that he or she is fully aware. The article contains useful details about the disorder and the problem of distinguishing it from a persistent vegetative state.

7. "Whose Body Is It, Anyway?" by Graham Lawton (*New Scientist*, March 21, 2009, 36–37), tells you how to create the illusion that you have three hands and how to get a glimpse of what an out-of-body experience is like.

KEY TERMS

agency 470
attention 467
brain interpreter 473
cataplexy 460
central executive network 463
dissociative identity disorder (DID) 474

insomnia 459
melatonin 450
narcolepsy 460
non-REM sleep 454
PGO waves 458
rapid eye movement (REM) sleep 453

REM sleep behavior disorder 461
salience network 463
slow-wave sleep 453
suprachiasmatic nucleus (SCN) 449
ultradian rhythm 451

 **SAGE edge**™　edge.sagepub.com/garrett5e

SAGE edge offers a robust online environment featuring an impressive array of free tools and resources for review, study, and further exploration, keeping both instructors and students on the cutting edge of teaching and learning.

15.1	Summarize the characteristics of the rhythms that occur during sleep and waking.	Science of Sleep: Circadian Rhythms
15.2	Describe the neural controls of sleep and waking rhythms.	Science of Sleep: Melatonin to Neural Pathways
15.3	Examine the functions of sleep and shorter rhythms.	Why Do We Sleep? / Sleep and Memory Consolidation
15.4	Assess the causes of sleep disorders.	Sleep Disorders
15.5	Explain how researchers are approaching the issue of consciousness.	The Quest to Understand Consciousness
15.6	Indicate the neural processes that contribute to consciousness.	What Is Consciousness?

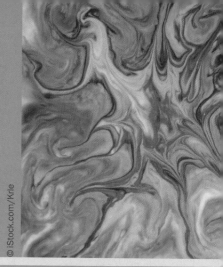

© iStock.com/Krle

PRACTICE AND APPLY WHAT YOU'VE LEARNED

▶ **edge.sagepub.com/garrett5e**

Glossary

aberrant salience hypothesis Heightened levels of dopamine increase attentional and motivational circuits to make ordinary environmental features seem significant.

ablation Removal of brain tissue.

absolute refractory period A brief period following the peak of the action potential when the sodium ion channels are inactivated and the neuron cannot be fired again.

absorptive phase The period of a few hours following a meal during which the body relies on the nutrients arriving from the digestive system.

accommodation Changing of the lens shape to focus light onto the retina; the ciliary muscles contract to make the lens rounder for a near object, and relax to flatten the lens for a far object.

action potential An all-or-none electrical signal of a neuronal membrane that contains an abrupt voltage depolarization and return to resting potential; allows the neuron to communicate over long distances.

activating effects Hormonal effects on sexual development that can occur at any time in an individual's life; their duration depends on the presence of the hormone.

acute Referring to symptoms that develop suddenly and are usually more responsive to treatment.

addiction A preoccupation with obtaining a drug, compulsive use of the drug in spite of adverse consequences, and a high tendency to relapse after quitting.

adequate stimulus The energy form for which a receptor is specialized.

ADHD See *attention-deficit/hyperactivity disorder.*

affective aggression Hostile or violent behavior that is characterized by impulsiveness and emotional arousal.

agency The sense that an action or effect is due to oneself rather than to another person or an external force.

aggression Hostile or violent behavior that is intended to harm another individual.

agonist Any substance that mimics or enhances the effect of a neurotransmitter.

agonist treatment Addiction treatment that replaces the addicting drug with another drug that has a similar effect.

agouti-related protein (AgRP) A transmitter released by NPY/AgRP neurons in the arcuate nucleus of the hypothalamus when nutrients diminish, which stimulates feeding.

agraphia The inability to write due to brain damage.

alcohol Ethanol, a drug fermented from fruits, grains, and other plant products, which acts at many brain sites to produce euphoria, anxiety reduction, motor incoordination, and cognitive impairment.

alexia The inability to read due to brain damage.

allele An alternate version of a gene; can be dominant or recessive.

all-or-none law The principle that an action potential occurs at full strength or it does not occur at all.

Alzheimer's disease A disorder characterized by progressive brain deterioration and impairment of memory and other mental abilities; the most common cause of dementia.

amino acids The building blocks of peptides, which in turn make up proteins. In digestion, the result of the breakdown of proteins.

amphetamine One of a group of synthetic drugs that produce euphoria and increase confidence and concentration.

amplitude The physical energy in a sound; the sound's intensity.

amygdala Limbic system structure located near the lateral ventricle in each temporal lobe that is involved with primarily negative emotions and with sexual behavior, aggression, and learning, especially in emotional situations.

analgesic Pain relieving.

androgen insensitivity syndrome A form of 46 XY difference in sexual development (DSD), involving insensitivity to androgen because of a genetic absence of androgen receptors. The person has male sex chromosomes and internal sex organs, but external sex characteristics are feminized or ambiguous.

androgens A class of hormones responsible for a number of male characteristics and functions.

angiotensin II A hormone that signals lowered blood volume and, thus, volemic thirst to the brain.

angular gyrus A gyrus at the border of the parietal and occipital lobes containing pathways that connect the visual area with auditory, visual, and somatosensory association areas in the temporal and parietal lobes. Damage results in alexia and agraphia.

anorexia nervosa An eating disorder in which the person restricts food intake to maintain weight at a level so low that it is threatening to health.

ANS See *autonomic nervous system.*

antagonist Any substance that reduces the effect of a neurotransmitter.

antagonist treatment A form of treatment for drug addiction using drugs that block the effects of the addicting drug.

antagonistic muscles Contractile tissues that produce opposite movements at a joint.

anterior Toward the front.

anterior cingulate cortex A part of the limbic system important in attention, cognitive processing, possibly consciousness, and emotion, including the emotion of pain.

anterograde amnesia An impairment in forming new memories.

antidrug vaccine A form of anti-addiction treatment using molecules that attach to the drug and stimulate the immune system to make antibodies that will break down the drug.

antisense RNA A technology that temporarily disables a targeted gene or reduces its effectiveness.

anxiolytic Anxiety reducing.

aphasia Language impairment caused by damage to the brain.

apotemnophilia See *body integrity identity disorder.*

arcuate nucleus A structure in the hypothalamus that monitors the body's nutrient condition and regulates eating behavior.

area postrema A brain area unprotected by the blood-brain barrier; blood-borne toxins entering here induce vomiting.

arousal theory The hypothesis that people behave in ways that keep them at their preferred level of arousal.

association area Cortical areas that carry out further processing beyond what the primary projection area does, often combining information from other senses.

associative long-term potentiation Strengthening of a weak synapse when it and a strong synapse on the same postsynaptic neuron are active simultaneously.

attention The brain's means of allocating its limited resources by focusing on some neural inputs to the exclusion of others.

attention-deficit/hyperactivity disorder (ADHD) A disorder that develops during childhood and is characterized by impulsiveness, inability to sustain attention, learning difficulty, and hyperactivity.

auditory cortex The area of cortex on the superior temporal gyrus, which is the primary projection area for auditory information.

auditory object A sound that we recognize as having an identity that is distinct from other sounds.

autism spectrum disorder A set of neurodevelopmental disorders characterized by social deficits, communication difficulties, and repetitive behaviors.

autistic savant An individual with autism with an isolated exceptional capability.

autoimmune disorder A disorder in which the immune system attacks the body's own cells.

autonomic nervous system (ANS) One of the two branches of the peripheral nervous system; composed of the sympathetic and parasympathetic nervous systems, which control smooth muscles, glands, and the heart and other organs.

autoradiography A technique for identifying brain structures involved in an activity; it involves injecting a radioactive substance (such as 2-DG) that will be absorbed most by the more active neurons, which then will show up on an X-ray image.

autoreceptor A receptor on a neuron terminal that senses the amount of transmitter in the synaptic cleft and reduces the presynaptic neuron's output when the level is excessive.

aversive treatment A form of addiction treatment that causes a negative reaction when the person takes the drug.

axon An extension from a neuron's cell body that carries information to other locations.

axon terminal A swelling on the branches at the end of a neuron that contains neurotransmitters; also called an end bulb.

B cell A type of immune cell that fights intruders by producing antibodies that attack a particular intruder.

barbiturate A class of drugs that act selectively on higher cortical centers, especially those involved in inhibiting behavior, so they produce talkativeness and increased social interaction. In higher doses, they act as sedatives and hypnotics. Used to treat anxiety, aid sleep, and prevent epileptic convulsions.

basal ganglia The caudate nucleus, putamen, and globus pallidus, located subcortically in the frontal lobes; they participate in motor activity by integrating and smoothing movements using information from the primary and secondary motor areas and the somatosensory cortex.

basal metabolism The amount of energy required to fuel the brain and other organs and to maintain body temperature.

basilar membrane The membrane in the cochlea that separates the cochlear canal from the tympanic canal, and on which the organ of Corti is located.

bath salts Any one of several synthetic derivatives of the *Catha edulis* plant that have amphetamine-like effects.

BDNF See *brain-derived neurotrophic factor.*

behavioral neuroscience The branch of psychology that studies the relationships between behavior and the body, particularly the brain.

benzodiazepine A class of drugs that produce anxiety reduction, sedation, and muscle relaxation by stimulating benzodiazepine receptors on the $GABA_A$ complex, facilitating GABA binding.

binaural Involving the use of both ears.

binding problem The question of how the brain combines all the information about an object into a unitary whole.

binge eating disorder A disorder characterized by frequent consumption of excessive amounts of food during a short interval of time and a feeling of loss of control over what and how much is eaten.

bipolar disorder Depression and mania that occur together in alternation.

blindsight The ability of cortically blind individuals to respond to visual stimuli that are outside conscious awareness.

blood-brain barrier The brain's protection from toxic substances and neurotransmitters in the bloodstream; the small openings in the capillary walls prevent large molecules from passing through unless they are fat soluble or carried through by special transporters.

BMI See *body mass index.*

body integrity identity disorder The desire, in individuals with no apparent brain damage or mental illness, to have a healthy limb amputated.

body mass index (BMI) The person's weight in kilograms divided by the squared height in meters; an indication of the person's deviation from the ideal weight for the person's height.

brain interpreter A hypothetical mechanism that integrates all the cognitive processes going on simultaneously in other modules of the brain.

brain-derived neurotrophic factor (BDNF) A protein that contributes to neuron growth and survival.

Broca's aphasia Language impairment caused by damage to Broca's area and surrounding cortical and subcortical areas.

Broca's area The area anterior to the precentral gyrus (motor cortex) that sends output to the facial motor area to produce speech and also provides grammatical structure to language.

bulimia nervosa An eating disorder involving bingeing on food, followed by purging by vomiting or using laxatives.

caffeine A drug that produces arousal, increased alertness, and decreased sleepiness; the active ingredient in coffee.

CAH See *congenital adrenal hyperplasia.*

cannabinoids A group of compounds that includes the active ingredient in marijuana (tetrahydrocannabinol) and the endogenous cannabinoid receptor ligands, anandamide, and 2-arachidonyl glycerol (2-Ara-Gl). Cannabinoids act as retrograde messengers.

cardiac muscles The strong contractile tissues that make up the heart.

castration Removal of the gonads (testes or ovaries).

cataplexy A disorder in which a person has a sudden loss of muscle strength (atonia) like that seen in REM sleep; the person may fall to the floor but remains awake.

CCK See *cholecystokinin.*

cell body The largest part of a neuron, which contains the cell's nucleus, cytoplasm, and structures that produce proteins, convert nutrients into energy, and eliminate waste materials. Also called the soma.

central executive network Pathways that are active when behaviors are goal and task oriented and externally directed; it is a part of the *salience network.*

central nervous system (CNS) The part of the nervous system made up of the brain and spinal cord.

central pattern generator (CPG) A neuronal network that produces a rhythmic pattern of motor activity, such as that involved in walking, swimming, flying, or breathing.

central sulcus The groove between the precentral gyrus and the postcentral gyrus that separates the frontal lobe from the parietal lobe in each hemisphere.

cerebellum A structure in the hindbrain that contributes the order of muscular contractions and their precise timing to intended movements and helps maintain posture and balance. It is also necessary for learning motor skills and contributes to nonmotor learning and cognitive activities.

cerebral hemispheres The large, wrinkled structures that are the dorsal or superior part of the brain and that are covered by the cortex.

cerebrospinal fluid Liquid in the ventricles and spinal canal that carries material from the blood vessels to the central nervous system and transports waste materials in the other direction. It also helps cushion the brain and spinal cord.

cholecystokinin (CCK) A peptide hormone released as food passes into the duodenum. CCK acts as a signal to the brain that reduces meal size.

chronic Referring to symptoms that develop gradually and persist for a long time with poor response to treatment.

chronic pain Pain that persists after healing has occurred, or beyond the time in which healing would be expected to occur.

circadian rhythm A rhythm that is a day in length, such as the wake-sleep cycle.

circannual rhythm A rhythm that is a year in length, such as migration and seasonal mood.

circuit formation The third stage of nervous system development, in which the developing neurons send processes to their target cells and form functional connections.

circuit pruning The fourth stage of nervous system development, in which neurons that are unsuccessful in finding a place on the appropriate target cell, or that arrive late, die and excess synapses are eliminated.

CNS See *central nervous system.*

cocaine A drug extracted from the South American coca plant; produces euphoria, decreased appetite, increased alertness, and relief from fatigue.

cochlea The snail-shaped structure where the ear's sound-analyzing structures are located.

cochlear canal The middle canal in the cochlea; contains the organ of Corti.

cocktail party effect The ability to sort out meaningful auditory messages from a complex background of sounds.

cognitive theory A theory that states that a person relies on a cognitive assessment of the stimulus situation to identify which emotion is being experienced; physiological arousal determines the intensity of the emotional experience.

coincidence detectors Neurons that fire most when they receive input from both ears at the same time; involved in sound localization.

color agnosia Loss of the ability to perceive colors due to brain damage.

color blindness Also called color vision deficiency; one or more color-sensitive cones is functionally impaired or absent.

color constancy The ability to recognize the natural color of an object regardless of the wavelength of illuminating light.

compensation A response to nervous system injury, in which surviving presynaptic neurons sprout new terminals, postsynaptic neurons add more receptors, or surrounding tissue takes over functions.

complementary colors Colors that cancel each other out to produce a neutral gray or white.

complex cell A type of cell in the visual cortex that continues to respond (unlike simple cells) when a line or an edge moves to a different location.

complex sound A sound composed of more than one pure tone.

computed tomography (CT) An imaging technique that produces a series of X-rays taken from different angles; these are combined by a computer into a three-dimensional image of the brain or other part of the body.

concordance rate The proportion of cases in which a pair of related individuals share a characteristic.

confabulation Fabrication of stories and facts, which are then accepted by the individual, to make up for those missing from memory.

congenital adrenal hyperplasia (CAH) A form of 46 XX difference in sexual development (DSD) characterized by XX chromosomes, female internal sex organs, and ambiguous or masculinized external sex characteristics. It is caused by excess production of androgens during prenatal development.

congenital insensitivity to pain A condition, present at birth, in which the person is insensitive to pain.

consolidation The process in which the brain forms a permanent representation of a memory.

Coolidge effect An increase in sexual activity when the variety of sexual partners increases; named after former president Calvin Coolidge.

corpus callosum The largest of the groups of neurons connecting the two cerebral hemispheres.

correlation The degree to which two variables are related, such as the IQs of siblings; it is measured by the correlation coefficient, a statistic that varies between the values of 0.0 and ±1.0.

correlational study A study in which the researcher does not control an independent variable but determines whether two variables are related to each other.

cortex The grayish 1.5- to 4-mm-thick surface of the hemispheres, composed mostly of cell bodies, where the highest-level processing occurs in the brain.

cortisol A hormone released by the adrenal glands that increases energy levels by converting proteins to glucose, increasing fat availability, and increasing metabolism. The increase is more sustained than that produced by epinephrine and norepinephrine.

cranial nerves The 12 pairs of axonal bundles that enter and leave the underside of the brain; part of the peripheral nervous system.

CT See *computed tomography.*

Dale's principle The theory that a neuron is able to release only one neurotransmitter.

db See *diabetes gene.*

DBS See *deep brain stimulation.*

deception In research, failing to tell the participants the exact purpose of the research or what will happen during the study, or actively misinforming them.

declarative memory The memory process that records memories of facts, people, and events that the person can verbalize, or *declare.*

deep brain stimulation (DBS) Electrical stimulation of the brain through implanted electrodes.

default mode network Portions of the frontal, parietal, and temporal lobes that are active when the brain is at rest or focused internally; its activity is thought to represent preparedness for action.

delirium tremens A reaction in some cases of withdrawal from alcohol, including hallucinations, delusions, confusion, and, in extreme cases, seizures and possible death.

dementia Substantial loss of memory and other cognitive abilities usually, but not necessarily, in the elderly.

dendrites Extensions that branch out from the neuron cell body and receive information from other neurons.

dendritic spines Outgrowths from the dendrites that partially bridge the synaptic cleft and make the synapse more sensitive.

deoxyribonucleic acid (DNA) A double-stranded chain of chemical molecules that looks like a ladder that has been twisted around itself; genes are composed of DNA.

depressant A drug that reduces central nervous system activity.

depression An intense feeling of sadness.

dermatome A segment of the body served by a spinal nerve.

diabetes An insulin disorder in which the person produces too little insulin (type 1), resulting in overeating with little weight gain, or the person's brain is insensitive to insulin (type 2), resulting in overeating with weight gain.

diabetes gene (db) A gene on chromosome 4 that produces diabetes and obesity; mice with the gene are insensitive to leptin.

dialect Difference in subtle aspects of a language within a population due to regional or cultural isolation from other speakers, resulting in different words for the same concept that are stable across generations. For example, calling a carbonated beverage either "pop" or "soda," or saying either "you all" or "y'all."

DID See *dissociative identity disorder.*

diffusion tensor imaging A variant of MRI that measures movement of water molecules to image brain pathways and quantify their quality.

dihydrotestosterone A derivative of testosterone that masculinizes the genitals of males.

disorders of sexual development (DSD) Due to a genetic, receptor, or hormonal abnormality, the individual develops outward sex characteristics that are atypical for the person's chromosomal sex. See *46 XX difference in sexual development* and *46 XY difference in sexual development.*

dissociative identity disorder (DID) The disorder previously known as multiple personality, which involves shifts in consciousness and behavior that appear to be distinct personalities or selves.

distributed A term referring to any brain function that occurs across a relatively wide area of the brain.

DNA See *deoxyribonucleic acid.*

dominant A term referring to an allele that will produce its effect regardless of which allele it is paired with in the fertilized egg.

dopamine hypothesis The hypothesis that schizophrenia involves excess dopamine activity in the brain.

dorsal Toward the back side of the body.

dorsal root The branch of a spinal nerve through which neurons enter the spinal cord.

dorsal stream The visual processing pathway that extends into the parietal lobes; it is especially concerned with the location of objects in space.

Down syndrome Intellectual disability characterized by IQs in the 40 to 55 range, usually caused by the presence of an extra 21st chromosome.

drive An aroused condition resulting from a departure from homeostasis, which impels the individual to take appropriate action, such as eating.

drive theory Hypothesis based on the assumption that an unmet need will result in behavior that will satisfy that need in order to maintain a condition of homeostasis.

drug Any substance that, on entering the body, changes the body or its functioning.

DSD See *disorders of sexual development.*

dualism The idea that the mind and the brain are separate.

duodenum The first section of the small intestine, where most digestion occurs.

dyslexia An impairment of reading, which can be developmental or acquired through brain damage.

ECT See *electroconvulsive therapy.*

EEG See *electroencephalogram.*

electrical stimulation of the brain (ESB) A procedure in which animals (or humans) learn to press a lever or perform some other action to deliver mild electrical stimulation to brain areas where the stimulation is rewarding.

electroconvulsive therapy (ECT) The application of 70–130 volts of electricity to the head of a lightly anesthetized patient, which produces a seizure and convulsions; a treatment for major depression.

electroencephalogram (EEG) A measure of brain activity recorded from two electrodes on the scalp over the area of interest and connected to an electronic amplifier; detects the combined electrical activity of all the neurons between the two electrodes.

electromagnetic spectrum A variety of energy forms, ranging from high-frequency gamma rays at one extreme to very-low-frequency electrical currents on the other.

electron microscope See *transmission electron microscope* and *scanning electron microscope*.

electrostatic pressure The force by which like-charged ions are repelled by each other and opposite-charged ions are attracted to each other.

embryo An organism in the early prenatal period; in humans, during the first eight weeks.

emotion A state of feelings accompanied by an increase or a decrease in physiological activity and, possibly, characteristic facial expression and behavior.

empiricism The procedure of obtaining information through observation.

endogenous Generated within the body; usually used to refer to natural ligands for neurotransmitter receptors.

endorphins Substances produced in the body that function both as neurotransmitters and as hormones and that act on opioid receptors in many parts of the nervous system.

epigenetic Referring to inheritable characteristics resulting from modifications in gene expression.

EPSP See *excitatory postsynaptic potential*.

equipotentiality The idea that the brain functions as a whole; opposite of localization.

ESB See *electrical stimulation of the brain*.

estrogen A class of hormones responsible for a number of female characteristics and functions; produced by the ovaries in women and, to a lesser extent, by the adrenal glands in males and females.

estrus A period when a nonhuman female animal is ovulating and sex hormone levels are high.

euphoria A sense of happiness or ecstasy; many abused drugs produce euphoria.

Eustachian tube The connection between the middle ear and the oral cavity, the function of which is to equalize air pressure differences between the outside of the head and the middle ear.

event-related potential An EEG technique for measuring the brain's responses to brief stimulation; it involves presenting a stimulus repeatedly and averaging the EEG over all the presentations to cancel out random activity,

leaving the electrical activity associated with the stimulus.

excitatory postsynaptic potential (EPSP) A hypopolarization (partial depolarization) of the dendrites and cell body, which makes the neuron more likely to fire.

experiment A study in which the researcher manipulates an independent variable and observes its effect on one or more dependent variables.

expression The translation of a gene's encoded information into the production of proteins, determining the gene's functioning.

fabrication In research, deliberately falsifying, altering, or manipulating data or results.

familial A term referring to a characteristic that occurs more frequently among relatives of a person with the characteristic than it does in the population.

family study A study of how strongly a characteristic is shared among relatives.

FAS See *fetal alcohol syndrome*.

fasting phase The period following the absorptive phase, when the glucose level in the blood drops and the body must rely on its energy stores.

fatty acids Breakdown product of fat, which supplies the muscles and organs of the body (except for the brain).

fetal alcohol syndrome A condition caused by the mother's use of alcohol during the third trimester of pregnancy; neurons fail to migrate properly, often resulting in intellectual disability; the leading cause of intellectual disability in the Western world.

fetus An organism after the initial prenatal period; in humans, after the first eight weeks.

FFA See *fusiform face area*.

fissure A deep groove between gyri of the cerebral hemispheres that is larger than a *sulcus*.

fMRI See *functional magnetic resonance imaging*.

force of diffusion The pressure exerted by ions from an area of greater concentration to an area where they are less concentrated.

form vision The detection of an object's boundaries and features, such as texture.

46 XX difference in sexual development A female fetus with two X sex chromosomes is masculinized (develops male characteristics) by abnormally high levels of androgen hormones.

46 XY difference in sexual development A genetic male with X and Y sex chromosomes is feminized (develops female characteristics) due to abnormally low levels of androgens or a lack of androgen receptors.

fovea A 1.5-mm-wide area in the middle of the retina in which cones are most concentrated and visual acuity and color discrimination are greatest.

fragile X syndrome A form of intellectual disability caused by excessive CGG repeats in the *FMR1* gene; IQ is typically below 75.

frequency A characteristic of sound; the number of cycles or waves of alternating compression and decompression of the

vibrating medium that occur in a second. For the psychological perception of frequency, see *pitch*.

frequency-place theory The hypothesis that frequency following individual neurons accounts for the discrimination of frequencies up to about 200 Hz, and higher frequencies are represented by the place of greatest activity on the basilar membrane.

frequency theory Any one of several hypotheses of auditory frequency analysis that state that the frequency of a sound is represented in the firing rate of each neuron or a group of neurons.

frontal lobe The area of each cerebral hemisphere anterior to the central sulcus and superior to the lateral fissure.

functional magnetic resonance imaging (fMRI) A brain-imaging procedure that measures brain activation by detecting the increase in oxygen levels in active neural structures.

fusiform face area (FFA) A part of the inferior temporal lobe important in face identification. See *prosopagnosia*.

ganglion A group of cell bodies in the peripheral nervous system.

gate control theory The hypothesis that pressure signals arriving in the brain trigger an inhibitory message that travels back down the spinal cord, where it closes a neural "gate" in the pain pathway.

gender The behavioral characteristics associated with being male or female.

gender dysphoria The distress that people may feel when their gender identity does not match their sex at birth.

gender identity The sex to which a person identifies as belonging.

gender nonconformity Sex-atypical mannerisms and dress, a tendency to engage in activities usually preferred by the other sex, and an atypical preference for other-sex playmates and companions while growing up.

gender role A set of behaviors society considers appropriate for members of the same sex.

gene The biological unit that directs cellular processes and transmits inherited characteristics.

gene therapy Treatment of a disorder by gene manipulation.

gene transfer Insertion of a gene from another organism into a recipient's cells, usually within a virus.

genetic engineering Manipulation of an organism's genes or their functioning.

genome The entire collection of genes in the chromosomes of a species.

genotype The combination of genes an individual has.

ghrelin A hormone released by the stomach during fasting; initiates eating.

glial cell A nonneural cell that provides several supporting functions to neurons, including myelination.

glucagon A hormone released by the pancreas that stimulates the liver to transform stored glycogen back into glucose during the fasting phase.

glucose One of the sugars; the body's main source of energy, reserved for the nervous system during the fasting phase; a major signal for hunger and satiation.

glutamate theory The hypothesis that NMDA receptor hypofunction results in glutamate and dopamine increases that produce positive and negative symptoms of schizophrenia.

glycerol A breakdown product of fats, which is converted to glucose for the brain during the fasting period.

glycogen The form in which glucose is stored in the liver and muscles during the absorptive phase; converted back to glucose for the brain during the fasting phase.

Golgi stain A staining method that randomly stains about 5% of neurons, which makes them stand out individually.

Golgi tendon organs Receptors that detect tension in a muscle.

gonads The primary reproductive organs; testes in the male or ovaries in the female. An individual can have only one of the two types of gonads.

graded potential A voltage change in a neuron that varies with the strength of the stimulus that initiated it.

growth cone A formation at the tip of a migrating neuron that samples the environment for directional cues.

gyrus A ridge in the cerebral cortex; the area between two sulci.

Hebb rule The principle stating that if an axon of a presynaptic neuron is active while the postsynaptic neuron is firing, the synapse between them will be strengthened.

heritability The percentage of the variation among individuals in a characteristic that can be attributed to heredity.

heroin A major drug of addiction synthesized from morphine.

heterozygous Having a pair of alleles for a specific characteristic that are different from each other.

hierarchical processing A type of processing in which lower levels of the nervous system analyze their information and pass the results on to the next higher level for further analysis.

homeostasis A body system seeks and maintains this condition of balance or equilibrium and has mechanisms to minimize changes to the system.

homozygous Having a pair of alleles for a specific characteristic that are identical with each other.

Human Connectome Project A large-scale cooperative effort to map the circuits in the human brain.

Human Genome Project An international project with the goal of mapping the location of all the genes on the human chromosomes and determining the base sequences of the genes.

Huntington's disease A degenerative disorder of the motor system involving cell loss in the striatum and cortex.

hydrocephalus A disorder in which cerebrospinal fluid fails to circulate and builds up in the cerebral ventricles, crowding out neural tissue and usually causing intellectual disability.

hyperpolarization A negative change in a neural membrane's voltage, which is inhibitory and makes an action potential less likely to occur. See *inhibitory postsynaptic potential* for the synaptic effect.

hypnotic Sleep inducing.

hypocretin See *orexin*.

hypopolarization A positive change in a neural membrane's voltage (also called partial depolarization), which is excitatory and makes an action potential more likely to occur. See *excitatory postsynaptic potential* for the synaptic effect.

hypothalamus A subcortical structure in the forebrain just below the thalamus that plays a major role in controlling emotion and motivated behaviors such as eating, drinking, and sexual activity.

hypothalamus-pituitary-adrenal axis A group of structures that help the body cope with stress.

hypovolemic thirst A fluid deficit that occurs when the blood volume drops due to a loss of extracellular water.

ID See *intellectual disability*.

IID See *interaural intensity difference*.

ILD See *interaural timing difference*.

immune system The cells and cell products that kill infected and malignant cells and protect the body against foreign substances, including bacteria and viruses.

immunocytochemistry A procedure for labeling cellular components such as receptors, neurotransmitters, or enzymes, using a dye attached to an antibody designed to attach the component.

impulsive aggression Hostile or violent behavior resulting from a threat (real or imagined) to the individual, characterized by heightened emotionality.

in situ hybridization A procedure for locating gene activity; involves constructing strands of complementary DNA that will dock with strands of messenger RNA. The complementary DNA is radioactive, so autoradiography can be used to locate the gene activity.

INAH 3 See *third interstitial nucleus of the anterior hypothalamus*.

incentive theory A theory that recognizes that people are motivated by external stimuli (incentives), not just internal needs.

inferior Below another structure.

inferior colliculi Part of the tectum in the brain stem that is involved in auditory functions such as locating the direction of sounds.

inferior temporal cortex An area in the lower part of the temporal lobe that plays a major role in the visual identification of objects.

informed consent Voluntary agreement to participate in a study after receiving full information about any risks, discomfort, or other adverse effects that might occur.

inhibitory postsynaptic potential (IPSP) A hyperpolarization of the dendrites and cell body, which makes a neuron less likely to fire.

inner hair cells A single row of about 3,500 hair cells located on the basilar membrane toward the inside of the cochlea's coil; they produce most, if not all, of the auditory signal.

insomnia The inability to sleep or to obtain quality sleep, to the extent that the person feels inadequately rested.

instinct A complex behavior that is automatic and unlearned and occurs in all the members of a species.

instrumental aggression Unprovoked and emotionless hostile or violent behavior intended to result in gain for the individual, such as to intimidate, rob, or kill the victim.

insulin A hormone secreted by the pancreas that enables entry of glucose into cells (not including the nervous system) during the absorptive phase and facilitates storage of excess nutrients.

intellectual disability (ID) Limitation in intellectual functioning (reasoning, learning, problem solving) and adaptive behavior that is developmental in origin.

intelligence The capacity for learning, reasoning, and understanding.

intelligence quotient (IQ) The measure typically used for intelligence.

intensity The physical energy in a sound; the sound's amplitude. For the psychological perception of intensity, see *loudness*.

interaural intensity difference (IID) A binaural cue to the location of a sound coming from one side that results from the sound shadow created by the head; most effective above 2000 to 3000 Hz.

interaural phase difference (IPD) A binaural cue to the location of a sound coming from one side due to the difference in the phase of the sound wave between the two ears.

interaural timing difference (ITD) A binaural cue to the location of a sound coming from one side due to the time the sound requires to travel the distance between the ears; most effective for low-frequency sounds.

interneuron A neuron that has a short axon or no axon at all and connects one neuron to another in the same part of the central nervous system.

iodopsin A group of three photopigments found in cones; one form is sensitive to red light, one is sensitive to green light, and one is sensitive to bluish-violet light.

ion An element or atom that is charged because it has lost or gained one or more electrons.

ionotropic receptor A receptor on a neuron membrane that opens ion channels directly and immediately to produce quick reactions.

IPD See *interaural phase difference*.

IPSP See *inhibitory postsynaptic potential*.

IQ See *intelligence quotient*.

James-Lange theory The idea that physiological arousal precedes and is the cause of an emotional experience and the pattern of arousal identifies the emotion.

knockout Genetic engineering technique in which a nonfunctioning gene mutation is inserted during the embryonic stage.

Korsakoff syndrome A form of dementia in which brain deterioration is almost always caused by chronic alcoholism.

L-dopa See *levodopa*.

language acquisition device A part of the brain hypothesized to be dedicated to learning and controlling language.

lateral Toward the side.

lateral fissure The fissure that separates the temporal lobe from the frontal and parietal lobes.

lateral hypothalamus A nucleus of the hypothalamus with roles in feeding and metabolism, aggression, and waking arousal.

lateral inhibition A method of enhancing neural information in which each neuron's activity inhibits the activity of its neighbors, and in turn its activity is inhibited by them.

learned taste aversion Learned avoidance of a food (based on its taste) eaten prior to becoming ill.

learned taste preference Preference for a food containing a needed nutrient (identified by the food's taste), learned, presumably, because the nutrient makes the individual feel better.

leptin A hormone secreted by fat cells, which is proportional to the percentage of body fat and which signals fat level to the brain.

lesion Damage to neural tissue. This can be brought about surgically for research or therapeutic reasons, or it can result from trauma, disease, or developmental error.

leukocytes White blood cells, which include macrophages, T cells, and B cells; part of the immune system.

levodopa (L-dopa) The precursor for dopamine; used to treat Parkinson's disease.

Lewy bodies Abnormal clumps of protein that form within neurons, found in some patients with Parkinson's disease and Alzheimer's disease.

limbic system A group of forebrain structures arranged around the upper brain stem that have roles in emotion, motivated behavior, and learning.

lithium A metal administered in the form of lithium carbonate; the medication of choice for treating bipolar disorder.

localization The idea that specific parts of the brain carry out specific functions.

longitudinal fissure The large fissure that extends the length of the brain, separating the two cerebral hemispheres.

long-term depression (LTD) Weakening of a synapse when stimulation of presynaptic neurons is insufficient to activate the postsynaptic neurons.

long-term potentiation (LTP) An increase in synaptic strength that occurs when presynaptic neurons and postsynaptic neurons are active simultaneously.

loudness The term for our *experience* of sound intensity.

LTD See *long-term depression*.

LTP See *long-term potentiation*.

macrophage A type of leukocyte that ingests intruders.

magnetic resonance imaging (MRI) An imaging technique that involves measuring the radiofrequency waves emitted by hydrogen atoms when they are subjected to a strong magnetic field. Because different structures have different concentrations of hydrogen atoms, the waves can be used to form a detailed image of the brain.

magnocellular system A division of the visual system, extending from the retina through the visual association areas, that is specialized for brightness contrast and movement.

major depressive disorder (MDD) A disorder involving feelings of sadness to the point of hopelessness for weeks at a time, along with slowness of thought, sleep disturbance, and loss of energy and appetite and the ability to enjoy life; in some cases, the person is also agitated or restless. Sometimes called unipolar depression.

mania A disorder involving excess energy and confidence that often leads to grandiose schemes, decreased need for sleep, increased sexual drive, and, often, abuse of drugs.

marijuana The dried and crushed leaves and flowers of the Indian hemp plant *Cannabis sativa*.

materialistic monism The view that the body and the mind and everything else are physical.

MDD See *major depressive disorder*.

medial Toward the middle.

medial amygdala Part of the amygdala that apparently responds to sexually exciting stimuli. In both male and female rats, it is active during copulation, and it causes the release of dopamine in the MPOA.

medial preoptic area (MPOA) A part of the preoptic area of the hypothalamus that appears to be important for sexual performance, but not sexual motivation, in male and female rats.

median preoptic nucleus A nucleus of the hypothalamus that initiates drinking in response to osmotic and volumetric deficits.

medulla The lower part of the hindbrain; its nuclei are involved with control of essential life processes such as cardiovascular activity and respiration.

melatonin A hormone secreted by the pineal gland that induces sleepiness; in the normal circadian rhythm, it is released about two hours before bedtime.

meninges A three-layered membrane that encloses and protects the brain.

mesocortical pathway A system that projects from dopamine neurons in the ventral tegmental area to the frontal cortex. See also *mesolimbocortical dopamine system*.

mesolimbic pathway A system that projects from dopamine neurons in the ventral tegmental area to the nucleus accumbens. See also *mesolimbocortical dopamine system*.

mesolimbocortical dopamine system A pathway including the ventral tegmental area, medial forebrain bundle, nucleus accumbens, and projections into prefrontal areas. The pathway is important in reward effects from drugs, electrical stimulation of the brain (ESB), and activities such as eating and sex.

messenger ribonucleic acid (mRNA) A copy of one strand of DNA that moves out of the nucleus to direct protein construction.

metabotropic receptor A receptor on a neuron membrane that opens ion channels slowly through a metabolic process and produces long-lasting effects.

methadone A synthetic opioid used as an agonist treatment for opiate addiction.

methylation Attachment of a methyl group to DNA, which suppresses a gene's activity. See also *epigenetic*.

microglia Glial cells that provide immune protection in the central nervous system by acting as macrophages.

midbrain The middle part of the brain, consisting of the tectum (roof) on the dorsal side and the tegmentum on the ventral side.

migration In brain development, movement of newly formed neurons from the ventricular zone to their final destinations.

mind-brain problem The issue of what the mind is and its relationship to the brain.

mirror neurons Cortical neurons that respond when engaging in an act and while observing the same act in others; found in the premotor cortex, supplementary motor area, primary somatosensory cortex, and inferior parietal cortex.

model A proposed mechanism for how something works.

modular processing The segregation of the various components of processing in the brain into separate locations.

monism The idea that the mind and the body consist of the same substance.

monoamine hypothesis The hypothesis that depression involves reduced activity at norepinephrine and serotonin synapses.

motivation The set of factors that initiate, sustain, and direct behavior.

motor cortex The area in the frontal lobes that controls voluntary (nonreflexive) body movements; the primary motor cortex is on the precentral gyrus.

motor neuron A neuron that carries commands to the muscles and organs.

movement agnosia Impaired ability to perceive movement.

MPOA See *medial preoptic area*.

MRI See *magnetic resonance imaging*.

Müllerian ducts Early structures that in the female develop into the uterus, fallopian tubes, and inner vagina.

Müllerian inhibiting hormone A hormone released in the male that causes the Müllerian ducts to degenerate.

multiple sclerosis A motor disorder caused by the deterioration of myelin (*demyelination*) and neuron loss in the central nervous system.

muscle spindles Receptors that detect stretching in muscles.

myasthenia gravis A disorder of muscular weakness caused by reduced numbers or sensitivity of acetylcholine receptors.

myelin A fatty tissue that wraps around an axon to insulate it from the surrounding fluid and from other neurons.

myelin stain A staining method that stains the fatty insulation on axons, thus identifying neural pathways.

narcolepsy A chronic neurological disorder in which individuals fall asleep suddenly during the daytime and go directly into REM sleep.

natural killer cell A type of immune cell that attacks and destroys certain kinds of cancer cells and cells infected with viruses.

natural selection The principle that those whose genes endow them with greater speed, intelligence, or health are more likely to survive and transmit their genes to more offspring.

nature versus nurture The issue of the relative importance of heredity (nature) and environment (nurture).

negative color aftereffect The experience of a color's complement following stimulation by the color.

negative symptoms Aspects of schizophrenia characterized by the absence or insufficiency of normal behaviors, including lack of affect (emotion), inability to experience pleasure, lack of motivation, poverty of speech, and impaired attention.

neglect A disorder in which the person ignores objects, people, and activity on the side opposite the brain damage.

nerve A bundle of axons running together in the peripheral nervous system.

neural network A group of neurons that function together to carry out a process.

neurofibrillary tangles Abnormal accumulations of the protein tau that develop inside neurons and are associated with the death of brain cells in people with Alzheimer's disease and Down syndrome.

neurogenesis The birth of new neurons.

neuroleptics Drugs that block dopamine receptors in the brain, decreasing many of the positive symptoms of schizophrenia; may cause tardive dyskinesia after prolonged use.

neuron A specialized cell that conveys sensory information into the brain, carries out the operations involved in thought and feeling and action, or transmits commands out into the body to control muscles and organs; a single neural cell, in contrast to a *nerve*.

neuropeptide Y (NPY) A transmitter released by NPY/AgRP neurons in the arcuate nucleus of the hypothalamus when nutrient levels diminish; it is a powerful stimulant for eating and conserves energy.

neurotoxin A neuron poison; a substance that impairs the functioning of a neuron.

neurotransmitter A chemical substance released by a neuron (usually at a synapse) that binds to receptors on the same neuron, nearby neurons, or other tissues such as muscles or organs.

neurotrophins Chemicals that enhance development and survival in neurons.

nicotine The primary psychoactive and addictive ingredient in tobacco.

Nissl stain A staining method that stains cell bodies.

node of Ranvier A gap in the myelin sheath covering an axon.

nondeclarative memory Non-statable memories that result from procedural or skills learning, emotional learning, and simple conditioning.

nondecremental A property of the action potential, which travels through the neuron without any decrease in size.

non-REM sleep The periods of sleep that are not rapid eye movement sleep.

NPY See *neuropeptide Y.*

NST See *nucleus of the solitary tract.*

nucleus (1) The part of every cell that contains the chromosomes and governs activity in the cell. (2) A group of neuron cell bodies in the central nervous system.

nucleus accumbens A forebrain structure that is part of the mesolimbocortical dopamine system and a potent center for reward.

nucleus of the solitary tract (NST) A part of the medulla that monitors several signals involved in the regulation of eating.

obesity gene (*ob*) A gene on chromosome 6 that causes obesity; in mice, it results in an inability to produce leptin.

object agnosia Impairment of the ability to recognize objects visually.

obsessive-compulsive disorder (OCD) A disorder consisting of obsessions (recurring thoughts) and compulsions (repetitive, ritualistic acts the person feels compelled to perform).

occipital lobe The most posterior part of each cerebral hemisphere, and the location of the visual cortex.

OCD See *obsessive-compulsive disorder.*

oligodendrocyte A type of glial cell that forms the myelin covering of neurons in the brain and spinal cord.

opiate Any drug derived from the opium poppy. The term is also used to refer to effects at opiate receptors, including those by endorphins.

opponent process theory A color vision theory that attempts to explain color vision in terms of opposing neural processes.

optogenetics Control of neurons by creating light-responsive ion channels in the cell membrane.

orexin A neuropeptide released by lateral hypothalamic neurons that increases feeding and arousal; also known as hypocretin.

organ of Corti The sound-analyzing structure on the basilar membrane of the cochlea; it consists of four rows of hair cells, their supporting cells, and the tectorial membrane.

organizing effects Hormonal effects of sexual development that occur during the prenatal period and shortly after birth and are permanent.

organum vasculosum lamina terminalis (OVLT) A structure bordering the third

ventricle that monitors fluid content in the cells and contributes to the control of osmotic thirst.

osmotic thirst Thirst that occurs when the fluid content is low inside the body's cells.

ossicles Tiny bones in the middle ear that operate in lever fashion to transfer vibration from the tympanic membrane to the cochlea; they also produce a slight amplification of the sound.

outer hair cells Three rows of about 12,000 cells located on the basilar membrane toward the outside of the cochlea's coil; they amplify the cochlea's output and sharpen frequency tuning, possibly by adjusting the tension of the tectorial membrane.

out-of-body experience A phenomenon, usually resulting from brain damage or epilepsy, in which the person hallucinates seeing his or her detached body from another location.

ovaries The female gonads, where the ova develop.

OVLT See *organum vasculosum lamina terminalis.*

oxytocin A neuropeptide hormone and neurotransmitter involved in lactation and orgasm; dubbed the "sociability molecule" because it affects social behavior and bonding.

PAG See *periaqueductal gray.*

parasympathetic nervous system The branch of the autonomic nervous system that slows the activity of most organs to conserve energy and activates digestion to renew energy.

paraventricular nucleus (PVN) A structure in the hypothalamus that monitors several signals involved in the regulation of eating, including input from the NST; it helps regulate metabolic processes.

parietal lobe The part of each cerebral hemisphere located above the lateral fissure and between the central sulcus and the occipital lobe; it contains the somatosensory cortex and visual association areas.

Parkinson's disease A movement disorder characterized by motor tremors, rigidity, loss of balance and coordination, and difficulty in moving, especially in initiating movements; caused by deterioration of the substantia nigra.

parvocellular system A division of the visual system, extending from the retina through the visual association areas, that is specialized for fine detail and color.

peptide YY$_{3-36}$ (PYY) An appetite-suppressing peptide hormone released in the intestines in response to food.

perception The interpretation of sensory information.

periaqueductal gray (PAG) A brain stem structure with numerous endorphin synapses; stimulation reduces pain transmission at the spinal cord level. The PAG also produces symptoms of drug withdrawal.

peripheral nervous system (PNS) The part of the nervous system made up of the cranial nerves and spinal nerves.

PET See *positron emission tomography.*

PGO waves Oscillations of excitation that flow from the pons through the lateral geniculate nucleus of the thalamus to the occipital area and appear to initiate the EEG desynchrony of REM sleep.

phantom pain Pain that seems to be in a missing limb.

phenotype In heredity, the characteristic of the individual.

phenylketonuria An inherited form of intellectual disability in which the body fails to metabolize the amino acid phenylalanine, which interferes with myelination during development.

pheromones Airborne chemicals released by an animal that have physiological or behavioral effects on another animal of the same species.

phonological hypothesis The idea that the fundamental problem in dyslexia is impaired phoneme processing.

photopigment A light-sensitive chemical in the visual receptors that initiates the neural response.

phototherapy A treatment for winter depression involving the use of high-intensity lights for a period of time each day.

phrenology The theory in the early 1900s that "faculties" of emotion and intellect were located in precise areas of the brain and could be assessed by feeling bumps on the skull.

pineal gland A gland located just posterior to the thalamus that secretes sleep-inducing melatonin; it controls seasonal cycles in nonhuman animals and participates with other structures in controlling daily rhythms in humans.

pinna The ear flap on each side of the head; the outer ear.

pitch The *experience* of the frequency of a sound.

place cells Cells in the hippocampus that increase their firing rate when the individual is in a specific location in the environment.

place theory A theory that states that the frequency of a sound is identified by the location of maximal vibration on the basilar membrane and which neurons are firing most.

plagiarism The theft of or use without permission of another's work or ideas.

planum temporale The area in each temporal lobe that is the location in the left hemisphere of Wernicke's area and that is larger on the left in most people.

plaques Clumps of amyloid, a type of protein, that cluster among axon terminals and interfere with neural transmission in the brains of people with Alzheimer's disease and Down syndrome.

plasticity The ability to be modified; a characteristic of the nervous system.

PNS See *peripheral nervous system.*

polarization A difference in electrical charge between the inside and outside of a neuron.

polygenic Determined by several genes rather than a single gene.

pons A part of the brain stem that contains centers related to sleep and arousal.

positive symptoms Symptoms of schizophrenia that involve the presence or exaggeration of behaviors, such as delusions,

hallucinations, thought disorder, and bizarre behavior.

positron emission tomography (PET) An imaging technique that reveals function. It involves injecting a radioactive substance into the bloodstream, which is taken up by parts of the brain according to how active they are; the scanner makes an image that is color coded to show the relative amounts of activity.

posterior Toward the rear.

posterior parietal cortex An association area that brings together the body senses, vision, and audition. It determines the body's orientation in space, the location of the limbs, and the location in space of objects detected by touch, sight, and sound.

postsynaptic A term referring to a neuron that receives transmission from another neuron.

posttraumatic stress disorder (PTSD) A prolonged stress reaction to a traumatic event; typically characterized by recurrent thoughts and images (flashbacks), nightmares, lack of concentration, and over-reactivity to environmental stimuli, such as loud noises.

precentral gyrus The gyrus anterior to, and extending the length of, the central sulcus; the location of the primary motor cortex.

predatory aggression Hostile or destructive behavior in which an animal attacks and kills its prey or a human engages in a premeditated, unprovoked, and similarly relatively emotionless attack.

prefrontal cortex The most anterior cortex of the frontal lobes; involved in working memory, planning and organization of behavior, and regulation of behavior in response to its consequences. It also integrates information about the body with sensory information from the world to select and plan movements.

premotor cortex An area anterior to the primary motor cortex that combines information from the prefrontal cortex and the posterior parietal cortex and begins the programming of a movement.

preoptic area A structure in the hypothalamus that contains warmth-sensitive cells and cold-sensitive cells and participates in the control of body temperature. See *medial preoptic area* regarding regulation of sexual behavior.

presynaptic A term referring to a neuron that transmits to another neuron.

presynaptic excitation Increased release of neurotransmitter from a neuron's terminal as the result of another neuron's release of neurotransmitter onto the terminal (an axoaxonic synapse).

presynaptic inhibition Decreased release of neurotransmitter from a neuron's terminal as the result of another neuron's release of neurotransmitter onto the terminal (an axoaxonic synapse).

primary motor cortex The area on the precentral gyrus responsible for the execution of voluntary movements.

primary somatosensory cortex The first stage in the cortical-level processing of somatosensory information, which is processed through the four subareas of the primary

somatosensory cortex and then passed on to the secondary somatosensory cortex.

proactive aggression See *instrumental aggression.*

proliferation The first stage of nervous system development, in which cells that will become neurons multiply at the rate of 250,000 new cells every minute.

proprioception The sense that informs us about the position and movement of the parts of the body.

prosody The use of intonation, emphasis, and rhythm to convey meaning in speech.

prosopagnosia The inability to visually recognize familiar faces.

psychedelic drug Any compound that causes perceptual distortions in the user.

psychoactive drug Any drug that has psychological effects, such as anxiety relief or hallucinations.

psychosis A severe mental disturbance of reality, thought, and orientation.

psychosurgery The use of surgical intervention to treat cognitive and emotional disorders.

PTSD See *posttraumatic stress disorder.*

pure tone A sound consisting of a single frequency.

PVN See *paraventricular nucleus.*

PYY See *peptide YY*$_{3-36}$.

radial glial cells Specialized glial cells that provide a scaffold for migrating neurons to climb to their destination.

rapid eye movement (REM) sleep The stage of sleep during which most dreaming occurs; research indicates that it is also a time of memory consolidation during which neural activity from the day is replayed.

rate law A principle that intensity of a stimulus is represented in an axon by the frequency of action potentials.

reactive aggression See *impulsive aggression.*

receptive field In vision, the area of the retina from which a cell in the visual system receives its input.

receptor A cell, often a specialized neuron, that is suited by its structure and function to respond to a particular form of energy, such as sound.

recessive A term referring to an allele that will have an influence only when it is paired with the same recessive allele on the other chromosome.

reflex A simple, automatic movement in response to a sensory stimulus.

regeneration The growth of severed axons; in mammals, it is limited to the peripheral nervous system.

relative refractory period The period during which a neuron can be fired again following an action potential, but only by an above-threshold stimulus.

REM See *rapid eye movement sleep.*

REM sleep behavior disorder A sleep disorder in which the person is physically active during REM sleep.

reorganization A shift in neural connections that changes the function of an area of the brain.

reserve hypothesis The hypothesis that individuals with greater cognitive or brain capacity are able to compensate for brain changes due to aging, brain damage, or disorders such as Alzheimer's.

resting potential The difference in charge between the inside and outside of the membrane of a neuron at rest.

reticular formation A collection of more than 90 nuclei running through the middle of the hindbrain and the midbrain with roles in sleep and arousal, attention, reflexes, and muscle tone.

retina The structure at the rear of the eye, which is made up of light-sensitive receptor cells and the neural cells that are connected to them.

retinal disparity A discrepancy in the location of an object's image on the two retinas; a cue to the distance of a focused object.

retinotopic map A map of the retina in the visual cortex, which results from adjacent receptors in the retina activating adjacent cells in the visual cortex.

retrieval The process of accessing stored memories.

retrograde amnesia The inability to remember events prior to impairment.

reuptake The process by which a neurotransmitter is taken back into the presynaptic terminals by transporters.

reward The positive effect on a user from a drug, electrical stimulation of the brain (ESB), sex, food, warmth, and so on.

rhodopsin The photopigment in rods that is sensitive to all wavelengths of visible light.

SAD See *seasonal affective disorder.*

salience network A cortical network that detects significant stimuli that require attention and switches between the resting default mode network and the goal-directed central executive network.

saltatory conduction The flow of electricity down the axon in which action potentials jump from one node of Ranvier to the next.

satiety Satisfaction of appetite.

scanning electron microscope A microscope that forms a three-dimensional image of up to 500,000 magnification by capturing electrons emitted by tissue when it is bombarded by a beam of electrons.

schizophrenia A disabling disorder characterized by perceptual, emotional, and intellectual deficits, loss of contact with reality, and an inability to function in life.

Schwann cell A type of glial cell that forms the myelin covering on neurons outside the brain and spinal cord.

SCN See *suprachiasmatic nucleus.*

SCR See *skin conductance response.*

SDN See *sexually dimorphic nucleus.*

seasonal affective disorder (SAD) Depression that is seasonal, being more pronounced in the summer in some people and in the winter in others.

secondary somatosensory cortex The part of the somatosensory cortex that receives information from the primary somatosensory cortex, from both sides of the body.

sedative A calming effect of a drug.

sensation The acquisition of sensory information.

sensory neuron A neuron that carries information from the body and from the outside world into the central nervous system.

sensory-specific satiety Decreased attractiveness of a food as the person or animal eats more of it.

set point A value in a control system that is the system's point of equilibrium or homeostasis; departures from this value initiate actions to restore the set-point condition.

sex The term for the biological characteristics that divide humans and other animals into the categories of male and female.

sexually dimorphic nucleus (SDN) A part of the MPOA important to male sexual behavior. It is larger in male rats, and their level of sexual activity depends on SDN size.

SFO See *subfornical organ.*

simple cell A cell in the visual cortex that responds to a line or an edge that is at a specific orientation and a specific place on the retina.

skeletal muscles The tissues that attach to bones and move the body and limbs.

skin conductance response (SCR) A measure of sweat gland activation and thus sympathetic nervous system activity.

skin senses Touch, warmth, cold, and pain (and, possibly, itch); the senses that arise from receptors in the skin.

slow-wave sleep Stages 3 and 4 of sleep, characterized by delta EEG and increased body activity; it appears to be a period of brain recuperation and may play a role in consolidation of declarative memory.

smooth muscles The tissues that control the contractions of internal organs other than the heart.

sodium-potassium pump Large protein molecules that move sodium ions through the neuron membrane to the outside and potassium ions back inside, helping to maintain the resting potential.

somatic nervous system The division of the peripheral nervous system that carries sensory information into the central nervous system (CNS) and motor commands from the CNS to the skeletal muscles.

somatosensory cortex The area in the parietal lobes that processes the skin senses and the senses that inform us about body position and movement, or proprioception; the primary somatosensory cortex is on the postcentral gyrus.

somatotopic map The form of topographic organization in the motor cortex and somatosensory cortex, such that adjacent body parts are represented in adjacent areas of the cortex.

spatial frequency theory The idea that visual cortical cells do a Fourier frequency analysis of the luminosity variations in a scene.

spatial summation The process of combining potentials that occur simultaneously at different locations on the dendrites and cell body.

spinal cord A part of the central nervous system; the spinal nerves, which communicate with the body below the head, enter and leave the spinal cord.

spinal nerves The peripheral axonal bundles that enter and leave the spinal cord at each vertebra and communicate with the body below the head.

stem cells Undifferentiated cells that can develop into specialized cells such as neurons, muscle, or blood.

stereotaxic instrument A device used for the precise positioning in the brain of an electrode or other device, such as a cannula.

stimulant A drug that activates the nervous system to produce arousal, increased alertness, and elevated mood.

stress A condition in the environment that makes unusual demands on the organism, such as threat, failure, or bereavement; the individual's negative response to a stressful situation.

striatum The caudate nucleus and putamen, both of the basal ganglia, and the nucleus accumbens.

stroke A medical condition caused by a loss of blood flow in the brain (also known as cerebrovascular accident).

subfornical organ (SFO) One of the structures bordering the third ventricle that increases drinking when stimulated by angiotensin II.

substance P A neuropeptide involved in pain signaling.

substantia nigra The nucleus that sends dopamine-releasing neurons to the striatum and that deteriorates in Parkinson's disease.

sudden cardiac death A fatal event when stress causes excessive sympathetic activity that sends the heart into fibrillation, contracting so rapidly that little or no blood is pumped.

sulcus A shallow groove or space between two *gyri*, not as deep as a *fissure.*

superior Above another structure.

superior colliculi Part of the tectum in the brain stem that is involved in visual functions such as guiding eye movements and fixation of gaze.

supplementary motor area The prefrontal area that assembles sequences of movements, such as those involved in eating or playing the piano, prior to execution by the primary motor cortex.

suprachiasmatic nucleus (SCN) A structure in the hypothalamus that (1) was found to be larger in gay men than in heterosexual men, (2) regulates the reproductive cycle in female rats, and (3) is the main biological clock, controlling several activities of the circadian rhythm.

sympathetic ganglion chain The structure running along each side of the spine through which most sympathetic neurons pass (and many synapses) on their way to and from the body's organs.

sympathetic nervous system The branch of the autonomic nervous system that activates the body in ways that help it cope with demands, such as emotional stress and physical emergencies.

synapse The structure in which a neuron passes electrical or chemical signals to another neuron, muscle, or organ.

synaptic cleft The small gap between a presynaptic neuron and a postsynaptic neuron.

synesthesia A condition in which stimulation in one sense triggers an experience in another sense, or a concept evokes an unrelated sensory experience.

T cell A type of leukocyte that attacks specific invaders.

tardive dyskinesia Tremors and involuntary movements caused by blocking of dopamine receptors in the basal ganglia due to prolonged use of drugs that block dopamine signals.

TBI See *traumatic brain injury.*

tectorial membrane A shelf-like membrane overlying the hair cells and the basilar membrane in the cochlea.

telephone theory A theory of auditory frequency analysis, which stated that the auditory neurons transmit the actual sound frequencies to the cortex.

temporal lobe The part of each cerebral hemisphere ventral to the lateral fissure; it contains the auditory cortex, visual and auditory association areas, and Wernicke's area.

temporal summation The process of combining potentials that arrive a short time apart on a neuron's dendrites and cell body.

terminal See *axon terminal.*

testes The male gonads that produce sperm.

testosterone The major sex hormone in males; a member of the class of androgens.

thalamus A forebrain structure lying just below the lateral ventricles, which receives information from all sensory systems except olfaction and relays it to the respective cortical projection areas. It has additional roles in movement, memory, and consciousness.

theory A system of statements that integrate and interpret diverse observations to explain some phenomenon.

theory of mind The ability to attribute mental states to oneself and to others.

third interstitial nucleus of the anterior hypothalamus (INAH3) A nucleus found to be half as large in gay men and heterosexual women as in heterosexual men, and similar in size in women and male-to-female transgender individuals.

TMS See *transcranial magnetic stimulation.*

tolerance After repeated drug use, the individual becomes less responsive and requires increasing amounts of a drug to produce the same results.

Tonotopically organized Neurons from adjacent receptor locations project to adjacent cells in the auditory cortex, forming a tonotopic map.

Tourette syndrome A disorder characterized by motor and phonic (sound) tics.

tract A bundle of axons in the central nervous system.

transcranial magnetic stimulation (TMS) A noninvasive stimulation technique that uses a magnetic coil to induce a voltage in brain tissue.

transgender An individual who believes he or she has been born into the wrong sex; the person may dress and live as the other sex and may undergo surgery for sex reassignment.

transmission electron microscope A magnification system that passes a beam of electrons through a thin slice of tissue onto a photographic film or a detector plate that connects to a computer monitor, forming an image magnified up to a million times.

traumatic brain injury (TBI) An injury caused by an external mechanical force such as a blow to the head, sudden acceleration or deceleration, or penetration.

trichromatic theory The hypothesis that three color processes account for all the colors we are able to distinguish.

tympanic membrane The eardrum, a very thin membrane stretched across the end of the auditory canal; its vibration transmits sound energy to the ossicles.

ultradian rhythm A rhythm with a length of less than a day, including the sleep stages and the basic rest and activity cycle during the day.

unipolar depression See *major depressive disorder.*

ventral Toward the stomach side.

ventral root The branch of each spinal nerve through which the motor neurons exit.

ventral stream The visual processing pathway that extends into the temporal lobes; it is especially concerned with the identification of objects.

ventral tegmental area A part of the mesolimbocortical dopamine system, which sends neurons to the nucleus accumbens and is a potent reward area.

ventricles Cavities in the brain filled with cerebrospinal fluid.

ventromedial hypothalamus An area in the hypothalamus important for sexual receptivity and copulation in female rats. It is also involved in eating behavior, and destruction in rats produces extreme obesity.

vesicle A membrane-enclosed container that stores neurotransmitter in the neuron terminal.

vestibular sense The sense that helps us maintain balance and that provides information about head position and movement; the receptors are located in the vestibular organs.

visual acuity The ability to distinguish visual details.

visual cortex Part of each occipital lobe where visual information is processed.

visual field The part of the environment that is being registered on the retina.

visual word form area (VWFA) An area in the human inferior temporal lobe involved in reading words.

VNO See *vomeronasal organ.*

volley theory Hypothesis of auditory frequency analysis that states that groups of neurons follow the frequency of a sound when the frequency exceeds the firing rate capability of a single neuron.

voltage The difference in electrical charge between two points.

vomeronasal organ (VNO) A cluster of receptors in the nasal cavity that detect pheromones.

vulnerability The idea that genes produce susceptibility to a disorder and that environmental challenges may combine with a person's biological susceptibility to exceed the threshold required to produce the disorder.

vulnerability model The idea that environmental challenges combine with a person's genetic vulnerability for a disease to exceed the threshold for the disease.

VWFA See *visual word form area.*

Wernicke's aphasia Language impairment resulting from damage to Wernicke's area; the person has difficulty understanding and producing spoken and written language.

Wernicke's area A brain area just posterior to the auditory cortex (in the left hemisphere in most people) that interprets spoken and written language input, and generates spoken and written language.

winter birth effect The tendency for more schizophrenics to be born during the winter and spring months than at any other time of the year.

Wisconsin Card Sorting Test A test of prefrontal functioning that requires the individual to sort cards using one criterion and then change to another criterion.

withdrawal A negative reaction that occurs when drug use is stopped.

Wolffian ducts The early structures that in the male develop into the seminal vesicles and the vas deferens.

working memory A form of short-term memory that provides a temporary "register" for information while it is being used.

X-linked In heredity, a condition in which a gene on the X chromosome is not paired with a gene on the shorter Y chromosome, so that a single recessive gene is adequate to produce a characteristic.

zygote A fertilized egg.

References

aan het Rot, M., Collins, K. A., Murrough, J. W., Perez, A. M., Reich, D. L., Charney, D. S., et al. (2010). Safety and efficacy of repeated-dose intravenous ketamine for treatment-resistant depression. *Biological Psychiatry, 15,* 139–145.

Abbot Laboratories agrees to withdraw its obesity drug Meridia. (2010, October 8). Retrieved from http://www.fda.gov/NewsEvents/Newsroom/Press Announcements/ucm228812.htm

Abe, K., Kroning, J., Greer, M. A., & Critchlow, V. (1979). Effects of destruction of the suprachiasmatic nuclei on the circadian rhythms in plasma corticosterone, body temperature, feeding and plasma thyrotropin. *Neuroendocrinology, 29,* 119–131.

Abel, E. L., & Sokol, R. J. (1986). Fetal alcohol syndrome is now leading cause of mental retardation. *Lancet, 2,* 1222.

Abelson, J. F., Kwan, K. Y., O'Roak, B. J., Baek, D. Y., Stillman, A. A., Morgan, T. M., et al. (2005). Sequence variants in *SLITRK1* are associated with Tourette's syndrome. *Science, 319,* 317–320.

Abi-Dargham, A., Rodenhiser, J., Printz, D., Zea-Ponce, Y., Gil, R., Kegeles, L. S., et al. (2000). Increased baseline occupancy of D$_2$ receptors by dopamine in schizophrenia. *Proceedings of the National Academy of Sciences, 97,* 8104–8109.

Abrahams, B. S., & Geschwind, D. H. (2008). Advances in autism genetics: On the threshold of a new neurobiology. *Nature Reviews Genetics, 9,* 341–355.

Abramowitz, J. S., Taylor, S., & McKay, D. (2009). Obsessive-compulsive disorder. *Lancet, 374,* 491–499.

A brighter day for Edward Taub. (1997). *Science, 276,* 1503.

Adams, D. B., Gold, A. R., & Burt, A. D. (1978). Rise in female-initiated sexual activity at ovulation and its suppression by oral contraceptives. *New England Journal of Medicine, 299,* 1145–1150.

Addolorato, G., Leggio, L., Ferrulli, A., Cardone, S., Bedogni, G., Caputo, F., Gasbarrini, G., Landolfi, R., & the Baclofen Study Group. (2011). Dose-response effect of baclofen in reducing daily alcohol intake in alcohol dependence: Secondary analysis of a randomized, double-blind, placebo-controlled trial. *Alcohol and Alcoholism, 46,* 312–317.

Adler, L. E., Olincy, A., Cawthra, E. M., McRae, K. A., Harris, J. G., Nagamoto, H. T., et al. (2004). Varied effects of atypical neuroleptics on P50 auditory gating in schizophrenia patients. *American Journal of Psychiatry, 161,* 1822–1828.

Adolphs, R., Damasio, H., Tranel, D., & Damasio, A. R. (1996). Cortical systems for the recognition of emotion in facial expressions. *Journal of Neuroscience, 16,* 7678–7687.

Adolphs, R., Tranel, D., & Damasio, A. R. (1998). The human amygdala in social judgment. *Nature, 393,* 470–474.

Agnew, B. (2000). Financial conflicts get more scrutiny in clinical trials. *Science, 289,* 1266–1267.

Agnew-Blais, J. C., Polanczyk, G. V., Danese, A., Wertz, J., Moffitt, T. E., & Arseneault, L. (2016). Evaluation of the persistence, remission, and emergence of attention-deficit/hyperactivity disorder in young adulthood. *JAMA Psychiatry, 73,* 713–720.

Ainsworth, C. (2009). Full without food: Can surgery cure obesity? *New Scientist,* September 2. Retrieved from www.newscientist.com/article/mg20327241.100-full-without-food-can-surgery-cure-obesity.html

Akbarian, S., Bunney, W. E., Potkin, S. G., Wigal, S. B., Hagman, J. O., Sandman, C. A., et al. (1993). Altered distribution of nicotinamide-adenine dinucleotide phosphate-diaphorase cells in frontal lobe of schizophrenics implies disturbances of cortical development. *Archives of General Psychiatry, 50,* 169–177.

Akbarian, S., Viñuela, A., Kim, J. J., Potkin, S. G., Bunney, W. E., & Jones, E. G. (1993). Distorted distribution of nicotinamide-adenine dinucleotide phosphate-diaphorase neurons in temporal lobe of schizophrenics implies anomalous cortical development. *Archives of General Psychiatry, 50,* 178–187.

Akeju, O., Loggia, M. L., Catana, C., Pavone, K. J., Vazquez, R., Rhee, J., et al. (2014). Disruption of thalamic functional connectivity is a neural correlate of dexmedetomidine-induced unconsciousness. *eLife, 3:* e04499. doi:10.7554/eLife.04499

Akil, O., Seal, R. P., Burke, K., Wang, C., Alemi, A., During, M., et al. (2012). Restoration of hearing in the VGLUT3 knockout mouse using virally mediated gene therapy. *Neuron, 75,* 283–293.

Alain, C., Arnott, S. R., Hevenor, S., Graham, S., & Grady, C. L. (2001). "What" and "where" in the human auditory system. *Proceedings of the National Academy of Sciences, 98,* 12301–12306.

Alaska Oil Spill Commission. (1990, February). *Final report: Details about the accident.* Retrieved from www.evostc.state.ak.us/facts/details.cfm

Alati, R., Mamun, A. A., Williams, G. M., O'Callaghan, M., Najman, J. M., & Bor, W. (2006). In utero alcohol exposure and prediction of alcohol disorders in early adulthood. *Archives of General Psychiatry, 63,* 1009–1016.

Albert, D. J., Walsh, M. L., Gorzalka, B. B., Siemens, Y., & Louie, H. (1986). Testosterone removal in rats results in a decrease in social aggression and a loss of social dominance. *Physiology and Behavior, 36,* 401–407.

Albrecht, D. G., De Valois, R. L., & Thorell, L. G. (1980). Visual cortical neurons: Are bars or gratings the optimal stimuli? *Science, 207,* 88–90.

Alexander, C. N., Langer, E. J., Newman, R. I., Chandler, H. M., & Davies, J. L. (1989). Transcendental meditation, mindfulness, and longevity: An experimental study with the elderly. *Journal of Personality and Social Psychology, 57,* 950–964.

Alexander, G. E., & Crutcher, M. D. (1990). Preparation for movement: Neural representations of intended direction in three motor areas of the monkey. *Journal of Neurophysiology, 64,* 133–150.

Alexander-Bloch, A. F., Reiss, P. T., Rapoport, J., McAdams, H., Giedd, J. N., Bullmore, E. T., et al. (2014). Abnormal cortical growth in schizophrenia targets normative modules of synchronized development. *Biological Psychiatry, 76,* 438–446.

Alkire, M. T., Haier, R. J., Fallon, J. H., & Cahill, L. (1998). Hippocampal, but not amygdala, activity at encoding correlates with long-term free recall of nonemotional information. *Proceedings of the National Academy of Sciences, 95,* 14506–14510.

Allegretta, M., Nicklas, J. A., Sriram, S., & Albertini, R. J. (1990). T cells responsive to myelin basic protein in patients with multiple sclerosis. *Science, 247,* 718–721.

Alliance for Regenerative Medicine. (2015a). The Alliance for Regenerative Medicine issues position statement regarding human embryo germline genome editing. Retrieved from http://alliancerm.org/press/alliance-regenerative-medicine-issues-position-statement-regarding-human-embryo-germline

Alliance for Regenerative Medicine. (2015b). Gene-editing summit supports some research in human embryos. Retrieved from http://alliancerm.org/news/gene-editing-summit-supports-some-research-human-embryos

Allison, T., & Cicchetti, D. V. (1976). Sleep in mammals: Ecological and constitutional correlates. *Science, 194,* 732–734.

Almeida, D. M., Jandacek, R. J., Weber, W. A., & McNamara, R. K. (2016). Docosahexaenoic acid biostatus is associated with event-related functional connectivity in cortical attention networks of typically developing children. *Nutritional Neuroscience, 20,* 246–254.

Altar, C. A., Laeng, P., Jurata, L. W., Brockman, J. A., Lemire, A., Bullard, J., et al. (2004). Electroconvulsive seizures regulate gene expression of distinct neurotrophic signaling pathways. *Journal of Neuroscience, 24,* 2667–2677.

Altena, E., Vrenken, H., Van Der Werf, Y. D., van den Heuvel, O. A., & Van Someren, E. J. W. (2010). Reduced orbitofrontal and parietal gray matter in chronic insomnia: A voxel-based morphometric study. *Biological Psychiatry, 67,* 182–185.

Alzheimer's Association. (2017). 2017 Alzheimer's disease facts and figures. Retrieved from http://www.alz.org/facts/overview.asp?sp=true

Amad, A., Ramoz, N., Thomas, P., Jardri, R., & Gorwood, P. (2014). Genetics of borderline personality disorder: Systematic review and proposal of an integrative model. *Neuroscience and Biobehavioral Reviews, 40,* 6–19.

Amado, D., Mingozzi, F., Hui, D., Bennicelli, J. L., Wei, Z., Chen, Y., et al. (2010). Safety and efficacy of subretinal readministration of a viral vector in large animals to treat congenital blindness. *Science Translational Medicine, 2(21),* 21ra16. doi:10.1126/scitranslmed.3000659

Amanzio, M., Pollo, A., Maggi, G., & Benedetti, F. (2001). Response variability to analgesics: A role for non-specific activation of endogenous opioids. *Pain, 90,* 205–215.

Ameis, S. H., Lerch, J. P., Taylor, M. J., Lee, W., Viviano, J. D., Pipitone, J., et al. (2016). A diffusion tensor imaging study in children with ADHD, autism spectrum disorder, OCD, and matched controls: Distinct and non-distinct white matter disruption and dimensional brain-behavior relationships. *American Journal of Psychiatry, 173,* 1213–1222.

American Academy of Sleep Medicine. (2010). "Sexsomnia" is common in sleep center patients, study finds. *Science Daily,* June 7. Retrieved from www.sciencedaily.com/releases/2010/06/100607065547.htm

American Medical Association. (1992). *Use of animals in biomedical research: The challenge and response.* Chicago: Author.

American Psychiatric Association. (2013). *Diagnostic and statistical manual of mental disorders* (5th ed.). Washington, DC: Author.

American Psychological Association. (2010). Ethical principles of psychologists and code of conduct. Retrieved from www.apa.org/ethics/code/index.aspx

Amrollahi, Z., Rezaei, F., Salehi, B., Modabbernia, A.-H., Maroufi, A., Esfandiari, G.-R., et al. (2011). Double-blind, randomized placebo-controlled 6-week study on the efficacy and safety of the tamoxifen adjunctive to lithium in acute bipolar mania. *Journal of Affective Disorders, 129*, 327–331.

Anaclet, C., Ferrari, L., Arrigoni, E., Bass, C. E., Saper, C. B., Lu, J., & Fuller, P. M. (2014). The GABAergic parafacial zone is a medullary slow wave sleep-promoting center. *Nature Neuroscience, 17*, 1217–1224.

Anagnostou, E., Soorya, L., Brian, J., Dupuis, A., Mankad, D., Smile, S., & Jacob, S. (2014). Intranasal oxytocin in the treatment of autism spectrum disorders: A review of literature and early safety and efficacy data in youth. *Brain Research.* doi:10.1016/j.brainres.2014.01.049

Anders, T. F., & Roffwarg, H. P. (1973). The effects of selective interruption and deprivation of sleep in the human newborn. *Developmental Psychobiology, 6*, 79–91.

Andersen, S., & Skorpen, F. (2009). Variation in the *COMT* gene: Implications for pain perception and pain treatment. *Summary Pharmacogenomics, 10*, 669–684.

Anderson, A. K., & Phelps, E. A. (2001). Lesions of the human amygdala impair enhanced perception of emotionally salient events. *Nature, 411*, 305–309.

Anderson, B., & Harvey, T. (1996). Alterations in cortical thickness and neuronal density in the frontal cortex of Albert Einstein. *Neuroscience Letters, 210*, 161–164.

Anderson, M., & Hanse, E. (2010). Astrocytes impose postburst depression of release probability at hippocampal glutamate synapses. *Journal of Neuroscience, 30*, 5776–5780.

Anderson, S. W., Bechara, A., Damasio, H., Tranel, D., & Damasio, A. R. (1999). Impairment of social and moral behavior related to early damage in human prefrontal cortex. *Nature Neuroscience, 2*, 1032–1037.

Ando, J., Ono, Y., & Wright, M. J. (2001). Genetic structure of spatial and verbal working memory. *Behavior Genetics, 31*, 615–624.

Ando, K., Laborde, Q., Lazar, A., Godefroy, D., Youssef, I., Amar, M., et al. (2014). Inside Alzheimer brain with CLARITY: Senile plaques, neurofibrillary tangles and axons in 3-D. *Acta Neuropathology, 128*, 457–459.

Andolfatto, P. (2005). Adaptive evolution of non-coding DNA in *Drosophila. Nature, 437*, 1149–1152.

Andrade, J. (1995). Learning during anaesthesia: A review. *British Journal of Psychology, 86*, 479–506.

Andreano, J. M., & Cahill, L. (2009). Sex influences on the neurobiology of learning and memory. *Learning and Memory, 16*, 248–266.

Andreasen, N. C. (1984). *The broken brain.* New York: Harper & Row.

Andreasen, N. C., Flaum, M., Swayze, V. W., II, Tyrrell, G., & Arndt, S. (1990). Positive and negative symptoms in schizophrenia: A critical reappraisal. *Archives of General Psychiatry, 47*, 615–621.

Andreasen, N. C., Rezai, K., Alliger, R., Swayzee, V. W., II, Flaum, M., Kirchner, P., et al. (1992). Hypofrontality in neuroleptic-naive patients and in patients with chronic schizophrenia: Assessment with xenon 133 single-photon emission computed tomography and the Tower of London. *Archives of General Psychiatry, 49*, 943–958.

Andrews-Hanna, J. R., Snyder, A. Z., Vincent, J. L., Lustig, C., Head, D., Raichle, M. E., et al. (2007). Disruption of large-scale brain systems in advanced aging. *Neuron, 56*, 924–935.

Anguera, J. A., Boccanfuso, J., Rintoul, J. L., Al-Hashimi, O., Faraji, F., Janowich, J., et al. (2013). Video game training enhances cognitive control in older adults. *Nature, 501*, 97–103.

Animal rights extremists increasingly targeting individuals. (2014). *ScienceInsider,* March 12. Retrieved from http://news.sciencemag.org/policy/2014/03/animal-rights-extremists-increasingly-targeting-individuals

Annese, J., Schenker-Ahmed, N. M., Bartsch, H., Maechler, P., Sheh, C., Thomas, N., et al. (2014). Postmortem examination of patient H.M.'s brain based on histological sectioning and digital 3D reconstruction. *Nature Communications, 5*, 3122. doi:10.1038/ncomms4122

Anney, R., Kiel, L., Pinto, D., Almeida, J., Bacchelli, E., Baird, G., et al. (2012). Individual common variants exert weak effects on the risk for autism spectrum disorders. *Human Molecular Genetics, 21*, 4781–4792.

Anonymous. (1970). Effects of sexual activity on beard growth in man. *Nature, 226*, 869–870.

Anson, P. (2017, March 20). New opioid relieves pain without the high. *Pain News Network.* Retrieved from https://www.painnewsnetwork.org/stories/2017/3/20/new-opioid-relieves-pain-without-the-high

Anthony, J. C., Warner, L. A., & Kessler, R. C. (1994). Comparative epidemiology of dependence on tobacco, alcohol, controlled substances, and inhalants: Basic findings from the national comorbidity survey. *Experimental and Clinical Psychopharmacology, 2*, 244–268.

Antilla, S. A., & Leinonen, E. V. (2001). A review of the pharmacological and clinical profile of mirtazapine. *CNS Drug Reviews, 7*, 249–264.

Aoki, Y., Abe, O., Nippashi, Y., & Yamasue, H. (2013). Comparison of white matter integrity between autism spectrum disorder subjects and typically developing individuals: A meta-analysis of diffusion tensor imaging tractography studies. *Molecular Autism, 4*, 25. doi:10.1186/2040-2392-4-25

Aoki, Y., Yahata, N., Watanabe, T., Takano, Y., Kawakubo, Y., Kuwabara, H., et al. (2014). Oxytocin improves behavioural and neural deficits in inferring others' social emotions in autism. *Brain, 137*, 3073–3086.

Apkarian, A. V., Sosa, Y., Krauss, B. R., Thomas, S. P., Fredrickson, B. E., Levy, R. E., et al. (2004). Chronic pain patients are impaired on an emotional decision-making task. *Pain, 108*, 129–136.

Apkarian, A. V., Sosa, Y., Sonty, S., Levy, R. M., Harden, R. N., Parrish, T. B., et al. (2004). Chronic back pain is associated with decreased prefrontal and thalamic gray matter density. *Journal of Neuroscience, 24*, 10410–10415.

Archer, J. (1991). The influence of testosterone on human aggression. *British Journal of Psychology, 82*, 1–28.

Archer, J., Graham-Kevan, N., & Davies, M. (2005). Testosterone and aggression: A reanalysis of Book, Starzyk, and Quinsey's (2001) study. *Aggression and Violent Behavior, 10*, 241–261.

Archer, S. N., Robillant, D. I., Shane, D. J., Smits, M., Williams, A., Arendt, J., et al. (2003). A length polymorphism in the circadian clock gene *Per3* is linked to delayed sleep phase syndrome and extreme diurnal preference. *Sleep, 26*, 413–415.

Arcila, V. (2016). Umbilical cord stem cells to treat acquired hearing loss in kids. CryoCell International. Retrieved from https://www.cryo-cell.com/blog/march-2016/acquired-hearing-loss-child-stem-cells

Arendt, J., Skene, D. J., Middleton, B., Lockley, S. W., & Deacon, S. (1997). Efficacy of melatonin treatment in jet lag, shift work, and blindness. *Journal of Biological Rhythms, 12*, 604–617.

Argiolas, A. (1999). Neuropeptides and sexual behavior. *Neuroscience and Biobehavioral Reviews, 23*, 1127–1142.

Arnold, P. D., & Richter, M. A. (2001). Is obsessive-compulsive disorder an autoimmune disease? *Canadian Medical Association Journal, 165*, 1353–1358.

Arnold, P. E., Zai, G., & Richter, M. A. (2004). Genetics of anxiety disorders. *Current Psychiatry Reports, 6*, 243–254.

Arnone, D., McIntosh, A. M., Ebmeier, K. P., Munafò, M. R., & Anderson, I. M. (2012). Magnetic resonance imaging studies in unipolar depression: Systematic review and meta-regression analyses. *European Neuropsychopharmacology, 22*, 1–16.

Arzy, S., Seeck, M., Ortigue, S., Spinelli, L., & Blanke, O. (2006). Induction of an illusory shadow person. *Nature, 443*(287), 287.

Asai, M., Ramachandrappa, S., Joachim, M., Shen, Y., Zhang, R., Nuthalapati, N., et al. (2013). Loss of function of the melanocortin 2 receptor accessory protein 2 is associated with mammalian obesity. *Science, 341*, 275–278.

Aschoff, J. (1984). Circadian timing. *Annals of the New York Academy of Sciences, 423*, 442–468.

Asher, J. E., Lamb, J. A., Brocklebank, D., Cazier, J. B., Maestrini, E., Addis, L., et al. (2009). A whole-genome scan and fine-mapping linkage study of auditory-visual synesthesia reveals evidence of linkage to chromosomes 2q24, 5q33, 6p12, and 12p12. *American Journal of Human Genetics, 84*, 279–285.

Ashour, M. H., Jain, S. K., Kattan, K. M., al-Daeef, A. Q., Abdal-Jabbar, M. S., al-Tahan, A. R., et al. (1995). Maximal thymectomy for myasthenia gravis. *European Journal of Cardio-thoracic Surgery, 9*, 461–464.

Asplund, C. L., Todd, J. J., Snyder, A. P., & Marois, R. (2010). A central role for the lateral prefrontal cortex in goal-directed and stimulus-driven attention. *Nature Neuroscience, 13*, 507–512.

Atkinson, R. L., Dhurandhar, N. V., Allison, D. B., Bowen, R. L., Israel, B. A., Albu, J. B., & Augustus, A. S. (2005). Human adenovirus-36 is associated with increased body weight and paradoxical reduction of serum lipids. *International Journal of Obesity, 29*, 281–284.

Attia, E. (2009). Anorexia nervosa: Current status and future directions. *Annual Review of Medicine, 61*, 425–435.

Avidan, G., & Behrmann, M. (2009). Functional MRI reveals compromised neural integrity of the face processing network in congenital prosopagnosia. *Current Biology, 19*, 1146–1150.

Ax, A. (1953). The physiological differentiation between fear and anger in humans. *Psychosomatic Medicine, 15*, 433–442.

Azevedo, F. A. C., Carvalho, L. R. B., Grinberg, L. T., Farfel, J. M., Ferretti, R. E. L., Leite, R. E. P., et al. (2009). Equal numbers of neuronal and nonneuronal cells make the human brain an isometrically scaled-up primate brain. *Journal of Comparative Neurology, 513*, 532–541.

Baaré, W. F. C., Pol, H. E. H., Boomsma, D. I., Posthuma, D., de Geus, E. J. C., Schnack, H. G., et al. (2001). Quantitative genetic modeling of variation in human brain morphology. *Cerebral Cortex, 11*, 816–824.

Baars, B. J. (2005). Global workspace theory of consciousness: Toward a cognitive neuroscience of human experience. In S. Laureys (Ed.), *The boundaries of consciousness: Neurobiology and neuropathology* (pp. 45–54). New York: Elsevier.

Bach, A. C., Clausen, B. H., Møller, M., Vestergaard, B., Chi, C. N., Round, A., et al. (2012). A high-affinity, dimeric inhibitor of PSD-95 bivalently interacts with PDZ1-2 and protects against ischemic brain damage. *Proceedings of the National Academy of Sciences, 109*, 3317–3322.

Bach-y-Rita, P. (1990). Brain plasticity as a basis for recovery of function in humans. *Neuropsychologia, 28*, 547–554.

BAC Measurement. (n.d.). Lifeloc Technologies. Retrieved from http://www.lifeloc.com/measurement.aspx

Baer, D. (2017, February 14). Rich people literally see the world differently. *New York Magazine*. Retrieved from http://nymag.com/scienceofus/2017/02/how-rich-people-see-the-world-differently.html

Bagni, C., & Greenough, W. T. (2005). From mRNP trafficking to spine dysmorphogenesis: The roots of fragile X syndrome. *Nature Reviews Neuroscience, 6,* 376–387.

Bailer, U. F., & Kaye, W. H. (2010, September 11). Serotonin: Imaging findings in eating disorders. In R. A. H. Adan & W. H. Kaye (Eds.), *Behavioral Neurobiology of Eating Disorders* (pp. 59–78). Retrieved from http://eatingdisorders.ucsd.edu/research/pdf_papers/2011/BailerKaye2011_PMID21243470.pdf

Bailer, U. F., Narendran, R., Frankle, W. G., Himes, M. L., Duvvuri, V., Mathis, C. A., & Kaye, W. H. (2012). Amphetamine induced dopamine release increases anxiety in individuals recovered from anorexia nervosa. *International Journal of Eating Disorders, 45,* 263–271.

Bailey, A., Le Couteur, A., Gottesman, I., Bolton, P., Simonoff, E., Yuzda, E., et al. (1995). Autism as a strongly genetic disorder: Evidence from a British twin study. *Psychological Medicine, 25,* 63–77.

Bailey, C. H., Bartsch, D., & Kandel, E. R. (1996). Toward a molecular definition of long-term memory storage. *Proceedings of the National Academy of Sciences, 93,* 13445–13452.

Bailey, J. M., & Bell, A. P. (1993). Familiality of female and male homosexuality. *Behavior Genetics, 23,* 313–322.

Bailey, J. M., & Benishay, D. S. (1993). Familial aggregation of female sexual orientation. *American Journal of Psychiatry, 150,* 272–277.

Bailey, J. M., Dunne, M. P., & Martin, N. G. (2000). Genetic and environmental influences on sexual orientation and its correlates in an Australian twin sample. *Journal of Personality and Social Psychology, 78,* 524–536.

Bailey, J. M., & Pillard, R. C. (1991). A genetic study of male sexual orientation. *Archives of General Psychiatry, 48,* 1089–1096.

Bailey, J. M., Pillard, R. C., Neale, M. C., & Agyei, Y. (1993). Heritable factors influence sexual orientation in women. *Archives of General Psychiatry, 50,* 217–223.

Baizer, J. S., Ungerleider, L. G., & Desimone, R. (1991). Organization of visual inputs to the inferior temporal and posterior parietal cortex in macaques. *Journal of Neuroscience, 11,* 168–190.

Bakermans-Kranenburg, M. J., & van IJzendoorn, M. H. (2008). Oxytocin receptor (OXTR) and serotonin transporter (5-HTT) genes associated with observed parenting. *Social Cognitive and Affective Neuroscience, 3,* 128–134.

Bakker, J., Honda, S.-I., Harada, N., & Balthazart, J. (2002). The aromatase knock-out mouse provides new evidence that estradiol is required during development in the female for the expression of sociosexual behaviors in adulthood. *Journal of Neuroscience, 22,* 9104–9112.

Bakker, J., Honda, S.-I., Harada, N., & Balthazart, J. (2003). The aromatase knock-out (ArKO) mouse provides new evidence that estrogens are required for the development of the female brain. *Annals of the New York Academy of Sciences, 1007,* 251–262.

Baliki, M. N., Chialvo, D. R., Geha, P. Y., Levy, R. M., Harden, R. N., Parrish, T. B., et al. (2006). Chronic pain and the emotional brain: Specific brain activity associated with spontaneous fluctuations of intensity of chronic back pain. *Journal of Neuroscience, 26,* 12165–12173.

Bao, A.-M., & Swaab, D. F. (2011). Sexual differentiation of the human brain: Relation to gender identity, sexual orientation and neuropsychiatric disorders. *Frontiers in Neuroendocrinology, 32,* 214–226.

Barinaga, M. (1996). Guiding neurons to the cortex. *Science, 274,* 1100–1101.

Barinaga, M. (1997). New imaging methods provide a better view into the brain. *Science, 276,* 1974–1981.

Barkley, R. A., Fischer, M., Smallish, L., & Fletcher, K. (2003). Does the treatment of attention-deficit/hyperactivity disorder with stimulants contribute to drug use/abuse? A 13-year prospective study. *Pediatrics, 111,* 97–109.

Barlassina, L., & Newen, A. (2013). The role of bodily perception in emotion: In defense of an impure somatic theory. *Philosophy and Phenomenological Research.* doi:10.1111/phpr.12041

Baron-Cohen, S., Johnson, D., Asher, J., Wheelwright, S., Fisher, S. E., Gregersen, P. K., & Allison, C. (2013). Is synaesthesia more common in autism? *Molecular Autism, 4,* 40. doi:10.1186/2040-2392-4-40

Bartlett, D. L., & Steele, J. B. (1979). *Empire: The life, legend, and madness of Howard Hughes.* New York: Norton.

Bartlett, E. L., Sadagopan, S., & Wang, X. (2011). Fine frequency tuning in monkey auditory cortex and thalamus. *Journal of Neurophysiology, 106,* 849–859.

Bartoshuk, L. M., Duffy, V. B., Hayes, J. E., Moskowitz, H. R., & Snyder, D. J. (2006). Psychophysics of sweet and fat perception in obesity: Problems, solutions and new perspectives. *Philosophical Transactions of the Royal Society: Biological Sciences, 361,* 1137–1148.

Barysheva, M., Jahanshad, N., Foland-Ross, L., Altshuler, L. L., & Thompson, P. M. (2013). White matter microstructural abnormalities in bipolar disorder: A whole brain diffusion tensor imaging study. *Neuroimage: Clinical, 2,* 558–568.

Basbaum, A. I., Bautista, D. M., Scherrer, G., & Julius, D. (2009). Cellular and molecular mechanisms of pain. *Cell, 139,* 267–284.

Basbaum, A. I., & Fields, H. L. (1984). Endogenous pain control systems: Brainstem spinal pathways and endorphin circuitry. *Annual Review of Neuroscience, 7,* 309–338.

Basbaum, A. I., & Jessell, T. M. (2000). The perception of pain. In E. R. Kandel, J. H. Schwartz, & T. M. Jessell (Eds.), *Principles of neural science* (4th ed., pp. 472–491). New York: McGraw-Hill.

Bassuk, A. G., Zheng, A., Li, Y., Tsang, S. H., & Mahajan, V. B. (2016). Precision medicine: Genetic repair of retinitis pigmentosa in patient-derived stem cells. *Scientific Reports, 6:*19969. doi:10.1038/srep19969

Bastiaansen, J. A. C. J., Thioux, M., & Keysers, C. (2009). Evidence for mirror systems in emotions. *Philosophical Transactions of the Royal Society B, 364,* 2391–2404.

Batista, A. P., Buneo, C. A., Snyder, L. H., & Andersen, R. A. (1999). Reach plans in eye-centered coordinates. *Science, 285,* 257–260.

Batterham, R. L., Cowley, M. A., Small, C. J., Herzog, H., Cohen, M. A., Dakin, C. L., et al. (2002). Gut hormone PYY$_{3-36}$ physiologically inhibits food intake. *Nature, 418,* 650–654.

Bauer, R. M. (1984). Autonomic recognition of names and faces in prosopagnosia: A neuropsychological application of the guilty knowledge test. *Neuropsychologia, 22,* 457–469.

Baulac, S., Huberfeld, G., Gourinkel-An, I., Mitropoulou, G., Beranger, A., Prud'homme, J.-F., et al. (2001). First genetic evidence of GABA$_A$ receptor dysfunction in epilepsy: A mutation in the γ2-subunit gene. *Nature Genetics, 28,* 46–48.

Baum, A., Gatchel, R. J., & Schaeffer, M. A. (1983). Emotional, behavioral, and physiological effects of chronic stress at Three Mile Island. *Journal of Consulting and Clinical Psychology, 51,* 565–572.

Baumesiter, J.-C., Papa, G., & Foroni, F. (2016). Deeper than skin deep: The effect of botulinum toxin-A on emotion processing. *Toxicon, 118,* 86–90.

Baumgart, M., Snyder, H. M., Carrillo, M. C., Fazio, S., Kim, H., & Johns, H. (2015). Summary of the evidence on modifiable risk factors for cognitive decline and dementia: A population-based perspective. *Alzheimer's & Dementia, 11,* 718–726.

Baumgartner, T., Heinrichs, M., Vonlanthen, A., Fischbacher, U., & Fehr, E. (2008). Oxytocin shapes the neural circuitry of trust and trust adaptation in humans. *Neuron, 58,* 639–650.

Baxter, L. R., Phelps, M. E., Mazziotta, J. C., Guze, B. H., Schwartz, J. M., & Selin, C. E. (1987). Local cerebral glucose metabolic rates in obsessive-compulsive disorder. *Archives of General Psychiatry, 44,* 211–218.

Baxter, L. R., Phelps, M. E., Mazziotta, J. C., Schwartz, J. M., Gerner, R. H., Selin, C. E., et al. (1985). Cerebral metabolic rates for glucose in mood disorders: Studies with positron emission tomography and fluorodeoxyglucose F 18. *Archives of General Psychiatry, 42,* 441–447.

Beauchamp, G. K., & Mennella, J. A. (2009). Early flavor learning and its impact on later feeding behavior. *Journal of Pediatric Gastroenterology and Nutrition, 48,* S25–S30.

Bechara, A., Damasio, H., Damasio, A. R., & Lee, G. P. (1999). Different contributions of the human amygdala and ventromedial prefrontal cortex to decision-making. *Journal of Neuroscience, 19,* 5473–5481.

Bechara, A., Damasio, H., Tranel, D., & Damasio, A. R. (1997). Deciding advantageously before knowing the advantageous strategy. *Science, 275,* 1293–1295.

Bechara, A., Tranel, D., Damasio, H., Adolphs, R., Rockland, C., & Damasio, A. R. (1995). Double dissociation of conditioning and declarative knowledge relative to the amygdala and hippocampus in humans. *Science, 269,* 1115–1118.

Beck, A., Wüstenberg, T., Gensuck, A., Wrase, J., Schiagenhauf, F., Smolka, M. N., et al. (2012). Effect of brain structure, brain function, and brain connectivity on relapse in alcohol-dependent patients. *Archives of General Psychiatry, 69,* 842–852.

Beck, A. T., & Galef, B. G. (1989). Social influences on the selection of a protein-sufficient diet by Norway rats (*Rattus norvegicus*). *Journal of Comparative Psychology, 103,* 132–139.

Becker, A. E., Burwell, R. A., Gilman, S. E., Herzog, D. B., & Hamburg, P. (2002). Eating behaviours and attitudes following prolonged exposure to television among ethnic Fijian adolescent girls. *British Journal of Psychiatry, 180,* 509–514.

Bedny, M., Kongle, T., Pelphrey, K., Saxe, R., & Pascual-Leone, A. (2010). Sensitive period for a multimodal response in human visual motion area MT/MST. *Current Biology, 20,* 1900–1906.

Beecher, D. K. (1956). Relationship of significance of wound to pain experienced. *Journal of the American Medical Association, 161,* 1609–1613.

Begley, S., & Biddle, N. A. (1996, February 26). For the obsesssed, the mind can fix the brain. *Newsweek,* p. 60.

Begré, S., & Koenig, T. (2008). Cerebral disconnectivity: An early event in schizophrenia. *Neuroscientist, 14,* 19–45.

Behrmann, M., Moscovitch, M., & Winocur, G. (1994). Intact visual imagery and impaired visual perception in a patient with visual agnosia. *Journal of Experimental Psychology: Human Perception and Performance, 20,* 1068–1087.

Bekar, L., Libionka, W., Tian, G. F., Xu, Q., Torres, A., Wang, X., et al. (2008). Adenosine is crucial for deep brain stimulation-mediated attenuation of tremor. *Nature Medicine, 14,* 75–80.

Békésy, G. von. (1951). The mechanical properties of the ear. In S. S. Stevens (Ed.), *The handbook of experimental psychology* (pp. 1075–1115). New York: Wiley.

Békésy, G. von. (1956). Current status of theories of hearing. *Science, 123,* 779–783.

Belfort, M. B., Anderson, P. J., Nowak, V. A., Lee, K. J., Molesworth, C., Thompson, D. K., et al. (2016). Breast milk feeding, brain development, and neurocognitive outcomes: A 7-year longitudinal study in infants born at less than 30 weeks' gestation. *Journal of Pediatrics, 177*, 133–139. doi:10.1016/j.jpeds.2016.06.045

Bell, A. P., Weinberg, M. S., & Hammersmith, S. K. (1981). *Sexual preference.* Bloomington: Indiana University Press.

Bellis, D. J. (1981). *Heroin and politicians: The failure of public policy to control addiction in America.* Westport, CT: Greenwood Press.

Benca, R. M., Obermeyer, W. H., Thisted, R. A., & Gillin, J. C. (1992). Sleep and psychiatric disorders: A meta-analysis. *Archives of General Psychiatry, 49*, 651–668.

Benedict, C., Axelsson, T., Söderberg, S., Larsson, A., Ingelsson, E., Lind, L., & Schiöth, H. B. (2014). Fat mass and obesity-associated gene (FTO) is linked to higher plasma levels of the hunger hormone ghrelin and lower serum levels of the satiety hormone leptin in older adults. *Diabetes, 63*, 3955–3959.

Bennett, I. J., & Madden, D. J. (2014). Disconnected aging: Cerebral white matter integrity and age-related differences in cognition. *Neuroscience, 276*, 187–205.

Bennett, M. V. L., & Zukin, S. (2004). Electrical coupling and neuronal synchronization in the mammalian brain. *Neuron, 41*, 495–511.

Benoit, E., & Dubois, J. M. (1986). Toxin I from the snake *Dendroaspis polylepsis polylepsis:* A highly specific blocker of one type of potassium channel in myelinated nerve fiber. *Brain Research, 377*, 374–377.

Benson, D. F., Djenderedjian, A., Miller, B. L., Pachana, N. A., Chang, L., Itti, L., et al. (1996). Neural basis of confabulation. *Neurology, 46*, 1239–1243.

Benton, A. L. (1980). The neuropsychology of facial recognition. *American Psychologist, 35*(10), 176–186.

Bentz, E.-K., Hefler, L. A., Kaufmann, U., Huber, J. C., Kolbus, A., & Tempfer, C. B. (2008). A polymorphism of the *CYP17* gene related to sex steroid metabolism is associated with female-to-male but not male-to-female transsexualism. *Fertility and Sterility, 90*, 56–59.

Ben Zion, I. Z., Tessler, R., Cohen, L., Lerer, E., Raz, Y., Bachner-Melman, R., et al. (2006). Polymorphisms in the dopamine D4 receptor gene (*DRD4*) contribute to individual differences in human sexual behavior: Desire, arousal and sexual function. *Molecular Psychiatry, 11*, 782–786.

Berenbaum, S. A., Duck, S. C., & Bryk, K. (2000). Behavioral effects of prenatal *versus* postnatal androgen excess in children with 21-hydroxylase-deficient congenital adrenal hyperplasia. *Journal of Clinical Endocrinology & Metabolism, 85*, 727–733.

Berglund, H., Lindström, P., Dhejne-Helmy, C., & Savic, I. (2008). Male-to-female transsexuals show sex-atypical hypothalamus activation when smelling odorous steroids. *Cerebral Cortex, 18*, 1900–1908.

Berlucchi, G., & Aglioti, S. (1997). The body in the brain: Neural bases of corporeal awareness. *Trends in Neurosciences, 20*, 560–564.

Berman, M., Gladue, B., & Taylor, S. (1993). The effects of hormones, Type A behavior pattern, and provocation on aggression in men. *Motivation and Emotion, 17*, 125–138.

Bernhardt, P. C., Dabbs, J. M., Jr., Fielden, J. A., & Lutter, C. D. (1998). Testosterone changes during vicarious experiences of winning and losing among fans at sporting events. *Physiological Behavior, 65*, 59–62.

Bernstein, D. M., Laney, C., Morris, E. K., & Loftus, E. F. (2005). False beliefs about fattening foods can have healthy consequences. *Proceedings of the National Academy of Sciences, 102*, 13724–13731.

Bernstein, I. L. (1978). Learned taste aversions in children receiving chemotherapy. *Science, 200*, 1302–1303.

Bernstein, L. J., & Robertson, L. C. (1998). Illusory conjunctions of color and motion with shape following bilateral parietal lesions. *Psychological Science, 9*, 167–175.

Berson, D. M., Dunn, F. A., & Takao, M. (2002). Phototransduction by retinal ganglion cells that set the circadian clock. *Science, 295*, 1070–1073.

Berthoud, H.-R., & Morrison, C. (2008). The brain, appetite, and obesity. *Annual Review of Psychology, 59*, 55–92.

Bervoets, L., Van Hoorenbeeck, K., Kortleven, I., Van Noten, C., Hens, N., Vael, C., et al. (2013). Differences in gut microbiota composition between obese and lean children: A cross-sectional study. *Gut Pathogens, 5*, 10.

Besnard, P., Passilly-Degrace, P., & Khan, N. A. (2016). Taste of fat: A sixth taste modality? *Physiology Review, 96*, 151–176.

Bessa, J. M., Ferreira, D., Melo, I., Marques, F., Cerqueira, J. J., Palha, J. A., et al. (2009). The mood-improving actions of antidepressant do not depend on neurogenesis but are associated with neuronal remodeling. *Molecular Psychiatry, 14*, 764–773.

Beveridge, T. J. R., Gill, K. E., Hanlon, C. A., & Porrino, L. J. (2008). Parallel studies of cocaine-related neural and cognitive impairment in humans and monkeys. *Philosophical Transactions of the Royal Society B, 363*, 3257–3266.

Bhola, R., Kinsella, E., Giffin, N., Lipscombe, S., Ahmed, F., Weatherall, M., & Goadsby, P. J. (2015). Single-pulse transcranial magnetic stimulation (sTMS) for the acute treatment of migraine: Evaluation of outcome data for the UK post market pilot program. *Journal of Headache and Pain.* doi:10.1186/s10194-015-0535-3

Bi, A., Cui, J., Ma, Y. P., Olshevskaya, E., Pu, M., Dizhoor, A. M., & Pan, Z. H. (2006). Ectopic expression of a microbial-type rhodopsin restores visual responses in mice with photoreceptor degeneration. *Neuron, 50*, 23–33.

Biederman, J. (2004). Impact of comorbidity in adults with attention-deficit/hyperactivity disorder. *Journal of Clinical Psychiatry, 65*, 3–7.

Biederman, J., & Faraone, S. V. (2005). Attention-deficit hyperactivity disorder. *Lancet, 366*, 237–248.

Bienvenu, O. J., Samuels, J. F., Wuyek, L. A., Liang, K. Y., Wang, Y., Grados, M. A., et al. (2012). Is obsessive-compulsive disorder an anxiety disorder, and what, if any, are spectrum conditions? A family study perspective. *Psychological Medicine, 42*, 1–13.

Bienvenu, O. J., Wang, Y., Shugart, Y. Y., Welch, J. M., Grados, M. A., Fyer, A. J., et al. (2008). *Sapap3* and pathological grooming in humans: Results from the OCD collaborative genetics study. *American Journal of Medical Genetics Part B, 150B*, 710–720.

Billington, C. J., & Levine, A. S. (1992). Hypothalamic neuropeptide Y regulation of feeding and energy metabolism. *Current Opinion in Neurobiology, 2*, 847–851.

Binder, E. B., Bradley, R. G., Liu, W., Epstein, M. P., Deveau, T. C., Mercer, K. B., et al. (2008). Association of *FKBP5* polymorphisms and childhood abuse with risk of posttraumatic stress disorder symptoms in adults. *Journal of the American Medical Association, 299*, 1291–1305.

Binet, S., & Simon, T. (1905). Méthodes nouvelles pour le diagnostic du niveau intellectuel des anormaux [New methods for the diagnosis of the intellectual level of subnormals]. *L'Année Psychologique, 12*, 191–244.

Birbaumer, N., Lutzenberger, W., Montoya, P., Larbig, W., Unerti, K., Töpfner, S., et al. (1997). Effects of regional anesthesia on phantom limb pain are mirrored in changes in cortical reorganization. *Journal of Neuroscience, 17*, 5503–5508.

Birney, R. C., & Teevan, R. C. (1961). *Instinct: An enduring problem in psychology.* Princeton, NJ: Van Nostrand.

Bittar, R. G., Kar-Purkayastha, I., Owen, S. L., Bear, R. E., Green, A., Wang, S. Y., et al. (2005). Deep brain stimulation for pain relief: A meta-analysis. *Journal of Clinical Neuroscience, 12*, 515–519.

Bitterman, Y., Mukamel, R., Malach, R., Fried, I., & Nelken, I. (2008). Ultra-fine frequency tuning revealed in single neurons of human auditory cortex. *Nature, 451*, 197–202.

Black, M. H., Sacks, D. A., Xiang, A. H., & Lawrence, J. M. (2013). The relative contribution of prepregnancy overweight and obesity, gestational weight gain, and IADPSG-defined gestational diabetes mellitus to fetal overgrowth. *Diabetes Care, 36*, 56–62.

Black, N., & Robertson, M. (2010). Midnight snack? Not quite. *ABC News/Health,* August 19. Retrieved from http://abcnews.com/Health/MedicalMysteries/story?id=5483978

Blaese, R. M., Culver, K. W., Miller, A. D., Carter, C. S., Fleisher, T., Clerici, M., et al. (1995). T lymphocyte-directed gene therapy for ADA–SCID: Initial trial results after 4 years. *Science, 270*, 475–480.

Blahak, C., Bazner, H., Capelle, H.-H., Wohrle, J., Weigel, R., Hennerici, M. G., et al. (2009). Rapid response of parkinsonian tremor to STN-DBS changes: Direct modulation of oscillatory basal ganglia activity? *Movement Disorders, 24*(8), 1221–1225.

Blake, M. (2014). Budget busting U.S. obesity costs climb past $300 billion a year. *Fiscal Times.* Retrieved from http://www.thefiscaltimes.com/Articles/2014/06/19/Budget-Busting-US-Obesity-Costs-Climb-Past-300-Billion-Year

Blanchard, D. C., & Blanchard, R. J. (1972). Innate and conditioned reactions to threat in rats with amygdaloid lesions. *Journal of Comparative and Physiological Psychology, 81*, 281–290.

Blanke, O., & Arzy, S. (2005). The out-of-body experience: Disturbed self-processing at the temporo-parietal junction. *Neuroscientist, 11*, 16–24.

Blehar, M. C., & Rosenthal, N. E. (1989). Seasonal affective disorders and phototherapy. *Archives of General Psychiatry, 46*, 469–474.

Bleuler, E. (1911). Dementia præcox, oder die Gruppe der Schizophrenien [Premature dementia, or the group of schizophrenias]. In G. Aschaffenburg (Ed.), *Handbuch der Psychiatrie.* Leipzig, Germany: Hälfte.

Blinder, B. J., Cumella, E. J., & Santhara, V. A. (2006). Psychiatric comorbidities of female inpatients with eating disorders. *Psychosomatic Medicine, 68*, 454–462.

Bliss, E. L. (1980). Multiple personalities: A report of 14 cases with implications for schizophrenia and hysteria. *Archives of General Psychiatry, 37*, 1388–1397.

Bloch, G. J., Butler, P. C., & Kohlert, J. G. (1996). Galanin microinjected into the medial preoptic nucleus facilitates female- and male-typical sexual behaviors in the female rat. *Physiology and Behavior, 59*, 1147–1154.

Bloch, G. J., Butler, P. C., Kohlert, J. G., & Bloch, D. A. (1993). Microinjection of galanin into the medial preoptic nucleus facilitates copulatory behavior in the male rat. *Physiology and Behavior, 54*, 615–624.

Blonder, L. X., Bowers, D., & Heilman, K. M. (1991). The role of the right hemisphere in emotional communication. *Brain, 114*, 1115–1127.

Bloom, F. E., & Lazerson, A. (1988). *Brain, mind and behavior* (2nd ed.). New York: W. H. Freeman.

Bloom, J. S., Garcia-Barrera, M. A., Miller, C. J., Miller, S. R., & Hynd, G. W. (2013). Planum temporale morphology in children with developmental dyslexia. *Neuropsychologia, 51*, 1684–1692.

Blum, D. (1994). *The monkey wars.* New York: Oxford.

Blum, K., Madigan, M. A., Fried, L., Braverman, E. R., Giordano, J., & Badgaiyan, R. (2017). Coupling genetic addiction risk score (GARS) and pro dopamine regulation (KB220) to combat substance use disorder. *Addiction & Rehabilitation Medicine, 11* (2). doi: 10.19080/GJARM.2017.01.555556

Bock, K. (2010). The efficacy of baclofen in reducing alcohol consumption and decreasing alcohol craving in alcohol dependent adults. *School of Physician Assistant Studies,* Paper 216. Retrieved from http://commons.pacificu.edu/pa//216

Bocklandt, S., Horvath, S., Vilain, E., & Hamer, D. H. (2006). Extreme skewing of X chromosome inactivation in mothers of homosexual men. *Human Genetics, 118,* 691–694.

Boecker, H., Dagher, A., Ceballos-Baumann, A. O., Passingham, R. E., Samuel, M., Friston, K. J., et al. (1998). Role of the human rostral supplementary motor area and the basal ganglia in motor sequence control: Investigations with H2 150 PET. *Journal of Neurophysiology, 79,* 1070–1080.

Boeve, B. F., Silber, M. H., Parisi, J. E., Dickson, D. W., Ferman, T. J., Benarroch, E. E., et al. (2003). Synucleinopathy pathology and REM sleep behavior disorder plus dementia or parkinsonism. *Neurology, 61,* 40–45.

Bogaert, A. F. (2004). Asexuality: Prevalence and associated factors in a national probability sample. *Journal of Sex Research, 41,* 279–287.

Bogardus, C., Lillioja, S., Ravussin, E., Abbott, W., Zawadzki, J. K., Young, A., et al. (1986). Familial dependence of the resting metabolic rate. *New England Journal of Medicine, 315,* 96–100.

Bohman, M. (1978). Some genetic aspects of alcoholism and criminality: A population of adoptees. *Archives of General Psychiatry, 35,* 269–276.

Boivin, D. B., Duffy, J. F., Kronauer, R. E., & Czeisler, C. A. (1996). Dose-response relationships for resetting of human circadian clock by light. *Nature, 379,* 540–542.

Bolles, R. C. (1975). *Theory of motivation.* New York: Harper & Row.

Bonda, E., Petrides, M., Frey, S., & Evans, A. (1995). Neural correlates of mental transformations of the body-in-space. *Proceedings of the National Academy of Sciences, 92,* 11180–11184.

Bonebakker, A. E., Bonke, B., Klein, J., Wolters, G., Stijnene, T., Passchier, J., et al. (1996). Information processing during general anesthesia: Evidence for unconscious memory. *Memory and Cognition, 24,* 766–776.

Bonnet, J., Yin, P., Ortiz, M. E., Subsoontorn, P., & Endy, D. (2013). Amplifying genetic logic gates. *Science, 340,* 599–603.

Bonnet, M. H., & Arand, D. L. (1996). Metabolic rate and the restorative function of sleep. *Physiology and Behavior, 59,* 777–782.

Bontempi, B., Laurent-Demir, C., Destrade, C., & Jaffard, R. (1999). Time-dependent reorganization of brain circuitry underlying long-term memory storage. *Nature, 400,* 671–675.

Bor, D. (2013). This is your brain on consciousness. *New Scientist, 218,* 32–34.

Bor, D., & Seth, A. K. (2012). Consciousness and the prefrontal parietal network: Insights from attention, working memory, and chunking. *Frontiers in Psychology, 3,* Article 63. Retrieved from http://journal.frontiersin.org/Journal/10.3389/fpsyg.2012.00063/abstract

Born, R. T., & Bradley, D. C. (2005). Structure and function of visual area MT. *Annual Review of Neuroscience, 28,* 157–189.

Borsook, D., Becerra, L., Fishman, S., Edwards, A., Jennings, C. L., Stojanovic, M., et al. (1998). Acute plasticity in the human somatosensory cortex following amputation. *Neuroreport, 9,* 1013–1017.

Bortsov, A. V., Platts-Mills, T. F., Peak, D. A., Jones, J. S., Swor, R. A., Domeier, R. M., et al. (2013). Pain distribution and predictors of widespread pain in the immediate aftermath of motor vehicle collision. *European Journal of Pain, 17*(8), 1243–1251.

Bortsov, A. V., Smith, J. E., Diatchenko, L., Soward, A. C., Ulirsch, J. C., Rossi, C., et al. (2013). Polymorphisms in the clucocorticoid receptor co-chaperone FKBP5 predict persistent musculoskeletal pain after traumatic stress exposure. *Pain, 154,* 1419–1426.

Bottini, G., Corcoran, R., Sterzi, R., Paulesu, E., Schenone, P., Scarpa, P., et al. (1994). The role of the right hemisphere in the interpretation of figurative aspects of language: A positron emission tomography activation study. *Brain, 117,* 1241–1253.

Botvinick, M. (2004). Probing the neural basis of body ownership. *Science, 305,* 782–783.

Bouchard, C. (1989). Genetic factors in obesity. *Medical Clinics of North America, 73,* 67–81.

Bouchard, C., Tremblay, A., Després, J.-P., Nadeau, A., Lupien, P. J., Thériault, G., et al. (1990). The response to long-term overfeeding in identical twins. *New England Journal of Medicine, 322,* 1477–1482.

Bouchard, M. F., Bellinger, D. C., Wright, R. O., & Weisskopf, M. G. (2010). Attention-deficit/hyperactivity disorder and urinary metabolites of organophosphate pesticides. *Pediatrics, 125,* e1270–e1277.

Bouchard, M. F., Chevrier, J., Harley, K. G., Kogut, K., Vedar, M., Calderon, N., et al. (2011). Prenatal exposure to organophosphate pesticides and IQ in 7-year-old children. *Environmental Health Perspectives, 119,* 1189–1195.

Bouchard, T. J. (1994). Genes, environment, and personality. *Science, 264,* 1700–1701.

Bouchard, T. J., Jr., & McGue, M. (1981). Familial studies of intelligence: A review. *Science, 212,* 1055–1059.

Bouchard, T. J., & Segal, N. L. (1985). Environment and IQ. In B. B. Wolman (Ed.), *Handbook of intelligence: Theories, measurements, and applications* (pp. 391–464). New York: Wiley.

Boulenguez, P., & Vinay, L. (2009). Strategies to restore motor functions after spinal cord injury. *Current Opinion in Neurobiology, 19,* 587–600.

Bourgeois, J.-P., & Rakic, P. (1993). Changes of synaptic density in the primary visual cortex of the macaque monkey from fetal to adult stage. *Journal of Neuroscience, 13,* 2801–2820.

Bouvier, S. E., & Engel, S. A. (2006). Behavioral deficits and cortical damage loci in cerebral achromatopsia. *Cerebral Cortex, 16,* 183–191.

Bowmaker, J. K., & Dartnall, H. J. A. (1980). Visual pigments of rods and cones in a human retina. *Journal of Physiology (London), 298,* 501–511.

Bozarth, M. A., & Wise, R. A. (1984). Anatomically distinct opiate receptor fields mediate reward and physical dependence. *Science, 224,* 516–517.

Bozarth, M. A., & Wise, R. A. (1985). Toxicity associated with long-term intravenous heroin and cocaine self-administration in the rat. *Journal of the American Medical Association, 254,* 81–83.

Braak, H., & Braak, E. (1991). Neuropathological stageing of Alzheimer-related changes. *Acta Neuropathology, 82,* 239–259.

Braak, H., Del Tredici, K., Rüb, U., de Vos, R. A. I., Steur, E. N. H. J., & Braak, E. (2003). Staging of brain pathology related to sporadic Parkinson's disease. *Neurobiology, 24,* 197–211.

Bracha, H. S., Torrey, E. F., Gottesman, I. I., Bigelow, L. B., & Cunniff, C. (1992). Second-trimester markers of fetal size in schizophrenia: A study of monozygotic twins. *American Journal of Psychiatry, 149,* 1355–1361.

Bradbury, J. (2003). Why do men and women feel and react to pain differently? *Lancet, 361,* 2052–2053.

Bradbury, T. N., & Miller, G. A. (1985). Season of birth in schizophrenia: A review of evidence, methodology, and etiology. *Psychological Bulletin, 98,* 569–594.

Branch, J. (2015, July 27). Dutee Chand, female sprinter with high testosterone level, wins right to compete. *New York Times.* Retrieved from https://www.nytimes.com/2015/07/28/sports/international/dutee-chand-female-sprinter-with-high-male-hormone-level-wins-right-to-compete.html?_r=0

Brang, D., & Ramachandran, V. S. (2011). Survival of the synesthesia gene: Why do people hear colors and taste words? *PLoS Biology, 9,* e1001205. Retrieved from http://www.plosbiology.org/article/info:doi/10.1371/journal.pbio.1001205

Brannon, E. M., & Terrace, H. S. (1998). Ordering of the numerosities 1 to 9 by monkeys. *Science, 282,* 746–749.

Braun, B. G. (1985). *Treatment of multiple personality disorder.* Washington, DC: American Psychiatric Press.

Braun, M., Wendt, A., Karanauskaite, J., Galvanovskis, J., Clark, A., MacDonald, P. E., & Rorsman, P. (2007). Corelease and differential exit via the fusion pore of GABA, serotonin, and ATP from LDCV in rat pancreatic β cells. *Journal of General Physiology, 129,* 221–231.

Braunschweig, D., Krakowiak, P., Duncanson, P., Boyce, R., Hansen, R. L., Ashwood, P., et al. (2013). Autism-specific maternal autoantibodies recognize critical proteins in developing brain. *Translational Psychiatry, 3,* e277. Retrieved from http://www.nature.com/tp/journal/v3/n7/full/tp201350a.html

Bray, G. A. (1992). Drug treatment of obesity. *American Journal of Clinical Nutrition, 55,* 538S–544S.

Breasted, J. H. (1930). *The Edwin Smith surgical papyrus.* Chicago: University of Chicago Press.

Brecher, E. M. (1972). *Licit and illicit drugs.* Boston: Little, Brown.

Breen, G., Webb, B. T., Butler, A. W., van den Oord, E. J. C. G., Tozzi, F., Craddock, N., et al. (2011). A genome-wide significant linkage for severe depression on chromosome 3: The depression network study. *American Journal of Psychiatry, 168,* 840–847.

Breitner, J. C., Folstein, M. E., & Murphy, E. A. (1986). Familial aggregation in Alzheimer dementia-1: A model for the age-dependent expression of an autosomal dominant gene. *Journal of Psychiatric Research, 20,* 31–43.

Bremer, J. (1959). *Asexualization: A follow-up study of 244 cases.* New York: Macmillan.

Bremner, J. D., Randall, P., Scott, T. M., Bronen, R. A., Seibyl, J. P., Southwick, S. M., et al. (1995). MRI-based measurement of hippocampal volume in patients with combat related posttraumatic stress disorder. *American Journal of Psychiatry, 152,* 973–981.

Bremner, J. D., Randall, P., Vermetten, E., Staib, L., Bronen, R. A., Mazure, C., et al. (1997). Magnetic resonance imaging-based measurement of hippocampal volume in posttraumatic stress disorder related to childhood physical and sexual abuse: A preliminary report. *Biological Psychiatry, 41,* 23–32.

Brenner, L. A., Ignacio, R. V., & Blow, F. C. (2011). Suicide and traumatic brain injury among individuals seeking Veterans Health Administration services. *Journal of Head Trauma and Rehabilitation, 26*(4), 257–264. doi:10.1097/HTR.0b013e31821fdb6e

Brent, D. A., & Melhem, N. (2008). Familial transmission of suicidal behavior. *Psychiaritc Clinics of North America, 31,* 157–177.

Breslow, J. M. (2015a). New: 87 deceased NFL players test positive for brain disease. *Frontline.* Retrieved from http://www.pbs.org/wgbh/frontline/article/new-87-deceased-nfl-players-test-positive-for-brain-disease/

Breslow, J. M. (2015b). NFL concussion settlement wins final approval from judge. *Frontline.* Retrieved from http://www.pbs.org/wgbh/frontline/article/nfl-concussion-settlement-wins-final-approval-from-judge/

Brewer, J. B., Zhao, Z., Desmond, J. E., Glover, G. H., & Gabrieli, J. D. E. (1998). Making memories: Brain activity that predicts how well visual experience will be remembered. *Science, 281,* 1185–1187.

Brickman, A. M., Khan, U. A., Provenzano, F. A., Yeung, L.-K., Suzuki, W., Schroeter, H., et al. (2014). Enhancing dentate gyrus function with dietary flavanols improves cognition in older adults. *Nature Neuroscience, 17,* 1798–1803.

Brikell, I., Kuja-Halkola, R., & Larsson, H. (2015). Heritability of attention-deficit hyperactivity disorder in adults. *American Journal of Medical Genetics, B, 168B,* 406–413.

Brimberg, L., Sadiq, A., Gregersen, P. K., & Diamond, B. (2013). Brain-reactive IgG correlates with autoimmunity in mothers of a child with an autism spectrum disorder. *Molecular Psychiatry, 18,* 1171–1177.

Brinkman, C. (1984). Supplementary motor area of the monkey's cerebral cortex: Short- and long-term deficits after unilateral ablation and the effects of subsequent callosal section. *Journal of Neuroscience, 4,* 918–929.

Britten, K. H. (2008). Mechanisms of self-motion perception. *Annual Review of Neuroscience, 31,* 389–410.

Britten, R. J. (2002). Divergence between samples of chimpanzee and human DNA sequences is 5%, counting indels. *Proceedings of the National Academy of Sciences, 99,* 13633–13635.

Broberg, D. J., & Bernstein, I. L. (1989). Cephalic insulin release in anorexic women. *Physiology and Behavior, 45,* 871–874.

Broberger, C., & Hökfelt, T. (2001). Hypothalamic and vagal neuropeptide circuitries regulating food intake. *Physiology and Behavior, 74,* 669–682.

Broca, P. (1861). Remarques sur le siège de la faculté du langage articulé, suivies d'une observation d'aphemie (perte de la parole). *Bulletin de la Société Anatomique (Paris), 36,* 330–357.

Broughton, R. (1975). Biorhythmic variations in consciousness and psychological functions. *Canadian Psychological Review, 16,* 217–239.

Broughton, R., Billings, R., Cartwright, R., Doucette, D., Edmeads, J., Edward, H. M., et al. (1994). Homicidal somnambulism: A case report. *Sleep, 17,* 253–264.

Brown, A. S., Begg, M. D., Gravenstein, S., Schaefer, C. A., Wyatt, R. J., Bresnahan, M., et al. (2004). Serologic evidence of prenatal influenza in the etiology of schizophrenia. *Archives of General Psychiatry, 61,* 774–780.

Brown, K., & Wald, G. (1964). Visual pigments in single rods and cones of the human retina. *Science, 143,* 45–52.

Brown, M. T., Murphy, F. T., Radin, D. M., Davignon, I., Smith, M. D., & West, C. R. (2013). Tanezumab reduces osteoarthritic hip pain. *Arthritis & Rheumatism, 65*(7), 1795–1803.

Brown, T. H., Chapman, P. F., Kairiss, E. W., & Keenan, C. L. (1988). Long-term synaptic potentiation. *Science, 242,* 724–727.

Broyd, S. J., Demanuele, C., Debener, S., Helps, S. K., James, C. J., & Sonuga-Barke, E. J. S. (2009). Default-mode brain dysfunction in mental disorders: A systematic review. *Neuroscience and Biobehavioral Reviews, 33,* 279–296.

Bruck, D. N. (2013). Decades-long social memory in bottlenose dolphins. *Proceedings of the Royal Society B, 280.* doi: 10.1098/rspb.2013.1726

Bucci, M. P., Bremond-Gignac, D., & Kapoula, Z. (2008). Latency of saccades and vergence eye movements in dyslexic children. *Experimental Brain Research, 188*(1), 1–12. doi:10.1007/s00221-008-1345-5

Buchanan, T. W., Lutz, K., Mirzazade, S., Specht, K., Shah, N. J., Zilles, K., et al. (2000). Recognition of emotional prosody and verbal components of spoken language: An fMRI study. *Cognitive Brain Research, 9,* 227–238.

Buchwald, H., Avidor, Y., Braunwald, E., Jensen, M. D., Pories, W., Fahrbach, K., et al. (2004). Bariatric surgery: A systematic review and meta-analysis. *Journal of the American Medical Association, 292,* 1724–1737.

Buchwald, H., Estok, R., Fahrbach, K., et al. (2009). Weight and type 2 diabetes after bariatric surgery: Systematic review and meta-analysis. *American Journal of Medicine, 122,* 248–256.

Buckley, N. A., Dawson, A. H., & Isbister, G. K. (2014). Serotonin syndrome. *British Medical Journal, 348,* 33–35.

Buckner, R. L., & Koutstaal, W. (1998). Functional neuroimaging studies of encoding, priming, and explicit memory retrieval. *Proceedings of the National Academy of Sciences, 95,* 891–898.

Buell, S. J., & Coleman, P. D. (1979). Dendritic growth in the aged human brain and failure of growth in senile dementia. *Science, 206,* 854–856.

Bufalino, C., Hepgul, N., Aguglia, E., & Pariante, C. M. (2013). The role of immune genes in the association between depression and inflammation: A review of recent clinical studies. *Brain, Behavior, and Immunity, 31,* 31–47.

Bufkin, J. L., & Luttrell, V. R. (2005). Neuroimaging studies of aggressive and violent behavior. *Trauma, Violence, and Abuse, 6,* 176–191.

Bulik, C. M., Devlin, B., Bacanu, S.-A., Thornton, L., Klump, K. L., Fichter, M. M., et al. (2003). Significant linkage on chromosome 10p in families with bulimia nervosa. *American Journal of Human Genetics, 72,* 200–207.

Bulik, C. M., Sullivan, P. F., Tozzi, F., Furberg, H., Lichtenstein, P., & Pedersen, N. L. (2006). Prevalence, heritability and prospective risk factors for anorexia nervosa. *Archives of General Psychiatry, 63,* 305–312.

Bulik, C. M., Sullivan, P. F., Wade, T. D., & Kendler, K. S. (2000). Twin studies of eating disorders: A review. *International Journal of Eating Disorders, 27,* 1–20.

Bunney, B. G., Li, J. Z., Walsh, D. M., Stein, R., Vawter, M. P., Cartagena, P., et al. (2014). Circadian dysregulation of clock genes: Clues to rapid treatments in major depressive disorder. *Molecular Psychiatry, 20,* 48–55.

Bunney, W. E., Jr., Murphy, D. L., Goodwin, F. K., & Borge, G. F. (1972). The "switch process" in manic-depressive illness: I. A systematic study of sequential behavioral changes. *Archives of General Psychiatry, 27,* 295–302.

Buñuel, L. (1983). *My last sigh.* New York: Knopf.

Bureau of the Census. (2001). *Population.* Retrieved from www.census.gov/prod/2001pubs/statab/sec01.pdf

Burgess, A., Dubey, S., Yeung, S., Hough, O., Eterman, N., Aubert, I., & Hynynen, K. (2014). Alzheimer disease in a mouse model: MR imaging-guided focused ultrasound targeted to the hippocampus opens the blood-brain barrier and improves pathologic abnormalities and behavior. *Radiology, 273,* 736–745.

Burke, S. N., & Barnes, C. A. (2006). Neural plasticity in the ageing brain. *Nature Reviews Neuroscience, 7,* 30–40.

Burkett, J. P., Andari, E., Johnson, Z. V., Curry, D. C., de Waal, F. B. M., & Young, L. J. (2016). Oxytocin-dependent consolation behavior in rodents. *Science, 351,* 375–378.

Buschman, T. J., & Miller, E. K. (2007). Top-down versus bottom-up control of attention in the prefrontal and posterior parietal cortices. *Science, 315,* 1860–1862.

Bushdid, C., Magnasco, M. O., Vosshall, L. B., & Keller, A. (2014). Humans can discriminate more than 1 trillion olfactory stimuli. *Science, 343,* 1370–1372.

Bushnell, I. W. (2001). Mother's face recognition in newborn infants: Learning and memory. *Infant and Child Development, 10,* 67–74.

Butterworth, B. (1999). A head for figures. *Science, 284,* 928–929.

Buxhoeveden, D. P., & Casanova, M. F. (2002). The minicolumn hypothesis in neuroscience. *Brain, 125,* 935–951.

Cabeza, R., Anderson, N. D., Locantore, J. K., & McIntosh, A. R. (2002). Aging gracefully: Compensatory brain activity in high-performing older adults. *NeuroImage, 17,* 1394–1402.

Caffeine prevents post-op headaches. (1996). *United Press International, MSNBC.* Retrieved from www.msnbc.com/news/36911.asp

Caggiula, A. R. (1970). Analysis of the copulation-reward properties of posterior hypothalamic stimulation in male rats. *Journal of Comparative and Physiological Psychology, 70,* 399–412.

Cahill, L., Haier, R. J., Fallon, J., Alkire, M. T., Tang, C., Keator, D., et al. (1996). Amygdala activity at encoding correlated with long-term, free recall of emotional information. *Proceedings of the National Academy of Sciences, 93,* 8016–8021.

Cajochen, C., Altanay-Ekici, S., Münch, M., Frey, S., Knoblauch, V., & Wirz-Justice, A. (2013). Evidence that the lunar cycle influences human sleep. *Current Biology, 23,* 1485–1488.

Caldwell, E. (2015, August 18). Scientist: Most complete human brain model to date is a "brain changer." Retrieved from https://news.osu.edu/news/2015/08/18/human-brain-model/

Callaway, E. (2012). Alzheimer's drugs take a new tack. *Nature News.* Retrieved from http://www.nature.com/news/alzheimer-s-drugs-take-a-new-tack-1.11343

Calles-Escandón, J., & Horton, E. S. (1992). The thermogenic role of exercise in the treatment of morbid obesity: A critical evaluation. *American Journal of Clinical Nutrition, 55,* 533S–537S.

Campbell, S. S., & Tobler, I. (1984). Animal sleep: A review of sleep duration across phylogeny. *Neuroscience and Biobehavioral Reviews, 8,* 269–300.

Camperio Ciani, A., Cermelli, P., & Zanzotto, G. (2008). Sexually antagonistic selection in human male homosexuality. *PLoS ONE, 3,* e2282. Retrieved from www.plosone.org/article/info%3Adoi%2F10.1371%2Fjournal.pone.0002282

Camperio Ciani, A., Corna, F., & Capiluppi, C. (2004). Evidence for maternally inherited factors favouring male homosexuality and promoting female fecundity. *Proceedings of the Royal Society of London B, 271,* 2217–2221.

Campfield, L. A., Smith, F. J., & Burn, P. (1998). Strategies and potential molecular targets for obesity treatment. *Science, 280,* 1383–1387.

Canavan, A. G. M., Sprengelmeyer, R., Diener, H.-C., & Hömberg, V. (1994). Conditional associative learning is impaired in cerebellar disease in humans. *Behavioral Neuroscience, 108,* 475–485.

Canli, T., Qiu, M., Omura, K., Congdon, E., Haas, B. W., Amin, Z., et al. (2006). Neural correlates of epigenesis. *Proceedings of the National Academy of Sciences, 103,* 16033–16038.

Cannon, M., Jones, P. B., & Murray, R. M. (2002). Obstetric complications and schizophrenia: Historical and meta-analytic review. *American Journal of Psychiatry, 159,* 1080–1092.

Cannon, W. B. (1942). "Voodoo" death. *American Anthropologist, 44,* 169–181.

Cantalupo, C., Oliver, J., Smith, J., Nir, T., Taglialatela, J. P., & Hopkins, W. D. (2009). The chimpanzee brain shows human-like perisylvian asymmetries in white matter. *European Journal of Neuroscience, 30,* 431–438.

Cao, Y. Q., Mantyh, P. W., Carlson, E. J., Gillespie, A. M., Epstein, C. J., & Basbaum, A. I. (1998). Primary afferent tachykinins are required to experience moderate-to-intense pain. *Nature, 392,* 390–394.

Caporale, N., Kolstad, K. D., Lee, T., Tochitsky, I., Dalkara, D., Trauner, D., et al. (2011). LiGluR restores visual responses in rodent models of inherited blindness. *Molecular Therapies, 19,* 1212–1219.

Caramazza, A., & Mahon, B. Z. (2006). The organisation of conceptual knowledge in the brain: The future's past and some future directions. *Cognitive Neuropsychology, 23,* 13–38.

Carelli, R. M. (2002). Nucleus accumbens cell firing during goal-directed behaviors for cocaine vs. "natural" reinforcement. *Physiology and Behavior, 76,* 379–387.

Carhart-Harris, R. L., Muthukumaraswamy, S., Roseman, L., Kaelen, M., Droog, W., Murphy, K., et al. (2016). Neural correlates of the LSD experience revealed by multimodal neuroimaging. *Proceedings of the National Academy of Sciences, 113*(17), 4853–4858. doi:www.pnas.org/cgi/doi/10.1073/pnas.1518377113

Cariani, P. A. (2004). Temporal codes and computations for sensory representation and scene analysis. *IEEE Transactions on Neural Networks, 15,* 1100–1111.

Carlezon, W. A., & Wise, R. A. (1996). Rewarding actions of phencyclidine and related drugs in nucleus accumbens shell and frontal cortex. *Journal of Neuroscience, 16,* 3112–3122.

Carlson, M. (1981). Characteristics of sensory deficits following lesions of Brodmann's areas 1 and 2 in the postcentral gyrus of Macaca mulatta. *Brain Research, 204,* 424–430.

Carlsson, H.-E., Hagelin, J., & Hau, J. (2004). Implementation of the Three Rs in biomedical research. *Veterinary Record, 154,* 467–470.

Carmichael, M. S., Warburton, V. L., Dixen, J., & Davidson, J. D. (1994). Relationships among cardiovascular, muscular, and oxytocin responses during human sexual activity. *Archives of Sexual Behavior, 23,* 59–79.

Carr, C. E., & Konishi, M. (1990). A circuit for detection of interaural time differences in the brain stem of the barn owl. *Journal of Neuroscience, 10,* 3227–3246.

Carr, K. W., White-Schwoch, T., Tierney, A. T., Strait, D. L., & Kraus, N. (2014). Beat synchronization predicts neural speech encoding and reading readiness in preschoolers. *Proceedings of the National Academy of Sciences, 111*(40), 14559–14564.

Carraher, T. N., Carraher, D. W., & Schliemann, A. D. (1985). Mathematics in the streets and in schools. *British Journal of Developmental Psychology, 3,* 21–29.

Carreiras, M., Lopez, J., Rivero, F., & Corina, D. (2005). Neural processing of a whistled language. *Nature, 433,* 31–32.

Carrera, M. R., Ashley, J. A., Parsons, L. H., Wirsching, P., Koob, G. F., & Janda, K. D. (1995). Suppresssion of psychoactive effects of cocaine by active immunization. *Nature, 378,* 727–730.

Carroll, J. B. (1993). *Human cognitive abilities: A survey of factor-analytic studies.* Cambridge, UK: University of Cambridge Press.

Cascio, C. J., Foss-Feig, J. H., Burnette, C. P., Heacock, J. L., & Cosby, A. A. (2012). The rubber hand illusion in children with autism spectrum disorders: Delayed influence of combined tactile and visual input on proprioception. *Autism, 16,* 406–419.

Caspi, A., McClay, J., Moffitt, T. E., Mill, J., Martin, J., Craig, I. W., et al. (2002). Role of genotype in the cycle of violence in maltreated children. *Science, 297,* 851–854.

Caspi, A., Sugden, K., Moffitt, T. E., Taylor, A., Craig, I. W., Harrington, H., et al. (2003). Influence of life stress on depression: Moderation by a polymorphism in the 5-HTT gene. *Science, 301,* 386–389.

Cassin, S., & von Ranson, K. (2005). Personality and eating disorders: A decade in review. *Clinical Psychology Review, 25,* 895–916.

Castellanos, F. X., & Tannock, R. (2002). Neuroscience of attention-deficit/hyperactivity disorder: The search for endophenotypes. *Nature Reviews Neuroscience, 3,* 617–628.

Castelli, F., Frith, C., Happé, F., & Frith, U. (2002). Autism, Asperger syndrome and brain mechanisms for the attribution of mental states to animated shapes. *Brain, 125,* 1839–1849.

Caster Semenya must wait for IAAF decision before competing. (2010, January 14). Retrieved from www.guardian.co.uk/sport/2010/jan/14/caster-semenya-iaaf-athletics-south-africa

Castro-Fornieles, J., Bargalió, N., Lázaro, L., Andrés, S., Falcon, C., Plana, M. T., & Junqué, C. (2009). A cross-sectional and follow-up voxel-based morphometric MRI study in adolescent anorexia nervosa. *Journal of Psychiatric Research, 43,* 331–340.

Cattaneo, A. (2010). Tanezumab, a recombinant humanized mAb against nerve growth factor for the treatment of acute and chronic pain. *Current Opinion in Molecular Therapeutics, 12,* 94–105.

Catterall, W. A. (1984). The molecular basis of neuronal excitability. *Science, 223,* 653–661.

Catterall, W. A. (2010). Ion channel voltage sensors: Structure, function, and pathophysiology. *Neuron, 67,* 915–928.

Caye, A., Rocha, T. B.-M., Anselmi, L., Murray, J., Menezes, A. M. B., Barros, F. D., et al. (2016). Attention-deficit/hyperactivity disorder trajectories from childhood to young adulthood: Evidence from a birth cohort supporting a late-onset syndrome. *JAMA Psychiatry, 73,* 705–712.

Ceci, S. J., & Liker, J. (1986). A day at the races: A study of IQ, expertise, and cognitive complexity. *Journal of Experimental Psychology: General, 115,* 255–266.

Cell Press. (2017, April 27). When students pay attention in class, their brains are in sync. *ScienceDaily.* Retrieved from www.sciencedaily.com/releases/2017/04/170427120908.htm

Centers for Disease Control and Prevention. (2015a). Leading causes of death. Retrieved from http://www.cdc.gov/nchs/fastats/leading-causes-of-death.htm

Centers for Disease Control and Prevention. (2015b). Smoking & tobacco use. Retrieved from http://www.cdc.gov/tobacco/data_statistics/fact_sheets/fast_facts/

Centers for Disease Control and Prevention. (2016a). Autism spectrum disorder (ASD). Retrieved from https://www.cdc.gov/ncbddd/autism/index.html

Centers for Disease Control and Prevention. (2016b). Measles cases and outbreaks. Retrieved from http://www.cdc.gov/measles/cases-outbreaks.html

Chai, G., Governale, L., McMahon, A. W., Trinidad, J. P., Staffa, J., & Murphy, D. (2012). Trends of outpatient prescription drug utilization in US children, 2002–2010. *Pediatrics, 130,* 23–31.

Chakrabarti, B., Bullmore, E., & Baron-Cohen, S. (2006). Empathizing with basic emotions: Common and discrete neural substrates. *Social Neuroscience, 1,* 364–384.

Chamberlain, S. R., Menzies, L., Hampshire, A., Suckling, J., Fineberg, N. A., de Campo, N., et al. (2008). Orbitofrontal dysfunction in patients with obsessive-compulsive disorder and their unaffected relatives. *Science, 321,* 421–422.

Chan, B. L., Witt, R., Charrow, A. P., Magee, A., Howard, R., & Pasquina, P. F. (2007). Mirror therapy for phantom limb pain. *New England Journal of Medicine, 357,* 2206–2207.

Chapman, P. F., White, G. L., Jones, M. W., Cooper-Blacketer, D., Marshall, V. J., Irizarry, M., et al. (1999). Impaired synaptic plasticity and learning in aged amyloid precursor protein transgenic mice. *Nature Neuroscience, 2,* 271–276.

Charman, T., Pickles, A., Simonoff, E., Chandler, S., Loucas, T., & Baird, G. (2011). IQ in children with autism spectrum disorders: Data from the Special Needs and Autism Project (SNAP). *Psychological Medicine, 41,* 619–627.

Chatelle, C., Thibaut, A., Gosseries, O., Bruno, M.-A., Demertzi, A., Bernard, C., et al. (2014). Changes in cerebral metabolism in patients with a minimally conscious state responding to zolpidem. *Frontiers in Human Neuroscience.* doi:10.3389/fnhum.2014.00917

Chau, A., Salazar, A. M., Kruege, F., Cristofori, I., & Grafman, J. (2015). The effect of claustrum lesions on human consciousness and recovery of function. *Consciousness and Cognition, 36,* 256–264.

Chaudhari, N., Pereira, E., & Roper, S. D. (2009). Taste receptors for umami: The case for multiple receptors. *American Journal of Clinical Nutrition, 90*(Suppl.), 738S–742S.

Chawla, D., Rees, G., & Friston, K. J. (1999). The physiological basis of attentional modulation in extrastriate visual areas. *Nature Neuroscience, 2,* 671–675.

Check, E. (2004). Cardiologists take heart from stem-cell treatment success. *Nature, 428,* 880.

Chemelli, R. M., Willie, J. T., Sinton, C. M., Elmquist, J. K., Scammell, T., Lee, C., et al. (1999). Narcolepsy in orexin knockout mice: Molecular genetics of sleep regulation. *Cell, 98,* 437–451.

Chen, D. F., Schneider, G. E., Martinou, J.-C., & Tonegawa, S. (1997). Bcl-2 promotes regeneration of severed axons in mammalian CNS. *Nature, 385,* 434–438.

Chen, G., Doumatey, A. P., Zhou, J., Lei, L., Bentley, A. R., Tekola-Ayele, F., et al. (2017). Genome-wide analysis identifies an African-specific variant in SEMA4D associated with body mass index. *Obesity, 2,* 794–800.

Chen, J., Yu, S., Fu, Y., & Li, X. (2014). Synaptic proteins and receptors defects in autism spectrum disorders. *Frontiers in Cellular Neuroscience, 8*(276), e1–13. doi:10.3389/fncel.2014.0027

Chen, J.-F., Xu, K., Petzer, J. P., Staal, R., Xu, Y.-H., Beilstein, M., et al. (2001). Neuroprotection by caffeine and A2a adenosine receptor inactivation in a model of Parkinson's disease. *Journal of Neuroscience, 21,* 1–6.

Chen, M. C., Hamilton, J. P., & Gotlib, I. H. (2010). Decreased hippocampal volume in healthy girls at risk of depression. *Archives of General Psychiatry, 67,* 270–276.

Chen, W., Jongkamonwiwat, N., Abbas, L., Eshtan, S. J., Johnson, S. I., Kuhn, S., et al. (2012). Restoration of auditory evoked responses by human ES-cell-derived otic progenitors. *Nature, 490,* 278–284.

Chen, X., Gabitto, M., Peng, Y., Ryba, N. J. P., & Zuker, C. S. (2011). A gustotopic map of taste qualities in the mammalian brain. *Science, 333,* 1262–1266.

Chen, Y.-C., Auer-Grumbach, M., Matsukawa, S., Zitzelsberger, M., Themistocleous, A. C., Strom, T. M., et al. (2015). Transcriptional regulator PRDM12 is essential for human pain perception. *Nature Genetics, 47*(7), 803–808.

Cherrier, M. M., Craft, S., & Matsumoto, A. H. (2003). Cognitive changes associated with supplementation of testosterone or dihydrotestosterone in mildly hypogonadal men: A preliminary report. *Journal of Andrology, 24,* 568–576.

Cherrier, M. M., Matsumoto, A. H., Amory, J. K., Ahmed, S., Bremner, W., Peskind, E. R., et al. (2005). The role of aromatization in testosterone supplementation. *Neurology, 64,* 290–296.

Chi, R. P., & Snyder, A. W. (2012). Brain stimulation enables the solution of an inherently difficult problem. *Neuroscience Letters, 515,* 121–124.

Chiang, M.-C., Barysheva, M., McMahon, K. L., de Zubicaray, G. I., Johnson, K., Montgomery, G. W., et al. (2012). Gene network effects on brain microstructure and intellectual performance identified in 472 twins. *Journal of Neuroscience, 32,* 8732–8745.

Chiang, M.-C., Barysheva, M., Shattuck, D. W., Lee, A. D., Madsen, S. K., Avedissian, C., et al. (2009). Genetics of brain fiber architecture and intellectual performance. *Journal of Neuroscience, 29,* 2212–2224.

Children's National Health System. (2017, May 4). Three of 48 fetuses exposed to Zika in utero had abnormal fetal MRIs: Long-term neurological fate of Zika-exposed infants with "normal" MRI remains uncertain. *ScienceDaily.* Retrieved from www.sciencedaily.com/releases/2017/05/170504131707.htm

Cho, A. K. (1990). Ice: A new dosage form of an old drug. *Science, 249,* 631–634.

Choi, S. H., Kim, Y. H., Hebisch, M., Sliwinski, C., Lee, S., D'Avanzo, C., et al. (2014). A three-dimensional human neural cell culture model of Alzheimer's disease. *Nature, 515,* 274–278.

Chomsky, N. (1980). *Rules and representations.* New York: Columbia University Press.

Chong, S. Y. C., Ptáček, L. J., & Fu, Y.-H. (2012). Genetic insights on sleep schedules: This time, it's *PER*sonal. *Cell, 28,* 598–605.

Chou, Y., Hickey, P. T., Sundman, M., Song, A. W., & Chen, N. (2015). Effects of repetitive transcranial magnetic stimulation on motor symptoms in Parkinson disease. *JAMA Neurology, 72,* 432–440.

Chowdhury, R., Guitart-Masip, M., Bunzeck, N., Dolan, R. J., & Düzel, E. (2012). Dopamine modulates episodic memory persistence in old age. *Journal of Neuroscience, 32,* 14193–14204.

Chronis, A. M., Lahey, B. B., Pelham, W. E., Jr., Kipp, H. L., Baumann, B. L., & Lee, S. S. (2003). Psychopathology and substance abuse in parents of young children with attention-deficit/hyperactivity disorder. *Journal of the American Academy of Child and Adolescent Psychiatry, 42,* 1424–1432.

Chuang, R. S.-I., Jaffe, H., Cribbs, L., Perez-Reyes, E., & Swartz, K. J. (1998). Inhibition of T-type voltage-gated calcium channels by a new scorpion toxin. *Nature Neuroscience, 1,* 668–674.

Chung, K., Wallace, J., Kim, S.-Y., Kalyanasundaram, S., Andalman, A. S., Davidson, T. J., et al. (2014). Advanced CLARITY for rapid and high-resolution imaging of intact tissues. *Nature Protocols, 9,* 1682–1697.

Church, T. S., Thomas, D. M., Tudor-Locke, C., Katzmarzyk, P. T., Earnest, C. P., Rodarte, R. Q., et al. (2011). Trends over 5 decades in U.S. occupation-related physical activity and their associations with obesity. *PLoS ONE, 6,* e19657.

Cicchetti, F., Seporta, S., Hauser, R. A., Parent, M., Saint-Pierre, M., Sanberg, P. R., et al. (2009). Neural transplants in patients with Huntington's disease undergo disease-like neuronal degeneration. *Proceedings of the National Academy of Sciences, 106,* 12483–12488.

Cima, M., Smeets, T., & Jelicic, M. (2008). Self-reported trauma, cortisol levels, and aggression in psychopathic and non-psychopathic prison inmates. *Biological Psychology, 78,* 75–86.

Ciompi, L. (1980). Catamnestic long-term study on the course of life and aging of schizophrenics. *Schizophrenia Bulletin, 6,* 607–618.

Cirelli, C., Gutierrez, C. M., & Tononi, G. (2004). Extensive and divergent effects of sleep and wakefulness on brain gene expression. *Neuron, 41,* 35–43.

Clark, J. T., Kalra, P. S., & Kalra, S. P. (1985). Neuropeptide Y stimulates feeding but inhibits sexual behavior in rats. *Endocrinology, 117,* 2435–2442.

Clarkson, A. N., Huang, B. S., MacIsaac, S. E., Mody, I., & Carmichael, T. (2010). Reducing excessive GABA-mediated tonic inhibition promotes functional recovery after stroke. *Nature, 468,* 305–309.

Clarren, S. K., Alvord, E. C., Sumi, S. M., Streissguth, A. P., & Smith, D. W. (1978). Brain malformations related to prenatal exposure to alcohol. *Journal of Pediatrics, 92,* 64–67.

Clayton, J. D., Kyriacou, C. P., & Reppert, S. M. (2001). Keeping time with the human genome. *Nature, 409,* 829–831.

Cleva, R. M., Gass, J. T., Widholm, J. J., & Olive, M. F. (2010). Glutamatergic targets for enhancing extinction learning in drug addiction. *Current Neuropharmacology, 8,* 394–408.

Cloninger, C. R. (1987). Neurogenetic adaptive mechanisms in alcoholism. *Science, 236,* 410–416.

Clopath, C. (2012). Synaptic consolidation: An approach to long-term learning. *Cognitive Neurodynamics, 6,* 251–257.

Cloutier, M., Aigbogun, M. S., Guerin, A., Nitulescu, R., Ramanakumar, A. B., Kamat, S. A., et al. (2016). The economic burden of schizophrenia in the United States in 2013. *Journal of Clinical Psychiatry, 77,* 764–771.

Coccaro, E. F., Lee, R., Groer, M. W., Can, A., Coussons-Reed, M., & Postolache, T. T. (2016). *Taxoplasma gondii* infection: Relationship with aggression in psychiatric subjects. *Journal of Clinical Psychiatry, 77,* 334–341.

Coccaro, E. F., Sripada, C. S., Yanowitch, R. N., & Phan, K. L. (2011). Corticolimbic function in impulsive aggressive behavior. *Biological Psychiatry, 69,* 1153–1159.

Coffee and Caffeine Genetics Consortium, Cornelis, M. C., Byrne, E. M., Esko, T., Nalls, M. A., Ganna, A., et al. (2015). Genome-wide meta-analysis identifies six novel loci associated with habitual coffee consumption. *Molecular Psychiatry, 20,* 647–656.

Coffman, B. A., Trumbo, M. C., & Clark, V. P. (2012). Enhancement of object detection with transcranial direct current stimulation is associated with increased attention. *BMC Neuroscience, 13,* 108. Retrieved from http://www.biomedcentral .com/1471-2202/13/108

Coghlan, A. (2017, April 22). Psychedelic drug ayahuasca improves hard-to-treat depression. *New Scientist.* Retrieved from https://www.newscientist.com/article/2127802-psychedelic-drug-ayahuasca-improves-hard-to-treat-depression/

Cognitive enhancement and relapse prevention in cocaine addiction. (2012, May 24). *ClinicalTrials.gov.* Retrieved from http://clinicaltrials.gov/ct2/show/NCT01067846

Cohen, J. D., & Tong, F. (2001). The face of controversy. *Science, 293,* 2405–2407.

Cohen, L. G., Celnik, P., Pascual-Leone, A., Corwell, B., Faiz, L., Dambrosia, J., et al. (1997). Functional relevance of cross-modal plasticity in blind humans. *Nature, 389,* 180.

Cohen, M. X., Schoene-Bake, J.-C., Elger, C. E., & Weber, B. (2009). Connectivity-based segregation of the human striatum predicts personality characteristics. *Nature Neuroscience, 12,* 32–34.

Cohen, N. J., Eichenbaum, H., Deacedo, B. S., & Corkin, S. (1985). Different memory systems underlying acquisition of procedural and declarative knowledge. *Annals of the New York Academy of Sciences, 444,* 54–71.

Cohen, P., & Friedman, J. M. (2004). Leptin and the control of metabolism: Role for stearoyl-CoA desaturase-1 (SCD-1). *Journal of Nutrition, 134,* 2455S–2463S.

Cohen, S., Frank, E., Doyle, W. J., Skoner, D. P., Rabin, B. S., & Gwaltney, J. M., Jr. (1998). Types of stressors that increase susceptibility to the common cold in healthy adults. *Health Psychology, 17,* 214–223.

Cohen, S., Tyrrell, D. A., & Smith, A. P. (1991). Psychological stress and susceptibility to the common cold. *New England Journal of Medicine, 325,* 606–612.

Cohen-Kettenis, P. T. (2005). Gender change in 46 XY persons with 5-alpha-reductase-2 deficiency and 17-beta-hydroxysteroid dehydrogenase-3 deficiency. *Archives of Sexual Behavior, 34,* 399–410.

Colapinto, J. (2004, June 3). Gender gap: What were the real reasons behind David Reimer's suicide? *Slate.* Retrieved from www.slate.com/id/2101678

Colby, C. L., & Goldberg, M. E. (1999). Space and attention in parietal cortex. *Annual Review of Neuroscience, 22,* 319–349.

Cole, J. (1995). *Pride and a daily marathon.* Cambridge, MA: MIT Press.

Cole, S. W., Kemeny, M. E., Fahey, J. L., Zack, J. A., & Naliboff, B. D. (2003). Psychological risk factors for HIV pathogenesis: Mediation by the autonomic nervous system. *Biological Psychiatry, 54,* 1444–1456.

Coleman, D. L. (1973). Effects of parabiosis of obese with diabetes and normal mice. *Diabetologia, 9,* 294–298.

Collaer, M. L., & Hines, M. (1995). Human behavioral sex differences: A role for gonadal hormones during early development? *Psychological Bulletin, 118,* 55–107.

Collaer, M. L., Reimers, S., & Manning, J. T. (2007). Visuospatial performance on an internet line judgment task and potential hormonal markers: Sex, sexual orientation, and 2D:4D. *Archives of Sexual Behavior, 36,* 177–192.

Collyer brothers. (n.d.). In *Wikipedia.* Retrieved from http://en.wikipedia.org/wiki/Collyer_brothers

Colman, R. J., Beasley, T. M., Kemnitz, J. W., Johnson, S. C., Weindruch, R., & Anderson, R. M. (2014). Caloric restriction reduces age-related and all-cause mortality in rhesus monkeys. *Nature Communications.* doi:10.1038/ncomms557

Colt, E. W. D., Wardlaw, S. L., & Frantz, A. G. (1981). The effect of running on plasma β-endorphin. *Life Sciences, 28,* 1637–1640.

Congressional Research Service. (2008). Genetic privacy laws. *National Conference of State Legislatures.* Retrieved from http://www.ncsl.org/research/health/genetic-privacy-laws.aspx

Considine, R. V., Sinha, M. K., Heiman, M. L., Kriauciunas, A., Stephens, T. W., Nyce, M. R., et al. (1996). Serum immunoreactive-leptin concentrations in normal-weight and obese humans. *New England Journal of Medicine, 334,* 292–295.

Constantinidis, C., & Steinmetz, M. A. (1996). Neuronal activity in posterior parietal area 7a during the delay periods of a spatial memory task. *Journal of Neurophysiology, 76,* 1352–1355.

Cook, T. B., Brenner, L. A., Cloninger, C. R., Langenberg, P., Igbide, A., Giegling, I., et al. (2015). "Latent" infection with Toxoplasma gondii: Association with trait aggression and impulsivity in healthy adults. *Journal of Psychiatric Research, 60,* 87–94. doi:10.1016/j.jpsychires.2014.09.019

Cooke, S. F., & Bliss, T. V. P. (2006). Plasticity in the human central nervous system. *Brain, 129,* 1659–1673.

Coolidge, F. L., Thede, L. L., & Young, S. E. (2002). The heritability of gender identity disorder in a child and adolescent twin sample. *Behavior Genetics, 32,* 251–257.

Coon, D. (2001). *Introduction to psychology: Gateways to mind and behavior* (with InfoTrac; 9th ed.). Belmont, CA: Wadsworth/Thomson Learning.

Corballis, M. C. (2002). *From hand to mouth: The origins of language.* Princeton, NJ: Princeton University Press.

Corbett, A., Owen, A., Hampshire, A., Grahn, J., Stenton, R., Dajani, S., et al. (2015). The effect of an online cognitive training package in healthy older adults: An online randomized controlled trial. *Journal of the American Medical Directors Association, 16,* 990–997.

Corbett, D., & Wise, R. A. (1980). Intracranial self-stimulation in relation to the ascending dopaminergic systems of the midbrain: A moveable electrode mapping study. *Brain Research, 185,* 1–15.

Corbetta, M., Miezin, F. M., Dobmeyer, S., Shulman, G. L., & Petersen, S. E. (1990). Attentional modulation of neural processing of shape, color, and velocity in humans. *Science, 248,* 1556–1559.

Corkin, S. (1984). Lasting consequences of bilateral medial temporal lobectomy: Clinical course and experimental findings in H. M. *Seminars in Neurology, 4,* 249–259.

Corkin, S. (2002). What's new with the amnesic patient H. M.? *Nature Reviews Neuroscience, 3,* 153–160.

Corkin, S., Amaral, D. G., González, R. G., Johnson, K. A., & Hyman, B. T. (1997). HM's medial temporal lobe lesion: Findings from magnetic resonance imaging. *Journal of Neuroscience, 17,* 3964–3979.

Cosgrove, G. R., & Eskandar, E. (1998). *Thalamotomy and pallidotomy.* Retrieved from www.neurosurgery.mgh.harvard.edu/functional/pallidt.htm

Cosmo, C., Ferreira, C., Miranda, J. G. V., do Rosário, R. S., Baptista, A. F., Montoya, P., & de Sena, E. P. (2015). Spreading effect of tDCS in individuals with attention-deficit/hyperactivity disorder as shown by functional cortical networks: A randomized, double-blind, sham-controlled trial. *Frontiers in Psychiatry, 6*, 111. doi:10.3389/fpsyt.2015.00111

Costall, B., & Naylor, R. J. (1992). Anxiolytic potential of 5-HT3 receptor antagonists. *Pharmacology and Toxicology, 70*, 157–162.

Courchesne, E., Pierce, K., Schumann, C. M., Redcay, E., Buckwalter, J. A., Kennedy, D. P., et al. (2007). Mapping early brain development in autism. *Neuron, 56*, 399–413.

Courtet, P., Gottesman, L. L., Jollant, F., & Gould, T. D. (2011). The neuroscience of suicidal behaviors: What can we expect from endophenotype strategies? *Translational Psychiatry, 1*, e7. doi:10.1038/tp.2011.6

Courtney, S. M., Ungerleider, L. G., Keil, K., & Haxby, J. V. (1997). Transient and sustained activity in a distributed neural system for human working memory. *Nature, 386*, 608–611.

Cox, D. J., Merkel, R. L., Kovatchev, B., & Seward, R. (2000). Effect of stimulant medication on driving performance of young adults with attention-deficit/hyperactivity disorder: A preliminary double-blind placebo controlled trial. *Journal of Nervous and Mental Disease, 188*, 230–234.

Cox, J. J., Reimann, F., Nicholas, A. K., Thornton, G., Roberts, E., Springell, K., et al. (2006). An SCN9A channelopathy causes congenital inability to experience pain. *Nature, 444*, 894–898.

Coyle, J. T. (2006). Glutamate and schizophrenia: Beyond the dopamine hypothesis. *Cellular and molecular neurobiology, 26*, 365–384.

Craig, I. W., & Halton, K. E. (2009). Genetics of human aggressive behaviour. *Human Genetics, 126*, 101–113.

Crane, G. E. (1957). Iproniazid (Marsilid*) phosphate, a therapeutic agent for mental disorders and debilitating diseases. *Psychiatry Research Reports, 8*, 142–152.

Crick, F. (1994). *The astonishing hypothesis: The scientific search for the soul.* New York: Scribner.

Crick, F. C., & Koch, C. (2005). What is the function of the claustrum? *Philosophical Transactions of the Royal Society of London, B, 360*, 1270–1279.

Criminologist believes violent behavior is biological. (2013). *NPR Books,* April 30. Retrieved from http://www.npr.org/2013/05/01/180096559/criminologist-believes-violent-behavior-is-biological

Cross-Disorder Group of the Psychiatric Genomics Consortium. (2013). Identification of risk loci with shared effects on five major psychiatric disorders: A genome-wide analysis. *Lancet, 381*, 1371–1379.

Crow, T. J. (1985). The two-syndrome concept: Origins and current status. *Schizophrenia Bulletin, 11*, 471–486.

Crowe, R. R. (1984). Electroconvulsive therapy: A current perspective. *New England Journal of Medicine, 311*, 163–167.

Culham, J., He, S., Dukelow, S., & Verstraten, F. A. J. (2001). Visual motion and the human brain: What has neuroimaging told us? *Acta Psychologica, 107*, 69–94.

Culp, R. E., Cook, A. S., & Housley, P. C. (1983). A comparison of observed and reported adult-infant interactions: Effects of perceived sex. *Sex Roles, 9*, 475–479.

Cummings, D. E., Clement, K., Purnell, J. Q., Vaisse, C., Foster, K. E., Frayo, R. S., et al. (2002). Elevated plasma ghrelin levels in Prader-Willi syndrome. *Nature Medicine, 8*, 643–644.

Cummings, D. E., Purnell, J. Q., Frayo, R. S., Schmidova, K., Wisse, B. E., & Weigle, D. S. (2001). A preprandial rise in plasma ghrelin levels suggests a role in meal initiation in humans. *Diabetes, 50*, 1714–1719.

Curcio, C. A., Sloan, K. R., Kalina, R. E., & Hendrickson, A. E. (1990). Human photoreceptor topography. *Journal of Comparative Neurology, 292*(4), 497–523.

Currie, P. J., & Coscina, D. V. (1996). Regional hypothalamic differences in neuropeptide Y-induced feeding and energy substrate utilization. *Brain Research, 737*, 238–242.

Currin, A., Korovin, K., Ababi, M., Roper, K., Kell, D. B., Day, P. J., & King, R. D. (2017). Computing exponentially faster: Implementing a non-deterministic universal Turing machine using DNA. *Journal of the Royal Society Interface, 14*, e20160990.

Curtis, M. A., Penney, E. B., Pearson, A. G., van Roon-Mom, W. M. C., Butterworth, N. J., Dragunow, M., et al. (2003). Increased cell proliferation and neurogenesis in the adult human Huntington's disease brain. *Proceedings of the National Academy of Sciences, 100*, 9023–9027.

Cutler, W. B., Friedmann, E., & McCoy, N. L. (1998). Pheromonal influences on sociosexual behavior in men. *Archives of Sexual Behavior, 27*, 1–13.

Czeisler, C. A., Duffy, J. F., Shanahan, T. L., Brown, E. N., Mitchell, J. F., Rimmer, D. W., et al. (1999). Stability, precision, and near-24-hour period of the human circadian pacemaker. *Science, 284*, 2177–2181.

Czeisler, C. A., Johnson, M. P., Duffy, J. F., Brown, E. N., Ronda, J. M., & Kronauer, R. E. (1990). Exposure to bright light and darkness to treat physiologic maladaptation to night work. *New England Journal of Medicine, 322*, 1253–1259.

Czeisler, C. A., Moore-Ede, M. C., & Coleman, R. M. (1982). Rotating shift work schedules that disrupt sleep are improved by applying circadian principles. *Science, 217*, 460–463.

Czeisler, C. A., Richardson, G. S., Coleman, R. M., Zimmerman, J. C., Moore-Ede, M. C., Dement, W. C., et al. (1981). Chronotherapy: Resetting the circadian clocks of patients with delayed sleep phase insomnia. *Sleep, 4*, 1–21.

Czeisler, C. A., Shanahan, T. L., Klerman, E. B., Martens, H., Brotman, D. J., Emens, J. S., et al. (1995). Suppression of melatonin secretion in some blind patients by exposure to bright light. *New England Journal of Medicine, 332*, 6–11.

Czeisler, C. A., Weitzman, E. D., & Moore-Ede, M. C. (1980). Human sleep: Its duration and organization depend on its circadian phase. *Science, 210*, 1264–1267.

Dabbs, J. M., Jr., Carr, T. S., Frady, R. L., & Riad, J. K. (1995). Testosterone, crime, and misbehavior among 692 male prison inmates. *Personality and Individual Differences, 18*, 627–633.

Dabbs, J. M., Jr., Frady, R. L., Carr, T. S., & Besch, N. F. (1987). Saliva testosterone and criminal violence in young adult prison inmates. *Psychosomatic Medicine, 49*, 174–182.

Dabbs, J. M., Jr., & Hargrove, M. F. (1997). Age, testosterone, and behavior among female prison inmates. *Psychosomatic Medicine, 59*, 477–480.

Dabbs, J. M., Jr., Jurkovic, G. J., & Frady, R. L. (1991). Salivary testosterone and cortisol among late adolescent male offenders. *Journal of Abnormal Child Psychology, 19*, 469–478.

Dabbs, J. M., Jr., & Mohammed, S. (1992). Male and female salivary testosterone concentrations before and after sexual activity. *Physiology and Behavior, 52*, 195–197.

Dacey, D. M., Llao, H.-W., Peterson, B. B., Robinson, F. R., Smith, V. C., Pokorny, J., et al. (2005). Melanopsin-expressing ganglion cells in primate retina signal colour and irradiance and project to the LGN. *Nature, 433*, 749–754.

Dalgleish, T. (2004). The emotional brain. *Nature Reviews Neuroscience, 5*, 582–589.

Dallos, P., & Cheatham, M. A. (1976). Production of cochlear potentials by inner and outer hair cells. *Journal of the Acoustical Society of America, 60*, 510–512.

Dalsgaard, S., Nielsen, H. S., & Simonsen, M. (2013). Five-fold increase in national prevalence rates of attention-deficit hyperactivity disorder medications for children and adolescents with autism spectrum disorder, attention-deficit/hyperactivity disorder, and other psychiatric disorders: A Danish register-based study. *Journal of Child and Adolescent Psychopharmacology, 23*, 432–439.

Dalsgaard, S., Østergaard, S. D., Leckman, J. F., Mortensen, P. B., & Pedersen, M. G. (2015). Mortality in children, adolescents, and adults with attention deficit hyperactivity disorder: A nationwide cohort study. *Lancet, 385*, 2190–2196.

Dalton, A. (2005, May/June). Sleeptalking: A child molester pleads unconsciousness. *Legal Affairs.* Retrieved from www.legalaffairs.org/issues/May-June-2005/scene_dalton_mayjun05.msp

Dalton, R. (2000). NIH cash tied to compulsory training in good behavior. *Nature, 408*, 629.

Daly, M., & Wilson, M. (1988). *Homicide.* New York: Aldine de Gruyter.

Damasio, A. (1994). *Descartes' error: Emotion, reason, and the human brain.* New York: Putnam.

Damasio, A. R. (1985). Prosopagnosia. *Trends in Neurosciences, 8*, 132–135.

Damasio, A. R., Grabowski, T. J., Bechara, A., Damasio, H., Ponto, L. L. B., Parvizi, J., et al. (2000). Subcortical and cortical brain activity during the feeling of self-generated emotions. *Nature Neuroscience, 3*, 1049–1056.

Damasio, H., Grabowski, T., Frank, R., Galaburda, A. M., & Damasio, A. R. (1994). The return of Phineas Gage: Clues about the brain from the skull of a famous patient. *Science, 264*, 1102–1105.

Damasio, H., Grabowski, T. J., Tranel, D., Hichwa, R. D., & Damasio, A. R. (1996). A neural basis for lexical retrieval. *Nature, 380*, 499–505.

Damsma, G., Pfaus, J. G., Wenkstern, D., & Phillips, A. G. (1992). Sexual behavior increases dopamine transmission in the nucleus accumbens and striatum of male rats: Comparison with novelty and locomotion. *Behavioral Neuroscience, 106*, 181–191.

Dandy, J., & Nettelbeck, T. (2002). The relationship between IQ, homework, aspirations and academic achievement for Chinese, Vietnamese and Anglo-Celtic Australian school children. *Educational Psychology, 22*, 267–276.

Dang-Vu, T. T., McKinney, S. M., Buxton, O. M., Solet, J. M., & Ellenbogen, J. M. (2010). Spontaneous brain rhythms predict sleep stability in the face of noise. *Current Biology, 20*, R626–R627.

Daniel, D., Weinberger, D. R., Jones, D. W., Zigun, J. R., Coppola, R., Handel, S., et al. (1991). The effect of amphetamine on regional cerebral blood flow during cognitive activation in schizophrenia. *Journal of Neuroscience, 11*, 1907–1917.

Dapretto, M., Davies, M. S., Pfeifer, J. H., Scott, A. A., Sigman, M., Bookheimer, S. Y., et al. (2006). Understanding emotions in others: Mirror neuron dysfunction in children with autism spectrum disorders. *Nature Neuroscience, 9*, 28–30.

DARPA Public Affairs. (2017, April 26). TNT researchers set out to advance pace and effectiveness of cognitive skills training. Retrieved from http://www.darpa.mil/news-events/2017-04-26

Dartnall, H. J. A., Bowmaker, J. K., & Mollon, J. D. (1983). Human visual pigments: Microspectrophotometric results from the eyes of seven persons. *Proceedings of the Royal Society of London, B, 220*, 115–130.

Darwin, C. (1859). *On the origin of species.* London: Murray.

Darwin, C. (1871). *The descent of man and selection in relation to sex*. London: Murray.

Das, A., & Gilbert, C. D. (1995). Long-range horizontal connections and their role in cortical reorganization revealed by optical recording of cat primary visual cortex. *Nature, 375,* 780–784.

David, A. S., & Prince, M. (2005). Psychosis following head injury: A critical review. *Journal of Neurology and Neurosurgical Psychiatry, 76,* i53–i60.

Davidson, J. M. (1966). Characteristics of sex behavior in male rats following castration. *Animal Behavior, 14,* 266–272.

Davidson, R. J. (1992). Anterior cerebral asymmetry and the nature of emotion. *Brain Cognition, 20,* 125–151.

Davidson, R. J., Pizzagalli, D., Nitschke, J. B., & Putnam, K. (2002). Depression: Perspectives from affective neuroscience. *Annual Review of Psychology, 53,* 545–574.

Davis, C. M. (1928). Self selection of diet in newly weaned infants: An experimental study. *American Journal of Diseases of Children, 36,* 651–679.

Davis, J. O., Phelps, J. A., & Bracha, H. S. (1995). Prenatal development of monozygotic twins and concordance for schizophrenia. *Schizophrenia Bulletin, 21,* 357–366.

Davis, K. D., Hutchison, W. D., Lozano, A. M., Tasker, R. R., & Dostrovsky, J. O. (2000). Human anterior cingulate cortex neurons modulated by attention-demanding tasks. *Journal of Neurophysiology, 83,* 3575–3577.

Davis, M. (1992). The role of the amygdala in fear and anxiety. *Annual Review of Neuroscience, 15,* 353–375.

Davis, S. W., Dennis, N. A., Daselaar, S. M., Fleck, M. S., & Cabeza, R. (2008). Qué PASA? The posterior-anterior shift in aging. *Cerebral Cortex, 18,* 1201–1209.

Deacon, T. W. (1990). Rethinking mammalian brain evolution. *American Zoologist, 30,* 629–705.

Dean, D. C., III, Jerskey, B. A., Chen, K., Protas, H., Thiyagura, P., Roontiva, A., et al. (2014). Brain differences in infants at differential genetic risk for late-onset Alzheimer disease: A cross-sectional imaging study. *JAMA Neurology, 71,* 11–22.

de Balzac, H. (1996). The pleasures and pains of coffee (Robert Onopa, Trans.). *Michigan Quarterly Review, 35,* 273–277. (Original work published 1839)

deCharms, R. C., Maeda, F., Glover, G. H., Ludlow, D., Pauly, J. M., Soneji, D., et al. (2005). Control over brain activation and pain learned by using real-time functional MRI. *Proceedings of the National Academy of Sciences, 102,* 18626–18631.

Dediu, D., & Levinson, S. C. (2013). On the antiquity of language: The reinterpretation of Neandertal linguistic capacities and its consequences. *Frontiers in Psychology, 4,* Article 397. Retrieved from http://www.frontiersin.org/Language_Sciences/10.3389/fpsyg.2013.00397/abstract

Deer, B. (2011). How the case against the MMR vaccine was fixed. *British Medical Journal, 342,* c5347. Retrieved from http://www.bmj.com/content/342/bmj.c5347

de Gelder, B., & Tamietto, M. (2007). Affective blindsight. *Scholarpedia, 2,* 3555. Retrieved from www.scholarpedia.org/article/Affective_blindsight

de Gonzalez, A. B., Hartge, P., Cerhan, J. R., Flint, A. J., Hannan, L., Cerhan, J. R., et al. (2010). Body-mass index and mortality among 1.46 million white adults. *New England Journal of Medicine, 363,* 2211–2219.

Degreef, G., Ashtari, M., Bogerts, B., Bilder, R. M., Jody, D. N., Alvir, J., et al. (1992). Volumes of ventricular system subdivisions measured from magnetic resonance images in first-episode schizophrenic patients. *Archives of General Psychiatry, 49,* 531–537.

Dehaene, S. (1997). *The number sense: How the mind creates mathematics.* New York: Oxford University Press.

Dehaene, S., & Cohen, L. (1997). Cerebral pathways for calculation: Double dissociation between rote verbal and quantitative knowledge of arithmetic. *Cortex, 33,* 219–250.

Dehaene, S., & Naccache, L. (2001). Towards a cognitive neuroscience of consciousness: Basic evidence and a workspace framework. *Cognition, 79,* 1–37.

Dehaene, S., Naccache, L., Cohen, L., Le Bihan, D., Mangin, J.-F., Poline, J.-B., et al. (2001). Cerebral mechanisms of word masking and unconscious repetition priming. *Nature Neuroscience, 4,* 752–758.

Dehaene, S., Spelke, E., Pinel, P., Stanescu, R., & Tsivkin, S. (1999). Sources of mathematical thinking: Behavioral and brain-imaging evidence. *Science, 284,* 970–974.

Deisseroth, K. (2015). Optogenetics: 10 years of microbial opsins in neuroscience. *Nature Neuroscience, 18,* 1213–1225.

de Jager, C. A., Oulhaj, A., Jacoby, R., Refsum, H., & Smith, A. D. (2012). Cognitive and clinical outcomes of homocysteine-lowering B-vitamin treatment in mild cognitive impairment: A randomized controlled trial. *International Journal of Geriatric Psychiatry, 27,* 592–600.

De Jager, P. L., Srivastava, G., Lunnon, K., Burgess, J., Schalkwyk, L. C., Yu, L., et al. (2014). Alzheimer's disease: Early alterations in brain DNA methylation at ANK1, BIN1, RHBDF2, and other loci. *Nature Neuroscience, 17,* 1156–1163.

de Jonge, F. H., Louwerse, A. L., Ooms, M. P., Evers, P., Endert, E., & Van de Poll, N. E. (1989). Lesions of the SDN-POA inhibit sexual behavior of male Wistar rats. *Brain Research Bulletin, 23,* 483–492.

de Jonge, F. H., Oldenburger, W. P., Louwerse, A. L., & Van de Poll, N. E. (1992). Changes in male copulatory behavior after sexual exciting stimuli: Effects of medial amygdala lesions. *Physiology and Behavior, 52,* 327–332.

Dekker, A. D., De Deyn, P. P., & Rots, M. G. (2014). Epigenetics: The neglected key to minimize learning and memory deficits in Down syndrome. *Neuroscience and Biobehavioral Reviews, 45,* 72–84.

de la Fuente-Fernández, R., Ruth, T. J., Sossi, V., Schulzer, M., Calne, D. B., & Stoessl, A. J. (2001). Expectation and dopamine release: Mechanism of the placebo effect in Parkinson's disease. *Science, 293,* 1164–1166.

De la Herran-Arita, A. K., Kornum, B. R., Mahlios, J., Jiang, W., Lin, L., Hou, T., et al. (2013). CD4 T cell autoimmunity to hypocretin/orexin and cross-reactivity to a 2009 H1N1 influenza A epitope in narcolepsy. *Science Translational Medicine, 5,* I216ra176. doi:10.1126/scitranslmed.3007762

DeLong, M. R. (2000). The basal ganglia. In E. R. Kandel, J. H. Schwartz, & T. M. Jessell (Eds.), *Principles of neural science* (4th ed., pp. 853–867). New York: McGraw-Hill.

DeLuca, G. C., Ebers, G. C., & Esiri, M. M. (2004). Axonal loss in multiple sclerosis: A pathological survey of the corticospinal and sensory tracts. *Brain, 127,* 1009–1018.

De Luca, V., Wang, H., Squassina, A., Wong, G. W. H., Yeomans, J., & Kennedy, J. L. (2004). Linkage of M5 muscarinic and a7-nicotinic receptor genes on 15q13 to schizophrenia. *Neuropsychobiology, 50,* 124–127.

De Luca, V., Wong, A. H. C., Muller, D. J., Wong, G. W. H., Tyndale, R. F., & Kennedy, J. L. (2004). Evidence of association between smoking and a7 nicotinic receptor subunit gene in schizophrenia patients. *Neuropsychopharmacology, 29,* 1522–1526.

Dement, W. (1960). The effect of dream deprivation. *Science, 131,* 1705–1707.

De Meyer, G., Shapiro, F., Vanderstichele, H., Vanmechelen, E., Engelborghs, S., et al. (2010). Diagnosis-independent Alzheimer disease biomarker signature in cognitively normal elderly people. *Archives of Neurology, 67,* 949–956.

Demicheli, V., Jefferson, T., Rivetti, A., & Price, D. (2005). Vaccines for measles, mumps and rubella in children. *The Cochrane Library.* Retrieved from www.mrw.interscience.wiley.com/cochrane/clsysrev/articles/CD004407/frame.html

Dempster, E., Viana, J., Pidsley, R., & Mill, J. (2013). Epigenetic studies of schizophrenia: Progress, predicaments, and promises for the future. *Schizophrenia Bulletin, 39,* 11–16.

Denissenko, M. F., Pao, A., Tang, M., & Pfeifer, G. P. (1996). Preferential formation of Benzo[a]pyrene adducts at lung cancer mutational hotspots in P53. *Science, 274,* 430–432.

Dennis, B. (2016, February 4). "We can do more," FDA says in announcing overhaul of approach to opioid painkillers. *Washington Post.* Retrieved from https://www.washingtonpost.com/news/to-your-health/wp/2016/02/04/we-can-do-more-fda-says-in-announcing-overhaul-of-its-approach-to-opioid-painkillers/?utm_term=.050b1187f7b1

Denyer, R., & Douglas, M. R. (2012). Gene therapy for Parkinson's disease. *Parkinson's Disease, 2012,* Article ID 757305.

Deol, M. S., & Gluecksohn-Waelsch, S. (1979). The role of inner hair cells in hearing. *Nature, 278,* 250–252.

Depression Guideline Panel. (1993). *Clinical practice guideline number 5: Depression in primary care II* (AHRQ Publication No. 93-0551). Rockville, MD: U.S. Department of Health and Human Services.

Depue, R. A., & Iacono, W. G. (1989). Neurobehavioral aspects of affective disorders. *Annual Review of Psychology, 40,* 457–492.

Derogatis, L. R., Abeloff, M. D., & Melisaratos, N. (1979). Psychological coping mechanisms and survival time in metastatic breast cancer. *Journal of the American Medical Association, 242,* 1504–1508.

DeSantis, A. D., Webb, E. M., & Noar, S. M. (2008). Illicit use of prescription ADHD medications on a college campus: A multimethodological approach. *Journal of American College Health, 57,* 315–324.

Descartes, R. (1984). Treatise on man (J. Cottingham, R. Stoothoff, & D. Murdoch, Trans.). *The philosophical writings of Descartes.* New York: Cambridge University Press. (Original work published about 1662)

De Silva, A., & Bloom, S. R. (2012). Gut hormones and appetite control: A focus on PYY and GLP-1 as therapeutic targets in obesity. *Gut and Liver, 6,* 10–20.

Desimone, R., Albright, T. D., Gross, C. G., & Bruce, C. (1984). Stimulus-selective properties of inferior temporal neurons in the macaque. *Journal of Neuroscience, 4,* 2051–2062.

D'Esposito, M., & Postle, B. R. (1999). The dependence of span and delayed response performance on prefrontal cortex. *Neuropsychologia, 37,* 1303–1315.

Desrivières, S., Lourdusamy, A., Tao, C., Toro, R., Jia, T., Loth, E., et al. (2014). Single nucleotide polymorphism in the neuroplastin locus associates with cortical thickness and intellectual ability in adolescents. *Molecular Psychiatry.* doi:10.1038/mp.2013.197

Dessens, A. B., Slijper, F. M. E., & Drop, S. L. S. (2005). Gender dysphoria and gender change in chromosomal females with congenital adrenal hyperplasia. *Archives of Sexual Behavior, 34,* 389–397.

De Stefano, N., Matthews, P. M., Filippi, M., Agosta, F., De Luca, M., Bartolozzi, M. L., et al. (2003). Evidence of early cortical atrophy in MS. *Neurology, 60,* 1157–1162.

Deutsch, J. A. (1983). The cholinergic synapse and the site of memory. In J. A. Deutsch (Ed.), *The physiological basis of memory* (pp. 367–386). New York: Academic Press.

Deutsch, S. I., Rosse, R. B., Schwartz, B. L., Weizman, A., Chilton, M., Arnold, D. S., et al. (2005). Therapeutic implications of a selective a7 nicotinic receptor abnormality in schizophrenics. *Israeli Journal of Psychiatry and Related Sciences, 42,* 33–44.

De Valois, R. L. (1960). Color vision mechanisms in the monkey. *Journal of General Physiology, 43,* 115–128.

De Valois, R. L., Abramov, I., & Jacobs, G. H. (1966). Analysis of response patterns of LGN cells. *Journal of the Optical Society of America, 56,* 966–977.

De Valois, R. L., Thorell, L. G., & Albrecht, D. G. (1985). Periodicity of striate-cortex-cell receptive fields. *Journal of the Optical Society of America, 2,* 1115–1123.

Devanand, D. P., Dwork, A. J., Hutchinson, E. R., Bolwig, T. G., & Sackeim, H. A. (1994). Does ECT alter brain structure? *American Journal of Psychiatry, 151,* 957–970.

Devane, W. A., Hanus, L., Breuer, A., Pertwee, R. G., Stevenson, L. A., Griffin, G., et al. (1992). Isolation and structure of a brain constituent that binds to the cannabinoid receptor. *Science, 258,* 1946–1949.

de Vivo, L., Bellesi, M., Marshall, W., Bushong, E. A., Ellisman, M. H., Tononi, G., & Cirelli, C. (2017). Ultrastructural evidence for synaptic scaling across the wake/sleep cycle. *Science, 355,* 507–510.

Devlin, B., Daniels, M., & Roeder, K. (1997). The heritability of IQ. *Nature, 388,* 468–471.

Devue, C., Collette, F., Balteau, E., Degueldre, C., Luxen, A., Maquet, P., et al. (2007). Here I am: The cortical correlates of visual self-recognition. *Brain Research, 1143,* 169–182.

Dew, M. A., Reynolds, C. F., III, Buysse, D. J., Houck, P. R., Hoch, C. C., Monk, T. H., et al. (1996). Electroencephalographic sleep profiles during depression: Effects of episode duration and other clinical and psychosocial factors in older adults. *Archives of General Psychiatry, 53,* 148–156.

DeWitt, I., & Rauschecker, J. P. (2012). Phoneme and word recognition in the auditory ventral stream. *Proceedings of the National Academy of Sciences, 109,* E505–E514.

DeWitt, S. J., Aslan, S., & Filbey, F. M. (2014). Adolescent risk-taking and resting state functional connectivity. *Psychiatry Research: Neuroimaging, 222,* 157–164.

Dhond, R. P., Buckner, R. L., Dale, A. M., Marinkovic, K., & Halgren, E. (2001). Spatiotemporal maps of brain activity underlying word generation and their modification during repetition priming. *Journal of Neuroscience, 21,* 3564–3571.

Diamond, J. (1992). Turning a man. *Discover, 13,* 71–77.

Diamond, M. (1965). A critical evaluation of the ontogeny of human sexual behavior. *Quarterly Review of Biology, 40,* 147–175.

Diamond, M., & Sigmundson, H. K. (1997). Sex reassignment at birth: Long-term review and clinical implications. *Archives of Pediatric and Adolescent Medicine, 151,* 298–304.

Diamond, M. C., Scheibel, A. B., Murphy, G. M., Jr., & Harvey, T. (1985). On the brain of a scientist: Albert Einstein. *Experimental Neurology, 88,* 198–204.

Dick, A. S., & Tremblay, P. (2012). Beyond the arcuate fasciculus: Consensus and controversy in the connectional anatomy of language. *Brain, 135,* 3529–3550.

Dick, D., & Agrawal, A. (2008). The genetics of alcohol and other drug dependence. *Alcohol Research and Health, 31,* 111–118.

Diderot, D. (1916). Letter on the blind for the use of those who see. In M. Jourdain (Ed. and Trans.), *Diderot's Early Philosophical Works.* Chicago: Open Court. (Original work published in 1749).

Dietis, N., Guerrini, R., Calo, G., Salvadori, S., Rowbotham, D. J., & Lambert, D. G. (2009). Simultaneous targeting of multiple opioid receptors: A strategy to improve side-effect profile. *British Journal of Anesthesia, 103,* 38–49.

Dietrich, T., Krings, T., Neulen, J., Willmes, K., Erberich, S., Thron, A., et al. (2001). Effects of blood estrogen level on cortical activation patterns during cognitive activation as measured by functional MRI. *NeuroImage, 13,* 425–432.

Dietz, V. (2009). Body weight supported gait training: From laboratory to clinical setting. *Brain Research Bulletin, 78,* i–vi.

Dietze, P., & Knowles, E. D. (2016). Social class and the motivational relevance of other human beings: Evidence from visual attention. *Psychological Science, 27*(11), 1517–1527. doi:10.1177/0956797616667721

DiFiglia, M., Sapp, E., Chase, K. O., Davies, S. W., Bates, G. P., Vonsattel, J. P., et al. (1997). Aggregation of huntingtin in neuronal intranuclear inclusions and dystrophic neurites in brain. *Science, 277,* 1990–1993.

Di Lorenzo, P. M., & Hecht, G. S. (1993). Perceptual consequences of electrical stimulation in the gustatory system. *Behavioral Neuroscience, 107,* 130–138.

Dilsaver, S. C. (2011). An estimate of the minimum economic burden of bipolar I and II disorders in the United States: 2009. *Journal of Affective Disorders, 129,* 79–83.

Di Marzo, V., Ligresti, A., & Cristino, L. (2009). The endocannabinoid system as a link between homeostatic and hedonic pathways involved in energy balance regulation. *International Journal of Obesity, 33,* S18–S24.

Dimitrijevic, M. R., Gerasimenko, Y., & Pinter, M. M. (1998). Evidence for a spinal central pattern generator in humans. *Annals of the New York Academy of Sciences, 860,* 360–376.

di Pellegrino, G., Fadiga, L., Fogassi, L., Gallese, V., & Rizzolatti, G. (1992). Understanding motor events: A neurophysiological study. *Experimental Brain Research, 91,* 176–180.

di Pellegrino, G., & Wise, S. P. (1993). Effects of attention on visuomotor activity in the premotor and prefrontal cortex of a primate. *Somatosensory and Motor Research, 10,* 245–262.

di Tomaso, E., Beltramo, M., & Piomelli, D. (1996). Brain cannabinoids in chocolate. *Nature, 382,* 677–678.

Dkhissi-Benyahya, O., Rieux, C., Hut, R. A., & Cooper, H. M. (2006). Immunohistochemical evidence of a melanopsin cone in human retina. *Investigative Ophthalmology & Visual Science, 47,* 1636–1641.

Doi, D., Morizane, A., Kikuchi, T., Onoe, H., Hayashi, T., Kawasaki, T., et al. (2012). Prolonged maturation culture favors a reduction in the tumorigenicity and the dopaminergic function of human ESC-derived neural cells in a primate model of Parkinson's disease. *Stem Cells, 30,* 935–945.

Dolak, K. (2012). "Bath salts": Use of dangerous drug increasing across U.S. *ABC News,* June 5. Retrieved from http://abcnews.go.com/Health/bath-salts-dangerous-drug-increasing-us/story?id=16496076

Dölen, G., Darvishzadeh, A., Huang, K. W., & Malenka, R. C. (2013). Social reward requires coordinated activity of nucleus accumbens oxytocin and serotonin. *Nature, 501,* 179–184.

Dollfus, S., Everitt, B., Ribeyre, J. M., Assouly-Besse, F., Sharp, C., & Petit, M. (1996). Identifying subtypes of schizophrenia by cluster analysis. *Schizophrenia Bulletin, 22,* 545–555.

Dom, G., Sabbe, B., Hulstijn, W., & van den Brink, W. (2005). Substance use disorders and the orbitofrontal cortex: Systematic review of behavioural decision-making and neuroimaging studies. *British Journal of Psychiatry, 187,* 209–220.

Dombeck, D. A., Khabbaz, A. N., Collman, F., Adelman, T. L., & Tank, D. W. (2007). Imaging large-scale neural activity with cellular resolution in awake, mobile, mice. *Neuron, 56,* 43–57.

Dominguez, J. M., & Hull, E. M. (2001). Stimulation of the medial amygdala enhances medial preoptic dopamine release: Implications for male rat sexual behavior. *Brain Research, 917,* 225–229.

Donnay, G. F., Rankin, S. K., Lopez-Gonzalez, M., Jiradejvong, P., & Limb, C. J. (2014). Neural substrates of interactive musical improvisation: An fMRI study of "Trading Fours" in jazz. *PLOS One, 9*(2), e88665.

Dörner, G. (1974). Sex-hormone-dependent brain differentiation and sexual functions. In G. Dörner (Ed.), *Endocrinology of sex* (pp. 30–37). Leipzig, Germany: J. A. Barth.

do Rosario-Campos, M. C., Leckman, J. F., Curi, M., Quatrano, S., Katsovitch, L., Miguel, E. C., et al. (2005). A family study of early-onset obsessive-compulsive disorder. *American Journal of Medical Genetics, Part B, 136,* 92–97.

Douaud, G., Refsum, H., de Jager, C. A., Jacoby, R., Nichols, T. E., Smith, S. M., & Smith, A. D. (2013). Preventing Alzheimer's disease-related gray matter atrophy by B-vitamin treatment. *Proceedings of National Academy of Sciences, 110,* 9523–9528.

Doucleff, M. (2013, September 17). Auto-brewery syndrome: Apparently you can make beer in your gut. NPR. Retrieved from http://www.npr.org/sections/thesalt/2013/09/17/223345977/auto-brewery-syndrome-apparently-you-can-make-beer-in-your-gut

Doughty, C. J., Wells, J. E., Joyce, P. R., & Walsh, A. E. (2004). Bipolar-panic disorder comorbidity within bipolar disorder families: A study of siblings. *Bipolar Disorders, 6,* 245–252.

Dowell, D., Haegerich, T. M., & Chou, R. (2016). CDC Guideline for prescribing opioids for chronic pain—United States. *Morbidity and Mortality Weekly Report, 65,* 1–49. doi:10.15585/mmwr.rr6501e1

Dowling, J. E., & Boycott, B. B. (1966). Organization of the primate retina. *Proceedings of the Royal Society of London, B, 166,* 80–111.

Downing, P. E., Jiang, Y., Shuman, M., & Kanwisher, N. (2001). A cortical area selective for visual processing of the human body. *Science, 293,* 2470–2473.

Dreifus, C. (1996, February 4). And then there was Frank. *New York Times Magazine,* 23–25.

Drevets, W. C. (2001). Neuroimaging and neuropathological studies of depression: Implications for the cognitive-emotional features of mood disorders. *Current Opinion in Neurobiology, 11,* 240–249.

Drevets, W. C., Price, J. L., Simpson, J. R., Todd, R. D., Reich, T., Vannier, M., et al. (1997). Subgenual prefrontal cortex abnormalities in mood disorders. *Nature, 386,* 824–827.

Drevets, W. C., & Raichle, M. E. (1995). Positron emission tomographic imaging studies of human emotional disorders. In M. S. Gazzaniga (Ed.), *The cognitive neurosciences* (pp. 1153–1164). Cambridge, MA: MIT Press.

Drevets, W. C., Videen, T. O., Price, J. L., Preskorn, S. H., Carmichael, S. T., & Raichle, M. E. (1992). A functional anatomical study of unipolar depression. *Journal of Neuroscience, 12,* 3628–3641.

Driver, J., & Mattingley, J. B. (1998). Parietal neglect and visual awareness. *Nature Neuroscience, 1,* 17–22.

Dronkers, N. F., Pinker, S., & Damasio, A. (2000). Language and the aphasias. In E. R. Kandel, J. H. Schwartz, & T. M. Jessell (Eds.), *Principles of neural science* (4th ed., pp. 1169–1187). New York: McGraw-Hill.

Drug Enforcement Administration. (2016). Established aggregate production quotas for Schedule I and II controlled substances and assessment of annual needs for the List I chemicals ephedrine, pseudoephedrine, and phenylpropanolamine for 2017. Retrieved from https://federalregister.gov/d/2016-23988

Drumi, C. (2009). Stem cell research: Toward greater unity in Europe? *Cell, 139,* 649–651.

Dryden, S., Wang, Q., Frankish, H. M., Pickavance, L., & Williams, G. (1995). The serotonin (5-HT) antagonist methysergide increases neuropeptide Y (NPY) synthesis and secretion in the hypothalamus of the rat. *Brain Research, 699,* 12–18.

Dudai, Y. (2004). The neurobiology of consolidations, or, how stable is the engram? *Annual Review of Psychology, 55,* 51–86.

Dudley, R. (2002). Fermenting fruit and the historical ecology of ethanol ingestion: Is alcoholism in modern humans an evolutionary hangover? *Addiction, 97,* 381–388.

Dujardin, K., Guerrien, A., & Leconte, P. (1990). Sleep, brain activation and cognition. *Physiology and Behavior, 47,* 1271–1278.

Dunbar, R. I. M. (1996). *Grooming, gossip and the evolution of language.* London: Faber & Faber.

Duncan, J., Seitz, R. J., Kolodny, J., Bor, D., Herzog, H., Ahmed, A., et al. (2000). A neural basis for general intelligence. *Science, 289,* 457–460.

Durand, J.-B., Nelissen, K., Joly, O., Wardak, C., Todd, J. T., Norman, J. F., et al. (2007). Anterior regions of monkey parietal cortex process visual 3D shape. *Neuron, 55,* 493–505.

Durand, V. M., & Barlow, D. H. (2006). *Essentials of abnormal psychology* (4th ed.). Belmont, CA: Thomson Wadsworth.

Durso, G. R. O., Luttrell, A., & Way, B. M. (2015). Over-the-counter relief from pains and pleasures alike: Acetaminophen blunts evaluation sensitivity to both negative and positive stimuli. *Psychological Science, 26,* 750–758.

Dutton, D. G., & Aron, A. P. (1974). Some evidence for heightened sexual attraction under conditions of high anxiety. *Journal of Personality and Social Psychology, 30,* 510–517.

Dworak, M., McCarley, R. W., Kim, T., Kalinchuk, A. V., & Basheer, R. (2010). Sleep and brain energy levels: ATP changes during sleep. *Journal of Neuroscience, 30,* 9007–9016.

Eagly, A. H. (1995). The science and politics of comparing women and men. *American Psychologist, 50,* 145–158.

Earnest, D. J., Liang, F.-Q., Ratcliff, M., & Cassone, V. M. (1999). Immortal time: Circadian clock properties of rat suprachiasmatic cell lines. *Science, 283,* 693–695.

Ecker, C., Suckling, J., Deoni, S. C., Lombardo, M. V., Bullmore, E. T., Baron-Cohen, S., et al. (2012). Brain anatomy and its relationship to behavior in adults with autism spectrum disorder: A multicenter magnetic resonance imaging study. *Archives of General Psychiatry, 69,* 195–209.

Edgerton, V. R., & Roy, R. R. (2009). Robotic training and spinal cord plasticity. *Brain Research Bulletin, 78,* 4–12.

Egger, K., Schocke, M., Weiss, E., Auffinger, S., Esterhammer, R., Goebel, G., et al. (2008). Pattern of brain atrophy in elderly patients with depression revealed by voxel-based morphometry. *Psychiatry Research, 164,* 237–244.

Ehrhardt, A. A., Meyer-Bahlburg, H. F. L., Rosen, L. R., Feldman, J. F., Veridiano, N. P., Zimmerman, I., & McEwen, B. S. (1985). Sexual orientation after prenatal exposure to exogenous estrogen. *Archives of Sexual Behavior, 14,* 57–77.

Ehrsson, H. H., Spence, C., & Passingham, R. E. (2004). That's my hand! Activity in premotor cortex reflects feeling of ownership of a limb. *Science, 305,* 875–877.

Ehtesham, M., Kabos, P., Kabosova, A., Neuman, T., Black, K. L., & Yu, J. S. (2002). The use of interleukin 12-secreting neural stem cells for the treatment of intracranial glioma. *Cancer Research, 62,* 5657–5663.

Einarsdottir, E., Carlsson, A., Minde, J., Toolanen, G., Svensson, O., Solders, G., et al. (2004). A mutation in the nerve growth factor beta gene *(NGFB)* causes loss of pain perception. *Human Molecular Genetics, 13,* 799–805.

Eksioglu, Y. Z., Scheffer, I. E., Cardenas, P., Knoll, J., DiMario, F., Ramsby, G., et al. (1996). Periventricular heterotopia: An x-linked dominant epilepsy locus causing aberrant cerebral cortical development. *Neuron, 16,* 77–87.

Elia, J., Gai, E. J., Xie, H. M., Perin, J. C., Geiger, E., Glessner, J. T., et al. (2010). Rare structural variants found in attention-deficit hyperactivity disorder are preferentially associated with neurodevelopmental genes. *Molecular Psychiatry, 15,* 637–646.

Elias, M. (2008, May 13). Another person with super-memory skills comes forward. *USA Today.* Retrieved from www.usatoday.com/news/health/2008-05-12-super-memory_N.htm

Elks, C. E., den Hoed, M., Zhao, J. H., Sharp, S. J., Wareham, N. J., Loos, R. J. F., & Ong, K. K. (2012). Variability in the heritability of body mass index: A systematic review and meta-regression. *Frontiers in Endocrinology, 3,* 1–16.

Ellis, L., & Ames, M. A. (1987). Neurohormonal functioning and sexual orientation: A theory of homosexuality-heterosexuality. *Psychological Bulletin, 101,* 233–258.

Ellison-Wright, I., & Bullmore, E. (2009). Meta-analysis of diffusion tensor imaging studies in schizophrenia. *Schizophrenia Research, 108,* 3–10.

Elman, J. A., Oh, H., Madison, C. M., Baker, S. I., Vogel, J. W., Marks, S. M., et al. (2014). Neural compensation in older people with brain amyloid-β deposition. *Nature Neuroscience, 17,* 1316–1318.

El Marroun, H., Schmidt, M. N., Franken, I. H. A., Jaddoe, V. W. V., Hofman, A., van der Lugt, A., et al. (2013). Prenatal tobacco exposure and brain morphology: A prospective study in young children. *Neuropsychopharmacology, 39,* 792–800.

Elmquist, J. K. (2001). Hypothalamic pathways underlying the endocrine, autonomic, and behavioral effects of leptin. *Physiology and Behavior, 74,* 703–708.

EMOTIV. (n.d.). Retrieved from https://www.emotiv.com/epoc/

Enard, W., Khaitovich, P., Klose, J., Zöllner, S., Heissig, F., Giavalisco, P., et al. (2002). Intra- and interspecific variation in primate gene expression patterns. *Science, 296,* 340–343.

ENCODE Project Consortium. (2012). An integrated encyclopedia of DNA elements in the human genome. *Nature, 489,* 57–74.

Eng, M. Y., Luczak, S. E., & Wall, T. L. (2007). ALDH2, ADH1B, and ADH1C genotypes in Asians: A literature review. *Alcohol Research and Health, 30,* 22–27.

Engel, A. K., König, P., Kreiter, A. K., & Singer, W. (1991). Interhemispheric synchronization of oscillatory neuronal responses in cat visual cortex. *Science, 252,* 1177–1179.

Engel, A. K., Kreiter, A. K., König, P., & Singer, W. (1991). Synchronization of oscillatory neuronal responses between striate and extrastriate visual cortical areas of the cat. *Proceedings of the National Academy of Sciences, 88,* 6048–6052.

Engel, S. M., Miodovnik, A., Canfield, R. L., Zhu, C., Silva, M. J., Calafat, A. M., et al. (2010). Prenatal phthalate exposure is associated with childhood behavior and executive functioning. *Environmental Health Perspectives.* Retrieved from http://ehp03.niehs.nih.gov/article/info%3Adoi%2F10.1289%2Fehp.0901470

Enoch, M.-A. (2006). Genetic and environmental influences on the development of alcoholism: Resilience *vs.* risk. *Annals of the New York Academy of Sciences, 1094,* 193–201.

Enriori, P. J., Evans, A. E., Sinnayah, P., Jobst, E. E., Tonelli-Lemos, L., Billes, S. K., et al. (2007). Diet-induced obesity causes severe but reversible leptin resistance in arcuate melanocortin neurons. *Cell Metabolism, 5,* 181–194.

Enserink, M. (2012). Fraud-detection tool could shake up psychology. *ScienceInsider,* July 3. Retrieved from http://news.sciencemag.org/scienceinsider/2012/07/fraud-detection-tool-could-shake.html?ref=em

Eppig, C., Fincher, C. L., & Thornhill, R. (2010). Parasite prevalence and the worldwide distribution of cognitive ability. *Proceedings of the Royal Society B.* Retrieved from http://rspb.royalsocietypublishing.org/content/early/2010/06/29/rspb.2010.0973.full.pdf+html

Epstein, R. H. (2010). Raiding the refrigerator but still asleep. *New York Times,* April 7. Retrieved from www.nytimes.com/2010/04/07/health/07eating.html

Ercan-Sencicek, A. G., Stillman, A. A., Ghosh, A. K., Bilguvar, K., O'Roak, B. J., Mason, C. E., et al. (2010). L-Histidine decarboxylase and Tourette's syndrome. *New England Journal of Medicine, 362,* 1901–1908.

Erickson, K. I., Colcombe, S. J., Wadhwa, R., Bherer, L., Peterson, M. S., Scalf, P. E., et al. (2007). Training-induced plasticity in older adults: Effects of training on hemispheric asymmetry. *Neurobiology of Aging, 28,* 272–283.

Ernst, M., Zametkin, A. J., Matochik, J. A., Jons, P. H., & Cohen, R. M. (1998). DOPA decarboxylase activity in attention-deficit/hyperactivity disorder adults: A [fluorine-18]fluorodopa positron emission tomographic study. *Journal of Neuroscience, 18,* 5901–5907.

Ernulf, K. E., Innala, S. M., & Whitam, F. L. (1989). Biological explanation, psychological explanation, and tolerance of homosexuals: A cross-national analysis of beliefs and attitudes. *Psychological Reports, 65,* 1003–1010.

Ersche, K. D., Jones, P. S., Williams, G. B., Robbins, T. W., & Bullmore, E. T. (2012). Cocaine dependence: A fast-track for brain ageing? *Molecular Psychiatry, 18,* 134–135.

Ersche, K. D., Jones, P. S., Williams, G. B., Turton, A. J., Robbins, T. W., & Bullmore, E. T. (2012). Abnormal brain structure implicated in stimulant drug addiction. *Science, 335,* 601–604.

Ethier, C., Oby, E. R., Bauman, M. J., & Miller, L. E. (2012). Restoration of grasp following paralysis through brain-controlled stimulation of muscles. *Nature, 485,* 368–371.

Etkin, A., & Wager, T. D. (2007). Functional neuroimaging of anxiety: A meta-analysis of emotional processing in PTSD, social anxiety disorder, and specific phobia. *American Journal of Psychiatry, 164,* 1476–1488.

Ettner, S. L., Huang, D., Evans, E., Ash, D. R., Hardy, M., Jourabchi, M., & Hser, Y.-I. (2006). Benefit-cost in the California Treatment Outcome Project: Does substance abuse treatment "pay for itself"? *Health Services Research, 41,* 192–213.

European Society of Human Genetics. (2012, June 23). Exome sequencing gives cheaper, faster diagnosis in heterogeneous disease; results from first use of this technique in the clinic. AlphaGalileo Foundation. Retrieved from http://www.alphagalileo.org/ViewItem.aspx?ItemId=121765&CultureCode=en

Evans, S. M., Haney, M., & Foltin, R. W. (2002). The effects of smoked cocaine during the follicular and luteal phases of the menstrual cycle in women. *Psychopharmacology* (Berlin), *159,* 397–406.

Evarts, E. V. (1979, March). Brain mechanisms of movement. *Scientific American, 241,* 164–179.

Faedda, G. L., Tondo, L., Teicher, M. H., Baldessarini, R. J., Gelbard, H. A., & Floris, G. F. (1993). Seasonal mood disorders: Patterns of seasonal recurrence in mania and depression. *Archives of General Psychiatry, 50,* 17–23.

Fahle, M., & Daum, I. (1997). Visual learning and memory as functions of age. *Neuropsychologia, 35,* 1583–1589.

Faigel, H. C., Szuajderman, S., Tishby, O., Turel, M., & Pinus, U. (1995). Attention-deficit disorder during adolescence: A review. *Journal of Adolescent Health, 16,* 174–184.

Falk, D. (2009). New information about Albert Einstein's brain. *Frontiers in Evolutionary Neuroscience, 1,* 1–6.

Falkner, A. L., & Lin, D. (2014). Recent advances in understanding the role of the hypothalamic circuit during aggression. *Frontiers in Systems Neuroscience, 8,* Article 168. doi:10.3389/fnsys.2014.00168

Falzi, G., Perrone, P., & Vignolo, L. A. (1982). Right-left asymmetry in anterior speech region. *Archives of Neurology, 39,* 239–240.

Fambrough, D. M., Drachman, D. B., & Satyamurti, S. (1973). Neuromuscular junction in myasthenia gravis: Decreased acetylcholine receptors. *Science, 182,* 293–295.

Fancher, R. E. (1979). *Pioneers of psychology.* New York: W. W. Norton.

Farina, D., Vujaklija, I., Sartori, M., Kapelner, T., Negro, F., Jiang, N., et al. (2017). Man/machine interface based on the discharge timings of spinal motor neurons after targeted muscle reinnervation. *Nature Biomedical Engineering, 1,* 0025. doi:10.1038/s41551-016-0025

Farooqi, I. S., Keogh, J. M., Yeo, G. S. H., Lank, E. J., Cheetham, T., & O'Rahilly, S. (2003). Clinical spectrum of obesity and mutations in the melanocortin 4 receptor gene. *New England Journal of Medicine, 348,* 1085–1095.

Farooqi, I. S., Matarese, G., Lord, G. M., Keogh, J. M., Lawrence, E., Agwu, C., et al. (2002). Beneficial effects of leptin on obesity, T cell hyporesponsiveness, and neuroendocrine/metabolic dysfunction of human congenital leptin deficiency. *Journal of Clinical Investigation, 110,* 1093–1103.

Farrer, C., Franck, N., Georgieff, N., Frith, C. D., Decety, J., & Jeannerod, M. (2003). Modulating the experience of agency. *NeuroImage, 18,* 324–333.

Farrer, C., Frey, S. H., Van Horn, J. D., Tunik, E., Turk, D., Inati, S., & Grafton, S. T. (2008). The angular gyrus computes action awareness representations. *Cerebral Cortex, 18,* 254–261.

Farrer, C., & Frith, C. D. (2002). Experiencing oneself vs another person as being the cause of an action: The neural correlates of the experience of agency. *NeuroImage, 15,* 596–603.

Fasano, A., Daniele, A., & Albanese, A. (2012). Treatment of motor and non-motor features of Parkinson's disease with deep brain stimulation. *Lancet, 11,* 429–442.

Fatemi, S. H., Earle, J. A., & McMenomy, T. (2000). Reduction in Reelin immunoreactivity in hippocampus of subjects with schizophrenia, bipolar disorder and major depression. *Molecular Psychiatry, 5,* 654–663.

Faul, M., Xu, L., Wald, M. M., & Coronado, V. G. (2010). *Traumatic brain injury in the United States.* Centers for Disease Control and Prevention. Retrieved from www.cdc.gov/traumaticbraininjury/pdf/blue_book.pdf

Fausto-Sterling, A. (1993, March/April). The five sexes: Why male and female are not enough. *The Sciences,* 20–25.

Fawzy, F. I., Fawzy, N. W., Hyun, C. S., Elashoff, R., Guthrie, D., Fahey, J. L., et al. (1993). Malignant melanoma: Effects of an early structured psychiatric intervention, coping, and affective state on recurrence and survival 6 years later. *Archives of General Psychiatry, 50,* 681–689.

Federal Bureau of Investigation. (2010). *Crime in the United States.* Retrieved from https://ucr.fbi.gov/crime-in-the-u.s/2010/crime-in-the-u.s.-2010/offenses-known-to-law-enforcement/expanded/expandhomicidemain

Feinberg, A. P., Irizarry, R. A., Fradin, D., Aryee, M. J., Murakami, P., Aspelund, T., et al. (2010). Personalized epigenomic signatures that are stable over time and covary with body mass index. *Science Translational Medicine, 2,* 49ra67.

Feinberg, T. E. (2001). *Altered egos: How the brain creates the self.* New York: Oxford University Press.

Feinstein, J. S., Adolphs, R., Damasio, A., & Tranel, D. (2011). The human amygdala and the induction and experience of fear. *Current Biology, 21,* 34–38.

Feinstein, J. S., Buzza, C., Hurlemann, R., Follmer, R. I., Dahdalch, N. S., & Coryell, W. H. (2013). Fear and panic in humans with bilateral amygdala damage. *Nature Neuroscience, 16,* 270–272.

Feldman, R., Weller, A., Zagoory-Sharon, O., & Levine, A. (2007). Evidence for a neuroendocrinological foundation of human affiliation: Plasma oxytocin levels across pregnancy and the postpartum period predict mother-infant bonding. *Psychological Science, 18,* 965–970.

Fenker, D. B., Frey, J. U., Schuetze, H., & Heipertz, D. (2008). Novel scenes improve recollection and recall of words. *Journal of Cognitive Neuroscience, 20*(7), 1250–1265.

Ferguson, J. N., Young, L. J., Hearn, E. F., Matzuk, M. M., Insel, T. R., & Winslow, J. T. (2000). Social amnesia in mice lacking the oxytocin gene. *Nature Genetics, 25,* 284–288.

Fergusson, D., Doucette, S., Glass, K. C., Shapiro, S., Healy, D., Hebert, P., et al. (2005). Association between suicide attempts and selective serotonin reuptake inhibitors: Systematic review of randomised controlled trials. *British Medical Journal, 330,* 396–402.

Fernández, G., Effern, A., Grunwald, T., Pezer, N., Lehnertz, K., Dümpelmann, M., et al. (1999). Real-time tracking of memory formation in the human rhinal cortex and the hippocampus. *Science, 285,* 1582–1585.

Fernàndez-Castillo, N., & Cormand, B. (2016). Aggressive behavior in humans: Genes and pathways identified through association studies. *American Journal of Medical Genetics Part B, 171B,* 676–696.

Fernández-Real, J. M., Ferri, M. J., Vendrell, J., & Ricart, W. (2007). Burden of infection and fat mass in healthy middle-aged men. *Obesity, 15,* 245–252.

Ferrarelli, F., Sarasso, S., Guller, Y., Riedner, B. A., Peterson, M. J., Bellesi, M., et al. (2012). Reduced natural oscillatory frequency of frontal thalamocortical circuits in schizophrenia. *Archives of General Psychiatry, 69,* 766–774.

Ferrari, P. F., Gallese, V., Rizzolatti, G., & Fogassi, L. (2003). Mirror neurons responding to the observation of ingestive and communicative mouth actions in the monkey ventral premotor cortex. *European Journal of Neuroscience, 17,* 1703–1714.

Fertuck, H. C., & Salpeter, M. M. (1974). Localization of acetylcholine receptor by 125I-labeled alpha-bungarotoxin binding at mouse motor endplates. *Proceedings of the National Academy of Sciences, 71,* 1376–1378.

Fibiger, H. C., LePiane, F. G., Jakubovic, A., & Phillips, A. G. (1987). The role of dopamine in intracranial self-stimulation of the ventral tegmental area. *Journal of Neuroscience, 7,* 3888–3896.

Field, A. E., Coakley, E. H., Must, A., Spadano, J. L., Laird, N., Dietz, W. H., et al. (2001). Impact of overweight on the risk of developing common chronic diseases during a 10-year period. *Archives of Internal Medicine, 161,* 1581–1586.

Fiez, J. (1996). Cerebellar contributions to cognition. *Neuron, 16,* 13–15.

Fike, M. L. (1990). Clinical manifestations in persons with multiple personality disorder. *American Journal of Occupational Therapy, 44,* 984–990.

Fink, D. J., Wechuck, J., Mata, M., Glorioso, J. C., Goss, J., Krisky, D., & Wolfe, D. (2011). Gene therapy for pain: Results of a phase I clinical trial. *Annals of Neurology, 70,* 207–212.

Fink, G., Pfaff, D., & Levine, J. (2012). *Handbook of Neuroendocrinology.* San Francisco: Elsevier.

Fink, G. R., Markowitsch, H. J., Reinkemeier, M., Bruckbauer, T., Kessler, J., & Heiss, W.-D. (1998). Cerebral representation of one's own past: Neural networks involved in autobiographical memory. *Journal of Neuroscience, 16,* 4275–4282.

Finn, E. S., Shen, X., Holahan, J. M., Scheinost, D., Lacadie, C., Papademetris, X., et al. (2014). Disruption of functional networks in dyslexia: A whole-brain, data-driven analysis of connectivity. *Biological Psychiatry, 76,* 397–404.

Fiorino, D. F., Coury, A., & Phillips, A. G. (1997). Dynamic changes in nucleus accumbens dopamine efflux during the Coolidge effect in male rats. *Journal of Neuroscience, 17,* 4849–4855.

Fischer, D. B., Boes, A. D., Demetzi, A., Evrard, H. C., Laureys, S., Edlow, B. L., et al. (2016). A human brain network derived from coma-causing brainstem lesions. *Neurology, 87,* 2427–2434.

Fischer, T. Z., & Waxman, S. G. (2010). Familial pain syndromes from mutations of the Na$_v$ 1.7 sodium channel. *Annals of the New York Academy of Sciences, 1184,* 196–207.

Fisher, P. M., Price, J. C., Meltzer, C. C., Moses-Kolko, E. L., Becker, C., Berga, S. L., & Hariri, A. R. (2011). Medial prefrontal cortex serotonin 1A and 2A receptor binding interacts to predict threat-related amygdala reactivity. *Biology of Mood & Anxiety Disorders, 1,* 2. Retrieved from http://www.biolmoodanxietydisord.com/content/1/1/2

Fiske, D. W., & Maddi, S. R. (1961). A conceptual framework. In D. W. Fiske & S. R. Maddi (Eds.), *Functions of varied experience* (pp. 11–56). Homewood, IL: Dorsey Press.

Fitzsimons, J. T. (1998). Angiotensin, thirst, and sodium appetite. *Physiological Reviews, 78,* 583–686.

Fitzsimons, J. T., & Moore-Gillon, M. J. (1980). Drinking and antidiuresis in response to reductions in venous return in the dog: Neural and endocrine mechanisms. *Journal of Physiology, 308,* 403–416.

Flanagin, V. L., Schörnich, S., Schranner, M., Hummel, N., Wallmeier, L., Wahlberg, M., et al. (2017). Human exploration of enclosed spaces through echolocation. *Journal of Neuroscience, 37*(6), 1614–1627. doi:10.1523/JNEUROSCI.1566-12.2016w

Flegal, K. M., Kruszon-Moran, D., Carroll, M. D., Fryar, C. D., & Ogden, C. L. (2016). Trends in obesity among adults in the United States, 2005–2014. *Journal of the American Medical Association, 315,* 2284–2291.

Fleming, R., Baum, A., Gisriel, M. M., & Gatchel, R. J. (1982). Mediating influences of social support on stress at Three Mile Island. *Journal of Human Stress, 8,* 14–22.

Flood, J. F., & Morley, J. E. (1991). Increased food intake by neuropeptide Y is due to an increased motivation to eat. *Peptides, 12,* 1329–1332.

Flor, H. (2008). Maladaptive plasticity, memory for pain and phantom limb pain: Review and suggestions for new therapies. *Expert Review of Neurotherapeutics, 8,* 809–818.

Flor, H., Braun, C., Elbert, T., & Birbaumer, N. (1997). Extensive reorganization of primary somatosensory cortex in chronic back pain patients. *Neuroscience Letters, 224,* 5–8.

Flor, H., Denke, C., Schaefer, M., & Grüsser, S. (2001). Effect of sensory discrimination training on cortical reorganisation and phantom limb pain. *Lancet, 357,* 1763–1764.

Flor, H., Diers, M., Christmann, C., & Koeppe, C. (2006). Mirror illusions of phantom hand movements: Brain activity mapped by fMRI. *NeuroImage, 31,* S159.

Flor, H., Elbert, T., Knecht, S., Wienbruch, C., Pantev, C., Birbaumer, N., et al. (1995). Phantom-limb pain as a perceptual correlate of cortical reorganization following arm amputation. *Nature, 375,* 482–484.

Flynn, J. R. (1987). Massive IQ gains in 14 nations: What IQ tests really measure. *Psychological Bulletin, 101,* 171–191.

Flynn, J. R., te Nijenhuis, J., & Metzen, D. (2014). The g beyond Spearman's g: Flynn's paradoxes resolved using four exploratory meta-analyses. *Intelligence, 44,* 1–10.

Foeli, J., Bekrater-Bodmann, R., Diers, M., & Flor, H. (2013). Mirror therapy for phantom limb pain: Brain changes and the role of body representation. *European Journal of Pain, 18*, 729–739.

Foerde, K., Steinglass, J. E., Shohamy, D., & Walsh, B. T. (2015). Neural mechanisms supporting maladaptive food choices in anorexia nervosa. *Nature Neuroscience, 18*, 1571–1573.

Ford, J. M., Mathalon, D. H., Whitfield, S., Faustman, W. O., & Roth, W. T. (2002). Reduced communication between frontal and temporal lobes during talking in schizophrenia. *Biological Psychiatry, 51*, 485–492.

Fotopoulou, A., Solms, M., & Turnbull, O. (2004). Wishful reality distortions in confabulation: A case report. *Neuropsychologia, 47*, 727–744.

Fournier, J. C., DeRubeis, R. J., Hollon, S. D., Dimidjian, S., Amsterdam, J. D., Shelton, R. C., & Fawcett, J. (2010). Antidepressant drug effects and depression severity. *Journal of the American Medical Association, 303*, 47–53.

Fouts, R. S., Fouts, D. S., & Schoenfeld, D. (1984). Sign language conversational interactions between chimpanzees. *Sign Language Studies, 42*, 1–12.

Fowler, C. D., Liu, Y., & Wang, Z. (2007). Estrogen and adult neurogenesis in the amygdala and hypothalamus. *Brain Research Reviews, 57*, 342–351.

Fowler, J. S., Logan, J., Wang, G.-J., Volkow, N. D., Telang, F., Zhu, W., et al. (2003). Low monoamine oxidase B levels in peripheral organs in smokers. *Proceedings of the National Academy of Sciences, 100*, 11600–11605.

Fowler, J. S., Volkow, N. D., Wang, G.-J., Pappas, N., Logan, J., MacGregor, R., et al. (1996). Inhibition of monoamine oxidase B in the brains of smokers. *Nature, 379*, 733–736.

Fowler, R. (1986, May). Howard Hughes: A psychological autopsy. *Psychology Today*, 22–33.

Fowles, D. C. (1992). Schizophrenia: Diathesis-stress revisited. *Annual Review of Psychology, 43*, 303–336.

Fox, J. W., Lamperti, E. D., Eksioglu, Y. Z., Hong, S. E., Feng, Y., Graham, D. A., et al. (1998). Mutations in *filamin 1* prevent migration of cerebral cortical neurons in human periventricular heterotopia. *Neuron, 21*, 1315–1325.

Fox, M. J. (2002). *Lucky man: A memoir*. New York: Hyperion.

Fralick, M., Thiruchelvam, D., Tien, H. C., & Redelmeier, D. A. (2016). Risk of suicide after a concussion. *Canadian Medical Association Journal, 188*(7), 497–504. doi:10.1503/cmaj.150790

Fraller, D. B. (2013). State of the science: Use of biomarkers and imaging in diagnosis and management of Alzheimer disease. *Journal of Neuroscience Nursing, 45*, 63–70.

Francis, H. W., Koch, M. E., Wyatt, J. R., & Niparko, J. K. (1999). Trends in educational placement and cost-benefit considerations in children with cochlear implants. *Archives of Otolaryngology: Head and Neck Surgery, 125*, 499–505.

Frankland, P. W., O'Brien, C., Ohno, M., Kirkwood, A., & Silva, A. J. (2001). α-CaMKII-dependent plasticity in the cortex is required for permanent memory. *Nature, 411*, 309–313.

Franklin, T. B., Russig, H., Weiss, I. C., Gräff, J., Linder, N., Michalon, A., et al. (2010). Epigenetic transmission of the impact of early stress across generations. *Biological Psychiatry, 68*, 408–415.

Fratiglioni, L., & Wang, H. X. (2000). Smoking and Parkinson's and Alzheimer's disease: Review of the epidemiological studies. *Behavioral Brain Research, 113*, 117–120.

Frayling, T. M., Timson, N. J., Weedon, M. N., Zeggini, E., Freathy, R. M., Lindgren, C., et al. (2007). A common variant in the *FTO* gene is associated with body mass index and predisposes to childhood and adult obesity. *Science, 316*, 889–894.

Freed, C. R., Greene, P. E., Breeze, R. E., Tsai, W.-Y., DuMouchel, W., Kao, R., et al. (2001). Transplantation of embryonic dopamine neurons for severe Parkinson's disease. *New England Journal of Medicine, 344*, 710–719.

Freed, W. J., de Medinaceli, L., & Wyatt, R. J. (1985). Promoting functional plasticity in the damaged nervous system. *Science, 227*, 1544–1552.

Freedman, M. S., Lucas, R. J., Soni, B., von Schantz, M., Muñoz, M., David-Gray, Z., et al. (1999). Regulation of mammalian circadian behavior by non-rod, non-cone ocular photoreceptors. *Science, 284*, 502–504.

Freer, R., Sormanni, P., Vecchi, G., Ciryam, P., Dobson, C. M., & Vendruscolo, M. (2016). A protein homeostasis signature in healthy brains recapitulates tissue vulnerability to Alzheimer's disease. *Science Advances, 2*(8), e1600947. doi:10.1126/sciadv.1600947

Freitag, C. M., Staal, W., Klauck, S. M., Duketis, E., & Waltes, R. (2010). Genetics of autistic disorders: Review and clinical applications. *European Child and Adolescent Psychiatry, 19*, 169–178.

French, E. D. (1994). Phencyclidine and the midbrain dopamine system: Electrophysiology and behavior. *Neurotoxicology and Teratology, 16*, 355–362.

French, S. J., & Cecil, J. E. (2001). Oral, gastric, and intenstinal influences on human feeding. *Physiology and Behavior, 74*, 729–734.

French roast. (1996, July). *Harper's Magazine, 293*, 28–30.

Freund, P., Schmidlin, E., Wannier, T., Bloch, J., Mir, A., Schwab, M. E., et al. (2006). Nogo-A-specific antibody treatment enhances sprouting and functional recovery after cervical lesion in adult primates. *Nature Medicine, 12*, 790–792.

Freund, P., Wannier, T., Schmidlin, E., Bloch, J., Mir, A., Schwab, M. E., et al. (2007). Anti-Nogo-A antibody treatment enhances sprouting of corticospinal axons rostral to a unilateral cervical spinal cord lesion in adult Macaque monkey. *Journal of Comparative Neurology, 502*, 644–659.

Fried, P., Watkinson, B., James, D., & Gray, R. (2002). Current and former marijuana use: Preliminary findings of a longitudinal study of effects on IQ in young adults. *Canadian Medical Association Journal, 166*, 887–891.

Fried, P. A. (1995). The Ottawa Prenatal Prospective Study (OPPS): Methodological issues and findings—it's easy to throw the baby out with the bath water. *Life Sciences, 56*, 23–24.

Friederici, A. D. (2006). The neural basis of language development and its impairment. *Neuron, 52*, 941–952.

Friedman, J. H. (2013). Pimavanserin for the treatment of Parkinson's disease psychosis. *Expert Opinion on Pharmacotherapy, 14*(14), 1969–1975.

Friedrich-Schiller-Universität Jena. (2010, August 9). Prosthesis with information at its fingertips: Hand prosthesis that eases phantom pain. *Science Daily*. Retrieved from www.sciencedaily.com/releases/2010/08/100806125508.htm

Frieling, H., Römer, K. D., Scholz, S., Mittelbach, F., Wilhelm, J., De Zwaan, M., et al. (2010). Epigenetic dysregulation of dopaminergic genes in eating disorders. *International Journal of Eating Disorders, 43*, 577–583.

Frings, L., Wagner, K., Unterrainer, J., Spreer, J., Halsband, U., & Schulze-Bonhage, A. (2006). Gender-related differences in lateralization of hippocampal activation and cognitive strategy. *Neuroreport, 17*, 417–421.

Frisén, L., Nordenström, A., Falhammar, H., Filipsson, H., Holmdahl, G., Janson, P. O., et al. (2009). Gender role behavior, sexuality, and psychosocial adaptation in women with congenital adrenal hyperplasia due to *CYP21A2* deficiency. *Journal of Clinical Endocrinology and Metabolism, 94*, 3432–3439.

Friston, K. J. (2009). Modalities, modes, and models in functional neuroimaging. *Science, 326*, 399–403.

Frith, U. (1993, June). Autism. *Scientific American, 268*, 108–114.

Frith, U., Morton, J., & Leslie, A. M. (1991). The cognitive basis of a biological disorder: Autism. *Trends in Neuroscience, 14*, 433–438.

Fritsch, G., & Hitzig, E. (1870). Über die elektrische Erregbarkeit des Grosshirns [Concerning the electrical stimulability of the cerebrum]. *Archiv für Anatomie Physiologie und Wissenschaftliche Medicin, 37*, 300–332.

Fritschy, J.-M., & Grzanna, R. (1992). Degeneration of rat locus coeruleus neurons is not accompanied by an irreversible loss of ascending projections. *Annals of the New York Academy of Sciences, 648*, 275–278.

From neurons to thoughts: Exploring the new frontier. (1998). *Nature Neuroscience, 1*, 1–2.

Fullerton, C. S., Ursano, R. J., Epstein, R. S., Crowley, B., Vance, K., Kao, T.-C., et al. (2001). Gender differences in posttraumatic stress disorder after motor vehicle accidents. *American Journal of Psychiatry, 158*, 1486–1491.

Furman, D. J., Hamilton, J. P., & Gotlib, I. H. (2011). Frontostriatal functional connectivity in major depressive disorder. *Biology of Mood & Anxiety Disorders, 1*, 11. Retrieved from http://www.biolmoodanxietydisord.com/content/1/1/11

Fuster, J., & Jervey, J. P. (1981). Inferotemporal neurons distinguish and retain behaviorally relevant features of visual stimuli. *Science, 212*, 952–955.

Fuster, J. M. (1989). *The prefrontal cortex: Anatomy, physiology, and neuropsychology of the frontal lobe* (2nd ed.). New York: Raven Press.

Gabrieli, J. D. E. (1998). Cognitive neuroscience of human memory. *Annual Review of Psychology, 49*, 87–115.

Gackenbach, J., & Bosveld, J. (1989). *Control your dreams*. New York: Harper & Row.

Gage, F. H. (2000). Mammalian neural stem cells. *Science, 287*, 1433–1438.

Gaillard, R., Dehaene, S., Adam, C., Clémenceau, S., Hasboun, D., Baulac, M., et al. (2009). Converging intracranial markers of conscious access. *PLoS Biology, 7*, e1000061. Retrieved from www.plosbiology.org/article/info:doi/10.1371/journal.pbio.1000061

Gaillard, R., Naccache, L., Pinel, P., Clémenceau, S., Volle, E., Hasboun, D., et al. (2006). Direct intracranial, fMRI, and lesion evidence for the causal role of left inferotemporal cortex in reading. *Neuron, 50*, 191–204.

Gainotti, G. (1972). Emotional behavior and hemispheric side of lesion. *Cortex, 8*, 41–55.

Gainotti, G., Caltagirone, C., & Zoccolotti, P. (1993). Left/right and cortical/subcortical dichotomies in the neuropsychological study of human emotions. *Cognition and Emotion, 7*, 71–94.

Galaburda, A. M. (1993). Neurology of developmental dyslexia. *Current Opinion in Neurobiology, 3*, 237–242.

Gale, J. T., Amirnovin, R., Roberts, D. W., Williams, Z. M., Blaha, C. D., & Eskandar, E. N. (2013). Electrical stimulation-evoked dopamine release in the primate striatum. *Stereotactic and Functional Neurosurgery, 91*, 355–363.

Gallese, V., & Goldman, A. (1998). Mirror neurons and the simulation theory of mindreading. *Trends in Cognitive Sciences, 2*, 493–501.

Gallup, G. G. (1983). Toward a comparative psychology of mind. In R. L. Mellgren (Ed.), *Animal cognition and behavior* (pp. 473–510). New York: North-Holland.

Gallup, G., Jr., & Povinelli, D. J. (1998, Winter). Can animals empathize? *Scientific American Presents*, 66–75.

Galton, F. (1883). *Inquiries into human faculty and its development*. London: Macmillan.

Gannon, P. J., Holloway, R. L., Broadfield, D. C., & Braun, A. R. (1998). Asymmetry of chimpanzee planum temporale: Human-like pattern of Wernicke's brain language area homolog. *Science, 279,* 220–222.

Ganzel, B. L., Kim, P., Glover, G. H., & Temple, E. (2008). Resilience after 9/11: Multimodal neuroimaging evidence for stress-related change in the healthy adult brain. *NeuroImage, 40,* 788–795.

Gao, Q., & Horvath, T. L. (2007). Neurobiology of feeding and energy expenditure. *Annual Review of Neuroscience, 30,* 367–398.

Garavan, H., Pankiewicz, J., Bloom, A., Cho, J.-K., Sperry, L., Ross, T. J., et al. (2000). Cue-induced cocaine craving: Neuroanatomical specificity for drug users and drug stimuli. *American Journal of Psychiatry, 157,* 1789–1798.

Garb, J. L., & Stunkard, A. J. (1974). Taste aversions in man. *American Journal of Psychiatry, 131,* 1204–1207.

Garcia, J. R., MacKillop, J., Aller, E. L., Merriwether, A. M., Wilson, D. S., & Lum, J. K. (2010). Associations between dopamine D4 receptor gene variation with both infidelity and sexual promiscuity. *PLoS ONE, 5,* e14162. doi:10.1371/journal.pone.0014162

Garcia-Falgueras, A., & Swaab, D. F. (2008). A sex difference in the hypothalamic uncinate nucleus: Relationship to gender identity. *Brain, 131,* 3132–3146.

Gardner, E. P., & Kandel, E. R. (2000). Touch. In E. R. Kandel, J. H. Schwartz, & T. M. Jessell (Eds.), *Principles of neural science* (4th ed., pp. 451–471). New York: McGraw-Hill.

Gardner, E. P., Martin, J. H., & Jessell, T. M. (2000). The bodily senses. In E. R. Kandel, J. H. Schwartz, & T. M. Jessell (Eds.), *Principles of neural science* (4th ed., pp. 430–450). New York: McGraw-Hill.

Gardner, G., & Halweil, B. (2000). *Overfed and underfed: The global epidemic of malnutrition.* Worldwatch Institute. Retrieved from www.worldwatch.org/system/files/EWP150.pdf

Gardner, H. (1975). *The shattered mind.* New York: Alfred A. Knopf.

Garrigan, P., Ratliff, C. P., Klein J. M., Sterling, P., Brainard, D. H., & Balasubramanian, V. (2010). Design of a trichromatic cone array. *PLoS Computational Biology, 6,* e1000677. Retrieved from http://www.ploscompbiol.org/article/info%3Adoi%2F10.1371%2Fjournal.pcbi.1000677

Gartrell, N. K. (1982). Hormones and homosexuality. In W. Paul, J. D. Weinrich, J. C. Gonsiorek, & M. E. Hotvedt (Eds.), *Homosexuality: Social, psychological, and biological issues* (pp. 169–182). Beverly Hills, CA: Sage.

Gasparini, F., Di Paolo, T., & Gomez-Mancilla, B. (2013). Metabotropic glutamate receptors for Parkinson's disease therapy. *Parkinson's Disease,* Article ID 196028. Retrieved from http://www.hindawi.com/journals/pd/2013/196028/

Gatchel, R. J. (1996). Psychological disorders and chronic pain: Cause-and-effect relationships. In R. J. Gatchel & D. C. Turk (Eds.), *Psychological approaches to pain management: A practitioner's handbook* (pp. 33–52). New York: Guilford Press.

Gates, G. J. (2011). How many people are lesbian, gay, bisexual, and transgender? Williams Institute. Retrieved from http://williamsinstitute.law.ucla.edu/wp-content/uploads/Gates-How-Many-People-LGBT-Apr-2011.pdf

Gauthier, I., Skudlarski, P., Gore, J. C., & Anderson, A. W. (2000). Expertise for cars and birds recruits brain areas involved in face recognition. *Nature Neuroscience, 3,* 191–197.

Gauthier, I., Tarr, M. J., Anderson, A. W., Skudlarski, P., & Gore, J. C. (1999). Activation of the middle fusiform "face area" increases with expertise in recognizing novel objects. *Nature Neuroscience, 2,* 568–573.

Gawin, F. H. (1991). Cocaine addiction: Psychology and neurophysiology. *Science, 251,* 1580–1586.

Gayán, J., & Olson, R. K. (2001). Genetic and environmental influences on orthographic and phonological skills in children with reading disabilities. *Developmental Neuropsychology, 20,* 483–507.

Gay and Lesbian Rights. (2016). Gallup. Retrieved from http://www.gallup.com/poll/1651/gay-lesbian-rights.aspx

Gazzaniga, M. S. (1967, August). The split brain in man. *Scientific American, 217,* 24–29.

Gazzaniga, M. S. (1970). *The bisected brain.* New York: Appleton-Century-Crofts.

Gazzaniga, M. S. (2002). The split brain revisited. *Scientific American, 12*(1), 27–31.

Gazzaniga, M. S., Ivry, R. B., & Mangun, G. R. (1998). *Cognitive neuroscience: The biology of the mind.* New York: Norton.

Gazzola, V., Aziz-Zadeh, L., & Keysers, C. (2006). Empathy and the somatotopic auditory mirror system in humans. *Current Biology, 16,* 1824–1829.

Gebhardt, C. A., Naeser, M. A., & Butters, N. (1984). Computerized measures of CT scans of alcoholics: Thalamic region related to memory. *Alcohol, 1,* 133–140.

Gefter, A. (2008, October 22). Creationists declare war over the brain. *New Scientist,* 46–47.

Gegenfurtner, K. R., & Kiper, D. C. (2003). Color vision. *Annual Review of Neuroscience, 26,* 181–206.

Geiger, A. (2016, October 12). Support for marijuana legalization continues to rise. FACTTANK. Retrieved from http://www.pewresearch.org/fact-tank/2016/10/12/support-for-marijuana-legalization-continues-to-rise/

Geiss, L. S., Wang, J., Cheng, Y. J., Thompson, T. J., Barker, L., Li, Y., et al. (2014). Prevalence and incidence trends for diagnosed diabetes among adults aged 20 to 79 years, United States, 1980–2012. *Journal of the American Medical Association, 312,* 1218–1226.

Gelosa, G., & Brooks, D. J. (2012). The prognostic value of amyloid imaging. *European Journal of Nuclear Medicine and Molecular Imaging, 39,* 1207–1219.

Genetic Information Nondiscrimination Act of 2008. (n.d.). *National Human Genome Research Institute.* Retrieved from http://www.genome.gov/10002328

Genoux, D., Haditsch, U., Knobloch, M., Michalon, A., Storm, D., & Mansuy, I. M. (2002). Protein phosphatase 1 is a molecular constraint on learning and memory. *Nature, 418,* 970–975.

Gentner, T. Q., Fenn, K. M., Margoliash, D., & Nusbaum, H. C. (2006). Recursive syntactic pattern learning by songbirds. *Nature, 440*(7088), 1204–1207.

Georgopoulos, A. P., Taira, M., & Lukashin, A. (1993). Cognitive neurophysiology of the motor cortex. *Science, 260,* 47–52.

Gérard, N., Pieters, G., Goffin, K., Bormans, G., & Van Laere, K. (2011). Brain type 1 cannabinoid receptor availability in patients with anorexia and bulimia nervosa. *Biological Psychiatry, 70,* 777–784.

Gerloff, C., Bushara, K., Sailer, A., Wasserman, E. M., Chen, R., Matsuoka, T., et al. (2006). Multimodal imaging of brain reorganization in motor areas of the contralesional hemisphere of well recovered patients after capsular stroke. *Brain, 129,* 791–808.

German education minister quits over PhD plagiarism. (2013, February 9). *The Guardian.* Retrieved from http://www.theguardian.com/world/2013/feb/09/german-education-minister-quits-phd-plagiarism

Gershon, E. S., Bunney, W. E., Leckman, J. F., Van Eerdewegh, M., & DeBauche, B. A. (1976). The inheritance of affective disorders: A review of data and of hypotheses. *Behavior Genetics, 6,* 227–261.

Gershoni, M., & Pietrokovski, S. (2017). The landscape of sex-differential transcriptome and its consequent selection in human adults. *BMC Biology, 15*(7). doi:10.1186/s12915-017-0352-z

Gertler, P., Heckman, J., Pinto, R., Zanolini, A., Vermeersch, C., Walker, S., et al. (2014). Labor market returns to an early childhood stimulation intervention in Jamaica. *Science, 344,* 998–1001.

Geschwind, N. (1970). The organization of language and the brain. *Science, 170,* 940–944.

Geschwind, N. (1972, April). Language and the brain. *Scientific American, 226*(4), 76–83.

Geschwind, N. (1979, September). Specializations of the human brain. *Scientific American, 241,* 180–199.

Geschwind, N., & Levitsky, W. (1968). Human brain: Left-right asymmetries in temporal speech region. *Science, 161,* 186–187.

Ghanizadeh, A., & Moghimi-Sarani, E. (2013). A randomized double blind placebo controlled clinical trial of N-acetylcysteine added to risperidone for treating autistic disorders. *BMC Psychiatry, 13,* 196. Retrieved from http://www.biomedcentral.com/1471-244X/13/196

Ghez, C., & Krakauer, J. (2000). The organization of movement. In E. R. Kandel, J. H. Schwartz, & T. M. Jessell (Eds.), *Principles of neural science* (4th ed., pp. 653–673). New York: McGraw-Hill.

Ghez, C., & Thach, W. T. (2000). The cerebellum. In E. R. Kandel, J. H. Schwartz, & T. M. Jessell (Eds.), *Principles of neural science* (4th ed., pp. 832–852). New York: McGraw-Hill.

Ghilardi, J. R., Röhrich, H., Lindsay, T. H., Sevcik, M. A., Schwei, M. J., Kubota, K., et al. (2005). Selective blockade of the capsaicin receptor TRPV1 attenuates bone cancer pain. *Journal of Neuroscience, 25,* 3126–3131.

Ghosh, A., & Sinha, A. K. (2007). A second Charak festival from Delhi. *Anthropologist, 9,* 289–294.

Gibbons, R. D., Brown, C. H., Hur, K., Marcus, S. M., Bhaumik, D. K., Erkens, J. A., et al. (2007). Early evidence on the effects of regulators' suicidality warnings on SSRI prescriptions and suicide in children and adolescents. *American Journal of Psychiatry, 164,* 1356–1363.

Giedke, H., & Schwarzler, F. (2002). Therapeutic use of sleep deprivation in depression. *Sleep Medicine Reviews, 6*(5), 361–377.

Gilad, Y., Wiebe, V., Przeworski, M., Lancet, D., & Pääbo, S. (2004). Loss of olfactory receptor genes coincides with the acquisition of full trichromatic vision in primates. *Public Library of Science Biology, 2,* 120–125.

Gilaie-Dolan, S., Tymula, A., Cooper, N., Kable, J. W., Glimcher, P. W., & Levy, I. (2014). Neuroanatomy predicts individual risk attitudes. *Journal of Neuroscience, 34,* 12394–12401.

Gilbertson, M. W., Shenton, M. E., Ciszewski, A., Kasai, K., Lasko, N. B., Orr, S. P., et al. (2002). Smaller hippocampal volume predicts pathologic vulnerability to psychological trauma. *Nature Neuroscience, 5,* 1242–1247.

Giles, D. E., Biggs, M. M., Rush, A. J., & Roffwarg, H. P. (1988). Risk factors in families of unipolar depression: I. Psychiatric illness and reduced REM latency. *Journal of Affective Disorders, 14,* 51–59.

Gilliland, F. D., Li, Y. F., & Peters, J. M. (2001). Effects of maternal smoking during pregnancy and environmental tobacco smoke on asthma and wheezing in children. *American Journal of Respiratory Critical Care Medicine, 163,* 429–436.

Gitlin, M. J., & Altshuler, L. L. (1997). Unanswered questions, unknown future for one of our oldest medications. *Archives of General Psychiatry, 54,* 21–23.

Giza, B. K., Scott, T. R., & Vanderweele, D. A. (1992). Administration of satiety factors and gustatory responsiveness in the nucleus tractus solitarius of the rat. *Brain Research Bulletin, 28,* 637–639.

Gizewski, E. R., Krause, E., Schlamann, M., Happich, F., Ladd, M. E., Forsting, M., et al. (2009). Specific cerebral activation due to visual erotic stimuli in male-to-female transsexuals compared with male and female controls: An fMRI study. *Journal of Sexual Medicine, 6,* 440–448.

Gladue, B. A., Beatty, W. W., Larson, J., & Staton, R. D. (1990). Sexual orientation and spatial ability in men and women. *Psychobiology, 18,* 101–108.

Gläscher, J., Rudrauf, D., Colom, R., Paul, L. K., Tranel, D., Damasio, H., et al. (2010). Distributed neural system for general intelligence revealed by lesion mapping. *Proceedings of the National Academy of Sciences, 107,* 4705–4709.

Glaser, R., Rice, J., Sheridan, J., Fertel, R., Stout, J., Speicher, C., et al. (1987). Stress-related immune suppression: Health implications. *Brain, Behavior, and Immunity, 1,* 7–20.

Glasner, A., Avraham, R., Rosenne, E., Benish, M., Zmora, O., Shemer, S., et al. (2010). Improving survival rates in two models of spontaneous postoperative metastasis in mice by combined administration of a beta-adrenergic antagonist and a cyclooxygenase-2 inhibitor. *Journal of Immunology, 184,* 2449–2457.

Glasson, B. I., Duda, J. E., Murray, I. V. J., Chen, Q., Souza, J. M., Hurtig, H. I., et al. (2000). Oxidative damage linked to neuro degeneration by selective a-synuclein nitration in synucleinopathy lesions. *Science, 290,* 985–989.

Glees, P. (1980). Functional cerebral reorganization following hemispherectomy in man and after small experimental lesions in primates. In P. Bach-y-Rita (Ed.), *Recovery of function: Theoretical considerations for brain injury rehabilitation* (pp. 106–125). Berne, Switzerland: Hans Huber.

Glenn, A. L., & Raine, R. (2014). Neurocriminology: Implications for the punishment, prediction and prevention of criminal behavior. *Nature Reviews Neuroscience, 15,* 54–63. doi:10.1038/nrn3640

Glezer, L. S., Jiang, X., & Riesenhuber, M. (2009). Evidence for highly selective neuronal tuning to whole words in the "visual word form area." *Neuron, 62,* 199–204.

Gloor, P., Olivier, A., Quesney, L. F., Andermann, F., & Horowitz, S. (1982). The role of the limbic system in experiential phenomena of temporal lobe epilepsy. *Annals of Neurology, 12,* 129–144.

Goate, A., Chartier-Harlin, M. C., Mullan, M., Brown, J., Crawford, F., Fidani, L., et al. (1991). Segregation of a missense mutation in the amyloid precursor protein gene with familial Alzheimer's disease. *Nature, 349,* 704–706.

Godfrey, K. M., Sheppard, A., Gluckman, P. D., Lillycrop, K. A., Burdge, G. C., et al. (2011). Epigenetic gene promoter methylation at birth is associated with child's later adiposity. *Diabetes, 60,* 1528–1534.

Gold, M. S. (1997). Cocaine (and crack): Clinical aspects. In J. H. Lowinson, P. Ruiz, R. B. Millman, & J. G. Langrod (Eds.), *Substance abuse: A comprehensive textbook* (pp. 181–199). Baltimore: Williams & Wilkins.

Gold, P. W., Goodwin, F. K., & Chrousos, G. P. (1988). Clinical and biochemical manifestations of depression: Relation to the neurobiology of stress. *New England Journal of Medicine, 319,* 348–353.

Goldberg, M., & Rosenberg, H. (1987). New muscle relaxants in outpatient anesthesiology. *Dental Clinics of North America, 31,* 117–129.

Goldberg, M. E., & Hudspeth, A. J. (2000). The vestibular system. In E. R. Kandel, J. H. Schwartz, & T. M. Jessell (Eds.), *Principles of neural science* (4th ed., pp. 801–815). New York: McGraw-Hill.

Goldman, N., Bertone, P., Chen, S., Desimoz, C., LeProust, E. M., Sipos, B., & Birney, E. (2013). Towards practical, high-capacity, low-maintenance information storage in synthesized DNA. *Nature, 494,* 77–80.

Goldman, N., Chen, M., Fujita, T., Xu, Q., Peng, W., Liu, W., et al. (2010). Adenosine A1 receptors mediate local anti-nociceptive effects of acupunctures. *Nature Neuroscience, 13* [electronic version]. Retrieved from www.nature.com/neuro/journal/vaop/ncurrent/full/nn.2562.html

Goldman-Rakic, P. S., Bates, J. F., & Chafee, M. V. (1992). The prefrontal cortex and internally generated motor acts. *Current Opinion in Neurobiology, 2,* 830–835.

Goldstein, E. B. (1999). *Sensation and perception* (5th ed.). Pacific Grove, CA: Brooks-Cole.

Goldstein, J. M., Scidman, L. J., Horton, N. J., Makris, N., Kennedy, D. N., Caviness, V. S., Jr., et al. (2001). Normal sexual dimorphism of the adult human brain assessed by *in vivo* magnetic resonance imaging. *Cerebral Cortex, 11,* 490–497.

Goldstein, R. Z., & Volkow, N. D. (2002). Drug addiction and its underlying neurobiological basis: Neuroimaging evidence for the involvement of the frontal cortex. *American Journal of Psychiatry, 10,* 1642–1652.

Gomez-Tortosa, E., Martin, E. M., Gaviria, M., Charbel, F., & Auman, J. I. (1995). Selective deficit of one language in a bilingual patient following surgery in the left perisylvian area. *Brain and Language, 48,* 320–325.

Gong, Y., Chang, L., Viola, K. L., Lacor, P. N., Lambert, M. P., Finch, C. E., et al. (2003). Alzheimer's disease-affected brain: Presence of oligomeric Ab ligands (ADDLs) suggests a molecular basis for reversible memory loss. *Proceedings of the National Academy of Sciences, 100,* 10417–10422.

González-Maeso, J., Ang, R. L., Yen, T., Chan, P., Weisstaub, N. V., López-Giménez, J. F., et al. (2008). Identification of a serotonin/glutamate receptor complex implicated in psychosis. *Nature, 452,* 93–99.

Goodell, E. W., & Studdert-Kennedy, M. (1993). Acoustic evidence for the development of gestural coordination in the speech of 2-year-olds: A longitudinal study. *Journal of Speech and Hearing Research, 36,* 707–727.

Goodman, D. C., Bogdasarian, R. S., & Horel, J. A. (1973). Axonal sprouting of ipsilateral optic tract following opposite eye removal. *Brain, Behavior, and Evolution, 8,* 27–50.

Goodwin, D. W. (1986). Heredity and alcoholism. *Annals of Behavioral Medicine, 8,* 3–6.

Gooley, J. J., Chamberlain, K., Smith, K. A., Khalsa, S. B. S., Rajaratnam, S. M. W., Van Reen, E., et al. (2011). Exposure to room light before bedtime suppresses melatonin onset and shortens melatonin duration in humans. *Journal of Clinical Endocrinology & Metabolism, 96,* E463–E472. doi:10.1210/jc.2010-2098

Gorelick, P. B., & Ross, E. D. (1987). The aprosodias: Further functional anatomical evidence for the organisation of affective language in the right hemisphere. *Journal of Neurology, Neurosurgery, and Psychiatry, 50,* 553–560.

Gorodetsky, E., Bevilacqua, L., Carli, V., Sarchiapone, M., Roy, A., Goldman, D., & Enoch, M.-A. (2014). The interactive effect of *MAOA-LPR* genotype and childhood physical neglect on aggressive behaviors in Italian male prisoners. *Genes, Brain and Behavior, 13,* 543–549.

Gorski, R. A. (1974). The neuroendocrine regulation of sexual behavior. In G. Newton & A. H. Riesen (Eds.), *Advances in psychobiology* (Vol. 2, pp. 1–58). New York: Wiley.

Gottesman, I. I. (1991). *Schizophrenia genesis: The origins of madness.* New York: Freeman.

Gottesman, I. I., & Bertelsen, A. (1989). Confirming unexpressed genotypes for schizophrenia. *Archives of General Psychiatry, 46,* 867–872.

Gottesman, I. I., McGuffin, P., & Farmer, A. E. (1987). Clinical genetics as clues to the "real genetics" of schizophrenia (a decade of modest gains while playing for time). *Schizophrenia Bulletin, 13,* 12–47.

Gougoux, F., Zatorre, R. J., Lassonde, M., Voss, P., & Lepore, F. (2005). A functional neuroimaging study of sound localization: Visual cortex activity predicts performance in early-blind individuals. *Public Library of Science Biology, 3,* 1–9.

Gould, E., & Gross, C. G. (2002). Neurogenesis in adult mammals: Some progress and problems. *Journal of Neuroscience, 22,* 619–623.

Gouras, P. (1968). Identification of cone mechanisms in monkey ganglion cells. *Journal of Physiology, 199,* 533–547.

Grace, A. A. (1991). Phasic versus tonic dopamine release and the modulation of dopamine system responsivity: A hypothesis for the etiology of schizophrenia. *Neuroscience, 41,* 1–24.

Grace, P. M., Strand, K. A., Galer, E. L., Urban, D. J., Wang, X., Baratta, M. V., et al. (2016). Morphine paradoxically prolongs neropathic pain in rats by amplifying spinal NLRP3 inflammasome activation. *Proceedings of the National Academy of Sciences, 113*(24), E3441–E3450. doi:10.1073/pnas.1602070113

Grant, B. F., Chou, S. P., Goldstein, R. B., Huang, B., Stinson, F. S., Saha, T. D., et al. (2008). Prevalence, correlates, disability, and comorbidity of DSM-IV borderline personality disorder: Results from the Wave 2 national epidemiologic survey on alcohol and related conditions. *Journal of Clinical Psychiatry, 69,* 533–545.

Grant, B. F., Stinson, F. S., Dawson, D. A., Chou, P., Dufour, M. C., Compton, W., et al. (2004a). Prevalence and co-occurrence of substance use disorders and independent mood and anxiety disorders. *Archives of General Psychiatry, 61,* 807–816.

Grant, B. F., Stinson, F. S., Dawson, D. A., Chou, S. P., Ruan, W. J., & Pickering, R. P. (2004b). Co-occurrence of 12-month alcohol and drug use disorders and personality disorders in the United States. *Archives of General Psychiatry, 61,* 361–368.

Grant, S., London, E. D., Newlin, D. B., Villemagne, V. L., Liu, X., Contoreggi, C., et al. (1996). Activation of memory circuits during cue-elicited cocaine craving. *Proceedings of the National Academy of Sciences, 93,* 12040–12045.

Gray, J. (1992). *Men are from Mars, women are from Venus: A practical guide for improving communication and getting what you want in your relationships.* New York: HarperCollins.

Gray, J. R., & Thompson, P. M. (2004). Neurobiology of intelligence: Science and ethics. *Nature Neuroscience, 5,* 471–482.

Gray, K., & Wegner, D. M. (2008). The sting of intentional pain. *Psychological Science, 19,* 1260–1262.

Graybiel, A. M. (1998). The basal ganglia and chunking of action repertoires. *Neurobiology of Learning and Memory, 70,* 119–136.

Graybiel, A. M., & Rauch, S. L. (2000). Toward a neurobiology of obsessive-compulsive disorder. *Neuron, 28,* 343–347.

Graziano, M. S. A., Cooke, D. F., & Taylor, C. S. R. (2000). Coding the location of the arm by sight. *Science, 290,* 1782–1786.

Graziano, M. S. A., Hu, X. T., & Gross, C. G. (1997). Visuospatial properties of ventral premotor cortex. *Journal of Neurophysiology, 77,* 2268–2292.

Graziano, M. S. A., Taylor, C. S. R., & Moore, T. (2002). Complex movements evoked by microstimulation of precentral cortex. *Neuron, 34,* 841–851.

Graziano, M. S. A., Yap, G. S., & Gross, C. G. (1994). Coding of visual space by premotor neurons. *Science, 266,* 1054–1057.

Greenamyre, J. T., & Hastings, T. G. (2004). Parkinson's: Divergent causes, convergent mechanisms. *Science, 304,* 1120–1122.

Greenberg, P. E., Kessler, R. C., Birnbaum, H. G., Leong, S. A., Lowe, S. W., Berglund, P. A., & Corey-Lisle, P. K. (2003). The economic burden of depression in the United States: How did it change between 1990 and 2000? *Journal of Clinical Psychiatry, 64,* 1465–1475.

Greene, P. E., & Fahn, S. (2002). Status of fetal tissue transplantation for the treatment of advanced Parkinson disease. *Neurosurgery Focus, 13,* 1–4.

Greenfeld, L. A., & Henneberg, M. A. (2001). Victim and offender self-reports of alcohol involvement in crime. *Alcohol Research and Health, 25,* 20–31.

Greenough, W. T. (1975). Experiential modification of the developing brain. *American Scientist, 63,* 37–46.

Greenwood, V. (2017). Put on telenovelas as you cook. *Scientific American Mind, 28*(8), 8.

Greer, S. (1991). Psychological response to cancer and survival. *Psychological Medicine, 21,* 43–49.

Greer, S. M., Goldstein, A. N., & Walker, M. P. (2013). The impact of sleep deprivation on food desire in the human brain. *Nature Communications, 4,* 2259. Retrieved from http://www.nature.com/ncomms/2013/130806/ncomms3259/full/ncomms3259.html#access

Gregory, S. G., Barlow, K. F., McLay, K. E., Kaul, R., Swarbreck, D., Dunham, A., et al. (2006). The DNA sequence and biological annotation of human chromosome 1. *Nature, 441,* 315–321.

Greimel, E., Nehrkorn, B., Schulte-Rüther, M., Fink, G. R., Nickl-Jockschat, T., Herpertz-Dahlmann, B., et al. (2013). Changes in grey matter development in autism spectrum disorder. *Brain Structure and Function, 218,* 929–942.

Gressens, P., Lammens, M., Picard, J. J., & Evrard, P. (1992). Ethanol-induced disturbances of gliogenesis and neurogenesis in the developing murine brain: An *in vitro* and an *in vivo* immunohistochemical and ultrastructural study. *Alcohol and Alcoholism, 27,* 219–226.

Grèzes, J., Armony, J. L., Rowe, J., & Passingham, R. E. (2003). Activations related to "mirror" and "canonical" neurones in the human brain: An fMRI study. *NeuroImage, 18,* 928–937.

Griffith, J. D., Cavanaugh, J., Held, J., & Oates, J. A. (1972). Dextroamphetamine: Evaluation of psychomimetic properties in man. *Archives of General Psychiatry, 26,* 97–100.

Griffiths, K. R., Grieve, S. M., Kohn, M. R., Clarke, S., Williams, L. M., & Korgaonkar, M. S. (2016). Altered gray matter organization in children and adolescents with ADHD: A structural covariance connectome study. *Translational Psychiatry, 6,* e947. doi:10.1038/tp2016.219

Grilo, C. M., & Pogue-Geile, M. F. (1991). The nature of environmental influences on weight and obesity: A behavior genetic anlaysis. *Psychological Bulletin, 110,* 520–537.

Grindlinger, H. M., & Ramsay, E. (1991). Compulsive feather-picking in birds. *Archives of General Psychiatry, 48,* 857.

Gross, C. G., Rocha-Miranda, C. E., & Bender, D. B. (1972). Visual properties of neurons in inferotemporal cortex of the macaque. *Journal of Neurophysiology, 35,* 96–111.

Grubb, M. A., Tymula, A., Gilaie-Dolan, S., Glimcher, P. W., & Levy, I. (2016). Neuroanatomy accounts for age-related changes in risk preferences. *Nature Communications.* doi:10.1038/ncomms13822

Gruenewald, D. A., & Matsumoto, A. M. (2003). Testosterone supplementation therapy for older men: Potential benefits and risks. *Journal of the American Geriatrics Society, 51,* 101–115.

Grueter, T. (2007, August/September). Forgetting faces. *Scientific American Mind,* 69–73.

Grüter, T., Grüter, M., & Carbon, C.-C. (2008). Neural and genetic foundations of face recognition and prosopagnosia. *Journal of Neuropsychology, 2,* 79–97.

Guerreiro, M., Castro-Caldas, A., & Martins, I. P. (1995). Aphasia following right hemisphere lesion in a woman with left hemisphere injury in childhood. *Brain and Language, 49,* 280–288.

Guidelines for ethical conduct in the care and use of animals. (n.d.). Retrieved from www.apa.org/science/anguide.html

Guidotti, A., Auta, J., Davis, J. M., Gerevini, V. D., Dwivedi, Y., Grayson, D. R., et al. (2000). Decrease in Reelin and glutamic acid decarboxylase67 (GAD67) expression in schizophrenia and bipolar disorder. *Archives of General Psychiatry, 57,* 1061–1069.

Gurd, J. M., & Marshall, J. C. (1992). Drawing upon the mind's eye. *Nature, 359,* 590–591.

Gusella, J. F., Wexler, N. S., Conneally, P. M., Naylor, S. L., Anderson, M. A., Tanzi, R. E., et al. (1983). A polymorphic DNA marker genetically linked to Huntington's disease. *Nature, 306,* 234–238.

Gustafson, D., Lissner, L., Bengtsson, C., Björkelund, C., & Skoog, I. (2004). A 24-year follow-up of body mass index and cerebral atrophy. *Neurology, 63,* 1876–1881.

Gustavson, C. R., Garcia, J., Hankins, W. G., & Rusiniak, K. W. (1974). Coyote predation control by aversive conditioning. *Science, 184,* 581–583.

Gustavson, C. R., Jowsey, J. R., & Milligan, D. N. (1982). A 3-year evaluation of taste aversion coyote control in Saskatchewan. *Journal of Range Management, 35,* 57–59.

Gustavson, C. R., Kelly, D. J., Sweeney, M., & Garcia, J. (1976). Prey lithium aversions I: Coyotes and wolves. *Behavioral Biology, 17,* 61–72.

Gustavson, D. E., Miyake, A., Hewitt, J. K., & Friedman, N. P. (2014). Genetic relations among procrastination, impulsivity, and goal-management ability: Implications for the evolutionary origin of procrastination. *Psychological Science, 25,* 1178–1188.

Guzowski, J. F., Knierim, J. J., & Moser, E. I. (2004). Ensemble dynamics of hippocampal regions of CA3 and CA1. *Neuron, 44,* 581–584.

György, B., Sage, C., Indzhykulian, A. A., Scheffer, D. I., Brisson, A. R., Tan, S., et al. (2017). Rescue of hearing by gene delivery to inner-ear hair cells using exosome-associated AAV. *Molecular Therapy, 25,* 379–391.

Haaxma, C., Bloem, B. R., Borm, G. F., Oyen, W. J. G., Leenders, K. L., Eshuis, S., et al. (2007). Gender differences in Parkinson's disease. *Journal of Neurology and Neurosurgical Psychiatry, 78,* 819–824.

Habib, M. (2000). The neurological basis of developmental dyslexia: An overview and working hypothesis. *Brain, 123,* 2373–2399.

Haier, R. J., Chueh, D., Touchette, P., Lott, I., Buchsbaum, M. S., MacMillan, D., et al. (1995). Brain size and cerebral glucose metabolic rate in nonspecific mental retardation and Down syndrome. *Intelligence, 20,* 191–210.

Haier, R. J., Jung, R. E., Yeo, R. A., Head, K., & Alkire, M. T. (2004). Structural brain variation and general intelligence. *NeuroImage, 23,* 425–433.

Haier, R. J., Jung, R. E., Yeo, R. A., Head, K., & Alkire, M. T. (2005). The neuroanatomy of general intelligence: Sex matters. *Neuroimage, 25,* 320–327.

Haier, R. J., Siegel, B., Tang, C., Abel, L., & Buchsbaum, M. S. (1992). Intelligence and changes in regional cerebral glucose metabolic rate following learning. *Intelligence, 16,* 415–426.

Haijma, S. V., Van Haren, N., Cahn, W., Kooschijn, C. M. P., Pol, H. E. H., & Kahn, R. S. (2012). Brain volumes in schizophrenia: A meta-analysis in over 18000 subjects. *Schizophrenia Bulletin, 39,* 1129–1138.

Hairston, I. S., & Knight, R. T. (2004). Sleep on it. *Nature, 430,* 27–28.

Halaas, J. L., Gajiwala, K. S., Maffei, M., Cohen, S. L., Chait, B. T., Rabinowitz, D., et al. (1995). Weight-reducing effects of the plasma protein encoded by the *obese* gene. *Science, 269,* 543–546.

Hall, M. H., Taylor, G., Salisbury, D. F., & Levy, D. L. (2010). Sensory gating event-related potentials and oscillations in schizophrenia patients and their unaffected relatives. *Schizophrenia Bulletin* (published online in advance of print April 2, 2010). doi:10.1093/schbul/sbq027

Haller, J. (2013). The neurobiology of abnormal manifestations of aggression—a review of hypothalamic mechanisms in cats, rodents, and humans. *Brain Research Bulletin, 93,* 97–109.

Hallmayer, J., Faraco, J., Lin, L., Hesselson, S., Winkelmann, J., Kawashima, M., et al. (2009). Narcolepsy is strongly associated with the T-cell receptor alpha locus. *Nature Genetics, 41,* 708–711.

Hamann, S. B., Ely, T. D., Grafton, S. T., & Kilts, C. D. (1999). Amygdala activity related to enhanced memory for pleasant and aversive stimuli. *Nature Neuroscience, 2,* 289–293.

Hamer, D. H. (1999). Genetics and male sexual orientation. *Science, 285,* 801–802.

Hamer, D. H., Hu, S., Magnuson, V. L., Hu, N., & Pattatucci, A. M. L. (1993). A linkage between DNA markers on the X chromosome and male sexual orientation. *Science, 261,* 321–327.

Hamilton, J. (2017, January 26). Art exhibit celebrates drawings by the founder of modern neuroscience [Radio broadcast]. NPR. Retrieved from http://www.npr.org/sections/healthshots/2017/01/26/511455876/art-exhibition-celebrates-drawings-by-the-founder-of-modern-Neuroscience

Hamza, T. H., Chen, H., Hill-Burns, E. M., Rhodes, S. L., Montimurro, J., Kay, D. M., et al. (2011). Genome-wide gene-environment study identifies glutamate receptor gene GRIN2A as a Parkinson's disease modifier gene via interaction with coffee. *PLOS Genetics, 7*(8), e1002237.

Han, F., Lin, L., Warby, S. C., Faraco, J., Li, J., Dong, S. X., An, P., et al. (2011). Narcolepsy onset is seasonal and increased following the 2009 H1N1 pandemic in China. *Annals of Neurology, 70,* 410–417.

Han, L., Ma, C., Liu, Q., Weng, H.-J., Cui, Y., Tang, Z., et al. (2012). A subpopulation of nociceptors specifically linked to itch. *Nature Neuroscience, 16,* 174–182.

Han, X., Chen, M., Wang, F., Windrem, M., Wang, B., Shanz, S., et al. (2013). Forebrain engraftment by human glial progenitor cells enhances synaptic plasticity and learning in adult mice. *Cell Stem Cell, 12,* 342–353.

Hanlon, E. M., & Bir, C. A. (2012). Real-time head acceleration measurement in girls' youth soccer. *Medicine & Science in Sports & Exercise, 44,* 1102–1108.

Hannibal, J., Hindersson, P., Knudsen, S. M., Georg, B., & Fahrenkrug, J. (2002). The photopigment melanopsin is exclusively present in pituitary adenylate cyclase-activating polypeptide-containing retinal ganglion cells of the retinohypothalamic tract. *Journal of Neuroscience, 22:RC191,* 1–7.

Hannula-Jouppi, K., Kaminen-Ahola, N., Taipale, M., Eklund, R., Nopola-Hemmi, J., Kääriäinen, H., & Kere, J. (2005). The axon guidance receptor gene ROBO1 is a candidate gene for developmental dyslexia. *PLoS Genetics, 1*(4), 467–474.

Happé, F., & Frith, U. (1996). The neuropsychology of autism. *Brain, 119,* 1377–1400.

Haqq, C. M., King, C.-Y., Ukiyama, E., Falsafi, S., Haqq, T. N., Donahoe, P. K., et al. (1994). Molecular basis of mammalian sexual determination: Activation of Müllerian inhibiting substance gene expression by SRY. *Science, 266,* 1494–1500.

Harada, C. N., Love, M. C. N., & Triebel, K. (2013). Normal cognitive aging. *Clinical Geriatric Medicine, 29,* 737–752.

Hare, L., Bernard, P., Sánchez, F. J., Baird, P. N., Vilain, E., Kennedy, T., & Harley, V. R. (2009). Androgen receptor repeat length polymorphism associated with male-to-female transsexualism. *Biological Psychiatry, 65,* 93–96.

Hariri, A. R., Mattay, V. S., Tessitore, A., Kolachana, B., Fera, F., Goldman, D., et al. (2002). Serotonin transporter genetic variation and the response of the human amygdala. *Science, 297,* 400–403.

Harmon, L. D., & Julesz, B. (1973). Masking in visual recognition: Effects of two-dimensional filtered noise. *Science, 180,* 1194–1197.

Harrington, G. S., & Farias, S. T. (2008). Sex differences in language processing: Functional MRI methodological considerations. *Journal of Magnetic Resonance Imaging, 27,* 1221–1228.

Harrison, P. J., Freemantle, N., & Geddes, J. R. (2003). Meta-analysis of brain weight in schizophrenia. *Schizophrenia Research, 64,* 25–34.

Harstall, C., & Ospina, M. (2003). How prevalent is chronic pain? *International Association for the Study of Pain: Clinical Updates, 11*(2), 1–4.

Hart, B. (1968). Role of prior experience on the effects of castration on sexual behavior of male dogs. *Journal of Comparative and Physiological Psychology, 66,* 719–725.

Hart, S. (2009). IAAF offers to pay for Caster Semenya's gender surgery if she fails verification test. *Telegraph* (UK), December 11. Retrieved from www.telegraph.co.uk/sport/othersports/athletics/6791558/IAAF-offers-to-pay-for-Caster-Semenyas-gender-surgery-if-she-fails-verification-test.html

Hartman, L. (1995). Cats as possible obsessive-compulsive disorder and medication models. *American Journal of Psychiatry, 152,* 1236.

Harvey, A. G., & Bryant, R. A. (2002). Acute stress disorder: A synthesis and critique. *Psychological Bulletin, 128,* 886–902.

Harvey, S. M. (1987). Female sexual behavior: Fluctuations during the menstrual cycle. *Journal of Psychosomatic Research, 31,* 101–110.

Hashimoto, M., Kato, S., Tanabe, Y., Katakura, M., Mamun, A. A., Ohno, M., et al. (2017). Beneficial effects of dietary docosahexaenoic acid intervention on cognitive function and mental health of the oldest elderly in Japanese care facilities and nursing homes. *Geriatrics and Gerontology International, 17,* 330–337. doi:10.1111/ggi.12691

Hassabis, D., Chu, C., Rees, G., Weiskopf, N., Molyneux, P. D., & Maguire, E. A. (2009). Decoding neuronal ensembles in the human hippocampus. *Current Biology, 19,* 546–554.

Hassan, T. H., Abdelrahman, H. M., Fattah, N. R. A., El-Masry, N. M., Hashim, H. M., El-Gerby, K. M., & Fattah, N. R. A. (2013). Blood and brain glutamate levels in children with autistic disorders. *Research in Autism Spectrum Disorders, 7,* 541–548.

Hastings, M. H., Reddy, A. B., & Maywood, E. S. (2003). A clockwork web: Circadian timing in brain and periphery, in health and disease. *Nature Reviews Neuroscience, 4,* 649–661.

Hattar, S., Liao, H.-W., Takao, M., Berson, D. M., & Yau, K.-W. (2002). Melanopsin-containing retinal ganglion cells: Architecture, projections, and intrinsic photosensitivity. *Science, 295,* 1065–1070.

Hauk, O., Johnsrude, I., & Pulvermüller, F. (2004). Somatotopic representation of action words in human motor and premotor cortex. *Neuron, 41,* 301–307.

Hauri, P. (1982). *Current concepts: The sleep disorders.* Kalamazoo, MI: Upjohn.

Hauser, M. D., MacNeilage, P., & Ware, M. (1996). Numerical representations in primates. *Proceedings of the National Academy of Sciences, 93,* 1514–1517.

Häusser, M., & Smith, S. L. (2007). Controlling neural circuits with light. *Nature, 446,* 617–619.

Hawass, Z. (2010). Ancestry and pathology in King Tutankhamun's family. *Journal of the American Medical Association, 303,* 638. doi:10.1001/jama.2010.121

Haworth, C. M. A., Wright, M. J., Luciano, M., Martin, N. G., de Geus, E. J. C., van Beijsterveld, C. E. M., et al. (2009). The heritability of general cognitive ability increases linearly from childhood to young adulthood. *Molecular Psychiatry.* Retrieved from www.nature.com/mp/journal/vaop/ncurrent/abs/mp200955a.html

Haxby, J. V., Gobbini, M. I., Furey, M. L., Ishai, A., Schouten, J. L., & Pietrini, P. (2001). Distributed and overlapping representations of faces and objects in ventral temporal cortex. *Science, 293,* 2425–2430.

Hayes, K. J., & Hayes, C. (1953). Picture perception in a home-raised chimpanzee. *Journal of Comparative and Physiological Psychology, 46,* 470–474.

He, Z., Ferguson, S. A., Cui, L., Greenfield, L. J., & Paule, M. G. (2013). Development of the sexually dimorphic nucleus of the preoptic area and the influence of estrogen-like compounds. *Neural Regeneration Research, 8,* 2763–2774.

Heath, R. G. (1964). *The role of pleasure in behavior.* New York: Harper & Row.

Hebb, D. O. (1940). *The organization of behavior.* New York: Wiley-Interscience.

Hebert, L. E., Weuve, J., Scherr, P. A., & Evans, D. A. (2013). Alzheimer disease in the United States (2010–2050) estimated using the 2010 census. *Neurology, 80,* 1778–1783.

Hécaen, H., & Angelergues, R. (1964). Localization of symptoms in aphasia. In A. V. S. de Reuck & M. O'Connor (Eds.), *Ciba Foundation symposium: Disorders of language* (pp. 223–260). Boston: Little, Brown.

Hedges, L. V., & Nowell, A. (1995). Sex differences in mental test scores, variability, and numbers of high-scoring individuals. *Science, 269,* 41–45.

Heilman, K. M., Watson, R. T., & Bowers, D. (1983). Affective disorders associated with hemispheric disease. In K. M. Heilman & P. Satz (Eds.), *Neuropsychology of human emotion* (pp. 45–64). New York: Guilford Press.

Heim, N. (1981). Sexual behavior of castrated sex offenders. *Archives of Sexual Behavior, 10,* 11–19.

Heller, A. S., Johnstone, T., Light, S. N., Peterson, M. J., Kolden, G. G., Kalin, N. H., & Davidson, R. J. (2013). Relationships between changes in sustained fronto-striatal connectivity and positive affect in major depression resulting from antidepressant treatment. *American Journal of Psychiatry, 170,* 197–206.

Heller, W., Miller, G. A., & Nitschke, J. B. (1998). Lateralization in emotion and emotional disorders. *Current Directions in Psychological Science, 1,* 26–32.

Helmholtz, H. von. (1852). On the theory of compound colors. *Philosophical Magazine, 4,* 519–534.

Helmholtz, H. von. (1948). *On the sensations of tone as a physiological basis for the theory of music* (A. J. Ellis, Trans.). New York: P. Smith. (Original work published 1863)

Helmuth, L. (2002). A generation gap in brain activity. *Science, 296,* 2131–2132.

Hemphill, J., & Deiters, A. (2013). DNA computation in mammalian cells: MicroRNA logic operations. *Journal of the American Chemical Society, 135,* 10512–10518.

Hendler, R. A., Ramchandani, V. A., Gilman, J., & Hammer, D. W. (2013). Stimulant and sedative effects of alcohol. *Current Topics in Behavioral Neuroscience, 13,* 489–509.

Heni, M., Kullmann, S., Ahlqvist, E., Wagner, R., Machicao, F., Staiger, H., et al. (2016). Interaction between the obesity-risk gene *FTO* and the dopamine D2 receptor gene *ANKK1/TaqIA* on insulin sensitivity. *Diabetologia, 59,* 2622–2631.

Hennenlotter, A., Dresel, C., Castrop, F., Ceballos Baumann, A. O., Wohlschläger, A. M., & Haslinger, B. (2009). The link between facial feedback and neural activity within central circuitries of emotion: New insights from botulinum toxin-induced denervation of frown muscles. *Cerebral Cortex, 19,* 537–542.

Hennevin, E., Hars, B., Maho, C., & Bloch, V. (1995). Processing of learned information in paradoxical sleep: Relevance for memory. *Behavioral Brain Research, 69,* 125–135.

Herbeck, D. (2015, December 26). Woman's body acts as "brewery," so judge dismisses DWI. *Buffalo News.* Retrieved from http://www.buffalonews.com/city-region/police-courts/womans-body-acts-as-brewery-so-judge-dismisses-dwi-20151226

Herbert, T. B., Cohen, S., Marsland, A. L., Bachen, E. A., Rabin, B. S., Muldoon, M. F., et al. (1994). Cardiovascular reactivity and the course of immune response to an acute psychological stressor. *Psychosomatic Medicine, 56,* 337–344.

Hering, E. (1878). *Zur lehre vom lichtsinne.* Vienna, Austria: Gerold.

Heritch, A. J. (1990). Evidence for reduced and dysregulated turnover of dopamine in schizophrenia. *Schizophrenia Bulletin, 16,* 605–615.

Herkenham, M. (1992). Cannabinoid receptor localization in brain: Relationship to motor and reward systems. *Annals of the New York Academy of Sciences, 654,* 19–32.

Herkenham, M. A., & Pert, C. B. (1982). Light microscopic localization of brain opiate receptors: A general autoradiographic method which preserves tissue quality. *Journal of Neuroscience, 2,* 1129–1149.

Hermann, L. (1870). Eine Erscheinung simultanen Contrastes. *Pflügers Archiv für die gesamte Physiologie, 3,* 13–15.

Hernán, M. A., Zhang, S. M., Lipworth, L., Olek, M. J., & Ascherio, A. (2001). Multiple sclerosis and age at infection with common viruses. *Epidemiology, 12,* 301–306.

Heron, M., Hoyert, D. L., Murphy, S. L., Xu, J., Kochanek, K. D., & Tejada-Vera, B. (2009). Deaths: Final data for 2006. *National Vital Statistics Reports, 57*(14). Retrieved from www.cdc.gov/nchs/data/nvsr/nvsr57/nvsr57_14.pdf

Herrera, B. M., Keildson, S., & Lindgren, C. M. (2011). Genetics and epigenetics of obesity. *Maturitas, 69,* 41–49.

Hervey, G. R. (1952). The effects of lesions in the hypothalamus in parabiotic rats. *Journal of Physiology, 145,* 336–352.

Herzog, D. B., Dorer, D. J., Keel, P. K., Selwyn, S. E., Ekeblad, E. R., Flores, A. T., et al. (1999). Recovery and relapse in anorexia and bulimia nervosa: A 7.5-year follow-up study. *Journal of the American Academy of Child and Adolescent Psychiatry, 38,* 829–837.

Herzog, H. A. (1998). Understanding animal activism. In L. A. Hart (Ed.), *Responsible conduct with animals in research* (pp. 165–184). New York: Oxford University Press.

Hesselbrock, V., Begleiter, H., Porjesz, B., O'Connor, S., & Bauer, L. (2001). P300 event-related potential amplitude as an endophenotype of alcoholism: Evidence from the collaborative study on the genetics of alcoholism. *Journal of Biomedical Science, 8,* 77–82.

Heston, L. L. (1970). The genetics of schizophrenic and schizoid disease. *Science, 167,* 249–256.

Hettema, J. M., Neale, M. C., & Kendler, K. S. (2001). A review and meta-analysis of the genetic epidemiology of anxiety disorders. *American Journal of Psychiatry, 158,* 1568–1578.

Hettema, J. M., Prescott, C. A., Myers, J. M., Neale, M. C., & Kendler, K. S. (2005). The structure of genetic and environmental risk factors for anxiety disorders in men and women. *Archives of General Psychiatry, 62,* 182–189.

Heywood, C. A., & Kentridge, R. W. (2003). Achromatopsia, color vision, and cortex. *Neurological Clinics of North America, 21,* 483–500.

Hickey, P., & Stacy, M. (2012). Adenosine A2A antagonists in Parkinson's disease: What's next? *Current Neurology and Neuroscience Reports, 12,* 376–385.

Hickok, G., Bellugi, U., & Klima, E. S. (1996). The neurobiology of sign language and its implications for the neural basis of language. *Nature, 381,* 699–702.

Hickok, G., & Poeppel, D. (2007). The cortical organization of speech processing. *Nature Reviews, 8,* 393–402.

Hicks, B. M., Bernat, E., Malone, S. M., Iacono, W. G., Patrick, C. J., Krueger, R. F., et al. (2007). Genes mediate the association between P3 amplitude and externalizing disorders. *Psychophysiology, 44,* 98–105.

Hier, D. B., & Crowley, W. F., Jr. (1982). Spatial ability in androgen-deficient men. *New England Journal of Medicine, 306,* 1202–1205.

Higley, J. D., Mehlman, P. T., Poland, R. E., Taub, D. M., Vickers, J., Suomi, S. J., et al. (1996). CSF testosterone and 5-HIAA correlate with different types of aggressive behaviors. *Biological Psychiatry, 40,* 1067–1082.

Higuchi, S., Usui, A., Murasaki, M., Matsushita, S., Nishioka, N., Yoshino, A., et al. (2002). Plasma orexin-A is lower in patients with narcolepsy. *Neuroscience Letters, 318,* 61–64.

Hill, J. O., & Peters, J. C. (1998). Environmental contributions to the obesity epidemic. *Science, 280,* 1371–1374.

Hill, J. O., Schlundt, D. G., Sbrocco, T., Sharp, T., Pope-Cordle, J., Stetson, B., et al. (1989). Evaluation of an alternating-calorie diet with and without exercise in the treatment of obesity. *American Journal of Nutrition, 50,* 248–254.

Hill, J. O., Wyatt, H. R., Reed, G. W., & Peters, J. C. (2003). Obesity and the environment: Where do we go from here? *Science, 299,* 853–855.

Hill, S. (1995). Neurobiological and clinical markers for a severe form of alcoholism in women. *Alcohol Health and Research World, 19*(3), 249–259.

Hill, S. Y., Muka, D., Steinhauer, S., & Locke, J. (1995). P300 amplitude decrements in children from families of alcoholic female probands. *Biological Psychiatry, 38,* 622–632.

Hillier, L. W., Coulson, A., & Murray, J. I. (2005). Genomics in C. elegans: So many genes, such a little worm. *Genome Research, 15,* 1651–1660.

Hines, D. J., Schmitt, L., Hines, R. M., Moss, S. J., & Haydon, P. G. (2013). Antidepressant effects of sleep deprivation require astrocyte-dependent adenosine mediated signaling. *Translational Psychiatry, 3,* e212. doi:10.1038/tp.2012.136. Retrieved from http://www.nature.com/tp/journal/v3/n1/full/tp2012136a.html

Hines, M. (1982). Prenatal gonadal hormones and sex differences in human behavior. *Psychological Bulletin, 92,* 56–80.

Hines, P. J. (1997). Noto bene: Unconscious odors. *Science, 278,* 79.

Hines, T. (1998). Further on Einstein's brain. *Experimental Neurology, 150,* 343–344.

Hochberg, L. R., Bacher, D., Jarosiewicz, B., Masse, N. Y., Simeral, J. D., Vogel, J., et al. (2012). Reach and grasp by people with tetraplegia using a neurally controlled robotic arm. *Nature, 485,* 372–377.

Hochberg, L. R., Serruya, M. D., Friehs, G. M., Muskand, J. A., Saleh, M., Caplan, A. H., et al. (2006). Neuronal ensemble control of prosthetic devices by a human with tetraplegia. *Nature, 442,* 164–171.

Hochner, H., Friedlander, Y., Calderon-Margalit, R., Meiner, V., Sagy, Y., Avgil-Tsadok, M., et al. (2012). Associations of maternal prepregnancy body mass index and gestational weight gain with adult offspring cardiometabolic risk factors. *Circulation, 125,* 1381–1389.

Hoebel, B. G., Monaco, A., Hernandes, L., Aulisi, E., Stanley, B. G., & Lenard, L. (1983). Self-injection of amphetamine directly into the brain. *Psychopharmacology, 81,* 158–163.

Hoffman, P. L., & Tabakoff, B. (1993). Ethanol, sedative hypnotics and glutamate receptor function in brain and cultured cells. *Alcohol and Alcoholism Supplement, 2,* 345–351.

Hohmann, A. G., Suplita, R. L., Bolton, N. M., Neely, M. H., Fegley, D., Mangieri, R., et al. (2005). An endocannabinoid mechanism for stress-induced analgesia. *Nature, 435,* 1108–1112.

Holden, C. (2004a). The origin of speech. *Science, 303,* 1316–1319.

Holden, C. (2004b). What's in a chimp's toolbox? *Science NOW.* Retrieved from sciencenow.sciencemag.org/cgi/content/full/2004/1007/2

Holloway, T., Moreno, J. L., Umali, A., Rayannavar, V., Hodes, G. E., Russo, S. J., & González-Maeso, J. (2013). Prenatal stress induces schizophrenia-like alterations of serotonin 2A and metabotropic glutamate 2 receptors in the adult offspring: Role of maternal immune system. *Journal of Neuroscience, 33,* 1088–1098.

Holstege, G., Georgiadis, J. R., Paans, A. M. J., Meiners, L. C., van der Graaf, F. H. C. E., & Reinders, A. A. T. S. (2003). Brain activation during human male ejaculation. *Journal of Neuroscience, 23,* 9185–9193.

Honea, R., Crow, T. J., Passingham, D., & MacKay, C. E. (2005). Regional deficits in brain volume in schizophrenia: A meta-analysis of voxel-based morphometry studies. *American Journal of Psychiatry, 162,* 2233–2245.

Hoogman, M., Bralten, J., Hibar, D. P., Mennes, M., Zwiers, M. P., Schweren, L. S., et al. (2017). Subcortical brain volume differences in participants with attention deficit hyperactivity disorder in children and adults: A cross-sectional mega-analysis. *Lancet Psychiatry, 4,* 310–319.

Hooks, B. M., & Chen, C. (2007). Critical periods in the visual system: Changing views for a model of experience-dependent plasticity. *Neuron, 56,* 312–326.

Hopkins, W. D., & Morris, R. D. (1993). Hemispheric priming as a technique in the study of lateralized cognitive processes in chimpanzees: Some recent findings. In H. L. Roitblat, L. M. Herman, & P. E. Nachtigall (Eds.), *Language and communication: Comparative perspectives* (pp. 293–309). Hillsdale, NJ: Lawrence Erlbaum.

Hopson, J. S. (1979). *Scent signals: The silent language of sex.* New York: Morrow.

Horgan, J. (1999). *The undiscovered mind.* New York: Free Press.

Horne, J. (1988). *Why we sleep: The functions of sleep in humans and other mammals.* New York: Oxford University Press.

Horne, J. (1992). Human slow wave sleep: A review and appraisal of recent findings, with implications for sleep functions, and psychiatric illness. *Experientia, 48,* 941–954.

Horne, J. A., & Harley, L. J. (1989). Human SWS following selective head heating during wakefulness. In J. Horne (Ed.), *Sleep '88* (pp. 188–190). New York: Gustav Fischer Verlag.

Horne, J. A., & Moore, V. J. (1985). Sleep EEG effects of exercise with and without additional body cooling. *Electroencephalography and Clinical Neurophysiology, 60,* 33–38.

Horner, P. J., & Gage, F. H. (2000). Regenerating the damaged central nervous system. *Nature, 407,* 963–970.

Horton, C., D'Zmura, M., & Srinivasan, R. (2013). Suppression of competing speech through entrainment of cortical oscillations. *Journal of Neurophysiology, 109,* 3082–3093.

Horvath, T. L., & Diano, S. (2004). The floating blueprint of hypothalamic feeding circuits. *Nature Reviews Neuroscience, 5,* 662–667.

Horvath, T. L., & Wikler, K. C. (1999). Aromatase in developing sensory systems of the rat brain. *Journal of Neuroendocrinology, 11,* 77–84.

Hosang, G. M., Shiles, C., Tansey, K. E., McGuffin, P., & Uher, R. (2014). Interaction between stress and the BDNF Val66Met polymorphism in depression: A systematic review and meta-analysis. *BMC Medicine, 12,* 7. Retrieved from http://www.biomedcentral.com/1741-7015/12/7

Hoshi, E., Shima, K., & Tanji, J. (2000). Neuronal activity in the primate prefrontal cortex in the process of motor selection based on two behavioral rules. *Journal of Neurophysiology, 83,* 2355–2373.

Hoshi, E., & Tanji, J. (2000). Integration of target and body-part information in the premotor cortex when planning action. *Nature, 408,* 466–470.

House, J. S., Landis, K. R., & Umberson, D. (1988). Social relationships and health. *Science, 241,* 540–545.

Howes, O. D., & Nour, M. N. (2016). Dopamine and the aberrant salience hypothesis of schizophrenia. *World Psychiatry, 15,* 3–4.

Howlett, A. C., Bidaut-Russell, M., Devane, W. A., Melvin, L. S., Johnson, M. R., & Herkenham, M. (1990). The cannabinoid receptor: Biochemical, anatomical and behavioral characterization. *Trends in Neurosciences, 13,* 420–423.

Hser, Y.-I., Hoffman, V., Grella, C. E., & Anglin, M. D. (2001). A 33-year follow-up of narcotics addicts. *Archives of General Psychiatry, 58,* 503–508.

Hsiao, S. S., O'Shaughnessy, D. M., & Johnson, K. O. (1993). Effects of selective attention on spatial form processing in monkey primary and secondary somatosensory cortex. *Journal of Neurophysiology, 70,* 444–447.

Hu, S., Pattatucci, A. M., Patterson, C., Li, L., Fulker, D. W., Cherny, S. S., et al. (1995). Linkage between sexual orientation and chromosome Xq28 in males but not in females. *Nature: Genetics, 11*(3), 248–256.

Hu, V. W., Sarachana, T., Sherrard, R. M., & Kocher, K. M. (2015). Investigation of sex differences in the expression of *RORA* and its transcriptional targets in the brain as a potential contributor to the sex bias in autism. *Molecular Autism, 6,* 7. doi:10.1186/2040-2392-6-7

Hubbard, E. M., Arman, A. C., Ramachandran, V. S., & Boyton, G. M. (2005). Individual differences among grapheme-color synesthetes: Brain-behavior correlations. *Neuron, 48,* 975–985.

Hubel, D. H. (1982). Exploration of the primary visual cortex, 1955–78. *Nature, 299,* 515–524.

Hubel, D. H., & Wiesel, T. N. (1959). Receptive fields of single neurons in the cat's striate cortex. *Journal of Physiology, 148,* 574–591.

Hubel, D. H., & Wiesel, T. N. (1974). Sequence regularity and geometry of orientation columns in the monkey striate cortex. *Journal of Comparative Neurology, 158,* 267–294.

Huber, G., Gross, G., Schüttler, R., & Linz, M. (1980). Longitudinal studies of schizophrenic patients. *Schizophrenia Bulletin, 6,* 593–605.

Huberman, A. D. (2007). Mechanisms of eye-specific visual circuit development. *Current Opinion in Neurobiology, 17,* 73–80.

Hudson, J. L., Hiripi, E., Pope, H. G., Jr., & Kessler, R. C. (2007). The prevalence and correlates of eating disorders in the National Comorbidity Survey replication. *Biological Psychiatry, 61,* 348–358.

Hudspeth, A. J. (1989). How the ear's works work. *Nature, 341,* 397–404.

Hudspeth, A. J. (2000). Hearing. In E. R. Kandel, J. H. Schwartz, & T. M. Jessell (Eds.), *Principles of neural science* (4th ed., pp. 590–613). New York: McGraw-Hill.

Hudspeth, A. J. (2008). Making an effort to listen: Mechanical amplification in the ear. *Neuron, 59,* 530–545.

Hull, C. L. (1951). *Essentials of behavior.* New Haven, CT: Yale University Press.

Hull, E. M., Lorrain, D. S., Du, J., Matuszewich, L., Lumley, L. A., Putnam, S. K., et al. (1999). Hormone-neurotransmitter interactions in the control of sexual behavior. *Behavioural Brain Research, 105,* 105–116.

Hulshoff Pol, H. E., Cohen-Kettenis, P. T., Van Haren, N. E. M., Peper, J. S., Brans, R. G. H., Cahn, W., et al. (2006). Changing your sex changes your brain: Influences of testosterone and estrogen on adult human brain structure. *European Journal of Endocrinology, 155,* S107–S114.

Humphries, C. (2015, July 7). Hugh Herr. *MIT Technology Review.* Retrieved from http://meche.mit.edu/people/hugh-herr

Hunt, G. L., & Hunt, M. W. (1977). Female-female pairing in western gulls *(Larus occidentalis)* in southern California. *Science, 196,* 1466–1467.

Hunt, G. L., Jr., Newman, A. L., Warner, M. H., Wingfield, J. C., & Kaiwi, J. (1984). Comparative behavior of male-female and female-female pairs among western gulls prior to egg laying. *The Condor, 86,* 157–162.

Huntington's Disease Collaborative Research Group. (1993). A novel gene containing a trinucleotide repeat that is expanded and unstable on Huntington's disease chromosomes. *Cell, 72,* 971–983.

Hurvich, L. M., & Jameson, D. (1957). An opponent-process theory of color vision. *Psychological Review, 64,* 384–404.

Husain, M., & Mehta, M. A. (2011). Cognitive enhancement by drugs in health and disease. *Trends in Cognitive Sciences, 15,* 28–36.

Hutchison, W. D., Davis, K. D., Lozano, A. M., Tasker, R. R., & Dostrovsky, J. O. (1999). Pain-related neurons in the human cingulate cortex. *Nature Neuroscience, 2,* 403–405.

Huttunen, M. (1989). Maternal stress during pregnancy and the behavior of the offspring. In S. Doxiadis (Ed.), *Early influences shaping the individual* (pp. 175–182). New York: Plenum Press.

Hyde, J. S. (1996). Where are the gender differences? Where are the gender similarities? In D. M. Buss & N. M. Malamuth (Eds.), *Sex, power, conflict: Evolutionary and feminist perspectives* (pp. 107–118). New York: Oxford University Press.

Hyde, J. S., Lindberg, S. M., Linn, M. C., Ellis, A. B., & Williams, C. C. (2008). Gender similarities characterize math performance. *Science, 321,* 494–495.

Hyman, B. T., Van Horsen, G. W., Damasio, A. R., & Barnes, C. L. (1984). Alzheimer's disease: Cell-specific pathology isolates the hippocampal formation. *Science, 225,* 1168–1170.

Hyman, S. E., & Malenka, R. C. (2001). Addiction and the brain: The neurobiology of compulsion and its persistence. *Nature Reviews: Neuroscience, 2,* 695–703.

Hyvärinen, J., & Poranen, A. (1978). Movement-sensitive cutaneous receptive fields in the hand area of the post-central gyrus in monkeys. *Journal of Physiology, 283,* 523–537.

Iacoboni, M., Molnar-Szakacs, I., Gallese, V., Buccino, G., Mazziotta, J. C., & Giacomo, R. (2005). Grasping the intentions of others with one's own mirror neuron system. *Public Library of Science Biology, 3,* 529–535.

Iacoboni, M., Woods, R. P., Brass, M., Bekkering, H., Mazziotta, J. C., & Rizzolatti, G. (1999). Cortical mechanisms of human imitation. *Science, 286,* 2526–2528.

Iacono, D., Markesbery, W. R., Gross, M., Pletnikova, O., Rudow, G., Zandi, P., et al. (2009). Clinically silent AD, neuronal hypertrophy, and linguistic skills in early life. *Neurology, 73,* 665–673.

Iacono, W. G., Carlson, S. R., Malone, S. M., & McGue, M. (2002). P3 event-related potential amplitude and the risk for disinhibitory disorders in adolescent boys. *Archives of General Psychiatry, 59,* 750–757.

Ichim, T. E., Solano, F., Lara, F., Paris, E., Ugalde, F., Rodriguez, J. P., et al. (2010). Feasibility of combination allogeneic stem cell therapy for spinal cord injury: A case report. *International Archives of Medicine, 3,* 30. Retrieved from http://www.intarchmed.com/content/3/1/30

Idänpään-Heikkilä, J., Alhava, E., Olkinuora, M., & Palva, I. P. (1977). Agranulocytosis during treatment with clozapine. *European Journal of Clinical Pharmacology, 11,* 193–198.

Iemmola, F., & Camperio Ciani, A. (2009). New evidence of genetic factors influencing sexual orientation in men: Female fecundity increase in the maternal line. *Archives of Sexual Behavior, 38,* 393–399.

Iijima, M., Arisaka, O., Minamoto, F., & Arai, Y. (2001). Sex differences in children's free drawings: A study on girls with congenital adrenal hyperplasia. *Hormones and Behavior, 40,* 99–104.

Immunization Safety Review Committee. (2004). *Immunization safety review: Vaccines and autism.* Institute of Medicine. Retrieved from www.nap.edu/catalog/10997.html

Imperato-McGinley, J., Peterson, R. E., Gautier, T., & Sturla, E. (1979). Androgen and the evolution of male-gender identity among male pseudohermaphrodites with 5a-reductase deficiency. *New England Journal of Medicine, 300,* 1233–1237.

Imperato-McGinley, J., Peterson, R. E., Stoller, R., & Goodwin, W. E. (1979). Male pseudohermaphroditism secondary to 17a-hydroxysteroid dehydrogenase deficiency: Gender role change with puberty. *Journal of Clinical Endocrinology and Metabolism, 49,* 391–395.

Imperato-McGinley, J., Pichardo, M., Gautier, T., Voyer, D., & Bryden, M. P. (1991). Cognitive abilities in androgen-insensitive subjects: Comparison with control males and females from the same kindred. *Clinical Endocrinology, 34,* 341–347.

Inda, M. C., Muravieva, E. V., & Alberini, C. M. (2011). Memory retrieval and the passage of time: From reconsolidation and strengthening to extinction. *Journal of Neuroscience, 31,* 1635–1643.

Ingalhalikar, M., Smith, A., Parker, D., Satterthwaite, T. D., Elliott, M. A., Ruparel, K., et al. (2014). Sex differences in the structural connectome of the human brain. *Proceedings of the National Academy of Sciences, 111,* 823–828.

Ingelfinger, F. J. (1944). The late effects of total and subtotal gastrectomy. *New England Journal of Medicine, 231,* 321–327.

Inouye, S.-I. T., & Kawamura, H. (1979). Persistence of circadian rhythmicity in a mammalian hypothalamic "island" containing the suprachiasmatic nucleus. *Proceedings of the National Academy of Sciences, 76,* 5962–5966.

Insel, T. (2015, May 15). Post by former NIMH director Thomas Insel: Mental Health Awareness Month: By the numbers. *National Institute of Mental Health.* Retrieved from https://www.nimh.nih.gov/about/directors/thomas-insel/blog/2015/mental-health-awareness-month-by-the-numbers.shtml

Insel, T. R. (1992). Toward a neuroanatomy of obsessive-compulsive disorder. *Archives of General Psychiatry, 49,* 739–744.

Insel, T. R., Zohar, J., Benkelfat, C., & Murphy, D. L. (1990). Serotonin in obsessions, compulsions, and the control of aggressive impulses. *Annals of the New York Academy of Sciences. Special Issue: The Neuropharmacology of Serotonin, 600,* 574–586.

Inta, D., Lima-Ojeda, J. M., Lau, T., Tang, W., Dormann, C., Sprengel, R., et al. (2013). Electroconvulsive therapy induces neurogenesis in frontal rat brain areas. *PLoS ONE, 8,* e69869. doi:10.1371/journal.pone.0069869

International Human Genome Sequencing Consortium. (2001). Initial sequencing and analysis of the human genome. *Nature, 409,* 860–921.

International Multiple Sclerosis Genetics Consortium. (2007). Risk alleles for multiple sclerosis identified by a genomewide study. *New England Journal of Medicine, 357,* 851–862.

Iossifov, I., Levy, D., Allen, J., Ye, K., Ronemus, M., Lee, Y., et al. (2015). Low load for disruptive mutations in autism genes and their biased transmission. *Proceedings of the National Academy of Sciences,* E5600–E5607. doi:10.1073/pnas.1516376112

Iqbal, N., & van Praag, H. M. (1995). The role of serotonin in schizophrenia. *European Neuropsychopharmacology Supplement, 5,* 11–23.

Ishihara, K., & Sasa, M. (1999). Mechanism underlying the therapeutic effects of electroconvulsive therapy (ECT) on depression. *Japanese Journal of Pharmacology, 80,* 185–189.

Iurato, S. (1967). *Submicroscopic structure of the inner ear.* Oxford, UK: Pergamon Press.

Iwamura, Y., Iriki, A., & Tanaka, M. (1994). Bilateral hand representation in the post-central somatosensory cortex. *Nature, 369,* 554–556.

Iwata, K. (1972). *A review of the literature on drunken syndromes due to yeasts in the gastrointestinal tract* (pp. 260–268). Tokyo: University of Tokyo Press.

Jackson, P. L., Meltzoff, A. N., & Decety, J. (2005). How do we perceive the pain of others? A window into the neural processes involved in empathy. *NeuroImage, 24,* 771–779.

Jacobs, B. L. (1987). How hallucinogenic drugs work. *American Scientist, 75,* 386–392.

Jacobs, B.L., van Praag, H., & Gage, F. H. (2000). Adult brain neurogenesis and psychiatry: A novel theory of depression. *Molecular Psychiatry, 5,* 262–269.

Jacobsen, J. H. W., Hutchinson, M. R., & Mustafa, S. (2016). Drug addiction: Targeting dynamic neuroimmune receptor interactions as a potential therapeutic strategy. *Current Opinion in Pharmacology, 26,* 131–137.

Jacquemont, S., Coe, B. P., Hersch, M., Duyzend, M. H., Krumm, N., Bergmann, S., et al. (2014). A higher mutational burden in females supports a "female protective model" in neurodevelopmental disorders. *American Journal of Human Genetics, 94,* 415–425.

Jaeggi, S. M., Buschkuehl, M., Jonides, J., & Shah, P. (2011). Short- and long-term benefits of cognitive training. *Proceedings of the National Academy of Sciences, 108,* 10081–10086.

Jain, M., Vélez, J. L., Acosta, M. T., Palacio, L. G., Balog, J., Roessler, E., et al. (2012). A cooperative interaction between *LPHN3* and 11q doubles the risk for ADHD. *Molecular Psychiatry, 17,* 741–747.

James, W. (1893). *Psychology.* New York: Henry Holt.

Janowsky, J. S., Oviatt, S. K., & Orwoll, E. S. (1994). Testosterone influences spatial cognition in older men. *Behavioral Neuroscience, 108,* 325–332.

Janszky, I., & Ljung, R. (2008). Shifts to and from daylight saving time and incidence of myocardial infarction. *New England Journal of Medicine, 359,* 1966–1968.

Jaretzki, A., III, Penn, A. S., Younger, D. S., Wolff, M., Olarte, M. R., Lovelace, R. E., et al. (1988). "Maximal" thymectomy for myasthenia gravis: Results. *Journal of Thoracic and Cardiovascular Surgery, 95,* 747–757.

Jarskog, L. F., Glantz, L. A., Gilmore, J. H., & Lieberman, J. A. (2005). Apoptotic mechanisms in the pathophysiology of schizophrenia. *Progress in Neuro-Psychopharmacology and Biological Psychiatry, 29,* 846–858.

Jeffords, J. M., & Daschle, T. (2001). Political issues in the genome era. *Science, 291,* 1249–1251.

Jeffress, L. A. (1948). A place theory of sound localization. *Journal of Comparative and Physiological Psychology, 41*(1), 35.

Jeffrey, S. (2010, January 22). FDA approves dalfampridine to improve walking in multiple sclerosis. *Medscape Medical News.* Retrieved from www.medscape.com/viewarticle/715722

Jensen, A. R. (1969). How much can we boost IQ and scholastic achievement? *Harvard Educational Review, 39,* 1–123.

Jensen, A. R. (1981). Raising the IQ: The Ramey and Haskins study. *Intelligence, 5,* 29–40.

Jensen, A. R. (1998). *The g factor.* Westport, CT: Praeger.

Jensen, T. S., Genefke, I. K., Hyldebrandt, N., Pedersen, H., Petersen, H. D., & Weile, B. (1982). Cerebral atrophy in young torture victims. *New England Journal of Medicine, 307,* 1341.

Jentsch, J. D., & Roth, R. H. (1999). The neuropsychopharmacology of phencyclidine: From NMDA receptor hypofunction to the dopamine hypothesis of schizophrenia. *Neuropsychopharmacology, 20,* 201–225.

Jin, K., Peel, A. L., Mao, X. O., Xie, L., Cottrell, B. A., Henshall, D. C., et al. (2004). Increased hippocampal neurogenesis in Alzheimer's disease. *Proceedings of the National Academy of Sciences, 101,* 343–347.

Joehanes, R., Just, A. C., Marioni, R. E., Pilling, L. C., Reynolds, L. M., Mandaviya, P. R., et al. (2016). Epigenetic signatures of cigarette smoking. *Circulation: Cardiovascular Genetics.* doi:10..1161//CIIRCGEENEETIICSS..116..001506

John, E. R. (2005). From synchronous neuronal discharges to subjective awareness? In S. Laureys (Ed.), *The boundaries of consciousness: Neurobiology and neuropathology* (pp. 143–171). New York: Elsevier.

Johnson, A., & Redish, A. D. (2007). Neural ensembles in CA3 transiently encode paths forward of the animal at a decision point. *Journal of Neuroscience, 27,* 12176–12189.

Johnson, C., Drgon, T., McMahon, F. J., & Uhl, G. R. (2009). Convergent genome wide association results for bipolar disorder and substance dependence. *American Journal of Medical Genetics, 150B,* 182–190.

Johnson, J. S., & Newport, E. L. (1989). Critical period effects in second language learning: The influence of maturational state on the acquisition of English as a second language. *Cognitive Psychology, 21,* 60–99.

Johnstone, T., Somerville, L. H., Alexander, A. L., Oakes, T. R., Davidson, R. J., Kalin, N. H., et al. (2005). Stability of amygdala BOLD response to fearful faces over multiple scan sessions. *NeuroImage, 25,* 1112–1123.

Jolles, D. D., van Buchem, M. A., Crone, E. A., & Rombouts, S. A. R. B. (2013). Functional brain connectivity at rest changes after working memory training. *Human Brain Mapping, 34,* 396–406.

Jones, H. M., & Pilowsky, L. S. (2002). Dopamine and antipsychotic drug action revisited. *British Journal of Psychiatry, 181,* 271–275.

Jones, J. G., Tansey, E. M., & Stuart, D. G. (2011). Thomas Graham Brown (1882–1965): Behind the scenes at the Cardiff Institute of Physiology. *Journal of the History of the Neurosciences, 20,* 188–209.

Jones, L. B., Stanwood, G. D., Reinoso, B. S., Washington, R. A., Wang, H.-Y., Friedman, E., et al. (2000). *In utero* cocaine-induced dysfunction of dopamine D1 receptor signaling and abnormal differentiation of cerebral cortical neurons. *Journal of Neuroscience, 20,* 4606–4614.

Jones, S., & Bonci, A. (2005). Synaptic plasticity and drug addiction. *Current Opinion in Pharmacology, 5,* 20–25.

Joseph, A. (2016, February 1). UK government agency approves editing genes in human embryos. *STAT.* Retrieved from https://www.statnews.com/2016/02/01/uk-gene-editing-embryos/

Joubert, B. R., Felix, J. F., Yousefi, P., Bakulski, K. M., Just, A. C., Breton, C., et al. (2016). DNA methylation in newborns and maternal smoking in pregnancy: Genome-wide consortium meta-analysis. *American Journal of Human Genetics, 98,* 680–696.

Judge, T. A., Ilies, R., & Zhang, Z. (2012). Genetic influences on core self-evaluations, job satisfaction, and work stress: A behavioral genetics mediated model. *Organizational Behavior and Human Decision Processes, 117,* 208–220.

Julien, R. M. (2008). *A primer of drug action* (11th ed.). New York: Worth.

Julius, D., & Basbaum, A. I. (2001). Molecular mechanisms of nociception. *Nature, 413,* 203–210.

Jung, R. (1974). Neuropsychologie und der Neurophysiologie des Kontur und Formsehens in Zeichnung und Malerei [Neuropsychology and neurophysiology of form vision in design and painting]. In H. H. Wieck (Ed.), *Psychopathologie musicher Gestaltungen* (pp. 29–88). Stuttgart, Germany: Schattauer.

Jung, R. E., & Haier, R. J. (2007). The Parieto-Frontal Integration Theory (P-FIT) of intelligence: Converging neuroimaging evidence. *Behavioral and Brain Sciences, 30,* 135–187.

Kahn, M. C., Hough, G. E., Ten Eyck, G., & Bingman, V. P. (2003). Internal connectivity of the homing pigeon (*Columba livia*) hippocampal formation: An anterograde and retrograde tracer study. *Journal of Comparative Neurology, 459,* 1227–1241.

Kaiser, J. (2012, August 24). U.S. appeals court upholds legality of stem cell research. *ScienceInsider.* Retrieved from http://news.sciencemag.org/scienceinsider/2012/08/us-appeals-court-upholds-legalit.html

Kaiser, J. (2016, May 6). Gene therapy halts rare brain disease in young boys. *ScienceInsider.* Retrieved from http://www.sciencemag.org/news/2016/05/gene-therapy-halts-rare-brain-disease-young-boys

Kaiser, T. S., Neumann, D., & Heckel, D. G. (2011). Timing the tides: Genetic control of diurnal and lunar emergence times is correlated in the marine midge *Clunio marinus. BMC Genetics, 12.* doi:10.1186/1471-2156-12-49

Kales, A., Scharf, M. B., Kales, J. D., & Soldatos, C. R. (1979). Rebound insomnia: A potential hazard following withdrawal of certain benzodiazepines. *Journal of the American Medical Association, 241,* 1692–1695.

Kamegai, J., Tamura, H., Shimizu, T., Ishii, S., Sugihara, H., & Wakabayashi, I. (2001). Chronic central infusion of ghrelin increases hypothalamic neuropeptide Y and agouti-related protein mRNA levels and body weight in rats. *Diabetes, 50,* 2438–2443.

Kanbayashi, T., Inoue, Y., Chiba, S., Aizawa, R., Saito, Y., Tsukamoto, H., et al. (2002). CSF hypocretin-1 (orexin-A) concentrations in narcolepsy with and without cataplexy and idiopathic hypersomnia. *Journal of Sleep Research, 11,* 91–93.

Kandel, E. R., & O'Dell, T. J. (1992). Are adult learning mechanisms also used for development? *Science, 258,* 243–245.

Kandel, E. R., & Siegelbaum, S. A. (2000a). Overview of synaptic transmission. In E. R. Kandel, J. H. Schwartz, & T. M. Jessell (Eds.), *Principles of neural science* (4th ed., pp. 175–186). New York: McGraw-Hill.

Kandel, E. R., & Siegelbaum, S. A. (2000b). Synaptic integration. In E. R. Kandel, J. H. Schwartz, & T. M. Jessell (Eds.), *Principles of neural science* (4th ed., pp. 207–228). New York: McGraw-Hill.

Kane, J. M. (1987). Treatment of schizophrenia. *Schizophrenia Bulletin, 13,* 133–156.

Kane, J. M., & Mertz, J. E. (2012). Debunking myths about gender and mathematics performance. *Notices of the AMS, 59,* 10–21.

Kanigel, R. (1988, October/November). Nicotine becomes addictive. *Science Illustrated,* 12–14, 19–21.

Kaplan, R., Adhikari, M. H., Hindriks, R., Mantini, D., Murayama, Y., Logothetis, N. K., & Deco, G. (2016). Hippocampal sharp-wave ripples influence selective activation of the default mode network. *Current Biology, 26,* 686–691.

Kapur, S., Zipursky, R. B., & Remington, G. (1999). Clinical and theoretical implications of 5-HT2 and D2 receptor occupancy of clozapine, risperidone, and olanzapine in schizophrenia. *American Journal of Psychiatry, 156,* 286–293.

Karg, K., Burmeister, M., Shedden, K., & Sen, S. (2011). The serotonin transporter promoter variant (5-HTTLPR), stress, and depression meta-analysis revisited: Evidence of genetic moderation. *Archives of General Psychiatry, 68*(5), 444–454.

Karnath, H.-O., & Baier, B. (2010). Right insula for our sense of limb ownership and self-awareness of actions. *Brain Structure and Function, 214,* 411–417.

Karni, A., Tanne, D., Rubenstein, B. S., Askenasy, J. J. M., & Sagi, D. (1994). Dependence on REM sleep of overnight improvement of a perceptual skill. *Science, 265,* 679–682.

Kasprian, G., Langs, G., Brugger, P. C., Bittner, M., Weber, M., Arantes, M., & Prayer, D. (2010). The prenatal origin of hemispheric asymmetry: An in utero neuroimaging study. *Cerebral Cortex, 21,* 1076–1083.

Kast, B. (2001). Decisions, decisions . . . *Nature, 411,* 126–128.

Katan, M., Moon, Y. P., Paik, M. C., Sacco, R. L., Wright, C. B., & Elkind, M. S. V. (2013). Infectious burden and cognitive function: The Northern Manhattan Study. *Neurology, 80,* 1209–1215.

Katz, J. (2016). *Speaking American: How y'all, youse, and you guys talk: A visual guide.* New York: Houghton Mifflin Harcourt.

Kaufman, J., & Charney, D. (2000). Comorbidity of mood and anxiety disorders. *Depression and Anxiety, 12*(Suppl. 1), 69–76.

Kausler, D. H. (1985). Episodic memory: Memorizing performance. In N. Charness (Ed.), *Aging and human performance* (pp. 101–139). New York: Wiley.

Kawai, N., & Matsuzawa, T. (2000). Numerical memory span in a chimpanzee. *Nature, 403,* 39–40.

Kaye, W., Gendall, K., & Strober, M. (1998). Serotonin neuronal function and selective serotonin reuptake inhibitor treatment in anorexia and bulimia nervosa. *Biological Psychiatry, 44,* 825–838.

Kaye, W. H., Berrettini, W., Gwirtsman, H., & George, D. T. (1990). Altered cerebrospinal fluid neuropeptide Y and peptide YY immunoreactivity in anorexia and bulimia nervosa. *Archives of General Psychiatry, 47,* 548–556.

Kaye, W. H., Fudge, J. L., & Paulus, M. (2009). New insights into symptoms and neurocircuit function of anorexia nervosa. *Nature Reviews of Neuroscience, 10,* 573–584.

Kayman, S., Bruvold, W., & Stern, J. S. (1990). Maintenance and relapse after weight loss in women: Behavioral aspects. *American Journal of Clinical Nutrition, 52,* 800–807.

Keele, S. W., & Ivry, R. (1990). Does the cerebellum provide a common computation for diverse tasks? A timing hypothesis. *Annals of the New York Academy of Sciences, 608,* 179–207.

Keenan, P. A., Ezzat, W. H., Ginsburg, K., & Moore, G. J. (2001). Prefrontal cortex as the site of estrogen's effect on cognition. *Psychoneuroendocrinology, 26,* 577–590.

Keesey, R. E., & Powley, T. L. (1986). The regulation of body weight. *Annual Review of Psychology, 37,* 109–133.

Kelleher, R. J., III, Govindarajan, A., & Tonegawa, S. (2004). Translational regulatory mechanisms in persistent forms of synaptic plasticity. *Neuron, 44,* 59–73.

Keller, K., & Menon, V. (2009). Gender differences in the functional and structural neuroanatomy of mathematical cognition. *Neuroimage, 47,* 342–352.

Kellner, C. H., Tobias, K. G., & Wiegand, J. (2010). Electrode placement in electroconvulsive therapy (ECT): A review of the literature. *Journal of ECT, 26,* 175–180.

Kellogg, W. N. (1968). Communication and language in the home-raised chimpanzee. *Science, 162,* 423–427.

Kelsey, J. E., Carlezon, W. A., Jr., & Falls, W. A. (1989). Lesions of the nucleus accumbens in rats reduce opiate reward but do not alter context-specific opiate tolerance. *Behavioral Neuroscience, 103,* 1327–1334.

Keltner, N. L., & Grant, J. S. (2006). Smoke, smoke, smoke that cigarette. *Biological Perspectives, 42,* 256–261.

Kendler, K. S., Gatz, M., Gardner, C. O., & Pedersen, N. L. (2006). A Swedish national twin study of lifetime major depression. *American Journal of Psychiatry, 163,* 109–114.

Kendler, K. S., MacLean, C., Neale, M., Kessler, R., Heath, A., & Eaves, L. (1991). The genetic epidemiology of bulimia nervosa. *American Journal of Psychiatry, 148,* 1627–1637.

Kendler, K. S., & Robinette, C. D. (1983). Schizophrenia in the National Academy of Sciences–National Research Council twin registry: A 16-year update. *American Journal of Psychiatry, 140,* 1551–1563.

Kennaway, D. J., & van Dorp, C. F. (1991). Free-running rhythms of melatonin, cortisol, electrolytes, and sleep in humans in Antarctica. *American Journal of Physiology, 260,* R1137–R1144.

Kennedy, B. K., Steffen, K. K., & Kaeberlein, M. (2007). Ruminations on dietary restriction and aging. *Cellular and Molecular Life Sciences, 64,* 1323–1328.

Kennerknecht, I., Grueter, T., Welling, B., Wentzek, S., Horst, J., Edwards, S., et al. (2006). First report of prevalence of non-syndromic hereditary prosopagnosia (HPA). *American Journal of Medical Genetics Part A, 140A,* 1617–1622.

Keown, C. L., Shih, P., Nair, A., Peterson, N., Mulvey, M. E., & Müller, R.-A. (2013). Local functional overconnectivity in posterior brain regions is associated with symptom severity in autism spectrum disorders. *Cell Reports, 5,* 1–6.

Kern, U., Busch, V., Rockland, M., Kohl, M., & Birklein, F. (2009). Prevalence and risk factors of phantom limb pain and phantom limb sensations in Germany: A nationwide field survey. *Schmerz, 23,* 479–488.

Kessler, R. C., Berglund, P., Demler, O., Jin, R., Merikangas, K. R., & Walters, E. E. (2005). Lifetime prevalence and age-of-onset distribution of DSM-IV disorders in the National Comorbidity Survey replication. *Archives of General Psychiatry, 62,* 593–602.

Kessler, R. C., Merikangas, K. R., & Wang, P. S. (2007). Prevalence, comorbidity, and service utilization for mood disorders in the United States at the beginning of the twenty-first century. *Annual Review of Clinical Psychiatry, 3,* 137–158.

Kessler, R. C., Petukhova, M., Sampson, N. A., Zaslavsky, A. M., & Wittchen, H.-U. (2012). Twelve-month and lifetime prevalence and lifetime morbid risk of anxiety and mood disorders in the United States. *International Journal of Methods in Psychiatric Research, 21,* 169–184.

Kessler, R. M., Hutson, P. H., Herman, B. K., & Potenza, M. N. (2016). The neurobiological basis of binge-eating disorder. *Neuroscience & Biobehavioral Reviews, 63,* 223–238.

Keverne, E. B. (1999). The vomeronasal organ. *Science, 286,* 716–720.

Khachaturian, Z. S. (1997, July/August). Plundered memories. *The Sciences,* 20–25.

Khalil, A. A., Davies, B., & Castagnoli, N., Jr. (2006). Isolation and characterization of a monoamine oxidase B selective inhibitor from tobacco smoke. *Bioorganic & Medicinal Chemistry, 14,* 3392–3398.

Khan, T. K., & Alkon, D. L. (2010). Early diagnostic accuracy and pathophysiologic relevance of an autopsy-confirmed Alzheimer's disease peripheral biomarker. *Neurobiology of Aging, 31,* 889–900.

Kiang, N. Y.-S. (1965). *Discharge patterns of single fibers in the cat's auditory nerve.* Cambridge, MA: MIT Press.

Kidd, B. L., & Urban, L. A. (2001). Mechanisms of inflammatory pain. *British Journal of Anaesthesiology, 87,* 3–11.

Kieseppä, T., Partonen, T., Haukka, J., Kaprio, J., & Lönnqvist, J. (2004). High concordance of bipolar I disorder in a nationwide sample of twins. *American Journal of Psychiatry, 161,* 1814–1821.

Kigar, D. L., Witelson, S. F., Glezer, I. I., & Harvey, T. (1997). Estimates of cell number in temporal neocortex in the brain of Albert Einstein. *Society for Neuroscience Abstracts, 23,* 213.

Killin, L. O. J., Starr, J. M., Shiue, I. J., & Russ, T. C. (2016). Environmental risk factors for dementia: A systematic review. *BMC Geriatrics, 16,* 175. doi:10.1186/s12877-016-0342-y

Kim, J. Y., Duan, X., Liu, C. Y., Jang, M.-H., Guo, J. U., Pow-anpongkul, N., et al. (2009). DISC1 regulates new neuron development in the adult brain via modulation of AKT-mTOR signaling through KIAA1212. *Neuron, 63,* 761–773.

Kim, K. H. S., Relkin, N. R., Lee, K.-M., & Hirsch, J. (1997). Distinct cortical areas associated with native and second languages. *Nature, 388,* 171–174.

Kimura, D., & Hampson, E. (1994). Cognitive pattern in men and women is influenced by fluctuations in sex hormones. *Current Directions in Psychological Science, 3,* 57–62.

King, F. A., Yarbrough, C. J., Anderson, D. C., Gordon, T. P., & Gould, K. G. (1988). Primates. *Science, 240,* 1475–1482.

King, J.-R., Sitt, J. D., Faugeras, F., Rohaut, B., El Karoui, I., Cohen, L., et al. (2013). Information sharing in the brain indexes consciousness in noncommunicative patients. *Current Biology, 23,* 1914–1919.

King, M.-C., & Wilson, A. C. (1975). Evolution at two levels in humans and chimpanzees. *Science, 188,* 107–116.

King, R. A., Leckman, J. F., Scahill, L. D., & Cohen, D. J. (1998). Obsessive-compulsive disorder, anxiety, and depression. In J. F. Leckman & D. J. Cohen (Eds.), *Tourette's syndrome tics, obsessions, compulsions: Developmental psychopathology and clinical care* (pp. 43–62). New York: Wiley.

Kinsey, A. C., Pomeroy, W. B., Martin, C. E., & Gebhard, P. H. (1953). *Sexual behavior in the human female.* Philadelphia: Saunders.

Kipman, A., Gorwood, P., Mouren-Simeoni, M. C., & Ad'es, J. (1999). Genetic factors in anorexia nervosa. *European Psychiatry, 14,* 189–198.

Kirk, K. M., Bailey, J. M., Dunne, M. P., & Martin, N. G. (2000). Measurement models for sexual orientation in a community twin sample. *Behavior Genetics, 30,* 345–356.

Kish, D. (2013, July 12). Experience: I taught myself to see. *The Guardian.* Retrieved from http://www.theguardian.com/lifeandstyle/2013/jul/13/experience-blindness-echolocation-daniel-kish

Kitamura, T., & Inokuchi, K. (2014). Role of adult neurogenesis in hippocampal-cortical memory consolidation. *Molecular Brain, 7,* 13. doi:10.1186/1756-6606-7-13

Klein, C., & Westenberger, A. (2012, January). Genetics of Parkinson's disease. *Cold Spring Harbor Perspectives in Medicine, 2,* a008888. Retrieved from http://www.ncbi.nlm.nih.gov/pmc/articles/PMC3253033/

Kleinman, J. C., Pierre, M. B., Jr., Madans, J. H., Land, G. H., & Schramm, W. F. (1988). The effects of maternal smoking on fetal and infant mortality. *American Journal of Epidemiology, 127,* 274–282.

Kline, P. (1991). *Intelligence: The psychometric view.* New York: Routledge.

Kloner, R. A., McDonald, S. A., Leeka, J., & Poole, W. K. (2011). Role of age, sex, and race on cardiac and total mortality associated with Super Bowl wins and losses. *Clinical Cardiology, 34,* 102–107.

Klump, K. L., Burt, A., McGue, M., & Iacono, W. G. (2007). Changes in genetic and environmental influences on disordered eating across adolescence. *Archives of General Psychiatry, 64,* 1409–1415.

Knafo, A., Iervolino, A. C., & Plomin, R. (2005). Masculine girls and feminine boys: Genetic and environmental contributions to atypical gender development in early childhood. *Journal of Personality and Social Psychology, 88,* 400–412.

Knecht, S., Dräger, B., Deppe, M., Bobe, L., Lohmann, H., Flöel, A., et al. (2000). Handedness and hemispheric language dominance in healthy humans. *Brain, 123,* 2512–2518.

Knowlton, B. J., Mangels, J. A., & Squire, L. R. (1996). A neostriatal habit learning system in humans. *Science, 273,* 1399–1402.

Koch, K., McLean, J., Segev, R., Freed, M. A., Berry, M. J., II, Balasubramanian, V., & Sterling, P. (2006). How much the eye tells the brain. *Current Biology, 16,* 1428–1434.

Koch, M., Varela, L., Kim, J. G., Kim, J. D., Hernández-Nuño, F., Simonds, S. E., et al. (2015). Hypothalamic POMC neurons promote cannabinoid-induced feeding. *Nature, 519,* 45–50. doi:10.1038/nature14260

Koenig, R. (1999). European researchers grapple with animal rights. *Science, 284,* 1604–1606.

Koeppen, B. M., & Stanton, B. A. (2008). *Berne & Levy physiology* (6th ed.). Maryland Heights, MO: Mosby/Elsevier.

Koester, J., & Siegelbaum, S. A. (2000). Local signaling: Passive electrical properties of the neuron. In E. R. Kandel, J. H. Schwartz, & T. M. Jessell (Eds.), *Principles of neural science* (4th ed., pp. 140–149). New York: McGraw-Hill.

Kojima, S., Nakahara, T., Nagai, N., Muranaga, T., Tanaka, M., Yasuhara, D., et al. (2005). Altered ghrelin and peptide YY responses to meals in bulimia nervosa. *Clinical Endocrinology, 62,* 74–78.

Komada, Y., Takaesu, Y., Matsui, K., Nakamura, M., Nishida, S., Kanno, M., et al. (2016). Comparison of clinical features between primary and drug-induced sleep-related eating disorder. *Neuropsychiatric Disease and Treatment, 12,* 1275–1280.

Komisaruk, B. R., Beyer, C., & Whipple, B. (2008). Orgasm. *Psychologist, 21,* 100–103.

Komisaruk, B. R., & Steinman, J. L. (1987). Genital stimulation as a trigger for neuroendocrine and behavioral control of reproduction. *Annals of the New York Academy of Sciences, 474,* 64–75.

Komisaruk, B. R., Whipple, B., Crawford, A., Grimes, S., Liu, W.-C., Kalnin, A., & Mosier, K. (2004). Brain activation during vaginocervical self-stimulation and orgasm in women with complete spinal cord injury: fMRI evidence of mediation by the vagus nerves. *Brain Research, 1024,* 77–88.

Kong, L.-C., Tap, J., Aron-Wisnewsky, J., Pelloux, V., Basdevant, A., Bouillot, J.-L., et al. (2013). Gut microbiota after gastric bypass in human obesity: Increased richness and associations of bacterial genera with adipose tissue genes. *American Journal of Clinical Nutrition, 98,* 16–24.

Koob, G. F., & Bloom, F. E. (1988). Cellular and molecular mechanisms of drug dependence. *Science, 242,* 715–723.

Kopelman, M. D. (1995). The Korsakoff syndrome. *British Journal of Psychiatry, 166,* 154–173.

Kordasiewicz, H. B., Stanek, L. M., Wancewicz, E. V., Mazur, C., McAlonis, M. M., Pytel, K. A., et al. (2012). Sustained therapeutic reversal of Huntington's disease by transient repression of huntingtin synthesis. *Neuron, 74,* 1031–1044.

Kosambi, D. D. (1967, February). Living prehistory in India. *Scientific American, 216,* 105–114.

Koscik, T., O'Leary, D., Moser, D. J., Andreasen, N. C., & Nopoulos, P. (2009). Sex differences in parietal lobe morphology: Relationship to mental rotation performance. *Brain and Cognition, 69,* 451–459.

Kosslyn, S. M., Ganis, G., & Thompson, W. L. (2001). Neural foundations of imagery. *Nature Reviews Neuroscience, 2,* 635–642.

Koubeissi, M. Z., Bartolomei, F., Beltagy, A., & Picard, F. (2014). Electrical stimulation of a small brain area reversibly disrupts consciousness. *Epilepsy & Behavior, 37,* 32–35.

Koulack, D., & Goodenough, D. R. (1976). Dream recall and dream recall failure: An arousal-retrieval model. *Psychological Bulletin, 83,* 975–984.

Koyama, T., Tanaka, Y., & Mikami, A. (1998). Nociceptive neurons in the macaque anterior cingulate activate during anticipation of pain. *NeuroReport, 9,* 2663–2667.

Kraemer, H. C., Becker, H. B., Brodie, H. K. H., Doering, C. H., Moos, R. H., & Hamburg, D. A. (1976). Orgasmic frequency and plasma testosterone levels in normal human males. *Archives of Sexual Behavior, 5,* 125–132.

Krakauer, J., & Ghez, C. (2000). Voluntary movement. In E. R. Kandel, J. H. Schwartz, & T. M. Jessell (Eds.), *Principles of neural science* (4th ed., pp. 756–781). New York: McGraw-Hill.

Krakowiak, P., Walker, C. K., Bremer, A. A., Baker, A. S., Ozonoff, S., Hansen, R. L., & Hertz-Picciotto, I. (2012). Maternal metabolic conditions and risk for autism and other neurodevelopmental disorders. *Pediatrics, 129,* 1–8.

Krause, J., Lalueza-Fox, C., Orlando, L., Enard, W., Green, R. E., Burbano, H. A., et al. (2007). The derived *FOXP2* variant of modern humans was shared with Neandertals. *Current Biology, 17,* 1908–1912.

Krause, K.-H., Dresel, S. H., Krause, J., Kung, H. F., & Tatsch, K. (2000). Increased striatal dopamine transporter in adult patients with attention-deficit/hyperactivity disorder: Effects of methylphenidate as measured by single photon emission computed tomography. *Neuroscience Letters, 285,* 107–110.

Kreiman, G., Koch, C., & Fried, I. (2000). Category-specific visual responses of single neurons in the human medial temporal lobe. *Nature Neuroscience, 3,* 946–953.

Kriegeskorte, N., Simmons, W. K., Bellgowan, P. S. F., & Baker, C. I. (2009). Circular analysis in systems neuroscience: The dangers of double dipping. *Nature Neuroscience, 12,* 535–540.

Kriegstein, K. V., & Giraud, A.-L. (2004). Distinct functional substrates along the right superior temporal sulcus for the processing of voices. *NeuroImage, 22,* 948–955.

Kripke, D. F., Garfinkel, L., Wingard, D. L., Klauber, M. R., & Marler, M. R. (2002). Mortality associated with sleep duration and insomnia. *Archives of General Psychiatry, 59,* 131–136.

Kripke, D. F., & Sonnenschein, D. (1973). A 90 minute daydream cycle [Abstract]. *Sleep Research, 70,* 187.

Kruijver, F. P. M., Zhou, J.-N., Pool, C. W., Hofman, M. A., Gooren, L. J. G., & Swaab, D. F. (2000). Male-to-female transsexuals have female neuron numbers in a limbic nucleus. *Journal of Clinical Endocrinology & Metabolism, 85,* 2034–2041.

Kuchinad, A., Schweinhardt, P., Seminowicz, D. A., Wood, P. B., Chizh, B. A., & Bushnell, M. C. (2007). Accelerated brain gray matter loss in fibromyalgia patients: Premature aging of the brain? *Journal of Neuroscience, 27,* 4004–4007.

Kudwa, A. E., Bodo, C., Gustafsson, J.-Å., & Rissman, E. F. (2005). A previously uncharacterized role for estrogen receptor: Defeminization of male brain and behavior. *Proceedings of the National Academy of Sciences, 102,* 4608–4612.

Kuepper, Y., Alexander, N., Osinsky, R., Mueller, E., Schmitz, A., Netter, P., et al. (2010). Aggression—interactions of serotonin and testosterone in healthy men and women. *Behavioural Brain Research, 206,* 93–100.

Kuffler, S. W. (1953). Discharge patterns and functional organization of mammalian retina. *Journal of Neurophysiology, 16,* 37–68.

Kumar, D., Kumar, V., Choi, S. H., Washicosky, K. J., Eimer, W. A., Tucker, S., et al. (2016). Amyloid-b peptide protects against microbial infection in mouse and worm models of Alzheimer's disease. *Science Translational Medicine, 8,* 340ra72. doi:10.1126/scitranslmed.aaf1059

Kumari, V., & Postma, P. (2005). Nicotine use in schizophrenia: The self-medication hypotheses. *Neuroscience and Biobehavioral Reviews, 29,* 1021–1034.

Kupfer, D. J. (1976). REM latency: A psychobiologic marker for primary depressive disease. *Biological Psychiatry, 11,* 159–174.

Kurihara, K., & Kashiwayanagi, M. (1998). Introductory remarks on umami taste. *Annals of the New York Academy of Sciences, 855,* 393–397.

Kutner, M. (2017, April 26). The Aaron Hernandez suicide: A football brain injury link? *Newsweek.* Retrieved from http://www.newsweek.com/aaron-hernandez-prison-suicide-cte-brain-injury-589819

Kuukasjärvi, S., Eriksson, C. J. P., Koskela, E., Mappes, T., Nissinen, K., & Rantala, M. J. (2004). Attractiveness of women's body odors over the menstrual cycle: The role of oral contraceptives and receiver sex. *Behavioral Ecology, 15,* 579–584.

Lafee, S. (2009, November 30). H. M. recollected. *San Diego Union-Tribune.* Retrieved from http://www.signonsandiego.com/news/2009/nov/30/hm-recollected-famous-amnesic-launches-bold-new-br/

Lai, C. S. L., Fisher, S. E., Hurst, J. A., Vargha-Khadem, F., & Monaco, A. P. (2001). A forkhead-domain gene is mutated in a severe speech and language disorder. *Nature, 413,* 519–523.

Lai, M.-C., Lombardo, M. V., Suckling, J., Rulgrok, A. N. V., Chakrabarti, B., Ecker, C., et al. (2013). Biological sex affects the neurobiology of autism. *Brain, 136,* 2799–2815.

Lam, P., Hong, C.-J., & Tsai. S.-J. (2005). Association study of A2a adenosine receptor genetic polymorhism in panic disorder. *Neuroscience Letters, 378,* 98–101.

LaMantia, A. S., & Rakic, P. (1990). Axon overproduction and elimination in the corpus callosum of the developing rhesus monkey. *Journal of Neuroscience, 10,* 2156–2175.

Lamb, T., & Yang, J. E. (2000). Could different directions of infant stepping be controlled by the same locomotor central pattern generator? *Journal of Neurophysiology, 83,* 2814–2824.

Lambe, E. K., Katzman, D. K., Mikulis, D. J., Kennedy, S. H., & Zipursky, R. B. (1997). Cerebral gray matter volume deficits after weight recovery from anorexia nervosa. *Archives of General Psychiatry, 54,* 537–542.

Lambert, J.-C., Ibrahim-Verbaas, C. A., Harold, D., Naj, A. C., Sims, R., Bellenguez, C., et al. (2013). Meta-analysis of 74,046 individuals identifies 11 new susceptibility loci for Alzheimer's disease. *Nature Genetics, 45,* 1452–1458.

LaMotte, S. (2015, December 31). Woman claims her body brews alcohol, has DUI charge dismissed. CNN. Retrieved from http://www.cnn.com/2015/12/31/health/auto-brewery-syndrome-dui-womans-body-brews-own-alcohol/

Lancaster, E. (1958). *The final face of Eve.* New York: McGraw-Hill.

Landry, D. W. (1997, February). Immunotherapy for cocaine addiction. *Scientific American, 276,* 42–45.

Landsness, E. C., Goldstein, M. R., Peterson, M. J., Tononi, G., & Benca, R. M. (2011). Antidepressant effects of selective slow wave sleep deprivation in major depression: A high-density EEG investigation. *Journal of Psychiatric Research, 45,* 1019–1026.

Langa, K. M. (2015). Is the risk of Alzheimer's disease and dementia declining? *Alzheimer's Research and Therapy, 7,* 34. doi:10.1186/s13195-015-0118-1

Langa, K. M., Larson, E. B., Crimmins, E. M., Faul, J. D., Levine, D. A., Kabeto, M. U., & Weir, D. R. (2017). A comparison of the prevalence of dementia in the United States in 2000 and 2012. *JAMA Internal Medicine, 177,* 51–58.

Lange, C., Deutschenbaur, L., Borgwardt, S., Lang, U. E., Walter, M., Huber, C. G., et al. (2017). Experimentally induced psychosocial stress in schizophrenia spectrum disorders: A systematic review. *Schizophrenia Research, 182,* 4–12.

Lange, C. G. (1885/2010). *Om Sindsbevaegelser.* Whitefish, MT: Kessinger.

Langer, N., Pedroni, A., Gianotti, L. R. R., Hänggi, J., Knoch, D., & Jäncke, L. (2012). Functional brain network efficiency predicts intelligence. *Human Brain Mapping, 33,* 1393–1406.

Langston, J. (2016, April 7). UW team stores digital images in DNA—and retrieves them perfectly. *UW Today.* Retrieved from http://www.washington.edu/news/2016/04/07/uw-team-stores-digital-images-in-dna-and-retrieves-them-perfectly/

Langström, N., Rahman, Q., Carlström, E., & Lichtenstein, P. (2010). Genetic and environmental effects on same-sex sexual behavior: A population study of twins in Sweden. *Archives of Sexual Behavior, 39,* 75–80.

Lanteaume, L., Khalfa, S., Régis, J., Marquis, P., Chauvel, P., & Bartolomei, F. (2007). Emotion induction after direct intracerebral stimulations of human amygdala. *Cerebral Cortex, 17,* 1307–1313.

Lapis, T. J., Penner, M. H., & Lim, J. (2016). Humans can taste glucose oligomers independent of the hT1R2/hT1R3 sweet taste receptor. *Chemical Senses.* doi:10.1093/chemse/bjw088

Laplane, D., Talairach, J., Meininger, V., Bancaud, J., & Orgogozo, J. M. (1977). Clinical consequences of corticectomies involving the supplementary motor area in man. *Journal of the Neurological Sciences, 34,* 301–314.

Larson, M. E., & Lesné, S. E. (2012). Soluble Aβ oligomer production and toxicity. *Journal of Neurochemistry, 120*(Suppl. 1), 125–139.

Lashley, K. (1929). *Brain mechanisms and intelligence: A quantitative study of injuries to the brain.* Chicago: University of Chicago Press.

Lau, B., Stanley, G. B., & Dan, Y. (2002). Computational subunits of visual cortical neurons revealed by artificial neural networks. *Proceedings of the National Academy of Sciences, 99,* 8974–8979.

Laureys, S. (2005). The neural correlate of (un)awareness: Lessons from the vegetative state. *Trends in Cognitive Sciences, 9,* 556–559.

Laureys, S., Owen, A. M., & Schiff, N. D. (2004). Brain function in coma, vegetative state, and related disorders. *Lancet Neurology, 3,* 537–546.

Lazarini, F., & Lledo, P.-M. (2011). Is adult neurogenesis essential for olfaction? *Trends in Neurosciences, 34,* 20–30.

Leavitt, I. (2016, November 10). Northbrook Cubs fan, 108, dies after team finally wins World Series. Fox News. Retrieved from http://www.foxnews.com/

us/2016/11/12/108-year-old-cubs-fan-dies-days-after-team-wins-world-series.html

Lecendreux, M., Bassetti, C., Dauvilliers, Y., Mayer, G., Neidhart, E., & Tafti, M. (2003). HLA and genetic susceptibility to sleepwalking. *Molecular Psychiatry, 8*, 114–117.

LeDoux, J. E. (1996). *The emotional brain.* New York: Simon & Schuster.

Lee, B. R., Ma, Y.-Y., Huang, Y. H., Wang, X., Otaka, M., Ishikawa, M., et al. (2013). Maturation of silent synapses in amygdala-accumbens projection contributes to incubation of cocaine craving. *Nature Neuroscience, 16*, 1644–1651.

Lee, D. S., Lee, J. S., Oh, S. H., Kim, S.-K., Kim, J.-W., Chung, J.-K., et al. (2001). Cross-modal plasticity and cochlear implants. *Nature, 409*, 149–150.

Lee, J. L. C. (2009). Reconsolidation: Maintaining memory relevance. *Trends in Neurosciences, 32*, 413–420.

Lee, K.-N., & Chirwa, S. (2015). Blocking dopaminergic signaling soon after learning impairs memory consolidation in guinea pigs. *PLOSone.* doi:10.1371/journal.pone.0135578

Lee, M., Zambreanu, L., Menon, D. K., & Tracey, I. (2008). Identifying brain activity specifically related to the maintenance and perceptual consequence of central sensitization in humans. *Journal of Neuroscience, 28*, 11642–11649.

Lee, S., Kim, K., & Zhou, Z. J. (2010). Role of ACh-GABA cotransmission in detecting image motion and motion direction. *Neuron, 68*, 1159–1172.

Lee, S.-Y., Kubicki, M., Asami, T., Seidman, L. J., Goldstein, J. M., Mesholam-Gately, R. I., et al. (2013). Extensive white matter abnormalities in patients with first-episode schizophrenia: A diffusion tensor imaging (DTI) study. *Schizophrenia Research, 143*, 231–238.

Lee, S. Y., Lee, A. R., Hwangbo, R., Han, J., Hong, M., & Bahn, G. H. (2015). Is oxy-tocin application for autism spectrum disorder evidence-based? *Experimental Neurobiology, 24*, 312–324.

Lefaucheur, J.-P., André-Obadia, N., Antal, A., Ayache, S. S., Baeken, C., & Benninger, D. H. (2014). Evidence-based guidelines on the therapeutic use of repetititve transcranial magnetic stimulation (rTMS). *Clinical Neurophysiology, 125*, 2150–2206.

Lehky, S. R., & Sejnowski, T. J. (1990). Neural network model of visual cortex for deter-mining surface curvature from images of shaded surfaces. *Proceedings of the Royal Society of London, B, 240*, 251–278.

Lehrman, S. (1999). Virus treatment questioned after gene therapy death. *Nature, 401*, 517–518.

Leibel, R. L., Rosenbaum, M., & Hirsch, J. (1995). Changes in energy expenditure resulting from altered body weight. *New England Journal of Medicine, 332*, 621–628.

Leibowitz, S. F., & Alexander, J. T. (1998). Hypothalamic serotonin in control of eating behavior, meal size, and body weight. *Biological Psychiatry, 44*, 851–864.

Leinenga, G., & Götz, J. (2015). Scanning ultrasound removes amyloid-β and restores memory in an Alzheimer's disease mouse model. *Science Translational Medicine, 7*(278), 278ra33. doi:10.1126/scitranslmed.aaa2512

Leinenga, G., Langton, C., Nisbet, R., & Götz, J. (2016) Ultrasound treatment of neurological diseases: Current and emerging applications. *Nature Reviews Neurology, 12*, 161–174.

Leland, J., & Miller, M. (1998, August 17). Can gays convert? *Newsweek*, 47–53.

Lenneberg, E. H. (1969). On explaining language. *Science, 164*, 635–643.

Lenzenweger, M. F., & Gottesman, I. I. (1994). Schizophrenia. In V. S. Ramachandran (Ed.), *Encyclopedia of human behavior.* San Diego, CA: Academic Press.

Leonard, H. L., Lenane, M. C., Swedo, S. E., Rettew, D. C., Gershon, E. S., & Rapoport, J. L. (1992). Tics and Tourette's disorder: A 2- to 7-year follow-up of 54 obsessive-compulsive children. *American Journal of Psychiatry, 149*, 1244–1251.

Leonard, H. L., Lenane, M. C., Swedo, S. E., Rettew, D. C., & Rapoport, J. L. (1991). A double-blind comparison of clomipramine and desipramine treatment of severe onychophagia (nail-biting). *Archives of General Psychiatry, 48*, 821–826.

Leopold, D. A., & Logothetis, N. K. (1996). Activity changes in early visual cortex reflect monkeys' percepts during binocular rivalry. *Nature, 379*, 549–553.

Leor, J., Poole, W. K., & Kloner, R. A. (1996). Sudden cardiac death triggered by an earthquake. *New England Journal of Medicine, 334*, 413–419.

LePort, A. K. R., Mattfeld, A. T., Dickinson-Anson, H., Fallon, J. H., Stark, C. E. L., Kruggel, F., et al. (2012). Behavioral and neuroanatomical investigation of highly superior autobiographical memory (HSAM). *Neurobiology of Learning and Memory, 98*, 78–92.

Leshner, A. I. (1997). Addiction is a brain disease, and it matters. *Science, 278*, 45–47.

Leucht, S., Corves, C., Arbter, D., Engel, R. R., Li, C., & Davis, J. M. (2009). Second-generation versus first-generation antipsychotic drugs for schizophrenia: A meta-analysis. *Lancet, 373*, 31–41.

LeVay, S. (1991). A difference in hypothalamic structure between heterosexual and homosexual men. *Science, 253*, 1034–1037.

LeVay, S. (1996). *Queer science: The use and abuse of research into homosexuality.* Cambridge, MA: MIT Press.

Levenson, R. W., Ekman, P., & Friesen, W. V. (1990). Voluntary facial action gener-ates emotion-specific autonomic nervous system activity. *Psychophysiology, 27*, 363–384.

Lévesque, M. F., Neuman, T., & Rezak, M. (2009). Therapeutic microinjection of autolo-gous adult human neural stem cells and differentiated neurons for Parkinson's disease: Five year post-operative outcome. *Open Stem Cell Journal, 1*, 20–29.

Levin, F. R., Evans, S. M., & Kleber, H. D. (1998). Methylphenidate treatment for cocaine abusers with adult attention-deficit/hyperactivity disorder: A pilot study. *Journal of Clinical Psychiatry, 59*, 300–305.

Levin, H. S., Culhane, K. A., Hartmann, J., Evankovich, K., Mattson, A. J., Harward, H., et al. (1991). Developmental changes in performance on tests of purported frontal lobe functioning. *Developmental Neuropsychology, 7*, 377–395.

Levin, N., Nelson, C., Gurney, A., Vandlen, R., & de Sauvage, F. (1996). Decreased food intake does not completely account for adiposity reduction after ob protein infusion. *Proceedings of the National Academy of Sciences, 93*, 1726–1730.

Levine, J. A., Eberhardt, N. L., & Jensen, M. D. (1999). Role of nonexercise activity ther-mogenesis in resistance to fat gain in humans. *Science, 283*, 212–214.

Levine, J. A., Lannigham-Foster, L. M., McCrady, S. K., Krizan, A. C., Olson, L. R., Kane, P. H., et al. (2005). Interindividual variation in posture allocation: possible role in human obesity. *Science, 307*, 584–586.

Levy, B. (1996). Improving memory in old age through implicit self-stereotyping. *Journal of Personality and Social Psychology, 71*, 1092–1107.

Levy, J. (1969). Possible basis for the evolution of lateral specialization of the human brain. *Nature, 224*, 614–615.

Levy, S., Sutton, G., Ng, P. C., Feuk, L., Halpern, A. L., Walenz, B. P., et al. (2007). The diploid genome sequence of an individual human. *PLoS Biology, 5*, article e254. Retrieved from www.plosbiology.org/article/info%3Adoi%2F10.1371%2Fjournal.pbio.0050254

Lewicki, P., Hill, T., & Czyzewska, M. (1992). Nonconscious acquisition of information. *American Psychologist, 47*, 796–801.

Lewin, R. (1980). Is your brain really necessary? *Science, 210*, 1232–1234.

Lewis, D. A., & Levitt, P. (2002). Schizophrenia as a disorder of neurodevelopment. *Annual Review of Neuroscience, 25*, 409–432.

Lewis, H. B., Goodenough, D. R., Shapiro, A., & Sleser, I. (1966). Individual differences in dream recall. *Journal of Abnormal Psychology, 71*, 52–59.

Lewis, J. W., Wightman, F. L., Brefczynski, J. A., Phinney, R. E., Binder, J. R., & DeYoc, E. A. (2004). Human brain regions involved in recognizing environmental sounds. *Cerebral Cortex, 14*, 1008–1021.

Lewis, M., & Brooks-Gunn, J. (1979). *Social cognition and the acquisition of self.* New York: Plenum Press.

Lewis, M. B., & Bowler, P. J. (2009). Botulinum toxin cosmetic therapy correlates with a more positive mood. *Journal of Cosmetic Dermatology, 8*, 24–26.

Lewis, P. D. (1985). Neuropathological effects of alcohol on the developing nervous sys-tem. *Alcohol and Alcoholism, 20*, 195–200.

Lewy, A. J., Sack, R. L., Miller, L. S., & Hoban, T. M. (1987). Antidepressant and circa-dian phase-shifting effects of light. *Science, 235*, 352–354.

Li, J. Z., Bunney, B. G., Meng, F., Hagenauer, M. H., Walsh, D. M., Vawter, M. P., et al. (2013). Circadian patterns of gene expression in the human brain and disruption in major depressive disorder. *Proceedings of the National Academy of Sciences, 110*, 9950–9955.

Li, S., Tian, J., Bauer, A., Huang, R., Wen, H., Li, M., et al. (2016). Reduced integrity of right lateralized white matter in patients with primary insomnia: A diffusion-tensor imaging study. *Radiology, 280*(2). doi:10.1148/radiol.2016152038

Li, Y., Liu, Y., Qin, W., Li, K., Yu, C., & Jiang, T. (2009). Brain anatomical network and intelligence. *PLoS Computational Biology, 5*, e1000395. Retrieved from http://www.ploscompbiol.org/article/info%3Adoi%2F10.1371%2Fjournal.pcbi.1000395

Li, Z., Chang, S., Zhang, L., Gao, L., & Wang, J. (2014). Molecular genetic studies of ADHD and its candidate genes: A review. *Psychiatry Research, 219*, 10–24.

Liang, P., Xu, Y., Zhang, X., Ding, C., Huang, R., Zhang, Z., et al. (2015). CRISPR/Cas9-mediated gene editing in human tripronuclear zygotes. *Protein Cell, 6*, 363–372.

Lichtman, S. W., Pisarska, K., Berman, E. R., Pestone, M., Dowling, H., Offenbacher, E., et al. (1992). Discrepancy between self-reported and actual caloric intake and exercise in obese subjects. *New England Journal of Medicine, 327*, 1893–1898.

Lieberman, H. R., Wurtman, J. J., & Chew, B. (1986). Changes in mood after carbo-hydrate consumption among obese individuals. *American Journal of Clinical Nutrition, 44*, 772–778.

Liechti, M. E., & Vollenweider, F. X. (2000). Acute psychological and physiological effects of MDMA ("ecstasy") after haloperidol pretreatment in healthy humans. *European Neuropsychopharmacology, 10*, 289–295.

Lim, A. S. P., Klein, H.-U., Yu, L., Chibnik, L. B., Ali, S., Xu, S., et al. (2017). Diurnal and seasonal molecular rhythms in human neocortex and their relation to Alzheimer's disease. *Nature Communications, 8*(14931), 1–16.

Lima, C., Pratas-Vital, J., Escada, P., Hasse-Ferreira, A., Capucho, C., & Peduzzi, J. D. (2006). Olfactory mucosa autografts in human spinal cord injury: A pilot clini-cal study. *Journal of Spinal Cord Medicine, 29*, 195–203.

Lin, L., Faraco, J., Li, R., Kadotani, H., Rogers, W., Lin, X., et al. (1999). The sleep dis-order canine narcolepsy is caused by a mutation in the hypocretin (orexin) receptor 2 gene. *Cell, 98*, 365–376.

Ling, V. J., Lester, D., Mortensen, P. B., Langenberg, P. W., & Postolache, T. T. (2011). Toxoplasma gondii seropositivity and suicide rates in women. *Journal of Nervous and Mental Disorders, 199*(7), 440–444. doi:10.1097/NMD.0b013e318221416e

Lipton, M. L., Kim, N., Zimmerman, M. E., Kim, M., Stewart, W. F., Branch, C. A., & Lipton, R. B. (2013). Soccer heading is associated with white matter microstructural and cognitive abnormalities. *Radiology, 268,* 850–857.

Lisman, J. E., Coyle, J. T., Green, R. W., Javitt, D. C., Benes, F. M., Heckers, S., & Grace, A. A. (2008). Circuit-based framework for understanding neurotransmitter and risk gene interactions in schizophrenia. *Trends in Neurosciences, 31,* 234–242.

Lisman, J., Grace, A. A., & Duzel, E. (2011). A neoHebbian framework for episodic memory: Role of dopamine-dependent late LTP. *Trends in Neurosciences, 34,* 536–547.

Lisman, J., & Morris, R. B. M. (2001). Why is the cortex a slow learner? *Nature, 411,* 248–249.

List of Countries by International Homicide Rate. (n.d.). In *Wikipedia.* Retrieved from http://en.wikipedia.org/wiki/List_of_countries_by_intentional_homicide_rate#cite_ref-geneva_5–0

Liu, J., Lee, H. J., Weitz, A. J., Fang, Z., Lin, P., Choy, M., et al. (2015). Frequency-selective control of cortical and subcortical networks by central thalamus. *eLife, 4,* e09215. doi:10.7554/eLife.09215

Liu, J., Yang, A. R., Kelly, T., Puche, A., Esoga, C., June, H. L., et al. (2012). Binge alcohol drinking is associated with GABA$_A$ α2-regulated toll-like receptor 4 (TLR4) expression in the central amygdala. *Proceedings of the National Academy of Sciences, 108,* 4465–4470.

Liu, Z., Li, S., Liang, Z., Zhao, Y., Zhang, Y., Yang, Y., et al. (2013). Targeting β-secretase with RNAi in neural stem cells for Alzheimer's disease therapy. *Neural Regeneration Research, 8,* 3095–3106.

Livingstone, D. (1971). *Missionary travels.* New York: Harper & Brothers. (Original work published 1858)

Livingstone, M., & Hubel, D. (1988). Segregation of form, color, movement, and depth: Anatomy, physiology, and perception. *Science, 240,* 740–749.

Livingstone, M. S., Rosen, G. D., Drislane, F. W., & Galaburda, A. M. (1991). Physiological and anatomical evidence for a magnocellular defect in developmental dyslexia. *Proceedings of the National Academy of Sciences, 88,* 7943–7947.

Locurto, C. (1991). *Sense and nonsense about IQ: The case for uniqueness.* New York: Praeger.

Loehlin, J. C., & Nichols, R. C. (1976). *Heredity, environment and personality: A study of 850 twins.* Austin: University of Texas Press.

Loewi, O. (1953). *From the workshop of discoveries.* Lawrence: University of Kansas Press.

Loftus, E. F. (1997, September). Creating false memories. *Scientific American, 277,* 70–75.

Logan, B. K., & Jones, A. W. (2000). Endogenous ethanol "auto-brewery syndrome" as a drunk-driving defence challenge. *Medicine, Science and the Law, 40,* 206–215.

Logothetis, N. K. (2002). The neural basis of the blood-oxygen-level-dependent functional magnetic resonance imaging signal. *Philosophical Transactions of the Royal Society B, 357,* 1003–1037.

Lomber, S. G., Meredith, M. A., & Kral, A. (2010). Cross-modal plasticity in specific auditory cortices underlies visual compensations in the deaf. *Nature Neuroscience, 13,* 1421–1427.

London, E. D., Cascella, N. G., Wong, D. F., Phillips, R. L., Dannals, R. F., Links, J. M., et al. (1990). Cocaine-induced reduction of glucose utilization in human brain. *Archives of General Psychiatry, 47,* 567–574.

Loos, R. J. F., Lindgren, C. M., Li, S., Wheeler, E., Zhao, J. H., Prokopenko, I., et al. (2008). Common variants near *MC4R* are associated with fat mass, weight and risk of obesity. *Nature Genetics, 40,* 768–775.

Lott, I. T. (1982). Down's syndrome, aging, and Alzheimer's disease: A clinical review. *Annals of the New York Academy of Sciences, 396,* 15–27.

Lotze, M., Grodd, W., Birbaumer, N., Erb, M., Huse, E., & Flor, H. (1999). Does use of a myoelectric prosthesis prevent cortical reorganization and phantom limb pain? *Nature Neuroscience, 2,* 501–502.

Lou, H. C., Changeux, J. P., & Rosenstand, A. (2016). Towards a cognitive neuroscience of self-awareness. *Neuroscience and Biobehavioral Reviews,* pii: S0149-7634(16)30041-0. doi:10.1016/j.neubiorev.2016.04.004

Lou, H. C., Luber, B., Stanford, A., & Lisanby, S. H. (2010). Self-specific processing in the default network: A single-pulse TMS study. *Experimental Brain Research, 207,* 27–38.

Louie, K., & Wilson, M. A. (2001). Temporally structured replay of awake hippocampal ensemble activity during rapid eye movement sleep. *Neuron, 29,* 145–156.

Lowenstein, R. J., & Putnam, F. W. (1990). The clinical phenomenology of males with MPD: A report of 21 cases. *Dissociation, 3,* 135–143.

Lowing, P. A., Mirsky, A. F., & Pereira, R. (1983). The inheritance of schizophrenia spectrum disorders: A reanalysis of the Danish adoptee study data. *American Journal of Psychiatry, 140,* 1167–1171.

Loy, B., Warner-Cyz, A. D., Tong, L., Tobey, E. A., & Roland, P. S. (2010). The children speak: An examination of the quality of life of pediatric cochlear implant users. *Otolaryngology—Head and Neck Surgery, 142,* 247–253.

Loyd, D. R., Wang, X., & Murphy, A. Z. (2008). Sex differences in μ-opioid receptor expression in the rat midbrain periaqueductal gray are essential for eliciting sex differences in morphine analgesia. *Journal of Neuroscience, 28,* 14007–14017.

Lu, T., Pan, Y., Kao, S.-Y., Li, C., Kohane, I., Chan, J., et al. (2004). Gene regulation and DNA damage in the ageing human brain. *Nature, 429,* 883–891.

Luber, B., Lou, H. C., Keenan, J. P., & Lisanby, S. H. (2012). Self-enhancement processing in the default network: A single-pulse TMS study. *Experimental Brain Research, 223,* 177–187.

Lucas, R. J., Freedman, M. S., Muñoz, M., Garcia-Fernández, J.-M., & Foster, R. G. (1999). Regulation of the mammalian pineal by non-rod, non-cone, ocular photoreceptors. *Science, 284,* 505–507.

Luciano, M., Wright, M., Smith, G. A., Geffen, G. M., Geffen, L. B., & Martin, N. G. (2001). Genetic covariance among measures of information processing speed, working memory, and IQ. *Behavior Genetics, 31,* 581–592.

Lupien, S. J., de Leon, M., de Santi, S., Convit, A., Tarshish, C., Thakur, M., et al. (1998). Cortisol levels during human aging predict hippocampal atrophy and memory deficits. *Nature Neuroscience, 1,* 69–73.

Lüscher, C. (2016). The emergence of a circuit model for addiction. *Annual Review of Neuroscience, 39,* 257–276.

Lüscher, C., & Malenka, R. C. (2012). NMDA receptor-dependent long-term potentiation and long-term depression (LTP/LTD). *Cold Springs Harbor Perspectives in Biology, 4,* (6). p ii: a005710. doi:10.1101/cshperspect.a005710

Ly, D. H., Lockhart, D. J., Lerner, R. A., & Schultz, P. G. (2000). Mitotic misregulation and human aging. *Science, 287,* 2486–2492.

Lynall, R. C., Clark, M. D., Grand, E. E., Stucker, J. C., Littleton, A. C., Aguilar, A. J., Petschauer, M. A., Teel, E. F., & Mihalik, J. P. (2016). Head impact biomechanics in women's college soccer. *Medicine & Science in Sports & Exercise.* Published online ahead of print. Retrieved from http://journals.lww.com/acsm-msse/Abstract/publishahead/Head_Impact_Biomechanics_in_Women_s_College.97509.aspx

Lyons, S. (2001, May 20). A will to eat, a fight for life. *San Luis Obispo Tribune,* p. A1.

Ma, Y.-Y., Lee, B. R., Wang, X., Guo, C., Liu, L., Cui, R., et al. (2014). Bidirectional modulation of incubation of cocaine craving by silent synapse-based remodeling of prefrontal cortex to accumbens projections. *Neuron, 83,* 1453–1467.

Maas, L. C., Lukas, S. E., Kaufman, M. J., Weiss, R. D., Daniels, S. L., Rogers, V. W., et al. (1998). Functional magnetic resonance imaging of human brain activation during cue-induced cocaine craving. *American Journal of Psychiatry, 155,* 124–126.

Maccoby, E. E., & Jacklin, C. N. (1974). *The psychology of sex differences.* Stanford, CA: Stanford University Press.

Mackey, A. P., Singley, A. T., & Bunge, S. A. (2013). Intensive reasoning training alters patterns of brain connectivity at rest. *Journal of Neuroscience, 33,* 4796–4803.

MacNeilage, P. F. (1998). The frame/content theory of evolution of speech production. *Behavioral and Brain Sciences, 21,* 499–511.

Macrae, J. R., Scoles, M. T., & Siegel, S. (1987). The contribution of Pavlovian conditioning to drug tolerance and dependence. *British Journal of Addiction, 82,* 371–380.

Macur, J. (2012, June 25). Sex-verification policy is criticized as a failure. *New York Times.* Retrieved from http://www.nytimes.com/2012/06/26/sports/olympics/critics-say-olympic-sex-verification-policy-is-a-failure.html?ref=castersemenya

Maddison, D., & Viola, A. (1968). The health of widows in the year following bereavement. *Journal of Psychosomatic Research, 12,* 297–306.

Maeder, P. P., Meuli, R. A., Adriani, M., Bellmann, A., Fornari, E., Thiran, J.-P., et al. (2001). Distinct pathways involved in sound recognition and localization: A human fMRI study. *NeuroImage, 14,* 802–816.

Maes, H. H. M., Neale, M. C., & Eaves, L. J. (1997). Genetic and environmental factors in relative body weight and human adiposity. *Behavior Genetics, 27,* 325–351.

Maffei, M., Halaas, J., Ravussin, E., Pratley, R. E., Lee, G. H., Zhang, Y., et al. (1995). Leptin levels in human and rodent: Measurement of plasma leptin and ob RNA in obese and weight-reduced subjects. *Nature Medicine, 1,* 1155–1161.

Magalhães, J. P., Wuttke, D., Wood, S. H., Plank, M., & Vora, C. (2011). Genome-environment interactions that modulate aging: Powerful targets for drug discovery. *Pharmacological Reviews, 64,* 88–101.

Magistretti, P. J., Pellerin, L., Rothman, D. L., & Shulman, R. G. (1999). Energy on demand. *Science, 283,* 496–497.

Maguire, E. A., Gadian, D. G., Johnsrude, I. S., Good, C. D., Ashburner, J., Frackowiak, R. S. J., et al. (2000). Navigation-related structural change in the hippocampi of taxi drivers. *Proceedings of the National Academy of Sciences, 97,* 4398–4403.

Maher, B. (2012, September 5). ENCODE: The human encyclopedia. *Nature.* Retrieved from http://www.nature.com/news/encode-the-human-encyclopaedia-1.11312

Maheshwari, P., & Eslick, G. D. (2015). Bacterial infection and Alzheimer's disease: A meta-analysis. *Journal of Alzheimer's Disease, 43,* 957–966.

Maheu, M. E., Devorak, J., Freibauer, A., Davoli, M. A., Turecki, G., & Mechawar, N. (2015). Increased doublecortin (DCX) expression and incidence of DCX-immunoreactive multipolar cells in the subventricular zone–olfactory bulb system of suicides. *Frontiers in Neuroanatomy, 9,* Article 74. Retrieved from http://journal.frontiersin.org/article/10.3389/fnana.2015.00074/full

Maier, M. A., Bennett, K. M., Hepp-Reymond, M. C., & Lemon, R. N. (1993). Contribution of the monkey corticomotoneuronal system to the control of force in precision grip. *Journal of Neurophysiology, 69,* 772–785.

Maier, S. F., Drugan, R. C., & Grau, J. W. (1982). Controllability, coping behavior, and stress-induced analgesia in the rat. *Pain, 12,* 47–56.

Mainz, V., Schulte-Rüther, M., Fink, G. R., Hepertz-Dahlmann, B., & Kornrad, K. (2012). Structural brain abnormalities in adolescent anorexia nervosa before and after weight recovery and associated hormonal changes. *Psychosomatic Medicine, 74*, 574–582.

Maison, S., Micheyl, C., & Collet, L. (2001). Influence of focused auditory attention on cochlear activity in humans. *Psychophysiology, 38*, 35–40.

Maki, P. M., Rich, J. B., & Rosenbaum, R. S. (2002). Implicit memory varies across the menstrual cycle: Estrogen effects in young women. *Neuropsychologia, 40*, 518–529.

Maliphol, A. B., Garth, D. J., & Medler, K. F. (2013). Diet-induced obesity reduces the responsiveness of the peripheral taste receptor cells. *PLoS ONE, 8*, e79403. Retrieved from http://www.plosone.org/article/info%3Adoi%2F10.1371%2Fjournal.pone.0079403

Malison, R. T., McDougle, C. J., van Dyck, C. H., Scahill, L., Baldwin, R. M., Seibyl, J. P., et al. (1995). [123I] β-CIT SPECT imaging of striatal dopamine transporter binding in Tourette's disorder. *American Journal of Psychiatry, 152*, 1359–1361.

Mameli, M., Halbout, B., Creton, C., Engblom, D., Parkitna, J. R., Spanagel, R., & Lüscher, C. (2009). Cocaine-evoked synaptic plasticity: Persistence in the VTA triggers adaptations in the NAC. *Nature Neuroscience, 12*, 1036–1041.

Mancuso, J. J., Kim, J., Lee, S., Tsuda, S., Chow, N. B. H., & Augustine, G. J. (2010). Optogenetic probing of functional brain circuitry. *Experimental Physiology, 96*, 26–33.

Mandel, H. (2010). *Here's the deal: Don't touch me.* New York: Bantam Press.

Manfredi, M., Bini, G., Cruccu, G., Accornero, N., Berardelli, A., & Medolago, L. (1981). Congenital absence of pain. *Archives of Neurology, 38*, 507–511.

Mann, J. J. (2003). Neurobiology of suicidal behaviour. *Nature Reviews Neuroscience, 4*, 819–828.

Mann, J. J., Arango, V., & Underwood, M. D. (1990). Serotonin and suicidal behavior. *Annals of the New York Academy of Sciences. Special Issue: The Neuropharmacology of Serotonin, 600*, 476–485.

Mansari, M., Sakai, K., & Jouvet, M. (1989). Unitary characteristics of presumptive cholinergic tegmental neurons during the sleep-waking cycle in freely moving cats. *Experimental Brain Research, 76*, 519–529.

Mantzoros, C., Flier, J. S., Lesem, M. D., Brewerton, T. D., & Jimerson, D. C. (1997). Cerebrospinal fluid leptin in anorexia nervosa: Correlation with nutritional status and potential role in resistance to weight gain. *Journal of Clinical Endocrinology and Metabolism, 82*, 1845–1851.

Mapes, G. (1990, April 10). Beating the clock: Was it an accident Chernobyl exploded at 1:23 in the morning? *Wall Street Journal*, p. A1.

Maquet, P., Laureys, S., Peigneux, P., Fuchs, S., Petiau, C., Phillips, C., et al. (2000). Experience-dependent changes in cerebral activation during human REM sleep. *Nature Neuroscience, 3*, 831–836.

Marczynski, T. J., & Urbancic, M. (1988). Animal models of chronic anxiety and "fearlessness." *Brain Research Bulletin, 21*, 483–490.

Marijuana legalized for fun in 4 more states and for medicine in 4 others. (2016, November 19). *Governing*. Retrieved from http://www.governing.com/topics/elections/gov-medical-recreational-marijuana-2016-state-ballot-measures.html

Marks, W. B., Dobelle, W. H., & MacNichol, E. F., Jr. (1964). Visual pigments of single primate cones. *Science, 143*, 1181–1183.

Marler, P. (1997). Three models of song learning: Evidence from behavior. *Journal of Neurobiology, 33*(5), 501–516.

Marler, P., & Tamura, M. (1964). Song "dialects" in three populations of white-crowned sparrows. *Science, 146*, 1483–1486.

Marshall, E. (2000a). Gene therapy on trial. *Science, 288*, 951–957.

Marshall, E. (2000b). How prevalent is fraud? That's a million-dollar question. *Science, 290*, 1662–1663.

Marshall, E. (2000c). Moratorium urged on germ line gene therapy. *Science, 289*, 2023.

Marshall, J. (2008, February 16). Forgetfulness is key to a healthy mind. *New Scientist*, 29–33.

Marshall, L., Helgadóttir, H., Mölle, M., & Born, J. (2006). Boosting slow oscillations during sleep potentiates memory. *Nature, 444*, 610–613.

Martin, A., Haxby, J. V., Lalonde, F. M., Wiggs, C. L., & Ungerleider, L. G. (1995). Discrete cortical regions associated with knowledge of color and knowledge of actions. *Science, 270*, 102–105.

Martin, A., Wiggs, C. L., Ungerleider, L. G., & Haxby, J. V. (1996). Neural correlates of category-specific knowledge. *Nature, 379*, 649–652.

Martin, D. S. (2008, May 16). Man's rare ability may unlock secret of memory. *CNN Health*. Retrieved from www.cnn.com/2008/HEALTH/conditions/05/07/miraculous.memory/index.html

Martin, J. B. (1987). Molecular genetics: Applications to the clinical neurosciences. *Science, 238*, 765–772.

Martin, M. J., Muotri, A., Gage, F., & Varki, A. (2005). Human embryonic stem cells express an immunogenic nonhuman sialic acid. *Nature Medicine, 11*, 228–232.

Martinez, D., & Trifilieff, P. (2014, October 14). Cocaine vaccine: Research review. *American Society of Addiction Medicine Magazine*. Retrieved from http://www.asam.org/magazine/read/article/2014/10/15/cocaine-vaccine-research-review

Martini, F. (1988). *Fundamentals of anatomy and physiology* (4th ed.). Upper Saddle River, NJ: Prentice Hall.

Martins, I. P., & Ferro, J. M. (1992). Recovery of acquired aphasia in children. *Aphasiology, 6*, 431–438.

Marty, N., Dallaporta, M., & Thorens, B. (2007). Brain glucose sensing, counterregulation, and energy homeostasis. *Physiology, 22*, 241–251.

Marucha, P. T., Kiecolt-Glaser, J. K., & Favagehi, M. (1998). Mucosal wound healing is impaired by examination stress. *Psychosomatic Medicine, 60*, 362–365.

Marx, J. (1998). New gene tied to common form of Alzheimer's. *Science, 281*, 507–509.

Marx, J. (2003). Cellular warriors at the battle of the bulge. *Science, 299*, 846–849.

Masica, D. N., Money, J., Ehrhardt, A. A., & Lewis, V. G. (1969). IQ, fetal sex hormones and cognitive patterns: Studies in the testicular feminizing syndrome of androgen insensitivity. *Johns Hopkins Medical Journal, 124*, 34–43.

Masters, W., & Johnson, V. (1966). *The human sexual response.* Boston: Little, Brown.

Masterton, B., Jane, J. A., & Diamond, I. T. (1966). Role of brainstem auditory structures in sound localization: I. Trapezoid body, superior olive, and lateral lemniscus. *Journal of Neurophysiology, 30*(2), 341–359.

Mateer, C. A., & Cameron, P. A. (1989). Electrophysiological correlates of language: Stimulation mapping and evoked potential studies. In F. Boller & J. Grafman (Eds.), *Handbook of neuropsychology* (Vol. 2, pp. 91–116). New York: Elsevier.

Matsuzaki, M., Honkura, N., Ellis-Davies, G. C. R., & Kasai, H. (2004). Structural basis of long-term potentiation in single dendritic spines. *Nature, 429*, 761–766.

Mattay, V. S., Berman, K. F., Ostrem, J. L., Esposito, G., Van Horn, J. D., Bigelow, L. B., et al. (1996). Dextroamphetamine enhances "neural network-specific" physiological signals: A positron-emission tomography rCBF study. *Journal of Neuroscience, 16*, 4816–4822.

Matthews, F. E., Stephan, B. C. M., Robinson, L., Jagger, C., Barnes, L. E., Arthur, A., et al. (2016). A two decade dementia incidence comparison from the cognitive function and ageing studies I and II. *Nature Communications, 11398*. doi:10.1038/ncomms11398

Matud, M. P. (2004). Gender differences in stress and coping styles. *Personality and Individual Differences, 37*, 1401–1415.

Matuszewich, L., Lorrain, D. S., & Hull, E. M. (2000). Dopamine release in the medial preoptic area of female rats in response to hormonal manipulation and sexual activity. *Behavioral Neuroscience, 114*, 772–782.

Maulik, P. K., Mascarenhas, M. N., Mathers, C. D., Dua, T., & Saxena, S. (2011). Prevalence of intellectual disability: A meta-analysis of population-based studies. *Research in Developmental Disabilities, 32*, 419–436.

Maurer, U., Bucher, K., Brem, S., Benz, R., Kranz, F., Schulz, E., et al. (2009). Neurophysiology in preschool improves behavioral prediction of reading ability throughout primary school. *Biological Psychiatry, 66*, 341–348.

Maya-Vetencourt, J. F., Ghezzi, D., Antognazza, M. R., Colombo, E., Mete, M., Feyen, P., et al. (2017). A fully organic retinal prosthesis restores vision in a rat model of degenerative blindness. *Nature Materials*. doi:10.1038/nmat4874

Mayer, E. A., Knight, R., Mazmanian, S. K., Cryan, J. F., & Tillisch, K. (2014). Gut microbes and the brain: Paradigm shift in neuroscience. *Journal of Neuroscience, 34*(46), 15490–15496. doi:10.1523/jneurosci.3299-14.2014

Mazur, A., & Lamb, T. A. (1980). Testosterone, status, and mood in human males. *Hormones and Behavior, 14*, 236–246.

Mazzocchi, F., & Vignolo, L. A. (1979). Localisation of lesions in aphasia: Clinical-CT scan correlations in stroke patients. *Cortex, 15*, 627–653.

McAllister, E. J., Dhurandhar, N. V., Keith, S. W., Aronne, L. J., Barger, J., Baskin, M., et al. (2009). Ten putative contributors to the obesity epidemic. *Critical Reviews in Food Science and Nutrition, 49*, 868–913.

McCandliss, B. D., & Noble, K. G. (2003). The development of reading impairment: A cognitive neuroscience model. *Mental Retardation and Developmental Disabilities Research Reviews, 9*, 196–205.

McCann, U. D., Lowe, K. A., & Ricaurte, G. A. (1997). Long-lasting effects of recreational drugs of abuse on the central nervous system. *Neuroscientist, 3*, 399–411.

McClearn, G. E., Johansson, B., Berg, S., Pedersen, N. L., Ahern, F., Petrill, S. A., et al. (1997). Substantial genetic influence on cognitive abilities in twins 80 or more years old. *Science, 276*, 1560–1563.

McClelland, J. L., McNaughton, B. L., & O'Reilly, R. C. (1995). Why there are complementary learning systems in the hippocampus and neocortex: Insights from the successes and failures of connectionist models of learning and memory. *Psychological Review, 102*, 419–457.

McCormick, C. M., & Witelson, S. F. (1991). A cognitive profile of homosexual men compared to heterosexual men and women. *Psychoneuroendocrinology, 16*, 459–473.

McCormick, D. A., & Thompson, R. F. (1984). Cerebellum: Essential involvement in the classically conditioned eyelid response. *Science, 223*, 296–299.

McCoy, N. L., & Davidson, J. M. (1985). A longitudinal study of the effects of menopause on sexuality. *Maturitas, 7*, 203–210.

McCoy, N. L., & Pitino, L. (2002). Pheromonal influences on sociosexual behavior in young women. *Physiology and Behavior, 75*, 367–375.

McDonald, J. W., Becker, D., Sadowsky, C. L., Jane, J. A., Conturo, T. E., & Schultz, L. M. (2002). Late recovery following spinal cord injury: Case report and review of the literature. *Journal of Neurosurgery: Spine, 97*, 252–265.

McDonald, J. W., Liu, X.-Z., Qu, Y., Liu, S., Mickey, S. K., Turetsky, D., et al. (1999). Transplanted embryonic stem cells survive, differentiate and promote recovery in injured rat spinal cord. *Nature Medicine, 5,* 1410–1412.

McDonald, R. J., & White, N. M. (1993). A triple dissociation of memory systems: Hippocampus, amygdala, and dorsal striatum. *Behavioral Neuroscience, 107,* 3–22.

McEvoy, S. P., Stevenson, M. R., McCartt, A. T., Woodward, M., Haworth, C., & Palamara, P. (2005). Role of mobile phones in motor vehicle crashes resulting in hospital attendance: A case-crossover study. *British Medical Journal, 331,* 428–432.

McGaugh, J. L. (2000). Memory: A century of consolidation. *Science, 287,* 248–251.

McGaugh, J. L., Cahill, L., & Roozendaal, B. (1996). Involvement of the amygdala in memory storage: Interaction with other brain systems. *Proceedings of the National Academy of Sciences, 93,* 13508–13514.

McGeoch, P. D., Brang, D., Song, T., Lee, R. R., Huang, M., & Ramachandran, V. S. (2009). Apotemnophilia: The neurological basis of a "psychological" disorder. *Nature Precedings.* Retrieved from http://precedings.nature.com/documents/2954/version/1

McGrath, C. L., Glatt, S. J., Sklar, P., Le-Niculescu, H., Kuczenski, R., Doyle, A. E., et al. (2009). Evidence for genetic association of *RORB* with bipolar disorder. *BMC Psychiatry, 9,* 70. Retrieved from http://www.biomedcentral.com/1471-244X/9/70

McGue, M., & Bouchard, T. J. (1998). Genetic and environmental influences on human behavioral differences. *Annual Review of Neuroscience, 21,* 1–24.

McGuffin, P., Rijsdijk, F., Andrew, M., Sham, P., Katz, R., & Cardno, A. (2003). The heritability of bipolar affective disorder and the genetic relationship to unipolar depression. *Archives of General Psychiatry, 60,* 497–502.

McGuire, P. K., Shah, G. M. S., & Murray, R. M. (1993). Increased blood flow in Broca's area during auditory hallucinations in schizophrenia. *Lancet, 342,* 703–706.

McGuire, P. K., Silbersweig, D. A., Wright, I., Murray, R. M., David, A. S., Frackowiak, R. S. J., et al. (1995). Abnormal monitoring of inner speech: A physiological basis for auditory hallucinations. *Lancet, 346,* 596–600.

McIntosh, A. R., Rajah, M. N., & Lobaugh, N. J. (1999). Interactions of prefrontal cortex in relation to awareness in sensory learning. *Science, 284,* 1531–1533.

McIntyre, C. C., Grill, W. M., Sherman, D. L., & Thakor, N. V. (2004). Cellular effects of deep brain stimulation: Model-based analysis of activation and inhibition. *Journal of Neurophysiology, 91,* 1457–1469.

McKeefry, D. J., Gouws, A., Burton, M. P., & Morland, A. B. (2009). The noninvasive dissection of the human visual cortex: Using fMRI and TMS to study the organization of the visual cortex. *Neuroscientist, 15,* 489–506.

McKeith, I. (2015, November 6). Robin Williams had dementia with Lewy Bodies—so what is it and why has it been eclipsed by Alzheimer's? *The Conversation.* Retrieved from https://theconversation.com/robin-williams-had-dementia-with-lewy-bodies-so-what-is-it-and-why-has-it-been-eclipsed-by-alzheimers-50221

McKenzie, S., & Eichenbaum, H. (2011). Consolidation and reconsolidation: Two lives of memories? *Neuron, 71,* 224–233.

McKeon, J., McGuffin, P., & Robinson, P. (1984). Obsessive-compulsive neurosis following head injury: A report of 4 cases. *British Journal of Psychiatry, 144,* 190–192.

McKinnon, W., Weisse, C. S., Reynolds, C. P., Bowles, C. A., & Baum, A. (1989). Chronic stress, leukocyte subpopulations, and humoral response to latent viruses. *Health Psychology, 8,* 389–402.

McLean, W. J., Yin, X., Lu, L., Lenz, D. R., McLean, D., Langer, R., et al. (2017). Clonal expansion of Lgr5-positive cells from mammalian cochlea and high-purity generation of sensory hair cells. *Cell Reports, 18,* 1917–1929.

McLellan, T. A., Lewis, D. C., O'Brien, C. P., & Kleber, H. D. (2000). Drug dependence, a chronic medical illness: Implications for treatment, insurance, and outcomes evaluation. *Journal of the American Medical Association, 284,* 1689–1695.

Mechoulam, R., Ben-Shabat, S., Hanus, L., Ligumsky, M., Kaminski, N. E., Schatz, A. R., et al. (1995). Identification of an endogenous 2-monoglyceride, present in canine gut, that binds to cannabinoid receptors. *Biochemical Pharmacology,* 83–90.

Medford, N., & Critchley, H. D. (2010). Conjoint activity of anterior insular and anterior cingulate cortex: Awareness and response. *Brain Structure and Function, 214,* 535–549.

Mednick, S., Nakayama, K., & Stickgold, R. (2003). Sleep-dependent learning: A nap is as good as a night. *Nature Neuroscience, 6,* 697–698.

Meier, M. H., Caspi, A., Ambler, A., Harrington, H., Houts, R., Keefe, R. S. E., et al. (2012). Persistent cannabis users show neuropsychological decline from childhood to midlife. *Proceedings of the National Academy of Sciences, 109,* E2657–E2664.

Meltzer, H. Y. (1990). Role of serotonin in depression. *Annals of the New York Academy of Sciences. Special Issue: The Neuropharmacology of Serotonin, 600,* 486–500.

Melzack, R. (1973). *The puzzle of pain.* New York: Basic Books.

Melzack, R. (1992, April). Phantom limbs. *Scientific American, 266,* 120–126.

Melzack, R., & Wall, P. D. (1965). Pain mechanisms: A new theory. *Science, 150,* 971–979.

Mendez-David, I., Hen, R., Gardier, A. M., & David, D. J. (2013). Adult hippocampal neurogenesis: An actor in the antidepressant-like action. *Annales Pharmaceutiques Françaises, 71,* 143–149.

Meng, M., Cherian, T., Singal, G., & Sinha, P. (2012). Lateralization of face processing in the human brain. *Proceedings of the Royal Society B: Biological Sciences, 279,* 2052–2061.

Meng, Q., Zhuang, Y., Ying, Z., Agrawal, R., Yang, X., & Gomez-Pinilla, F. (2017). Traumatic brain injury induces genome-wide transcriptomic, methylomic, and network perturbations in brain and blood predicting neurological disorders. *EBioMedicine, 16,* 184–194.

Mennella, J. A., Jagnow, C. P., & Beauchamp, G. K. (2001). Prenatal and postnatal flavor learning by human infants. *Pediatrics, 107,* E88. Retrieved from http://www.pediatricsdigest.mobi/content/107/6/e88.full

Menon, V., Rivera, S. M., White, C. D., Glover, G. H., & Reiss, A. L. (2000). Dissociating prefrontal and parietal cortex activation during arithmetic processing. *NeuroImage, 12,* 357–365.

Merlin, M. D. (2003). Archeological evidence for the tradition of psychoactive plant use in the Old World. *Economic Botany, 57,* 295–323.

Merzenich, M. M., Knight, P. L., & Roth, G. L. (1975). Representation of cochlea within primary auditory cortex in the cat. *Journal of Neurophysiology, 61,* 231–249.

Meston, C. M., & Frohlich, P. F. (2000). The neurobiology of sexual function. *Archives of General Psychiatry, 57,* 1012–1030.

Mesulam, M. M. (1981). Dissociative states with abnormal temporal lobe EEG: Multiple personality and the illusion of possession. *Archives of Neurology, 38,* 176–181.

Mesulam, M.-M. (1986). Frontal cortex and behavior. *Annals of Neurology, 19,* 320–325.

Meyer, H. C., & Bucci, D. J. (2016). Imbalanced activity in the orbitofrontal cortex and nucleus accumbens impairs behavioral inhibition. *Current Biology, 26,* 2834–2839.

Meyer-Bahlburg, H. F. L. (1984). Psychoendocrine research on sexual orientation: Current status and future options. *Progress in Brain Research, 61,* 375–398.

Meyer-Bahlburg, H. F. L. (2005). Gender identity outcome in female-raised 46,XY persons with penile agenesis, cloacal exstrophy of the bladder, or penile ablation. *Archives of Sexual Behavior, 34,* 423–438.

Meyer-Bahlburg, H. F. L., Ehrhardt, A. A., Rosen, L. R., Gruen, R. S., Veridiana, N. P., Vann, F. H., et al. (1995). Prenatal estrogens and the development of homosexual orientation. *Developmental Psychobiology, 31,* 12–21.

Meyer-Lindberg, A. S., Olsen, R. K., Kohn, P. D., Brown, T., Egan, M. F., Weinberger, D. R., et al. (2005). Regionally specific disturbance of dorsolateral prefrontal-hippocampal functional connectivity in schizophrenia. *Archives of General Psychiatry, 62,* 379–386.

Mickey, B. J., Zhou, Z., Heitzeg, M. M., Heinz, E., Hodgkinson, C. A., Hsu, D. T., et al. (2011). Emotion processing, major depression, and functional genetic variation of neuropeptide Y. *Archives of General Psychiatry, 68,* 158–166.

Mignot, E. (1998). Genetic and familial aspects of narcolepsy. *Neurology, 50*(Suppl. 1), S16–S22.

Mikelberg, F. S., Drance, S. M., Schulzer, M., Yidegiligne, H. M., & Wels, M. M. (1989). The normal human optic nerve: Axon count and axon diameter distribution. *Ophthalmology, 96*(9), 1325–1328.

Miklowitz, D. J., & Johnson, S. L. (2006). The psychopathology and treatment of bipolar disorder. *Annual Review of Clinical Psychology, 2,* 199–235.

Millar, J. K., Pickard, B. S., Mackie, S., James, R., Christie, S., Buchanan, S. R., et al. (2005). DISC1 and PDE4B are interacting genetic factors in schizophrenia that regulate cAMP signaling. *Science, 310,* 1187–1191.

Millar, J. K., Wilson-Annan, J. C., Anderson, S., Christie, S., Taylor, M. S., Semple, C. A., et al. (2000). Disruption of two novel genes by a translocation co-segregating with schizophrenia. *Human Molecular Genetics, 9,* 1415–1423.

Miller, A. (1967). The lobotomy patient—a decade later: A follow-up study of a research project started in 1948. *Canadian Medical Association Journal, 96,* 1095–1103.

Miller, B., Messias, E., Miettunen, J., Alaräisänen, A., Järvelin, M.-R., Koponen, H., et al. (2010). Meta-analysis of paternal age and schizophrenia risk in male versus female offspring. *Schizophrenia Bulletin* (published online in advance of print). Retrieved from http://schizophreniabulletin.oxfordjournals.org/cgi/content/abstract/sbq011v1

Miller, B. L., Boone, K., Cummings, J. L., Read, S. L., & Mishkin, F. (2000). Functional correlates of musical and visual ability in frontotemporal dementia. *British Journal of Psychiatry, 176,* 458–463.

Miller, B. L., Cummings, J., Mishkin, F., Boone, K., Prince, F., Ponton, M., et al. (1998). Emergence of artistic talent in frontotemporal dementia. *Neurology, 51,* 978–982.

Miller, D. S., & Parsonage, S. (1975). Resistance to slimming: Adaptation or illusion? *Lancet, 1,* 773–775.

Miller, E. K., Erickson, C. A., & Desimone, R. (1996). Neural mechanisms of visual working memory in prefrontal cortex of the Macaque. *Journal of Neuroscience, 16,* 5151–5167.

Miller, G. (2008). Scientists targeted in California firebombings. *Science, 321,* 755.

Miller, G. (2010). Beyond *DSM*: Seeking a brain-based classification of mental illness. *Science, 327,* 1437.

Miller, N. F. (1985). The value of behavioral research on animals. *American Psychologist, 40,* 423–440.

Miller, T. Q., Smith, T. W., Turner, C. W., Guijarro, M. L., & Hallet, A. J. (1996). A meta-analytic review of research on hostility and physical health. *Psychological Bulletin, 119,* 322–348.

Milner, B. (1970). Memory and the temporal regions of the brain. In K. H. Pribram & D. E. Broadbent (Eds.), *Biology and memory* (pp. 29–50). New York: Academic Press.

Milner, B. (1974). Hemispheric specialization: Scope and limits. In F. O. Schmitt & F. G. Worden (Eds.), *The neurosciences: Third study program* (pp. 75–89). Cambridge, MA: MIT Press.

Milner, B., Corkin, S., & Teuber, H.-L. (1968). Further analysis of the hippocampal amnesic syndrome: 14-year follow-up study of HM. *Neuropsychologia, 6,* 215–234.

Milner, P. (1977, June). How much distraction can you hear? *Stereo Review,* 64–68.

Miltner, W. H. R., Braun, C., Arnold, M., Witte, H., & Taub, E. (1999). Coherence of gamma-band EEG activity as a basis for associative learning. *Nature, 397,* 434–436.

Mineur, Y. S., Abizaid, A., Rao, Y., Salas, R., DiLeone, R. J., Gündisch, D., et al. (2011). Nicotine decreases food intake through activation of POMC neurons. *Science, 332,* 1330–1332.

Ming, G. L., & Song, H. (2011). Adult neurogenesis in the mammalian brain: Significant answers and significant questions. *Neuron, 70,* 687–702.

Mintun, M. A., LaRossa, G. N., Sheline, Y. I., Dence, C. S., Lee, S. Y., Mach, R. H., et al. (2006). [¹¹C]PIB in a nondemented population: Potential antecedent marker of Alzheimer disease. *Neurology, 67,* 446–452.

Miranda, A., & Taca, A. (2017). Neuromodulation with percutaneous electrical nerve field stimulation is associated with reduction in signs and symptoms of opioid withdrawal: A multisite, retrospective assessment. *American Journal of Drug and Alcohol Abuse.* doi:10.1080/00952990.2017.1295459

Mischkowski, D., Crocker, J., & Way, B. M. (2016). From painkiller to empathy killer: Acetaminophen (paracetamol) reduces empathy for pain. *Social Cognitive and Affective Neuroscience, 11,* 1345–1353.

Mishra, S. K., & Hoon, M. A. (2013). The cells and circuitry for itch responses in mice. *Science, 340,* 968–971.

Mitchell, K. S., Neale, M. C., Bulik, C. M., Aggen, S. H., Kendler, K. S., & Mazzeo, S. E. (2010). Binge eating disorder: A symptom-level investigation of genetic and environmental influences on liability. *Psychological Medicine, 40,* 1899–1906.

Mitchell, S. W. (1866, July). The case of George Dedlow. *Atlantic Monthly, 18,* 1–11.

Mitka, M. (2006). Surgery useful for morbid obesity, but safety and efficacy questions linger. *Journal of the American Medical Association, 296,* 1575–1577.

Mitler, M. M., Carskadon, M. A., Czeisler, C. A., Dement, W. C., Dinges, D. F., & Graeber, R. C. (1988). Catastrophes, sleep, and public policy: Consensus report. *Sleep, 11,* 100–109.

Miyashita, Y. (1993). Inferior temporal cortex: Where visual perception meets memory. *Annual Review of Neuroscience, 16,* 245–263.

Miyashita, Y., & Chang, H. S. (1988). Neuronal correlate of pictorial short-term memory in the primate temporal cortex. *Nature, 331,* 68–70.

Moffat, S. D., Zonderman, A. B., Metter, E. J., Blackman, M. R., Harman, S. M., & Resnick, S. M. (2002). Longitudinal assessment of serum-free testosterone concentration predicts memory performance and cognitive status in elderly men. *Journal of Clinical Endocrinology and Metabolism, 87,* 5001–5007.

Mogilner, A., Grossman, J. A. I., Ribary, U., Jolikot, M., Volkmann, J., Rapaport, D., et al. (1993). Somatosensory cortical plasticity in adult humans revealed by magnetoencephalography. *Proceedings of the National Academy of Sciences, 90,* 3593–3597.

Moir, H. M., Jackson, J. C., & Windmill, J. F. C. (2013). Extremely high frequency sensitivity in a "simple" ear. *Biology Letters, 9,* e20130241.

Moldin, S. O., Reich, T., & Rice, J. P. (1991). Current perspectives on the genetics of unipolar depression. *Behavior Genetics, 21,* 211–242.

Monai, H., Ohkura, M., Tanaka, M., Oe, Y., Konno, A., Hirai, H., et al. (2016). Calcium imaging reveals glial involvement in transcranial direct current stimulation-induced plasticity in mouse brain. *Nature Communications, 7,* 11100. doi:10.1038/ncomms11100

Mondal, K., Ramachandran, D., Patel, V. C., Hagen, K. R., Bose, P., Cutler, D. J., & Zwick, M. E. (2012). Excess variants in AFF2 detected by massively parallel sequencing of males with autism spectrum disorder. *Human Molecular Genetics, 21,* 4356–4364.

Money, J. (1968). *Sex errors of the body and related syndromes: A guide to counseling children, adolescents, and their families.* Baltimore: Paul H. Brookes.

Money, J., Devore, H., & Norman, B. F. (1986). Gender identity and gender transposition: Longitudinal outcome study of 32 male hermaphrodites assigned as girls. *Journal of Sex and Marital Therapy, 12,* 165–181.

Money, J., & Ehrhardt, A. A. (1972). *Man and woman, boy and girl.* Baltimore: Johns Hopkins University Press.

Money, J., Schwartz, M., & Lewis, V. G. (1984). Adult erotosexual status and fetal hormonal masculinization and demasculinization: 46, XX congenital virilizing adrenal hyperplasia and 46, XY androgen-insensitivity syndrome compared. *Psychoneuroendocrinology, 9,* 405–414.

Monteith, S. J., Gwinn, R., & Newell, D. W. (2015). A brain surgery revolution: Using sound instead of scalpels. *Scientific American Mind.* Retrieved from http://www.scientificamerican.com/article/a-brain-surgery-revolution-using-sound-instead-of-scalpels/

Monti, M. M., Vanhaudenhuyse, A., Coleman, M. R., Boly, M., Pickard, J. D., Tshibanda, L., et al. (2010). Willful modulation of brain activity in disorders of consciousness. *New England Journal of Medicine, 362,* 579–589.

Montoya, E. R., Terburg, D., Bos, P. A., & van Honk, J. (2012). Testosterone, cortisol, and serotonin as key regulators of social aggression: A review and theoretical perspective. *Motivation and Emotion, 36,* 65–73.

Mora, F. (2013). Successful brain aging: Plasticity, environmental enrichment, and lifestyle. *Dialogues in Clinical Neuroscience, 15*(1), 45–52.

Moreno, J. L., Kurita, M., Holloway, T., López, J., Cadagan, R., Martínez-Sobrido, L., et al. (2011). Maternal influenza viral infection causes schizophrenia-like alterations of 5-HT2A and mGlu2 receptors in the adult offspring. *Journal of Neuroscience, 31,* 1863–1872.

Moretto, A., & Colosio, C. (2013). The role of pesticide exposure in the genesis of Parkinson's disease: Epidemiological studies and experimental data. *Toxicology, 307,* 24–34.

Morey, R. A., Gold, A. L., LaBar, K. S., Beall, S. K., Brown, V. M., Haswell, C. C., et al. (2012). Amygdala volume changes in posttraumatic stress disorder in a large case-controlled veterans group. *Archives of General Psychiatry, 69,* 1169–1178.

Morizane, A., Doi, D., Kikuchi, T., Okita, K., Hotta, A., Kawasaki, T., et al. (2013). Direct comparison of iPSC-derived neural cells in the brain of a nonhuman primate. *Stem Cell Reports, 1,* 283–292.

Morrel-Samuels, P., & Herman, L. M. (1993). Cognitive factors affecting comprehension of gesture language signs: A brief comparison of dolphins and humans. In H. L. Roitblat, L. M. Herman, & P. E. Nachtigall (Eds.), *Language and communicaton: Comparative perspectives* (pp. 311–327). Hillsdale, NJ: Lawrence Erlbaum.

Morris, J. M. (1953). The syndrome of testicular feminization in male pseudohermaphrodites. *American Journal of Obstetrics and Gynecology, 65,* 1192–1211.

Morris, M., Lack, L., & Dawson, D. (1990). Sleep-onset insomniacs have delayed temperature rhythms. *Sleep, 13,* 1–14.

Morris, M. C., Evans, D. A., Tangney, C. C., Bienias, J. L., & Wilson, R. S. (2005). Fish consumption and cognitive decline with age in a large community study. *Archives of Neurology, 62,* 1–5.

Morris, N. M., Udry, J. R., Khan-Dawood, F., & Dawood, M. Y. (1987). Marital sex frequency and midcycle female testosterone. *Archives of Sexual Behavior, 16,* 27–37.

Morrison, S. F. (2016). Central neural control of thermoregulation and brown adipose tissue. *Autonomic Neuroscience, 196,* 14–24.

Mountcastle, V. B., & Powell, T. P. S. (1959). Neural mechanisms subserving cutaneous sensibility, with special reference to the role of afferent inhibition in sensory perception and discrimination. *Bulletin of the Johns Hopkins Hospital, 105,* 201–232.

Mouritsen, H., Janssen-Bienhold, U., Liedvogel, M., Feenders, G., Stalleicken, J., Dirks, P., et al. (2004). Cryptocromes and neuronal-activity markers colocalize in the retina of migratory birds during magnetic orientation. *Proceedings of the National Academy of Sciences, 101,* 14297.

Mpakopoulou, M., Gatos, H., Brolis, A., Paterakis, K. N., & Fountas, K. N. (2008). Stereotactic amygdalotomy in the management of severe aggressive behavioral disorders. *Neurosurgery Focus, 42:* E3. doi:10.3171/2016.10.FOCUS16411

Mühleisen, T. W., Leber, M., Schulze, T. G., Strohmaier, J., Degenhardt, F., Treutlein, J., et al. (2014). Genome-wide association study reveals two new risk loci for bipolar disorder. *Nature Communications, 5,* 3339. Retrieved from http://www.nature.com/ncomms/2014/140311/ncomms4339/full/ncomms4339.html

Mujica-Parodi, L. R., Strey, H. H., Frederick, B., Savoy, R., Cox, D., Botanov, Y., et al. (2009). Chemosensory cues to conspecific emotional stress activate amygdala in humans. *PLoS One, 4,* e6415. Retrieved from www.plosone.org/article/info:doi%2F10.1371%2Fjournal.pone.0006415

Mulle, J. G., Pulver, A. E., McGrath, J. A., Wolyniec, P. S., Dodd, A. F., Cutler, D. J., et al. (2014). Reciprocal duplication of the Williams-Beuren syndrome deletion on chromosome 7q11.23 is associated with schizophrenia. *Biological Psychiatry, 75,* 371–377.

Muraro, P. A., Pasquini, M., Atkins, H. L., Bowen, J. D., Farge, D., Fassas, A., et al. (2017). Long-term outcomes after autologous hematopoietic stem cell transplantation for multiple sclerosis. *JAMA Neurology.* doi:10.1001/jamaneurol.2016.5867

Murphy, F. C., Nimmo-Smith, I., & Lawrence, A. D. (2003). Functional neuroanatomy of emotions: A meta-analysis. *Cognitive, Affective, and Behavioral Neuroscience, 3,* 207–233.

Murphy, G. (1949). *Historical introduction to modern psychology.* New York: Harcourt, Brace & World.

Murphy, M. R., Checkley, S. A., Seckl, J. R., & Lightman, S. L. (1990). Naloxone inhibits oxytocin release at orgasm in man. *Journal of Clinical Endocrinology and Metabolism, 71,* 1056–1058.

Murphy, S. L., Xu, J., & Kochanek, K. D. (2013). Deaths: Final data for 2010. *National Vital Statstics Reports, 61.* Retrieved from http://www.cdc.gov/nchs/data/nvsr/nvsr61/nvsr61_04.pdf

Murray, J. B. (2002). Phencyclidine (PCP): A dangerous drug, but useful in schizophrenia research. *Journal of Psychology, 136,* 319–327.

Murrell, J., Farlow, M., Ghetti, B., & Benson, M. D. (1991). A mutation in the amyloid precursor protein associated with hereditary Alzheimer's disease. *Science, 254,* 97–99.

Murrough, J. W., Iosifescu, D. V., Chang, L. C., Al Jurdi, R. K., Green, C. E., Perez, A. M., et al. (2013). Antidepressant efficacy of ketamine in treatment-resistant major depression: A two-site randomized controlled trial. *American Journal of Psychiatry, 170*(10), 1134–1142.

Must, A., Spadano, J., Coakley, E. H., Field, A. E., Colditz, G., & Dietz, W. H. (1999). The disease burden associated with overweight and obesity. *Journal of the American Medical Association, 282,* 1523–1529.

Mustanski, B. S., DuPree, M. G., Nievergelt, C. M., Bocklandt, S., Schork, N. J., & Hamer, D. H. (2005). A genomewide scan of male sexual orientation. *Human Genetics, 116,* 272–278.

Nader, K., Schafe, G. E., & LeDoux, J. E. (2000). Fear memories require protein synthesis in the amygdala for reconsolidation after retrieval. *Nature, 406,* 722–726.

Naeser, M. A., Alexander, M. P., Helm-Estabrooks, N., Levine, H. L., Laughlin, S. A., & Geschwind, N. (1982). Aphasia with predominantly subcortical lesion sites. *Archives of Neurology, 39,* 2–14.

Naglieri, J. A., & Ronning, M. E. (2000). Comparison of white, African American, Hispanic, and Asian children on the Naglieri nonverbal ability test. *Psychological Assessment, 12,* 328–334.

Nair, A., Treiber, J. M., Shukla, D. K., Shih, P., & Müller, R.-A. (2013). Impaired thalamocortical connectivity in autism spectrum disorder: A study of functional and anatomical connectivity. *Brain, 136,* 1942–1955.

Nairne, J. S. (2000). *Psychology: The adaptive mind* (2nd ed.). Belmont, CA: Wadsworth/Thomson Learning.

Nakashima, T., Pierau, F. K., Simon, E., & Hori, T. (1987). Comparison between hypothalamic thermoresponsive neurons from duck and rat slices. *Pflugers Archive: European Journal of Physiology, 409,* 236–243.

Naliboff, B., Berman, S., Chang, L., Derbyshire, S., Suyenobu, B., Vogt, B., et al. (2003). Sex-related differences in IBS patients: Central processing of visceral stimuli. *Gastroenterology, 124,* 1738–1747.

Nanda, P., Tandon, N., Mathew, I. T., Giakoumatos, C. I., Abhishekh, H. A., Clementz, B. A., et al. (2014). Local gyrification index in probands with psychotic disorders and their first-degree relatives. *Biological Psychiatry, 76,* 447–455.

Narr, K. L., Woods, R. P., Thompson, P. M., Szeszko, P., Robinson, D., Dimtcheva, T., et al. (2007). Relationships between IQ and regional cortical gray matter thickness in healthy adults. *Cerebral Cortex, 17,* 2163–2171.

Nash, J. M., Park, A., & Willwerth, J. (1995, July 17). "Consciousness" may be an evanescent illusion. *Time,* p. 52.

Nathan, D. (2011). *Sybil exposed.* Free Press: New York.

National Highway Traffic Safety Administration. (2015). Traffic safety facts 2014 data: Alcohol-impaired driving. Retrieved from https://crashstats.nhtsa.dot.gov/Api/Public/ViewPublication/812231

National Human Genome Research Institute. (2016, January 7). *The Genotype-Tissue Expression Project (GTEx).* Retrieved from https://www.genome.gov/gtex/

National Institute of Mental Health. (1986). *Schizophrenia: Questions and answers* (DHHS Publication No. ADM 86-1457). Washington, DC: U.S. Government Printing Office.

National Institute on Alcohol Abuse and Alcoholism. (2016, January). Alcohol facts and statistics. Retrieved from https://www.niaaa.nih.gov/alcohol-health/overview-alcohol-consumption/alcohol-facts-and-statistics

National Institute on Drug Abuse. (2012, October). Drug facts: Understanding drug abuse and addiction. Retrieved from http://www.drugabuse.gov/publications/drugfacts/understanding-drug-abuse-addiction

National Institute on Drug Abuse. (2014). Principles of adolescent substance use disorder treatment: A research guide. Retrieved from https://www.drugabuse.gov/publications/principles-adolescent-substance-use-disorder-treatment-research-based-guide/evidence-based-approaches-to-treating-adolescent-substance-use-disorders/addiction-medications

National Institute on Drug Abuse. (2015, December). Overdose death rates. Retrieved from https://www.drugabuse.gov/related-topics/trends-statistics/overdose-death-rates

National Institutes of Health. (2015, November 18). NIH will no longer support biomedical research on chimpanzees. Retrieved from https://www.nih.gov/about-nih/who-we-are/nih-director/statements/nih-will-no-longer-support-biomedical-research-chimpanzees

National Institutes of Health. (2016). National Human Genome Research Institute (NHGRI). Retrieved from https://www.nih.gov/about-nih/what-we-do/nih-almanac/national-human-genome-research-institute-nhgri

National Sleep Foundation. (2002). *2002 "Sleep in America" poll.* Retrieved from www.sleepfoundation.org/site/c.huIXKjM0IxF/b.2417355/k.143E/2002_Sleep_in_America_Poll.htm

NCD Risk Factor Collaboration. (2016). Trends in adult body-mass index in 200 countries from 1975 to 2014: A pooled analysis of 1698 population-based measurement studies with 19.2 million participants. *Lancet, 387,* 1377–1396.

Nebes, R. D. (1974). Hemispheric specialization in commissurotomized man. *Psychological Bulletin, 81,* 1–14.

Neisser, U., Boodoo, G., Bouchard, T. J., Jr., Boykin, A. W., Brody, N., Ceci, S. J., et al. (1996). Intelligence: Knowns and unknowns. *American Psychologist, 51,* 77–101.

Nelson, L. (2004). Venomous snails: One slip, and you're dead . . . *Nature, 429,* 798–799.

Nelson, R. J., & Trainor, B. C. (2007). Neural mechanisms of aggression. *Nature Reviews Neuroscience, 8,* 536–546.

Nemade, R., & Dombeck, M. (2009, August 7). Schizophrenia symptoms, patterns and statistics and patterns. *MentalHelp.net.* Retrieved from https://www.mentalhelp.net/articles/schizophrenia-symptoms-patterns-and-statistics-and-patterns/

Nervaes, R., & de Almeida, R. M. M. (2014). Aggressive behavior and three neurotransmitters: Dopamine, GABA, and serotonin—a review of the last 10 years. *Psychology & Neuroscience, 7,* 601–607.

Nestler, E. J. (2005). The neurobiology of cocaine addiction. *Science & Practice Perspectives, 3,* 4–10.

Netter, F. H. (1983). *CIBA collection of medical illustrations: Vol. 1. Nervous system.* New York: CIBA.

Neville, H. J., Bavelier, D., Corina, D., Rauschecker, J., Karni, A., Lalwani, A., et al. (1998). Cerebral organization for language in deaf and hearing subjects: Biological constraints and effects of experience. *Proceedings of the National Academy of Sciences, 95,* 922–929.

Newbury, D. F., Fisher, S. E., & Monaco, A. P. (2010). Recent advances in the genetics of language impairment. *Genome Medicine, 2*(6). Retrieved from http://genomemedicine.com/content/2/1/6

Newhouse, P. A., Potter, A., Corwin, J., & Lenox, R. (1992). Acute nicotinic blockade produces cognitive impairment in normal humans. *Psychopharmacology, 108,* 480–484.

Newman, A. (2006, July 5). "Collyers' Mansion" is code for firefighters' nightmare. *New York Times.* Retrieved from www.nytimes.com/2006/07/05/nyregion/05hoard.html

Newman, E. A. (2003). New roles for astrocytes: Regulation of synaptic transmission. *Trends in Neurosciences, 26,* 536–542.

New method to manage stress responses for more successful tumor removal. (2012, January 30). *American Friends Tel Aviv University.* Retrieved from http://www.aftau.org/site/News2?page=NewsArticle&id=15919

Newport, F. (2015, May 21). Americans greatly overestimate percent gay, lesbian in U.S. *Gallup.* Retrieved from http://www.gallup.com/poll/183383/americans-greatly-overestimate-percent-gay-lesbian.aspx

Ng, S. W., & Popkin, B. M. (2012). Time use and physical activity: A shift away from movement across the globe. *Obesity Reviews, 13,* 659–680.

Ngun, T. C., Guo, W., Ghahramani, N. M., Purkayastha, K., Conn, D., Sanchez, F. J., et al. (2015). PgmNr 95: A novel predictive model of sexual orientation using epigenetic markers. Paper presented at the annual meeting of the American Society of Human Genetics, Baltimore, MD, October 6–10, 2015.

Ngun, T. C., & Vilain, E. (2014). The biological basis of human sexual orientation: Is there a role for epigenetics? *Advances in Genetics, 86,* 167–184.

Nichelli, P., Grafman, J., Pietrini, P., Clark, K., Lee, K. Y., & Miletich, R. (1995). Where the brain appreciates the moral of a story. *Neuroreport, 6,* 2309–2313.

Nicoll, R. A., & Madison, D. V. (1982). General anesthetics hyperpolarize neurons in the vertebrate central nervous system. *Science, 217,* 1055–1057.

Nield, D. (2016, June 3). The first gene therapy for children has just been approved in Europe. *ScienceAlert.* Retrieved from http://www.sciencealert.com/first-gene-therapy-for-children-is-approved-in-europe

Nielsen, A. S., Mortensen, P. B., O'Callaghan, E., Mors, O., & Ewald, H. (2002). Is head injury a risk factor for schizophrenia? *Schizophrenia Research, 55,* 93–98.

Nigg, J. T., Elmore, A. L., Natarjan, N., Friderici, K. H., & Nikolas, M. A. (2016). Variation in an iron metabolism gene moderates the association between blood lead levels and attention-deficit/hyperactivity disorder in children. *Psychological Science, 27,* 257–269.

Nigg, J. T., Nikolas, M., Knottnerus, G. M., Cavanagh, K., & Friderici, K. (2010). Confirmation and extension of association of blood lead with attention-deficit/hyperactivity disorder (ADHD) and ADHD symptom domains at population-typical exposure levels. *Journal of Child Psychology and Psychiatry, 51,* 58–65.

Niimura, Y., Matsui, A., & Touhara, K. (2016). Extreme expansion of the olfactory receptor gene repertoire in African elephants and evolutionary dynamics of orthologous gene groups in 13 placental mammals. *Genome Research.* doi:10.1101/gr.169532.113

Niiyama, Y., Kawamata, T., Yamamoto, J., Furuse, S., & Namiki, A. (2009). SB366791, a TRPV1 antagonist, potentiates analgesic effects of systemic morphine in a murine model of bone cancer pain. *British Journal of Anesthesia, 102,* 251–258.

Nimkarn, S., & New, M. I. (2010). Congenital adrenal hyperplasia due to 21-hydroxylase deficiency: A paradigm for prenatal diagnosis and treatment. *Annals of the New York Academy of Sciences, 1192,* 5–11.

Nisbett, R. E. (2005). Heredity, environment, and race differences in IQ: A commentary on Rushton and Jensen. *Psychology, Public Policy, and Law, 11,* 302–310.

Nishitani, N., Avikainen, S., & Hari, R. (2004). Abnormal imitation-related cortical activation sequences in Asperger's syndrome. *Annals of Neurology, 55,* 558–562.

Nobili, L., Ferrillo, F., Besset, A., Rosadini, G., Schiavi, G., & Billiard, M. (1996). Ultradian aspects of sleep in narcolepsy. *Neurophysiologie Clinique, 26,* 51–59.

Nottebohm, F. (1977). Asymmetries in neural control of vocalization in the canary. In S. Harnad, R. W. Doty, L. Goldstein, J. Jaynes, & G. Krauthamer (Eds.), *Lateralization in the nervous system* (pp. 23–44). New York: Academic Press.

Novin, D., VanderWeele, D. A., & Rezek, M. (1973). Infusion of 2-deoxy d-glucose into the hepatic portal system causes eating: Evidence for peripheral glucoreceptors. *Science, 181,* 858–860.

Nulman, I., Rovet, J., Greenbaum, R., Loebstein, M., Wolpin, J., Pace-Asciak, P., et al. (2001). Neurodevelopment of adopted children exposed in utero to cocaine: The Toronto Adoption Study. *Clinical and Investigative Medicine, 24,* 129–137.

Nunn, J. A., Gregory, L. J., Brammer, M., Williams, S. C. R., Parslow, D. M., Morgan, M. J., et al. (2002). Functional magnetic resonance imaging of synesthesia: Activation of V4/V8 by spoken words. *Nature Neuroscience, 5,* 371–375.

Nussbaum, R. L., & Ellis, C. E. (2003). Alzheimer's disease and Parkinson's disease. *New England Journal of Medicine, 348,* 1356–1364.

Oberman, L. M., Winkielman, P., & Ramachandran, V. S. (2007). Face to face: Blocking facial mimicry can selectively impair recognition of emotional expressions. *Social Neuroscience, 2,* 167–178.

Oberman, L. M., Winkielman, P., & Ramachandran, V. S. (2009). Slow echo: Facial EMG evidence for the delay of spontaneous, but not voluntary, emotional mimicry in children with autism spectrum disorders. *Developmental Science, 12,* 510–520.

O'Brien, C. P. (1997). A range of research-based pharmacotherapies for addiction. *Science, 278,* 66–70.

O'Brien, N. L., Way, M. L., Kandaswamy, R., Fiorentino, A., Sharp, S. I., Wuadri, G., et al. (2014). The functional GRM3 Kozak sequence variant rs148754219 affects the risk of schizophrenia and alcohol dependence as well as bipolar disorder. *Psychiatric Genetics, 24,* 277–278.

O'Connor, D. H., Fukui, M. M., Pinsk, M. A., & Kastner, S. (2002). Attention modulates responses in the human lateral geniculate nucleus. *Nature Neuroscience, 5,* 1203–1209.

Ogden, C. L., Carroll, M. D., Lawman, H. G., Fryar, C. D., Kruszon-Moran, D., et al. (2016). Trends in obesity prevalence among children and adolescents in the United States, 1988–1994 through 2013–2014. *Journal of the American Medical Association, 315,* 2292–2299.

Ogden, J. (1989). Visuospatial and other "right-hemispheric" functions after long recovery periods in left-hemispherectomized subjects. *Neuropsychologia, 27,* 765–776.

Ojemann, G. A. (1983). Brain organization for language from the perspective of electrical stimulation mapping. *Behavioral and Brain Sciences, 2,* 189–230.

O'Keane, V., & Dinan, T. G. (1992). Sex steroid priming effects on growth hormone response to pyridostigmine throughout the menstrual cycle. *Journal of Clinical Endocrinology and Metabolism, 75,* 11–14.

Okita, K., Shiina, A., Nakazato, M., & Iyo, M. (2013). Tandospirone, a 5-HT1A partial agonist is effective in treating anorexia nervosa: A case series. *Annals of General Psychiatry, 12*(7). doi:10.1186/1744-859X-12-7

Okubo, Y., Suhara, T., Suzuki, K., Kobayashi, K., Inoue, O., Terasaki, O., et al. (1997). Decreased prefrontal dopamine D1 receptors in schizophrenia revealed by PET. *Nature, 385,* 634–636.

Okun, M. S., Foote, K. D., Wu, S. S., Ward, H. E., Bowers, D., Rodriguez, R. L., et al. (2013). A trial of scheduled deep brain stimulation for Tourette syndrome. *JAMA Neurology, 70,* 85–94.

Olanow, C. W., & Tatton, W. G. (1999). Etiology and pathogenesis of Parkinson's disease. *Annual Review of Neuroscience, 22,* 123–144.

Olender, T., Waszak, S. M., Viavant, M., Khen, M., Ben-Asher, E., Reyes, A., et al. (2012). Personal receptor repertoires: Olfaction as a model. *BMC Genomics, 13*(414). Retrieved from http://www.biomedcentral.com/1471-2164/13/414

Oliet, S. H. R., Piet, R., & Poulain, D. A. (2001). Control of glutamate clearance and synaptic efficacy by glial coverage of neurons. *Science, 292,* 923–925.

Olshansky, S. J., Antonucci, T., Berkman, L., Binstock, R. H., Boersch-Supan, A., Cacioppo, J. T., et al. (2012). Differences in life expectancy due to race and educational differences are widening, and many may not catch up. *Health Affairs, 31,* 1803–1813.

Olson, B. R., Freilino, M., Hoffman, G. E., Stricker, E. M., Sved, A. F., & Verbalis, J. G. (1993). C-fos expression in rat brain and brainstem nuclei in response to treatments that alter food intake and gastric motility. *Molecular and Cellular Neuroscience, 4,* 93–106.

Olson, E. J., Boeve, B. F., & Silber, M. H. (2000). Rapid eye movement sleep behaviour disorder: Demographic, clinical and laboratory findings in 93 cases. *Brain, 123,* 331–339.

Olulade, O. A., Napollelo, E. M., & Eden, G. F. (2013). Abnormal visual motion processing is not a cause of dyslexia. *Neuron, 79,* 180–190.

Ong, J. L., Lo, J. C., Chee, I. Y. N., Santostasi, G., Paller, K. A., Zee, P. C., & Chee, M. W. L. (2016). Effects of phase-locked acoustic stimulation during a nap on EEG spectra and declarative memory consolidation. *Sleep Medicine, 20,* 88–97.

Ong, W. Y., & Mackie, K. (1999). A light and electron microscopic study of the CB1 cannabinoid receptor in primate brain. *Neuroscience, 92,* 1177–1191.

Onstad, S., Skre, I., Torgersen, S., & Kringlen, E. (1991). Twin concordance for DSM-III-R schizophrenia. *Acta Psychiatria Scandinavica, 83,* 395–401.

O'Reilly, I. (2010). *Gender testing in sport: A case for treatment?* BBC News, February 15. Retrieved from http://news.bbc.co.uk/2/hi/8511176.stm

Orexigen has another go at FDA approval of obesity drug Contrave. (2013, December 12). *thepharmaletter.* Retrieved from http://www.thepharmaletter.com/article/orexigen-has-another-go-at-fda- approval-of-obesity-drug-contrave

Orexigen Therapeutics, Inc. (OREX) Contrave(R) obesity research phase 3 program meets co-primary and key secondary endpoints: Exceeds FDA efficacy benchmark for obesity treatments. (2009, July 21). Retrieved from www.biospace.com/news_story.aspx?NewsEntityid-150551

Orlans, F. B. (1993). *In the name of science.* New York: Oxford University Press.

Orlovska, S., Pedersen, M. S., Benros, M. R., Mortensen, P. B., Agerbo, E., & Nordentoft, M. (2014). Head injury as risk factor for psychiatric disorders: A nationwide register-based follow-up study of 113,906 persons with head injury. *American Journal of Psychiatry, 171*(4), 463–469.

O'Rourke, D., Wurtman, J. J., Wurtman, R. J., Chebli, R., & Gleason, R. (1989). Treatment of seasonal depression with *d*-fenfluramine. *Journal of Clinical Psychiatry, 50,* 343–347.

Ortiz-Catalan, M., Guðmundsdóttir, R. A., Kristoffersen, M. B., Zepeda-Echavarria, A., Caine-Winterberger, K., Kulbacka-Ortiz, K., et al. (2016). Phantom motor execution facilitated by machine learning and augmented reality as treatment for phantom limb pain: A single group, clinical trial in patients with chronic intractable phantom limb pain. *Lancet, 388,* 2885–2894.

Osvath, M. (2009). Spontaneous planning for future stone throwing by a male chimpanzee. *Current Biology, 19,* R190–R191.

Oveido-Joekes, E., Guh, D., Brissette, S., Marchand, K., MacDonald, S., Lock, K., et al. (2016). Hydromorphone compared with diacetylmorphine for long-term opioid dependence: A randomized trial. *JAMA Psychiatry, 73,* 447–455.

Overberg, J., Hummel, T., Krude, H., & Weigand, S. (2012). Differences in taste sensitivity between obese and non-obese children and adolescents. *Archives of Disease in Childhood, 97,* 1048–1052.

Owens, N., & McGorry, P. D. (2003). Seasonality of symptom onset in first-episode schizophrenia. *Psychological Medicine, 33,* 163–167.

Paean to Nepenthe. (1961, November 24). *Time,* p. 68.

Pagnin, D., de Queiroz, V., Pini, S., & Cassano, G. B. (2004). Efficacy of ECT in depression: A meta-analytic review. *Journal of Electroconvulsive Therapy, 20,* 13–20.

Palfi, S., Gurruchaga, J. M., Ralph, G. S., Lepetit, H., Lavisse, S., Buttery, P. C., et al. (2014). Long-term safety and tolerability of ProSavin, a lentiviral vector-based gene therapy for Parkinson's disease: A dose escalation, open-label, phase 1/2 trial. *Lancet, 383,* 1138–1146.

Palmer, A. R. (1987). Physiology of the cochlear nerve and cochlear nucleus. In M. P. Haggard & E. F. Evans (Eds.), *Hearing* (pp. 838–855). Edinburgh, UK: Churchill Livingstone.

Panda, S., Nayak, S. K., Campo, B., Walker, J. R., Hogenesch, J. B., & Jegla, T. (2005). Illumination of the melanopsin signaling pathway. *Science, 307,* 600–604.

Pandey, M., Zhang, J.-H., Mishra, S. K., Adikaram, P. R., Harris, B., Kahler, J. F., et al. (2017). A central role for R7bp in the regulation of itch. *Pain, 158*(5), 931–944.

Papalambros, N. A., Santostasi, G., Malkani, R. G., Braun, R., Weintraub, S., Paller, K. A., & Zee, P. C. (2017). Acoustic enhancement of sleep slow oscillations and concomitant memory improvement in older adults. *Frontiers in Human Neuroscience, 11,* 109. doi:10.3389/fnhum.2017.00109

Pappone, P. A., & Cahalan, M. D. (1987). *Pandinus imperator* scorpion venom blocks voltage-gated potassium channels in nerve fibers. *Journal of Neuroscience, 7,* 3300–3305.

Parent, J. M. (2003). Injury-induced neurogenesis in the adult mammalian brain. *Neuroscientist, 9,* 261–272.

Parikshak, N. N., Luo, R., Zhang, A., Won, H., Lowe, J. K., Chandran, V., et al. (2013). Integrative functional genomic analyses implicate specific molecular pathways and circuits in autism. *Cell, 155,* 1008–1021.

Park, D. C., Lodi-Smith, J., Drew, L., Haer, S., Hebrank, A., Bischof, G. N., & Aamodt, W. (2014). The impact of sustained engagement on cognitive function in older adults: The synapse project. *Psychological Science, 25,* 103–112.

Park, J., Park, D. C., & Polk, T. A. (2012). Parietal functional connectivity in numerical cognition. *Cerebral Cortex, 23,* 2127–2135.

Park, M. (2010, February 2). Medical journal retracts study linking autism to vaccine. *CNN Health.* Retrieved from http://www.cnn.com/2010/HEALTH/02/02/lancet.retraction.autism/index.html

Park, M. (2012, September 5). Using chemical castration to punish child sex crimes. *CNN Health.* Retrieved from http://www.cnn.com/2012/09/05/health/chemical-castration-science/

Parker, E. S., Cahill, L., & McGaugh, J. L. (2006). A case of unusual autobiographical remembering. *Neurocase, 12,* 35–49.

Parker, J. (2003). Computing with DNA. *European Molecular Biology Organization Reports, 4,* 7–10

Parker, S. E., Mai, C. T., Canfield, M. A., Rickard, R., Wang, Y., Meyer, R. E., et al. (2010). Updated national birth prevalence estimates for selected birth defects in the United States, 2004–2006. *Birth Defects Research A: Clinical and Molecular Teratology, 88,* 1008–1016.

Pascual-Leone, A., & Torres, F. (1993). Plasticity of the sensorimotor cortex representation of the reading finger in Braille readers. *Brain, 116,* 39–52.

Pastalkova, E., Itskov, V., Amarasingham, A., & Buzsáki, G. (2008). Internally generated cell assembly sequences in the rat hippocampus. *Science, 321,* 1322–1327.

Patel, A. (2009). The cost of mood disorders. *Psychiatry, 8,* 76–80.

Patel, A. J., Honoré, E., Lesage, F., Fink, M., Romey, G., & Lazdunski, M. (1999). Inhalational anesthetics activate two-pore-domain background K⁺ channels. *Nature Neuroscience, 2*, 422–426.

Patel, A. N., Vina, R. F., Geffner, L., Kormos, R., Urschel, H. C., Jr., & Benetti, F. (2004, April 25). *Surgical treatment for congestive heart failure using autologous adult stem cell transplantation: A prospective randomized study.* Presented at the 84th annual meeting of the American Association for Thoracic Surgery, Toronto, Ontario, Canada.

Patihis, L., Frenda, S. J., LePort, A. K. R., Petersen, N., Nichols, R. M., Stark, C. E. L., et al. (2013). False memories in highly superior autobiographical memory individuals. *Proceedings of the National Academy of Sciences, 110*(52), 20947–20952.

Patoine, B., & Bilanow, T. (n.d.). Alzheimer's approved drugs. Retrieved from www.alzinfo.org/alzheimers-treatment-cognitive.asp

Paulesu, E., Démonet, J. F., Fazio, F., McCrory, E., Chanoine, V., Brunswick, N., et al. (2001). Dyslexia: Cultural diversity and biological unity. *Science, 291*, 2165–2167.

Pavlopoulos, E., Jones, S., Kosmidis, S., Close, M., Kim, C., Kovalerchik, O., et al. (2013). Molecular mechanism for age-related memory loss: The histone-binding protein RbAp48. *Science Translational Medicine, 5*, 200ra115. Retrieved from http://stm.sciencemag.org/content/5/200/200ra115

Pearlson, G. D., Kim, W. S., Kubos, K. L., Moberg, P. J., Jayaram, G., Bascom, M. J., et al. (1989). Ventricle-brain ratio, computed tomographic density, and brain area in 50 schizophrenics. *Archives of General Psychiatry, 46*, 690–697.

Peeters, R., Simone, L., Nelissen, K., Fabbri-Destro, M., Vanduffel, W., Rizzolatti, G., et al. (2009). The representation of tool use in humans and monkeys: Common and uniquely human features. *Journal of Neuroscience, 29*, 11523–11539.

Pellegrino, L. J., Pellegrino, A. S., & Cushman, A. J. (1979). *A stereotaxic atlas of the rat brain* (2nd ed.). New York: Plenum Press.

Penfield, W. (1955). The permanent record of the stream of consciousness. *Acta Psychologica, 11*, 47–69.

Penfield, W. (1958). *The excitable cortex in conscious man.* Springfield, IL: Charles C Thomas.

Penfield, W., & Rasmussen, T. (1950). *The cerebral cortex of man.* New York: Macmillan.

Penke, L., Maniega, S. M., Bastin, M. E., Hernández, M. C. V., Murray, C., Royle, N. A., et al. (2012). Brain white matter tract integrity as a neural foundation for general intelligence. *Molecular Psychiatry, 17*, 1026–1030.

Pennacchio, L. A., Ahituv, N., Moses, A. M., Prabhakar, S., Nobrega, M. A., Shoukry, M., et al. (2006). *In vivo* enhancer analysis of human conserved non-coding sequences. *Nature, 444*, 499–502.

Pennisi, E. (2012, September 5). Human genome is much more than just genes. *Science Now.* Retrieved from http://news.sciencemag.org/sciencenow/2012/09/human-genome-is-much-more-than-j.html?ref=em

Pentel, P. R., Malin, D. H., Ennifar, S., Hieda, Y., Keyler, D. E., Lake, J. R., et al. (2000). A nicotine conjugate vaccine reduces nicotine distribution to brain and attenuates its behavioral and cardiovascular effects in rats. *Pharmacology, Biochemistry, and Behavior, 65*, 191–198.

Pepperberg, I. M. (1993). Cognition and communication in an African grey parrot *(Psittacus erithacus):* Studies on a nonhuman, nonprimate, nonmammalian subject. In H. L. Roitblat, L. M. Herman, & P. E. Nachtigall (Eds.), *Language and communication: Comparative perspectives* (pp. 221–248). Hillsdale, NJ: Lawrence Erlbaum.

Perera, F. P., Chang, H., Tang, D., Roen, E. L., Herbstman, J., Margolis, A., et al. (2014). Early-life exposure to polycyclic aromatic hydrocarbons and ADHD behavior problems. *PLOSone, 9*, e111670. doi:10.1371/journal.pone.0111670

Perkel, D. J., & Farries, M. A. (2000). Complementary "bottom-up" and "top-down" approaches to basal ganglia function. *Current Opinion in Neurobiology, 10*, 725–731.

Perkins, A., & Fitzgerald, J. A. (1992). Luteinizing hormone, testosterone, and behavioral response of male-oriented rams to estrous ewes and rams. *Journal of Animal Science, 70*, 1787–1794.

Perlis, M. L., Smith, M. T., Andrews, P. J., Orff, H., & Giles, D. E. (2001). Beta/gamma EEG activity in patients with primary and secondary insomnia and good sleeper controls. *Sleep, 24*, 110–117.

Perrin, J. S., Merz, S., Bennett, D. M., Currie, J., Steele, D. J., Reid, I. C., & Schwarzbauer, C. (2012). Electroconvulsive therapy reduces frontal cortical connectivity in severe depressive disorder. *Proceedings of the National Academy of Sciences, 109*, 5464–5468.

Perry, D. (2000). Patients' voices: The powerful sound in the stem cell debate. *Science, 287*, 1423.

Pert, C. B., & Snyder, S. H. (1973). Opiate receptor: Demonstration in nervous tissue. *Science, 179*, 1011–1014.

Petersen, M. R., Beecher, M. D., Zoloth, S. R., Moody, D. B., & Stebbins, W. C. (1978). Neural lateralization of species-specific vocalizations by Japanese Macaques *(Macaca fuscata). Science, 202*, 324–326.

Petersen, S. E., Fox, P. T., Snyder, A. Z., & Raichle, M. E. (1990). Activation of extrastriate and frontal cortical areas by visual words and word-like stimuli. *Science, 249*, 1041–1044.

Peterson, B. S., Skudlarski, P., Gatenby, J. C., Zhang, H., Anderson, A. W., & Gore, J. C. (1999). An fMRI study of Stroop word-color interference: Evidence for cingulate

subregions subserving multiple distributed attentional systems. *Biological Psychiatry, 45*, 1237–1258.

Peterson, B. S., Warner, V., Bansal, R., Zhu, H., Hao, X., Liu, J., et al. (2009). Cortical thinning in persons at increased familial risk for major depression. *Proceedings of the National Academy of Sciences, 106*, 6273–6278.

Petitto, L. A., Holowka, S., Sergio, L. E., & Ostry, D. (2001). Language rhythms in baby hand movements. *Nature, 413*, 35–36.

Petitto, L. A., & Marentette, P. F. (1991). Babbling in the manual mode: Evidence for the ontogeny of language. *Science, 251*, 1493–1496.

Petitto, L. A., Zatorre, R. J., Gauna, K., Nikelski, E. J., Dostie, D., & Evans, A. C. (2000). Speech-like cerebral activity in profoundly deaf people processing signed languages: Implications for the neural basis of human language. *Proceedings of the National Academy of Sciences, 97*, 13961–13966.

Petkov, C. I., Kayser, C., Steudel, T., Whittingstall, K., Augath, M., & Logothetis, N. K. (2008). A voice region in the monkey brain. *Nature Neuroscience, 11*, 367–374.

Petrovic, P. (2005). Opioid and placebo analgesia share the same network. *Seminars in Pain and Medicine, 3*, 31–36.

Petrovic, P., Kalso, E., Petersson, K. M., & Ingvar, M. (2002). Opioid and placebo analgesia: Imaging a shared neuronal network. *Science, 295*, 1737–1740.

Peuskens, H., Sunaert, S., Dupont, P., Van Hecke, P., & Orban, G. A. (2001). Human brain regions involved in heading estimation. *Journal of Neuroscience, 21*, 2451–2461.

Pew Research Center. (2015, April 14). In debate over legalizing marijuana, disagreement over drug's dangers. Retrieved from http://www.people-press.org/2015/04/14/in-debate-over-legalizing-marijuana-disagreement-over-drugs-dangers/

Pezawas, L., Meyer-Lindenberg, A., Drabant, E. M., Verchinski, B. A., Munoz, K. E., Kolachana, B. S., et al. (2005). 5-HTTLPR polymorphism impacts human cingulate-amygdala interactions: A genetic susceptibility mechanism for depression. *Nature Neuroscience, 8*, 828–834.

Pezawas, L., Meyer-Lindenberg, A., Goldman, A. L., Verchinski, B. A., Chen, G., Kolachana, B. S., et al. (2008). Evidence of biologic epistasis between BDNF and SLC6A4 and implications for depression. *Molecular Psychiatry, 13*, 709–716.

Pfaff, D. W., & Sakuma, Y. (1979). Deficit in the lordosis reflex of female rats caused by lesions in the ventromedial nucleus of the hypothalamus. *Journal of Physiology, 288*, 203–210.

Pfaus, J. G., Kleopoulos, S. P., Mobbs, C. V., Gibbs, R. B., & Pfaff, D. W. (1993). Sexual stimulation activates c-fos within estrogen-concentrating regions of the female rat forebrain. *Brain Research, 624*, 253–267.

Pfrieger, F. W., & Barres, B. A. (1997). Synaptic efficacy enhanced by glial cells in vitro. *Science, 277*, 1684–1687.

Phan, K. L., Wager, T., Taylor, S. F., & Liberzon, I. (2002). Functional neuroanatomy of emotion: A meta-analysis of emotion activation studies in PET and fMRI. *NeuroImage, 16*, 331–348.

Phillips, A. G., Coury, A., Fiorino, D., LePiane, F. G., Brown, E., & Fibiger, H. C. (1992). Self-stimulation of the ventral tegmental area enhances dopamine release in the nucleus accumbens. *Annals of the New York Academy of Sciences, 654*, 199–206.

Phillips, R. J., & Powley, T. L. (1996). Gastric volume rather than nutrient content inhibits food intake. *American Journal of Regulatory, Integrative, and Comparative Physiology, 271*, R766–R779.

Picciotto, M. R. (2013). Nicotine, food intake, and activation of POMC neurons. *Neuropsychopharmacology, 38*, 245.

Pickar, D. (1995). Prospects for pharmacotherapy of schizophrenia. *Lancet, 345*, 557–562.

Pickens, C. L., Theberge, A. M., Fanous, S., Hope, B. T., & Shaham, Y. (2011). Neurobiology of the incubation of drug craving. *Trends in Neurosciences, 34*, 411–420.

Pietiläinen, K. H., Kaprio, J., Borg, P., Plasqui, G., Yki-Järvinen, H., Kujala, U. M., et al. (2008). Physical inactivity and obesity: A vicious circle. *Obesity, 16*, 409–414.

Pietschnig, J., Penke, L., Wicherts, J. M., Zeiler, M., & Voracek, M. (2015). Meta-analysis of associations between human brain volume and intelligence differences: How strong are they and what do they mean? *Neuroscience and Biobehavioral Reviews, 57*, 411–432.

Pihl, R. O., & Peterson, J. B. (1993). Alcohol, serotonin, and aggression. *Alcohol Health and Research World, 17*, 113–116.

Pillay, P., & Manger, P. R. (2007). Order-specific quantitative patterns of cortical gyrification. *European Journal of Neuroscience, 25*, 2705–2712.

Pilowsky, L. S., Costa, D. C., Eli, P. J., Murray, R. M., Verhoeff, N. P., & Kerwin, R. W. (1993). Antipsychotic medication, D₂ dopamine receptor blockade and clinical response: A ¹²³I-IBZM SPET (single photon emission tomography) study. *Psychological Medicine, 23*, 791–799.

Pinker, S. (1994). *The language instinct.* New York: Morrow.

Pinker, S. (2001). Talk of genetics and vice versa. *Nature, 413*, 465–466.

Pinyon, J. L., Tadros, S. F., Froud, K. E., Wong, A. C. Y., Tompson, I. T., Crawford, E. N., et al. (2014). Close-field electroporation gene delivery using the cochlear implant electrode array enhances the bionic ear. *Science Translational Medicine, 6*(233), 233ra54.

Pi-Sunyer, X. (2003). A clinical view of the obesity problem. *Science, 299*, 859–860.

Pi-Sunyer, X., Kissileff, H. R., Thornton, J., & Smith, G. P. (1982). C terminal octapeptide of cholecystokinin decreases food intake in obese men. *Physiology and Behavior, 29,* 627–630.

Platje, E., Popma, A., Vermeiren, R. R. J. M., Doreleijers, T. A. H., Meeus, W. H. J., van Lier, P. A. C., et al. (2015). Testosterone and cortisol in relation to aggression in a non-clinical sample of boys and girls. *Aggressive Behavior, 41,* 478–487.

Plomin, R. (1990). The role of inheritance in behavior. *Science, 248,* 183–188.

Plomin, R., & McClearn, G. E. (Eds.). (1993). *Nature, nurture, and psychology.* Washington, DC: American Psychological Association.

Plomin, R., Owen, M. J., & McGuffin, P. (1994). The genetic basis of complex human behaviors. *Science, 264,* 1733–1739.

Plotnik, J. M., de Waal, F. B. M., & Reiss, D. (2006). Self recognition in an Asian elephant. *Proceedings of the National Academy of Sciences, 103,* 17053–17057.

Poggio, G. F., & Poggio, T. (1984). The analysis of stereopsis. *Annual Review of Neuroscience, 7,* 379–412.

Policies on the use of animals and humans in neuroscience research. (n.d.). Retrieved from www.sfn.org/index.aspx?pagename=guidelinesPolicies_UseOfAnimalsandHumans

Pollock, K., Dahlenburg, H., Nelson, H., Fink, K. D., Cary, W., Hendrix, K., et al. (2016). Human mesenchymal stem cells genetically engineered to overexpress brain-derived neurotrophic factor improve outcomes in Huntington's disease mouse models. *Molecular Therapy, 24,* 965–977.

Porto, P. R., Oliveira, L., Mari, J., Volchan, E., Figueira, I., & Ventura, P. (2009). Does cognitive therapy change the brain? A systematic review of neuroimaging in anxiety disorders. *Journal of Neuropsychiatry and Clinical Neuroscience, 21,* 114–125.

Posner, M. I., & Rothbart, M. K. (1998). Attention, self-regulation and consciousness. *Philosophical Transactions of the Royal Society of London B, 353,* 1915–1927.

Posthuma, D., De Geus, E. J., & Boomsma, D. I. (2001). Perceptual speed and IQ are associated through common genetic factors. *Behavior Genetics, 31,* 593–602.

Potter, W. Z., & Rudorfer, M. V. (1993). Electroconvulsive therapy: A modern medical procedure. *New England Journal of Medicine, 328,* 882–883.

Pournaras, D. J., & le Roux, C. W. (2009). Obesity, gut hormones, and bariatric surgery. *World Journal of Surgery, 33,* 1983–1988.

Power, R. A., Steinberg, S., Bjornsdottir, G., Rietveld, C. A., Abdellaoui, A., Nivard, M. M., et al. (2015). Polygenic risk scores for schizophrenia and bipolar disorder predict creativity. *Nature Neuroscience, 18,* 953–955.

Powers, J. (2010, July 9). Gender issue finally resolved. *Boston Globe.* Retrieved from www.boston.com/sports/other_sports/olympics/articles/2010/07/09/gender_issue_finally_resolved

Prabhakar, S., Visel, Z., Akiyama, J. A., Shoukry, M., Lewis, K. D., Holt, A., et al. (2008). Human-specific gain of function in a developmental enhancer. *Science, 321,* 1346–1350.

Prather, J. F., Peters, S., Nowicki, S., & Mooney, R. (2008). Precise auditory-vocal mirroring in neurons for learned vocal communication. *Nature, 415,* 305–310.

Prehn-Kristensen, A., Munz, M., Göder, R., Wilhelm, I., Korr, K., Vahl, W., et al. (2014). Transcranial oscillatory direct current stimulation during sleep improves declarative memory consolidation in children with attention-deficit/hyperactivity disorder to a level comparable to healthy controls. *Brain Stimulation, 7,* 793–799.

Preston, J. D., O'Neal, J. H., & Talaga, M. C. (2013). *Handbook of clinical psychopharmacology for therapists* (7th ed). Oakland CA: New Harbinger Publications.

Preti, G., Cutler, W. B., Garcia, C. R., Huggins, G. R., & Lawley, H. J. (1986). Human axillary secretions influence women's menstrual cycles: The role of donor extract of females. *Hormones and Behavior, 20,* 474–482.

Preti, G., Wysocki, C. J., Barnhart, K. T., Sondheimer, S. J., & Leyden, J. J. (2003). Male axillary extracts contain pheromones that affect pulsatile secretion of luteinizing hormone and mood in women recipients. *Biology of Reproduction, 68,* 2107–2113.

Price, D. D. (2000). Psychological and neural mechanisms of the affective dimension of pain. *Science, 288,* 1769–1772.

Price, J. (1968). The genetics of depressive behavior. *British Journal of Psychiatry* (Special Publication No. 2), 37–45.

Price, R. A., Kidd, K. K., Cohen, D. J., Pauls, D. L., & Leckman, J. F. (1985). A twin study of Tourette syndrome. *Archives of General Psychiatry, 42,* 815–820.

Prior, H., Schwarz, A., & Güntürkün, O. (2008). Mirror-induced behavior in the magpie (*Pica pica*): Evidence of self-recognition. *PLoS Biology, 6*(8), e202. Retrieved from www.plosbiology.org/article/info:doi/10.1371/journal.pbio.0060202

Proal, E., Reiss, P. T., Klein, R. G., Mannuzza, S., Gotimer, K., Ramos-Olazagasti, M. A., et al. (2011). Brain gray matter deficits at 33-year follow-up in adults with attention-deficit/hyperactivity disorder established in childhood. *Archives of General Psychiatry, 68,* 1122–1134.

Proof? The joke was on Bischoff, but too late. (1942, March). *Scientific American, 166*(3), 145.

Prospective Studies Collaboration. (2009). Body-mass index and cause-specific mortality in 900 000 adults: Collaborative analyses of 57 prospective studies. *Lancet, 373,* 1083–1096.

Prufer, K., Munch, K., Hellmann, I., Akagi, K., Miller, J. R., Walenz, B., et al. (2012). The bonobo genome compared with the chimpanzee and human genomes. *Nature, 486*(7404), 527–531.

Public Health Service policy on humane care and use of laboratory animals. (2015). Retrieved from http://grants.nih.gov/grants/olaw/references/phspol.htm

Pujol, J., López, A., Deus, J., Cardoner, N., Vallejo, J., Capdevila, A., et al. (2002). Anatomical variability of the anterior cingulate gyrus and basic dimensions of human personality. *NeuroImage, 15,* 847–855.

Putnam, F. W. (1991). Recent research on multiple personality disorder. *Psychiatric Clinics of North America, 14,* 489–502.

Puts, D. A., McDaniel, M. A., Jordan, C. L., & Breedlove, S. M. (2008). Spatial ability and prenatal androgens: Meta-analyses of congenital adrenal hyperplasia and digit ratio (2D:4D) studies. *Archives of Sexual Behavior, 37*(1), 100–111.

Pyter, L. M., Pineros, V., Galang, J. A., McClintock, M. K., & Prendergast, B. J. (2009). Peripheral tumors induce depressive-like behaviors and cytokine production and alter hypothalamic-pituitary-adrenal axis regulation. *Proceedings of the National Academy of Sciences, 106,* 9069–9074.

Qadri, Y. J., Bortsov, A. V., Swor, R. A., Peak, D. A., Jones, J. S., Rathlev, N. K., et al. (2012). Genetic polymorphisms in the dopamine receptor D2 are associated with acute pain severity after motor vehicle collision. Paper presented at the annual meeting of the American Society of Anesthesiologists, October 16, 2012, Washington, DC.

Qin, Y.-L., McNaughton, B. L., Skaggs, W. E., & Barnes, C. A. (1997). Memory reprocessing in corticocortical and hippocampocortical neuronal ensembles. *Philosophical Transactions of the Royal Society of London, B, 352,* 1525–1533.

Qiu, X., Kumbalasiri, T., Carlson, S. M., Wong, K. Y., Krishna, V., Provencio, I., et al. (2005). Induction of photosensitivity by heterologous expression of melanopsin. *Nature, 433,* 745–749.

Quian Quiroga, R., Kraskov, A., Koch, C., & Fried, I. (2009). Explicit encoding of multimodal percepts by single neurons in the human brain. *Current Biology, 19*(15), 1308–1313.

Quian Quiroga, R., Kraskov, A., Mormann, F., Fried, I., & Koch, C. K. (2014). Single-cell responses to face adaptation in the human medial temporal lobe. *Neuron, 84,* 363–369.

Raboch, J., & Stárka, L. (1973). Reported coital activity of men and levels of plasma testosterone. *Archives of Sexual Behavior, 2,* 309–315.

Ragozzino, M. E. (2007). The contribution of the medial prefrontal cortex, orbitofrontal cortex, and dorsomedial striatum to behavioral flexibility. *Annals of the New York Academy of Sciences, 1121,* 355–375.

Ragsdale, D. S., McPhee, J. C., Scheuer, T., & Catterall, W. A. (1994). Molecular determinants of state-dependent block of Na+ channels by local anesthetics. *Science, 265,* 1724–1728.

Rahman, Q., Abrahams, S., & Wilson, G. D. (2003). Sexual-orientation-related differences in verbal fluency. *Neuropsychology, 17,* 240–246.

Raine, A. (2013, April 26). The criminal mind. *Wall Street Journal.* Retrieved from http://online.wsj.com/article/SB10001424127887323335404578444682892520530.html

Raine, A., Meloy, J. R., Bihrle, S., Stoddard, J., LaCasse, L., & Buchsbaum, M. S. (1998). Reduced prefrontal and increased subcortical brain functioning assessed using positron emission tomography in predatory and affective murderers. *Behavioral Science and Law, 16,* 319–332.

Raine, A., Yang, Y., Narr, K. L., & Toga, A. W. (2009, December 22). Sex differences in orbitofrontal gray as a partial explanation for sex differences in antisocial personality. *Molecular Psychiatry.* doi:10.1038/mp.2009.136

Rainer, G. S., Rao, S. C., & Miller, E. K. (1999). Prospective coding for objects in primate prefrontal cortex. *Journal of Neuroscience, 19,* 5493–5505.

Rainville, P., Duncan, G. H., Price, D. D., Carrier, B., & Bushnell, M. C. (1997). Pain affect encoded in human anterior cingulate but not somatosensory cortex. *Science, 227,* 968–971.

Rais, Y., Zviran, A., Geula, S., Gafni, O., Chomsky, E., Viukov, S., et al. (2013). Deterministic direct reprogramming of somatic cells to pluripotency. *Nature, 502,* 65–70.

Raja, S. N., Meyer, R. A., Ringkamp, M., & Campbell, J. N. (1999). Peripheral neural mechanisms of nociception. In P. D. Wall & R. Melzack (Eds.), *Textbook of pain* (pp. 11–57). Edinburgh: Churchill Livingstone.

Rakic, P. (1985). Limits of neurogenesis in primates. *Science, 227,* 1054–1056.

Ramachandran, V. S., & Altschuler, E. L. (2009). The use of visual feedback, in particular mirror visual feedback, in restoring brain function. *Brain, 132,* 1693–1710.

Ramachandran, V. S., & Blakeslee, S. (1998). *Phantoms in the brain.* New York: Morrow.

Ramey, C. T., Campbell, F. A., Burchinal, M., Skinner, M. L., Gardner, D. M., & Ramey, S. L. (2000). Persistent effects of early childhood education on high-risk children and their mothers. *Applied Developmental Science, 4,* 2–14.

Ramón y Cajal, S. (1928). *Degeneration and regeneration of the nervous system.* New York: Hafner.

Ramón y Cajal, S. (1989). *Recollections of my life* (E. H. Craigie & J. Cano, Trans.). Cambridge, MA: MIT Press. (Original work published 1937)

Ramus, F., Rosen, S., Dakin, S. C., Day, B. L., Castellote, J. M., White, S., et al. (2003). Theories of developmental dyslexia: Insights from a multiple case study of dyslexic adults. *Brain, 126,* 841–865.

Rao, S. C., Rainer, G., & Miller, E. K. (1997). Integration of what and where in the primate prefrontal cortex. *Science, 276,* 821–824.

Rapoport, J. L. (1991). Recent advances in obsessive-compulsive disorder. *Neuropsychopharmacology, 5,* 1–10.

Rasmussen, T., & Milner, B. (1977). The role of early left-brain injury in determining lateralization of cerebral speech functions. *Annals of the New York Academy of Sciences, 299,* 355–369.

Ratliff, C. P., Borghuis, B. G., Kao, Y.-H., Sterling, P., & Balasubramanian, V. (2010). Retina is structured to process an excess of darkness in natural scenes. *Proceedings of the National Academy of Sciences, 107,* 17368–17373.

Ratliff, F., & Hartline, H. K. (1959). The responses of Limulus optic nerve fibers to patterns of illumination on the receptor mosaic. *Journal of General Physiology, 42,* 1241–1255.

Rauch, V., Arunajadai, S., Horton, M., Perera, F., Hoepner, L., Barr, D. B., & Whyatt, R. (2011). Seven-year neurodevelopmental scores and prenatal exposure to chlorpyrifos, a common agricultural pesticide. *Environmental Health Perspectives, 119,* 1196–1201.

Rauschecker, J. P., & Tian, B. (2000). Mechanisms and streams for processing of "what" and "where" in auditory cortex. *Proceedings of the National Academy of Sciences, 97,* 11800–11806.

Ravelli, G. P., Stein, Z. A., & Susser, M. W. (1976). Obesity in young men after famine exposure in utero and early infancy. *New England Journal of Medicine, 295,* 349–353.

Raven, J. C. (2003). *Standard Progressive Matrices (Manual).* San Antonio, TX: PsychCorp/Pearson.

Ray, L. A., & Hutchison, K. E. (2004). A polymorphism of the μ-opioid receptor gene (*OPRM1*) and sensitivity to the effects of alcohol in humans. *Alcoholism Clinical and Experimental Research, 28,* 1789–1795.

Ray, S., Britschgi, M., Herbert, C., Takeda-Uchimura, Y., Boxer, A., Blennow, K., et al. (2007). Classification and prediction of clinical Alzheimer's diagnosis based on plasma signaling proteins. *Nature Medicine, 13,* 1359–1362.

Ray, W. J. (2014). *Abnormal Psychology.* Los Angeles: Sage.

Raznahan, A., Toro, R., Daly, E., Robertson, D., Murphy, C., Deeley, Q., et al. (2010). Cortical anatomy in autism spectrum disorder: An in vivo MRI study on the effect of age. *Cerebral Cortex, 20,* 1332–1340.

Recht, L. D., Lew, R. A., & Schwartz, W. J. (1995). Baseball teams beaten by jet lag. *Nature, 377,* 583.

Redcay, E., & Courchesne, E. (2005). When is the brain enlarged in autism? A meta-analysis of all brain size reports. *Biological Psychiatry, 58,* 1–9.

Redelmeier, D. A., & Tibshirani, R. J. (1997). Association between cellular telephone calls and motor vehicle collisions. *New England Journal of Medicine, 336,* 453–458.

Reed, J. J., & Squire, L. R. (1998). Retrograde amnesia for facts and events: Findings from four new cases. *Journal of Neuroscience, 18,* 3943–3954.

Reed, T. E., & Jensen, A. R. (1992). Conduction velocity in a brain nerve pathway of normal adults correlates with intelligence level. *Intelligence, 16,* 259–272.

Reichenberg, A., Caspi, A., Harrington, H., Houts, R., Keefe, R. S. E., Murray, R. M., et al. (2010). Static and dynamic cognitive deficits in childhood preceding adult schizophrenia: A 30-year study. *American Journal of Psychiatry, 167,* 160–169.

Reiman, E. M., Armstrong, S. M., Matt, K. S., & Mattox, J. H. (1996). The application of positron emission tomography to the study of the normal menstrual cycle. *Human Reproduction, 11,* 2799–2805.

Reinders, A. A., Nijenhuis, E. R., Quak, J., Korf, J., Haaksma, J., Paans, A. M., et al. (2006). Psychobiological characteristics of dissociative identity disorder: A symptom provocation study. *Biological Psychiatry, 60,* 730–740.

Reiner, W. G., & Gearhart, J. P. (2004). Discordant sexual identity in some genetic males with cloacal exstrophy assigned to female sex at birth. *New England Journal of Medicine, 350,* 333–341.

Reinisch, J. M. (1981). Prenatal exposure to synthetic progestins increases potential for aggression in humans. *Science, 211,* 1171–1173.

Reisberg, B., Doody, R., Stöffler, A., Schmitt, F., Ferris, S., & Möbius, H. J. (2003). Memantine in moderate-to-severe Alzheimer's disease. *New England Journal of Medicine, 348,* 1333–1341.

Reiss, D., & Marino, L. (2001). Mirror self-recognition in the bottlenose dolphin: A case of cognitive convergence. *Proceedings of the National Academy of Sciences, 98,* 5937–5942.

Remondes, M., & Schuman, E. M. (2004). Role for a cortical input to the hippocampal area CA1 in the consolidation of a long-term memory. *Nature, 431,* 699–703.

Rempel-Clower, N. L., Zola, S. M., Squire, L. R., & Amaral, D. G. (1996). Three cases of enduring memory impairment after bilateral damage limited to the hippocampal formation. *Journal of Neuroscience, 16,* 5233–5255.

Ren, J., Tate, B. A., Sietsma, D., Marciniak, A., Snyder, E. Y., & Finklestein, S. P. (2000, November). *Co-administration of neural stem cells and BFGF enhances functional recovery following focal cerebral infarction in rat.* Poster session presented at the annual meeting of the Society for Neuroscience, New Orleans, LA.

Renault, B., Signoret, J.-L., Debruille, B., Breton, F., & Bolger, F. (1989). Brain potentials reveal covert facial recognition in prosopagnosia. *Neuropsychologia, 27,* 905–912.

Renier, L. A., Anurova, I., De Volder, A. G., Carlson, S., VanMeter, J., & Rauschecker, J. P. (2010). Preserved functional specialization for spatial processing in the middle occipital gyrus of the early blind. *Cell, 68,* 138–148.

Research involving human subjects. (n.d.). National Institutes of Health. Retrieved from http://grants.nih.gov/grants/policy/hs/index.htm

RetroSense Therapeutics doses first patient in phase I/II clinical trial for lead compound RST-001. (2016, March 21). BusinessWire. Retrieved from http://www.businesswire.com/news/home/20160321005376/en

Ribary, U. (2005). Dynamics of thalamo-cortical network oscillations and human perception. In S. Laureys (Ed.), *The boundaries of consciousness: Neurobiology and neuropathology* (pp. 127–142). New York: Elsevier.

Ribeiro, S., Gervasoni, D., Soares, E. S., Zhou, Y., Lin, S.-C., Pantoja, J., et al. (2004). Long-lasting novelty-induced neuronal reverberation during slow-wave sleep in multiple forebrain areas. *PLoS Biology, 2,* 126–137.

Ribiez, S. R., Duran, F., Oliviera, M. C., Bezerra, D., Castro, C. C., Steffens, D. C., et al. (2013). Structural brain changes as biomarkers and outcome predictors in patients with late-life depression: A cross-sectional and prospective study. *PLoS One, 8*(11), e80049.

Rice, F., Harold, G. T., Bolvin, J., Hay, D. F., van den Bree, M., & Thapar, A. (2009). Disentangling prenatal and inherited influences in humans with an experimental design. *Proceedings of the National Academy of Sciences, 106,* 2464–2467.

Rice, M. L., Smith, S. D., & Gayán, J. (2009). Convergent genetic linkage and associations to language, speech and reading measures in families of probands with specific language impairment. *Journal of Neurodevelopmental Disorders, 1,* 264–282.

Rice, W. R., Friberg, U., & Gavrilets, S. (2012). Homosexuality as a consequence of epigenetically canalized sexual development. *Quarterly Review of Biology, 87,* 343–368.

Richardson, C., Glenn, S., Nurmikko, T., & Horgan, M. (2006). Incidence of phantom phenomena including phantom limb pain 6 months after major lower limb amputation in patients with peripheral vascular disease. *Clinical Journal of Pain, 22,* 353–358.

Ridaura, V. K., Faith, J. J., Rey, F. E., Cheng, J., Duncan, A. E., Kau, A. L., et al. (2013). Gut microbiota from twins discordant for obesity modulate metabolism in mice. *Science, 341,* 6150. Retrieved from http://www.sciencemag.org/content/341/6150/1241214.abstract

Riedel, G., Micheau, J., Lam, A. G. M., Roloff, E. V. L., Martin, S. J., Bridge, H., et al. (1999). Reversible neural inactivation reveals hippocampal participation in several memory processes. *Nature Neuroscience, 2,* 898–905.

Rieger, G., Linsenmeier, J. A. W., Gygax, L., & Bailey, J. M. (2008). Sexual orientation and childhood gender nonconformity: Evidence from home videos. *Developmental Psychology, 44,* 46–58.

Riehle, A., & Requin, J. (1989). Monkey primary motor and premotor cortex: Single-cell activity related to prior information about direction and extent of an intended movement. *Journal of Neurophysiology, 61,* 534–549.

Rijlaarsdam, J., Cecil, C. A. M., Walton, E., Mesirow, M. S. C., Relton, C. L., Gaunt, T. R., et al. (2017). Prenatal unhealthy diet, insulin-like growth factor 2 gene (*IGF2*) methylation, and attention deficit hyperactivity disorder symptoms in youth with early-onset conduct problems. *Journal of Child Psychology and Psychiatry, 58,* 19–27.

Riley, K. P., Snowdon, D. A., Desrosiers, M. F., & Markesbery, W. R. (2005). Early life linguistic ability, late life cognitive function, and neuropathology: Findings from the nun study. *Neurobiology of Aging, 26,* 341–347.

Rimmele, U., Hediger, K., Heinrichs, M., & Klaver, P. (2009). Oxytocin makes a face in memory familiar. *Journal of Neuroscience, 29,* 38–42.

Ritchie, J. M., & Rogart, R. B. (1977). Density of sodium channels in mammalian myelinated nerve fibers and nature of the axonal membrane under the myelin sheath. *Proceedings of the National Academy of Sciences, 74,* 211–215.

Ritter, S., & Taylor, J. S. (1990). Vagal sensory neurons are required for lipoprivic but not glucoprivic feeding in rats. *American Journal of Physiology, 258,* R1395–R1401.

Ritterband-Rosenbaum, A., Nielsen, J. B., & Christensen, M. S. (2014). Sense of agency is related to gamma band coupling in an inferior parietal-preSMA circuitry. *Frontiers in Human Neuroscience, 16*(8), 510. doi:10.3389/fnhum.2014.00510

Roberts, A. I., Vick, S.-J., Roberts, S. G. B., Buchanan-Smith, H. M., & Zuberbühler, K. (2012). A structure-based repertoire of manual gestures in wild chimpanzees: Statistical analyses of a graded communication system. *Evolution and Human Behavior, 33,* 578–589.

Roberts, G. W. (1990). Schizophrenia: The cellular biology of a functional psychosis. *Trends in the Neurosciences, 13,* 207–211.

Robinson, T. E., Gorny, G., Mitton, E., & Kolb, B. (2001). Cocaine self-administration alters the morphology of dendrites and dendritic spines in the nucleus accumbens and neocortex. *Synapse, 39,* 257–266.

Robinson, T. E., & Kolb, B. (1997). Persistent structural modifications in nucleus accumbens and prefrontal cortex neurons produced by previous experience with amphetamine. *Journal of Neuroscience, 17,* 8491–8497.

Rodin, J., Schank, D., & Striegel-Moore, R. (1989). Psychological features of obesity. *Medical Clinics of North America, 73,* 47–66.

Rodriguez, A., & Bohlin, G. (2005). Are maternal smoking and stress during pregnancy related to ADHD symptoms in children? *Journal of Child Psychology and Psychiatry, 46,* 246–254.

Rodriguez, I. (2004). Pheromone receptors in mammals. *Hormones and Behavior, 46,* 219–230.

Rodriguez-Raecke, R., Niemeier, A., Ihle, K., Ruether, W., & May, A. (2009). Brain gray matter decrease in chronic pain is the consequence and not the cause of pain. *Journal of Neuroscience, 29,* 13746–13750.

Roenneberg, T., Kuehnle, T., Pramstaller, P. P., Ricken, J., Havel, M., Guth, A., et al. (2004). A marker for the end of adolescence. *Current Biology, 14,* R1038–R1039.

Roffwarg, H. P., Muzio, J. N., & Dement, W. C. (1966). Ontogenetic development of the human sleep-dream cycle. *Science, 152,* 604–619.

Rogan, M. T., Stäubli, U. V., & LeDoux, J. E. (1997). Fear conditioning induces associative long-term potentiation in the amygdala. *Nature, 390,* 604–607.

Rogers, G., Elston, J., Garside, R., Roome, C., Taylor, R., Younger, P., et al. (2009). The harmful health effects of recreational ecstasy: A systematic review of observational evidence. *Health Technology Assessment, 13*(6). Retrieved from www.hta .ac.uk/fullmono/mon1306.pdf

Rolls, B. J., Rolls, E. T., Rowe, E. A., & Sweeney, K. (1981). Sensory-specific satiety in man. *Physiology and Behavior, 27,* 137–142.

Rolls, B. J., Rowe, E. A., & Turner, R. C. (1980). Persistent obesity in rats following a period of consumption of a mixed, high-energy diet. *Journal of Physiology, 298,* 415–427.

Rosa, R. R., & Bonnet, M. H. (2000). Reported chronic insomnia is independent of poor sleep as measured by electroencephalography. *Psychosomatic Medicine, 62,* 474–482.

Rose, J. E., Brugge, J. F., Anderson, D. J., & Hind, J. E. (1967). Phase-locked response to low-frequency tones in single auditory nerve fibers of the squirrel monkey. *Journal of Neurophysiology, 30,* 769–793.

Rose, R. J. (1995). Genes and human behavior. *Annual Review of Psychology, 46,* 625–654.

Roselli, C. E., Larkin, K., Resko, J. A., Stellflug, J. N., & Stormshak, F. (2004). The volume of a sexually dimorphic nucleus in the ovine medial preoptic area/anterior hypothalamus varies with sexual partner preference. *Endocrinology, 145,* 478–483.

Rose'Meyer, R. (2013). A review of the serotonin transporter and prenatal cortisol in the development of autism spectrum disorders. *Molecular Autism, 4,* 37. Retrieved from http://www.molecular autism.com/content/4/1/37

Rosen, S. (1999). Most—but not all—regions see food gains. *FoodReview, 22,* 13–19.

Rosenberg, E., & Schweber, N. (2016, July 13). 33 suspected of overdosing on synthetic marijuana in Brooklyn. *New York Times,* p. A17.

Rosenkranz, M. A., Jackson, D. C., Dalton, K. M., Dolski, I., Ryff, C. D., Singer, B. H., et al. (2003). Affective style and *in vivo* immune response: Neurobehavioral mechanisms. *Proceedings of the National Academy of Sciences, 100,* 11148–11152.

Rosenthal, N. E., Sack, D. A., Carpenter, C. J., Parry, B. L., Mendelson, W. B., & Wehr, T. A. (1985). Antidepressant effects of light in seasonal affective disorder. *American Journal of Psychiatry, 142,* 163–170.

Rösler, A., & Witztum, E. (1998). Treatment of men with paraphilia with a long-acting analogue of gonadotropin-releasing hormone. *New England Journal of Medicine, 338,* 416–422.

Rösler, F., Heil, M., & Henninghausen, E. (1995). Distinct cortical activation patterns during long-term memory retrieval of verbal, spatial and color information. *Journal of Cognitive Neuroscience, 7,* 51–65.

Ross, C. A., Miller, S. C., Reagor, P., Bjornson, L., Fraser, G. A., & Anderson, G. (1990). Structured interview data on 102 cases of multiple personality disorder from four centers. *American Journal of Psychiatry, 147,* 596–601.

Ross, E. D., Homan, R. W., & Buck, R. (1994). Differential hemispheric lateralization of primary and social emotions. *Neuropsychiatry, Neuropsychology, and Behavioral Neurology, 7,* 1–19.

Ross, G. W., Abbott, R. D., Petrivotch, H., Morens, D. M., Grandinetti, A., Tung, K.-H., et al. (2000). Association of coffee and caffeine intake with the risk of Parkinson disease. *Journal of the American Medical Association, 283,* 2674–2679.

Rossi, G. S., & Rosadini, G. (1967). Experimental analysis of cerebral dominance in man. In C. Millikan & F. L. Darley (Eds.), *Brain mechanisms underlying speech and language* (pp. 167–184). New York: Grune & Stratton.

Rothe, C., Gutknecht, L., Freitag, C., Tauber, R., Mössner, R., Franke, P., et al. (2004). Association of a functional 1019C>G 5-HT1A receptor gene polymorphism with panic disorder with agoraphobia. *International Journal of Neuropsychopharmacology, 7,* 189–192.

Rothman, J. M., Van Soest, P. J., & Pell, A. N. (2006). Decaying wood is a sodium source for mountain gorillas. *Biology Letters, 2,* 321–324.

Rouw, R., & Scholte, S. (2007). Increased structural connectivity in grapheme-color synesthesia. *Nature Neuroscience, 10,* 792–797.

Rowe, M. L., & Goldin-Meadow, S. (2009). Differences in early gesture explain SES disparities in child vocabulary size at school entry. *Science, 323,* 951–953.

Rowland, L. P. (2000a). Diseases of chemical transmission at the nerve-muscle synapse: Myasthenia gravis. In E. R. Kandel, J. H. Schwartz, & T. M. Jessell (Eds.), *Principles of neural science* (4th ed., pp. 298–309). New York: McGraw-Hill.

Rowland, L. P. (2000b). Diseases of the motor unit. In E. R. Kandel, J. H. Schwartz, & T. M. Jessell (Eds.), *Principles of neural science* (4th ed., pp. 695–712). New York: McGraw-Hill.

Rowland, L. P., Hoefer, P. F. A., & Aranow, H., Jr. (1960). Myasthenic syndromes. *Research Publications—Association for Research in Nervous and Mental Disease, 38,* 547–560.

Roy, A., DeJong, J., & Linnoila, M. (1989). Cerebrospinal fluid monoamine metabolites and suicidal behavior in depressed patients: A 5-year followup study. *Archives of General Psychiatry, 46,* 609–612.

Rozin, P. (1967). Specific aversions as a component of specific hungers. *Journal of Comparative and Physiological Psychology, 64,* 237–242.

Rozin, P. (1969). Adaptive food sampling patterns in vitamin deficient rats. *Journal of Comparative and Physiological Psychology, 69,* 126–132.

Rozin, P. (1976). The selection of foods by rats, humans, and other animals. *Advances in the Study of Behavior, 6,* 21–76.

Rubens, A. B. (1977). Anatomical asymmetries of human cerebral cortex. In S. Harnad, R. W. Doty, L. Goldstein, J. Jaynes, & G. Krauthamer (Eds.), *Lateralization in the nervous system* (pp. 503–516). New York: Academic Press.

Rubino, F., Nathan, D. M., Eckel, R. H., Schauer, P. R., Alberti, K. G. M. M., Zimmet, P. Z., et al. (2016). Metabolic surgery in the treatment algorithm for Type 2 diabetes: A joint statement by international diabetes organizations. *Diabetes Care, 39,* 861–877.

Rudd, R. A., Paulozzi, L. J., Bauer, M. J., Burleson, R. W., Carlson, R. E., Dao, D., et al. (2014). Increases in heroin overdose deaths—28 states, 2010 to 2012. *Morbidity and Mortality Weekly Report, 63*(39), 849–854.

Rudorfer, M. V., Henry, M. E., & Sackeim, H. A. (1997). Electroconvulsive therapy. In A. Tasman, J. Kay, & J. A. Lieberman (Eds.), *Psychiatry* (pp. 1535–1556). Philadelphia: W. B. Saunders.

Rushton, J. P., Fulker, D. W., Neale, M. C., Nias, D. K. B., & Eysenck, H. J. (1986). Altruism and aggression: The heritability of individual differences. *Journal of Personality and Social Psychology, 50,* 1192–1198.

Rushton, J. P., & Jensen, A. R. (2005). Thirty years of research on race differences in cognitive ability. *Psychology, Public Policy, and Law, 11,* 235–294.

Rutherford, W. (1886). The sense and hearing. *Journal of Anatomy and Physiology, 21,* 166–168.

Rutter, M. (1983). Cognitive deficits in the pathogenesis of autism. *Journal of Child Psychology and Psychiatry, 24,* 513–531.

Rutter, M. (2005). Incidence of autism spectrum disorders: Changes over time and their meaning. *Acta Paediatrica, 94,* 2–15.

Rutz, C., Klump, B. C., Komarczyk, L., Leighton, R., Kramer, J., Wischnewski, S., et al. (2016). Discovery of species-wide tool use in the Hawaiian crow. *Nature, 537,* 403–407.

Rzhetsky, A., Bagley, S. C., Wang, K., Lyttle, C. S., Cook, E. H., Jr., Altman, R. B., & Gibbons, R. D. (2014). Environmental and state-level regulatory factors affect the incidence of autism and intellectual disability. *PLoS Computational Biology, 10,* e1003518. Retrieved from http://www.ploscompbiol.org/article/info%3Adoi%2F10.1371%2Fjournal.pcbi.1003518

Saalmann, Y. B., Pigarev, I. N., & Vidyasagar, T. R. (2007). Neural mechanisms of visual attention: How top-down feedback highlights relevant locations. *Science, 316,* 1612–1615.

Sabesan, R., Schmidt, B. P., Tuten, W. S., & Roorda, A. (2016). The elementary representation of spatial and color vision in the human retina. *Science Advances, 2,* e1600797.

Sacco, K. A., Bannon, K. L., & George, T. P. (2004). Nicotinic receptor mechanisms and cognition in normal states and neuropsychiatric disorders. *Journal of Psychopharmacology, 18,* 457–474.

Sacco, K. A., Termine, A., Seyal, A., Dudas, M. M., Vessicchio, J. C., Krishnan-Sarin, S., et al. (2005). Effects of cigarette smoking on spatial working memory and attentional deficits in schizophrenia. *Archives of General Psychiatry, 62,* 649–659.

Sachs, B., & Meisel, R. L. (1994). The physiology of male sexual behavior. In J. D. Neill & E. Knobil (Eds.), *The physiology of reproduction* (Vol. 2, pp. 3–106). New York: Raven Press.

Sack, A. T., Kohler, A., Bestmann, S., Linden, D. E. J., Dechent, P., Goebel, R., et al. (2007). Imaging the brain activity changes underlying impaired visuospatial judgments: Simultaneous fMRI, TMS, and behavioral studies. *Cerebral Cortex, 17,* 2841–2852.

Sack, D. A., Nurnberger, J., Rosenthal, N. E., Ashburn, E., & Wehr, T. A. (1985). Potentiation of antidepressant medications by phase advance of the sleep-wake cycle. *American Journal of Psychiatry, 142,* 606–608.

Sackeim, H. A., Luber, B., Katzman, G. P., Moeller, J. R., Prudic, J., Devanand, D. P., et al. (1996). The effects of electroconvulsive therapy on quantitative electroencephalograms: Relationship to clinical outcome. *Archives of General Psychiatry, 53,* 814–823.

Sackeim, H. A., Prohovnik, I., Moeller, J. R., Brown, R. P., Apter, S., Prudic, J., et al. (1990). Regional cerebral blood flow in mood disorders: I. Comparison of major depressives and normal controls at rest. *Archives of General Psychiatry, 47,* 60–70.

Sackeim, H. A., Prudic, J., Devanand, D. P., Kiersky, J. E., Fitzsimons, L., Moody, B. J., et al. (1993). Effects of stimulus intensity and electrode placement on the efficacy and cognitive effects of electroconvulsive therapy. *New England Journal of Medicine, 328,* 839–846.

Sacks, J. J., Gonzales, K. R., Bouchery, E. E., Tomedi, L. E., & Brewer, R. D. (2015). 2010 national and state costs of excessive alcohol consumption. *American Journal of Preventive Medicine, 49,* e73–e79.

Sacks, O. (1990). *The man who mistook his wife for a hat and other clinical tales.* New York: HarperPerennial.

Sacks, O. (1995). *An anthropologist on Mars.* New York: Vintage Books.

Sacks, O., & Wasserman, R. (1987, November 19). The case of the color-blind painter. *New York Review of Books, 34,* 25–34.

Safavi-Hemani, H., Gajewiak, J., Karanth, S., Robinson, S. D., Ueberheide, B., Douglass, A. D., et al. 2015. Specialized insulin is used for chemical warfare by fish-hunting cone snails. *Proceedings of the National Academy of Sciences, 112,* 1743–1748.

Saha, S., Chant, D., & McGrath, J. (2005). A systematic review of the prevalence of schizophrenia. *PLoS Medicine, 2,* 413–433.

Sairanen, M., Lucas, G., Ernfors, P., Castrén, M., & Castrén, E. (2005). Brain-derived neurotrophic factor and antidepressant drugs have different but coordinated effects on neuronal turnover, proliferation, and survival in the adult dentate gyrus. *Journal of Neuroscience, 25,* 1089–1094.

Sakata, H., Takaoka, Y., Kawarasaki, A., & Shibutani, H. (1973). Somatosensory properties of neurons in the superior parietal cortex (area 5) of the rhesus monkey. *Brain Research, 64,* 85–102.

Sakurai, T. (2007). The neural circuit of orexin (hypocretin): Maintaining sleep and wakefulness. *Nature Reviews Neuroscience, 8,* 171–181.

Salamy, J. (1970). Instrumental responding to internal cues associated with REM sleep. *Psychonomic Science, 18,* 342–343.

Salehi, A., Faizi, M., Colas, D., Valletta, J., Laguna, J., Takimoto-Kimura, R., et al. (2009). Restoration of norepinephrine-modulated contextual memory in a mouse model of Down syndrome. *Science Translational Medicine, 1,* 7–17. Retrieved from http://stm.sciencemag.org/content/1/7/7ra17.full.pdf

Salomons, T. V., Coan, J. A., Hunt, S. M., Backonja, M.-M., & Davidson, R. J. (2008). Voluntary facial displays of pain increase suffering in response to nociceptive stimulation. *Journal of Pain, 9,* 443–448.

Salthouse, T. A. (2006). Mental exercise and mental aging: Evaluating the validity of the "use it or lose it" hypothesis. *Perspectives on Psychological Science, 1*(1), 68–87.

Salthouse, T. A., & Babcock, R. L. (1991). Decomposing adult age differences in working memory. *Developmental Psychology, 27,* 763–776.

Sanacora, G., Mason, G. F., Rothman, D. L., Hyder, F., Ciarcia, J. J., Osroff, R. B., et al. (2003). Increased cortical GABA concentrations in depressed patients receiving ECT. *American Journal of Psychiatry, 160,* 577–579.

Sanders, A. R., Martin, E. R., Beecham, G. W., Guo, S., Dawood, K., Rieger, G., et al. (2015). Genome-wide scan demonstrates significant linkage for male sexual orientation. *Psychological Medicine, 45,* 1379–1388.

Sandin, S., Lichtenstein, P., Kuja-Halkota, R., Larsson, H., Hultman, C. M., & Reichenberg, A. (2014). The familial risk of autism. *Journal of the American Medical Association, 311,* 1770–1777.

Santarelli, L., Saxe, M., Gross, C., Surget, A., Battaglia, F., Dulawa, S., et al. (2003). Requirement of hippocampal neurogenesis for the behavioral effects of antidepressants. *Science, 301,* 805–809.

Santini, E., Muller, R. U., & Quirk, G. J. (2001). Consolidation of extinction learning involves transfer from NMDA-independent to NMDA-dependent memory. *Journal of Neuroscience, 21,* 9009–9017.

Sanz, C., Cali, J., & Morgan, D. (2009). Design complexity in termite-fishing tools of chimpanzees (*Pan troglodytes*). *Biology Letters, 5,* 293–296.

Saper, C. B., Chou, T. C., & Elmquist, J. K. (2002). The need to feed: Homeostatic and hedonic control of eating. *Neuron, 36,* 199–211.

Saper, C. B., Fuller, P. M., Pedersen, N. P., Lu, J., & Scammell, T. E. (2010). Sleep state switching. *Neuron, 68,* 1023–1042.

Saper, C. B., Iverson, S., & Frackowiak, R. (2000). Integration of sensory and motor function. In E. R. Kandel, J. H. Schwartz, & T. M. Jessell (Eds.), *Principles of neural science* (4th ed., pp. 349–380). New York: McGraw-Hill.

Sapolsky, R. M., Uno, H., Rebert, C. S., & Finch, C. E. (1990). Hippocampal damage associated with prolonged glucocorticoid exposure in primates. *Journal of Neuroscience, 10,* 2897–2902.

Sar, V., Unal, S. N., & Ozturk, E. (2007). Frontal and occipital perfusion changes in dissociative identity disorder. *Psychiatry Research: Neuroimaging, 156,* 217–223.

Sarachana, T., & Hu, V. W. (2013). Genome-wide identification of transcriptional targets of RORA reveals direct regulation of multiple genes associated with autism spectrum disorder. *Molecular Autism, 4,* 14. Retrieved from http://www.molecularautism.com/content/4/1/14

Saraswat, A., Weinand, J. D., & Safer, J. D. (2015). Evidence supporting the biologic nature of gender identity. *Endocrine Practice, 21,* 199–204.

Sáry, G., Vogels, R., & Orban, G. A. (1993). Cue-invariant shape selectivity of macaque inferior temporal neurons. *Science, 260,* 995–997.

Sata, R., Maloku, E., Zhubi, A., Pibiri, F., Hajos, M., Costa, E., et al. (2008). Nicotine decreases DNA methyltransferase 1 expression and glutamic acid decarboxylase 67 promoter methylation in GABAergic interneurons. *Proceedings of the National Academy of Sciences, 105,* 16356–16361.

Sato, M. (1986). Acute exacerbation of methamphetamine psychosis and lasting dopaminergic supersensitivity: A clinical survey. *Psychopharmacology Bulletin, 22,* 751–756.

Savage-Rumbaugh, E. S., Murphy, J., Sevcik, R. A., Brakke, K. E., Williams, S. L., & Rumbaugh, D. M. (1993). Language comprehension in ape and child. *Monographs of the Society for Research in Child Development, 58,* 1–222.

Savage-Rumbaugh, S. (1987). A new look at ape language: Comprehension of vocal speech and syntax. *Nebraska Symposium on Motivation, 35,* 201–255.

Savage-Rumbaugh, S., McDonald, K., Sevcik, R. A., Hopkins, W. D., & Rubert, E. (1986). Spontaneous symbol acquisition and communicative use by pygmy chimpanzees *(Pan paniscus)*. *Journal of Experimental Psychology: General, 115,* 211–235.

Savic, I., Berglund, H., & Lindström, P. (2005). Brain response to putative pheromones in homosexual men. *Proceedings of the National Academy of Sciences, 102,* 7356–7361.

Savic, I., & Lindström, P. (2008). PET and MRI show differences in cerebral asymmetry and functional connectivity between homo- and heterosexual subjects. *Proceedings of the National Academy of Sciences, 105,* 9403–9408.

Savica, R. (2014, June 18). Silenced by dementia: What happened to Casey Kasem. *University of Utah HealthFeed.* Retrieved from http://healthcare.utah.edu/healthfeed/postings/2014/06/061814_kasem.silenced.php

Savin-Williams, R. C. (1996). Self-labeling and disclosure among gay, lesbian, and bisexual youths. In J. Laird & R.-J. Green (Eds.), *Lesbians and gays in couples and families: A handbook for therapists* (pp. 153–182). San Francisco: Jossey-Bass.

Sawa, A., & Snyder, S. H. (2002). Schizophrenia: Diverse approaches to a complex disease. *Science, 296,* 692–695.

Sawchenko, P. E. (1998). Toward a new neurobiology of energy balance, appetite, and obesity: The anatomists weigh in. *Journal of Comparative Neurology, 402,* 435–441.

Saxe, G. N., Vasile, R. G., Hill, T. C., Bloomingdale, K., & Van der Kolk, B. A. (1992). SPECT imaging and multiple personality disorder. *Journal of Nervous and Mental Disease, 180,* 662–663.

Saygin, Z. M., Norton, E. S., Osher, D. E., Beach, S. D., Cyr, A. B., Ozernov-Palchik, O., et al. (2013). Tracking the roots of reading ability: White matter volume and integrity correlate with phonological awareness in prereading and early-reading kindergarten children. *Journal of Neuroscience, 33,* 13251–13258.

Scahill, L., Bitsko, R. H., Visser, S. N., & Blumberg, S. J. (2009). Prevalence of diagnosed Tourette syndrome in persons aged 6–17 years—United States, 2007. *Morbidity and Mortality Weekly Report.* Retrieved from http://www.cdc.gov/mmwr/preview/mmwrhtml/mm5821a1.htm

Scarr, S., & Carter-Saltzman, L. (1982). Genetics and intelligence. In R. J. Sternberg (Ed.), *Handbook of human intelligence* (pp. 792–896). New York: Cambridge University Press.

Scarr, S., Pakstis, A. J., Katz, S. H., & Barker, W. B. (1977). Absence of a relationship between degree of white ancestry and intellectual skills within a black population. *Human Genetics, 39,* 69–86.

Scarr, S., & Weinberg, R. A. (1976). IQ test performance of black children adopted by white families. *American Psychologist, 31,* 726–739.

Scerri, T. S., & Schulte-Körne, G. (2010). Genetics of developmental dyslexia. *European Child and Adolescent Psychiatry, 19,* 179–197.

Schachter, S., & Singer, J. E. (1962). Cognitive, social, and physiological determinants of emotional state. *Psychological Review, 69,* 379–399.

Schacter, D. L., Alpert, N. M., Savage, C. R., Rauch, S. L., & Albert, M. S. (1996). Conscious recollection and the human hippocampal formation: Evidence from positron emission tomography. *Proceedings of the National Academy of Sciences, 93,* 321–325.

Schacter, D. L., & Wagner, A. D. (1999). Remembrance of things past. *Science, 285,* 1503–1504.

Schaie, K. W. (1994). The course of adult intellectual development. *American Psychologist, 49,* 304–311.

Scheele, D., Wille, A., Kendrick, K. M., Stoffel-Wagner, B., Becker, B., Güntürkün, O., et al. (2013). Oxytocin enhances brain reward system responses in men viewing the face of their female partner. *Proceedings of the National Academy of Sciences.* doi:10.1073/pnas.1314190110

Schein, S. J., & Desimone, R. (1990). Spectral properties of V4 neurons in the macaque. *Journal of Neuroscience, 10,* 3369–3389.

Schelling, T. C. (1992). Addictive drugs: The cigarette experience. *Science, 255,* 430–433.

Schenck, C. H., Milner, D. M., Hurwitz, T. D., Bundlie, S. R., & Mahowald, M. W. (1989). A polysomnographic and clinical report on sleep-related injury in 100 adult patients. *American Journal of Psychiatry, 146,* 1166–1173.

Scherag, S., Hebebrand, J., & Hinney, A. (2009). Eating disorders: The current status of molecular genetic research. *European Child and Adolescent Psychiatry.* doi:10.1007/s00787-009-0085-9

Scherf, S., Behrmann, M., Minshew, N., & Luna, B. (2008). Atypical development of face and greeble recognition in autism. *Journal of Child Psychiatry, 49,* 838–847.

Schiermeier, Q. (1998). Animal rights activists turn the screw. *Nature, 396,* 505.

Schiff, N. D., Giacino, J. T., Kalmar, K., Victor, J. D., Baker, K., Gerber, M., et al. (2007). Behavioral improvements with thalamic stimulation after severe traumatic brain injury. *Nature, 448,* 600–604.

Schildkraut, J. J. (1965). The catecholamine hypothesis of affective disorders: A review of supporting evidence. *American Journal of Psychiatry, 122,* 509–522.

Schiller, D., Monfils, M.-H., Raio, C. M., Johnson, D. C., LeDoux, J. E., & Phelps, E. A. (2010). Preventing the return of fear in humans using reconsolidation update mechanisms. *Nature, 463,* 49–53.

Schiller, P. H., & Logothetis, N. K. (1990). The color-opponent and broadband channels of the primate visual system. *Trends in Neurosciences, 13,* 392–398.

Schizophrenia Working Group of the Psychiatric Genomics Consortium. (2014). Biological insights from 108 schizophrenia-associated genetic loci. *Nature, 511,* 421–427.

Schmidt, S. L., Harmon, K. A., Sharp, T. A., Kealey, E. H., & Bessesen, D. H. (2012). The effects of overfeeding on spontaneous physical activity in obesity prone and obesity resistant humans. *Obesity, 20,* 2186–2193.

Schmidt, S. L., Keialey, E. H., Horton, T. J., VonKaenel, S., & Bessesen, D. H. (2013). The effects of short-term overfeeding on energy expenditure and nutrient oxidation in obesity-prone and obesity-resistant individuals. *International Journal of Obesity, 37,* 1192–1197.

Schmidt, W. T. (2015, December 14). 2015 Top 10 retinal-research advances. *Eye On the Cure Blog.* Retrieved from http://www.blindness.org/blog/index .php/2015-top-10-retinal-research-advances-2

Schnakers, C., Vanhaudenhuyse, A., Giacino, J., Ventura, M., Boly, M., Majerus, S., et al. (2009). Diagnostic accuracy of the vegetative and minimally conscious state: Clinical consensus versus standardized neurobehavioral assessment. *BMC Neurology, 9,* 35. Retrieved from www.biomedcentral.com/1471-2377/9/35

Schnider, A. (2003). Spontaneous confabulation and the adaptation of thought to ongoing reality. *Nature Reviews Neuroscience, 4,* 662–671.

Schnider, A., & Ptak, R. (1999). Spontaneous confabulators fail to suppress currently irrelevant memory traces. *Nature Neuroscience, 2,* 677–681.

Schobel, S. A., Lewandowski, N. M., Corcoran, C. M., Moore, H., Brown, T., Malaspina, D., et al. (2009). Differential targeting of the CA1 subfield of the hippocampal formation by schizophrenia and related psychotic disorders. *Archives of General Psychiatry, 66,* 938–946.

Schober, M. E., Requena, D. F., Abdullah, O. M., Casper, T. C., Beach, J., Malleske, D., & Pauly, J. R. (2016). Dietary docosahexaenoic acid improves cognitive function, tissue sparing, and magnetic resonance imaging indices of edema and white matter injury in the immature rat after traumatic brain injury. *Journal of Neurotrauma, 33*(4), 390–402. doi:10.1089/neu.2015.3945

Schoenfeld, M. A., Neuer, G., Tempelmann, C., Schübler, K., Noesselt, T., Hopf, J.-M., et al. (2004). Functional magnetic resonance tomography correlates of taste perception in the human primary taste cortex. *Neuroscience, 127,* 347–353.

Schreiber, R., Melon, C., & DeVry, J. (1998). The role of 5-HT receptor subtypes in the anxiolytic effects of selective serotonin reuptake inhibitors in the rat ultrasonic vocalization test. *Psychopharmacology, 135,* 383–391.

Schreiweis, C., Bornschein, U., Burguiere, E., Kerimoglu, C., Schreiter, S., Dannemann, M., et al. (2014). Humanized Foxp2 accelerates learning by enhancing transitions from declarative to procedural performance. *Proceedings of the National Academy of Sciences, 111*(39), 14253–14258.

Schuckit, M. A. (1994). Low level of response to alcohol as a predictor of future alcoholism. *American Journal of Psychiatry, 151,* 184–189.

Schull, W. J., Norton, S., & Jensh, R. P. (1990). Ionizing radiation and the developing brain. *Neurotoxicology and Teratology, 12,* 249–260.

Schulsinger, F., Parnas, J., Petersen, E. T., Schulsinger, H., Teasdale, T. W., Mednick, S. A., et al. (1984). Cerebral ventricular size in the offspring of schizophrenic mothers. *Archives of General Psychiatry, 41,* 602–606.

Schultz, W. (2016). Dopamine reward prediction error coding. *Dialogues in Clinical Neuroscience, 18,* 23–32.

Schwartz, J. M., Stoessel, P. W., Baxter, L. R., Martin, K. M., & Phelps, M. E. (1996). Systematic changes in cerebral glucose metabolic rate after successful behavior modification treatment of obsessive-compulsive disorder. *Archives of General Psychiatry, 53,* 109–113.

Schwartz, M. S. (1994). Ictal language shift in a polyglot. *Journal of Neurology, Neurosurgery, and Psychiatry, 57,* 121.

Schwartz, M. W., & Morton, G. J. (2002). Keeping hunger at bay. *Nature, 418,* 595–597.

Schwartz, M. W., & Seeley, R. J. (1997). The new biology of body weight regulation. *Journal of the American Dietetic Association, 97,* 54–58.

Schwartz, R. (2015, June 9). Breakthrough lets amputees "feel" their artificial limbs. *The Daily Good.* Retrieved from https://www.good.is/articles/ prosthetic-limb-lets-amputees-feel-ends-phantom-limb-pain

Schwartz, W. J., & Gainer, H. D. (1977). Suprachiasmatic nucleus: Use of 14C-labeled deoxyglucose uptake as a functional marker. *Science, 197,* 1089–1091.

Scott, E. M., & Verney, E. L. (1947). Self-selection of diet: VI. The nature of appetites for B vitamins. *Journal of Nutrition, 34,* 471–480.

Scott, T. R. (2011). Learning through the taste system. *Frontiers in Systems Neuoscience, 5,* Article 8. Retrieved from http://www.ncbi.nlm.nih.gov/pmc/articles/ PMC3222881/

Sedaris, D. (1998). *Naked.* Boston: Little, Brown.

Seeing color in sounds has genetic link. (2009, February 9). Retrieved from http:// www.cnn.com/2009/HEALTH/02/09/synesthesia.genes/index.html

Seeman, P., Lee, T., Chau-Wong, M., & Wong, K. (1976). Antipsychotic drug doses and neuroleptic/dopamine receptors. *Nature, 261,* 717–719.

Sekiguchi, A., Kotozaki, Y., Sugiura, M., Nouchi, R., Takeuchi, H., Hanawa, S., et al. (2014). Resilience after 3/11: Structural brain changes 1 year after the Japanese earthquake. *Molecular Psychiatry, 20,* 553–554.

Sekiguchi, A., Sugiura, M., Taki, Y., Kotozaki, Y., Nouchi, R., Takeuchi, H., et al. (2013). Brain structural changes as vulnerability factors and acquired signs of post-earthquake stress. *Molecular Psychiatry, 18,* 618–623.

Selfe, L. (1977). *Nadia: A case of extraordinary drawing ability in children.* London: Academic Press.

Selkoe, D. J. (1997). Alzheimer's disease: Genotypes, phenotype, and treatments. *Science, 275,* 630–631.

Sellers, E. W., Ryan, D. B., & Hauser, C. K. (2014). Noninvasive brain-computer interface enables communication after brainstem stroke. *Science Translational Medicine, 6*(257), 257re7. doi:10.1126/scitranslmed.3007801

Sendt, K.-V., Giaroli, G., & Tracy, D. K. (2012). Beyond dopamine: Glutamate as a target for future antipsychotics. *ISRN Pharmacology, 2012,* 427267. Retrieved from http://www.ncbi.nlm.nih.gov/pmc/articles/PMC3399404/

Senghas, A., Kita, S., & Özyürek, A. (2004). Children creating core properties of language: Evidence from an emerging sign language in Nicaragua. *Science, 305,* 1779–1782.

Senju, A., Maeda, M., Kikuchi, Y., Hasegawa, T., Tojo, Y., & Osanai, H. (2007). Absence of contagious yawning in children with autism spectrum disorder. *Biology Letters.* doi:10.1098/rsb1.2007.0337

Sergent, C., Baillet, S., & Dehaene, S. (2005). Timing of the brain events underlying access to consciousness during the attentional blink. *Nature Neuroscience, 8,* 1391–1400.

Sevigny, J., Chiao, P., Bussière, T., Weinreb, P. H., Williams, L, Maier, M., et al. (2016). The antibody aducanumab reduces Aβ plaques in Alzheimer's disease. *Nature, 537,* 50–56.

Shaffery, J. P., Roffwarg, H. P., Speciale, S. G., & Marks, G. A. (1999). Ponto-geniculo-occipital-wave suppression amplifies lateral geniculate nucleus cell-size changes in monocularly deprived kittens. *Brain Research. Developmental Brain Research, 114,* 109–119.

Shah, A., & Lisak, R. P. (1993). Immunopharmacologic therapy in myasthenia gravis. *Clinical Neuropharmacology, 16,* 97–103.

Shalev, A. Y., Peri, T., Brandes, D., Freedman, S., Orr, S. P., & Pittman, R. K. (2000). Auditory startle response in trauma survivors with posttraumatic stress disorder: A prospective study. *American Journal of Psychiatry, 157,* 255–261.

Sham, P. C., O'Callaghan, E., Takei, N., Murray, G. K., Hare, E. H., & Murray, R. M. (1992). Schizophrenia following pre-natal exposure to influenza epidemics between 1939 and 1960. *British Journal of Psychiatry, 160,* 461–466.

Shapiro, C. M., Bortz, R., Mitchell, D., Bartel, P., & Jooste, P. (1981). Slow-wave sleep: A recovery period after exercise. *Science, 214,* 1253–1254.

Shapiro, M. L., Tanila, H., & Eichenbaum, H. (1997). Cues that hippocampal place cells encode: Dynamic and hierarchical representation of local and distal stimuli. *Hippocampus, 7,* 624–642.

Sharma, A., & Shaw, S. R. (2012). Efficacy of risperidone in managing maladaptive behaviors for children with autistic spectrum disorder: A meta-analysis. *Journal of Pediatric Health Care, 26,* 291–299.

Shearman, L. P., Sriram, S., Weaver, D. R., Maywood, E. S., Chaves, I., Zheng, B., et al. (2000). Interacting molecular loops in the mammalian circadian clock. *Science, 288,* 1013–1019.

Sheehan, W., Thurber, S., & Sewall, B. (2006). Dissociative identity disorder and temporal lobe involvement: Replication and a cautionary note. *Australian & New Zealand Journal of Psychiatry, 40,* 374–375.

Shepard, R. N. (1990). *Mind sights: Original visual illusions, ambiguities, and other anomalies, with a commentary on the play of mind in perception in art.* New York: W. H. Freeman & Co.

Sherva, R., Wilhelmsen, K., Pomerleau, C. S., Chasse, S. A., Rice, J. P., Snedecor, S. M., et al. (2008). Association of a single nucleotide polymorphism in neuronal acetylcholine receptor subunit alpha 5 (CHRNA5) with smoking status and with "pleasurable buzz" during early experimentation with smoking. *Addiction, 103,* 1544–1552.

Sherwin, B. B. (2003). Estrogen and cognitive functioning in women. *Endocrine Reviews, 24,* 133–151.

Sherwin, B. B., & Gelfand, M. M. (1987). The role of androgen in the maintenance of sexual functioning in oophorectomized women. *Psychosomatic Medicine, 49,* 397–409.

Sheth, S. A., Neal, J., Tangherlini, F., Mian, M. K., Gentil, A., Cosgrove, G. R., et al. (2013). Limbic system surgery for treatment-refractory obsessive-compulsive disorder: A prospective long-term follow-up of 64 patients. *Journal of Neurosurgery, 118,* 491–497.

Shibata, D. K. (2007). Differences in brain structure in deaf persons on MR imaging studied with voxel-based morphometry. *American Journal of Neuroradiology, 28,* 243–249.

Shifren, J. L., Braunstein, G. D., Simon, J. A., Casson, P. R., Buster, J. E., Redmond, G. P., et al. (2000). Transdermal testosterone treatment in women with impaired sexual function after oophorectomy. *New England Journal of Medicine, 343,* 682–688.

Shiiya, T., Nakazato, M., Mizuta, M., Date, Y., Mondal, M. S., Tanaka, M., et al. (2009). Plasma ghrelin levels in lean and obese humans and the effect of glucose on ghrelin secretion. *Journal of Clinical Endocrinology and Metabolism, 87,* 240–244.

Shima, K., & Tanji, J. (2000). Neuronal activity in the supplementary and presupplementary motor areas for temporal organization of multiple movements. *Journal of Neurophysiology, 84,* 2148–2160.

Shimura, T., & Shimokochi, M. (1990). Involvement of the lateral mesencephalic tegmentum in copulatory behavior of male rats: Neuron activity in freely moving animals. *Neuroscience Research, 9,* 173–183.

Shin, L. M., & Liberzon, I. (2010). The neurocircuitry of fear, stress, and anxiety disorders. *Neuropsychopharmacology Reviews, 35,* 169–191.

Shouse, M. N., & Siegel, J. M. (1992). Pontine regulation of REM sleep components in cats: Integrity of the pedunculopontine tegmentum (PPT) is important for phasic events but unnecessary for atonia during REM sleep. *Brain Research, 571,* 50–63.

Shu, J.-J., Wang, Q.-W., Yong, K.-Y., Shao, F., & Lee, K. J. (2015). Programmable DNA-mediated multitasking processor. *Journal of Physical Chemistry B, 119,* 5639–5644.

Shuai, Y., Lu, B., Hu, Y., Wang, L., Sun, K., & Zhong, Y. (2010). Forgetting is regulated through Rac activity in *Drosophila. Cell, 140,* 579–589.

Shulgin, A., & Shulgin, A. (1991). *Pihkal: A chemical love story.* Lafayette, CA: Transform Press.

Shulgin, A., & Shulgin, A. (1997). *TIHKAL: The continuation.* Berkeley, CA: Transform Press.

Siclari, F., Baird, B., Perogamvros, L., Bernardi, G., LaRocque, J., Riedner, B., et al. (2017). The neural correlates of dreaming. *Nature Neuroscience, 20,* 872–878.

Siegel, S. (1984). Pavlovian conditioning and heroin overdose: Reports by overdose victims. *Bulletin of the Psychonomic Society, 22,* 428–430.

Siegel, S., Hinson, R. E., Krank, M. D., & McCully, J. (1982). Heroin "overdose" death: Contribution of drug-associated environmental cues. *Science, 216,* 436–437.

Siepel, A., Bejerano, G., Pedersen, J. S., Hinrichs, A. S., Hou, M., Rosenbloom, K., et al. (2005). Evolutionarily conserved elements in vertebrate, insect, worm, and yeast genomes. *Genome Research, 15,* 1034–1050.

Siever, L. J., Kahn, R. S., Lawlor, B. A., Trestman, R. L., Lawrence, T. L., & Coccaro, E. F. (1991). II. Critical issues in defining the role of serotonin in psychiatric disorders. *Pharmacological Reviews, 43,* 509–525.

Silbersweig, D. A., Stern, E., Frith, C., Cahill, C., Homes, A., Grootoonk, S., et al. (1995). A functional neuroanatomy of hallucinations in schizophrenia. *Nature, 378,* 176–179.

Silinsky, E. M. (1989). Adenosine derivatives and neuronal function. *Seminars in the Neurosciences, 1,* 155–165.

Simner, J., Mulvenna, C., Sagiv, N., Tsakanikos, E., Witherby, S. A., Fraser, C., et al. (2006). Synesthesia: The prevalence of atypical cross-modal experiences. *Perception, 35,* 1024–1033.

Simos, P. G., Castillo, E. M., Fletcher, J. M., Francis, D. J., Maestu, F., Breier, J. I., et al. (2001). Mapping of receptive language cortex in bilingual volunteers by using magnetic source imaging. *Journal of Neurosurgery, 95,* 76–81.

Simpson, J. B., Epstein, A. N., & Camardo, J. S., Jr. (1978). Localization of receptors for the dipsogenic action of angiotensin II in the subfornical organ of rat. *Journal of Comparative and Physiological Psychology, 92,* 581–601.

Simpson, J. L., Ljungqvist, A., de la Chapelle, A., Ferguson-Smith, M. A., Genel, M., Carlson, A. S., et al. (1993). Gender verification in competitive sports. *Sports Medicine, 16,* 305–315.

Singer, T., O'Doherty, S. B., Kaube, H., Dolan, R. J., & Frith, C. D. (2004). Empathy for pain involves the affective but not sensory components of pain. *Science, 303,* 1157–1162.

Singer, W. (1995). Development and plasticity of cortical processing architectures. *Science, 270,* 758–764.

Siniscalco, D., Cirillo, A., Bradstreet, J. J., & Antonucci, N. (2013). Epigenetic findings in autism: New perspectives for therapy. *International Journal of Environmental Research and Public Health, 10,* 4261–4273.

Sivian, L. J., & White, S. D. (1933). On minimum audible fields. *Journal of the Acoustical Society of America, 4,* 288–321.

Sizemore, C. C. (1989). *A mind of my own.* New York: William Morrow.

Sjöström, L., Narbro, K., Sjöström, D., Karason, K., Larsson, B., Wedel, H., et al. (2007). Effects of bariatric surgery on mortality in Swedish obese subjects. *New England Journal of Medicine, 357,* 741–752.

Slimp, J. C., Hart, B. L., & Goy, R. W. (1978). Heterosexual, autosexual and social behavior of adult male rhesus monkeys with medial preoptic–anterior hypothalamic lesions. *Brain Research, 142,* 105–122.

Small, S. A., Stern, Y., Tang, M., & Mayeux, R. (1999). Selective decline in memory function among healthy elderly. *Neurology, 52,* 1392–1396.

Small, furry . . . and smart. (2009). *Nature, 461,* 862–864.

Smalley, S. L. (1997). Genetic influences in childhood-onset psychiatric disorders: Autism and attention-deficit/hyperactivity disorder. *American Journal of Human Genetics, 60,* 1276–1282.

Smith, C. (1995). Sleep states and memory processes. *Behavioural Brain Research, 69,* 137–145.

Smith, C. (1996). Sleep states, memory processes and synaptic plasticity. *Behavioural Brain Research, 78,* 49–56.

Smith, C. N., & Squire, L. R. (2009). Medial temporal lobe activity during retrieval of semantic memory is related to the age of the memory. *Journal of Neuroscience, 29,* 930–938.

Smith, D. M., & Atkinson, R. M. (1995). Alcoholism and dementia. *International Journal of Addiction, 30,* 1843–1869.

Smith, D. M., & Mizumori, S. J. Y. (2006). Hippocampal place cells, context, and episodic memory. *Hippocampus, 16,* 716–729.

Smith, J., Cianflone, K., Biron, S., Hould, F. S., Lebel, S., Marceau, S., et al. (2009). Effects of maternal surgical weight loss in mothers on intergenerational transmission of obesity. *Journal of Clinical Endocrinology and Metabolism, 94,* 4275–4283.

Smith, M. A., Brandt, J., & Shadmehr, R. (2000). Motor disorder in Huntington's disease begins as a dysfunction in error feedback control. *Nature, 403,* 544–549.

Smith, M. J., Keel, J. C., Greenberg, B. D., Adams, L. F., Schmidt, P. J., Rubinow, D. A., et al. (1999). Menstrual cycle effects on cortical excitability. *Neurology, 53,* 2069–2072.

Smith, T. (2013, December 12). Newtown parents seek a clear window into violent behavior. *NPR Morning Edition.* Retrieved from http://www.npr.org/2013/12/12/250287971/newtown-parents-seek-a-clearer-window-into-violent-behavior

Smucny, J., Stevens, K. E., Olincy, A., & Tregellas, J. R. (2015). Translational utility of rodent hippocampal auditory gating in schizophrenia research: A review and evaluation. *Translational Psychiatry, 5,* e587.

Smythies, J., Edelstein, L., & Ramachandran, V. (2012). Hypotheses relating to the function of the claustrum. *Frontiers in Integrative Neuroscience, 6,* 53. doi:10.3389/fnint.2012.00053

Smythies, J., Edelstein, L., & Ramachandran, V. (2014). Hypotheses relating to the function of the claustrum II: Does the claustrum use frequency codes? *Frontiers in Integrative Neuroscience, 8(7),* 1–3. doi:10.3389/fnint.2014.0000

Sneaky DNA analysis to be outlawed. (2006, August 29). *New Scientist,* 6–7.

Snowball, A., Tachtsidis, I., Popescu, T., Thompson, J., Delazer, M., Zamarian, L., et al. (2013). Long-term enhancement of brain function and cognition using cognitive training and brain stimulation. *Current Biology, 23,* 987–992.

Snyder, A. (2009). Explaining and inducing savant skills: Privileged access to lower level, less-processed information. *Philosophical Transactions of the Royal Society B, 364,* 1399–1405.

Snyder, A. W., & Mitchell, D. J. (1999). Is integer arithmetic fundamental to mental processing? The mind's secret arithmetic. *Proceedings of the Royal Society of London B, 266,* 587–592.

Snyder, S. H. (1972). Catecholamines in the brain as mediators of amphetamine psychosis. *Archives of General Psychiatry, 27,* 169–179.

Snyder, S. H. (1984). Drug and neurotransmitter receptors in the brain. *Science, 224,* 22–31.

Snyder, S. H. (1997). Knockouts anxious for new therapy. *Nature, 388,* 624.

Snyder, S. H., Banerjee, S. P., Yamamura, H. I., & Greenberg, D. (1974). Drugs, neurotransmitters, and schizophrenia. *Science, 184,* 1243–1253.

Söderland, J., Schröder, J., Nordin, C., Samuelsson, M., Walther-Jallow, L., Karlsson, H., et al. (2009). Activation of brain interleukin-1b in schizophrenia. *Molecular Psychiatry, 14,* 1069–1071.

Sohl-Dickstein, J., Teng, S., Gaub, B. M., Rodgers, C. C., Li, C., DeWeese, M. R., & Harper, N. S. (2015). A device for human ultrasonic echolocation. *IEEE Transactions on Biomedical Engineering, 62(6),* 1526–1534.

Soliman, F., Glatt, C. E., Bath, K. G., Levita, L., Jones, R. M., Pattwell, S. S., et al. (2010). A genetic variant BDNF polymorphism alters extinction learning in both mouse and human. *Science, 327,* 863–866.

Sommer, I. E. C., Aleman, A., Bouma, A., & Kahn, R. S. (2004). Do women really have more bilateral language representation than men? A meta-analysis of functional imaging studies. *Brain, 127,* 1845–1852.

Soria, V., Martinez-Amorós, È., Crespo, J. M., Martorell, L., Vilella, E., Labad, A., et al. (2010). Differential association of circadian genes with mood disorders: CRY1 and NPAS2 are associated with unipolar major depression and CLOCK and VIP with bipolar disorder. *Neuropsychopharmacology, 35,* 1279–1289.

Sotiriadis, A., & Makrydimas, G. (2012). Neurodevelopment after prenatal diagnosis of isolated agenesis of the corpus callosum: An integrative review. *American Journal of Obstetrics & Gynecology, 206,* 337.e1–337e5. Retrieved from http://www.ajog.org/article/S0002-9378(11)02432-X/

Soto-Otero, R., Méndez-Alvarez, E., Sánchez-Sellero, J., Cruz-Landeira, A., & López-Rivadulla, L. M. (2001). Reduction of rat brain levels of the endogenous dopaminergic proneurotoxins 1,2,3,4-tetrahydroisoquinoline and 1,2,3,4-tetrahydro-beta-carboline by cigarette smoke. *Neuroscience Letters, 298,* 187–190.

Sowell, E. R., Thompson, P. M., Holmes, C. J., Jernigan, T. L., & Toga, A. W. (1999). *In vivo* evidence for post-adolescent brain maturation in frontal and striatal regions. *Nature Neuroscience, 2,* 859–861.

Spalding, K. L., Bergmann, O., Alkass, K., Bernard, S., Salehpour, M., Huttner, H. B., et al. (2013). Dynamics of hippocampal neurogenesis in adult humans. *Cell, 153,* 1219–1227.

Spanos, N. P. (1994). Multiple identity enactments and multiple personality disorder: A sociocognitive perspective. *Psychological Bulletin, 116,* 143–165.

Sparing, R., & Mottaghy, F. M. (2008). Noninvasive brain stimulation with transcranial magnetic or direct current stimulation (TMS/tDCS)—from insights into human memory to therapy of its dysfunction. *Methods, 44,* 329–337.

Speakman, J. R., Rance, K. A., & Johnstone, A. M. (2008). Polymorphisms of the FTO gene are associated with variation in energy intake but not energy expenditure. *Obesity, 16,* 1961–1965.

Spence, S., Shapiro, D., & Zaidel, E. (1996). The role of the right hemisphere in the physiological and cognitive components of emotional processing. *Psychophysiology, 33,* 112–122.

Spence, S. A., Brooks, D. J., Hirsch, S. R., Liddle, P. F., Mechan, J., & Grasby, P. (1997). A PET study of voluntary movement in schizophrenic patients experiencing passivity phenomena (delusions of alien control). *Brain, 120,* 1997–2011.

Spencer, K. M., Nestor, P. G., Permutter, R., Nizmikiewicz, M. A., Klump, M. C., Frumin, M., et al. (2004). Neural synchrony indexes disordered perception and cognition in schizophrenia. *Proceedings of the National Academy of Sciences, 101,* 17288–17293.

Spencer, K. M., Niznikiewicz, M. A., Nestor, P. G., Shenton, M. E., & McCarley, R. W. (2009). Left auditory cortex gamma synchronization and auditory hallucination symptoms in schizophrenia. *BMC Neuroscience.* Retrieved from www.biomedcentral.com/1471-2202/10/85

Sperry, R. W. (1943). Effect of 180 degrees rotation of the retinal field on visuomotor coordination. *Journal of Experimental Zoology, 92,* 263–279.

Sperry, R. W. (1945). Restoration of vision after crossing of optic nerves and after contralateral transplantation of eye. *Journal of Neurophysiology, 8,* 15–28.

Spiegel, D. (1996). Cancer and depression. *British Journal of Psychiatry, 168,* 109–116.

Spillantini, M. G., Schmidt, M. L., Lee, V. M.-Y., Trojanowski, J. Q., Jakes, R., & Goedert, M. (1997). a-Synuclein in Lewy bodies. *Nature, 388,* 839–840.

Spinney, L. (2002, September 21). The mind readers. *New Scientist,* 38–41.

Spreux-Varoquaux, O., Alvarez, J.-C., Berlin, I., Batista, G., Despierre, P.-G., Gilton, A., et al. (2001). Differential abnormalities in plasma 5-HIAA and platelet serotonin concentrations in violent suicide attempters: Relationships with impulsivity and depression. *Life Sciences, 69,* 647–657.

Springen, K. (2004, December 6). Using genes as medicine. *Newsweek,* p. 55.

Spurzheim, J. G. (1908). *Phrenology* (Rev. ed.). Philadelphia: Lippincott.

Squire, L. R., & Alvarez, P. (1995). Retrograde amnesia and memory consolidation: A neurobiological perspective. *Current Opinion in Neurobiology, 5,* 169–177.

Squire, L. R., Amaral, D. G., & Press, G. A. (1990). Magnetic resonance imaging of the hippocampal formation and mammillary nuclei distinguish medial temporal lobe and diencephalic amnesia. *Journal of Neuroscience, 10,* 3106–3117.

Squire, L. R., Amaral, D. G., Zola-Morgan, S., Kritchevsky, M., & Press, G. (1989). Description of brain injury in the amnesic patient N.A. based on magnetic resonance imaging. *Experimental Neurology, 105,* 23–35.

Squire, L. R., Ojemann, J. G., Miezin, F. M., Petersen, S. E., Videen, T. O., & Raichle, M. E. (1992). Activation of the hippocampus in normal humans: A functional anatomical study of memory. *Proceedings of the National Academy of Sciences, 89,* 1837–1841.

Srivastava, S. (2003, September). Fear not traveling salesmen, DNA computing is here to save the day. *Journal of Young Investigators, 8*(2). Retrieved from http://www.jyi.org/volumes/volume8/issue2/features/srivastava.html

Stahre, M., Roeber, J., Kanny, D., Brewer, R. D., & Zhang, X. (2014). Contribution of excessive alcohol consumption to deaths and years of potential life lost in the United States. *Preventing Chronic Disease, 11,* 130293.

Stanley, B. G., Kyrkouli, S. E., Lampert, S., & Leibowitz, S. F. (1986). Neuropeptide Y chronically injected into the hypothalamus: A powerful neurochemical inducer of hyperphagia and obesity. *Peptides, 7,* 1189–1192.

Stanley, M., Stanley, B., Traskman-Bendz, L., Mann, J. J., & Meyendorff, E. (1986). Neurochemical findings in suicide completers and suicide attempters. *Suicide and Life-Threatening Behavior, 16,* 286–299.

Starr, C., & Taggart, R. (1989). *Biology: The unity and diversity of life.* Pacific Grove, CA: Brooks/Cole.

St. Clair, D., Xu, M., Wang, P., Yu, Y., Fang, Y., Zhang, F., et al. (2005). Rates of adult schizophrenia following prenatal exposure to the Chinese famine of 1959–1961. *Journal of the American Medical Association, 294,* 557–562.

Stein, J. (2001). The magnocellular theory of developmental dyslexia. *Dyslexia, 7,* 12–36.

Stein, J. L., Medland, S. E., Vasquez, A. A., Hibar, D. P., Senstad, R. E., Winkler, A. M., et al. (2012). Identification of common variants associated with human hippocampal and intracranial volumes. *Nature Genetics, 44,* 552–561.

Stein, P. K., Soare, A., Meyer, T. E., Cangemi, R., Holloszy, J. O., & Fontana, L. (2012). Caloric restriction may reverse age-related autonomic decline in humans. *Aging Cell, 11,* 644–650.

Steinberg, E. E., Christoffel, D. J., Deisseroth, K., & Malenka, R. C. (2015). Illuminating circuitry relevant to psychiatric disorders with optogenetics. *Current Opinion in Neurobiology, 30,* 9–16.

Stellar, J. R., & Stellar, E. (1985). *The neurobiology of motivation and reward.* New York: Springer-Verlag.

Stem Cells Portal. (2017, March 20). Phase 1 enrollment completed in groundbreaking stem cell trial for Alzheimer's disease. Retrieved from https://stemcellsportal.com/news/phase-1-enrollment-completed-groundbreaking-stem-cell-trial-alzheimers-disease

Stephan, F. K., & Nunez, A. A. (1977). Elimination of circadian rhythms in drinking, activity, sleep, and temperature by isolation of the suprachiasmatic nuclei. *Behavioral Biology, 20,* 1–16.

Stephen Wiltshire MBE—Biography. (n.d.). Retrieved from http://www.stephenwiltshire.co.uk/biography.aspx

Stephens, D. N., & Duka, T. (2008). Cognitive and emotional consequences of binge drinking: Role of amygdala and prefrontal cortex. *Philosophical Transactions of the Royal Society B, 363,* 3169–3179.

Steriade, M., Paré, D., Bouhassira, D., Deschênes, M., & Oakson, G. (1989). Phasic activation of lateral geniculate and perigeniculate thalamic neurons during sleep with ponto-geniculo-occipital waves. *Journal of Neuroscience, 9,* 2215–2229.

Stern, K., & McClintock, M. K. (1998). Regulation of ovulation by human pheromones. *Nature, 392,* 177–179.

Stern, Y. (2012). Cognitive reserve in ageing and Alzheimer's disease. *Lancet Neurology, 11,* 1006–1012.

Sternbach, R. A. (1968). *Pain: A psychophysiological analysis.* New York: Academic Press.

Sternberg, R. J. (1988). *The triarchic mind: A new theory of human intelligence.* New York: Viking.

Sternberg, R. J. (2000). The holey grail of general intelligence. *Science, 289,* 399–401.

Stewart, J. E., Feinle-Bisset, C., Golding, M., Delahunty, C., Clifton, P. M., & Keast, R. S. J. (2010). Oral sensitivity to fatty acids, food consumption and BMI in human subjects. *British Journal of Nutrition, 104,* 145–152.

Stickgold, R., Hobson, J. A., Fosse, R., & Fosse, M. (2001). Sleep, learning, and dreams: Off-line memory reprocessing. *Science, 294,* 1052–1057.

Stickgold, R., Whidbee, D., Schirmer, B., Patel, V., & Hobson, J. A. (2000). Visual discrimination task improvement: A multi-step process occurring during sleep. *Journal of Cognitive Neuroscience, 12,* 246–254.

Stingl, K., Bartz-Schmidt, K. U., Besch, D., Braun, A., Bruckmann, A., Gekeler, F., et al. (2013). Artificial vision with wirelessly powered subretinal electronic implant Alpha-IMS. *Proceedings of the Royal Society B, 280,* 20130077. doi:10.1098/rspb.2013.0077

Strack, F., Martin, L. L., & Stepper, S. (1988). Inhibiting and facilitating conditions of the human smile: A nonobtrusive test of the facial feedback hypothesis. *Journal of Personality and Social Psychology, 54,* 768–777.

Strakowski, S. (2011). Structural imaging of bipolar illness. In M. Shenton & B. Turetsky (Eds.), *Understanding neuropsychiatric disorders: Insights from neuroimaging.* New York: Cambridge University Press.

Strakowski, S. M., Adler, C. M., Holland, S. K., Mills, N., & DelBello, M. P. (2004). A preliminary FMRI study of sustained attention in euthymic, unmedicated bipolar disorder. *Neuropsychopharmacology, 29,* 1734–1740.

Strang, J., Babor, T., Caulkins, J., Fischer, B., Foxcroft, D., & Humphreys, K. (2012). Drug policy and the public good: Evidence for effective interventions. *Lancet, 379,* 71–83.

Stratigopoulos, G., Carli, J. F. M., O'Day, D. R., Wang, L., LeDuc, C. A., Lanzano, P., et al. (2014). Hypomorphism for *RPGRIP1L*, a ciliary gene vicinal to the *FTO* locus causes increased adiposity in mice. *Cell Metabolism, 19,* 767–779.

Streissguth, A. P., Barr, H. M., Bookstein, F. L., Sampson, P. D., & Olson, H. C. (1999). The long-term neurocognitive consequences of prenatal alcohol exposure: A 14-year study. *Psychological Science, 10,* 186–190.

Stricker, E. M., & Sved, A. F. (2000). Thirst. *Nutrition, 16,* 821–826.

Studer, B., Manes, F., Humphreys, G., Robbins, T. W., & Clark, L. (2015). Risk-sensitive decision-making in patients with posterior parietal and ventromedial prefrontal cortex injury. *Cerebral Cortex, 25,* 1–9.

Studte, S., Bridger, E., & Mecklinger, A. (2015). Nap sleep preserves associative but not item memory preference. *Neurobiology of Learning and Memory, 120,* 84–93.

Suddath, R. L., Casanova, M. F., Goldberg, T. E., Daniel, D. G., Kelsoe, J. R., & Weinberger, D. R. (1989). Temporal lobe pathology in schizophrenia: A quantitative magnetic resonance imaging study. *American Journal of Psychiatry, 146,* 464–472.

Suddath, R. L., Christison, G. W., Torrey, E. F., Casanova, M. F., & Weinberger, D. R. (1990). Anatomical abnormalities in the brains of monozygotic twins discordant for schizophrenia. *New England Journal of Medicine, 322,* 789–794.

Sullivan, P. F. (1995). Mortality in anorexia nervosa. *American Journal of Psychiatry, 152,* 1073–1074.

Supa, M., Cotzin, M., & Dallenbach, K. M. (1944). "Facial vision": The perception of obstacles by the blind. *American Journal of Psychology, 57,* 133–183.

Supekar, K., Uddin, L. Q., Khouzam, A., Phillips, J., Gaillad, W. D., Kenworthy, L. E., et al. (2013). Brain hyperconnectivity in children with autism and its links to social deficits. *Cell Reports, 5,* 738–747.

Supreme Court rules that religious group can use illegal drug in their worship services. (2006, February 21). Pew Research Center. Retrieved from http://www

.pewforum.org/2006/02/21/supreme-court-rules-that-religious-group-can-use-illegal-drug-in-their-worship-services

Surén, P., Roth, C., Bresnahan, M., Haugen, M., Hornig, M., Hirtz, D., et al. (2013). Association between maternal use of folic acid supplements and risk of autism in children. *Journal of the American Medical Association, 309,* 570–577.

Susser, E., Neugebauer, R., Hoek, H. W., Brown, A. S., Lin, S., Labovitz, D., et al. (1996). Schizophrenia after prenatal famine: Further evidence. *Archives of General Psychiatry, 53,* 25–31.

Sutcliffe, J. S. (2008). Insights into the pathogenesis of autism. *Science, 321,* 208–209.

Suvisaari, J. M., Haukka, J. K., Tanskanen, A. J., & Lönnqvist, J. K. (1999). Decline in the incidence of schizophrenia in Finnish cohorts born from 1954 to 1965. *Archives of General Psychiatry, 56,* 733–740.

Suzdak, P. D., Glowa, J. R., Crawley, J. N., Schwartz, R. D., Skolnick, P., & Paul, S. M. (1986). A selective imidazobenzodiazepine antagonist of ethanol in the rat. *Science, 234,* 1243–1247.

Suzuki, A., Stern, S. A., Bozdagi, O., Huntley, G. W., Walker, R. H., Magistretti, P. J., & Alberini, C. M. (2011). Astrocyte-neuron lactate transport is required for long-term memory formation. *Cell, 144,* 810–823.

Svensson, T. H., Grenhoff, J., & Aston-Jones, G. (1986). Midbrain dopamine neurons: Nicotinic control of firing pattern. *Society for Neuroscience Abstracts, 12,* 1154.

Swaab, D. F. (1996). Desirable biology. *Science, 382,* 682–683.

Swaab, D. F., & Hofman, M. A. (1990). An enlarged suprachiasmatic nucleus in homosexual men. *Brain Research, 537,* 141–148.

Swaab, D. F., Slob, A. K., Houtsmuller, E. J., Brand, T., & Zhou, J. N. (1995). Increased number of vasopressin neurons in the suprachiasmatic nucleus (SCN) of "bisexual" adult male rats following perinatal treatment with the aromatase blocker ATD. *Developmental Brain Research, 85,* 273–279.

Swank, M. W., & Sweatt, D. (2001). Increased histone acetyltransferase and lysine acetyltransferase activity and biphasic activation of the ERK/RSK cascade in insular cortex during novel taste learning. *Journal of Neuroscience, 21,* 3383–3391.

Swedo, S. E., Rapoport, J. L., Leonard, H. L., Lenane, M., & Cheslow, D. (1989). Obsessive-compulsive disorder in children and adolescents: Clinical phenomenology of 70 consecutive cases. *Archives of General Psychiatry, 46,* 335–341.

Swedo, S. E., Rapoport, J. L., Leonard, H. L., Schapiro, M. B., Rapoport, S. I., & Grady, C. L. (1991). Regional cerebral glucose metabolism of women with trichotillomania. *Archives of General Psychiatry, 48,* 828–833.

Swedo, S. E., Schapiro, M. B., Grady, C. L., Cheslow, D. L., Leonard, H. L., Kumar, A., et al. (1989). Cerebral glucose metabolism in childhood-onset obsessive-compulsive disorder. *Archives of General Psychiatry, 46,* 518–523.

Sylvester, C. M., Corbetta, M., Raichle, M. E., Rodebaugh, T. L., Schlaggar, B. L., Sheline, Y. I., et al. (2012). Functional network dysfunction in anxiety and anxiety disorders. *Trends in Neurosciences, 35,* 527–535.

Szalavitz, M. (2000). Drugs to fight drugs. *HMS Beagle.* Retrieved from www.news.bmn.com/hmsbeagle/91/notes/feature1

Szeszko, P. R., Ardekani, B. A., Ashtari, M., Malhotra, A. K., Robinson, D. G., Bilder, R. M., et al. (2005). White matter abnormalities in obsessive-compulsive disorder: A diffusion tensor imaging study. *Archives of General Psychiatry, 62,* 782–790.

Tabrizi, S. J., Cleeter, M. W., Xuereb, J., Taanman, J. W., Cooper, J. M., & Schapira, A. H. (1999). Biochemical abnormalities and excitotoxicity in Huntington's disease brain. *Annals of Neurology, 45,* 25–32.

Tadic, A., Rujescu, D., Szegedi, A., Giegling, I., Singer, P., Möller, H.-J., et al. (2003). Association of a *MAOA* gene variant with generalized anxiety disorder, but not with panic disorder or major depression. *American Journal of Medical Genetics Part B, 117B,* 1–6.

Taheri, S., Lin, L., Austin, D., Young, T., & Mignot, E. (2004). Short sleep duration is associated with reduced leptin, elevated ghrelin, and increased body mass index. *Public Library of Science Medicine, 1,* 210–217.

Takayanagi, Y., Spira, A. P., Roth, K. B., Gallo, J. J., Eaton, W. W., & Mojtabai, R. (2014). Accuracy of reports of lifetime medical and physical disorders: Results from the Baltimore epidemiological catchment area study. *JAMA Psychiatry, 71*(3), 273–280.

Talbot, J. D., Marrett, S., Evans, A. C., Meyer, E., Bushnell, M. C., & Duncan, G. H. (1991). Multiple representations of pain in human cerebral cortex. *Science, 251,* 1355–1358.

Tam, N., & Noakes, T. D. (2013). The quantification of body fluid allostasis during exercise. *Sports Medicine, 43,* 1289–1299.

Tamietto, M., Castelli, L., Vighetti, S., Perozzo, P., Geminiani, G., Weiskrantz, L., et al. (2009). Unseen facial and bodily expressions trigger fast emotional reactions. *Proceedings of the National Academy of Sciences, 106,* 17661–17666.

Tamietto, M., Cauda, F., Corazzini, L. L., Savazzi, S., Marzi, C. A., Goebel, R., et al. (2010). Collicular vision guides nonconscious behavior. *Journal of Cognitive Neuroscience, 22,* 888–902.

Tan, R., & Goldman, M. S. (2015). Exposure to female fertility pheromones influences men's drinking. *Experimental & Clinical Psychopharmacology, 23*(3), 139–146.

Tanaka, K. (1996). Inferotemporal cortex and object vision. *Annual Review of Neuroscience, 19,* 109–139.

Tanaka, K. (2003). Columns for complex visual object features in the inferotemporal cortex: Clustering of cells with similar but slightly different stimulus selectivities. *Cerebral Cortex, 13,* 90–99.

Tanda, G., Munzar, P., & Goldberg, S. R. (2000). Self-administration behavior is maintained by the psychoactive ingredient of marijuana in squirrel monkeys. *Nature Neuroscience, 3,* 1073–1074.

Tanda, G., Pontieri, F. E., & Di Chiara, G. (1997). Cannabinoid and heroin activation of mesolimbic dopamine transmission by a common μ1 opioid receptor mechanism. *Science, 276,* 2048–2050.

Tang, H., Hammack, C., Ogden, S. C., Wen, Z., Qian, X., Li, Y., et al. (2016). Zika virus infects human cortical neural progenitors and attenuates their growth. *Cell Stem Cell, 18,* 1–4. doi:10.1016/j.stem.2016.02.016

Tanji, J., & Shima, K. (1994). Role for supplementary motor area cells in planning several movements ahead. *Nature, 371,* 413–416.

Tanner, C. M., Ottman, R., Goldman, S. M., Ellenberg, J., Chan, P., Mayeux, R., et al. (1999). Parkinson disease in twins: An etiologic study. *Journal of the American Medical Association, 281,* 341–346.

TauRx Therapeutics. (n.d.). About LMTX™ for Alzheimer's. Retrieved from http://taurx.com/lmtx-for-ad.html

Taylor, D. (2009). Withdrawal of rimonabant: Walking the tightrope of 21st century pharmaceutical regulation? *Current Drug Safety, 4,* 2–4.

Taylor, D. N. (1995). Effects of a behavioral stress-management program on anxiety, mood, self-esteem, and T-cell count in HIV-positive men. *Psychological Reports, 76,* 451–457.

Taylor, L. E., Swerdfeger, A. L., & Eslick, G. D. (2014). Vaccines are not associated with autism: An evidence-based meta-analysis of case-control and cohort studies. *Vaccine, 32,* 3623–3629.

Taylor, S. (2013). Molecular genetics of obsessive-compulsive disorder: A comprehensive meta-analysis of genetic association studies. *Molecular Psychiatry, 18,* 799–805.

Taylor, V. H., Curtis, C. M., & Davis, C. (2009). The obesity epidemic: The role of addiction. *Canadian Medical Association Journal.* doi:10.1503/cmaj.091142

Tellegen, A., Lykken, D. T., Bouchard, T. J., Wilcox, K. J., Segal, N. L., & Rich, S. (1988). Personality similarity in twins reared apart and together. *Journal of Personality and Social Psychology, 54,* 1031–1039.

Telzer, E. H., Ichien, N. T., & Qu, Y. (2015). Mothers know best: Redirecting adolescent reward sensitivity toward safe behavior during risk taking. *Social Cognitive and Affective Neuroscience, 10,* 1383–1391.

Temoshok, L. (1987). Personality, coping style, emotion and cancer: Towards an integrative model. *Cancer Survivor, 6,* 545–567.

Tepas, D. I., & Carvalhais, A. B. (1990). Sleep patterns of shiftworkers. *Occupational Medicine, 5,* 199–208.

Terrace, H. S., Petitto, L. A., Sanders, R. J., & Bever, T. G. (1979). Can an ape create a sentence? *Science, 206,* 891–901.

Tessier-Lavigne, M., & Goodman, C. S. (1996). The molecular biology of axon guidance. *Science, 274,* 1123–1132.

Tessmar-Raible, K., Raible, F., & Arboleda, E. (2011). Another place, another timer: Marine species and the rhythms of life. *Bioessays, 33,* 165–172.

Thaler, L., Arnott, S. R., & Goodale, M. A. (2011). Neural correlates of natural human echolocation in early and late blind echolocation experts. *PLoS ONE, 6,* e20162. doi:10.1371/journal.pone.0020162

Thallmair, M., Metz, G. A. S., Z'Graggen, W. J., Raineteau, O., Kartje, G. L., & Schwab, M. E. (1998). Neurite growth inhibitors restrict plasticity and functional recovery following corticospinal tract lesions. *Nature Neuroscience, 1*(2), 124–131.

Thambisetty, M., Beason-Held, L., An, Y., Kraut, M. A., & Resnick, S. M. (2010). *APOE ε4* genotype and longitudinal changes in cerebral blood flow in normal aging. *Archives of Neurology, 67,* 93–98.

Therapy setback. (2005, February 12). *New Scientist, 185,* 6.

These 5 weight-loss drugs really work—but here's what else you need to know. (2016, June 22). *Women'sHealth.* Retrieved from http://www.womenshealthmag.com/weight-loss/fda-approved-weight-loss-prescriptions

Thibaut, F., Cordier, B., & Kuhn, J.-M. (1996). Gonadotrophin hormone releasing hormone agonist in cases of severe paraphilia: A lifetime treatment? *Psychoneuroendocrinology, 21,* 411–419.

Thiele, A., Henning, P., Kubischik, M., & Hoffmann, K.-P. (2002). Neural mechanisms of saccadic suppression. *Science, 295,* 2460–2462.

Thier, P., Haarmeier, T., Chakraborty, S., Lindner, A., & Tikhonov, A. (2001). Cortical substrates of perceptual stability during eye movements. *NeuroImage, 14,* S33–S39.

Thigpen, C. H., & Cleckley, H. M. (1957). *The three faces of Eve.* London: Secker & Warburg.

Thomas, R., Sanders, S., Doust, J., Beller, E., & Glasziou, P. (2015). Prevalence of attention-deficit/hyperactivity disorder: A systematic review and meta-analysis. *Pediatrics, 135,* e994–e1001. doi:10.1542/peds2014-3482

Thompson, P. M., Cannon, T. D., Narr, K. L., van Erp, T., Poutanen, V.-P., Huttunen, M., et al. (2001). Genetic influences on brain structure. *Nature Neuroscience, 4,* 1253–1258.

Thompson, P. M., Vidal, C., Giedd, J. N., Gochman, P., Blumenthal, J., Nicolson, R., et al. (2001). Mapping adolescent brain change reveals dynamic wave of accelerated gray matter loss in very early-onset schizophrenia. *Proceedings of the National Academy of Sciences, 98,* 11650–11655.

Thomson, S. N., Avidan, N., Lee, K., Sarma, A. K., Tushe, R., Milewicz, D. M., et al. (2011). The genetics of colored sequence synesthesia: Suggestive evidence of linkage to 16q and genetic heterogeneity for the condition. *Behavioural Brain Research, 223*, 48–52.

Thrasher, T. N., & Keil, L. C. (1987). Regulation of drinking and vasopressin secretion: Role of organum vasculosum laminae terminalis. *American Journal of Physiology, 253*, R108–R120.

Tobi, E. W., Lumey, L. H., Talens, R. P., Kremer, D., Putter, H., Stein, A. D., et al. (2009). DNA methylation differences after exposure to prenatal famine are common and timing- and sex-specific. *Human Molecular Genetics, 18*, 4046–4053.

Tobi, E. W., Slagboom, P. E., van Dongen, J., Kremer, D., Stein, A. D., Putter, H., et al. (2012). Prenatal famine and genetic variation are independently and additively associated with DNA methylation at regulatory loci within *IGF2/H19*. *PLoS ONE, 7*, e37933. Retrieved from http://www.plosone.org/article/info%3Adoi%2F10.1371%2Fjournal.pone.0037933

Tohen, M. (2015). Cariprazine in bipolar disorders. *Journal of Clinical Psychiatry, 73*(3), e368–e370.

Tolin, D. F., Stevens, M. C., Villavicencio, A. L., Norberg, M. M., Calhoun, V. D., Frost, R. O., et al. (2012). Neural mechanisms of decision making in hoarding behavior. *Archives of General Psychiatry, 69*, 832–841.

Tomasi, D., & Volkow, N. D. (2012). Laterality patterns of brain functional connectivity: Gender effects. *Cerebral Cortex, 201*, 1455–1462.

Tomer, R., Ye, L., Hsueh, B., & Deisseroth, K. (2014). Advanced CLARITY for rapid and high-resolution imaging of intact tissues. *Nature Protocols, 9*, 1682–1697. doi:10.1038/nprot.2014.123

Tong, F. (2003). Primary visual cortex and visual awareness. *Nature Reviews Neuroscience, 4*, 219–229.

Toni, N., Buchs, P.-A., Nikonenko, I., Bron, C. R., & Muller, D. (1999). LTP promotes formation of multiple spine synapses between a single axon terminal and a dendrite. *Nature, 402*, 421–425.

Tononi, G. (2005). Consciousness, information integration, and the brain. In S. Laureys (Ed.), *The boundaries of consciousness: Neurobiology and neuropathology* (pp. 109–126). New York: Elsevier.

Tononi, G. (2008). Consciousness as integrated information: A provisional manifesto. *Biological Bulletin, 215*, 216–242.

Tononi, G., & Cirelli, C. (2013). Perchance to prune. *Scientific American, 309*, 34–39.

Tononi, G., & Cirelli, C. (2014). Sleep and the price of plasticity: From synaptic and cellular homeostasis to memory consolidation and integration. *Cell, 81*, 1–34.

Tootell, R. B. H., Silverman, M. S., Switkes, E., & De Valois, R. L. (1982). Deoxyglucose analysis of retinotopic organization in primate striate cortex. *Science, 218*, 902–904.

Topol, A., Zhu, S., Hartley, B. J., English, J., Hauberg, M. E., Tran, N., et al. (2016). Dysregulation of miRNA-9 in a subset of schizophrenia patient-derived neural progenitor cells. *Cell Reports, 15*, 1024–1036.

Torgerson, C. M., Irimia, A., Goh, S. Y. M., & Van Horn, J. D. (2015). The DTI connectivity of the human claustrum. *Human Brain Mapping, 36*, 827–838.

Torii, M., Hashimoto-Torii, K., Levitt, P., & Rakic, P. (2009). Integration of neuronal clones in the radial cortical columns by EphA and ephrin-A signalling. *Nature, 461*, 524–530.

Torrey, E. F., Bartko, J. J., & Yolken, R. H. (2012). Toxoplasma gondii and other risk factors for schizophrenia: An update. *Schizophrenia Bulletin, 38*(3), 642–647. doi:10.1093/schbul/sbs043

Toshitani, K., Kobayashi, T., Osawa, T., Kato, S., Eto, S., & Ojima, T. (2006). Is the incidence of schizophrenia declining? An investigation of the examination rates in the psychiatric clinics of a medical school hospital and a general hospital. *Seishin shinkeigaku zasshi, 108*, 694–704.

Toso, L., Cameroni, I., Roberson, R., Abebe, D., Bissell, S., & Spong, C. Y. (2008). Prevention of developmental delays in a Down syndrome mouse model. *Obstetrics and Gynecology, 112*, 1242–1251.

Townsend, J., Courchesne, E., Covington, J., Westerfield, M., Harris, N. S., Lyden, P., et al. (1999). Spatial attention deficits in patients with acquired or developmental cerebellar abnormality. *Journal of Neuroscience, 19*, 5632–5643.

Trace, S. E., Baker, J. H., Peñas-Lledó, E., & Bulik, C. M. (2013). The genetics of eating disorders. *Annual Review of Clinical Psychology, 9*, 589–620.

Tracey, I., Ploghaus, A., Gati, J. S., Clare, S., Smith, S., Menon, R. S., et al. (2002). Imaging attentional modulation of pain in the periaqueductal gray in humans. *Journal of Neuroscience, 22*, 2748–2752.

Tracy, T. E., Sohn, P. D., Minami, S. S., Wang, C., Min, S. W., Li, Y., et al. (2016). Acetylated tau obstructs KIBRA-mediated signaling in synaptic plasticity and promotes tauopathy-related memory loss. *Neuron, 90*, 245–260.

Tranel, D., & Damasio, A. R. (1985). Knowledge without awareness: An autonomic index of facial recognition by prosopagnosics. *Science, 228*, 1453–1454.

Tranel, D., Damasio, A. R., & Damasio, H. (1988). Intact recognition of facial expression, gender, and age in patients with impaired recognition of face identity. *Neurology, 38*, 690–696.

Träskman, L., Åsberg, M., Bertilsson, L., & Sjöstrand, L. (1981). Monoamine metabolites in CSF and suicidal behavior. *Archives of General Psychiatry, 38*, 631–635.

Trautmann, A. (1983). Tubocurarine, a partial agonist for cholinergic receptors. *Journal of Neural Transmission. Supplementum, 18*, 353–361.

Trautmann, S., Rehm, J., & Wittchen, H. (2016). The economic costs of mental disorders. *EMBO Reports, 17*, 1245–1249.

Treffert, D. A., & Christensen, D. D. (2006, June/July). Inside the mind of a savant. *Scientific American Mind, 17*, 50–55.

Tregellas, J. R., Tanabe, J. L., Martin, L. F., & Freedman, R. (2005). fMRI of response to nicotine during a smooth pursuit eye movement task in schizophrenia. *American Journal of Psychiatry, 162*, 391–393.

Treger, J. (2015). Single-molecule fluorimetry and gating currents inspire an improved optical voltage indicator. *eLife, 4*, e10482. doi:10.7554/eLife.10482

Trepanowski, J. F., Canale, R. E., Marshall, K. E., Kabir, M. M., & Bloomer, R. J. (2011). Impact of caloric and dietary restriction regimens on markers of health and longevity in humans and animals: A summary of available findings. *Nutrition Journal, 10*, 107. Retrieved from http://www.nutritionj.com/content/10/1/107

Trial of Ibudilast for methamphetamine dependence (IBUD ph II). (2016, January 26). *ClinicalTrials.gov.* Retrieved from https://clinicaltrials.gov/ct2/show/NCT01860807?intr=ibudilast&rank=5

Trinko, R., Sears, R. M., Guarnieri, D. J., & DiLeone, R. J. (2007). Neural mechanisms underlying obesity and drug addiction. *Physiology and Behavior, 91*, 499–505.

Tripp, G., & Wickens, J. R. (2009). Neurobiology of ADHD. *Neuropharmacology, 57*, 579–589.

Trudeau, L.-É. (2004). Glutamate co-transmission as an emerging concept in monoamine neuron function. *Reviews in Psychiatric Neuroscience, 29*, 296–310.

Trulson, M. E., Crisp, T., & Trulson, V. M. (1984). Activity of serotonin-containing nucleus centralis superior (raphe medianus) neurons in freely moving cats. *Experimental Brain Research, 54*, 33–44.

Tsai, G. E., Condie, D., Wu, M. T., & Chang, I.-W. (1999). Functional magnetic resonance imaging of personality switches in a woman with dissociative identity disorder. *Harvard Review of Psychiatry, 7*, 119–122.

Tsai, G., Gastfriend, D. R., & Coyle, J. T. (1995). The glutamatergic basis of human alcoholism. *American Journal of Psychiatry, 152*, 332–340.

Tsai, S.-J., Hong, C.-J., & Liou, Y.-J. (2011). Recent molecular genetic studies and methodological issues in suicide research. *Progress in Neuro-Psychopharmacology & Biological Psychiatry, 35*, 809–817.

Tsankova, N., Renthal, W., Kumar, A., & Nestler, E. J. (2007). Epigenetic regulation in psychiatric disorders. *Nature Reviews Neuroscience, 8*, 355–367.

Tsend-Ayush, E., He, C., Myers, M. A., Andrikopoulos, S., Wong, N., Sexton, P. M., et al. (2016). Monotreme *glucagon-like peptide-1* in venom and gut: One gene—two very different functions. *Scientific Reports, 6*, 37744. doi:10.1038/srep37744

Tsuang, M. T., Gilbertson, M. W., & Faraone, S. V. (1991). The genetics of schizophrenia: Current knowledge and future directions. *Schizophrenia Research, 4*, 157–171.

Tsujino, N., & Sakurai, T. (2009). Orexin/hypocretin: A neuropeptide at the interface of sleep, energy homeostasis, and reward system. *Pharmacological Reviews, 61*, 162–176.

Tuiten, A., Van Honk, J., Koppeschaar, H., Bernaards, C., Thijssen, J., & Verbaten, R. (2000). Time course of effects of testosterone administration on sexual arousal in women. *Archives of General Psychiatry, 57*, 149–153.

Tun, H. M., Konya, T., Takaro, T. K., Brook, J. R., Chari, R., Field, C. J., et al. (2017). Exposure to household furry pets influences the gut microbiota of infants at 3–4 months following various birth scenarios. *Microbiome, 5*, 40–54. doi:10.1186/s40168-017-0254-x

Turkheimer, E. (1991). Individual and group differences in adoption studies of IQ. *Psychological Bulletin, 110*, 392–405.

Turner, M. S., Cipolotti, L., Yousry, T. A., & Shallice, T. (2008). Confabulation: Damage to a specific inferior medial prefrontal system. *Cortex, 44*, 637–648.

Tuszynski, M. H., & Nagahara, A. H. (2016). NGF and BDNF gene therapy for Alzheimer's disease. In M. H. Tuszynski (Ed.), *Translational Neuroscience* (pp. 33–64). New York: Springer.

Tuszynski, M. H., Yang, J. H., Barba, D., H. S., U., Bakay, R. A., Pay, M. M., et al. (2015). Nerve growth factor gene therapy: Activation of neuronal responses in Alzheimer disease. *JAMA Neurology, 72*, 1139–1147.

Tuvblad, C., & Baker, L. A. (2011). Human aggression across the lifespan: Genetic propensities and environmental moderators. *Advances in Genetics, 75*, 171–214.

Uddin, L. O., (2015). Salience processing and insular cortical function and dysfunction. *Nature Reviews Neuroscience, 16*, 55–61.

Uhl, G. R., & Grow, R. W. (2004). The burden of complex genetics in brain disorders. *Archives of General Psychiatry, 61*, 223–229.

Uhlhaas, P. J., & Singer, W. (2010). Abnormal neural oscillations and synchrony in schizophrenia. *Nature Reviews Neuroscience, 11*, 100–113.

Ulanovsky, N., & Moss, C. F. (2008). What the bat's voice tells the bat's brain. *Proceedings of the National Academy of Sciences, 105*(25), 8491–8498.

Ullian, E. M., Sapperstein, S. K., Christopherson, K. S., & Barres, B. A. (2001). Control of synapse number by glia. *Science, 291*, 657–660.

Ullman, M. T. (2001). A neurocognitive perspective on language: The declarative/procedural model. *Nature Reviews Neuroscinece, 2*, 717–726.

Uncapher, M. R., Otten, L. J., & Rugg, M. D. (2006). Episodic encoding is more than the sum of its parts: An fMRI investigation of multifeatural contextual encoding. *Neuron, 52*, 547–556.

Underwood, E. (2016, April 12). European mental health project targets biological roots of social withdrawal. Retrieved from http://www.sciencemag.org/news/2016/04/european-mental-health-project-targets-biological-roots-social-withdrawal

Ungerleider, L. G., & Haxby, J. V. (1994). "What" and "where" in the human brain. *Current Opinion in Neurobiology, 4*, 157–165.

Ungerleider, L. G., & Mishkin, M. (1982). Two cortical visual systems. In D. J. Ingle, M. A. Goodale, & R. J. W. Mansfield (Eds.), *Analysis of visual behavior* (pp. 549–586). Cambridge, MA: MIT Press.

Uno, H., Tarara, R., Else, J. G., Suleman, M. A., & Sapolsky, R. M. (1999). Hippocampal damage associated with prolonged and fatal stress in primates. *Journal of Neuroscience, 9*, 1705–1711.

Unternaehrer, E., Luers, P., Mill, J., Meyer, A. H., Staehli, S., Lieb, R., et al. (2012). Dynamic changes in DNA methylation of stress-associated genes (*OXTR, BDNF*) after acute psychological stress. *Translational Psychiatry, 2*, e150. Retrieved from http://www.nature.com/tp/journal/v2/n8/pdf/tp201277a.pdf

U.S. Congress Office of Technology Assessment. (1986). *Alternatives to animal research in testing and education.* Washington, DC: U.S. Government Printing Office.

U.S. Department of Health and Human Services. (2012). Overweight and obesity statistics. Retrieved from http://win.niddk.nih.gov/publications/PDFs/stat904z.pdf

U.S. Food and Drug Administration. (2003, October 17). FDA approves memantine (Namenda) for Alzheimer's disease. Retrieved from www.fda.gov/bbs/topics/NEWS/2003/NEW00961.html

U.S. Food and Drug Administration. (2009). FDA approves humanitarian device exemption for deep brain stimulator for severe obsessive-compulsive disorder. Retrieved from http://www.fda.gov/NewsEvents/Newsroom/PressAnnouncements/ucm149529.htm

U.S. Food and Drug Administration. (2010, May 26). FDA drug safety communication: Completed safety review of Xenical/Alli (orlistat) and severe liver injury. Retrieved from http://www.fda.gov/Drugs/DrugSafety/PostmarketDrugSafetyInformationforPatientsandProviders/ucm213038.htm

U.S. Food and Drug Administration. (2012, July 2). FDA drug safety communication: Seizure risk for multiple sclerosis patients who take Ampyra (dalfampridine). Retrieved from http://www.fda.gov/Drugs/DrugSafety/ucm312846.htm

U.S. government shuts down Pennsylvania gene therapy trials. (2000). *Nature, 403*, 354–355.

Vaaga, C. E., Borisovska, M., & Westbrook, G. L. (2014). Dual-transmitter neurons: Functional implications of co-release and co-transmission. *Current Opinion in Neurobiology, 29*, 25–32.

Vaccine court finds no link to autism. (2010, March 12). *CNN Health.* Retrieved from http://www.cnn.com/2010/HEALTH/03/12/vaccine.court.ruling.autism/index.html

Vaina, L. M. (1998). Complex motion perception and its deficits. *Current Opinion in Neurobiology, 8*, 494–502.

Vaina, L. M., Solomon, J., Chowdhury, S., Sinha, P., & Belliveau, J. W. (2001). Functional neuroanatomy of biological motion perception in humans. *Proceedings of the National Academy of Sciences, 98*, 11656–11661.

Valenstein, E. S. (1986). *Great and desperate cures.* New York: Basic Books.

van Amelsvoort, T., Compton, J., & Murphy, D. (2001). *In vivo* assessment of the effects of estrogen on human brain. *Trends in Endocrinology & Metabolism, 12*, 273–276.

Van Anders, S. M., Goldey, K. L., & Kuo, P. X. (2011). The steroid/peptide theory of social bonds: Integrating testosterone and peptide responses for clarifying social behavioral contexts. *Psychoneuroendocrinology, 36*, 1265–1275.

van den Brand, R., Heutschi, J., Barraud, Q., DiGiovanna, J., Bartholdi, K., Huerlimann, M., et al. (2012). Restoring voluntary control of locomotion after paralyzing spinal cord injury. *Science, 336*, 1182–1185.

van der Veen, F. M., Nijhuis, F. A. P., Tisserand, D. J., Backes, W. H., & Jolles, J. (2006). Effects of aging on recognition of intentionally and incidentally stored words: An fMRI study. *Neuropsychologia, 44*, 2477–2486.

Vandewalle, G., Collignon, O., Hull, J. T., & Daneault, V. (2013). Blue light stimulates cognitive brain activity in visually blind individuals. *Journal of Cognitive Neurosciences, 25*(12), 2072–2085.

Van Dongen, H. P. A., Maislin, G., Mullington, J. M., & Dinges, D. F. (2003). The cumulative cost of additional wakefulness: Dose-response effects on neurobehavioral functions and sleep physiology from chronic sleep restriction and total sleep deprivation. *Sleep, 26*, 117–126.

Van Essen, D. C., Anderson, C. H., & Felleman, D. J. (1992). Information processing in the primate visual system: An integrated systems perspective. *Science, 255*, 419–423.

Van Essen, D. C., Smith, S. M., Barch, D. M., Behrens, T. E. J., Yacoub, E., Ugurbil, K., et al. (2013). The WU-Minn Human Connectome Project: An overview. *NeuroImage, 62*, 2222–2231.

Van Horn, J. D., Irimia, A., Torgerson, C. M., Chambers, M. C., Kikinis, R., & Toga, A. W. (2012). Mapping connectivity damage in the case of Phineas Gage. *PLoS One, 7*, e37454. doi:10.1371/journal.pone.0037454

van Os, J., & Selten, J. (1998). Prenatal exposure to maternal stress and subsequent schizophrenia: The May 1940 invasion of the Netherlands. *British Journal of Psychiatry, 172*, 324–326.

Van Wyk, P. H., & Geist, C. S. (1984). Psychosocial development of heterosexual, bisexual, and homosexual behavior. *Archives of Sexual Behavior, 13*, 505–544.

Vargha-Khadem, F., Gadian, D. G., Copp, A., & Mishkin, M. (2005). *FOXP2* and the neuroanatomy of speech and language. *Nature Reviews Neuroscience, 6*, 131–138.

Varnum, M. E. W., Blais, C., & Brewer, G. A. (2016). Social class affects mu-suppression during action observation. *Social Neuroscience, 11*(4), 449–454. doi:10.1080/17470919.2015.1105865

Vauzour, D. (2014). Effect of flavonoids on learning, memory and neurocognitive performance: Relevance and potential implications for Alzheimer's disease pathophysiology. *Journal of the Science of Food and Agriculture, 94*(6), 1042–1056.

Venter, J. C. (and 273 others). (2001). The sequence of the human genome. *Science, 291*, 1304–1351.

Vermetten, E., Schmahl, C., Lindner, S., Loewenstein, R. J., & Bremner, J. D. (2006). Hippocampal and amygdalar volumes in dissociative identity disorder. *American Journal of Psychiatry, 163*, 630–636.

Vernes, S. C., Newbury, D. F., Abrahams, B. S., Winchester, L., Nicod, J., Groszer, M., et al. (2008). A functional genetic link between distinct developmental language disorders. *New England Journal of Medicine, 359*, 2337–2345.

Vgontzas, A. N., Bixler, E. O., Lin, H. M., Prolo, P., Mastorakos, G., Vela-Bueno, A., et al. (2001). Chronic insomnia is associated with nyctohemeral activation of the hypothalamic-pituitary-adrenal axis: Clinical implications. *Journal of Clinical Endocrinology and Metabolism, 86*, 3787–3794.

Vikingstad, E. M., Cao, Y., Thomas, A. J., Johnson, A., Malik, G. M., & Welch, K. M. A. (2000). Language hemispheric dominance in patients with congenital lesions of eloquent brain. *Neurosurgery, 47*, 562–570.

Villafuerte, S., Heitzeg, M. M., Foley, S., Yau, W.-Y., Majczenko, K., Zubieta, J.-K., et al. (2012). Impulsiveness and insula activation during reward anticipation are associated with genetic variants in GABRA$_2$ in a family sample enriched for alcoholism. *Molecular Psychiatry, 17*, 511–519.

Villalobos, M. E., Mizuno, A., Dahl, B. C., Kemmotsu, N., & Müller, R.-A. (2005). Reduced functional connectivity between V1 and inferior frontal cortex associated with visuomotor performance in autism. *NeuroImage, 25*, 916–925.

Vincent, A. S., Roebuck-Spencer, T. M., & Cernich, A. (2014). Cognitive changes and dementia risk after traumatic brain injury: Implications for aging military personnel. *Alzheimer's & Dementia, 10*, S174–S187.

Virkkunen, M., Goldman, D., & Linnoila, M. (1996). Serotonin in alcoholic violent offenders. In *Genetics of criminal and antisocial behaviour. Ciba Foundation Symposium 194* (pp. 168–182). Chichester, UK: Wiley.

Virkkunen, M., & Linnoila, M. (1993). Brain serotonin, Type II alcoholism and impulsive violence. *Journal of Studies of Alcohol Supplement, 11*, 163–169.

Visser, S. N., Danielson, M. L., Bitsko, R. H., Holbrook, J. R., Kogan, M. D., Ghandour, R. M., et al. (2014). Trends in the parent-report of health care provider-diagnosed and medicated attention-deficit/hyperactivity disorder: United States, 2003–2011. *Journal of the American Academy of Child & Adolescent Psychiatry, 53*, 34–46.

Vissers, L. E. L. M., Gilissen, C., & Veitman, J. A. (2016). Genetic studies in intellectual disability and related disorders. *Nature Reviews Genetics, 17*, 9–18.

Vogel, G. (1998). Penetrating insight into the brain. *Science, 282*, 39.

Vogel, G. W., Buffenstein, A., Minter, K., & Hennessey, A. (1990). Drug effects on REM sleep and on endogenous depression. *Neuroscience and Biobehavioral Review, 14*, 49–63.

Vogel, J. M., Bowers, C. A., & Vogel, D. S. (2003). Cerebral lateralization of spatial abilities: A meta-analysis. *Brain and Cognition, 52*, 197–204.

Vogels, R. (1999). Categorization of complex visual images by rhesus monkeys: Part 2. Single-cell study. *European Journal of Neuroscience, 11*, 1239–1255.

Voineagu, I., Wang, X., Johnston, P., Lowe, J. K., Tian, Y., Horvath, S., et al. (2011). Transcriptomic analysis of autistic brain reveals convergent molecular pathology. *Nature, 474*, 380–386.

Volk, H. E., Lurmann, F., Penfold, B., Hertz-Picciotto, I., & McConnell, R. (2014). Traffic-related air pollution, particulate matter, and autism. *JAMA Psychiatry, 70*, 71–77.

Volkow, N. D., & Fowler, J. S. (2000). Addiction, a disease of compulsion and drive: Involvement of the orbitofrontal cortex. *Cerebral Cortex, 10*, 318–325.

Volkow, N. D., Fowler, J. S., & Wang, G.-J. (2003). The addicted human brain: Insights from imaging studies. *Journal of Clinical Investigation, 111*, 1444–1451.

Volkow, N. D., Fowler, J. S., & Wang, G.-J. (2004). The addicted human brain viewed in the light of imaging studies: Brain circuits and treatment strategies. *Neuropharmacology, 47*(Suppl.), 3–13.

Volkow, N. D., Fowler, J. S., Wang, G.-J., & Swanson, J. M. (2004). Dopamine in drug abuse and addiction: Results from imaging studies and treatment implications. *Molecular Psychiatry, 9*, 557–569.

Volkow, N. D., Fowler, J. S., Wolf, A. P., Hitzemann, R., Dewey, S., Bendriem, B., et al. (1991). Changes in brain glucose metabolism in cocaine dependence and withdrawal. *American Journal of Psychiatry, 148*, 621–626.

Volkow, N. D., Wang, G.-J., Fischman, M. W., Foltin, R. W., Fowler, J. S., Abumrad, N. N., et al. (1997). Relationship between subjective effects of cocaine and dopamine transporter occupancy. *Nature, 386*, 827–830.

Volkow, N. D., Wang, G.-J., Fowler, J. S., Hitzemann, R., Angrist, B., Gatley, S. J., et al. (1999). Association of methylphenidate-induced craving with changes in right striato-orbitofrontal metabolism in cocaine abusers: Implications in addiction. *American Journal of Psychiatry, 156,* 19–26.

Volkow, N. D., Wang, G.-J., Fowler, J., & Telang, F. (2008). Overlapping neuronal circuits in addiction and obesity: Evidence of systems pathology. *Philosophical Transactions of the Royal Society of London B, 363,* 3191–3200.

Volkow, N. D., Wang, G.-J., Tomasi, D., & Baler, R. D. (2013). The addictive dimensionality of obesity. *Biological Psychiatry, 73,* 811–818.

Volkow, N. D., & Wise, R. A. (2005). How can drug addiction help us understand obesity? *Nature Neuroscience, 8,* 555–560.

Volpe, B. T., LeDoux, J. E., & Gazzaniga, M. S. (1979). Information processing of visual stimuli in an "extinguished" field. *Nature, 282,* 722–724.

von der Heydt, R., Peterhans, E., & Dürsteler, M. R. (1992). Periodic pattern-selective cells in monkey visual cortex. *Journal of Neuroscience, 12,* 1416–1434.

von der Heydt, R., Peterhans, E., & Baumgartner, G. (1984). Illusory contours and cortical neuron responses. *Science, 224,* 1260–1262.

Vorel, S. R., Liu, X., Hayes, R. J., Spector, J. A., & Gardner, E. L. (2001). Relapse to cocaine-seeking after hippocampal theta burst stimulation. *Science, 292,* 1175–1178.

Voyer, D., Voyer, S., & Bryden, M. P. (1995). Magnitude of sex differences in spatial abilities: A meta-analysis and consideration of critical variables. *Psychological Bulletin, 117,* 250–270.

Vu, E. T., Mazurek, M. E., & Kuo, Y.-C. (1994). Identification of a forebrain motor programming network for the learned song of zebra finches. *Journal of Neuroscience, 14*(11), 6924–6934.

Vul, E., Harris, C., Winkielman, P., & Pashler, H. (2009). Puzzlingly high correlations in fMRI studies of emotion, personality, and social cognition. *Perspectives on Psychological Science, 4,* 274–290.

Wada, J. A., Clarke, R., & Hamm, A. (1975). Cerebral hemispheric asymmetry in humans: Cortical speech zones in 100 adult and 100 infant brains. *Archives of Neurology, 32,* 239–246.

Wade, J. A., Garry, M., Read, J. D., & Lindsay, S. (2002). A picture is worth a thousand lies. *Psychonomic Bulletin Reviews, 9,* 597–603.

Wagner, D., Becker, B., Koester, P., Gouzoulis-Mayfrank, E., & Daumann, J. (2013). A prospective study of learning, memory, and executive function in new MDMA users. *Addiction, 108,* 136–145.

Wagner, H. J., Hennig, H., Jabs, W. J., Sickhaus, A., Wessel, K., & Wandinger, K. P. (2000). Altered prevalence and reactivity of anti-Epstein-Barr virus antibodies in patients with multiple sclerosis. *Viral Immunology, 13,* 497–502.

Wakefield, A. J., Murch, S. H., Anthony, A., Linnell, J., Casson, D. M., Malik, M., et al. (1998). Ileal-lymphoid-nodular hyperplasia, non-specific colitis, and pervasive developmental disorder in children. *Lancet, 351,* 637–641.

Walker, E. F., Lewine, R. R. J., & Neumann, C. (1996). Childhood behavioral characteristics and adult brain morphology in schizophrenia. *Schizophrenia Research, 22,* 93–101.

Walker, F. O. (2007). Huntington's disease. *Lancet, 369,* 2–26.

Walker, M. P., & Robertson, E. M. (2016). Memory processing: Ripples in the resting brain. *Current Biology, 26,* R229–R246.

Walsh, B. T., & Devlin, M. J. (1998). Eating disorders: Progress and problems. *Science, 280,* 1387–1390.

Waltes, R., Chiocchetti, A. G., & Freitag, C. M. (2016). The neurobiological basis of human aggression: A review on genetic and epigenetic mechanisms. *American Journal of Medical Genetics Part B, 171B,* 650–675.

Wan, F.-J., Berton, F., Madamba, S. G., Francesconi, W., & Siggins, G. R. (1996). Low ethanol concentrations enhance GABAergic inhibitory postsynaptic potentials in hippocampal pyramidal neurons only after block of GABAB receptors. *Proceedings of the National Academy of Sciences, 93,* 5049–5054.

Wang, A., Costello, S., Cockburn, M., Zhang, X., Bronstein, J., & Ritz, B. (2011). Parkinson's disease risk from ambient exposure to pesticides. *European Journal of Epidemiology, 26,* 547–555.

Wang, B. (2017, April 28). DARPA and ASU electrical brain stimulation could boost learning and memory by 30 percent. Retrieved from http://www.nextbigfuture .com/2017/04/darpa-and-asu-electrical-brain-stimulation-could-boost-learning-and-memory-by-30-percent.html

Wang, B., Zhou, S., Hong, F., Wang, J., Liu, X., Cai, Y., et al. (2012). Association analysis between the tag SNP for sonic hedgehog rs9333613 polymorphism and male sexual orientation. *Journal of Andrology, 33,* 951–964.

Wang, J., Korczykowski, M., Rao, H., Fan, Y., Pluta, J., Gur, R. C., et al. (2007). Gender difference in neural response to psychological stress. *Social, Cognitive and Affective Neuroscience, 2,* 227–239.

Wang, J. C., Kapoor, M., & Goate, A. M. (2012). The genetics of substance dependence. *Annual Review of Genomics and Human Genetics, 13,* 241–261.

Wang, R., Chen, C.-C., Hara, E., Rivas, M. V., Roulhac, P. L., Howard, J. T, Chakraborty, M., et al. (2014). Convergent differential regulation of SLIT-ROBO axon guidance genes in the brains of vocal learners. *Journal of Comparative Neurology, 523,* 892–906.

Wang, S., Tudusciuc, O., Mamelak, A. N., Ross, I. B., Adolphs, R., & Rutishauser, U. (2014). Neurons in the human amygdala selective for perceived emotion.

Proceedings of the National Academy of Sciences, E3110–E3119. Retrieved from http://www.pnas.org/content/111/30/E3110.full.pdf

Wang, S.-H., Redondo, R. L., & Morris, R. G. M. (2010). Relevance of synaptic tagging and capture to the persistence of long-term potentiation and everyday spatial memory. *Proceedigs of the National Academy of Sciences, 107,* 19537–19542.

Wang, Y., Qian, Y., Yang, S., Shi, H., Liao, C., Zheng, H.-K., et al. (2005). Accelerated evolution of the pituitary adenylate cyclase-activating polypeptide precursor gene during human origin. *Genetics, 170,* 801–806.

Warner, R. (2005). *Recovery from schizophrenia: Psychiatry and political economy.* Abingdon, UK: Routledge.

Warren, S., Hämäläinen, H. A., & Gardner, E. P. (1986). Objective classification of motion- and direction-sensitive neurons in primary somatosensory cortex of awake monkeys. *Journal of Neurophysiology, 56,* 598–622.

Watanabe, T., Kuroda, M., Kuwabara, H., Aoki, Y., Iwashiro, N., Tatsunobu, N., et al. (2015). Clinical and neural effects of six-week administration of oxytocin on core symptoms of autism. *Brain, 138,* 3400–3412.

Waterland, R. A., & Jirtle, R. L. (2003). Transposable elements: Targets for early nutritional effects on epigenetic gene regulation. *Molecular and Cellular Biology, 23,* 5293–5300.

Waters, A. J., Jarvis, M. J., & Sutton, S. R. (1998). Nicotine withdrawal and accident rates. *Nature, 394,* 137.

Watkins, L. R., & Mayer, D. J. (1982). Organization of endogenous opiate and nonopiate pain control systems. *Science, 216,* 1185–1192.

Watson, C. G., Kucala, T., Tilleskjor, C., & Jacobs, L. (1984). Schizophrenic birth seasonality in relation to the incidence of infectious diseases and temperature extremes. *Archives of General Psychiatry, 41,* 85–90.

Watson, J. D., & Crick, F. H. C. (1953). Genetical implications of the structure of deoxyribonucleic acid. *Nature, 171,* 964–967.

Wattles, J. (2016, April 17). Medical marijuana now legal in 24 states. Retrieved from http://money.cnn.com/2016/04/17/news/economy/medical-marijuana-pennsylvania/

Waxman, S. G., & Ritchie, J. M. (1985). Organization of ion channels in the myelinated nerve fiber. *Science, 228,* 1502–1507.

Webb, W. B. (1974). Sleep as an adaptive response. *Perceptual and Motor Skills, 38,* 1023–1027.

Weeks, D., Freeman, C. P., & Kendell, R. E. (1980). ECT: II: Enduring cognitive deficits? *British Journal of Psychiatry, 137,* 26–37.

Wehr, T. A., Jacobsen, F. M., Sack, D. A., Arendt, J., Tamarkin, L., & Rosenthal, N. E. (1986). Phototherapy of seasonal affective disorder: Time of day and suppression of melatonin are not critical for antidepressant effects. *Archives of General Psychiatry, 43,* 870–875.

Weight loss drugs: Pros and cons of 5 approved prescriptions. (2015, August 18). *LIVESCIENCE.* Retrieved from http://www.livescience.com/51896-weight-loss-drugs-pros-cons.html

Weight loss surgery insurance coverage and costs. (2016, September 20). *Obesity Coverage.* Retrieved from http://www.obesitycoverage.com/weight-loss-surgery-insurance-coverage-and-costs/

Weill Cornell Medical College. (2014, July 16). Weill Cornell presents updated results from phase 3 trial of IVIG for Alzheimer's disease. Retrieved from http://weill .cornell.edu/news/pr/2013/07/weill-cornell-presents-updated-results-from-phase-3-trial-of-ivig-for-alzheimers-disease.html

Weinberg, R. A. (1989). Intelligence and IQ: Landmark issues and great debates. *American Psychologist, 44,* 98–104.

Weinberg, R. A., Scarr, S., & Waldman, I. D. (1992). The Minnesota Transracial Adoption Study: A follow-up of IQ test performance at adolescence. *Intelligence, 16,* 117–135.

Weinberger, D. R. (1987). Implications of normal brain development for the pathogenesis of schizophrenia. *Archives of General Psychiatry, 44,* 660–669.

Weinberger, D. R., Berman, K. F., Suddath, R., & Torrey, E. F. (1992). Evidence of dysfunction of a prefrontal-limbic network in schizophrenia: A magnetic resonance imaging and regional cerebral blood flow study of discordant monozygotic twins. *American Journal of Psychiatry, 149,* 890–897.

Weinberger, D. R., Berman, K. F., & Zec, R. F. (1986). Physiologic dysfunction of dorsolateral prefrontal cortex in schizophrenia: I. Regional cerebral blood flow evidence. *Archives of General Psychiatry, 43,* 114–124.

Weinberger, D. R., & Lipska, B. K. (1995). Cortical maldevelopment, antipsychotic drugs, and schizophrenia: A search for common ground. *Schizophrenia Research, 16,* 87–110.

Weinberger, D. R., & Wyatt, R. J. (1983). Enlarged cerebral ventricles in schizophrenia. *Psychiatric Annals, 13,* 412–418.

Weiner, R. D., & Krystal, A. D. (1994). The present use of electroconvulsive therapy. *Annual Review of Medicine, 45,* 273–281.

Weingarten, H. P., Chang, P. K., & McDonald, T. J. (1985). Comparison of the metabolic and behavioral disturbances following paraventricular- and ventromedial-hypothalamic lesions. *Brain Research Bulletin, 14,* 551–559.

Weinstein, G., Beiser, A. S., Choi, S. H., Preis, S. R., Chen, T. C., Vorgas, D., et al. (2014). Serum brain-derived neurotrophic factor and the risk for dementia: The Framingham Heart Study. *JAMA Neurology, 71,* 55–61.

Weinstein, S. (1968). Intensive and extensive aspects of tactile sensitivity as a function of body part, sex, and laterality. In D. R. Kenshalo (Ed.), *The skin senses* (pp. 195–222). Springfield, IL: Thomas.

Weir, A. A. S., Chapell, J., & Kacelnik, A. (2002). Shaping of hooks in New Caledonian crows. *Science, 297,* 981.

Weiser, M. J., Butt, C. M., & Hasan Mohajeri, M. (2016). Docosahexaenoic acid and cognition throughout the lifespan. *Nutrients, 8*(2), 99. doi:10.3390/nu8020099

Weiss, K. J. (2010). Hoarding, hermitage, and the law: Why we love the Collyer brothers. *Journal of the American Academy of Psychiatry and Law, 38,* 251–257.

Wekerle, H. (1993). Experimental autoimmune encephalomyelitis as a model of immune-mediated CNS disease. *Current Opinion in Neurobiology, 3,* 779–784.

Welch, B. T., Coelho Prabhu, N., Walkoff, L., & Trenkner, S. W. (2016). Auto-brewery syndrome in the setting of long-standing Crohn's disease: A case report and review of the literature. *Journal of Crohn's and Colitis, 10,* 1448–1450.

Welch, J. M., Lu, J., Rodriguiz, R. M., Trotta, N. C., Peca, J., Ding, J.-D., et al. (2007). Cortico-striatal synaptic defects and OCD-like behaviours in *Sapap3*-mutant mice. *Nature, 448,* 894–901.

Weltzin, T. E., Hsu, L. K., Pollice, C., & Kaye, W. H. (1991). Feeding patterns in bulimia nervosa. *Biological Psychiatry, 30,* 1093–1110.

Wen, W., Zhu, W., He, Y., Kochan, N. A., Reppermund, S., Slavin, M. J., et al. (2011). Discrete neuroanatomical networks are associated with specific cognitive abilities in old age. *Journal of Neuroscience, 31,* 1204–1212.

Wender, P. H., Rosenthal, D., Kety, S. S., Schulsinger, F., & Welner, J. (1974). Cross-fostering: A research strategy for clarifying the role of genetic and experiential factors in the etiology of schizophrenia. *Archives of General Psychiatry, 30,* 121–128.

Wender, P. H., Wolf, L. E., & Wasserstein, J. (2001). Adults with ADHD: An overview. *Annals of the New York Academy of Sciences, 931,* 1–16.

Wennberg, P., Berglund, K., Berggren, U., Balldin, J., & Fahlke, C. (2014). The Cloninger TypeI/TypeII typology: Configurations and personality profiles in socially stable alcohol dependent patients. *Advances in Psychiatry,* Article ID 346157. doi:10.1155/2014/346157

West, D. B., Fey, D., & Woods, S. C. (1984). Cholecystokinin persistently suppresses meal size but not food intake in free-feeding rats. *American Journal of Physiology, 246,* R776–R787.

Westerberg, C. E., Florczak, S. M., Weintraub, S., Mesulam, M.-M., Marshall, L., Zee, P. C., & Paller, K. A. (2015). Memory improvement via slow-oscillatory stimulation during sleep in older adults. *Neurobiology of Aging, 36,* 2577–2586.

Wever, E. G. (1949). *Theory of hearing.* New York: Wiley.

Wever, E. G., & Bray, C. W. (1930). The nature of acoustic response: The relation between sound frequency and frequency of impulses in the auditory nerve. *Journal of Experimental Psychology, 13,* 373–387.

Wheaton, K. J., Thompson, J. C., Syngeniotis, A., Abbott, D. F., & Puce, A. (2004). Viewing the motion of human body parts activates different regions of premotor, temporal, and parietal cortex. *NeuroImage, 22,* 277–288.

Wheeler, M. A., Stuss, D. T., & Tulving, E. (1997). Toward a theory of episodic memory: The frontal lobes and autonoetic consciousness. *Psychological Bulletin, 121,* 331–354.

Wheeler, M. E., Petersen, S. E., & Buckner, R. L. (2000). Memory's echo: Vivid remembering reactivates sensory-specific cortex. *Proceedings of the National Academy of Sciences, 97,* 11125–11129.

Whipple, B., & Komisaruk, B. R. (1988). Analgesia produced in women by genital self-stimulation. *Journal of Sex Research, 24,* 130–140.

Whiteside, S. P., Port, J. D., & Abramowitz, J. S. (2004). A meta-analysis of functional neuroimaging in obsessive-compulsive disorder. *Psychiatry Research, 132,* 69–79.

Whitney, D., Elison, A., Rice, N. J., Arnold, D., Goodale, M., Walsh, V., et al. (2007). Visually guided reaching depends on motion area MT+. *Cerebral Cortex, 17,* 2644–2649.

Wichmann, T., Bergman, H., & DeLong, M. R. (1994). The primate subthalamic nucleus: III. Changes in motor behavior and neuronal activity in the internal pallidum induced by subthalamic inactivation in the MPTP model of parkinsonism. *Journal of Neurophysiology, 72,* 521–530.

Wichmann, T., & DeLong, M. R. (2016). Deep brain stimulation for movement disorders of basal ganglia origin: Restoring function or functionality. *Neurotherapeutics, 13,* 264–283.

Wickelgren, I. (1997). Getting a grasp on working memory. *Science, 275,* 1580–1582.

Wierenga, C. E., Bischoff-Grethe, A., Melrose, A. J., Irvine, Z., Torres, L., Bailer, U. F., et al. (2014). Hunger does not motivate reward in women remitted from anorexia nervosa. *Biological Psychiatry, 77,* 642–652.

Wierzynski, C. M., Lubenov, E. V., Gu, M., & Siapas, A. G. (2009). State-dependent spike-timing relationships between hippocampal and prefrontal circuits during sleep. *Neuron, 61,* 587–596.

Wiesel, T. N., & Hubel, D. H. (1966). Spatial and chromatic interactions in the lateral geniculate body of the rhesus monkey. *Journal of Neurophysiology, 29,* 1115–1156.

Wilbert-Lampen, U., Leistner, D., Greven, S., Tilmann, P., Sper, S., Völker, C., et al. (2008). Cardiovascular events during world cup soccer. *New England Journal of Medicine, 358,* 475–483.

Wilens, T. E., Faraone, S. V., Biederman, J., & Gunawardene, S. (2003). Does stimulant therapy of attention-deficit/hyperactivity disorder beget later substance abuse? A meta-analytic review of the literature. *Pediatrics, 111,* 179–185.

Wiles, N., Thomas, L., Abel, A., Ridgway, N., Turner, N., Campbell, J., et al. (2013). Cognitive behavioral therapy as an adjunct to pharmacotherapy for primary care based patients with treatment resistant depression: Results of the CoBalT randomised controlled trial. *Lancet, 381,* 375–384.

Wilkins, J., & Hill, S. (2006). *Food in the ancient world.* Malden, MA: Wiley-Blackwell.

Wilkinson, M., Wang, R., van der Kouwe, A., & Takahashi, E. (2016). White and gray matter fiber pathways in autism spectrum disorder revealed by ex vivo diffusion MR tractography. *Brain and Behavior, 6,* e00483. doi:10.1002/brb3.483

Willerman, L., Schultz, R., Rutledge, J. N., & Bigler, E. D. (1991). In vivo brain size and intelligence. *Intelligence, 15,* 223–228.

Willerman, L., Schultz, R., Rutledge, J. N., & Bigler, E. D. (1994). Brain structure and cognitive function. In C. R. Reynolds (Ed.), *Cognitive assessment: A multidisciplinary perspective* (pp. 35–55). New York: Plenum Press.

Williams, F. (2016, January). This is your brain on nature. *National Geographic.* Retrieved from http://www.nationalgeographic.com/magazine/2016/01/call-to-wild/

Williams, H., Crane, L. A., Hale, T. K., Esposito, M. A., & Nottebohm, F. (1992). Right-side dominance for song control in the zebra finch. *Journal of Neurobiology, 23*(8), 1006–1020.

Williams, J. H. G. (2008). Self-other relations in social development and autism: Multiple roles for mirror neurons and other brain bases. *Autism Research, 1,* 73–90.

Williams, J. H. G., Whiten, A., Suddendorf, T., & Perrett, D. I. (2001). Imitation, mirror neurons and autism. *Neuroscience and Biobehavioral Reviews, 25,* 287–295.

Williams, N. M., Zaharieva, I., Martin, A., Langley, K., Mantripragada, K., Fassdal, R., et al. (2010). Rare chromosomal deletions and duplications in attention-deficit hyperactivity disorder: A genome-wide analysis. *Lancet, 376,* 1401–1408.

Williams, R. W., Ryder, K., & Rakic, P. (1987). Emergence of cytoarchitectonic differences between areas 17 and 18 in the developing rhesus monkey. *Abstracts of the Society for Neuroscience, 13,* 1044.

Williams, T. J., Pepitone, M. E., Christensen, S. E., Cooke, B. M., Huberman, A. D., Breedlove, N. J., et al. (2000). Finger-length ratios and sexual orientation. *Nature, 404,* 455–456.

Willie, J. T., Chemelli, R. M., Sinton, C. M., & Yanagisawa, M. (2001). To eat or to sleep? Orexin in the regulation of feeding and wakefulness. *Annual Review of Neuroscience, 24,* 429–458.

Wilson, A. (1998, September 4). Gray matters memory: How much can we remember? And why is it necessary to forget? *Orange County Register,* p. E1.

Wilson, F. A. W., Ó Scalaidhe, S. P., & Goldman-Rakic, P. S. (1993). Dissociation of object and spatial processing domains in primate prefrontal cortex. *Science, 260,* 1955–1958.

Wilson, M. A., & McNaughton, B. L. (1993). Dynamics of the hippocampal ensemble code for space. *Science, 261,* 1055–1058.

Wilson, R. I., & Nicoll, R. A. (2001). Endogenous cannabinoids mediate retrograde signalling at hippocampal synapses. *Nature, 410,* 588–592.

Wise, R. A. (2002). Brain reward circuitry: Insights from unsensed incentives. *Neuron, 36,* 229–240.

Wise, R. A. (2004). Dopamine, learning, and motivation. *Nature Reviews: Neuroscience, 5,* 1–12.

Witelson, S. F., Kigar, D. L., & Harvey, T. (1999). The exceptional brain of Albert Einstein. *Lancet, 353,* 2149–2153.

Witte, A. V., Fobker, M., Gellner, R., Knecht, S., & Flöel, A. (2009). Caloric restriction improves memory in elderly humans. *Proceedings of the National Academy of Sciences, 106,* 1255–1260.

Witthoft, N., Nguyen, M. L., Golarai, G., LaRocque, K. F., Liberman, A., Smith, M. E., & Grill-Spector, K. (2013). Where is human V4? Predicting the location of hV4 and VO1 from cortical folding. *Cerebral Cortex.* doi:10.1093/cercor/bht092

Wolff, J. J., Gu, H., Gerig, G., Elison, J. T., Styner, M., Gouttard, S., et al. (2012). Differences in white matter fiber tract development present from 6 to 24 months in infants with autism. *American Journal of Psychiatry, 169,* 589–600.

Wollberg, Z., & Newman, J. D. (1972). Auditory cortex of squirrel monkey: Response patterns of single cells to species-specific vocalizations. *Science, 175,* 212–214.

Wood, D. L., Sheps, S. G., Elveback, L. R., & Schirger, A. (1984). Cold pressor test as a predictor of hypertension. *Hypertension, 6,* 301–306.

Woods, B. T. (1998). Is schizophrenia a progressive neurodevelopmental disorder? Toward a unitary pathogenetic mechanism. *American Journal of Psychiatry, 155,* 1661–1670.

Woods, C. G. (2004). Crossing the midline. *Science, 304,* 1455–1456.

Woods, S. C. (2004). Gastrointestinal satiety signals: I. An overview of gastrointestinal signals that influence food intake. *American Journal of Physiology, 286,* G7–G13.

Woodworth, R. S. (1941). *Heredity and environment: A critical survey of recently published material on twins and foster children* (A report prepared for the Committee on Social Adjustment). New York: Social Science Research Council.

Woogh, C. (2001). Is schizophrenia on the decline in Canada? *Canadian Journal of Psychiatry, 46,* 61–67.

Woolf, C. J., & Salter, M. W. (2000). Neuronal plasticity: Increasing the gain in pain. *Science, 288,* 1765–1768.

Woollett, K., & Maguire, E. A. (2011). Acquiring "the knowledge" of London's layout drives structural brain changes. *Current Biology, 21,* 2109–2114.

World Health Organization. (2002). Self-directed violence. In *World report on violence and health.* Geneva, Switzerland: Author.

World Health Organization. (2008). *The global burden of disease: 2004 update; annex A.* Geneva, Switzerland: Author. Retrieved from www.who.int/healthinfo/global_burden_disease/GBD_report_2004update_AnnexA.pdf

World Health Organization. (2013). *Visual impairment and blindness.* Retrieved from http://www.who.int/mediacentre/factsheets/fs282/en/

Worley, P. F., Heller, W. A., Snyder, S. H., & Baraban, J. M. (1988). Lithium blocks a phosphoinositide-mediated cholinergic response in hippocampal slices. *Science, 239,* 1428–1429.

Wray, N. R., & Visscher, P. M. (2010). Narrowing the boundaries of the genetic architecture of schizophrenia. *Schizophrenia Bulletin, 36,* 14–23.

Wright, J. D., Kennedy-Stephenson, J., Wang, C. Y., McDowell, M. A., & Johnson, C. L. (2004, February 6). Trends in intake of energy and macronutrients—United States, 1971–2000. *Morbidity and Mortality Weekly Report, 53*(4), 80–82.

Wu, C.-S., Jew, C. P., & Lu, H.-C. (2011). Lasting impacts of prenatal cannabis exposure and the role of endogenous cannabinoids in the developing brain: Adverse effect of prenatal exposure to marijuana. *Medscape Education.* Retrieved from http://www.medscape.org/viewarticle/745279_2

Wu, G., Arbuckle, R., Liu, B., Tao, H. W., & Zhang, L. I. (2008). Lateral sharpening of cortical frequency tuning by approximately balanced inhibition. *Neuron, 58,* 132–143.

Wu, J. C., & Bunney, W. E. (1990). The biological basis of an antidepressant response to sleep deprivation and relapse: Review and hypothesis. *American Journal of Psychiatry, 147,* 14–21.

Wurtman, J. J., Wurtman, R. J., Reynolds, S., Tsay, R., & Chew, B. (1987). Fenfluramine suppresses snack intake among carbohydrate cravers but not among noncarbohydrate cravers. *International Journal of Eating Disorders, 6,* 687–699.

Wyatt, T. D. (2015). The search for human pheromones: The lost decades and the necessity of returning to first principles. *Proceedings of the Royal Society, 282,* e20142994

Wynn, K. (1992). Addition and subtraction by human infants. *Nature, 358,* 749–750.

Wynn, K. (1998). Psychological foundations of number: Numerical competence in human infants. *Trends in Cognitive Sciences, 2,* 296–303.

Wysocki, C. J., & Preti, G. (2004). Facts, fallacies, fears, and frustrations with human pheromones. *Anatomical Record Part A, 281A,* 1201–1211.

Xiao, C., Cho, J. R., Zhou, C., Treweek, J. B., Chan, K., McKinney, S. L., et al. (2016). Cholinergic mesopontine signals govern locomotion and reward through dissociable midbrain pathways. *Neuron, 90,* 333–347.

Xiao, Z., & Suga, N. (2002). Modulation of cochlear hair cells by the auditory cortex in the mustached bat. *Nature Neuroscience, 5,* 57–63.

Xie, L., Kang, H., Xu, Q., Chen, M. J., Lia, Y., Thiyagaparajan, M., et al. (2013). Sleep drives metabolite clearance from the adult brain. *Science, 342,* 373–377.

Xu, Y., Padiath, Q. S., Shapiro, R. E., Jones, C. R., Wu, S. C., Saigoh, N., et al. (2005). Functional consequences of a *CKId* mutation causing familial advanced sleep phase syndrome. *Nature, 434,* 640–644.

Yacoub, E., Harel, N., & Ugurbil, K. (2008). High-field fMRI unveils orientation columns in humans. *Proceedings of the National Academy of Sciences, 105,* 10607–10612.

Yam, P. (1998, Winter). Intelligence considered. *Scientific American Presents,* 6–11.

Yamada, M., Yamada, M., & Higuchi, T. (2005). Remodeling of neuronal circuits as a new hypothesis for drug efficacy. *Progress in Neuro-Psychopharmacology and Biological Psychiatry, 29,* 999–1009.

Yanagisawa, T., Fukuma, R., Seymour, B., Hosomi, K., Kishima, H., Shimizu, T., et al. (2016). Induced sensorimotor brain plasticity controls pain in phantom limb patients. *Nature Communications, 7,* 13209. doi:10.1038/ncomms13209

Yang, W., Kelly, T., & He, J. (2007). Genetic epidemiology of obesity. *Epidemiologic Review, 29,* 49–61.

Yang, Y., Raine, A., Lencz, T., Bihrle, S., LaCasse, L., & Colletti, P. (2005). Volume reduction in prefrontal gray matter in unsuccessful criminal psychopaths. *Biological Psychiatry, 57,* 1103–1108.

Yang, Z., & Schank, J. C. (2006). Women do not synchronize their menstrual cycles. *Human Nature, 17,* 433–447.

Yates, F. A. (1966). *The art of memory.* Abingdon, UK: Routledge.

Yau, S. Y., Li, A., & So, K. F. (2015). Involvement of adult hippocampal neurogenesis in learning and forgetting. *Neural Plasticity,* e717958.

Yehuda, R. (2001). Are glucocorticoids responsible for putative hippocampal damage in PTSD? How and when to decide. *Hippocampus, 11,* 85–89.

Yeni-Komshian, G. H., & Benson, D. A. (1976). Anatomical study of cerebral asymmetry in the temporal lobe of humans, chimpanzees, and rhesus monkeys. *Science, 192,* 387–389.

Yip, M., Jin, R., Nakajima, H. H., Stankovic, K. M., & Chandrakasan, A. P. (2015). A fully-implantable cochlear implant SoC with piezoelectric middle-ear sensor and arbitrary waveform neural stimulation. *IEEE Journal of Solid-State Circuits, 50*(1), 214–229.

Yong, E. (2016, July). Breast-feeding the microbiome. *The New Yorker.* Retrieved from http://www.newyorker.com/tech/elements/breast-feeding-the-microbiome

You, J. S., Hu, S. Y., Chen, B., & Zhang, H. G. (2005). Serotonin transporter and tryptophan hydroxylase gene polymorphisms in Chinese patients with generalized anxiety disorder. *Psychiatric Genetics, 15,* 7–11.

Youdim, M. B. H., & Riederer, P. (1997, January). Understanding Parkinson's disease. *Scientific American, 276,* 52–58.

Young, E. (2014, June 3). Brain stimulation: The military's mind-zapping project. *BBC Future.* Retrieved from http://www.bbc.com/future/story/20140603-brain-zapping-the-future-of-war

Young, E. J., Aceti, M., Griggs, E. M., Fuchs, R. A., Zigmond, Z., Rumbaugh, G., & Miller, C. A. (2014). Selective, retrieval-independent disruption of methamphetamine-asociated memory by actin depolymerization. *Biological Psychiatry, 75,* 96–104.

Young, L. J., & Wang, Z. (2004). The neurobiology of pair bonding. *Nature Neuroscience, 10,* 1048–1054.

Young, M. P., & Yamane, S. (1992). Sparse population coding of faces in the inferotemporal cortex. *Science, 256,* 1327–1331.

Yu, X., Ye, Z., Houston, C. M., Franks, N. P., Brickley, S. G., & Wisden, W. (2015). Wakefulness is governed by GABA and histamine cotransmission. *Neuron, 87,* 164–178.

Yücel, M., Solowij, N., Respondek, C., Whittle, S., Fornito, A., Pantelis, C., et al. (2008). Regional brain abnormalities associated with long-term heavy cannabis use. *Archives of General Psychiatry, 65,* 694–701.

Zadka, L. (2015). Effectiveness of psychopharmacology in anorexia nervosa treatment. *Current Issues in Pharmacy and Medical Sciences, 28,* 69–71.

Zai, L., Ferrari, C., Dice, C., Subbaiah, S., Havton, L. A., Coppola, G., et al. (2011). Inosine augments the effects of a Nogo receptor blocker and of environmental enrichment to restore skilled forelimb use after stroke. *Journal of Neuroscience, 31,* 5977–5988.

Zalesky, A., Solowij, N., Yücel, M., Lubman, D. I., Takagi, M., Harding, I. H., et al. (2012). Effect of long-term cannabis use on axonal fibre connectivity. *Brain, 135,* 2245–2255.

Zanos, P., Moaddel, R., Morris, P. J., Georgiou, P., Fischell, J., Elmer, G. I., et al. (2016). NMDAR inhibition-independent antidepressant actions of ketamine metabolites. *Nature, 26,* 481–486.

Zeki, S. (1983). Colour coding in the cerebral cortex: The reaction of cells in monkey visual cortex to wavelengths and colours. *Journal of Neuroscience, 9,* 741–765.

Zeki, S. (1992, September). The visual image in mind and brain. *Scientific American, 267,* 69–76.

Zepelin, H., & Rechtshaffen, A. (1974). Mammalian sleep, longevity, and energy metabolism. *Brain, Behavior and Evolution, 10,* 425–470.

Zerbo, O., Qian, Y., Yoshida, C., Grether, J. K., Van de Water, J., & Croen, L. A. (2015). Maternal infection during pregnancy and autism spectrum disorders. *Journal of Autism and Developmental Disorders, 45,* 4015–4125.

Zhang, F., Vierock, J., Yizhar, O., Fenno, L. E., Tsunoda, S., Kianianmomeni, A., et al. (2011). The microbial opsin family of optogenetic tools. *Cell, 147,* 1446–1457.

Zhang, J. (2003). Evolution of the human ASPM gene, a major determinant of brain size. *Genetics, 165,* 2063–2070.

Zhang, J., Zhu, Y., Zhan, G., Fenik, P., Panossian, L., Wang, M. M., et al. (2014). Extended wakefulness: Compromised metabolics in and degeneration of locus ceruleus neurons. *Journal of Neuroscience, 34,* 4418–4431.

Zhang, Y., Proenca, R., Mafei, M., Barone, M., Leopold, L., & Friedman, J. M. (1994). Positional cloning of the mouse *obese* gene and its human homologue. *Nature, 335,* 311–317.

Zhou, J. N., Hofman, M. A., Gooren, L. J., & Swaab, D. F. (1995). A sex difference in the human brain and its relation to transsexuality. *Nature, 378,* 68–70.

Zhou, W., Yang, X., Chen, K., Cai, P., He, S., & Jiang, Y. (2014). Chemosensory communication of gender through two human steroids in a sexually dimorphic manner. *Cell, 24,* 1091–1095.

Zhou, Y., Kierans, A., Kenul, D., Ge, Y., Rath, J., Reaume, J., et al. (2013). Mild traumatic brain injury: Longitudinal regional brain volume changes. *Radiology, 267,* 880–890.

Zhou-Hao, L., Yip, P. K., Priestley, J. V., & Michael-Titus, A. T. (2017). A single dose of docosahexaenoic acid increases the functional recovery promoted by rehabilitation after cervical spinal cord injury in the rat. *Journal of Neurotrauma.* doi:10.1089/neu.2016.4556

Zhu, Q., Song, Y., Hu, S., Li, X., Tian, M., Zhen, Z., et al. (2010). Hereditability of the specific cognitive ability of face perception. *Current Biology, 20,* 137–142.

Zihl, J., von Cramon, D., & Mai, N. (1983). Selective disturbance of movement vision after bilateral brain damage. *Brain, 106,* 313–340.

Zillmer, E. A., & Spiers, M. V. (2001). *Principles of neuropsychology.* Belmont, CA: Wadsworth.

Zimmerman, C. A., Lin, Y.-C., Leib, D. E., Guo, L., Huey, E. L., Daly, G. E., et al. (2016). Thirst neurons anticipate the homeostatic consequences of eating and drinking. *Nature, 537,* 680–684.

Zion Golumbic, E. M., Ding, N., Bickel, S., Lakatos, P., Schevon, C. A., McKhann, G. M., et al. (2013). Mechanisms underlying selective neuronal tracking of attended speech at a "cocktail party." *Neuron, 77,* 980–991.

Zola-Morgan, S., Squire, L. R., & Amaral, D. G. (1986). Human amnesia and the medial temporal region: Enduring memory impairment following a bilateral lesion limited to field CA1 of the hippocampus. *Neuroscience, 6,* 2950–2967.

Zollinger, S. A., & Suthers, R. A. (2004). Motor mechanisms of a vocal mimic: Implications for birdsong production. *Proceedings of the Royal Society of London B: Biological Sciences, 271,* 483–491.

Zou, K., Deng, W., Li, T., Zhang, B., Jiang, L., Huang, C., et al. (2010). Changes of brain morphometry in first-episode, drug naïve, non-late-life adult patients with major depression: An optimized voxel-based morphometry study. *Biological Psychiatry, 67,* 186–188.

Zubenko, G. S., Hughes, H. B., Stiffler, J. S., Zubenko, W. N., & Kaplan, B. B. (2002). Genome survey for susceptibility loci for recurrent, early-onset major depression: Results at 10cM resolution. *American Journal of Medical Genetics, 114,* 413–422.

Zubenko, G. S., Maher, B. S., Hughes, H. B., III, Zubenko, W. N., Stiffler, J. S., & Marazita, M. L. (2004). Genome-wide linkage survey for genetic loci that affect the risk of suicide attempts in families with recurrent, early-onset, major depression. *American Journal of Medical Genetics B, 129,* 47–54.

Zubin, J., & Spring, B. (1977). Vulnerability: A new view of schizophrenia. *Journal of Abnormal Psychology, 86,* 103–126.

Zucker, K. J., & Bradley, S. J. (1995). *Gender identity disorder and psychosexual problems in children and adolescents.* New York: Guilford Press.

Zuckerman, M. (1971). Dimensions of sensation seeking. *Journal of Consulting and Clinical Psychology, 36,* 45–52.

Author Index

Money, J., 193, 196, 197, 198
Monfils, M.-H., 360, 434
Monk, T. H., 427
Monteith, S. J., 74
Montgomery, G. W., 382
Monti, M. M., 468
Montimurro, J., 334
Montoya, E. R., 230, 232
Montoya, P., 97, 324, 326
Moody, B. J., 426
Moody, D. B., 267
Moon, Y. P., 386
Mooney, R., 268
Moore, G. J., 388
Moore, H., 415
Moore, T., 331
Moore, V. J., 454
Moore-Ede, M. C., 450, 459, 460
Moore-Gillon, M. J., 148
Moos, R. H., 182
Mora, F., 360, 361
Moreno, J. L., 418, 419
Morens, D. M., 334
Moretto, A., 334
Morey, R. A., 434
Morgan, D., 381
Morgan, M. J., 305
Morgan, T. M., 440
Morizane, A., 334, 335
Morland, A. B., 306
Morley, J. E., 156
Mormann, F., 301
Morrel-Samuels, P., 267
Morris, E. K., 360
Morris, J. M., 196
Morris, M., 459
Morris, M. C., 387
Morris, N. M., 182
Morris, P. J., 424
Morris, R. B. M., 357
Morris, R. D., 267
Morris, R. G. M., 350
Morrison, C., 158
Morrison, S. F., 148
Mors, O., 418
Mortensen, P. B., 229, 397, 418
Morton, G. J., 158
Morton, J., 392
Moscovitch, M., 301
Moser, D. J., 193, 379
Moser, E. I., 351
Moses, A. M., 10
Moses-Kolko, E. L., 173
Mosier, K., 184, 185
Moss, C. F., 254
Moss, S. J., 428
Mössner, R., 433
Mottaghy, F. M., 97
Mountcastle, V. B., 317
Mouren-Simeoni, M. C., 172
Mouritsen, H., 90

Mpakopoulou, M., 229
Mueller, E., 231
Mühleisen, T. W., 423
Mujica-Parodi, L. R., 186
Mukamel, R., 247
Muldoon, M. F., 222
Mullan, M., 363, 389
Mulle, J. G., 410
Muller, D., 356
Muller, D. J., 417
Müller, R.-A., 392, 393
Muller, R. U., 358
Mullington, J. M., 454
Mulvenna, C., 305
Mulvey, M. E., 393
Munafò, M. R., 430
Munch, K., 265
Münch, M., 450
Muñoz, M., 451
Munz, M., 97
Munzar, P., 129
Muotri, A., 109
Murakami, P., 164
Muranaga, T., 171
Muraro, P. A., 338
Murasaki, M., 461
Muravieva, E. V., 360
Murayama, Y., 456
Murphy, A. Z., 322
Murphy, C., 392
Murphy, D., 388, 397
Murphy, D. L., 429, 438
Murphy, F. C., 215, 216
Murphy, F. T., 320
Murphy, G., 3
Murphy, G. M., 376
Murphy, J., 266
Murphy, M. R., 187
Murphy, S. L., 72, 361
Murray, C., 378
Murray, I. V. J., 334
Murray, J., 398
Murray, J. B., 127
Murray, J. I., 9
Murray, R. M., 412, 417, 418, 420
Murrell, J., 389
Murrough, J. W., 424
Muskand, J. A., 78
Must, A., 160
Mustafa, S., 134
Mustanski, B. S., 201
Muzio, J. N., 455
Myers, J. M., 433
Myers, M. A., 161

Naccache, L., 302, 464
Nadeau, A., 166
Nader, K., 359
Naeser, M. A., 257, 366
Nagahara, A. H., 365
Nagai, N., 171

Nagamoto, H. T., 417
Naglieri, J. A., 384
Nair, A., 393
Naj, A. C., 364
Najman, J. M., 122
Nakahara, T., 171
Nakajima, H. H., 250
Nakamura, M., 461
Nakashima, T., 148
Nakayama, K., 456
Naliboff, B., 193
Naliboff, B. D., 225
Namiki, A., 320
Nanda, P., 416
Napollelo, E. M., 260
Narbro, K., 169
Narendran, R., 173
Narr, K. L., 229
Nash, J. M., 463
Natarjan, N., 400
Nathan, D., 474
Nathan, D. M., 169
Nayak, S. K., 451
Naylor, R. J., 434
Naylor, S. L., 11
Neal, J., 438
Neale, M., 172
Neale, M. C., 8, 163, 172, 192, 200, 433
Nebes, R. D., 60
Neely, M. H., 322
Nehrkorn, B., 392
Neidhart, E., 460
Neisser, U., 374, 384
Nelissen, K., 281, 381
Nelken, I., 247
Nelson, C., 168
Nelson, H., 337
Nelson, L., 28
Nelson, R. J., 229, 231
Nemade, R., 407
Nervaes, R., 232
Nestler, E. J., 131, 411
Nestor, P. G., 417
Netter, P, 231
Neuer, G., 151
Neugebauer, R., 165, 419
Neulen, J., 388
Neuman, T., 109, 334
Neumann, C., 420
Neumann, D., 450
Neville, H. J., 263
New, M. I., 196
Newbury, D. F., 268
Newell, D. W., 74
Newen, A., 213
Newhouse, P. A., 364
Newlin, D. B., 124, 132
Newman, A., 439
Newman, A. L., 202
Newman, E. A., 36

Subject Index